The Oxford Handbook of
Organizational Psychology

OXFORD LIBRARY OF PSYCHOLOGY

Editor in Chief PETER E. NATHAN

Editor, Organizational Psychology STEVE W. J. KOZLOWSKI

The Oxford Handbook of Organizational Psychology

Edited by

Steve W. J. Kozlowski

VOLUME 2

OXFORD
UNIVERSITY PRESS

OXFORD
UNIVERSITY PRESS

Oxford University Press, Inc., publishes works that further
Oxford University's objective of excellence
in research, scholarship, and education.

Oxford New York
Auckland Cape Town Dar es Salaam Hong Kong Karachi
Kuala Lumpur Madrid Melbourne Mexico City Nairobi
New Delhi Shanghai Taipei Toronto

With offices in
Argentina Austria Brazil Chile Czech Republic France Greece
Guatemala Hungary Italy Japan Poland Portugal Singapore
South Korea Switzerland Thailand Turkey Ukraine Vietnam

Copyright © 2012 by Oxford University Press, Inc.

Published by Oxford University Press, Inc.
198 Madison Avenue, New York, New York 10016
www.oup.com

Oxford is a registered trademark of Oxford University Press

Library of Congress Cataloging-in-Publication Data
The Oxford handbook of organizational psychology / edited by Steve W.J. Kozlowski.
    p. cm. — (Oxford library of psychology)
  ISBN-13: 978–0–19–992828–6 (acid-free paper)
  1. Psychology, Industrial—Handbooks, manuals, etc.
  2. Organizational behavior—Handbooks, manuals, etc. I. Kozlowski, Steve W. J.
  HF5548.8.O94 2012
  302.3'5—dc23
  2011037047

9 8 7 6 5 4 3 2
Printed in the United States of America
on acid-free paper

SHORT CONTENTS

OXFORD LIBRARY OF PSYCHOLOGY

The *Oxford Library of Psychology,* a landmark series of handbooks, is published by Oxford University Press, one of the world's oldest and most highly respected publishers, with a tradition of publishing significant books in psychology. The ambitious goal of the *Oxford Library of Psychology* is nothing less than to span a vibrant, wide-ranging field and, in so doing, to fill a clear market need.

Encompassing a comprehensive set of handbooks, organized hierarchically, the *Library* incorporates volumes at different levels, each designed to meet a distinct need. At one level are a set of handbooks designed broadly to survey the major subfields of psychology; at another are numerous handbooks that cover important current focal research and scholarly areas of psychology in depth and detail. Planned as a reflection of the dynamism of psychology, the *Library* will grow and expand as psychology itself develops, thereby highlighting significant new research that will impact on the field. Adding to its accessibility and ease of use, the *Library* will be published in print and, later on, electronically.

The *Library* surveys psychology's principal subfields with a set of handbooks that capture the current status and future prospects of those major subdisciplines. This initial set includes handbooks of social and personality psychology, clinical psychology, counseling psychology, school psychology, educational psychology, industrial and organizational psychology, cognitive psychology, cognitive neuroscience, methods and measurements, history, neuropsychology, personality assessment, developmental psychology, and more. Each handbook undertakes to review one of psychology's major subdisciplines with breadth, comprehensiveness, and exemplary scholarship. In addition to these broadly-conceived volumes, the *Library* also includes a large number of handbooks designed to explore in depth more specialized areas of scholarship and research, such as stress, health and coping, anxiety and related disorders, cognitive development, or child and adolescent assessment. In contrast to the broad coverage of the subfield handbooks, each of these latter volumes focuses on an especially productive, more highly focused line of scholarship and research. Whether at the broadest or most specific level, however, all of the *Library* handbooks offer synthetic coverage that reviews and evaluates the relevant past and present research and anticipates research in the future. Each handbook in the *Library* includes introductory and concluding chapters written by its editor to provide a roadmap to the handbook's table of contents and to offer informed anticipations of significant future developments in that field.

An undertaking of this scope calls for handbook editors and chapter authors who are established scholars in the areas about which they write. Many of the nation's and world's most productive and best-respected psychologists have agreed to edit *Library* handbooks or write authoritative chapters in their areas of expertise.

For whom has the *Oxford Library of Psychology* been written? Because of its breadth, depth, and accessibility, the *Library* serves a diverse audience, including graduate students in psychology and their faculty mentors, scholars, researchers, and practitioners in psychology and related fields. Each will find in the *Library* the information they seek on the subfield or focal area of psychology in which they work or are interested.

Befitting its commitment to accessibility, each handbook includes a comprehensive index, as well as extensive references to help guide research. And because the *Library* was designed from its inception as an online as well as a print resource, its structure and contents will be readily and rationally searchable online. Further, once the *Library* is released online, the handbooks will be regularly and thoroughly updated.

In summary, the *Oxford Library of Psychology* will grow organically to provide a thoroughly informed perspective on the field of psychology, one that reflects both psychology's dynamism and its increasing interdisciplinarity. Once published electronically, the *Library* is also destined to become a uniquely valuable interactive tool, with extended search and browsing capabilities. As you begin to consult this handbook, we sincerely hope you will share our enthusiasm for the more than 500-year tradition of Oxford University Press for excellence, innovation, and quality, as exemplified by the *Oxford Library of Psychology.*

Peter E. Nathan
Editor-in-Chief
Oxford Library of Psychology

Steve W. J. Kozlowski

Dr. Kozlowski is a recognized authority in human learning, team effectiveness, and multilevel theory. His research is focused on the design of active learning systems and the use of "synthetic experience" to train adaptive skills, the development of systems to enhance team learning and team effectiveness, and the critical role of team leaders in the development of adaptive teams. The goal of his programmatic research is to generate actionable theory, research-based principles, and deployable tools to facilitate the development of adaptive individuals, teams, and organizations. His work has generated over $7 million in funded research. He has published over 80 books, chapters, and articles and has delivered over 200 refereed and invited presentations. Dr. Kozlowski is the Editor (and a former Associate Editor) for the *Journal of Applied Psychology* and serves as the Editor for the *Oxford Series in Organizational Psychology*. He serves on the Editorial Boards of *Current Directions in Psychological Science* and the *Journal of Management*, and he has previously served on the Editorial Boards of the *Academy of Management Journal, Human Factors*, the *Journal of Applied Psychology*, and *Organizational Behavior and Human Decision Processes*. He is a Fellow of the American Psychological Association, the Association for Psychological Science, the International Association for Applied Psychology, and the Society for Industrial and Organizational Psychology. Dr. Kozlowski received his B.A. in psychology from the University of Rhode Island, and his M.S. and Ph.D. degrees in organizational psychology from The Pennsylvania State University.

CONTRIBUTORS

Linda Argote
Tepper School of Business
Carnegie Mellon University
Pittsburgh, PA

Tammy D. Allen
Department of Psychology
University of South Florida
Tampa, FL

Zeynep Aycan
Department of Psychology
Koc University
Istanbul, Turkey

Bradford S. Bell
Department of Human Resource Studies
Cornell University
Ithaca, NY

Sabrina Blawath
School of Management
University of St. Gallen
St. Gallen, Switzerland

Walter C. Borman
PDRI
University of South Florida
Tampa, FL

Daniel J. Brass
LINKS Center for Social Network Analysis
University of Kentucky
Lexington, KY

Laura L. Koppes Bryan
School of Psychological and Behavioral Sciences
University of West Florida
Pensacola, FL

Daniel M. Cable
Kenan-Flagler Business School
University of North Carolina at Chapel Hill
Chapel Hill, NC

John P. Campbell
Department of Psychology
University of Minnesota
Minneapolis, MN

Georgia T. Chao
The Eli Broad Graduate School of Management
Michigan State University
East Lansing, MI

Gilad Chen
Department of Management and Organization
University of Maryland
College Park, MD

Adrienne J. Colella
A. B. Freeman School of Business
Tulane University
New Orleans, LA

Jason A. Colquitt
Terry College of Business
University of Georgia
Athens, GA

John Cordery
UWA Business School
University of Western Australia
Perth, Australia

Reeshad S. Dalal
Department of Psychology
George Mason University
Fairfax, VA

Shanna R. Daniels
A. B. Freeman School of Business
Tulane University
New Orleans, LA

David V. Day
UWA Business School
University of Western Australia
Perth, Australia

Richard P. DeShon
Department of Psychology
Michigan State University
East Lansing, MI

Deborah DiazGranados
Department of Psychology
University of Central Florida
Orlando, FL

Lillian T. Eby
Department of Psychology
University of Georgia
Athens, GA

J. Kevin Ford
Department of Psychology
Michigan State University
East Lansing, MI

Stephen M. Fiore
Department of Philosophy and Institute for
Simulation and Training
University of Central Florida
Orlando, FL

Pennie Foster-Fishman
Department of Psychology
Michigan State University
East Lansing, MI

Michael Frese
NUS Business School
National University of Singapore
Singapore
Leuphana University of Lueneburg
Lueneburg, Germany

Michele J. Gelfand
Department of Psychology
University of Maryland
College Park, MD

Cristina B. Gibson
Management and Organisations
The University of Western Australia
Crawley, WA

Lucy L. Gilson
School of Business
Department of Management
University of Connecticut
Storrs, CT

Jonathan Grudin
Microsoft Research
Redmond, WA

Paul J. Hanges
Department of Psychology
University of Maryland
College Park, MD

Jerry W. Hedge
Survey Research Division
RTI International
Research Triangle Park, NC

David A. Hofmann
Kenan-Flagler Business School
University of North Carolina at Chapel Hill
Chapel Hill, NC

John R. Hollenbeck
The Eli Broad Graduate School of Management
Michigan State University
East Lansing, MI

Charles L. Hulin
Department of Psychology
University of Illinois
Champaign, IL

Timothy A. Judge
Mendoza College of Business
University of Notre Dame
Notre Dame, IN

Ruth Kanfer
School of Psychology
Georgia Institute of Technology
Atlanta, GA

Kwanghyun Kim
Korea University Business School
Korea University
Seoul, Korea

Bradley L. Kirkman
Mays Business School
Texas A&M University
College Station, TX

Alex Kirlik
Departments of Computer Science, Psychology,
and the Beckman Institute
University of Illinois at Urbana-Champaign
Urbana, IL

Steve W. J. Kozlowski
Department of Psychology
Michigan State University
East Lansing, MI

Manuel London
College of Business
State University of New York at
Stony Brook
Stony Brook, NY

John E. Mathieu
School of Business
Department of Management
University of Connecticut
Storrs, CT

Patrick F. McKay
School of Management and Labor Relations
Rutgers University
Piscataway, NJ

Cheri Ostroff
Department of Psychology
University of Maryland
College Park, MD

Sharon K. Parker
UWA Business School
University of Western Australia
Perth, Australia

José M. Peiró
Department of Social Psychology
University of Valencia
Valencia, Spain

Robert E. Ployhart
The Moore School of Business
Department of Management
University of South Carolina
Columbia, SC

Steven E. Poltrock
Bellevue, WA and Padova, Italy

Quinetta M. Roberson
School of Business
Villanova University
Villanova, PA

Michael A. Rosen
Department of Psychology
University of Central Florida
Orlando, FL

Ann Marie Ryan
Department of Psychology
Michigan State University
East Lansing, MI

Sara L. Rynes
Tippie College of Business
University of Iowa
Iowa City, IA

Paul R. Sackett
Department of Psychology
University of Minnesota
Minneapolis, MN

Eduardo Salas
Institute for Simulation & Training and
Department of Psychology
University of Central Florida
Orlando, FL

Marissa L. Shuffler
Department of Psychology
University of Central Florida
Orlando, FL

Sloane M. Signal
A. B. Freeman School of Business
Tulane University
New Orleans, LA

James W. Smither
School of Business
Department of Management
La Salle University
Philadelphia, PA

Scott A. Snell
Darden School of Business
University of Virginia
Charlottesville, VA

Charles C. Snow
Department of Management and Organization
The Pennsylvania State University
University Park, PA

Sabine Sonnentag
Department of Psychology
University of Mannheim
Mannheim, Germany

Matthias Spitzmuller
The Eli Broad Graduate School of Management
Michigan State University
East Lansing, MI

Paul Tesluk
Department of Management and Organization
University of Maryland
College Park, MD

Lois E. Tetrick
Department of Psychology
George Mason University
Fairfax, VA

Andrew J. Vinchur
Department of Psychology
Lafayette College
Easton, PA

Mo Wang
Warrington College of Business Administration
University of Florida
Gainesville, FL

Sallie J. Weaver
Department of Psychology
University of Central Florida
Orlando, FL

Kang Yang Trevor Yu
College of Business (Nanyang Business School)
Nanyang Technological University
Singapore

Dov M. Zohar
William Davidson Faculty of Industrial
    Engineering and Management
Technion – Israel Institute of Technology
Technion City, Haifa, Israel

CONTENTS

PART 6

Work Teams in Organizations

Team Structure: Tight Versus Loose Coupling in Task-Oriented Groups

John R. Hollenbeck *and* Matthias Spitzmuller

Abstract

By definition, teams are made up of multiple, interdependent individuals. The individuals within a team are separate and holistic units with their own identity, but this interdependence also means that the team is a holistic unit with its own separate identity. The dual set of identities embodied in teams creates an inherent figure versus ground confusion. In this chapter we use the concept of loosely structured systems (Weick, 1976) to help unravel this figure versus ground paradox. We show how the literature has operationalized four specific dimensions of structural interdependence: (a) task allocation structure (horizontal interdependence), (b) decision-making structure (vertical interdependence), (c) reward structure (outcome interdependence), and (d) communication structure (spatial interdependence). The literature reveals that organizations can no longer compete successfully via uncoupled structures, but at the same time, organizations resist the formation of tightly coupled systems. We discuss the virtues and liabilities of each of the four types of interdependence in teams, and describe why loose coupling may be a normative, and not just a descriptive, practice of organizations.

Key Words: Team design, team structure, team interdependence, team decision making, teams as loosely coupled systems

Introduction

Teams have been defined as "small groups of *interdependent individuals* who share responsibility for specific outcomes," and team-based structures have played an increasingly important role in contemporary organizations (Ilgen, Hollenbeck, Johnson, & Jundt, 2005). Longitudinal surveys of Fortune 1,000 firms have shown a steady increase in the use of team-based structures moving from less than 20% in 1980, to roughly 50% in 1990, to over 80% in 2000 (Garvey, 2002). Although organizations are now quick to create teams, they are still reluctant to totally overhaul their human resource management systems, which have been traditionally been oriented toward individuals. That is, even organizations that report relying heavily on teams fail to report that they complement their team-based

structures with team-level performance evaluation systems, team-based training programs, or team-based compensation practices (Devine, Clayton, Philips, Dunford, & Melner 1999). Thus, there is somewhat of a disconnect between what organizations say and what they do with respect to teams, and perhaps this should not be surprising, given the nature of team-based structures.

By definition, teams are composed of *individuals*, and each individual on a team is a living organism with his or her own unique and holistic identity. Because of this, these individuals are always in a position to make their own decisions and execute their own actions, unconstrained by the decisions and actions of other people. Even in team contexts, some degree of personal identity and personal freedom of individuals is maintained. If the level of this identity and freedom become extreme, people are essentially uncoupled, and they are a team in name only. The perception experienced by an observer of a five-person team that was a team in name only would lead that observer to "see" the five separate units but not the single unit that is the team.

However, also by definition, teams are made up of multiple individuals who are linked to each other, and this connection of separate but holistically identifiable individuals creates *interdependence*. This interdependence may dictate the decisions and actions of multiple people who are yoked, in that their decisions differ from those that any one individual would make if he or she were truly alone. Thus, although these individuals can make their own decisions and execute their own behaviors, when embedded in teams, individuals may voluntarily surrender their own independence, and may allow themselves to be influenced by other people. In extreme cases, individuals who are part of tightly coupled and cohesive teams may even lose much of their own personal identity in the service of the larger group identity. In this case, the perceptual experience of an observer of such a five-person team would be such that she can only "see" the single unit that is the team and may struggle to see the five separate units that constitute the team.

Thus, much like a perceptual illusion in which figure-ground confusion can create different perceptual experiences for different observers, teams can be conceptualized as a paradox of holistic identity. At one extreme, when the team members are uncoupled, the separate individuals become the figure, and the team becomes the ground. At the other extreme, when the team members are tightly coupled, the team itself becomes the figure, and the multiple individuals that make up the team become the ground. As we have noted, however, in real world organizations, few teams reside at either of these two extremes, and thus researchers who study teams are constantly struggling with the figure-ground paradox created by the fact that people in teams tend to be loosely coupled.

In the field of organization theory, Weick (1976) used the term *loosely coupled systems* to convey the image that organizations can be conceived as holistic units that are collectively responsive, but that each element of the holistic system preserves its own unique identity, as well as its own physical and logical separateness. At the organizational level, this image captures the paradox that each subunit of the organization is its own unique holistic unit that retains much of its own identity, even though

it is simultaneously part of a larger holistic unit that has a separate identity. Within this framework, coupling is a multidimensional concept that allows subunits to be simultaneously tightly coupled on one dimension, but uncoupled on another dimension at the same time. Coupling is also a dynamic concept that allows one subunit to be tightly coupled to another at one moment in time, but uncoupled at other times. Conceptualizing organizations as loosely coupled systems had a powerful impact on theory-building in organization theory, and the two primary articles that introduced and refined this concept (Weick, 1976; Orton & Weick, 1990) have been cited over 1,100 times.

Clearly, if one substitutes *individuals* for *subunits* and *teams* for *organizations*, the image of teams as loosely coupled systems is an image that helps to resolve the "figure-ground" problem that one experiences when observing teams. It also helps one to understand the slightly schizophrenic manner in which organizations have embraced and, at the same time, rejected team-based structures. In addition, if one construes teams as loosely coupled systems at a lower level of analysis, much of what has been learned by examining organizations from this lens becomes a set of working hypotheses that can be used for theory-building and empirical testing in the area of teams. For example, Orton and Weick (1990) proposed that organizational subunits in loosely coupled structures will find it easier to scan their respective environments and to adapt to changes in these environments. Similarly, it is likely that loosely coupled individuals serve as a more effective system for sensing the environment when compared to tightly coupled individuals.

The key to effectively employing this lens, however, is the ability to articulate the dimensions of coupling that matter most when it comes to helping shape when teams versus individuals become figure versus ground. As Orton and Weick (1990) stated, "it is not a trivial matter to specify which elements are coupled" and that using this image "puts pressure on the investigator to specify clearly the identity, separateness, and boundaries of the elements coupled" (p. 4). Thus, to effectively appreciate the nature of teams, it is critical to understand the many different ways that people within teams can be coupled or uncoupled. In terms of the paradox identified above, this means describing the variables where high or low values promote the perception of the team as figure and individuals as ground, or vice versa. The purpose of this chapter is to leverage the existing literature on team structure toward this end.

Dimensions of Team Interdependence

As we will see throughout this chapter, although there is agreement that team structure is the means of defining the linkages between team members, there has been a great deal of variability on the dimensions on which researchers have focused, and hence the phrase *team structure* has taken on different meanings for different researchers. We will examine four specific dimensions where coupling may occur: (a) task allocation structure, (b) decision-making structure, (c) reward structure, and (d) communication structure, summarizing the research that has been conducted on each dimension. If one conceptualizes teams as loosely coupled systems, these are the four primary dimensions that serve as coupling opportunities.

This decoupling of coupling mechanisms that comprise the larger construct of interdependence encourages two different types of theorizing and empirical testing. First, this creates an opportunity for a unidimensional approach to structure, in which each and every team can be placed on a bipolar scale anchored at one end by "tightly coupled" and at the other end by "decoupled," where "loosely coupled" serves as the midpoint. This allows structure to be used as a simple, single variable in theories of teams, where it can play the role of cause, effect, or boundary condition for other cause-and-effect relationships. At a more refined level, by identifying the multiple dimensions that serve as coupling opportunities, this creates the ability to establish a multidimensional construct in which any one team can be tightly coupled on dimension A while being loosely coupled on dimension B and totally uncoupled on dimension C. This team could then be compared to a team that is tightly coupled on dimension C, loosely coupled on dimension B, and uncoupled on dimension A. These two teams may have identical scores when structure is considered as a unidimensional construct, but operate quite differently because of the unique aspects of being coupled on different dimensions. Since most teams in real-world contexts tend to be "loosely coupled," this allows researchers to make more refined differentiations between two different loosely coupled teams that vary on how and where they are coupled. Currently, when researchers claim that team members are interdependent, the dimensions on which they are coupled are all treated as synonymous, and therefore we are not able to delineate different antecedents and consequences of unique forms of coupling.

Although there are an infinite number of potential dimensions whereby individuals in teams might

be coupled, as we noted above, we have decided to focus on four specific dimensions of team interdependence. These are: (a) task allocation structure (e.g., functional versus divisional); (b) decision-making structure (e.g., hierarchical or self-managed); (c) reward structures (e.g., cooperative versus competitive); and (d) communication structures (e.g., face-to-face versus virtual). We have chosen to focus on these four dimensions of interdependence for three reasons. First, these four dimensions are theoretically appealing because they are all related to three critical processes, which, according to Deutsch (1949), generally result from social interdependence among individuals. These three processes (cf. Johnson, 2003) are: substitutability (the degree to which actions of one person substitute for actions of other person(s); cathexis (the degree to which individuals are willing to invest psychological energy in objects and person outside of oneself); and inducibility (the degree to which individuals are open to being influenced and to influencing others).

Second, the four dimensions of interdependence demonstrate similar, yet not identical relationships with these three critical processes. This reiterates the need for a multidimensional approach to team interdependence. For example, all four dimensions of team interdependence increase (in varying degrees) inducibility in work groups; that is, they increase the extent to which individuals are willing to influence others and to be influenced by others. The four dimensions of interdependence are, however, differentially related with substitutability, that is, with the extent to which the actions of one person substitute for the actions of another person. Horizontal interdependence results in greater individual specialization, which reduces the capability of individuals to substitute for others' job. Communication interdependence, on the other hand, increases the mutual awareness of individuals' tasks and responsibilities, thereby also increasing substitutability. Finally, we view vertical interdependence as unrelated to substitutability in teams, since the extent to which teams depend on hierarchical leaders in their decision-making process is not related to the extent to which team members specialize in specific functions and tasks and how they increase their awareness of each others' tasks and responsibilities.

Third, three of the four dimensions have been extensively investigated over the last decades and draw from major theories in the organization sciences. For example, Burns and Stalker (1961) discussed departmentation (similar to our conceptualization of horizontal interdependence) and centralization (similar to our conceptualization of vertical interdependence) as two central dimensions of organizing. Similarly, Johnson et al. (2006) discuss centralization, departmentation, and reward structure (similar to our conceptualization of outcome interdependence) as three central structural dimensions in their structural adaptation theory. In addition to the three structural dimensions discussed in structural adaptation theory, we have chosen to add communication interdependence as a fourth structural dimension in order to reflect the changing nature of work, which has dramatically increased reliance on virtual team and communication structures.

Like the figure-ground paradox that underlies the holistic "interdependence" construct, coupling on each of these subdimensions constrains individual team members from making some decisions and executing some behaviors but, at the same time, also frees them from having to make other decisions or engage in other behaviors. Indeed, this simultaneous constraint/freedom tension can be a metaphor that helps elucidate where, when, and with whom coupling takes place, as well as why. Over the last ten years, there has been considerable research on team structure on each of these dimensions, and we will review this research in order to build a theory of team structure that uses the loosely coupled system metaphor to describe structure's role as cause, effect, and boundary condition for other cause-effect relationships in team contexts.

The remainder of this chapter is structured around these four different dimensions of team interdependence introduced above. We start each section by providing a practical example of a student team that faces different constraints and opportunities as a consequence of the specific structure in which the team is operating. This practical example will be followed by a brief introduction and definition of the respective dimension of team interdependence. The main focus will then be placed on a discussion of relevant previous research. Our intent is to summarize and integrate previous research on team structure into one coherent whole. As such, our chapter critically reviews previous research studies and evaluates their potential contributions to developing an integrated theory of team structure. We conclude with a discussion of research implications. In doing so, we first outline a theoretically driven research agenda to investigate the broader nomological network of team interdependence. Second, we discuss the extent to which loosely coupled team structures may provide a viable solution to the dilemmas that

teams in both tightly coupled and uncoupled structures face.

Horizontal Interdependence: Team Task Allocation Structures
Practical Example

Imagine a set of four students who have been formed into one team to conduct four case studies that involve four separate industries, in which each case study has four parts. Each case study consists of: (a) a research component that involves collecting raw qualitative information and quantitative data from the library and the web; (b) a data analytic component that involves statistical analysis of the raw data used to support specific inferences; (c) a written component that weaves the qualitative information and data analysis into a coherent eight-page report; and (d) a formal, multimedia presentation of that report presented in front of a critical audience.

Although there are an infinite number of ways in which the four members of this team could break down this task into smaller parts that can be allocated to different members, most of these can be contrasted by the degree to which they create *horizontal interdependence* between the members. For example, the team could decide to decompose the task so that each member does one functionally specific aspect of the task. That is, one team member would do the research for all four cases, another member would do the data analysis for all four cases, yet another team member would do all the written reports, and the final member would do all four multimedia presentations. Alternatively, each team member could decide to take an industry-specific approach, and do all four parts of each report (research, analysis, writing, presentation) for one of the cases. These two alternatives have been referred to as functional versus divisional approaches to task allocation, respectively, and each choice can be conceived as a complex constraint/freedom package for the team members (Hollenbeck et al., 2002).

The choice to adopt a functional approach creates a certain freedom for the members (the most introverted member is freed from having to perform a stressful public defense of the report, while the most extroverted member is freed from toiling alone in anonymity in the stacks of the library), but at the same time creates a set of constraints as well. Those who write up and present the research can only work with the information collected and analyzed by others, and the sequential nature of the tasks makes them vulnerable to slow or poor performance of others. Thus, the functional approach creates a tight coupling between each of the four members, who are tightly yoked, and thus horizontally interdependent (Morgeson & Humphrey, 2006; Wageman, 1999). In this case, the team is likely to be seen as figure and not ground.

The choice to adopt a divisional structure, on the other hand, creates a much looser coupling of individuals who can go off on their own and do all four parts of their own case, such that individuals are likely to be seen as figure in this case, and the team as ground. The team is still interdependent in the sense that the four completed cases need to be grafted together at the end, and this will entail some editing to create a consistent style, but the level of horizontal interdependence is lower relative to the team that chose a functional structure. The members of these divisional teams are freed from the sequential interdependence created by the functional structure, but are constrained to do all four parts of the project, regardless of their skills or preferences for specific tasks.

Construct Definition

Our definition of horizontal interdependence among team members coincides with earlier definitions of task interdependence. Thompson (1967) argued that high task interdependence poses critical contingencies for all team members that must be resolved before the team can complete their work. He refers to this type of interdependence as reciprocal interdependence and contrasts it with other types of task interdependence on a lower level of complexity, such as pooled or sequential interdependence. Similarly, Kiggundu (1981) proposed that high task interdependence implies a broad scope in connections among individuals, an intensive exchange of resources and expertise among individuals, and high criticality in these connections among individuals. Consistent with these definitions, we view the intensity, the depth, the criticality, and the functional specialization among several individuals as defining elements of horizontal interdependence in teams. We have chosen to refer to this type of interdependence as horizontal interdependence in order to emphasize the contrast between horizontal interdependence and vertical interdependence. Specifically, we conceptualize horizontal interdependence as a form of social interdependence among individuals operating on the same hierarchical level in an organization, whereas vertical interdependence describes social interdependence in manager-subordinate relationships.

After defining horizontal/task interdependence, we now turn to our review and discussion of relevant research on this important dimension of task interdependence. We begin this section with a discussion of research that investigates the general implications of horizontal interdependence for team processes and performance. Next, we summarize recent research on specific aspects of task design that are particularly salient for horizontal interdependence in teams, such as transactive memory systems, cross-functional team compositions, and intrapersonal cross-functionality. During this discussion, it will become clear that high levels of horizontal interdependence generally allow the efficient distribution and utilization of information and expertise in teams, but they also imply higher potential for conflict in teams. We suggest that this dilemma has to be managed in an effective manner in order to align teams with their task environment.

Task Decomposition

As noted earlier, in functionally structured groups, individuals in the team all focus on specializing in one element of the task (or a few elements), whereas in divisional structures, each member performs a wider variety of tasks, centered on a unique and holistic product. For our discussion of horizontal interdependence, this differentiation is meaningful because functional structures imply narrow and specialized roles characterized by tight coupling and high interdependence among team members. Also, the differentiation between a functional and divisional structure is practically meaningful, as managers must decide which structure best capitalizes on individual differences in teams and the environment in which the team operates.

Consistent with this idea, Hollenbeck and colleagues (2002) adapted structural contingency theory to a team context, investigating how the influence of individual differences on team performance is moderated by the structure as well as by the task environment in which teams perform. Specifically, Hollenbeck and colleagues (2002) found, in a laboratory study of 80 teams, that functional structures were superior to divisional structures in predictable environments, but that divisional structures outperformed functional structures when the task was unpredictable. In addition, they found that individual differences predicted team performance in a higher scope, divisional task characterized by low horizontal interdependence, but not in narrower functional task. For example, Hollenbeck and colleagues (2002) demonstrated that team member cognitive ability was a strong predictor of team performance when the divisional structure was aligned with its environment, that is, in a dynamic task environment. In addition, team level emotional stability emerged as a critical factor in a divisional structure in a task environment that was not aligned with team structure. The fact that the yoking associated with tightly coupled functional structures reduces the impact of individual differences shows directly how the team becomes the figure and the individuals ground when this type of structure is employed.

The flip side of this finding is demonstrated by a recent meta-analysis on teamwork processes by LePine, Piccolo, Jackson, Mathieu, and Saul (2008), who found that team-level processes play a more critical role in tasks characterized by high horizontal interdependence, such as in a functional structure. That is, the relationship between team-level processes such as strategy formulation, coordination, and conflict management were higher when horizontal interdependence was high relative to when teams were less tightly coupled. This finding coincides with the previously discussed study by Hollenbeck et al. (2002), who find that individual-level factors play a larger role in a divisional structure, whereas team-level factors play a larger role in more tightly coupled functional structures.

Stewart and Barrick (2000) also found contingencies associated with horizontal structure in a field study of 45 production teams. Specifically, they found that the effect of horizontal interdependence on team performance is moderated by task type, such that high interdependence exhibits a U-shaped relationship with team performance for teams engaged primarily in conceptual tasks, whereas interdependence exhibits an inversely U-shaped relationship with performance for behavioral task. The reason for this was that for conceptual tasks, extremely low levels of interdependence led to less conflict, and extremely high levels of horizontal interdependence promoted communication, and both of these processes were positively related to performance on conceptual tasks. In contrast, for behavioral tasks, moderate levels of horizontal interdependence promoted performance but, as Stewart and Barrick (2000) note, "the intrateam process measures included in this study were generally unrelated to performance for teams performing these tasks, thereby providing little insight into the mechanisms that might explain…the direction of the relationships" (p. 144). We suspect that since horizontal interdependence is just one of the dimensions of coupling, a full appreciation of the level of interdependence associated with these teams cannot truly be known.

Results from a three-year quasi-experimental field study by Parker (2003) further attest to the multifaceted nature of horizontal interdependence in teams. In her study, Parker (2003) investigated the effect of lean production practices on work perceptions and attitudes. For the purpose of our discussion of horizontal interdependence in teams, lean production practices can be characterized as implying high degrees of horizontal interdependence for teams, such that individual group members assume highly specialized roles. Lean production practices are frequently used in mass production in order to increase system stability and efficiency. At the same time, they reduce cognitive demands for individual jobs. Interestingly, however, Parker (2003) demonstrated that the increased efficiency in work structures that imply high horizontal interdependence comes at a cost, as they lead to declines in perceived work characteristics, such as job autonomy, skill utilization, and participation in decision making. These perceptions in turn were found to result in lower organizational commitment and role breadth self-efficacy, while increasing job depression.

Just as Parker (2003) was able to identify negative consequences that tight horizontal coupling can have for team functioning, Drach-Zahavy (2004) demonstrated that too little horizontal interdependence can also be detrimental for teams. In her study on job enrichment practices, Drach-Zahavy (2004) argued that decreased horizontal interdependence among individuals in teams will be associated with decreased team support, as individuals no longer feel accountable for the team as a whole. Indeed, one of the liabilities of loosely structured divisional teams is that individuals become the figure and the team becomes the ground, and hence, helping behavior directed at others is not necessarily legitimated the same way as it is in tightly coupled structures.

It is likely that high levels of horizontal interdependence will often be associated with a high degree of formalization in work teams. In fact, the study by Parker (2003) provides a good example for this association. In a sample of customer service technicians, Gilson, Mathieu, Shalley, and Ruddy (2005) found that high levels of standardization in interdependent work teams has both positive and negative effects for teams. Work standardization was found to lead to higher levels of customer satisfaction, but it also neutralized the positive effect of creative team environments on team performance. Gilson and colleagues (2005) suggested that established practices and documented procedures are well-received by customers as they remove ambiguity, but that they also constrain the creative potential of teams. Similarly, Janz, Colquitt, and Noe (1997) argued that horizontal interdependence constrains the different ways in which individuals can perform their work, such that the positive influence of autonomy on work motivation gets neutralized.

So far, our discussion has treated horizontal interdependence in work teams mostly as a dichotomous variable, differentiating between autonomous, divisionally organized teams and interdependent, functionally specialized teams. Even though this reflects the way in which interdependent task structures have often been investigated (cf. Hollenbeck et al., 2002), it is important to note that the two structures can also be blended in one approach. For example, Ellis et al. (2003) found in a command and control context that both a functional and a divisional structure were associated with inferior team learning for different reasons. In a largely uncoupled structure, the learning task was too big and complex for individuals to comprehend, which resulted in less learning. In a tightly structured system, the learning task was reduced in scope; however, the specialization of team members made it impossible to double-check or replicate what was learned by any one person. In contrast, a hybrid structure that created "learning partners" in which two individuals shared expertise and information-processing responsibilities was associated with superior learning outcomes.

The findings of Ellis et al. (2003) may also explain the curvilinear effects that Stewart and Barrick (2000) found for behavioral tasks; in general, these findings reflect the larger literature that suggests that there are negative features associated with either very tightly coupled teams (low team member autonomy and satisfaction, less creativity, higher conflict) and highly uncoupled teams (less standardization and customer satisfaction, less communication and helping, more variability caused by individual differences) when it comes to task allocation structures. Overall, these results suggest that the effectiveness of horizontal interdependence and autonomy should always be evaluated with respect to the specific criteria at hand, but that in most cases, it seems that loosely coupled teams will probably be the safest bet in terms of avoiding well-documented problems of alternative task allocation structures.

Although not directly investigating horizontal task structure per se, several research streams within the teams literature have investigated the role of functional specialization and how this is associated with team functioning. In the following three sections, we review research on three related topics relevant to functional specialization in teams: transactive memory systems (TMS), cross-functional team compositions, and intrapersonal cross-functionality. We have identified these topics as emerging research streams in which researchers have made significant advances over the last decade, justifying a systematic review.

Transactive Memory Systems

Consistent with the idea to assign functionally specialized roles to individual team members, transactive memory systems (TMS) seek to better coordinate and use expertise in teams in order to solve complex problems (Austin, 2003). Building on the work of Wegner (1986, 1995), Austin (2003) conceptualized transactive memory systems as being composed of four distinct aspects: knowledge stock, knowledge specialization, transactive memory consensus, and transactive memory accuracy. Knowledge stock refers to the absolute amount of knowledge that is available to a team. As such, it captures the unique individual knowledge that is represented in a team. Knowledge specialization refers to the degree to which members' knowledge overlaps with knowledge of other group members. The smaller the overlap between group members' knowledge, the more knowledge specialization occurs. Transactive memory consensus is a third, important aspect of transactive memory systems, describing the extent to which group members agree about who has what knowledge. Finally, transactive memory accuracy specifies the extent to which mental representations of knowledge distributions overlap with actual knowledge distributions in teams. Transactive memory consensus can be viewed as a necessary, but not sufficient prerequisite for transactive memory accuracy.

Clearly, teams that develop highly specialized and refined transactive memory systems become a tightly coupled unit, and in a study of 27 teams structured around different product lines, Austin (2003) found that the development of transactive memory systems predicted group goal performance, external group evaluations, and internal group evaluations. On the other hand, these kinds of highly specialized and interdependent teams were found by Hollenbeck, Ilgen, Sego, Hedlund, and Major

(1995) to be much more negatively impacted by turnover or the momentary loss of access to any one team member, making them highly unstable in terms or their performance.

Even though TMS is conceptualized as a dynamic concept, most research has failed to acknowledge how TMS develops over time. In a conceptual article, Brandon and Hollingshead (2004) made a first step in this direction, suggesting that task type is an important factor in influencing how TMS develops over time. According to Brandon and Hollingshead (2004), teams must converge in their TMS in order to promote team efficiency and effectiveness. They introduce the notions of task representation and the task-expertise-person (TEP) unit as basic constructs involved in transactive memory development, and they provide a dynamic model of how TEP units are constructed, evaluated, and utilized. Over time, high performing teams converge on an optimal state in which there is a high level of accuracy and shared information regarding who is an expert on different elements of the larger overall task.

Even though convergence in TMS is a desirable end state, it is important to note that the process of reaching convergence in TMS can be a difficult one. In order to reach convergence in TMS, team members must be willing to reexamine their individual representations of team knowledge structures in a continuous dialogue with group members. Often, this process will be accompanied by conflict, as diverging mental representations of team knowledge or responsibilities will become apparent. Even though early research on conflict suggested that such a task-focused type of conflict can be beneficial for team functioning (cf. Jehn, 1994), more recent research negates this finding. A recent meta-analysis conducted by De Dreu and Weingart (2003) revealed that task type is moderately and negatively associated with team performance. For the study of TMS, this implies that teams have to engage in a constructive negotiation of individual representations of team knowledge structures in order to avoid the negative effect of task conflict on team performance. Only then will the development of converging TMS outweigh the costs associated with it. In other words, teams need to develop an atmosphere in which team members find it acceptable to engage in task-related conflict.

Consistent with this idea, Lovelace, Shapiro, and Weingart (2001) found that the negative effect of task disagreement was attenuated by the extent to which group members felt confident to express task-related doubts and how these doubts were expressed in teams. The importance of developing TMS through a positive communication atmosphere has been reaffirmed in a recent conceptual article by Brodbeck, Kerschreiter, Mojzisch, and Schulz-Hardt (2007). They argue that the development of TMS will reduce asymmetries in information processing that can undermine effective group decision making. Hence, they suggest that teams should develop team norms according to which team members try to gather all available information as accurately and completely as possible.

Van der Vegt and Bunderson (2005) further suggested that collective identification can serve as a buffer against the negative impact of different knowledge structures in teams. Investigating the effect of expertise diversity in multidisciplinary teams, they found that team identification moderated the effect of expertness diversity on team learning and performance. Specifically, expertness diversity was negatively related to team learning and performance when team identification was low, but exhibited a positive effect when team identification was high.

Gurtner, Tschan, Semmer, and Naegele (2007) investigated the extent to which teams can be trained in how they reflect on team processes. Administering a reflexivity intervention to hierarchically structured teams, they find that higher reflexivity is associated with improved communication, similarity in mental models, and ultimately, performance. Overall, the previous findings suggest that teams can develop convergence in TMS, without necessarily creating a destructive task or relationship conflict. In doing so, careful reflection on and management of communication norms, decision procedures, and collective identification are critical.

Failure to establish convergence in TMS and to resolve conflict has several negative consequences for teams. For example, Langfred (2007) suggests that team conflict not only has negative process-related effects, but also structure-related effects. Specifically, he finds that increased team conflict is associated with lower intrateam team trust. This effect will, in turn, loosen future task interdependencies in teams. As such, conflict not only leads to poor processes and performance, but it also destroys the structural foundations on which the team has been built. Interestingly, this sets the stage of employing coupling as a dependent variable, in the sense that over time, team members may reevaluate the constraint/freedom balance associated with any one task structure, and then choose to decouple based on that analysis. Thus, the gains/losses associated with the freedoms/constraints of either tight or loose coupling over time are being constantly evaluated by team members, who adjust their coupling based on their experience, which again, suggests a movement to loosely coupled ties, as opposed to tight coupling or uncoupling.

Cross-Functional Teams

Transactive memory systems are typically built from relatively homogeneous and flexible members who opt to specialize in different directions for efficiency purposes, and subsequently these individuals take off in different developmental trajectories. In many organizational contexts, however, this specialization is already embodied in individuals who are chosen to perform unique and specialized roles in teams. Specifically, cross-functional teams are composed of group members with different functional backgrounds or research disciplines, such as marketing, finance, or human resource management (Keller, 2001). This diverse background implies an inevitable horizontal interdependence among highly specialized group members.

Cross-functional teams try to capitalize on multiple sources of information and perspective that result from members' diverse functional backgrounds, making them the "method of choice by which high-technology organizations generate and deploy new products and processes" (Keller, 2001, p. 547). And indeed, cross-functional teams have been found to increase schedule and budget performance in 93 research and new product development teams (Keller, 2001). This positive effect was mediated through external communication, operationalized as the amount of task-related communication with individuals outside the research and new product development team. In other words, the diverse background of team members with different areas of expertise and unique external social networks improves external communication and ultimately team outcomes. Interestingly, however, the positive effects of functional diversity also appear to have their price: in the same study, Keller (2001) found that functional diversity was also associated with increased job stress and reduced group cohesiveness.

In a study of the effects of individual self-management on team effectiveness, Uhl-Bien and Graen (1998) further argued that the highly interdependent nature of group processes in cross-functional teams requires a high degree of individual commitment to high technical standards and teamwork. Uhl-Bien and Graen (1998) defined self-management as the extent to which individuals monitor and manage their own work, irrespective of interdependencies in a team. As such, individual self-management is different from team self-management in which team members self-manage team processes such as hiring, firing, scheduling, operating procedures, or disciplining. They predicted and found that self-management was beneficial for functional teams, but not for cross-functional teams. In fact, self-management even exerted a weak, negative effect on team effectiveness in cross-functional teams, again illustrating how tight coupling reduces the impact of individual differences. Despite their negative effect on team effectiveness, cross-functional teams were associated with lower perceptions of bureaucratic obstacles in the organization. This finding is consistent with Keller's (2001) finding that cross-functional teams are associated with improved external communication. By interacting with diverse organizational units, cross-functional units appear to be more flexible and adaptive to environmental changes, relying much less on the regulating influence of the organizational bureaucracy.

Cross-Functionality as Intrapersonal Dimension

Bunderson and Sutcliffe (2002) made a compelling case for differentiating among different types of functional diversity in research on management teams. Bunderson and Sutcliffe (2002) note that most research had explicitly or implicitly conceptualized functional diversity as the degree to which people differ from one another in their functional background. This ignores the possibility that individual team members often bring a diverse functional background to their team. Bunderson and Sutcliffe (2002) referred to the interpersonal type of diversity as *dominant function* diversity, whereas *intrapersonal functional* diversity refers to the degree to which individual group members unite diverse functional backgrounds in one person. According to Bunderson and Sutcliffe (2002), dominant function diversity exacerbates demands for team communication and coordination, making it difficult for teams to exploit the unique knowledge and background of all team members. Conversely, they suggested that teams characterized by high intrapersonal functional diversity may exploit their diverse backgrounds by enabling team members to relate to the background of other team members. As such, intrapersonal functional diversity creates a shared language in cross-functional teams that transcends traditional functional boundaries.

Marks, Sabella, Burke, and Zaccaro (2002) further found, in two experiments, that cross-training in shared knowledge structures enhanced the development of shared team-interaction models, coordination, and team performance. By using the typology of Bunderson and Sutcliffe (2002), we can view these studies as an experimental manipulation of intrapersonal functional diversity in teams. Both the studies of Marks and colleagues (2002) and Bunderson and Sutcliffe (2002) emphasize the positive effect of intrapersonal functional diversity on shared team-interaction models, which allow teams to capitalize on the entire range of functional diversity represented in teams. By creating a shared language among team members, intrapersonal functionality will also reduce the potential for team conflict.

It is important to note, however, that there are limits to the degree to which team members in functionally diverse teams can acquire knowledge of the functional background of all other team members. Today's project teams in organizations are often composed of members with highly specialized backgrounds. Believing that all team members can be familiarized with the entire inventory of knowledge, skills, and experiences is unrealistic. There are clear limits with respect to the intrapersonal functional diversity that can be obtained in teams. For example, it is unrealistic to expect a pediatric anesthetist to fully acquire the knowledge of a pediatric brain surgeon, and vice versa. Thus, we again see how tight horizontal coupling can both constrain and free individuals at the same time. The brain surgeon is free to devote a lifetime to the study of his or her craft, without devoting his or lifetime to the craft of anesthesiology, but at the same time, during actual surgery, his actions and decisions are constrained by the presence of a cross-sectional, tightly linked team member.

Vertical Interdependence: Team Decision-making Structures
Practical Example

Earlier, in the process of defining and illustrating the concept of horizontal interdependence and task allocation structure, we used the example of a set of four students who have been formed into one team to conduct four case studies that involve four separate industries, where each case study has four parts. We confronted this team with a choice to employ a tightly coupled functional structure, high in specialization and high in coordination requirements, or a loosely coupled divisional structure,

low in specialization but also low in coordination requirements. We also showed how this basic choice regarding tight versus loose coupling constrains and frees individual members at the same time, and how this serves as a key element of task decomposition processes, transactional memory systems, and cross-functional teams. We also showed that there is no "one-best-way" to structure teams along this dimension, but instead, the literature is littered with curvilinear and contingency effects that make choosing a specific structure a complicated decision.

In the face of this literature or, perhaps based on their own previous experience working in teams structured in alternative ways, it is easy to imagine how this set of four students might disagree on which of the two task allocation structures to choose. Student A may prefer the functional structure, whereas Student B might prefer the divisional approach. Student C might argue for a hybrid structure in which the research and analysis tasks are combined into a single role, but the writing and presentation are combined into a second unique role. Student D may argue for combining the writing and presentation roles into a single role, but keeping the research and analysis roles separate, and then adding a new "coordinator or leader role" for overseeing the whole process, ensuring standardization and seamless integration of the different roles.

In the face of this total lack of agreement regarding task allocation structure, how should this team decide how to go forward? Clearly, in any team context, there must be some mechanism in place to resolve these discrepant views, merging the four sets of different preferences into a single decision that will be implemented by the team. Thus, just as task allocation structure has to be addressed when breaking down a mission too large for any one individual to perform, so too, collective decision-making structures must be set in place for the inevitable situation in which team members disagree with respect to the best course of action.

Construct Definition

Again, although there are an infinite number of ways to accomplish this objective, two alternatives stand out when one examines the literature on this concept. These include hierarchical decision-making structures, in which a formal leader has unilateral authority to make decisions for the team after seeking input from the team members (Bonaccio & Dalal, 2006; Hollenbeck et al., 1995), or self-managing teams that resolve their own discrepancies via either consensus or, if this breaks down, voting procedures.

In defining vertical interdependence, we draw on previous research on team self-management, which describes self-managing teams as work structures in which employees have "discretion over such decisions as methods of work, task schedules, and assignment of members to different tasks; and compensation and feedback for the performance for the group as a whole" (Hackman, cited in Manz & Sims, 1987, p. 106).

As such, team members with hierarchical leaders are freed from the necessity of battling out each and every disagreement whether large or small, but are constrained from making their own decisions, and may be forced to implement a decision that they would have not made on their own. Teams with powerful centralized leadership are tightly coupled in the sense that they can move quickly as one; however, some individuals may be bound to decisions that may differ from what they would have chosen based on their own individual volition. In this case, it is more difficult to see individual team members as the "figure," and they revert to the "ground" in one's perceptual experience.

The only manner for teams to arrive at collective decisions that do not force one member to implement a decision that he or she does not support is to arrive at consensus. If consensus is achieved, then the team is loosely coupled in the sense that each member has been convinced that the course of action is the one she would have chosen on her own, and hence the link between the team's action and her own personal volition is not severed, as it could be with a decision made by a hierarchical leader. Moreover, the discussion and debate process used to arrive at consensus makes each person's inputs and viewpoints highly salient, and thus it is much easier to see individuals as the "figure" and the team as "ground." Whereas self-managing teams are not constrained by a hierarchical leader and are free to voice their own opinions, if they strive for consensus they may be constrained by time limits that run out prior to ever having reached consensus.

Short of consensus, the team could vote on the decision, which still leaves the team decoupled from an external leader, and thus somewhat loosely structured. Indeed, if the voting process has members "raise their hands," then the individuals quickly become the "figure" and the team becomes the "ground," and the divisions within the overall team may even promote the perceptions of subgroups and faultiness (Homan et al., 2008; Lau & Murnighan,

2005). When those who lose out in the voting fail to rally behind the majority decision, the team as "figure" is lost altogether, and one instead perceives the existence of two teams. Thus, as a collective decision-making mechanism, voting comes with its own set of freedoms and constraints. The team is freed from endless discussions and not yoked to the decisions of uncompromising members who cannot be moved from their own viewpoint. However, voting blocks can constrain the decision-making effectiveness of teams by overruling or out-voting some well-informed set of minority dissenters, who, over time, may disengage from the team. Thus, voting systems lie somewhere between tightly coupled hierarchical systems and less tightly coupled consensus structures when it comes to decision-making interdependence.

Comparing Self-managing Teams with Hierarchical Teams

Although there has been a great deal of research on self-managing teams, most of this research contrasts hierarchical or externally led teams on the one hand, with self-managed teams on the other hand. Research has not differentiated between self-managed teams that resolve disagreements by requiring a consensus-building process versus self-managed teams that vote for different decision options. Instead, the extant research has focused on the role that external leaders play in decoupling self-managing teams from other teams and the larger organizational context. Thus, this research shows that external leadership still plays an important role for self-managing teams, even though self-managing teams can substitute for some of the functions traditionally performed by formal leaders. For example, Griffin, Patterson, and West (2001) found that supervisory support exhibited a smaller effect on job satisfaction in companies with high levels of teamwork, compared to companies with low levels of teamwork. This finding suggests that high levels of teamwork shift team members' focus from organizational leaders to the team, thereby substituting the motivating influence that leadership often performs for individuals at work.

It is likely, however, that self-managing teams have to undergo a transition period until they can function effectively. For example, Douglas and Gardner (2004) argued that managers often find it difficult to relinquish control over decision-making processes to self-managing teams. In a study of self-managing teams in a major aluminum products manufacturer, they found that managers relied too heavily on hard influence tactics (i.e., coalition building, legitimating, and pressure) after the organization had adopted self-directed work teams, even though soft influence tactics (i.e., inspirational appeals and ingratiation) would have been more appropriate. By using soft influence tactics, Douglas and Gardner (2004) argued, managers can communicate trust in the ability of a team to self-manage, whereas hard influence tactics are associated with low collective efficacy, subordinate conformity, and a lack of trust in management, all of which are detrimental for self-managing teams. Over time, however, managers decreased their use of hard influence tactics such that the fit between influence tactics and decision-making structure was gradually improved.

External Leadership for Self-Managing Teams

The two studies by Griffin and colleagues (2001) and Douglas and Gardner (2004) suggest that external leadership of self-managing teams is either not very important, or that it is most effective when it uses a hands-off approach that does not interfere with the autonomy of the team. There is, however, also a large literature documenting the critical role that leadership plays for self-managing teams. This literature suggests that self-managing teams do not operate in a vacuum. Instead, self-managing teams are influenced by the extent to which external leaders (leaders to whom a team reports; they are not members of the work team) and internal leaders (leaders who are members of the work team) create interdependencies with other organizational units or managerial levels in the organization. Self-managing teams can have internal leadership, external leadership, and a combination of both internal and external leadership.

Tesluk and Mathieu (1999) argued that external leaders can provide important resources that shield the team and free them from resource dependencies in the organization. In terms of coupling, this implies that if teams are going to be making their own decisions, they need to be buffered, and essentially uncoupled, from other teams and the task environment by their external leader. Thus, the freedom that self-managing teams have regarding decision making must be supported by a buffering mechanism that decouples them from other self-managing teams in order to have coordination at the organizational level, and this seems to be the critical role for external leaders of self-managing teams. External leaders can also further influence goals, directions, and decisions in self-managing teams so that the decisions they render will be consistent with larger organizational objectives. They can help formulate team objectives, which self-managing teams then refine by deciding how to pace work, allocate tasks, schedule work, or implement work and problem-solving procedures.

Reaffirming the influence of external leaders, internal leaders can encourage other team members to plan their own work, to set performance goals, and to monitor their own as well as others' performance. In their study of 88 maintenance and construction road crews, Tesluk and Mathieu (1999) found a moderately strong, positive correlation between external and internal leadership of self-managing teams. This suggests that external leaders are generally supported in their efforts to encourage team self-management by internal team leaders. In this study, both external and internal leadership also exhibited a positive effect on the frequency with which teams engaged in problem management actions and strategies in order to remove performance barriers. Interestingly, however, only external leadership was positively associated with team performance, whereas internal leadership was associated with a strong increase in team viability, operationalized as team cohesion, team satisfaction, and the intention to remain a team member. The positive effect on team viability did not occur for external leadership. Apparently, internal leadership plays a more important role in determining how team members evaluate their team, both in cognitive and affective terms. On the other hand, external leadership appears to lay important foundations for team self-management, without influencing team members' cognitions and feelings about their team. These results suggest that both internal and external leadership of self-managing teams are important and that they can reinforce each other to create an environment in which self-managing teams can function effectively.

Based on in-depth critical incident interviews, Druskat and Wheeler (2003) further elaborated on the role of external leaders in self-managing teams. They argued that the role of an external leader is particularly complex when compared with the role of traditional team leaders. For example, external team leaders have only little legitimate control over decision-making processes in teams. Hence, they must identify different mechanisms through which they can influence self-managing teams, such as referent or expert power. The leadership role of external leaders is further complicated by the fact that they are equipped with little legitimate power, while overseeing a large number of teams at the same time. Druskat and Wheeler (2003) noted that the transition to the role of an external leader is often associated with role ambiguity for leaders, as their traditional understanding of team leadership is no longer applicable to their current position. All of these factors add to the high levels of complexity that external leaders face.

According to Druskat and Wheeler (2003), however, the most important factor contributing to the complexity of the external leadership role is the requirement to connect largely autonomous teams with the overall organization. Specifically, external leaders are required to span the boundary of the team with the organization. Druskat and Wheeler (2003) emphasized that this task is particularly challenging because external leaders are often not co-located with the teams whose goals and actions they are supposed to align with the overall strategy of the organization. This requires them to continuously switch between a team leader role and an outsider role while working with important constituents of their teams. In their role as team leader, they influence team members such that team actions are consistent with the overall strategy of the organization. They build relationships with team members and give and seek information to and from team members, thereby raising their awareness of strengths and developmental opportunities of group members. In addition, they empower teams to make decisions, while coaching them in critical stages of the decision-making process.

In their organizational role, external leaders develop a sense for social and political developments in the organization that are relevant for their teams. External leaders also seek to clarify the strategic direction of the organization in order to understand how individual teams can contribute to organizational effectiveness. In order to enable their teams to function effectively, external leaders also must ensure that decision makers in the organization provide necessary resources for the team. Overall, the findings from this case study conducted by Druskat and Wheeler (2003) reiterate that external team leadership is not only a hands-off approach, a conclusion that could be drawn from earlier studies on self-managing teams. Instead, external leaders perform both active and observing roles in the teams that they lead, buffering these self-managed teams from having to integrate their efforts into the larger organizational context in which they are embedded.

The notion that leaders should play a more active role in self-managing teams is consistent with research on team empowerment. Kirkman and Rosen (1997) posited that for self-managing teams to be effective, they require more than mere decision-making authority. Kirkman and Rosen (1997) suggested that self-managing teams also have to experience feelings of collective efficacy, meaningfulness, and impact, all of which are states that can be enhanced by the boundary-spanning functions which external team leaders perform, according to the model developed by Druskat and Wheeler (2003). In a study of 111 work teams in four organizations, Kirkman and Rosen (1999) found additional support for the important role that external leaders can play in self-managing teams. They found that external leaders can contribute to the effectiveness of self-managing work teams by using team members' ideas and suggestions in decisions, by encouraging teams to set goals and to monitor individual and team performance, and by providing genuine trust to the team. Overall, these findings are consistent with the results by Druskat and Wheeler (2003).

The study by Kirkman and Rosen (1999), however, also established an important link between the role of external team leaders and critical team states, such as experienced potency, meaningfulness, autonomy, and impact. Moreover, Kirkman and Rosen (1999) demonstrated that these critical team states are in turn related to a number of important criteria, such as team productivity, team proactivity, customer service quality, job satisfaction, and organizational and team commitment. As such, their study sheds light on the mediating mechanisms through which the external leadership of self-managing teams enhances superior team performance (cf. our discussion of Tesluk & Mathieu, 1999).

Mathieu, Gilson, and Ruddy (2006) further elaborated the model proposed by Kirkman and Rosen (1999). Utilizing a structural model, they proposed that external team leadership will enhance perceptions of team empowerment, which will in turn lead to improved team processes, and ultimately customer satisfaction and quantitative performance. Overall, the previously discussed studies emphasize the important role of external leadership in self-managing teams. Consistent with Mathieu et al. (2006), we conclude that effective external leadership is an important facilitator for team empowerment, whereas "a lack of effective external leader support can result in teams that feel 'abandoned' by their organizations" (Mathieu et al., 2006; p. 100), where "abandoned" implies being decoupled.

Team Self-Management as an Emergent Property

Even though the use of self-managing teams is generally conceptualized as a dichotomy—organizations use them or they do not—there is also evidence that self-management can occur in traditional team structures. For example, Cohen, Chang, and Ledford (1997) found that self-managing leadership behaviors were perceived as occurring only slightly more frequently in self-managing teams, when compared to traditional work teams. They reported that the factor structure of self-management was largely unaffected by whether teams were self-managing or were organized in traditional team structures. Moreover, self-managing leadership behaviors in either team structure (self-managing or traditional) were associated with higher perceived quality of work life and self-rated effectiveness. Based on these findings, Cohen et al. (1997) concluded that self-managing leadership behaviors exhibit very similar relationships to outcomes in both self-managing and traditional team structures. Hence, self-managing leadership behaviors are not only the result of team empowerment, but also of the degree to which team members feel that it is appropriate to self-manage. This can in turn be a function of cultural norms and values.

Consistent with this idea, Kirkman and Shapiro (1997) developed a conceptual model in which cultural values determine the extent to which individuals resist the implementation of self-management and the introduction of teamwork. For example, individuals high in power distance desire a strong leader figure who directs team actions. The notion of self-management is in stark contrast to this desire. Similarly, individuals with a low doing orientation that is associated with a weaker work ethic will find it difficult to adapt to self-management in the workplace, as they dislike engaging in persistent, goal-directed behavior. Individuals high in determinism generally doubt that their fate is within their own control. Hence, the concept of self-management, in which individuals take control of their own work, is antithetical to their self-understanding. Kirkman and Shapiro (1997) further proposed that cultural values will influence the degree to which employees oppose the concept of teamwork, suggesting that employees with a strong individualistic orientation are more likely to perceive group-based rewards as unfair and to resist the introduction of teamwork. According to Kirkman and Shapiro (1997), both resistance to self-management and resistance to the introduction of teams will in turn be negatively associated with team effectiveness. Overall, this model strongly suggests that the effectiveness of self-managing work teams will depend on cultural values in the countries where they are implemented.

By drawing on these conceptual arguments, Drach-Zahavy (2004) conducted an empirical test of how cultural values influence the degree to which individuals support teams. Specifically, she investigated how cultural values moderate the effect of job enrichment on team support. Job enrichment constitutes a procedure in which individuals are awarded greater job autonomy, control, and skill variety in their work. In short, job enrichment creates complete jobs with high individual autonomy and accountability, which run counter to the interdependencies typically found in teamwork. Based on these arguments, Drach-Zahavy (2004) hypothesized and found that job enrichment practices are negatively associated with team support, but that this effect can be attenuated by enforcing a low power distance culture and collectivistic values, which remind individuals of the larger objectives of the entire work team and organization.

Providing further support for the important role of collectivistic cultural values in the context of self-managing teams, Man and Lam (2003) found that the relationship of group autonomy with group cohesiveness was contingent upon such values. Man and Lam (2003) proposed that increasing group autonomy will make group behavior more salient, an effect that is going to be particularly pronounced in individualistic countries, where collectives generally have a lower meaning than in collectivistic cultures. In other words, individuals will already feel a strong sense of commitment and ownership to their team in collectivistic cultures, irrespective of the degree of autonomy awarded to this team. Thus, an increase in group autonomy will not dramatically increase feelings of commitment to the team, which were already high to begin with. Conversely, individuals in individualistic cultures start with low commitment to their team, but are particularly affected by the increase in group autonomy, which puts group processes suddenly center stage.

This finding appears to contradict the moderating influence of collectivistic values on the relationship of job enrichment with team support reported by Drach-Zahavy (2004), where collectivistic values were found to contribute to higher team support. A closer look at the investigated relationships, however, can resolve this seeming contradiction. The study of Drach-Zahavy (2004) was interested in the influence of job enrichment practices on team support, defining job enrichment practices as a procedure that created larger individual autonomy and accountability. As such, job enrichment decreases horizontal interdependence. On the other hand, the study by Man and Lam (2003) takes group autonomy as its starting point, a concept that is negatively associated with job enrichment practices.

The Role of HR Practices for Team Self-Management

As we noted at the outset of this chapter, although teams are increasingly using team-based structures, there has been a reluctance to fully realign the HR practice of organizations that are still grounded in the treatment of individuals as individuals. Some of the research on self-managing teams has addressed this issue. Kirkman and Rosen (1999) were among the first to discuss the role of HR practices for team self-management. They argued that the introduction of team-based rewards, the experience of receiving or delivering cross-training, and the opportunity to make important staff decisions will enhance the experience of critical team states, such as team potency and perceived meaningfulness of work, which are in turn related to successful team empowerment. Kirkman and Rosen (1999) found support for this prediction in their study of 111 work teams in four organizations. In a similar vein, Mathieu et al. (2006) proposed that providing teams with the necessary skills and abilities to handle the task and decisions at hand constitutes a critical task for HR departments. They further suggested that HR departments should provide feedback to self-managing teams in order to ensure that teams can learn from past experiences. Both of these predictions were supported in a sample of 121 service technician teams.

An Integrated Contingency View of Horizontal and Vertical Autonomy

To this point, we have treated vertical interdependence as a unique dimension of coupling separate from horizontal interdependence, but several studies in the literature can be identified that have either integrated or confounded the two dimensions. Individuals in teams that are tightly coupled on both dimensions lose a great deal of their own individual autonomy in the sense that (a) they depend a great deal on other team members to do elements of the task that they lack the ability or interest to

do, and (b) they are dependent upon a team leader to make decisions for the team that may or may not reflect what individual team members would do if they were acting alone. In contrast, when both vertical and horizontal interdependence are low, individuals may have great freedom, and one may start to struggle to find the team in that specific instance of figure-ground confusion. Finally, the two dimensions need not be aligned at all, and team members might be tightly coupled horizontally and loosely coupled vertically, and vice versa.

Langfred (2000) proposed an integrated contingency view of horizontal and vertical autonomy, and found empirically that individual autonomy (low horizontal coupling) exerted a positive effect on group effectiveness in a military setting characterized by tight vertical coupling (i.e., clear lines of decision-making authority). In the same sample, however, group autonomy (low vertical coupling) was negatively associated with group effectiveness. In contrast, within a different sample of groups working in a social service agency, Langfred (2000) obtained the opposite pattern of results. In this context, where the team members were loosely coupled vertically, individual autonomy was negatively related to group effectiveness, whereas group autonomy was positively related to group effectiveness.

Providing further support to this contingency model of autonomy, Uhl-Bien and Graen (1998) predicted and found that *individual* self-management (loose vertical coupling) was beneficial for functional teams (tight horizontal coupling), but not for cross-functional teams characterized by a high degree of horizontal interdependence. In fact, self-management even had a small negative effect on group effectiveness in cross-functional teams. It is important to note that these findings provide a contrast to the long-standing assumption in the work design literature that individual autonomy is generally beneficial for performance (Hackman & Oldham, 1976), and illustrate that tightly coupled structures, which place the team as figure and individuals as ground, reduce the role of individual-level work characteristics in terms of predicting team-level performance.

Apart from their effect on work group effectiveness, horizontal and vertical autonomy also exerted differential effects on group cohesiveness. In the previously discussed study, Langfred (2000) found that group autonomy had a positive effect on group cohesiveness, whereas individual autonomy had a negative effect on this same outcome. Sewell (1998) further elaborated on the concept of group autonomy and pointed to potential negative effects that team self-management (loose vertical coupling) can have in modern work structures. Based on qualitative data, he suggested that today's electronic surveillance systems, which deliver precise data on the productivity of individual team members, may undermine lateral trust among team members in self-managed teams. In other words, the availability of data on minute differentials in individuals' contributions to team outcomes leads team members to internalize organizational norms and objectives. As such, self-managed teams establish powerful horizontal control processes that replace traditional forms of control in organizations.

Sewell (1998) summarizes this paradox by noting that "the constant and supportive interaction of electronic surveillance and the peer group scrutiny allows organizations to cede a degree of discretion to teams while increasing the probability that it is then exercised in line with the organization's goals and objectives" (p. 422). Sewell's (1998) article is unique in research on team autonomy, as it goes beyond functional arguments explaining the emergence and superiority of self-managed teams. Instead, he provides a powerful account of how the emergence of self-managed teams changes the very nature of how team members conceptualize their individual role in their team and organization.

More recently, Langfred (2004) investigated the moderating role of trust and monitoring on the relationship of individual autonomy with group performance. He found that high trust in teams will make team members more reluctant to monitor other group members. Monitoring activities, however, were found to be an important boundary condition for the effect of individual autonomy on team performance. Specifically, for teams with high trust and little monitoring, individual autonomy was negatively associated with team performance. These findings further attest to the power of peer monitoring for teams, as proposed by Sewell (1998).

While this research tries to separate the unique and distinctive aspects of horizontal versus vertical interdependence, other research seems to confound the two dimensions. Consistent with Langfred (2000), Drach-Zahavy and Freund (2007) adopted a contingency perspective on team structure in their investigation of how different types of stress influence team effectiveness in teams characterized by different levels of individual and group autonomy. Specifically, Drach-Zahavy and Freund (2007) differentiated between mechanistic team structures

and organic team structures. They characterized mechanistic team structures as having largely routinized jobs, pervasive rules, and a high degree of formalization and record keeping. Organic structures, on the other hand, are described as providing rich job feedback, task identity, and [individual] autonomy. Drach-Zahavy and Freund (2007) found that mechanistic structures thrived on quantitative stress, whereas organic structures produced better results when facing high levels of qualitative stress. They argue that mechanistic structures are primarily designed to increase the efficiency of operations, which explains why they are amenable to high quantitative stress. Conversely, qualitative stress increases the demand for teamwork, which makes organic structures the better fit for task environments characterized by high qualitative stress.

Even though Drach-Zahavy and Freund's (2007) hypotheses were generally supported in a sample of 73 health care teams, we see their study as a prime example of how extant research has sometimes failed to differentiate between horizontal and vertical autonomy. Their operationalization of organic structures focuses exclusively on individual jobs, ignoring the social embeddedness of work. Specifically, this study does not measure the extent to which teams self-manage, that is, it does not measure the extent to which teams assume control over important teamwork processes such as staffing, disciplining, communicating, information processing, or rewarding. These issues, however, should be discussed in modern conceptualizations of organic structures, given the fact that work is increasingly structured around self-managed teams. In other words, research should no longer ignore the social embeddedness of team structure. Only by integrating these social components of autonomy can we differentiate meaningfully between the effects of individual self-management/horizontal autonomy and team self-management/vertical autonomy on team processes and team performance

Outcome Interdependence: Team Reward Structures
Practical Example

In introducing our discussion of horizontal and vertical interdependence, we used the example of a set of four students who have been formed into one team to conduct four case studies that involve four separate industries, where each case study has four parts. We showed how horizontal and vertical interdependence are separate dimensions of coupling that can be conceptualized in 2 x 2 terms.

Tightly coupled teams employ functional structures and centralized decision-making structures that make it easy to see the team, but difficult to see the individuals in the figure-ground paradox of teams. Thus, a tightly coupled team in this context might have team members who specialize in separate components of the task (research, analysis, and writing/presenting) that are sequentially handed off from one person to the next, and resolve any disagreements by having some emergent leader unilaterally make the team's decision.

Alternatively, loosely coupled teams employ divisional structures and collective decision-making processes that emphasize consensus-building systems (of voting procedures) that make it easy to see individuals as "figure" (especially uncompromising members who can bring the process to a standstill) but more difficult to see the team as a holistic identity. Thus, in a loosely coupled student team, each member would go off and do all four parts of the assignment on their own, eliminating the need for sequential handoffs. When it came time to integrate the distinct reports, if there were disagreement about how to best merge these four subreports into one seamless report, the team would debate the merits of each, trying to unify all the individual preferences into one single preference.

Separate from how each person is coupled in terms of task allocation and decision-making authority, however, is the degree to which the students' grades are based on individual versus group-level outcomes. In this running example, the question becomes, regardless of how the team does the task, how will they be graded? On the one hand, one could totally ignore individual contributions and just give all students the exact same grade for the entire report, which results in a tightly coupled set of outcomes. On the other hand, one might try to assign grades to these four students so that each student is graded solely on that part of the project for which they were responsible. This would result in four different grades for each student, implying a loose coupling of outcomes.

Construct Definition

We will define *outcome interdependence* as the extent to which group members share the same goals and rewards for the work which they perform together, recognizing that even though goals and rewards may be directly coupled in many instances, this is not necessarily the case (Knight, Durham, & Locke, 2001). For example, as stated previously, many organizations have shifted toward more fluid, team-based work structures. In order to shift the focus of individuals' attention to team outcomes, organizations have started to use team-based goals in order to align individual actions with team objectives. Interestingly, however, the change to collective goal systems has often not been accompanied with an according change in reward structures—and instead, organizations offer only small incentives for team performance, despite a strong reliance on team goals. In fact, many organizations employ annual merit-based pay systems that actually place team members in competition with one another for variations in pay around a fixed unit average increase.

We now continue with a review and discussion of relevant research in this area. In this section, we review recent research that has identified positive aspects of outcome interdependence, such as its positive effect on collaboration, constructive controversy, conflict efficacy, and transactive memory systems. This will be followed by a discussion of research that demonstrates that outcome interdependence can also be a burden for teams, for example by decreasing the speed with which teams perform, or by increasing the risk of social loafing. As we have seen throughout this chapter, the research seems to warn against both uncoupled systems and tightly coupled systems, pointing to the need for balance and loosely coupled systems.

Positive Aspects of Outcome Interdependence

In a field study of 34 self-managing teams, Wageman (2001) investigated several structural team design features as predictors of team self-management and team effectiveness, the latter being operationalized as team performance, quality of group processes, and team member satisfaction. By drawing on Hackman's (1987) conceptual model of work-team effectiveness, Wageman (2001) differentiated between four structural team design variables that leaders can manipulate in an ideal setting: first, establishing a real team with clear and stable membership; second, giving teams a clear direction by developing a clear statement of purpose; third, providing teams with an enabling structure by choosing the appropriate team size, skill diversity, task interdependence, task goals, and strategy norms; fourth, providing teams with a supportive organizational context that recognizes and rewards excellent team performance. We view a clear direction, task goals, and group reward systems as three factors which, taken together, coincide with our definition of outcome interdependence, as provided earlier. For our discussion of the effect of outcome interdependence on team behavior, this study is important because it discusses both the absolute effect of goal structure and reward mechanisms on team processes and outcomes, as well as the relative magnitude of these effects when compared to other team design features.

Wageman's (2001) results identify outcome interdependence as one of the most powerful, if not the most powerful, structural team design feature. For example, team performance was most strongly associated with a clear direction, group rewards, and task interdependence, the first two reflecting outcome interdependence as we have defined it in this chapter. Similarly, the quality of group processes was best predicted by a clear direction, group rewards, strategy norms, and task objectives. Three of these four variables (with the exception of strategy norms) are again indicative of the outcome interdependence in teams. A clear direction and group rewards were also the two factors with the highest predictive validity for team self-management. Wageman (2001), however, also emphasized that team leaders often cannot control the team's purpose or the ways in which rewards are allocated. Instead, environmental and institutional forces would often determine these factors. This qualifies the large impact that outcome interdependence has for team outcomes—outcome interdependence presents a powerful leverage for team design, but only to the extent that it can be manipulated by team leaders.

The importance of outcome interdependence for group processes and outcomes was also demonstrated in a study of 88 three-person student teams by Harrison, Price, Gavin, and Florey (2002). The study found that outcome interdependence exhibited a positive effect on team collaboration, that is, the time team members spend in interactions. Collaboration then moderated the effects of different types of diversity on team social integration. By differentiating between surface- (demographic) and deep-level (psychological) diversity, the study showed that collaboration increased the salience of deep-level diversity over time, such that high levels of collaboration enhanced the negative effect of deep-level diversity on team social integration. The opposite effect was found for surface-level diversity, where high levels of collaboration weakened the negative effect of surface-level diversity on team social integration. In other words, surface-level diversity had a smaller negative effect on team social integration for teams with high levels of collaboration, when compared to teams with low levels of

collaboration. Team social integration in turn was positively associated with task performance. On the one hand, this study has a positive message by suggesting that outcome interdependence can alleviate the negative effects of demographic diversity on social integration and, ultimately, team performance. On the other hand, the findings of this study also suggest that outcome interdependence can be a double-edged sword by enhancing the negative effects of deep-level diversity (mediated by collaboration) on team social integration and team performance. We will return to the potentially negative effects of outcome interdependence later in this section.

The findings of Harrison et al. (2002) have been discussed extensively (Van Knippenberg & Schippers, 2007), in part because subsequent studies failed to replicate the differentiating moderating role of outcome interdependence for particular types of diversity. In particular, other studies contested the negative role of outcome interdependence for the effect of deep-level diversity on team social integration and team performance. For example, Alper, Tjosvold, and Law (1998) found in a study of 60 self-managing teams that cooperative goals were associated with constructive controversy in teams, such that team members were more willing to "share information, acknowledge each other's perspectives, communicate and influence effectively, exchange resources, assist and support each other, discuss opposing ideas openly, and use higher-quality reasoning" (p. 36). This finding suggests that cooperative goals can also be beneficial for teams characterized by high deep-level diversity—relying on higher quality reasoning and open discussions that establish a constructive team climate in which differences in values, beliefs, or personality can more easily be overcome. Indeed, Alper et al. (1998) reported that constructive controversy mediated the effect of cooperative goals on team confidence, which in turn promoted team effectiveness. Conversely, competitive team goals were found to be negatively related to constructive controversy, confidence, and effectiveness.

A related study by the same authors of 61 self-managing teams produced similar results (Alper, Tjosvold, & Law, 2000). In this study, Alper et al. (2000) investigated the effect of cooperative approaches to conflict on conflict efficacy and supervisory team performance ratings. Cooperative approaches to conflict were operationalized as an emphasis on mutual goals, understanding everyone's views, a focus on collective rewards, and incorporating different positions when developing joint solutions. Compared to the earlier study, this study takes a broader approach by defining outcome interdependence as only one of several aspects of a cooperative team environment. Similar to their findings obtained in the 1998 study, the authors reported a positive effect of a cooperative conflict approach on conflict efficacy, and, ultimately, supervisory effectiveness ratings.

Utilizing an input-process-output model, Zhang, Hempel, Han, and Tjosvold (2007) investigated the effect of cooperative goal interdependence on team performance, mediated by transactive memory system. Consistent with the findings reported by Alper et al. (1998, 2000) and Wageman (2001), Zhang et al. (2007) found a positive effect of cooperative goal interdependence on team performance. Interestingly, cooperative goal interdependence was strongly associated with transactive memory systems, exhibiting higher validities than the other two predictors included in the model (task interdependence and support for innovation). As suggested by Wageman (2001), this finding further attests to the important role of outcome interdependence for team design.

By adopting a motivated information-processing perspective, De Dreu (2007) predicted and found empirically that cooperative outcome interdependence is associated with improved information sharing, learning, and team effectiveness. Hence, cooperative outcome interdependence helps to uncover hidden profiles in groups. The positive effect of cooperative outcome interdependence on information sharing, learning, and team effectiveness were especially pronounced when team reflexivity was high.

It is important to note that the positive effect of outcome interdependence on team performance will not generalize to all task contexts. Investigating the moderating influence of outcome interdependence on emergent states in teams and team outcomes, Schippers, Hartog, Koopman, and Wienk (2003) predicted that outcome interdependence moderates the effect of team diversity on team reflexivity, satisfaction, commitment, and performance. Consistent with their predictions, they found that teams high on outcome interdependence are more reflexive when they are more diverse, whereas teams that were low on interdependence were found to be more reflexive when they were less diverse. Moreover, the effect of diversity on satisfaction and performance was also moderated by outcome interdependence, such that team outcomes were positively affected when groups were diverse and outcome interdependence was low, or when groups were highly diverse and outcome interdependence was high.

Also, Deutsch (1949) and Wageman (1995) suggested that collaborative rewards should be utilized in settings characterized by high task interdependence, whereas competitive rewards should be utilized in settings in which individuals work independently. Given that most organizations have started to organize their work around teams in which individuals work interdependently on their tasks, it is not surprising that the more recent studies on this topic have largely reported positive effects of outcome interdependence on team performance. This well-established finding suggests that one should match the degree of outcome interdependence with the level of task interdependence when designing teams.

Negative Aspects of Outcome Interdependence

More recent research, however, comes to a more nuanced conclusion. By investigating the effects of outcome interdependence on different performance criteria, Beersma et al. (2003) were able to demonstrate that outcome interdependence has both positive and negative consequences for team outcomes. Specifically, they found that teams perform better in terms of accuracy under a cooperative reward structure, whereas a competitive reward structure was associated with higher speed. This finding lends support to a contingency view of outcome interdependence, suggesting that the dimension of a task (speed vs. accuracy) that is most relevant in a specific setting should be matched with the corresponding reward structure (competitive vs. cooperative). Moreover, Beersma et al. (2003) found that the effect of outcome interdependence on team performance is contingent upon the interpersonal orientation of team members: extraverted and agreeable team members were found to enhance team performance under a cooperative reward structure, whereas teams with introverted and disagreeable team members performed better in a competitive setting. Interestingly, outcome interdependence had a particularly strong impact for team members with low performance, such that their speed was increased in a competitive structure and their accuracy was increased in a cooperative structure.

More recently, other more critical findings have been reported regarding the role of outcome interdependence in team settings, suggesting that outcome interdependence can in fact be a double-edged sword for teams. In a study of 144 student teams working together over the course of one semester, Price, Harrison, and Gavin (2006) investigated the role of identifiability of individual contributions for social loafing behavior. This study draws on a long tradition of research that has consistently shown that the identifiability of individual contributions to team performance reduces social loafing behavior in teams (Latané, Williams, & Harkins, 1979). As we have noted, when teams are tightly coupled in terms of horizontal and vertical interdependence, this yoking may make it difficult to see individuals as figures and instead place them in the ground. A tightly coupled structure reduces the identifiability of individual contributions and diffuses decision-making responsibility in a manner that promotes finger pointing when a group fails to accomplish its objectives. Similarly, collective goals and a collective reward structure imply reduced identifiability of individual contributions to teamwork, which should in turn increase social loafing in teams. With respect to social loafing, Price et al. (2006) reported a moderating effect, such that the relationship between dispensability and social loafing behavior was strengthened when the identifiability of individual contributions was rated as low. In other words, the absence of an individual evaluation structure is problematic when team members feel that their individual contributions are dispensable.

This finding seems to suggest that both individual-based and team-based evaluation structures should be employed in team design in order to capitalize on the advantages of each approach. Providing feedback to individual team members on their individual performance increases the identifiability of individual contributions, while simultaneously provided team feedback ensures the consistency of individuals' actions and goals with team objectives. Unfortunately, however, this conclusion oversimplifies the multiple-goal, multilevel character of team behavior. DeShon, Kozlowski, Schmidt, Milner, and Wiechmann (2004) found, in a laboratory study of 79 teams, that individuals in teams struggle if they receive feedback for both their individual and their team performance.

DeShon et al. (2004) argued that team members face a trade-off between maximizing individual goals or team goals. Empirical results provided support for this proposition: if team members were only provided with individual feedback, they focused their attention on individual performance, a decision that translated into the highest levels of individual performance. If team members were only provided

with team-level feedback, they focused on maximizing team performance, which was associated with the highest team-oriented performance. Combining both individual- and team-level feedback, however, was not associated with superior performance on any level, indicating that team members could not capitalize on multiple-goal feedback. Both the findings of Price et al. (2006) and DeShon et al. (2004) raise the question how teams can be designed such that individuals' performance is maximized, while at the same time securing alignment of individual actions with team objectives.

Barnes, Hollenbeck, Wagner, DeRue, Nahrgang, and Schwind (2008) addressed this conundrum by investigating how team members' decisions to engage in backing-up behavior affects their own performance, the performance of the beneficiary of backing-up behavior, as well as team performance. Prior research on teams portrayed backing-up behavior primarily as performance-enhancing (Porter 2005; Porter et al., 2003), but the study by Barnes et al. (2008) demonstrates that backing-up behavior can be costly for teams. Specifically, providers of backing-up behavior were found to neglect some of their own task duties, and beneficiaries of backing-up behavior were found to reduce their task work in a subsequent task. This effect was particularly pronounced when workload was distributed evenly among team members. This study provides further support to the notion that team members struggle when aligning individual behavior with team objectives, while at the same time trying to maintain the maximum level of performance in their individual work. This finding is largely consistent with the findings reported by DeShon et al. (2004), according to which team members were unable to capitalize on individual- and team-level feedback.

The majority of the previously discussed studies on outcome interdependence (or some variation of this construct) investigated the main effect of outcome interdependence on individual and team performance. A different approach was taken by Van der Vegt and his colleagues (2001), who investigated goal interdependence as a moderator of the effect of task interdependence on job satisfaction and team satisfaction (Van der Vegt, Emans, Van de Vliert, 2001). Their findings reaffirm the important role of outcome interdependence for team design: when goal interdependence was low, task interdependence did not predict job satisfaction and team satisfaction, whereas high goal interdependence was associated with a positive relationship between task interdependence and job and team satisfaction. In other words, the combination of high task interdependence and high goal interdependence is associated with maximum levels of job and team satisfaction.

In a related study, Van der Vegt, Van de Vliert, and Oosterhof (2003) examined the moderating effect of goal interdependence and task interdependence on the relationship of informational dissimilarity and both team identification and organizational citizenship behavior, positing that it is the configuration of task interdependence and outcome interdependence that matters for the relationship of informational dissimilarity with team identification and OCBs. Indeed, their study of 20 multidisciplinary project teams revealed that low task interdependence paired with high outcome interdependence (and vice versa) is detrimental for teams with high informational dissimilarity. Conversely, congruent combinations of low task interdependence and low outcome interdependence and high task interdependence and high outcome interdependence were associated with an insignificant relationship of informational dissimilarity with team identification and OCBs. A different approach was taken by Van der Vegt, Emans, and Van de Vliert (2001), who investigated goal interdependence as a moderator of the effect of task interdependence on job satisfaction and team satisfaction. Two teams could both be "loosely coupled" or at some middle value on a unidimensional measure of interdependence, but this middle value may or may not represent a "fit" between two dimensions that need to go together.

Spatial Interdependence: Team Communication Structures
Practical Example

Our student team that we have been using as part of our running example may be part of a distance learning program, where they live in four separate time zones and interact via a social networking site, but never face-to-face. In contrast, they could all be living together in the same apartment and share a common office space at work. Individuals in loosely coupled communication structures do not occupy the same space and are less distracted. Whereas spatial independence leaves them free to devote their attention to uninterrupted information processing, these same individuals may be constrained in their effort to get needed information from other team members at certain times. This creates a tension between *information exchange*, a staple when one considers the team as "figure" and the individual as "ground," and *information processing*, a central aspect of human behavior when one considers the individual as "figure" and the team as "ground."

Construct Definition

Although groups have often been conceptualized as information-processing vehicles, this is a dangerous reification where the individuals in the group are treated as background, and not figure. Information processing is inherently an individual-level phenomenon. What passes for "group-level information processing" is not really the processing of information, but rather the *exchange of information* between individuals, which is subsequently processed by those individuals and then, perhaps, re-exchanged in the group context. In this section, we introduce spatial interdependence as the fourth facet of interdependence in teams.

We define spatial interdependence as the degree to which the team context facilitates direct, reciprocal, frequent, and face-to-face interpersonal communication in teams. As such, our definition of spatial/communication interdependence draws on research on media richness. According to this research, rich media provide instant feedback, utilize multiple cues such as body language, and use natural language rather than numbers (McGrath & Hollingshead, 1994; Trevino, Lengel, & Daft, 1987). Team members are tightly coupled when they share a small physical space where any one team member can communicate to another whenever he or she would like. Team members in tightly coupled communication structures are free to exchange information easily, but left unchecked, this can become a constraint on information-processing capacity when social interruptions disrupt individual contemplation and reflection that might be needed to ascertain what this information means in terms of task accomplishment.

Spatial interdependence does not focus on individuals' contributions to a task, but on the way in which team members interact to accomplish their tasks. In other words, communication interdependence refers to the degree to which communication structures affect the nature and the richness of interpersonal communication in teams. In a tightly coupled communication structure, an individual may not be able to concentrate and "turn off" social interactions, but in a loosely coupled system, one can ignore and buffer oneself from social distractions. Of course, in interdependent team contexts, one person's social distraction is another person's required information exchange, thus pointing to another paradox in which alternative structural options simultaneously free and constrain individuals.

In our review of research on communication structure, we focus on two central topics. First, we review research that discusses implications of different communication channels for team behavior and team performance, differentiating between virtual and face-to-face communication. Numerous studies in this area consistently point to the challenges that virtual communication imposes on teams. After reviewing these studies, we identify potential solutions to these challenges. Second, we review recent empirical work on network structures on teams as they influence the nature, the amount, and the frequency of communication of team members with each other, as well as with individuals outside the team.

Although a large number of studies have discussed the role of communication in teams (cf. Ilgen et al., 2005), most of this research ignores the implications that different communication structures have for the interdependence among team members. For example, there is a rich literature on the effects of virtual and face-to-face communication channels on team processes and team outcomes, discussing the effects of virtual communication structures on team behavior and performance (i.e., Tangirala & Alge, 2006). Unfortunately, this research rarely discusses the substantive differences between these different communication modes. We assert in this chapter that future research should view communication modes as one theoretically meaningful aspect of interdependence in teams. That is, we propose to conceptualize communication modes as a structural dimension of team design that determines the richness of social contact between team members, the immediacy of communication, as well as the duration and the frequency with which communication occurs in teams. Similarly, network structures in teams can be described in terms of their implications for communication interdependence.

Communication Structure
LIABILITIES OF VIRTUAL COMMUNICATION STRUCTURES

The two-sided nature of the impact that alternative communication structures can have on team processes and team performance was documented by Hedlund, Ilgen, and Hollenbeck (1998), who investigated the differential effects of computer-mediated and face-to-face communication on decision accuracy in teams. Overall, they found a slight superiority for face-to-face communication relative to virtual communication with respect to higher decision-making accuracy in teams, but this belied complex positive and negative paths that ran from communication structure to overall team outcomes. The modest positive effect in favor of face-to-face teams was mediated by team informity and staff validity, such that face-to-face communication was associated with a more effective exchange of information among team members, which ensured that team members were better informed and that team members made more accurate recommendations to their team leaders. Interestingly, however, this study also found that computer-mediated communication in teams is associated with improved hierarchical sensitivity in teams; that is, team leaders in more sterile, computer-mediated communication environments find it easier to abstract the relevant content of the message from the emotionally laden content of communication with staff members. Thus, the attention-intensive task that required formal leaders to discern which staff members were most and least accurate was facilitated by the leader's separation from the group.

This study relates communication mode to conceptually meaningful emergent states in teams, such as team informity, staff validity, and hierarchical sensitivity. As such, this study fills the concept of communication modes with theoretical meaning—something that has generally been missing in research on this topic. Second, this study points to the complex relationship of communication interdependence with team outcomes, demonstrating both positive and negative effects of communication modes for team behavior and performance that relate directly to information exchange versus information processing. This finding is interesting, given the fact that other empirical research on communication modes has consistently reported negative consequences of computer-mediated communication for team processes and performance. We will review this research in the following section of this chapter.

In a case study of 13 geographically dispersed teams relying on computer-mediated communication, Cramton (2001) asserted that it is a critical challenge for such teams to establish and maintain mutual knowledge. Drawing on the work of Krauss and Fussell (1990), she proposed that firsthand experience with individuals and direct interaction among team members help to establish mutual knowledge in teams, both of which are less likely to happen in geographically dispersed, computer-mediated teams. If mutual knowledge cannot be established in teams, hidden profiles will emerge, which will eventually lead to communication failures in teams. Cramton (2001) further proposed that individuals in geographically dispersed teams will rely more strongly on social categorization processes when such communication failures occur. A stronger reliance on social categorization processes in teams increases the likelihood of dispositional attributions in such teams, which has detrimental consequences for both team cohesion and team learning.

Tangirala and Alge (2006) further noted that unfair events have a higher significance for members of computer-mediated teams than they do for teams who communicate face-to-face. They argued that individuals in computer-mediated groups receive less cues about the quality of their social relationships with other team members. Members of face-to-face teams are generally better able to correctly assess the quality of their interpersonal relationships with other group members. As such, events that are perceived as unfair will be interpreted as only one of many components which constitute the perceived quality of interpersonal relationships. Members of computer-mediated teams, however, lack such social information about other group members, and thus their reactions to unfair events are magnified. Interestingly, Tangirala and Alge (2006) also showed that this effect increases over time: members of computer-mediated teams react even more negatively to unfair events as time elapses.

In an experimental study of 60 teams, Hambley, O'Neill, and Kline (2007) showed that the communication mode of teams also has important implications for team interaction styles and outcomes. Specifically, they found that face-to-face communication was associated with more constructive interaction among team members, when compared to videoconferencing or text-based chat. Consistent with this idea, they further reported that team cohesion was higher in face-to-face teams. These findings further attest to the importance of communication mode for team communication and interpersonal relationships among team members. Interestingly, however, communication mode was not associated with team performance in this study.

In a conceptual article, Hinds and Bailey (2003) further discussed the critical challenges that distributed teams in organizations face. They define *distributed teams* as teams in which members are either separated by a large distance or in which members rely on computer-mediated communication. They proposed that distributed teams will lack a shared context because members of distributed teams are likely to have different perspectives and norms. Such teams will generally be more heterogeneous than face-to-face teams, characterized by lower levels of familiarity and weaker friendship ties. Consistent with these arguments, they further predicted that distributed teams will be less cohesive and that they have a weaker collective identity than face-to-face teams. Distributed teams can further be expected to experience difficulties in transferring relevant information to all team members and to coordinate team actions effectively. Overall, Hinds and Bailey (2003) conclude that face-to-face teams can be expected to experience much higher levels of task, affective, and process conflict than distributed teams, an effect that will in turn reduce the performance potential of distributed teams.

BENEFITS OF VIRTUAL COMMUNICATION STRUCTURES

Based on the previously discussed articles, a rather gloomy picture emerges for distributed teams in organizations, but such a conclusion would be premature. Wilson, Straus, and McEvily (2006) aptly pointed out that previous research on computer-mediated teams had largely relied on studies that provided only a snapshot of computer-mediated teams, ignoring how computer-mediated teams perform over longer periods of time when compared to face-to-face teams. Indeed, they found that computer-mediated teams had lower levels of trust at the beginning, but eventually reached comparable levels of trust and cooperation at the end of their three-week experiment when compared to face-to-face teams. By conducting a post hoc content-analysis of communication of teams in their experiment, Wilson et al. (2006) further showed that computer-mediated teams tend to rely more heavily on offensive language early on, an effect that was also associated with the lower values in trust and cooperation in these teams. Over time, however, computer-mediated teams decreased the use of inflammatory communication, which was in turn associated with higher levels of trust and cooperation. Based on these findings, Wilson et al. (2006) call for an integrated theory of technology-mediated communication that considers how the content of communication influences relational development over time.

In a similar vein, Alge, Wiethoff, and Klein (2003) argued that the extent to which teams have a common history or expect to have a common future affects the effectiveness of communication media. In a laboratory study of 66 teams, they found partial support for their arguments: compared to face-to-face teams, computer-mediated teams exhibited lower values of openness/trust and were less likely to share information when teams lacked a common history, an effect which was not sustained for teams that could draw on a common history. Interestingly, however, the same effect was not found for team member exchange: here, face-to-face teams exhibited higher quality team member relationships than computer-mediated teams, irrespective of the temporal scope of teams. This supports the notion that some differences in emergent states between face-to-face teams and computer-mediated teams will eventually even out over time, whereas other differences will be sustained over time.

In another experiment, Montoya-Weiss, Massey, and Song (2001) further investigated the importance of temporal coordination mechanisms for virtual teams. They proposed that the relationship between conflict management strategies and team performance would be moderated by temporal coordination mechanisms, defined as a process structure that directs the form and timing of communication in teams. Their study of 35 five-person teams in the United States and Japan provided partial support for this prediction: temporal coordination mechanisms moderated the effect of two conflict management strategies on virtual team performance. Specifically, temporal coordination mechanisms weakened the negative influence of avoidance conflict management behaviors and compromise conflict management behaviors on virtual team performance, but they did not influence the effectiveness of the other three conflict management strategies: accommodation behaviors, competition behaviors, and collaborative behaviors.

Kirkman, Rosen, Tesluk, and Gibson (2004) adopted a different approach in their investigation of how the effectiveness of virtual teams can be enhanced. They proposed and found in a study of 35 sales and service virtual teams that team empowerment was beneficial for team process improvement and customer satisfaction. They further predicted that team empowerment was especially salient for teams who met less, rather than more, frequently, arguing that teams who do not meet frequently have a tendency to become passive if they lack feelings of potency, meaningfulness, autonomy, and impact. Such teams are more likely to rely on their team leaders, instead of trusting in the capabilities of the team. Indeed, they found that for virtual teams that

met less frequently face-to-face, team empowerment was associated with a dramatic increase in process improvements. It is important to note, however, that empowerment in virtual teams should have a somewhat different focus from empowerment in co-located teams. Kirkman et al. (2004) suggested that for virtual teams, it is especially critical that all team members are informed about organizational objectives and procedures, and that all team members have a high proficiency in using modern means of communication that facilitate communication across distances. We view this study as a particularly important contribution to research on computer-mediated teams. Not only does it identify an important boundary condition for virtual teams to perform effectively, but it also adopts a more precise operationalization of the concept of computer-mediated communication in teams, acknowledging that computer-mediated communication does not occur as a dichotomy (entirely computer-mediated or face-to-face), but rather on a continuum, ranging from "with little frequency—very rarely" to "with high frequency—very often."

Consistent with this idea, Maznevski and Chudoba (2000) investigated, in an intensive case study of three virtual teams, how teams adapt their communication patterns to the requirements of the task and the decision process. Based on a content analysis of communication in these teams, the authors proposed that effective virtual teams will rely on richer communication media when confronted with higher level decision processes. For example, effective virtual teams will rely on face-to-face communication when generating decision alternatives, a decision process categorized as a higher level decision process, whereas computer-mediated communication will be more appropriate for such teams when confronted with lower level decision processes, such as executing a predefined sequence of actions. Maznevski and Chudoba (2000) further predicted that the more complex the content of a message, the more appropriate it is for virtual teams to rely on rich media of communication. By observing the three teams over a 21-month period, Maznevski and Chudoba (2000) further proposed that effective virtual teams develop a rhythmic temporal pattern of communication, alternating between face-to-face communication and remote communication. They devote their face-to-face meetings to higher level decision processes, whereas simple messages and lower level decision processes are exchanged and decided via remote communication. This research shows how the key to team effectiveness is having a tightly coupled communication structure at one time and with one task, but then a decoupled communication structure at a later time with a different task. The most effective communication structure is thus "loosely coupled" when averaged over multiple performance episodes.

Network Structure
CLOSURE AND BRIDGING RELATIONSHIPS

In this section, we turn to network structure as a second important dimension of communication interdependence in teams. Contrary to communication structure, network structure does not address the channels through which team members communicate with each other. Instead, network structure focuses on the number and the intensity of social ties that team members share with each other, as well as with individuals in the larger organizational context. Drawing from the work of Burt (2000), Oh, Chung, and Labianca (2004) differentiated between intragroup closure relationships and bridging relationships that transcend the boundary of the team. Closure in a group ensures that all team members are connected with each other, whereas bridging emphasizes relationships among otherwise heterogeneous people in organizations.

Both of these conduits have potential advantages: closure relationships reduce the need to engage in monitoring activities and increase team cohesiveness, whereas bridging conduits ensure that individuals receive timely and diverse information on organizational matters. It is important to note that developing one type of conduit generally happens at the expense of the other conduit. For example, if team members seek to connect themselves with other individuals in the organization, they will have less time to develop closure relationships within their team. Acknowledging this inherent tension and trade-off between closure and bridging conduits, Oh et al. (2004) proposed that teams should seek to balance closure and bridging relationships in order to reap the benefits of both, thereby maximizing team effectiveness. Their field study of 60 teams in Korea provided support for this prediction.

NETWORK CENTRALITY

Even though the study by Oh et al. (2004) provides important insights on how teams should manage their internal and external social relationships, it cannot explain why some individuals in teams assume more central network positions than others. This, however, is pivotal to our understanding of communication interdependencies in teams. In a field study of 96 teams, Klein, Lim, Saltz, and Mayer (2004) attempted to answer the question of how individuals acquire central positions in team networks, differentiating between advice centrality, friendship centrality, and adversarial centrality. They hypothesized that demographics, values, and personality characteristics determine network centrality in teams. Among all the variables included in their study, education and neuroticism emerged as powerful predictors of network centrality, exhibiting significant relationships with all three facets of network centrality.

Klein et al. (2004) argued that this finding supports the notion that team members establish social relationships with other team members if they offer opportunities for benefits (education) that can be attained at little cost (neuroticism). Results from their study further established personal values as important antecedents of network centrality. Activity preference, tradition, and hedonism all exhibited significant relationships with two of three facets of network centrality. Moreover, drawing on similarity-attraction theory, Klein et al. (2004) investigated the extent to which similarity in demographics and values influence network centrality. They reported that similarity in hedonistic and tradition values were associated with higher advice and friendship centrality in teams. Consistent with the model of surface and deep-level diversity of Harrison et al. (2002), the effects of demographic similarity were overshadowed by the effect of value similarity.

Further extending the nomological network of network centrality, Baldwin, Bedell, and Johnson (1997) investigated consequences of network centrality for attitudinal and performance outcomes in a field study of 250 MBA students. They found that communication centrality and friendship centrality predicted perceptions of learning and enjoyment of the MBA program. Also, communication centrality was associated with higher grades of students. Consistent with their predictions, Baldwin et al. (1997) further showed that adversarial centrality is negatively related to satisfaction with teams and the MBA program.

NETWORK BREADTH

Gargiulo and Benassi (2000) argued that managers face an inherent trade-off between developing cohesive relationships with other individuals in the organization and filling positions in an organizational network which connect otherwise separate clusters in an organization, also referred to as structural holes. That is, team managers have to balance network closure with network bridging. In a field study of managers employed by an Italian subsidiary of a multinational computer firm, the authors showed that network bridging is especially important for managers in a period of organizational change. During such times, cohesive ties functioned as a source of structural rigidity that prevented managers from coordinating complex tasks successfully. Conversely, entering cooperative relationships with individuals who were not part of a manager's established network allowed these managers to attain the flexibility required to coordinate complex organizational change processes. This finding is consistent with the previously discussed finding obtained by Oh et al. (2004), who investigated the optimal configuration of closure and bridging conduits on the team level of analysis. Both studies emphasize that closure conduits are associated with increased safety, whereas bridging conduits provide additional flexibility.

The importance of remote social ties in an organization has further been attested by Lawrence (2006), who introduced the concept of organizational reference groups. Lawrence (2006) defined organizational reference groups as "the set of people an individual perceives as belonging to his or her work environment that defines the social world of work in which he or she engages" (p. 80). This includes individuals with whom one shares no immediate social contact—individuals who are merely known through company newsletters or gossip. Results obtained in an extensive field study showed that organizational reference groups can guide individuals' career referent selection and can help individuals identify expected achievement—results that could not have been obtained if only the immediate social network of individuals in an organization would have been examined, as is the case in traditional social network analysis.

A common pattern of the two previously discussed studies is the inherent tension and trade-off between network density and network breadth. Investing time into the development of cohesive relationships with other group members will ultimately be at the expense of developing a broad social network in the larger organization, and vice versa. It is important to note, however, that social relationships within teams can also be narrow or broad in nature: team members develop strong relationships with some team members, whereas they interact only sporadically with others, beyond the immediate requirements of their task. This raises the question of whether teams should create homogeneous and dense patterns of interaction among team members, or whether such heterogeneous relationships can in fact be desirable for teams.

Reagans and Zuckerman (2001) investigated this question in a study of 224 research development (R&D) teams in 29 organizations. Their findings suggest that R&D teams with more dense networks of interaction were more productive than R&D teams with sparse interaction networks. Interestingly, however, Reagans and Zuckerman (2001) also found that teams which exhibit more contact between team members of the same organizational tenure were less productive than teams with strong links between members of different organizational tenure. This finding suggests that team members should establish deep relationships with other team members, while at the same ensuring that their relationships are not restricted to demographically similar team members.

This finding raises the question of whether managers should attempt to influence communication links by managing team members' demographic characteristics, or whether team managers should rather focus on managing team members' social networks. In a follow-up study of 1,518 project teams, Reagans, Zuckerman, and McEvily (2004) investigated this question. They argued that an approach which focuses on demographic characteristics has ambiguous performance implications because demographic diversity exhibits differential relationships with two central social network variables: internal density and external range (or external breadth). Reagans et al. (2004) predicted and found that demographic diversity is associated with an increase in external network range, that is, with a larger pool of contacts that teams can access, while at the same time decreasing the internal network density of teams by reducing the intensity of within-team relationships. Internal network density and external network range are in turn positively associated with team performance, which renders the overall effect of demographic diversity on team performance ambiguous. This finding strongly underlines the importance of network structures for team design, and the need for coupling both within and between teams. As we saw earlier in summarizing the literature on self-managed teams, external leaders are often most adept at managing the "between team" aspects of coupling, whereas emergent, internal team leaders may be best able to manage the "within-team" aspects of coupling.

Discussion

We began this chapter by defining teams as "small groups of *interdependent individuals* who share responsibility for specific outcomes" (Ilgen, 1999), and then described four specific, but different ways that individuals could be interdependent on other people in team contexts. Each of these potential forms of interdependence was conceptualized as a linkage where one person could be tightly coupled, loosely coupled, or uncoupled to others, and that these bonds form what we commonly refer to as *team structure*. Teams that are tightly structured have individuals who are specialized and horizontally dependent; the members often surrender decision-making authority to formal leaders; the members all experience the same outcomes for success and failure; and they all occupy a small physical space that promotes constant, unrestricted communication. The tight yoking of individuals to one another makes it easy to see the team as "figure," and individuals as "ground."

At the other extreme, when individuals are totally uncoupled on all four of these dimensions, each person does his own holistic task, makes his own decisions, receives his own rewards, and can shut himself off from unwanted communication and social interruptions; there is no team at all. The lack of interdependence on those four dimensions violates the very definition of team. Thus, this perspective helps add specificity to the definition of team which, on the one hand, includes interdependence as a requirement, but then after this, differentiates one team from one another in terms of being "high" or "low" in interdependence. How can a team be low in interdependence if one has to have interdependence to meet the definition of being a team? By specifying in greater detail the four dimensions of structure, one can see that a team could be coupled on one, two, three, or all four dimensions. Thus, a team could meet the definition of being team, but still be high, medium, or low in interdependence, as long as they are not uncoupled on all four dimensions. The definition snaps, however, once all four dimensions are uncoupled, and we observe a person who is doing work that one person can do all by himself or herself, totally disconnected from others. That person might be part of some organizational unit, such as

the accounting department, but this department is not a team.

Implications for Research: Relating Team Interdependence to Its Nomological Network

In this chapter, we conceptualize the four dimensions of team interdependence as distinct, yet related facets of team interdependence. Up to this point, however, there is relatively little research that has investigated the relationship of different dimensions of social interdependence empirically. Therefore, it is critical that additional empirical research investigates the uniqueness and utility of the different facets of interdependence in order to provide additional support for our theoretical model. In particular, such a research program would have to address the following questions.

First, how strongly related are the individual facets of team interdependence? Are we dealing with indicators of the same latent construct, or are the different facets of interdependence distinct concepts? This necessitates an examination of the factor structure underlying the different dimensions of team interdependence.

Second, do certain pairs of dimensions seem to go naturally together, as in the case of divisional structures that tend to be decentralized (a configuration referred to as *organic*) and functional structures that tend to be centralized (a configuration referred to as *mechanistic*)? In addition, some of the research discussed here implies normatively that if a team is high on one dimension, they ought to be high on all (i.e., if a team is high on horizontal interdependence, then it ought also to be high on outcome interdependence). If, as we have seen, organizations tend to shy away from creating "tightly coupled" structures, this suggests that relationships among other dimensions may be weaker than one might expect, based solely on theories that specify a need for "fit" or alignment of dimensions. If teams do indeed rely on different configurations of team interdependence, then a multidimensional approach to team interdependence can provide a more complete understanding of the structural antecedents of team behavior and team performance. Cluster analyzing teams from a variety of industries and settings could demonstrate empirically how teams rely on different configurations of team interdependence.

Third, in order to substantiate the utility of a multidimensional model of team interdependence, future research must demonstrate that the different facets of team interdependence exhibit differential relationships with meaningful outcomes on the individual- and team-level of analysis. Any such investigation into the broader nomological network of team interdependence should be theory-driven. Restated, the selection of important individual- and team-level outcomes, as well as the predicted relationships, should logically follow from a theoretical framework that can explain how individuals behave and interact in socially interdependent settings.

Fourth, the interaction between various structures and individual differences needs to be examined to see if certain people are differentially attracted to or perform differentially in alternative structures. For example, a common theme in our literature review on team structure is that tightly coupled team structures and decoupled team structures both impose important freedoms and restrictions on individuals at the same time. Generally, decoupled structures allow individuals to maintain their personal identities to a larger extent, whereas tightly coupled structures emphasize and enforce a collective group identity. At the same time, however, tightly coupled structures give individuals the freedom to assume a more specialized role that emphasizes their individual preferences and abilities, whereas tightly coupled team structures force team members to assume a narrower role in which they easily lose track of the dynamics of the larger social system. Thus, overall, individuals in tightly coupled and in decoupled team structures constantly face the challenge of balancing the uniqueness and distinctiveness of their identity with the need to be similar to other group members and to be assimilated.

Optimal distinctiveness theory (ODT; Brewer, 1991) is a theoretical framework which can help to develop a systematic investigation into the nomological network of these kinds of individual differences. OPT argues that individuals have a simultaneous need to be assimilated and similar to relevant others, yet at the same time to be sufficiently distinct and unique. Brewer (1991) posits that deviations from an optimal balance between distinctiveness and assimilation lead to negative effects for psychological well-being, for individuals' conceptualization of their roles in the group, and for group functioning. By relating the four facets of team interdependence to feelings of distinctiveness/uniqueness and assimilation/similarity, we can use optimal distinctiveness theory to derive theoretically driven predictions on the relationships between different facets of team interdependence and individual- and team-level outcomes, allowing us to investigate the broader

nomological network of team interdependence in a systematic manner.

Implications for Research: Loosely Coupled Team Structures as the Solution?

As we have seen, the complexity of contemporary organizational missions that demand both efficiency and flexibility in the face of dynamically changing task environments and competitive landscapes is making it increasingly difficult to structure organizations around decoupled individuals. Hence, the evidence is clear that more organizations are turning to team-based structures, and indeed, it is difficult to find anyone who argues for the value of totally decoupled, individually based systems in either the academic literature or the popular press. At the same time, however, we noted that most forms of coupling come with their own unique set of freedoms and constraints, and the mixed set of virtues and liabilities associated with different forms of interdependence make it difficult for organizations to create tightly structured teams.

In addition, since individuals have their own separate uniqueness, identity, and, ultimately, volition, organizations as a whole tend to develop a separate relationship with each person above and beyond their membership in any one team. Hence, in many organizations, HR departments, who manage the transactional relationship between individuals and the organization, also stand in the way of any move to create tightly structured teams. Although many view HR departments as obstacles to team-based structures, in fact, as we have seen throughout this review, the literature seems to speak against tight coupling on all dimensions at all times, and hence the preference for loosely structured teams in organizations may be normative as well as descriptive.

As Weick (1976) argued in the context of organization theory, there are many advantages associated with loose coupling of subunits within an organization, and many of these virtues seem to translate well to the team-level of analysis. Loose coupling partially separates the individual from the team, allowing each individual her own personal identity, a sense of self-determination, and her own developmental trajectory, where the team serves as a vehicle for, rather than a barrier to, personal expression. Tightly coupled teams create high needs for coordination, which may take the form of long, frequent, and potentially contentious meetings that become social interruptions that disrupt actual work activity. The only means for avoiding this type of costly mutual adjustment is to put power in the hands of one centralized individual or to create highly formalized and standardized work rules that destroy individual initiative and team flexibility.

Loosely coupled individuals also serve as a more effective system for sensing the environment and collecting information, because the unique perspective of each individual increases the probability of sensing important changes that are likely to be missed if each person narrowly focuses on a small part of the overall task environment. This is especially the case if individuals are attached to multiple different social networks, in which case the collective sensing of the team is multiplied exponentially. A tightly coupled and cohesive team is often described as "being of *one* mind," but the requisite variety of the task environment often demands a number larger than this.

When the perceptual diversity created by loosely structured teams is combined with decentralized decision-making authority, this also promotes swift and local adaptation to conditions that might be highly desirable, but impossible in the time that it would take to convince leaders or develop consensus of the whole team. Loose coupling also promotes experimentation by individuals who may see and exploit some innovation first in their own work, thus economically building their own set of empirical data regarding its effectiveness, prior to trying to diffusing the new technique to all parts of the team. In a similar manner, loose coupling also prevents some breakdown by any one individual on the team from spreading quickly throughout the whole team. Like compartments in a submarine, individual problems can be sealed off and the damage contained in a way that would not be possible in a tightly coupled system. An old proverb notes that "for want of a nail, the horseshoe was lost; for want of a horse, the leader was lost; for want of the leader, the battle was lost; for want of the battle, the war was lost." If indeed, one loses a war for "want of a nail," then perhaps this system was too tightly coupled.

Thus, rather than strive to create increasingly tighter coupling of teams on all dimensions, the literature reviewed as part of this chapter seems to suggest a need for an optimum level of loose coupling, or a balance that simultaneously blends tight coupling on one dimension, with loose coupling on another; or tight coupling at one moment with loose coupling at another moment. With respect to horizontal interdependence, for example, for tasks that demand efficiency, the team might coalesce around a tightly structured functional task decomposition process that highlights specialization and leverages each person's current stock of knowledge and set of skills. In contrast, for tasks that demand creativity, the team may reconfigure along broader, more self-determined roles that allow for more experimentation, which may expand their current stock of knowledge and set of skills. In terms of vertical interdependence, a team could be loosely structured to make decision by consensus in non-emergency situations, but then revert to a more tightly structured, hierarchically led structure when confronted with time pressure. When it comes to rewards, individual pay could be loosely structured at the end of the year, when annual individual performance appraisal is attached to some kind of merit raise, but also rewarded via tightly coupled team bonuses at the end of specific team-based projects. Rather than trying to resolve the figure/ground perceptual problem, this framework embraces this perceptual illusion, and isolates specific angles and perspectives that make it easier to see either the team or the individuals as "figure or ground" as the situation demands.

Of course, structural reconfiguration, like that described above, creates its own sets of challenges, and recent research on structural adaptation theory suggests that movement in some structural directions is easier or more natural, relative to movement in other directions (Beersma, et al. 2009; Ellis, Li, Hollenbeck, Ilgen, & Humphrey, 2006; Johnson et al. 2006; Moon et al, 2004). Specifically, this research indicates that the virtues and liabilities traditionally associated with alternative structures based upon cross-sectional studies only seem to manifest themselves when structures move toward looser, relative to tighter forms of coupling. That is, Moon et al. (2004) showed that teams that changed from functional to divisional structures acted much like teams who were always arrayed in divisional structures, but that divisional teams that restructured along functional lines struggled to adapt in this direction, and performed worse relative to pure functional teams. Johnson et al. (2006) found that teams that moved from cooperative to competitive structures acted much like teams that were always arrayed in competitive structures, but that teams that switched from competitive to cooperative structures failed to conform to the behaviors typically revealed in cooperative teams that never experienced competition. Ellis et al. (2006) found that teams that transitioned from centralized to decentralized decision-making structures acted very much like pure decentralized teams, but that teams that moved in the opposite direction experienced all the liabilities of centralized structures, but none of their benefits. These documented asymmetries in structural movement all imply that moving toward more tightly coupled structures is less natural for people relative to movement in the other direction, which perhaps should not be surprising, given the proclivity of individuals to become "ground" rather than "figure" when placed in tightly coupled systems.

Indeed, one theme that runs throughout this review is that tightly coupled systems tend to mute the effects of individual differences when it comes to predicting team-level outcomes from individual measures. When individuals do more parts of the task, when they make their own decisions, when they strive for their own personal rewards, and when they are left uninterrupted from social intrusions, the link between individual-level compositional factors (like cognitive ability, emotional stability, and other dispositional characteristics) is stronger than when the same individuals get tightly yoked to others as part of tightly coupled systems. Indeed, in tightly coupled contexts, it is often the conjunctive operationalization (the lowest scoring team member) of team composition that seems to best represent the team (LePine, Hollenbeck, Ilgen, & Hedlund, 1997). In contrast, LePine et al. (2008) showed meta-analytically how the predictive value of traditional measures of group processes tends to get muted when teams are loosely coupled. Much of the variance in loosely coupled teams reverts back to dispositional characteristics at the individual level of analysis in this case, as the members become "figure" and the team becomes "ground."

Conclusion

Thus, when all of this research is taken together, it becomes clear that, rather than confronting uncoupled individuals or tightly coupled teams, most researchers and practitioners in organizational contexts are likely to encounter loosely coupled teams. In this situation, one can take the sum of the levels of interdependence across the four dimensions, treat it as a unidimensional construct, and then place any one team on some continuum of overall tightness or looseness of structure. This overall construct of tightness/looseness could then be used as a continuous variable that could be used as cause, effect, or moderator of cause-effect relationships in theories of team behavior. There would be real value in developing this unidimensional and continuous measure of structure in terms of developing a more coherent and cumulative body of literature on structure. This would definitely improve the situation relative to the

current milieu, which tends to create a large number of unrelated categorical typologies of team types that collapse across various dimensions (Cunha & Chia, 2007; Devine et al., 1999; Fisher & Fisher, 2001; Lickel, Hamilton, & Sherman, 2001; Loo & Loewen, 2003; Moorehead, Neck, & West, 1998; Steiner, 1972; Stewart & Manz, 1995). Categorical systems such as this are a good start at differentiation, but most of these systems are hard to compare to one another and struggle in their ability to accommodate the clear classifications of the myriad forms that real-world teams can take. Stewart and Barrick (2000, p. 137) summarize the problems associated with typologies for team behavior quite eloquently in their discussion of task classifications:

> However, one problem with task classifications in actual work situations is that a team rarely performs only one type of task (Argote & McGrath, 1993; Goodman, 1986). In fact, McGrath (1984) suggested that teams perform tasks associated with all four of his categories, but with unequal frequency. This means that it may be inappropriate to classify the multidimensional tasks of actual work teams into mutually exclusive categories. An alternative, and often more appropriate, approach is to arrange tasks along a continuum like the behavioral-conceptual dimension.

Even though this comment addresses task typologies (and not typologies of interdependence), we echo its criticism of the application of simple typologies applied to complex multilevel systems such as teams. Thus, we propose to allow for more flexibility in the way that researchers and practitioners can describe team interdependence. At the same time, however, we also caution that the unidimensional approach to structure is also unable to portray the vast multiplicity of structural forms present in real-world organizations, and because most teams, for the reasons laid out above, are going to be "loosely structured," will wind up near the midpoint of this unidimensional measure. Yet two teams that receive similar overall scores near the middle of this tight/loose structure variable can get to this midpoint in different ways. This review has shown clearly that their unique processes and outcomes associated with specific dimensions of coupling, such that a loosely coupled team that is tightly structured on one pair of dimensions (horizontal and rewards) but loosely structured on the other two dimensions (vertical and spatial) will differ from another team for which the reverse is true. A multidimensional approach to structure, which keeps information on the four separate dimensions distinct, could lead to a better cumulation of results across studies, since currently, the term *interdependence* is often being used without reference to the specific dimension where people are coupled.

Indeed, just as the concept of teams as loosely coupled structures allows one to flexibly move back and forth from perceiving figure/ground relationships when observing teams of individuals, an approach to measurement that allows for both unidimensional and multidimensional conceptualizations of tight versus loose coupling also provides flexibility. In research contexts where structure is not central to the theorizing, but one wants to either control for variation or simply describe the nature of the teams to help place them in the larger literature, grosser unidimensional measures of structural tightness might be used. When structure is central to the theory, on the other hand, a more refined approach that distinguishes specific dimensions of coupling might be required in order to capture more subtle nuances of alternative forms of interdependence. In either case, the ability to more systematically define what is meant by the terms *team structure* and *interdependence* will be helpful as researchers attempt to expand the knowledge base on teams, as well as the individuals from whom teams are constructed.

References

Alge, B. J., Wiethoff, C., & Klein, H. J. (2003). When does the medium matter? Knowledge-building experiences and opportunities in decision-making teams. *Organizational Behavior and Human Decision Processes, 91,* 26–37.

Alper, S., Tjosvold, D., & Law, K. S. (1998). Interdependence and controversy in group decision making: Antecedents to effective self-managing teams. *Organizational Behavior and Team Decision Processes, 74,* 33–52.

Alper, S., Tjosvold, D., & Law, K. S. (2000). Conflict management, efficacy, and performance in organizational teams. *Personnel Psychology, 53,* 625–642.

Argote, L., & McGrath, J. E. (1993). Group processes in organizations: Continuity and change. In C. L. Cooper & I. T. Robertson (Eds.), *International review of industrial and organizational psychology* (Vol. 8, pp. 333–389). New York: Wiley.

Austin, J. R. (2003). Transactive memory in organizational groups: The effects of content, consensus, specialization, and accuracy on group performance. *Journal of Applied Psychology, 88,* 866–878.

Baldwin, T. T., Bedell, M. D., & Johnson, J. L. (1997). The social fabric of a team-based MBA program: Network effects on student satisfaction and performance. *Academy of Management Journal, 40,* 1369–1397.

Barnes, C. M., Hollenbeck, J. R., Wagner, D. T., DeRue, S. D., Nahrgang, J. D., & Schwind, K. (2008). Harmful help: The costs of backing-up behavior in teams. *Journal of Applied Psychology, 93,* 529–539.

Beersma, B., Hollenbeck, J. R., Conlon, D. E., Humphrey, S. E., Moon, H., & Ilgen, D. R. (2009). Cutthroat cooperation: The effects of team role decisions on adaptation to alternative reward structures. *Organizational Behavior and Human Decision Processes, 108,* 131–142.

Beersma, B., Hollenbeck, J. R., Humphrey, S. E., Moon, H., Conlon, D. E., & Ilgen, D. R. (2003). Cooperation, competition, and team performance: Toward a contingency approach. *Academy of Management Journal, 46,* 572–590.

Bonaccio, S., & Dalal, R. S. (2006). Advice-taking and decision-making: An integrative literature review, and implications for the organizational sciences. *Organizational Behavior and Human Decision Processes, 101,* 127–151.

Brandon, D. P., & Hollingshead, A. B. (2004). Transactive memory systems in organizations: Matching tasks, expertise, and people. *Organization Science, 15,* 633–644.

Brewer, M. B. (1991). The social self: On being the same and different at the same time. *Personality and Social Psychology Bulletin, 17,* 475–482.

Brodbeck, F. C., Kerschreiter, R., Mojzisch, A., & Schulz-Hardt, S. (2007). Group decision making under conditions of distributed knowledge: The information asymmetries model. *Academy of Management Review, 32,* 459–479.

Bunderson, J. S., & Sutcliffe, K. M. (2002). Comparing alternative conceptualizations of functional diversity in management teams: Process and performance effect. *Academy of Management Journal, 45,* 875–893.

Burns, T., & Stalker, G. M. (1961). *The management of innovation.* London: Tavistock.

Burt, R. S. (2000). The network structure of social capital. *Research in Organizational Behavior, 22,* 345–423.

Cohen, S. G., Chang, L., & Ledford, G. E. (1997). A hierarchical construct of self-management leadership and its relationship to quality of work life and perceived work group effectiveness. *Personnel Psychology, 50,* 275–308.

Cramton, C. D. (2001). The mutual knowledge problem and its consequences for dispersed collaboration. *Organization Science, 12,* 346–371.

Cunha, M. P., & Chia, R. (2007). Using teams to avoid peripheral blindness. *Long Range Planning, 40,* 559–573.

De Dreu, C. K. W. (2007). Cooperative outcome interdependence, task reflexivity, and team effectiveness: A motivated information processing perspective. *Journal of Applied Psychology, 92,* 628–638.

De Dreu, C. K. W., & Weingart, L. R. (2003). Task versus relationship conflict, team performance, and team member satisfaction: A meta-analysis. *Journal of Applied Psychology, 88,* 741–749.

DeShon, R. P., Kozlowski, S. W. J., Schmidt, A. M., Milner, K. R., & Wiechmann, D. (2004). A multiple-goal, multilevel model of feedback effects on the regulation of individual and team performance. *Journal of Applied Psychology, 89,* 1035–1056.

Deutsch, M. (1949). A theory of co-operation and competition. *Human Relations, 2,* 129–152.

Devine, D. J., Clayton, L. D., Philips, J. L., Dunford, B. B., & Melner, S. B. (1999). Teams in organizations: Prevalence, characteristics, and effectiveness. *Small Group Research, 30,* 678–711.

Douglas, C., & Gardner, W. L. (2004). Transition to self-directed work teams: Implications of transition time and self-monitoring for managers' use of influence tactics. *Journal of Organizational Behavior, 25,* 47–65.

Drach-Zahavy, A. (2004). The proficiency trap: How to balance enriched job designs and the team's need for support. *Journal of Organizational Behavior, 25*, 979–996.

Drach-Zahavy, A., & Freund, A. (2007). Team effectiveness under stress: A structural contingency approach. *Journal of Organizational Behavior, 28*, 423–450.

Druskat, V. U., & Wheeler, J. V. (2003). Managing from the boundary: The effective leadership of self-managing work teams. *Academy of Management Journal, 46*, 435–457.

Ellis, A. P. J., Hollenbeck, J. R., Ilgen, D. R., Porter, C. O. L. H., West. B. J., & Moon, H. (2003). Team learning: Collectively connecting the dots. *Journal of Applied Psychology, 88*, 821–835.

Ellis, A. P. J. Li, A., Hollenbeck, J. R., Ilgen, D. R., & Humphrey, S. E. (2006). *The asymmetrical nature of structural changes in teams.* Paper presented at the 20th Annual Conference of the Society for Industrial and Organizational Psychology, Dallas, TX.

Fisher, K., & Fisher, M. D. (2001). *The distance manager: A hands-on guide to managing off-site employees and virtual teams.* New York: McGraw-Hill.

Gargiulo, M., & Benassi, M. (2000). Trapped in your own net? Network cohesion, structural holes, and the adaptation of social capital. *Organization Science, 11*, 183–196.

Garvey, C. (2002). Steer teams with the right pay. *HR Magazine,* 19–20.

Gilson, L. L., Mathieu, J. E., Shalley, C. E., & Ruddy, T. M. (2005). Creativity and standardization: Complementary or conflicting drivers of team effectiveness? *Academy of Management Journal, 48*, 521–531.

Goodman, P. S. (1986). Impact of task and technology on group performance. In P. S. Goodman (Ed.), *Designing effective work groups* (pp. 120–167). San Francisco: Jossey-Bass.

Griffin, M. A., Patterson, M. G., & West. M. A. (2001). Job satisfaction and teamwork: The role of supervisor support. *Journal of Organizational Behavior, 22*, 537–550.

Gurtner, A., Tschan, F., Semmer, N. K., & Naegele, C. (2007). Getting groups to develop good strategies: Effects of reflexivity interventions on team process, team performance, and shared mental models. *Organizational Behavior and Human Decision Processes, 102*, 127–142.

Hackman, J. R., & Oldham, G. R. (1976). Motivation through the design of work: Test of a theory. *Organizational Behavior and Human Performance, 16*, 250–279.

Hackman, J. R. (1987). The design of work teams. In J. Lorsch (Ed.), *Handbook of organizational behavior* (pp. 315–342). Englewood Cliffs, NJ: Prentice Hall.

Hambley, L. A., O'Neill, T. A., & Kline, T. J. B. (2007). Virtual team leadership: The effects of leadership style and communication medium on team interaction styles and outcomes. *Organizational Behavior and Human Decision Processes, 103*, 1–20.

Harrison, D. A., Price, K. H., Gavin, J. H., & Florey, A. T. (2002). Time, teams, and task performance: Changing effects of surface- and deep-level diversity on group functioning. *Academy of Management Journal, 45*, 1029–1045.

Hedlund, J., Ilgen, D. R., & Hollenbeck, J. R. (1998). Decision accuracy in computer-mediated versus face-to-face decision-making teams. *Organizational Behavior and Human Decision Processes, 76*, 30–47.

Hinds, P. J., & Bailey, D. E. (2003). Out of sight, out of sync: Understanding conflict in distributed teams. *Organization Science, 14*, 615–632.

Hollenbeck, J. R., Ilgen, D. R., Sego, D. J., Hedlund, J., & Major, D. A. (1995). Multilevel theory of team decision-making: decision performance in teams incorporating distributed expertise. *Journal of Applied Psychology, 80*, 292–316.

Hollenbeck, J. R., Moon, H., Ellis, A. P. J., West, B. J., Ilgen, D. R., Sheppard, L., Porter, C. O. L. H., & Wagner, J. A. (2002). Structural contingency theory and individual differences: Examination of external and internal person-team fit. *Journal of Applied Psychology, 87*, 599–607.

Homan, A. C., Hollenbeck, J. R., Humphrey, S. E., Van Knippenberg, D., Ilgen, D. R., & Van Kleef, G. A. (2008). Facing differences with an open mind: Openness to experience, salience of intragroup differences, and performance of diverse work groups. *Academy of Management Journal, 51*, 1204–1222.

Ilgen, D. R. (1999). Teams embedded in organizations. *American Psychologist, 54*, 129–139.

Ilgen, D. R., Hollenbeck, J. R., Johnson, M., & Jundt, D. (2005). Teams in organizations: From I-P-O Models to IMOI models. *Annual Review of Psychology, 56*, 517–543.

Janz, B. D., Colquitt, J. A., & Noe, R. A. (1997). Knowledge worker team effectiveness: The role of autonomy, interdependence, team development, and contextual support variables. *Personnel Psychology, 50*, 877–904.

Jehn, K. A. (1994). Enhancing effectiveness: An investigation of advantages and disadvantages of value-based intragroup conflict. *International Journal of Conflict Management, 5*, 223–238.

Johnson, D. W. (2003). Social interdependence: Interrelationships among theory, research, and practice. *American Psychologist, 58*, 133–154.

Johnson, M. D., Hollenbeck, J. R., Humphrey, S. E., Ilgen, D. R., Jundt, D., & Meyer, C. (2006). Cutthroat cooperation: Asymmetrical adaptation to changes in team reward structure. *Academy of Management Journal, 49*, 103–119.

Keller, R. T. (2001). Cross-functional project groups in research and new product development: Diversity, communications, job stress, and outcomes. *Academy of Management Journal, 44*, 547–555.

Kiggundu, M. N. (1981). Task interdependence and the theory of job design. *Academy of Management Review, 6*, 499–508.

Kirkman, B. L., & Rosen, B. (1997). A model of work team empowerment. In W. A. Pasmore & R. W. Woodman (Eds.), *Research in organizational change and development* (Vol. 10, pp. 131–167). Greenwich, CT: Elsevier Science/JAI Press.

Kirkman, B. L., & Rosen, B. (1999). Beyond self-management: Antecedents and consequences of team empowerment. *Academy of Management Journal, 42*, 58–74.

Kirkman, B. L., Rosen, B., Tesluk, P., & Gibson, C. B. (2004). The impact of team empowerment on virtual team performance: The moderating role of face-to-face interaction. *Academy of Management Journal, 47*, 175–192.

Kirkman, B. L., & Shapiro, D. L. (1997). The impact of cultural values on employee resistance to teams: Toward a model of globalized self-managing work team effectiveness. *Academy of Management Review, 22*, 730–757.

Klein, K. J., Lim, B. C., Saltz, J. L., & Mayer, D. M. (2004). How do they get there? An examination of the antecedents of network centrality in team networks. *Academy of Management Journal, 47*, 952–963.

Knight, D., Durham, C. C., & Locke, E. A. (2001). The relationship of team goals, incentives, and efficacy to strategic risk, tactical implementation, and performance. *Academy of Management Journal, 44,* 326–338.

Krauss, R. M., & Fussell, S. R. (1990). Mutual knowledge and communication effectiveness. In J. Galegher, R. E. Kraut, & C. Egido (Eds.), *Intellectual teamwork: Social and technological foundations for cooperative work* (pp. 111–145). Hillsdale, NJ: Erlbaum.

Langfred, C. W. (2000). The paradox of self-management: Individual and group autonomy in work groups. *Journal of Organizational Behavior, 21,* 563–585.

Langfred, C. W. (2004). Too much of a good thing? Negative effects of high trust and individual autonomy in self-managing teams. *Academy of Management Journal, 47,* 385–399.

Langfred, C. W. (2007). The downside of self-management: A longitudinal study of the effects of conflict on trust, autonomy, and task interdependence self-managing teams. *Academy of Management Journal, 50,* 885–900.

Latané, B., Williams, K., & Harkins, S. (1979). Many hands make light the work: The causes and consequences of social loafing. *Journal of Personality and Social Psychology, 37,* 822–832.

Lau, D. C., & Murnighan, J. K. (2005). Interactions within groups and subgroups: The effects of demographic faultlines. *Academy of Management Journal, 48,* 645–659.

Lawrence, B. S. (2006). Organizational reference groups: A missing perspective on social context. *Organization Science, 17,* 80–100.

LePine, J. A., Hollenbeck, J. R., Ilgen, D. R., & Hedlund, J. (1997). Effects of individual differences on the performance of hierarchical decision-making teams: Much more than g. *Journal of Applied Psychology, 82,* 803–811.

LePine, J. A., Piccolo, R. F., Jackson, C. L., Mathieu, J. E., & Saul, J. R. (2008). A meta-analysis of teamwork processes: Tests of a multidimensional model and relationships with team effectiveness criteria. *Personnel Psychology, 61,* 273–308.

Lickel, B., Hamilton, D. L., & Sherman, S. J. (2001). Elements of a lay theory of groups. Types of groups, relationship styles, and the perception of group entitativity. *Personality and Social Psychology Review, 5,* 129–140.

Loo, R., & Loewen, P. (2003). The typology of self-managed teams based upon team climate: Examining stability and change in typologies. *Team Performance Management, 9,* 59–68.

Lovelace, K., Shapiro, D. L., & Weingart, L. R. (2001). Maximizing cross-functional new product teams' innovativeness and constraint adherence: A conflict communications perspective. *Academy of Management Journal, 44,* 779–793.

Man, D. C., & Lam, S. K. (2003). The effects of job complexity and autonomy on cohesiveness and collectivistic and individualistic work groups: A cross-cultural analysis. *Journal of Organizational Behavior, 24,* 979–1001.

Manz, C. C., & Sims, H. P. (1987). Leading workers to lead themselves. The external leadership of self-managing work teams. *Administrative Science Quarterly, 32,* 106–129.

Marks, M. A., Sabella, M. J., Burke, S. J., & Zaccaro, S. J. (2002). The impact of cross-training on team effectiveness. *Journal of Applied Psychology, 87,* 3–13.

Mathieu, J. E., Gilson, L. L., & Ruddy, T. M. (2006). Empowerment and team effectiveness: An empirical test of an integrated model. *Journal of Applied Psychology, 91,* 97–108.

Maznevski, M. L., & Chudoba, K. M. (2000). Bridging space over time: Global virtual team dynamics and effectiveness. *Organization Science, 11,* 473–492.

McGrath, J. E. (1984). *Groups: Interaction and performance.* Upper Saddle River, NJ: Prentice Hall.

McGrath, J. E., & Hollingshead, A. B. (1994). *Groups interacting with technology.* Newbury Park, CA: Sage.

Montoya-Weiss, M. M., Massey, A. P., & Song, M. (2001). Getting it together: Temporal coordination and conflict management in global virtual teams. *Academy of Management Journal, 44,* 1251–1261.

Moon, H., Hollenbeck, J. R., Humphrey, S. E., Ilgen, D. R., West, B., Ellis, A. P. J., Porter, C. O. L. H. (2004). Asymmetric adaptability: Dynamic team structure as oneway streets. *Academy of Management Journal, 47,* 681–695.

Moorehead, G., Neck, C. P., & West, M. S. (1998). The tendency toward defective decision making within self-managing teams: The relevance of groupthink for the 21st century. *Organizational Behavior and Human Decision Processes. Special Issue: Theoretical perspectives on groupthink: A twenty-fifth anniversary appraisal, 73,* 327–351.

Morgeson, F. P., & Humphrey, S. E. (2006). The work design questionnaire (WDQ): Developing and validating a comprehensive measure for assessing job design and the nature of work. *Journal of Applied Psychology, 91,* 1321–1339.

Oh, H., Chung, M. H., & Labianca, G. (2004). Group social capital and group effectiveness: The role of informal socializing ties. *Academy of Management Journal, Special Research Forum: Building Effective Networks, 47,* 860–875.

Orton, J. D., & Weick, K. E. (1990). Loosely coupled systems: A reconceptualization. *Academy of Management Review, 15,* 203–223.

Parker, S. K. (2003). Longitudinal effects of lean production on employee outcomes and the mediating role of work characteristics. *Journal of Applied Psychology, 88,* 620–634.

Porter, C. O. L. H. (2005). Goal orientation: Effects on backing-up behavior, performance efficacy, and commitment in teams. *Journal of Applied Psychology, 90,* 811–818.

Porter, C. O. L. H., Hollenbeck, J. R., Ilgen, D. R., Ellis, A. P. J., West, B. J., & Moon, H. (2003). Backing-up behavior in teams: The role of personality and legitimacy of need. *Journal of Applied Psychology, 88,* 391–403.

Price, K. H., Harrison, D. A., & Gavin, J. H. (2006). Withholding inputs in team contexts: Member composition, interaction processes, evaluation structure, and social loafing. *Journal of Applied Psychology, 91,* 1375–1384.

Reagans, R., & Zuckerman, E. W. (2001). Networks, diversity, and productivity: The social capital of corporate R&D teams. *Organization Science, 12,* 502–517.

Reagans, R., Zuckerman, E. W., & McEvily, B. (2004). How to make the team: Social networks vs. demography as criteria for designing effective teams. *Administrative Science Quarterly, 49,* 101–133.

Schippers, M. C., Hartog, D. N., Koopman, P. L., & Wienk, J. A. (2003). Diversity and team outcomes: The moderating effects of outcome interdependence and group longevity and the mediating effect of reflexivity. *Journal of Organizational Behavior, 24,* 779–802.

Sewell, G. (1998). The discipline of teams: The control of team-based industrial work through electronic and peer surveillance. *Administrative Science Quarterly, 43,* 397–428.

Steiner, I. D. (1972). *Group process and productivity.* New York: Academic Press.

Stewart, G. L., & Barrick, M. R. (2000). Team structure and performance: Assessing the mediating role of intrateam process and the moderating role of task type. *Academy of Management Journal, 43*, 135–148.

Stewart, G. L., & Manz, C. C. (1995). Leadership for self-managing work teams: A typology and integrative model. *Human Relations, 48*, 747–770.

Tangirala, S., & Alge, B. J. (2006). Reactions to unfair events in computer-mediated groups: A test of uncertainty management theory. *Organizational Behavior and Human Decision Processes, 100*, 1–20.

Tesluk, P., & Mathieu, J. E. (1999). Overcoming roadblocks to effectiveness: Incorporating management of performance barriers into models of work group effectiveness. *Journal of Applied Psychology, 84*, 200–217.

Thompson, J. D. (1967). *Organizations in action*. New York: McGraw Hill.

Trevino, L. K., Lengel, R. H., & Daft, R. L. (1987). Media symbolism, media richness, and media choice in organizations: A symbolic interactionist perspective. *Communication Research, 14*, 553–574.

Uhl-Bien, M., & Graen, G. B. (1998). Individual self-management: Analysis of professionals' self-managing activities in functional and cross-functional work teams. *Academy of Management Journal, 41*, 340–350.

Van der Vegt, G. S., & Bunderson, J. S. (2005). Learning and performance in multidisciplinary teams: The importance of collective team identification. *Academy of Management Journal, 48*, 532–547.

Van der Vegt, G. S., Emans, B. J. M., & Van de Vliert, E. (2001). Patterns of interdependence in work teams: A two-level investigation of the relations with job and team satisfaction. *Personnel Psychology, 54*, 51–69.

Van der Vegt, G. S., Van de Vliert, E., & Oosterhof, A. (2003). Informational dissimilarity and organizational citizenship behavior: The role of intrateam interdependence and team identification. *Academy of Management Journal, 46*, 715–722.

Van Knippenberg, D., & Schippers, M. C. (2007). Work group diversity. *Annual Review of Psychology, 58*, 515–541.

Wageman, R. (1995). Interdependence and group effectiveness. *Administrative Science Quarterly, 40*, 145–180.

Wageman, R. (1999). Task design, outcome interdependence, and individual differences: Their joint effects on effort in task-performing teams (Commentary on Huguet et al., 1999). *Group Dynamics: Theory, Research, and Practice, 3*, 132–137.

Wageman, R. (2001). How leaders foster self-managing team effectiveness: Design choices versus hands-on coaching. *Organization Science, 12*, 559–577.

Wegner, D. M. (1986). Transactive memory: A contemporary analysis of the group mind. In B. Mullen & G. R. Goethals (Eds.), *Theories of group behavior* (pp. 185–205). New York: Springer.

Wegner, D. M. (1995). A computer network model of human transactive memory. *Social Cognition, 13*, 1–21.

Weick, K. E. (1976). Educational organizations as loosely coupled systems. *Administrative Science Quarterly, 21*, 1–19.

Wilson, J. M., Straus, S. G., & McEvily, B. (2006). All in due-time: The development of trust in computer-mediated and face-to-face teams. *Organizational Behavior and Human Decision Processes, 99*, 16–33.

Zhang, Z. X, Hempel, P., Han, Y. L., & Tjosvold, D. (2007). Transactive memory system links work team characteristics and performance. *Journal of Applied Psychology, 92*, 1722–1730.

Team Participation and Empowerment: A Multilevel Perspective

Gilad Chen *and* Paul Tesluk

Abstract

In this chapter, we review and integrate the literatures on team empowerment and team participation. We first delineate the individual and collective phenomena that underlie team empowerment and participation, and suggest that the two constructs collectively capture psychological and behavioral aspects of team engagement, respectively. Second, we delineate a multilevel framework that includes individual-level, team-level, and organizational-level antecedents and outcomes of team empowerment and participation. In building this framework, we propose that adopting a multilevel perspective that considers both emergent and contextual phenomena can enhance our understanding of the bases for, as well as nature and function of, team empowerment and participation. Following this framework, we end the chapter by suggesting a set of research questions that can help extend the current state of knowledge pertaining to team empowerment and participation.

Key Words: Teams, empowerment, participation, engagement, motivation, levels of analysis

Scholars in the industrial-organizational psychology and related fields have long been interested in employee empowerment and participation. Indeed, this interest can be traced as far back as Kurt Lewin's classic research on leadership styles (Lewin, Lippitt, & White, 1939), as well as the Hawthorne studies of the 1930s (Roethlisberger & Dickson, 1939). At the individual level, a long history of studying agency needs (e.g., need for control, need for achievement; Kanfer, 1990) indicates the motivating potential of employee involvement and empowerment (Tesluk, Vance, & Mathieu, 1999). From an organizational perspective, employee involvement practices can not only serve to motivate employees, but can ensure further that employees contribute effectively to crucial organizational functions (Lawler, 1992). In the 1980s and 1990s, the increased reliance on self-managed and empowered teams has led to further interest in empowerment and participation (Kirkman & Rosen, 1997, 1999; Manz &

Sims, 1987). The current emphasis on knowledge-based work and utilizing highly specialized forms of employee expertise, along with a decided trend toward flatter and more organic organizational structure (DeNisi, Hitt, & Jackson, 2003), also highlight the role of empowerment and participation (Lawler, Mohrman, & Benson, 2001). Although much has been learned about the value of empowering and involving employees (see Spreitzer, 2008), as well as about work group and teams (Kozlowski & Bell, 2003; Mathieu, Maynard, Rapp, & Gilson, 2008), open questions remain regarding team participation and empowerment.

The present chapter builds on and extends prior work on employee involvement, participation, and empowerment in teams in two important ways. First, we seek to clarify similarities and distinctions between the empowerment and participation constructs, as well as related constructs. In so doing, we will develop a more integrative understanding of the psychological and behavioral attributes underlying team empowerment and participation, and propose a richer conceptualization of team engagement. Second, we will delineate a multilevel framework of the individual-level, team-level, and organizational-level antecedents and outcomes of team empowerment and participation. This framework integrates across literatures that, to date, have been somewhat disparate, yet which have several natural linkages that, if brought together, may provide a more unified perspective. We focus primarily on extant research on individual attributes, job design, team structure and design, leadership, and organizational-level high performance work systems that likely influence the emergence of empowerment and participation in teams. Thus, we aim to clarify core constructs and processes underlying team participation and empowerment, and to develop a better understanding of how these phenomena operate in a multilevel system involving individual team members, the team itself, and the organizational contexts within which the team operates.

In this chapter, we define teams as "a distinguishable set of two or more people who interact, dynamically, interdependently, and adaptively toward a common and valued goal/objective/mission, who have each been assigned specific roles or functions to perform, and who have a limited lifespan of membership" (Salas, Dickinson, Converse, & Tannenbaum, 1992, p. 4). Consistent with others (e.g., Kozlowski & Bell, 2003), we use the terms *teams* and *groups* interchangeably throughout the chapter. However, we recognize that the term *group* is broader and more inclusive than *team* (e.g., it can reflect a broad "racial group" in addition to a narrower "work group"), and that interdependencies are typically higher in teams than in groups.

Team Empowerment and Participation: Conceptual Similarities and Distinctions

In this section, we first review the literatures on empowerment and participation, and offer conceptual definitions of each. We then clarify how the two constructs are similar to and different from each other and related constructs. Finally, we discuss level issues pertaining to the meaning, structure, and function of each construct (cf. Morgeson & Hofmann, 1999). That is, we clarify the rationale for why and how empowerment and participation likely emerge as meaningful team-level constructs. Thus, in this section we hope to establish a conceptual basis on which a multilevel, system-based conceptual framework of team empowerment and

participation can be developed in later sections of the chapter.

Team Empowerment

In the past 20 years, the concept of empowerment has emerged from prior theories of leadership, work design, and motivation (for historical review, see Spreitzer, 2008). As reviewed by Spreitzer (2008), the literature has formed two overarching views of empowerment: (a) *structural empowerment*, which focuses on socio-technical forces that enable employee empowerment (e.g., Liden & Arad, 1996; Mills & Ungson, 2003), and (b) *psychological empowerment*, or employees' actual sense of being empowered. In this section, we focus primarily on employees' subjective feeling or sense of empowerment (i.e., psychological empowerment). We consider structural aspects of empowerment more in later sections, when examining multilevel antecedents of team empowerment.

At the individual level of analysis, scholars have conceptualized psychological empowerment as a multidimensional construct consisting of a set of beliefs or states—autonomy, meaning, competence, and impact (Spreitzer, 1995, 1996; Thomas & Velthouse, 1990). First, emanating from earlier work on the job characteristics model (Hackman & Oldham, 1976) and self-determination theory (Deci, Connell, & Ryan, 1989), *autonomy* involves employees' sense that they have the latitude to choose how and where to get their work done (e.g., which tasks to work on, what methods or procedures to apply at work, when to arrive and leave work, etc.). Second, also based on the job characteristics model, *meaning* captures how much employees intrinsically care about and identify with their work roles and tasks, or whether they believe they are performing worthwhile work. Third, *competence*, which is equivalent to self-efficacy (Bandura, 1997), captures the belief that employees possess in their capabilities to perform effectively work tasks and roles. Finally, *impact* involves a belief that one can make a difference in the workplace (e.g., by influencing decisions, processes, and outcomes in one's organization). Thus, empowered employees believe that they have the competence and autonomy to perform meaningful and impactful tasks.

Although several components of psychological empowerment emanate from the job characteristics model (Hackman & Oldham, 1976), there are two key differences between the two theoretical frameworks. First, in line with the distinction between structural and psychological empowerment, the job characteristics model emphasizes work and job dimensions that give rise to empowerment and related states (akin to structural empowerment), whereas the main focus of psychological empowerment is on the psychological reactions to job characteristics and other empowerment-related inputs (Chen & Klimoski, 2003; Liden, Wayne, & Sparrow, 2000). Second, although the job characteristics model also considers psychological states resulting from core job dimensions (i.e., experienced meaningfulness, experienced responsibility, and knowledge of results), an explicit assumption made by this model is that these psychological reactions operate separately from each other (i.e., are triggered by distinct antecedents and uniquely predict outcomes). In contrast, the four dimensions of psychological empowerment are assumed to reflect a higher order, unified construct, and hence are assumed to be functionally similar (cf. Law, Wong, & Mobley, 1998). That is, the four dimensions of empowerment are expected to be positively related, and to operate similarly (i.e., to be predicted by similar antecedents and to influence similar outcomes). Moreover, by definition, empowerment is high to the extent to which employees score highly on all four dimensions, such that experiencing a lower level of any one empowerment dimension reduces from one's overall empowerment experience (Spreitzer, 2008). Indeed, there is evidence supporting the functional similarity among the four empowerment dimensions (Chen & Klimoski, 2003; Spreitzer, 1995, 1996).

Much of the empowerment research has been conducted at the individual level of analysis. However, work by Kirkman and Rosen (1997, 1999) suggested that empowerment is also meaningful at the team level of analysis. According to Kirkman and Rosen (1997, 1999), team members can share the belief that their team is empowered. In particular, similar to individual-level conceptualization of empowerment, members can share beliefs regarding the extent to which their team has autonomy, performs meaningful task, is competent, and makes an impact. That is, Kirkman and Rosen (1997, 1999) argued that team empowerment consists of the same underlying dimensions as individual (psychological) empowerment.

Three important assumptions underlie team empowerment. First, it is assumed that core empowerment dimensions—autonomy, meaningfulness, competence, and impact—are isomorphic (i.e., capture the same conceptual meaning; cf. Kozlowski & Klein, 2000) across the individual and team level.

That is, the key difference between individual and team empowerment is the level or referent (individual vs. team) of the phenomenon, as opposed to the phenomenon itself. Indeed, measures of individual and team empowerment often differ only with respect to the referent of the items, not the content of the items—for example, "I am confident about my ability to do my job" reflects individual competence (Spreitzer, 1995), whereas "my team believes it can be very productive" reflects team competence (Kirkman, Rosen, Tesluk, & Gibson, 2004).

Second, team empowerment is assumed to be shared among team members, such that it reflects a shared experience among members, as opposed to an idiosyncratic experience that could differ across members (Chen, Mathieu, & Bliese, 2004). According to Seibert, Silver, and Randolph (2004), members of teams experience common collective interactions among members; exposure to common goals, tasks, and task procedures; and consistent leadership and managerial practices. Through such shared experiences, team members likely develop a shared sense of team empowerment (Kirkman & Rosen, 1999; Kirkman et al., 2004). That is, individual members' perceptions of team empowerment likely converge over time, to reflect what has been termed a *referent-shift consensus* compositional model, in which individuals share perceptions of team-level attributes (Chan, 1998; Kozlowski & Klein, 2000).

Finally, while clearly related to individual empowerment, team empowerment is assumed to be distinct from individual empowerment. Specifically, team members may differ in how psychologically empowered they feel personally, and yet simultaneously share a sense of how empowered their team is. Thus, team members who believe that their team is highly empowered may not necessarily feel personally empowered, and, likewise, team members who believe that their team has low levels of team empowerment can still personally maintain high levels of psychological empowerment.

In support of the first two assumptions, there is evidence that: (a) the four team empowerment dimensions are positively and significantly correlated, (b) team members share perceptions of team empowerment, and (c) average levels of team empowerment can be used to reliably differentiate between teams (Chen, Kirkman, Kanfer, Allen, & Rosen, 2007; Kirkman & Rosen, 1999; Kirkman & Shapiro, 2001; Kirkman et al., 2004). Furthermore, in support of the third assumption, Chen et al. (2007) found that, despite a significant positive correlation between team empowerment and psychological empowerment ($r = .57$, $p < .05$), there was stronger support for aggregating perceptions of team empowerment to the team level, than for aggregating perceptions of psychological empowerment. Moreover, Chen et al. (2007) found that individual and team empowerment contributed uniquely to the prediction of individual and team performance, respectively. In sum, team empowerment parallels psychological empowerment in terms of its conceptual meaning, but the two constructs reside at distinct levels of analysis.

Team Participation

A closely related concept to empowerment, participation captures more behavioral aspects of employee involvement. Specifically, Locke, Alavi, and Wagner (1997, p. 323) posit that "participation is best viewed as a process of information exchange and knowledge transfer." Employee participation involves contributions to work-related decisions and processes. Relative to empowerment, there has been a far longer tradition of theory and research on participation. Ironically, however, as we note below, the concept of *team participation* is relatively less well-developed than the relatively newer concept of team empowerment. Instead, as we next explain, team participation and related phenomena (e.g., involvement) have been considered in three streams of research: (a) participation in decision making (PDM), (b) proactive and citizenship behaviors, and (c) self-management/autonomous work teams. We next briefly review the relevance of these literatures to the concept of team participation. Building on these literatures, we then offer a more concrete conceptual definition of team participation.

PARTICIPATION IN DECISION MAKING

As reviewed by Locke and Schweiger (1979) and Locke et al. (1997), PDM research can be traced back to classic research on democratic/participative versus autocratic/directive leadership and management practices (e.g., Lewin et al., 1939; Roethlisberger & Dickson, 1939). The core underlying assumption of PDM is that encouraging and allowing employees to be involved in decision-making processes motivate employees and promote decision quality and outcomes. However, Locke et al. (1997, p. 304) concluded in their review of the PDM literature that "its effects, as it has been studied to date, are neither large nor consistent." Instead, it is important to consider mediators (e.g., perceived fairness; Roberson, Moye, & Locke, 1999) and moderators

(e.g., nature of the task and employee knowledge; Vroom & Yetton, 1973) that explain how and when PDM is related to performance and motivation outcomes, as well as the larger set of interrelated ways in which PDM is exercised in a given organizational setting (e.g., task forces, suggestion programs, quality improvement teams) rather than a single, limited area (Ledford & Lawler, 1994). Similar conclusions have been reached in research on participation in goal setting (Latham, Erez, & Locke, 1988), according to which participation in goal setting promotes motivation and performance under certain conditions but not others (e.g., when performing more challenging rather than simpler tasks) and is best understood and applied by adapting to the specific organizational context (e.g., linking to superordinate organizational goals; Latham, 2001).

Importantly, although PDM research is often conducted in the context of groups or teams, teams and teamwork have often been given a more secondary role relative to the concepts of participation and decision making. Moreover, akin to the notion of structural empowerment, PDM research has been mainly focused on social and structural conditions (e.g., leadership styles, organizational and job design) that encourage participation, rather than on participation in and of itself (Locke et al., 1997). Thus, although clearly informative for participation processes in teams, with few exceptions (e.g., Sonnentag, 2001), prior PDM research has not explicitly defined or measured team participation outside the decision making domain.

PROACTIVE AND CITIZENSHIP BEHAVIORS

Unlike work on PDM, which has tended to emphasize antecedents of participation, theorizing and research on employee proactive and citizenship behaviors have more explicitly and directly mapped participation-related behaviors and processes. In particular, individual-level research on personal initiative (e.g., Frese & Fay, 2001), voice (Van Dyne & LePine, 1998), and citizenship behaviors (e.g., Podsakoff, MacKenzie, Paine, & Bachrach, 2000) has more directly considered employees' active and proactive engagement at work (for review and integration of these literatures, see Griffin, Neal, & Parker, 2007). Common to these individual-level behaviors is the notion that employees choose—as well as can be encouraged—to actively participate in and contribute to important organizational activities and processes. For instance, research on voice by Tangirala and Ramanujam (2008) has shown that employees are especially likely to engage in voice behavior when they perceive that they have a high level of personal control, and identify strongly with their organization. These findings also suggest that there is a likely connection between psychological empowerment (as reflected by personal control) and participation behavior.

Although most research on proactive and citizenship behaviors to date has been conducted at the individual level of analysis, there is also more recent work on such behaviors in the context of teams. In particular, team researchers have examined team member backup behavior, which includes assisting other members to perform their role in the team and stepping in to fulfill roles that should otherwise be performed by other members (Marks, Mathieu, & Zaccaro, 2001; Porter, Hollenbeck, Ilgen, Ellis, West, & Moon, 2003), as well as broader sets of group-level organizational citizenship behaviors (Ehrhart, 2004). A recent meta-analysis conducted by LePine, Piccolo, Jackson, Mathieu, and Saul (2008) found that backup behaviors relate to other effective teamwork processes (e.g., coordination, conflict management), as well as to improved team effectiveness.

Thus, unlike PDM research, research on proactive and citizenship behaviors in general, and backup behavior in particular, has focused more explicitly on participation-like behaviors and processes. However, like PDM research, team participation has not been explicitly considered or defined in the literature on proactive and citizenship behaviors. Moreover, the bulk of this research has been conducted at the individual level of analysis, and has not considered how such behaviors emerge and aggregate to form the broader concept of team participation.

PARTICIPATION IN SELF-MANAGED, AUTONOMOUS WORK TEAMS

A third literature relevant to the concept of team participation has focused on self-managed, or autonomous work teams. Members of self-managing work teams are encouraged to be involved and to participate "in making decisions that were formerly the province of supervisors and managers" (Cohen & Bailey, 1997, p. 242). Although self-managed teams involve team design (akin to structural empowerment), this literature has emphasized the importance of members' active participation in key team decision and processes. That is, members in such teams assume and share leadership functions and responsibilities. According to Manz and Sims (1987), many PDM principles are applicable

at the team level. In particular, in self-managed teams, members are encouraged to set team goals, decide on role assignments, and even make staffing decision (Manz & Sims, 1987). Indeed, work on shared leadership (Carson, Tesluk, & Marrone, 2007; Pearce, & Sims, 2002) suggests that teams whose members actively participate in such leadership responsibilities and decisions tend to be more effective.

Relative to research on PDM and proactive and citizenship behaviors, the self-managing teams literature has more explicitly focused on the team level, and has considered the value of involving team members and encouraging participation in teams. However, like research on PDM, the main focus in the self-managing teams literature has been on antecedents of team participation (namely, team design and leadership principles that encourage and promote participation), as opposed to more directly on team participation processes.

DEFINING TEAM PARTICIPATION

All three literatures reviewed above highlight the importance of participation in teams, behaviors reflecting members' participation, and socio-technical conditions that likely induce and stimulate team participation. However, all three literatures fall short of directly conceptualizing *team participation*. Despite lack of clarity regarding the content and nature of team participation, the review above indicates that team participation entails greater engagement of team members in processes contributing to team success. Hence, to understand better what collective behaviors team participation entails, we need to consider the specific team processes that likely contribute to team effectiveness.

A comprehensive review of the team literature conducted by Marks et al. (2001) has identified three main types of team processes: (a) *transition processes* (i.e., mainly decision-making processes involving scanning the team's internal and external environment and the generation of team task strategies, goals, and plans); (b) *action processes* (i.e., processes by which teams coordinate and regulate collective effort in pursuit of team goals and objectives, or decision-implementation processes); and (c) *interpersonal processes* (i.e., processes in which teams manage affective and motivational states, such as managing conflict or morale in the team). Thus, we submit that *team participation involves the extent to which team members collectively and actively engage in such team processes*. That is, team processes reflect the targeted collective behaviors that emerge when team members engage in greater levels of participation.

Team participation may not necessarily mean that members are engaging in such processes effectively or accurately, although empirical evidence suggests that more frequent and more active engagement in team processes tends to lead to more effective and accurate execution of these processes. For example, a study by Marks, Sabella, Burke, and Zaccaro (2002) reported that expert ratings of team coordination frequency (i.e., how *frequently* team members engaged in coordination activities) correlated .90 with team coordination quality (i.e., how *effectively* team members engaged in coordination activities). Thus, although team participation is more congruent with the frequency by which team members engaged in team processes than with the quality of team processes, team process frequency and quality are likely highly related. In other words, team participation is likely to be highly beneficial for team functioning and effectiveness (cf. LePine et al., 2008).

Of course, individual differences in how team members contribute to team processes are possible. For example, some members may be more likely to "socially loaf" than others, or to allocate less effort toward the accomplishment of team tasks (Karau & Williams, 1993). Also, due to the fact that many teams are structured such that different members fulfill different roles, members may contribute equally to team processes and success in different ways, consistent with their unique and different roles (e.g., a pilot and a copilot likely need to perform different functions for the flight team to coordinate and communicate effectively). However, in line with Chen and Kanfer's (2006) systems-based view of team motivation, we argue that team participation is higher when all members are fully engaged in performing their individual roles in the team, as well as in allocating greater effort toward the execution of team processes.

Empowerment and Participation: An Integration

The literature review above indicates that little effort to date has attempted to integrate team empowerment and team participation. Our review, however, indicates that there are three important similarities between conceptualizations of these two constructs. First, both empowerment and participation assume that involving team members in core team functions would lead to improved team effectiveness. More specifically, both assume that teams with greater levels of empowerment and participation will be able to transform their internal and external resources (e.g., members' capabilities, financial resources) into improved team outcomes, leading teams to be more productive, more viable over time, and to have more satisfied members (cf. Hackman, 1987). Second, and related, the assumption behind team empowerment and team participation is that both would not only be satisfying for team members, but would further motivate them to be more engaged at work. As stated by Brown (1996), involving employees "can enhance organizational effectiveness and productivity by engaging employees more completely in their work and making work a more meaningful and fulfilling experience" (p. 235). Thus, the assumption is that team empowerment and team participation both enable and motivate greater member involvement, leading to more effective team functioning.

A third similarity between the empowerment and participation literatures is that they both capture aspects of employee and team *engagement*. Indeed, researchers have argued that the concept of engagement, which has emerged as a popular construct in the industrial-organizational psychology literature, contains both psychological (i.e., feelings of energy and absorption) and behavioral (i.e., extra-role behaviors) components that correspond closely to empowerment and participation (see Macey & Schneider, 2008). Thus, empowerment and participation collectively capture important aspects of engagement.

However, there are also two key differences between team empowerment and team participation. First, team empowerment has been conceptualized as a collection of four "emergent states"—(i.e., shared *perceptions* regarding the team that both influence and are influenced by team activities and outcomes; Marks et al., 2001). In contrast, team participation involves the extent to which team members actually engage in *behaviors* that contribute to team functions and outcomes, and hence are more akin to the notion of "team processes" than team emergent states (Marks et al., 2001). In other words, team empowerment captures a collective *psychological engagement* among team members (i.e., team members' sense of engagement), whereas team participation involves collective *behavioral engagement* of team members (i.e., team members' actual engagement in team processes). This distinction, again, is consistent with a recent framework of employee engagement suggested by Macey and Schneider (2008), which has also distinguished between psychological and behavioral aspects of engagement (albeit their focus was on the individual level of analysis).

A second distinction is that scholars have been far clearer regarding the dimensionality and content of team empowerment than for team participation. Team empowerment is a relatively narrower construct than is team participation. Specifically, as discussed above, team empowerment is a multidimensional construct, with four well-established dimensions that, when aggregated, represent team empowerment (Kirkman & Rosen, 1997, 1999). In contrast, the teams and related literatures are far less clear with respect to specific behavioral indicators of team participation. Our definition of team participation as engagement in team processes helps reduce some of this ambiguity, by emphasizing Marks et al.'s (2001) typology of team processes as the key targets of team participation (i.e., teams may differ in the extent to which they engage or participate in different team processes identified by Marks et al., 2001). However, team participation remains a broader concept than team empowerment, as it can involve teams' engagement in a large variety of team processes (e.g., voice, boundary spanning, internal leadership).

Given their similar assumptions and shared focus on collective team members' engagement, it is likely that team empowerment and team participation are positively and strongly related. That is, more empowered team members are more likely to actively participate in and contribute to team processes, and vice versa. Indeed, according to Chen and Kanfer (2006), team empowerment reflects motivational states that drive and sustain the collective effort that team members devote toward generation and accomplishment of team goals. Thus, together, team empowerment and team participation likely capture a boarder "construct space" of team members' collective engagement (cf. Macey & Schneider, 2008). Although we are not aware of any empirical evidence for the relationship between team empowerment and team participation, there is evidence that team emergent states positively and strongly relate to team processes (for reviews, see Chen & Kanfer, 2006; Marks et al., 2001; Mathieu et al., 2008). Also, as noted earlier, individual-level research on voice has found that constructs similar to empowerment (i.e., personal control) and participation (i.e., voice) are positively related (Tangirala & Ramanujam, 2008).

Empowerment and Participation: Cross-Level Relationships

The discussion above indicated that empowerment and participation reflect "emergent phenomena," which originate in individual-level cognitions and behaviors and aggregate to form meaningful collective constructs (Kozlowski & Klein, 2000). The emergent nature of team empowerment and participation also means that empowerment and participation at the team level are likely to be related to empowerment and participation at the individual level. That is, individual-level and team-level empowerment and participation "exist" in an open social system, in which individual cognitions and behaviors influence the emergence of shared (or collective) cognitions and behaviors, which in turn are also likely to impact individual cognitions and behaviors (see Chen & Kanfer, 2006; Chen et al., 2007; Seibert et al., 2004).

Thus, the interconnectedness between empowerment and participation across levels reflect both "bottom-up" and "top-down" processes, through which individual members influence their team, and the team influences individual members, respectively. For example, individual team members' sense of personal empowerment and active participation likely spreads across members, as individuals observe others on their team take greater initiative and engage more in team activities (e.g., as a result of greater autonomy), project confidence in their capabilities, and discuss their attitudes pertaining to task meaningfulness and impact. In addition, when the team as a whole engages in tasks consistently over time, it likely signals to each individual member that participation is encouraged and expected (reflecting social learning and other normative influences on individuals in the team; cf. Hackman, 1992).

The interconnectedness of individual-level and team-level empowerment and participation also means that antecedents affecting individual empowerment and participation likely emerge to influence team empowerment and participation, and vice versa. This is important, because it suggests that models of team empowerment and participation can be expanded by adopting a multilevel perspective. To date, there has been very little attempt to examine multilevel models of team empowerment and participation (two recent exceptions, which we discuss further below, include Chen et al., 2007, and Seibert et al., 2004). Accordingly, we posit that a multilevel perspective is needed to better understand how team empowerment and participation evolve as a function of individual-, team-, and organizational-level influences.

Multilevel Antecedents of Team Empowerment and Participation

In the sections that follow, we discuss multilevel (individual-, team-, and organizational-level) antecedents of team empowerment and participation. Rather than focusing on a comprehensive and specific list of all possible antecedents, we focus primarily on delineating a framework for identifying likely antecedents at each level. We believe that such a framework can help researchers identify different antecedents in different contexts, where different research purposes might be more salient. We do, however, provide examples of various antecedents at different levels, to illustrate and support the framework. Also, given the likely strong relationship between team empowerment and team participation, we do not attempt to identify separate antecedents for team empowerment and team participation, but, rather, focus on more powerful antecedents that likely affect both constructs. In doing so, our framework focuses on *both* psychological and behavioral aspects of team engagement. Thus, we aim to delineate a general framework for the multilevel bases of team empowerment and participation.

Individual-Level Antecedents

Teams consist of a social system of interdependent individual members—that is, individual team members cannot accomplish their roles effectively, and the team as a whole cannot function effectively, unless members work together in coordinated fashion (Kozlowski & Bell, 2003). Yet, despite the notion that team behavior is highly dependent on individual member behavior, the vast majority of team empowerment and participation research to date has ignored individual-level predictors. Focusing on individual-level empowerment, Spreitzer (2008) has suggested that individual differences may influence empowerment either directly, or by moderating other influences on empowerment. According to Chen and Kanfer's (2006) multilevel theory of motivated behavior in teams, individual-oriented inputs—or antecedents that can differentially affect members within the same team—can influence team-level motivational states (e.g., team empowerment) and processes (e.g., participation) in two distinct ways: (a) via indirect or mediated processes; and (b) via moderated processes. Chen and Kanfer

(2006) proposed that such individual-oriented inputs may include individual differences (e.g., personality, values, or expertise), as well as social influences directed at specific individuals (e.g., individualized feedback, leader-member relationship). We next discuss these distinct processes through which individual-level antecedents likely influence team empowerment and participation.

INDIRECT AND MEDIATED INFLUENCES

Individual-level antecedents can exert indirect "bottom-up" influences on team empowerment and participation through two mechanisms. First, antecedents can influence individual members' empowerment and participation, which, in turn, aggregates to influence shared perceptions of team empowerment and collective, team-level participation. Indeed, there is empirical evidence that individual and team empowerment are positively related (Chen et al., 2007; Seibert et al., 2004). Second, antecedents can aggregate to the team level, and then directly influence team empowerment and participation. This mediated effect through aggregation is especially likely to occur when predictors involve individual difference in personality, values, and expertise, which have been shown to relate to team effectiveness when aggregated to the team level (Bell, 2007). Thus, as summarized in Figure 24.1, individual-level inputs can influence individual-level empowerment and participation, which then aggregate to influence team empowerment and participation, or influence team empowerment and participation directly, after they aggregate to the team level. Stated another way, the indirect nature of these effects occur as either the mediators (individual empowerment and participation) or the inputs themselves aggregate to the team level.

Research on psychological empowerment found three types of individual-level antecedents. First, there is evidence that positive self-views, including self-esteem (Spreitzer, 1995) and general self-efficacy (Chen & Klimoski, 2003), are positively related to psychological empowerment. Such individual differences likely lead individuals to interpret work experience more positively, as well as to be more proactive at work, and hence enhance the likelihood of being more empowered by their supervisors. Of course, other individual difference constructs yet to be studied can also predict individual empowerment. For example, the need for achievement and openness (which are highly related to general self-efficacy) and emotional stability (which is highly

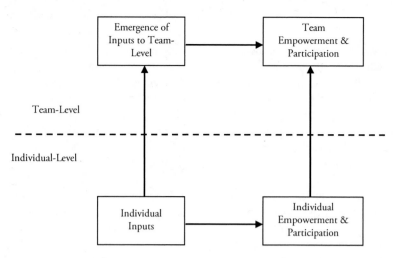

Figure 24.1 Mediated Individual-Level Influences on Team Empowerment and Participation.

related to self-esteem) are also likely to positively relate to individual empowerment.

A second set of individual-level antecedents of empowerment involve various characteristics of jobs to which employees are exposed. Spreitzer (1996), for example, found that employees had higher levels of psychological empowerment when their job was less ambiguous, when they worked in larger work units, and when they had access to more information at work. Further, studies by Chen and Klimoski (2003) and Liden et al. (2000) showed that core job characteristics—including greater skill variety, task identity, autonomy, task significance, and job feedback—positively related to employees' psychological empowerment. Together, these sets of findings suggest that richer, more complex, and enriched jobs and work assignments lend themselves to—or even require—greater levels of employee empowerment.

Finally, a third individual-level antecedent of employee empowerment involves the quality of relationships that employees develop with their supervisor and coworkers. As suggested by Spreitzer (1996), higher quality relationships at work lead employees to gain greater social support, and hence feel more empowered. Moreover, leaders are more likely to empower followers with whom they have better relationships, and hence in whom they trust (Chen & Klimoski, 2003). In support, studies have found positive relationships between employees' psychological and perceived social support (Spreitzer, 1996) and perceived quality of relationships with one's leader and coworkers (Chen & Klimoski, 2003; Liden et al., 2000).

The research reviewed above has thus linked three types of individual-level inputs (positive self-views, work characteristics, and social relationships) and individual-level empowerment. However, most of this research has not tested whether empowerment at the individual level mediates between such antecedents and *team* empowerment. In one exception, a study by Chen et al. (2007) did not only link between perceptions of leader-member relationships and individual empowerment, but also between individual and team empowerment (suggesting an indirect, leader-member relationship → individual empowerment → team empowerment relationship). Multilevel studies by Chen and Bliese (2002) and Jex and Bliese (1999), focusing on efficacy beliefs (which capture one of four empowerment components), also indicated that self-efficacy can link between individual-level antecedents (e.g., experience, job characteristics) and team-level efficacy beliefs. Thus, there is support for the notion that psychological empowerment can mediate between individual-level antecedents and team empowerment. In a similar fashion, there is evidence for individual team member participation serving to link individual-level antecedents and team-level participation. For instance, Marrone, Tesluk, and Carson (2007) found that team members' efficacy in engaging in boundary-spanning activities and self-defined role expectations were related to their team's level of participation in boundary-spanning behaviors through individual engagement in boundary spanning. Hence, while the research relating individual-level antecedents to empowerment and participation at the team level is scant, the limited work to date encourages the exploration of such relationships.

Relative to the evidence cited above, there is far less empirical evidence in support of indirect effects of individual-level antecedents on team empowerment through aggregation of inputs to the team-level, or any effects of such antecedents on team participation. However, there is support of this expected indirect effect in the broader teams and proactive behavior literatures. In particular, Porter et al. (2003) found that members with higher levels of conscientiousness and emotional stability were more likely to engage in backup behaviors. In addition, Jackson, Colquitt, Wesson, & Zapata-Phelan (2006) found that team members with higher levels of collectivism (i.e., those who place greater value in being a member of a group, as well as in achieving group-oriented outcomes) exhibited greater engagement in team-oriented behaviors, and performed better in the context of their team. Moreover, there is evidence that, at the team level, team composition of members' personality (Barrick, Stewart, Neubert, & Mount, 1998) and more direct measures of team personality (Hofmann & Jones, 2005) are associated with team processes and outcomes.

MODERATED INFLUENCES

Individual-level antecedents can also impact team empowerment and participation via moderating influences. In particular, certain individual-level inputs can attenuate, or moderate, the extent to which interventions directed at empowering and involving individuals and teams would be successful (Spreitzer, 2008). In other words, certain individual-level attributes are likely to make individuals more receptive, or instead resistant, to empowerment and involvement practices and interventions. In particular, as summarized below, likely moderators include motivational attributes, cultural differences, employee expertise, and the quality of leader-member relationships.

First, according to the job characteristics model, more enriched and complex job characteristics have more motivating effects for individuals higher on growth need strength, defined as one's "desire to obtain 'growth' satisfaction from his or her work" (Hackman & Oldham, 1975, pp. 162–163). Likewise, Chen and Kanfer (2006) proposed that team members with a higher need for achievement are more likely to embrace motivational interventions, such as empowering and involvement practices. An open question, which has yet to be addressed in prior research, is whether teams

composed of members with higher levels of motivational traits and tendencies also collectively react more positively to team-oriented empowering and involvement practices.

Second, according to Spreitzer (2008), culture seems to be an important boundary condition affecting empowerment interventions. As a recent review of the cross-cultural organizational behavior literature concluded, "empowering employees… can be effective when it is congruent with values in the cultural context" (Gelfand, Erez, & Aycan, 2007, p. 484). In the context of teams, greater levels of empowerment and participation means that team members are encouraged to (a) share power and decision authority with each other and with the team's leader(s), and (b) work collectively to develop and implement team goals. Consistent with this, Kirkman and Shapiro (1997, 2001) theorized and empirically found that team members with low levels of power distance (who value flatter organizational structures, and who believe that power is best shared between superiors and followers) and high levels of collectivism (who value group work and care about group success and well-being) are more likely to embrace self-management in teams than are those with high power distance and low collectivism levels. Thus, employees' cultural values, particularly power distance and collectivism, likely moderate the extent to which team members embrace empowerment and participation in teams.

Third, research by Ahearne, Mathieu, and their colleagues suggests further that team members' expertise (i.e., their work-related knowledge, skills, and experience) can moderate influences of empowering leadership behaviors. In particular, in two studies (Ahearne, Mathieu, & Rapp; 2005; Mathieu, Ahearne, & Taylor, 2007), these researchers found that empowering leadership leads to higher levels of self-efficacy and adaptability among employees with low, rather than high, levels of expertise. These results suggest that employees with lower levels of expertise are especially likely to benefit from empowering practices, implying that the empowering practices can help develop expertise as well as motivate employees to utilize their expertise.

Finally, according to Chen et al. (2007), the quality of leader-member relationships is likely to interact with empowerment-related interventions to affect psychological empowerment. Specifically, "members with more positive [leader-member relationships] are more likely to believe further that the leader would also empower them personally more relative to other members, given their particularly high levels of mutual trust and respect" (Chen et al., 2007, p. 334). Stated another way, individual team members who have better relationships with their team leader are more likely to embrace empowering leadership practices, because they believe that they will not lose personal power—and in fact may gain more personal power—when their team as a whole becomes more empowered. Chen et al.'s (2007) study supported this assertion.

SUMMARY

In sum, individual-level input variables can influence team empowerment and participation in two ways. First, individual-level inputs may influence team empowerment and participation through their influence on individual empowerment (which in turn aggregates to influence team empowerment), or through their emergence to the team level, where they in turn directly influence team empowerment and participation. Second, individual-level inputs can moderate the extent to which team members find team empowerment and involvement practices motivating and rewarding. Our review has identified three kinds of individual-level antecedents that can contribute to team empowerment participation: (a) *team member attributes* (including personality, self-views, cultural values, and expertise); (b) *job and work characteristics* (e.g., the extent to which jobs and work assignments are rich and complex); and (c) *relationships with leaders and coworkers* (which include better access to a supportive social network).

Although individual-level inputs are unlikely to directly influence team empowerment and participation, they can certainly explain an important piece of the team empowerment and participation puzzle. In particular, better understanding of the impact of individual-level inputs can make two important contributions. First, it can help organizations and managers enhance team empowerment and participation by employing individual-oriented practices (e.g., staffing, training, leadership), to complement or even enhance team-oriented practices. Second, it can inform managers of likely reasons that some individual team members embrace empowerment more than others, and hence can identify ways of reducing members' resistance for empowerment and participation.

Team-Level Antecedents

Not surprisingly, relative to individual-level antecedents, which have rarely been linked directly to team empowerment and participation, more conceptual and empirical work has considered team-level antecedents of team empowerment and participation. As reviewed by Locke et al. (1997) and Spreitzer (2008), the literature has identified a variety of antecedents of both team participation and empowerment. In line with socio-technical approaches to the study of organizational behavior (Salancik & Pfeffer, 1978; Trist & Bamforth, 1951), as well as with the social-structural view of empowerment (Mills & Ungson, 2003), we propose that team-level antecedents can be classified as either *social-oriented inputs* or *structure-oriented inputs*. We next review prior theorizing and empirical research in support of this classification of team-level antecedents. Since team-level antecedents of team empowerment and participation have been discussed extensively elsewhere (e.g., Kirkman & Rosen, 1997, 1999; Locke et al., 1997), our review below is fairly brief.

SOCIAL-ORIENTED INPUTS

Social-oriented inputs include inputs such as leadership behaviors and climate, which exert social influences on teams. Indeed, as reviewed by Locke et al. (1997) and Locke and Schweiger (1979), the majority of PDM research has focused on participative leadership practices, which involve employees in core leadership functions. Likewise, according to Kirkman and Rosen's (1997) theoretical model of team empowerment, as well as Manz and Sims's (1987) work on self-management teams, empowering leadership practices play a major role in allowing, encouraging, and enabling team empowerment and participation. Empowering leadership behaviors encourage team members to set their own goals, delegate high responsibility to the team, enhance team members' sense of control and autonomy, and raise team members' expectations regarding team outcomes (Kirkman & Rosen, 1997).

Another social-oriented input, which is closely related to empowering and participative leadership, is empowerment climate. Seibert et al. (2004, p. 334) defined empowerment climate as "a shared perception regarding the extent to which an organization makes use of structures, policies, and practices supporting employee empowerment." In particular, empowerment climate consists of shared perceptions regarding practices that encourage information sharing, autonomy, and team accountability. Although climate can operate at multiple levels of analysis (e.g., psychological, team/unit, organization), Seibert et al. (2004) have argued that empowerment climate is most meaningful at the team level of analysis, since team members are most likely to experience empowerment practices in the context of their team, often as executed and "translated" by their immediate team leader (for similar arguments, see Zohar, 2000). In fact, Chen et al. (2007) have argued that empowering leadership is highly related to team-level empowerment climate, since both capture "ambient leadership behaviors (cf. Hackman, 1992), which are directed at the team as a whole and have the potential of developing shared, team-level empowerment" (p. 333). Thus, social-oriented inputs consist of team members' shared perceptions regarding leadership and managerial practices that empower and involve team members in core team functions.

STRUCTURE-ORIENTED INPUTS

Structure-oriented inputs include team-related human resource management policies and practices and team structure and design features. Team-oriented human resource management policies and practices include team-based rewards and feedback, team staffing, and team training (e.g., cross-training of members in the team; Kirkman & Rosen, 1997). Relevant team structure and design features include team work characteristics (analogous to individual job characteristics, but also including the extent to which roles in the team are interdependent), enabling team communication technologies (e.g., teleconferencing), and the extent to which team members are supported by the organization and have access to information critical to their mission (Campion, Medsker, & Higgs, 1993; Kirkman & Rosen, 1997; Locke et al., 1997). In line with the notion of structural empowerment (Mills & Ungson, 2003), these team structural features are designed to encourage and enable greater team empowerment and more effective team participation.

EMPIRICAL SUPPORT FOR TEAM-LEVEL ANTECEDENTS

Several team-level studies have provided support for both social-oriented and structure-oriented team antecedents of team empowerment and participation. In a study of teams in manufacturing and insurance companies, Kirkman and Rosen (1999) found that empowering leadership behaviors, design features that encourage self-management (which they dubbed production/service responsibilities), team-oriented human resources policies, and supportive team environment all positively related to team empowerment. Empowering leadership behaviors also related positively to team

empowerment in Chen et al.'s (2007) study of service teams. Evidence linking leadership to team participation comes from Tesluk and Mathieu (1999), who found that both internal and external forms of empowering leadership predicted the degree to which teams collectively engaged in problem management strategies, which, in turn, was related to the ability of teams to minimize work constraints and improve their performance and viability. In addition, although they did not explicitly measure team empowerment, Seibert et al. (2004) found that the empowerment climate positively related to average levels of psychological empowerment in the team, as well as to team performance. Finally, in a study of customer service engineers (Mathieu, Gilson, & Ruddy, 2006), training supports, organizational supports, and team-oriented work design positively and uniquely related to team empowerment. Mathieu et al. (2006) also found that training supports positively related to the extent to which teams engaged in effective team processes both directly and through team empowerment, and that organizational supports and team design related to team processes through their relationships with team empowerment.

SUMMARY

As discussed above, team-level antecedents of empowerment and participation consist of a confluence of social and structural forces that encourage and enable members to feel collectively empowered and to collectively participate in teamwork processes. Given that these antecedents are at the team level, and are more directly targeting team empowerment and participation, they likely exert more powerful and direct effects than do either individual-level or organizational-level antecedents. This is consistent with multilevel principles which argue that influences that emanate within the same level of a phenomenon tend to be more immediate and powerful than those emanating from antecedents that originate at different levels of analysis (Kozlowski & Klein, 2000). Furthermore, as we alluded to earlier, and will discuss further below, team-level antecedents can mediate the influences of individual-level and organizational-level antecedents on team empowerment and participation.

It should be noted that other social-oriented inputs besides empowering leadership and empowering climate are also possible. For instance, group norms that encourage employee involvement and team composition on certain attributes noted earlier can also promote team empowerment and participation. However, we are not aware of any previous studies considering social-oriented input other than leadership and climate. In contrast, researchers have identified a more comprehensive list of team structure-oriented inputs.

Organizational-Level Antecedents

Thus far, we have considered antecedents of team empowerment and participation that reside at the team- and individual-level. However, teams operate in a broader organizational context, in which they are exposed to organizational-level phenomena (Ilgen, 1999). As such, it is highly likely that organizational-level antecedents also influence team empowerment and participation. In particular, various contextual features at the organizational level of analysis can both facilitate and impede the emergence of empowerment and participation at the team level of analysis. By organizational-level, we broadly refer to any collective unit that resides above the team level, and under which multiple teams are nested (e.g., the organization as a whole, as well as strategic business units, divisions, establishments, or departments within the organization).

Indeed, there is evidence that organizational-level features impact team functioning and effectiveness. For instance, Ancona and Caldwell (1992) found that teams functioned more effectively when their members engaged with top managers at higher organizational levels, and with members from different teams. In addition, a study by Griffin and Mathieu (1997) demonstrated that team leadership, climate, and processes at one organizational level can cascade downward to influence team leadership, climate, and processes at lower organizational levels. Although we are not aware of any research that has explicitly linked organizational-level antecedents with team empowerment or team participation, we propose two types of organizational-level antecedents that parallel team-level antecedents: high performance work systems and organizational climate (see also Spreitzer, 2008).

HIGH PERFORMANCE WORK SYSTEMS (HPWS)

According to Spreitzer (2008), HPWS have been the focus of much of the research to date that has centered on structural aspects of empowerment. HPWS involve a coherent system of human resource management (HRM) practices that enhances the organization's workforce (a) *ability* to perform (e.g., through integrated job analysis, recruitment, staffing, and training systems), and (b) *motivation* to perform (e.g., through well-aligned compensation, performance

management, job design, and employee development systems; Huselid, 1995). Although other labels and conceptualizations of HRM systems have been proposed in the strategic HRM literature (e.g., high commitment systems, high involvement systems), a review by Lepak, Liao, Chung, and Harden (2006) indicated that these systems largely share the same set of HRM practices, as well as a common emphasis on a well-integrated and a well-aligned set of HRM practices that enhance employee ability and motivation. Moreover, a study by Lepak and Snell (2002) found that HRM practices that target ability/productivity are highly related to those targeting commitment/motivation. Providing support for the utility of HPWS, a meta-analysis by Combs, Liu, Hall, and Ketchen (2006) found that such systems are positively related firm-level performance.

We are not aware of any research to date that either proposed or tested cross-level effects of firm-level HPWS and team-level empowerment and participation. Nonetheless, there are two main reasons that HPWS would be positively related to team empowerment and participation. First, as found by Lepak et al.'s (2006) review, HPWS often include HRM practices that specifically target employee empowerment and participation, such as information sharing, participative decision making, and flexible scheduling practices. Second, and related to the first point, HPWS have been found to positively promote social exchanges and the emergence of a climate supportive of employees in organizations (Takeuchi, Chen, & Lepak, 2009; Takeuchi, Lepak, Wang, & Takeuchi, 2007). Thus, HPWS likely enable and motivate team empowerment and participation, by creating a context conducive for employee involvement.

ORGANIZATIONAL CLIMATE

Takeuchi et al.'s (2007, 2009) findings suggest that climate may be another important organizational-level antecedent. Indeed, research has indicated that climate can exert meaningful influences at different organizational levels (for review, see Ostroff, Kinicki, & Tamkins, 2003). As such, organizational-level climate—in addition to team-level climate—can promote team empowerment and participation. In particular, we suspect that organizational-level climate can capture similar aspects to those of team-level empowerment climate (cf. Seibert et al., 2004). At the organizational level, empowerment climate can reinforce team-level empowerment climate, but can also facilitate other mechanisms that likely promote team empowerment and participation (e.g., it can facilitate greater cooperation, coordination, and communication between teams).

Similarly, in a study of participation in an employee involvement initiative in a large state agency, Tesluk et al. (1999) found evidence of a cascading relationship between leader support for employee involvement, participative climates, and employee participation and work attitudes across district, unit, and individual levels of analysis. Specifically, they found that when top-level district managers strongly supported employee involvement, districts had more practices in place supporting employee involvement and had more participative climates, which were then, in turn, related to the support for employee involvement provided by unit-level managers and the resulting climates for participation at the unit level. Employee participation was greatest when both their unit climate and their district climate supported employee involvement.

SUMMARY

In addition to individual-level and team-level antecedents, organizational-level antecedents can also promote team empowerment and participation. Similar to our classification of team-level antecedents, the discussion above suggests that organizational-level antecedents include both *social-oriented inputs* (i.e., organizational climate) and *structure-oriented inputs* (i.e., HPWS). Unlike team-level inputs, however, these organizational-level inputs create a broader organizational context that can empower and encourage participation in multiple teams within the organization. Such context can, of course, serve to also reinforce team-level inputs. Indeed, team-level inputs are likely to be influenced by organizational-level inputs, as well as mediate (at least in part) between organizational-level inputs and team empowerment and participation.

Multilevel Outcomes of Team Empowerment and Participation

Given that teams operate in a multilevel system, team empowerment and participation likely exert influences that transcend levels, and are not just affected by multilevel antecedents. Thus, a more complete understanding of the function of team empowerment and participation requires understanding of their impact across levels. Accordingly, we now discuss the influences of team empowerment and participation on outcomes residing at the team as well as individual and organizational levels. We begin our discussion with team-level outcomes, since such outcomes have been the most widely theorized and studied to date, and since these outcomes can also mediate the influences of team empowerment and participation on outcomes at higher (organizational) and lower (individual) levels. As in our discussion of antecedents, we do not separate between outcomes of team empowerment and team participation below.

Team-Level Outcomes

In their conceptual model of team empowerment, Kirkman and Rosen (1997) proposed that team empowerment would positively promote a host of positive team outcomes, including team members' satisfaction and commitment, team productivity and proactivity, reduced resistance to change in the team, and improved customer service provided by the team. These proposed effects were largely supported in follow-up studies. For instance, Hyatt and Ruddy (1997) reported a positive relationship between empowerment and performance at the team level. Using an expanded set of performance criteria, Kirkman and Rosen (1999) found team empowerment to be related to team productivity, team proactivity, the quality of service that teams provided their customers, as well as affective reactions of team members (i.e., team commitment, organizational commitment, and job satisfaction).

Although review of the PDM literature indicated mixed support for participation on attitudinal and behavioral outcomes, there is considerable research demonstrating the importance of team processes (e.g., backup behaviors, intrateam communication, team member coordination) on team performance (for review, see Marks et al., 2001). In fact, a recent meta-analysis by LePine et al. (2008) found that team transition, action, and interpersonal processes all positively related to team performance and average member satisfaction in teams (ρ = .29 to .46). Boundary spanning and other externally directed processes have also shown to be important, and lead to improved team performance (Ancona & Caldwell, 1992; Marrone et al., 2007).

One outcome that has not been studied in the team empowerment and participation literature, and, for that matter, was largely neglected in the broader team literature, is *team viability*. Team viability involves the extent to which teams can enhance their capacity to function and be productive over time (Hackman, 1987). Indeed, there is evidence that teams exhibit systematic differences in performance trajectories over time—some teams improve their performance, while others exhibit performance declines (Landis, 2001; Mathieu & Rapp, 2009). Team empowerment and participation likely promote team viability, since more empowered and engaged teams are more able and motivated to learn from prior performance, and to identify ways of using performance feedback toward developing improved work strategies and processes. However, these theoretical possibilities remain to be tested empirically.

MEDIATED AND MODERATED PROCESSES

While both the empowerment and participation literatures have demonstrated clear associations with team-level outcomes, there has been little attempt to integrate and understand how empowerment and participation may work together to influence outcomes at the team level of analysis. In the empowerment literature, more recent work seeking to understand the potential linkages between empowerment and critical team outcomes such as performance has suggested one potentially important means of integration between empowerment and participation. Specifically, Mathieu et al. (2006) found, using a sample of customer service technician teams, that a composite assessment of transition, action, and interpersonal processes fully mediated the relationship between team empowerment and customer satisfaction and team performance (an index of machine reliability, repair response time, and parts expense management). This study offers one potentially fruitful way to take an integrated approach, and is consistent with the argument presented earlier that team empowerment provides an important motivational mechanism activating team member engagement in team processes that facilitate performance. At the same time, it should be noted that, in Mathieu et al.'s (2006) study, team empowerment only partially mediated relationships between team design features and organizational supports on outcomes, suggesting that models of team effectiveness need to also consider direct relationships and other potential mediating mechanisms besides empowerment and participation.

Research in both the empowerment and participation literatures has also suggested potential boundary conditions that may influence the relationships that these two team-level constructs share with team outcomes. For example, Kirkman et al. (2004) found that when team members interacted with each other more in virtual modes (i.e., through less face-to-face interaction), team empowerment was more strongly (positively) related to team performance. Further, Chen et al. (2007) found that team empowerment positively related to team performance in highly interdependent teams, but not in low interdependent teams. Moreover, there is evidence suggesting that certain forms of participation may require specific conditions. As an example, DeDreu and West (2001) found that team member participation was more strongly related to team innovation when minority options in the decision-making process were actively expressed.

SUMMARY

The research summarized above indicates that team empowerment and participation are associated with a host of positive attitudinal and behavioral indices of team effectiveness, including team performance, member attitudes, and likely even team viability. However, relatively less is known about the mechanisms through which team empowerment and participation influence team outcomes, and the moderators that serve as boundary conditions for their effects. In the sections that follow, we consider how team empowerment and participation can also influence individual-level and organizational-level outcomes.

Individual-Level Outcomes

The empirical evidence that team empowerment and participation positively relate to team performance and member attributes may tempt the reader to conclude that there are direct, cross-level linkages between team empowerment and participation and individual-level attitudes and performance. However, such cross-level influences are in fact more complex. Instead of direct effects, initial cross-level research has indicated that team empowerment and participation relate to individual performance and attitudes only indirectly. Specifically, Seibert et al. (2004) found evidence suggesting that individuals whose teams collectively feel more empowered experience greater levels of empowerment themselves, which, in turn, was related to feeling greater levels of job satisfaction and to higher levels of job performance. Similarly, Chen and colleagues (2007) found that individual-level empowerment mediated between team-level empowerment and individual performance.

However, Chen et al. (2007) also found that team empowerment moderated the relationship between individual-level empowerment and employee performance. In their study, Chen et al. (2007) found that individual empowerment related more positively to individual performance when team empowerment was low, and that individuals maintained a high level of performance irrespective of individual empowerment when team empowerment was high. Thus, high levels of team empowerment can compensate for low levels of individual empowerment.

Empirical evidence for the positive relationship between team empowerment and individual empowerment indicates further that team empowerment could also indirectly relate to a host of other individual-level outcomes, such as lower turnover intentions (Chen, 2005), and employee attitudes other than satisfaction, such as organizational commitment (Liden et al., 2000). Thus, there is evidence that team empowerment creates an environment that promotes several positive individual-level outcomes. Although we are not aware of any cross-level research that directly examined team participation, there are reasons to believe that team participation will also promote positive individual-level outcomes. For instance, Chen and Kanfer's (2006) theory suggests that team motivation processes (e.g., team transition and action processes) positively promote individual-level motivation and performance. A recent study of simulated flight and radar teams provided empirical evidence for these proposed cross-level effects, in finding that team action processes positively related to individual performance, even when taking individual-level motivational processes into account (Chen, Kanfer, DeShon, Mathieu, & Kozlowski, 2009).

Organizational-Level Outcomes

Research on organizational-level outcomes of team empowerment and participation has been scant. Yet, we posit that team empowerment and participation can impact organizational-level outcomes such as firm performance and firm innovation through three mechanisms. First, team empowerment and participation may exert direct, upward cross-level influences with organizational-level outcomes for teams that potentially have control or "line of sight" over organizational-level outcome. In particular, such direct effects are plausible in top management teams (TMTs), who directly manage and control outcomes at the organizational level. Second, empowerment and participation may exert influences on organizational-level outcomes via emergence to the organizational level. For example, an empowerment climate can emerge to the organizational level, where it may be either directly or indirectly related to organizational-level

outcomes. Third, team empowerment and participation can also indirectly relate to organizational-level outcomes through their impact on team-level outcomes that, in turn, aggregate in some manner into organizational-level outcomes. As an example, team participation could influence customer satisfaction at that team level, which in aggregate results in sales growth and market position at the organizational level.

The research to date has been primarily in the first form of influence noted above. Specifically, Hambrick (1994) suggested that behavioral integration, which is composed of the quality and quantity of information exchange, collaborative behavior, and joint decision making in the TMT, is related to organizational performance. In more recent empirical work, behavioral integration in TMTs has been associated with firm performance (Barrick, Bradley, Kristof-Brown, & Colbert, 2007; Lubatkin, Simsek, Ling, & Veiga, 2006) and decision quality and organizational decline (Carmeli & Schaubroeck, 2006). Thus, there is indirect evidence that constructs similar to team empowerment and participation (i.e., team behavioral integration) can directly impact firm-level outcomes, albeit only among TMTs.

Summary

We began this chapter by discussing and integrating among conceptualizations of team empowerment and participation. We proposed that empowerment and participation capture psychological and behavioral components of engagement (respectively), and hence offer a more comprehensive understanding of what engagement in and of teams entails. Building on this integrative conceptualization, we then delineated a multilevel model, in which team empowerment and participation reside in a multilevel system, which includes individual-level, team-level, and organizational-level antecedents and outcomes. Figure 24.2 provides a heuristic framework that summarizes this multilevel model. However, as explained earlier, several of the multilevel antecedents and outcomes that we have delineated entail more complex relationships than those depicted in Figure 24.2 (e.g., moderating influences of individual-level antecedents).

Agenda for Future Research

We view the model delineated in Figure 24.2 as a mere stepping stone for enhancing our understanding of the complex, multilevel system within which team empowerment and participation reside. Indeed, much remains to be learned about team

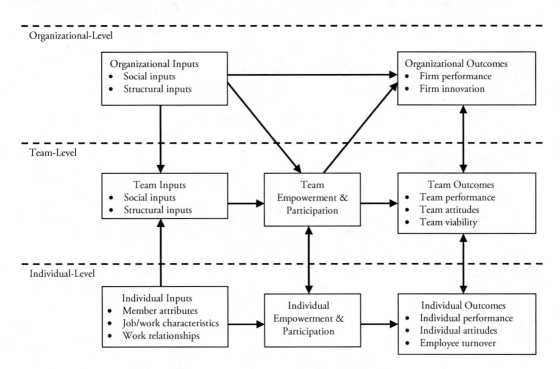

Figure 24.2 Multilevel Model of Team Empowerment and Participation.

empowerment and participation. Accordingly, we conclude the chapter by discussing several ways in which future research can extend our understanding of team empowerment and participation. Our proposed agenda for future research is summarized in Table 24.1.

First, an assumption that we have made earlier in this chapter is that team empowerment and participation largely share the same nomological network of multilevel antecedents and outcomes, and that these two constructs collectively capture the concept of *team engagement*. Although we offered some support for this assertion in several previous sections, we encourage researchers to test more explicitly whether the nomological networks of team empowerment and team participation are equivalent. Likewise, researchers should consider whether team empowerment and participation can indeed be combined to form the construct of team engagement. Unfortunately, to date, the term *engagement* has been used rather loosely in the team and motivation literatures (e.g., Blader & Tyler's [2009] model of group engagement focuses on *individual-level* social identity and extra-role behavior), and evidence regarding what it may actually entail at the team level is scant. Through systematic comparison of the team empowerment and participation constructs, researchers may identify points of convergences

and differentiation between the two constructs. For example, it is possible that team empowerment is more strongly related to attitudinal outcomes (e.g., team member satisfaction) than is team participation, whereas team participation is more strongly related to behavioral criteria (e.g., team productivity) than is team empowerment. More importantly, perhaps, more research is needed to clarify how the two constructs might operate in concert, and hence whether or how the two constructs may combine to form the team engagement construct. As an example, researchers should continue to explore whether team empowerment mediates (partially or fully) between antecedents and team participation, and whether team participation exerts more proximal influences on outcomes than does team empowerment (cf. Mathieu et al., 2006).

A second avenue for future research involves a more fine-grained analysis of the antecedents we identified, as well as other likely antecedents beyond those we explicitly considered. It is particularly important to examine the unique influences of different antecedents—both within and across levels. For example, do social inputs at the organizational level (e.g., empowerment climate at the organizational level) directly relate to team empowerment, or is this cross-level relationship mediated through team-level social inputs (e.g., team-level empowerment

Table 24.1 Summary of Directions for Future Research

Research Domain	Research Questions and Directions
Construct Clarification Issues	Explore the unique and similar aspects in the nomological network of team empowerment and participation. That is, what is similar and what is different about these constructs? Develop better understanding of whether and how team empowerment and participation may in fact combine to form a single, team engagement construct; or, alternatively, whether the two constructs are better kept separate.
Antecedents of Team Empowerment and Participation	Identify additional antecedents of team empowerment and participation, beyond the variables (and classes of variables) that have been studied to date. Consider the relative influences of top-down (contextual) and bottom-up (emergent) antecedents on team empowerment and participation, as well as moderators that dictate when bottom-up influences are more likely to occur, relative to top-town influences.
Variability in Team Empowerment and Participation Across Members	Explore the extent to which variability in team empowerment and participation across members moderates relationships involving empowerment and participation.
Boundary Conditions for Team Empowerment and Participation Effects	Identify possible boundary conditions that moderate the function of team empowerment and participation. That is, in what situations would team empowerment and participation be most likely to be beneficial for performance outcomes?

climate)? Also, how does the potency of bottom-up influences of individual-level antecedents compare with the top-down influences of organizational-level antecedents? Multilevel principles suggest that top-down influences are more powerful and immediate than bottom-up influences (Kozlowski & Klein, 2000), but this principle has yet to be tested in team empowerment and participation research (and, in fact, has rarely been tested elsewhere in the broader team literature). Along these lines, it is also possible that certain boundary conditions exist that dictate *when* bottom-up influences are likely to be more powerful, such as earlier stages of team formation, or periods that follow major changes in an organization or in a team (e.g., following membership change; see Chen, 2005; Chen et al., 2009). Researchers should thus consider both simple and complex ways in which multiple antecedents at multiple levels of analysis combine to influence team empowerment and participation.

Third, building on previous research on climate strength (e.g., Schneider, Salvaggio, & Subirats, 2002), it is important to study the extent to which within-team agreement or dispersion on empowerment and participation may moderate the influences of team empowerment and participation on outcomes. For example, do *all* team members need

to participate or feel empowered, or is one subset of engaged members sufficient, to reap the maximum benefits of team empowerment and participation? Importantly, such studies could also shed more light on the emergence of shared leadership in teams, and the nature of the leadership-sharing process. For example, based on work demonstrating that empowerment appears to activate team processes (Chen & Kanfer, 2006; Mathieu et al., 2006), we might hypothesize that team members who individually feel more psychologically empowered will be more likely to emerge as internal team leaders and will occupy a more central role within the team's network structure. The degree to which leadership is shared among a larger number of team members might depend in part on the extent to which all (or most) team members view the team as empowered. By the same token, perhaps the coupling between team empowerment and team participation is stronger when team members share team empowerment perceptions to a larger extent, relative to when such perceptions are shared to a lesser extent among members.

Finally, we also believe that research should identify critical boundaries for the function of team empowerment and participation. To begin with, is team participation different in different team contexts, such that participation consists of different team processes for different types of teams? For example, do members of decision-making teams versus action teams "participate differently," via engagement of different team processes? For instance, boundary-spanning processes seem more important for teams that are highly dependent on external resources, support, or externally derived knowledge and information, such as project teams or TMTs, but such processes are perhaps less critical for some service and production teams. Likewise, decision-making processes are more important in TMTs and other knowledge-intensive teams (e.g., R&D or project teams), but perhaps less critical among action teams, in which decision implementation or action processes are more critical (Chen & Kanfer, 2006). Furthermore, as we noted earlier, team type and the level at which teams reside within the organization can serve as important boundary conditions to the extent to which team empowerment and participation directly (or, rather, indirectly) impact organizational-level outcomes. Moreover, given that cultural values seem to play a nontrivial role in members' reactions to practices directed at enhancing team empowerment and participation, researchers should examine the extent to which models of team empowerment and participation generalize across countries and cultures. For example, it could be that team empowerment and participation are more central to employee, team, and organizational effectiveness in cultures that place greater value on employee involvement (i.e., low power distance cultures).

Conclusion

As we stated at the outset of this chapter, empowerment and participation have been central in multiple literatures within the I/O psychology and related fields for quite some time. With the ever increasing complexities faced by twenty-first century work organizations, we predict that empowerment and participation will only continue to gain import in I-O Psychology theories, as it is through these processes that organizations leverage their human resources to meet complex challenges. With this in mind, we have proposed in this chapter that team empowerment and participation capture an essential part within a complex, multilevel system of psychological and behavioral engagement. Beyond reviewing and integrating the existing literatures on empowerment and participation, we hope that the integrative multilevel framework we have developed will encourage and stimulate additional research that

will yield greater understanding of team empowerment and participation.

References

Ahearne, M. J., Mathieu, J. E., & Rapp, A. (2005). To empower or not to empower your sales force? An empirical examination of the influence of empowering leader behaviors on customer satisfaction and performance. *Journal of Applied Psychology, 90*, 945–955.

Ancona, D. G., & Caldwell, D. F. (1992). Bridging the boundary: External activity and performance in organizational teams. *Administrative Science Quarterly, 37*, 634–665.

Bandura, A. (1997). *Self-efficacy: The exercise of control.* New York: Freeman.

Barrick, M. R., Bradley, B. H., Kristof-Brown, A. L., & Colbert, A. E. (2007). The moderating role of top management team interdependence: Implications for real teams and working groups. *Academy of Management Journal, 50*, 544–557.

Barrick, M. R., Stewart, G. L., Neubert, M. J., & Mount, M. K. (1998). Relating member ability and personality to work-team processes and team effectiveness. *Journal of Applied Psychology, 83*, 377–391.

Bell, S. T. (2007). Deep-level composition variables as predictors of team performance: A meta-analysis. *Journal of Applied Psychology, 92*, 595–615.

Blader, S. L., & Tyler, T. R. (2009). Testing and extending the group engagement model: Linkages between social identity, procedural justice, economic outcomes, and extrarole behavior. *Journal of Applied Psychology, 94*, 445–464.

Brown, S. P. (1996). A meta-analysis and review of organizational research on job involvement. *Psychological Bulletin, 120*, 235–255.

Campion, M. A., Medsker, G. J., & Higgs, A. C. (1993). Relations between work group characteristics and effectiveness: Implications for designing effective work groups. *Personnel Psychology, 46*, 823–850.

Carmeli, A., & Schaubroeck, J. (2006). Top management team behavioral integration, decision quality, and organizational decline. *Leadership Quarterly, 17*, 441–453.

Carson, J. B., Tesluk, P. E., & Marrone, J. A. (2007). Shared leadership in teams: An investigation of antecedent conditions and performance. *Academy of Management Journal, 50*, 1217–1234.

Chan, D. (1998). Functional relations among constructs in the same content domain at different levels of analysis: A typology of composition models. *Journal of Applied Psychology, 83*, 234–246.

Chen, G. (2005). Newcomer adaptation in teams: Multilevel antecedents and outcomes. *Academy of Management Journal, 48*, 101–116.

Chen, G., & Bliese, P. D. (2002). The role of different levels of leadership in predicting self and collective efficacy: Evidence for discontinuity. *Journal of Applied Psychology, 87*, 549–556.

Chen, G., & Kanfer, R. (2006). Toward a systems theory of motivated behavior in work teams. *Research in Organizational Behavior, 27*, 223–267.

Chen, G., Kanfer, R., DeShon, R. P., Mathieu, J. E., & Kozlowski, S. W. J. (2009). The motivating potential of teams: A test and extension of Chen & Kanfer's (2006) model. *Organizational Behavior and Human Decision Processes, 110*, 45–55.

Chen, G., Kirkman, B. L., Kanfer, R., Allen, D., & Rosen, B. (2007). A multilevel study of leadership, empowerment, and performance in teams. *Journal of Applied Psychology, 92*, 331–346.

Chen, G., & Klimoski, R. J. (2003). The impact of expectations on newcomer performance in teams as mediated by work characteristics, social exchanges, and empowerment. *Academy of Management Journal, 46*, 591–607.

Chen, G., Mathieu, J. E., & Bliese, P. D. (2004). A framework for conducting multilevel construct validation. In F. J. Yammarino & F. Dansereau (Eds.), *Research in multilevel issues: Multilevel issues in organizational behavior and processes* (Vol. 3, pp. 273–303). Oxford: Elsevier.

Cohen, S. G., & Bailey, D. E. (1997). What makes teams work: Group effectiveness research from the shop floor to the executive suite. *Journal of Management, 23*, 239–290.

Combs, J., Liu, Y., Hall, A., & Ketchen, D. (2006). How much do high-performance work practices matter? A meta-analysis of their effects on organizational performance. *Personnel Psychology, 59*, 501–528.

Deci, E. L., Connell, J. P., & Ryan, R. M. (1989). Self-determination in a work organization. *Journal of Applied Psychology, 74*, 580–590.

DeDreu, C. K. W., & West, M. A. (2001). Minority dissent and team innovation: The importance of participation in decision making. *Journal of Applied Psychology, 86*, 1191–1201.

DeNisi, A. S., Hitt, M. A., & Jackson, S. E. (2003). The knowledge-based approach to sustainable competitive advantage. In S. E. Jackson, M. A. Hitt, & A. S. DeNisi (Eds.), *Managing knowledge for sustained competitive advantage* (pp. 3–33). San Francisco: Jossey-Bass.

Ehrhart, M. G. (2004). Leadership and procedural justice climate as antecedents of unit-level organizational citizenship behavior. *Personnel Psychology, 57*, 61–94.

Frese, M., & Fay, D. (2001). Personal initiative: An active performance concept for work in the 21st century. *Research in Organizational Behavior, 23*, 133–187.

Gelfand, M. J., Erez, M., & Aycan, Z. (2007). Cross-cultural approaches to organizational behavior. *Annual Review of Psychology, 58*, 479–515.

Griffin, M. A., & Mathieu, J. E. (1997). Modeling organizational processes across hierarchical levels: Climate, leadership, and group process in work groups. *Journal of Organizational Behavior, 18*, 731–744.

Griffin, M. A., Neal, A., & Parker, S. K. (2007). A new model of work role performance: Positive behavior in uncertain and interdependent contexts. *Academy of Management Journal, 50*, 327–347.

Hackman, J. R. (1987). The design of work teams. In J. W. Lorsch (Ed.), *Handbook of organizational behavior* (pp. 315–342). Englewood Cliffs, NJ: Prentice-Hall.

Hackman, J. R. (1992). Group influences on individuals in organizations. In M. D. Dunnette & L. M. Hough (Eds.), *Handbook of industrial and organizational psychology* (Vol. 3, pp. 199–267). Palo Alto, CA: Consulting Psychologists Press.

Hackman, J. R., & Oldham, G. R. (1975). Development of the Job Diagnostic Survey. *Journal of Applied Psychology, 60*, 159–170.

Hackman, J. R., & Oldham, G. R. (1976). Motivation through the design of work: Test of a theory. *Organizational Behavior and Human Performance, 16*, 250–279.

Hambrick, D. C. (1994). Top management groups: A conceptual integration and reconsideration of the team label. *Research in Organizational Behavior, 16*, 171–214.

Hofmann, D. A., & Jones, L. M. (2005). Leadership, collective personality, and performance. *Journal of Applied Psychology, 90*, 509–522.

Huselid, M. A. (1995). The impact of human resource management practices on turnover, productivity, and corporate financial performance. *Academy of Management Journal, 38*, 635–672.

Hyatt, D. E., & Ruddy, T. M. (1997). An examination of the relationship between work group characteristics and performance: Once more into the breech. *Personnel Psychology, 50*, 553–585.

Ilgen, D. R. (1999). Teams embedded in organizations: Some implications. *American Psychologist, 54*, 129–139.

Jackson, C. L., Colquitt, J. A., Wesson, M. J., & Zapata-Phelan, C. P. (2006). Psychological collectivism: A measurement validation and linkage to group member performance. *Journal of Applied Psychology, 91*, 884–899.

Jex, S. M., & Bliese, P. D. (1999). Efficacy beliefs as a moderator of the impact of work-related stressors: A multilevel study. *Journal of Applied Psychology, 84*, 349–361.

Kanfer, R. (1990). Motivation theory and industrial and organizational psychology. In M. D. Dunnette & L. M. Hough (Eds.), *Handbook of industrial and organizational psychology* (2nd ed., Vol. 1, pp. 75–170). Palo Alto, CA: Consulting Psychologists Press.

Karau, S. J., & Williams, K. D. (1993). Social loafing: A meta-analytic review and theoretical integration. *Journal of Personality and Social Psychology, 65*, 681–706.

Kirkman, B. L., & Rosen, B. (1997). A model of work team empowerment. *Research in Organizational Change and Development, 10*, 131–167.

Kirkman, B. L., & Rosen, B. (1999). Beyond self-management: Antecedents and consequences of team empowerment. *Academy of Management Journal, 42*, 58–74.

Kirkman, B. L., Rosen, B., Tesluk, P. E., & Gibson, C. B. (2004). The impact of team empowerment on virtual team performance: The moderating role of face-to-face interaction. *Academy of Management Journal, 47*, 175–192.

Kirkman, B. L., & Shapiro, D. L. (1997). The impact of cultural values on employee resistance to teams: Toward a model of globalized self-managing work team effectiveness. *Academy of Management Review, 22*, 730–757.

Kirkman, B. L., & Shapiro, D. L. (2001). The impact of cultural values on job satisfaction and organizational commitment in self-managing work teams: The mediating role of employee resistance. *Academy of Management Journal, 44*, 557–569.

Kozlowski, S. W. J., & Bell, B. S. (2003). Work groups and teams in organizations. In W. C. Borman, D. R. Ilgen, & R. J. Klimoski (Eds.), *Comprehensive handbook of psychology*, Volume 12, *Industrial and organizational psychology* (pp. 333–375). New York: Wiley.

Kozlowski, S. W. J., & Klein, K. J. (2000). A multilevel approach to theory and research in organizations: Contextual, temporal, and emergent processes. In K. J. Klein & S. W. J. Kozlowski (Eds.), *Multilevel theory, research, and methods in organizations: Foundations, extensions, and new directions* (pp. 3–90). San Francisco: Jossey-Bass.

Landis, R. S. (2001). A note on the stability of team performance. *Journal of Applied Psychology, 86*, 446–450.

Latham, G. P. (2001). The importance of understanding and changing employee outcome expectancies for gaining commitment to an organizational goal. *Personnel Psychology, 54*, 707–716.

Latham, G. P., Erez, M., & Locke, E. A. (1988). Resolving scientific disputes by the joint design of crucial experiments by the antagonists: Application to the Erez-Latham dispute regarding participation in goal setting. *Journal of Applied Psychology, 73*, 753–772.

Law, K. S., Wong, C. S., & Mobley, W. H. (1998). Toward a taxonomy of multidimensional constructs. *Academy of Management Review, 23*, 741–755.

Lawler, E. E., III. (1992). *The ultimate advantage: Creating the high involvement organization.* San Francisco: Jossey-Bass.

Lawler, E. E., III., Mohrman, S. A., & Benson, G. (2001). *Organizing for high performance: Employee involvement, TQM, reengineering, and knowledge management in the Fortune 1000.* San Francisco: Jossey-Bass.

Ledford, G. E., & Lawler, E. E., III. (1994). Research on employee participation: Beating a dead horse? *Academy of Management Review, 19*, 633–636.

Lepak, D. P., Liao, H., Chung, Y., & Harden, E. E. (2006). A conceptual review of human resource management systems in strategic human resource management research. In J. J. Martocchio (Ed.), *Research in personnel and human resources management* (Vol. 25, pp. 217–271). Greenwich, CT: JAI Press.

Lepak, D. P., & Snell, S. A. (2002). Examining the human resource architecture: The relationships among human capital, employment, and human resource configurations. *Journal of Management, 28*, 517–543.

LePine, J. A., Piccolo, R. F., Jackson, C. L., Mathieu, J. E., & Saul, J. R. (2008). A meta-analysis of teamwork processes: Tests of a multidimensional model and relationships with team effectiveness criteria. *Personnel Psychology, 61*, 273–307.

Lewin, K., Lippitt, R., & White, R. K. (1939). Patterns of aggressive behavior in experimentally created "social climates." *Journal of Social Psychology, 10*, 271–308.

Liden, R. C., & Arad, S. (1996). A power perspective of empowerment and work groups: Implications for human resources management research. *Research in Personnel and Human Resources Management, 14*, 205–251.

Liden, R. C., Wayne, S. J., & Sparrow, R. T. (2000). An examination of the mediating role of psychological empowerment on the relations between the job, interpersonal relationships, and work outcomes. *Journal of Applied Psychology, 85*, 407–416.

Locke, E. A., Alavi, M., & Wagner, J. A. (1997). Participation in decision making: An information exchange perspective. *Research in Personnel and Human Resources Management, 15*, 293–331.

Locke, E. A., & Schweiger, D. M. (1979). Participation in decision-making: One more look. *Research in Organizational Behavior, 1*, 265–339.

Lubatkin, M. H., Simsek, Z., Ling, Y., & Veiga, J. F. (2006). Ambidexterity and performance in small- to medium-sized firms: The pivotal role of top management team behavioral integration. *Journal of Management, 32*, 646–672.

Macey, W. M., & Schneider, B. (2008). The meaning of employee engagement. *Industrial and Organizational Psychology, 1*, 3–30.

Manz, C. C., & Sims, H. P. (1987). Leading workers to lead themselves: The external leadership of self-managing work teams. *Administrative Science Quarterly, 32*, 106–129.

Marks, M. A., Mathieu, J. E., & Zaccaro, S. J. (2001). A conceptual framework and taxonomy of team processes. *Academy of Management Review, 26*, 356–376.

Marks, M. A., Sabella, M. J., Burke, C. S., & Zaccaro, S. J. (2002). The impact of cross-training on team effectiveness. *Journal of Applied Psychology, 87*, 3–13.

Marrone, J. A., Tesluk, P. E., & Carson, J. B. (2007). A multilevel investigation of antecedents and consequences of team member boundary-spanning behavior. *Academy of Management Journal, 50*, 1423–1439.

Mathieu, J. E., Ahearne, M. J., & Taylor, S. R. (2007). A longitudinal cross-level model of leader and salesperson influences on sales force technology use and performance. *Journal of Applied Psychology, 90*, 528–537.

Mathieu, J. E., Gilson, L. L., & Ruddy, T. M. (2006). Empowerment and team effectiveness: An empirical test of an integrated model. *Journal of Applied Psychology, 91*, 97–108.

Mathieu, J. E., Maynard, M. T., Rapp, T. L., & Gilson, L. L. (2008). Team effectiveness 1997–2007: A review of recent advancements and a glimpse into the future. *Journal of Management, 34*, 410–476.

Mathieu, J. E., & Rapp, T. L. (2009). Laying the foundation for successful team performance trajectories: The roles of team charters and performance strategies. *Journal of Applied Psychology, 94*, 90–103.

Mills, P. K., & Ungson, G. R. (2003). Reassessing the limits of structural empowerment: Organizational constitution and trust as controls. *Academy of Management Review, 28*, 143–153.

Morgeson, F. P., & Hofmann, D. A. (1999). The structure and function of collective constructs: Implications for multilevel research and theory development. *Academy of Management Review, 24*, 249–265.

Ostroff, C., Kinicki, A. J., & Tamkins, M. M. (2003). Organizational culture and climate. In W. C. Borman, D. R. Ilgen, & R. J. Klimoski (Eds.), *Handbook of psychology* (Vol. 12, pp. 565–593). Hoboken, NJ: Wiley.

Pearce, C. L., & Sims, H. P. (2002). The relative influence of vertical vs. shared leadership on the longitudinal effectiveness of change management teams. *Group Dynamics: Theory, Research, and Practice, 6*, 172–197.

Podsakoff, P. M., MacKenzie, S. B., Paine, J. B., & Bachrach, D. G. (2000). Organizational citizenship behaviors: Critical review of the theoretical and empirical literature and suggestions for future research. *Journal of Management, 26*, 513–563.

Porter, C. O. L. H., Hollenbeck, J. R., Ilgen, D. R., Ellis, A. P. J., West, B. J., & Moon, H. (2003). Backing up behaviors in teams: The role of personality and legitimacy of need. *Journal of Applied Psychology, 88*, 391–403.

Roberson, Q. M., Moye, N. A., & Locke, E. A. (1999). Identifying a missing link between participation and satisfaction: The mediating role of procedural justice perceptions. *Journal of Applied Psychology, 84*, 585–593.

Roethlisberger, F. J., & Dickson, W. J. (1939). *Management and the worker.* Cambridge, MA: Harvard University Press.

Salancik, G. J., & Pfeffer, J. (1978). A social information processing approach to job attitudes and task design. *Administrative Science Quarterly, 23*, 224–253.

Salas, E., Dickinson, T. L., Converse, S. A., & Tannenbaum, S. I. (1992). Toward an understanding of team performance and training. In R. W. Swezey & E. Salas (Eds.), *Teams: Their training and performance* (pp. 3–29). Norwood, NJ: Ablex.

Schneider, B., Salvaggio, A. N., & Subirats, M. (2002). Climate strength: A new direction for climate research. *Journal of Applied Psychology, 87,* 220–229.

Seibert, S. E., Silver, S. R., & Randolph, W. A. (2004). Taking empowerment to the next level: A multiple-level model of empowerment, performance, and satisfaction. *Academy of Management Journal, 47,* 332–349.

Sonnentag, S. (2001). High performance and meeting participation: An observational study in software design teams. *Group Dynamics: Theory, Research, and Practice, 5,* 3–18.

Spreitzer, G. M. (1995). Psychological empowerment in the workplace: Dimensions, measurement, and validation. *Academy of Management Journal, 38,* 1442–1465.

Spreitzer, G. M. (1996). Social structural characteristics of psychological empowerment. *Academy of Management Journal, 39,* 483–504.

Spreitzer, G. M. (2008). Taking stock: A review of more than twenty years of research on empowerment at work. In J. L. Barling & C. Cooper (Eds.), *The Sage handbook of organizational behavior* (pp. 54–72). Thousand Oaks, CA: Sage.

Takeuchi, R., Chen, G., & Lepak, D. P. (2009). Through the looking glass of a social system: Cross-level effects of high performance work systems on employees' attitudes. *Personnel Psychology, 62,* 1–29.

Takeuchi, R., Lepak, D. P., Wang, H., & Takeuchi, K. (2007). An empirical examination of the mechanisms mediating between high performance work systems and the performance of Japanese organizations. *Journal of Applied Psychology, 92,* 1069–1083.

Tangirala, S., & Ramanujam, R. (2008). Exploring non-linearity in employee voice: The effects of personal control and organizational identification. *Academy of Management Journal, 51,* 1189–1203.

Tesluk, P. E., & Mathieu, J. E. (1999). Overcoming road blocks to effectiveness: Incorporating management of performance barriers into model of work group effectiveness. *Journal of Applied Psychology, 84,* 200–217.

Tesluk, P. E., Vance, R. J., & Mathieu, J. E. (1999). Examining employee involvement in the context of participative work environments. *Group & Organization Management, 24,* 271–299.

Thomas, K. W., & Velthouse, B. A. (1990). Cognitive elements of empowerment: An "interpretive" model of intrinsic task motivation. *Academy of Management Review, 15,* 666–681.

Trist, E. L., & Bamforth, K. W. (1951). Some social and psychological consequences of the Longwall method of coal-getting. *Human Relations, 4,* 3–38.

Van Dyne, L., & LePine, J. A. (1998). Helping and voice extra-role behaviors: Evidence of construct and predictive validity. *Academy of Management Journal, 41,* 108–119.

Vroom, V. H., & Yetton, P. W. (1973). *Leadership and decision making.* Pittsburgh, PA: University of Pittsburgh Press.

Zohar, D. (2000). A group-level model of safety climate: Testing the effect of group climate on microaccidents in manufacturing jobs. *Journal of Applied Psychology, 85,* 587–596.

Across Borders and Technologies: Advancements in Virtual Teams Research

Bradley L. Kirkman, Cristina B. Gibson, *and* Kwanghyun Kim

Abstract

Research on virtual teams continues to grow as this form of teaming is increasingly adopted by organizations worldwide. To comprehensively analyze the growing literature on virtual teams, we reviewed 197 articles published between 1986 and 2008. We organize our review both by level of analysis (i.e., individual, group, and organization) and by relevance to the input-emergent state-process-output (IEPO) framework, yielding 12 theoretically meaningful categories of research. We summarize and synthesize this research over the last 22 years in each of these 12 areas, and we conclude with directions for future research related to five overarching themes: (a) the conceptualization of virtuality; (b) team development; (c) virtual team leadership; (d) levels of analysis; and (e) multidisciplinary approaches.

Key Words: virtual teams, computer-mediated communication, knowledge work, virtuality, teams

Over the last two decades, as the quality of technology-mediated communication has continued to improve and has been adopted by organizations worldwide, there has been a tremendous increase in both the use of virtual teams and scholarly attention devoted to understanding how to make virtual teams more effective (see Stanko & Gibson, 2009; Hertel, Geister, & Konradt, 2005; and Martins, Gilson, & Maynard, 2004, for reviews). Virtual teams are variously defined as groups of interdependent coworkers who are geographically dispersed (i.e., consisting of members spread across more than one location), electronically dependent (i.e., communicating using electronic tools such as e-mail or knowledge repositories), structurally dynamic (i.e., in which change occurs frequently among members, their roles, and relationships to each other), or nationally diverse (i.e., consisting of members with more than one national or cultural background; Gibson & Gibbs, 2006; Griffith, Sawyer, & Neale, 2003; Kirkman & Mathieu, 2005; Martins et al., 2004). These dimensions are often related, such that when teams are geographically dispersed and electronic dependence is high, teams are often also nationally diverse (although this is not always necessarily the case).

What is exciting about virtual teams is both their practical potential as well as their theoretical "messiness." When utilized successfully, they bring great promise because they allow organizations worldwide to include members with the most relevant expertise, regardless of their physical location. Under the best of circumstances, this can enable integration of information, knowledge, and resources from a broad variety of contexts within the same team. Yet, teams with a high degree of "virtuality" are not without their challenges (Kirkman & Mathieu, 2005), and when managed poorly, they often underperform face-to-face (FTF) teams (Stanko & Gibson, 2009).

At the same time, they surface fascinating theoretical issues which call into question traditional models of team effectiveness, such as: Where do the boundaries of a team begin and end? How might technology overcome limitations posed by traditional group biases such as risky shift (or exacerbate them)? What degree of local responsiveness is ideal when balanced with needs for global integration? Despite the prevalence of teams with some degree of virtuality worldwide and the important implications of research investigating them for theory development, we could find only three published reviews (Hertel et al., 2005; Martins et al., 2004; Stanko & Gibson), and these reviews focused more on virtual working in general. Thus, our purpose is to review the growing theoretical and empirical literature specifically on *virtual teams*. In doing so, we hope to assist both researchers and practitioners to fine tune their efforts in understanding and enhancing the functioning of virtual teams worldwide.

Scope and Framework Used to Organize the Review

The scope of this review includes any scholarly journal articles published on virtual teams between 1986 and 2008. We used library search engines such as ABI-Inform and EbscoHost and searched high-quality empirical journals within the fields of management (e.g., *Academy of Management Journal, Administrative Science Quarterly, Organization Science*), psychology (e.g., *Journal of Applied Psychology, Personnel Psychology, Small Group Research*), information technology (IT)/information systems (IS; e.g., *MIS Quarterly, Information Systems Research, Journal of Management Information Systems*), and communication (e.g., *Journal of Communication, Communication Monographs, Human Communication Research*). We used key words such as *virtual teams, virtuality, virtualness*, and *computer-mediated communication* to guide our search. Using this methodology, our search resulted in an initial total of 537 articles. Next, we omitted research in related fields such as virtual gaming, virtual reality, immersive collaborative virtual environments (e.g., Second Life), online communities, research related to technology acceptance in the IT field, or individual differences related to communication media preferences in the communication field, thus restricting our review to virtual *teams* and *groups*. After eliminating works falling outside our criteria, we retained a total of 197 articles in our review. As another way

to bound our review, we focused almost exclusively on articles published in scholarly journals rather than book chapters, conference papers, or working papers. To maintain comprehensiveness and consistency, we have incorporated articles included in Martins et al.'s (2004) review, but we have added approximately 100 more articles published mostly since 2004.

To organize our review and building on Martins et al. (2004), we use a revised version of the classic input-process-output (IPO) framework (Hackman & Morris, 1975; McGrath, 1984) applied in hundreds of team studies over the last few decades (see Mathieu, Maynard, Rapp, & Gilson, 2008, for a recent review). Inputs are typically factors that are controllable by organizations and managers such as leader behaviors, team composition, human resource policies, and job design. Team processes are "interdependent team activities that orchestrate taskwork in employees' pursuit of goals" (Marks, Mathieu, & Zaccaro, 2001, p. 358). Team outputs include performance (e.g., quality, productivity), attitudes (e.g., job satisfaction, organizational commitment), and behaviors (e.g., turnover, absenteeism; Cohen & Bailey, 1997).

In addition to inputs, processes, and outputs, we also include team emergent states, defined as "constructs that characterize properties of the team that are typically dynamic in nature and vary as a function of team context, inputs, processes, and outcomes" (Marks et al., 2001, p. 357). Emergent states represent important mediational influences with explanatory power accounting for variability in team performance, which scholars have suggested are critical in addressing the limitations of IPO models. (See Ilgen, Hollenbeck, Johnson, & Jundt's [2005] discussion of more inclusive input-mediator-output, [i.e., IMO] models.) We consider each of the input-emergent state-process-output (IEPO) domains at three different levels of analysis used in virtual teams research including: individual, team, and organizational; and hence our review categorizes research into 12 discrete categories. In doing so, we extend previous reviews of the virtual teams literature that did not include attention to emergent states or different levels of analysis. Researchers can use our framework to quickly identify areas of research that need more attention and also areas that may be particularly saturated. Note also that we do not explicitly discuss every article identified in our review; rather, we discuss particularly compelling studies that can be considered representative of a category. For more detail, Appendices A–D includes all 197 articles we reviewed (organized by level of analysis), addressing the sample, methodology, variables (categorized as inputs, emergent states, processes, and outputs), theories/models used, and key findings. Our appendices show that many articles included multiple types of variables in the modified IEPO framework, and thus our categorizations below generally consider the main variable(s) focused on in a given article. Table 25.1 provides an abbreviated version of the Appendices by showing the citations for the articles included in each of the review categories and providing key lessons learned.

Individual-Level Virtual Teams Research
Inputs

Several researchers have investigated the role of team inputs in virtual team models at the individual level of analysis, with research clustering around four themes: effects of communication medium/technology; relational demography (e.g., on cultural values, country of origin, gender, etc.); individual differences; and task type/characteristics. Given the rise in the use of collaborative tools in the workplace that promote the creation of virtual alter egos (e.g., avatars in Second Life), some of the most interesting research investigating inputs has examined the role of anonymity. For example, in two laboratory experiments with university students in Germany, Sassenberg and Boos (2003) found that high anonymity (compared to low anonymity) as well as computer-mediated communication (CMC; compared to FTF communication) cause more conformity to individual needs or goals when personal identity was salient; and higher conformity to a socially shared superordinate category norm was the result when social identity was salient. Regarding the use of electronic communication more generally, Aiello and Kolb (1995) compared the effects of individual- and work group–level electronic performance monitoring on participants working on a data entry task alone, in non-interacting groups, and cohesive groups, finding that highly skilled, monitored participants keyed more entries than highly skilled, unmonitored participants, with the opposite pattern for low-skilled participants; no signs of social loafing were detected among group-monitored participants; and unmonitored workers and members of cohesive groups felt the least stressed.

In the domain of relational demography, researchers have investigated how virtual team diversity affects individual expectations about teamwork. For example, in a case study of two virtual teams based in Sweden, Bosch-Sijtsema (2007) found that when members of virtual teams are heterogeneous in organizational and cultural background, have little history of working previously together, and have different experiences working in teams, members often bring widely different expectations to the team, compared to FTF teams. Expectation mismatches led to motivational problems, dissatisfaction, and lower performance in these teams, but did result in more individual learning.

Individual differences have also been investigated in a number of studies, including personality characteristics such as extraversion (Straus, 1996), internal locus of control (Lee-Kelley, 2006), focus immersion (i.e., the level of attention focus and engagement; Rutkowski, Saunders, Vogel, & van Genuchten, 2007), self-efficacy (Staples & Webster, 2007), cultural values/country of origin (Hardin, Fuller, & Davison, 2007; Tan, Wei, Watson, Clapper, & McLean, 1998), and gender (Bhappu, Griffith, & Northcraft, 1997; Palomares, 2004). For example, among 261 information system virtual team members in a large financial institution, Workman, Kahnweiler, and Bommer (2003) found that individuals' commitment to virtual teams was stronger when they had cognitive styles characterized as external (i.e., preferring group, rather than individual, problem solving), conservative (i.e., preferring structure, compliance with existing rules and procedures, familiarity, and minimal change), and global (i.e., having mental representations that have thin or fuzzy boundaries). The relationships between both external and conservative cognitive styles and commitment to virtual teams were stronger when individuals reported using richer, rather than leaner, communication media.

Research investigating task type or characteristics as inputs has focused on norms and the degree of routineness. For example, among 44 individuals in a university student laboratory experiment, Walther and Bunz (2005) found that the degree of self-reported adherence to a set of team work rules (i.e., start immediately, communicate frequently, acknowledge others, explicitness, multitasking, and observe deadlines) was related to a host of positive individual outcomes including trust, task attraction, social attraction, and self-rated task success.

Table 25.1 Organizing Framework for the Virtual Teams Review

	Inputs	Emergent States	Processes	Outputs
Individual-Level Features Investigated	Communication medium/technology (e.g., Sassenberg & Boos, 2003); Member heterogeneity (e.g., Bosch-Sijtsema, 2007); Personality (e.g., Straus, 1996); Locus of control (e.g., Lee-Kelley, 2006); Focus immersion (e.g., Rutkowski et al., 2007); Self-efficacy (e.g., Staples & Webster, 2007); Cultural values (e.g., Hardin et al., 2007); Gender (e.g., Bhappu et al., 1997); Adherence to team work rules (e.g., Walther & Bunz, 2005); Reward structure (e.g., Ferrin & Dirks, 2003); Group size (e.g., Gallupe et al., 1992)	Trust (e.g., Aubert & Kelsey, 2003; Ferrin & Dirks, 2003; Morris et al., 2002); Group self-efficacy/group potency (e.g., Hardin et al., 2007)	De-individuation or depersonalization (e.g., Lea & Spears, 1992; Lee, 2004); Information processing (e.g., Griffith & Sawyer, 2006; Belanger, Watson-Manheim, 2006); Goal commitment and setting (e.g., Forester et al., 2007); Communication (e.g., Anawati & Craig, 2006; Walther & Bazarova, 2007); Socialization (e.g., Ahuja & Galvin, 2003; Tanis & Postmes, 2003); Majority influence (Tan et al., 1998)	Satisfaction (e.g., Gallupe et al., 1992; Mejias, 2007); Idea generation (e.g., Jessup & Tansik, 1991); Customer service (Froehle, 2006)
Individual-Level Key Findings	Self-efficacy for teamwork is particularly important in virtual teams and higher among individualists (Staples & Webster, 2007).	Different emergent states are related to affective vs. performance outcomes (e.g., Morris et al., 2002).	Depersonalization increases conformity to group norms due to effects on identity (e.g., Lee, 2004).	CMC (particularly anonymous CMC) is positively related to # of ideas, and self-ratings of contributions and negatively related to production blocking and evaluation apprehension (e.g., Gallupe et al. 1992)
Team-Level Features Investigated	Communication medium/technology (e.g., Andres, 2002; Schmidt et al., 2001); Group/team composition (e.g., Gefen & Straub, 1997; Paul et al., 2004); Geographic dispersion (e.g., Gibson & Gibbs, 2006; Metiu, 2006); Team size (e.g., Bradner et al., 2005; Zhou & Zhang, 2006); Team leadership (e.g., Alge et al., 2004; Sosik et al., 1998); Team training (e.g., Kirkman et al., 2006; Tan et al., 2000); Team structure (e.g., Timmerman & Scott, 2006); Status difference (e.g., Hollingshead, 1996); Team task types (e.g., Straus & McGrath, 1994)	Trust (e.g., Jarvenpaa et al., 2004; Stewart & Gosain, 2006); Team potency/collective efficacy (e.g., Dennis & Garfield, 2003; Fuller et al., 2007); Cohesion (Beal et al., 2003; Gonzalez et al., 2003); Group identity (e.g., Bouas & Arrow, 1996); Team empowerment (e.g., Kirkman et al., 2004); Communication climate (e.g., Gibson & Gibbs, 2006); Psychological safety (e.g., Van den Bossche et al., 2006)	Acquisition and sharing of knowledge (e.g., Rafaeli & Ravid, 2003; Sole & Edmondson, 2002); Team development (e.g., Massey et al., 2003; Maznevski & Chudoba, 2000); Cognitive convergence process (e.g., Baba et al., 2004); Goal setting structure (e.g., Huang et al., 2002); Communication (e.g., Rains, 2007; Yoo & Kanawattanachai, 2001); Conflict (e.g., Montoya-Weiss et al., 2001; Watson et al., 1988); Team commitment (Bradner et al., 2005)	Team performance (e.g., Connolly et al., 1990; May & Carter, 2001); Team member satisfaction (e.g., Lurey & Raisinghani, 2001); Idea generation (e.g., Shepherd et al., 1996); Group creativity (Sosik et al., 1998)

Team-Level Key Findings	Larger teams more productive (Lowry et al. 2006) but have worse affective outcomes (Valacich et al. 1992). Geographic dispersion negatively related to communication, coordination, trust, innovation effectiveness (e.g., Gibson & Gibbs, 2006). Formal roles, boundary permeability, group incentives, positively related to performance (Workman, 2005).	Trust positively related to performance (Paul & McDaniel, 2004) Potentcy/collective efficacy positively related to performance (e.g., Hardin et al. 2006). Group cohesion and identity lag initially but increase equal to FTF over time (e.g., Dennis & Garfield, 2003).	Volume of communication affected by communication media and stage of development (e.g., Rasters et al. 2002) Creativity highest with moderately frequent communication (Leenders et al. 2003). Competition and collaboration conflict handling strategies positively related to performance (Montoya-Weiss et al. 2001). Conflict more detrimental to CMC then FTF teams (Mortensen & Hinds, 2001); this effect is contingent on task complexity and conflict resolution approach (Kankanhalli et al. 2007). Lack of immediacy of feedback contributes to task conflict (Kankanhalli et al. 2007).	Virtual team outcomes are more complex than originally proposed in early research and contingent on factors such as tool use (e.g., Potter & Balthazard, 2002) and macro factors such as norms, time pressure, team climate and shared understanding (e.g., Ocker, 2005)
Organizational-Level Features Investigated	Communication medium (e.g., Andersen, 2005); Social context- culture, power distribution, social norms (e.g., Zack & McKenney, 1995); Geographic dispersion and virtuality (McDonough et al., 2001)	NA	Decision making (e.g., Anderson, 2005); Communication (e.g., Zack & McKenney, 1995)	Firm performance (e.g., Andersen, 2005; McDonough et al., 2001)
Organizational-Level Key Findings	Social context influences technology use (Zack & McKenney, 1995).	NA	Decision making is more strongly related to firm performance with greater CMC use; CMC related to firm performance (Anderson, 2005).	Use of global teams is more detrimental to firm performance than collocated or virtual teams (McDonough et al. 2001)

Using 263 individuals working in 54 global virtual teams, Majchrzak, Malhotra, and John (2005) found that when individuals perceive their task as non-routine, there is a positive relationship between an individual's perceived degree of IT support for communicating context information and his or her collaboration know-how development; however, when individuals perceive their task as routine, partial IT support for contextualization is associated with lower levels of collaboration know-how development.

Emergent States

Fewer researchers have investigated the role of team emergent states in virtual team models at the individual level of analysis; and those who have tend to focus on trust (e.g., Aubert & Kelsey, 2003). For example, among 158 survey responses from IT consultants and developers, Morris, Marshall, and Rainer (2002) found that both user satisfaction and trust are positively related to job satisfaction in virtual teams. Examining antecedents of trust with 224 U.S. undergraduate students using CMC in a laboratory experiment, Ferrin and Dirks (2003) found that the effects of different types of team-based rewards (i.e., cooperative, competitive, or mixed) on individual trust in team members was mediated by perceived partner motives and performance and own information sharing.

Processes

Research investigating team processes can be categorized in terms of action (i.e., periods of time when teams are engaged in acts that contribute directly to goal accomplishment), transition (i.e., periods of time when teams focus primarily on evaluation and/or planning activities to guide their accomplishment of a team goal or objective), or interpersonal (i.e., processes that teams use to manage interpersonal relationships; Marks et al., 2001).

Regarding action processes, several researchers have examined the effects of de-individuation or depersonalization (i.e., the process of reducing individual identity salience) on action processes in virtual teams (e.g., Lea & Spears, 1992; Spears, Lea, & Lee, 1990). This work is exemplified in a series of experiments conducted by Lee (2004, 2005, 2006, 2007a, 2007b). For example, using a series of university student laboratory experiments, Lee (2004) found that when the group level of self-identity was salient, uniform virtual appearance of CMC partners (i.e., using computer-rendered symbols) triggered depersonalization and heightened conformity behavior; however, when virtual appearance of CMC partners was distinct, conformity actually decreased; and depersonalization enhanced adherence to group norms directly and through its effects on group identification.

Several studies examined information processing in virtual teams (e.g., Griffith & Sawyer, 2006; Heninger, Dennis, & Hilmer, 2006). For example, Belanger and Watson-Manheim (2006) examined how virtual team members structure their use of multiple media to attain strategic goals in complex work environments, based on interviews with 40 information technology workers in two organizations. Results identified two primary structures that individuals employ when using multiple media (i.e., sequential and concurrent) and indicated that individuals strategically use multiple media to accomplish specific communication goals beyond simply transmitting the message, such as message acknowledgment, enhancement of mutual understanding, and participation in multiple communication interactions.

Regarding transition processes, Forester, Thoms, and Pinto (2007), using 82 participants from 12 virtual teams in an international engineering and construction company, found that goal commitment was significantly positively related to both perceived task outcome and psychosocial outcomes, whereas quality of goal setting was related only to perceived task outcome, suggesting that goal setting is related to perceptions of outcomes in virtual teams.

Regarding interpersonal processes, not surprisingly, most of the existing research has examined communication (e.g., Anawati & Craig, 2006; Zhou & Zhang, 2007), led by Walther and colleagues (e.g., Walther, 1994, 1997; Walther & Bazarova, 2007; Walther & Burgoon, 1992). For example, among over 150 individuals in a university student laboratory experiment, Tidwell and Walther (2002) found that individuals interacting in CMC exhibited a greater proportion of more direct and intimate uncertainty-reduction behaviors than FTF participants did, and demonstrated significantly greater gains in attributional confidence over the course of the conversations; they also found that the use of direct strategies by CMC individuals resulted in judgments of greater conversational effectiveness by partners.

Socialization has also been examined. For example, using a case study of one virtual team in the field, Ahuja and Galvin (2003) examined socialization processes by content, analyzing members' e-mail over a three-month period, and found that, as expected, newcomers exhibited an information-seeking mode, while established members exhibited an information-providing mode. While newcomers also actively engaged in discussions regarding cognitive information (i.e., construction of task-based information based on the social reality of the group) via e-mail, the medium did not facilitate the exchange of normative (i.e., understanding what the group values or expects) or regulative (i.e., structure, procedures, or processes that currently exist within a group) information. In a second example, Tanis and Postmes (2003) conducted a series of laboratory experiments with university students in the Netherlands and found that the limited availability of social cues (independent of the communication medium) negatively affected individuals' ability to reduce ambiguity and make positive impressions on collaboration partners; and that the effects of the limited capacity to convey social cues on selecting collaboration partners depended on the social identity of the parties involved.

Outputs

Several researchers investigated outputs in virtual team models at the individual level of analysis, including satisfaction, idea generation, and customer service (e.g., Gallupe et al., 1992; Jessup & Tansik, 1991; Weisband & Atwater, 1999). For example, among 167 students in a university laboratory experiment, Mejias (2007) found that process losses have negative effects on two dimensions of meeting satisfaction (i.e., process and outcome satisfaction) only in identified CMC environments, but not in anonymous CMC settings. Conversely, process gains generate positive effects on both outcome and process satisfaction, regardless of anonymity levels. As a second example, Froehle (2006) found that among survey responses from over 2,000 customers of a large Internet service provider, three customer service representative characteristics typically associated with satisfaction in FTF encounters (i.e., courtesy, professionalism, and attentiveness) had no effect on customer satisfaction in either telephone or CMC contexts.

Summary of Research Accomplishments

We believe that some of the most important advancements at the individual level of analysis have been made in identifying relationships that look very different in highly virtual teams than in more traditional teams that meet FTF. For example, most FTF research has demonstrated that collectivists are typically more comfortable, have less social loafing, and are more productive in team-based settings than are individualists (Earley & Gibson, 1998; Oyserman, Coon, & Kemmelmeier, 2002). However, Hardin et al. (2007) found that team members from individualistic cultures reported higher levels of self-efficacy for working in groups and virtual teams than did team members from collectivistic cultures. This finding is critical, given that Staples and Webster (2007) found that self-efficacy for teamwork was important for virtual teams (even more so than FTF teams). Similarly, like research on FTF teams, emergent state research at the individual level of analysis provides some clues that there may be different antecedents to affective- and performance-oriented outcomes. While trust was found to be positively related to job satisfaction in virtual teams in one study (Morris et al., 2002), it was not related to virtual team performance in another (Aubert & Kelsey, 2003). Such differences are common in teams research (see Cohen & Bailey, 1997; Kozlowski & Bell, 2003; and Mathieu et al., 2008, for reviews), but scholars have only recently been examining these issues in virtual teams.

Important advancements have also been made in the domain of processes at the individual level of analysis. The studies examining the impact of reducing individual identity salience in virtual teams have found that depersonalization increases conformity to group norms, typically through its effects on group identity, more so for women than for men (Lee, 2004, 2005). Some research also found that depersonalization induced greater polarization and extreme perceptions of group norms, especially when group identity, rather than individual identity, was more salient (Lee, 2006, 2007b; Spears et al., 1990). Several studies have also found beneficial effects for the use of CMC as compared to FTF on individual-level outcomes, including: number of ideas, less production blocking, and less evaluation apprehension, although studies are mixed with regard to levels of satisfaction (Gallupe et al., 1992; Jessup & Tansik, 1991).

Anonymous CMC brainstorming appears to have more advantages than identified CMC brainstorming for individual outputs (Jessup & Tansik; Mejias, 2007). A danger of CMC groups, however, is that self-ratings of contribution are typically more inflated and less accurate than in FTF groups; and, on the contrary, rating biases stemming from liking are evident in ratings of others in FTF groups but not in CMC groups (Weisband & Atwater, 1999).

Team-Level Virtual Team Research
Inputs

Not surprisingly, many researchers have investigated the role of team inputs in virtual team models at the team level of analysis. Features examined can be organized into one of seven categories: effects of communication medium/technology; group/team composition (e.g., on cultural values, country of origin, gender, etc); geographic dispersion; team size; team leadership; team training; and team structure.

EFFECTS OF COMMUNICATION MEDIUM/TECHNOLOGY

The communication medium has received the lion's share of attention as an input at the team level of analysis by virtual team researchers, especially those in both the IT and communication fields (e.g., Andres, 2002; Burgoon et al., 2002; Cappel & Windsor, 2000; Chidambaram & Tung, 2005; Daly, 1993; Dennis & Garfield, 2003; Dubrovsky, Kiesler, & Sethna, 1991; El-Shinnawy & Vinze, 1998; Finholt & Sproull, 1990; Graetz, Boyle, Kimble, Thompson, & Garloch, 1998; Hedlund, Ilgen, & Hollenbeck, 1998; Hiltz, Johnson, & Turoff, 1986; Hinds & Kiesler, 1995; Hollingshead, 1996; Hollingshead, McGrath, & O'Connor, 1993; Huang, Hung, & Yen, 2007; Jarvenpaa, Rao, & Huber, 1988; Lebie, Rhoades, & McGrath, 1996; McLeod, Baron, Marti, & Yoon, 1997; Pensendorfer & Koeszegi, 2006; Reid & Reid, 2005; Roch & Ayman, 2005; Schmidt, Montoya-Weiss, & Massey, 2001; Shepherd, Briggs, Reinig, Yen, & Nunamaker, 1996; Siegel, Dubrovsky, Kiesler, & McGuire, 1986; Stanton, Ashleigh, Roberts, & Xu, 2003; Straus & McGrath, 1994; Thompson & Coovert, 2002, 2003; Valacich, Dennis, & Connolly, 1994; Valacich & Schwenk, 1995; Walther, 1995; Warkentin, Sayeed, & Hightower, 1997; Weisband, 1992; Weisband, Schneider, & Connolly, 1995; Zigurs, Poole, & DeSanctis, 1988).

Two recent meta-analyses compared FTF versus CMC interaction. For example, using studies of 48 experiments of CMC and FTF groups, Rains (2005) found that CMC groups experience greater participation and influence equality, generate a larger amount of unique ideas, and experience less member dominance than do groups meeting FTF. In another meta-analysis of 145 experiments that used communication mode as the independent variable, Fjermestad (2004) found that the modal outcome for CMC compared to FTF methods is "no difference," while the overall percentage of positive effects (i.e., decision quality, depth of analysis, equality of participation, and satisfaction) for results that compare CMC to FTF is 29.2% in favor of CMC. Additionally, more detailed analysis suggests that task type, CMC type, and their interaction have a moderating effect on adaptation and outcome factors. Specifically, groups working on idea generation tasks using CMC improve to 39.6% over FTF. Conversely, asynchronous CMC groups working on decision-making tasks improved to 46.4% over FTF. FTF groups show higher levels of consensus and perceived quality, communicate more, and are more efficient (i.e., requiring less time to complete the tasks). No differences, however, were observed between FTF and group support systems groups on satisfaction and usability.

A typical example of research in this domain is a study conducted with 79 university student teams in a laboratory experiment by Colquitt, Hollenbeck, Ilgen, LePine, and Sheppard (2002), who found that access to CMC improved decision making in teams, but only when those teams were characterized by high levels of openness to experience. A second example is a study conducted by Campbell and Stasser (2006) with 95 three-person groups of university students, comparing CMC and FTF groups on a decision-making task in which time was either restricted or ample, and the task was one to solve or judge. Findings showed that solution rates were highest, and repeating and recall of unshared information greatest, in CMC groups given ample time and instructions to solve rather than judge.

Increasingly, the research comparing FTF and CMC groups has become more sophisticated, introducing cultural features and multiple outcome measures. For example, among 23 four-five person groups in a university student laboratory experiment in Taiwan, Li (2007) found that FTF groups, compared to CMC groups, performed better on critical functions, such as problem analysis and criteria establishment, and were more efficient in communication effectiveness; however, there were no significant differences on most objective and perceived group outcomes. Likewise, Daily and Teich (2000) found that among 27 four-five person multicultural groups in a university student laboratory experiment involving perceptions of contributions such as ratings of self, ratings of others, and ratings by others, ratings were higher in a non-group decision support system (GDSS) environment compared to a GDSS-supported environment; ethnic minorities' ratings of self were significantly lower than ethnic minorities' ratings of others in the non-GDSS environment but not in the GDSS environment; and the average number of ideas generated were greater in the GDSS environment.

Beyond the studies examining only CMC versus FTF collaboration, other researchers have compared the effects of a wider array of communication media on group processes and outcomes. For example, among 64 three-four person teams in a university laboratory experiment, Baker (2002) found no decision quality differences between teams using text-only or audio-only CMC, and the addition of video to audio-only CMC resulted in significant improvement to teams strategic decision quality. Using 30 three-person groups in a university student laboratory experiment, Kahai and Cooper (2003) found that richer media facilitate social perceptions (i.e., total socio-emotional communication and positive socio-emotional climate) and perceived ability to evaluate others' deception and expertise; leaner media (i.e., electronic mail and electronic conferencing) facilitate communication clarity when participants have less task-relevant knowledge; richer media can have significantly positive impacts on decision quality when participants' task-relevant knowledge is high; and the effects of participant deception can be mitigated by employing richer media. Among over 400 students in a university laboratory experiment, Lowry, Roberts, Romano, Cheney, and Hightower (2006) compared groups of three and six members each with three media options (i.e., FTF without CMC support, FTF with CMC support, and virtual with CMC support). Results indicated that smaller groups establish and maintain higher levels of communication quality, and FTF with CMC support groups have higher levels of communication quality than virtual with CMC

support groups; however, no significant difference between traditional FTF groups and virtual groups with CMC support was found. Finally, a few researchers have examined predictors of media use by virtual team members. For example, in a sample of teams in sales divisions of two Fortune 100 companies in the IT industry, Watson-Manheim and Belanger (2007) found that repertoires of communication media use are influenced by institutional conditions (e.g., incentives, trust, and physical proximity) and situational conditions (e.g., urgency, task, etc.) and by routine use of the media over time.

TEAM COMPOSITION

Most of the team composition studies at the team level of analysis examined the effects of gender differences (e.g., Gefen & Straub, 1997; Lind, 1999; Nowak, 2003; Savicki, Kelley, & Lingenfelter, 1996). Indicative of this research, Ocker (2007) examined the emergence of dominance in virtual teams using in-depth case studies of eight teams in a university setting, finding that the dominant individual belonged to the majority sex in each team; dominance was driven by a combination of a few team member status traits; and when one or more status markers belonged to a single person—the dominant member—and were absent in other team members, dominance was most pronounced.

Beyond gender, research on the cultural values/country of origin composition of teams has received increasing attention (e.g., Paul, Seetharaman, Samarah, & Mykytyn, 2004; Zhang, Lowry, Zhou, & Fu, 2007). For example, among 22 groups in a university student laboratory experiment in India and the United States, Paul, Samarah, Seetharaman, and Mykytyn (2005) found that cultural diversity moderated the relationship between collaborative conflict and performance such that the effects are stronger for culturally heterogeneous rather than homogeneous groups. Staples and Zhao (2006) compared homogeneous and heterogeneous groups (i.e., based on individualism/collectivism values, different languages spoken, country of birth, and nationality) using 79 four-five person university student groups, and found that heterogeneous teams were less satisfied and cohesive and had more conflict than the homogeneous teams, and that within just the heterogeneous teams, the performance of the virtual teams was superior to that of the FTF teams.

Illustrative of other individual differences examined in virtual team composition studies (e.g., Krebs, Hobman, & Bordia, 2006; Potter & Balthazard, 2002), Haas (2005) examined the impact of team composition in 96 global virtual project teams in an international development agency in terms of the number of cosmopolitan members (i.e., individuals with broad experience in many countries) and local members (i.e., individuals with deep experience in the project country), finding that both cosmopolitans and locals helped to increase internal knowledge (i.e., knowledge possessed by members themselves), that cosmopolitans (but not locals) helped to increase external knowledge (i.e., knowledge from sources outside the team), and that a mix of both locals and cosmopolitans was optimal for GVT performance.

GEOGRAPHIC DISPERSION

Despite the fact that many virtual teams are geographically dispersed, at the time of our review only a handful of studies have examined the effects of geographic dispersion at the team level of analysis (e.g., Burgoon et al., 2002; Pena, Walther, & Hancock, 2007; Valacich, George, Nunamaker, & Vogel, 1994). For example, among 218 members of 39 software development work teams, Cramton and Webber (2005) found that geographic dispersion significantly and negatively related to work processes (i.e., communication, coordination) and team effectiveness, and work processes partially mediated the relationship between geographic dispersion and team effectiveness. Chudoba, Wynn, Lu, and Watson-Manheim (2005), in a sample of surveys obtained from over 1,000 worldwide employees of the Intel Corporation, found that being distributed had no impact on self-assessed team performance. Using 56 global virtual engineering teams in the aerospace defense industry, Gibson and Gibbs (2006) found that geographic dispersion was negatively related to virtual team innovation, but the effects were less negative in teams with higher psychological safety. In an in-depth ethnographic study of a single GVT containing members from both a U.S. and Indian information technology organization, Metiu (2006) found that geographical dispersion exacerbated processes related to status closure (i.e., the monopolization of opportunities of higher status groups at the expense of lower status groups), and status closure resulted in less intragroup cooperation within the overall GVT.

TEAM SIZE

The size of virtual teams has received some attention in the literature (e.g., Lowry et al., 2006; Zhou & Zhang, 2006), with the earlier studies tending to focus on electronic brainstorming (e.g., Gallupe et al., 1992; Valacich, Dennis, & Nunamaker, 1992). For example, using surveys from 109 team members in a large multinational technology manufacturing company, Bradner, Mark, and Hertel (2005) found that, compared to members of larger teams, members of smaller teams participated more actively, were more committed to their team, were more aware of the goals of the team, had greater awareness of other team members, and were in teams with higher levels of rapport; larger teams were more conscientious than smaller teams in preparing meeting agendas; team size was also associated with different technology choice—larger teams adopted technology to support the coordination of asynchronous work, while smaller teams adopted technology that primarily supported collaboration.

TEAM LEADERSHIP

Given the importance of leadership to virtual team success (Bell & Kozlowski, 2002), we were very surprised by the small number of studies examining this aspect of virtual teams (e.g., Alge, Ballinger, & Green, 2004; Hambley, O'Neill, & Klein, 2007; Sosik, Avolio, & Kahai, 1998). Typical of research in this category, Kayworth and Leidner (2000) identified four critical success factors for virtual team leadership—communication, culture, technology, and project management—among 12 five-seven person teams in a university student quasi-experiment. Carte, Chidambaram, and Becker (2006) found, in a longitudinal study of university student virtual teams in North America, that the most successful teams displayed significantly more concentrated leadership behavior focused on performance (i.e., "producer" behavior) and more shared leadership behavior focused on keeping track of group work (i.e., "monitor" behavior) than the lower performing teams; these behaviors emerged strongly during the first half of the groups' life span, and remained throughout the life of the groups, but steadily dissipated in strength over time.

Case studies also dominate virtual team leadership research (e.g., Johnson, Suriya, Yoon, Berrett, & La Fleur, 2002; Pauleen, 2004). For example, in an in-depth case study of a single virtual team in the aerospace industry, Malhotra, Majchrzak,

Carman, and Lott (2001) identified several key leadership practices for managing successful virtual teams, including: establishing virtual team strategy initially, encouraging the use of knowledge management/collaborative tools, and restructuring work without changing core creative needs. Similarly, Suchan and Hayzak (2001) found in a case study of a single customer support virtual team in a Fortune 500 consulting organization, that to build and maintain team trust, the virtual team leader used an FTF, three-day project kick-off, a mentoring program, and a culture that promoted information sharing, team-based rewards, and employee development. Likewise, using case studies of four virtual team leaders from four international organizations, Sivunen (2006) identified four different leadership tactics employed in enhancing identification with the team: catering to the individual, giving positive feedback, bringing out common goals and talking up the team activities, and FTF meetings.

TEAM TRAINING

The tactics and training tools used to facilitate virtual teamwork have received modest attention in the literature (e.g., Chen, Liou, Wang, Fan, & Chi, 2005; Warkentin & Beranek, 1999). For example, among 75 individuals arrayed into five-person teams in a university student longitudinal laboratory experiment, Tan, Wei, Huang, and Ng (2000) found that virtual teams that were first trained in the use of a dialogue technique (i.e., engaging in small talk, discussing good communication practices, and building a team mental model of good communication practices) exhibited stronger cohesion, collaboration, perceived decision quality, and decision satisfaction during subsequent interactions. Cornelius and Boos (2003), using 240 individuals in 80 three-person groups in a university student laboratory experiment in Germany, examined the impact of training on CMC use and found the best performance scores in the FTF condition, performance scores in CMC with training approximating those of the FTF condition, and the lowest performance scores in CMC without training. Finally, Kirkman, Rosen, Tesluk, and Gibson (2006) found that among 40 virtual teams from a high technology service organization, virtual team CD-ROM–based training proficiency was more strongly related to customer satisfaction when teams had higher levels of trust and technology support, and when team leaders had longer, rather than shorter, tenure with their teams.

TEAM STRUCTURE

Some research has investigated various elements of virtual team structure (e.g., Suchan & Hayzak, 2001). Notable among these is the work of Timmerman and Scott (2006), who examined a comprehensive model of virtual team performance using key informants from 98 organizational teams. The authors investigated the impact of both communication (e.g., communication styles, channel selection) and structural (e.g., size, number of member locations and time zones, organization type) factors on actual technology use and virtual team performance finding that structural features primarily related to technology use, whereas communication considerations were associated more with team outcomes. Likewise, Workman (2005) gathered data from 436 virtual team projects over a 27-month period in a global information technology firm headquartered in France, and found that team boundary permeability strengthens the positive effects of various aspects of virtual team culture on team performance. Examining the impact of roles, Strijbos, Martens, Jochems, and Broers (2004) found that in a sample of 33 students in a university laboratory experiment in the Netherlands, CMC groups with formally designated roles, versus those in a non-role condition, have higher team coordination, a larger amount of task-content focused statements, and increased member awareness of team efficiency. A final example is a study conducted by Barkhi (2005) using 24 four-person groups in a university student laboratory experiment to examine the interactive effects of communication medium (i.e., FTF-GDSS vs. distributed GDSS) and incentive structure (i.e., individual- vs. group-based) on group performance, finding that groups with group-based incentives engage in free-riding behavior by selecting low effort levels less often in FTF-GDSS groups than in distributed-GDSS groups; however, the performance difference between FTF-GDSS groups and distributed-GDSS groups is not statistically significant when the incentive is individual-based.

Emergent States

Like the individual level studies reviewed earlier, trust is the emergent state that has by far received the most attention by virtual team researchers at the team level (e.g., Kanawattanachai & Yoo, 2002; Paul & McDaniel, 2004). This may not be too surprising, given the early focus on trust in the virtual teams practitioner literature (Handy, 1995), with some calling it the "glue of the global workspace" (O'Hara-Devereaux & Johansen, 1994, p. 243). Research on virtual team trust usually falls into two categories: trust as a predictor of virtual team outcomes, and antecedents of trust in virtual teams. Indicative of research in which trust is a predictor, Jarvenpaa, Shaw, and Staples (2004) found that among 42 six-person teams in a university student laboratory experiment, early in a team's existence, a member's trusting beliefs have a direct positive effect on his or her trust in the team and perceptions of team cohesiveness; later on, however, a member's trust in his team operates as a moderator, indirectly affecting the relationships between team communication and perceptual outcomes. Using case studies of five virtual teams in a large petrochemical company, Baskerville and Nandhakumar (2007) found that personal trust is most effectively established or reinvigorated through geographically co-located social interaction; personal trust is an antecedent to the activation and operation of effective virtual teams; abstract trust (i.e., trust based on shared organizational norms and expertise) is an alternative to personal trust as an antecedent to the activation and operation of effective, short-term virtual teams; and personal trust gradually dissipates over time without co-located social interaction.

Regarding the antecedents of trust in virtual teams (e.g., Jarvenpaa, Knoll, & Leidner, 1998; Jarvenpaa & Leidner, 1999; Krebs et al., 2006; Piccoli & Ives, 2003), recent research suggests that different sets of actions and behaviors are linked to building trust early in global virtual teams (e.g., social communication, communication conveying enthusiasm, individual initiative) than are involved in maintaining trust at later stages (e.g., substantive and timely response, leadership). For example, in a set of surveys obtained from 38 senior managers in new product development manufacturing firms in the United Kingdom and a smaller set of more in-depth case studies, Sharifi and Pawar (2002) summarized the many challenges associated with building and maintaining virtual teams—specifically, trust is essential to virtual team success, with co-location as a necessary but not sufficient ingredient for building trust. Using surveys of student teams participating in online courses, Coppola, Hiltz, and Rotter (2004) found that leaders of virtual groups build swift trust by establishing early communication, developing a positive social atmosphere, reinforcing predictable patterns, and

involving team members in tasks. Stewart and Gosain (2006) found that among 67 established open source software project teams, adhering to the ideological tenets of the open source software community (i.e., values, norms, and beliefs) positively affected both trust and communication quality which, in turn, affected team performance. Using 45 university student virtual teams, Polzer, Crisp, Jarvenpaa, and Kim (2006) examined the effects of a combination of different types of physical co-location and different configurations of nationality composition on team trust. The lowest levels of trust occurred in virtual teams consisting of two same-nationality co-located subgroups, providing evidence for fault-line effects along nationality.

OTHER EMERGENT STATES

In addition to trust, a wide variety of emergent states have been examined by virtual team researchers with team potency/collective efficacy and cohesion receiving the most attention (e.g., Chidambaram, 1996; Gonzalez, Burke, Santuzzi, & Bradley, 2003; Hardin, Fuller, & Valacich, 2006). For example, among 75 teams of university students in the Netherlands, Van den Bossche, Gijselaers, Segers, and Kirschner (2006) found that: interdependence, task cohesion, group potency, and psychological safety were all related to team learning behaviors; task cohesion was positively related to mutually shared cognition; and task cohesion and group potency were positively related to team effectiveness. Fuller, Hardin, and Davison (2007) found that, among 52 virtual teams comprising 318 university students from the United States, Great Britain, and Hong Kong, group potency and computer collective efficacy act as antecedents to virtual team efficacy. Virtual team efficacy in turn predicted both perceptual and objective measures of performance; and effort fully, and communication partially, mediated the effects of virtual team efficacy on performance. Using six medical project teams in a field study, Dennis and Garfield (2003) compared scores on satisfaction, cohesion, and perceived effectiveness over a seven-week period, finding that attitudes in the CMC groups, which were initially lower than FTF groups, increased positively over time to reach FTF group levels.

In addition to potency, collective efficacy, and cohesion, a small amount of attention has been given to group identity, team empowerment, and communication climate. For example, using 31 stable and 29 reconfigured university student groups meeting and working over a seven-week period, Bouas and Arrow (1996) found that: group identity was significantly lower for CMC versus FTF groups; the effects were stronger in the reconfigured groups; but the differences between groups in identity narrowed over the course of the study. Using 35 virtual teams in a field study of a high technology travel company, Kirkman, Rosen, Tesluk, and Gibson (2004) found that team empowerment was related to both process improvement and customer satisfaction, but that team empowerment was more important for virtual teams that met FTF less, rather than more. In a comprehensive examination of 56 global virtual engineering teams in the aerospace defense industry, Gibson and Gibbs (2006) found that a psychologically safe communication climate mitigated the negative effects of virtuality on innovation.

Processes

Several researchers investigated the role of team processes in virtual team models at the team level of analysis. As was the case in the individual-level section, team process studies included action, transition, and interpersonal processes. Regarding action processes, the bulk of the studies can be divided into two main groups: those dealing with aspects of knowledge management, such as acquisition and sharing, and those dealing with various stages of virtual team development. For example, in the area of knowledge management, in a longitudinal qualitative field study of seven cross-functional virtual teams, Sole and Edmondson (2002) found that, while virtual teams can easily access and use unique locale-specific knowledge resources to resolve problems that arise in those same locales, they encounter difficulties in uncovering and sharing situated knowledge (i.e., knowledge embedded in the work practices of a particular organizational site). Rafaeli and Ravid (2003), using 76 four-person teams of executive education students participating in a simulation in Israel, found that teams that used e-mail to share more information performed better than teams who shared less information. From in-depth case studies of 12 virtual teams in a university setting in Norway and the United States, Sarker, Sarker, Nicholson, and Joshi (2005) found that the volume of communication, the credibility of the communicator, and the nature of cultural values (i.e., collectivism) held by the communicator were found to significantly predict the extent of knowledge transferred;

however, capability was not found to have a significant influence.

Regarding stages of group development (e.g., Bordia, DiFonzo, & Chang, 1999; Kanawattanachai & Yoo, 2007; Massey, Montoya-Weiss, & Hung, 2003; Nemiro, 2002; Qureshi, Liu, & Vogel, 2006), Maznevski and Chudoba (2000) conducted a multimethod, in-depth field study of three GVTs in a high technology manufacturing organization, and found that virtual team dynamics were characterized by both: (a) a series of interaction incidents incorporating a set of decision processes using a particular medium that are shaped by a limited set of structural characteristics; and (b) repeating temporal patterns of regular FTF meetings in which the intensity of interaction is extremely high, followed by a period of some weeks in which interaction incidents are less intense. Drawing upon adaptive structuration theory, the authors suggest that within interaction incidents the medium and form are selected to match the function, but across incidents over time, the function is modified to match the medium and form. In a similar in-depth case study of a single virtual team over a 10-month period, Majchrzak, Rice, Malhotra, King, and Ba (2000) found that to address misalignment between the organizational environment, group structure, and technology, group members initially modified their environment and group structures, whereas later in the team's life span, group members modified all three aspects, including technology. Using a multimethod study of five virtual team projects in five different organizations, Ratcheva and Vyakarnam (2001) found that virtual teams follow self-energizing developmental processes that are non-linear and are not consistent with existing developmental models for FTF teams. Using surveys and interviews of seven virtual teams of five-six members engaged in distance learning in a university setting, Johnson et al. (2002) found that the developmental pattern of the teams followed Tuckman's (1965) forming-storming-norming-performing model, but the teams moved through the stages very quickly, did not experience the storming stage, and encountered a conflict resolution stage between the performing and forming stage in an interactive fashion.

Regarding transition processes, using 48 groups in a university student laboratory experiment, Huang, Wei, Watson, and Tan (2002) found that CMC groups with an embedded goal-setting structure had higher cohesion, better team commitment, better collaboration climate, perceived decision quality, and more decision alternatives than CMC groups without a goal-setting structure. In a case study of one virtual team in a Fortune 500 manufacturing and sales organization, Baba, Gluesing, Ratner, and Wagner (2004) found that the process of cognitive convergence (i.e., increasing similarity of individual cognitive structures through information sharing) was related to virtual team performance only when patterns of cognitive divergence were also reversed. Facilitators of the relationship between cognitive convergence also included: similar experiences in a common context, surfacing hidden truths through knowledge brokering, and shifts in agent self-interest and negotiation of task interdependence. Using an exploratory study of virtual teams in a university setting over a two-week period in Norway and the United States, Munkvold and Zigurs (2007) found that swift-starting virtual teams need to structure their interaction from the onset, including introducing team members' background and competence, discussing project goals and deliverables, defining roles and responsibilities, and setting milestones; they have to pay immediate attention to familiarizing themselves with and integrating available technology, and agreeing on preferred communication media and frequency.

Research on virtual team interpersonal processes at the team level falls mainly into two categories: communication (e.g., Crowston, Howison, Masango, & Eseryel, 2007; Leenders, van Engelen, & Kratzer, 2003; Murthy & Kerr, 2002; Pauleen & Yoong, 2001; Rains, 2007; Reinig & Mejias, 2004; Sproull & Kiesler, 1986) and conflict management (e.g., Rutkowski et al., 2007). Within each of these categories, both communication and conflict have been treated as either a predictor or criterion variable.

COMMUNICATION

Exemplifying research in which communication is a predictor variable, Saphiere (1996) found, in a sample of 12 global business teams in three U.S.-based corporations, that the most successful teams communicated more often in informal, social ways; utilized more task and affect behaviors; frequently disagreed with one another, critically analyzing issues in meetings and focusing on task in a positive manner in writing; acted as cultural interpreters and mediators; and unanimously desired to work together again in the future. With

longitudinal data from 38 teams of university students, Yoo and Kanawattanachai (2001) found that the influence of a team's early communication volume on team performance decreases as teams develop transactive memory systems and a collective mind. Using the electronic communication records of 13 teams of university graduate students, Cramton (2001) identified five key GVT interpersonal process problems—failure to communicate and retain contextual information, unevenly distributed information, differences in the salience of information, relative differences in speed of access to information, and interpreting the meaning of silence—that contribute to a lack of mutual knowledge among team members; structural and task-related factors (e.g., feedback lags, task interdependence, tight time frames) exacerbate the relationship between the five key interpersonal problems and GVT performance. In an example of research in which communication was treated as a criterion variable, Rasters, Vissers, and Dankbaar (2002) found, in an in-depth case study of a single virtual team based in Europe, that virtual team communication was affected far more by the stage of group development (using Gersick's, 1988, punctuated equilibrium model) than by the particular communication media used.

CONFLICT

Illustrative of research in which conflict is a predictor variable, using a subset of data from university student laboratory experiments run by Watson, DeSanctis, and Poole (1988), Poole, Holmes, and DeSanctis (1991) found that the introduction of a CMC tool had no direct effect on team outcomes (i.e., group consensus), but the effects were mediated by how the groups adapted the tools to either promote, or inhibit, productive conflict management. Montoya-Weiss, Massey, and Song (2001), in a field experiment using 35 five-person university student virtual teams in the United States and Japan, found that certain conflict-handling strategies (i.e., competition, collaboration) were positively related to virtual team performance, while others (i.e., avoidance, compromise) were negatively related. Introducing a formal, structured plan for managing team time and activities weakened the negative effects of avoidance and compromise on virtual team performance. Using 24 product development teams in five organizations, Mortensen and Hinds (2001) found that conflict was slightly more detrimental to CMC team performance than FTF team performance.

Regarding conflict as a criterion variable, in a study just discussed, Mortensen and Hinds (2001) found that shared team identity was associated with less task and affective conflict in CMC but not in FTF teams. In an in-depth case study of three global virtual teams from North America, Europe, and Asia in a university setting, Kankanhalli, Tan, and Wei (2007) examined antecedents to conflict and found that: cultural diversity is likely to contribute to both task and relationship conflict, while functional diversity may result in task conflict; large volumes of electronic communication and lack of immediacy of feedback in asynchronous media can contribute to task conflict; the relationship between task conflict and team performance is likely to be contingent upon task complexity and conflict resolution approach. The influence of relationship conflict on performance may depend on task interdependence and conflict resolution approach. The conflict resolution approach may in turn be determined by the nature of conflict attribution.

Besides communication and conflict, a handful of additional studies examined other facets of interpersonal processes in virtual teams (e.g., Alge, Wiethoff, & Klein, 2003; Easley, Devaraj, & Crant, 2003). For example, using eight virtual teams in a university student laboratory experiment in England and the United States, Walther, Slovacek, and Tidwell (2001) found that in new, unacquainted teams, seeing one's partner (in a photograph) promotes affection and social attraction, but in long-term virtual teams, the same type of photograph dampens affinity. In a sample of 47 individuals in eight virtual teams in a university setting in England and Hong Kong, Panteli and Davison (2005) found that subgroups exert different degrees of impact on the team as a whole; where the impact was high, boundaries were created between team members in different subgroups while the development of team cohesiveness was restricted; and all teams were able to produce high-quality outcomes, suggesting that the emergence of subgroups may not always have a negative influence on team performance.

Outputs

Several researchers investigated the role of team outputs in virtual team models at the team level of analysis (Connolly, Jessup, & Valacich, 1990; Geister, Konradt, & Hertel, 2006; Jarman, 2005;

Ocker, 2005; Potter & Balthazard, 2002; Rutkowski et al., 2007). A noteworthy example is an examination of an in-depth case study of a European based automotive manufacturing team, in which May and Carter (2001) found that the introduction of video conferencing, shared whiteboard, application sharing, and product data management tools increased team efficiency and flexibility, including time savings, sales volume, and reduced costs. Using an in-depth case study of a single virtual team in the aerospace industry, Malhotra et al. (2001) examined how an interorganizational virtual team was able to produce radical innovation. Using surveys of 67 virtual team members representing 12 teams in eight different organizations, Lurey and Raisinghani (2001) found that teams' processes and team members' relations were strongly positively related to team performance and team member satisfaction; selection procedures and executive leadership styles were moderately associated; and design process, other internal group dynamics, and additional external support mechanisms were only weakly related. Another comprehensive study involved 493 project teams that ranged in the degree of physical dispersion over a five-year period in a professional service organization, in which Boh, Ren, Kiesler, and Bussjaeger (2007) found that dispersed projects garnered higher net earnings than local projects when there was a better match of scarce expertise to project requirements; and a curvilinear relationship was observed, such that a very high percentage of dispersed experts on a project increased coordination costs and reduced net earnings.

Summary of Research Accomplishments

Beyond the meta-analyses and follow-up studies comparing FTF to CMC use, there has been increasing attention to team composition on a variety of dimensions, including size, location, country of origin, cultural values, gender, and personality. From a productivity standpoint (e.g., number of ideas, idea uniqueness), larger CMC teams are typically better than smaller teams (Gallupe et al., 1992; Lowry et al., 2006; Valacich et al., 1992); however, when considering affective outcomes (e.g., satisfaction, participation, commitment, awareness of goals, awareness of other members), smaller teams seem to have better results (Bradner et al., 2005; Valacich et al.). Almost all of the studies to date have found negative effects of geographic dispersion on team processes and outcomes, including: reduced communication, coordination, and trust (Burgoon et al., 2002; Cramton & Webber, 2005); lower innovation (Gibson & Gibbs, 2006); the dominance of certain members over others (Metiu, 2006; Pena et al., 2007); and lower overall team effectiveness (Cramton & Webber). Regarding team structure, researchers have found positive team performance effects for formally designated roles (Strijbos et al., 2004), team boundary permeability (Workman, 2005), and group-based incentives (Barkhi, 2005). Suchan and Hayzak (2001) found that corporate mission, strategy, tasks, reward systems, and attitudes toward technology supported virtual team structure; and Timmerman and Scott (2006) found that virtual team structure was a key determinant of technology use.

As at the individual level, trust is the most frequently studied emergent state at the team level of analysis, and most of the studies have found positive relationships with performance (Baskerville & Nandhakumar, 2007; Coppola et al., 2004; Kanawattanachai & Yoo, 2002; Paul & McDaniel, 2004). As an alternative to swift trust (which received much attention in prior reviews, as exemplified by Jarvenpaa & Leidner, 1999), Baskerville and Nandhakumar found that abstract trust (i.e., trust based on shared organizational norms and expertise) is critical to the activation and operation of effective, short-term virtual teams. Unlike swift trust, which is characterized by beliefs in the care of collaborators, suspension of uncertainty, risk taking, and expected benefits, trust based on abstract systems is not premised on urgent, short-term goals.

Besides trust, the other emergent states receiving the most attention are team potency/collective efficacy and cohesion. Paralleling the FTF team meta-analytic research on potency/collective efficacy (Gully, Incalaterra, Joshi, & Beaubien, 2002) and cohesion (Beal, Cohen, Burke, & McLendon, 2003), virtual team research has supported the positive effects of both potency/collective efficacy (Gonzalez et al., 2003; Hardin et al., 2006, Hardin et al., 2007; Van den Bossche et al., 2006) and cohesion (Gonzalez et al.; Van den Bossche et al.) for virtual team performance. Research comparing cohesion between FTF and CMC groups found that while initially lagging behind FTF groups, cohesion in CMC groups typically increases and equals that of FTF groups over time (Chidambaram, 1996; Dennis & Garfield, 2003).

The same held true for group identity over time (Bouas & Arrow, 1996).

With regard to team-level processes, while it might be tempting to conclude from most virtual team studies that the more communication, the better the team performance (and the richer the communication, even better; Pauleen &Yoong, 2001; Saphiere, 1996), a closer examination of several studies provides a more nuanced view of the effects of communication in virtual teams. For example, the volume of communication may depend to some extent on the stage of the team's life cycle, as Yoo and Kanawattanachai (2001) found that the relationship between a team's early communication volume and team performance decreases as teams develop transactive memory systems and a collective mind. Similarly, Rasters et al. (2002) found that virtual team communication was affected far more by the stage of group development than by the particular communication media used. The amount of communication may also depend on the type of outcome under consideration, as Leenders et al. (2003) found that team creativity is highest with a moderate frequency of communication and a low level of communication centralization. Crowston et al. (2007) found that open source software development team members generally do not meet FTF until the project is well under way.

In addition to communication, research on conflict management in virtual teams has also yielded important advancements. For example, Montoya-Weiss et al. (2001) found that certain conflict-handling strategies (i.e., competition, collaboration) were positively related to virtual team performance, while others (i.e., avoidance, compromise) were negatively related, and that a temporal coordination mechanism weakened the negative effects of avoidance and compromise on virtual team performance. Mortensen and Hinds (2001) found that conflict was slightly more detrimental to CMC team performance than FTF team performance, and that shared team identity was associated with less task and affective conflict in CMC but not in FTF teams. More recently, Kankanhalli et al. (2007) found that large volumes of electronic communication and lack of immediacy of feedback in asynchronous media can contribute to task conflict; the relationship between task conflict and team performance is likely to be contingent upon task complexity and conflict resolution approach.

Regarding virtual team outputs at the team level of analysis, researchers have moved beyond more simplistic comparisons of the outputs of CMC and FTF teams (e.g., Potter & Balthazard, 2002) to more complex models of virtual team performance. For example, May and Carter (2001) found that the introduction of video conferencing, shared whiteboard, application sharing and product data management tools increased team efficiency and flexibility. In a comprehensive model, Ocker (2005) found that significant inhibitors to the creative performance of virtual teams included dominance, domain knowledge, downward norm setting, lack of shared understanding, time pressure, and technical difficulties; and significant enhancers to creativity included stimulating colleagues, the existence of a variety of social influences, a collaborative team climate, and both the surfacing and reduction of equivocality.

Organization-Level Virtual Team Research

We found only three studies that investigated virtual teams at the organizational level of analysis. In a case study of two newspaper publishing organizations, Zack and McKenney (1995) found that the inputs of social context (i.e., the culture, distribution of power, and the social norms, habits, practices, expectations, and preferences held by a group regarding its present and past interaction) influenced each group's use of e-mail and FTF communication such that there was greater similarity of interaction within groups across communication mode than within communication mode across groups. Examining team processes in a variety of manufacturing organizations, Andersen (2005) found that the use of CMC moderated the relationship between decentralized strategic decision making and firm performance such that the relationship was stronger with greater, rather than less, use of CMC; and that CMC was also positively related to firm performance. Finally, McDonough, Kahn, and Barczak (2001) found that among 100 firms in new product development, global teams presented companies with many more challenges than either co-located or virtual teams, and that performance is also lower for these types of teams.

Discussion

Our review of almost 200 articles on virtual teams demonstrates that multiple academic fields (i.e., management, psychology, information technology,

and communication) have made progress in better understanding virtual team functioning and performance. We summarize below what we believe will be the most important directions for future research over the next decade, addressing both theoretical and methodological implications in each of five areas: (a) conceptualization of virtuality; (b) team development; (c) virtual team leadership; (d) levels of analysis; and (e) multidisciplinary approaches. Several of these were domains identified in prior reviews (Hertel et al. 2005; Martins et al. 2004; Stanko & Gibson, 2009); we review progress in these domains since that time, and then address other unique areas that we have identified in our own review. We hope that this summary provides an impetus for moving virtual teams research in directions that are sorely needed for a better understanding of the dynamics so crucial to virtual team success.

Conceptualizing Virtuality

All three prior reviews noted the continuing pattern of researchers comparing CMC and FTF groups and teams looking for differences in emergent states, processes, and outcomes. Such comparisons provide, at best, a modest degree of theoretical advancement for virtual team performance in general. Clearly, most teams in industry lie on a continuum somewhere between completely virtual and completely FTF, an acknowledgment that is not new (Bell & Kozlowski, 2002; Griffith et al., 2003; Kirkman & Mathieu, 2005; Martins et al., 2004) but has still gone largely unheeded. To artificially separate teams into completely virtual and completely FTF ignores the important nuances that accompany teams using a variety of different communication tools in their collaborative efforts. Examining extremes has its place in research, of course, but we believe (as others do) that continuing to pursue these comparative studies oversimplifies the complexities inherent in teams with a sometimes unlimited array of communication options.

In an effort to remedy this problem to some degree, more recent research has begun to add communication technology options beyond simply one type of CMC and FTF (e.g., Becker-Beck, Wintermantel, & Borg, 2005; Huang et al., 2007; Lowry et al., 2006; Murthy & Kerr, 2004; Simon, 2006). While broadening the array of communication tools available to collaborators is admirable and parallels the increasing availability of technologies in industry, research still tends to simply compare virtual team processes and outcomes for those using different tools (e.g., bulletin board, chat, e-mail, etc.). Clearly, virtual team members use a variety of communication tools simultaneously (or more often in quick succession) and are not isolated to one tool for particular tasks (Driskell, Radtke, & Salas, 2003). We applaud efforts to better understand theoretically how and why virtual team members select particular media configurations, particularly those that propose more complex, non-linear approaches such as behavioral complexity theory (Shachaf & Hara, 2007).

In addition, none of the aforementioned research incorporates the element of time or stages of team development; thus we have little understanding of the interaction of communication tool use and team development. Perhaps certain communication tools are more important at different stages of a team's life cycle (Kirkman & Mathieu, 2005; Nemiro, 2002). Research that incorporates the examination of teams using multiple media at different points in time and to varying degrees should help to better understand the role of technology in virtual team success (see Shim, Warkentin, Courtney, Power, Sharda, & Carlsson, 2002, for a review of technology-based communication research). Clearly, our recommendation here would necessitate the use of longitudinal designs, a refrain often heard in teams research in general.

Various theoretical conceptualizations of virtuality also exist (Bell & Kozlowski, 2002; Griffith & Neale, 2001; Griffith et al., 2003). For example, Kirkman and Mathieu (2005) developed a three-dimensional model of team virtuality including: the extent to which team members utilize virtual tools to coordinate and execute team processes (versus working and meeting face-to-face); the amount of informational value provided by such tools (i.e., how important each tool is to accomplishing work, akin to communication richness for communication tools); and the synchronicity of team member virtual interaction (i.e., whether or not communication or work occurs in real time between sender and receiver). Gibson and Gibbs (2006) conceptualize virtuality along four dimensions: geographic dispersion; electronic dependence; dynamic structural arrangements (i.e., frequent changes in team members, their roles, and relationships to each other); and nationality diversity. Common to these conceptualizations is the degree to which teams use CMC; however, debate remains about what constitutes virtuality versus its antecedents (Kirkman & Mathieu, 2005). We

believe that researchers should continue to debate and refine the conceptualization of virtuality. In addition, there is a need for more empirical attention to understanding the potentially differential impact of the various dimensions on virtual team outcomes (see Stanko & Gibson, 2009, for a review).

Regarding the geographic dispersion dimension of virtuality, O'Leary and Cummings (2007) conceptualize it along three dimensions: spatial (i.e., geographic distance among team members); temporal (i.e., time difference among team members); and configurational (i.e., location where team members work, including the uneven distribution of team members). Such a conceptualization of geographic dispersion means that researchers will also have to move beyond simple treatments of geographic dispersion in terms of miles or time zones and perhaps make different predictions for each of these three dimensions. Each of the dimensions is likely to be associated with different team outcomes, and the dimensions are likely to have different antecedents as well (O'Leary & Cummings). For example, Cummings, Espinosa, and Pickering's (2009) recent work indicates that time zone dispersion is more impactful on team coordination than mileage dispersion (i.e., it matters more how many time zones are crossed by members when they collaborate than how many miles they cross).

Team Development in Virtual Settings

There has been a general lack of attention to time and stages of development in virtual teams research (beyond interactions with communication technology). Although this issue is not addressed by either Stanko and Gibson (2009) or Martins et al. (2004), Hertel et al. (2005) organized their entire virtual teams review around a life cycle model of team development. They concluded that "...many disadvantages of virtual teams that are suggested by experimental research with ad hoc teams seem to diminish when a longer temporal scope is taken into account..." and "longitudinal studies are desirable to address these issues, and also to acknowledge the developmental aspects of virtual teams" (p. 89). We could not agree more with these statements.

Our review of the literature has shown very little progress in examining developmental models of virtual teams over time. A notable exception is the work of Walther and Burgoon (1992), who found that CMC groups could attain various relational aspects equal to that of FTF groups over time, and argued that previous findings failed to detect these trends because they were cross-sectional. Such findings suggest that relationship building may take more time in CMC versus FTF groups, but there may be no eventual differences in relationship quality. Ahn, Lee, Cho, and Park (2005) theoretically show how the utilization and creation of knowledge along the virtual team life cycle can be enhanced by considering the knowledge context. Saunders and Ahuja (2006) offer a framework for understanding the differences between temporary and ongoing virtual teams' structure, processes, and outcomes, suggesting that ongoing virtual teams must tackle more process and structural issues than temporary teams. While some theoretical progress has been made, more empirical research to test these theoretical assertions is needed.

One way to perhaps accelerate CMC relationship quality and informal communication is to generate expectations of long-term working arrangements and group identity (Walther, 1994, 1997). In addition, the negative effects of limited social cues on relationship building in CMC groups depend, to some extent, on the social identities of the parties involved (Tanis & Postmes, 2003) and the willingness of communication partners to adapt their behavior to recognize different religious beliefs and time zone differences (Anawati & Craig, 2006). Likewise, we view as promising research that compares teams with different temporal expectations. For example, Alge et al. (2003) compared both CMC and FTF teams that were ad hoc (i.e., had no prior history of working together or expectation of working together in the future), past (i.e., teams with a prior history of working together but no future expectation of working together), or future (i.e., teams that had not worked together previously but expected to work together in the future). Past teams, with a history of knowledge-building experiences, eliminated media differences with respect to communication effectiveness, and although future teams were not able to eliminate media differences, they demonstrated the highest levels of information sharing.

Further, while some research has found that virtual teams can follow developmental cycles associated with FTF teams (Bordia et al., 1999), most of the remaining research suggests that virtual teams do not follow the most prevalent, existing models of team development, such as Tuckman's (1965) forming-storming-norming-performing-adjourning model or Gersick's (1988) punctuated equilibrium model (Johnson et al., 2002; Maznevski & Chudoba, 2000). For example, while one study found that the developmental pattern of CMC groups was very similar to that of FTF groups (Bordia et al.), most of the studies examining virtual team development have found key differences compared to FTF team development (Johnson et al.; Maznevski & Chudoba; Ratcheva & Vyakarnam, 2001). Virtual team development is described as non-linear and often dependent on other aspects of team functioning, such as communication media used (Nemiro, 2002), temporal coordination mechanisms (Massey et al., 2003), transactive memory systems (Kanawattanachai & Yoo, 2007), and the alignment between organizational environment, group structure, and technology (Majchrzak et al., 2000).

Consistent with the team developmental work of Marks et al. (2001), Maznevski and Chudoba (2000) found that virtual teams go through repeating temporal patterns of regular FTF meetings in which the intensity of interaction is extremely high (i.e., action), followed by a period of some weeks in which interaction incidents are less intense (i.e., transition). Likewise, Ratcheva and Vyakarnam (2001) found that virtual teams follow self-energizing developmental processes that are non-linear and are not consistent with existing developmental models for FTF teams. In a longitudinal study of medical project teams, Dennis and Garfield (2003) found that while FTF teams developed conservative projects that met unstated project criteria, CMC teams developed projects more closely aligned with team member interests.

The challenge here is threefold: (1) there is not enough research to understand how virtual team development differs from FTF team development; (2) we do not know whether or not developmental cycles differ within different types of virtual teams performing different tasks (Bell & Kozlowski, 2002), which is true for teams research in general; and (3) most of the existing developmental virtual teams research is based almost entirely on case studies of very small numbers of teams. While we in no way disparage case study research, more multimethod studies are needed to fully understand the complexity inherent in virtual team life cycles. In addition, since virtual teams often have more dynamic structural arrangements (i.e., changing membership) than traditional, FTF teams (Gibson & Gibbs, 2006), virtual team researchers will need to map developmental models that incorporate frequently changing members. Such models are not likely to be linear or "stage" models and are more likely to be dynamic life-cycle models (see Hertel et al., 2005). In their review of the last decade of teams research, Mathieu et al. (2008, p. 461) urge researchers to "embrace the complexity" in their pursuit of scholarly understanding of team functioning and performance. We argue that nowhere is this truer than in the virtual teams arena. We also agree with Mathieu et al. that highly dynamic team environments may create the need for adapting or perhaps even moving beyond more static IPO or IEPO models. Perhaps more qualitative or ethnographic research is needed to create a baseline understanding of team development in virtual teams.

Virtual Team Leadership

In their article on factors contributing to virtual team success, Blackburn, Furst, and Rosen (2003, p. 102) conclude, "The number one key success factor for virtual teams is strong leadership." Among the studies we reviewed, transformational and transactional leadership has received some attention. For example, Sosik et al. (1998) found that the inspirational leadership dimension of transformational leadership was positively related, and the intellectual stimulation and individualized consideration dimensions were negatively related, to CMC group creativity; and Hambley et al. (2007) found that the effects of transactional and transformational leadership on team interaction and performance did not differ with changes in the richness of the communication media (i.e., FTF, videoconferencing, chat). In contrast to a single, assigned leader, Johnson et al. (2002) found that successful virtual teams had shared leadership rather than a single, emergent leader; and Carte et al. (2006) found that the most successful virtual teams had formal leaders who focused on performance issues and shared leadership that focused on keeping track of group work.

Highlighting the far-reaching importance of leadership, virtual team researchers have generally found positive effects for training on both taskwork (Chen et al., 2005; Cornelius & Boos, 2003) and teamwork (Tan et al., 2000; Warkentin

& Beranek, 1999), but Kirkman et al. (2006) found no effects for teamwork training on customer satisfaction in virtual teams unless the teams had a high level of trust and technology support and team leaders with longer, rather than shorter, team leader tenure. Paralleling dyadic leadership research, more interest in contingency-based approaches might uncover more interesting findings.

While some leader actions for virtual teams might be "inferred" from existing research that does not explicitly address leadership, we agree with the previous reviews (Hertel et al., 2005; Martins et al., 2004) that not nearly enough has been done to understand virtual team leadership. Bell and Kozlowski (2002) provide a theoretically grounded, contingency model of team leadership, but to our knowledge there has been no empirical research on the model. In their review of the teams literature, Kozlowski and Bell (2003) argue that most team leadership theories and models simply borrow from dyadic models and apply findings from these models to teams. We agree that such application is problematic, particularly for virtual teams. Almost 20 years ago, Hirschhorn (1991) argued that team leaders have to pay attention to a "triangle" of relationships when leading their teams: (a) a leader's relationship to each individual member; (b) a leader's relationship to the team as a whole; and (c) each member's relationship to the team as a whole. Thus, team leadership is likely to be many more times as complex as dyadic leadership. Compounding this complexity is the fact that virtual team leaders will not have the degree of face-to-face contact typical of traditional teams, depending on the team's level of virtuality.

Similar to the research on virtual team development, virtual team leadership research is primarily case study driven or laboratory based using student samples. Thus, we recommend that virtual team leadership be studied in the real-world context in which it occurs: organizations. We also caution researchers to avoid knee-jerk use of existing leadership constructs and models such as transformational-transactional leadership (Hambley et al., 2007; Sosik et al., 1998). The radically different environment in which virtual team leaders lead will likely call for novel leadership theories and models that may be specific to virtual teams (see Schiller & Mandviwalla, 2007, for a discussion of theories that have been applied in virtual teams research). Due to geographic dispersion, the concept of shared leadership is likely to be relevant (Johnson et al., 2002). Thus, a singular focus on the "leader" of virtual teams might be erroneous in many cases. Finally, in keeping with our call for more research on team development, virtual team leadership models will have to be contingency based, in part, relying on development cycles to uncover key leadership behaviors (see Carte et al., 2006). Such an approach will make research offering "lists" of virtual team leader behaviors obsolete (e.g., Kayworth & Leidner, 2000; Malhotra et al., 2001; Pauleen, 2004; Sivunen, 2006; Suchan & Hayzak, 2001).

Levels of Analysis

In the management and psychology literatures in general, there is a growing interest in examining organizational phenomena at multiple levels of analysis, as well as relationships across levels, as evidenced by several recent special issues of our key journals. This is in part due to the recognition that many features of organizational life have individual, team, and organizational level analogues (i.e., self-efficacy, group efficacy, collective efficacy), but also due to the availability of specific methodological techniques, such as hierarchical linear modeling, which help to isolate variance at different levels as well as modeling cross-level relationships. Yet, most of the research we reviewed is being conducted at the team level, without acknowledging important features and phenomena at other levels.

Because virtual teams are clearly composed of individuals, who are often from different countries and cultures, understanding the impact of individual differences and the resulting individual-level outcomes, such as satisfaction and commitment, is extremely important. While individual level inputs and outputs have received considerable attention in the FTF teams literature (Cohen & Bailey, 1997; Kozlowski & Bell, 2003; Mathieu et al., 2008), our review shows that many gaps remain in understanding the role of the individual in virtual teams. Indeed, while some individual differences, such as extraversion, individualism-collectivism, and gender, have received some attention, there are literally hundreds of other individual differences that have gone unexplored.

Noticeably absent is a substantial body of research investigating individual cultural value differences in virtual teams. To our knowledge, only a handful of studies have actually measured individual cultural features (e.g., cultural values; Hardin et al., 2007; Paul et al., 2005; Staples & Zhao, 2006; Swigger, Alpaslan, Brazile, & Monticino, 2004; Zhang et al., 2007), and all of these are laboratory experiments conducted with student teams. Further, although Hardin et al. (2007) measured individualism-collectivism, these assessments were not used to compose teams or test hypotheses (in fact, team composition is not clear, but the authors imply that teams in their study had Hong Kong and U.S. participants). This dearth of research is surprising, given that many researchers have suggested that members of highly virtual teams often represent different nations or cultural contexts, which likely give rise to individual cultural differences within the team that may affect emergent states or processes. Some researchers include national heterogeneity, or assume it, but do not measure the underlying cultural features that they claim explain the effect of national differences. Hence, there is a major disconnect between theory and research evidence in this regard.

For example, Shin (2004) theoretically argued that certain individual differences contribute to person-group fit in virtual teams including: willingness to trust, trustworthiness, lateral skills, and virtual communication skills; Brown, Poole, and Rodgers (2004) developed a model that proposes that personality type affects individuals' disposition to trust, perceived trustworthiness, communication, willingness to collaborate, and the sustainability and productivity of the collaboration; and Fiol and O'Connor (2005) theoretically posit both antecedents (e.g., need for uncertainty reduction, communication context) and moderators (e.g., tolerance for ambiguity, experienced media richness) of individual identification in virtual teams. To our knowledge, none of these individual differences have been empirically examined, but they will clearly be relevant to team staffing (see Harvey, Novicevic, & Garrison, 2004).

Further, it is rare that researchers attempt to understand individual-level components that underlie collective phenomena in virtual teams. For example, Gibson and Gibbs (2006) found that a collective psychologically safe communication climate moderates the negative effect of several features of virtuality on team innovation, indicating that communication climate is an important point of leverage for virtual teams. But how do individual members' communication behaviors combine to create a psychologically safe communication climate? We understand little about these generative individual-level processes. We see as equally promising research that investigates individual cognitive reactions to a variety of media. For example, Kock (2004), drawing on Darwinian theory, introduced a psychobiological model of CMC that proposes a negative causal link between the naturalness of a CMC medium (i.e., the similarity of the medium to FTF) and the cognitive effort required from an individual using the medium for knowledge transfer, and that this causal link depends on both schema alignment (i.e., the similarity between the mental schemas of an individual and those of other participants) and cognitive adaptation (i.e., an individual's level of schema development associated with the use of a particular medium). We believe that such work inspires not only a much more fine-grained analysis, but also cross-level insights into CMC use in virtual teams.

At the team level of analysis, although a great deal has been accomplished (and the research is accelerating exponentially), there are still a multitude of research challenges. Many researchers have investigated the emergent state of trust, indicating that it is important for virtual teams, yet there are an endless number of other emergent states that might be relevant. The small number of studies on psychological safety (Gibson & Gibbs, 2006; Van den Bossche et al., 2006) and team empowerment (Kirkman et al., 2004) in virtual teams suggests that these might be fruitful avenues for future research. If researchers do engage in research on emergent states in virtual teams, the role of the developmental life cycle of teams is likely to be critical (e.g., Jarvenpaa et al., 2004), again making longitudinal studies of paramount importance. Also, researchers need to consider whether existing measures of trust (developed mostly in FTF team contexts) are sufficient for virtual teams research (see Sarker, Valacich, & Sarker, 2003, for a specific measure of virtual team trust). We see as equally promising research on knowledge-management processes, a gap identified by Martins et al. (2004) and in several theoretical frameworks (e.g.,

Cramton & Hinds, 2005; Griffith & Neale, 2001; Griffith et al., 2003; Hinds & Bailey, 2003). Sole and Edmondson (2002) found that virtual team members encounter difficulties using knowledge situated in one location to solve problems located in another; however, Sarker et al. (2005) found that extent of knowledge transferred was positively influenced by volume of communication, the credibility of the communicator, and the collectivism level of the communicator. Likewise, in a case study of a global science/technology company, Griffith and Sawyer (2006) found that attendance at FTF community of practice meetings, use of searchable archives, video-on-demand, and full-text search of video-on-demand all positively predict knowledge attainment in virtual environments. Additional research addressing these issues might yield interesting, added-value contributions to a seemingly saturated area of research.

We were particularly dismayed at the lack of research at the organizational level. Many organizations make firm-wide decisions about the degree to which their employees will work virtually. We understand very little about the reasons that such decisions are made, the infrastructure that supports the implementation (or does not), and the firm-level implications of such strategies (Furst, Blackburn, & Rosen, 1999). Investigating such issues will likely require the use of archival data and objective measures of firm performance, and involve research designs that are common to the strategy arena but less represented in organizational behavior or psychology studies. Gibson, Porath, Benson, and Lawler (2007) utilized such an approach to investigate the differential impact of firm empowerment practices on three indicators of firm-level outcomes (i.e., financial performance, customer satisfaction, and quality) among the Fortune 500. Examining firm-level outcomes associated with the implementation of virtual teams would be a welcome extension of this research, providing insights into the payoff of investment in virtual work.

Multidisciplinary Approaches

As we mentioned, our review has covered research published in the fields of management, psychology, IT, and communication. An important observation is that researchers in each of these fields tend to limit their focus to certain issues and questions, and limit their process of inquiry to only certain methodologies. For example, it is rare for researchers publishing in the psychology journals to consider contextual features of the organization in their models and to implement designs that can assess such features; researchers publishing in management journals sometimes utilize simplistic conceptualizations and operationalizations of communication-related variables (e.g., frequency of communication); research published in information systems journals rarely takes into account underlying motivational or psychological processes. Yet, we believe it is at the nexus of these issues where the real insights will occur in future research—hence the need for multidisciplinary studies. This can only occur when scholars in one area take the time to become familiar with research conducted in another area and then incorporate key ideas from outside their disciplines. Perhaps even more promising, however, is multidisciplinary collaboration on research among scholars from the domains reviewed here.

Further, as discussed above, most of the virtual teams research is still laboratory based using student samples, or case study driven using very small numbers of teams, despite Stanko and Gibson's (2009), Hertel et al.'s (2005), and Martins et al.'s (2004) call for virtual teams researchers to move out of the laboratory and into the field of actual organizations. This is particularly important, given the contrasting patterns of findings that we see in the lab and in the field, perhaps most evident in the research investigating virtual team performance. As noted by Stanko and Gibson, many of the studies in which a negative relationship between virtuality and performance has been found have involved field research with team members from corporate organizations. In contrast, nearly all of the studies that found a positive relationship between virtuality and performance, and several studies that found no relationship or mixed results, involved student subjects in the laboratory. We echo Martins et al.'s acknowledgment that virtual teams research in the field is necessarily messy and complicated (similar to Mathieu et al.'s, 2008, acknowledgment of this fact in teams research in general). Getting organizations to grant access to a large set of virtual teams, with members spread out in dozens of countries, is fraught with obstacles and challenges (see Espinosa, Cummings, Wilson, & Pearce, 2003,

for a discussion of additional methodological challenges to studying global virtual teams and potential solutions).

However, to more fully understand this complex form of teaming, researchers need access to real team members in real organizations. This is particularly important given recent meta-analytic findings that the effects of CMC over FTF are not uniform but depend on the nature of the task and the specific technology used. Specifically, asynchronous CMC groups working on decision-making tasks actually benefited more from this form of electronic collaboration than groups working on idea-generation tasks using GDSS decision-room technology (although both improvements were large). At the same time, FTF groups show higher levels of consensus and perceived quality, communicate more, and require less time to complete tasks, with no differences on satisfaction. Thus, the choice to use CMC versus FTF collaboration will need to depend, to a certain extent, on which outcomes are most important to team members and leaders.

Conclusion

We have reviewed almost 200 articles that have been published on virtual teams over the last two decades. In doing so, we have noted considerable progress in a few areas and fragmentation and lack of development in many others. Our knowledge of team-level processes in particular is much richer as a result of the plethora of studies examining communication and conflict when members are electronically dependent and/or geographically dispersed. Unfortunately, we have not witnessed the acceleration of high-quality virtual teams research that we expected since the most recent reviews were published. While not discounting the contributions of existing research, we view as promising research that addresses more complex models identifying contingencies, moderators, and mediating effects, at levels other than the team level of analysis or across levels. Importantly, we encourage research that investigates virtual teams in organizational settings, examining individual- and firm-level features and outcomes. Like virtual teams themselves, to advance the domain we need to move beyond traditional boundaries to develop and integrate knowledge across multiple disciplines and space and time.

Appendix A Article Summaries, Individual Level of Analysis

Author(s)	Sample	Method	Variable(s)	Theories/Models	Key Findings
Ahuja & Galvin (2003)	98 SOAR groups	Survey (content analysis of e-mail communication)	Membership status-tenure (I*); Information exchange (P)	Socialization	Both newcomers' information seeking and established members' providing behaviors contributed to the effective utilization of knowledge and information in virtual work groups. Information seeking exchanges had much lower normative content than either regulative or cognitive ones.
Aiello & Kolb (1995)	202 undergraduate students in the U.S.	Lab Experiment	Social context (alone, aggregate, group), electronic performance monitoring condition (none, individual, work group) (I); Stress, task performance (O)	Social facilitation	Electronic monitoring intensified performance in accordance with preexisting ability levels. High-ability workers who were electronically monitored showed strong performance, whereas low-ability workers who were electronically monitored showed poorer performance. Unmonitored participants and members of cohesive groups felt the least stressed.
Anawati & Craig (2006)	122 employees working in 17 countries	Survey (explanatory case study)	Methods of communication, awareness of culture, virtual team training (I); Spoken vs. written communication, concerning behavior (P)	Behavioral adaptation	Members in cross-cultural virtual teams could adapt their behaviors in both spoken and written communication, as well as allowing for religious beliefs and time zone differences.
Aubert & Kelsey (2003)	68 undergraduate students in Canada	Experiment	Trust in other members (E); Team performance (O)	Agency theory	One's belief in other team members' ability, integrity, and propensity to trust were all positively related to his or her trust in the team members in virtual teams. However, trust was not related to team performance. Information symmetry and good communication distinguished high performance teams from low performance teams.
Belanger & Watson-Manheim (2006)	40 information technology workers in 2 organizations	Case Study	Media combination selection (P)	Communication media usage	When using multiple media, virtual team members employed two primary structures (i.e., sequential and concurrent). Individuals strategically used multiple media to accomplish specific communication goals beyond simply transmitting the message, such as message acknowledgment, enhancement of mutual understanding, and participation in multiple communication interactions.

Citation	Sample	Method	Variables	Theory	Findings
Bhappu et al. (1997)	17 6-person undergraduate teams in the U.S.	Experiment	Gender, media type (I); Differential attention and influence (P)	Social identity	Individuals in FTF (Face-to-face) groups paid more attention to in-group/out-group differences in terms of gender than those in CMC (computer mediated communication) groups, even when gender could be identified in the latter groups.
Bosch-Sijtsema (2007)	2 virtual teams in Sweden	Case Study	Expectation mismatches (I); Satisfaction, performance, learning (P)	Psychological contract, conflicts, and learning	Because members of virtual teams are heterogeneous in organizational and cultural backgrounds, have little history of previously working together, and have different experiences of working in teams, they often bring widely different expectations to the team compared to FTF teams. Expectation mismatches led to motivational problems, dissatisfaction, and lower performance in these teams, but did result in more individual learning.
Ferrin & Dirks (2003)	112 undergraduate dyads in the U.S.	Lab Experiment	Reward structure (I); Information sharing, cooperation (P); Individual's trust in a partner (E)	Attribution theory	The effects of different types of team-based rewards (i.e., cooperative, competitive, or mixed) on individual trust in team member were mediated by perceived partner motives and performance and own information sharing.
Forester et al. (2007)	82 employee participants from 12 virtual teams in 6 countries	Survey	Quality of goal setting, goal commitment (P); Perceived task and psychological outcomes of virtual teams (O)	Goal setting	Goal commitment was significantly positively related to both perceived task and psychosocial outcomes, whereas quality of goal setting was related only to perceived task outcome, suggesting that goal setting is related to perceptions of outcomes in virtual teams.
Froehle (2006)	2001 customers of a larger Internet service provider in the U.S.	Survey	Customer service representative characteristics, communication medium (I); Customer satisfaction (O)	Media richness	Customer service representative (CSR) characteristics influenced customer service satisfaction similarly across all three technology-mediated contexts (i.e., telephone, e-mail, online chat). Three CSR characteristics typically associated with satisfaction in FTF encounters (i.e., courtesy, professionalism, and attentiveness) had no effect on customer satisfaction in either telephone or CMC contexts.

(Continued)

Appendix A (Continued)

Author(s)	Sample	Method	Variable(s)	Theories/Models	Key Findings
Gallupe et al. (1992)	264 undergraduate students from 46 groups in Canada and the U.S.	Lab Experiment	Group size, technology (I); Idea generation and satisfaction (O)	Electronic brainstorming	Participants in brainstorming studies perceived less production blocking, had less evaluation apprehension, and were more satisfied when using electronic, versus FTF, brainstorming.
Griffith & Sawyer (2006)	336 employees in a global science company	Case Study and Survey	Technology and practice use, attendance of community of practice meetings (P)	Knowledge transfer	Attendance at FTF community of practice meetings, use of searchable archives, video-on-demand, and full-text search of video-on-demand all positively predicted knowledge attainment in virtual environments.
Hardin et al. (2007)	243 students in teams from the U.S. and Hong Kong	Survey	Team member's national culture (I); Group self-efficacy, virtual team self-efficacy, computer collective efficacy; virtual team efficacy, group potency (E)	Collective efficacy	Regardless of cultural origin, team members reported less confidence in their ability to work in virtual team environments than FTF environments; team members from individualistic cultures (i.e., the U.S.) reported higher self-efficacy beliefs (both group self-efficacy and virtual team self-efficacy) than team members from collectivist cultures (i.e., Hong Kong); and when the reference for efficacy beliefs changed from the individual to the group, the magnitude of change was greater for the collectivist versus individualistic team members.
Heninger et al. (2006)	102 undergraduates in the U.S.	Lab Experiment	Task interference (I); Information processing (P); Decision quality (O)	Cognitive interference in decision making	Dual-task interference (i.e., the need to concurrently process new information from others while also contributing one's own information) significantly reduced participants' information processing and led to lower decision quality when using CMC.
Jessup & Tansik (1991)	20 4-person groups of university students	Lab Experiment	Comments generated during group problem sessions, overall satisfaction, perceived system effectiveness (O)	Human information processing	Group members working anonymously and apart generated more comments, and working in the same room increased satisfaction; the highest levels of perceived system effectiveness were reported under anonymity.

Lea & Spears (1992)	72 undergraduates and employees in Europe	Lab Experiment	Different cue type, group salience, de-individualization (P)	Social cues and identity	Communicators rated their partners differently depending on the content of their paralanguage (i.e., symbols, codes, and other cues used to convey meaning), and de-individuated subjects for whom group identity was made salient evaluated users of paralanguage more positively than when group salience was low, suggesting that social context need not be dramatically reduced in groups using CMC.
Lee (2004)	60 undergraduate students in the U.S.	Lab Experiment	Depersonalization, perceived similarity to self, conformity (P)	Social identity	When the group level of self-identity was salient, uniform virtual appearance of CMC partners (i.e., using computer-rendered symbols) triggered depersonalization and heightened conformity behavior; however, when distinct virtual appearance of CMC partners was used, conformity actually decreased; and depersonalization enhanced adherence to group norms directly and through its effects on group identification.
Lee (2005)	269 undergraduate students in the U.S.	Lab Experiment	Participants' sex, character, self-confidence (I); Sex inference, perceive confidence, conformity (P)	Informational social influence	When a communication partner's confidence was presented in quantitative form, its effect on conformity was more pronounced among men than among women, whereas verbally expressed confidence induced stronger effects among women than among men.
Lee (2006)	217 undergraduate students in the U.S.	Lab Experiment	Individuating information, need for public individuation (I); Group identification, extremity of group norms, conformity (P); Perceived quality of arguments, message recall (O)	Social identity	Depersonalization led to a more extreme perception of the group norm, better recall of the interactants' arguments, and more positive evaluations of the interactants' arguments through group identification, albeit only for women; depersonalization was more likely to facilitate conformity to group norms among those with higher need for public individuation and among women; and group identification and extremity of the perceived group norm mediated the effects of depersonalization on conformity.

(Continued)

Appendix A (Continued)

Author(s)	Sample	Method	Variable(s)	Theories/Models	Key Findings
Lee (2007a)	193 undergraduate students in the U.S.	Lab Experiment	Participant gender, gendered language style, personalizing information, gender-role orientation (I); Conformity, gender inference (P)	Social identity	Those who did not exchange brief personal profiles with their partner (i.e., depersonalization) were more likely to infer their partner's gender from the language cues than those who did. Depersonalization, however, facilitated stereotype-consistent conformity behaviors only among gender-typed individuals; that is, participants conformed more to their masculine- than feminine-comment partners, and men were less conforming than were women, only when they were both gender-typed and depersonalized.
Lee (2007b)	104 undergraduate students in the U.S.	Lab Experiment	Group identification and polarization, perceived quality of the discussion partners' arguments, public self-awareness (P)	Group identification	De-individuation (i.e., when individuals did not share personal information before engaging in CMC discussion) fostered greater group identification with the partners and induced greater opinion polarization, partly by heightening concerns about public evaluations, although participants rated the partners' arguments more positively when they identified with the partners, perceived argument quality did not significantly affect post-discussion opinion shift, and de-individuation did not lower private self-awareness, nor did private-self-awareness significantly influence opinion polarization.
Lee-Kelley (2006)	108 members of virtual teams from a defense organization in the UK	Survey	Locus of control (I)	Reinforcement & learning theory	For those with an internal locus of control, there was a negative relationship between role conflict and job satisfaction, a finding opposite to studies of FTF teams.
Majchrzak et al. (2005)	263 individuals working in 54 global virtual teams	Survey	Degree of IT support for contextualization, task non-routineness (I); Collaboration know-how development (P)	Knowledge sharing	When individuals perceived their task as non-routine, there was a positive relationship between an individual's perceived degree of IT support for communicating context information and his/her collaboration know-how development; however, when individuals perceived their task as routine, partial IT support for contextualization was associated with lower levels of collaboration and know-how development.

Author (Year)	Sample	Method	Variables	Theory	Findings
Mejias (2007)	167 students in the U.S.	Lab Experiment	Group process gains and losses (P); Meeting satisfaction (O)	Group process gains/losses	Process losses had negative effects on two dimensions of meeting satisfaction (i.e., process and outcome satisfaction) only in identified CMC environments, not in anonymous CMC settings. Conversely, process gains generated positive effects upon both outcome and process satisfaction regardless of anonymity levels.
Morris et al. (2002)	158 IT consultants and developers in the U.S.	Survey	Trust in other team members (E)	Transaction cost economics	Both user satisfaction and trust were positively related to job satisfaction in virtual teams.
Palomares (2004)	210 Undergraduates in the U.S.	Lab Experiment	Gender, gender schematicity, gender identity salience (I)	Self-categorization theory	When using CMC, gender schematic individuals (i.e., those whose cognitive structures predispose them to process information in terms of the cultural definitions of gender) whose gender was also salient used typical gender-linked language (e.g., men used male language), whereas in the low gender salience condition, individuals used countertypical gender-linked language (e.g., men used female language).
Sassenberg & Boos (2003)	145 undergraduate students in Germany	Lab Experiment	Communication media (CMC vs. FTF), salient level of identity (personal vs. social) (I); Attitude change (P)	Social influence	High anonymity (compared to low anonymity) as well as CMC (compared to FTF communication) caused more conformity to individual needs or goals when personal identity was salient. Higher conformity to a socially shared superordinate category norm was the result when social identity was salient.
Spears et al. (1990)	48 students in Europe	Lab Experiment	Group immersion, de-individuation, norm reference (P)	De-individuation, group polarization	Group polarization was strongest in de-individuated (i.e., physically separate member) CMC groups in which group identity was salient compared to de-individuated CMC groups in which individual identity was salient.
Staples & Webster (2007)	6 best practices teams and 493 working adults in a variety of organizations	Case Study and Survey	Teamwork self-efficacy (I); Individual's perceptions of team effectiveness (O)	Social cognitive theory	Self-efficacy for teamwork was more important for virtual teams compared to the TFT and hybrid teams.

(Continued)

Appendix A (Continued)

Author(s)	Sample	Method	Variable(s)	Theories/Models	Key Findings
Straus (1996)	54 3-undergraduate student teams in the U.S.	Lab Experiment	Communication media (FTF vs. CMC), information distribution, extraversion (I); Participation (P); Satisfaction, performance (O)	Equalization effect	Extraversion was positively related to participation in CMC groups. Compared to FTF groups, overall patterns of interaction and performance were very similar in CMC groups; however, there was more equal participation in CMC groups, and CMC participants were less satisfied with the process.
Tan et al. (1998)	119 university students in Singapore and the U.S.	Lab Experiment	National culture, task type, communication medium (I); Majority influence (P)	Majority influence	In the individualistic culture (i.e., the U.S.), participants challenged majority positions more than those in the collectivistic culture (i.e., Singapore).
Tanis & Postmes (2003)	106 undergraduate students in Netherlands	Lab Experiment	Group membership, social cues (I): Ambiguity of impressions, positivity of impression, identification with the in-group or with the out-group (P)	Social information theory, social identity	The limited availability of social cues (independent of the communication medium) negatively affected individuals' ability to reduce ambiguity and made positive impressions on collaboration partners. The negative effects of limited social cues on relationship building in CMC groups depended, to some extent, on the social identities of the parties involved.
Tidwell & Walther (2002)	158 students in the U.S.	Lab Experiment	Media types (I); Interactive uncertain reduction strategy, social disclosure, attributional confidence, conversational effectiveness (P)	Social information processing theory, uncertainty reduction theory	Individuals interacting in CMC exhibited a greater proportion of more direct and intimate uncertainty reduction behaviors than FTF participants did, and they demonstrated significantly greater gains in attributional confidence over the course of the conversations; and the use of direct strategies by CMC individuals resulted in judgments of greater conversational effectiveness by partners.
Walther (1994)	114 students in the U.S.	Lab Experiment	Assignment type, communication medium (I); Partners' anticipation of future interaction, relational communication (P)	Uncertainty reduction theory	The assignment of long-term versus short-term partnerships (i.e. belief in extent of future interaction) had a larger impact on anticipated future interaction reported by CMC, rather than FTF, partners. The group's belief of future interactions had a more significant influence on the extent of informal communication exchanged than did the medium of communication.

Author (year)	Sample	Method	Variables	Theory	Findings
Walther (1997)	54 undergraduate students in the U.K. and U.S.	Lab Experiment	Long- vs. short-term partnership, social vs. individual identity (I): Intimacy/affection, social and physical attractiveness, study effort (P)	Information richness theory, social identification/de-individuation	For subjects using CMC, long-term versus short-term partnership assignment interacted with identity (i.e., individual vs. group) such that affective partner ratings (e.g., affection, attractiveness) were highest in the long-term/group condition, but no such interactions occurred in the FTF comparison groups.
Walther & Bazarova (2007)	237 students arrayed into 63 3- or 4-person groups in the U.S. and Canada	Lab Experiment	Team distribution condition, inferential goal inductions (I); Self/other dispositional attributions for poor performance, self/other distributions to other group members (P)	Attribution theory	Attributions for participants' own poor performance reflected a self-serving bias in completely distributed groups, whose members eschewed personal responsibility and blamed their partners more than in co-located groups. An externally imposed observational goal mitigated attributional bias among distributed members by raising awareness of the sociotechnical effects of communication medium among those for whom the goal was successfully induced.
Walther & Bunz (2005)	44 undergraduate students in the U.S.	Lab Experiment	Rule adherence (I); Communication behaviors (P); Performance (O)	Social information processing theory	The degree of self-reported adherence to a set of team work rules (i.e., start immediately; communicate frequently; acknowledge others, explicitness, multitasking, and observe deadlines) was related to a host of positive individual outcomes including trust, task attraction, social attraction, and self-rated task success.
Walther & Burgoon (1992)	96 undergraduate students arrayed into 32 3-person groups in the U.S.	Lab Experiment	Communication medium (I); Relational communication (P)	Social presence theory, social penetration theory	The relational dimensions of CMC groups (e.g., affection, relaxation, equality, trust) increased over time to the level of FTF groups.
Weisband & Atwater (1999)	105 university students in the U.S.	Lab Experiment	Communication mode (I); Self-ratings of contribution, ratings of others' contribution, actual contribution of self and others (P)	Performance appraisal	Self-ratings of contribution were more inflated and less accurate in CMC groups than in FTF groups. Liking accounted for significant variance in ratings of others' contributions in FTF groups, whereas actual contribution accounted for significant variance in ratings of others in CMC groups.

(Continued)

Appendix A (Continued)

Author(s)	Sample	Method	Variable(s)	Theories/Models	Key Findings
Workman et al. (2003)	261 information system virtual team members in a large financial institution	Survey	Cognitive styles and scope, learning styles, media types (I); Commitment to virtual team and telework (P)	Information richness and cognitive style theory	Individuals' commitment to virtual teams was stronger when they had cognitive styles characterized as external (i.e., preferring group, rather than individual, problem solving), conservative (i.e., preferring structure, compliance with existing rules and procedures, familiarity, and minimal change), and global (i.e., having mental representations that have thin or fuzzy boundaries). The relationships between both external and conservative cognitive styles and commitment to virtual teams were stronger when individuals reported using richer, rather than leaner, communication media.
Zhou & Zhang (2007)	40 undergraduate students in the U.S.	Lab Experiment	Media modality, message veracity (I); Deception detection (P)	Social presence theory, information manipulation theory, interpersonal deception theory	The accuracy of and confidence in deception detection in the messaging (i.e., a sequence of messages is presented in the order of being received) and chatting (i.e., combination of messaging and typing) modes were significantly higher than those in the typing mode (i.e., the message is seen as it is typed). User satisfaction with deception detection process and perceived information usefulness were the highest in the chatting mode, followed by the messaging mode, and the lowest in the typing mode.

* I = Input; E = Emergent State; P = Process; O = Output

Appendix B: Article Summaries, Team Level of Analysis

Author(s)	Sample	Method	Variable(s)	Theories/Models	Key Findings
Alge et al. (2003)	198 undergraduates from 66 teams in the U.S.	Experiment	Team temporal scope, communication media, task interdependence (I*); Openness/trust (E); TMX, information sharing (P); Decision-making effectiveness (O)	Team temporal scope (future, past, and ad hoc teams)	Media differences existed for teams lacking a history, with face-to-face teams exhibiting higher openness/trust and information sharing than computer-mediated teams. However, computer-mediated teams with a history were able to eliminate these differences.
Alge et al. (2004)	90 undergraduate students in the U.S.	Lab Experiment	Team leaders' decisions to electronically monitor their subordinates (I)	Control and agency theory, resource dependence perspective	Team leaders electronically monitored subordinates more intensely when dependence on subordinates was high or future performance expectation was low. Team leaders were more likely to monitor in secret when dependence was high or propensity to trust was low.
Andres (2002)	192 undergraduates from 48 teams in the U.S.	Experiment	Virtual team vs. FTF setting (I); Interaction quality, process satisfaction (P); Team productivity (O)	Social presence, media richness, time, interaction, and performance theory	FTF groups were more productive and had higher interactive quality than those using videoconferencing, but there were no differences on group process satisfaction.
Baba et al. (2004)	1 globally distributed team (20 members in 7 countries)	Qualitative Analysis (interview, observation, etc.)	Learning experience, evaluative knowledge and associated beliefs among members of a GDT, geopolitics of leader behavior on a GDT (I); Cognitive convergence process (P); Team performance (O)	Shared cognition & knowledge sharing	The process of cognitive convergence (i.e., increasing similarity of individual cognitive structures through information sharing) was related to virtual team performance only when patterns of cognitive divergence were also reversed. Beyond the influence of direct knowledge sharing, the process of cognitive convergence was influenced by other factors, such as separate but parallel or similar learning experiences in a common context, the surfacing of hidden knowledge at remote sites by third-party mediators or knowledge brokers, and shifts in agent self-interest that motivate collaboration and trigger the negotiation of task interdependence. Globally distributed teams could be effective, as they bring together team members' divergent points of view to produce new organizational capabilities. However, for such a benefit to occur, teams should recognize the existence of differences and validate them early and explicitly.

(Continued)

Appendix B (Continued)

Author(s)	Sample	Method	Variable(s)	Theories/Models	Key Findings
Baker (2002)	64 undergraduate teams in the U.S.	Experiment	Collaborative technology (I); Decision outcome (O)	Social presence, media richness, media synchronicity	No significant difference was found between the qualities of decisions for teams using text-only versus audio-only communication, but the addition of video to audio-only communication resulted in significant improvement in the quality of the teams' strategic decisions.
Barkhi (2005)	24 four-person undergraduate teams in the U.S.	Experiment	Communication channel, incentive structure (I); Information change, frustration with the process (P); Team performance (O)	Game theory	Groups with group-based incentives engaged in free-riding behavior by selecting low effort levels less often in FTF-Group Decision Support System (GDSS) groups than in distributed-GDSS groups. However, the performance difference between FTF-GDSS groups and distributed-GDSS groups was not statistically significant when the incentive was individual-based.
Baskerville & Nandhakumar (2007)	5 virtual teams projects in a large petrochemical company	Interpretive Case Study	Personal and abstract trust (E), Team effectiveness (O)	Trust perspective & switching logic perspective	Personal trust is most effectively established or reinvigorated through geographically co-located social interaction; personal trust was an antecedent to the activation and operation of effective virtual teams; abstract trust (i.e., trust based on shared organizational norms and expertise) was an alternative to personal trust as an antecedent to the activation and operation of effective, short-term virtual teams; and personal trust gradually dissipated over time without co-located social interaction.
Becker-Beck et al. (2005)	18 4-person undergraduate teams in Germany	Lab Experiment	Modality of communication (I), Interaction behaviors and referential level (P); Group satisfaction and performance (O)	Cues-filtered-out theories, social information processing perspective	Significant different interaction styles (e.g, task-orientation, socio-emotional orientation) existed between the FTF and asynchronous CMC, but there were few differences between FTF and synchronous CMC. There were no differences in member satisfaction between the three modalities of communication (FTF, asynchronous CMC, synchronous CMC), but group performance was judged better in the FTF condition versus both CMC conditions.

Study	Sample	Method	Variables	Topic	Findings
Boh et al. (2007)	493 project teams in the U.S.	Quantitative Analysis (with coding object data) supplemented by Interviews	Project member expertise, project requirement, match of project member expertise with project requirements, cross-site connections, project team size (I); Project outcomes (O)	Dispersed collaboration, social ties	Managers created dispersed projects comparatively rarely; they did so when scarce expertise from other sites was needed to match customers' project requirements. Dispersed projects garnered higher net earnings than local projects when there was a better match of scarce expertise to project requirements; and a curvilinear relationship was observed, such that a very high percentage of dispersed experts on a project increased coordination costs and reduced net earnings.
Bordia et al. (1999)	14 informal teams	Content Analysis	Characteristics of group development stages (P)	Group development	In terms of group communication, computer-mediated groups followed highly similar developmental patterns (i.e, dependency and inclusion, counterdependency and fight, trust and structure, work, termination) as those described in the FTF groups literature.
Bouas & Arrow (1996)	60 student groups in the U.S.	Survey	Media type, temporal factor, original vs. reconfigured group, demographic diversity (I); Group identity (E)	Group identity	Group identity was significantly lower for CMC versus FTF groups, the effects were stronger in the reconfigured groups, but the differences between groups in identity narrowed over the course of the study.
Bradner et al. (2005)	109 team members in a large multinational company	Survey	Team size (I); Team participation and commitment (P)	Distributed team size	Compared to members of larger teams, members of smaller teams participated more actively on their team, were more committed to their team, were more aware of the goals of the team, had greater awareness of other team members, and were in teams with higher levels of rapport; larger teams are more conscientious than smaller teams in preparing meeting agendas; team size was also associated with different technology choice: larger teams adopted technology to support the coordination of asynchronous work, while smaller teams adopted technology that primarily supported collaboration.
Burgoon et al. (2002)	80 undergraduates in the U.S.	Lab Experiment	Proximal vs. distal interactions (I); Social judgment, task outcomes (O)	Interactivity principle	Proximity increased interactivity and fostered more favorable social judgments but did not affect performance. Proximal text and distributed audio were the most advantageous, with distributed video the least so, for promoting trust, sociability, and other favorable social judgments. Videoconferencing outperformed FTF interaction but not the other mediated conditions.

(Continued)

Appendix B (Continued)

Author(s)	Method	Sample	Variable(s)	Theories/Models	Key Findings
Campbell & Stasser (2006)	Lab Experiment	95 3-person undergraduate groups in the U.S.	FTF vs. CMC group condition (I); Decision quality (O)	Hidden-profile paradigm in decision making	Solution rates were highest, and repeating and recall of unshared information greatest, in CMC groups given ample time and instructions to solve rather than to judge.
Cappel & Windsor (2000)	Experiment	12 IT professional groups in the U.S.	Computer-supported vs. FTF group (I); Choice shift, decision polarity, group consensus, group member reactions (P)	Group ethical decision making	Compared to CMC groups engaged in an ethical decision-making task, FTF groups reached their decisions more quickly, were more successful in attaining group consensus, and evaluated FTF communication more favorably on perceived group processes and satisfaction.
Carre et al. (2006)	Experiment	22 undergraduate teams in the U.S.	Leadership behaviors (I); Performance (O)	Leadership effectiveness in self-managed teams	High-performing self-managed virtual teams displayed significantly more concentrated leadership behavior focused on performance, and shared leadership behavior focused on keeping track of group work than the lower performing teams. These behaviors emerged strongly during the first half of the groups' life span, and stayed throughout the life of the groups, but steadily dissipated in strength over time.
Chen et al. (2005)	Experiment	4-person groups in Taiwan and the U.S.	Creative problem solving training (I); Creativity performance (O)	Web-based group problem-solving system	Giving creative problem-solving training to team members had positive impacts on team performance, and that users who received brief "TeamSpirit" training were able to design and facilitate virtual meetings by themselves and achieved better team performance than control groups.
Chidambaram (1996)	Experiment	28 5-person undergraduate teams in the U.S.	Anonymity, simultaneity, electronic recording and display, process structuring (I); Cohesiveness (E); Group process (P); Satisfaction with outcomes (O)	Social information processing theory	Attitudes in the CMC groups, which were initially lower than FTF groups, increased positively over time to reach FTF group levels.
Chidambaram & Tung (2005)	Experiment	40 undergraduate teams in the U.S.	Group size, group dispersion (I), Quantity and quality of ideas, decision quality (O)	Social loafing, dilution effect, & immediacy gap	Compared to CMC groups, FTF group members contributed visibly more on a brainstorming task (i.e., there was less social loafing in FTF groups) but there were no significant differences in group outcomes.

Chudoba et al. (2005)	1,269 worldwide employees of a multinational company	Survey	Virtuality, social interactivity, knowledge networking, work predictability (I); Team performance (O)	Discontinuities, changes in expected conditions	There were no effects of geographic dispersion on self-assessed team performance. Being distributed had no impact on self-assessed team performance.
Colquitt et al. (2002)	79 undergraduate teams in the U.S.	Experiment	Working condition (computer-assisted vs. verbal communication), openness to experience (I); Efficiency in integrating verbal and computerized communication (P); Team decision-making performance (O)	Personality	Access to CMC improved decision making in teams but only when those teams were characterized by high levels of openness to experience.
Connolly et al. (1990)	24 3-undergraduate teams in the U.S.	Experiment	Anonymity, evaluative tone (I); Group process (P); Effectiveness of idea generation, participant satisfaction (O)	Balance of forces	Groups produced the greatest number of original solutions and overall comments when members were anonymous and groups had a critical confederate, but produced the lowest number of original solutions and overall comments in identified groups with a supportive confederate. The latter groups, however, had the highest levels of member satisfaction and perceived effectiveness.
Coppola et al. (2004)	Over 1,300 students in the U.S.	Survey (exploratory content analysis)	Swift trust (E); Teaching effectiveness (O)	Trust development	Establishing swift trust at the beginning of an online course was related to instructors' subsequent course success.
Cornelius & Boos (2003)	80 3-student groups in Germany	Experiment	Communication training (I); Group process and satisfaction (P)	Group decision making	The best performance scores were found in the FTF condition; performance scores in CMC with training approximated those of the FTF condition; and the lowest performance scores were found in CMC without training.

(Continued)

Appendix B (Continued)

Author(s)	Sample	Method	Variable(s)	Theories/Models	Key Findings
Cramton (2001)	13 6-student teams (members from more than 10 countries)	Case Analysis	Use of technology-mediated communication, geographic dispersion, task characteristics (I); Cohesion (E); Use of communication media, information exchange, viability of collaboration (P); Performance (O)	Knowledge sharing	Five key GVT interpersonal process problems that contribute to a lack of mutual knowledge among team members were identified problems (failure to communicate and retain contextual information, unevenly distributed information, differences in the salience of information, relative differences in speed of access to information, and interpreting the meaning of silence); structural and task-related factors (e.g., feedback lags, task interdependence, tight time frames) exacerbated the relationship between the five key interpersonal problems and GVT performance.
Cramton & Webber (2005)	39 software development work teams in Europe and the U.S.	Survey	Geographic dispersion (I); Group processes (P); Team performance (O)	Sociotechnical perspective	Geographic dispersion significantly and negatively related to work processes (i.e., communication, coordination) and team effectiveness and work processes partially mediated the relationship between geographic dispersion and team effectiveness.
Crowston et al. (2007)	22 virtual project teams engaged in open source software development	Interview and Observations	Opportunities for FTF meetings (I); Benefits of FTF meetings (P & O)	Hybrid mode virtual teams	Contrary to conventional wisdom about distributed teams, open source software development team members generally did not meet FTF until the project was well under way; and an additional benefit of FTF meetings was time away from a regular job and speed of interaction for certain kinds of tasks.
Daily & Teich (2000)	27 4- or 5-undergraduate multicultural groups	Experiment	Communication media type (I); Idea generation (O)	Group decisions in multicultural groups	Compared to a GDSS-supported environment, perceptions of contributions involving ratings of self, ratings of others, and ratings by others, ratings were higher in a non-GDSS environment; ethnic minorities' ratings of self was significantly lower than ethnic minorities' ratings of others in the non-GDSS environment but not the GDSS environment; and the average number of ideas generated were greater in the GDSS environment.

Study	Method	Variables	Theory	Findings
Daly (1993)	Experiment	Communication channel (I); Decision making outcomes (O)	Computer supported cooperative work	CMC was superior to FTF for generating correct solutions to the rule induction task, whereas FTF was superior to CMC for assisting groups in deciding among proposed solutions; and fewer comments were exchanged and more time was required for groups communicating using CMC.
64 4-undergraduate groups in the U.S.				
Dennis & Garfield (2003)	Field Experiment	GSS (Group Support System) appropriation (I); Leadership and decision processes (P); Team cohesion (E); Team performance (O)	Adaptive structuration theory	While FTF teams developed conservative projects that met unstated project criteria, CMC teams developed projects more closely aligned with team member interests.
6 medical project teams				
Dubrovsky et al. (1991)	Lab Experiment	Communication media type, status difference (I); Equalization (P)	Equalization phenomenon in group decision making	Compared to FTF groups, CMC groups of mixed status exhibited fewer status and expertise inequalities in participation among members.
24 4-person MBA student groups in the U.S.				
Easley et al. (2003)	Survey	Teamwork quality, task type (I); Technology use (P); Creative and decision making performance (O)	Collaborative systems	Teamwork quality was positively associated with usage of CMC and usage of CMC was in turn positively associated with team performance for supported tasks, but not with team performance for unsupported tasks.
24 MBA student teams in the U.S.				
El-shinnawy & Vinze (1998)	Lab Experiment	Task characteristics, communication medium, group composition (I); Polarization and persuasive arguments (P)	Group polarization, theory of persuasive arguments	CMC groups had lower levels of polarization than FTF groups. Communication media and task type interacted in multiple ways to affect both polarization and the number of persuasive arguments.
65 student groups in the U.S.				
Finholt & Sproull (1990)	Survey	Computer-based communication technology, group attributes (I); Group processes (P)	Group communication	Electronic group mail was used throughout the organization for many kinds of group communication. At least some of the groups behaved like real social groups despite the fact that they shared no physical space, their members were invisible, and their interaction was asynchronous.
96 employees in a Fortune 500 office products firm				

(Continued)

Appendix B (Continued)

Author(s)	Sample	Method	Variable(s)	Theories/Models	Key Findings
Fuller et al. (2007)	52 student project teams from the U.S., U.K., and Hong Kong	Survey	Group potency, computer collective efficacy, virtual team efficacy (E); Team effort, communication level (P); Group outcomes perceptions, actual performance (O)	Efficacy within groups	Group potency and computer collective efficacy acted as antecedents to virtual team efficacy. Virtual team efficacy was in turn predictive of perceptual and objective measures of performance; and effort fully, and communication partially, mediated the effects of virtual team efficacy on performance.
Gefen & Straub (1997)	392 airline company knowledge workers in North America, Asia, and Europe	Survey	Gender (I); Social presence, perceived usefulness of e-mail, perceived ease of use of e-mail, use of e-mail (O)	IT diffusion process model	Women viewed e-mail as having greater usefulness and higher social presence than men, but there were no gender differences in levels of usage.
Geister et al. (2006)	52 2-undergraduate student teams in Germany	Lab Experiment	Team process feedback, motivation of team members (P); Team member's satisfaction with a team; Team performance (O)	Motivation, feedback	Team process feedback (i.e., regarding motivation, task-related aspects, and relationship-related aspects) resulted in higher team performance and was associated with greater satisfaction and motivation for less motivated members.
Gibson & Gibbs (2006)	443 employees in 70 teams from more than 18 countries	Qualitative Analysis and Survey	Virtuality (I); Psychologically safe communication climate (E); Team innovation (O)	Virtual innovation	The negative effect of geographic dispersion on team innovation was less for the teams with psychologically safe communication.
Gonzalez et al. (2003)	71 groups engaged in distance learning in a Mexican university	Survey	Interpersonal attraction, task cohesion (I); Collective efficacy (E); Team and peer facilitation (P); Group effectiveness (O)	Distance collaboration group effectiveness	Task cohesion mediated the relation between collective efficacy and group effectiveness. Team and peer facilitation served only as a direct antecedent to group effectiveness.

Study	Method	Sample	Variables	Topic	Findings
Graetz et al. (1998)	Lab Experiment	37 student groups in the U.S.	Communication condition (FTF, telephone, electronic) (I); Time to decision, subjective mental workload, impressions of the group, recorded discussions (P)	Information sharing	Cognitive workload was significantly higher and fewer correct decisions were obtained in the electronic chat condition versus FTF and teleconference. The electronic chat medium limited participants' ability to coordinate and verify information.
Haas (2005)	Survey	96 global virtual project teams	Number of cosmopolitans and locals within a team (I); Project quality (O)	Knowledge acquisition and application	Both cosmopolitans (i.e., individuals with broad experience in many countries) and locals (i.e., individuals with deep experience in the project country) helped to increase internal knowledge (i.e., knowledge possessed by members themselves), while cosmopolitans, but not locals, helped to increase external knowledge (i.e., knowledge from sources outside the team). A mix of both locals and cosmopolitans was optimal for GVT performance.
Hambley et al. (2007)	Lab Experiment	228 undergraduates from 60 teams in Canada	Leadership style, communication media type (I); Team interaction style (P); Team cohesion (E); Task performance (O)	Virtual team leadership	The effects of transactional and transformational leadership on team interaction and performance did not differ with changes in the richness of the communication media (i.e., FTF, videoconferencing, chat). Team interactions were more constructive and cohesion was higher in teams using richer communication media.
Hardin et al. (2006)	Survey	15 undergraduate student teams in the U.S.	Group efficacy (E); Group outcome perceptions, team performance (O)	Group efficacy	The consensus-based method resulted in significantly higher scores in group potency and virtual team efficacy than the aggregation method. The aggregation method was more strongly related to group outcomes than the consensus method.
Hedlund et al. (1998)	Lab Experiment	64 4-undergraduate teams (half CMC, half FTF) in the U.S.	Communication medium (I); Team infirmity, staff validity, hierarchical sensitivity (P); Decision accuracy (O)	Multilevel theory of team decision	Members of FTF teams were better informed and made recommendations that were more predictive of the correct team decision, but leaders of CMC teams were better able to differentiate staff members on the quality of their decisions.

(Continued)

Appendix B (Continued)

Author(s)	Sample	Method	Variable(s)	Theories/Models	Key Findings
Hiltz et al. (1986)	80 students from 16 teams in the U.S.	Lab Experiment	Communication mode, task type (I); Interaction process, inequality of participation (P); Quality of decision, agreement (O)	Group decision making	In FTF, versus CMC groups, there was a higher quantity of communication, a higher likelihood of reaching agreement, and fewer types of task-oriented communication; however, there were no differences in quality of group decisions across the groups.
Hinds & Kiesler (1995)	Using the communication logs of 88 employees in a large telecommunications firm	Survey	Communication type (I); Use of communication technology (P)	Boundary spanning	There were differences in communication media use when comparing administrative employees versus technical employees. For asynchronous communication, technical employees tended to use e-mail, while administrative employees used voice; extra-departmental communication was almost all phone-based; and technical employees tended to have more lateral communication than administrative employees, but all lateral communication by both types of employees was phone-based.
Hollingshead (1996)	53 3-undergraduate groups in the U.S.	Lab Experiment	Status differences among members, communication media (I); Information exchange, perceived influence (P); Group decision quality (O)	Social status	CMC suppressed information exchange and the perceived influence of group members. Mixed-status groups made poorer decisions and made fewer references to critical information than equal-status groups, regardless of the communication medium.
Hollingshead et al. (1993)	22 student groups in a university	Lab Experiment	Task type, communication medium, experience with technology (I); Members' perceptions of effective group process (P); Satisfaction with task performance, group task performance (O)	Task-media fit	FTF groups performed better on negotiation and intellective tasks than did CMC groups; there were no performance differences on generate or decision-making tasks; and the novelty of using certain CMC media contributed to poorer performance of CMC groups on certain tasks.

Huang et al. (2002)	48 student groups	Lab Experiment	Communication setting (i.e., FTF vs. virtual), goal setting structure (I); Team cohesion, collaborative climate (E); team commitment, (P); Perceived decision quality, number of decision alternatives generated (O)	Team-building	CMC groups with an embedded goal-setting structure had higher cohesion, better team commitment, better collaboration climate, perceived decision quality, and more decision alternatives than CMC groups without a goal-setting structure.
Huang et al. (2007)	44 2-student teams in the U.S.	Lab Experiment	Communication mode (I); Task effectiveness and satisfaction, (O)	Group problem solving	Teams using e-mail generated more ideas than teams using instant messaging, although there were no significant differences on task difficulty, playfulness, or ease of use.
Jarman (2005)	2 teams in Australia	Case Study	Productivity, growth, and well-being of team members, technological outcomes, perceptions of success (O)	Adaptive structuration theory	Team members' subjective assessments of performance were not consistent with more objective indicators of virtual team performance.
Jarvenpaa et al. (1988)	3 teams in an IT organization	Field Experiment	Communication medium (I); Communication thoroughness, equality of participation (P); Team performance and satisfaction (O)	Ill-structured problem solving	Few differences existed on equality and perceived equity of participation or satisfaction for groups using different communication media (i.e., FTF, electronic blackboards, and networked workstations). However, quality of team performance was enhanced in the CMC conditions, while communication thoroughness was higher in the FTF condition.
Jarvenpaa et al. (1998)	73 graduate student teams around the world	Survey	Members' own propensity to trust, other team members' perceived ability, integrity, and benevolence, temporal factor (I); Team trust (E)	Trust development	Two-week trust-building exercises had a significant effect on the team members' perceptions of the other members' ability, integrity, and benevolence; in the early phases of teamwork, team trust was predicted strongest by perceptions of other team members' integrity, and weakest by perceptions of their benevolence; the effect of other members' perceived ability on trust decreased over time; and the members' own propensity to trust had a significant, though unchanging, effect on trust.

(Continued)

Appendix B (Continued)

Author(s)	Sample	Method	Variable(s)	Theories/Models	Key Findings
Jarvenpaa et al. (2004)	42 6-student teams from 13 countries	Lab Experiment	Initial trustworthiness, communication level (I); Cohesiveness, trust development (E); Subjective outcome quality, task performance (O)	Trust development	Early in a team's existence, a member's trusting beliefs had a direct positive effect on his or her trust in the team and perceptions of team cohesiveness; later on, however, a member's trust in his team operated as a moderator, indirectly affecting the relationships between team communication and perceptual outcomes; trust affected virtual teams differently in different situations.
Jarvenpaa & Leidner (1999)	12 teams of graduate business students around the world	Case Study	Team member's cultural values, international experience, initial trust facilitating communication behaviors (I); Trust in teams (E)	Trust development	GVTs could develop a form of swift trust rather quickly, but such forms of trust were often fragile and temporal. Different sets of actions and behaviors were linked to building trust early in GVTs (e.g., social communication, communication conveying enthusiasm, individual initiative) and maintaining trust at later stages (e.g., substantive and timely response, leadership).
Johnson et al. (2002)	7 virtual teams engaged in distance learning in the U.S.	Case Study	Team leadership (I); Team development (P)	Group development	Virtual learning groups could collaborate effectively from a distance to accomplish group tasks. Most of the virtual teams had shared leadership rather than a single, emergent leader.
Kahai & Cooper (2003)	30 3-person undergraduate groups in the U.S.	Lab Experiment	Media type (I); Socio-emotional climate (E); Task-oriented communication (P); Decision quality (O)	Media richness	Richer media facilitated social perceptions (total socio-emotional communication and positive socio-emotional climate) and perceived ability to evaluate others' deception and expertise; leaner media (electronic mail and electronic conferencing) facilitated communication clarity when participants had less task-relevant knowledge; richer media could have significantly positive impacts on decision quality when participants' task relevant knowledge was high; and the effects of participant deception could be mitigated by employing richer media.
Kanawattanachai & Yoo (2002)	36 4-person MBA student teams of 10 different nationalities	Lab Experiment	Team performance level, temporal factor (I); Cognition- and affect-based trust (E)	Trust development	Both high- and low-performing teams started with similar levels of trust in both cognitive and affective dimensions; high-performing teams were better at developing and maintaining the trust level throughout the project life; and virtual teams relied more on a cognitive than an affective element of trust.

Study	Sample	Method	Variables	Key construct	Findings
Kanawattanachai & Yoo (2007)	38 MBA student teams of 10 different nationalities	Lab Experiment	Task oriented-communication, transactive memory system (P); Team performance (O)	Transactive memory	In the early stage of the project, the frequency and volume of task-oriented communications among team members played an important role in forming expertise location and cognition-based trust; however, once transactive memory systems were established, task-oriented communication became less important and task-knowledge coordination emerged as a key construct that influences team performance, mediating the impact of all other constructs.
Kankanhalli et al. (2007)	3 master student GVTs from North America, Europe, and Asia	Case Study	Team diversity, communication technology (I); Task and relationship conflict (P); Team performance (O)	Team conflict	Cultural diversity is likely to contribute to both task and relationship conflict, while functional diversity may result in task conflict; large volumes of electronic communication and lack of immediacy of feedback in asynchronous media can contribute to task conflict; the relationship between task conflict and team performance is likely to be contingent upon task complexity and conflict resolution approach. The influence of relationship conflict on performance may depend on task interdependence and conflict resolution approach. The conflict resolution approach may in turn be determined by the nature of conflict attribution.
Kayworth & Leidner (2000)	12 student GVTs from Europe, Mexico, and the U.S.	Field Experiment	Virtual team leadership (I); Successful design and deployment of virtual teams (O)		Four critical success factors for virtual team leadership were identified: communication, culture, technology, and project management (leadership).
Kirkman et al. (2004)	35 teams in a high-tech service organization	Survey	Team empowerment (E); Team performance (O)	Team empowerment	Team empowerment was related to both process improvement and customer satisfaction, but team empowerment was more important for virtual teams that met FTF less, rather than more.
Kirkman et al. (2006)	40 virtual teams from a high technology service organization	Survey	Virtual team training (I); Customer satisfaction (O)	Team training	Virtual team CD-ROM–based training proficiency was more strongly related to customer satisfaction when teams had high levels of trust and technology support, and when team leaders had longer, rather than shorter, tenure with their teams. There were no effects for teamwork training on customer satisfaction in virtual teams unless the teams had high level of trust and technology support and team leaders with longer, rather than shorter, team leader tenure.

(Continued)

Appendix B (Continued)

Author(s)	Sample	Method	Variable(s)	Theories/Models	Key Findings
Krebs et al. (2006)	50 3–4 student groups in Australia	Lab Experiment	Demographic dissimilarity, communication media type (I); Trust in group members (E)	Trust	Age dissimilarity was negatively related to trust in FTF groups but not in CMC groups, and birthplace dissimilarity was positively related to trust in CMC groups.
Lebie et al. (1996)	30 student groups in the U.S.	Lab Experiment	Media type (I); Team interaction (P)	Production blocking, impersonality, communication difficulty	Members communicated less in CMC versus FTF groups overall. CMC groups spent less time discussing non-task matters than FTF groups.
Leenders et al. (2003)	44 new product development teams in 11 companies	Survey	Communication frequency and centralization (P); Team creativity (O)	Distraction-conflict theory	Team creativity was optimal with a moderate frequency of communication and a low level of communication centralization.
Li (2007)	23 4–5 undergraduate groups in Taiwan	Field Experiment	Communication type (FTF vs. CMC) (I); Communication quality (P); Group outcomes (O)	A functional perspective	FTF groups, compared to CMC groups, performed better on critical functions such as problem analysis and criteria establishment, and were more efficient in communication effectiveness; however, there were no significant differences on most objective and perceived group outcomes.
Lind (1999)	In Mexico and the U.S.	Lab Experiment	Gender (I); Group cohesion (E); Group conflict (P); Group performance (O)	Gender impact of virtual collaboration	Women in virtual groups perceived that the group stuck together more and helped each other more than did the men; the women were more satisfied with the virtual group than men and felt that group conflict was readily resolved; and the FTF women were less satisfied with the group experience than their virtual counterparts and perceived that conflict was smoothed over.
Lowry et al. (2006)	474 undergraduate students in the U.S.	Lab Experiment	Process structure conditions, team size (I); Communication quality (P); Group performance (O)	Impact of process structure on virtual collaborative writing teams	Smaller groups established and maintained higher levels of communication quality. FTF with CMC support groups had higher levels of communication quality than virtual with CMC support groups. However, no significant difference between traditional FTF groups and virtual groups with CMC support was found.

Study	Sample	Method	Variables	Theory	Findings
Lurey & Raisinghani (2001)	12 teams in 8 different organizations from U.S., Europe, and Asia	Survey	Job characteristics, executive leadership style, external support mechanisms (I); Internal group dynamics (P); Team performance and satisfaction (O)	Best practices approach	Teams' processes and team members' relations were strongly positively related to team performance and team member satisfaction; selection procedures and executive leadership styles were moderately associated; and internal group dynamics, and additional external support mechanisms were only weakly related
Majchrzak et al. (2000)	An inter-organizational virtual team tasked with creating a highly innovative product	Case Study	Group developmental process (P)	Adaptive structuration theory	To address misalignment between the organizational environment, group structure, and technology, group members initially modified their environment and group structures, whereas later in its life span, group members modified all three aspects including technology.
Malhotra et al. (2001)	A single virtual team in the aerospace industry	Case Study	Team objectives, development of shared understanding, frequent opportunities for interaction with team members, role definition, coordination norms	Supply-chain collaboration	Several key leadership practices for managing successful virtual teams were identified: establish virtual team strategy initially, encourage the use of knowledge management/collaborative tools, and restructure work without changing core creative needs.
Massey et al. (2003)	36 MBA student teams in Japan and the U.S.	Lab Experiment	Temporal coordination mechanisms (I); Team interaction process (P); Team performance (O)	Time-interaction-performance theory	Temporal coordination mechanisms (i.e., schedule deadlines, coordinated pace of effort within and between members, and specification of time spent on specific tasks) were associated with higher team performance through their effects on team interaction behaviors (e.g., informational, decisional, and interpersonal behaviors).
May & Carter (2001)	A European-based automotive manufacturing team	Case Study	Advanced information technology and telecommunication (I); Team efficiency and flexibility (O)		The introduction of video conferencing, shared whiteboard, application sharing, and product data management tools increased team efficiency and flexibility, including time savings, sales volume, and reduced costs.

(Continued)

Appendix B (Continued)

Author(s)	Sample	Method	Variable(s)	Theories/Models	Key Findings
Maznevski & Chudoba (2000)	3 GVTs in the high tech industry	Case Study	Structural characteristics (task, group, technology) (I); Social interaction (P); Decision and action quality (O)	Adaptive structuration theory	Virtual team dynamics were characterized by both: (a) a series of interaction incidents incorporating a set of decision processes using a particular medium that are shaped by a limited set of structural characteristics; and (b) repeating temporal patterns of regular FTF meetings in which the intensity of interaction is extremely high, followed by a period of some weeks in which interaction incidents are less intense.
McLeod et al. (1997)	59 4-student groups	Lab Experiment	Communication medium type (I); Minority information expression, attention to minority information, minority information influence (P)	Minority influence in group discussion	While the use of CMC allowed minority opinion holders to express their arguments most frequently, the influence of the minority arguments on private opinions and on group decisions was highest under FTF communication.
Metiu (2006)	A single GVT containing members from both a U.S. and Indian information technology organization	In-depth Ethnographic Study	Status differentials, geographical distance (I) ; Informal closure (P); Effects of information closures (O)	Status Closure	Geographical dispersion exacerbated processes related to status closure (i.e., the monopolization of opportunities of higher status groups at the expense of lower status groups), and how status closure resulted in less intragroup cooperation within the overall GVT.
Montoya-Weiss et al. (2001)	35 5-graduate student groups in Japan and the U.S.	Field Experiment	Conflict management behaviors (P); Team performance (O)	Effects of temporal coordination on VTs	Certain conflict-handling strategies (i.e., competition, collaboration) were positively related to virtual team performance, while others (i.e., avoidance, compromise) were negatively related. Introducing a formal, structured plan for managing team time and activities weakened the negative effects of avoidance and compromise on virtual team performance.
Mortensen & Hinds (2001)	24 product development teams in 5 organizations	Survey	Geographic dispersion, cultural heterogeneity (I); Shared team identity (E); Task and affective conflict (P); Team performance (O)	Conflict and shared identity	Conflict was slightly more detrimental to CMC team performance than FTF team performance.

Study	Sample	Method	Variables	Theory	Findings
Munkvold & Zigurs (2007)	5 graduate student teams in Norway and the U.S.	Exploratory Qualitative Study	Factors influencing team process and outcomes (e.g., trust among team members, well-defined task structure, time differences, mismatch in expectations, cultural differences)	Time-interaction-performance theory	Swift-starting virtual teams need to structure their interaction from the onset, including introducing team members' background and competence, discussing project goals and deliverables, defining roles and responsibilities, and setting milestones; they have to pay immediate attention to familiarizing themselves with and integrating available technology, and agreeing on preferred communication media and frequency.
Murthy & Kerr (2002)	19 4-person teams in the U.S.	Lab Experiment	Communication mode (I); Communication process goal (P); Group performance and satisfaction with performance (O)	Media synchronicity theory	When the goal of the communication process was conveyance of information, CMC and FTF teams performed equally well; however, when the communication process goal involved convergence, FTF communication resulted in better performance than CMC.
Murthy & Kerr (2004)	35 4-graduate student teams in the U.S.	Lab Experiment	Interaction mode (I); Problem-solving performance (O)	Task-technology fit	Teams performing audit work using a bulletin board tool outperformed teams using either FTF or chat (with no significant differences between FTF and chat).
Nemiro (2002)	9 organizational virtual teams	Qualitative Study	Work nature, communication method, geographic dispersion (I); Creative process stages (P)		The creative process in virtual teams moved through several recognizable stages (i.e., idea generation, development, finalization and closure, and evaluation), teams used different communication media at different stages of the creative process, and knowledge repositories allowed members to review team interactions to improve the creative process in the future.
Nowak (2003)	42 undergraduate students in the U.S.	Lab Experiment	Perceived virtual partner sex (I), Virtual partner's social presence, involvement, and credibility (P)	Sex categorization	Even if people are making perceptions of gender online, these perceptions did not really influence social judgment. Regardless of the participants' perceptions of the sex of the person they were interacting with, there were no significant differences in perceived involvement, credibility, or social presence.

(Continued)

Appendix B (Continued)

Author(s)	Sample	Method	Variable(s)	Theories/Models	Key Findings
Ocker (2005)	10 graduate student teams in the U.S.	Case Study of Lab Experiments	Individual and group characteristics (I); Group interaction (P); Creative performance (O)	Social influences	Significant inhibitors to the creative performance of virtual teams included dominance, domain knowledge, downward norm setting, lack of shared understanding, time pressure, and technical difficulties; and significant enhancers to creativity included stimulating colleagues, the existence of a variety of social influences, a collaborative team climate, and both the surfacing and reduction of equivocality.
Ocker (2007)	8 graduate student teams in the U.S.	Case Study of Lab Experiment	Team composition (I); Patterns of dominance (P)	Status characteristics theory	The emergence of a dominant individual in a virtual team was associated with that member being from the majority sex in each team; dominance was driven by a combination of a few team member status traits; and when one or more status markers belonged to a single person—the dominant member—and were absent in other team members, dominance was pronounced.
Panteli & Davison (2005)	8 student GVTs from England and Hong Kong	Case Study	Geographical and cultural dispersion, inter- and intra-organizational homogeneity, temporality (I); Communication patterns and interactions (P)	Subgroup impact	Subgroups exert different degrees of impact on the team as a whole. Where the impact was high, boundaries were created between team members in different subgroups, while the development of team cohesiveness was restricted. All teams were able to produce high-quality outcomes, suggesting that the emergence of subgroups may not always have a negative influence on team performance.
Paul & McDaniel (2004)	10 virtual team projects in the health care industry	Case Study	Interpersonal trust (E); Virtual collaborative relationship performance (P)	Interpersonal trust	Three types of interpersonal trust—calculative, competence, and relational—were all positively related to virtual collaborative relationship performance.
Paul et al. (2004)	16 student groups in India and the U.S.	Lab Experiment	Group heterogeneity (I); Collaborative conflict management style; satisfaction with decision making process, perceived participation (P); Decision quality (O)	Team diversity	Collaborative conflict management style positively impacted satisfaction with the decision-making process, perceived decision quality, and perceived participation of the virtual teams, but collaborative conflict style was not significantly associated with group heterogeneity.

Study	Method	Sample	Topic	Variables	Findings
Paul et al. (2005)	Lab Experiment	22 MBA student groups in India and the U.S.	Team diversity	Team's cultural orientation, team heterogeneity (I); Group member participation, group agreement (P); Decision quality (O)	More individualistic groups had lower levels of collaborative conflict management. Cultural diversity moderated the relationship between collaborative conflict and performance such that the effects are stronger for culturally heterogeneous rather than homogeneous groups
Pauleen (2004)	Case Study	7 virtual team leaders in New Zealand	Virtual team leadersip	Virtual team leadership (I); Relationship development (P)	Leaders built personal relationships with their virtual team members before starting a virtual working relationship that includes three steps: assessing conditions, targeting level of relationship, and creating strategies.
Pauleen & Yoong (2001)	In-depth Interviews	7 organizations using virtual teams in New Zealand	Team building	Communication channels in online relationships among virtual team members (P)	Building and maintaining virtual team relationships was facilitated by richer communication media such as FTF, videoconferencing, and telephone.
Pena et al. (2007)	Lab Experiment	65 student groups in North America	Dominance in teams	Geographic location, communication medium (I); Dominance perception (P); Group cohesiveness (E)	Dominance perceptions were more extreme in distributed, compared to co-located groups; co-located groups showed greater convergence between self and partner dominance perceptions than distributed groups, suggesting more symmetrical perceptions. More symmetrical groups exhibited more attraction and cohesion than less symmetrical groups.
Pensendorfer & Koeszegi (2006)	Lab Experiment	50 dyads in Austria and Taiwan	De-individuation	Communication mode (I); Communication behaviors in negotiation, satisfaction with negotiation process (P); Satisfaction with negotiation outcome (O)	A synchronous negotiation mode led to less friendly, more affective, and more competitive negotiation behavior; in the asynchronous communication mode, negotiators exchanged more private and task-oriented information and were friendlier; and negotiators in the asynchronous mode were more satisfied with the process and outcome of the negotiation.

(Continued)

Appendix B (Continued)

Author(s)	Sample	Method	Variable(s)	Theories/Models	Key Findings
Piccoli & Ives (2003)	51 student teams from the U.S., Europe, and New Zealand	Lab Experiment	Trust (E)	Control theory	The behavior control mechanisms typically used in traditional teams had a significant negative effect on trust in virtual teams. Trust decline in virtual teams was rooted in instances of reneging and incongruence. Behavior control mechanisms increased vigilance and made instances when individuals perceive team members to have failed to uphold their obligations (i.e., reneging and incongruence) salient. Heightened vigilance and salience increased the likelihood that team members' failure to fulfill their obligations would be detected, thus contributing to trust decline.
Polzer et al. (2006)	45 graduate student virtual teams in 10 countries	Lab Experiment	Physical co-location type, nationality heterogeneity (I); Trust (E); Team conflict (P)	Subgroup fault-line	The lowest levels of trust occurred in virtual teams consisting of two same-nationality co-located subgroups providing evidence for fault-lines effects along nationality.
Poole et al. (1991)	40 student groups	Lab Experiment	Technological support, conflict potential, context (group size, task) (I); Conflict interaction process, conflict outcomes (i.e., change in consensus) (P)	Team conflicts in decision making	There were differences in the level of conflict in GDSS-supported and unsupported groups, and in conflict management behaviors adopted by the different conditions. Moreover, there were differences in the impacts of GDSS for different groups, which contributed to consensus change.
Potter & Balthazard (2002)	252 teams	Lab Experiment	Group interaction style, extraversion (I); Group cohesion (E); Group effectiveness (O)	Human interaction	1st Study: Interaction style predicted task performance outcomes and process outcomes in virtual teams in ways very similar to those seen in face-to-face teams. 2nd study: Virtual teams were less successful than FTF teams on most outcome measures. Interaction styles explained much more variance of process outcomes than does communication mode. 3rd study: Extraversion begot a productive interaction style but a difference in extraversion between team members led to a negative style.
Qureshi et al. (2006)	21 student teams in Netherlands and Hong Kong	Case Study	Communication, coordination, adaptation (P)		A model of electronic collaboration was developed, integrating three key elements for virtual team success: communication, coordination, and adaptation.

Study	Method	Sample	Variables	Theory	Findings
Rafaeli & Ravid (2003)	Lab Experiment	76 4-person teams of executive education students in Israel	Information sharing (P); Team performance (O)	Information sharing	Teams that used e-mail to share more information performed better than teams who shared less information.
Rains (2007)	Lab Experiment	164–7 undergraduate student teams in the U.S.	Anonymity in communication (I); Source credibility and influence (P)	Adaptive structuration theory	Anonymity provided by electronic meeting systems undermined source credibility and influence, supporting the discount hypothesis of anonymity effects.
Rasters et al. (2002)	Case Study	A European research project	Group formation and composition (I); Virtual team communication (P)	Media richness theory	Virtual team communication was affected far more by the stage of group development (using Gersick's [1988] punctuated equilibrium model) than by the particular communication media used.
Ratcheva & Vyakarnam (2001)	Case Study	5 virtual team projects	Factors influencing team development in virtual settings (P)	Group development	Virtual teams followed self-energizing developmental processes that were non-linear and not consistent with existing developmental models for FTF teams.
Reid & Reid (2005)	Lab Experiment	16 3-undergraduate student groups in the U.K.	Communication condition (I): Group interaction (P); Idea generation (O)	Focus group discussion	After controlling for the greater number of contributions made by participants in FTF marketing focus groups, more ideas and answers were generated in CMC than in FTF discussions, and participants showed equal liking for each medium.
Reinig & Mejias (2004)	Lab Experiment	39 6–7 person groups of university students located in both the U.S. and Hong Kong	Group anonymity, group's national culture (I); flame and critical comments in GSS-supported discussions (P)	Anonymity and group norm influence	Both anonymous groups and individualistic (i.e., U.S.) groups produced more critical comments than identified or collectivistic (i.e., Hong Kong) groups, but there were no significant effects on flaming comments.
Roch & Ayman (2005)	Lab Experiment	74 3-undergraduate student groups	Communication condition, perceived group competence (I); Decision success (O)	Elaboration likelihood model	CMC group members' success perceptions significantly predicted their group's performance, but FTF group members' perceptions did not; only CMC group members' judgments regarding their group's problem-solving ability significantly predicted their group's decision success; and judgments of decision success mediated the relationship between perceptions of members' problem-solving ability and decision success only for CMC group members.

(Continued)

Appendix B (Continued)

Author(s)	Sample	Method	Variable(s)	Theories/Models	Key Findings
Rutkowski et al. (2007)	118 university students (13 teams) from Netherlands, Hong Kong, and the U.S.	Lab Experiment	Focus immersion, temporal disassociation (I); Interpersonal conflict (P); Subjective performance (O)	Focus immersion, temporal disassociation	Individuals with a higher focus immersion (i.e., the level of attention focus and engagement) rated asynchronous technologies as more useful, while individuals with higher temporal dissociation (i.e., time distortion or losing track of time) rated synchronous technologies as more useful. Virtual teams with higher levels of focus immersion and temporal dissociation had higher levels of interpersonal conflict.
Saphiere (1996)	12 global business teams in 3 U.S.-based corporations	Survey, Interviews, Observation, Content Analysis	Communication, task and affective behaviors, disagreement, cultural interpretation and mediation (P); Productivity (O)		The most successful teams communicated more often in informal, social ways; utilized more task and affect behaviors; frequently disagreed with one another, critically analyzing issues in meetings and focusing on task in a positive manner in writing; acted as cultural interpreters and mediators; and unanimously desired to work together again in the future.
Sarker et al. (2003)	14 4–5 member virtual teams of university students in Canada and the U.S.	Lab Experiment	Measure development of virtual team trust	Virtual team trust	A measure of virtual team trust with five subfactors were developed and validated: unit grouping, reputation categorization, physical appearance/behavior-based stereotyping, message-based stereotyping, and technology-related.
Sarker et al. (2005)	12 virtual teams in a university setting in Norway and the U.S.	Case Study	Communication (P); Knowledge transfer (O)	Knowledge management	The volume of communication, the credibility of the communicator, and the nature of cultural values held (i.e., collectivism) by the communicator were found to significantly predict the extent of knowledge transferred; however, capability was not found to have a significant influence.
Savicki et al. (1996)	12 undergraduate students in the U.S.	Lab Experiment	Group composition, task type (I); Participation, group development, conflict (P); Performance accuracy, group task discrepancy (O)	Group Composition	Female-only CMC groups sent more words per message, were more satisfied with the group process, and reported higher levels of group development than either mixed-gender or male-only CMC groups; mixed-gender groups communicated more frequently that same-gender groups; and members of male-only groups used more argumentative language than female-only groups.

Citation	Sample	Method	Variables	Theory/Focus	Findings
Schmidt et al. (2001)	171 individuals and 65 teams of university students in the U.S.	Lab Experiment	Working condition (I); Team performance (O)	Comparing performance of individuals, face-to-face teams, and virtual teams	Virtual (i.e., asynchronous CMC) new product development teams outperformed FTF teams.
Sharifi & Pawar (2002)	38 senior managers in new product development manufacturing firms in the U.K.	Survey and Case Study	Benefits and problems experienced by firms on adopting either physical virtual team co-location (e.g., building relationships, time reductions, reduction in reiteration of designs, better product quality)	Collaboration	Many challenges associated with building and maintaining virtual teams were summarized. Specifically, trust was essential to virtual team success with co-location as a necessary but not sufficient ingredient for building trust.
Shepherd et al. (1996)	93 student groups	Lab Experiment	Anonymity, social comparison (I); Idea Generation (O)	Social comparison in brainstorming	Social comparisons enabled by technology reduced the effects of social loafing (thereby increasing productivity) in electronic brainstorming groups.
Siegel et al. (1986)	48 3-person student groups in the U.S.	Lab Experiment	Computer-mediated communication condition (I); Participation, interpersonal behavior (P); Group decision (O)	Group decision making	CMC group members, compared to FTF, made fewer remarks, took longer to make group decisions, participated more equally, exhibited more uninhibited behavior in the form of inflammatory remarks, and produced decisions that shifted further away from group members' initial choices.
Simon (2006)	75 undergraduate dyads in the U.S.	Lab Experiment	Communication modes (I); Task satisfaction and performance (O)	Median naturalness theory	Satisfaction with communication medium was lower among those dyads communicating through an instant-messaging system than among those interacting face to face or through videoconferencing, although there were no differences in task performance.
Sivunen (2006)	4 virtual team leaders from 4 international organizations	Case Study	Virtual team leadership (I)	Team identity	Four different leadership tactics employed to enhance identification with the team were identified: catering to the individual, giving positive feedback, bringing out common goals and workings, and talking up team activities and FTF meetings.

(Continued)

Appendix B (Continued)

Author(s)	Sample	Method	Variable(s)	Theories/Models	Key Findings
Sole & Edmondson (2002)	7 cross-functional virtual teams	Qualitative Field Study	Dispersed team learning from situated knowledge (P)	Team learning	While virtual teams could easily access and use unique locale-specific knowledge resources to resolve problems that arise in those same locales, they encountered difficulties in uncovering and sharing situated knowledge (i.e., knowledge embedded in the work practices of a particular organizational site).
Sosik et al. (1998)	36 4–5 undergraduate student teams in the U.S.	Lab Experiment	Perceived leadership style, identified/anonymous GDSS setting (I); Group creativity (O)	Group brainstorming	Certain elements of transformational leadership were positively (i.e., inspirational leadership) and others negatively (i.e., intellectual stimulation and individualized consideration) related to CMC group creativity. Transactional goal setting was positively related to CMC group creativity; and the effects were generally stronger in anonymous, rather than identified, CMC groups. The inspirational leadership dimension of transformational leadership was positively, and the intellectual stimulation and individualized consideration dimensions were negatively, related to CMC group creativity
Sproull & Kiesler (1986)	96 employees in a Fortune 500 office equipment company	Survey	Electronic communication (I); Absorption effects, status equalization effects, uninhibited behavior (P)	Social context cues	Using CMC reduced social context cues, provided information that was relatively self-absorbed, undifferentiated by status, uninhibited, and provided information that would not have been obtained using another medium.
Stanton et al. (2003)	24 4-student groups in England	Lab Experiment	Communication condition (I); Group identity (E); Group effectiveness (O)	Human supervisory control	FTF groups in a low fidelity simulation generated more reduced costs, greater group identity, enhanced motivation and greater tactical control than those using CMC.
Staples & Zhao (2006)	79 student teams in Canada	Lab Experiment	Cultural diversity, communication mode (I); Team cohesion (E); Conflict (P) Team performance (O)	Team diversity	Heterogeneous teams were less satisfied and cohesive and had more conflict than the homogeneous teams. Within just the heterogeneous team, the performance of the virtual teams was superior to that of the FTF teams.

Study	Method	Sample	Variables	Theory	Findings
Stewart & Gosain (2006)	Survey	67 open source software project teams	Team member's adherence to norms, beliefs, and values (I); Affective and cognitive trust among team members (E); Communication quality (P); Team effectiveness (O)	Ideology's impact on team effectiveness	Adhering to the ideological tenets of the open source software community (i.e., values, norms, and beliefs) positively affected both trust and communication quality which, in turn, affected team performance.
Straus & McGrath (1994)	Lab Experiment	72 3-person undergraduate groups in the U.S.	Communication media, task type (I); Group performance (O)	Information richness	While there were no differences in the quality of work performance by CMC and FTF groups, FTF groups were more productive, especially for more interdependent tasks.
Strijbos et al. (2004)	Lab Experiment	33 students distributed over 19 groups in Netherlands	Role vs. non-role (I); Collaboration, team development, group process satisfaction, intergroup conflict (P)	Collaborative learning	CMC groups with formally designated roles, versus those in a non-role condition, have higher team coordination, a larger amount of task-content focused statements, and increased member awareness of team efficiency.
Suchan & Hayzak (2001)	Case Study	A single customer support virtual team in a Fortune 500 consulting organization	Virtual team structure (I)		Corporate mission, strategy, tasks, reward systems, and attitudes toward technology supported virtual team structure. To build and maintain team trust, the virtual team leader used a FTF, three-day project kickoff, a mentoring program, and a culture that promoted information sharing, team-based rewards, and employee development.
Swigger et al. (2004)	Case Study	55 teams composed of the U.S. and Turkey students	Cultural attributes (I); Team performance (O)		Teams' cultural composition was a significant predictor of team performance.
Tan et al. (2000)	Lab Experiment	75 undergraduates arrayed into 5-person team	Dialogue technique training (I); Team cohesion (E); Collaboration (P); Decision quality and satisfaction (O)	Dialogue theory	Virtual teams trained in using a dialogue technique (i.e., engaging in small talk, discussing good communication practices, and building a team mental model of good communication practices) before interacting exhibited stronger cohesion, collaboration, perceived decision quality, and decision satisfaction.

(Continued)

Appendix B (Continued)

Author(s)	Sample	Method	Variable(s)	Theories/Models	Key Findings
Thompson & Coovert (2002)	80 4-person student teams in the U.S.	Lab Experiment	Decision making technique, communication media type (I); Team member influence (P); Team solution quality (O)	Decision making	The stepladder technique (i.e., introducing additional team members in team decision making, one-by-one, in stages) improved FTF, but not CMC, team decision quality. FTF participants felt more influential and satisfied than CMC participants, regardless of decision technique.
Thompson & Coovert (2003)	40 4-person student teams in the U.S.	Lab Experiment	Communication medium (I); Team discussion time, process satisfaction (P); Team effectiveness (O)	Information richness	CMC teams viewed their discussions as more confusing and less satisfying, spent more time devising decisions, and felt less content with their outcomes than FTF teams. Discussion time mediated the relationship between the communication medium and outcome satisfaction.
Timmerman & Scott (2006)	Informants from 98 organizational teams	Survey	Communication and structural factors (I); Communication technology use (P); Virtual team outcomes (O)	Adaptive Structuration theory, dual captivity theory of media use	Structural features primarily related to technology use, whereas communication considerations were associated more with team outcomes.
Valacich et al. (1992)	22 student CMC groups (12 3- and 10 9-member teams) in the U.S.	Lab Experiment	Anonymity and group size (I); Participation (P); Team Effectiveness (O)	Information richness	Larger groups generated significantly more and higher quality ideas than smaller groups, and members of small identified CMC groups were the most satisfied and rated themselves as more effective than the other conditions.
Valacich et al. (1994)	64 students teams in the U.S.	Lab Experiment	Electronic braining storming vs. nominal groups, group size (I); Idea quantity and quality (O)	Information richness	CMC groups produced more ideas as the size of the groups increased and outperformed nominal groups of the same size and attributed their findings to less production blocking in CMC groups.
Valacich et al. (1994)	128 student teams arrayed into 12 4-member and 10 8-member CMC groups in the U.S.	Lab Experiment	Group size and group member proximity (I); Idea quantity and quality (O)	Information richness	CMC groups that were dispersed (i.e., not in the same room) outperformed co-located CMC groups in terms of total number of unique, total quality, and number of high quality ideas generated.

Study	Sample	Method	Variables	Theory	Findings
Valacich & Schwenk (1995)	42 5-person undergraduate groups in the U.S.	Lab Experiment	Communication medium, decision making method (I); Decision making performance (O)	Group decision making method	Using the devil's advocate procedure in CMC groups resulted in more solution alternatives on a decision-making task, more voting rounds to reach agreement and higher satisfaction with the process, compared to FTF groups.
Van den Bossche et al. (2006)	75 teams of undergraduate students in the Netherlands	Survey	Psychological safety, task and social cohesion, group potency, shared cognition (E); Team learning behavior (P); Team effectiveness (O)	Team learning	Interdependence, task cohesion, group potency, and psychological safety were all related to team learning behaviors; task cohesion was positively related to mutually shared cognition; and task cohesion and group potency were positively related to team effectiveness.
Walther (1995)	32 3-person undergraduate student groups in the U.S.	Lab Experiment	Communication medium (I); Relational communication (P)	Social presence, media richness, and social information processing theory	FTF was not more intimate and sociable than CMC over time. CMC was more dominant than FTF in initial conversations alone, but the difference dissipated thereafter. CMC groups became less formal and less task-oriented over time. Regarding formality and receptivity, groups using either CMC or FTF reached levels of relational communication similar to the other medium over time. In other cases, there were differences between CMC and FTF across time, and, in each case, CMC was more relationally positive.
Walther et al. (2001)	24 students from the England and U.S. arrayed into 8 international virtual groups	Lab Experiment	Team longevity, physical presence, communication medium (I); Intimacy, social and physical attraction, self-presentation (P)	Social presence theory, social information processing theory	In new, unacquainted teams, seeing one's partner (in a photograph) promoted affection and social attraction, but in long-term virtual teams, the same type of photograph dampened affinity.
Warkentin et al. (1997)	24 student teams in the U.S.	Lab Experiment	Communication medium (I); Group cohesiveness (E); Group interaction process, information exchange (P); Group outcomes (O)	Time-Interaction-Performance theory	Both CMC and FTF teams exhibited similar levels of communication effectiveness and performance, but FTF team members reported higher levels of satisfaction.

(Continued)

Appendix B (Continued)

Author(s)	Sample	Method	Variable(s)	Theories/Models	Key Findings
Warkentin & Beranek (1999)	12 graduate student groups in the U.S.	Lab Experiment	Virtual team communication training (I); Team trust (E); Commitment to team goals and objectives, open and frank idea expression (P)	Media richness theory and social presence theory	Teams that were given appropriate training exhibited improved perceptions of the interaction process over time, specifically with regard to trust, commitment and frank expression between members.
Watson et al. (1988)	82 3- or 4-person student groups	Lab Experiment	Decision aid (baseline vs. manual vs. computer) (I); Attitudes toward group process, equality of influence, group consensus (P)	Group decision support systems	The introduction of a CMC tool had no direct effect on team outcomes (i.e., group consensus), but the effects were mediated by how the groups adapted the tools to either promote, or inhibit, productive conflict management.
Watson-Manheim & Belanger (2007)	30 individuals in 2 Fortune 100 IT companies	Case Study	Institutional and situational factors influencing communication media usage (I)		Repertoires of communication media use were influenced by institutional conditions (e.g., incentives, trust, and physical proximity) and situational conditions (e.g., urgency, task, etc.), and by routine use of the media over time.
Weisband (1992)	24 3-person student groups in the U.S.	Lab Experiment	Communication mode (FTF vs. electronic mail) (I); Group process (P); Group outcomes (O)	First advocate effect	Compared to FTF groups, CMC took almost four times as long to reach consensus, had more direct arguing and conflict; discussion contained significantly more implicit preferences and explicit proposals, as well as more social pressure remarks, more uninhibited behavior, and more task-irrelevant remarks.
Weisband et al. (1995)	156 student groups	Lab Experiment	Communication modality, majority condition (I); Group participation and influence (P)	Social influence (based on status difference)	Medium of communication (CMC versus FTF) had no effect on the impact of member status on team member participation and influence, demonstrating that status differences can persist in teams using CMC.
Workman (2005)	436 virtual team projects in a global IT firm	Survey	Virtual team culture (I); Schedule and quality performance (O)	Social influence and social identity theory	Team boundary permeability strengthened the positive effects of various aspects of virtual team culture on team performance.

Study	Sample	Method	Variables	Theory	Findings
Yoo & Kanawattanachai (2001)	38 MBA student teams of 10 nationalities	Quasi-experiment	Communication volume of virtual team members, transactive memory system development (P); Team performance (O)	Transactive memory systems	The influence of a team's early communication volume on team performance decreased as teams developed transactive memory systems and a collective mind.
Zhang et al. (2007)	183 groups in university in China and the U.S.	Lab Experiment	Degree of collectivism, social presence, group diversity (cultural heterogeneity) (I); Majority influence (P)	Convergent-divergent theory; social identity theory; social presence theory	Majority influence on collectivistic group minorities was manifested more strongly than that on individualistic group minorities; minorities in FTF groups experienced a higher level of majority influence than FTF with CMC support groups and distributed CMC groups; however, there was no significant difference between FTF-CMC groups and distributed CMC groups, and majority influence was manifested more strongly on Chinese minorities in heterogeneous groups than in homogeneous Chinese groups in a distributed CMC setting.
Zhou & Zhang (2006)	68 students arrayed into 16 CMC dyads and 12 CMC triads in the U.S.	Lab Experiment	Communication intent (deceptive vs. truthful), group size (dyad vs. triadic) (I)	Interpersonal deception theory	Those engaging in deceptive behavior showed a lower level of pleasantness and language complexity only in dyads, whereas a higher level of cognitive complexity and initiation only in triadic groups.
Zigurs et al. (1988)	32 undergraduate student groups in the U.S.	Lab Experiment	Communication media type (GDSS vs. FTF) (I); Influence behavior (P); Group outcome (O)	Group decision making	No significant difference was found between the overall amount of influence behavior attempted in CMC versus FTF groups, while significant differences were found in the pattern of influence behaviors (e.g., more time spent discussing procedures, more initiation and process behavior), with more equal participation occurring in CMC versus FTF groups.

* I = Input; E = Emergent State; P = Process; O = Output

Appendix C Article Summaries, Organizational Level of Analysis

Author(s)	Sample	Method	Variable(s)	Theories/Models	Key Findings
Andersen (2005)	101 manufacturing firms in North America	Survey	Communication media (I); Firm profitability (O)	Decentralized strategic decision making	Computer-mediated communication between middle managers located in different functional areas in the firm increased firm performance.
McDonough et al. (2001)	103 firms in new product development	Survey	Geographic dispersion and virtuality (I); Project performance (O)		Global teams presented companies with many more challenges than either co-located or virtual teams, and that performance was also lower for these types of team.
Zack & McKenney (1995)	2 editorial management groups at 2 newspaper publishing organizations	Case Study	Social context (communication norms, power and control, philos), social structure (patterns of interaction) (I), Communication (P)	Adaptive structuration theory, social information processing theory	Social context (i.e., the culture, distribution of power, and the social norms, habits, practices, expectations and preferences held by a group regarding its present and past interaction) influenced each group's use of e-mail and FTF communication such that there was greater similarity of interaction within group across communication mode than within communication mode across group.

* I = Input; E = Emergent State; P = Process; O = Output

Appendix D Meta-Analyses of Virtual Teams Research

Author(s)	Sample	Method	Variable(s)	Theories/Models	Key Findings
Fjermestad (2004)	145 experiments that used communication mode as an independent variable	Meta-Analysis	Communication mode (I*); Group adaptation process, group gains/losses, intermediate role outcomes (P); Consensus, efficiency and effective measures, satisfaction and usability measures (O)	Input-Process-Output model for analyzing group support systems	The modal outcome for CMC compared to FTF methods was "no difference," while the overall percentage of positive effects for results that compare CMC to FTF was 29.2%. The results suggest that the use of CMC improves decision quality, depth of analysis, equality of participation, and satisfaction over manual methods. Additionally, more detailed analysis suggests that task type, CMC type, and the interaction of both have a moderating effect on adaptation and outcome factors. Specifically, groups working on idea-generation tasks using CMC improved to 39.6% over FTF. Conversely, asynchronous CMC groups working on decision-making tasks improved to 46.4% over FTF. FTF groups showed higher levels of consensus and perceived quality, communicate more, and are more efficient (requiring less time to complete the tasks). No differences, however, were observed between FTF and GSS groups on satisfaction and usability.
Rains (2005)	48 experiments of groups using CMC and FTF	Meta-Analysis	Group support systems use (I); Participation equality, influence equality, dominance, unique information, normative influence, decision shifts (P)		Groups using CMC experienced greater participation and influenced equality, generated a larger amount of unique ideas, and experienced less member dominance than do groups meeting FTF.

* I = Input; E = Emergent State; P = Process; O = Output

References*

Ahn, H. J., Lee, H. J., Cho, K., & Park, S. J. (2005). Utilizing knowledge context in virtual collaborative work. *Decision Support Sciences, 39,* 563–582.

*Ahuja, M. K., & Galvin, J. E. (2003). Socialization in virtual groups. *Journal of Management, 29,* 161–185.

*Aiello, J. R., & Kolb, K. J. (1995). Electronic performance monitoring and social context: Impact on productivity and stress. *Journal of Applied Psychology, 80,* 339–353.

*Alge, B. J., Ballinger, G. A., & Green, S. G. (2004). Remote control: Predictors of electronic intensity and secrecy. *Personnel Psychology, 57,* 377–410.

*Alge, B. J., Wiethoff, C., & Klein, H. J. (2003). When does the medium matter? Knowledge-building experiences and opportunities in decision-making teams. *Organizational Behavior and Human Decision Processes, 91,* 26–37.

*Anawati, D., & Craig, A. (2006). Behavioral adaptation within cross-cultural virtual teams. *IEEE Transactions on Professional Communication, 49,* 44–56.

*Andersen, T. J. (2005). The performance effect of computer-mediated communication and decentralized strategic decision making. *Journal of Business Research, 58,* 1059–1067.

*Andres, H. P. (2002). A comparison of face-to-face and virtual software development teams. *Team Performance Management, 8,* 39–48.

*Aubert, B. A., & Kelsey, B. L. (2003). Further understanding of trust and performance in virtual teams. *Small Group Research, 34,* 575–618.

*Baba, M. L., Gluesing, J., Ratner, H., & Wagner, K. H. (2004). The contexts of knowing: Natural history of a globally distributed team. *Journal of Organizational Behavior, 25,* 547–587.

*Baker, G. (2002). The effects of synchronous collaborative technologies on decision making: A study of virtual teams. *Information Resources Management Journal, 15,* 79–93.

*Barkhi, R. (2005). Information exchange and induced cooperation in group decision support systems. *Communication Research, 32,* 646–678.

*Baskerville, R., & Nandhakumar, J. (2007). Activating and perpetuating virtual teams: Now that we're mobile, where do we go? *IEEE Transactions on Professional Communication, 50,* 17–34.

Beal, D. J., Cohen, R. R., Burke, M. J., & McLendon, C. L. (2003). Cohesion and performance in groups: A meta-analytic clarification of construct relations. *Journal of Applied Psychology, 88,* 989–1004.

*Becker-Beck, U., Wintermantel, M., & Borg, A. (2005). Principles in regulating interaction in teams practicing face-to-face communication versus teams practicing computer-mediated communication. *Small Group Research, 36,* 499–536.

*Belanger, F., & Watson-Manheim, M. B. (2006). Virtual team and multiple media: Structuring media use to attain strategic goals. *Group Decision and Negotiation, 15,* 299–321.

Bell, B. S., & Kozlowski, S. W. J. (2002). A typology of virtual teams: Implications for effective leadership. *Group & Organization Management, 27,* 14–49.

*Bhappu, A. D., Griffith, T. L., & Northcraft, G. B. (1997). Media effects and communication bias in diverse groups. *Organizational Behavior and Human Decision Processes, 70,* 199–205.

Blackburn, R. S., Furst, S. A., & Rosen, B. (2003). Building a winning virtual team. In C. B. Gibson & S. G. Cohen (Eds.), *Virtual teams that work: Creating the conditions for virtual team effectiveness* (pp. 95–120). San Francisco: Jossey-Bass.

*Boh, W. F., Ren, Y., Kiesler, S., & Bussjaeger, R. (2007). Expertise and collaboration in the geographically dispersed organization. *Organization Science, 18,* 595–612.

*Bordia, P., DiFonzo, N., & Chang, A. (1999). Rumor as group problem solving: Development patterns in informal computer-mediated groups. *Small Group Research, 30,* 8–28.

*Bosch-Sijtsema, P. (2007). The impact of individual expectations and expectation conflict on virtual teams. *Group & Organization Management, 32,* 358–388.

*Bouas, K. S., & Arrow, H. (1996). The development of group identity in computer and face-to-face groups with membership change. *Computer Supported Cooperative Work, 4,* 153–178.

*Bradner, E., Mark, G., & Hertel, T. D. (2005). Team size and technology fit: Participation, awareness, and rapport in distributed teams. *IEEE Transactions on Professional Communication, 48,* 68–77.

Brown, H. G., Poole, M. S., & Rodgers, T. L. (2004). Interpersonal traits, complementarity, and trust in virtual collaboration. *Journal of Management Information Systems, 20,* 115–137.

*Burgoon, J. K., Bonito, J. A., Ramirez, A., Jr., Dunbar, N. E., Kam, K., & Fischer, J. (2002). Testing the interactivity principle: Effects of mediation, propinquity, and verbal and nonverbal modalities in interpersonal interaction. *Journal of Communication, 52,* 657–677.

*Campbell, J., & Stasser, G. (2006). The influence of time and task demonstrability on decision making in computer-mediated and face-to-face groups. *Small Group Research, 37,* 271–294.

*Cappel, J. J., & Windsor, J. C. (2000). Ethical decision making: A comparison of computer-supported and face-to-face group. *Journal of Business Ethics, 28,* 95–107.

*Carte, T. A., Chidambaram, L., & Becker, A. (2006). Emergent leadership in self-managed virtual teams. *Group Decision and Negotiation, 15,* 323–343.

*Chen, M., Liou, Y., Wang, C. W., Fan, Y. W., & Chi, Y. P. J. (2005). TeamSpirit: Design, implementation, and evaluation of a web-based group decision support system. *Decision Support Systems, 43,* 1186–1202.

*Chidambaram, L. (1996). Relational development in computer-supported groups. *MIS Quarterly, 20,* 143–165.

*Chidambaram, L., & Tung, L. L. (2005). Is out of sight, out of mind? An empirical study of social loafing in technology-supported groups. *Information Systems Research, 16,* 149–168.

*Chudoba, K. M., Wynn, E., Lu, M., & Watson-Manheim, M. B. (2005). How virtual are we? Measuring virtuality and understanding its impact in a global organization. *Information Systems Journal, 15,* 279–306.

Cohen, S. G., & Bailey, D. E. (1997). What makes teams work: Group effectiveness research from the shop floor to the executive suite. *Journal of Management, 23,* 239–290.

*Colquitt, J. A., Hollenbeck, J. R., Ilgen, D. R., LePine, J. A., & Sheppard, L. (2002). Computer-assisted communication and team decision-making performance: The moderating effect of openness to experience. *Journal of Applied Psychology, 87,* 402–410.

*Connolly, T., Jessup, L. M., & Valacich, J. S. (1990). Effects of anonymity and evaluative tone on idea generation in computer-mediated groups. *Management Science, 36,* 689–703.

*Coppola, N. W., Hiltz, S. R., & Rotter, N. G. (2004). Building trust in virtual teams. *IEEE Transactions on Professional Communication*, *47*, 95–104.

*Cornelius, C., & Boos, M. (2003). Enhancing mutual understanding in synchronous computer-mediated communication by training. *Communication Research*, *30*, 147–177.

*Cramton, C. D. (2001). The mutual knowledge problem and its consequences for dispersed collaboration. *Organization Science*, *12*, 346–371.

Cramton, C. D., & Hinds, P. (2005). Subgroup dynamics in internationally distributed teams: Ethnocentrism or cross-national learning. In B. M. Staw & R. M. Kramer (Eds.), *Research in organizational behavior* (Vol. 26, pp. 231–263). Greenwich, CT: JAI Press.

*Cramton, C. D., & Webber, S. S. (2005). Relationships among geographic dispersion, team processes, and effectiveness in software development work teams. *Journal of Business Research*, *58*, 758–765.

*Crowston, K., Howison, J., Masango, C., & Eseryel, U. Y. (2007). The role of face-to-face meetings in technology-supported self-organizing distributed teams. *IEEE Transactions on Professional Communication*, *50*, 185–203.

Cummings, J. N., Espinosa, J. A., & Pickering, C. K. (2009). Crossing spatial and temporal boundaries in globally distributed projects: A relational model of coordination delay. *Information Systems Research*, *20*, 420–439.

*Daily, B. F., & Teich, J. E. (2000). Perceptions of contributions in multi-cultural groups in non-GDSS and GDSS environments. *European Journal of Operational Research*, *134*, 70–83.

*Daly, B. L. (1993). The influence of face-to-face versus computer-mediated communication channels on collective induction. *Accounting, Management, and Information Technology*, *3*, 1–22.

*Dennis, A. R., & Garfield, M. J. (2003). The adoption and use of GSS in project teams: Toward more participative processes and outcomes. *MIS Quarterly*, *27*, 289–323.

Driskell, J. E., Radtke, P. H., & Salas, E. (2003). Virtual teams: Effects of technological mediation on team performance. *Group Dynamics: Theory, Research, and Practice*, *7*, 297–323.

*Dubrovsky, V., Kiesler, S., & Sethna, B. (1991). The equalization phenomenon: Status effects in computer-mediated and face-to-face decision making groups. *Human Computer Interaction*, *6*, 119–146.

Earley, P. C., & Gibson, C. B. (1998). Taking stock in our progress on individualism-collectivism: 100 years of solidarity and community. *Journal of Management*, *24*, 265–304.

*Easley, R. F., Devaraj, S., & Crant, J. M. (2003). Relating collaborative technology use to teamwork quality and performance: An empirical analysis. *Journal of Management Information Systems*, *19*, 247–268.

*El-Shinnawy, M., & Vinze, A. S. (1998). Polarization and persuasive argumentation: A study of decision making in group settings. *MIS Quarterly*, *22*, 165–198.

Espinosa, J. A., Cummings, J. N., Wilson, J. M., & Pearce, B. M. (2003). Team boundary issues across multiple global firms. *Journal of Management Information Systems*, *19*, 157–190.

*Ferrin, D. L., & Dirks, K. T. (2003). The use of rewards to increase and decrease trust: Mediating processes and differential effects. *Organization Science*, *14*, 18–31.

*Finholt, T., & Sproull, L. S. (1990). Electronic groups at work. *Organization Science*, *1*, 41–64.

Fiol, C. M., & O'Connor, E. J. (2005). Identification in face-to-face, hybrid, and pure virtual teams: Untangling the contradictions. *Organization Science*, *16*, 19–32.

*Fjermestad, J. (2004). An analysis of communication mode in group support systems research. *Decision Support Systems*, *37*, 239–263.

*Forester, G. L., Thoms, P., & Pinto, J. K. (2007). Importance of goal setting in virtual project teams. *Psychological Reports*, *100*, 270–274.

*Froehle, C. M. (2006). Service personnel, technology, and their interaction in influencing customer satisfaction. *Decision Sciences*, *37*, 5–38.

*Fuller, M. A., Hardin, A. M., & Davison, R. M. (2007). Efficacy in technology-mediated distributed teams. *Journal of Management Information Systems*, *23*, 209–235.

Furst, S., Blackburn, R., & Rosen, B. (1999). Virtual team effectiveness: A proposed research agenda. *Information Systems Journal*, *9*, 249–269.

*Gallupe, R. B., Dennis, A. R., Cooper, W. H., Valacich, J. S., Bastianutti, L. M., & Nunamaker, J. F. (1992). Electronic brainstorming and group size. *Academy of Management Journal*, *35*, 350–369.

*Gefen, D., & Straub, D. W. (1997). Gender differences in the perception and use of e-mail: An extension to the technology acceptance model. *MIS Quarterly*, *21*, 389–400.

*Geister, S., Konradt, U., & Hertel, G. (2006). Effects of process feedback on motivation, satisfaction, and performance in virtual teams. *Small Group Research*, *37*, 459–489.

Gersick, C. J. G. (1988). Time and transition in work teams: Toward a new model of group development. *Academy of Management Journal*, *31*, 9–41.

*Gibson, C. B. & Gibbs, J. L. (2006). Unpacking the concept of virtuality: The effects of geographic dispersion, electronic dependence, dynamic structure, and national diversity on team innovation. *Administrative Science Quarterly*, *51*, 451–495.

Gibson, C. B., Porath, C. L., Benson, G. S., & Lawler, E. E., III. (2007). What results when firms implement practices: The differential relationship between specific practices, firm financial performance, customer service, and quality. *Journal of Applied Psychology*, *92*, 1467–1480.

*Gonzalez, M. G., Burke, M. J., Santuzzi, A. M., & Bradley, J. C. (2003). The impact of group process variables on the effectiveness of distance collaboration groups. *Computers in Human Behavior*, *19*, 629–648.

*Graetz, K. A., Boyle, E., Kimble, C., Thompson, P., & Garloch, J. (1998). Information sharing in face-to-face, teleconferencing and electronic chat groups. *Small Group Research*, *29*, 714–743.

Griffith, T. L., & Neale, M. A. (2001). Information processing in traditional, hybrid, and virtual teams: From nascent knowledge to transactive memory. In B. M. Staw & R. L. Sutton (Eds.), *Research in organizational behavior* (Vol. 23, pp. 379–421). Greenwich, CT: JAI Press.

*Griffith, T. L., & Sawyer, J. E. (2006). Supporting technologies and organizational practices for the transfer of knowledge in virtual environments. *Group Decision and Negotiation*, *15*, 407–423.

Griffith, T. L., Sawyer, J. E., & Neale, M. A. (2003). Virtualness and knowledge in teams: Managing the love triangle of organizations, individuals, and information technology. *MIS Quarterly*, *27*, 265–287.

Gully, S. M., Incalaterra, K. A., Joshi, A., & Beaubien, J. M. (2002). A meta-analysis of team efficacy, potency, and performance: Interdependence and level of analysis as moderators of observed relationships. *Journal of Applied Psychology, 87,* 819–832.

*Haas, M. R. (2005). Acquiring and applying knowledge in transnational teams: The roles of cosmopolitans and locals. *Organization Science, 17,* 367–384.

Hackman, J. R., & Morris, C. G. (1975). Group tasks, group interaction process, and group performance effectiveness: A review and proposed integration. In L. Berkowitz (Ed.), *Advances in experimental social psychology* (Vol. 8, pp. 47–101). New York: Academic Press.

*Hambley, L. A., O'Neill, T. A., & Klein, T. J. B. (2007). Virtual team leadership: The effects of leadership style and communication medium on team interaction styles and outcomes. *Organizational Behavior and Human Decision Processes, 103,* 1–20.

Handy, C. (1995). Trust and the virtual organization. *Harvard Business Review, 73(9),* 40–48

*Hardin, A. M., Fuller, M. A., & Davison, R. M. (2007). I know I can, but can we? Culture and efficacy beliefs in global virtual teams. *Small Group Research, 38,* 130–155.

*Hardin, A. M., Fuller, M. A., & Valacich, J. S. (2006). Measuring group efficacy in virtual teams: New questions in an old debate. *Small Group Research, 37,* 65–85.

Harvey, M., Novicevic, M. M., & Garrison, G. (2004). Challenges to staffing global virtual teams. *Human Resource Management Review, 14,* 275–294.

*Hedlund, J., Ilgen, D. R., & Hollenbeck, J. R. (1998). Decision accuracy in computer-mediated versus face-to-face decision-making teams. *Organizational Behavior and Human Decision Processes, 76,* 30–47.

*Heninger, W. G., Dennis, A. R., & Hilmer, K. M. (2006). Individual cognition and dual task interference in group support systems. *Information Systems Research, 17,* 415–424.

Hertel, G., Geister, S., & Konradt, U. (2005). Managing virtual teams: A review of current empirical research. *Human Resource Management Review, 15,* 69–95.

*Hiltz, S. R., Johnson, K., & Turoff, M. (1986). Experiments in group decision making: Communication process and outcome in face-to-face versus computerized conferences. *Human Communication Research, 13,* 225–252.

Hinds, P. J., & Bailey, D. E. (2003). Out of sight, out of sync: Understanding conflict in distributed teams. *Organization Science, 14,* 615–632.

*Hinds, P. J., & Kiesler, S. (1995). Communication across boundaries: Work, structure, and use of communication technologies in a large organization. *Organization Science, 6,* 373–393.

Hirschhorn, L. (1991). *Managing in the new team environment: Skills, tools, and methods.* Reading, MA: Addison-Wesley.

*Hollingshead, A. B. (1996). Information suppression and status persistence in group decision making. *Human Communication Research, 23,* 193–219.

*Hollingshead, A. B., McGrath, J. E., & O'Connor, K. M. (1993). Group task performance and communication technology: A longitudinal study of computer-mediated versus face-to-face work groups. *Small Group Research, 24,* 307–333.

*Huang, A. H., Hung, S. Y., & Yen, D. C. (2007). An exploratory investigation of two internet-based communication modes. *Computer Standards & Interfaces, 29,* 238–243.

*Huang, W. W., Wei, K. K., Watson, R. T., & Tan, B. C. Y. (2002). Supporting virtual team-building with a GSS: An empirical investigation. *Decision Support Systems, 34,* 359–367.

Ilgen, D. R., Hollenbeck, J. R., Johnson, M., & Jundt, D. (2005). Teams in organizations: From input-process-output models to IMOI models. *Annual Review of Psychology, 56,* 517–543.

*Jarman, R. (2005). Why success isn't everything: Case studies of two virtual teams. *Group Decision and Negotiation, 14,* 333–354.

*Jarvenpaa, S. L., Knoll, K., & Leidner, D. E. (1998). Is anybody out there? Antecedents of trust in global virtual teams. *Journal of Management Information Systems, 14,* 29–64.

*Jarvenpaa, S. L., & Leidner, D. E. (1999). Communication and trust in global virtual teams. *Organization Science, 10,* 791–815.

*Jarvenpaa, S. L., Rao, V. S., & Huber, G. P. (1988). Computer support for meetings of groupsworking on unstructured problems: A field experiment. *MIS Quarterly, 12,* 645–666.

*Jarvenpaa, S. L., Shaw, T. R., & Staples, D. S. (2004). Toward contextualized theories of trust: The role of trust in global virtual teams. *Information Systems Research, 15,* 250–267.

*Jessup, L. M., & Tansik, D. A. (1991). Decision making in an automated environment: The effects of anonymity and proximity with a group decision support system. *Decision Sciences, 22,* 266–279.

*Johnson, S. D., Suriya, C., Yoon, S. W., Berrett, J. V., & La Fleur, J. (2002). Team development and group processes of virtual learning teams. *Computers & Education, 39,* 379–393.

*Kahai, S. S., & Cooper, R. B. (2003). Exploring the core concepts of media richness theory: The impact of cue multiplicity and feedback immediacy on decision quality. *Journal of Management Information Systems, 20,* 263–299.

*Kanawattanachai, P., & Yoo, Y. (2002). Dynamic nature of trust in virtual teams. *Journal of Strategic Information Systems, 11,* 187–213.

*Kanawattanachai, P., & Yoo, Y. (2007). The impact of knowledge coordination on virtual team performance over time. *MIS Quarterly, 31,* 783–808.

*Kankanhalli, A., Tan, B. C. Y., & Wei, K. K. (2007). Conflict and performance in global virtual teams. *Journal of Management Information Systems, 23,* 237–274.

*Kayworth, T., & Leidner, D. (2000). The global virtual manager: A prescription for success. *European Management Journal, 18,* 183–194.

Kirkman, B. L., & Mathieu, J. E. (2005). The dimensions and antecedents of team virtuality. *Journal of Management, 31,* 700–718.

*Kirkman, B. L., Rosen, B., Tesluk, P. E., & Gibson, C. B. (2004). The impact of team empowerment on virtual team performance: The moderating role of face-to-face interaction. *Academy of Management Journal, 47,* 175–192.

*Kirkman, B. L., Rosen, B., Tesluk, P. E., & Gibson, C. B. (2006). Enhancing the transfer of computer-assisted training proficiency in geographically-distributed teams. *Journal of Applied Psychology, 91,* 706–716.

Kock, N. (2004). The psychobiological model: Towards a new theory of computer-mediated communication based on Darwinian evolution. *Organization Science, 15,* 327–348.

Kozlowski, S. W. J., & Bell, B. S. (2003). Work groups and teams in organizations. In W. C. Borman, D. R. Ilgen, & R. J. Klimoski (Eds.), *Handbook of psychology: Industrial and organizational psychology* (Vol. 12, pp. 333–375). London: Wiley.

*Krebs, S. A., Hobman, E. V., & Bordia, P. (2006). Virtual teams and group member dissimilarity: Consequences for the development of trust. *Small Group Research, 37,* 721–741.

*Lebie, L., Rhoades, J. A., & McGrath, J. E. (1996). Interaction process in computer-mediated and face-to-face groups. *Computer Supported Cooperative Work, 4*, 127–152.

*Lea, M., & Spears, R. (1992). Paralanguage and social perception in computer-mediated communication. *Journal of Organizational Computing, 2*, 321–341.

*Lee, E. J. (2004). Effects of visual representation on social influence in computer-mediated communication: Experimental tests of the social identity model of deindividuation effects. *Human Communication Research, 30*, 234–259.

*Lee, E. J. (2005). Effects of the influence agent's sex and self-confidence on informational social influence in computer-mediated communication: Quantitative versus verbal presentation. *Communication Research, 32*, 29–58.

*Lee, E. J. (2006). When and how does depersonalization increase conformity to group norms in computer-mediated communication? *Communication Research, 33*, 423–447.

*Lee, E. J. (2007a). Effects of gendered language on gender stereotyping in computer-mediated communication: The moderating role of depersonalization and gender-role orientation. *Human Communication Research, 33*, 515–535.

*Lee, E. J. (2007b). Deindividuation effects on group polarization in computer-mediated communication: The role of group identification, public-self-awareness, and perceived argument quality. *Journal of Communication, 57*, 385–403.

*Lee-Kelley, L. (2006). Locus of control and attitudes to working in virtual teams. *International Journal of Project Management, 24*, 234–243.

*Leenders, R. T., van Engelen, J., & Kratzer, J. (2003). Virtuality, communication, and new product team creativity: A social network perspective. *Journal of Engineering and Technology Management, 20*, 69–92.

*Li, S. S. (2007). Computer-mediated communication and group decision making: A functional perspective. *Small Group Research, 38*, 593–614.

*Lind, M. R. (1999). The gender impact of temporary virtual work groups. *IEEE Transactions on Professional Communication, 42*, 276–285.

*Lowry, P. B., Roberts, T. L., Romano, N. C., Jr., Cheney, P. D., & Hightower, R. T. (2006). The impact of group size and social presence on small-group communication: Does computer-mediated communication make a difference? *Small Group Research, 37*, 631–661.

*Lurey, J. S., & Raisinghani, M. S. (2001). An empirical study of best practices in virtual teams. *Information & Management, 38*, 523–544.

*Majchrzak, A., Malhotra, A., & John, R. (2005). Perceived individual collaboration know-how development through information technology-enabled contextualization: Evidence from distributed teams. *Information Systems Research, 16*, 9–27.

*Majchrzak, A., Rice, R. E., Malhotra, A., King, N., & Ba, S. (2000). Technology adaptation: The case of a computer-supported inter-organizational virtual team. *MIS Quarterly, 24*, 569–600.

*Malhotra, A., Majchrzak, A., Carman, R., & Lott, V. (2001). Radical innovation without collocation: A case study at Boeing-Rocketdyne. *MIS Quarterly, 25*, 229–249.

Marks, M. A., Mathieu, J. E., & Zaccaro, S. J. (2001). A temporally based framework and taxonomy of team processes. *Academy of Management Review, 26*, 356–376.

Martins, L. L., Gilson, L. L., & Maynard, M. T. (2004). Virtual teams: What do we know and where do we go from here? *Journal of Management, 30*, 805–835.

*Massey, A. P., Montoya-Weiss, M. M., & Hung, Y. T. (2003). Because time matters: Temporal coordination in global virtual project teams. *Journal of Management Information Systems, 19*, 129–155.

Mathieu, J. E., Maynard, M. T., Rapp, T., & Gilson, L. L. (2008). Team effectiveness 1997–2007: A review of recent advancements and a glimpse into the future. *Journal of Management, 34*, 410–476.

*May, A., & Carter, C. (2001). A case study of virtual teams working in the European automotive industry. *International Journal of Industrial Ergonomics, 27*, 171–186.

*Maznevski, M. L., & Chudoba, K. M. (2000). Bridging space over time: Global virtual-team dynamics and effectiveness. *Organization Science, 11*, 473–492.

*McDonough, E. F., III., Kahn, K. B., & Barczak, G. (2001). An investigation of the use of global, virtual, and colocated new product development teams. *The Journal of Product Innovation Management, 18*, 110–120.

McGrath, J. E. (1984). *Groups, interaction and performance.* Englewood Cliffs, NJ: Prentice-Hall.

*McLeod, P., Baron, R., Marti, M., & Yoon, K. (1997). The eyes have it: Minority influence in face-to-face and computer-mediated group discussion. *Journal of Applied Psychology, 82*, 706–718.

*Mejias, R. J. (2007). The interaction of process losses, process gains, and meeting satisfaction within technology-supported environments. *Small Group Research, 38*, 156–194.

*Metiu, A. (2006). Owning the code: Status closure in distributed groups. *Organization Science, 17*, 418–435.

*Montoya-Weiss, M. M., Massey, A. P., & Song, M. (2001). Getting it together: Temporal coordination and conflict management in global virtual teams. *Academy of Management Journal, 44*, 1251–1262.

*Morris, S. A., Marshall, T. E., & Rainer, R. K., Jr. (2002). Impact of user satisfaction and trust on virtual team members. *Information Resources Management Journal, 15*, 22–30.

*Mortensen, M., & Hinds, P. J. (2001). Conflict and shared identity in geographically distributed teams. *International Journal of Conflict Management, 12*, 212–238.

*Munkvold, B. E., & Zigurs, I. (2007). Process and technology challenges in swift-starting virtual teams. *Information & Management, 44*, 287–299.

*Murthy, U. S., & Kerr, D. S. (2002). Decision making performance of interacting groups: An experimental investigation of the effects of task type and communication mode. *Information & Management, 40*, 351–360.

*Murthy, U. S., & Kerr, D. S. (2004). Comparing audit team effectiveness via alternative modes of computer-mediated communication. *Auditing: A Journal of Practice & Theory, 23*, 141–152.

*Nemiro, J. E. (2002). The creative process in virtual teams. *Creativity Research Journal, 14*, 69–83.

*Nowak, K. L. (2003). Sex categorization in computer mediated communication (CMC): Exploring the utopian promise. *Media Psychology, 5*, 83–103.

*Ocker, R. J. (2005). Influences on creativity in asynchronous virtual teams: A qualitative analysis of experimental teams. *IEEE Transactions on Professional Communication, 48*, 22–39.

*Ocker, R. J. (2007). A balancing act: The interplay of status effects on dominance in virtual teams. *IEEE Transactions on Professional Communication, 50*, 204–218.

O'Hara-Devereaux, M., & Johansen, B. (1994). *Global work: Bridging distance, culture, and time.* San Francisco: Jossey-Bass

O'Leary, M. B., & Cummings, J. N. (2007). The spatial, temporal, and configurational characteristics of geographic dispersion in teams. *MIS Quarterly, 31,* 433–452.

Oyserman, D., Coon, H. M., & Kemmelmeier, M. (2002). Rethinking individualism and collectivism: Evaluation of theoretical assumptions and meta-analysis. *Psychological Bulletin, 128,* 3–72.

*Palomares, N. A. (2004). Gender schematicity, gender identity salience, and gender-linked language use. *Human Communication Research, 30,* 556–588.

*Panteli, N., & Davison, R. M. (2005). The role of subgroups in the communication patterns of global virtual teams. *IEEE Transactions on Professional Communication, 48,* 191–200.

*Paul, D. L., & McDaniel, R. R., Jr. (2004). A field study of the effect of interpersonal trust on virtual collaborative relationship performance. *MIS Quarterly, 28,* 183–227.

*Paul, S., Samarah, I. M., Seetharaman, P., & Mykytyn, P. P., Jr. (2005). An empirical investigation of collaborative conflict management style in group support system-based global virtual teams. *Journal of Management Information Systems, 21,* 185–222.

*Paul, S., Seetharaman, P., Samarah, I., & Mykytyn, P. P. (2004). Impact of heterogeneity and collaborative conflict management style on the performance of synchronous global virtual teams. *Information & Management, 41,* 303–321.

*Pauleen, D. J. (2004). An inductively derived model leader-initiated relationship building with virtual team members. *Journal of Management Information Systems, 20,* 227–256.

*Pauleen, D. J., & Yoong, P. (2001). Facilitating virtual team relationships via Internet and conventional communication channels. *Internet Research, 11,* 190–202.

*Pena, J., Walther, J. B., & Hancock, J. T. (2007). Effects of geographic distribution on dominance perceptions in computer-mediated communication. *Communication Research, 34,* 313–331.

*Pensendorfer, E. M., & Koeszegi, S. T. (2006). Hot versus cool behavioural styles in electronic negotiations: The impact of communication mode. *Group Decision & Negotiations, 15,* 141–155.

*Piccoli, G., & Ives, B. (2003). Trust and the unintended effects of behavior control in virtual teams. *MIS Quarterly, 27,* 365–395.

*Polzer, J. T., Crisp, C. B., Jarvenpaa, S. L., & Kim, J. W. (2006). Extending the faultline model to geographically dispersed teams: How collocated subgroups can impair group functioning. *Academy of Management Journal, 49,* 679–692.

*Poole, M. S., Holmes, M., & DeSanctis, G. (1991). Conflict management in a computer-supported meeting environment. *Management Science, 37,* 926–953.

*Potter, R. E., & Balthazard, P. A. (2002). Understanding human interaction and performance in the virtual team. *Journal of Information Technology Theory and Application, 4,* 1–23.

*Qureshi, S., Liu, M., & Vogel, D. (2006). The effects of electronic collaboration in distributed project management. *Group Decision and Negotiation, 15,* 55–75.

*Rafaeli, S., & Ravid, G. (2003). Information sharing as enabler for the virtual team: An experimental approach to assessing the role of electronic mail in disintermediation. *Information Systems Journal, 13,* 191–206.

*Rains, S. A. (2005). Leveling the organizational playing field—virtually: A meta-analysis of experimental research assessing the impact of group support system use on member influence behaviors. *Communication Research, 32,* 193–234.

*Rains, S. A. (2007). The impact of anonymity on perceptions of source credibility and influence in computer-mediated group communication: A test of two competing hypotheses. *Communication Research, 34,* 100–125.

*Rasters, G., Vissers, G., & Dankbaar, B. (2002). An inside look: Rich communication through lean media in a virtual research team. *Small Group Research, 33,* 718–754.

*Ratcheva, V., & Vyakarnam, S. (2001). Exploring team formation processes in virtual partnerships. *Integrated Manufacturing Systems, 12,* 512–523.

*Reid, D. J., & Reid, F. J. M. (2005). Online focus groups: An in-depth comparison of computer-mediated and conventional focus group discussions. *International Journal of Market Research, 47,* 131–162.

*Reinig, B. A., & Mejias, R. J. (2004). The effects of national culture and anonymity on flaming and criticalness in GSS-supported discussions. *Small Group Research, 35,* 698–723.

*Roch, S. G., & Ayman, R. (2005). Group decision making and perceived decision success: The role of communication medium. *Group Dynamics: Theory, Research, and Practice, 9,* 15–31.

*Rutkowski, A. F., Saunders, C., Vogel, D., & van Genuchten, M. (2007). "Is it already 4 a.m. in your time zone?" Focus immersion and temporal disassociation in virtual teams. *Small Group Research, 38,* 98–129.

* Saphiere, D. M. H. (1996). Productive behaviors of global business teams. *International Journal of Intercultural Relations, 20,* 227–259.

*Sarker, S., Sarker, S., Nicholson, D. B., & Joshi, K. D. (2005). Knowledge transfer in virtual systems development teams: An exploratory study of four key enablers. *IEEE Transactions on Professional Communication, 48,* 201–218.

*Sarker, S., Valacich, J. S., & Sarker, S. (2003). Virtual team trust: Instrument development and validation in an IS educational environment. *Information Resources Management Journal, 16,* 35–55.

*Sassenberg, K., & Boos, M. (2003). Attitude change in computer-mediated communication: Effects of anonymity and category norms. *Group Process & Intergroup Relations, 6,* 405–422.

*Saunders, C. S., & Ahuja, M. K. (2006). Are all distributed teams the same? Differentiating between temporary and ongoing distributed teams. *Small Group Research, 37,* 662–700.

*Savicki, V., Kelley, M., & Lingenfelter, D. (1996). Gender and group composition in small task groups using computer-mediated communication. *Computers in Human Behavior, 12,* 209–224.

Schiller, S. Z., & Mandviwalla, M. (2007). Virtual team research: An analysis of theory use and a framework for theory appropriation. *Small Group Research, 38,* 12–59.

*Schmidt, J. B., Montoya-Weiss, M. M., & Massey, A. P. (2001). New product development decision-making effectiveness: Comparing individuals, face-to-face teams, and virtual teams. *Decision Sciences, 32,* 575–600.

Shachaf, P., & Hara, N. (2007). Behavioral complexity theory of media selection: A proposed theory for global virtual teams. *Journal of Information Science, 33,* 63–75.

*Sharifi, S., & Pawar, K. S. (2002). Virtually co-located product design teams: Sharing teaming experiences after the event? *International Journal of Operations & Production Management, 22,* 656–679.

*Shepherd, M. M., Briggs, R. O., Reinig, B. A., Yen, J., & Nunamaker, J. F., Jr. (1996). Invoking social comparison to improve electronic brainstorming: Beyond anonymity. *Journal of Management Information Systems, 12,* 155–170.

Shim, J. P., Warkentin, M., Courtney, J. F., Power, D. J., Sharda, R., & Carlsson, C. (2002). Past, present, and future of decision support technology. *Decision Support Systems, 33,* 111–126.

Shin, Y. (2004). A person-environment fit model for virtual organizations. *Journal of Management, 30,* 725–743.

*Siegel, J., Dubrovsky,V., Kiesler, S., & McGuire, T. (1986). Group processes in computer-mediated communication. *Organizational Behavior and Human Decision Processes, 37,* 157–187.

*Simon, A. F. (2006). Computer-mediated communication: Task performance and satisfaction. *The Journal of Social Psychology, 146,* 349–379.

*Sivunen, A. (2006). Strengthening identification with the team in virtual teams: The leaders' perspective. *Group Decision and Negotiation, 15,* 345–366.

*Sole, D., & Edmondson, A. (2002). Situated knowledge and learning in dispersed team. *British Journal of Management, 13,* 17–34.

*Sosik, J. J., Avolio, B. J., & Kahai, S. S. (1998). Inspiring group creativity: Comparing anonymous and identified electronic brainstorming. *Small Group Research, 29,* 3–31.

*Spears, R., Lea, M., & Lee, S. (1990). De-individuation and group polarization in computer-mediated communication. *British Journal of Social Psychology, 29,* 121–134.

*Sproull, L., & Kiesler, S. (1986). Reducing social context cues: Electronic mail in organizational communication. *Management Science, 32,* 1492–1512.

Stanko, T. L., & Gibson, C. B. (2009). The role of cultural elements in virtual teams. In R. S. Bhagat & R. M. Steers (Eds.), *Cambridge handbook of culture, organization, and work* (pp. 272–304). Cambridge: Cambridge University Press.

*Stanton, N. A., Ashleigh, M. J., Roberts, A. D., & Xu, F. (2003). Virtuality in human supervisory control: Assessing the effects of psychological and social remoteness. *Ergonomics, 46,* 1215–1232.

*Staples, D. S., & Webster, J. (2007). Exploring traditional and virtual team members' "best practices": A social cognitive theory perspective. *Small Group Research, 38,* 60–97.

*Staples, D. S., & Zhao, L. (2006). The effects of cultural diversity in virtual teams versus face-to-face teams. *Group Decision and Negotiation, 15,* 389–406.

*Stewart, K. J., & Gosain, S. (2006). The impact of ideology on effectiveness in open source software development teams. *MIS Quarterly, 30,* 291–314.

*Straus, S. G. (1996). Getting a clue: The effects of communication media and information distribution on participation and performance in computer-mediated and face-to-face groups. *Small Group Research, 27,* 115–142.

*Straus, S. G., & McGrath, J. E. (1994). Does the medium matter? The interaction of task type and technology on group performance and member reactions. *Journal of Applied Psychology, 79,* 87–97.

*Strijbos, J. W., Martens, R. L., Jochems, W. M. G., & Broers, N. J. (2004). The effect of functional roles on group efficiency: Using multilevel modeling and content analysis to investigate computer-supported collaboration in small groups. *Small Group Research, 35,* 195–229.

*Suchan, J., & Hayzak, G. (2001). The communication characteristics of virtual teams: A case study. *IEEE Transactions on Professional Communication, 44,* 174–186.

*Swigger, K., Alpaslan, F., Brazile, R., & Monticino, M. (2004). Effects of culture on computer-supported international collaborations. *International Journal of Human-Computer Studies, 60,* 365–380.

*Tan, B. C. Y., Wei, K., Huang, W. W., & Ng, G. N. (2000). A dialogue technique to enhance electronic communication in virtual teams. *IEEE Transactions on Professional Communication, 43,* 153–165.

*Tan, B. C. Y., Wei, K., Watson, R. T., Clapper, D. L., & McLean, E. R. (1998). Computer-mediated communication and majority influence: Assessing the impact in an individualistic and collectivistic culture. *Management Science, 44,* 1263–1278.

*Tanis, M., & Postmes, T. (2003). Social cues and impression formation in CMC. *Journal of Communication, 53,* 676–693.

*Thompson, L. F., & Coovert, M. D. (2002). Stepping up to the challenge: A critical examination of face-to-face and computer-mediated team decision making. *Group Dynamics: Theory, Research, and Practice, 6,* 52–64.

*Thompson, L. F., & Coovert, M. D. (2003). Teamwork online: The effects of computer conferencing on perceived confusion, satisfaction, and post-discussion accuracy. *Group Dynamics: Theory, Research, and Practice, 7,* 135–151.

*Tidwell, L. C., & Walther, J. B. (2002). Computer-mediated communication effects on disclosure, impressions, and interpersonal evaluations: Getting to know one another a bit at a time. *Human Communication Research, 28,* 317–348.

*Timmerman, C. E., & Scott, C. R. (2006). Virtually working: Communicative and structural predictors of media use and key outcomes in virtual work teams. *Communication Monographs, 73,* 108–136.

Tuckman, B. W. (1965). Development sequence in small groups. *Psychological Bulletin, 63,* 384–399.

*Valacich, J. S., Dennis, A. R., & Connolly, T. (1994). Idea generation in computer-based groups: A new ending to an old story. *Organizational Behavior and Human Decision Processes, 57,* 448–467.

*Valacich, J. S., Dennis, A. R., & Nunamaker, J. F., Jr. (1992). Group size and anonymity effects on computer-mediated idea generation. *Small Group Research, 23,* 49–73.

*Valacich, J. S., George, J. F., Nunamaker, J. F., Jr., & Vogel, D. R. (1994). Physical proximity effects on computer-mediated group idea generation. *Small Group Research, 25,* 83–104.

*Valacich, J. S., & Schwenk, C. (1995). Devil's advocacy and dialectical inquiry effects on face-to-face and computer mediated group decision making. *Organizational Behavior and Human Decision Processes, 63,* 158–173.

*Van den Bossche, P., Gijselaers, W. H., Segers, M., & Kirschner, P. A. (2006). Social and cognitive factors driving teamwork in collaborative learning environments: Team learning beliefs and behaviors. *Small Group Research, 37,* 490–521.

*Walther, J. B. (1994). Anticipated ongoing interaction versus channel effects on relational communication in computer-mediated interaction. *Human Communication Research, 20,* 473–501.

*Walther, J. B. (1995). Relational aspects of computer-mediated communication: Experimental observations over time. *Organization Science, 6,* 186–203.

*Walther, J. B. (1997). Group and interpersonal effects in international computer-mediated collaboration. *Human Communication Research, 23*, 342–369.

*Walther, J. B., & Bazarova, N. N. (2007). Misattribution in virtual groups: The effects of member distribution on self-serving bias and partner blame. *Human Communication Research, 33*, 1–26.

*Walther, J. B., & Bunz, U. (2005). The rules of virtual groups: Trust, liking, and performance in computer-mediated communication. *Journal of Communication, 55*, 828–846.

*Walther, J. B., & Burgoon, J. K. (1992). Relational communication in computer-mediated interaction. *Human Communication Research, 19*, 50–88.

*Walther, J. B., Slovacek, C. L., & Tidwell, L. C. (2001). Is a picture worth a thousand words? Photographic images in long-term and short-term computer-mediated communication. *Communication Research, 28*, 105–134.

*Warkentin, M. E., & Beranek, P. M. (1999). Training to improve virtual team communication. *Information Systems Journal, 9*, 271–289.

*Warkentin, M. E., Sayeed, L., & Hightower, R. (1997). Virtual teams versus face-to-face teams: An exploratory study of a web-based conference system. *Decision Sciences, 28*, 975–996.

*Watson, R. T., DeSanctis, G., & Poole, M. S. (1988). Using a GDSS to facilitate group consensus: Some intended and unintended consequences. *MIS Quarterly, 12*, 463–480.

*Watson-Manheim, M. B., & Belanger, F. (2007). Communication media repertoires: Dealing with the multiplicity of media choices. *MIS Quarterly, 31*, 267–293.

*Weisband, S. P. (1992). Group discussion and first advocacy effects in computer-mediated and face-to-face decision making groups. *Organizational Behavior and Human Decision Processes, 53*, 352–380.

*Weisband, S. P., & Atwater, L. (1999). Evaluating self and others in electronic and face-to-face groups. *Journal of Applied Psychology, 84*, 632–639.

*Weisband, S. P., Schneider, S. K., & Connolly, T. (1995). Computer-mediated communication and social information: Status salience and status differences. *Academy of Management Journal, 38*, 1124–1151.

*Workman, M. (2005). Virtual team culture and the amplification of team boundary permeability on performance. *Human Resource Development Quarterly, 16*, 435–458.

*Workman, M., Kahnweiler, W., & Bommer, W. (2003). The effects of cognitive style and media richness on commitment to telework and virtual teams. *Journal of Vocational Behavior, 63*, 199–219.

*Yoo, Y., & Kanawattanachai, P. (2001). Developments of transactive memory systems and collective mind in virtual teams. *International Journal of Organizational Analysis, 9*, 187–208.

*Zack, M. H., & McKenney, J. L. (1995). Social context and interaction in ongoing computer-supported management groups. *Organization Science, 6*, 394–422.

*Zhang, D., Lowry, B. J., Zhou, L., & Fu, X. (2007). The impact of individualism-collectivism, social presence, and group diversity on group decision making under majority influence. *Journal of Management Information Systems, 23*, 53–80.

*Zhou, L., & Zhang, D. (2006). A comparison of deception behavior in dyad and triadic group decision making in synchronous computer-mediated communication. *Small Group Research, 37*, 140–164.

*Zhou, L., & Zhang, D. (2007). Typing or messaging? Modality effect on deception detection in computer-mediated communication. *Decision Support Systems, 44*, 188–201.

*Zigurs, I., Poole, M. S., & DeSanctis, G. L. (1988). A study of influence in computer-mediated group decision making. *MIS Quarterly, 12*, 625–644.

*Indicates article/chapter included in review

Team Learning: A Theoretical Integration and Review

Bradford S. Bell, Steve W. J. Kozlowski, *and* Sabrina Blawath

Abstract

With the increasing emphasis on work teams as the primary architecture of organizational structure, scholars have begun to focus attention on team learning, the processes that support it, and the important outcomes that depend on it. Although the literature addressing learning in teams is broad, it is also messy and fraught with conceptual confusion. This chapter presents a theoretical integration and review. The goal is to organize theory and research on team learning, identify actionable frameworks and findings, and emphasize promising targets for future research. We emphasize three theoretical foci in our examination of team learning, treating it as multilevel (individual *and* team, not individual *or* team), dynamic (iterative and progressive; a *process* not an *outcome*), and emergent (outcomes of team learning can manifest in different ways over time). The integrative theoretical heuristic distinguishes team learning process theories, supporting emergent states, team knowledge representations, and respective influences on team performance and effectiveness. Promising directions for theory development and research are discussed.

Key Words: team learning, team action regulation, group information processing, collective knowledge, macrocognition

Over two decades have passed since Senge (1990) proclaimed that teams, not individuals, are the fundamental learning unit in modern organizations. During this time, there has been an ongoing shift from work organized around individual jobs to team-based work systems (Devine, Clayton, Phillips, Dunford, & Melner, 1999; Lawler, Mohrman, & Ledford, 1995). This transformation in organizational work structures has occurred as organizations have increasingly turned to teams as a means of addressing a variety of emerging pressures and challenges. Teams bring together the diverse skills, expertise, and experience needed to tackle increasingly complex and dynamic organizational problems. They enable more rapid and flexible responses to the technological, economic, and political pressures faced by modern organizations. In addition, teams facilitate collaboration and knowledge sharing across organizational, cultural, and spatio-temporal boundaries.

The emergence of teams as the basic building blocks of organizations has been accompanied by growing interest in the topic of team learning. As teams have grown more central to organizational functioning, there has been a natural interest in understanding the factors that influence team effectiveness (Ilgen, Hollenbeck, Johnson, & Jundt, 2005; Kozlowski & Bell, 2003; Kozlowski & Ilgen, 2006). Team learning has been identified as an important mechanism through which teams develop their performance capabilities, adapt to changes in their environment, and renew and sustain their performance over time. In addition, interest in team learning has been driven by its important role in organizational learning. Research has begun to identify the conditions under which team learning translates into organizational learning (Edmondson, 2002) and has examined the impact of factors within the team environment on learning behavior within organizations. Overall, the growing literature in this area has established support for Senge's claim that teams represent the nexus of learning in modern organizations.

Although we have gained significant insight into team learning over the past two decades, research in this area has been plagued by conceptual ambiguities and the absence of a coherent theoretical framework. Wilson, Goodman, and Cronin (2007), for example, recently highlighted inconsistencies in the conceptualization of team learning across studies and "the disjointed treatment of this fundamental construct" (p. 1054). Similarly, Edmondson, Dillon, and Roloff (2007) argued that research on team learning falls into three distinct bodies of work that address different fundamental questions and offer different conceptualizations of the construct. In addition to these inconsistencies, prior research has not been clear about issues concerning levels of analysis, the processes that underlie team learning, or the distinction between team learning and team performance (Kozlowski & Ilgen, 2006; Wilson et al., 2007). Although examining team learning from different perspectives and research traditions may be generative (Edmondson et al., 2007), there is also agreement that greater consistency and clarity around the constructs and measures used in team learning research are needed to systematically advance knowledge in this area.

Our goal in the current chapter is to provide a review and integration of the research that has been conducted on team learning over the past two decades. We seek to illuminate what we know about the process of team learning, the outcomes of this process, and the factors that shape it. In particular, our review makes a clear distinction between team learning *processes,* and the knowledge and other emergent states that result from the process, which ultimately shape team effectiveness.

Review Structure and Focus

Given the different conceptualizations of team learning that have been introduced in the literature and the divergent perspectives that have been used to explore the construct, it is important to clarify the scope and structure of our review. Our purpose is to review the literature that has examined the learning, development, and adaptation of teams, which

have been defined by Kozlowski and Bell (2003, p. 334) as:

> two or more individuals who (a) exist to perform organizationally relevant tasks, (b) share one more common goals, (c) interact socially, (d) exhibit task interdependencies (i.e., work flow, goals, outcomes), (e) maintain and manage boundaries, and (f) are embedded in an organizational context that sets boundaries, constrains the team, and influences exchanges with other units in the broader entity.

Although we adopt a multilevel perspective of team learning and acknowledge its connections with individual and organizational learning, our focus is on teams; we do not review work specifically focused on the role of team learning in organizational learning, nor do we discuss research that has examined individual learning in the context of groups (e.g., collaborative learning) or the individual characteristics that may influence team learning and adaptation (e.g., Ployhart & Bliese, 2006; Pulakos, Arad, Donovan, & Plamondon, 2000). Likewise, we review a variety of team processes, emergent states, and outcomes in this chapter, but our focus is on how these mechanisms and outcomes relate to team learning; we do not intend to provide a comprehensive review of the team effectiveness literature.

The theoretical heuristic presented in Figure 26.1 provides an overview of the structure and focus of our review. In the following section, we begin by discussing the theoretical considerations that form the foundation of our perspective on team learning. These considerations emphasize the multilevel, emergent, and dynamic nature of team learning, and we use these foci to guide our analysis of the team learning literature. The core of our review examines three models—goal and action regulation, information processing, and macrocognition—that have been used to examine the processes involved in team learning. Each of these models offers a distinct conceptual lens through which to understand the theoretical "engine" of team learning. We then review research that has examined emergent states, such as psychological safety and team efficacy, which support and enable team learning. Our review highlights the dynamic relationship that exists between these states and team learning processes; they are reciprocally entwined and emergent. Finally, we discuss research that has examined the outcomes of team learning, including collective knowledge, shared cognition (e.g., transactive memory, team mental models), team knowledge emergence, and—ultimately—team performance.

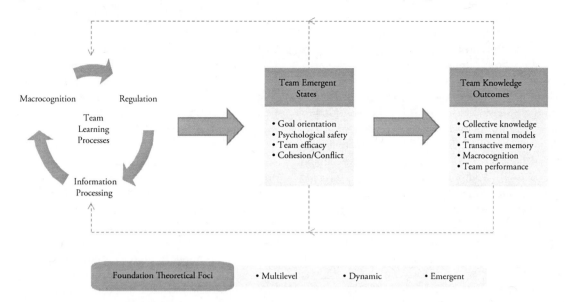

Figure 26.1 Theoretical Integration of Team Learning
© 2011 B. S. Bell & S. W. J. Kozlowski. All rights reserved worldwide. Used with permission.

Foundation Theoretical Foci

There are three primary theoretical foci that form the foundation for our perspective on team learning. We use these theoretical foci to guide the identification of material to review (i.e., models of team learning, knowledge outcomes, emergent states, and antecedents). We also use them as critical guides to help highlight where we have made progress and where research attention should be devoted to make advances. First, team learning is *multilevel* in nature, encompassing individual-level processes and, simultaneously, team-level processes. Second, team learning is not a fixed and static phenomenon; rather, it is a *dynamic process*. Third, team learning is *emergent*. It is not purely "holistic." It does not just magically manifest as a collective property; it develops, evolves, and emerges over time at the team level. Although these primary considerations are obviously intertwined, there are key aspects of each that merit highlighting.

TEAM LEARNING IS MULTILEVEL

Learning is a process of acquiring knowledge, skill, attitudes, or other characteristics that change the potential for behavior (Ford & Kraiger, 1995). It is axiomatic that learning is a psychological phenomenon and, as such, originates within the individual as entwined cognitive, motivational-affective, and behavioral processes (Kozlowski & Bell, 2003, 2008). One of the key challenges of conceptualizing learning as a collective process is bridging the gap

between the origin of learning as a psychological phenomenon and its manifestation in the higher level entity.

Some approaches simply extrapolate from our knowledge of learning as a psychological phenomenon, and assert a parallel process that exists at the team or collective level (e.g., Hinsz, Tindale, & Vollrath, 1997; Walsh & Ungson, 1991). Sometimes, such extrapolation is based on metaphor, which is a weak form of theorizing (Pinder & Bourgeois, 1982); other times, it may be based on a more formal analogy, but this too, though useful, is not the strongest foundation for theory. Sometimes, such extrapolations are characterized as holistic, unique, and indivisible systems. The argument is made that any attempt to decompose the collective phenomenon risks reductionism and should be avoided (von Bertalanffy, 1972). However, we view argument by mere metaphor or analogy as conceptually vague and the holism of general systems thinking to be overstated. The challenge is not to be reductionist, assuming that learning can only be psychological, while also eschewing holism, assuming that systems cannot be meaningfully decomposed (Simon, 1973). The challenge is to conceptualize team learning in a way that encompasses both levels—individual and team—simultaneously.

This is the province of multilevel theory. Rather than the holistic perspective of general systems theory (von Bertalanffy, 1972), multilevel theory is based on more contemporary concepts emanating from complexity theory (Kozlowski & Klein, 2000). Complexity theory is concerned with understanding how complex, system-level phenomena can emerge from the dynamic interactions of system elements. As Kozlowski (2012) notes, "The focus is on the emergence of complex system behavior, but the focus on the basic elements, entities, or agents is not reductionism. Rather, it is an effort to understand how the 'wholeness' arises without reifying it" (p. 265). From a multilevel theory perspective, team learning is not just about individuals learning together or a team learning as a holistic and indivisible entity, it is about the interplay between and within the levels: the way that the team context influences and shapes individual learning and the way that learning simultaneously forms, evolves, and emerges at the team level—not either/or, but both.

TEAM LEARNING IS DYNAMIC

Learning is a complex process that also encompasses motivation and performance. Learning, motivation, and performance are entwined. As a process, it is axiomatic that learning is dynamic and there are two key dynamic aspects that merit discussion: (a) the process is iterative, and (b) it evidences developmental progression.

First, it is a near-universal assumption across learning theories that the process is cyclical and iterative. Classical conditioning, operant theory, subjective expected utility theory (and its variants, like valence-instrumentality-expectancy theory), and self-regulation theory (and its variants of control theory and social-cognitive theory), among others, all incorporate feedback loops that have implications for subsequent cycles of iteration. For example, a simple regulation heuristic asserts a goal—a desired performance standard—as an energizer of the system. The goal, possibly guided by a strategy, serves to direct effort toward goal accomplishment. Some level of performance results, and feedback is compared to the goal standard. Unless the goal is exceptionally simple, performance is typically below standard. Perceptions of progress (e.g., satisfaction) and capability (e.g., efficacy), among other factors, influence subsequent effort and/or strategy modification. If progress and capability are adequate, effort is maintained or increased, whereas if progress or capability is inadequate, effort and attention are withdrawn. This cyclic dynamic has rather obvious implications for learning. Kozlowski and Bell (2008) characterize the interconnected iterative cycles of individual and team regulation as the theoretical "engine" of team learning.

Second, learning processes entail a developmental progression. One has to learn simple basics before one can master more complex material. This dynamic progression is another near-universal aspect of learning and skill acquisition theory (e.g., Anderson, 1987; Fitts and Posner, 1967; Ford & Kraiger, 1995). For example, as shown in Figure 26.2, Kozlowski and Bell (2007) formulated a progressive model of knowledge compilation. The model sequences from basic to more advanced knowledge (i.e., facts → conditional rules → synthesis → generalization). More important, it integrates qualitatively different learning processes to the progressive phases of knowledge compilation. Learning processes for basic knowledge acquisition entail rehearsal and memorization; advanced knowledge compilation necessitates exploration,

Basic	**Knowledge and Skill Complexity**		*Advanced*

Knowledge Type	Declarative Knowledge [DATA]	Procedural Knowledge & Skill [INFORMATION]	Strategic Knowledge & Skill [KNOWLEDGE]	Adaptive Knowledge & Skill [ADAPTATION]
Knowledge Capability	Facts, concepts, rules; Definition, meaning (*What?*)	Contexualized rule application; Conditional if-then rules (*How?*)	Synthesis; Task contingencies; Selective resource allocation (*When, Where, Why?*)	Generalization of task rules, principles, & contingencies to new situations (*What now, What next?*)

Figure 26.2 Knowledge Compilation

Adapted with permission from Kozlowski, S. W. J., & Bell. B. S. (2007). A theory-based approach for designing distributed learning systems. In S. M. Fiore & E. Salas (Eds.), *Where is the learning in distance learning? Toward a science of distributed learning and training* (pp. 15–39). Washington, DC: APA Books. © 2002, 2010 S. W. J. Kozlowski and B. S. Bell. All rights reserved worldwide. Adapted with permission.

variability, and reflection. The authors assert, "The acquisition of basic knowledge necessitates encoding and is memory intensive, whereas advanced knowledge and skill acquisition require higher-level self-regulatory and metacognitive processes with an emphasis on integrating cognitive and behavioral skill" (p. 21). The key points that we advance are that learning as a dynamic process cycles and iterates, and the nature of learning as a process progressively evolves as knowledge and skills compile.

TEAM LEARNING IS EMERGENT

In a team context, individuals engage in a domain, learn, and acquire progressively more complex knowledge and skill. However, they do not learn in a social vacuum. They are both influenced by and influence the learning processes of their teammates. Individual learning shapes and is shaped by team learning as an emergent phenomenon. "A phenomenon is emergent when it originates in the cognition, affect, behaviors, or other characteristics of individuals, is amplified by their interactions, and manifests as a higher-level, collective phenomenon" (Kozlowski & Klein, 2000, p. 55).

Teams learn as members exchange ideas, information, and insights, building collaborative knowledge. The process is shaped by the formal workflow structure that necessitates the sharing of relevant information and by informal social exchange as members negotiate their roles. Teams learn as the knowledge acquired via individual learning is shared, exchanged, and transmitted. Collaborative learning and the knowledge acquired shapes subsequent individual learning. Team learning is emergent (Kozlowski & Bell, 2008; Kozlowski & Chao, 2012). Team knowledge that emerges via dynamic team learning processes can manifest as qualitatively different types, composition, or compilation, which represent opposing poles of a continuum of emergence (Kozlowski & Klein, 2000). Composition constructs emerge via linear, convergent processes, and compilation forms emerge via divergent, configural, or patterned processes.

Composition types of emergence apply to phenomena that manifest through convergent processes by which essentially the same content becomes held or shared across all team members. Composition constructs are isomorphic, in that it is essentially the same construct at the individual and team levels of analysis. The content is the same, the structure is the same, but the referent—individual or team—is different. Composition constructs are structurally equivalent (i.e., identical elemental content) and functionally equivalent (i.e., assume the same role in a model) at both levels of analysis (Kozlowski & Klein, 2000; Morgeson & Hofmann, 1999). For example, in terms of team knowledge developed through team learning, theorists have speculated that teams acquire shared mental models of the team, task, equipment, and pattern of exchange that allow team members to coordinate implicitly (Cannon-Bowers, Salas, & Converse, 1993). Shared mental models emerge as composition constructs.

Compilation types of emergence apply to phenomenon that manifest through divergent processes by which diverse content is combined across team members to form a configuration or pattern. One can liken this configuration to puzzle pieces or to the nodes and links of a network. The unique content fits together to form a meaningful whole. Compilation constructs are functionally, but not structurally, equivalent across levels (Kozlowski & Klein, 2000; Morgeson & Hofmann, 1999). Thus, for example, theorists have postulated that teams can create a networked memory system—transactive memory—in which distinct knowledge and expertise can be accessed by the team. Team members possess knowledge of each member's unique expertise that enables the team to collectively access knowledge as needed (Mohammed & Dumville, 2001). Transactive memory emerges as a compilation construct in which the pattern of individual team member knowledge comprises the structure of team memory.

Team Learning Process Models

As we noted in the previous section, team learning processes are multilevel, dynamic, and emergent. In addition, learning is a fundamental human experience—whether we learn as individuals or as co-acting members of small groups—that is inextricably entwined with the fundamentals of motivation and performance. The models that we review in this section emphasize some of these aspects more than others. However, in our view, all of the approaches are consistent with our theoretical foci and provide insights into a useful conceptualization of team learning processes. The models that we examine include models of goal and action regulation, information processing, and macrocognition. Finally, we should note that this section is by no means intended to capture every possible model that has ever been used in an effort to understand team learning processes. Rather, we have focused our review on those models with a stream of systematic theory development, supportive empirical findings, and/or emerging theory that promises new insights and research opportunities.

Regulation Models
OVERVIEW

Regulatory models are dynamic in that they are cyclical and iterative. At the individual level, regulatory models are the dominant models of learning, motivation, and performance (Kanfer, Chen, & Pritchard, 2008; Karoly, 1993). There have been several notable extensions to the team level that we review in the material that follows in this section. One important issue to recognize about these models is that there are several key components of the regulatory process—goals, goal commitment, strategies, effort, performance, feedback, comparison, and reactions—and different models tend to emphasize some components of the process to a greater extent than others. Obviously, more inclusive models are likely to be more useful. A second, and related, issue is that while there is a substantial amount of heuristic-level commonality among the models, there are some important theoretical distinctions that result from the different emphases of the models. Although these differences have resulted in vigorous conceptual disagreements in individual-level research (i.e., Bandura & Locke, 2003; Vancouver, 2005), these points have not permeated team-level research (at least, not yet).

At the highest heuristic level, Kanfer (1990) has distinguished between *goal setting* and *goal striving* processes. Models that emphasize goal setting tend to focus on goal choice (i.e., level of goal difficulty), the nature of goals (e.g., goal content oriented toward learning vs. performance), and goal acceptance (i.e., commitment). Models that emphasize goal striving focus more on action regulation and the cyclical dynamics as one reacts to goal progress, modifies effort and strategies, and further strives to attain the objective. Ultimately, both goal setting and goal striving processes are important for understanding team learning. From our view, an important value of the regulatory approach to team learning is that it is explicitly multilevel, dynamic, and emergent.

GROUP GOAL SETTING

Research on group goal setting represents some of the earliest efforts to apply individual motivation theory to the group level. Although these early efforts were not theoretically deep, the findings from individual-level research were by then well established by meta-analytic support (Mento, Steel, & Karren, 1987), and the early work represented simple extensions to the team level. At the individual level, the central tenets of goal setting are that goals should be difficult to achieve, specific, and accepted (Locke & Latham, 1990). Goal difficulty has an orienting property for effort, and specificity is critical for establishing a reference standard so that progress toward goal accomplishment can be monitored. It is also important that individuals commit to investing effort to accomplish the goal. Finally, although it is not a central tenet of goal-setting theory, social cognitive theory (Bandura, 1991) places considerable emphasis on the agency provided by self-perceptions of efficacy to support effort investment and task persistence. Some early pioneering research extended the social cognitive framework to the team level of analysis (Prussia & Kinicki, 1996). However, the most influential aspect of social cognitive theory with respect to team learning has been the considerable work on the concept of collective efficacy, as we shall describe in a subsequent section that addresses *emergent states*.

An early meta-analysis of group goal-setting research (based on 26 effect sizes from 10 studies) reported that, compared to no or low group goals, group goals yielded an effect size equivalent to about a one standard deviation improvement in group performance—a substantial effect (O'Leary-Kelly, Martocchio, & Frink, 1994). Unfortunately, the pool of qualified primary studies for this early meta-analysis was too small to allow for an examination of moderators that would evaluate the central tenets of goal setting (and other moderators) at the group level of analysis. Nonetheless, a qualitative assessment generally concluded that there was support for expected effects of goals at the group level.

Given that it has been over a decade and a half since this study was published, it is remarkable that it is only recently that the findings of this meta-analysis have been updated. This more recent meta-analysis, based on 30 studies with 76 independent effect sizes, concluded that there was an overall relationship of group goals with group performance ($d = 0.56 \pm 0.19$, $k = 49$) and that specific/difficult group goals were associated with higher performance than were non-specific goals ($d = 0.80 \pm 0.35$, $k = 23$) (Kleingeld, van Mierlo, & Arends, 2011). The analysis also revealed that individually oriented goals (i.e., targeted on individual performance) had a negative effect ($d = -1.75 \pm 0.60$, $k = 6$), whereas group-oriented goals (i.e., targeted on the individual's contribution to group performance) were positively related to group performance ($d = 1.20 \pm 1.03$, $k = 4$). Although these latter findings are to be expected, they are based on relatively few studies. Surprisingly, an examination of moderating effects for task interdependence, complexity, and participation were null.

Although the findings of Kleingeld et al. (2011) help to clarify the extent to which central tenets of goal setting generalize to the team level, there are additional contingencies that also need to be examined. For example, teams tend to be utilized when tasks are complex, a condition that makes team learning central and salient. At the individual level, there has been a stream of research demonstrating that learning goals (i.e., goals that target specific learning objectives) are superior to performance goals (i.e., difficult and specific performance levels) when individuals must acquire complex skills (e.g., Kozlowski & Bell, 2006; Seijts, Latham, Tasa, & Latham, 2004; Winters & Latham, 1996). Efforts to examine these contingencies on the effectiveness of goals at the team level have been relatively rare (e.g., Weingart, 1992). Similarly, it is also remarkable that there is very little research that examines the effects of individual-level and team-level feedback on individual and team performance (DeShon, Kozlowski, Schmidt, Milner, & Wiechmann, 2004). Perhaps this is because feedback does not generate much attention in goal-setting research (which tends to be static in orientation), although it is central to the dynamic, iterative, and cyclical aspects of regulation during goal striving. More recent research focused on action regulation has sought to examine a more complex and dynamic interplay among goals, strategies, feedback, and reactions across the individual and team levels of analysis.

TEAM ACTION REGULATION, LEARNING, AND PERFORMANCE

Models that focus on action-regulation processes have tended to be less concerned with the central tenets of goal setting (i.e., the characteristics of goals) and more concerned with: (a) the linkages among key components of the broader regulatory process, including goals, commitment, strategies, effort, performance, feedback, comparison, and reactions; (b) the dynamics of the process as it iterates over time; and (c) the multilevel and emergent aspects of team regulation. DeShon et al. (2004) advanced a multiple goal, multilevel model of individual and team regulation (as a parallel emergent process) in an effort to capture this complexity. Here we describe the theoretical underpinnings of their approach to model team learning and skill acquisition as a dynamic multilevel process.

Teams, of course, can be structured in a variety of different ways that have implications for the nature of the linkage between individual and team goals and performance. For example, in *additive tasks*, team performance results from a simple pooling of individual contributions such that individuals striving to accomplish their own goals are also contributing to team goal accomplishment (Steiner, 1972). This is the weakest form of team interdependence. In contrast, *discretionary tasks* entail distinct individual and team goals and an interdependent structure such that team members cannot simultaneously strive to accomplish individual and team goals. In other words, team members have considerable latitude in the extent to which they allocate personal resources to accomplish team objectives, by assisting or backing up a teammate, at the expense of their own goal striving. This is viewed as the most general type of team task structure (Steiner, 1972) and would be consistent with the interdependence structure of many types of project, research, and decision-making teams.

Such team task structures entail multiple goals—distinct individual and team goals—that team members must strive to accomplish and necessitates a more complex regulatory model that incorporates distinct goal-feedback loops governing the regulation of individual attention and resource allocation. A heuristic model, shown on the left side in Figure 26.3, illustrates the interplay of the dual goal-feedback loops that regulate individual and team resource allocation. Resources cannot be allocated to both feedback loops simultaneously and, thus, the loops vie for behavioral control. Each goal-feedback loop monitors discrepancies (i.e., comparison) between current performance and their respective goal states and activates behaviors (i.e., strategies, effort) to reduce the discrepancy. Because individual and team performance are distinct in the discretionary task structure, a choice to devote resources toward one feedback loop necessitates the withdrawal of resources devoted to the other loop. Thus, minimizing discrepancies on one loop will increase the magnitude of discrepancies on the other loop. All things being equal and assuming equivalent commitment to both goals, the self-regulation system will monitor both loops and dynamically switch control to the loop that accumulates discrepancies beyond a trigger value (Kernan & Lord, 1990). In this conceptualization, team regulation is energized by a dynamic process of

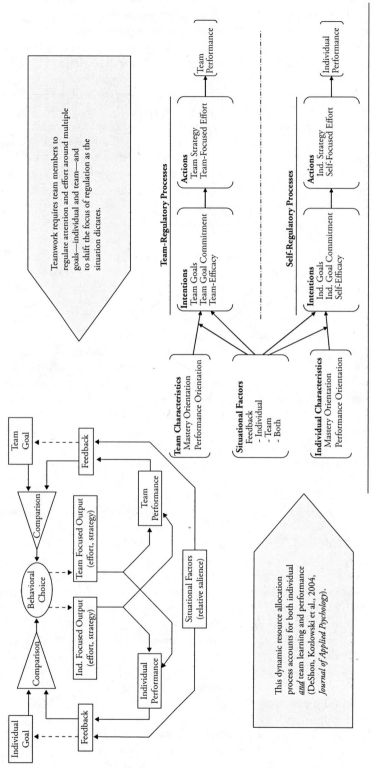

Figure 26.3 A Multiple Goal, Multilevel Model of Individual and Team Regulation

Adapted with permission from DeShon, R. P., Kozlowski, S. W. J., Schmidt, A. M., Milner, K. R., & Wiechmann, D. (2004). A multiple goal, multilevel model of feedback effects on the regulation of individual and team performance. *Journal of Applied Psychology, 89,* 1035–1056.

NOTE: Constructs above dashed line represent *team*-level constructs. Constructs below line represent *individual*-level constructs.

individual-level goal switching. Of course, the environmental context within which the team is embedded may sensitize team members to discrepancies on a particular goal-feedback loop, thereby creating an allocation bias of regulatory resources to either the individual or team-level goal.

DeShon et al. (2004) put the dual goal-feedback loop model into action and extrapolated the implications of the dynamic goal-switching process for the emergence of a homologous multilevel model that represented parallel individual and team regulatory processes, illustrated on the right side in Figure 26.3. Kozlowski and Klein (2000) have indicated that validating a multilevel homology necessitates: (a) conceptually parallel individual and team constructs that meet composition criteria for representation at the team level, and (b) functionally equivalent relations linking the parallel constructs at both levels of analysis. Experimental data in which feedback was manipulated to influence the relative salience of the dual feedback loops (i.e., individual feedback, team feedback, or both) provided support for the homologous multilevel model and, by inference, the underlying dynamic multiple goal heuristic. Thus, the processes of action regulation responsible for individual resource allocation, learning, and performance also emerge and substantially hold at the team level, making multilevel regulation a very basic and useful team learning process

model—one that is consistent with our theoretical foci of multilevel, dynamic, and emergent.

Whereas DeShon et al. (2004) focused on multilevel regulation during learning and skill acquisition, Chen, Thomas, and Wallace (2005) focused on multilevel regulation processes at the end of training as a mediator of the relationship between roughly parallel training outcomes at the individual and team levels (i.e., knowledge, skill, and efficacy) and adaptive performance (i.e., an additional performance trial that involved greater component complexity or difficulty relative to prior training). The focus is still on learning, although with emphasis on generalization of skill. As shown in Figure 26.4, their conceptual model represents a synthesis between Kanfer's (1990) heuristic of goal choice and goal striving phases of *self*-regulation, coupled with a parallel distinction made by Marks, Mathieu, and Zaccaro (2001) between *team* transition processes (e.g., goal and strategy selection) and *team* action processes (e.g., monitoring progress toward goals, coordinating effort, correcting errors). Although the model was not posited as a strict multilevel homology, in part due to measurement differences in parallel constructs across levels, aspects of the framework were intended to be conceptually parallel. The results were complex, but in general indicated that viewing regulation as a multilevel process was a useful way to represent the process of skill generalization at the individual and team levels.

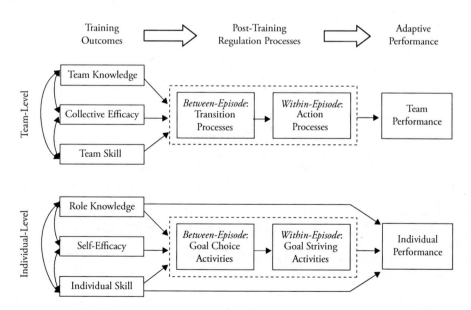

Figure 26.4 A Multilevel Model of Training Outcomes and Post-training Adaptive Performance Reprinted with permission from Chen, G., Thomas, B., & Wallace, J. C. (2005). A multilevel examination of the relationships among training outcomes, mediating regulatory processes, and adaptive performance. *Journal of Applied Psychology, 90*, 827–841.

Both prior models of individual and team action regulation focused on the multilevel character of the process as team members strive to accomplish individual and team objectives. The emphasis is on a dynamic interplay across the levels with respect to parallelism in constructs and processes. We do not mean to minimize this contribution because we think it is vitally important as a fundamental approach to conceptualizing team learning. However, only so much can be accomplished in any one study, and in focusing on the parallelism inherent in multilevel models, the prior research has neglected the cross-level linkages that also bind individual and team regulation. From a cross-level perspective, team phenomena—once they have emerged—serve to shape and constrain subsequent individual level phenomena. Process begets structure which constrains subsequent processes (Katz & Kahn, 1966; Kozlowski & Klein, 2000).

Building on this perspective, Chen and Kanfer (2006) posited a theoretical model of motivation in teams that places emphasis on this cross-level interplay. Research by Chen, Kanfer, DeShon, Mathieu, and Kozlowski (2009) evaluated that model and extended it by also focusing on the dynamics of these cross-level regulatory relations. The study reanalyzed the data reported by Chen et al. (2005) and DeShon et al. (2004) to provide replicated evaluations of the model. Whereas the original research had focused on the parallel, multilevel aspects of regulatory processes, these new analyses examined the effects of the cross-level linkages on shaping individual regulation that had not been previously examined (see Figure 26.5). The researchers found consistent support for their hypotheses linking the levels of the regulation system, and emphasizing the team as a context for individual regulatory processes and outcomes. In combination with the prior research, we think that this consistent support for the value of an integrated, multilevel, and cross-level individual and team regulatory process as a means to conceptualize learning, motivation, and performance is very promising.

Finally, although its genesis is independent of the theory and research previously described, Pritchard and colleagues (Pritchard, Jones, Roth, Stuebing, & Ekeberg, 1988) developed an application described as the Productivity Measurement and Enhancement System (ProMES) that instantiates, in essence, a team-level goal-setting and regulatory system to facilitate team productivity. The ProMES system installs the regulatory components of goals, feedback, and incentives that are defined in ways meaningful to team members. The initial validation effort for the ProMES application reported substantial improvements in productivity, compared to baseline performance, as each of the components was installed. Feedback was implemented first, yielding a 50% improvement. Goal setting was next, yielding a 75% improvement. Finally, incentives were added for a 76% improvement in productivity. Recently, a meta-analysis was conducted to summarize 83 ProMES implementations (Pritchard, Harrell, DiazGranados, & Guzman, 2008). The researchers

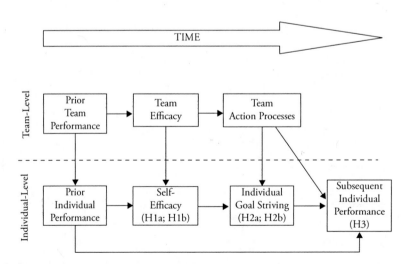

Figure 26.5 Hypothesized Multilevel Model of Motivation and Performance in Teams

Reprinted with permission from Chen, G., Kanfer, R., DeShon, R. P., Mathieu, J. E., & Kozlowski, S. W. J. (2009). The motivating potential of teams: Test and extension of Chen and Kanfer's (2006) cross-level model of motivation in teams. *Organizational Behavior and Human Decision Processes, 110,* 45–55.

concluded that the overall effects of ProMES on productivity improvement across a wide range of organizations and different team tasks were substantial and the improvements were potent, in some cases persisting over years.

ACTION REGULATION AND EMERGENT TEAM PROCESSES

A related theoretical perspective takes as its starting point the concept of iterative, episodic task cycles and uses those dynamics to infer *which* team behavioral processes are relevant and *when* they are relevant during team action regulation (Marks et al., 2001). Task episodes are conceptualized as a linked sequence of *transition* and *action* phases. Transition phases represent periods before or after action (between episodes), when the team is preparing for an upcoming engagement (e.g., planning, anticipating strategies, and setting goals) or evaluating the effectiveness of their action following an engagement. Action phases represent periods when team members are engaged in goal striving (within episodes), by monitoring the overall situation, progress toward goals, coordination, and member actions (e.g., correcting errors, sharing the load, cooperating). There are also interpersonal processes—motivation, conflict management, and affect management—that are important across both phases.

Their conceptualization of team tasks as episodic in nature is consistent with the previously discussed models of team action regulation (e.g., DeShon et al., 2004) and with models that emphasize team learning cycles as the core mechanism of team development and adaptation (Kozlowski, Gully, McHugh, Salas, & Cannon-Bowers, 1996; Kozlowski, Gully, Salas, & Cannon-Bowers, 1996), which we highlight in the next section. However, there are two novel and important aspects of the Marks et al. (2001) conceptualization. First, task episodes are viewed as multifaceted in that teams can be engaged in multiple, distinct transition-action sequences with different rhythms that have to be monitored simultaneously. This adds substantial complexity to the process of team action regulation. Second, Marks et al. use the distinct foci of transition and action phases to structure when particular team "emergent states" or processes are relevant. The processes that they consider are synthesized from a stream of prior research on team performance functions (see Fleishman & Zaccaro, 1992, for a summary) and related research on team behaviors that underlie effectiveness (Marks et al., 2001). This is a parsimonious organizing framework that helps to identify which team behaviors are important, when they are important, and why they are important.

Subsequent meta-analytic research has built on this conceptual framework to propose a hierarchical model such that the specific team behavioral processes proposed by Marks et al. (2001) would form first-order factors; loading onto second-order transition, action, and interpersonal factors; under an overall team-process factor (LePine, Piccolo, Jackson, Mathieu, & Saul, 2008). A meta-analytic confirmatory factor analysis based on 138 studies using 1,507 correlations from 147 independent samples provided empirical support for this conceptual structure. In addition, LePine et al. (2008) examined the meta-analytic relationship between the first- and second-order team processes with team performance. They reported corrected correlations, for the first-order processes and performance that ranged from .17 (systems monitoring) to .35 (strategy formulation). Of the 10 first-order processes, 9 evidenced corrected correlations, with performance in excess of .25, with one-half of them greater than or equal to .30. As would be expected, the second- and third-order factors also related to team performance. Finally, they also examined the relationships between the second-order factors—transition, action, and interpersonal processes—and what Marks et al. (2001) refer to as "emergent states" of team cohesion and group potency. The corrected correlations were substantial (cohesion: .60, .61, .53; potency: .63, .65, .70).

When considered in conjunction with the theoretical and empirical support highlighted in the prior section, we conclude that there is solid support for action regulation as a basic theoretical engine of team learning processes, that team action regulation behaviors are associated with motivational and affective emergent states (cohesion, potency), and that team action regulation behaviors contribute to team performance. Although it is somewhat more speculative to presume that team action regulation contributes to other cognitive and motivational-affective team processes (emergent states), we think that is likely to be the case. For example, action regulation is known to shape the development of team efficacy (e.g., Chen et al., 2009; DeShon et al., 2004). In addition, there is some evidence that action regulation leads to the development of shared mental models (Mohammed, Ferzandi, & Hamilton, 2010). In concert, we view the regulatory perspective on team learning to be highly promising.

TEAM REGULATION, LEARNING, AND DEVELOPMENT

A series of integrated theoretical frameworks created by Kozlowski and colleagues (Kozlowski, Gully, McHugh et al., 1996; Kozlowski, Gully, Salas et al., 1996; Kozlowski, Gully, Nason, & Smith, 1999; Kozlowski, Watola, Jensen, Kim, & Botero, 2009) characterize how individual and team regulatory processes, as we have described in detail above, function as the theoretical "engine" of team learning. Regulation processes propel a developmental sequence of increasing knowledge and skill capability across focal levels—individual, dyadic, and team—that ultimately culminates in an adaptive, regulating, collective entity. In addition, a key aspect of their approach is the principle that team leaders should play a central role in energizing the regulatory learning process and shaping developmental progression. The cyclical, episodic nature of team tasks provides an opportunity for team leaders to harness task cycles and to focus regulation and learning around specific, phased developmental goals. As team members acquire basic proficiencies, the team leader transitions the team to focus learning and development on more complex skills sets. As team-level capabilities emerge, the team becomes a self-regulating entity, and the leader is able to shift to boundary and environmental monitoring (see also Day, chapter 22 of this handbook). This meta-theoretical perspective has three primary conceptual underpinnings: (a) team tasks are episodic and can be explicitly linked to a regulation cycle; (b) teams, like individuals, progress through a series of phases during which they learn and compile increasingly complex knowledge and skill; and (c) as teams develop, the focal level of learning transitions from individuals becoming proficient to dyads negotiating role exchanges to the team network mapping out a repertoire of its adaptive capabilities.

First, as noted previously, team tasks exhibit episodic dynamics, cycling from low engagement prior to the task to high as the team engages the task, and back to low as the cycle concludes. As shown in Figure 26.6, this episodic dynamic enables a three-part regulatory process that sets desired learning goals during low load, monitors team learning and performance during task engagement, and then facilitates process feedback and reflection as the team transitions from task engagement back to low load (Kozlowski, Gully, McHugh et al., 1996; Kozlowski, Gully, Salas et al., 1996; Kozlowski et al., 2009). Although this model was developed independently

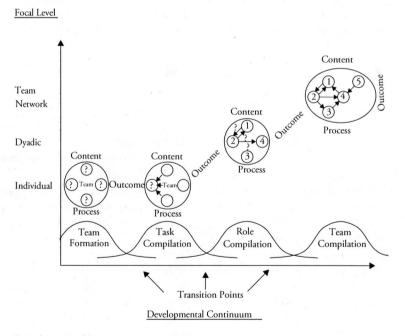

Figure 26.6 Team Compilation Model

of the Marks et al. (2001) episodic model and typology, the frameworks are compatible. With repeated episodes, regulation focused on individual learning and skill acquisition proficiency begins to emerge as a multilevel—individual and team—regulation process that encompasses team learning, skill acquisition, and performance (Kozlowski, Gully, Nason, et al., 1999).

Second, similar to the way in which individual learning compiles increasingly complex skills, the theorists posit that teams progress through a series of modal learning phases that involve qualitatively distinct learning content and outcomes. Regulation is the engine that enables within-phase learning and a transition to more complex skill acquisition. Third, this is viewed as a process of building and compiling knowledge and skill that also shift across focal levels of emergence from individuals to dyads to teams. Initially, during *team formation*, new members engage in informal socialization processes to define social structure and space, establishing norms, goals, and a sense of mission. During *task compilation*, they focus on regulating their individual performance and building their own task proficiency. As they begin to master their own capabilities, they shift to a *role compilation* process as team members focus on task-driven dyadic interactions to identify role sets, negotiate exchanges, and establish routines to guide interdependence. As teams transition to the last phase in the meta-model, *team compilation*, members focus on the team network of interdependencies and begin to develop a repertoire of alternative, reconfigurable linkages that enable them to continuously improve for the expected and provide the underpinnings for adaption to the unexpected. Although there are no direct evaluations of this meta-theory, which is synthesized from a broad literature, there is support for the regulatory mechanisms (Chen et al., 2005; Chen et al., 2009; DeShon et al., 2004; Mathieu, Gilson, & Ruddy, 2006), and there is some support for the principle that progressive shifts in the focal level of development—individual to team—contributes to team adaptability (DeShon, Kozlowski, Schmidt, Wiechmann, & Milner, 2001).

CONCLUSION

Self-regulation, in its various incarnations, is the dominant model of individual-level learning, motivation, and performance; it has amassed a substantial supporting empirical foundation; and some of its basic principles have been extended in an effort to provide insights about team learning processes.

Overall, we think that the application of regulation models to the team level evidences considerable promise. As our review documents, we know that difficult and specific team goals prompt similar effects on increasing team performance as those observed at the individual level (O'Leary-Kelly et al., 1994; Pritchard et al., 2008). Remarkably, although there is voluminous research on individual goal setting, research on the effects of team goal setting are still quite limited. Not only is there a small empirical foundation overall, it is also remarkable that there is very little team-level research examining the major moderating contingency factors (e.g., goal specificity, goal content) of goal setting. O'Leary-Kelly et al. (1994) could not examine these contingency effects in their meta-analysis because there were an insufficient number of primary studies. In the preceding 17 years, little has changed. Although research on these relationships may not be viewed as plowing new conceptual turf, they are nonetheless important principles to generalize—or to demonstrate boundary conditions in their generalization—to the team level. Conducting the basic work to map the generalization of goal-setting principles to the team level is an obvious research target.

Goals, however, are only one part of the learning process. Feedback also plays a critical role in self-regulation. Indeed, there is no process to regulate without feedback to influence subsequent effort and strategy adaptations across goal-striving iterations. Yet, remarkably, there is also surprisingly little research on the effects of feedback on regulation, learning, and performance at the team level, as documented by DeShon et al. (2004). Is it better to give team feedback, individual feedback, or both types? In the DeShon et al. (2004) study, individual feedback (only) led to the best individual performance, team feedback (only) led to the best team performance, and those teams receiving both types (individual and team) could not maximize performance on both goal-feedback loops. It is likely that there are ways to augment raw outcome feedback that could help to maximize performance on both goal-feedback loops. Understanding how to better deliver feedback to support individual *and* team performance is another rather obvious target for systematic research.

Our review also described a set of related "meta" theoretical frameworks on team learning that extends action regulation to understand: (a) team developmental processes, and (b) how they can be shaped by team leaders. This meta-theory addresses distinctive learning processes and outcomes, and is constructed on a broad base of conceptual integration and related empirical findings. We think it is promising, but it needs to be evaluated, refined, and extended. The meta-theory incorporates "core" principles that can be used to evaluate the usefulness of the overall frameworks. The team development models by Kozlowski and colleagues focus on regulation as a theoretical engine for team learning, developmental transitions across time and focal levels, and the potential for leaders to shape developmental processes. These core principles are key research foci for evaluating the frameworks. As we highlighted in the review, there is emerging support for multilevel regulation as an engine of team learning. Subsequent research should focus on developmental transitions, shifts in the focal level of development, and the ability of leaders to augment these developmental transitions. In addition to core principles, the meta-models can also be used to generate numerous more specific, contextualized models in which specific hypotheses can be examined and boundary conditions established.

Finally, Pritchard et al. (2008) have shown that the ProMES application of principles that underlie action regulation are potent ways to shape team members' abilities to improve performance. We presume that learning as a process, collaboration and/or supporting "emergent states," and knowledge components underlie this improvement. Thus, while there is evidence showing the effectiveness of ProMES, we think that basic research to unpack its mechanisms would enhance understanding and would advance applications.

Information-Processing Models
OVERVIEW

Early efforts to conceptualize learning at higher levels of analysis relied heavily on information-processing theory that grew out of the post–World War II explosion of interest in the science of cybernetics (Wiener, 1948), which also prompted the cognitive revolution in psychology (e.g., Miller, Galanter, & Pribram, 1960; Shiffrin & Schneider, 1977). Cybernetic control systems are based on the negative feedback loop and hierarchically nested layers of control loops (e.g., Carver & Scheier, 1981; Powers, 1973). This is the same basic system architecture as in self-regulation models, albeit self-regulation models focus more on psychological processes implicated by the control loop, and information-processing models focus more on the functional components of system control.

In organizational psychology and behavior, information processing was used as a heuristic to understand organizational learning and decision making (e.g., Cyert & March, 1963). In his review, Huber (1991) described four processes that underlie organizational learning—knowledge acquisition, information distribution, information interpretation, and organizational memory—each associated with a set of subprocesses. For example, organizations may acquire knowledge through a variety of activities and behaviors, including experiential learning, vicarious learning, and searching. Together, these processes and subprocesses are proposed to influence the breadth, elaborateness, and thoroughness of organizational learning. Unfortunately, much of the "theory" that underlies this domain is largely based on metaphor and analogies that seek to instantiate information-processing components and mechanisms in ephemeral organizational systems and structures (Huber, 1991; Walsh & Ungson, 1991). There have been, however, more focused efforts to apply the information-processing perspective to groups and teams as a framework to understand learning and decision making.

GROUPS AS INFORMATION PROCESSORS

In his review of managerial and organizational cognition, Walsh (1995) notes, "The key challenge in considering knowledge structures at the supra-individual level of analysis is to account for the role of social processes in the acquisition, retention, and retrieval of information" (p. 291). Indeed, most information-processing or cognitive theories of team learning have focused significant attention on delineating these social and interpersonal processes. Hinsz et al. (1997) provided a narrative review of research that has examined how task-performing groups process information. They suggest that information processing at the group level "involves the degree to which information, ideas, or cognitive processes are shared, and are being shared, among the group members and how this sharing of information affects both individual- and group-level outcomes" (p. 43). Thus, information exchange and transfer among group members is central to their conceptualization of group information processing. In addition, they acknowledge the fact that information processing in groups is inherently a multilevel process; group-level processing is dependent on individual-level processing, and individual-level processing is influenced by group-level processes. For example, group information processing can be influenced by the focus of members' attention (e.g., internally vs. externally), and aspects of the group context (e.g., group size) and interactions (e.g., time pressure) can similarly influence what information becomes the focus of members' attention. Although they highlight some notable interdependencies and interactions across these levels, the review focuses primarily on extending information-processing theory to the group level, rather than delineating these multilevel processes.

Hinsz et al. (1997) organize their review based on a generic information-processing model that has emerged from individual-level research in cognitive psychology. Although they acknowledge distinct differences in how individuals and groups process information, they argue that the components of the model serve as a useful framework for examining how small groups process relevant and available information to perform cognitive tasks. Thus, they extrapolate the individual-level model of information processing to explore parallel processes at the group level. The first component of the model, *processing objective*, recognizes the fact that groups, like individuals, process information in terms of objectives, tasks, missions, or collective goals derived from the context. In the *attention* phase of information processing, group members attend to particular information in order to process it. This information is then evaluated, interpreted, and transformed into a representation through an *encoding* process that enables the information to enter group memory through the *storage* process. The *retrieval* process allows groups to search for and recall necessary information. In the *processing work space*, groups combine, integrate, and process information on the basis of various rules, strategies, and procedures. Finally, after information is processed, a *response* is produced that represents the collective will of the group, and often the response generates *feedback* about changes in the situation. After reviewing group research related to each of these components of information processing, they discuss four dimensions of variability that may influence group information processing. For example, they examine how group information processing is influenced by variability in group members' access to a piece of information (i.e., commonality/uniqueness of information dimension) and variability in cognitive representations among group members (i.e., convergence/diversity of ideas dimension). Ultimately, they argue that group information processing can be conceptualized as a process through which the individual contributions (e.g., information, ideas, cognitive processes) of group members are combined through interaction to produce the group-level outcome.

Building on the work of Hinsz et al. (1997), Ellis and Bell (2005) present an information-processing model of team learning (see Figure 26.7), which they define as "*a relatively permanent change in the team's collective level of knowledge and skill produced by the shared experience of the team members*" (italics in original, p. 6). However, rather than providing a detailed examination of each component of the model, they focus on describing three conditions that must exist for team learning to occur. The first condition, *capacity*, refers to the cognitive resources that the team brings to the situation. Teams composed of members with higher levels of cognitive

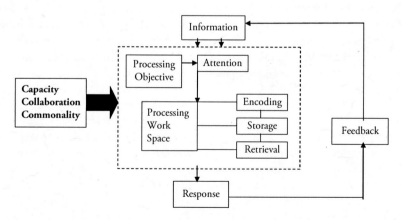

Figure 26.7 An Information-Processing Model of Team Learning
Adapted with permission from Ellis, A. P. J., & Bell, B. S. (2005). Capacity, collaboration, and commonality: A framework for understanding team learning. In L. L. Neider & C. A. Shriesheim (Eds.), *Understanding teams: A volume in research in management* (pp. 1–25). Greenwich, CT: Information Age.

ability should have greater capacity to collectively process information. The second critical condition for team learning is effective *collaboration*, which refers to the sharing of knowledge, experience, or ideas within the team. This condition captures the social aspect of learning in teams; collaboration can be influenced by not only the personalities of individual members but also interventions such as team training. The final condition, *commonality*, suggests that team members must have a common frame of reference or language in order to collaborate effectively and engage in collective learning. Commonality can be influenced by selecting team members who are familiar with one another or by developing shared mental models. Overall, the capacity-collaboration-commonality framework serves to highlight several potential antecedents of information processing in teams.

In a recent article, Wilson et al. (2007) proposed a cognitive theory of group learning. Similar to Huber (1991), they treat group learning as an outcome that can be defined as "a change in the group's repertoire of potential behavior" (p. 1044). In addition, they argue that *sharing, storage,* and *retrieval* represent the processes through which group learning occurs. Sharing is the process through which knowledge is distributed within the group and members develop an understanding that others have the same knowledge. New knowledge must not only be shared within the team, but it must also be stored and retained so that it can be exploited over time. The final group learning process is retrieval, which means that group members are able to find and access stored knowledge for subsequent use. Wilson et al. (2007) examine not only the independent effects of each of these processes on group learning but also the relationships among these processes. For example, they argue that increasing the breadth of sharing enhances the robustness of group learning by allowing learning to be stored across multiple members' memories and by expanding the number of group members who are able to recognize and respond to retrieval cues.

INFORMATION SHARING

Each of the conceptual frameworks described above emphasizes the importance of communication and information sharing in team learning. These processes distribute new knowledge among group members so that it can become a shared property of the group. Research by Stasser and his colleagues, however, has demonstrated that discussion in groups is often biased in favor of shared information

that all members know, instead of unshared information that only a single member knows (Stasser & Titus, 1985, 1987). Research on this phenomenon has relied primarily on the hidden profile task, in which information that supports an inferior decision is predominantly shared, whereas information that supports the superior decision is unshared (i.e., unique information is distributed across members).

Group discussion often favors shared information because it has a statistical sampling advantage and a recognition and recall advantage over unshared information (Stasser, Taylor, & Hanna, 1989). In addition, research has found that members often face social costs associated with establishing the credibility and relevance of unique information (Stasser & Titus, 2003; Wittenbaum & Park, 2001). Given the implications of biased information sampling for group decision making, and potentially group learning, research has focused attention on identifying the factors that influence information sharing. A number of variables within the temporal (e.g., length of discussion), social (e.g., status, expertise, leadership), and task environment (e.g., information load) have been shown to impact the information-sharing process (Wittenbaum & Park, 2001; Wittenbaum & Stasser, 1996).

In their review of this literature, Mohammed and Dumville (2001) note that there have been few conceptual advances beyond the original information-sampling model proposed by Stasser and Titus, and they also highlight the need to expand the research to intact organizational teams. Responding to this call, De Dreu (2007) applied a motivated information-processing perspective (e.g., De Dreu & Carnevale, 2003) to examine information sharing in management and cross-functional teams and found that perceived cooperative outcome interdependence related positively to information sharing, team learning, and team effectiveness, but only when task reflexivity (i.e., systematic information processing) was high. The authors conclude that cooperation facilitates the constructive exchange of information, but deliberate and systematic information processing is needed to help team members combine and integrate this information to make better decisions and create new problem solutions.

CONCLUSION

Expansion of information-processing theory to the team level has helped to elucidate the cognitive processes that underlie team learning and the conditions (e.g., individual characteristics, interventions) that shape these processes. It has also highlighted the important role of communication and information sharing in group learning (Wilson et al., 2007) and has demonstrated that group members often fail to share unique information or to systematically process the information that is exchanged within the group (De Dreu, 2007). However, the information-processing approach to understanding team learning has also been criticized on several grounds. Johnson and Hollenbeck (2007), for example, argue that the extrapolation of individual-level models to understand team-level information processing and learning fails to account for the challenges of learning at the team level. Accordingly, they suggest that "a true team-level model of learning must incorporate not only the cognitive and affective *intra*personal factors that affect the learning process, but also the social *inter*personal factors that exist at the team level" (italics in original, p. 319). Critics have also cited the use of metaphorical explanations of collective learning processes, such as dialogue, as vague and superficial (e.g., Rowe, 2008), and others have called for more attention to the dynamics that characterize the diffusion of individual knowledge to the collective (e.g., Tompkins, 1995).

There is some evidence that research has begun to address these issues. The cognitive theory of group learning presented by Wilson and colleagues (2007) is more explicit about issues surrounding levels of analysis and time. They argue that group learning should be conceptualized and measured at the group level of analysis and that treatments of group learning need to examine changes over time so as to be able to examine important learning processes (e.g., forgetting) and to distinguish group learning from related constructs (e.g., decision making). This is a step in the right direction and future work should continue to develop a multilevel, dynamic theory of information processing in teams. Given that past research on information processing and information sharing has focused primarily on small, ad hoc groups performing cognitive tasks, it will also be important to expand work in this area to different types of teams situated in organizational settings. Sole and Edmondson (2002), for instance, examined how geographically dispersed, cross-functional development teams access, combine, and apply situated knowledge, or knowledge that is grounded in site-specific work practices. They found that situated knowledge plays a critical role in dispersed team learning, but the ease of accessing this information varies, depending on whether the information is situated locally (i.e., at the same site as the problem) or remotely (i.e., located elsewhere). By studying teams outside the laboratory, we can begin to identify the barriers that different types of teams face in the sharing and processing of information.

Macrocognition

OVERVIEW

The term *macrocognition* was coined by Cacciabue and Hollnagel (1995) to describe cognitive functioning in naturalistic decision-making contexts (Klein, Ross, Moon, Klein, Hoffman, & Hollnagel, 2003) and is a concept with roots in human factors and cognitive engineering psychology. In this conception, macrocognition is contrasted with the *microcognition* of "standard laboratory paradigms for psychological research" (p. 81). Much like the distinction between naturalistic decision making and classical decision making (Salas, Rosen, & DiazGranados, chapter 41 of this handbook), the primary distinctions that are emphasized are: (a) naturalistic, situated cognition and decision making in field settings versus contrived cognition and decision making in the lab; (b) decision making that is complex, time pressured, with ill-defined goals, and high uncertainty versus decision making that conforms to well-defined, reductionist, and rational theoretical models; and (c) the use of naturalistic observation-description and qualitative analysis versus experimentation and quantitative analysis (Klein et al., 2003). These authors frame macro- and microcognition as complementary, but with distinct differences in their paradigms, methodologies, and research foci.

Klein et al. (2003) also note that macrocognition is often collaborative, in that decisions are made in team contexts, and is dynamic and emergent over time, although these themes are not explicitly developed. Given our theoretical foci, we think that macrocognition and microcognition need not be regarded as distinct paradigms or locations for research, but rather as different, but complementary, levels in a complex multilevel system of situated individual cognition and emergent team cognitive processes that underlie collaborative decision making in teams.

MACROCOGNITIVE KNOWLEDGE-BUILDING PROCESSES

Theorists have recently begun to hone this perspective. In particular, Fiore, Rosen, Smith-Jentsch, Salas, Letsky, and Warner (2010; see also Fiore, Smith-Jentsch, Salas, Warner, & Letsky, 2010) developed a theoretical framework, a "meta-model," for understanding team macrocognitive processes in complex collaborative decision making. What makes this macrocognitive theory useful for understanding team learning is that it focuses on knowledge-building processes—the acquisition, transformation, and adaptation of knowledge in teams—and its use to solve unique, complex, and challenging problems. Another important aspect of the model is that it distinguishes learning processes and the knowledge that results from that process. Thus, it is consistent with our "meta" perspective. Moreover, it is conceptually consistent with our theoretical foci in that it is explicitly multilevel, dynamic, and emergent.

Fiore et al. (2010) define macrocognition as a process whereby *internalized knowledge* that has been acquired by individual team members is transformed through collaborative knowledge building into *externalized knowledge* that is shared by all team members. Their meta-model is shown in Figure 26.8. This transformation process is multilevel. *Individual knowledge building processes* (i.e.,

learning as a process) yield *internalized knowledge* held by team members. *Team knowledge building processes* transform that internally held knowledge into *externalized team knowledge* that can be applied to solving the problem. In other words, knowledge is first acquired and learned by individual team members and then, through collaboration, sharing, and externalization, it is acquired and held by the team as a collective. The process is dynamic, with multiple feedback loops, as individual knowledge building and team knowledge building and externalization incrementally build the knowledge capacity of the team. And, the process is emergent as individual knowledge is shared, acquired by other team members, and then manifests as externalized team knowledge.

The framework also incorporates a series of problem-solving phases as teams transition across knowledge construction, problem model development, team consensus, and outcome evaluation and revision (Letsky, Warner, Fiore, Rosen, & Salas,

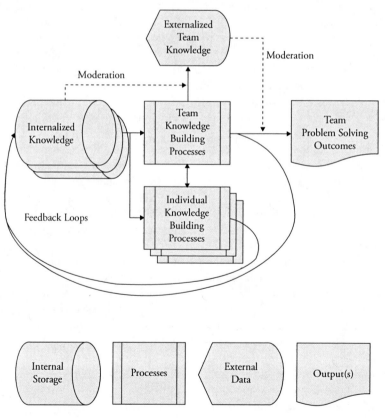

Figure 26.8 Meta-model of team macrocognition

Note: Multiple overlapping symbols indicate representations for multiple team members. Reprinted with permission from Fiore, S. M., Rosen, M. A., Smith-Jentsch, K. A., Salas, E., Letsky, M., & Warner, N. (2010). Toward an understanding of macrocognition in teams: Predicting processes in complex collaborative contexts. *Human Factors, 52,* 203–224.

2007). Their conceptualization of these transitions as phases (rather than stages) is consistent with Kozlowski, Gully, Nason, et al. (1999). That is, the transitions across phases are viewed as continuous, with partial overlap at transition points, rather than the hard discontinuous shifts of stages. Phases describe modal activity and allow for some movement back and forth. In their model, the *knowledge construction* phase centers on the acquisition of relevant problem-domain information by team members, the *problem model development* phase addresses the development of shared understanding, the *team consensus* phase is focused on achieving agreement on a solution, and the *outcome evaluation and revision phase* concerns validating the agreed-upon solution and making adjustments as necessary.

CONCLUSION

Although there are not as yet direct empirical tests of the meta-model, phase model, or the derived propositions, the frameworks are intended to organize a broad-based program of multidisciplinary research on collaborative, macrocognitive team decision making (see Letsky & Warner, 2008). In addition, there are several research thrusts that encompass, for example, communication processes (Cooke, Gorman, & Preston, 2008), shared mental model convergence (McComb, 2008), and meaning creation (Rentsch, Delise, & Hutchinson, 2008). More recently, Kozlowski and Chao (2012) and their research team (Kozlowski, Chao, Grand, Keeney, Braun, & Kuljanin, 2011) have developed a macrocognitive knowledge typology that is designed to capture the key process components of the macrocognition meta-model. We will describe the measurement typology in a subsequent section on team knowledge outcomes and representations. However, the key point is that their typology is explicitly designed to capture team knowledge development as a multilevel, dynamic, and emergent phenomenon that results from macrocognitive processes. This macrocognitive framework can synthesize regulation-based learning and progressive knowledge development, it examines the dynamics and emergence of knowledge from the individual to the team level, and it can capture different forms of team knowledge emergence, ranging from composition to compilation forms.

Collectively, we think that this research program has great promise for building an integrated theory, a coupled research paradigm, and an aligned measurement system that can address macrocognition as a multilevel, dynamic, and emergent phenomenon—our foundation theoretical foci. One key aspect of the team knowledge-building conceptualization is its emphasis on the process of externalization. Externalization encompasses what might be considered "typical" processes like communication and information exchange, but it also considers "artifacts" that team members create to help capture knowledge and foster shared meaning. For example, in an effort to promote understanding of a problem space, a team member might draw a map; another might notate information on the map in way that contextualizes it; and another member might use that contextualized information to infer new knowledge and create shared meaning. This sort of collaborative and iterative conceptualization of team learning and meaning creation is relatively unique to macrocognition and it brings a novel and valuable perspective to the set of learning process models that we have reviewed. Overall, we think that this approach is conceptually quite promising. We hope to see a stream of systematic empirical research, tools, and applications unfold in the not too distant future.

Team Emergent States

In this section, we examine the team emergent states that support the theoretical engines of team learning, development, and adaptation reviewed above. How teams regulate their actions, share and process information, and construct shared meaning is shaped by the team context or climate, in particular the motivational and affective states that emerge within the team over time. Emergent states, such as team goal orientation and team efficacy, represent compositional properties of a team that shape the processes (e.g., information sharing, experimentation) that underlie team learning. At the same time, these states emerge from the interactions and iteration dynamics inherent in team learning that then support or constrain learning processes and knowledge outcomes. An overreliance on cross-sectional designs has meant that past research has typically focused on how these states impact team learning and performance. However, there are emerging efforts to explore, both conceptually and empirically, the dynamic and cyclical relationships between team learning and the emergence of these states. In the sections that follow, we examine four emergent states that have received considerable attention in the team learning literature, are supported by a stream of systematic theory development, and are generating a growing body of empirical findings.

Goal Orientation

Goal orientation is a construct that originated in the educational literature to explain differences in how individuals approach achievement situations (e.g., Dweck, 1986). The original theory proposed two independent types of goal orientation: learning and performance. A learning orientation is characterized by a desire to increase one's competence by developing new skills and mastering new situations. Individuals with a learning orientation tend to pursue what researchers have called an adaptive response pattern, characterized by persistence in the face of failure, feedback seeking, the use of more complex learning strategies, and the pursuit of difficult and challenging tasks (Bell & Kozlowski, 2002). In contrast, a performance orientation reflects a desire to demonstrate one's competence and to be positively evaluated by others (Farr, Hofmann, & Ringenbach, 1993). Performance orientation is often associated with a maladaptive response pattern in which individuals are more likely to withdraw from tasks in the face of failure, have less interest in difficult tasks, and exhibit a tendency to seek less challenging tasks in which success is likely. Subsequent work integrated traditional conceptualizations of mastery and performance goals with classic achievement motivation theories, which differentiate between activities that are oriented toward the attainment of success (approach) and those that are directed toward the avoidance of failure. The result has been the separation of performance orientation into two distinct motivational orientations, one focused on approaching success (performance-approach orientation) and the other focused on avoiding failure (performance-avoid orientation) (e.g., Elliot & Church, 1997; VandeWalle, 1997).

Over the years, there has been considerable debate around whether goal orientation should be conceptualized as a trait or a state. The emerging consensus is that it is both. Individuals possess dispositional goal orientations characterized by the chronic pursuit of a particular type of goal (e.g., learning, performance-avoid) in different situations across time (DeShon & Gillespie, 2005). However, the goals that individuals adopt during an achievement situation can also be influenced by situational factors. As Button, Mathieu, and Zajac (1996, p. 28) state, "Dispositional goal orientation will predispose individuals to adopt particular response patterns across situations, but situational characteristics may cause them to adopt a different or less acute response pattern for a particular situation."

Situational factors, such as goals or task framing, can induce different types of goal orientation, and these situational inducements often interact with individuals' dispositional goal orientation to influence individuals' learning processes and outcomes (Bell & Kozlowski, 2008; Kozlowski & Bell, 2006).

A recent meta-analysis by Payne, Youngcourt, and Beaubien (2007) provided convincing evidence of the importance of goal orientation for learning and performance. In general, learning orientation demonstrated a positive relationship and performance-avoid orientation a negative relationship with self-regulatory constructs, such as self-efficacy and learning strategies. In addition, learning orientation was positively related to learning, academic performance, and job performance, and performance-avoid orientation was negatively related to learning and task performance. The relationships between performance-approach orientation and self-regulation and learning were more mixed, but the consequences of performance-approach orientation were generally trivial.

Although goal orientation has historically been studied at the individual level of analysis, these findings have attracted the interest of team effectiveness researchers and have sparked efforts to extend goal orientation to higher levels of analysis (Gully & Phillips, 2005). It is important to note that researchers have adopted two different approaches to examining goal orientation within teams (Porter, 2007). The first approach treats goal orientation as a team composition variable. These studies measure individual team members' goal orientations, aggregate these scores to the team level, and examine how these scores relate to team processes and performance. This is a bottom-up approach that assumes that team members' goal orientations combine to create a compositional property of the team. The second approach examines goal orientation as a collective, emergent state (Porter, 2007). These studies often rely on the same measures used in the compositional studies, but shift the referent to the team level. Thus, collective goal orientation is viewed as a shared, team-level perception—a climate-like construct—that influences team process and performance. It is assumed that collective goal orientation emerges through both top-down (e.g., organizational climate) and bottom-up (e.g., interactions between team leaders and members) processes (Gully & Phillips, 2005; Porter, 2007), although these processes have received little research attention to date. Below, we briefly review the findings from studies that have examined goal orientation in teams from these two different perspectives.

One of the first studies to examine goal orientation as a team composition variable was conducted by Porter (2005), who examined the relationship between goal orientation in teams and several team processes and outcomes. The study involved four-person student teams performing a command and control simulation, and goal orientation was measured at the individual level and mean scores were used to aggregate learning and performance orientation to the team level. The results revealed that learning orientation was significantly and positively related to collective efficacy, team commitment, and backing up behavior, but did not exhibit a significant relationship with task performance. The effects of performance orientation were contingent on the team's task performance and the outcome examined. Specifically, performance orientation was negatively related to efficacy among teams that performed poorly, but was unrelated to efficacy among teams that performed well. However, performance orientation was positively related to commitment among teams that performed well and unrelated to commitment among those teams that performed poorly. LePine (2005) examined how team goal orientation (again using the mean of individual member scores) influenced the adaptation of three-person student teams performing a decision-making simulation. Halfway through the experiment, a communication channel between two team members deteriorated, which necessitated that the teams adapt their role structures in order to perform effectively. The results revealed that adaptation was influenced by a combination of team goal difficulty and team goal orientation. In particular, when teams had difficult goals, they were especially likely to adapt when comprising members with high learning orientation and especially unlikely to adapt when comprising members with high performance orientation. Supplemental analyses suggested that teams composed of members with high levels of learning orientation were more likely to adapt because they were more cooperative and more likely to engage in constructive learning activities (e.g., sharing problem information, analyzing alternative ways to approach the task) during the change.

Several studies have also examined team goal orientation as a shared, team-level perception that reflects an aspect of group climate. Bunderson and Sutcliffe (2003) examined the effects of team learning orientation on the performance of 44 business unit management teams in a Fortune 100 consumer products company. In this study, team learning orientation was measured by asking team members to assess the extent to which their team engages in various learning-related activities, such as taking risks on new ideas. The results revealed that the effect of team learning orientation on performance was inverse curvilinear, indicating that learning orientation improves performance to a point beyond which too much emphasis on learning begins to compromise team effectiveness. In addition, they found that the effects of learning orientation on performance were moderated by a team's past performance, such that teams with low performance benefit more from a stronger learning orientation than do teams with high performance. These findings are consistent with the notion that low-performing teams should use learning activities to find new solutions, whereas high-performing teams should continue to exploit those solutions that have worked in the past. DeShon et al. (2004) examined the effects of team learning and performance orientation on the regulation activities of 79 three-person student teams performing a simulated radar task. They found that team learning orientation was positively related to team goal commitment and team efficacy, and this positive effect was stronger for those teams that received team feedback (either alone or combined with individual feedback). Team performance orientation had a significant, positive relationship with team efficacy, although this relationship was weaker for those teams that received both individual and team feedback. Finally, a recent study by Porter, Webb, and Gogus (2010) examined the effects of team learning and performance orientation on the adaptive performance of teams performing a command-and-control simulation. The authors found that when teams had slack resources, team learning orientation led to performance improvements across the three trials, but team performance orientation only led to smaller improvements between the second and third performance trials. For those teams that did not have slack resources, team learning and performance orientations interacted to affect performance. Specifically, team learning orientation had little effect on performance improvements for those teams low in performance orientation. But, among those teams that were high on performance orientation, team learning orientation was negatively related to initial performance improvements but positively related to later performance improvements.

CONCLUSION

Overall, these studies provide preliminary evidence that goal orientation has an important influence on team learning, performance, and adaptability, yet there remain a number of important questions surrounding team goal orientation. One important issue that warrants greater attention concerns the effects of goal orientation on team learning and performance over time. Several of the studies reviewed above either showed that the effects of team goal orientation vary across time (e.g., Porter et al., 2010) or mentioned time as a potential boundary condition of their findings. Bunderson and Sutcliffe (2003), for example, note that the effects of team learning orientation may be different when examined over longer time frames. High-performing teams that emphasize learning may compromise some efficiency in the near term, but will be better equipped to respond to market shifts and environmental challenges over the long term. In addition, future research should focus on elaborating a multilevel model of team goal orientation that includes consideration of potential cross-level effects (Gully & Phillips, 2005). For instance, a recent study by Hirst, Van Knippenberg, and Zhou (2009) found that individual goal orientation and team learning behavior interacted to influence the individual creativity of employees in research and development teams. Team learning behavior activated the creative tendencies of those dispositionally inclined to learn, which led to higher levels of employee creativity. However, similar to the findings of Bunderson and Sutcliffe (2003), they found that learning orientation has diminishing returns for individual creativity above a certain point. Future research should also explore the contingencies that influence the effects of learning and performance orientation. The studies reviewed above suggest that team feedback, goal difficulty, prior performance, and resources all have the potential to shape the effects of team goal orientation on team learning, performance, and adaptation. These and other potential moderators need to be integrated into a systematic theory that can be subjected to targeted research designed to provide insight into the factors that serve as contingencies of the team goal orientation–team learning relationship. Finally, future research needs to further examine the implications of conceptualzing team goal orientation as a compositional variable versus as a shared, emergent state and should also consider the potential interactive effects of these two types of team goal orientation on learning and performance.

Psychological Safety

Because much of the early research on team learning was conducted in the laboratory, very little attention was focused on understanding how learning processes in teams are affected by managerial and contextual factors (Edmondson et al., 2007). However, as studies sought to extend these laboratory findings to real work groups in field settings, researchers began to investigate the role of leader behavior and group climate in shaping team learning. One of the constructs to emerge from this work was team psychological safety, which is defined as "a shared belief that the team is safe for interpersonal risk taking" (Edmondson, 1999, p. 354). Psychological safety creates a supportive interpersonal climate that enables team members to engage in critical learning behaviors, such as raising concerns, experimenting, sharing information, and revealing mistakes. Cannon and Edmondson (2001), for example, argue that two capabilities increase the chances that teams will learn from failure: members must be able and willing to take risks, and they must be able to confront failure directly rather than covering it up. Similarly, Burke, Salas, Wilson-Donnelly, and Priest (2004, p. i101) state, "The ability to speak up in a non-threatening and respectful manner (deference to expertise) is a hallmark of learning organizations and the teams within them."

The importance of psychological safety in shaping team learning was first discussed by Edmondson (1996) in a study in which she examined group-level factors that affect drug error rates in hospital units. Contrary to expectations, quantitative survey data revealed that unit error rates were positively associated with nurse manager direction setting and coaching, members' perceptions of unit performance, and the quality of interpersonal relationships in the unit. Edmondson proposed that these unexpected results may be due to the fact that better teams have created a climate of openness that facilitates the discussion of error, which would increase reported error rates. Qualitative interview and observational data provided support for this hypothesis and suggested that nurse manager behaviors may be particularly important for creating a team climate in which members can openly discuss and learn from their own and others' mistakes.

In a subsequent study designed to further explore these findings, Edmondson (1999) used quantitative and qualitative data gathered from 51 work teams in a manufacturing company to test a model of team learning. This study formally introduced the construct of team psychological safety and positioned it as a key mediator of the relationship between structural team inputs and team learning behaviors. The results revealed that both context support (i.e., adequate resources, information, and rewards) and team leader coaching influenced psychological safety, which in turn was associated with learning behaviors indicative of a team learning process. In addition, these learning behaviors mediated the relationship between team psychological safety and team performance.

The fact that these early studies pointed to leaders as having a critical influence on team learning led to research aimed at further exploring leader actions that promote and inhibit team psychological safety. Edmondson, Bohmer, and Pisano (2001), for example, studied 16 hospitals implementing a new technology for cardiac surgery. Although senior management support was not associated with implementation success, they found that team leaders (i.e., surgeons) played a critical role in facilitating a successful team learning process. In particular, effective team leaders encouraged speaking up by reducing power differences in the team and motivated effort by framing the technology as a team innovation project and conveying the benefits of the new technology for patients (see also Edmondson, 2003). In another study, Nembhard and Edmondson (2006) examined the effects of leader inclusiveness, or the extent to which leaders invite and appreciate others' contributions, on psychological safety in neonatal intensive care units. The results revealed that team members perceived higher levels of psychological safety when physician leaders were seen as more inclusive and welcoming of others' ideas. In addition, higher status medical professionals (e.g., physicians) perceived greater psychological safety than lower status professionals (e.g., nurses and respiratory therapists). However, leader inclusiveness moderated the effects of professional status on psychological safety, such that the disparity in psychological safety between high- and low-status professionals was greater when leader inclusiveness was low. Finally, the authors found that psychological safety mediated the relationship between leader inclusiveness and team engagement in quality improvement work.

CONCLUSION

Together, these studies have solidified the importance of members' perceptions of psychological safety for team learning and performance and have also demonstrated the important role of leaders in shaping these perceptions. As work in this area continues, one issue worth examining concerns the importance of psychology safety for learning across different types of teams. Edmondson (2003), for example, suggested that psychological safety may be particularly important for learning and performance in interdisciplinary action teams (e.g., surgical teams), because the expertise and power differences inherent in such teams have the potential to undermine the coordination that is essential to team success. In addition, researchers have proposed that team trust, which is related to but distinct from psychological safety, may be particularly important for learning and performance in geographically dispersed teams (e.g., Cohen & Gibson, 2003; Kirkman, Rosen, Tesluk, & Gibson, 2006). However, in a study that examined collective learning across five different types of teams (e.g., production teams, middle management teams), Edmondson (2002) concluded that team type was not associated with team learning patterns and that members' interpersonal perceptions were uniformly an important predictor of learning and change across the different types of teams. Thus, more research is needed to determine whether the effects of psychological safety on team learning are dependent on the team and task context (Edmondson et al., 2007). Future research also needs to devote greater attention to understanding the temporal dynamics that surround the development of psychological safety in teams. Edmondson (1999), for example, proposed a self-perpetuating cycle in which perceptions of psychological safety make team members more willing to report and discuss errors in the future, which in turn should reinforce the belief that mistakes will not be held against them. However, the cross-sectional design of the study did not allow for a formal test of this feedback loop. Edmondson and colleagues (2001) used qualitative techniques to examine how activities at different stages of the implementation process contributed to the development of psychological safety, but research has not yet conducted an empirical test of their conclusions. Future research that uses quantitative data to examine psychological safety over time has the potential to contribute valuable insight into the dynamics that surround the emergence of psychological safety perceptions, as well the critical antecedents and consequences of these perceptions at different stages of a team's life cycle.

Team Efficacy

Self-efficacy refers to an individual's belief in his or her capability to perform a specific task (Bandura, 1977; Gist, 1987). It represents a comprehensive judgment of beliefs in one's capability to mobilize the motivation, cognitive resources, and actions needed to achieve a particular level of performance in goal accomplishment (Bandura, 1997). Self-efficacy is important because it leads to upward goal revision after initial goal levels are accomplished (Phillips, Hollenbeck, & Ilgen, 1996), it boosts persistence in the face of difficulties and challenges, and it fosters adaptation to increasing task complexity (Kozlowski, Gully, Brown, et al., 2001). Meta-analytic findings have shown that self-efficacy is a strong predictor of individual task performance across a variety of domains (Stajkovic & Luthans, 1998). Given these important findings for self-efficacy at the individual level of analysis, parallel concepts of team efficacy (sometimes referred to as *collective efficacy*) and group potency have been proposed.

Team efficacy refers to a team's belief that it can successfully perform a specific task (Lindsley, Brass, & Thomas, 1995). Self- and team efficacy are distinct in their unit of focus (Gully, Incalcaterra, Joshi, & Beaubien, 2002). However, team efficacy is not simply an aggregate of self-efficacy across team members; rather, it represents a team-level property that is shared, consensual, and held in common across group members, and it may be different from individuals' own self-perceptions of competence (Kozlowski & Ilgen, 2006). Bandura (1997) proposed that, similar to self-efficacy, team efficacy influences what a team chooses to do, how much effort is devoted to the activity, and the persistence of the team in the face of failure. Group potency has been defined as a generalized collective belief that the group can be effective (Shea & Guzzo, 1987). Most researchers acknowledge that team efficacy and group potency are similar constructs. However, whereas team efficacy is task specific, group potency represents a shared belief about the general effectiveness of the group across multiple tasks and contexts. A meta-analysis by Gully et al. (2002) found that both team efficacy and group potency had a positive relationship with team performance and that effect sizes were comparable across the two constructs. In addition, the relationship of team efficacy with team performance was stronger when it was appropriately examined at the team level rather than the individual level of analysis. Moreover, team interdependence

moderated the team efficacy-performance relationship, such that team efficacy was a more important contributor to team performance when interdependence was high than when interdependence was low. The relationship between group potency and performance, however, was not moderated by team interdependence.

Although most of the research on team efficacy has focused on its relationship with team performance, researchers have recently begun to explore the role of team efficacy as a potential enabler of team learning. Edmondson (1999) suggested that team members may only be motivated to reveal errors and to speak up when they believe that the team is capable of using this new information to generate useful results. In addition, it has been argued that team efficacy should influence a team's ability to regulate team processes and share and process information (DeShon et al., 2004; Gully et al., 2002; Van den Bossche, Gijselaers, Segers, & Kirschner, 2006). Yet, empirical research examining the relationship between team efficacy and team learning has failed to yield a clear pattern of results. Edmondson (1999), for example, found some support for a positive relationship between team efficacy and team learning behavior, but the significance of this relationship depended on the measure of team learning behavior (self-reported vs. observer-assessed) and the other antecedents included in the model (e.g., psychological safety). In addition, she failed to find evidence that team efficacy mediates the effects of context support and leader behavior on team learning. Van den Bossche et al. (2006) found that group potency was significantly and positively related to the learning behaviors of 75 student project teams. However, these results must be interpreted cautiously, since both group potency and team learning behaviors were assessed through self-report measures collected on a single survey administered at the end of the course. In a study examining student learning groups in a college software class, Hsu, Chen, Chiu, and Ju (2007) found that task-specific computer collective efficacy (assessed through a consensus measure) had a significant and positive effect on the teams' software learning performance, after controlling for prior team performance and general computer collective efficacy. In contrast to the studies reviewed above, however, the authors did not examine team learning behaviors, and it is, therefore, unclear whether the effect of collective efficacy on team performance was due to differences in learning behavior or other team processes.

Researchers have also examined the relationship between team efficacy and emergent outcomes of team learning, such as shared mental models, again with somewhat mixed results. Peterson, Mitchell, Thompson, and Burr (2000) examined collective efficacy and shared mental models among 26 college student groups. The results revealed that collective efficacy measured early in the semester was positively related to shared mental models later in the semester, but the extent to which mental models were shared among members early in the semester did not predict collective efficacy later in the semester. Mathieu, Rapp, Maynard, and Mangos (2010) suggest that shared mental models may not have predicted collective efficacy in the Peterson et al. (2000) study because the students had no history of working together and many were unfamiliar with the task that they performed. Thus, the student teams may not have had enough opportunity for shared mental models to develop early in the semester. Indeed, using a sample of 43 U.S. air-traffic control teams, who on average had worked together for over six years, Mathieu et al. (2010) showed that shared task mental models significantly predicted collective efficacy and that collective efficacy mediated the relationship between shared task mental models and team effectiveness. It is important to note, however, that shared team mental models were unrelated to collective efficacy.

CONCLUSION

The research reviewed above provides some preliminary evidence that team efficacy may represent an important enabling condition for team learning. Yet, the mixed findings of these studies also highlight the need for more work in this area. Emerging research suggests that there are both similarities and dissimilarities in the antecedents and outcomes of efficacy beliefs across different levels of analysis. Goal orientation, past performance, and achievement motivation–team drive, for example, have been shown to predict efficacy at both the individual and team level (Chen et al., 2002; Chen et al., 2009; DeShon et al., 2004). Yet, Chen et al. (2002) also found that experience positively predicted self-efficacy, but team expertise did not relate to team efficacy. Thus, although the findings of individual-level research on the efficacy-learning relationship may serve as a valuable guide for research in this area, we need to be careful about generalizing these findings to the team level. For example, feedback has been identified as having an important influence on efficacy and learning at both the individual and team level of analysis (e.g., DeShon et al., 2004; London & Sessa, 2006). However, different types of feedback (e.g., public vs. private, team vs. individual) may have different effects on efficacy and learning at the individual and team level (c.f., Deshon et al., 2004). Another important direction for future research is to examine team efficacy–team learning relations over time. Not only is longitudinal research important for establishing causal relationships between team efficacy and team learning, but it can also provide insight into reciprocal relationships that may exist between team efficacy and emergent team learning outcomes, such as shared mental models and collective knowledge.

Cohesion and Conflict

Research on team cohesion dates to the early work of Festinger (1950), who defined cohesiveness as "the resultant of all the forces acting on the members to remain in the group" (p. 274). Festinger also suggested that there are three facets that comprise cohesion: member attraction (i.e., interpersonal attraction), group activities (i.e., task commitment), and prestige or group pride. Research findings have provided support for this multidimensional view of cohesion and have demonstrated the importance of cohesion for team effectiveness. A meta-analysis by Beal, Cohen, Burke, and McLendon (2003) found that all three dimensions of cohesion were significantly related to group performance, and the effect sizes for the different dimensions were not significantly different from each other. In addition, cohesion was more strongly related to performance behaviors than performance outcomes and was more strongly related to measures of performance efficiency than measures of performance effectiveness. Moreover, the cohesion-performance relationship became stronger as team workflow (i.e., interdependence) increased. Another recent meta-analysis by Chiocchio and Essiembre (2009) provides some preliminary evidence that cohesion-performance relationships may vary across different types of teams (e.g., project vs. product teams) and team settings (e.g., organizational vs. academic). However, more research is needed to tease apart the effects of team type and team setting on the relationship between different types of cohesion and team performance.

Whereas cohesion has generally been found to enhance team performance, research has offered somewhat mixed perspectives on the effects of conflict on team effectiveness. On the one hand, it has been argued that conflict and divisiveness have the potential to undermine team member satisfaction, interfere with team information processing, and hinder team performance (e.g., Carnevale & Probst, 1998; Lau & Murnighan, 1998). On the other hand, some research suggests that moderate levels of conflict that is focused on the task (rather than interpersonal relationships) may be functional in that it leads to different perspectives and ideas that can help teams avoid groupthink and enhance their performance, particularly on non-routine and creative tasks (Amason, 1996; Jehn, 1995). However, a recent meta-analysis by De Dreu and Weingart (2003) showed that both task and relationship conflict are negatively associated with team member satisfaction and team performance. In addition, they found that the negative relationship between conflict and team performance was stronger for teams performing complex, uncertain, rather than simple and routine, tasks. Kozlowski and Ilgen (2006) note that due to several unresolved issues, such as the causal ambiguity in the conflict-performance relationship, more work is needed to better specify the effects of conflict on team performance.

Although much of the research on cohesion and conflict has examined their effects on team performance, emerging work has begun to explore the implications of these emergent states for learning in teams. Interest in these constructs has been driven, in part, by their potential to facilitate or inhibit critical team learning processes, such as collaboration and communication (Ellis & Bell, 2005). Wong (2004) argued that stronger group cohesion should foster team learning "by increasing the motivation, trust, and cognitive familiarity for productive inquiry" (p. 647). In addition, researchers have posited that cohesion and conflict may be critical to deciphering the effects of diversity on team learning. It has been argued that teams whose members are heterogeneous with regard to background and perspective have the potential to pool their diverse knowledge and viewpoints, thereby facilitating team learning (Argote, Gruenfeld, & Naquin, 2001). However, to realize this potential, diverse teams must overcome the disruptive effects of their differences (Mannix & Neale, 2005). In particular, diversity can create social divisions that result in poor social integration and cohesion and lead to higher levels of conflict in teams (Roberson, Bell, & Porter, 2008). Thus, diversity may lead to greater team learning, but only if teams are able to build a collective identity and

effectively manage conflict when it occurs (Van der Vegt & Bunderson, 2005).

Several articles provide evidence that cohesion is an important supporting condition for team learning. Wong (2004) examined both local team learning (i.e., learning within the group) and distal team learning (i.e., learning with individuals external to the group) among 78 teams drawn from four different organizations. Her results revealed a positive, linear relationship between group cohesion and distal learning. However, there was an inverted U-shaped relationship between group cohesion and local learning, suggesting that very high levels of social integration diminished learning among team members. These results contradict the popular belief that high levels of group cohesion may insulate a group from external ideas, and suggest that excessive levels of trust and cognitive familiarity may undermine important team learning processes (e.g., knowledge exchange, exploring new ideas). Van der Vegt and Bunderson (2005) examined the relationship of expertise diversity with team learning and team performance in multidisciplinary teams in the oil and gas industry. They found that these relationships were moderated by collective team identification, such that expertise diversity was negatively related to team learning and performance when collective identification was low, but these relationships were positive when collective team identification was high. These results suggest that diversity can be positively related to team learning, but only when members identify with their teams. It is important to note, however, that even under conditions of high collective interdependence, moderate levels of expertise diversity stimulated greater team learning than very high levels of diversity (i.e., inverted curvilinear relationship). Finally, a study by Kane, Argote, and Levine (2005) examined the effects of social identity on knowledge transfer across groups. The authors found that when a new member rotated into a group, the group was more likely to adopt his or her knowledge when the routine of the new member was superior to their own and both shared a superordinate identity (i.e., viewed themselves as part of a larger, shared group). When groups did not share a superordinate identity with the rotating member, they rarely adopted his or her routine, even when it represented superior knowledge.

Although a number of studies have examined the relationship between diversity and team learning processes and outcomes (e.g., Gibson & Vermeulen, 2003; Drach-Zahavy & Somech, 2001; Somech & Drach-Zahavy, 2007; van Offenbeek, 2001), very few studies have directly explored the relationship between conflict and team learning. One exception is a study by Rau (2005), which examined relationship conflict as a moderator of the relationship between transactive memory and the performance of top management teams. The results revealed that the shared awareness of the location of expertise in the team was positively related to team performance when relationship conflict was low but was unrelated to performance under high levels of relationship conflict. These results suggest that high levels of relationship conflict may prevent members from leveraging the expertise distributed throughout the team.

In a related stream of research, several studies have examined the effects of cooperation on team learning. Tjosvold, Yu, and Hui (2004), for example, examined the effects of different types of goals on the learning behaviors of teams drawn from a variety of Chinese organizations. They found evidence that cooperative goals are positively related to group problem solving and learning from mistakes, whereas competitive and independent goals are positively related to blaming within groups. It should be noted that the effects of blaming on reported team learning were mixed, with correlational analyses revealing a non-significant relationship but structural equation analyses suggesting a significant, positive relationship between blaming and learning from mistakes. As noted earlier, De Dreu (2007) found that team members' perceptions of cooperative outcome interdependence were positively related to information sharing, team learning, and team effectiveness. However, cooperative outcome interdependence was only related to these outcomes when task reflexivity was high, suggesting that learning requires teams to not only cooperate but also to engage in the systematic processing of information. These results may help explain why, in the study by Wong (2004) discussed above, the teams with very high levels of cohesion (which may prevent critical analysis of information) failed to engage in mutual learning. Finally, Ellis et al. (2003) found that teams with higher levels of average agreeableness evidenced lower levels of team learning. Mirroring the arguments of De Dreu (2007), they conclude that high levels of agreeableness may lead to cohesion but also prevent a team from critically evaluating different opinions or conflicting pieces of information.

CONCLUSION

In summary, these studies suggest a complex relationship between cohesion, conflict, and team learning. The studies reviewed above generally suggest that cohesion enhances team learning processes and outcomes. At the same time, there is evidence that learning may be impeded when teams are characterized by excessive social integration or when cohesion is not supplemented with processes that facilitate the critical processing of information (e.g., team reflexivity, constructive conflict). These findings suggest that future research should focus on how to effectively manage cohesion and conflict toward promoting team learning (Kozlowski & Ilgen, 2006). London, Polzer, and Omoregie (2005) present a model of group learning that suggests that team members engage in identity negotiation behaviors (e.g., sharing information about themselves), which influence interpersonal congruence (i.e., group members seeing themselves similarly) and ultimately group learning. They argue that interventions organized by the team leader or facilitator, such as multisource feedback, can strengthen the relationship between identity negotiation and interpersonal congruence. Gibson and Vermeulen (2003) empirically demonstrated that the presence of moderately strong subgroups stimulated team learning behavior, whereas very weak or very strong subgroups inhibited team learning behavior. In addition, they found that the effects of organizational design features, such as performance management by an external team leader, had different effects on team learning behavior, depending on the strength of subgroups within the team. These findings suggest that different strategies may be needed to promote team learning, depending on where a team falls on the continuum between being highly cohesive and highly fractured. A study by Zellmer-Bruhn and Gibson (2006) extends these findings by showing that team learning is shaped by not only these micro-contextual features (e.g., team leadership) but also macro-aspects of the context. Based on data collected from teams in the subsidiaries of several multinational organizations, they found that organizational contexts emphasizing global integration hindered team learning, whereas those emphasizing responsiveness and knowledge management increased team learning. These findings suggest that macro-contextual features, such as strategy, culture, and resources, may play a role in promoting or inhibiting a supportive context for team learning. Overall, future work needs to explore how these micro- and macro-elements can be used to shape cohesion and conflict so as to create a supportive environment for team learning.

Team Learning Outcomes: Team Knowledge and Team Performance

In this section, we review research that has examined the outcomes of team learning, with particular emphasis on the cognitive and knowledge-based outcomes that represent the most salient manifestations of learning as a psychological process. These outcomes include collective knowledge, shared cognition (transactive memory, team mental models), and macrocognition and team knowledge emergence. In addition, we discuss the findings of research that has examined the relationship between team learning and team performance. Prior research has tended to focus either on the process of team learning (e.g., team learning behaviors) or the outcomes of team learning, with few studies having integrated these two foci to examine the linkages between indicators of team learning processes and team learning outcomes. Our goal is to review the outcome representations of team learning and to conceptually explore their linkages to the processes and emergent states reviewed above.

Collective Knowledge

Cognitive theories of team learning generally argue that the sharing or exchange of information within a team should lead to a change in the collective knowledge of the group (Ellis & Bell, 2005; Wilson et al., 2007). New knowledge, behaviors, or routines become distributed among the members of the group and are stored either in the memories of members or in different types of technological (e.g., databases) or structural repositories (e.g., rules and procedures). Accordingly, a number of researchers have defined team learning as a change in a team's collective level of knowledge and skills (e.g., Ellis et al., 2003), which expands on traditional conceptualizations of learning at the individual level.

Although conceptually changes in collective knowledge represent a direct indication that team learning has taken place, very little empirical research has examined collective knowledge as an outcome of team learning. As Kozlowski and Ilgen (2006) note, past research, rather than directly measuring team learning, instead has inferred it from changes in team performance. Thus, few studies on team learning directly assess changes in collective knowledge. For example, Argote, Insko, Yovetich, and Romero (1995) conducted a laboratory study to examine the effects of turnover and task complexity on group performance. Three-person groups were asked to perform a production-task over six trials, and the results revealed that group performance followed a learning curve trajectory, such that output improved significantly over time, and this increase occurred at a decreasing rate. In addition, they found that groups not experiencing turnover outperformed those groups experiencing turnover and that the gap in performance was amplified over time and was greater for the simple than the complex task. Based on these findings, the authors suggest that turnover depletes the collective knowledge of a group, which undermines performance. In addition, they argue that turnover had less of an effect on groups performing the complex tasks because these groups produced innovations that made some of the knowledge of experienced members obsolete. Individual training of new team members failed to mitigate the effects of turnover, which they argue suggests that the knowledge that members developed of their group's structure, culture, and work procedures (i.e., social knowledge) was more important for performance than task-specific knowledge. However, since the knowledge of group members was never measured, it is impossible to know whether the effects of turnover were due to changes in collective knowledge. It may be that turnover impacted team performance via mechanisms other than learning, such as by undermining coordination or communication processes (Kozlowski & Bell, 2008).

More recent theoretical and empirical work has attempted to focus more direct attention on collective knowledge and its antecedents and consequences. Zellmer-Bruhn (2003) examined the effects of interruptions on team knowledge acquisition. Using data from 46 operational teams in the pharmaceutical and medical products industry, the author found that teams that experienced more interruptive events (e.g., loss of a member, changes in machines, tools, or other technology) acquired more knowledge in the form of new routines. In addition, the results revealed that the effects of interruptions on team knowledge acquisition could be partially explained by the fact that interruptions led the teams to devote more effort to knowledge transfer activities, such as searching for new practices. Finally, exploratory analyses suggested that different types of interruptions may have differential effects on knowledge transfer effort and acquisition. For instance, changes in team structure positively affected team knowledge acquisition, whereas unusually disruptive events had a negative effect on knowledge acquisition. Griffith, Sawyer, and Neale (2003) proposed that team context, in particular a team's level of virtuality, may also influence collective knowledge, which they defined as tacit team knowledge. Because interpersonal interaction is critical to the development of tacit knowledge, they argue that highly virtual teams may have difficulty forming collective knowledge unless they are able to use media or other means to engage in rich communication. In addition, they suggest that the collective knowledge generated by virtual teams is more likely to be captured and made accessible through technology tools than the collective knowledge generated by less virtual teams, which is likely to remain more tacit. Unfortunately, very little research has examined the storage of knowledge in teams, and more work is needed to understand the most effective means for different types of teams to store different types of knowledge (Wilson et al., 2007). As noted earlier, research on macrocognition has begun to explore this issue by exploring the concept of externalized knowledge that may be captured by the team in the artifacts that they create (Fiore et al., 2010).

Some recent work has also started to explore the consequences of membership changes for a team's collective knowledge and the subsequent implications for team performance. Although it has been argued that new members can be beneficial for a team because they increase the group's knowledge stock, research also suggests that there are a number of factors that determine whether groups incorporate and leverage the knowledge of new members. Kane et al. (2005) conducted a laboratory study in which three-person groups performed a production task (constructing origami sailboats). Midway through the task, a member from a different group rotated into each group. As noted earlier, they found that groups were more likely to adopt the routine of the rotating member when both shared a superordinate identity (i.e., they viewed themselves as part of a larger, shared group) and when the rotating member possessed a superior routine (i.e., a more efficient production routine than the one currently used by the group). In addition, they found that groups that shared a superordinate identity with the new member were likely to adopt a superior routine and to reap the performance benefits, whereas groups that did not share a superordinate identity with the new member rarely adopted the superior routine and did not improve their performance. A recent laboratory study by Lewis, Belliveau, Herndon, and Keller (2007) further illustrates the challenges that teams face in leveraging the knowledge of new members. Three-person groups were trained to perform a telephone assembly task and then were brought back one week later for a performance session. In the performance session, groups were assigned to one of three membership change conditions, which left the original group either fully intact, partially intact (two members from the original group and one new member), or reconstituted (three members, each trained with a different group). They found that transactive memory system structure stability was greater in partially intact groups than in the reconstituted groups. In other words, groups with partial membership changes were more likely to rely on the TMS structure developed by old-timers, and newcomers were more likely to adapt to the existing structure. They also found evidence that this pattern was detrimental to performance because it created inefficient TMS processes in partially-intact groups relative to intact groups. In a supplemental study, they found that asking old-timers to deliberately reflect on their collective knowledge (i.e., the breadth and depth of their own and other old-timer's knowledge) made them more likely to adjust their specializations when new members were added. This led to a more elaborated TMS structure, improved TMS process efficiency, and generated higher levels of performance. It is important to note that the intervention did not change the overall structure of the group's expertise. Rather, the results suggest that forcing existing team members to evaluate their collective knowledge in the wake of a membership change allows for greater flexibility in integrating newcomer's expertise into the TMS structure.

CONCLUSION

Although recent work has begun to focus more attention on collective knowledge as an important outcome of team learning, there remain several unaddressed issues. One important issue concerns the implications of using different methods to aggregate individual knowledge to create a team-level construct. One approach has been to operationalize collective knowledge as either the sum or average of individual team members' knowledge. Ellis et al. (2003), for instance, assessed the collective knowledge of teams in their study by summing the efficiency and effectiveness with which individual team members engaged unknown tracks. Teams that performed better on this measure could be inferred as having shared more information with one another about the unknown tracks. However, recent research suggests that, in some cases, the average level of knowledge in a team may be less important than how that knowledge is distributed within a team. That is, the effects of collective knowledge may sometimes depend on exactly who knows what. Ellis, Bell, Ployhart, Hollenbeck, and Ilgen (2005) found that the knowledge of critical team members, or those who were central to the workflow of the team, had a greater impact on team performance than the knowledge of less critical team members. The uniqueness of team members' knowledge may also be important, as this determines how much of the knowledge space is covered by the collective knowledge of the team (Hinsz, 1990). We address these distributional properties of collective knowledge in more detail below, in our discussion of shared mental models and transactive memory systems. However, given that collective knowledge is often considered in conjunction with these structural elements of team knowledge (e.g., Lewis et al., 2007), it raises the question as to whether collective knowledge represents a meaningful outcome of team learning in its own right. A second important issue concerns the effects of different types of collective knowledge on team performance. Reagans, Argote, and Brooks (2005) found that surgical teams that had more relationship-specific knowledge (operationalized as the average amount of experience that team members had working with each other) took less time to complete their procedures. However, cumulative individual knowledge (operationalized as the average number of times each member of a team had performed a procedure) had a curvilinear relationship with completion times. Initial increases in individual experience hampered team performance, but continued increases in individual experience eventually reduced procedure completion time. These results suggest that the effects of collective knowledge on team performance may depend on how collective knowledge is conceptualized and operationalized. A final issue concerning collective knowledge is that it has been studied almost exclusively in the laboratory, using small groups performing production tasks. More studies similar to the one conducted by Zellmer-Bruhn (2003) are needed that use field study methods to examine knowledge acquisition among real teams performing different types of tasks.

Team Mental Models

Team mental models represent team members' shared, organized understanding and mental representation of knowledge or beliefs about key elements within a team's relevant environment (Klimoski & Mohammed, 1994). They are shared, compositional, emergent characteristics that derive from the cognition of individual team members but manifest at the collective level (Kozlowski &

Chao, 2011; Kozlowski & Klein, 2000; Marks et al., 2001). Cannon-Bowers et al. (1993) originally proposed four non-independent content domains of team mental models. These domains include: (a) knowledge of the equipment or tools used by the team (equipment model); (b) understanding of the team's task, including its goals or performance requirements and the problems facing the team (task model); (c) awareness of team member characteristics, including their knowledge, skills, preferences, and habits (team or member model); and (d) team members' knowledge or beliefs regarding appropriate or effective team processes (teamwork or team interaction model). Team mental models can be distinguished from other forms of team cognition by their incorporation of a broader array of cognitive content (e.g., taskwork and teamwork) and their focus on the structure of the content (Mohammed et al., 2010).

The formation of shared team mental models is typically viewed as an important indicator of team development. Interest in team mental models grew out of research suggesting that teams whose members share models of both taskwork and teamwork will be better equipped to implicitly coordinate their behavior and improve their performance (Cannon-Bowers et al., 1993). Although much of the early work on team mental models was conceptual, Mohammed et al. (2010) note in their recent review that there has been a proliferation of empirical studies on the construct conducted over the past 15 years. Much of this research has examined the relationship between team mental model sharedness/convergence and team performance. For instance, Mathieu, Heffner, Goodwin, Salas, and Cannon-Bowers (2000) examined the effects of shared mental models on team processes and performance among 56 dyads performing a flight simulation. They found that team mental model convergence had a significant and positive effect on team performance, and this effect was fully mediated by team processes (e.g., strategy formation, coordination, cooperation, and communication). However, they found that task mental model convergence did not significantly affect team performance, although it did have a positive influence on team processes, suggesting an indirect effect. In another study, Waller, Gupta, and Giambatista (2004) examined shared mental model development among 14 nuclear power plant control room crews performing simulations. They found that when crews were faced with non-routine situations, high-performing crews were more likely to act to develop a shared understanding of the situation or response than were lower performing crews. However, during monitoring or routine situations, there was no significant difference in the mental modeling activities of high and low performing crews. These results suggest that the ability to formulate shared understanding in abnormal, high workload situations may represent a key differentiator of high and low performing crews. Smith-Jentsch, Mathieu, and Kraiger (2005) examined the relationship between two types of shared mental models—team interaction model and task model—and team effectiveness in an air traffic control environment. Although neither type of mental model demonstrated a linear relationship with tower safety or efficiency, the two shared mental models interacted to predict effectiveness. In particular, tower safety and efficiency were highest when the air traffic controllers exhibited consistent team interaction *and* task shared mental models. It is interesting to note, however, that this interactive pattern was not found when the shared mental models were indexed in terms of agreement rather than consistency. Although most studies in this area have focused on the effects of team mental model sharedness or convergence, a growing number of studies have examined the effects of team mental model accuracy. The basic argument underlying this stream of research is that team mental models must be not only shared but also accurate if they are to have beneficial effects on team processes and performance. However, Mohammed et al. (2010) note that research on the effects of accuracy have yielded inconsistent findings, with some studies finding team mental model accuracy to be a stronger predictor of team performance than similarity (e.g., Edwards et al., 2006), and others failing to find a significant relationship between accuracy and performance (e.g., Mathieu, Heffner, Goodwin, Cannon-Bowers, & Salas, 2005). One of the big challenges with the issue of accuracy is that one needs to have a indisputable mental model structure as the target criterion; outside laboratory tasks (and they are problematic, too!), this criterion is difficult to establish with certainty.

Recent qualitative (e.g., Mohammed et al., 2010) and quantitative (e.g., DeChurch & Mesmer-Magnus, 2010b) reviews have concluded that the research in this area has firmly established a positive relationship between team mental models and team processes and performance. DeChurch and Mesmer-Magnus (2010b) recently conducted a meta-analysis to examine the relationship between team cognition and team performance, and the overall findings revealed that team cognition has a strong positive relationship with team behavioral processes, motivational states, and performance. Based on these findings, the authors conclude that "there is clearly a cognitive foundation to teamwork" (p. 44). However, they also note that the effects of team cognition varied, based on three classes of moderators: cognitive underpinnings, task features, and study characteristics. For instance, they found that the effects of cognition on behavioral processes and team performance were stronger when emergence is represented through compilation (consistent with the transactive memory tradition) than composition (consistent with the shared mental model tradition). They suggest that the patterned knowledge that emerges through compilation offers greater predictive power because it is non-isomorphic to the individual-level cognitive content. In addition, they found that the effects of cognition depend on the type of tasks that teams perform. Compositional cognition, for example, was more predictive of team process in action teams than in decision-making teams, and was more predictive of performance in project and decision-making teams than in action teams. In sum, the meta-analysis further demonstrates that, although the effects of team cognition are generally positive, the magnitude of the effect often depends on the type of cognition being examined as well as the nature of the team, the tasks being performed, and the outcomes under investigation.

Having shown that team mental models predict process and performance, there is an emerging body of work that aims to understand the factors that influence the development of team mental models. The shared and complimentary cognitions that form the basis of these models emerge from the exchange of information, ideas, knowledge, and insights within a team over time (Kozlowski & Bell, 2008). This exchange may occur through a variety of mechanisms, including informal and social interaction, shared task experiences, and formal interventions. Pearsall, Ellis, and Bell (2010) recently showed that the number of role identification behaviors (e.g., sharing or requesting information about roles) exhibited by a team during the early stages of their development was positively related to the development of team-interaction mental models. Similarly, Levesque, Wilson, and Wholey (2001) found that as role differentiation increased in software development teams, there was a decline in shared mental models. They argue that, as members' roles became increasingly specialized, there was a corresponding decrease in interaction in the group, which led to a divergence in mental models over time.

Mohammed et al. (2010) suggest that the drivers of team mental models can be organized into three broad categories. The first category is team member characteristics and includes variables such as age, gender, and tenure. For example, Smith-Jentsch, Campbell, Milanovich, and Reynolds (2001) examined the similarity among the teamwork mental models of 176 U.S. Navy personnel. They found that there was greater similarity among high-ranking (vs. low-ranking) groups and among those groups that had high time in service (vs. low time in service). These results are consistent with the notion that mental models will become more similar and accurate as individuals gain experience. The second category of antecedents is team interventions, such as planning, reflexivity, and training. Gurtner, Tschan, Semmer, and Nägele (2007), for example, examined the effect of guided reflection on the similarity of team interaction models. Three-person teams were asked to perform a military simulation and were assigned to either a control condition or one of two reflexivity conditions (individual or group). Participants in the reflexivity conditions were instructed to engage in guided reflection on teamwork and the task. They found that the team interaction mental models were more similar in the individual and group reflexivity conditions than in the control conditions and that there was no significant difference between the two reflexivity conditions. A number of studies have found that various types of training, such as team self-correction and cross-training, can also increase team mental model similarity or accuracy (Cannon-Bowers, 2007; Marks, Sabella, Burke, & Zaccaro, 2002; Smith-Jentsch, Cannon-Bowers, Tannenbaum, & Salas, 2008). Moreover, Kozlowski and Ilgen (2006) suggest that leaders can play a central role in shaping the formation of team mental models. The final category mentioned by Mohammed et al. (2010) focuses on contextual factors that can influence team mental models, including stress, workload, and the novelty of the environment. Ellis (2006), for example, found that acute stress had a negative effect on both the accuracy and similarity of team interaction mental models. In addition, he found that team interaction mental models partially mediated the negative relationship between acute stress and team performance.

CONCLUSION

Although the research on team mental models has matured more rapidly than in other areas of team cognition (Kozlowski & Bell, 2003), there remain a number of issues to address moving forward. One issue that has always plagued this literature concerns the measurement of team mental models (e.g., Mohammed, Klimoski, & Rentsch, 2000). As Mohammed et al. (2010) note, "Because of their context-dependent nature, there is no consistent methodology that has been used to measure TMMs" (p. 884). Fortunately, some recent work has examined the implications associated with different measurement techniques. DeChurch and Mesmer-Magnus (2010a) conducted a meta-analysis to examine how the measurement of shared mental models influences relationships with team process and performance. Their results revealed that shared mental models only predict team process when the measurement techniques enable the representation of the structure or organization of knowledge, as is the case when similarity ratings (with Pathfinder network analysis for structural representation), concept mapping, or card sorting is used. When traditional rating scale techniques were used (e.g., rating scales or questionnaires), the relationship between shared mental models and team process was small and negative. However, shared mental models positively predicted team performance regardless of which measurement strategy was used, although the magnitude of the relationships differed across measurement method. Based on these findings, the authors conclude that whereas knowledge structure is predictive of both team process and performance, knowledge content is only predictive of team performance. A recent study by Resick et al. (2010) compared the validity of three team mental model measurement approaches: structural networks, priority rankings, and importance ratings. The authors found little convergent and considerable discriminant validity across the three measurement approaches, suggesting that the metrics measure different underlying constructs. In addition, they found that the structural networks approach predicted team adaptation and performance, whereas the other two approaches did not. Finally, they found that the quality of team member structural networks had a significant, positive effect on team adaptation and performance, whereas the similarity of structural networks did not. Yet, similarity moderated the effect of quality on adaptation, such that quality was most strongly related to adaptation when members had *less similar* structural networks. These studies, along with other qualitative reviews of different measurement approaches (e.g., Langan-Fox, Code, & Langfield-Smith, 2000; Mohammed et al., 2000), have begun to highlight some basic guidelines that researchers can follow when choosing a measurement approach, such as using a methodology that is capable of mapping the structure of the knowledge and aligning the measurement technique with the research question and team context under examination.

A second issue involves examining the relationship between team learning processes and team mental models. Although team mental models have long been viewed as an important indicator of team development, few studies have directly examined how different team learning processes foster the development of team mental models. Often, these processes are inferred rather than directly assessed. For example, Rentsch and Klimoski (2001) found that team size was negatively related to teamwork schema agreement. They argue that team size serves as a rough estimate of team member interaction opportunity, but they do not study these interaction and communication processes directly. However, some recent work has proposed theoretical frameworks for the development of team mental models (e.g., Langan-Fox, 2003; McComb, 2008), and empirical studies have started to focus more specifically on the processes that influence the development of mental models (e.g., Pearsall et al., 2010). We believe that more work is needed in this area. As Mohammed et al. (2010) note, "Much remains to be known about the developmental processes by which TMMs evolve over time" (p. 901).

Finally, there is a need for research that challenges the presumption that an increased sharing of knowledge among team members is always necessary or beneficial. As Kozlowski and Ilgen (2006) suggest, "Although the notion of a common or shared team mental model has tended to dominate the research, there is recognition that team mental models may be more complex" (p. 83). In particular, it is important to recognize that team members may not necessarily need to have identical knowledge structures, but rather may possess some sharing and also some unique structural information based on role distinctions. Thus, it is important to examine what roles in the teams may benefit from greater convergence of knowledge and which may be better served by complementary or distributed mental models (Mohammed et al., 2010). This conceptualization

of distributed or networked knowledge is similar to the notion of transactive memory, which we turn to next.

Transactive Memory

The concept of transactive memory was introduced to explain how intimate relationships foster the development of common memory (Wegner, Giuliano, & Hertel, 1985). Accordingly, transactive memory has often been studied within dyads, although over the past decade the construct has increasingly been applied to groups and teams. Within teams, transactive memory represents a group-level shared system for encoding, storing, and retrieving information that is distributed across group members (Wegner, 1986, 1995; Wegner et al., 1985). This distributed pattern suggests that transactive memory represents a compilation form of emergence (DeChurch & Mesmer-Magnus, 2010b; Kozlowski & Chao, 2011). It is conceptualized as a set of distributed, individual memory systems that combine two components: (a) internal memory, or the knowledge possessed by particular team members; and (b) external memory, or the shared awareness of who knows what (Peltokorpi, 2008; Wegner, 1995). A transactive memory system functions through transactive processes, including directory updating, information allocation, and retrieval coordination (Lewis, Lange, & Gillis, 2005; Wegner, 1986). Although past research has sometimes blurred the distinction between team mental models and transactive memory (Kozlowski & Ilgen, 2006), there are a few features that distinguish transactive memory from other team cognitive constructs. Whereas shared mental models typically emphasize the overlap among team member knowledge (Mohammed & Dumville, 2001), transactive memory focuses on the distribution or network of knowledge in the team (Kozlowski & Ilgen, 2006). In addition, transactive memory is unique in its emphasis on the shared awareness of expertise and its focus on critical learning processes, particularly the retrieval of information (Mohammed & Dumville, 2001; Peltokorpi, 2008).[1]

The emergence of transactive memory systems represents an important manifestation of team learning processes (Kozlowski & Bell, 2008). These systems develop as groups gain experience and members communicate and update the information they have about other members' unique knowledge. Members keep track of other members' expertise, direct incoming information to those individuals with matching domain expertise, and use that tracking to access information from others in the system (Mohammed & Dumville, 2001; Wegner, 1995). In essence, team members cultivate one another as external memory aids, thereby creating a compatible and differentiated memory system that is useful to the team (Kozlowski & Bell, 2003). In addition to representing an emergent outcome of team learning, researchers have noted that transactive memory systems facilitate team learning. During the initial stages of transactive memory system development, a shared awareness of expertise allows individual members to specialize in different areas, which not only makes the group's knowledge more differentiated but also provides the freedom for members to develop more knowledge in their specialty areas (Lewis et al., 2005). In addition, as groups perform their tasks and engage in learning by doing, the transactive memory system is further refined to include higher order knowledge structures and stable patterns of interacting that allow learning to be transferred across functionally similar tasks. Thus, when viewed from a dynamic perspective, transactive memory serves as both an outcome of team learning processes and as a driver of team learning and transfer.

One of the first studies to examine the development of transactive memory systems in teams was conducted by Liang, Moreland, and Argote (1995), who compared the performance of groups whose members were trained individually to that of groups whose members were trained together on a radio assembly task. They found that groups whose members were trained together recalled more about the assembly procedure and produced higher quality radios than those groups whose members were trained alone. Based on an analysis of videotaped data, they concluded that the performance benefits of group training were primarily due to the fact that it fostered the development of transactive memory among group members. Specifically, groups whose members were trained together exhibited greater memory differentiation, task coordination, and task credibility (trust in other members' expertise), and a composite of these three factors mediated the relationship between group training and performance. Several follow-up studies were conducted using the radio assembly paradigm to further test the role of transactive memory in explaining the benefits of group training. Moreland and Myaskovsky (2000) examined whether the benefits of group training may instead be due to improved communication among group members. They found that groups

whose members were not allowed to communicate during training but received information about one another's skills performed equally as well as those groups trained together, and both of these groups outperformed the groups whose members were trained individually. These findings, combined with the fact that the training method did not impact members' ratings of communication, suggest that the performance benefits of group training are due to transactive memory, not improved communication. In another study using the same experimental task, Rulke and Rau (2000) employed qualitative methods to examine the encoding process of transactive memory development during group training. Their findings revealed that groups with strong transactive memory (those in the group training condition) spent more time in the early periods of group interaction identifying who had what expertise in what domains. In addition, they found evidence that transactive encoding occurs through short, recurring encoding cycles and that the frequency of the different cycle elements (e.g., declaring expertise) vary over time.

Subsequent research has identified a number of other factors that influence the development of transactive memory systems. Several studies have shown that face-to-face communication is important for the emergence and refinement of transactive memory systems, but computer-mediated communication can present barriers to the development of transactive memory systems (Hollingshead, 1998a, 1998b; Lewis, 2004). Pearsall et al. (2010) also found that communication about roles and responsibilities early in a team's development was positively related to the development of transactive memory. Together, these studies suggest that co-presence and communication are important to the development and modification of transactive memory systems (Brandon and Hollingshead, 2004). Several studies have also shown that changes in team membership (i.e., turnover) can have a detrimental effect on transactive memory systems (Akgün, Byrne, Keskin, Lynn, & Imamoglu, 2005; Moreland, Argote, & Krishnan, 1996). As discussed earlier, Lewis et al. (2005) showed that having remaining team members reflect on their collective knowledge may be beneficial to transactive memory system processes following turnover. Research has also shown that transactive memory development is influenced by task and outcome interdependence (Hollingshead, 2001; Lewis, 2003; Zhang, Hempel, Han, & Tjosvold, 2007), acute stress (Ellis, 2006), and team member personality (Pearsall & Ellis, 2006).

The development of transactive memory systems is important, as conceptually such systems should offer teams the advantage of cognitive efficiency. Through the encoding and information allocation processes, individual knowledge becomes progressively more specialized and differentiated. The knowledge specialization that team members develop within a transactive memory system reduces cognitive load, increases the knowledge stock of the team, and reduces redundancy of effort (Hollingshead, 1998b). However, the complexity of transactive memory can create confusion, such as when important information is not captured or is directed to the wrong team member (Wegner, 1986; Pearsall, Ellis, & Bell, 2008). In addition, potential delays associated with retrieving information can negatively affect team effectiveness in time-critical situations (Kozlowski & Bell, 2003). These challenges are likely more salient for larger teams.

Empirical research has generally found support for a positive relationship between transactive memory and team effectiveness (e.g., Ellis, 2006; Pearsall & Ellis, 2006; Pearsall et al., 2010; Zhang et al., 2007). Austin (2003), for instance, examined the effects of different dimensions of transactive memory on the performance of 27 groups in an apparel and sporting goods company. He found that transactive memory accuracy and specialization were significantly and positively related to internal and external performance evaluations, and accuracy also predicted external ratings of group goal attainment. Lewis et al. (2005) found that a developed transactive memory allows groups to develop abstract knowledge of the task domain after experience with several tasks, which can facilitate the transfer of learning to functionally similar tasks. Finally, using computational modeling to run virtual experiments, Ren, Carley, and Argote (2006) found that transactive memory enhances the quality of performance for small groups and improves the efficiency of performance for large groups and groups operating in dynamic task environments and volatile knowledge environments.

CONCLUSION

Kozlowski and Ilgen (2006) note that research on transactive memory is still in its infancy. Although recent studies have helped to expand our understanding of transactive memory systems, more work is needed in this area. Although measurement of transactive memory has not garnered much attention in the literature, we think it is an important issue that merits examination. At its conceptual roots, transactive memory is a distributed memory structure (i.e., unique knowledge linked in a network) and, in that sense, it is a compilation construct (Kozlowski & Klein, 2000). Yet, the instrument used to assess it most often (i.e., Lewis, 2003) does not assess that distributed structure directly. Rather, team member perceptions of knowledge distribution are assessed, ratings are examined for restricted within-group variance (i.e., justification for aggregating a *composition* construct; Kozlowski & Klein, 2000), and the mean ratings are used as indicators of transactive memory facets. Although the facets—specialization, credibility, and coordination—are consistent with the underlying theoretical *content* of transactive memory (Liang et al., 1995), and meta-analytic evidence shows that they relate to team performance (DeChurch & Mesmer-Magnus, 2010b), this conceptual inconsistency (i.e., structure vs. content; compilation conceptualization vs. composition operationalization) creates questions as to what is actually being captured by the measure (Kozlowski & Chao, 2011). Given the different findings for content versus structure (DeChurch & Mesmer-Magnus, 2010b), this issue merits more research attention.

Another important issue that needs to be examined concerns the development of transactive memory in geographically distributed or virtual teams. As noted above, several studies have found that computer-mediated communication impedes the development of transactive memory systems. Future work is needed to understand the mechanisms that explain these effects and to identify strategies for inducing the co-presence and communication cues necessary to develop transactive memory through remote communication (Kozlowski & Ilgen, 2006). In addition, future research must continue to examine the role of the team and task context in shaping transactive memory. Peltokorpi (2008) notes that the transactive memory literature often assumes that groups members have egalitarian relationships and are motivated to share their knowledge. Yet, conflict, power differentials, and hierarchy can influence the dynamics of information sharing within teams, and research on hidden profiles suggests that unshared information does not automatically emerge through communication (Stasser & Titus, 2003). In addition, several of the studies reviewed above suggest that role interdependencies influence the importance of knowledge distribution in teams. Thus, research is needed that examines the contingencies that influence both the development of transactive memory as well as its importance to team effectiveness.

Macrocognition and Team Knowledge Emergence

The last form of team knowledge representation that we address in this section is a conceptual typology that is based on the macrocognition meta-model (Fiore et al., 2010) described previously as a team learning process. Kozlowski and Chao (2012) and their research team (Kozlowski et al., 2011) have developed a *team knowledge typology* that is designed to capture knowledge resulting from the key process components of the macrocognition meta-model. Their typology is a conceptual framework for representing macrocognitive team knowledge that explicitly incorporates our theoretical foci—it is multilevel, dynamic, and emergent—and, while it is not an explicit integration, it also incorporates aspects of each of the prior forms of team knowledge reviewed in this section—collective knowledge, team mental models, and transactive memory.

First, like collective knowledge, it is focused on the pool of relevant knowledge that teams acquire as they endeavor to perform their task, solve the problem, or make a decision. However, unlike collective knowledge, there is an explicit focus on understanding how individual knowledge contributes to the collective pool. Second, like team mental models, it is concerned with shared team knowledge. However, unlike team mental models, it is explicitly concerned with how knowledge becomes shared—how it moves from the individual to the team level. And, third, like transactive memory, it is focused on the distribution of knowledge. However, unlike transactive memory, it is explicitly concerned with how uniquely held knowledge (specific to a team member) and common knowledge (available to all team members) emerge to form a shared pool that the team can apply to perform, problem solve, or render a decision.

As noted previously, the conceptual foundation for the team knowledge typology is formulated around our core theoretical foci—multilevel, dynamic, and emergent. It is a synthesis of regulatory processes that underlie individual and team learning (DeShon et al., 2004), progressive knowledge compilation (Fiore et al., 2010; Kozlowski & Bell, 2008), and composition and compilation forms of knowledge emergence across levels (Kozlowski & Klein, 2000). The theoretical driver of the typology is the macrocognition meta-model shown in Figure 26.8 (Fiore et al., 2010). The learning process

of *individual knowledge building* yields *internalized knowledge*, which is the knowledge that individual team members acquire and the knowledge that the team possesses collectively. Internalized knowledge influences both subsequent individual knowledge building and *team knowledge building*, which represents team-level learning processes that yield *externalized team knowledge*. It is externalized knowledge in the sense that it has to be made tangible; it is explicitly communicated, discussed, and shared—perhaps used to create an artifact (a note, a posting to a map)—and is available to be acquired by other team members who did not previously know it. Thus, it influences subsequent individual learning, is captured as internalized knowledge, and can influence subsequent team knowledge building and externalized team knowledge. In the macrocognition meta-model, learning and knowledge representation are intertwined, such that team knowledge building and externalized team knowledge influence team problem-solving effectiveness.

From this synthesis, the typology captures forms of knowledge that emerge from macrocognitive processes that represent: (a) *pools* of individual and collective team knowledge; (b) *configurations* in the knowledge pool that represent patterns of distinct individual, dyadic, and collective knowledge; and (c) *variance* in the rates of knowledge acquisition and its emergence at the team level, both within and across teams. The typology is a conceptual model; thus the operationalization of a knowledge type must be grounded in a specific task and knowledge domain. In that sense, it is designed to provide measurement comparability across qualitatively different collaborative team tasks.

An assumption inherent in this framework is that each team member can acquire both common (available to all) and unique knowledge (specific to team member expertise) that represent the problem space. Thus, the sum of the total pool of common and unique knowledge specifies all the knowledge relevant for solving the problem or making a decision. For example, one could have a product design team composed of a design engineer, production manager, and market researcher, each with common knowledge about a new product and also access to specialized knowledge about product features, production capabilities, and consumer preferences, respectively. How can these individual and team patterns of knowledge be captured, and how can changes in these patterns be represented as team members discuss the problem and collaborate to make a decision?

Figure 26.9 illustrates the typology and defines the knowledge types. The most basic type captures *individual knowledge* as the proportion of the total pool of knowledge relevant to solving the problem or making a decision that is possessed by one team member at any one point in time (individual level, internalized knowledge). It captures individual-level knowledge, but it does not account for any redundancy among team members. The *knowledge pool* accounts for this overlap and captures the proportion of the total pool held by the team as a whole (team-level *composition* measure, internalized and externalized knowledge). Although this represents what is known collectively, it is not diagnostic of how the knowledge is distributed across individuals, dyads, and the team as a collective. The *knowledge configuration* metrics capture this distribution as a set of proportions (team-level *compilation* measures, internalized and externalized knowledge). As team members acquire information about the problem space, and share their knowledge, the patterns of knowledge held across members are dynamic and evolve. These dynamics and the emergence of knowledge can be captured as *knowledge acquisition,* or the rate of growth of individual knowledge (i.e., how rapidly the Venn diagram expands for a team member; individual-level internalized and externalized knowledge). Of course, numerous factors, including individual differences, team composition, and the context, will influence the rate of individual learning, how much individuals share what they learn, and how well team members will learn from one another. These factors yield *knowledge variability* in the within-team rates of acquisition (team-level internalized and externalized knowledge acquisition).

Knowledge Metrics	Brief Description	Example	
Individual Knowledge	The proportion of the total pool of possible knowledge possessed by each team member separately		The amount of knowledge individuals i, j and k each possess within the problem space
Knowledge Pool	The proportion of the total pool of possible knowledge possessed by each team member collectively		The proportion of the total knowledge among individual team members accounting for overlap
Knowledge Configuration	The proportion of the total pool shared in common by team members and the pattern of unique knowledge held across individuals		Understanding what is common and what is unique knowledge among team members
Knowledge Acquisition	The rate of knowledge compiled by each team member over time		How fast an individual learns (expands a circle in above venn diagrams)
Knowledge Variability	Within team variance in the rates of knowledge acquisition		Different rates of knowledge acquisition can affect a team's learning
Knowledge Emergence (with in team)	The rates of growth for Knowledge Pool and Knowledge Configuration		Changes over time
Knowledge Emergence (between)	Comparing growth rates for Knowledge Variability, Knowledge Pool, and Knowledge Configuration across teams		

Figure 26.9 Team Knowledge Typology

As Kozlowski and Chao (2012) note, "A basic principle of team learning (Kozlowski & Bell, 2008) is that the most rapid rates of knowledge acquisition with low *within team variance*, yields optimum team learning. Thus, within team variance in the rates of knowledge acquisition is likely to impede team knowledge building processes, the development of externalized team knowledge, and team problem solving outcomes" (p. 33; team level internalized and externalized knowledge). Finally, *knowledge emergence* can be captured within and between teams by tracking the rates of growth for the knowledge pool, knowledge configuration, and knowledge variability (between team only). As dynamic indices, they provide metrics to represent how quickly team members internalize, share, and externalize knowledge relevant to the problem at hand. In complex, ill-defined, time-pressured situations (Klein et al., 2003), teams that can better build and externalize relevant knowledge are more likely to make effective decisions.

CONCLUSION

The macrocognition meta-model and the linked team knowledge typology are recent conceptual developments, so there is very little direct research at this point that can be used to evaluate their merit. However, they have some novel conceptual features that we think will contribute to a better understanding of team learning processes and knowledge outcomes. First, these models explicitly incorporate our theoretical foci; they are explicitly multilevel, dynamic, and emergent. We believe that all three theoretical foci are essential to unpack team learning, so the models are constructed on a solid theoretical foundation. Second, the macrocognition meta-model makes a clear distinction between learning processes and learning outcomes, and the team knowledge typology provides metrics to capture knowledge outcomes. Research is underway to validate the meta-model and the linked metrics. Third, we believe that efforts to examine the models will necessitate research advances that, thus far, have only been lightly probed in industrial and organizational psychology. In particular, the research will have to address the dynamics of emergence (see DeShon, chapter 4 of this handbook; Kozlowski, 2012). Imagine that, rather than a collage of snapshots (single shot, cross-sectional designs), our understanding of team learning and knowledge emergence was a movie (multilevel, longitudinal).[2] That is where this research is headed.

Team Performance

The ultimate goal of team learning is an improvement in team performance or effectiveness. Indeed, if we view learning as an expansion in a team's repertoire of potential behaviors, and collective knowledge as an instantiation of learning potential, then it follows that this potential must be realized in performance improvement, capacity, and adaptation. Thus, it is surprising that few studies have focused attention on the relationship between team learning and performance. This is not to say that performance has been ignored within this literature; many studies of team learning have measured team performance. However, in the majority of these studies, team learning is inferred from changes in team performance (Kozlowski & Ilgen, 2006; Stagl, Salas, & Day, 2008). That is, research has used improvements in team performance as evidence that team learning has occurred, which confounds team learning and team performance and often makes it impossible to tie the performance improvements to the team learning processes or the emergent states that we have discussed.

One area in which this practice has been common is in research that has examined learning curves within teams. Studies within the learning-curve tradition have typically been designed to document and explain differences in rates of performance improvement across teams (Edmondson et al., 2007). Teams have been studied in a variety of different field settings, including manufacturing and service, and performance efficiency is typically measured in terms of cost, productivity, or time. Edmondson et al. (2007) note that the research is this area possesses many strengths, including its use of objective outcome variables and its focus on challenges in real work settings and organizations. However, studies within this tradition typically do not measure the mechanisms that are thought to explain the performance differences across teams. For example, Darr et al. (1995) examined learning among 36 pizza stores owned by 10 different franchises. They found that as the stores gained experience (produced more pizzas), the cost of production decreased at a decreasing rate (i.e., a learning curve), but there were also significant differences in learning across stores. They found evidence that stores were able to learn from the knowledge gained by other stores in the same franchise but not stores owned by other franchisees, and they suggest that these differences may be due to the more frequent communication that occurred in same-owned stores in the form of phone calls, personal acquaintances, and meetings. However, communication was never measured, and the authors note that, "a greater understanding of the micro processes underlying the transfer of knowledge is needed" (p. 1761).

One of the problems of using performance as a proxy for team learning is that researchers have noted that teams can learn yet not experience any changes in their performance. Likewise, performance can change without any learning actually taking place, and sometimes learning can result in dysfunctional outcomes. Wilson et al. (2007), for example, explain that a team can learn something but be unable to apply the learning in a way that impacts its performance, team performance can improve due to environmental changes (having nothing to do with learning), and teams can engage in superstitious learning that has negative implications for team functioning. Edmondson (2002) also notes that team learning does not always translate into organizational learning. Groups may fail to communicate what they have learned with others in the organization, or may be unable to convince others to adopt the new work practices. The underlying message is that changes in team or organizational performance do not always serve as an accurate indicator of team learning.

In recent years, a growing body of research has examined the relationship between team learning and performance. These studies differ in that some examine team learning as a process (e.g., by measuring specific team learning behaviors), whereas others examine it as an outcome (e.g., collective knowledge or skills). This dual-conceptualization of team learning is characteristic of the broader literature (Edmondson et al., 2007). However, in these studies performance is measured separately from team learning, so the relationship between the two constructs can be tested. Although this represents an important step toward understanding the outcomes of team learning, it is important to note that these studies have often suffered from other methodological limitations. A number of studies have used self-report data to assess both team learning and performance (e.g., Jeong, Lee, Kim, Lee, & Kim, 2006; Van den Bossche et al., 2006), which raises concerns about whether common method bias may be inflating observed relationships. In addition, a number of studies have examined the link between team learning and team performance using individual-level data (e.g., Chan, Pearson, & Entrekin, 2003; Jeong et al., 2006; Yeh & Chou, 2005). The use of single

respondents raises concerns about the reliability of the ratings of team learning and performance, and this practice also ignores the nesting that is often inherent within the data (e.g., respondents nested within teams and/or departments/units).

Despite some limitations, this body of work provides evidence that team learning is positively associated with team performance. Van der Vegt and Bunderson (2005) examined the effects of team learning behaviors on the performance of multidisciplinary teams in the oil and gas industry. They found that team learning was positively associated with supervisor ratings of team performance and that team learning mediated the effect of expertise diversity and collective identification on team performance. Ellis et al. (2003) reported that team learning behaviors were positively related to the performance of four-person teams performing a military command-and-control simulation. Druskat and Kayes (2000) also found a moderate, positive relationship between team learning behaviors and the performance of MBA project teams. However, the relationship did not achieve significance, likely due to the small number of teams included in the study ($n = 26$). A number of field studies using qualitative methods have also provided evidence of a connection between team learning behaviors and team performance outcomes (e.g., Bondarouk & Sikkel, 2005; Mittendorff, Geijsel, Hoeve, de Laat, & Nieuwenhuis, 2006).

As noted above, a number of studies have also examined the relationship between team learning, measured as an outcome, and team performance. Hirschfeld, Jordan, Feild, Giles, and Armenakis (2006), for example, studied 92 teams participating in a U.S. Air Force officer development program aimed at developing transportable teamwork knowledge and skills. They found that the average teamwork knowledge within a team was positively related to the team's performance in a variety of tasks (e.g., field operations, problem-solving exercises, physical tasks), as well as observer ratings of effective teamwork. Further, they found that average teamwork knowledge significantly predicted teamwork ratings, even after controlling for task proficiency.

CONCLUSION

Although these studies suggest that there generally exists a positive relationship between team learning and team performance, there is also emerging evidence that this relationship may be moderated by a number of factors. Kirkman et al. (2006) studied 40 geographically distributed teams in the travel industry. During the launch of these teams, members participated in an online training program designed to enhance their teamwork skills and allow them to deliver better customer service through teamwork. The authors discovered a complex relationship between teams' average training proficiency and team performance (customer satisfaction). Specifically, average training proficiency had positive associations with customer satisfaction when team trust and technology support were higher, rather than lower, and when team leaders had longer, rather than shorter, tenure. Consistent with our discussion earlier in this chapter, these results suggest that teams may only be able to apply their learning when certain conditions are present (e.g., trust, support). In another study, Wong (2004) examined the effects of team learning activities across 78 teams from four different firms. As noted earlier, she found that local team learning (i.e., learning with individuals in the immediate team) was significantly and positively related to group efficiency, whereas distal team learning (i.e., learning with individuals external to the group) was significantly and positively related to group innovativeness. In addition, she found that local learning was significantly associated with group efficiency when distal learning was low or moderate, but unrelated to efficiency when distal learning was high. These results suggest that there may exist performance trade-offs associated with focusing on either local or distal learning, and that attempts to emphasize both may undermine the benefits of local learning for group efficiency. Although these studies provide important insight into the effects of team learning, more research is needed to identify the conditions under which team learning enhances team effectiveness.

Discussion

In this chapter, we have reviewed roughly two decades of literature addressing the phenomenon of team learning, with the goal of providing an integrative understanding of where the field has made conceptual advances and research progress and where new theoretical developments and research resources can be profitably applied. Unlike many reviews of this domain, our review is founded on a clear distinction between team learning as a *process* and the team knowledge *outcomes* that emerge from learning, which are often confabulated with learning and/or team performance. Moreover, we

conceptualized team emergent states (or "processes" like collective efficacy and cohesion) as supportive, reciprocal emergent phenomena that arise from the learning processes, but also feed forward to shape team learning. Collectively and dynamically, these team learning processes, reciprocal emergent states, and team knowledge outcomes influence team effectiveness (see Figure 26.1). Consistent with our integrative heuristic, our review highlighted three foundational theoretical foci that we believe are essential for advancing understanding of team learning as a complex, systems phenomenon. Team learning is multilevel, dynamic, and emergent. Taking these theoretical foci to heart will necessitate advances in theory and the use of new, creative, and sophisticated research methodologies. In this final section we highlight key conceptual insights, research findings, and future research foci to better illuminate the nature of team learning, its outcomes, and its implications for team effectiveness.

Team Learning Process Models

Table 26.1 summarizes the results of our review of several team learning process models that have received significant attention within this literature and/or hold the potential to offer new insights and research opportunities. We reviewed a number of different models and approaches, which can be categorized under three broad theoretical umbrellas—regulation, information processing, and macrocognition. Although each of the models offers a different theoretical lens through which to interpret team learning processes, we view these different perspectives as complementary and synergistic, rather than competing, and believe that together they offer a rich conceptual foundation for future work in this area.

It is important to note that some of these models and approaches have received greater research support than others. The regulation models have received the greatest research attention to date. There is meta-analytic support for the models of group goal setting and action regulation/emergent team processes, and in recent years we have witnessed a growing base of theory and primary studies for the model of team action regulation and the model of team learning and development. The information-processing models also represent a popular approach to understanding the functional process mechanisms of team learning. Yet, research aimed at understanding information processing in teams has often suffered from conceptual and methodological inconsistencies, as well as segregation across

Table 26.1 Team Learning Process Models: Support and Recommendations

Model/Approach	Support	Comments and Recommendations
Regulation Models		
Group goal setting	Meta-analytic support for the effect of group goals on performance	Needs research examining contingencies (e.g., difficulty, goal content, feedback) that influence the effectiveness of group goal setting
Team action regulation, learning, and performance	Preliminary empirical support for models of team action regulation	Initial research promising; additional research needed on multilevel and cross-level regulation process during learning and skill acquisition
Action regulation and emergent team processes	Meta-analytic support for multidimensional theory of teamwork processes	Need to examine linkages between action regulation behaviors and other cognitive and motivational-affective team processes (e.g., team efficacy, shared mental models)
Team regulation, learning, and development	Indirect support for the regulatory mechanisms and team learning phases	Needs direct evaluations of the core principles (e.g., regulatory mechanisms, developmental transitions, leader influence) of the meta-theoretical framework
Information Processing Models		
Groups as information processors	Support limited by conceptual and measurement inconsistencies	Promising new theoretical models; continuing research to refine a multilevel, dynamic theory of information processing in teams; research on neglected processes (e.g., group-level storage and retrieval)
Information sharing	Body of systematic theory and laboratory research	Conceptual advances beyond information sampling model needed; continue to expand research to intact organizational teams
Macrocognition		
Macrocognitive knowledge building processes	Indirect support but no direct tests of the meta-model	Conceptual framework is promising and offers a novel perspective; systematic empirical research is needed to refine and apply the model

disciplines or research thrusts. Research on information sharing in teams has been more systematic, but this approach has been criticized for being conceptually stagnant (Mohammed & Dumville, 2001). Fortunately, researchers have recently introduced new, integrative models of group information processing (Wilson et al., 2007) and have provided novel insights into information sharing (De Dreu, 2007), which bode well for the future. The final model, which focuses on macrocognitive knowledge building processes, is derived from established research in areas such as macrocognitive team decision making

and team communication processes, but the meta-model has not yet been subjected to direct empirical tests. Although future research is needed to refine and apply the model, this framework offers a novel perspective and is conceptually very promising.

An evaluation of the different process models using our three theoretical foci reveals significant advances in recent years. Research on team action regulation has moved from focusing on the parallelism inherent in multilevel models of action regulation to examining the cross-level linkages that bind individual and team regulation. There has also been greater emphasis on modeling the episodic dynamics involved in the emergence of teamwork processes and team development activities. More recent models of group information processing have demonstrated renewed attention to issues surrounding levels of analysis and time, and the macrocognition meta-model is explicitly designed to capture team knowledge development as a multilevel, dynamic, and emergent phenomenon. Given these recent developments, we believe that these different models offer a robust theoretical platform on which to build a greater understanding of team learning as a multilevel, dynamic, and emergent process.

Team Emergent States

Table 26.2 summarizes the results of our review of team emergent states that can support and shape the team learning process. All four of the emergent states we addressed—team goal orientation, psychological safety, team efficacy, and cohesion/conflict—arise from learning and also have the potential to influence how teams regulate their actions, process and share information, and capture knowledge and foster shared meaning. Yet, the relationship between these states and team learning is also dynamic and iterative, such that the states not only shape and support team learning but also emerge from the interactions inherent in team learning that support or constrain learning processes and knowledge generation.

Our review reveals that the volume and nature of research support varies across the four emergent states. Although team goal orientation and psychological safety have received significant attention in recent years, these are relatively newer constructs that have not been studied as extensively as team efficacy, cohesion, and conflict. However, psychological safety has been studied almost exclusively in the context of team learning, and there is growing support that links team goal orientation to team learning and adaptation. In contrast, there is a voluminous and systematic body of evidence that links team efficacy, cohesion, and conflict to team performance, but few studies that have examined the relationship between these states and team learning. Thus, the research recommendations are somewhat

Table 26.2 Team Emergent States: Support and Recommendations

Emergent State	Support	Comments and Recommendations
Goal orientation	Preliminary support for effects on team processes, performance, and adaptation	Need to examine the effects of goal orientation over time and across levels, identify contingencies within the team and task context, and better understand the implications of conceptualizing and measuring team goal orientation as a compositional variable vs. as a shared, climate-like state
Psychological safety	Quantitative and qualitative support for effects on team learning behaviors and performance; leader actions identified as key antecedent	Need to extend research to different team and task contexts and to examine temporal dynamics underlying emergence of psychological safety perceptions and critical antecedents and consequences over time
Team efficacy	Meta-analytic support for effect on team performance; inconsistent support for link to team learning behaviors and outcomes	Continuing research to refine and extend individual-level findings to team-level; need longitudinal research to examine reciprocal relationships between efficacy and emergent team learning outcomes (e.g., shared mental models)
Cohesion and conflict	Meta-analytic support for link to team performance; preliminary evidence suggests a complex relationship between cohesion, conflict, and team learning	Additional research needed to clarify the effects of cohesion and conflict on team learning; need to examine effects of both micro- and macro-contextual features on cohesion, conflict, and team learning

different across these areas. In terms of team goal orientation and psychological safety, there is a need for continuing research that refines our understanding of how these states relate to team learning. Future research needs to identify the contingencies within both the team and task context that shape the relationships between these states and team learning. In contrast, prior work provides valuable information about the contingencies that shape the effects of team efficacy, conflict, and cohesion, but there exists a need to evaluate the extent to which these findings generalize when team learning is the outcome of interest. The findings of individual-level research and studies that have explored linkages between these states and team performance can serve as a valuable guide for research in this area. Yet, preliminary evidence also suggests that different patterns of results may emerge when these states are examined across levels of analysis and in the context of team learning, which implies caution in overextending past findings.

There is also a need for future research on these emergent states to more explicitly incorporate our key theoretical foci. Future studies in this area need

to focus greater attention on multilevel issues, such as the implications of measuring and conceptualizing team goal orientation as a compositional variable as opposed to a shared, climate-like state, the similarities and dissimilarities in the antecedents and consequences of efficacy beliefs across levels of analysis, and the effects of both micro- and macro-contextual features on the relationship between cohesion/conflict and team learning. Similarly, we need a better understanding of the dynamic and emergent relationships that exist between these states and team learning. Research should examine the temporal dynamics that underlie the emergence of psychological safety perceptions and the critical antecedents and consequences of these perceptions at different stages in a team's life cycle. Similarly, research should further explore the reciprocal relationships that likely exist between team efficacy and emergent team outcomes, such as shared mental models.

Team Knowledge Outcomes

Table 26.3 summarizes our review of research that has examined the knowledge outcomes of team

Table 26.3 Team Knowledge Outcomes: Support and Recommendations

Emergent State	Support	Comments and Recommendations
Collective knowledge	Changes in collective knowledge often not examined; theory and emerging research examining antecedents and consequences of collective knowledge and team knowledge acquisition	Continuing research to refine theory; need to examine different conceptualizations and operationalizations of collective knowledge and implications for team performance; needs more field-based investigations
Team mental models	Body of systematic theory and research; meta-analytic findings	Continuing research to refine measurement guidelines and understand development processes; need to examine different mental model structures (e.g., complementary and distributed mental models)
Transactive memory	Theory and emerging research examining antecedents and consequences	Initial research promising; needs continued research across different team and task contexts
Macrocognition and team knowledge emergence	No direct tests of conceptual typology	Needs research to validate the typology and the linked metrics
Team performance	Often used as a surrogate for team learning; direct examinations of relationship between team learning and team performance are rare but supportive	Needs targeted research on the conditions (e.g., trust) and factors (e.g., type of team learning) that serve as contingencies of team learning—performance relationship

learning. Although we placed particular emphasis on the cognitive and knowledge-based outcomes that represent the most salient manifestations of team learning, we also reviewed research that examined the effects of team learning on team performance. As noted previously, research examining the outcomes of team learning has suffered from several limitations, including the confabulation of team learning, team knowledge, and team performance and the failure to clearly establish the distinctiveness of specific knowledge-based outcomes of team learning. Yet, when the research on these different outcomes is compiled, there is convincing evidence that team learning is an important driver of team effectiveness.

As with the other areas that we have covered, there exist varying levels of support for the different team learning outcomes. Research in the area of shared cognition (i.e., team mental models and transactive memory) has matured more rapidly than research in some of the other areas. Recent meta-analyses (DeChurch & Mesmer-Magnus, 2010a, 2010b) have established the relationship between shared cognition and team processes and performance, have highlighted the moderators of these relationships, and have demonstrated the implications of different approaches to measuring shared cognition. Future research can further refine these findings by examining the effects of different mental model structures and extending research on transactive memory across different team and task contexts. There also exists some emerging research that has examined the antecedents and consequences of collective knowledge and team knowledge acquisition. Yet, more work is needed in this area to refine existing theory, to examine different conceptualizations and operationalizations of collective knowledge and the implications for team learning and performance, and to focus on the dynamic aspects of how individual learning and knowledge building emerge dynamically to shape multilevel configurations of team knowledge and its application to problem solving and performance. This is the promise of research on team macrocognition and macrocognitive team knowledge representations. Although there is yet very little direct research on the macrocognition meta-model and the linked team knowledge typology, these frameworks incorporate novel features that we believe have the potential to expand our understanding of knowledge outcomes. In particular, these frameworks explicitly incorporate our theoretical foci; they are multilevel, dynamic, and emergent. Accordingly, they can help unpack team

learning and create a clear distinction between learning processes and learning outcomes, which is essential for understanding the consequences of team learning for team effectiveness. Finally, direct examinations of the relationship between team learning and team performance are rare but generally supportive. Future research that disentangles the team learning process from team learning outcomes is needed, along with targeted investigations of the conditions (e.g., trust) and factors (e.g., type of team learning) that serve as contingencies of the team learning–performance relationship.

Conclusion

The intended purpose of this chapter was to organize, synthesize, and integrate the diffuse literature addressing team learning that has developed in organizational science over the last two to three decades. Our review sought to balance breadth of coverage (capturing a range of useful conceptualizations) and depth (focusing our attention on conceptualizations that are most relevant, best supported by the research, and most promising for future advances). Although much progress has been made in the last 20 years, it is also the case that team learning is a diverse, sprawling, and messy conceptual domain. We believe that the organization and integration inherent in our heuristic synthesis offered by our review of the literature, and, in particular, the conceptual contribution of our foundational theoretical foci—that team learning is multilevel, emergent, and dynamic—offer novel and exciting prospects for future theoretical, empirical, and application advances in this important domain.

Acknowledgment

Steve W. J. Kozlowski gratefully acknowledges the Office of Naval Research (ONR), Command Decision Making (CDM) Program (N00014-09-1-0519, S. W. J. Kozlowski and G. T. Chao, Principal Investigators) and the National Aeronautics and Space Administration (NASA, NNX09AK47G, S. W. J. Kozlowski, Principal Investigator) for support that, in part, assisted the composition of this chapter. Any opinions, findings, and conclusions or recommendations expressed are those of the authors and do not necessarily reflect the views of ONR or NASA.

Notes

1. Mohammed et al. (2010) note that researchers have debated the importance of shared awareness in the development

of team mental models and that this issue warrants additional conceptual and empirical attention.

2. This metaphor is adapted from a talk by Dinges (2010).

References

Akgün, A. E., Byrne, J., Keskin, H., Lynn, G. S., & Imamoglu, S. Z. (2005). Knowledge networks in new product development projects: A transactive memory perspective. *Information & Management, 42,* 1105–1120.

Amason, A. C. (1996). Distinguishing the effects of functional and dysfunctional conflict on strategic decision making: Resolving a paradox for top management teams. *Academy of Management Journal, 39*(1), 123–148.

Anderson, J. R. (1987). Skill acquisition: Compilation of weak-method problem situations. *Psychological Review, 94*(2), 192–210.

Argote, L., Gruenfeld, D. H., & Naquin, C. (2001). Group learning in organizations. In M. Turner (Ed.), *Groups at work: Theory and research* (pp. 369–411). Mahwah, NJ: Lawrence Erlbaum Associates.

Argote, L., Insko, C. A., Yovetich, N., & Romero, A. A. (1995). Group learning curves: The effects of turnover and task complexity on group performance. *Journal of Applied Social Psychology, 25,* 512–529.

Austin, J. R. (2003). Transactive memory in organizational groups: The effects of content, consensus, specialization, and accuracy on group performance. *Journal of Applied Psychology, 88*(5), 866–878.

Bandura, A. (1977). Self-efficacy: Toward a unifying theory of behavioral change. *Psychological Review, 84*(2), 191–215.

Bandura, A. (1991). Social cognitive theory of self-regulation. *Organizational Behavior and Human Decision Processes, 50,* 248–287.

Bandura, A. (1997). *Self-efficacy: The exercise of control.* New York: Freeman.

Bandura, A., & Locke, E. A. (2003). Negative self-efficacy and goal effects revisited. *Journal of Applied Psychology, 88*(1), 87–99.

Beal, D. J., Cohen, R. R., Burke, M. J., & McLendon, C. L. (2003). Cohesion and performance in groups: A meta-analytic clarification of construct relations. *Journal of Applied Psychology, 88*(6), 989–1004.

Bell, B. S., & Kozlowski, S. W. J. (2002). Adaptive guidance: Enhancing self-regulation, knowledge, and performance in technology-based training. *Personnel Psychology, 55*(2), 267–306.

Bell, B. S., & Kozlowski, S. W. J. (2008). Active learning: Effects of core training design elements on self-regulatory processes, learning, and adaptability. *Journal of Applied Psychology, 93,* 296–316.

Bondarouk, T., & Sikkel, K. (2005). Explaining IT implementation through group learning. *Information Resources Management Journal, 18*(1), 42–60.

Brandon, D. P., & Hollingshead, A. B. (2004). Transactive memory systems in organizations: Matching tasks, expertise, and people. *Organization Science, 15*(6), 633–644.

Bunderson, J. S., & Sutcliffe, K. A. (2003). Management team learning orientation and business unit performance. *Journal of Applied Psychology, 88,* 552–560.

Burke, C. S., Salas, E., Wilson-Donnelly, K., & Priest, H. (2004). How to turn a team of experts into an expert medical team: guidance from the aviation and military communities. *Quality and Safety in Health Care, 13,* i96-i104.

Button, S. B., Mathieu, J. E., & Zajac, D. M. (1996). Goal orientation in organizational research: A conceptual and empirical foundation. *Organizational Behavior and Human Decision Processes, 67,* 26–48.

Cacciabue, P. C., & Hollnagel, E. (1995). Simulation of cognition: Applications. In J. M. Hoc, P. C. Cacciabue, & E. Hollnagel (Eds.), *Expertise and technology: Cognition and human-computer cooperation* (pp. 55–73). Mahwah, NJ: Lawrence Erlbaum Associates.

Cannon, M. D., & Edmondson, A. C. (2001). Confronting failure: Antecedents and consequences of shared beliefs about failure in organizational work groups. *Journal of Organizational Behavior, 22,* 161–177.

Cannon-Bowers, J. A. (2007). Fostering mental model convergence through training. In F. Dansereau & F. Yammarino (Eds.), *Multi-level issues in organizations and time* (pp. 149–157). San Diego, CA: Elsevier.

Cannon-Bowers, J. A., Salas, E., & Converse, S. A. (1993). Shared mental models in expert team decision making. In N. J. Castellan (Ed.), *Individual and group decision making: Current issues* (pp. 221–246). Hillsdale, NJ: LEA.

Carnevale, P. J., & Probst, T. M. (1998). Social values and social conflict in creative problem solving and categorization. *Journal of Personality and Social Psychology, 74,* 1300–1309.

Carver, C. S., & Scheier, M. F. (1981). *Attention and self-regulation: A control-theory approach to human behavior.* New York: Springer-Verlag.

Chan, C. C. A., Pearson, C., & Entrekin, L. (2003). Examining the effects of internal and external team learning on team performance. *Team Performance Management, 9,* 174–181.

Chen, G., & Kanfer, R. (2006). Toward a systems theory of motivated behavior in work teams. *Research in Organizational Behavior, 27,* 223–267.

Chen, G., Kanfer, R., DeShon, R. P., Mathieu, J. E., & Kozlowski, S. W. J. (2009). The motivating potential of teams: Test and extension of Chen and Kanfer's (2006) cross-level model of motivation in teams. *Organizational Behavior and Human Decision Processes, 110,* 45–55.

Chen, G., Thomas, B., & Wallace, J. C. (2005). A multilevel examination of the relationships among training outcomes, mediating regulatory processes, and adaptive performance. *Journal of Applied Psychology, 90,* 827–841.

Chen, G., Webber, S. S., Bliese, P. D., Mathieu, J. E., Payne, S. C., Born, D. H., & Zaccaro, S. J. (2002). Simultaneous examination of the antecedents and consequences of efficacy beliefs at multiple levels of analysis. *Human Performance, 15,* 381–409.

Chiocchio, F., & Essiembre, H. (2009). Cohesion and performance: A meta-analytic review of disparities between project teams, production teams, and service teams. *Small Group Research, 40*(4), 382–420.

Cohen, S. G., & Gibson, C. B. (2003). In the beginning: Introduction and framework. In C. B. Gibson & S. G. Cohen (Eds.), *Virtual teams that work: Creating conditions for virtual team effectiveness* (pp. 1–13). San Francisco: Jossey-Bass.

Cooke, N. J., Gorman, J. C., & Preston, K. A. (2008). Communication as team-level cognitive processing. In M. P. Letsky, N. W. Warner, S. M. Fiore, & C. A. P. Smith (Eds.), *Macrocognition in teams: Theories and methodologies* (pp. 51–64). Burlington, VT: Ashgate Publishing.

Cyert, R., & March, J. (1963). *Behavioral theory of the firm.* Oxford: Blackwell.

Darr, E. D., Argote, L., & Epple, D. (1995). The acquisition, transfer, and depreciation of knowledge in service organizations: Productivity in franchises. *Management Science, 41*(11), 1750–1762.

De Dreu, C. K. W. (2007). Cooperative outcome interdependence, task reflexivity, and team effectiveness: A motivated information processing perspective. *Journal of Applied Psychology, 92*(3), 628–638.

De Dreu, C. K. W., & Carnevale, P. J. D. (2003). Motivational bases for information processing and strategic choice in conflict and negotiation. In M. P. Zanna (Ed.), *Advances in experimental social psychology* (Vol. 35, pp. 235–291). New York: Academic Press.

De Dreu, C. K. W., & Weingart, L. R. (2003). Task versus relationship conflict, team performance, and team member satisfaction: A meta-analysis. *Journal of Applied Psychology, 88*(4), 741–749.

DeChurch, L. A., & Mesmer-Magnus, J. R. (2010a). Measuring shared team mental models: A meta-analysis. *Group Dynamics: Theory, Research, and Practice, 14,* 1–14.

DeChurch, L. A., & Mesmer-Magnus, J. R. (2010b). The cognitive underpinnings of effective teamwork: A meta-analysis. *Journal of Applied Psychology, 95*(1), 32–53.

DeShon, R. P., & Gillespie, J. Z. (2005). A motivated action theory account of goal orientation. *Journal of Applied Psychology, 90*(6), 1096–1127.

DeShon, R. P., Kozlowski, S. W. J., Schmidt, A. M., Milner, K. R., & Wiechmann, D. (2004). A multiple goal, multilevel model of feedback effects on the regulation of individual and team performance. *Journal of Applied Psychology, 89,* 1035–1056.

DeShon, R. P., Kozlowski, S. W. J., Schmidt, A. M., Wiechmann, D., & Milner, K. A. (2001). *Developing team adaptability: Shifting regulatory focus across levels.* Paper presented at the 16th Annual Conference of the Society for Industrial and Organizational Psychology, San Diego.

Devine, D. J., Clayton, L. D., Phillips, J. L., Dunford, B. B., & Melner, S. B. (1999). Teams in organizations: Prevalence, characteristics, and effectiveness. *Small Group Research, 30*(6), 678–711.

Dinges, D. (December, 2010). Maintaining human behavioral capability: Where biology meets technology. Keynote address presented at *Human-Systems Integration at the National Academies: A celebration of 30 years (1980–2010).* Committee on Human-Systems Integration, National Research Council. Washington, DC.

Drach-Zahavy, A., & Somech, A. (2001). Understanding team innovation: The role of team processes and structures. *Group Dynamics: Theory, Research, and Practice, 5*(2), 111–123.

Druskat, V. U, & Kayes, D. C. (2000). Learning versus performance in short-term project teams. *Small Group Research, 31*(3), 328–353.

Dweck, C. S. (1986). Motivational processes affecting learning. *American Psychologist, 41*(10), 1040–1048.

Edmondson, A. C. (1996). Learning from mistakes is easier said than done: Group and organizational influences on the detection and correction of human error. *Journal of Applied Behavioral Science, 32,* 5–28.

Edmondson, A. C. (1999). Psychological safety and learning behavior in work teams. *Administrative Science Quarterly, 44,* 350–383.

Edmondson, A. C. (2002). The local and variegated nature of learning in organizations: A group-level perspective. *Organization Science, 13*(2), 128–146.

Edmondson, A. C. (2003). Speaking up in the operating room: How team leaders promote learning in interdisciplinary action teams. *Journal of Management Studies, 40*(6), 1419–1452.

Edmondson, A. C., Bohmer, R. M., & Pisano, G. P. (2001). Disrupted routines: Team learning and new technology implementation in hospitals. *Administrative Science Quarterly, 46,* 685–716.

Edmondson, A. C., Dillon, J. R., & Roloff, K. S. (2007). Three perspectives on team learning. *The Academy of Management Annuals, 1,* 269–314.

Edwards, B. D., Day, E. A., Arthur, W., & Bell, S. T. (2006). Relationships among team ability composition, team mental models, and team performance. *Journal of Applied Psychology, 91,* 727–736.

Elliot, A. J., & Church, M. A. (1997). A hierarchical model of approach and avoidance achievement motivation. *Journal of Personality and Social Psychology, 72,* 218–232.

Ellis, A. P. J. (2006). System breakdown: The role of mental models and transactive memory in the relationship between acute stress and team performance. *Academy of Management Journal, 49*(3), 576–589.

Ellis, A. P. J., & Bell, B. S. (2005). Capacity, collaboration, and commonality: A framework for understanding team learning. In L. L. Neider & C. A. Shriesheim (Eds.), *Understanding teams: A volume in research in management* (pp. 1–25). Greenwich, CT: Information Age.

Ellis, A. P. J., Bell, B. S., Ployhart, R. E., Hollenbeck, J. R., & Ilgen, D. R. (2005). An evaluation of generic teamwork skills training with action teams: Effects on cognitive and skill-based outcomes. *Personnel Psychology, 58,* 641–672.

Ellis, A. P. J., Hollenbeck, J. R., Ilgen, D. R., Porter, C. O. L. H., West, B. J., & Moon, H. (2003). Team learning: Collectively connecting the dots. *Journal of Applied Psychology, 88*(5), 821–835.

Farr, J. L., Hofmann, D. A., & Ringenbach, K. L. (1993). Goal orientation and action control theory: Implications for industrial and organizational psychology. In C. L. Cooper & I. T. Robertson (Eds.), *International review of industrial and organizational psychology* (pp. 193–232). New York: Wiley.

Festinger, L. (1950). Informal social communication. *Psychological Review, 57,* 271–282.

Fiore, S. M., Rosen, M. A., Smith-Jentsch, K. A., Salas, E., Letsky, M., & Warner, N. (2010). Toward an understanding of macrocognition in teams: Predicting processes in complex collaborative contexts. *Human Factors, 52,* 203–224.

Fiore, S. M., Smith-Jentsch, K. A., Salas, E., Warner, N., & Letsky, M. (2010). Toward an understanding of macrocognition in teams: Developing and defining complex collaborative processes and products. *Theoretical Issues in Ergonomic Science, 11,* 250–271.

Fitts, P. M., & Posner, M. I. (1967). *Human performance.* Oxford: Brooks/Cole.

Fleishman, E. A., & Zaccaro, S. J. (1992). Toward a taxonomy of team performance functions. In R. W. Swezey & E. Salas (Eds.), *Teams: Their training and performance* (pp. 31–56). Norwood, NJ: Ablex.

Ford, J. K., & Kraiger, K. (1995). The application of cognitive constructs and principles to the instructional systems model of training: Implications for needs assessment, design, and transfer. In C. L. Cooper & I. T. Robertson (Eds.), *International review of industrial and organizational psychology* (vol. 10, pp. 1–48). New York: Wiley.

Gibson, C., & Vermeulen, F. (2003). A healthy divide: Subgroups as a stimulus for team learning behavior. *Administrative Science Quarterly, 48*, 202–239.

Gist, M. E. (1987). Self-efficacy: Implications for organizational behavior and human resource management. *Academy of Management Review, 12*, 472–485.

Griffith, T. L., Sawyer, J. E., & Neale, M. A. (2003). Virtualness and knowledge in teams: Managing the love triangle of organizations, individuals, and information technology. *MIS Quarterly, 27*(2), 265–287.

Gully, S. M., Incalcaterra, K. A., Joshi, A., & Beaubien, J. M. (2002). A meta-analysis of team-efficacy, potency, and performance: Interdependence and level of analysis as moderators of observed relationships. *Journal of Applied Psychology, 87*(5), 819–832.

Gully, S. M., & Phillips, J. M. (2005). A multilevel application of learning and performance orientations to individual, group, and organizational outcomes. *Research in Personnel and Human Resources Management, 24*, 1–51.

Gurtner, A., Tschan, F., Semmer, N. K., & Nägele, C. (2007). Getting groups to develop good strategies: Effects of reflexivity interventions on team process, team performance, and shared mental models. *Organizational Behavior and Human Decision Processes, 102*, 127–142.

Hinsz, V. B. (1990). Cognitive and consensus processes in group recognition memory performance. *Journal of Personality and Social Psychology, 59*, 705–718.

Hinsz, V. B., Tindale, R. S., & Vollrath, D. A. (1997). The emerging conceptualization of groups as information processors. *Psychological Bulletin, 121*(1), 43–64.

Hirschfeld, R. R., Jordan, M. H., Feild, H. S., Giles, W. F., & Armenakis, A. A. (2006). Becoming team players: Team members' mastery of teamwork knowledge as a predictor of team task proficiency and observed teamwork effectiveness. *Journal of Applied Psychology, 91*(2), 467–474.

Hirst, G., Van Knippenberg, D., & Zhou, J. (2009). A cross-level perspective on employee creativity: Goal orientation, team learning behavior, and individual creativity. *Academy of Management Journal, 52*(2), 280–293.

Hollingshead, A. B. (1998a). Communication, learning, and retrieval in transactive memory systems. *Journal of Experimental Social Psychology, 34*, 423–442.

Hollingshead, A. B. (1998b). Retrieval processes in transactive memory systems. *Journal of Personality and Social Psychology, 74*, 659–671.

Hollingshead, A. B. (2001). Cognitive interdependence and convergent expectations in transactive memory. *Jounal of Personality and Social Psychology, 81*, 1080–1089.

Hsu, M., Chen, I. Y., Chiu, C., & Ju, T. L. (2007). Exploring the antecedents of team performance in collaborative learning of computer software. *Computer & Education, 48*, 700–718.

Huber, G. P. (1991). Organizational learning: The contributing processes and the literatures. *Organization Science, 2*(1), 88–115.

Ilgen, D. R., Hollenbeck, J. R., Johnson, M., & Jundt, D. (2005). Teams in organizations: From i-p-o models to imoi models. *Annual Review of Psychology, 56*, 517–543.

Jehn, K. A. (1995). A multimethod examination of the benefits and detriments of intragroup conflict. *Administrative Science Quarterly, 40*(2), 256–282.

Jeong, S. H., Lee, T., Kim, I. S., Ha, M., & Kim, M. J. (2007). The effect of nurses' use of the principles of learning organization on organizational effectiveness. *Journal of Advanced Nursing, 58*(1), 53–62.

Johnson, M. D., & Hollenbeck, J. R. (2007). Collective wisdom as an oxymoron: Team-based structures as impediments to learning. In J. Langan-Fox, C. L. Cooper, & R. J. Klimoski (Eds.), *Research companion to the dysfunctional workplace* (pp. 319–331). Northampton, MA: Edward Elgar.

Kane, A. A., Argote, L., & Levine, J. M. (2005). Knowledge transfer between groups via personnel rotation: Effects of social identity and knowledge quality. *Organizational Behavior and Human Decision Processes, 96*, 56–71.

Kanfer, R. (1990). Motivation theory and industrial and organization psychology. In M. D. Dunnette & L. M. Hough (Eds.), *Handbook of industrial and organizational psychology* (2nd ed., Vol. 1, pp. 75–170). Palo Alto, CA: Consulting Psychologists Press.

Kanfer, R., Chen, G., & Pritchard, R. (2008). The three C's of work motivation: Content, context, and change. In R. Kanfer, G. Chen, & R. D. Pritchard (Eds.), *Work motivation: Past, present, and future* (pp. 1–16). New York: Routledge Academic.

Karoly, P. (1993). Mechanisms of self-regulation: A systems view. *Annual Review of Psychology, 44*, 23–52.

Katz, D., & Kahn, R. L. (1966). *The social psychology of organizations.* New York: Wiley.

Kernan, M. C., & Lord, R. G. (1990). Effects of valence, expectancies, and goal-performance discrepancies in single and multiple goal environments. *Journal of Applied Psychology, 75*, 194–203.

Kirkman, B. L., Rosen, B., Tesluk, P. E., & Gibson, C. B. (2006). Enhancing the transfer of computer-assisted training proficiency in geographically distributed teams. *Journal of Applied Psychology, 91*(3), 706–716.

Klein, G. Ross, K., Moon, B. M., Klein, D. E., Hoffman, R. R., & Hollnagel, E. (2003). Macrocognition. *IEEE Intelligent Systems*, May/June, 81–84.

Kleingeld, A., van Mierlo, H., & Arends, L. (2011). The effect of goal setting on group performance: A meta-analysis. *Journal of Applied Psychology, 96*, 1289–1304.

Klimoski, R. J., & Mohammed, S. (1994). Team mental model: Construct or metaphor? *Journal of Management, 20*, 403–437.

Kozlowski, S. W. J. (2012). Groups and teams in organizations: Studying the multilevel dynamics of emergence. In A. B. Hollingshead & M. S. Poole (Eds.), *Methods for studying small groups: A behind-the-scenes guide* (pp. 260–283). New York: Routledge Academic.

Kozlowski, S. W. J., & Bell, B. S. (2003). Work groups and teams in organizations. In W. C. Borman, D. R. Ilgen & R. J. Klimoski (Eds.), *Handbook of psychology: Industrial and organizational psychology* (Vol. 12, pp. 333–375). London: Wiley.

Kozlowski, S. W. J., & Bell, B. S. (2006) Disentangling achievement orientation and goal setting: Effects on self-regulatory processes. *Journal of Applied Psychology, 91*, 900–916.

Kozlowski, S. W. J., & Bell, B. S. (2007). A theory-based approach for designing distributed learning systems. In S. M. Fiore & E. Salas (Eds.), *Toward a science of distributed learning* (pp. 15–39). Washington, DC: APA.

Kozlowski, S. W. J., & Bell, B. S. (2008). Team learning, development, and adaptation. In V. I. Sessa & M. London (Eds.), *Work group learning* (pp. 15–44). Mahwah, NJ: LEA.

Kozlowski, S. W. J. & Chao, G. T. (2012). Macrocognition, team learning, and team knowledge: Origins, emergence, and measurement. In E. Salas, S. Fiore, & M. Letsky (Eds.),

Theories of team cognition: Cross-disciplinary perspectives (pp. 19–48). New York: Routledge Academic.

Kozlowski, S. W. J. & Chao, G. T. (2011). The dynamics of emergence: Cognition and cohesion in work teams. *Managerial and Decision Economics*. Manuscript under review.

Kozlowski, S. W. J., Chao, G. T., Grand, J., Keeney, J., Braun, M., & Kuljanin, G. (2011, April). Macrocognition and teams: The emergence and measurement of team knowledge. In G. T. Chao & S. W. J. Kozlowski (Chairs), *Macrocognition: The next frontier for team cognition research*. Symposium presented at the 26th Annual Conference of the Society for Industrial and Organizational Psychology, Chicago.

Kozlowski, S. W. J., Gully, S. M., Brown, K. G., Salas, E., Smith, E. M., & Nason, E. R. (2001). Effects of training goals and goal orientation traits on multidimensional training outcomes and performance adaptability. *Organizational Behavior and Human Decision Processes, 85,* 1–31.

Kozlowski, S. W. J., Gully, S. M., McHugh, P. P., Salas, E., & Cannon-Bowers, J. A. (1996). A dynamic theory of leadership and team effectiveness: Developmental and task contingent leader roles. In G. R. Ferris (Ed.), *Research in personnel and human resource management* (Vol. 14, pp. 253–305). Greenwich, CT: JAI Press.

Kozlowski, S. W. J., Gully, S. M., Nason, E. R., & Smith, E. M. (1999). Developing adaptive teams: A theory of compilation and performance across levels and time. In D. R. Ilgen & E. D. Pulakos (Eds.), *The changing nature of work performance: Implications for staffing, personnel actions, and development* (pp. 240–292). San Francisco: Jossey-Bass.

Kozlowski, S. W. J., Gully, S. M., Salas, E., & Cannon-Bowers, J. A. (1996). Team leadership and development: Theory principles, and guidelines for training leaders and teams. In M. Beyerlein, D. Johnson & S. Beyerlein (Eds.), *Advances in interdisciplinary studies of work teams: Team leadership* (Vol. 3, pp. 251–289). Greenwich, CT: JAI Press.

Kozlowski, S. W. J., & Ilgen, D. R. (2006). Enhancing the effectiveness of work groups and teams. *Psychological Science, 7*(3), 77–124.

Kozlowski, S. W. J., & Klein, K. J. (2000). A multilevel approach to theory and research in organizations: Contextual, temporal, and emergent processes. In K. J. Klein & S. W. J. Kozlowski (Eds.), *Multilevel theory, research, and methods in organizations: Foundations, extensions, and new directions* (pp. 3–90). San Francisco: Jossey-Bass.

Kozlowski, S. W. J., Watola, D., Jensen, J. M., Kim, B., & Botero, I. (2009). Developing adaptive teams: A theory of dynamic team leadership. In E. Salas, G. F. Goodwin, & C. S. Burke (Eds.), *Team effectiveness in complex organizations: Cross-disciplinary perspectives and approaches* (pp. 109–146). New York: Routledge Academic.

Langan-Fox, J. (2003). Skill acquisition and the development of the team mental model: An integrative approach to analyzing organizational teams. In M. West, D. Tjosvold, & K. G. Smith (Eds.), *International handbook of organizational teamwork and co-operative working* (pp. 321–360). London: Wiley.

Langan-Fox, J., Code, S., & Langfield-Smith, K. (2000). Team mental models: Techniques, methods, and analytic approaches. *Human Factors, 42*(2), 242–271.

Lau, D. C., & Murnighan, J. K. (1998). Demographic diversity and faultlines: The compositional dynamics of organizational groups. *Academy of Management Review, 23*(2), 325–340.

Lawler, E. E., Mohrman, S. A., & Ledford, G. E. (1995). *Creating high performance organizations: Practices and results of employee involvement and total quality management in Fortune 1000 companies*. San Francisco: Jossey-Bass.

LePine, J. A. (2005). Adaptation of teams in response to unforeseen change: Effects of goal difficulty and team composition in terms of cognitive ability and goal orientation. *Journal of Applied Psychology, 90*(6), 1153–1167.

LePine, J. A., Piccolo, R. F., Jackson, C. L., Mathieu, J. E., & Saul, J. R. (2008). A meta-analysis of teamwork processes: Tests of a multidimensional model and relationships with team effectiveness criteria. *Personnel Psychology, 61,* 273–307.

Letsky, M., Warner, N., Fiore, S. M., Rosen, M. A., & Salas, E. (2007). Macrocognition in complex team problem solving. In *Proceedings of the 12th International Command and Control Research and Technology Symposium*. Washington, DC: U.S. Department of Defense Command and Control Research Program. Retrieved from http://www.dodccrp.org/events/12th_ICCRTS/CD/html/papers/239.pdf.

Letsky, M. P., & Warner, N. W. (2008). Macrocognition in teams. In M. P. Letsky, N. W. Warner, S. M. Fiore, & C. A. P. Smith (Eds.), *Macrocognition in teams: Theories and methodologies* (pp. 1–13). Burlington, VT: Ashgate Publishing.

Levesque, L. L., Wilson, J. M., & Wholey, D. R. (2001). Cognitive divergence and shared mental models in software development project teams. *Journal of Organizational Behavior, 22,* 135–144.

Lewis, K. (2003). Measuring transactive memory systems in the field: Scale development and validation. *Journal of Applied Psychology, 88*(4), 587–604.

Lewis, K. (2004). Knowledge and performance in knowledge-worker teams: A longitudinal study of transactive memory systems. *Management Science, 50*(11), 1519–1533.

Lewis, K., Belliveau, M., Herndon, B., & Keller, J. (2007). Group cognition, membership change, and performance: Investigating the benefits and detriments of collective knowledge. *Organizational Behavior and Human Decision Processes, 103,* 159–178.

Lewis, K., Lange, D., & Gillis, L. (2005). Transactive memory systems, learning, and learning transfer. *Organization Science, 16*(6), 581–598.

Liang, D. W., Moreland, R. L., & Argote, L. (1995). Group versus individual training and group performance: The mediating role of transactive memory. *Personality and Social Psychology Bulletin, 21,* 384–393.

Lindsley, D. H., Brass, D. J., & Thomas, J. B. (1995). Efficacy-performance spirals: A multilevel perspective. *Academy of Management Review, 20,* 645–678.

Locke, E. A., & Latham, G. P. (1990). *A theory of goal-setting and task performance*. Englewood Cliffs, NJ: Prentice-Hall.

London, M., Polzer, J. T., & Omoregie, H. (2005). Interpersonal congruence, transactive memory, and feedback processes: An integrative model of group learning. *Human Resource Development Review, 4*(2), 114–135.

London, M., & Sessa, V. I. (2006). Group feedback for continuous learning. *Human Resource Development Review, 5*(3), 303–329.

Mannix, E., & Neale, M. A. (2005). What differences make a difference? The promise and reality of diverse teams in organizations. *Psychological Science in the Public Interest, 6,* 31–55.

Marks, M. A., Sabella, M. J., Burke, C. S., & Zaccaro, S. J. (2002). The impact of cross-training on team effectiveness. *Journal of Applied Psychology, 87*(1), 3–13.

Marks, M. A., Mathieu, J. E., & Zaccaro, S. J. (2001). A temporally based framework and taxonomy of team processes. *Academy of Management Review, 26*(3), 356–376.

Mathieu, J. E., Gilson, L. L., & Ruddy, T. M. (2006). Empowerment and team effectiveness: An empirical test of an integrated model. *Journal of Applied Psychology, 91*(1), 97–108.

Mathieu, J. E., Heffner, T. S., Goodwin, G. F., Cannon-Bowers, J. A., & Salas, E. (2005). Scaling the quality of teammates' mental models: equifinality and normative comparisons. *Journal of Organizational Behavior, 26*, 37–56.

Mathieu, J. E., Heffner, T. S., Goodwin, G. F., Salas, E., & Cannon-Bowers, J. A. (2000). The influence of shared mental models on team process and performance. *Journal of Applied Psychology, 85*(2), 273–283.

Mathieu, J. E., Rapp, T. L., Maynard, M. T., & Mangos, P. M. (2010). Interactive effects of team and task shared mental models as related to air traffic controllers' collective efficacy and effectiveness. *Human Performance, 23*, 22–40.

McComb, S. A. (2008). Shared mental models and their convergence. In M. P. Letsky, N. W. Warner, S. M. Fiore, & C. A. P. Smith (Eds.), *Macrocognition in teams: Theories and methodologies* (pp. 35–50). Burlington, VT: Ashgate Publishing.

Mento, A. J., Steel, R. P., & Karren, R. J. (1987). A meta-analytic study of the effects of goal-setting on task performance: 1966–1984. *Organizational Behavior and Human Decision Processes, 39*(1), 52–83.

Miller, G. A., Galanter, E., & Pribram, K. H. (1960). *Plans and the structure of behavior.* New York: Henry Holt.

Mittendorff, K., Geijsel, F., Hoeve, A., de Laat, M., & Nieuwenhuis, L. (2006). Communities of practice as stimulating forces for collective learning. *Journal of Workplace Learning, 18*(5), 298–312.

Mohammed, S., & Dumville, B. C. (2001). Term mental models in a team knowledge framework: Expanding theory and measurement across disciplinary boundaries. *Journal of Organizational Behavior, 22*, 89–106.

Mohammed, S., Ferzandi, L., & Hamilton, K. (2010). Metaphor no more: A 15-year review of the team mental model construct. *Journal of Management, 36*(4), 876–910.

Mohammed, S., Klimoski, R. J., & Rentsch, J. R. (2000). The measurement of team mental models: We have no shared schema. *Organizational Research Methods, 3*(2), 123–165.

Moreland, R. L., Argote, L., & Krishnan, R. (1996). Socially shared cognition at work: Transactive memory and group performance. In J. L. Nye & A. M. Brower (Eds.), *What's social about social cognition? Research on socially shared cognition in small groups* (pp. 57–84). Thousand Oaks, CA: Sage.

Moreland, R. L., & Myaskovsky, L. (2000). Exploring the performance benefits of group training: Transactive memory or improved communication? *Organizational Behavior and Human Decision Processes, 82*(1), 117–133.

Morgeson, F. P., & Hofmann, D. A. (1999). The structure and function of collective constructs: Implications for research and theory development. *Academy of Management Review, 24*, 249–265.

Nembhard, I. M., & Edmondson, A. C. (2006). Making it safe: The effects of leader inclusiveness and professional status on psychological safety and improvement efforts in health care teams. *Journal of Organizational Behavior, 27*, 941–966.

O'Leary-Kelly, A. M., Martocchio, J. J., & Frink, D. D. (1994). A review of the influence of group goals on group-performance. *Academy of Management Journal, 37*(5), 1285–1301.

Payne, S. C., Youngcourt, S. S., & Beaubien, J. M. (2007). A meta-analytic examination of the goal orientation nomological net. *Journal of Applied Psychology, 92*(1), 128–150.

Pearsall, M. J., & Ellis, A. P. J. (2006). The effects of critical team member assertiveness on team performance and satisfaction. *Journal of Management, 32*(4), 575–594.

Pearsall, M. J., Ellis, A. P. J., & Bell, B. S. (August, 2008). Slippage in the system: The effects of errors in transactive memory behavior on team performance. *Academy of Management Annual Meeting Proceedings.*

Pearsall, M. J., Ellis, A. P. J., & Bell, B. S. (2010). Building the infrastructure: The effects of role identification behaviors on team cognition development and performance. *Journal of Applied Psychology, 95*, 192–200.

Peltokorpi, V. (2008). Transactive memory systems. *Review of General Psychology, 12*(4), 378–394.

Peterson, E., Mitchell, T. R., Thompson, L., & Burr, R. (2000). Collective efficacy and aspects of shared mental models as predictors of performance over time in work groups. *Groups Processes & Intergroup Relations, 3*(3), 296–316.

Phillips, J. M., Hollenbeck, J. R., & Ilgen, D. R. (1996). The prevalence and prediction of positive discrepancy creation: An integration of episodic and non-episodic theories of motivation. *Journal of Applied Psychology, 81*, 498–511.

Pinder, C. C., & Bourgeois, V. W. (1982). Controlling tropes in administrative science. *Administrative Science Quarterly, 27*(4), 641–652.

Ployhart, R. E., & Bliese, P. D. (2006). Individual adaptability (I-ADAPT) theory: Conceptualizing the antecedents, consequences, and measurement of individual differences in adaptability. In S. Burke, L. Pierce, & E. Salas (Eds.), *Understanding adaptability: A prerequisite for effective performance within complex environments* (pp. 3–39). Oxford: Elsevier.

Porter, C. O. L. H. (2005). Goal orientation: Effects on backing up behavior, performance, efficacy, and commitment in teams. *Journal of Applied Psychology, 90*, 811–818.

Porter, C. O. L. H. (2007). A multilevel, multiconceptualization perspective of goal orientation in teams. In V. L. Sessa & M. London (Eds.), *Work group learning: Understanding, improving & assessing how groups learn in organizations* (pp. 149–173). New York: Erlbaum.

Porter, C. O. L. H., Webb, J. W., & Gogus, C. I. (2010). When goal orientations collide: Effects of learning and performance orientation on team adaptability in response to workload imbalance. *Journal of Applied Psychology, 95*(5), 935–943.

Powers, W. T. (1973). *Behavior: The control of perception.* Chicago: Aldine.

Pritchard, R. D., Jones, S. D., Roth, P. L., Stuebing, K. K., & Ekeberg, S. E. (1988). The effects of feedback, goal setting, and incentiveson organizational productivity. *Journal of Applied Psychology, 73*, 337–358.

Pritchard, R. D., Harrell, M. M., DiazGranados, D., & Guzman, M. J. (2008). The productivity measurement and enhancement system: A meta-analysis. *Journal of Applied Psychology, 93*(3), 540–567.

Prussia, G. E., & Kinicki, A. J. (1996). A motivational investigation of group effectiveness using social-cognitive theory. *Journal of Applied Psychology, 81*(2), 187–198.

Pulakos, E. D., Arad, S., Donovan, M. A., & Plamondon, K. E. (2000). Adaptability in the workplace: Development of a taxonomy of adaptive performance. *Journal of Applied Psychology, 85*(4), 612–624.

Rau, D. (2005). The influence of relationship conflict and trust on the transactive memory: Performance Relation in top management teams. *Small Group Research, 36*(6), 746–771.

Reagans, R., Argote, L., & Brooks, D. (2005). Individual experience and experience working together: Predicting learning rates from knowing who knows what and knowing how to work together. *Management Science, 51*(6), 869–881.

Ren, Y., Carley, K. M., & Argote, L. (2006). The contingent effects of transactive memory: When is it more beneficial to know what others know? *Management Science, 52*(5), 671–682.

Rentsch, J. R., Delise, L. A., & Hutchinson, S. (2008). Transferring and developing cognitive similarity in decision-making teams: Collaboration and meaning analysis process. In M. P. Letsky, N. W. Warner, S. M. Fiore, & C. A. P. Smith (Eds.), *Macrocognition in teams: Theories and methodologies* (pp. 127–142). Burlington, VT: Ashgate Publishing.

Rentsch, J. R., & Klimoski, R. J. (2001). Why do 'great minds' think alike?: Antecedents of team member schema agreement. *Journal of Organizational Behavior, 22,* 107–120.

Resick, C. J., Murase, T., Bedwell, W. L., Sanz, E., Jiménez, M., & DeChurch, L. A. (2010). Mental model metrics and team adaptability: A multi-facet multi-method examination. *Group Dynamics: Theory, Research, and Practice, 14*(4), 332–349.

Roberson, Q. M., Bell, B. S., & Porter, S. C. (2008). The language of bias: A linguistic approach to understanding intergroup relations. In K. Phillips (Ed.), *Research in managing groups and teams: Diversity & groups* (Vol. 11, pp. 267–294). Bingley, UK: Emerald.

Rowe, A. (2008). Unfolding the dance of team learning: A metaphorical investigation of collective learning. *Management Learning, 39*(1), 41–56.

Rulke, D. L., & Rau, D. (2000). Investigating the encoding process of transactive memory development in group training. *Group and Organizational Management, 25,* 373–396.

Seijts, G. H., Latham, G. P., Tasa, K., & Latham, B. W. (2004). Goal setting and goal orientation: An integration of two different yet related literatures. *Academy of Management Journal, 47,* 227–239.

Senge, P. M. (1990). *The fifth discipline: The art and practice of the learning organization.* New York: Doubleday.

Shea, G. P., & Guzzo, R. A. (1987). Groups as human resources. In K. M. Rowland & G. R. Ferris (Eds.), *Research in personnel and human resource management* (Vol. 5, pp. 323–356). Greenwich, CT: JAI Press.

Shiffrin, R. M., & Schneider, W. (1977). Controlled and automatic human information processing: II. Perceptual learning, automatic attending, and a general theory. *Psychological Review, 84*(2), 127–190.

Simon, H. A. (1973). The organization of complex systems. In H. H. Pattee (Ed.), *Hierarchy theory* (pp. 1–27). New York: Braziller.

Smith-Jentsch, K. A., Campbell, G. E., Milanovich, D. M., & Reynolds, A. M. (2001). Measuring teamwork mental models to support training needs assessment, development, and evaluation: two empirical studies. *Journal of Organizational Behavior, 22,* 179–194.

Smith-Jentsch, K. A., Cannon-Bowers, J. A., Tannenbaum, S. I., & Salas, E. (2008). Guided team self-correction: Impacts on team mental models, processes, and effectiveness. *Small Group Research, 39,* 303–327.

Smith-Jentsch, K. A., Mathieu, J. E., & Kraiger, K. (2005). Investigating linear and interactive effects of shared mental models on safety and efficiency in a field setting. *Journal of Applied Psychology, 90*(3), 523–535.

Sole, D., & Edmondson, A. (2002). Situated knowledge and learning in dispersed teams. *British Journal of Management, 13,* S17–S34.

Somech, A., & Drach-Zahavy, A. (2007). Schools as team-based organizations: A structure-process-outcomes approach. *Group Dynamics: Theory, Research, and Practice, 11*(4), 305–320.

Stagl, K. C., Salas, E., & Day, D. V. (2008). Assessing team learning outcomes: Improving team learning and performance. In V. I. Sessa & M. London (Eds.), *Work group learning* (pp. 367–390). Mahwah, NJ: LEA.

Stajkovic, A. D., & Luthans, F. (1998). Self-efficacy and work-related performance: A meta-analysis. *Psychological Bulletin, 124*(2), 240–261.

Stasser, G., Taylor, L. A., & Hanna, C. (1989). Information sampling in structured and unstructured discussions of three- and six-person groups. *Journal of Personality and Social Psychology, 57,* 67–78.

Stasser, G., & Titus, W. (1985). Pooling of unshared information in group decision making: Biased information sampling during discussion. *Journal of Personality and Social Psychology, 48,* 1467–1478.

Stasser, G., & Titus, W. (1987). Effects of information load and percentage of shared information on the dissemination of unshared information during group discussion. *Journal of Personality and Social Psychology, 53,* 81–93.

Stasser, G., & Titus, W. (2003). Hidden profiles: A brief history. *Psychological Inquiry, 14*(3/4), 304–313.

Steiner, I. D. (1972). *Group process and productivity.* New York: Academic Press.

Tompkins, T. C. (1995). Role of diffusion in collective learning. *International Journal of Organizational Analysis, 3*(1), 69–85.

Tjosvold, D., Yu, Z., & Hui, C. (2004). Team learning from mistakes: The contribution of cooperative goals and problem-solving. *Journal of Management Studies, 41,* 1223–1245.

Vancouver, J. B. (2005). The depth of history and explanation as benefit and bane of psychological control theories. *Journal of Applied Psychology, 90*(1), 38–52.

Van den Bossche, P., Gijselaers, W. H., Segers, M., & Kirschner, P. A. (2006). Social and cognitive factors driving teamwork in collaborative learning environments: Team learning beliefs and behaviors. *Small Group Research, 37*(5), 490–521.

Van der Vegt, G. S., & Bunderson, J. S. (2005). Learning and performance in multidisciplinary teams: The Importance of collective team identification. *Academy of Management Journal, 48,* 532–547.

Van Offenbeek, M. (2001). Processes and outcomes of team learning. *European Journal of Work and Organizational Psychology, 10*(3), 303–317.

VandeWalle, D. (1997). Development and validation of a work domain goal orientation instrument. *Educational and Psychological Measurement, 57,* 995–1015.

Von Bertalanffy, L. (1972). The history and status of general systems theory. *Academy of Management Journal, 15*(4), 407–426.

Waller, M. J., Gupta, N., & Giambatista, R. C. (2004). Effects of adaptive behaviors and shared mental models on control crew performance. *Management Science, 50*(11), 1534–1544.

Walsh, J. P. (1995). Managerial and organizational cognition: Notes from a trip down memory lane. *Organization Science, 6*(3), 280–321.

Walsh, J. P., & Ungson, G. R. (1991). Organizational memory. *Academy of Management Review, 16*(1), 57–91.

Wegner, D. M. (1986). Transactive memory: A contemporary analysis of the group mind. In B. Mullen & G. R. Goethals (Eds.), *Theories of group behavior* (pp. 185–205). New York: Springer-Verlag.

Wegner, D. M. (1995). A computer network model of human transactive memory. *Social Cognition, 13*, 319–339.

Wegner, D. M., Giuliano, T., & Hertel, P. (1985). Cognitive interdependence in close relationships. In W. J. Ickes (Ed.), *Compatible and incompatible relationships* (pp. 253–276). New York: Springer-Verlag.

Weingart, L. R. (1992). Impact of group goals, task component complexity, effort, and planning on group performance. *Journal of Applied Psychology, 77*(5), 682–693.

Wiener, N. (1948). *Cybernetics: Control and communication in the animal and machine.* Paris: Hermann & Cie.

Wilson, J. M., Goodman, P. S., & Cronin, M. A. (2007). Group learning. *Academy of Management Review, 32*, 1041–1059.

Winters, D., & Latham, G. P. (1996). The effect of learning versus outcome goals on a simple versus a complex task. *Group & Organization Management, 21*, 236–250.

Wittenbaum, G. M., & Park, E. S. (2001). The collective preference for shared information. *Current Directions in Psychological Science, 10*(2), 70–73.

Wittenbaum, G. M., & Stasser, G. (1996). Management of information in small groups. In J. L. Nye & A. M. Brower (Eds.), *What's social about social cognition? Social cognition research in small groups* (pp. 3–28). Thousand Oaks, CA: Sage.

Wong, S. (2004). Distal and local group learning: Performance trade-offs and tensions. *Organization Science, 15*(6), 645–656.

Yeh, Y., & Chou, H. (2005). Team composition and learning behaviors in cross-functional teams. *Social Behavior and Personality, 33*(4), 391–402.

Zellmer-Bruhn, M. E. (2003). Interruptive events and team knowledge acquisition. *Management Science, 49*(4), 514–528.

Zellmer-Bruhn, M., & Gibson, C. (2006). Multinational organization context: Implications for team learning and performance. *Academy of Management Journal, 49*(3), 501–518.

Zhang, Z., Hempel, P. S., Han, Y, & Tjosvold, D. (2007). Transactive memory system links work team characteristics and performance. *Journal of Applied Psychology, 92*(6), 1722–1730.

Criteria Issues and Team Effectiveness

John E. Mathieu *and* Lucy L. Gilson

Abstract

Despite the proliferation of research about teams in the past few decades, relatively little attention has been devoted to understanding the criteria domain of team effectiveness. Accordingly, we identify two fairly general forms of criteria, namely *tangible outputs* and *members' reactions*. We further differentiate three types of tangible outcomes: (a) *productivity*; (b) *efficiency*; and (c) *quality*, and also distinguish between team-level member reactions (i.e., *emergent states*) and individual-level *attitudes, reactions, behaviors,* and *personal development*. We illustrate alternative assessment schemes for each type of criteria. Finally, we discuss how gaining an appreciation for four temporal-related factors—(a) postdictive versus predictive designs; (b) aggregation lags and periods; (c) episodic cycles; and (d) developmental processes—will enhance our understanding of the team effectiveness criteria construct.

Key Words: Team effectiveness, performance, quality, member reactions, criteria

The past 20 years have shown a resurgence in the importance of teamwork to organizations. As numerous reviews well document, the 1990s saw researchers in industrial/organizational (I/O) psychology and organizational behavior pick up the "teams torch" that had been dropped by social psychologists in the 1970s and 1980s (Sanna & Parks, 1997; Sundstrom, McIntyre, Halfhill, & Richards, 2000). This momentum has shown no signs of waning in the first decade of the twenty-first century, as numerous recent reviews attest to the continual importance of teams as the basic building block of modern-day organizations (cf., Ilgen, Hollenbeck, Johnson, & Jundt, 2005; Kozlowski & Ilgen, 2006; Mathieu, Maynard, Rapp, & Gilson, 2008). This burgeoning literature has identified a number of important drivers of team effectiveness, as well as illuminating various mechanisms through which they exert such influence. Here, it is widely agreed that teams exist to perform tasks

and that "performance is the most widely studied criterion variable in the organizational behavior and human resource management literatures" (Bommer, Johnson, Rich, Podsakoff, & MacKenzie, 1995, p. 587). Interestingly however, in the teams research arena, the focus to date has predominantly been on *who* is a member of the team, *how* they work together, and *what* they do to perform their work— hence, the construct of performance has been "less systematically addressed" (Ilgen, 1999, p. 131). In other words, team effectiveness itself has received relatively little attention and remains the Achilles' heel of such work.

Accordingly, the primary focus of this chapter will be on the construct of team effectiveness. Given the enormity of the extant literature, as well as the excellent review of work conducted through the 1990s by Sundstrom and colleagues (2000) with a particular emphasis on team outcomes, we will focus our attention on research conducted over the past 10 years or so, with only passing reference to particularly relevant earlier work. The chapter begins with a definition of teams and a brief discussion of the evolution of the input-process-outcome (IPO) framework for studying team effectiveness. Using this as our foundation, we next detail the multidimensional nature of team effectiveness. This detail is necessary in order to move forward onto a discussion that differentiates between team effectiveness indicators, and to review research exemplars that have employed each type. Following that, we consider issues regarding measurement as related to each type of indicator. We then overlay the importance of temporal considerations, in terms of the functioning of IPO-style frameworks, as well as in terms of dynamic team criteria. In conclusion, recommendations for future research are offered in terms of better specification of the team criteria domain, as well as means for advancing dynamic models of team effectiveness.

Defining Teams

Teams, groups, and other forms of collectives have been defined in different ways over the years. These definitions share many attributes, while at the same time possessing a number of subtle differences. Given that our focus herein is on work teams, we adopt the conception advanced by Kozlowski and Bell (2003), who defined teams as collectives "…who exist to perform organizationally relevant tasks, share one or more common goals, interact socially, exhibit task interdependencies, maintain and manage boundaries, and are embedded in an organizational context that sets boundaries, constrains the team, and influences exchanges with other units in the broader entity" (p. 334). We use this definition because of its focus on the fact that work teams have some level of interdependence and operate in an organizational context that influences their functioning.

When considering team effectiveness and outcomes, there are a few other important definitional components that need to be considered, such as the fact that teams are used for various reasons and consequently face distinct demands and therefore may be designed and may function quite differently. Specifically, this means that teams are sometimes configured based upon the nature of the task they are to perform or the environment in which they operate (i.e., customer service teams, flight crews, emergency response teams). To this end, some teams operate in intense and complex environments, while others perform in fairly stable

environments. In other instances, teams may need to be configured to act quickly, with all members quickly moving into their predetermined roles (e.g., trauma teams); other teams may be able to learn the task together and evolve their roles as the work progresses (e.g., quality improvement teams). Finally, teams can be distinguished based upon member composition, how long they are together as a team, and the fluidity of their membership. In trying to delineate team types, researchers have proposed a number of useful taxonomies (e.g., Cohen & Bailey, 1997; Devine, 2002; Hackman, 1990). These taxonomies clearly illustrate that not all teams are alike; however, it is important to appreciate that the categories themselves are simply proxies for more substantive issues—namely, the team task and work context.

Team Effectiveness Framework

The primary framework used for studying teams is the input-process-outcome (IPO) framework developed by McGrath (1964) and refined by Steiner (1972), Hackman (1987) and others. Within this framework, *inputs* describe antecedent factors that enable and constrain how members will work together. These include *individual team member characteristics* (e.g., competencies, personalities), *team-level factors* (e.g., task structure, external leader influences), and *organizational and contextual factors* (e.g., organizational design features, environmental complexity). The antecedents combine to drive team *processes*, which describe members' interactions directed toward task accomplishment. Processes are important because they describe how team inputs are transformed into outcomes. *Outcomes* are the results and by-products of team activity that are valued by one or more constituencies (Mathieu, Heffner, Goodwin, Salas, & Cannon-Bowers, 2000).

To date, the IPO model has served as a valuable research guide, although, not surprisingly, it has also been modified and extended in several ways (e.g., Cohen & Bailey, 1997; Hackman & Morris, 1975; Ilgen et al., 2005; McGrath, Arrow, & Berdahl, 2000; Salas, Dickinson, Converse, & Tannenbaum, 1992). Specifically, theorists have sought to place the IPO model within a larger context, emphasizing temporal elements, or uncovering more subtle aspects of the model that have gone overlooked, such as the delineation of team processes into three distinct phases: planning/transition, action, and interpersonal (Marks, Mathieu, & Zaccaro, 2001). To this end, there is now agreement that, while the IPO framework is a useful starting place, its single linear path is not truly representative of teams in organizations (Ilgen et al., 2005)

Numerous authors also have emphasized that time plays a critical role in team functioning that is not adequately depicted in a typical unidirectional I→P→O framework (Ancona & Chong, 1996; Kozlowski, Gully, Nason, & Smith, 1999; Marks et al., 2001; McGrath, 1991). The past decade has seen a much greater appreciation of temporal dynamics in teamwork. Although time can be depicted in a number of ways (Ancona, Goodman, Lawrence, & Tushman, 2001; Ancona, Okhuysen, & Perlow, 2001), two of the more prominent approaches are: (a) developmental models; and (b) episodic approaches. The *developmental models* illustrate how teams qualitatively change and are differentially influenced by various factors as they mature over time (Kozlowski, Gully, McHugh, Salas, & Cannon-Bowers, 1996; Kozlowski et al., 1999). In contrast, the *episodic approaches* argue that teams must execute different processes at different times, depending on task demands that recur in a cyclical fashion (cf., Marks et al., 2001; McGrath, 1984). Naturally, the two temporal processes may align with one another, particularly with newly formed teams. However, the distinction is that developmental processes accumulate over chronological time, whereas episodic processes reoccur as triggered by some temporal, task, or member-triggered transition event.

Figure 27.1 depicts the traditional IPO model with the inclusion of time. As shown by the solid line running at the bottom of the figure, developmental processes unfold over time as teams mature. Also depicted are feedback loops, which represent the more cyclical or episodic processes. Ilgen et al.

(2005) recognized this feature as well and refined the IPO framework into one that they labeled IMOI, or input-mediator-outcome-input, to represent both a broad range of mediators as well as the inherent cyclical nature of team functioning. Therefore the more inclusive "mediators" term replaces the more limit "process" label, as show in Figure 27.1. The solid line from outcomes to mediators, within Figure 27.1, suggests that feedback of this type is likely to be quite influential, while the dashed line suggests that the influence of outcomes and processes on inputs would likely be less potent. This follows from the fact that team states are likely to be readily influenced by their progress over time, and teams may readily adopt different processes as a function of outcomes. Alternatively, the influence of team outcomes or mediators on subsequent member composition, team structure, organizational contextual factors, or other inputs is likely to be less immediate or malleable. The small arrows shown within the inputs section of Figure 27.1 illustrate the nested arrangements of such antecedents. The solid arrows imply the likely more potent influence of top→down effects (e.g., organizational context → teams; team properties → member characteristics), whereas the dotted lines imply the potential for somewhat less potent upward influences (e.g., individual members → team properties; team properties → organizational characteristics).

In considering the team effectiveness framework, it is interesting to note that the majority of empirical work, as well as a number of recent meta-analyses (Bell, 2007; Burke et al., 2006; De Dreu, & Weingart, 2003; Gully, Incalcaterra, Joshi, & Beaubien, 2002; LePine, Piccolo, Jackson, Mathieu,

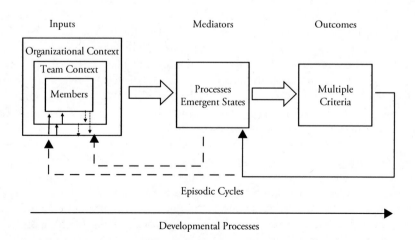

Figure 27.1 Team Effectiveness Framework.

& Saul, 2008; Stewart, 2006) and many of the chapters in this handbook, are dedicated to examining the antecedents of team success (inputs and processes). However, much less attention has been given to the team outcomes themselves, which is somewhat surprising given that outcomes are often the driving force behind why organization employ teams and why researchers study them; as stated by Ilgen, "it is their raison d'etre" (1999, p. 130).

Team Effectiveness

Historically, team outcomes have been defined primarily as *performance* (e.g., quality and quantity) and members' *affective* reactions (e.g., satisfaction, commitment, viability; McGrath, 1964). Further delineation has consisted predominantly of expanding these two components into three (Cohen & Bailey, 1997; Hackman, 1987). The three components, as suggested by Hackman, were: (a) *performance* as rated by relevant others outside the team; (b) *meeting team-member* needs; and (c) *viability*, or the willingness of members to continue to work together as a team (Hackman, 1987). Building on these facets, Cohen and Bailey (1997), in their review of the teams literature, categorized effectiveness into the following three categories: (a) *performance,* within which they grouped efficiency, productivity, responsiveness, quality, customer satisfaction, and innovation; (b) *attitudes,* which included satisfaction, commitment, and trust; and (c) *behaviors,* which entailed absenteeism, turnover, and safety issues. Each of these categories is extremely broad and all encompassing, as illustrated by Sundstrom and colleagues (2000), whose review listed over 20 types of outcomes studied between the 1980s and 1990s.

In a recent review of the teams literature, Mathieu and colleagues (2008) posited that work in the past decade has expanded the range of team effectiveness criteria moving beyond performance quantity and quality to also consider: (a) knowledge accumulation and management; (b) strategic decision making; (c) customer relations; and (d) creativity, among others. In addition, they concluded that, while the traditional member viability criterion remains frequently employed, it has been operationalized in a myriad of ways and at different levels of analysis, resulting in fragmented findings.

Synthesizing the above and other reviews, it appears that a fine-grained approach to team effectiveness is not a viable option, as too many categories emerge, such that meaning is hard to assign to all of them. Thus, we propose that team outcomes can be broadly characterized in terms of two general types: (a) *tangible outputs, or products of team interaction*; and (b) *influences on team members*. This distinction is consistent with that advocated by Mathieu et al. (2000), who defined team outcomes as "...results and by-products of team activity that are valued by one or more constituencies" (p. 273). In this sense, we wish to establish a distinction between related, but different types of constructs. First, we differentiate team outcomes from team members' *actions*. For example, in a meta-analysis of the relationship between cohesion and team performance, Beal, Cohen, Burke, and McLendon (2003) distinguished *performance behaviors* from *performance outcomes*. Behaviors are actions that are relevant to achieving goals, whereas outcomes are the actual consequences or results of performance behaviors. Examples of performance behaviors include team process improvement, learning behaviors, and cognitive task performance. Team process improvements have been measured using feedback seeking, error discussion, and experimentation, which have been argued as critical in giving teams the ability to adapt and improve (Kirkman, Rosen, Tesluk, & Gibson, 2006). Similarly, Edmondson (1999) examined team learning behaviors, while Jehn and Shah (1997) assessed team cognitive task performance, or the degree to which a team's decision matches those of an expert committee. Finally, Kirkman and Rosen (1999) had team leaders rate teams' levels of proactivity, which encompassed behaviors such as whether the team could fix things and whether they were always looking for better ways to do something.

The important point of distinction here is that certain team behaviors are thought to result in valued team outcomes. However, such behaviors are not outcomes themselves per se. In fact, a close inspection of "performance behaviors" reveals them to have far more in common with what are commonly referred to as team processes (i.e., intermember actions) than with the by-products of members' interactions. Consequently, in order to minimize construct confusion and overlap, we believe that team member performance-related behaviors are better conceived as mediators linking antecedents with team outcomes, rather than as criteria.

Mathieu et al. (2000) also described team outcomes as by-products that are valued by one or more constituencies. Therein resides the second part of our distinction, in that for team outcomes there are two primary constituencies: (a) team members; and (b) other parties who have a vested interest in how the team functions. The latter group would include other collectives who rely on the outcomes of a team, such as external stakeholders, other teams, and customers, to give but a few examples (in short, anyone outside the team who has a value stake in the team's functioning). In addition, collectively members are an important constituency, as their willingness to work together again, their commitment to the team and to the organization, and their personal reactions are all important outcomes to consider (Hackman & Morris, 1975). Moreover, individual members have a vested interest in the functioning of their team, as they stand to reap rewards, gain valuable experience, learn new things and develop new skills, operate in an enriched environment, and so forth. Accordingly, team functioning influences members both as a collective and as a set of individuals, and these experiences constitute an important aspect of team effectiveness.

Before moving forward and to ensure clarity in a field where outcomes vary greatly, we would like to reiterate that we are defining team outcomes as being broadly characterized in terms of two general types: (a) *tangible outputs, or products of team interaction*; and (b) *influences on team members*. Table 27.1 provides a summary of these two broad types and subcategories, which are described below.

Tangible Outputs

Tangible outcomes can be further classified into three types: (a) productivity; (b) efficiency; and (c) quality. *Productivity* is defined in terms of quantitative counts of some unit that a team produces. Here, examples could include items made, sales logged, clients served, or engagements completed. *Efficiency* is a related concept, but is defined in terms of quantitative counts of units produced relative to some standard or benchmark. Some examples would include

Table 27.1 Team Effectiveness Criteria

Tangible Outputs	Members' Reactions
– Productivity	– Collective Emergent States
– Efficiency	– Individual-Level
– Quality	– Attitudes
	– Reactions
	– Behaviors
	– Personal Development

products relative to raw materials consumed, time required to reach a decision versus time allocated, sales relative to quotas, and average call duration as compared to prior standards. *Quality* represents an assessment of the value or worth of outputs, and might be gauged in terms of product rejection rates, decision quality, customer satisfaction, referrals, and safety rates. In the sections that follow, we detail and provide some highlights of investigations that have employed such criteria measures.

PRODUCTIVITY

The success of many teams is defined by the quantifiable outcome of something that they do or produce. To this end, the productivity dimension of effectiveness captures the notion of "how many." In lab and simulation studies, productivity is the most frequently used measure of team effectiveness because outcomes such as the number of planes or tanks destroyed, enemies eliminated, shots fired, or vehicles lost to friendly fire are easily accounted for (e.g., Bass, Avolio, Jung, & Berson, 2003; Chen, 2005; Marks, Zaccaro, & Mathieu, 2000). Likewise, when student samples are used, productivity is probably the most frequently used effectiveness measure. For example, Lester, Meglino, and Korsgaard (2002) calculated the dollar sales of 32 student teams running companies. Similarly, the numbers of models produced (Jehn & Shah, 1997), team grades (Brown, 2003), number of games won by hockey teams (Feltz & Lirgg, 1998), or points scored and points lost (Porter, 2005) all are quantifiable productivity measures that allow for the performance of one team to be seemingly objectively compared to those of others in the same study. Hence, when trying to understand what helps one team outperform another, having a productivity outcome is a good criterion that ensures a level of similarity, enabling comparisons using other variables of interest. Further, productivity is meaningful, easily explained and understood. The team that scores the most goals wins; the troop that shoots the most targets is the best; the group that has the highest grade is the best performer. Productivity outcomes are usually fairly unambiguous.

Productivity is also used extensively in field studies where, not surprisingly, given the variety of tasks that teams perform, research has assessed a broad range of measures. For example, in a study of 92 groups from a household moving company Jehn, Northcraft, and Neale (1999) measured both team member perceptions of how productive their teams were and computerized departmental performance records. The two measures of productively (perceptual and objective) were significantly correlated with each other, suggesting that teams actually were aware of their productivity levels. Tesluk and Mathieu (1999) asked managers to assess the performance of construction and maintenance road crews, whereas the number of innovations generated by teams was the productivity measure employed by De Dreu and West (2001). While the measures considered thus far assume that more is better, in a study of 47 air traffic control towers, Smith-Jentsch, Mathieu, and Kraiger (2005) examined the number of aviation safety incidents, where obviously fewer incidents were associated with superior performance. While these productivity measures are vastly different from one another, they are all relevant to the teams and organization in which the work was conducted. Further, as discussed with regard to the productivity measures used in lab studies, or with student samples, all of these tangible productivity outcomes allow for one team to be directly compared to another on a criterion that "makes sense" and is quantifiable—regardless of whether more or less is better.

For some teams, productivity is directly related to the number of items they produce or ideas they generate, whereas for other teams, productivity might be a more distal measure such as firm performance. While the previous examples of field-based teams all use more proximal productivity measures, there are several good examples of more distal productivity measures as well. For instance, Barrick, Bradley, Kristof-Brown, and Colbert (2007) measured team productivity through firms' financial ratios, which was an applicable measure given that the teams in their study were top management teams (TMTs). Similarly, Srivastava, Bartol, and Locke (2006) used organizationallevel hotel data to assess the productivity of management teams.

One area that we have not yet discussed—which will be covered indepth later in this chapter, but bears note here—is that productivity also can be ascertained using archival data (e.g., Barrick et al., 2007; Smith-Jentsch et al., 2005; Raver & Gelfand, 2005), computer-generated results (Chen et al., 2002; Porter, 2005), supervisor ratings (Barrick Stewart, Neubert, & Mount 1998; De Dreu & West, 2001), employee ratings, and teacher or instructor evaluations. Regardless of the source of the productivity data, the advantages of it remain the same—the results yield a nice clean number or series of data points that allow for comparisons between teams. The difficulty with productivity is that it does not take other drivers of quantitative counts into effect; hence we move to efficiency.

EFFICIENCY

In organizational environments, the most commonly used measure of team effectiveness is efficiency—usually simply labeled as *performance*. In part, this is because efficiency is a related concept, meaning that what is produced, made, sold, or used is compared to either organizationally relevant goals or external benchmarks. In effect, the comparative nature of the measure is believed to give it better grounding and a more reliable way to access superior performance; for example, how can we tell if a team that produces 50 washing machines is in fact performing well? Using the productivity criteria discussed above, we would say that a team producing 50 machines is superior to one that produces 30; however, is 50 a marker of good performance, or did the teams produce 55 and 60, respectively, the year before? Another related question is: Are all washing machines the same? Here, one team may only produce 10 machines, but they are highly complex, top-of-the-line, high-profit-margin machines. In contrast, another team may produce 80 machines, but theirs are very simple low-end types from which the organization does not make much money. Has the team that made 10 performed less well or better than that which produced 80? What if the team producing more is using newer or better technology than the lesser producing team?

What the efficiency component of the performance metric gives us is the standard from which more accurate evaluations and interpretations can be made. In other words, productivity values are adjusted for extenuating circumstances to yield a "fair playing field" for comparative purposes. Productivity measures may simply not be completely under the control of the team members. For example, in a study of service technician teams, Gilson, Mathieu, Shalley, and Ruddy (2005) compared three months of data on breakdowns, parts expenditure, and time between service calls to the goals set for each team. In this study, goals were set based on equipment history, machine type, usage, and age making an efficiency score a much better predictor of performance than a productivity score would have been. Some teams with high parts expenditure (negative absolute productivity) may have in fact had more complex or older equipment on their territories and thus, when performance was compared to the goal, their performance was actually very good; this would not have been reflected in the simple productivity measure.

Other examples of efficiency abound, but a few exemplars include work that has examined flight delays as compared to scheduled arrivals and departures (Smith-Jentsch et al., 2005); firm performance as it compares to major competitors with regard to growth, sales revenue, and return to shareholders (Simsek, Veiga, Lubatkin, & Dino, 2005); and profitability relative to targeted profitability for the survey year (Bunderson & Sutcliffe, 2003). Efficiency is also used in student teams in which team decisions have been compared to correct decisions across multiple trials in military command- and control-type tasks (Colquitt, Hollenbeck, Ilgen, LePine, & Sheppard, 2002).

As with productivity, efficiency measures can be obtained from multiple different sources, such as archival (Bunderson & Sutcliffe, 2003; Mathieu, Gilson, & Ruddy, 2006), supervisors, managers, and instructor ratings (Bass et al., 2003; Kirkman & Rosen, 1999; Lester et al., 2002; Tesluk & Mathieu, 1999), as long as there are prior data, goals, or a standard against which the measure can be compared. As with productivity, what determines efficiency can be either proximal or more distal to the team depending on the type of team in question. While efficiency offers the benefit of comparing current outcomes, it does not take into account the value of the outcome; thus, we move to a discussion of outcome quality.

QUALITY

The final tangible outcome in our typology is quality. Quality in this context refers to the value or worth of the outputs delivered by the team. Using our simplistic washing machine example above, if many of the machines produced failed to operate properly or are returned by customers, then productivity does not translate in to effectiveness. Furthermore, even if the adjusted efficiency rates appear promising, poor quality and high returns serve to undermine effectiveness.

One of the most popular ways to assess quality is through customer satisfaction ratings. Kirkman and Rosen (1999) had external team leaders assess organizational customer service indicators, such as whether the team produced high-quality products and satisfactory levels of customer service. Mathieu and colleagues (2006) used three months of organizational customer satisfaction survey results to determine the quality of the performance between teams. Quality also can be used as a measure to

ascertain whether team performance is superior to that of individuals (Janssen, Van de Vliert, & Veenstra, 1999), performance of experts (Jehn & Shah, 1997), or ratings by supervisors who are directly asked about the quality and accuracy of the work completed by the team (Langfred, 2000). In short, obviously it is not only important to generate a high quantity of outcomes, whatever they may be, but the quality of the products produced, services rendered, and so forth matters greatly. Clearly, what constitutes quality in one context may not generalize to other contexts, but the general idea of the quality component of team effectiveness matters and must be considered in concert with productivity or efficiency indices. This perspective suggests the potential value of combining individual indices into effectiveness composites.

Effectiveness Composites

In the preceding sections we have sought to highlight the fact that team outcomes come in many different forms. However, researchers often seek to synthesize such information into a single overall effectiveness composite score. A *composite* measure of team effectiveness is one in which various tangible outcomes (i.e., productivity and quality) are combined with affective outcomes (i.e., member commitment to the project) to form an all-encompassing outcome measured. For instance, in a sample of high school junior achievement student companies, Lester and colleagues (2002) defined performance as meeting constituent needs, achieving objectives, and recognizing key survival factors. Likewise, Hiller, Day, and Vance (2006) studied Department of Transportation road maintenance crews and had supervisors rate their performance based on planning, problem solving, support and consideration, mentoring and development, and overall effectiveness. Similarly, Van der Vegt and Bunderson (2005) had supervisors rate efficiency, quality, overall achievement, productivity, and mission fulfillment of multidisciplinary teams in the oil and gas industry. Elsewhere, Barrick and colleagues (1998) included knowledge, quality, quantity, initiative, interpersonal skills, planning, and overall commitment in their measure of performance.

Given that teams often must carry out multiple functions and that their overall success is based on how well they carry out *all* functions rather than just one, a blended composite measure may very well be a better or more accurate indicator of team effectiveness than a measure of any one aspect. In effect, composite measures may more closely map onto work that utilizes a balanced scorecard approach (e.g., Kirkman, Rosen, Tesluk, & Gibson, 2004). Interestingly, while the balanced scorecard remains a popular practitioner tool, it is not used frequently in the academic literature.

In the academic world, a systematic approach to composite measures is cumbersome. To be effective, these measures need to be multidimensional and indexed by multiple different constitutes. A good example of this approach is the work by Pritchard and his colleagues (Pritchard, 1992; Pritchard, Jones, Roth, Stuebing, & Ekeberg, 1988) who asked teams to identify their key outcomes and to estimate how each contributed to their effectiveness. In turn, the weights and indices were used to derive an overall productivity measure (ProMES). This approach addresses both organizational relevance as well as the multiple functions performed by teams. Unfortunately, because both measure development and assessment are cumbersome and time consuming, it has not been used often. Nevertheless, there have been other applications that have employed specific weighting schemes, such as a balanced scorecard approach (see Kirkman et al., 2004), which explicitly articulate and justify the relative importance of different criteria as a function of organizational priorities. Whereas such explicit approaches are far preferable to simply undifferentiated combinations, composite approaches to tangible outcomes still run the risk of losing important nuances between outcomes and may result in distorted conclusions and interpretations of the findings.

SUMMARY REGARDING TANGIBLE OUTPUTS

One of our goals in this section has been to outline the fact that team effectiveness is a multidimensional construct with subtle, yet important, differences. Moving forward, we urge researchers to pay careful attention to whether their metric of effectiveness makes the most sense for the teams they are accessing. Further, we advocate that careful consideration be given to whether the outcome(s) that is(are) most relevant for the teams in questions are ones of productivity, efficiency, or quality. All are informative and important measures of team performance, but they are substantively different. We find numerous studies that have blended two or three of the types with little rationale as to why. As we discussed earlier, this may in fact be a very appropriate measure; however, careful attention needs to be given to the team type, task, and context to substantiate the justification, along with the rationale for aggregation.

For example, if quality and efficiency are all combined into one measure of team effectiveness, how can we determine what inputs or processes are driving the quality of the outputs rather than the tangible outcomes? Alternatively, given that most teams are responsible for simultaneously meeting multiple goals, does distilling out any particular component for focus and scrutiny necessarily yield a deficient criterion? We advocate that, based on a thorough understanding of the criteria domain for any given application, that researchers employ multiple measures of tangible outcomes as appropriate. They can then test empirically whether certain antecedent factors differentially predict the different criteria, while also having the option of deriving higher-order composites if desired.

Influences on Team Members

The second general category of team outcomes can be defined in terms of influences on members. In a general sense, this category can be conceived as collective or individualistic outcomes. The collective level of analysis includes shared experiences, such as cohesion or psychological safety, which conceptually are experienced similarly by all members. The collective level also includes descriptive characteristics of the whole that are not necessarily shared by all members but are also not reducible to individual member attributes or reactions (e.g., diversity, faultlines). In contrast, the individual level outcomes refer to attitudes, reactions, and behaviors of individuals that may vary not only between teams, but also within teams. Both of these themes are developed further below.

TEAM EMERGENT STATES

Marks and her colleagues (2001) defined emergent states as "constructs that characterize properties of the team that are typically dynamic in nature and vary as a function of team context, inputs, processes, and outcomes. Emergent states describe cognitive, motivational, and affective states of teams as opposed to the nature of their member interaction" (p. 358). They further submitted that... "[a]lthough researchers have not typically classified them as such, emergent states can be considered as both team inputs and proximal outcomes.... Emergent states do not represent team interaction or team actions that lead toward outcomes. Rather, they are products of team experiences (including team processes) and become new inputs to subsequent processes and outcomes" (Marks et al., p. 358). In other words, team states such as collective efficacy, cohesion, shared mental models, and so forth may follow from previous team actions and outcomes, while also leading to, or influencing, subsequent team actions and outcomes.

Whether team emergent states are considered as antecedents, correlates, or consequences of team interactions is determined, in large part, by the design that researchers employ. Psychological states require some period of time and experience to develop and to crystallize, particularly if they describe collective properties (Morgeson & Hofmann, 1999). In this regard, states are dynamic entities that change over time. For example, team efficacy has been shown to be a significant predictor of subsequent team performance, yet such performance will also impact future states of efficacy (Stajkovic, Lee, & Nyberg, 2009). Whether efficacy is an antecedent or outcome is a function of its dynamic quality and when it is measured relative to performance.

Team viability (see, e.g., Barrick et al., 2007), while conceptually distinct from emergent states, is often combined with collective climate or attitudinal type measures in meta-analytical work. For example, Balkundi and Harrison (2006, p. 57) hypothesize team viability but capture in their methodology "group member satisfaction, team climate or atmosphere, team commitment, or indicators of group cohesion were assessed as a team outcome." There are several studies that have used supervisor ratings (e.g., Barrick et al., 2007; Hiller et al., 2006; Lester et al., 2002; Stewart & Barrick, 2000) of both viability and affective outcomes but found that they lack discriminant validity from team performance. This finding is likely due to some sort of a "halo effect" or measurement artifact leading researchers to employ composite approaches, as discussed previously.

The dynamic feature of emergent states and similar collective constructs highlights the fact that indices of team effectiveness inherently imply a temporal relationship, where team characteristics (inputs [I]) and mediators (M) precede and potentially influence outcomes (O) of team interactions (i.e., IPO models). By the same token, however, team outcomes from earlier periods may well influence subsequent team-related variables. This is easily seen in the case of emergent states, but in reality may be conveyed through other mechanisms. For example, a well performing team, gauged in terms of customers served and their satisfaction, may well be granted greater empowerment in the future. They may choose to coordinate their activities differently, their leaders might adopt different behaviors, and their membership may even change as some of their members

might be better utilized elsewhere. In other words, many variables that have traditionally been viewed as relatively fixed team inputs (e.g., work design, external leadership, team composition) may actually be driven by previous team outcomes. This leads to an unwieldy situation in which any variable might be considered an antecedent, mediator, or outcome of team activity as a consequence of when, in the sequence of events, a researcher chooses to anchor his or her investigation. However, if one adopts a more episodic view of team functioning (e.g., Marks et al., 2001; McGrath, 1991), then it makes sense to sort variables in terms of their temporal precedence and to reserve the term *outcomes* to refer to the results and by-products of team activity that are valued by one or more constituencies as indexed at the end of any given performance episode. Given that team emergent states may be considered as important variables throughout the typical IPO framework, along with the fact that other chapters of this handbook deal specifically with them in greater depth, we will not further chronicle them as outcomes here. Rather, we turn our attention to individual-level outcomes of team functioning.

INDIVIDUAL LEVEL OUTCOMES

Since well before even the Hawthorne studies, groups have been viewed as important drivers of individuals' attitudes, reactions, and behaviors. Hackman (1976, 1992) has long chronicled the influences of team factors on individual members. At issue is the fact that team functioning and tangible outcomes represent particularly salient types of stimuli for individual members. More recently, Chen and Kanfer (2006) advanced a systems theory of individuals' motivated behavior in teams. In both Hackman's (1976, 1992) and Chen and Kanfer's (2006) theories, the logic is that team membership represents a particularly salient context that has potent influences on individual members' attitudes, reactions, and behaviors. Consequently, this type of phenomenon represents a classic cross-level direct or mediated-style relationship (cf., Mathieu & Taylor, 2007) of team influences on individual level outcomes.

At the individual level, team activities may have important influences on members' affective states, work attitudes, and motivation. To this end, it is important for researchers and practitioners alike to be able to determine whether a team's functioning and performance results in members who are satisfied with their team, willing to give increased effort to see their team perform well in the future, and feel a sense of commitment to their team and organization. Team member individual reactions are important as drivers of tangible outcomes such as increased individual effort or, alternatively, social loafing (Price, Harrison, & Gavin, 2006). To this end, there are a number of studies that have considered team, job, and organizational satisfaction (e.g., Janz, Colquitt, & Noe, 1997; Kirkman & Rosen, 1999; Tesluk & Mathieu, 1999), along with team and organizational commitment (e.g., Janz et al., 1997; Jehn et al., 1999; Kirkman & Rosen, 1999; Tesluk & Mathieu, 1999). Elsewhere, Maynard, Mathieu, Marsh, and Ruddy (2007) examined team empowerment climate and team processes as influences on individual members' resistance to empowerment. An interesting perspective on affective outcomes was adopted by Janssen and colleagues (1999), who asked members to evaluate whether their team exhibited a good atmosphere and if they were treated with respect.

We would also like to highlight a particularly neglected criterion of team effectiveness that we believe warrants greater attention in the future. Long ago, McGrath (1964) and Hackman and Morris (1975) suggested that individual members' degree of personal development represents an important aspect of the success of a team. This concept sometimes gets confused or confounded with individual-level team viability. Whereas individual viability refers to whether or not a member wishes to remain on their current team in the future, their degree of personal development refers to the extent to which individuals grow and develop as a consequence of participating in a team. Given the fluidity of current organizational designs, we believe that members' personal development represents a far more important criterion than has been recognized previously. Organizational members often participate in multiple teams simultaneously. To the extent that they develop, as members of one team, new skills or attitudes that can transfer and apply to other situations, a positive team experience can have a "multiplier effect" in organizations. Moreover, organizations rapidly create and dismantle teams for a wide variety of reasons. To the extent that individual members have a positive experience and develop as a consequence of working on a team, the overall human capital of the entire organization rises and can be redeployed and leveraged in the future. In short, the notion of individual member development as a salient criterion of effectiveness underscores the fact that "success" may not be apparent as related to the outcomes of a given team, but may

only be manifest via its impact on other teams on which members are working—currently or in the future. Although conveyed through individual personal development, notably this suggests that teams may yield additional benefits at the organizational level via compilational processes (Kozlowski & Salas, 1997).

Group factors may also exert influence directly on individual members' behaviors. For example, Mathieu and Kohler (1990) employed a cross-level design and illustrated that team absence behaviors exhibited a significant cross-level influence on subsequent individual absence behaviors beyond that accounted for by previous individual absences. Similarly, Blau (1995) used a cross-level design to illustrate the effects of group lateness on individual lateness behavior. Xie and Johns (2000) found that absence culture salience and group cohesiveness interacted to predict individual-level absence behavior in a Chinese context. Recently, Chen, Kanfer, DeShon, Mathieu, and Kozlowski (2009) reported a two sample test whereby team-level motivational processes were shown to drive subsequent individual-level motivational processes and performance along the lines of Chen and Kanfer's (2006) multilevel theory. They illustrated complex meditational effects that operated both within the team and at individual levels, as well as traversing downward in a cross-level fashion (i.e., complex cross-level mediation effects; see Mathieu & Taylor, 2007). Importantly, all of these studies examined such effects in a multilevel framework and associated team-level antecedents with individual-level criteria. This meso-paradigm offers a potentially fruitful area for future research.

SUMMARY REGARDING INFLUENCES ON MEMBERS

In sum, it is clear that team-level variables constitute important sources of influence on individual members' attitudes and behaviors. Notably, such effects manifest themselves primarily in a downward cross-level framework. This does not, however, preclude the potential reciprocal influences on individuals' attitudes and behaviors on subsequent team processes and effectiveness (cf., Chen & Kanfer, 2006; Hackman, 1976, 1992). Indeed, such lagged upward influences represent an important avenue for future research. Yet, for current purposes, we wish to reiterate the importance of considering members' individual outcomes as important by-products of team activity.

Sources of Team Effectiveness Criteria

Researchers are faced with the challenge of collecting indices of team effectiveness while balancing a number of seemingly competing demands. Naturally, one prefers to collect thorough, reliable, construct valid, and meaningful data. Moreover, there is a natural desire to collect such data over time at a minimum cost and with as little intrusion into the workplace as possible. In addition, there is always the preference for gathering multiple sources of information for any important variable in one's study. Yet, the realities of conducting research in the "real" world place limits on what can and cannot be done. Teams are not always accessible, practitioners desire minimal disruption to work routines, raters have limited information, and a wide variety of different biases leak into any subjective assessment of team effectiveness. Although archival measures have the allure of "objectivity" and ease, they are not always sensitive to team actions, are frequently contaminated by other influences, and are often a deficient representation of the outputs of team activity. The choice of measurement sources is a complicated one, and one that we believe ought to be guided first and foremost by theory.

As shown in Table 27.2, we believe that certain outcomes are better assessed by certain sources or measurement methods. Tesluk, Zaccaro, Marks, and Mathieu (1997) have previously advocated a similar approach. For example, indices of productivity and efficiency are well gauged by organizational records or archival counts of tangible outcomes. As an example, Gilson et al. (2005) used multiple indices of machine output and technician responsiveness to index service team performance. Raver and Gelfand (2005) assessed team performance using financial performance data. Smith-Jentsch et al. (2005) associated air traffic controllers' shared mental models with outcome indices of tower efficiency and safety that were gathered from publicly available databases maintained by the Federal Aviation Association (FAA) and the National Transportation Safety Bureau (NTSB). Archival indices also may be valuable in determining the quality of team outputs. For example, time to job completion, rejection rates, scrap material produced, and similar indices may all yield informative indices of team performance quality.

Industrial/organizational psychology has a long history of employing archival indices of individuals' behaviors such as absenteeism, turnover, and, in many cases, job performance. Human resource systems routinely track individual job performance, as well as certifications or other measures of individual

Table 27.2 Sources of Information Regarding Different Aspects of Team Effectiveness

	Archives	Subjective Evaluations			
		Members	Observers	Managers	Customers
Tangible Outputs					
Productivity	XX	X	X	X	
Efficiency	XX	X	X	X	
Quality	X	X	X	X	XX
Influence on Members					
Team Emergent States		XX	X	X	X
Individual Reactions		XX			
Individual Attitudes		XX			X
Individual Behavior	XX	X	X	X	X
Individual Development	XX	XX	X	X	

Note: XX signifies a primary source of such information; X signifies a secondary source of such information development. In the context of teams, such performance metrics are becoming more commonplace, particularly with the advent of performance-monitoring systems, global position satellite monitoring, digital portable systems, and so forth. For example, in a study of sales team effectiveness, Ahearne, MacKenzie, Podsakoff, Mathieu, and Lam (2010) were able to leverage team members' service rates as an index of productivity while also using sales relative to quotas as an index of efficiency. Moreover, modern-day team laboratory simulations often provide abundant indices of tangible outputs, such as performance (Chen et al., 2002; Marks et al., 2002), targets neutralized (DeShon, Kozlowski, Schmidt, Milner, & Wiechmann, 2004), decision quality (Colquitt et al., 2002; Jehn et al., 1999), and financial performance relative to competitors (Mathieu & Rapp, 2009).

In the absence of archival counts of team outcomes, researchers must rely on some form of subjective evaluation of effectiveness. The issues are: What types of constructs are under consideration, and which individuals are best positioned to provide such ratings? In this sense, we are paralleling the logic of 360-degree feedback systems, where the question is: What types of behaviors are apparent to which source(s) of rating? Naturally, team members are privy to all aspects of team functioning and provide a valuable source of information. However, members also have a biased view of themselves and tend to engage in attributional biases when it comes to the evaluation of their own behaviors (Martell, Guzzo, & Willis, 1995). At issue, then, is: What types of constructs are best evaluated by members?

We submit that team members are the most appropriate source of information for assessing internal psychological states and reactions. Presumably, they are better aware of how they feel, whether that be a collective state such as cohesion or an individual attitude such as commitment or satisfaction, than are external observers. This is not to preclude the possibility that others can accurately perceive individuals' psychological states, as previous research has shown that they often can (cf., Schneider, White, & Paul, 1998). But, it is to say that asking individuals to report on their own psychological processes is not only appropriate but, we submit, the preferred source of such information. By the same token, members' attributional biases are likely to be most acute if asked to rate their own individual- or team-level outcomes. Consequently, while members are still a viable source of ratings for performance outcomes, we believe that there are better alternatives. With that said, research in the domain of top management teams is often forced to rely on chief executive officers or members to provide information about company performance (see Simsek et al., 2005). In such instances, it is certainly preferable to try to separate the rating of performance from the assessment of other team variables. For example, the financial performance of the organization is perhaps best evaluated by the chief financial officer, whereas the functioning of the team as a whole could perhaps be rated by other team members. Similarly, the creativity literature has often argued that individuals are in the best position to evaluate creative processes, as creativity entails taking risks and trying new things, behaviors that might be kept out of view from supervisors, who may only see the end product (Janssen, 2000). That said, self-report measures have been found to correlate with supervisory ratings of creativity (Axtell, Holman, & Unsworth, 2000).

Beyond team members, others are often well positioned to rate team effectiveness. Notably, higher-level supervisors or managers of teams are often sampled to supply team effectiveness ratings. For example, Austin (2003) had managers rate their team effectiveness with regard to their success in fulfilling company objectives, which were to: (a) increase company responsiveness to changing market demands for their products; and (b) improve cross-functional communication in the merchandising process. Stewart and Barrick (2000) had supervisors rate eight dimensions of team performance that included: (a) knowledge of tasks; (b) quality of work; (c) quantity of work; (d) initiative; (e) interpersonal skills; (f) planning and allocation; (g) commitment to the team; and (h) overall performance. Finally, Hiller and colleagues (2006) had supervisors from the Department of Transportation rate the planning, problem solving, support and consideration, development and mentoring, and overall performance of 52 winter road teams.

In some instances, there are external observers who are not responsible for the team functioning but who are well positioned to evaluate the team's functioning or performance. Course instructors would represent this perspective for measurement in research conducted with student teams performing classroom projects or exercises (Barry & Stewart, 1997, Lester et al., 2002). In training applications, there are often instances when teams perform capstone exercises that are watched and critiqued by external observers. For example, the first author is currently involved in a project in which Army Transition Teams perform high-fidelity simulations at the end of a two-month training period before being deployed in theater. The exercises are watched and scored by highly trained observers for both feedback and evaluation purposes. Kirkman, Mathieu, Cordery, Rosen and Kukenberger (2011) reported a study in which the effectiveness of organizational communities of practice (OCoPs, similar to virtual teams) were assessed by two organizational members who were responsible for maintaining an organizational program. In other words, these two individuals had the responsibility to monitor and provide support for all OCoPs in the company and knew the strengths and weakness of each one better than anyone else. In sum, external observers are a valuable source of information in many instances, provided that they have sufficient opportunity to witness critical team functioning.

Last, customers can provide keen insights regarding the operations of many teams, especially ones that provide services. For example, Mathieu et al. (2006) used customer evaluations of the service teams' timeliness and work quality. Kirkman et al. (2006) indexed team performance using three months of averaged customer ratings of service and support. Following the logic outlined earlier, customers themselves are naturally the prime source of information about their satisfaction. They may also be a valuable gauge of service quality and timeliness, particularly if teams operate outside the purview of organizational members (e.g., sales teams).

Summary Regarding Sources of Team Criteria Measures

In summary, naturally it is ideal to have multiple sources of team effectiveness information. However, we submit that some sources of information are better suited for providing information of certain types. The ideal configuration of measurement sources for any application will be a function of the type of team(s) being studied, resource availability, logistical challenges, and a host of other considerations. However, we encourage researchers to move beyond members' self-assessments and a relative overreliance on managerial ratings, and to employ a wider variety of measures including archival traces, customer evaluations, and neutral observer ratings whenever available.

Temporal Issues

It is widely accepted that teams are dynamic entities that have a past, present, and future (McGrath, Arrow, & Berdahl, 2000). Gully (2000) submitted that "[t]o fully understand work teams, researchers must investigate how team dynamics develop and change over time" (p. 35). Time can be conceived in several different fashions (see Ancona, Okhuysen, et al., 2001). At issue for our present purposes are four related factors: (a) postdictive versus predictive research designs; (b) aggregation lags and periods; (c) episodic cycles; and (d) developmental processes. The first two factors represent primarily methodological concerns. At issue is how the outcome measures relate in time to when various team activities occurred and whether the period of outcome observation is sufficient for making important distinctions.

The latter two temporal features are more substantive in nature and suggest that researchers should consider the relationships between their outcome measures and teams' episodic periods (Marks et al., 2001) or developmental stages (Kozlowski et al., 1999). A misalignment between when various team phenomena actually occur and when they are measured could easy lead to a misrepresentation of relationships. Appreciation of these four temporal factors highlights the fact that decisions concerning what outcome(s) to measure, when to collect them, and for how long should be guided by the team task and performance environment and ones' extant theory. Accordingly, each of the four temporal factors, as related to team effectiveness criteria, is elaborated upon below.

Postdictive Versus Predictive Research Designs

It seems obvious to even say that predictive measures should be collected prior to one's criteria, but close examination of the literature reveals many instances in which this was not the case. Many authors frame their study as a cross-sectional design if their predictor measures are collected at the same time as their criteria. However, even with that caveat, the situation may actually be postdictive. For example, typically one collects information about team composition and mediators (e.g., emergent states or processes) from members while perhaps asking their supervisors to rate the team's effectiveness. No doubt the researcher wishes to justify depicting a causal order of team composition → team mediators → team outcomes. Given that compositional factors are typically based on member traits and characteristics, it is probably the case that the composition → mediator portion of such a model is easily defendable (see Mathieu & Taylor, 2007). This ordering would be less convincing, however, if the team composition was based on members' attitudes. However, the team mediators → outcome ordering is more problematic.

For sake of argument, let us say that the team mediators were measured using members' survey responses at the end of the first quarterly performance period. Most likely, members' responses would reflect recent team activities unless survey items specifically referred to a designated time period (e.g., "Rate your team processes over the past three months"). What would be the salient period of performance for an external manager when it comes to rating the team's performance? Most likely it would be an extended period of performance dating back further than the past quarter. And, even if framed in terms of the "past three months," there would not likely be an alignment between the temporal focus of members' process responses and managers' effectiveness ratings. Assuming some ebb and flow between team processes and effectiveness over time, there is no way to ensure that the temporal focus of members is consistent with the temporal focus of managers. The bottom line is that if team processes take some time to generate team effectiveness, then having members or their managers focus on the same period of time is more likely to yield process scores that are consequent to earlier team effectiveness than it is the reverse. Thus, the standard cross-sectional design is quite likely to yield postdictive data. The situation is only exacerbated if researchers were to associate team members' response gathered in the first quarter with existing performance evaluations or organizational archives—which naturally would reflect earlier performance periods.

More generally, the problem outlined above is referred to as endogeniety in the strategic management literature (Hamilton & Nickerson, 2003). In brief, the endogeniety problem suggests that one's predictor variables may actually be the product, to varying degrees, of earlier states of one's outcome variable. Applied to this context, if previous team performance (i.e., t0) generates future team states (e.g., team efficacy, t1), and team performance is fairly consistent over time, one might easily observe an illusionary correlation between team efficacy and subsequent (i.e., t2) team performance. This follows from the fact that the observed efficacy (t1)–performance (i.e., t2) correlation really emanates from their common roots in earlier performance (i.e., t0). Hamilton and Nickerson (2003), as well as Maxwell and Cole (2007), outline different ways

in which the endogeniety threat to causal inferences may be addressed.

Aggregation Lags and Periods

The previous section made the point that criteria measures should represent outcomes that followed from earlier team activities. While the point may appear to be self-evident, it becomes tricky to implement in practice. At issue are two related factors: (a) when would outcomes becomes manifest; and (b) how long should criteria be accumulated (i.e., aggregated)? As for the first point, consider a study in which some intervention is introduced (e.g., external leader training) in the hopes of significantly improving team functioning and thereby team effectiveness. Assuming for the moment that the intervention worked and was powerful, how long would it take for leaders' behaviorstoward the team to change? How long would it take for the team members to notice such changes and to begin acting differently? And then, how long would it take for their different team behaviors to result in changes in effectiveness indicators, whether those are productivity counts or customer reactions? Collectively, we submit, such potent intervention changes may take several weeks or months to manifest changes in criteria measures. Therefore, an intervention introduced in the first quarter of the year may not begin to show its effects until the second quarter or even later. A tally of effectiveness indicators gathered immediately following the intervention may well miss such effects. In short, there is very little in the literature that addresses the appropriate time lag to employ between team influences and their effects. And, we further submit that such lags may well differ, depending on the nature of the intervention and the type of effectiveness indicator being considered. We urge researchers to consider such relationships, and to justify the lag periods that they employ.

The second point concerns how long a period of aggregation should be employed for the outcome measures. Note that this issue is pertinent no matter what method of measurement is used. Good survey measures direct the respondent to a particular timeframe (e.g., "Rate the quality of the team's performance over the past three months"). Aggregation of archival indices and other types of measures also requires some specific timeframe. Given that team criteria are often dynamic entities (Landis, 2001), the choice of aggregation period becomes particularly important. On one hand, the aggregation period should be sufficiently long so as to yield a psychometrically stable composite. On the other hand, the aggregation period should not be so long as to become susceptible to other sources of contamination. Here again, the ideal period of time may well differ from one situation to another, and as a function of the criterion measure employed. In any event, it is important for researchers to articulate the rationale for the aggregation period(s) that they employ.

We should mention briefly one other temporal-related methodological concern, namely seasonal trends. If performance values, customer preferences, and other elements are susceptible to factors that change systematically over time, one may fall prey to illusionary increasing or decreasing outcome patterns over time. Various forms of norming (e.g., efficiency rates) may help to control for such factors, such as considering performance relative to quotas, comparing quarterly performance against the same period in previous years, or making within-period comparisons across teams. In short, researchers may have to recalibrate outcome indicators to yield a "level playing field" for criteria measures over time.

Episodic Cycles

Teams may well exhibit different processes over time attributable to substantive matters. For example, Marks et al. (2001) advanced an episodic model of team processes and argued that "work teams strive toward collective goals that incorporate time as a component....Time-based rhythms act to shape how teams manage their behavior" (pp. 358–359). Episodic theories of team processes hinge on the notion of performance episodes, which serve as demarcation points for recurring cycles of task accomplishment (Marks et al., 2001). Similar notions were advanced by Kozlowski et al. (1999) and McGrath and Rotchford (1983), who discussed recurrent periodicity, and Ancona, Goodman, et al. (2001), who addressed repeated activity mapping. The general idea is that longer-term efforts are broken down into more operational and meaningful subperiods. "Episodes' durations stem largely from the nature of the tasks that teams perform and the technology that they employ, and from the manner in which members choose to complete work. Episodes are most easily identified by goals and goal accomplishment periods" (Marks et al., 2001, p. 359). For example, year-long performance targets can be partitioned or "chunked" into quarterly, or even weekly, goals and monitored at a more fine-grained level. Production teams may chunk activities into periods that correspond to different product runs, shift changes, or other times that are

meaningful to them. The point is simply that linear clock time is partitioned into recurring chunks that have meaning to members—usually in terms of being tied to goals and/or feedback delivery. This implies a natural nesting of phenomena where faster cycling team processes and performance outcomes unfold episodically within the context of longer time periods. In this sense, the episodic processes are nested within teams over time, in what amounts to a hierarchical multilevel design.

Cyclical models such as Marks et al.'s (2001) suggest that different team outcomes will be salient at different times. Decision timeliness, the quality of strategies and plans, and so forth would constitute suitable criteria for teams in the transition stage. Alternatively, performance metrics, efficiencies, customer reactions, and the like would be more suitable criteria for teams performing in action phases. Traditionally, various effectiveness indices are aggregated over time, as described above. However, in so doing, important relationships and temporal variance may be obscured. For example, using students competing in a business simulation, Mathieu and Schulze (2006) found that unpacking transition-action periods led to far more significant results than when data were aggregated across episodes over time.

In sum, cyclical theories of team activity raise issues surrounding the pace and frequency of performance episodes. Researchers need to discern the most appropriate temporal "chunks" or units of time to consider. Cyclical theories also highlight the fact that teams are doing different things at different times, and therefore the relevant indicators of effectiveness differ across time. Aligning their research designs and analyses with such cycles represents a challenge for researchers, as well as an opportunity for new insights.

Developmental Processes

The extant team literature is replete with models of how teams develop and change over time. Developmental theories suggest that teams go through a series of phases as members seek to understand their task environment and get to know one another. Team development is described as "the path a [team] takes over its life-spantoward the accomplishment of its main tasks" (Gersick, 1988, p. 9), and many models of such processes exist (e.g., Ancona & Chong, 1996; Gersick, 1988; Kozlowski et al., 1996; Tuckman, 1965). For example, the well-known developmental model advanced by Tuckman suggests that, in general, teams go through a series of *forming*, *storming*, *norming*, *performing*, and *adjourning* stages. Similar to the cyclical theories of team functioning, the developmental approaches suggest that teams are accomplishing different things at different times. However, rather than repeating in a predictable cycle of phases, the developmental models suggest that teams evolve over time from birth to death.

The developmental models suggest that what constitutes effectiveness may radically change over time. For example, we are currently involved in a study in which a regional grocery store has launched a quality circle–style initiative. Each store in the chain has constituted a team whose members follow a general protocol to propose process improvements. During the initial stages, not only do members need to understand one another, their strengths and weakness, but the team must also identify a set of initiatives that they might work on. At this stage, effectiveness is gauged primarily in terms of the number of potential initiatives that are identified and how well they are framed. The second stage involves the development of various initiatives to the point at which the team can choose one initiative on which to focus in the future. In short, the primary index of effectiveness at this stage, roughly halfway through the process, is a well-defined problem or innovation that the team will address.

The third stage of the process involves members researching the selected problem space, developing ideas and proposals, and refining their proposed intervention or innovation. Often, the teams discover dead-ends during this phase and must cycle back to phase two and select a different project to pursue. Inevitably, the teams close out this third phase with a proposal for what they think should be done. The extent to which the teams' proposals are thoroughly researched, have identified the costs and benefits of proposed courses of action, and so forth, represents effectiveness at this point. In the final stage, the team presents their ideas to a review panel, receives feedback, and submits a final written proposal. The ultimate criteria following this stage are whether the teams' proposals are creative, are implemented, and the extent to which they yield a positive cost/benefit ratio.

As detailed in the example above, what constitutes team effectiveness changed over time, with the success of latter stages dependent, in part, on the success of earlier stages. Importantly, given that the nature of effectiveness qualitatively changed over time, temporal-based comparisons become far more difficult, as compared to those of teams who perform the same tasks over time (e.g., production teams). While researchers may choose to employ fairly generic indices (e.g., observers' ratings of "overall effectiveness") in an effort to have comparable indices over time, the disadvantage of that approach is less sensitive and valid measures of effectiveness at any given phase. Alternatively, researchers may use earlier indices of effectiveness as predictors of later team states, processes, and effectiveness. Of course, this strategy presents serious logistical challenges if different teams are at different developmental stages during any calendar periods. In other words, adopting this phase-sensitive approach would mean that data collection efforts would need to be yoked to the developmental stage of each and every team. While this would help to align data collection with team developmental processes, it represents a daunting logistical challenge. For example, we adopted such an approach in the grocery store study described above, which necessitated nearly daily data collection efforts for almost a year to gather information for approximately 35 teams.

Summary of Temporal Issues

Criteria issues are typically discussed in terms of what should be measured and how it should be indexed. However, temporal issues play a large role in the value of the resulting indices. We summarize our recommendations in terms of incorporating temporal issues in team effectiveness research in Table 27.3. Two of the factors that we discussed were primarily methodological in nature. Criteria measures should be postdictive of team effectiveness predictors, and they should be collected at and for the proper duration of time in order to be valuable. We also discussed two more substantive temporal factors. We noted that teams often function in a cyclical fashion through episodes, rendering some types of effectiveness measures particularly suitable at some times, yet other indices more applicable at other times. In a similar vein, teams develop over time and have a lifecycle. Consequently, the nature of what constitutes effectiveness often qualitatively changes over time and should be accounted for in any investigation that considers developmental processes.

Overall Conclusions

Although research on teams has gained renewed interest in recent decades, the bulk of attention has been focused on antecedents and mediating mechanisms predicting effectiveness. Far less attention has been devoted to understanding the

Table 27.3 Recommendations for Addressing Temporal Issues in Team Criteria

1. Utilize postdictive versus concurrent (or predictive) designs
   a. Do the criteria occur after the predictive factors?
   b. When would changes in the criteria become evident?
2. Select appropriate aggregation periods that are:
   a. Sufficiently long enough to provide stable criteria estimates
   b. Not so long as to become overly susceptible to contamination
3. Formally incorporate episodic processes into research designs:
   a. How frequently do episodes cycle?
   b. What triggers or marks episodic transitions?
   c. Align the collection of predictor and criteria variables with episodic phases
4. Formally incorporate developmental processes into research designs
   a. How lengthy is the team life cycle?
   b. When are transition phases likely to occur?
   c. What are the salient criteria for each stage of development?

criteria domain of team effectiveness. Accordingly, we first described a general team effectiveness framework. This framework served to illustrate the general causal flow of team phenomena, but also illustrated the fact that what constitute criteria at one point in time may well serve as antecedents to later team functioning. The take-away point from that discussion is that criteria measures stem not only from one's guiding theory, but also from the research design that one employs and the purpose of the investigation.

We next turned our attention to a detailed examination of the types and measurement of team outcomes. We identified two fairly general forms of effectiveness criteria, namely *tangible outputs* and *members' reactions*. We further differentiated three types of tangible outcomes: (a) *productivity*; (b) *efficiency*; and (c) *quality*. Our intention was to provide a categorization scheme such that researchers can more clearly articulate the nature of the criteria that they are using, and why they are particularly suitable for their investigation. Such a framework may also prove useful for future reviews and meta-analyses that seek to balance the specificity of the criteria domain with a desire to have more inclusive categories to facilitate comparisons of results across different investigations.

We also distinguished between team-level member reactions, in the form of *emergent states*, as well as individual-level *attitudes, reactions, behaviors*, and *personal development* as criteria of team functioning. We argued that emergent states, in particular, have been employed as predictors, mediators, and outcomes in models of team effectiveness. Here again, the research design employed and the

purpose of the investigation help to clarify the role of such variables. We also revisited the role that team factors have on members' individual-level attitudes, reactions, behaviors, and development. Despite the emergence of multilevel theories, designs, and analyses in recent years, the cross-level influences of team factors on individuals have seemingly dropped out of favor. We believe that the individual-level criteria warrant renewed attention in the years to come. Given that individuals are often simultaneously members of multiple teams, as well as the fact that teams reconstitute and reform over time, the individual-level criteria may gain far greater importance in the years to come. Individuals' reactions and development stemming from any given team experience may well taint, or serve as a catalyst, for their attitudes toward, and their motivation and participation in, future teams.

We also discussed the relative suitability of alternative assessment schemes for each type of criteria. We noted that some types of criteria are simply more validly assessed using certain methods or sources of information. Whereas concerns about "methods effects" are naturally salient for any investigation, researchers should appreciate that some constructs are simply better addressed in certain fashions (e.g., customer reactions from customers, productivity from archival counts, members' reactions from members' self-reports, etc.).

Finally, we illustrated how gaining an appreciation for four temporal-related factors—(a) postdictive versus predictive designs; (b) aggregation lags and periods; (c) episodic cycles; and (d) developmental processes—will enhance our understanding of the team effectiveness criteria construct. Notably, the first two temporal factors are more methodological in nature and focus on ensuring an accurate depiction of the causal order of phenomena, as well as having a reliable and representative criterion measure. The latter two temporal factors are more substantive in nature and illustrate that team effectiveness criteria are dynamic entities. While episodic models imply that different criteria will be salient at different times in a fairly predictable sequence, developmental processes suggest that the nature of team effectiveness may well qualitatively change over time. Both of these approaches, particularly when combined with the methodological concerns, suggest that the criteria of team effectiveness are far more fluid and complex than researchers have typically implied. We encourage future work to embrace such complexity, as we believe that developing a better understanding of the team effectiveness criteria domain offers many insights for the advancement of our theories and the application of our work.

References

Ahearne, M., MacKenzie, S. B., Podsakoff, P. M., Mathieu, J. E., & Lam, S. K. (2010). The role of consensus in sales team performance. *Journal of Marketing Research, 47*, 458–469.

Ancona, D., & Chong, C. L. (1996). Entrainment: Pace, cycle, and rhythm in organizational behavior. *Research in Organizational Behavior, 18*, 251–284.

Ancona, D. G., Goodman, P. S., Lawrence, B. S., & Tushman, M. L. (2001). Time: A new research lens. *Academy of Management Review, 26*(4), 645–663.

Ancona, D. G., Okhuysen, G. A., & Perlow, L. A. (2001). Taking time to integrate temporal research. *Academy of Management Review, 26*(4), 512–529.

Austin, J. R. (2003). Transactive memory in organizational groups: The effects of content, consensus, specialization, and accuracy on group performance. *Journal of Applied Psychology, 88*, 866–878.

Axtell, C. M., Holman, D., & Unsworth, K. L. (2000). Shopfloor innovation: Facilitating the suggestion and implementation of ideas. *Journal of Occupational and Organizational Psychology, 73*, 265–285.

Balkundi, P., & Harrison, D. A. (2006). Ties, leaders, and time in teams: Strong inference about network structure's effects on team viability and performance. *Academy of Management Journal, 49*(1), 49–68.

Barrick, M. B., Bradley, B. H., Kristof-Brown, A. L., & Colbert, A. E. (2007). The moderating role of top management team interdependence: Implications for real teams and working groups. *Academy of Management Journal, 50*, 544–557.

Barrick, M. R., Stewart, G. L., Neubert, J. M., & Mount, M. K. (1998). Relating member ability and personality to work team processes and team effectiveness. *Journal of Applied Psychology, 83*, 377–391.

Barry, B., & Stewart, G. L. (1997). Composition, process, and performance in self-managed groups: The role of personality. *Journal of Applied Psychology, 82*, 62–78.

Bass, B. M., Avolio, B. J., Jung, D. I., & Berson, Y. (2003). Predicting unit performance by assessing transformational and transactional leadership. *Journal of Applied Psychology, 88*, 207–218.

Beal, D. J., Cohen, R. R., Burke, M. J., & McLendon, C. L. (2003). Cohesion and performance in groups: A meta-analytic clarification of construct relations. *Journal of Applied Psychology, 88*, 989–1004.

Bell, S. T. (2007). Deep-level composition variables as predictors of team performance: A meta-analysis. *Journal of Applied Psychology, 92*, 595–615.

Blau, G. (1995). Influence of group lateness on individual lateness: A cross-level examination. *Academy of Management Journal, 38*(5), 1483–1496.

Bommer, W. H., Johnson, J. L., Rich, G. A., Podsakoff, P. M., & MacKenzie, S. B. (1995). On the interchangeability of objective and subjective measures of employee performance: A meta-analysis. *Personnel Psychology, 48*, 587–605.

Brown, T. C. (2003). The effect of verbal self-guidance training on collective efficacy and team performance. *Personnel Psychology, 56*(4), 935–964.

Bunderson, J. S., & Sutcliffe, K. M. (2003). Management team learning orientation and business unit performance. *Journal of Applied Psychology, 88*, 552–560.

Burke, C. S., Stagl, K. C., Klein, C., Goodwin, G. F., Salas, E., & Halpin, S. M. (2006). What types of leadership behaviors are functional in teams? A meta-analysis. *Leadership Quarterly, 17*, 288–307.

Chen, G. (2005). Newcomer adaptation in teams: Multilevel antecedents and outcomes. *Academy of Management Journal, 48*, 101–116.

Chen, G., & Kanfer, R. (2006). Toward a systems theory of motivated behavior in work teams. *Research in Organizational Behavior: An Annual Series of Analytical Essays and Critical Reviews, 27*, 223–267.

Chen, G., Kanfer, R., DeShon, R. P., Mathieu, J. E., & Kozlowski, S. W. J. (2009). The motivating potential of teams: Test and extension of Chen & Kanfer's (2006) cross-level model of motivation in teams. *Organizational Behavior and Human Decision Processes, 110*, 45–55.

Chen, G., Webber, S. S., Bliese, P. D., Mathieu, J. E., Payne, S. C., Born, D. H., & Zaccaro, S. J. (2002). Simultaneous examination of the antecedents and consequences of efficacy beliefs at multiple levels of analysis. *Human Performance, 15*(4), 381–409.

Cohen, S. G., & Bailey, D. E. (1997). What makes teams work: Group effectiveness research from the shop floor to the executive suite. *Journal of Management, 23*, 239–290.

Colquitt, J. A., Hollenbeck, J. R., Ilgen, D. R., LePine, J. A., & Sheppard, L. (2002). Computer-assisted communication and team decision-making performance: The moderating effect of openness to experience. *Journal of Applied Psychology, 87*, 402–410.

De Dreu, C. K. W., & Weingart, L. R. (2003). Task versus relationship conflict: Team performance, and team member satisfaction: A meta-analysis. *Journal of Applied Psychology, 88*, 741–749.

De Dreu, C. K. W., & West, M. A. (2001). Minority dissent and team innovation: The importance of participation in decision making. *Journal of Applied Psychology, 86*, 1191–1201.

DeShon, R. P., Kozlowski, S. W. J., Schmidt, A. M., Milner, K. R., & Wiechmann, D. (2004). A multiple-goal, multilevel model of feedback effects on the regulation of individual and team performance. *Journal of Applied Psychology, 89*, 1035–1056.

Devine, D. J. (2002). A review and integration of classification systems relevant to teams in organizations. *Group Dynamics-Theory Research and Practice, 6*(4), 291–310.

Edmondson, A. (1999). Psychological safety and learning behavior in work teams. *Administrative Science Quarterly, 44*, 350–383.

Feltz, D. L., & Lirgg, C. D. (1998). Perceived team and player efficacy in hockey. *Journal of Applied Psychology, 83*, 557–564.

Gersick, C. (1988). Time and transition in work teams: Toward a model of group development. *Academy of Management Journal, 31*, 9–42.

Gilson, L. L., Mathieu, J. E., Shalley, C. E., & Ruddy, T. M. (2005). Creativity and standardization: Complementary or conflicting drivers of team effectiveness. *Academy of Management Journal, 48*, 521–531.

Gully, S. M. (2000). Work teams research: Recent findings and future trends. In M. M. Beyerlein (Ed.), *Work teams: Past, present, and future* (pp. 25–44). Netherlands: Kluwer.

Gully, S. M., Incalcaterra, K. A., Joshi, A., & Beaubien, J. M. (2002). A meta-analysis of team-efficacy, potency, and performance: Interdependence and level of analysis as moderators of observed relationships. *Journal of Applied Psychology, 87*, 819–832.

Hackman, J. R. (1976). Group influences on individuals. In M. D. Dunnette (Ed.), *Handbook of industrial and organizational psychology* (pp. 1455–1525). Chicago: Rand-McNally.

Hackman, J. R. (1987). The design of work teams. In J. Lorsch (Ed.), *Handbook of organizational behavior* (pp. 315–342). Englewood Cliffs, NJ: Prentice Hall.

Hackman, R. (1990). *Groups that work and those that don't.* San Francisco: Jossey-Bass.

Hackman, J. R. (1992). Group influences on individuals in organizations. In M. D. Dunnette & L. M. Hough (Eds.), *Handbook of industrial and organizational psychology* (2nd ed., Vol. 3, pp. 199–267). Chicago: Rand-McNally.

Hackman, J. R., & Morris, C. G. (1975). Group tasks, group interaction processes, and group performance effectiveness: A review and proposed integration. *Advances in Experimental Social Psychology, 8*, 45–99.

Hamilton, B. H., & Nickerson, J. A. (2003). Correcting for endogeneity in strategic management research. *Strategic Organization, 1*, 51–78.

Hiller, N. J., Day, D. V., & Vance, R. J. (2006). Collective enactment of leadership roles and team effectiveness: A field study. *Leadership Quarterly, 17*, 387–397.

Ilgen, D. R. (1999). Teams embedded in organizations: Some implications. *American Psychologist, 54*(2), 129–139.

Ilgen, D. R., Hollenbeck, J. R., Johnson, M., & Jundt, D. (2005). Teams in organizations: From input-process-output models to IMOI models. *Annual Review of Psychology, 56*, 517–543.

Janssen, O. (2000). Job demands, perceptions of effort-reward fairness and innovative work behaviors. *Journal of Occupational and Organizational Psychology, 73*, 287–302.

Janssen, O., Van de Vliert, E., & Veenstra, C. (1999). How task and person conflict shape the role of positive interdependence in management teams. *Journal of Management, 25*, 117–141.

Janz, B. D., Colquitt, J. A., & Noe, R. A. (1997). Knowledge worker team effectiveness: The role of autonomy, interdependence, team development, and contextual support variables. *Personnel Psychology, 50*, 877–904.

Jehn, K. A., & Shah, P. P. (1997). Interpersonal relationships and task performance: An examination of mediation processes in friendship and acquaintance groups. *Journal of Personality and Social Psychology, 72*, 775–790.

Jehn, K. A., Northcraft, G. B., & Neale, M. A. (1999). Why differences make a difference: A field study of diversity, conflict, and performance in workgroups. *Administrative Science Quarterly, 44*, 741–763.

Kirkman, B. L., Mathieu, J. E., Cordery, J. L., Kukenberger, M. R. & Rosen, B. (2011). Managing a New Collaborative Entity in Business Organizations: Understanding Organizational Communities of Practice Effectiveness. *Journal of Applied Psychology. 96* (6), 1234–1245.

Kirkman, B. L., & Rosen, B. (1999). Beyond self-management: Antecedents and consequences of team empowerment. *Academy of Management Journal, 42*, 58–74.

Kirkman, B. L., Rosen, B., Tesluk, P. E., & Gibson, C. B. (2004). The impact of team empowerment on virtual team performance: The moderating role of face-to-face interaction. *Academy of Management Journal, 47*(2), 175–192.

Kirkman, B. L., Rosen, B., Tesluk, P. E., & Gibson, C. B. (2006). Enhancing the transfer of computer-assisted training proficiency in geographically distributed teams. *Journal of Applied Psychology, 91*(3), 706–716.

Kozlowski, S. W. J., & Bell, B. S. (2003). Work groups and teams in organizations. In W. C. Borman, D. R. Ilgen, & R. J. Klimoski (Eds.), *Handbook of psychology: Industrial and organizational psychology* (Vol. 12, pp. 333–375). London: Wiley.

Kozlowski, S. W. J., & Ilgen, D. R. (2006). Enhancing the effectiveness of work groups and teams. *Psychological Science in the Public Interest, 7*, 77–124.

Kozlowski, S. W. J., Gully, S. M., McHugh, P. P., Salas, E., & Cannon-Bowers, J. A. (1996). A dynamic theory of leadership and team effectiveness: Developmental and task contingent leader roles. *Research in Personnel and Human Resources Management, 14*, 253–305.

Kozlowski, S. W. J., Gully, S. M., Nason, E. R., & Smith, E. M. (1999). Developing adaptive teams: A theory of compilation and performance across levels and time. In D. R. Ilgen & E. D. Pulakos (Eds.), *The changing nature of work performance: Implications for staffing, personnel actions, and development* (pp. 240–292). San Francisco: Jossey-Bass.

Kozlowski, S. W. J., & Salas, E. (1997). A multilevel organizational systems approach for the implementation and transfer of training. In J. K. Ford, S. W. J. Kozlowski, K. Kraiger, E. Salas, & M. Teachout (Eds.), *Improving training effectiveness in work organizations* (pp. 247–287). Mahwah, NJ: Erlbaum.

Landis, R. S. (2001). A note on the stability of team performance. *Journal of Applied Psychology, 86*, 446–450.

Langfred, C. W. (2000). Work-group design and autonomy: A field study of the interaction between task interdependence and group autonomy. *Small Group Research, 31*(1), 54–70.

LePine, J. A., Piccolo, R. F., Jackson, C. L., Mathieu, J. E., & Saul, J. R. (2008). A meta-analysis of teamwork processes: Tests of a multidimensional model and relationships with team effectiveness criteria. *Personnel Psychology, 61*, 273–307.

Lester, S. W., Meglino, B. M., & Korsgaard, M. A. (2002). The antecedents and consequences of group potency: A longitudinal investigation of newly formed work groups. *Academy of Management Journal, 45*, 352–368.

Marks, M. A., Mathieu, J. E., & Zaccaro, S. J. (2001). A temporally based framework and taxonomy of team processes. *Academy of Management Review, 26*(3), 356–376.

Marks, M. A., Sabella, M. J., Burke, C. S., & Zaccaro, S. J. (2002). The impact of cross-training on team effectiveness. *Journal of Applied Psychology, 87*, 3–13.

Marks, M. A., Zaccaro, S. J., & Mathieu, J. E. (2000). Performance implications of leader briefings and team-interaction training for team adaptation to novel environments. *Journal of Applied Psychology, 85*(6), 971–986.

Martell, R. E., Guzzo, R. A., & Willis, C. E. (1995). A methodological and substantive note on the performance-cue effect in ratings of work-group behavior. *Journal of Applied Psychology, 80*, 191–195.

Mathieu, J. E., Gilson, L. L., & Ruddy, T. M. (2006). Empowerment and team effectiveness: An empirical test of an integrated model. *Journal of Applied Psychology, 91*, 97–108.

Mathieu, J. E., Heffner, T. S., Goodwin, G. F., Salas, E., & Cannon-Bowers, J. A. (2000). The influence of shared mental models on team process and performance. *Journal of Applied Psychology, 85*, 273–283.

Mathieu, J. E., & Kohler, S. S. (1990). A cross-level examination of group absence influences on individual absence. *Journal of Applied Psychology, 75*, 217–220.

Mathieu, J. E., Maynard, M. T., Rapp, T. L., & Gilson, L. L. (2008). Team effectiveness 1997–2007: A review of recent advancements and a glimpse into the future. *Journal of Management, 34*, 410–476.

Mathieu, J. E., & Rapp, T. L. (2009). Laying the foundation for successful team performance trajectories: The roles of team charters and performance strategies. *Journal of Applied Psychology, 94*(1), 90–103.

Mathieu, J. E., & Schulze, W. (2006). The influence of team knowledge and formal plans on episodic team process-performance relationships. *Academy of Management Journal, 49*, 605–619.

Mathieu, J. E., & Taylor, S. (2007). A framework for testing meso-mediational relationships in organizational behavior. *Journal of Organizational Behavior, 28*, 141–172.

Maxwell, S. E., & Cole, D. A. (2007). Bias in cross-sectional analyses of longitudinal mediation. *Psychological Methods, 12*, 23–44.

Maynard, M. T., Mathieu, J. E., Marsh, W. M., & Ruddy, T. (2007). A multi-level investigation of the influences of employees' resistance to teams and empowerment. *Human Performance, 20*(2), 147–171.

McGrath, J. E. (1964). *Social psychology: A brief introduction.* New York: Holt.

McGrath, J. E. (1984). *Groups: Interaction and performance.* Englewood Cliffs, NJ: Prentice-Hall.

McGrath, J. E. (1991). Time, interaction, and performance (TIP): A theory of groups. *Small Group Research, 22*, 147–174.

McGrath, J. E., Arrow, H., & Berdahl, J. L. (2000). The study of groups: Past, present, and future. *Personality & Social Psychology Review, 4*(1), 95–105.

McGrath, J. E., & Rotchford, N. L. (1983). Time and behavior in organizations. *Research in Organizational Behavior, 5*, 57–101.

Morgeson, F. P., & Hofmann, D. A. (1999). The structure and function of collective constructs: Implications for multilevel research and theory development. *Academy of Management Review, 24*, 249–265.

Porter, C. (2005). Goal orientation: Effects on backing up behavior, performance, efficacy, and commitment in teams. *Journal of Applied Psychology, 90*(4), 811–818.

Price, K. H., Harrison, D. A., & Gavin, J. H. (2006). Withholding inputs in team contexts: Member composition, interaction processes, evaluation structure, and social loafing. *Journal of Applied Psychology, 91*, 1375–1384.

Pritchard, R. D. (1992). Organizational productivity. In M. D. Dunnette & L. M. Hough (Eds.), *Handbook of industrial and organizational psychology* (Vol. 2, pp. 443–471). Palo Alto, CA: Consulting Psychologists Press.

Pritchard, R. D., Jones, S., Roth, P., Stuebing, K., & Ekeberg, S. (1988). Effects of group feedback, goal setting, and incentives on organizational productivity. *Journal of Applied Psychology, 73*, 337–358.

Raver, J. L., & Gelfand, M. J. (2005). Beyond the individual victim: Linking sexual harassment, team processes, and team performance. *Academy of Management Journal, 48*, 387–400.

Salas, E., Dickinson, T. L., Converse, S. A., & Tannenbaum, S. I. (1992). Toward an understanding of team performance and training. In R. W. Swezey & E. Salas (Eds.), *Teams: Their training and performance* (pp. 3–29). Norwood, NJ: Ablex.

Sanna, L. J., & Parks, C. D. (1997). Group research trends in social and organizational psychology: Whatever happened to intragroup research? *Psychological Science, 8*(4), 261–267.

Schneider, B., White, S. S., & Paul, M. C. (1998). Linking service climate and customer perceptions of service quality: Test of a causal model. *Journal of Applied Psychology, 83*, 150–163.

Simsek, Z., Veiga, J. F., Lubatkin, M. H., & Dino, R. N. (2005). Modeling the multilevel determinants of top management team behavioral integration. *Academy of Management Journal, 48*, 69–84.

Smith-Jentsch, K. A., Mathieu, J. E., & Kraiger, K. (2005). Investigating linear and interactive effects of shared mental models on safety and efficiency in a field setting. *Journal of Applied Psychology, 90*, 523–535.

Srivastava, A., Bartol, K. M., & Locke, E. A. (2006). Empowering leadership in management teams: Effects on knowledge sharing, efficacy, and performance. *Academy of Management Journal, 49*, 1239–1251.

Stajkovic, A. D., Lee, D., & Nyberg, A. J. (2009). Collective efficacy, group potency, and group performance: Meta-analyses of their relationships and test of a mediation model. *Journal of Applied Psychology, 94*, 814–828.

Steiner, I. D. (1972). *Group process and productivity.* New York: Academic Press.

Stewart, G. L. (2006). A meta-analytic review of relationships between team design features and team performance. *Journal of Management, 32*, 29–54.

Stewart, G. L., & Barrick, M. R. (2000). Team structure and performance: Assessing the mediating role of intrateam process and the moderating role of task type. *Academy of Management Journal, 43*, 135–148.

Sundstrom, E., McIntyre, M., Halfhill, T., & Richards, H. (2000). Work groups: From Hawthorne studies to work teams of the 1990s and beyond. *Group Dynamics: Theory, Research, and Practice, 4*(1), 44–67.

Tesluk, P. E., & Mathieu, J. E. (1999). Overcoming roadblocks to effectiveness: Incorporating management of performance barriers into models of work group effectiveness. *Journal of Applied Psychology, 84*, 200–217.

Tesluk, P., Zaccaro, S., Marks, M., & Mathieu, J. (1997). Task and aggregation issues in the analysis and assessment of team performance. In M. Brannick & E. Salas (Eds.), *Team performance assessment and measurement: Theory, methods, and applications* (pp. 197–226). Mahwah, NJ: Erlbaum.

Tuckman, B. W. (1965). Developmental sequence in small groups. *Psychological Bulletin, 63*, 384–399.

Van Der Vegt, G. S., & Bunderson, J. S. (2005). Learning and performance in multidisciplinary teams: The importance of collective team identification. *Academy of Management Journal. 48*, 532–547.

Xie, J. L., & Johns, G. (2000). Interactive effects of absence culture salience and group cohesiveness: A multi-level and cross-level analysis of work absenteeism in the Chinese context. *Journal of Occupational and Organizational Psychology, 73*, 31–52.

PART 7

Organizational Learning, Development, and Adaptation

Organizational Learning and Knowledge Management

Linda Argote

Abstract

Research on organizational learning and knowledge management has increased dramatically over the last 20 years. This chapter discusses reasons for the surge in research, describes approaches to defining organizational learning and knowledge, and discusses levels at which learning occurs. It presents major findings about creating, retaining, and transferring knowledge, identifying gaps in our understanding as well as directions for future research. Because organizational learning and effective knowledge management are sources of performance improvements in organizations, a greater understanding of these topics has the potential to advance practice as well as theory.

Key Words: organizational learning, learning curves, knowledge management, knowledge transfer, organizational memory, creativity, innovation

Research on organizational learning and knowledge management has flourished during the last 20 years. Questions of how and when organizations learn from their experience and manage the knowledge they acquire have generated much excitement. The ability to create and transfer knowledge has been identified as a source of competitive advantage for organizations.

Research articles, special issues of journals, and books appeared at an increasing rate on organizational learning, beginning in the late 1980s. Levitt and March (1988) published an influential theory piece on organizational learning in 1988. Special issues of *Organization Science* (Cohen & Sproull, 1991; Lampel, Shamsie, & Shapira, 2009) and the *Journal of Management Studies* (Easterby-Smith, Crossan, & Nicolini, 2000) were devoted to organizational learning. Books and handbooks were also published by many researchers, including Argyris (1990), Easterby-Smith and Lyles (2003), Garvin (2000), Greve (2003), Lipshitz, Freedman, and Popper (2007), and Senge (1990).

In the mid-1990s, interest in organizational learning broadened to include the outcome of learning—knowledge. Several influential books were prepared on knowledge (Davenport & Prusak, 1998; Leonard-Barton, 1995; Nonaka & Takeuchi, 1995). Other books were published that combined organizational learning and knowledge (Argote, 1999; Gherardi, 2006). Special issues of *Organizational Behavior and Human Decision Processes* (Argote, Ingram, Levine, & Moreland, 2000), *Organization Science* (Grandori & Kogut, 2002), *Management Science* (Argote, McEvily, & Reagans, 2003), and *Strategic Management Journal* (Helfat, 2000; Spender & Grant, 1996) were developed on managing knowledge in organizations.

Organizational learning and knowledge management are central to the performance and long-run success of organizations. Learning from experience is a mechanism through which organizations develop capabilities (Salvato, 2009), improve their performance, and adapt to their environments. Organizations that are able to create new knowledge, retain that knowledge and transfer it throughout their establishments are more likely to prosper than their counterparts that are less adept at organizational learning and knowledge management (Argote & Ingram, 2000; Spender & Grant, 1996; Teece, Pisano, & Shuen, 1997).

Yet organizations vary dramatically in their ability to learn. Some exhibit remarkable performance improvements with experience, while others evidence little or no learning. For example, Starbuck (2009) described how a law firm learned from its experience and developed new business strategies that enabled it to improve its performance. This example contrasts with the example of NASA; the 2003 *Columbia* disaster shared many similarities with the 1986 *Challenger* disaster, suggesting that NASA did not learn from its experience (Starbuck, 2009). Clearly, a failure to learn can have significant consequences for organizations and their members.

Similarly, organizations vary in the extent to which they retain and transfer knowledge successfully (Argote, 1999; Szulanski, 1996). Concerning knowledge retention, some organizations are successful in retaining knowledge and exhibit little knowledge decay, such as the Israeli kibbutzim studied by Ingram and Simons (2002). Other organizations are less successful in retaining knowledge and exhibit rapid knowledge decay, such as the fast food franchises analyzed by Darr, Argote, and Epple (1995).

Concerning knowledge transfer, considerable evidence of transfer has been found in organizations such as franchises where one unit can learn from the experience of another (Darr et al., 1995; Knott, 2001). Yet, the extent of transfer varies widely (Szulanski, 1996), and knowledge that would benefit other units often remains in the unit where it originated. For example, Argote and Kane (2009) pointed out that members of Sony's tape recorder division resisted sharing knowledge with the headphone division until the company's cofounder and honorary chairman intervened (Nayak & Ketteringham, 1986).

In the sections that follow, I discuss why research on organizational learning and knowledge management has surged in recent years. I then describe approaches to defining organizational learning and knowledge, and discuss levels at which learning and knowledge management occur. Research on organizational learning has generally focused on process or flow aspects of learning, while research on knowledge has typically emphasized managing the stock of knowledge. This chapter describes a theoretical framework that integrates organizational learning and knowledge, presenting major findings about knowledge creation, retention, and transfer. Gaps in our understanding are identified, and suggestions for future research are developed.

Reasons for Increased Research

Important practical concerns contributed to the rise in research on organizational learning and knowledge management that began in the late 1980s. Many organizations, especially in the United States (Krugman, 1991), experienced major productivity problems in the 1980s (Minabe, 1986). Understanding why some organizations were more productive than others became the subject of much debate and analysis. Because organizational learning is an important source of performance improvements in organizations, research on organizational learning was conducted to understand why some organizations were more productive than others.

Concerns about innovation also became paramount during this period. Innovation is increasingly seen as resulting from recombining knowledge in new ways (Fleming, 2001; Kogut & Zander, 1992; Murray & O'Mahony, 2007; Nickerson & Zenger, 2004). For example, the combination of knowledge from the headphone and the tape recorder divisions at Sony ultimately resulted in a very successful project, the Walkman (Nayak & Ketteringham, 1986). Thus, in order to understand how firms innovate, researchers analyzed how firms combine and manage knowledge.

With the anticipated retirement of the baby boomer generation, issues of knowledge retention also became central concerns in many organizations. Although developments in information systems can be helpful in retaining and transferring knowledge, they do not provide a complete solution because organizational members are more likely to seek knowledge from other individuals than from technology (Cross, Parker, Prusak, & Borgatti, 2001). Thus, research was initiated to understand how social and psychological as well as technological factors affected knowledge retention.

Knowledge transfer also attracted considerable attention. New organizational forms require knowledge transfer to be effective. Firms are increasingly distributing work around the globe to take advantage of differences in labor costs, expertise, and product demand that exist across countries. Not only is this distribution taking place for manufacturing ("Survey of Manufacturing," 1998), it is also occurring for product development and research

(Anderson, Davis-Blake, Erzurumlu, Joglekar & Parker, 2008). The distribution of employees across spatial, temporal, and organizational boundaries poses challenges to knowledge transfer. Yet, in order for these distributed work arrangements to be effective, knowledge transfer must occur.

The multiunit, multimarket organizational form, which includes franchises and chains, also benefits from and poses challenges to knowledge transfer (Darr et al., 1995). This form is increasingly prevalent in many industries, in both manufacturing and service sectors such as hospitality and health care (Baum & Greve, 2001). Multiunit organizations operate in different markets yet standardize their activities. Because the various units of the organizations are producing the same product or delivering the same service, there are enormous opportunities to transfer knowledge acquired at one establishment to improve the performance of others. At the same time, because the environments in which the units operate may differ, knowledge transfer is not straightforward. Understanding how to transfer knowledge and improve the performance of multiunit organizations has generated much interest.

Other organizational forms that benefit from knowledge transfer include interorganizational relationships such as mergers, joint ventures, and alliances. To the extent that organizations experience multiple instances of these relationships, there are opportunities to learn from one instance of the relationship and transfer the knowledge to subsequent instances (e.g., Lavie & Miller, 2008; Zollo & Reuer, 2010). In order for these relationships to realize their full potential, knowledge must transfer from one organizational unit to another. For example, Szulanski (2000) described how a bank managed knowledge transfer successfully in the firms that it acquired and increased the return on assets of the acquired firms.

Conceptual/Measurement Approaches

Organizational learning is a change in the organization's knowledge that occurs as a function of experience (Fiol & Lyles, 1985). The knowledge can be explicit, or it can be tacit and difficult to articulate. The knowledge can be embedded in individuals, or it can be embedded in other repositories such as routines, practices, and databases. The knowledge might not manifest itself immediately in behavioral change (Huber, 1991).

A variety of approaches have been taken to assessing organizational learning and measuring knowledge in organizations. Just as researchers of individual learning assess learning by measuring changes in cognitions and/or behaviors associated with experience (Hilgard & Bower, 1975; Wingfield, 1979), researchers of organizational learning and knowledge generally take cognitive or behavioral approaches. On the cognitive side, researchers have assessed the cognitions of organization members (e.g., see Huff & Jenkins, 2002). On the behavioral side, researchers have studied how organizational routines or practices change as a function of experience (Levitt & March, 1988). Another behavioral approach for assessing organizational learning involves analyzing how characteristics of performance, such as speed or accuracy, change as a function of experience (Argote & Epple, 1990; Dutton & Thomas, 1984). Researchers have also measured knowledge by measuring characteristics of an organization's products or services (Amabile, 1983) or its patent stock (Alcacer & Gittleman, 2006).

The measurement approach that is most useful, of course, depends on the purpose and empirical context of the research. In using any of the measures, one needs to assess how the measure changes as a function of experience in order to determine whether organizational learning occurred. Further, one needs to control for factors besides experience in order to rule out alternative explanations to learning as a driver of changes observed in the organization (Argote, 1999).

Levels of Analysis

Learning occurs at different levels of analysis in organizations: individual, group, organizational and interorganizational (Kozlowski, Chao & Jensen, 2010). For example, in a study of hospital surgical teams, Reagans, Argote, and Brooks (2005) found that learning occurred at the levels of individuals within the team, the team, and the hospital organization. Processes of individual learning that are relevant for organizational learning are incorporated in this review. Reviewing the voluminous literature on individual learning, however, is beyond the scope of this chapter. Similarly, reviewing the literature on population-level learning (Miner & Anderson, 1999; Miner & Haunschild, 1995) or learning through interorganizational relationships is beyond the scope of this chapter (see Ingram, 2002, for a review of the literature on interorganizational learning).

Although the focus of this chapter is on organizational learning, relevant research at the group as well as the organizational level of analysis is included. Certain groups, such as top management teams, have a major influence on organizations (Cho & Hambrick, 2006), including what they learn. Further, many of the processes that occur in organizations, such as communication, coordination, and influence, take place in groups, so they serve as microcosms of organizations (see Cohen & Bacdayan, 1994, for an example). Because groups are generally smaller than organizations (McGrath, 1984), learning processes may be more visible in groups than in organizations and hence more tractable to analyze.

More generally, groups share important defining characteristics with organizations. Most definitions of groups emphasize that they are collections of individuals who perform interdependent tasks, who see themselves and are seen by others as social entities, and who are embedded in a larger social system (Cohen & Bailey, 1997; Guzzo & Dickson, 1996). Similarly, definitions of organizations emphasize that they are composed of individuals and groups who perform interdependent tasks in order to achieve goals via differentiated functions over time (Porter, Lawler, & Hackman, 1975). Thus, interdependence is key to definitions of both groups and organizations.

The distinction between groups and organizations is less sharp now than in the past. With groups increasingly being geographically dispersed, experiencing membership change and having members who belong to multiple groups, entities generally considered to be groups may not meet the criterion that members see themselves and are seen by others as intact social entities. This suggests that the extents to which groups are intact or are seen as social entities should be treated as variables rather than as criteria. Similarly, many organizations are becoming less differentiated and more temporary, which suggests that these features should be treated as interesting variables to study, rather than cut-off criteria. Thus, research on group learning that helps us understand organizational learning will be included in this chapter (see Argote, Gruenfeld, & Naquin, 2001; Edmondson, Dillon, & Roloff, 2007; Kozlowski & Bell, 2008, for reviews).

Although group and organizational learning share many processes, group and organizational learning differ from individual learning. The knowledge that individuals acquire has to be embedded in a supra-individual repository in order for group or organizational learning to occur. Thus, although individuals are generally the media through which groups and organizations learn, individual learning does not necessarily imply that the organization has acquired knowledge. In order for organizational learning to occur, the individual would have to share knowledge with other individuals and embed it in a repository such as a database, routine, or transactive memory system that other members could use.

A Theoretical Framework

Argote and Miron-Spektor (2011) have developed a framework for analyzing organizational learning and knowledge. Their framework is briefly described because it is used as an organizing device to present major findings on organizational learning and knowledge in this chapter. According to their framework, experience interacts with the organizational context to produce knowledge.

Experience

Organizational learning begins with experience. Experience is what occurs in the organization as it performs its task—what transpires as it accomplishes its purpose. Experience can be measured by the total or cumulative number of task performances up to the present time. For example, in a hospital emergency unit, experience would be measured by the cumulative number of patients the unit has treated. The more patients the unit treats, the more experience it accumulates.

Because different types of experience can have different effects on learning processes and outcomes, researchers have argued for the benefits of characterizing experience at a fine-grained level (Argote & Ophir, 2002; Argote & Todorova, 2007; Ingram, 2002; Schulz, 2002). I find it useful to distinguish between types of experience and dimensions of experience. A particular unit of experience can be one type or the other. For example, experience can be acquired directly from the focal unit's own experience or vicariously (Bandura, 1977) from the experience of other units (Baum & Ingram, 1998; Bresman, 2010; Darr et al., 1995; Wong, 2004). As an example, a hospital emergency unit could learn from its own experience or from the experience of other hospital emergency units. Both direct and indirect types of experience can vary along several dimensions.

Table 28.1 depicts the type of experience (direct versus indirect) crossed by various dimensions. Dimensions are of two forms.

Several dimensions characterize a particular unit of experience, such as its novelty; other dimensions characterize cumulative experience, such as its heterogeneity. The former dimensions, which apply to a particular unit of experience, can be aggregated

Table 28.1 Organizational Experience: Types and Dimensions

Dimensions	Experience Type	
	Direct (Own Units)	Indirect (Other Units)
Particular Unit of Experience		
Novelty		
Ambiguity		
Degree of Success		
Timing		
Geographic Location		
Cumulative Units of Experience		
Amount		
Heterogeneity		
Pace		

to characterize the cumulative experience of the organization.

As can be seen from Table 28.1, a particular unit of experience can be characterized in terms of its novelty, ambiguity, success, timing, and geographic location. For example, experience can be acquired from a patient with unusual symptoms not seen before in the unit or from one with symptoms seen repeatedly (Garud, Dunbar, & Bartel, 2011) Katila & Ahuja, 2002). Experience can vary in its ambiguity, ranging, for example, from a patient with symptoms that are readily diagnosed to a patient with symptoms that are difficult to diagnose (Bohn, 1994; Repenning & Sterman, 2002). Experience can be acquired from successful or unsuccessful units of task performance (Denrell & March, 2001; Kim, Kim, & Miner, 2009; Sitkin, 1992). In the hospital context, members might learn from a patient who was successfully treated for an allergic reaction or from one whose allergic reaction escalated into anaphylactic shock.

Concerning timing, experience can be acquired before (Pisano, 1994), during, or after task performance (Ellis & Davidi, 2005). An emergency unit that simulates a disaster to increase its preparedness would be an example of learning before doing. A unit that conducts an after-action review about how a case was handled would be learning after doing.

A unit of experience can be acquired with members who are geographically close or geographically distant (Cramton, 2001; Cummings, 2004; Gibson & Gibbs, 2006). As an example, contrast a team in an emergency unit diagnosing a patient face-to-face versus a team remotely diagnosing a patient who appeared in a satellite clinic (e.g., see Coff, Coff, & Eastvold, 2006).

Concerning cumulative experience, the most fundamental dimension is the cumulative amount of experience that the organizations have acquired. Heterogeneity is another dimension along which the overall cumulative experience can vary, ranging from a case mix of patients with similar symptoms to a mix of patients with very different symptoms (Haunschild & Sullivan, 2002; Schilling, Vidal, Ployhart, & Marangoni, 2003). Cumulative experience can also vary in its pace (Argote, Beckman, & Epple, 1990; Herriott, Levinthal, & March, 1985; Levinthal & March, 1981). Some units might experience patients at a steady rate, while others might experience patients more sporadically.

Context

Organizational learning occurs in a context. The context includes the organization, the environment in which the organization is embedded, and relationships with other organizations. The context affects the experience that the organization acquires. For example, a hospital emergency unit located in a particular environment would receive certain kinds of patients. Decisions the hospital has made about whether it specializes in the treatment of particular patients, such as burn victims or high-risk infants, would also affect the patients it receives.

Argote and Miron-Spektor (2011) distinguished between the active context through which learning occurs and a latent context. The active context includes the basic elements of organizations, members, and tools that interact with the task. The latent context includes characteristics of the organization such as its culture, structure, or technology. The latent context affects the basic elements of the organization by influencing who are members of organizations, what tools they have, and which tasks they perform.

This conceptualization of the active context draws on a theoretical framework of the basic elements of organizations developed by McGrath and colleagues (Arrow, McGrath, & Berdahl, 2000; McGrath & Argote, 2001). According to this framework, the basic elements of organizations are members, tools, and tasks. The basic elements combine to form networks. The member-member network is the organization's social network. The task-task and the tool-tool networks define the interrelationships within tasks and tools, respectively. The member-task network is the organization's division of labor; it maps members onto tasks. The member-tool network specifies which tools are used to perform which tasks. The member-task-tool network identifies which members perform which tasks with which tools. These elements of members, tools, and tasks are the primary mechanisms in organizations through which organizational learning occurs and knowledge is retained and transferred.

Organizational Learning Processes

Organizational learning processes translate experience into knowledge. Organizational learning can be conceived as having three interrelated subprocesses: creating, retaining, and transferring knowledge. These subprocesses can be characterized along several dimensions.

A dimension of organizational learning processes that has received considerable attention is "mindfulness." Weick and Sutcliffe (2006) argued for the benefits of mindful or attentive processes, while Levinthal and Rerup (2006) advocated for the advantages of less mindful or routine processes. Mindful processes are analogous to controlled processes in the psychological literature, while less mindful processes are analogous to automatic ones (Shiffrin & Schneider, 1977). Dialogic practices (Tsoukas, 2009) are an example of mindful processes for creating knowledge. Stimulus-response learning is an example of a less mindful process for creating knowledge.

In addition to characterizing knowledge creation subprocesses according to their mindfulness, the subprocesses of knowledge retention and transfer can also be characterized by their degree of mindfulness. For example, knowledge retention subprocesses can

range from deliberate or mindful attempts to codify knowledge (Zollo & Winter, 2002) to less mindful attempts. Similarly, knowledge transfer approaches can be mindful processes that involve adapting the knowledge to the new context, or less mindful processes such as "copy exactly" approaches (Williams, 2007).

The learning subprocesses of knowledge creation, retention, and transfer also vary in the extent to which they are distributed across organizational members. In organizations with well-developed transactive memory systems, the subprocesses of creating, retaining, and transferring knowledge are distributed across organizational members. A transactive memory system is a collective system for storing and distributing information (Brandon & Hollingshead, 2004; Wegner, 1986) through which members specialize in learning and remembering different pieces of information. Further, members possess meta-knowledge of who knows what, which facilitates knowledge transfer.

Organizational Knowledge

Knowledge acquired through learning flows back into the organization and affects the basic elements of members, tools, and tasks and their networks. Knowledge in products or services also flows out of the organization into the environment. Knowledge can be characterized along several dimensions (see Alavi & Leidner, 2001, for a discussion of knowledge taxonomies). The dimension of knowledge that has received the most attention is its tacitness. Knowledge ranges from explicit knowledge that can be codified (Vaast & Levina, 2006; Zander & Kogut, 1995) to tacit knowledge that is difficult to articulate (Berry & Broadbent, 1984, 1987; Nonaka & von Krogh, 2009; Polanyi, 1962). A related dimension is whether the knowledge is declarative versus procedural (Singley & Anderson, 1989)—whether it is "know what" or "know how" (Edmondson, Pisano, Bohmer & Winslow, 2003; Lapré, Mukherjee, & Van Wassenhove, 2000). The former is explicit, while the later has a significant tacit component.

Key findings on knowledge creation, retention, and transfer are now presented. Suggestions for fruitful future research on knowledge creation, retention, and transfer are offered in each section. The chapter concludes with a discussion of future research directions that cut across knowledge creation, retention, and transfer. Although studying organizational learning requires time series data, static studies will be included in the review if they advance theory about organizational learning and knowledge management.

Knowledge Creation

Knowledge creation occurs when a unit generates knowledge that is new to it. Organizational learning involves some degree of knowledge creation because the focal unit generates knowledge that is new to it. Research on creativity that examines how creativity is affected by experience is relevant for understanding organizational learning (e.g., Taylor & Greve, 2006). Research on how different types of experience affect knowledge creation is reviewed and research that examines how the latent or background context affects knowledge creation is discussed. Following this, research on how the active context affects knowledge creation is described.

Experience

Although experience can sometimes constrain creativity, on balance, the evidence indicates that experience improves creativity (Amabile, 1997; Audia & Goncalo, 2007; Shane, 2000). A promising recent trend in research on creativity is distinguishing between different types of experience. For example, Gino, Argote, Miron-Spektor, and Todorova (2010) distinguished between direct and indirect experience and found that direct experience with the task was more conducive to creativity than indirect task experience. Audia and Goncalo (2007) differentiated between successful and unsuccessful experience and found that successful experience increased the number of ideas generated but decreased the extent to which the ideas were radical.

Context

Many dimensions of the context have been shown to affect knowledge creation. Several studies have examined how an organization's structure affects organizational learning and knowledge creation. A structural dimension that has received considerable attention is whether the organization is a specialist organization, focusing on a narrow range of products or services, or a generalist organization, focusing on a broad range of products or services. Specialist organizations generally learn more from experience than generalist organizations because they acquire deeper experience (Haunschild & Sullivan, 2002; Ingram & Baum, 1997).

Another structural dimension that has received considerable attention is the extent to which the organization is decentralized (Ethiraj & Levinthal, 2004; Siggelkow & Levinthal, 2003; Siggelkow & Rivkin, 2005). Decentralization generally enables the organization to explore solutions and thereby prevents it from prematurely converging on a suboptimal solution, which is especially valuable in changing environments. Jansen, Van Den Bosch, and Volberda (2006) differentiated between explorative and exploitative innovation and found that decentralization increased explorative innovation and had no effect on exploitative innovation. Fang, Lee, and Schilling (2010) found that semi-isolated subgroups with moderate cross-group links promoted the greatest organizational learning. The semi-isolation of subgroups fostered the diversity of ideas, while the connections between groups fostered knowledge transfer across them.

Research has examined the effects of additional structural dimensions on learning and innovation. Bunderson and Boumgarden (2010) found that team structures characterized by specialization, formalization, and hierarchy increased team learning because they increased information sharing and reduced conflict. Jansen et al. (2006) found that formalization enhanced a unit's exploitative innovation and had no effect on explorative innovation, while densely connected social relations within units positively enhanced both explorative and exploitative innovation. Sorenson (2003) found that interdependence engendered by vertical integration slowed the rate of learning in firms in stable environments. In contrast, in volatile environments, vertically integrated firms learned faster than less interdependent firms, arguably because they contained relevant components within their boundaries.

The effect of organizational slack on learning and creativity has received considerable research attention. Starting with Cyert and March's (1963) *A Behavioral Theory of the Firm*, researchers have examined whether slack resources increase creativity and the functional form of the relationship between slack and creativity (Greve, 2003; Gulati & Nohria, 1996). For example, Wiersma (2007) found that slack resources increased experimentation and improved organizational learning.

Dimensions of an organization's culture have also been found to affect organizational learning. A culture of psychological safety has been shown to promote team learning (Edmondson, 1999). A "learning" orientation, as opposed to a "performing" orientation, has been shown to facilitate learning, at least up to a point (Bunderson & Sutcliffe, 2003). Some researchers have found that cohesion or liking among members of the group facilitates organizational learning (Wong, 2004). Other researchers have found that individualist groups are more creative than collectivist groups (Goncalo & Staw, 2006).

Rewards and incentives also affect learning and knowledge creation. Creativity has been shown to be enhanced by both intrinsic (Amabile, 1997) and extrinsic (Eisenberger & Rhoades, 2001) rewards. Future research is needed to determine the best mix of rewards to increase learning and creativity,

Research on the effects of feedback on organizational learning and knowledge creation has yielded somewhat mixed results (Greve, 2003). Delays in feedback have been found to hinder learning from experience (Diehl & Sterman, 1995; Gibson, 2000; Rahmandad, 2008). When actions do not have direct payoffs but are part of a sequence with an overall payoff, learning is also impaired, especially when turnover occurs (Denrell, Fang & Levinthal, 2004). High feedback specificity has been found to initially improve learning but negatively affect exploratory behavior over the long run (Goodman, Wood, & Hendrickx, 2004). Rick and Weber (2010) found that withholding feedback led to deeper deliberation and more meaningful learning processes than providing feedback. Although individual feedback has been found to reinforce the negative effects of power differences on learning (e.g., see Edmondson, 2002), group feedback has been found to transform those differences into opportunities for learning (Van der Vegt, de Jong, Bunderson, & Molleman, 2010). More research is needed on the conditions under which feedback enhances organizational learning and the type of feedback that is most effective.

The interrelationships among the knowledge elements of an organization also affect knowledge creation. Yayavaram and Ahuja (2008) argued that knowledge elements can vary from fully decomposable, where the knowledge base is composed of distinct clusters of knowledge elements with no ties between them, to nearly decomposable, where knowledge clusters are discernible but connected through ties, to non-decomposable, where no clusters emerge because the ties between all knowledge elements are so dense. Yayavaram and Ahuja (2008) found that a nearly decomposable knowledge base generated more useful innovations than either a tightly integrated knowledge base or non-decomposable knowledge base. Further, decomposable knowledge bases enhanced absorptive capacity and facilitated non-local search.

Miller, Fern, and Cardinal (2007) compared the effect of different knowledge sources on innovation. They found that the use of knowledge from other divisions within an organization had a more positive effect on innovation than the use of knowledge either from within the same division or from outside the organization.

The background dimensions of the context affect learning through their effects on the active elements of members, tools, and tasks. The context determines the organization's task and affects the tools available to perform the task. The context also affects which members perform the organization's task and their abilities, motivations, and opportunities. For example, the background context, including rewards, goals, norms, culture, and job design, affects individuals' motivations. Their abilities are affected by factors such as selection processes, training, feedback, and their previous experience. Members' opportunities to learn and to create knowledge are affected by dimensions of the context such as the organization's structure, social networks, and technologies.

Members

Organizational learning is affected by qualities of members who do the learning, including their abilities, motivations, and opportunities (Argote et al., 2003). General cognitive ability and intelligence have been shown to benefit the performance of a wide range of tasks (Ree, Earles, & Teachout, 1994). Individual experience, especially when measured by the amount of task experience, has also been found to be generally beneficial for individual performance (see Quiñones, Ford, & Teachout, 1995, and Tesluk & Jacobs, 1998, for reviews). Training can also have positive effects on members' learning abilities (Bell & Kozlowski, 2008; Ford & Kozlowski, 1996).

Members' motivations also affect learning and creativity. Motivation affects which activities members choose to perform, how much effort they expend and how long they persist in various activities. Members' aspiration levels affect creativity and innovation (Bromiley, 1991; Cyert & March, 1963; Lant, 1992). Members in a learning orientation are more likely to learn than those in a performing orientation (Bunderson & Sutcliffe, 2003). Members in a promotion focus (Higgins, 1997), who are motivated to attain rewards, are more likely to be creative than those in a prevention focus, who are motivated to avoid punishment (Friedman & Förster, 2001; Kark & Van Dijk, 2007).

Members' emotions have also been found to affect knowledge creation. Many studies have found that individuals perform better on creative tasks when they are in positive moods (see Davis, 2009, for a review). The simultaneous occurrence of negative and positive emotions has also been shown to enhance creativity (Amabile, Barsade, Mueller, & Staw, 2005; Fong, 2006; George & Zhou, 2007).

The distribution of member characteristics affects knowledge creation. Heterogeneous groups composed of members with diverse characteristics have been found to be more creative than homogeneous groups composed of similar members (Bantel & Jackson, 1989; Dunbar, 1995; Hambrick, Cho, & Chen, 1996; Lant, Milliken, & Batra, 1992). The dimension of heterogeneity that has been shown to be most beneficial for creativity is functional heterogeneity or diversity in backgrounds (Williams & O'Reilly, 1998). Further, this heterogeneity is most valuable in environments of rapid environmental change (Eisenhardt & Tabrizi, 1995; Moorman & Miner, 1997).

Dimensions of the context have been found to interact with member characteristics, such as member heterogeneity, to predict learning outcomes. For example, transformational leadership (Shin & Zhou, 2007) and a shared team identity (Van der Vegt & Bunderson, 2005) have been found to moderate the relationship between member heterogeneity and performance. Transformational leadership and a shared identity enable groups to realize the potential benefits of member heterogeneity on performance.

Moving members across groups can stimulate the creation of new knowledge. Gruenfeld, Martorana, and Fan (2000) found that new knowledge was generated in groups when their members returned from assignments to other groups. Choi and Thompson (2005) found that groups with changing membership were more creative than groups with stable membership. Wiersma (2007) found that a moderate number of temporary workers increased the learning rate of organizations. Thus, groups with changing membership, whose members have been exposed to other ways of working, have greater opportunities to learn than their more stable counterparts.

Member-Member Network

The member-member or the social network also affects knowledge creation. Ties that bridge "structural holes" or otherwise unconnected parts of a network facilitate creativity (Burt, 2004). Tortoriello and Krackhardt (2010) found that bridging ties that span boundaries increase innovation when the ties are "Simmelian" or are characterized by a common third-party tie. Strong ties can constrain creativity when they are formed with similar individuals and thus limit members' exposure to new information (Perry-Smith, 2006; Perry-Smith & Shalley, 2003). When strong ties, however, are maintained with members who themselves are disconnected, creativity has been found to increase (McFadyen, Semadeni, & Cannella, 2009). More research on the ways in which social networks affect creativity is needed. Distinguishing between the effects of networks on member motivation and their effects on exposure to information is likely to advance research on the effects of social networks on knowledge creation.

Tasks and Task Network

Some degree of task heterogeneity is valuable for organizational learning and knowledge creation. Schilling et al. (2003) found that groups learn more from performing tasks that are related than from performing tasks that are either identical or very different. Wiersma (2007) found that organizations with a diverse product mix had higher rates of learning than those with a similar product mix. The degree of diversity that is most beneficial is likely to depend on the nature of the task. Some degree of diversity appears to be valuable in enhancing understanding of the task and increasing creativity.

Routines specify relationships among tasks and are thus part of the task-task network. Early work on routines focused on how they can impair learning. For example, Argyris and Schon (1978) showed how defensive routines prevent learning. Viewing routines as a source of inertia, Benner and Tushman (2003) also argued that routines reduce variation and flexibility in organizations and thereby impede innovation.

More recent work, however, demonstrates that routines can be a source of change (Feldman, 2004) as well as stability. A current research thrust is identifying the characteristics of routines that promote learning and innovation as well as the characteristics that impede learning and innovation (Miron, Erez, & Naveh, 2004; Naveh & Erez, 2004). For example, Paulus and Yang (2000) found that interaction routines that exposed group members to the ideas of others while allowing them to generate their own ideas and maintain their own identity enhanced creativity.

Tools and Tool Network

Research is beginning to address how tools and the tool-tool network affect the creation of knowledge in organizations. Alavi and Leidner (2001) noted that electronic mail and group support systems increase the number of weak ties in organizations, which in turn can enhance knowledge creation. Boland, Tenkasi, and Te'eni (1994) described an information system that provided an environment for exchanging ideas, which in turn increased knowledge creation. Ashworth, Mukhopadhyay, and Argote (2004) demonstrated that the introduction of information technology in a bank increased the rate of organizational learning.

Zammuto, Griffith, Majchrzak, Dougherty, and Faraj (2007) identified various affordances that technology provides organizations. These affordances are not automatic but rather result from the interaction of tools and the organization. The five affordances identified by Zammuto et al. (2007) hold promise for facilitating knowledge creation: visualizing entire work processes; real-time product and service innovation; virtual collaboration; mass collaboration; and synthetic reality.

There is debate about whether organizations should use multiple types of information system tools to support learning or should use one type of information system based on a contingency approach (Kane & Alavi, 2007). Arguing for the contingency approach, Hansen, Nohria, and Tierney (1999) suggested that when work is standardized, developing detailed databases or repositories of knowledge about customers, suppliers, competitors, products, projects and industries is valuable. In contrast, when work is customized, detailed databases are less valuable than yellow pages or directories that identify the expertise of organization members.

Kane and Alavi (2007) examined in a simulation the separate and combined effects of three knowledge management tools on organizational learning: knowledge repositories/portals; team rooms; and electronic communities of practice. Both knowledge repositories/portals and team rooms yielded immediate performance benefits that leveled off over time. In contrast, the benefits of electronic communities of practice were slower initially but did not level off and ultimately surpassed the benefits of the other tools. Further, knowledge repositories/portals produced the same performance with or without augmentation by other tools. When other tools were added to the team room, however, the combined configuration did not plateau but rather continued to improve and ultimately outperformed the electronic communities of practice. On the other hand, adding other tools to electronic communities of practice detracted from their performance.

Thus, when the predominant tool is a team room, the other tools complement it. In contrast, when the predominant tool is an electronic community of practice, the other tools detract from it.

Member-Task Network

A transactive memory system (TMS) is an example of a member-task network (Wegner, 1986). As members acquire experience working together, they learn who is good at what and they assign members to tasks for which they are best suited. Transactive memory systems have been found to improve group performance for virtual (Kanawattanachai & Yoo, 2007) as well as co-located groups (Austin, 2003; Hollingshead, 1998; Lewis, 2004; Liang, Moreland, & Argote, 1995).

Although early work on transactive memory systems examined their effects on knowledge retention (e.g., Liang et al., 1995), more recent research examines the effects of transactive memory systems on knowledge creation. Gino et al. (2010) found that transactive memory systems improved creativity on a product development task. Further, the researchers found that transactive memory systems mediated the relationship between experience and creativity. The more beneficial effects of direct, relative to indirect, experience on team creativity were due to the operation of transactive memory systems.

Although transactive memory systems have primarily been discussed in terms of knowing who is good at which task, transactive memory systems can be generalized to include knowledge of who is good at using which tools. Thus, research findings about transactive memory are also relevant for the member-tool network.

In summary, research on knowledge creation has begun to characterize experience at a fine-grained level, which is a promising trend. Considerable research has been done on how structural dimensions of the latent context affect learning; more research is needed on how other dimensions of the latent context affect learning. Concerning the active context, comparatively more research has been devoted to how characteristics of members affect knowledge creation than to how characteristics of other elements of the active context affect knowledge creation. The element that has received the next most attention is the social, or member-member network. Research on how task networks and tools affect learning and creativity has increased in recent years. Research has also begun on how the member-task network affects creativity. These are promising trends. More research on how the member-member, member-task, member-tool, and tool networks affect knowledge creation is needed.

Research on knowledge creation would also be advanced by examining the interactions across the elements of the context. For example, do certain characteristics of members interact with characteristics of the social network or the task network to promote knowledge creation? Do the characteristics reinforce each other and interact in a complementary fashion, or do they serve as substitutes for each other? In addition to examining how the elements of organizations interact among themselves, examining how the basic elements interact with various types of experience would also move research forward.

Knowledge Retention

Research on knowledge retention examines whether knowledge acquired by organizations persists through time or whether organizations "forget" (de Holan & Phillips, 2004). There is considerable evidence that knowledge depreciates in organizations (Argote et al., 1990: Benkard, 2000; Darr et al., 1995; Ingram & Baum, 1997; Thompson, 2007). That is, knowledge does not persist indefinitely through time but rather decays. For example, in his discussion of NASA, Starbuck (2009) noted that many employees who were involved with the *Challenger* disaster in 1986 were no longer with NASA in 2003 when the *Columbia* accident occurred. The repeat of the disaster with many common features suggests that lessons learned by the employees in the aftermath of the 1986 disaster were not retained in the organization.

Organizations vary in the extent to which they retain knowledge. Some organizations show little evidence of knowledge decay, while others show dramatic depreciation. In the sections that follow, I discuss how characteristics of experience, the latent context, and the active context affect knowledge retention.

Experience

Most of the research on knowledge retention analyzes whether cumulative experience decays or depreciates. This research takes advantage of variation in the rate of output or interruptions in production to assess whether cumulative experience or depreciated experience is the better predictor of current performance (e.g., see Argote et al., 1990; Benkard, 2000; Darr et al., 1995). A recent study by Madsen and Desai (2010) took a more fine-grained approach to characterizing experience

and contrasted the effects of success experience and the effects of failure experience on knowledge depreciation. The researchers found that knowledge generated from failure experience decayed more slowly than knowledge generated from success experience.

Context

The aspects of the background context that have received the most attention in analyses of knowledge retention are the organization's structure and technology. Structure can buffer the organization from the deleterious effects of turnover. Similarly, technology can minimize knowledge depreciation. Because structures and technologies directly affect the elements of the active context, the effects of structures and technologies are discussed in the context of those elements.

Members

The feature of members that has received the most attention in analyses of knowledge retention is their turnover. If knowledge is embedded in members, their turnover would subtract knowledge from the organization's memory. Hollenbeck et al. (1995) found, in an experimental study of decision making, that turnover reduced decision accuracy by harming leaders' abilities to weight members' contributions appropriately. Similarly, in a laboratory study of a production task, Argote, Insko, Yovetich, and Romero (1995) found that member turnover harmed task performance.

The effect of turnover observed in the field has been found to depend on important contingencies. For example, the effect of turnover has been found to depend on the quality of replacement members (Trow, 1960). The effect of turnover has also been found to depend on the member-member network, the task network, and the member-task network. Each of these effects is discussed in subsequent sections.

Member-Member Network

In the context of knowledge retention, the member-member network has been investigated as a variable that moderates the effect of turnover on learning outcomes. For example, although teams learn better and faster than hierarchies, hierarchies are less affected by turnover than teams (Carley, 1992). Similarly, turnover has been found to have a less harmful effect in highly structured groups than in less structured groups (Rao & Argote, 2006). In highly structured organizations, a significant amount of the organization's knowledge is embedded in the structure, which buffers the organization from the effect of turnover.

An individual's position in a social network also conditions the effect of turnover on organizational learning. For example, whether an employee bridges a structural hole (Burt, 1992) has been found to affect the relationship between turnover and performance. The departure of employees with many redundant communication links in a network has been found to harm performance less than the departure of those who occupy structural holes or bridge otherwise open links in the network (Shaw, Duffy, Johnson, & Lockhart, 2005).

Tasks and Task Network

The effect of turnover also depends on characteristics of the organization's task. Argote et al. (1995) found that turnover was less harmful on complex tasks that involved innovation than on simple tasks that did not. Thus, if the task involves innovation, the departure of experienced members whose knowledge may have become obsolete may be less harmful than when the task does not involve innovation. Several field studies have found that when the task involves innovation, turnover can even have a positive effect on performance. For example, Wells and Pelz (1966) found that turnover among scientists improved the performance of research teams. Similarly, Virany, Tushman, and Romanelli (1992) found that executive turnover was associated with improved organizational performance in the computer industry.

In addition to analyzing tasks as a moderator of the relationship between turnover and learning, task networks are also analyzed as a knowledge repository because knowledge can be embedded in task networks or routines (Cyert & March, 1963; Nelson & Winter, 1982). Argote et al. (1990) found evidence of both a permanent and transient component of knowledge in organizations and suggested that the relatively permanent component was embedded in organizational routines. Cohen and Bacdayan (1994) found that knowledge embedded in routines was not affected by task-performance interruptions. Similarly, Ton and Huckman (2008) found that in organizations where members conformed to task processes, turnover had less of an effect on performance than in organizations where members did not conform to processes.

Tools and Tool Network

Embedding knowledge in tools and the tool network also promotes its retention. Alavi and Leidner (2001) indicated that computer storage technology and retrieval techniques can enhance organizational memory. Ashworth et al. (2004) found that the introduction of new information technology at a bank reduced knowledge decay.

Kane and Alavi (2007) examined in a simulation how tools interact with member turnover to affect organizational learning and knowledge retention. Results indicate that the performance of electronic communities of practice was more affected by turnover than the performance of knowledge repositories/portals or team rooms. Under conditions of no turnover, electronic communities of practice performed better than the other tools. The performance of electronic communities, however, decreased as turnover increased and fell below knowledge repositories/portals and team rooms at moderate levels of turnover.

Kane and Alavi (2007) also examined how the effectiveness of the tools varied as a function of environmental turbulence. Knowledge repositories/portals and team rooms were susceptible to the negative effects of environmental turbulence: their performance deteriorated as environmental turbulence increased and the knowledge held in the tools became obsolete. In contrast, the performance of electronic communities of practice was less affected by environmental turbulence than was the performance of knowledge repositories/portals and team rooms.

Member-Task Network

Transactive memory systems serve as a knowledge repository because knowledge acquired from experience is embedded in the systems (Austin, 2003; Hollingshead, 1998; Lewis, Lange, & Gillis, 2005; Liang et al., 1995). Transactive memory systems are especially valuable under changing conditions (Ren, Carley, & Argote, 2006). Communication among team members (Kanawattanachai & Yoo, 2007), task characteristics (Zhang, Hempel, Han, & Tjosvold, 2007), stress (Pearsall, Ellis, & Stein, 2009), and social identity and the interaction of social identity and motivation (Todorova, Argote, & Reagans, 2008) have been shown to affect the development of transactive memory systems.

In summary, much of the research on knowledge retention has focused on estimating the extent of knowledge retention, or its inverse, knowledge depreciation, in different settings. Research has begun to address the important issue of whether knowledge generated from different types of experience decays differently. Research has also begun to address whether knowledge embedded in different elements of the organizational context decays at different rates, but more work is needed on this important topic. Considerable progress has been made in understanding how and when member turnover affects knowledge retention. Research on transactive memory and routines has also increased in recent years, which is a very promising trend. More work is needed on how these and other elements of organizations affect knowledge retention. Research is also needed on whether the different knowledge repositories serve as substitutes or complements for each other.

Knowledge Transfer

Knowledge transfer is the process through which one unit is influenced by the experience of another (Argote & Ingram, 2000). Knowledge transfer is also referred to as vicarious learning (Bandura, 1977). Knowledge transfer can occur at different levels: from one member to another, from one group to another, or from one organization to another. Consistent with the emphasis of this chapter, I focus on knowledge transfer across groups or organizational units. Research on knowledge transfer analyzes whether organizations learn indirectly or vicariously from the experience of other organizations. For example, Bresman (2010) analyzed whether pharmaceutical licensing teams learned from the experiences of other teams as well as from their own experience. The more a team was able to learn from its own experience, the more effective it was at learning from the experience of other teams.

An issue that many firms face, especially for-profit firms, is how to facilitate knowledge transfer inside the firm and block its transfer or spillover to other firms (Argote & Ingram, 2000; Kogut & Zander, 1992; Rivkin, 2001). This issue is especially challenging because some approaches that facilitate the internal transfer of knowledge (which generally improves organizational performance) can also facilitate external spillover (which may harm organizational performance). Argote and Ingram (2000) argued that embedding knowledge in networks involving members is a way to manage this tension because knowledge in networks involving members transfers more readily within than between organizations.

Experience

Just as an organization's own experience can be characterized at a fine-grained level, the experience of other organizations can also be characterized at a fine-grained level. Research that characterizes the experience of others at a more fine-grained level is in its infancy. For example, Weigelt and Sarkar (2009) studied the diversity of experience of a firm's suppliers.

Context

The extent to which knowledge depends on the context affects its transfer. Williams (2007) found that firms replicate, or copy exactly, less and adapt more when knowledge depends on the context. Szulanski and Jensen (2006) argued that conservative approaches to adaptation, which involve only modest modifications of the original practice, are more effective than approaches that involve significant adaptation of the practice.

Several dimensions of the context have been found to affect knowledge transfer. One important dimension of the context is whether the organization is part of a multiunit firm such as a franchise or chain. Knowledge transfer has been found to be greater across units of a multiunit organization than across independent organizations (Baum & Ingram, 1998; Darr et al., 1995; Ingram & Simons, 2002). Being a part of a multiunit organization is likely to increase motivation to share knowledge because all the units benefit from the excellent performance of a focal unit—either directly because they have a reward structure in which they share in the profits or indirectly because they benefit from the positive reputation of a unit that shares their name. Belonging to a multiunit organization is also likely to increase opportunities to transfer knowledge because there are more units from which to learn. Being a member of a multiunit organization may increase ability due to more training opportunities, including those offered at the corporate office.

The organizational structure has also been found to affect knowledge transfer. Based on data from a large multiunit company, Tsai (2002) found that social interaction facilitated knowledge transfer across units, while centralization impeded knowledge transfer. Further, external market competition facilitated knowledge transfer between units and interacted with centralization and social interaction to predict knowledge transfer. Decentralization and social interaction were especially effective in facilitating knowledge transfer across units that compete with each other in the market.

Human resource practices have been shown to affect the extent of knowledge transfer. Collins and Smith (2006) found that commitment-based human resource practices such as group incentives, training, and performance approaches based on growth were positively related to a social climate of trust, cooperation, and shared language. Further, a firm's social climate affected knowledge transfer, which in turn affected firm performance.

The similarity of the units involved in the transfer also affects its success. Knowledge is more likely to transfer across similar than dissimilar units (Baum & Berta, 1999; Darr & Kurtzberg, 2000; Tsai, 2002). Knowledge acquired in dissimilar contexts is less likely to be relevant for a focal unit and may even harm the unit's performance (Baum & Ingram, 1998; Greve, 1999).

The geographic distance of units can also affect the success of transfer. While some studies have found that geographic distance impedes transfer (e.g., Galbraith, 1990; Tsai, 2002), others have not found an effect of distance (Darr & Kurtzberg, 2000). Interestingly, Borgatti and Cross (2003) found that the effect of distance on knowledge transfer was mediated by knowledge of what others know and being able to access that knowledge. Thus, the effect of distance can be overcome by a transactive memory system.

Characteristics of organizational units such as their "absorptive capacity" (Cohen & Levinthal, 1990) or status have been found to affect knowledge transfer. Units high in absorptive capacity are more likely to transfer knowledge successfully than units low in absorptive capacity (Szulanski, 1996). Similarly, previous experience in knowledge transfer increases the success of knowledge transfer attempts (Galbraith, 1990). Knowledge developed in a high-status organization is more likely to be used by a focal firm than knowledge created by a low-status organization (Sine, Shane, & Di Gregorio, 2003). Knowledge generated by rivals is more likely to be used when the rival is external rather than internal to the organization (Menon, Thompson, & Choi, 2006).

Members

Moving members has been shown to be an effective mechanism for transferring knowledge between groups (Kane, Argote & Levine, 2005) and organizations (Almeida & Kogut, 1999). An advantage of moving members is that they can transfer tacit as well as explicit knowledge to new contexts (see Berry & Broadbent, 1984, 1987). Members have been shown to be an especially effective knowledge transfer mechanism when the organizational units share a superordinate identity (Kane et al., 2005).

Member-Member Network

How the member-member or social network affects knowledge transfer has received considerable research attention recently. Hansen (1999) found that weak ties between members facilitated the transfer of codified or explicit knowledge, while strong ties facilitated the transfer of tacit knowledge. Reagans and McEvily (2003) focused on how network structure affects knowledge transfer and found that social cohesion and range facilitated transfer over and above tie strength.

Tasks and Task Network

Moving task networks or routines from one social unit to another is also a mechanism for the transfer of knowledge (Kane et al., 2005). For example, Darr et al. (1995) found that an innovative routine transferred across the units of fast food franchises.

Tools and Tool Network

Knowledge also transfers by moving tools from one context to another (Galbraith, 1990) because tools have knowledge embedded in them. Transferring knowledge through moving tools enables knowledge to transfer consistently and on a large scale. For example, Ashworth et al. (2004) found that the introduction of new information technology in six geographically distributed units of a bank facilitated knowledge transfer across the units. Moving members along with tools is an approach for moving tacit knowledge along with explicit knowledge and is generally more effective than moving tools alone (Galbraith, 1990).

Although many attempts to transfer knowledge through tools involve only explicit knowledge, some tools enable the transfer of tacit knowledge as well. Alavi and Leidner (2001) noted that online communities, corporate directories, and discussion groups facilitate connections between people and, thereby, enable the transfer of tacit as well as explicit knowledge. Coff et al. (2006) described how the introduction of information technology enabled engineers to monitor data from multiple plants at a central location and thereby facilitated knowledge transfer across the plants. The engineers were not required to make their own knowledge explicit and appeared to rely on tacit knowledge to identify patterns and problems in the data they received through the tool.

Haas and Hansen (2005) analyzed the effectiveness of a tool (a knowledge management system) at a consulting firm. The system consisted of document libraries on various topics and industries linked by a search engine. The researchers found a negative main effect for the number of documents used from the knowledge management system on consulting team performance, as well as an interaction between the number of documents utilized and team experience. As the level of team experience increased, the more documents a team utilized from the knowledge management system, the worse its performance. Further, an interaction was found between the number of competitors and the amount of knowledge used from the system: as the number of competitors increased, greater utilization of documents from the knowledge management system decreased team performance. Thus, using electronic documents from a knowledge management system was more likely to impair team performance when the team was experienced and faced a competitive environment than when the team was inexperienced or did not face a competitive environment.

Kim (2008) also found that the effect of a knowledge management system on performance was contingent on users' alternative sources of knowledge and the external environment. In contrast to Haas and Hansen's (2005) results, Kim (2008) found that the impact of a knowledge management system on the performance of stores in a retail grocery chain was generally positive. Further, the magnitude of the impact of using the knowledge management system on performance was greater for managers with fewer alternative sources of knowledge, for managers who were remotely located, and for those who dealt primarily with products that did not become obsolete quickly. Thus, in these two studies, knowledge management systems served as substitutes for experience (Haas & Hansen, 2005) or for other sources of knowledge (Kim, 2008).

Member-Task Network

Research on transactive memory provides insights into the extent to which the member-task network transfers to new people or to new tasks. Lewis and her colleagues studied transactive memory under conditions of changing membership and changing tasks. Although changing membership disrupted the transactive memory system, a transactive memory developed in a group with one set of members was useful when some members changed, as long as the new members had skills similar to those of departing members (Lewis, Belliveau, Herndon, & Keller, 2007). Similarly, a transactive memory developed on one task can transfer to another task and improve performance, as long as the tasks have common elements (Lewis et al.,

2007). Thus, transactive memory systems were useful knowledge transfer mechanisms under particular conditions.

In summary, research on knowledge transfer is starting to take a fine-grained approach to characterizing the experience of other organizations, which is a promising trend. More research is needed that compares the effectiveness of the elements of the context as knowledge transfer mechanisms. Relatedly, research is needed to determine whether the elements operate as substitutes or as complements for each other. Research on how different dimensions of the experience of others interact with each other and with the elements of the organizational context to affect knowledge transfer is needed.

Future Directions

Although significant progress has been made in our understanding of organizational learning and knowledge management, additional research would further our understanding of these important topics. Promising research directions within each area of knowledge creation, retention, and transfer have been described in the preceding sections. This section identifies fruitful research directions that cut across the subprocesses of knowledge creation, retention, and transfer.

As noted previously, because the effects of different types of experience on organizational learning processes and outcomes can differ, research is advanced by a fine-grained characterization of experience. More progress has been made in the study of how different dimensions of experience affect knowledge creation than in the study of knowledge retention and transfer. Understanding these latter subprocesses of organizational learning would also be advanced by research that characterizes experience at a fine-grained level. Research is also needed on whether and when the different types of experience serve as complements or substitutes for each other. That is, we need to determine if the types of experience interact positively or negatively in affecting organizational learning processes and outcomes.

Research has been done on how the elements of the context affect organizational learning. Table 28.2 provides an overview of the research and identifies where we have made significant progress and where more research is needed. Table 28.2 catalogs research findings according to whether they pertain to the organizational learning subprocesses of creating, retaining, and transferring knowledge, and which component of the context they examine. As can be

Table 28.2 Organizational Learning Research: Contributions and Opportunities

Components of the Organizational Context

Organizational Learning Subprocesses	Members	Tasks	Tools	Member-Member Network (Social)	Task-Task Network (Routines)	Tool-Tool Network	Member-Task Network	Member–Tool Network	Member-Task-Tool Network
Creating knowledge	***	**	*	**	*	*	*	*	*
Retaining knowledge	**	*	*	*	**	*	**	*	*
Transferring knowledge	**	*	**	**	*	**	*	*	*

***Considerable research
**Some research
*Little or no research

seen from Table 28.2, we know comparatively more about the effect of members on organizational learning subprocesses and outcomes than the effects of the other elements of the context. The social network is the next most researched element of the context. The social network has been studied more in regard to knowledge creation and knowledge transfer than knowledge retention. The task-task network and the member-task network have been studied more with respect to knowledge retention than knowledge creation or transfer, although research has begun on the latter subprocess.

More research is needed on all the elements of the organizational context and their interrelationships. The question of substitutes and complements arises here as well as in our analysis of experience. When do the elements of the organization's context substitute for each other as knowledge repositories or knowledge transfer mechanisms, and when do they complement each other? For example, moving members may be complementary to moving tools as a knowledge transfer mechanism: members and tools positively reinforce each other. In contrast, transactive memory systems may substitute for tools as knowledge repositories. These issues seem worthy of future research.

Research is also needed on the relationships among the learning subprocesses of creating, retaining, and transferring knowledge. The factors that enhance one subprocess may differ from those that enhance another. For example, personnel movement enhances knowledge creation and transfer but detracts from knowledge retention. How organizations manage these learning tensions would benefit from additional research. This research may be enriched by work on organizational ambidexterity that addresses how organizations manage tensions (Raisch, Birkinshaw, Probst, & Tushman, 2009).

Characterizing the organizational learning subprocesses would also benefit from further research. Several dimensions of the learning processes have been discussed, such as their mindfulness or the extent to which they are distributed. Measuring less mindful learning processes is challenging because these processes are not amenable to being captured through surveys and verbal protocols. Developments in neuroscience and physiology as well as practice theory (Gherardi, 2006) may further our understanding of organizational learning processes.

In addition to refining conceptual and measurement approaches to organizational learning processes, research is needed on substantive and theoretical issues about these processes. For example,

a greater understanding of when mindful processes facilitate learning and when less mindful processes are advantageous is needed. Although it is tempting to equate mindful processes with good processes, less mindful or automatic processes have many advantages. They save time, capture lessons from the past, and conserve cognitive capacity for novel situations (Levinthal & Rerup, 2006). Research is needed on the relationship between the learning processes and the conditions under which each process leads to positive learning outcomes.

Conclusion

This chapter has aimed to integrate recent research findings about organizational learning and knowledge management, to identify gaps in our understanding, and to suggest fruitful research directions. Hopefully, the chapter will serve as a repository of findings on organizational learning and knowledge management, as a mechanism to transfer knowledge to others, and as a catalyst for other researchers to create new knowledge about the important topics of organizational learning and knowledge management. A greater understanding of organizational learning has the potential to improve the performance of organizations and to enhance the well-being of their members. With shorter product life cycles, more rapid technological change, greater globalization, and changing demographics, the ability to learn and effectively manage knowledge is more important now than ever for organizations.

Author's Note

I wish to thank Steve Kozlowski for his comments on the manuscript and Jennifer Kukawa and Jonathan Kush for their help in preparing it.

References

Alavi, M., & Leidner, D. E. (2001). Review: Knowledge management and knowledge management systems: Conceptual foundations and research issues. *MIS Quarterly*, *25*(1), 107–136.

Alcacer, J., & Gittleman, M. (2006). Patent citations as a measure of knowledge flows: The influence of examiner citations. *The Review of Economic Statistics*, *88*(4), 774–779.

Almeida, P., & Kogut, B. (1999). Localization of knowledge and the mobility of engineers in regional networks. *Management Science*, *45*(7), 905–917.

Amabile, T. M. (1983). The social psychology of creativity: A componential conceptualization. *Journal of Personality and Social Psychology*, *45*, 357–377.

Amabile, T. (1997). Motivating creativity in organizations: On doing what you love and loving what you do. *California Management Review*, *40*, 39–58.

Amabile, T. M., Barsade, S. G., Mueller, J. S., & Staw, B. M. (2005). Affect and creativity at work. *Administrative Science Quarterly, 50*, 367–403.

Anderson, E. G., Davis-Blake, A., Erzurumlu, S. S., Joglekar, N. R., & Parker, G. G. (2008). The effects of outsourcing, offshoring, and distributed product development organization on coordinating the NPD process. In C. Loch & S. Kavadiae (Eds.), *Handbook of new product development management* (pp. 259–289). Burlington, MA: Elsevier.

Argote, L. (1999). *Organizational learning: Creating, retaining and transferring knowledge.* Norwell, MA: Kluwer.

Argote, L., Beckman, S., & Epple, D. (1990). The persistence and transfer of learning in industrial settings. *Management Science, 36*, 140–154.

Argote, L., & Epple, D. (February 23, 1990). Learning curves in manufacturing. *Science, 247*, 920–924.

Argote, L., Gruenfeld, D., & Naquin, C. (2001). Group learning in organizations. In M. E. Turner (Ed.), *Groups at work* (pp. 369–411). Mahwah, NJ: Erlbaum.

Argote, L., & Ingram, P. (2000). Knowledge transfer in organizations: A basis for competitive advantage in firms. *Organizational Behavior and Human Decision Processes, 82*, 150–169.

Argote, L., Ingram, P., Levine, J. M., & Moreland, R. L. (2000). Knowledge transfer in organizations: Learning from the experiences of others. *Organizational Behavior and Human Decision Processes, 82*(1), 1–8.

Argote, L., Insko, C., Yovetich, N., & Romero, A. (1995). Group learning curves: The effect of turnover, task complexity and training on group performance. *Journal of Applied Social Psychology, 25*, 512–529.

Argote, L., & Kane, A. A. (2009). Superordinate identity and knowledge creation and transfer in organizations. In N. Foss & S. Michaelova (Eds.), *Knowledge governance* (pp. 166–190). Oxford: Oxford University Press.

Argote, L., McEvily, B., & Reagans, R. (2003). Managing knowledge in organizations: An integrative framework and review of emerging themes. *Management Science, 49*, 571–582.

Argote, L., & Miron-Spektor, E. (2011). Organizational learning: From experience to knowledge. *Organization Science, 22*, 1123–1137.

Argote, L., & Ophir, R. (2002). Intraorganizational learning. In J. A. C. Baum (Ed.), *Companion to organizations* (pp. 181–207). Oxford, UK: Blackwell.

Argote, L., & Todorova, G. (2007). Organizational learning: Review and future directions. In G. P. Hodgkinson & J. K. Ford (Eds.), *International review of industrial and organizational psychology* (pp. 193–234). New York: Wiley.

Argyris, C. (1990) *Overcoming organizational defenses: Facilitating organizational learning.* Boston: Allyn and Bacon.

Argyris, C., & Schon, P. (1978). *Organizational learning.* Reading, MA: Addison-Wesley.

Arrow, H., McGrath, J. E., & Berdahl, J. L. (2000). *Small groups as complex systems: Formation, coordination, development, and adaptation.* Thousand Oaks, CA: Sage.

Ashworth, M., Mukhopadhyay, T., & Argote, L. (2004). Information technology and organizational learning: An empirical analysis. *Proceedings of the 25th Annual International Conference on Information Systems (ICIS)*, 11–21.

Audia, P. G., & Goncalo, J. A. (2007). Success and creativity over time: A study of inventors in the hard-disk drive industry. *Management Science, 53*, 1–15.

Austin, J. R. (2003). Transactive memory in organizational groups: The effects of content, consensus, specialization, and accuracy on group performance. *Journal of Applied Psychology, 88*(5), 866–878.

Bandura, A. (1977). *Social learning theory.* Englewood Cliffs, NJ: Prentice-Hall.

Bantel, K. A., & Jackson, S. E. (1989). Top management and innovations in banking: Does the composition of the top team make a difference? *Strategic Management Journal, 10*, 107–124.

Baum, J. A. C., & Berta, W. B. (1999). Sources, dynamics and speed: Population-level learning by organizations in a longitudinal behavioral simulation. *Advances in Strategic Management, 16*, 155–184.

Baum, J. A. C., & Greve, H. R. (Eds.). (2001). *Multiunit organizations and multiunit strategy: Advances in strategic management* (Vol. 18). Oxford: Elsevier.

Baum, J. A. C., & Ingram, P. (1998). Survival-enhancing learning in the Manhattan hotel industry, 1898–1980. *Management Science, 44*, 996–1016.

Bell, B. S., & Kozlowski, S. W. J. (2008). Active learning: Effects of core training design elements on self-regulatory processes, learning, and adaptability. *Journal of Applied Psychology, 93*(2), 296–316.

Benkard, C. L. (2000). Learning and forgetting: The dynamics of aircraft production. *American Economic Review, 90*(4), 1034–1054.

Benner, M. J., & Tushman, M. L. (2003). Exploitation, exploration, and process management: The productivity dilemma revisited. *Academy of Management Review, 28*(2), 238–256.

Berry, D., & Broadbent, D. E. (1984). On the relationship between task performance and associated verbalizable knowledge. *Quarterly Journal of Experimental Psychology, 36*, 209–231.

Berry, D., & Broadbent, D. E. (1987). The combination of implicit and explicit knowledge in task control. *Psychological Research, 49*, 7–15.

Bohn, R. E. (1994). Measuring and managing technological knowledge. *Sloan Management Review, 36*(1), 61–73.

Boland, R. J., Tenkasi, R. V., & Te'eni, D. (1994). Designing information technology to support distributed cognition. *Organization Science, 5*(3), 456–475.

Borgatti, S. P., & Cross, R. (2003). A relational view of information seeking and learning in social networks. *Management Science, 49*(4), 432–445.

Brandon, D. P., & Hollingshead, A. B. (2004). Transactive memory systems in organizations: Matching tasks, expertise and people. *Organization Science, 15*, 633–644.

Bresman, H. (2010). External learning activities and team performance: A multimethod field study. *Organization Science, 21*, 81–96.

Bromiley, P. (1991). Testing a causal model of corporate risk taking and performance. *Academy of Management Journal, 34*(1), 37–59.

Bunderson, J. S., & Boumgarden, P. (2010). Structure and learning in self-managed teams: Why "bureaucratic" teams can be better learners. *Organization Science, 21*, 609–624.

Bunderson, J. S., & Sutcliffe, K. M. (2003). Management team learning orientation and business unit performance. *Journal of Applied Psychology, 88*(3), 552–560.

Burt, R. S. (1992). *Structural holes.* Cambridge, MA: Harvard University Press.

Burt, R. S. (2004). Structural holes and good ideas. *American Journal of Sociology, 110*, 349–399.

Carley, K. (1992). Organizational learning and personnel turnover. *Organization Science, 3*(1), 20–46.

Cho, T. S., & Hambrick, D. C. (2006). Attention as the mediator between top management team characteristics and strategic change: The case of airline deregulation. *Organization Science, 17*(4), 453–469.

Choi, H. S., & Thompson, L. (2005). Old wine in a new bottle: Impact of membership change on group creativity. *Organization Behavior and Human Decision Processes, 98*, 121–132.

Coff, R. W., Coff, D. C., & Eastvold, R. (2006). The knowledge of leveraging paradox: How to achieve scale without making knowledge imitable. *Academy of Management Review, 31*(2), 452–465.

Cohen, M. D., & Bacdayan, P. (1994). Organizational routines are stored as procedural memory: Evidence from a laboratory study. *Organization Science, 5*, 554–568.

Cohen, M. D., & Sproull, L. S. (Eds.). (1991). Special issue. *Organization Science, 2*(1).

Cohen, S. G., & Bailey, D. E. (1997). What makes teams work: Group effectiveness research from the shop floor to the executive suite. *Journal of Management, 23*, 239–290.

Cohen, W., & Levinthal, D. (1990). Absorptive capacity: A new perspective on learning and innovation. *Administrative Science Quarterly, 35*, 128–152.

Collins, C. J., & Smith, K. G. (2006). Knowledge exchange and combination: The role of human resource practices in the performance of high-technology firms. *Academy of Management Journal, 49*(3), 544–560.

Cramton, C. D. (2001). The mutual knowledge problem and its consequences in geographically dispersed teams. *Organization Science, 12*(3), 346–371.

Cross, R., Parker, A., Prusak, L., & Borgatti, S. P. (2001). Knowing what we know: Supporting knowledge creation and sharing in social networks. *Organizational Dynamics, 30*(2), 100–120.

Cummings, J. N. (2004). Work groups, structural diversity, and knowledge sharing in a global organization. *Management Science, 50*(3), 352–364.

Cyert, R. M., & March, J. G. (1963). *A behavioral theory of the firm.* Englewood Cliffs, NJ: Prentice-Hall.

Darr, E., Argote, L., & Epple, D. (1995). The acquisition, transfer and depreciation of knowledge in service organizations: Productivity in franchises. *Management Science, 41*, 1750–1762.

Darr, E. D., & Kurtzberg, T. R. (2000). An investigation of partner similarity dimensions on knowledge transfer. *Organizational Behavior and Human Decision Processes, 82*, 28–44.

Davenport, T., & Prusak, L. (1998). *Working knowledge: How organizations manage what they know.* Boston, MA: Harvard Business School Press.

Davis, M. A. (2009). Understanding the relationship between mood and creativity: A meta-analysis. *Organizational Behavior and Human Decision Processes, 108*, 25–38.

de Holan, P. M., & Phillips, N. (2004). Remembrance of things past? The dynamics of organizational forgetting. *Management Science, 50*(11), 1603–1613.

Denrell, J., Fang, C., & Levinthal, D. A. (2004). From t-mazes to labyrinths: Learning from model-based feedback. *Management Science, 50*(10), 1366–1378.

Denrell, J., & March, J. G. (2001). Adaptation as information restriction: The hot stove effect. *Organization Science, 12*(5), 523–538.

Diehl, E., & Sterman, J. D. (1995). Effects of feedback complexity on dynamic decision making. *Organizational Behavior and Human Decision Processes, 62*, 198–215.

Dunbar, K. (1995). How scientists really reason: Scientific reasoning in real-world laboratories. In R. J. Sternberg & J. E. Davidson (Eds.), *The nature of insight* (pp. 365–395). Cambridge, MA: MIT Press.

Dutton, J. M., & Thomas, A. (1984). Treating progress functions as a managerial opportunity. *Academy of Management Review, 9*, 235–247.

Easterby-Smith, M., Crossan, M., & Nicolini, D. (2000). Organizational learning: Debates past, present and future. *Journal of Management Studies, 37*(6), 783–796.

Easterby-Smith, M. P. V., & Lyles, M. (Eds.). (2003). *The Blackwell handbook of organizational learning and knowledge management.* Oxford: Blackwell.

Edmondson, A. (1999). Psychological safety and learning behavior in work teams. *Administrative Science Quarterly, 44*(4), 350–383.

Edmondson, A. C. (2002). The local and variegated nature of learning in organizations: A group-level perspective. *Organization Science, 13*(2), 128–146.

Edmondson, A. C., Dillon, J. R., & Roloff, K. (2007). Three perspectives on team learning: Outcome improvement, task mastery, and group process. In J. P. Walsh & A. P. Brief (Eds.), *The Academy of Management Annals* (pp. 269–314). Florence, KY: Psychology Press.

Edmondson, A., Pisano, G. P., Bohmer, R., & Winslow, A. (2003). Learning how and learning what: Effects of tacit and codified knowledge on performance improvement following technology adoption. *Decision Sciences, 34*, 197–223.

Eisenberger, R., & Rhoades, L. (2001). Incremental effects of awards on creativity. *Journal of Personality and Social Psychology, 4*, 728–741.

Eisenhardt, K. M., & Tabrizi, B. N. (1995). Accelerating adaptive processes: Product innovation in the global computer industry. *Administrative Science Quarterly, 40*(1), 84–110.

Ellis, S., & Davidi, I. (2005). After-event reviews: Drawing lessons from successful and failed experience. *Journal of Applied Psychology, 90*(5), 857–871.

Ethiraj, S., & Levinthal, D. (2004). Bounded rationality and the search for organizational architecture: An evolutionary perspective on the design of organizations and their evolvability. *Administrative Science Quarterly, 49*, 404–437.

Fang, C., Lee, J., & Schilling, M. A. (2010). Balancing exploration and exploitation through structural design: The isolation of subgroups and organizational learning. *Organization Science, 21*, 625–642.

Feldman, M. S. (2004). Resources in emerging structures and processes of change. *Organization Science, 15*(3), 295–309.

Fiol, C. M., & Lyles, M. A. (1985). Organizational learning. *Academy of Management Review, 10*, 803–813.

Fleming, L. (2001). Recombinant uncertainty in technological search. *Management Science, 47*(1), 117–132.

Fong, C. T. (2006). The effects of emotional ambivalence on creativity. *Academy of Management Journal, 49*, 1016–1030.

Ford, J. K., & Kozlowski, S. W. J. (1996). *Improving training effectiveness in work organizations.* Mahwah, NJ: Erlbaum.

Friedman, R. S., & Förster, J. (2001). The effects of promotion and prevention cues on creativity. *Journal of Personality and Social Psychology, 81*(6), 1001–1013.

Galbraith, C. S. (1990). Transferring core manufacturing technologies in high-technology firms. *California Management Review, 32*, 56–70.

Garud, R., Dunbar, R., & Bartel, C. (2011). Dealing with unusual experiences: A narrative perspective on organizational learning. *Organization Science, 22*, 587–601.

Garvin, D. A. (2000). *Learning in action: A guide to putting the learning organization to work*. Boston, MA: Harvard Business School Press.

George, J. M., & Zhou, J. (2007). Dual tuning in a supportive context: Joint contributions of positive mood, negative mood, and supervisory behaviors to employee creativity. *Academy of Management Journal, 50*, 605–622.

Gherardi, S. (2006). *Organizational knowledge: The texture of workplace learning*. Malden, MA: Blackwell.

Gibson, C. B., & Gibbs, J. L. (2006). Unpacking the concept of virtuality: The effects of geographic dispersion, electronic dependence, dynamic structure, and national diversity on team innovation. *Administrative Science Quarterly, 51*, 451–495.

Gibson, F. P. (2000). Feedback delays: How can decision makers learn not to buy a new car every time the garage is empty? *Organizational Behavior and Human Decision Processes, 83*(1), 141–166.

Gino, F., Argote, L., Miron-Spektor, E., & Todorova, G. (2010). First get your feet wet: The effects of learning from direct and indirect experience on team creativity. *Organizational Behavior and Human Decision Processes, 111*(2), 102–115.

Goncalo, J. A., & Staw, B. M. (2006). Individualism-collectivism and group creativity. *Organizational Behavior and Human Decision Processes, 100*, 96–109.

Goodman, J. S., Wood, R. E., & Hendrickx, M. (2004). Feedback specificity, exploration and learning. *Journal of Applied Psychology, 89*(2), 248–262.

Grandori, A., & Kogut, B. (2002). Dialogue on organization and knowledge. *Organization Science, 13*(3), 224–231.

Greve, H. (2003). *Organizational learning from performance feedback*. Cambridge, UK: Cambridge University Press.

Greve, H. R. (1999). Branch systems and nonlocal learning in populations. In A. Miner & P. Anderson (Eds.), *Advances in strategic management* (Vol. 16, pp. 57–80). Cambridge, MA: Emerald Group Publishing.

Gruenfeld, D., Martorana, P. V., & Fan, E. T. (2000). What do groups learn from their worldliest members? Direct and indirect influence in dynamic teams. *Organizational Behavior and Human Decision Processes, 82*, 60–74.

Gulati, R., & Nohria, N. (1996). Is slack good or bad for innovation? *Academy of Management Journal, 39*, 1245–1264.

Guzzo, R. A., & Dickson, M. W. (1996). Teams in organizations: Recent research on performance and effectiveness. *Annual Review of Psychology, 47*, 307–338.

Haas, M. R., & Hansen, M. T. (2005). When using knowledge can hurt performance: The value of organizational capabilities in a management consulting company. *Strategic Management Journal, 26*, 1–24.

Hambrick, D. C., Cho, T. S., & Chen, M. J. (1996). Top management team heterogeneity and competitive behaviors of the firm. *Administrative Science Quarterly, 41*, 659–684.

Hansen, M. (1999). The search transfer problem: The role of weak ties in sharing knowledge across organization subunits. *Administrative Science Quarterly, 44*, 82–111.

Hansen, M. T., Nohria, N., & Tierney, T. (1999). What's your strategy for managing knowledge. *Harvard Business Review, 77*(2), 106–115.

Haunschild, P., & Sullivan, B. (2002). Learning from complexity: Effects of airline accident/incident heterogeneity on subsequent accident/incident rates. *Administrative Science Quarterly, 47*, 609–643.

Helfat, C. (Ed.). (2000). Guest editor's introduction to the special issue: The evolution of firm capabilities. *Strategic Management Journal, 21*(10/11), 955–959.

Herriott, S. R., Levinthal, D., & March, J. G. (1985). Learning from experience in organizations. *American Economic Review, 75*(2), 298–302.

Higgins, E. T. (1997). Beyond pleasure and pain. *American Psychology, 52*, 1280–1300.

Hilgard, E. R., & Bower, G. H. (1975). *Theories of learning* (4th ed.). Englewood Cliffs, NJ: Prentice-Hall.

Hollenbeck, J. R., Ilgen, D. R., Sego, D. J., Hedlund, J., Major, D. A., & Philips, J. (1995). Multilevel theory of team decision making: Decision performance in teams incorporating distributed expertise. *Journal of Applied Psychology, 80*, 292–316.

Hollingshead, A. B. (1998). Retrieval processes in transactive memory systems. *Journal of Personality and Social Psychology, 74*, 659–671.

Huber, G. P. (1991). Organizational learning: The contributing processes and the literatures. *Organization Science, 2*, 88–115.

Huff, A., & Jenkins, M. (Eds.). (2002). *Mapping strategic knowledge*. Thousand Oaks, CA: Sage.

Ingram, P. (2002). Interorganizational learning. In J. A. C. Baum (Ed.), *The Blackwell companion to organizations* (pp. 642–663). Oxford: Blackwell Business.

Ingram, P., & Baum, J. A. C. (1997). Opportunity and constraint: Organizations' learning from the operating and competitive experience of industries. *Strategic Management Journal, 18*, 75–98.

Ingram, P., & Simons, T. (2002). The transfer of experience in groups of organizations: Implications for performance and competition. *Management Science, 48*, 1517–1533.

Jansen, J. P. J., Van Den Bosch, F. A. J., & Volberda, H. W. (2006). Exploratory innovation, and performance: Effects of organizational antecedents and environmental moderators. *Management Science, 52*(11), 1661–1674.

Kanawattanachai, P., & Yoo, Y. (2007). The impact of knowledge coordination on virtual performance over time. *MIS Quarterly, 31*(4), 783–808.

Kane, A. A., Argote, L., & Levine, J. M. (2005). Knowledge transfer between groups via personnel rotation: Effects of social identity and knowledge quality. *Organizational Behavior and Human Decision Processes, 96*, 56–71.

Kane, G. C., & Alavi, M. (2007). Information technology and organizational learning: An investigation of exploration and exploitation processes. *Organization Science, 18*(5), 796–812.

Kark, R., & Van Dijk, D. (2007). Motivation to lead motivation to follow: The role of the self-regulatory focus in leadership processes. *Academy of Management Review, 32*(2), 500–528.

Katila, R., & Ahuja, G. (2002). Something old, something new: A longitudinal study of search behavior and new product introductions. *Academy of Management Journal, 45*(6), 1183–1194.

Kim, J., Kim, J., & Miner, A. S. (2009). Organizational learning from extreme performance experience: The impact of success and recovery experience. *Organization Science, 20*(6), 958–978.

Kim, S. H. (2008). An empirical assessment of knowledge management systems. Ph.D. dissertation, Carnegie Mellon University.

Knott, A. M. (2001). The dynamic value of hierarchy. *Management Science, 47*(3), 430–448.

Kogut, B., & Zander, U. (1992). Knowledge of the firm, combinative capabilities and the replication of technology. *Organization Science, 3*, 383–397.

Kozlowski, S. W. J., & Bell, B. S. (2008). Team learning, development and adaptation. In V. I. Sesso & M. London (Eds.), *Group learning* (pp. 15–44). Mahwah, NJ: Erlbaum.

Kozlowski, S.W. J., Chao, G. T., & Jensen, J. M. (2010). Building an infrastructure for organizational learning: A multilevel approach. In S. W. J. Kozlowski & E. Salas (Eds.), *Learning, training and development in organizations* (pp. 361–400). New York: Routledge Academic.

Krugman, P. A. (November 8, 1991). Myths and realities of U.S. competitiveness. *Science, 254*, 811–815.

Lampel, J., Shamsie, J., & Shapira, Z. (2009). Experiencing the improbable: Rare events and organizational learning. *Organization Science, 20*, 835–845.

Lant, T. K. (1992). Aspiration level adaptation: An empirical exploration. *Management Science, 38*, 623–644.

Lant, T. K., Milliken, F. J., & Batra, B. (1992). The role of managerial learning and interpretation in strategic persistence and reorientation: An empirical exploration. *Strategic Management Journal, 13*, 585–608.

Lapré, M. A., Mukherjee, A. S., & Van Wassenhove, L. N. (2000). Behind the learning curve: Linking learning activities to waste reduction. *Management Science, 46*(5), 597–611.

Lavie, D., & Miller, S. (2008). Alliance portfolio internationalization and firm performance. *Organization Science, 19*, 623–646.

Leonard-Barton, D. A. (1995). *Wellsprings of knowledge: Building and sustaining the sources of innovation.* Boston: Harvard Business School Press.

Levinthal, D. A., & March, J. G. (1981). A model of adaptive organizational search. *Journal of Economic Behavior in Organizations, 2*, 307–333.

Levinthal, D., & Rerup, C. (2006). Crossing an apparent chasm: Bridging mindful and less-mindful perspectives on organizational learning. *Organizational Science, 17*, 502–513.

Levitt, B., & March, J. G. (1988). Organizational learning. *Annual Review of Sociology, 14*, 319–340.

Lewis, K. (2004). Knowledge and performance in knowledge-worker teams: A longitudinal study of transactive memory systems. *Management Science, 50*(11), 1519–1533.

Lewis, K., Belliveau, M., Herndon, B., & Keller, J. (2007). Group cognition, membership change, and performance: Investigating the benefits and detriments of collective knowledge. *Organizational Behavior and Human Decision Processes, 103*(2), 159–178.

Lewis, K., Lange, D., & Gillis, L. (2005). Transactive memory systems, learning, and learning transfer. *Organization Science, 16*(6), 581–598.

Liang, D. W., Moreland, R., & Argote, L. (1995). Group versus individual training and group performance: The mediating role of transactive memory. *Personality and Social Psychology Bulletin, 21*, 384–393.

Lipshitz, R., Freedman, V., & Popper, M. (2007). *Demystifying organizational learning.* San Francisco: Sage.

Madsen, P., & Desai, V. (2011). Failing to learn? The effects of failure and success on organizational learning in the global orbital launch vehicle industry. *Academy of Management Journal, 53*(3), 451–476.

McFadyen, M. A., Semadeni, M., & Cannella, A. A. (2009). Value of strong ties to disconnected others: Examining knowledge creation in biomedicine. *Organization Science, 20*, 552–564.

McGrath, J. E. (1984). *Groups: Interaction and performance.* Englewood Cliffs, NJ: Prentice-Hall.

McGrath, J. E., & Argote, L. (2001). Group processes in organizational contexts. In M. A. Hogg & R. S. Tindale (Eds.), *Blackwell handbook of social psychology,* Vol. 3: *Group processes* (pp. 603–627). Oxford: Blackwell.

Menon, T., Thompson, L., & Choi, H. (2006). Tainted knowledge vs. tempting knowledge: People avoid knowledge from internal rivals and seek knowledge from external rivals. *Management Science, 52*(8), 1129–1144.

Miller, D. J., Fern, M. J., & Cardinal, L. B. (2007). The use of knowledge for technological innovation within diversified firms. *Academy of Management Journal, 50*(2), 308–326.

Minabe, S. (July 18, 1986). Japanese competitiveness and Japanese management. *Science, 233*, 301–304.

Miner, A. S., & Anderson, P. (1999). Interorganizational and population level learning: Engines of industry transformation. *Advances in Strategic Management, 16*, 1–30.

Miner, A. S., & Haunschild, P. R. (1995). Population level learning. In L. L. Cummings & B. M. Staw (Eds.), *Research in organizational behavior* (pp. 115–166). Greenwich, CT: JAI Press.

Miron, E., Erez, M., & Naveh, E. (2004). Do personal characteristics and cultural values that promote innovation, quality, and efficiency compete or complement each other? *Journal of Organizational Behavior, 25*(2), 175–199.

Moorman, C., &. Miner, A. S. (1997). The impact of organizational memory in new product performance and creativity. *Journal of Marketing Research, 34*, 91–106.

Murray, F., & O'Mahony, S. (2007). Exploring the foundations of cumulative innovation: Implications for organization science. *Organization Science, 18*, 1006–1021.

Naveh, E., & Erez, M. (2004). Innovation and attention-to-detail in the quality improvement paradigm. *Management Science, 50*(11), 1576–1586.

Nayak, P., & Ketteringham, J. (1986). *Breakthroughs.* New York: Rawson Associates.

Nelson, R. R., & Winter, S. G. (1982). *An evolutionary theory of economic change.* Boston: Belkman.

Nickerson, J. A., & Zenger, T. R. (2004). A knowledge-based theory of the firm: The problem-solving perspective. *Organization Science, 15*, 617–632.

Nonaka, I., & Takeuchi, H. (1995). *The knowledge creating company.* New York: Oxford University Press.

Nonaka, I., & von Krogh, G. (2009). Perspective-tacit knowledge and knowledge conversion: Controversy and advancement in organizational knowledge creation theory. *Organization Science, 20*, 635–652.

Paulus, P. B., & Yang, H. C. (2000). Idea generation in groups: A basis for creativity in organizations. *Organizational Behavior and Human Decision Processes, 82*, 76–87.

Pearsall, M. J., Ellis, A. P. J., & Stein, J. H. (2009). Coping with challenge and hindrance stressors in teams: Behavioral, cognitive, and affective outcomes. *Organizational Behavior and Human Decision Processes, 109*, 18–28.

Perry-Smith, J. (2006). Social yet creative: The role of social relationships in facilitating individual creativity. *Academy of Management Journal, 49*, 85–101.

Perry-Smith, J., & Shalley, C. E. (2003). The social side of creativity: A static and dynamic social network perspective. *Academy of Management Review, 28,* 89–106.

Pisano, G. P. (1994). Knowledge, integration, and the locus of learning: An empirical analysis of process development. *Strategic Management Journal, 15,* 85–100.

Polanyi, M. (1962). *Personal knowledge: Towards a post-critical philosophy.* New York: Harper & Row.

Porter, L. W., Lawler, E. E., & Hackman, J. R. (1975). *Behavior in organizations.* New York: McGraw-Hill.

Quiñones, M. A., Ford, J. K., & Teachout, M. S. (1995). The relationship between work experience and job performance: A conceptual and meta-analytic review. *Personnel Psychology, 48,* 887–910.

Rahmandad, H. (2008). Effects of delays on complexity of organizational learning. *Management Science, 54*(7), 1297–1312.

Raisch, S., Birkinshaw, J., Probst, G., & Tushman, M. L. (2009). Organizational ambidexterity: Balancing exploitation and exploration for sustained performance. *Organization Science, 20,* 685–695.

Rao, R., & Argote, L. (2006). Organizational learning and forgetting: The effects of turnover and structure. *European Management Review, 3,* 77–85.

Reagans, R., Argote, L., & Brooks, D. (2005). Individual experience and experience working together: Predicting learning rates from knowing what to do and knowing who knows what. *Management Science, 51,* 869–881.

Reagans, R., & McEvily, B. (2003). Network structure and knowledge transfer: The effects of cohesion and range. *Administrative Science Quarterly, 48,* 240–267.

Ree, M. J., Earles, J. A., & Teachout, M. S. (1994). Predicting job performance: Not much more than g. *Journal of Applied Psychology, 79,* 518–524.

Ren, Y., Carley, K. M., & Argote, L. (2006). The contingent effects of transactive memory: When is it more beneficial to know what others know? *Management Science, 52,* 671–682.

Repenning, N., & Sterman, J. (2002). Capability traps and self-confirming attribution errors in the dynamics of process improvement. *Administrative Science Quarterly, 47,* 265–295.

Rick, S., & Weber, R. A. (2010). Meaningful learning and transfer learning in games played repeatedly without feedback. *Games and Economic Behavior, 68,* 716–730.

Rivkin, J. (2001). Reproducing knowledge: Replication without imitation at moderate complexity. *Organization Science, 12,* 274–293.

Salvato, C. (2009). Capabilities unveiled: The role of ordinary activities in the evolution of product development processes. *Organization Science, 20,* 384–409.

Schilling, M. A., Vidal, P., Ployhart, R. E., & Marangoni, A. (2003). Learning by doing something else: Variation, relatedness, and the learning curve. *Management Science, 49*(1), 39–56.

Schulz, M. (2002). Organizational learning. In J. A. C. Baum (Ed.), *The Blackwell companion to organizations* (pp. 416–441). Oxford: Blackwell Business.

Senge, P. M. (1990). *The fifth discipline: The art and practice of the learning organization.* New York: Currency Doubleday.

Shane, S. (2000). Prior knowledge and the discovery of entrepreneurial opportunities. *Organization Science, 11*(4), 448–469.

Shaw, J. D., Duffy, M. K., Johnson, J. J., & Lockhart, D. (2005). Turnover, social capital losses, and performance. *Academy of Management Journal, 48,* 594–606.

Shiffrin, R. M., & Schneider, W. (1977). Controlled and automatic human information processing: II. Perceptual learning, automatic attending, and a general theory. *Psychological Review, 84,* 127–190.

Shin, S. J., & Zhou, J. (2007). When is educational specialization heterogeneity related to creativity in research and development teams? Transformational leadership as a moderator. *Journal of Applied Psychology, 92*(6), 1709–1721.

Siggelkow, N., & Levinthal, D. A. (2003). Temporarily divide to conquer: Centralized, decentralized, and reintegrated organizational approaches to exploration and adaptation. *Organization Science, 14,* 650–669.

Siggelkow, N., & Rivkin, J. W. (2005). Speed and search: Designing organizations for turbulence and complexity. *Organization Science, 16,* 101–122.

Sine, W. D., Shane, S., & Di Gregorio, D. (2003). The halo effect and technology licensing: The influence of institutional prestige on the licensing of university inventions. *Management Science, 49*(4), 478–496.

Singley, M. K., & Anderson, J. R. (1989). *The transfer of cognitive skill.* Cambridge, MA: Harvard University Press.

Sitkin, S. B. (1992). Learning through failure: The strategy of small losses. *Research on Organizational Behavior, 14,* 231–266.

Sorenson, O. (2003). Interdependence and adaptability: Organizational learning and the long-term effect of integration. *Management Science, 49*(4), 446–463.

Spender, J.-C, & Grant, R. M. (1996). Knowledge and the firm: Overview. *Strategic Management Journal, 17,* 5–10.

Starbuck, W. H. (2009). Perspective-cognitive reactions to rare events: Perceptions, uncertainty, and learning. *Organization Science, 20,* 925–937.

A survey of manufacturing: Meet the global factory. (June 20, 1998). *The Economist,* M1-M18.

Szulanski, G. (1996). Exploring internal stickiness: Impediments to the transfer of best practice within the firm. *Strategic Management Journal, 17,* 27–43.

Szulanski, G. (2000). Appropriability and the challenge of scope: Bank One routinizes replication. In G. Dosi, R. Nelson, & S. Winter (Eds.), *The nature and dynamics of organizational capabilities* (pp. 69–98). New York: Oxford University Press.

Szulanski, G., & Jensen, R. J. (2006). Presumptive adaptation and the effectiveness of knowledge transfer. *Strategic Management Journal, 27*(10), 937–957.

Taylor, A., & Greve, H. R. (2006). Superman or the Fantastic Four? Knowledge combination and experience in innovative teams. *Academy of Management Journal, 49*(4), 723–740.

Teece, D. J., Pisano, G., & Shuen, A. (1997). Dynamic capabilities and strategic management. *Strategic Management Journal, 18*(7), 509–533.

Tesluk, P. E., & Jacobs, R. J. (1998). Toward an integrated model of work experience. *Personnel Psychology, 51,* 321–355.

Thompson, P. (2007). How much did the Liberty shipbuilders forget? *Management Science, 53,* 908–918.

Todorova, G., Argote, L., & Reagans, R. (2008). Working alone or working together: The effects of individual motivation and group identification on transactive memory systems and team performance. *Best Paper Proceedings of the Academy of Management.*

Ton, Z., & Huckman, R. S. (2008). Managing the impact of employee turnover on performance: The role of process conformance. *Organization Science, 19,* 56–68.

Tortoriello, M., & Krackhardt, D. (2010). Activating cross-boundary knowledge: Simmelian ties and the generation of innovation. *Academy of Management Journal, 53*(1), 167–181.

Trow, D. B. (1960). Membership succession and team performance. *Human Relations, 13*, 259–269.

Tsai, W. (2002). Social structure of "coopetition" within a multiunit organization: Coordination, competition, and intraorganizational knowledge sharing. *Organization Science, 13*(2), 179–190.

Tsoukas, H. (2009). A dialogical approach to the creation of new knowledge in organizations. *Organization Science, 20*, 941–957.

Vaast, E., & Levina, N. (2006). Multiple faces of codification: Organizational redesign in an IT organization. *Organization Science, 17*(2), 190–201.

Van der Vegt, G. S., & Bunderson, J. S. (2005). Learning and performance in multidisciplinary teams: The importance of collective team identification. *Academy of Management Journal, 48*, 532–547.

Van der Vegt, G. S., de Jong, S. B., Bunderson, J. S., & Molleman, E. (2010). Power asymmetry and learning in teams: The moderating role of performance feedback. *Organization Science, 21*, 347–361.

Virany, B., Tushman, M. L., & Romanelli, E. (1992). Executive succession and organizational outcomes in turbulent environments: An organizational approach. *Organization Science, 3*, 72–91.

Wegner, D. M. (1986). Transactive memory: A contemporary analysis of the group mind. In B. Millen & G. R. Goethals (Eds.), *Theories of group behavior* (pp. 185–205). New York: Springer-Verlag.

Weick, K. E., & Sutcliffe, K. M. (2006). Mindfulness and the quality of organizational attention. *Organization Science, 17*(4), 514–524.

Weigelt, C., & Sarkar, M. (2009). Learning from supply-side agents: The impact of technology solution providers' experiential diversity on clients' innovation adoption. *Academy of Management Journal, 52*(1), 37–60.

Wells, W. P., & Pelz, D. C. (1966). *Scientists in organizations.* New York: Wiley.

Wiersma, E. (2007). Conditions that shape the learning curve: Factors that increase the ability and opportunity to learn. *Management Science, 53*(12), 1903–1915.

Williams, C. (2007). Transfer in context: Replication and adaptation in knowledge transfer relationships. *Strategic Management Journal, 28*, 867–889.

Williams, K. Y., & O'Reilly, C. A. (1998). Demography and diversity in organizations: A review of 40 years of research. *Research in Organizational Behavior, 20*, 77–140.

Wingfield, A. (1979). *Human learning and memory: An introduction.* New York: Harper & Row.

Wong, S. (2004). Distal and local group learning: Performance trade-offs and tensions. *Organization Science, 15*, 645–656.

Yayavaram, S., & Ahuja, G. (2008). Decomposability in knowledge structures and its impact on the usefulness of inventions and knowledge-base malleability. *Administrative Science Quarterly, 53*(2), 333–362.

Zammuto, R. F., Griffith, T. L., Majchrzak, A., Dougherty, D. J., & Faraj, S. (2007). Information technology and the changing fabric of organizations. *Organization Science, 18*(5), 749–762.

Zander, U., & Kogut, B. (1995). Knowledge and the speed of the transfer and imitation of organizational capabilities: An empirical test. *Organization Science, 6*, 76–92.

Zhang, Z. X., Hempel, P. S., Han, Y. L., & Tjosvold, D. (2007). Transactive memory system links work team characteristics and performance. *Journal of Applied Psychology, 92*, 1722–1730.

Zollo, M., & Reuer, J. (2010). Experience spillovers across corporate development activities. *Organization Science, 21*, 1195–1212.

Zollo, M., & Winter, S. (2002). Deliberate learning and the evolution of dynamic capabilities. *Organization Science, 13*, 339–351.

Organizational Development and Change: Linking Research from the Profit, Nonprofit, and Public Sectors

J. Kevin Ford *and* Pennie Foster-Fishman

Abstract

We review the organizational psychology, community psychology, and organizational behavior literatures in order to provide an integrated perspective to change and the factors that impact the success or failure of organizational change initiatives. This chapter provides a historical context for the changing focus and key tensions in the field; describes key change theories that help us understand change processes; and reviews empirical work in the for-profit, nonprofit, and public sectors relevant to understanding core concepts of readiness for change, change capacity, and organizational learning. We identify recent conceptual and methodological approaches that bring a systems perspective to the study of change. The chapter concludes with thoughts on the sustainability of change and the identification of needed research that can inform practice.

Key Words: Change theories, readiness for change, change capability, organizational learning, systems thinking, and sustainability

A manufacturing company of gears decides that there is a need to move from its long-standing traditional assembly line system to a team-based cellular, decentralized manufacturing process. A police chief sees the need to transform a police department from a reactive enforcement focus that has generated a large number of citizen complaints to a community policing perspective with an emphasis on proactively working with citizens to solve long-standing problems and issues in the community. A state governmental agency pushes to enhance the effectiveness of human resource services by moving from a transactional to a transformational, consultative approach to developing human resources. The plan calls for human resource personnel to become strategic business partners and agents for change within the various agencies in the state government. A nonprofit hospital system sees the need to develop a new vision for health. The vision involves collaboration with various health-related systems and schools to develop and implement a community-based health initiative to proactively address issues such as obesity, diabetes, and smoking within their community. Organizational change is inevitable and is all around us.

This review examines the literature on organizational development (OD) that has attempted to understand change processes and the factors that impact the success or failure of organizational change initiatives. This chapter reviews what we know, and what we should know more about, relevant to organizational change. Such a review of the field of OD is a bit daunting. Kahn (1974) noted that OD is only a "convenient label for a bunch of activities" (p. 486). Mirvis (1988), in his review of OD practices in the 1960s, 1970s, and 1980s, noted that "it is always a problem to precisely define OD" (p. 4). Similarly, Beer and Walton (1987) declared that the "field no longer has professional boundaries" (p. 340). Weick and Quinn (1999) concluded their review that "the sheer sprawl of the change literature is a continuing challenge to investigators who thrive on frameworks" (p. 364).

The "continual sprawl" of interesting theoretical and empirically driven research on change since Weick and Quinn's (1999) review provides a great opportunity to gain some understanding and appreciation of research efforts focused on planned change efforts. As noted by Macy, Farias, Rosa, and Moore (2007), the "search for innovative ways to improve organizational performance is central to the work of a large number of scholars and practitioners" (p. 338). In that sense, we feel relieved that our focus on a variety of change related concepts, the complexity of change processes, the diversity of methods used to study those processes, and the many frameworks or lens for looking at OD change can provide a window for understanding what we know and what we still have to learn about organizational change efforts.

The review integrates research in organizational psychology, community psychology, and organizational behavior around organizational development and change. These areas of research provide unique perspectives to understanding change that need to be considered to provide an integrated perspective to change. In particular, this review has four main purposes: (a) to provide a historical context of the changing focus of the OD field by examining major reviews that have already been completed; (b) to describe key change theories that have emerged in the field; (c) to review empirical research across a variety of settings (profit, not for profit, public) over the last 10 years around core concepts that are advancing the field; and (d) to emphasize taking a systems based approach to change based on this analysis and our own experiences in change efforts, which is then used to guide future research directions.

Historical Trends and Foundations of OD

The field of organizational development and change (OD) has often been described as having its beginnings in the theoretical work of Lewin (1947), the empirical work on participation and change by Coch and French (1948), and the development of the laboratory training methodology (see Highhouse, 2002 for a review) in the late 1940s. As noted by French and Bell (1973), while it is unclear who coined the term *organizational development*, it seems to have emerged from the works of Blake, Mouton, Douglas McGregor, and other pioneers working to improve the welfare of

employees through efforts such as treating workers as adults rather than as children (Argyris, 1957, 1973), moving an organization from a Theory X to a Theory Y perspective (McGregor, 1960) and intervening to change an organization from a Level 1 (exploitive authoritative) to a Level 4 (participative) type organization (Likert, 1961, 1967). In a conversation with French and Bell (1995), Beckard discussed working with McGregor on a project at General Mills in the late 1940s. He noted that "we clearly didn't want to call it management development because it was total organization-wide...so we labeled the program organizational development meaning system-wide change effort" (p. 47).

Since these early works, the field has evolved into a major area of research and practice. One way to understand advances to a field of inquiry is to examine and analyze previous reviews in the area. We have used six major reviews in the *Annual Review of Psychology* from 1974 to 1999 to delineate how the focus and scope of the field has changed and expanded into the 1990s. We then talk about key foundations and continual tensions in the field that emerge from this historical review before discussing change theories and recent empirical research.

Reviews of OD

Friedlander and Brown (1974) provided one of the first systematic reviews of what they call the emerging interdisciplinary field of organizational development. They defined OD as a method for facilitating change and development in people (styles, values, and skills), in technology (greater simplicity or complexity), and within organizational processes and structures (relationships and roles), with the goal of human fulfillment and optimizing task accomplishment. They provided a framework of thinking about planned change that focused on techno-structural changes such as job enlargement, job enrichment, and socio-technical systems and human-process oriented changes such as t-groups, team building, and survey-feedback approaches. They noted that the field tended to focus on humanistic and democratic values and valued open communication and problem solving, locating decision making as close to the information sources as possible, building trust and collaboration and enhancing self-control and direction (Theory Y). They cited research on interventions that pointed to the importance of strong internal and external pressure for change, the gradual involvement of many levels in the diagnosis and change activities, and shared decision making around the change. They also highlighted that unambiguous evaluations of the success of various change interventions are few and are difficult to conduct.

Alderfer (1977) noted that OD seeks to understand planned change processes, to assess the effects of efforts to promote social change, and to evolve better theories of change processes. In contrast to Friedlander and Brown (1974), he highlighted the variety of value conflicts characteristic of the field, including the historically strong force in the field to "humanize" organizations to be more responsive to human concerns rather than just developing technologies to improve organizational effectiveness. He questioned whether OD practitioners actually advance humane values, as much effort seems to be on developing methods to solve organizational problems. His review focused on the interdependencies among applied problems, technological developments, values, and research. The review highlighted two major trends in the field: (a) expansion of the kinds of organizational settings in which traditional OD techniques were being used (e.g., multinational companies, public sector entities such as policing, and nonprofits such as community mental health); and (b) elaboration of the kinds of techniques that are being developed by practitioners that are a result of the challenges faced when attempting to solve enduring organizational problems. He notes in the review that there had been little empirical research that carefully evaluated these new methods or interventions. At the same time, there was some evidence for more sophistication in research design, measurement, and theory (e.g., examination of alpha, beta, gamma change).

Faucheux, Amado, and Laurent (1982) provided a multicultural perspective to the field by describing research being conducted in Europe and other parts of the world. They stressed that the field of OD must be seen as more than a management tool and must be viewed as a total organizational process that meets employee and organizational needs. The scope of their review went beyond OD as a field to include what they saw as the more general issues of organizational change—even questioning whether the term *organizational development* is adequate to describe the various developments taking place in the field. Their suggestion was to change labels to more encompassing terms such as *quality of working life*. They noted how different approaches to change had emerged in the United States and Europe—with Europe focusing on a more holistic approach to jobs

and considering intergroup and worker participation issues and the joint influence of both technological and social requirements—a socio-technical approach. The United States was seen as focusing more on specific issues and problems within group as well as interpersonal issues relevant to change. The major contribution of the review was on examining the many different cultural contexts in which change can take place and questioning the assumptions in OD that ideas and methods can easily be applied to organizations in different cultures. They cautioned that cross-cultural transfer of change technology has proved to be difficult and slow. They concluded that the evaluation research to date indicated little evidence for the efficacy of OD, as it did not seem to make people more satisfied, and group-level process variables seemed to change less than half the time they were measured. There was also limited evidence for the overall impact on organizational processes, with better results for participative methods and socio-technical systems than for group-level interventions.

Beer and Walton (1987) contended in their review that the field of OD had continued to be consultant centered and that there had been no significant breakthroughs in intervention methodologies. In addition, they saw the greatest advance in understanding of key concepts for change as coming from the general management literature on culture and leadership, rather than from the OD field itself. In fact, Beer and Walton (1987) argued that the general management literature had by that time absorbed many of the concepts, values, and methods of OD (e.g., participative management, use of problem-solving task forces, collaborative approaches, and mission-building sessions). This absorption led to questioning what was the unique contribution of the OD field to understanding and improving organizational life for employees as well as organizational effectiveness. They also noted more emphasis on issues with system-wide implications, such as the need for revitalization and turnaround as well as innovation. These needs were seen to require more system dynamics thinking, which included understanding stakeholder issues and network concepts crucial for creating and maintaining change. They also saw an increased emphasis on understanding alternative structural arrangements such as parallel and matrix organizations and the decentralization and flattening of organizational hierarchies. In terms of the consultant role, Beer and Walton (1987) saw a need to be less value laden (e.g., focused on democracy) and advocacy oriented.

They also contended that OD must broaden itself to move away from programs in which the consultant develops interventions to more systematic and collaborative approaches in which mangers, staff members, and consultants work together to manage change to redirect efforts and performance.

In their review, Porras and Silvers (1991) distinguished between traditional organizational development activities that focused on improving organizations and organizational transformation efforts that emphasized creating a new vision for an organization and new work setting arrangements so as to help the organization better fit with the changing realities of the organization's environment. This movement toward organizational transformations (similar to the theme raised by Beer & Walton, 1987) required an examination of deeper level issues of organizational beliefs, purpose, mission, and vision, rather than the typical OD emphasis on changing work settings or dealing with group problems. They noted the need for more research and practice efforts aimed at understanding planned change activities that help make organizations more responsive to external environmental shifts and the need to take a contingency perspective to understanding change. They saw organizational transformation research as at the cutting edge of planning change, calling for the development of the capacity for continuous self-diagnosis and change—explicitly linking the emerging organizational learning perspective to the field of organizational development (Cyert & March, 1963; Fiol & Lyles, 1985; March & Simon, 1958). They highlighted the development of new methods such as appreciative inquiry (Cooperrider & Srivastva, 1987) and stream analysis (Porras, 1987), in which problems are mapped onto a change model. They also noted the shift in research from individual and group process issues to more structural arrangements and reward systems that take a more organizational level orientation. They described advances in the evaluation of alpha, beta, and gamma change. Nevertheless, they concluded their review that "although there are some innovative areas of OD research in the period reviewed, no fundamental new paradigms have been developed and embraced by the field and major new insights are rare" (p. 74).

The review by Weick and Quinn (1999) extends the perspective taken by Porras and Silvers (1991) that planned change is usually needed because of the failure of people to create continuously adaptive organizations. They noted that research had begun to rely more on systems theory and learning about the environment. Practice was seen as more participant centered rather than researcher centered. They cautioned that change is more often spiral or open-ended, rather than linear, and that the chains of causality are much longer and less determinate than is often anticipated by researchers and practitioners. They highlighted the importance of sense making during change efforts. Weick and Quinn (1999) saw more practice efforts of whole-scale change in which large numbers of employees and key stakeholders would help plan for change within a concentrated period of time. These methods include interventions such as real time strategic change (Jacobs, 1994), whole-scale systems change (Bunker & Alban, 1997), and fast-cycle full-participation organization design (Manning & Binzagr, 1996).

Tensions in the Field

The six reviews of the OD literature from 1974 to 1999 highlight at least three broad themes and tensions in the field. The first issue is the interplay of science/research and practice in OD. In 1974, Friedlander and Brown described a hope that theory and practice could become part of a broader, far-reaching, and relevant field of planned change. They also warned, though, that research would either come to play a far more crucial role in the advancement of the field or would become an increasingly irrelevant side to the advancement of the field. Alderfer (1977) noted in his review that OD at that point in history was dominated by the values of practice, and that developments in the field revolved more around new interventions arising out of the challenges to practitioners, induced by the real problems of clients within complex organizational systems struggling to be effective. This emphasis on methods and techniques led Beer and Walton (1987) to note that theory building in OD has always been weak. They noted the need for contingency perspectives to change, as well as the need to incorporate time more explicitly into planned change models. They concluded that research and theory have historically fallen behind the leads coming from practice. Porras and Silvers (1991) concluded that planned changes should be guided by generally accepted and unified theories of organizations and organizational change—neither of which currently exists. The goal of the scientist-practitioner model of research driving best practices, with practice leading to important research questions, has clearly not been met.

A second tension is how to accumulate knowledge about change processes and outcomes. Early reviews bemoaned the limited number of empirically based studies on the effectiveness of change interventions such as team building, survey feedback, and job redesign. Faucheux et al. (1982) lamented how few evaluation studies (35 of 160 studies) satisfied even the basic criteria of scientific rigor. Beer and Walton (1987) noted that Guzzo, Jette, and Katzell (1983) did find evidence that psychologically based productivity studies led to worker productivity increases of one-half a standard deviation. Macy and Izumi (1993) did find some evidence for impacts on productivity but not on job attitudes, satisfaction, and work involvement. Nevertheless, Beer and Walton (1987) concluded that the research on interventions are limited by time horizons, are context poor in terms of describing and understanding change, and that there seems to be a focus on greater research precision at the expense of conducting research that creates knowledge that can lead to direct transfer to improving practice. They go so far as to say that OD research had reached a turning point: "As long as OD researchers emulate traditional science methodology, they will confine themselves to isolated episodes of change. By evaluating a specified intervention, they neglect the interrelatedness of elements in a system so that exogenous variables will prevent any powerful conclusions" (p. 344). They stressed that, rather than attempt to find the perfect quantitative methodology to prove its worth, OD must build a different model for the accumulation of knowledge than the dominant positivist paradigm. Instead, they argued that there was a need for a return to action research traditions with full participation of the client in the research, but with much longer time frame and inclusion of rich descriptions of content and system dynamics. Similarly, Porras and Silvers (1991) contended that there was a need for more systems-oriented research that indicates how change cascades throughout the organizational system.

A third tension is the focus or goal of organizational change initiatives. Mirvis (1988) provided a detailed analysis of the evolving nature of the field of organizational development (OD) relevant to the overall goals of change initiatives. He noted that in the early days (up to the 1960s), the field reflected a humanistic philosophy or set of beliefs about people and organizations. The field focused on human potential and how change can help people—similar to Maslow's self-actualization process of becoming more of who they could be. Friedlander and Brown (1974) cited the dual tracking goals of OD by stating that the goal of change is toward human

fulfillment and optimizing task accomplishment. By the 1980s, the focus became more on the strategic management of change and optimizing task accomplishment to deal with more turbulent environments. The goal of change interventions has become more focused on organizational member achievement, aligned toward the new strategic focus rather than on human expression and fulfillment. Burnes (2009) contends that the current focus on profit maximization and self-interest must return to the Lewinian values of ethical and participatory change and socially responsible behavior.

In many ways, these tensions continue today. As we will illustrate below, the OD field continues to need to promote better and more effective integration of scientist/practitioner fields, needs to heed more attention to conceptual fit between research methods used and the phenomenon studied, and needs to recognize the implications and the potential risks of the targeted goals and the underlying values of the change endeavors. The current context of today highlights, in many ways, the criticality and dynamic interplay across these three tensions.

Theories of Change

As noted by Beer and Walton (1987), OD had been historically weak on theory development. Nevertheless, an underlying foundation of organizational development has been systems theory. Systems theory involves consideration of the interdependency, interconnectedness, and interrelatedness of the parts within the organization that constitutes the whole. An organizational system can be characterized by a continuous cycle of input, transformation, output, and feedback, whereby one element of experience influences the next (Katz & Kahn, 1978). Thus, systems thinking is the process of seeing the whole, including the underlying structures in complex situations (Senge, 1990). There are four key consequences of viewing organizations from a systems perspective. First, issues, events, forces, and incidents are not viewed as isolated phenomena but are seen in relation to other issues, events, and forces. Second, there is an analysis of events in terms of multiple causation rather than a single cause. Third, one cannot change one part of a system without influencing other parts in some ways. Fourth, if one wants to change a system, one changes the system, not just its component parts. While systems thinking pervades organizational development and change frameworks, we agree with the contention by Kozlowski and Klein (2000) that the influence of systems thinking in the organizational sciences—and in our case, in this review of OD—has been primarily at the metaphorical level. Below, we discuss key change theories that provide different perspectives for understanding change while having a common root within the metaphor of systems.

Since the early conception of change as freezing, moving, and refreezing (Coch & French, 1948; Lewin, 1947), a number of frameworks for change have been developed to provide researchers and practitioners with a wider variety of perspectives that one could take to understand the process of change. These theories of change have direct implications for research as well as for practice. We have chosen what we see as some key change theories to illustrate the advances made to the theoretical development of the OD field. The theories emphasize different aspects relevant to change. Some theories speak more to understanding and describing the types of change possible (Argyris, 1985; Bartunek & Moch, 1987), while others describe more fully the process of change (e.g., Gersick, 1991). Still others focus more on the form of the interventions needed for change (e.g., Huy, 2001).

Argyris (1976, 1985, 1990) and Argyris and Schon (1974) describe organizational learning systems of change from a conceptual perspective and provide a practical model of what needs to change. They conceptualize change as consisting of single loop and double loop learning. Single loop learning is oriented to maintaining the current state around an equilibrium point and the detection and correction of an error. Similar to the idea of a thermostat, single loop learning focuses on moving toward and maintaining the achievement of a particular goal. Double loop learning is focused on questioning assumptions and moving beyond the status quo. For example, one could question why the goal is set at the point it is, or reflect on whether the existing strategy is effective in reaching a goal, or even whether there should be a goal at all. One attempts to scan and monitor and test ideas in order to continually learn and grow as a person. Argyris and Schon (1974) also highlight the practical barriers that inhibit learning. They describe a Model I theory in use, in which the governing variables and actions strategies are focused on controlling and winning, as well as the displaying of defensive routines that are designed to protect oneself or others. They argue that these actions of control and defensive routines are the typical way we in which go about our world, leading us to single loop learning as the "theory in use." Nevertheless, individuals espouse a theory of action that does not acknowledge this reality, but instead state that they

hold values (importance of collaboration, being honest); that is, their espoused theory is quite different from their theory in use. Model I theory in use leads to predictable observable consequences such as miscommunication, self-fulfilling prophecies, and escalating error. Yet, people are often not aware of this disconnect between theory in use and espoused theory, thus staying within a single loop learning paradigm. Argyris argues for the need to move to Model II theory in use, in which the governing variables of action are valid information and free and informed choice, which leads to combining learning and inquiry when advocating for a position. This type of Model II theory in use can lead to double loop learning, which can lead to effective problem solving and reduction of the self-fulfilling, error-escalating process.

Bartunek and Moch (1987) distinguished between incremental and transformational change. They took a cognitive-based perspective by focusing on schemata relevant to three types of change—first, second, and third order change. The change involves individual-level schemata (organizing frameworks for understanding events and giving meaning to behavior/actions) and organizational schemata (shared meaning across the organization as a whole that help members interpret the environment, select priorities, and allocate resources). With first order change, problems are identified and targeted for resolution. This type of incremental change does not require any change in schemata; in fact, because the changes enacted are consistent with present organizational schemata, they actually legitimize and reinforce current understandings. Second order change is transformative, as there is a conscious modification of the present schemata in a particular direction—usually as a function of a change agent leading the process. With third order change, organizational members have the capacity to recognize when the current framework is not working and they choose to alter the framework (i.e., choose another schemata for interpreting events and selecting priorities). A strength of this change theory is that it provides a cognitive approach to understanding individual and organizational functioning. In addition, the theory acknowledges the complexity of change, the potential shifting of schemata, and the important role of sense making by individuals in organizations. It provides a focus on how an organization can adapt to changing realities, as well as what to look for with change, by paying attention to linguistic symbols such as stories, myths, rites, and language as windows into individual and organizational schemata.

Some limitations of this framework are that there is not a full discussion of how to identify and measure schemata within an organization, how a change agent can enact second order change, or how third order change can occur when there are different or competing interests across organizational levels and/or functions.

Gersick (1991) provided a more process-oriented perspective to transformative change through her discussion of the punctuated equilibrium model. She argues that organizations seek some equilibrium point at which the basic patterns within the organization stay the same. These basic patterns affect what is given attention and what choices are made. The need for equilibrium leads over time to inertia, where organizational forces resist changes to the underlying deep structure—the network of fundamental, interdependent choices about how units will be organized and what activity patterns are needed to maintain its survival. At some point, this equilibrium is not adaptable to changing realities, thus requiring a revolution in which the old deep structure is challenged and comes apart until the natural process of equilibrium forms around a new deep structure. During the revolutionary phase, there comes recognition that maintaining the status quo is not possible (a point of clarity called *symmetry breaking*). This episodic model of change is consistent with the frameworks developed by Bartunek and Moch (1987) and by Lewin (1947). According to these frameworks, fundamental change cannot be accomplished piecemeal or gradually, but instead is dramatic, infrequent, and often driven by external changes. Also consistent with Bartunek and Moch (1987), transformative change leads to cognitive restructuring and new standards of judgment and decision making within the organization. There is literature across many disciplines that support this change paradigm as well as its explanatory framework for system-level resistance. The theory also acknowledges both internal as well as external forces for change, as well as adding a time component to change. A limitation of this theory is that it is more of a descriptive model of change rather than a model that generates predictions of when change might occur and what factors might impact the success of the change process. Measurement of such concepts of deep structure and equilibrium is challenging.

Brown and Eisenhardt (1997) provide a theory that emphasizes the continuous nature of change in organizations. Continuous change is defined as change that is non-episodic, frequent, regular, and common within an organization—in other words,

the opposite of a punctuated, episodic framework of change (Weick & Quinn, 1999). This model highlights a number of key concepts of change, including semi-structures, links in time, sequenced steps, and probing. Semi-structures highlight that organizations have some well-defined features, such as task responsibilities and functions that are fairly stable, and also have more flexible or less rigid components, such as teamwork and communication patterns. Links in time are practices in which the organization attends to the needed transitions of the present and the future by also considering the past. Sequenced steps are the actions taken to affect change in the organization. Probing involves actively identifying and then preparing for environmental changes and exploring multiple options for dealing with those changes. The incremental change model emphasizes that sense making and "controlled improvisation," along with probing and links in time, lead to constant changes to daily contingencies. One strength of this theory is that change is thought of as evolving and cumulative, as work processes and interaction patterns are modified through emergent and self-organizing processes. Thus, continuous change is more than simply a reactive change in response to events as implied by episodic change frameworks. A limitation of the theory is that there is little attempt to understand how to facilitate this process and no compelling reconciliation with the episodic change theory. Nevertheless, there are compelling reasons to think of each theory as having some validity (Tushman & Romanelli, 1985). For example, one could imagine that the self-organizing processes that occur in continuous change processes happen because of some threat to current equilibriums and a need to reshift as a new "attractor" emerges to which a subsystem must respond. From this perspective, some subsystems could experience a punctuated equilibrium process, while other subsystems are going through the change process in a more steady or consistent way.

Some research has been done to examine issues of incremental and more episodic change. For example, Amis, Slack, and Hinings (2004) presented a study that examined the pace, sequence, and linearity of change. Pace focuses on the question of how fast change is to be implemented—rapidly or incrementally. The sequence of change concerns the question of which part of the organization should be changed and when; that is, is the change about the entire organization, or is it focused on high-impact parts? The linearity of change explores the question of whether change is thought of as linear or non-linear, with delays, reversals, and oscillations. With radical change, they note that there is a shift from "one archetypal configuration to another or a transition from a design that can be identified with no single archetype to one that has clear archetypal status" (p. 16). They define archetypes as a collection of values and beliefs that are made manifest through particular structural arrangements. In this large-scale study of various organizations, Amis et al. (2004) found that there were no significant differences between the amount of early change that took place in those organizations that successfully completed the radical change process and those that did not. Fast pace change across an organization early in the transition process is not sufficient to bring about lasting, long-term transformation. The results also indicated that radical change is more likely if early changes are made to an organization's high-impact elements. In addition, radical change is likely to lead to a non-linear process characterized by delays, reversals, and oscillations.

Thietart and Forgues (1995) and others have applied concepts from chaos theory to organizational life and change. They stress that embedded in organizations is a continuous process of convergence and divergence. From this perspective, organizations are seen as non-linear dynamic systems, subject to forces of stability (planning, structuring) and instability (innovation, experimentation) that push them toward chaos. They contend that the path from organizational stability to chaos follows a discrete process of change. With the move to the level of chaotic domain, small changes can have big consequences that cannot be predicted in the long term. From this chaos, new stabilities emerge from attractor patterns (organizations attracted to an identifiable configuration) and assimilated into this new organizational reality. A model of change from this perspective includes a process of stability, environmental disturbance, amplification, instability, reconfiguration, order, and stability (Wheatley, 1992). Chaos theories of change view organizations as open systems that shape themselves to account for environmental disturbances. An important implication of this theoretical perspective is that organizational crises may be more a function of the complex, tightly coupled relationships among elements in an organization, in a continual process of convergence and divergence, than the result of inadequate actions on the part of organizational members. In addition, it is unlikely that a chaotic system ever finds itself twice in the same situation—this implies that the similar actions that an organization takes in one situation and point in time may lead to failure at a different point in time. As they note, "to rely on successful practices as a basis to manage in a different context can only lead to deception" (p. 27).

An integrative approach to understanding change theories has been attempted by Van de Ven and Poole (1995). While acknowledging the theoretical advances that have been made, they also contend that it is the interplay among different perspectives of change that can help one gain a more comprehensive understanding of organizational change. They stress that an integrative perspective is possible if the different change theories are viewed as providing "alternative pictures of the same organizational processes without nullifying each other" (p. 511). Based on their analysis of change approaches, they describe four basic types of change process theories to explain how and why change unfolds.

The life cycle theory views change as organic growth that occurs in a prescribed sequence of stages, whereby each stage must occur prior to the next stage. The characteristics acquired in the earlier stages are retained in the later stages, and each stage is derived from a common underlying logic or process. The cyclical pattern of start-up, growth, harvest, terminate, and repeat is linear and irreversible.

Teleological theories of change focus on the repetitive sequence of goal formulation, implementation, evaluation, and modification of goals, based on what was learned or intended by the organization. This model provides a standard for judging change by comparing the current state to the end state. The theory contends that there is a recurrent and discontinuous sequence of goal setting, implementation, and adaptation to reach desired end states.

The dialectic theory views change as occurring when opposing values, forces, or events (antithesis) gain sufficient power to confront and engage the status quo (thesis), which can set the stage for producing a synthesis. The synthesis in time becomes the next thesis. The dialectical approach also acknowledges that there may be sufficient power to suppress any opposing entity and thus maintain the status quo. This theory of change, then, emphasizes the discontinuous sequence of confrontation, conflict, and synthesis of contradictory values and ideas.

The evolutionary theory views the environment as the main engine for change through the repetitive sequence of variation, selection, and retention among entities in a designated population (e.g., department, organization). Variation occurs through random chance, selection occurs through the competition for scarce resources, and the environment selects the best fit entities. Retention processes maintain the entities and counteract variation and selection. If the organization meets the requirements of the environment, it will survive.

Van de Ven and Poole (1995) examine the similarities and differences of these four change theories. They note that, with life cycle and teleology approaches, there is a single entity promoting change—the changes comes from within, and environmental influences are seen as secondary influences. The evolution and dialectic change processes are seen as having multiple entities, as the push for change comes from competition and conflict between two or more entities. The mode of change can be prescribed through pre-specified direction (life cycle and evolution) or construction—often discontinuous and unpredictable (teleological and dialectic). Thus, the prescribed mode focuses on the incremental and continuous change processes, while the constructive model focuses on radical and episodic change. They then go on to describe "hybrid" change theories that are various combinations of these four ideal types of change.

Huy (2001) provides a theory of change that directly incorporates time and temporal capability into an understanding of planned change. He notes four types of change interventions—commanding, engineering, teaching, and socializing—and connects these interventions to quantitative time (time as a scarce commodity) and inner or qualitative time (time experienced at the individual level of consciousness). Each type of intervention is characterized by different processes and time considerations, with different implications for the role of change agents. With the commanding intervention, the focus is on quantitative time and strict compliance to the change agent in order to make change happen quickly. The engineering intervention also involves quantitative time and the analysis of work processes and reengineering. The change agent acts in this case as an analyst of the needed change. The teaching intervention focuses on inner or qualitative time, as leaders act as teachers of vision and facilitate the change process. The socializing intervention involves qualitative time, with a democratic community of semi-autonomous work groups, where the change agent acts as a role model.

Perhaps the greatest challenge for change researchers and practitioners is that, while effective organizational change requires simultaneous attention to context, process, content, and the temporal nature of change (Pettigrew, Woodman, & Cameron (2001),

no theories to date have successfully integrated these four dimensions. In addition, though most of the above theories provide useful heuristic value, in that they promote insights into understanding the change process, few offer explanatory value.

Key Concepts and Advances in the Field

Planned organizational change must face the double hurdle of scholarly quality and practical relevance (Austin & Bartunek, 2003). While concerns over the future of OD continue (e.g., see Worley & Feyerherm, 2003), Pettigrew et al. (2001) note that progress is being made in terms of understanding contextual factors, time, and process issues revolving around change. While Pettigrew et al. (2001) contend that more frameworks are needed that simultaneously attend to all these dimensions, more efforts are being conducted to view change as a process rather than an event. Change theories have enhanced our understanding of different ways of thinking about change. In addition, empirical work has advanced our understanding of factors impacting change efforts. Research has also examined the effectiveness of various strategies for change, including structural and technological change (Drazin, Glynn & Kazanjian, 2004; Pugh, Hickson, & Hinings, 1969; Thompson, 1967), socio-technical change (Shani & Elliott, 1989; Trist & Bamforth, 1951), and cultural change (Cameron & Quinn, 1999; Schein, 2009).

We focus on three key advances that have occurred in the last 10 years that we believe have provide significant insights into the assessment, design, and delivery of planned change efforts, regardless of the particular organizational strategy: the readiness for change; change capacity; and organizational learning. We review the literature in each area and provide our analysis of key advances as well as future research needs.

Readiness for Change

Readiness for change is recognized as one of the most important factors influencing employees' support for a change endeavor (Armenakis, Harris, & Feild, 1999; Armenakis, Harris, & Mossholder, 1993). Readiness for change refers to the "cognitive precursors to the behaviors of either resistance to, or support for, a change effort" (Armenakis et al., 1993, pp. 681–682). In general, it refers to the extent to which employees believe that change is necessary, feasible, and desirable, in that the change is needed to improve current conditions, is possible to happen within the current context, and is likely to lead to positive outcomes for themselves and the larger organization (Armenakis et al., 1993; Eby, Adams, Russell, & Gaby, 2000; Holt, Armenakis, Feild, & Harris, 2007; Miller, Johnson, & Grau, 1994). In many ways, readiness for change captures Lewin's (1947) concept of "unfreezing" in that it recognizes that before significant change can occur, individuals must first accept that the status quo is untenable and that a new reality must be created. As a psychological phenomenon, readiness for change primes employees to either support or resist a change pursuit (Armenakis et al., 1993). In fact, when organizations fail to create within their employees the necessary levels of readiness for change, they are more likely to encounter significant resistance when launching a change effort and the endeavor is more likely to fail (Schein, 1987, 1999). Overall, this suggests that change agents and organizational leaders interested in pursuing change should assess current levels of readiness and pursue strategies that promote readiness for change before implementing a change effort (Holt et al., 2007).

A growing body of research has provided strong evidence for the importance of readiness for change. Researchers have demonstrated that higher levels of readiness for change are predictive of engagement in redesign efforts (Cunningham et al., 2002), use of new technologies (Jones, Jimmieson, & Griffiths, 2005), and satisfaction with change initiatives (Jones et al., 2005).

While the concept of readiness has been around for over 50 years (e.g., Jacobson, 1957), researchers in the past decade have just begun to unpack this construct. In particular, the past decade has shown significant advancements in two areas within the field of readiness for change: (a) conceptualization and measurement; and (b) the identification of antecedent and intervening conditions. These empirical advancements are important steps toward helping leaders, researchers, and change agents understand how to identify and create readiness for change (Cummings & Worley, 2005).

CONCEPTUALIZATION AND MEASUREMENT ADVANCEMENTS

While there appears to be strong agreement that readiness is a critical component within the overall change process, there is less agreement around its conceptualization and measurement. This lack of agreement highlights the different conceptual approaches that have been taken in the past. Below, we review and compare three divergent approaches to readiness to change that appear within the literature: a manifest approach, a developmental approach, and a conceptual domain approach.

Organizational researchers who ascribe to the manifest approach to readiness frame this construct as a general belief in the possibility of and intention to change. The aim in this approach is to directly measure the extent of this belief within an employee or organizational system. For example, Eby et al. (2000) defined readiness as the extent to which individuals viewed their organization as ready to take on a large-scale change effort. They assumed that employees would vary in this perception, since employees' perceptions of organizational life are developed through their unique personal history with and position/role within the organization (Wheatley, 1992). Thus, some employees may perceive their organization as having a high readiness for change; others may perceive a lower level of readiness. To assess this range of readiness, Eby and her colleagues (2000) used items that measured individuals' perceptions of their colleagues' general attitudes about change (e.g., employees here are resistant to change; employees here act as agents of change).

Jones et al. (2005) adopted a similar approach to assessing readiness to change. They defined readiness for change as the extent to which change is possible and the targeted change is viewed as desirable. Their measurement scale assessed the extent to which employees within a government agency viewed themselves as open or resistant to change and if they were positive about the specific changes. Overall, they found that levels of readiness influenced employees' perceptions of and satisfaction with the change effort and their use of the new technology.

While the manifest approach provides a direct and relatively simple approach to measuring the belief in the possibility of change, there is some concern that this approach minimizes the conceptual complexity present within the readiness construct (Holt et al., 2007; Jones et al., 2005). The other two approaches to readiness—the development and concept-domain approach—address this concern.

Some organizational researchers have adopted a developmental model to readiness for change, building upon Prochaska's work. Prochaska and colleagues found that individuals proceed through a series of readiness stages when pursuing significant change, such as quitting smoking (Prochaska, Norcross, & DiClemente, 1994; Prochaska, Redding, & Evers, 1997). By assessing an individual's stage of readiness before and throughout a change effort, practitioners are better positioned to tailor intervention efforts and to promote an individual's progression through the readiness phases. Overall, Prochaska's model proposes five readiness stages: pre-contemplative (the need for change is not acknowledged); contemplative (individuals consider but do not initiate change); preparatory (individuals are planning to change); action (behavioral change is happening); and maintenance (individuals are trying to sustain change).

Cunningham et al. (2002) applied Prochaska's model to their longitudinal assessment of readiness for change within a large health care setting. Readiness for change was assessed in a scale designed to measure the five readiness stages. Overall, Cunningham et al. (2002) found that employees who were more ready to change (and thus further along in Prochaska's readiness stages) prior to the introduction of the change effort participated in more reengineering activities during the year-long change effort.

Researchers who ascribe to the content domain approach to readiness view it as a multidimensional latent construct (e.g., Holt, Armenakis, Harris, & Feild, 2006). For example, Holt and colleagues (2007), based upon their extensive review of the literature, developed a conceptual framework and a corresponding measurement instrument that defined readiness as a "comprehensive attitude that is influenced simultaneously by the *content* (i.e., what is being changed), the *process* (i.e., how the change is being implemented), the *context* (i.e., circumstances under which the change is occurring), and the *individuals* (i.e., characteristics of those being asked to change) involved. Furthermore, readiness collectively reflects the extent to which an individual or individuals are cognitively and emotionally inclined to accept, embrace, and adopt a particular plan to purposefully alter the status quo" (p. 235). What is important to note about this framework is its recognition that readiness for change is both content and context specific; in other words, an organizational setting may be ready for one change effort and yet highly resistant to another. This approach can be contrasted with that adopted by some of the process researchers identified above, who viewed readiness as more of a general attitude about change, rather than as a specific belief related to a particular change effort.

Another important distinction between these approaches to readiness for change concerns the boundaries around the readiness construct. Researchers who use a content-domain approach to readiness tend to adopt a more comprehensive approach and include within the readiness construct elements that process/developmental researchers are more apt to define as antecedents to readiness to change. For example, several process researchers have defined leadership support for change and self-efficacy to implement change as important antecedents to readiness for change (e.g., Eby et al., 2000; Jones et al., 2005) and have demonstrated that these factors are related to employees' beliefs about their organization's ability to implement change.

Meanwhile, content-domain researchers have incorporated these elements within their definitions and measurements of readiness for change (Holt et al., 2006; Armenakis et al., 1999). For example, Holt et al. (2002) developed an integrated conceptual framework and corresponding measurement instrument for readiness that included five factors:

- Organizational valence: change would benefit the organization
- Personal valence: change would be personally beneficial
- Management support: organizational leaders are committed to the change
- Discrepancy: change is necessary
- Self-efficacy: change is feasible and employees can implement the new behaviors required by the change effort.

Armenakis and his colleagues (1999) also developed a framework and corresponding measurement instrument designed to assess what they labeled "organization change recipients belief scale." While this scale was designed to assess employees' beliefs about the change process throughout all phases of a change effort, including readiness, adoption, and institutionalization, it targets all of the components highlighted in Holt and colleagues' (2002) framework, with the addition of a scale that targets the appropriateness of the change, or the extent to which the proposed change will address the need. Tested on different organizational sectors, including private and public organizations, both Holt's and Armenakis's measurement instruments demonstrated strong psychometric properties and produced support for their proposed multidimensional view of readiness.

Together, these conceptual frameworks and their corresponding measurement instruments provide strong support for the view that readiness for change is a multifaceted construct that requires attention to employees' beliefs about discrepancy, appropriateness, efficacy, leader support, and valence, and that these beliefs play an important role in promoting employee buy-in and support of a change effort. While future research in other organizational settings is needed to more fully examine the generalizability of the proposed conceptual frameworks, the instruments provided significant advancements in the measurement of readiness for change. Prior to the work of Holt and Armenakis, several other readiness assessment instruments had been developed (e.g., Cunningham et al., 2002; Jones et al., 2005; Weeks, Roberts, Chonko, & Jones, 2004), though most lacked the conceptual robustness and/or the psychometric properties needed for a valid, comprehensive assessment of readiness (see Holt et al., 2006, for a more detailed discussion and assessment of 32 readiness instruments).

CONCEPTUAL CONTRIBUTIONS FROM THE COMMUNITY CHANGE FIELD

Another conceptual approach to readiness for change, which has important implications for the organizational sciences, has emerged in the community change literature. Edwards, Jumper-Thurman, Plested, Oetting, and Swanson (2000) have created a Community Readiness to Change framework that integrates the developmental and conceptual-domain approaches described above. Drawing on Prochasks's model of individual readiness for change, their model recognizes that communities, and even different stakeholder groups and organizations within a community, are at different stages of readiness and that these readiness stages (and the variability across a community) have significant implications for the success of a community change effort, such as a health promotion or prevention initiative. Thus, in their readiness assessment efforts, they categorize communities—and even groups of stakeholders and community organizations—into different stages of readiness and use this information to identify the interventions needed to build the necessary levels of readiness before a change effort is launched. This readiness assessment includes consideration of several dimensions found in Holt and Armenakis's frameworks including: (a) *discrepancy*, particularly the recognition that a problem exists; (b) *efficacy* to address the problem, including current capacities such as knowledge and skills, and historical approaches to and success with change; and (c) *formal and informal leader support* for the change. Interestingly, this framework also includes what organizational researchers refer to as "reshaping capabilities" (e.g., Turner & Crawford, 1998), or characteristics that help entities manage change

effectively: (a) development capabilities—the availability of resources to support the change; and (b) engagement capabilities—the involvement of residents in decision making. Numerous researchers across a variety of disciplines have applied the Community Readiness for Change framework to their prevention and social change work within communities, and have found that a community's level of readiness is predictive of a community's effectiveness at implementing a variety of social programs (Engstrom, Jason, Townsend, Pokorny, & Curie, 2002; Jason, Pokorny, Kunz, & Adams, 2004) and creating comprehensive community change (Foster-Fishman et al., 2006).

While community readiness research varies from organizational readiness research in its level of analysis and scale and scope of the targeted change, the conceptual model adopted by community researchers provides an integrative approach that we feel could be fruitful for organizational change researchers. For example, community readiness researchers pay particular attention to the community's capacity to implement the targeted change, highlighting the extent to which the targeted community has the knowledge, skills sets, and relational structures needed to pursue and support the new behaviors required by the change effort. While most readiness models within the organizational sciences highlight the "feasibility of change," which is often measured by the perceived self-efficacy of employees to implement the change, community researchers move beyond the subjective assessment of individual or team efficacy ("I could do this" or "we can do this") to the presence of the actual skills, knowledge, and relational sets needed to successfully implement a new change. While attention to efficacy is important, since individuals are more inclined to pursue a change if they feel they are likely to succeed at it (Bandura, 1986), this assessment can miss the identification of the specific capacities needed to ensure a successful change endeavor. Thus, one potential area for future readiness research within the organizational sciences includes the consideration of the full array of capacities needed to support the targeted change endeavor.

Another potential contribution from the community change area involves the conceptualization of readiness for change as a dynamic construct that should be continually assessed and promoted throughout the duration of a change endeavor. Within the organizational change field, readiness for change is typically viewed as an initial step in the overall change process. However, some research within the community change field suggests that readiness for change can promote the sustainability of change efforts because it helps to create a context capable of change, and thus should be a continued target of intervention efforts throughout a change effort. For example, Jason and his colleagues (Jason et al., 2004) found that communities that had made the largest changes in community readiness to enforce youth access to tobacco laws during the three-year intervention were the ones most likely to continue enforcement activities into the follow-up period.

IDENTIFYING ANTECEDENTS TO READINESS FOR CHANGE

Significant research has emerged around the identification of the antecedents to readiness to change, promoting better understanding of the individual and organizational conditions that prime one to be more or less ready to pursue change.

There is a growing body of evidence to suggest that employees are more open and ready for change when they have the capacities to support a change endeavor, including a problem-solving orientation (Cunningham et al., 2002), job knowledge and skills, effective job performance (Hanpachern, Morgan, & Griego, 1998), and higher levels of organizational commitment (Madsen, Miller, & John, 2005). High job satisfaction has also been linked to readiness for change (McNabb & Sepic, 1995). More mixed results have emerged around the linkage of demographic variables and readiness for change. Some researchers have found that job position and length of employment are related to readiness levels (e.g., Hanpachern, 1997) while age, gender, and marital status have been unassociated with this construct (Cunningham et al., 2002; Hanpachern, 1997; Weber & Weber, 2001).

Active jobs that provide employees with more decision-making latitude and control over complex tasks appear to promote readiness for change. For example, Cunningham et al. (2002) found that active jobs were one of the strongest predictors of readiness for organizational change within a sample of health care employees. In addition, positive relationships with coworkers appear to foster beliefs in the possibility for change. For example, employees who have stronger and more positive interpersonal relationships with their coworkers (Hanpachern, 1997; Madsen, et al., 2005; McNabb & Sepic, 1995) or who trust their peers (Eby et al., 2000) have higher levels of readiness for change.

Several researchers have demonstrated that employees are more ready for change (and thus less resistant) when they work within a setting that has a supportive, flexible work culture. Eby et al. (2000) found that employees reported more readiness to change when they worked within units that had flexible policies and procedures. Jones et al. (2005) found higher levels of readiness within employees who described their units as having strong human relations values; readiness levels, in turn, were related to the use of the new technology on the job. Similarly, employees have reported lower levels of resistance to change when their organization has a supportive and participative culture (Burnes & James, 1995).

The extent to which organizations openly share information with their employees about change efforts also influences readiness for change. For example, Miller et al. (1994) and colleagues found employees within a national insurance company were more ready for change when they had received high levels of information about the impending change.

Finally, organizations that have the capacity to promote change, or what Turner and Crawford (1998) refer to as reshaping capabilities, are better positioned to promote readiness for change because employees perceive that their organization has the resources, the support, and the operations in place to make change happen. For example, Jones and his colleagues (2005) found that employees who rated their government agency unit as high in reshaping capabilities were also more likely to report more readiness for change.

FUTURE DIRECTIONS IN READINESS FOR CHANGE

Readiness for change has grown increasingly important as a construct for research and intervention. With the widespread recognition that organizational change can happen only with the active support of employees, and that a critical precursor to this support is readiness to change, researchers and change agents have worked to better understand how to define, assess, and promote employee readiness for change. Recent contributions made by Holt, Armenakis, and their colleagues have provided conceptually robust definitions and frameworks for this construct, as well as validated assessment tools. Future research needs to examine the utility of these measures in other organizational contexts and to more fully link readiness to a range of change outcomes. In addition, more research is needed around the antecedents of readiness for change, linking the more complex definitions with the findings that individual, job, social, and organizational conditions influence readiness for change.

Another issue that future researchers could explore concerns the potential multileveled character of readiness for change. To date, researchers have confined this construct to the individual level of analysis. However, readiness for change is likely to have important characteristics and implications at the unit and organizational level as well. For example, many change endeavors are multileveled, directly or indirectly targeting shifts in employee behaviors, unit activities, and overall organizational performance indices. The extent to which these different levels are ready to accept, support, and pursue these new behaviors has important implications for the overall success of this effort. However, to date, the readiness for change construct has limited its conceptualization and measurement to the individual level of analysis. Future researchers could develop conceptual and measurement models that consider readiness for change as a multileveled construct.

Finally, while important developments have been made around the conceptualization and measurement of readiness to change, there is still much to be learned about how to promote readiness within employees. With more precise measurement instruments now available, researchers and practitioners may be better positioned to identify the specific components of readiness that need to be fostered and to assess their development over time. Longitudinal research is also needed to test the effectiveness of readiness interventions on the different readiness components of discrepancy, efficacy, appropriateness, valence, and support.

Change Capability

Beer and Nohria (2000) discussed how OD has struggled around whether the focus should be on meeting humane values of freedom and collaboration or on the economic–oriented, bottom-line focus. They note that a third "way" is to view OD as an inherently capacity-building process (or intervention). Traditionally, research in OD has stressed that increased involvement and participation of people can energize performance, produce better solutions to problems, and greatly enhance acceptance of decisions. In a transformation process, a number of positive outcomes can arise from involving employees in resolving organizational issues and problems. These include increased trust and confidence between supervisors and employees,

increased communication and information flow, more effective decision making, increased self-control, enhanced problem solving, and higher performance and quality goals (see Lawler, 1992). This capacity-building function of empowerment has a relatively long history now in OD (Belasco, 1990).

More recent efforts have focused on expanding this idea of building capacity through collaborative efforts and aligning systems. For example, Trickett (2009) notes in his review of community psychology that capacity building is a critical component in the success of change efforts. Capacity building in community settings has typically been defined as efforts to increase resources available for problem solving and community improvement. He cites research on building capacity within organizational groups and building capacity at the community level. For example, Foster-Fishman, Cantillon, Pierce, and Van Egeren (2007) focused on building community capacity for change by focusing on the structures and processes in place to help mobilize community residents for change in their neighborhoods. They considered capacity as the knowledge, skills, relationships, leadership, and resources present to support a specific change initiative. In a study of 460 residents in seven neighborhoods, resident perceptions of neighborhood readiness (collective efficacy) and capacity for change (social ties, leadership) were strongly related to resident involvement in individual and collective action in the neighborhood. More broadly, Foster-Fishman, Berkowitz, Lounsbury, Jacobson, and Allen (2001) reviewed 80 articles, chapters, and practice guides to develop an integrative framework on the core processes and competencies needed to build collaborative capacity within an interorganizational alliance. The framework described four levels of collaborative capacity—member capacity, relational capacity, organizational capacity, and programmatic capacity (the capacity to design and implement impactful programs).

Another lens for examining capacity building is the utilization of evidence-based knowledge to improve organizational functioning and impact. This orientation focuses on the capacity of an organization to recognize the value of new knowledge/best practices, assimilate it, and use new knowledge to enhance innovation and improvement (Cohen & Levinthal, 1990).

This capability to value, assimilate, and use new knowledge has been called the absorptive capacity of an organization or organizational subunit. Lane, Koka, and Pathak (2006) note that absorptive capacity has become one of the most popular constructs within the field of organizational sciences, including strategic management, organizational economics, and technology management. We see much value in applying this concept of absorptive capacity to link the focus on evidence-based management and organizational change.

Cohen and Levinthal (1990) argue that absorptive capacity is critical to an organization's innovative capabilities. Absorptive capacity emerges in settings that include the operational, relational, and learning systems to promote the exploration and application of new knowledge (Koza & Lewin, 1998; Lane et al., 2006). Research within the organizational sciences provides evidence that the strength of absorptive capacity affects an organization's ability to adopt and implement new ideas and practices (Szulanski, 1996; Zahra & George, 2002). This construct has potential for great utility within the OD field, as theorists have long highlighted the importance of learning within organizational settings as well as the need for mechanisms and processes that promote the integration of new evidence-based ideas and knowledge (e.g., Lasker & Weiss, 2003).

The value dimension focuses on the capacity (skills and motivation) to identify and acquire externally generated knowledge that may be critical to an organization's effectiveness. Settings vary considerably in their desire and ability to access external research information (or diffuse internal best practices; Honig & Coburn, 2008), with factors such as resources (time, dedicated personnel), information availability (access to journals, professional associations, and perceived importance of external information) influencing the likelihood of a search.

Assimilation refers to the organization's process that allows it to analyze, process, interpret, and ultimately understand, the research evidence. Spillane, Reiser, & Reimer (2002) noted that this "sense making" is a critical step in the process of deciding to use new knowledge and is necessarily a highly social endeavor, often involving numerous meetings and informal conversations (Hannaway, 1989; Spillane, 2002). In fact, when organizational settings create participatory processes in which members can openly explore and assess external or internal best practice evidence, organization members are more likely to develop shared understandings about the evidence, promoting broader support for the new knowledge and implementation decisions (e.g., Hannaway, 1989). Overall, the assimilation process can require a transformation in the way that the organization sees itself and its efforts, particularly when the research evidence significantly challenges existing understandings and perspectives (Zahra & George, 2002).

Use or exploitation emphasizes the capacity to apply new knowledge or research evidence within the organization setting. In this way, the organization leverages existing competencies or creates new ones to transform new knowledge into day-to-day operations. Researchers have found that organizations are more likely to adopt and implement new knowledge when it only requires the use of existing capacities or it represents something that organizational members believe they could implement well (e.g., Hannaway, 1989; Honig, 2003; Spillane, 2000).

Szulanski (1996) examined absorptive capacity as a predictor of effective transfer of best practices within an organization. The results across multiple organizations showed that low levels of absorptive capacity in some parts or across most of the organization led to difficulties in imitating best practices throughout the organization. In addition, while they did not explicitly use the construct of absorptive capacity to explain their findings, several educational researchers have found that school districts are more likely to use best practice evidence to guide their decisions when they have the capacity to acquire and make sense of this evidence (e.g., Honig, 2003; Honig & Coburn, 2008; Spillane, 1998; Spillane et al., 2002).

THE ANTECEDENTS OF ABSORPTIVE CAPACITY

Absorptive capacity is recognized as a dynamic capability that can be affected by a number of factors that promote the building of capabilities (Lane et al., 2006; Zahra & George, 2002). As noted by Lane et al. (2006), the key is examining how these different factors affect knowledge transfer, sharing, and integration. These antecedent factors are described below.

In many ways, an organization's capacity to identify, assimilate, and apply external knowledge is a function of the "sociological" interactions and collaborative processes that the organizational members develop over time (Dyer & Singh, 1998). In fact, research has shown that when knowledge flows across network members, individuals and organizations are more likely to decide to adopt the new idea (Frank, Krause, & Penuel, 2009; Frank, Zhao, & Borman, 2004; Penuel, Riel, Krause, & Frank, 2009). Of particular importance is the extent to which the social network within an organization fosters the development of shared meaning and understanding. Such knowledge integration helps organizations to adopt external information more successfully (Henderson, 1994). In addition, such knowledge integration is particularly critical where stakeholders often have access to unique sets of information given their specific role or position within the organization or community. When individual knowledge sets are relatively unshared across setting members, decision-making effectiveness is greatly affected by the ability of the setting to foster knowledge sharing and integration (e.g., Feighery & Rogers, 1990; Wischnowski & McCollum, 1995; Wittenbaum & Bowman, 2005).

Drawing from social network theory, it is clear that the level of absorptive capacity is impacted by the extent and character of social ties within the coalition. Social ties, particularly the degree of trust, can promote or hinder the sharing of information, and thus impact the amount of research evidence that flows into the system (Spillane & Thompson, 1997). Deeper, trusting social ties can also promote or hinder the adoption and use of new ideas and practices through their normative social influence (Bryk & Schneider, 2002; Frank et al., 2004); when individuals trust each other, they are more inclined to support a viewpoint held by their peers (Rogers, 2003), facilitating the development of shared understanding and meaning across coalition members. When social ties are weak and mostly distrustful, coalition members will be less inclined to act on collective information, and thus the link between absorptive capacity and research use will be weakened (Macy, 1991).

Another key factor involved in the development of absorptive capacity is the creation of internal information and decision-making routines that guide how information should be discussed and decisions made (e.g., see Winder, 2000). As noted by Strong, Davenport and Prusak (2008), many organizations make substantial investments in knowledge and learning functions only to not realize an optimal level of return due to poor governance structures around learning and knowledge creation and dissemination. Along a similar line, several studies have found that one of the most reported barriers to implementing research evidence within the field is the lack of sufficient time to think and talk about the idea (e.g., Humphris, Littlejohns, Victor, O'Halloran, & Peacock, 2000; Retsas, 2000).

Researchers have documented that organizations require routines that are designed to organize discussion and decision-making processes in a productive manner (e.g., Goodman, Wandersman, Chinman, Imm, & Morrissey, 1996; Roussos & Fawcett, 2000; Wandersman, Goodman, & Butterfoss, 1997). Effective internal knowledge management routines include having formalized processes and procedures in place that allocate agenda time for the consideration of research information (Foster-Fishman et al., 2001) and that provide guidance on the material that should be considered when assessing research information when making decisions. For example, Davenport, Eccles, and Prusak (1992) found that learning benefits are more likely to accrue when there are clear boundaries for how decisions are made and how to utilize resources to take advantage of new knowledge. Strong et al. (2008) highlight the need to specify decision points around identifying the desired outcomes and budgeting for the new approach. In addition, reporting guidelines must be established and standards must be defined for determining the value of the new approach and the processes for getting to the desired outcomes and evaluating success. Overall, the extent to which organizations create opportunities for and routines around the discussion and assessment of research evidence and best practices will significantly influence the level of absorptive capacity (Honig & Coburn, 2008).

THE MODERATING ROLE OF INNOVATION CHARACTERISTICS

The research on absorptive capacity has also focused on how the characteristics of the new knowledge may help or hinder the actual use of information (e.g., Todorova & Durisin, 2007). Research within the diffusion of innovation field strongly supports this premise; how individuals perceive a new innovation has been found to be significantly related to adoption and implementation rates across a wide variety of innovations and technologies, including public health campaigns (Goldman, 1994), information systems (Agarwal & Prasad, 1997; Moore & Benbasat, 1991), e-learning systems (Liao, Lu, & Yi, 2007), software applications (Van Slyke, Lou, & Day, 2002) and use of the world-wide web (Agarwal & Prasad, 1997). In fact, how settings evaluate the idea can significantly determine if their understanding of the idea (absorptive capacity) actually leads to adoption and use (Rogers, 2003).

Diffusion of innovation scholars have typically emphasized three characteristics of innovations and have found that these characteristics predict both the intention and the actual use of innovations (Moore & Benbasat, 1991; Rogers, 2003). First, the compatibility of the innovation with the existing knowledge and practices within an organization—the degree of fit—can significantly impact adoption and use (Lane & Lubatkin, 1998). For example, Todorova and Durisin (2007) highlighted that the degree of fit between new knowledge and member cognitive structures can have important implications for the success or failure of adopting a best practice. They stressed that there are two types of change that can occur in a setting with new research knowledge. When a new idea fits the existing cognitive schemas well—either because it naturally fits or can be easily modified to fit—it can be easily incorporated into the existing cognitive structure, representing a fairly straightforward adoption and use process. A more transformative (and hence more difficult) process will need to occur when the new idea does not easily fit into existing schemata and the idea cannot be easily shifted to make this fit. In this case, the cognitive structures of organizational members must be transformed in order for adoption and use of the new idea to occur. A logical conclusion from this conceptual framework is that resistance to a new idea might be stronger in the face of a need for transformative change. Research, though, is needed to explore this process in cases where adoption is not so straightforward.

Second, the ease of use of the new knowledge/best practice (e.g., the number of interdependent technologies, routines, and resources linked to the new knowledge/best practice) can also be an important moderating factor. As knowledge becomes more complex, organizations need to absorb more areas of knowledge content as well as understand the linkages between different content areas (Garud & Nayyar, 1994). This complexity may tax the system beyond its comfort zone and thus lead to non-adoption (Rogers, 2003).

Third, the relative advantage of the new knowledge/best practice must also be considered. Systems are more likely to decide to use a new idea when it appears to be better than existing practices and programs (Moore & Benbasat, 1991; Rogers, 2003). In fact, innovation researchers have found relative advantage to be one of the best predictors of the rate of adoption within a targeted system (Rogers, 2003). This construct fit wells within the context of settings where resources are often tight and funders expect outcomes; thus any new idea or program needs to have the promise for improving organizational conditions.

Organizational Learning

Various private- and public-sector organizations have acknowledged the importance of learning and knowledge creation as a key method for improving productivity and for delivering effective services (Senge, 1990). In order to thrive, organizations need to learn and adapt at an increasingly rapid rate (Rousseau, 1997). In this section, we provide a historical perspective as to the growth in our understanding of organizational learning and change, highlighting key conceptual and methodological advances. The section concludes with a discussion of advances in our understanding of how to build a learning culture within an organization.

HISTORICAL PERSPECTIVE

The pioneering efforts regarding the concept of organizational learning as an adaptive process toward greater organizational effectiveness have been discussed since at least the 1960s (e.g., Argyris & Schon, 1978; Cangelosi & Dill, 1965; Hedberg, 1981; March & Olsen, 1975; Michael, 1973; Starbuck & Hedberg, 1977). This literature grew out of contingency perspectives to organizational theory, which specified that organizational structures (e.g., mechanistic and organic) and processes must match environmental conditions (stable, unstable). A major premise of this contingency perspective is that the environment surrounding organizations is becoming more complex, where the rate of change is increasing, and where the scarcity of information about the changes could lead to organizational failure if organizations retain their mechanistic structures and rigid organizational processes. Not surprisingly, early efforts to understand learning focused on the reactive and proactive processes by which knowledge is used to improve the fit between an organization and its changing external environment (e.g., Starbuck, 1976).

By the 1980s, there was expanded conceptual work on understanding the individual learner within an organizational system, the transmission of knowledge across people and systems within an organization, and the sensing and adoption of new policies, practices, and technologies to better match an organization and its changing environment. The "state of the art" at this time was captured by a conference at Carnegie Mellon in 1989, with papers published in a special 1991 issue of *Organization Science* and a compilation of published articles and chapters in a book by Cohen & Sproull (1996).

This emerging literature focused on learning from an open systems perspective (Katz & Kahn, 1978). From this open systems perspective, learning within an organization was viewed not as a mechanism for self-stabilization but as a critical mechanism for questioning, reorienting, and changing an organization to met changing realities (Hedberg, 1981; March, 1991). This led to bringing systems thinking into the core of the organizational learning discussion, including issues of knowledge acquisition, information distribution, information interpretation, organizational memory issues, and feedback loops (Huber, 1991; Weick, 1991). This cognitive-based perspective (attention processes, mental maps, sense making, informational overload) was in contrast to the focus of learning at that time on behaviorism-based stimulus-response models (Hedberg, 1981; Huber, 1991).

Learning was also conceptualized as a social rather than a solitary phenomenon (Simon, 1991). Thus, organizational learning was seen as not simply the sum of individual-level learning (Hedberg, 1981). Rather, organizations were seen as having customs, worldviews, and cognitive systems, as well as norms and values, that impact learning processes within an organization and the transmission of these systems to newcomers. Learning was also seen as part of an ongoing organizational system of norms, strategies, and assumptions that governs activities and that impacts the sensing and transmitting of information (Argyris & Schon, 1978). Thus, existing systems within organizations can lead to where the "whole" (in terms of learning) is less than the sum of its parts (March & Olsen, 1975).

The literature also highlighted the multiple modes or type of learning that can occur in organizations. For example, Huber (1991) talked about subprocesses of congenital learning (the impact of founders on subsequent learning processes), experiential learning, vicarious learning, and grafting (acquiring new members with different knowledge bases from those currently in the organization). Hedberg (1981) noted three modes: adjustment learning, turnover learning, and turnaround learning. Adjustment learning—similar to Argyris's (1985) single loop learning as well as Bartunek and Moch's (1987) first order change—is the adjustments of rules or procedures that do not require major changes in the organization. These changes are relatively easy and are often routinized over time by organizations. Turnover learning—similar to Argyris's (1985) double loop learning and Bartunek and Moch's (1987) second order change—consists of substantial changes that are made by revising the current "theory of action" in the organization. This calls for more transformative changes in underlying values and assumptions. The third mode, or turnaround learning, occurs when significant changes are needed that require the unlearning or discarding of obsolete or misleading knowledge, leading to replacement of behaviors of the past with new behavior patterns that deal more effectively with the performance needs of the organization, given changing realties and new opportunities. Finally, March (1991) noted that organizational learning processes can be focused on exploration (searching for opportunities, taking risks, discovering) and exploitation (refining what is already being done well, making choices from current practices, becoming more efficient). March (1991) posited that a key to adaptability is the ability of an organization to balance these two processes so that short-term gains are not made to the detriment of long-term survival and growth.

The concept of a learning organization captured much attention with practitioners due to Senge's book *The Fifth Discipline* (1990). His work focused on the factors that can lead to the building of a learning organization where "people continually expand their capacity to create the results they truly desire, where new and expansive patterns of thinking are nurtured, where collective aspiration is set free, and where people are continually learning how to learn together" (p. 3). Senge (1990) presented the five disciplines of a learning organization: systems thinking; personal mastery; mental models (implicit assumptions and worldviews); building a shared vision; and team learning. He saw systems thinking as the key discipline that fused the other disciplines into a coherent body of theory and practice. While not focused on measurement as much as the mind shift needed in organizations, Senge (1990) does discuss system archetypes and modeling the non-linear relationships among organizational processes, rather than conducting what he calls "piecemeal" research that fragments our understanding of the complex phenomenon that we are hoping to better understand.

The emphasis in the practice literature on organizational learning has been on ways to create learning cultures. With learning cultures, teamwork, collaboration, creativity, and knowledge processes have a collective meaning and value (Confessore & Kops, 1998). Underlying these ideas is the fundamental notion that a learning culture strives to continuously change the organization's capacity for doing something new (Goldstein & Ford, 2002; Tannenbaum, 1997). Zollo and Winter (2002) described the modification of existing routines as an organization's dynamic capability to integrate, build, and reconfigure internal competencies and operations to address changing environments. They provided a cyclical evolutionary view of organizational knowledge that includes scanning for new information, evaluating the legitimacy of the information, sharing the information across the organization, and enacting and routinizing a new set of policies, procedures, and actions.

From this perspective, although data are crucial to becoming a learning organization, they remain useless until turned into knowledge. In order for data to be turned into shared knowledge, organizational members need to interpret and then agree on the meaning of the data. Researchers have noted that tacit individual information or data are more likely to be transformed into shared organizational knowledge when organizational members engage in discovery processes in which they, together, challenge existing assumptions, explore patterns and inconsistencies within the data, and co-generate new meaning (e.g., Argyris & Schon, 1996; Swan & Scarbrough, 2001). Some argue that the best forum for creating such discovery is through the intentional development of learning communities, or communities of practice, where peers, such as coworkers, spend time together examining their current realities and relevant data to improve their practice (Wenger, 1999; Wenger, McDermoot, & Snyder, 2002). Recent advances suggest that settings are more likely to acquire and assimilate information/research evidence to guide their behavior when they have developed a strong learning culture in which individuals are working together across organizational boundaries to solve problems and to create innovative solutions (Senge, 2006). Overall, a learning culture supports the gathering of data, the sharing of knowledge, and the taking of collective action to improve system functioning (Cuther-Gershenfeld & Ford, 2005).

CONCEPTUAL ADVANCES

Given momentum from these pioneering efforts, the 1990s and beyond have focused on conceptual advances, as well as some empirical studies of the antecedents and outcomes of organizational learning. One conceptual advance focuses on the process of organizational learning and understanding how learning crosses organizational levels. A second conceptual advance focuses on the facets of organizational learning in order to develop an integrative framework of factors needed to facilitate learning. Both approaches attempt to understand how learning, which is an individual-level phenomenon, becomes something more than individual insight

and innovation. There have also been attempts to better understand types of learning (vicarious learning and grafting), barriers to learning, and organizational unlearning processes.

Crossan, Lane, and White (1999) defined organizational learning as the principal means of achieving the strategic renewal of an organization. They acknowledge as a foundational premise the work by March (1991) that organizational learning involves the tension between exploration or the assimilation and utilization of existing knowledge and the exploration or the creation of new knowledge to develop strategic initiatives. They acknowledge that organizational learning is a multilevel phenomenon across individuals, groups, and the organization. The framework also describes the underlying processes that cut across these multiple levels—intuiting, interpreting, integrating, and institutionalizing. Intuiting (recognizing) and interpreting (sense making) are viewed as mainly individual-level phenomenon, while integrating (shared knowledge) mainly occurs at the group level. Institutionalization, or the process of embedding learning at the individual and group levels, involves systems, structures, policies, and procedures that change as a function of this learning. Kozlowski, Chao, and Jensen (2010) have expanded our understanding of the levels issues inherent in the framework by Crossan et al. (1999). They developed an explicit multilevel framework that is described as an "infrastructure" for organizational learning, which integrates multiple levels, formal processes, informal processes, and outcomes.

Crossan et al. (1999) also provide a dynamic, time-oriented perspective to the framework by incorporating the tensions of exploration and exploitation. They use the concept of feedback from the organizational level down to the group and then individual level to visualize how an organization exploits existing "learnings" that are embedded in systems, processes, and procedures by conveying these down levels (from institutionalizing to integrating to interpreting to intuiting) and attempting to create consensus around thinking and acting across people to exploit the organization's advantages around current knowledge. "Feed forward" is the process of exploration in which individuals recognize new knowledge and potential innovation and these insights are then conveyed up the learning levels (from intuiting to interpreting to integrating to institutionalizing). Subsequent conceptual work has linked strategic leadership theory (transformational and transactional leadership) with this organizational learning framework (Vera & Crossan,

2004) as well as power and politics (Lawrence, Mauws, Dyck, & Kleysen, 2005). For example, Vera and Crossan (2004) propose that transformational leaders can have a positive impact on "feed forward" learning that challenges institutional learning, while transactional leadership will have a positive impact on the feedback learning that reinforces institutional learning. Lawrence et al. (2005) add issues of influence and force to the "feed forward" process and issues of discipline and domination to the feedback processes to help understand the realities underlying organizational learning processes within organizations.

Schilling and Kluge (2009) used the framework of Crossan et al. (1999) and reviewed the literature on organizational learning in order to create a list of barriers that either prevent learning or impede its practicality in organizations at the intuiting, interpreting, integrating, and institutionalizing processes. They categorized barriers for each process across levels that they call *actional-personal, structural-organizational*, and *societal-environmental*, which are similar to the three levels presented by Crossan et al. (1999). For example, lack of motivation would be an actional-personal barrier to intuition, while lack of clear measurable goals would be a structural-organizational barrier to intuition. Based on the categorization of barriers across processes, they developed 15 research propositions. As an illustration, one proposition is that a restrictive management style and "blame" culture would be related to a lack of psychological safety, which, in turn, would lead to a suppression of novel insights and new ideas. The contribution of the paper is that it explicitly shows how barriers are interlinked and interrelated within and across the four learning processes, as well as providing at least a beginning framework for generating specific and concrete hypotheses.

Popper and Lipschitz (1998) proposed that there are two forms of organizational learning: learning in organizations, and learning by organizations. Learning in organizations is learning by individuals within the organizational context. Learning by organizations involves learning processes outside the individual in which organizations codify behaviors and values and then transmit these preferred behaviors and values through policies, procedures, routines, and strategies. They develop the concept of organizational learning mechanisms as a way of delineating the institutionalized arrangements that "allow organizations to systematically collect, analyze, store, disseminate, and use information relevant to the performance of the organization" (p. 170).

The two facets discussed are the structural facet and the cultural facet. The structural facet includes the roles, functions, and procedures that allow members to collect, analyze, store, disseminate, and use information relevant to performance and innovation. The cultural facet involves the norms and shared values that can lead to productive (or unproductive) learning, such as transparency, integrity, inquiry, and accountability system within an organization. Lipschitz, Popper, and Friedman (2002) expanded this notion of facets and added the psychological facet of learning (psychological safety and organizational commitment), the policy facet (commitment to learning, tolerance for error), and the contextual facet of learning (environmental uncertainty, error criticality). They note that each facet contributes toward increasing (or decreasing) the likelihood of organizational learning. Thus, the model provides practitioners with some ideas as to where the focus energies to build a learning organization.

EMPIRICAL STUDIES

Much of the excitement around organizational learning has been due to prescriptive writings on the value of learning to adapt to rapidly changing conditions. There have also been attempts to measure the impact of human resource practices (that overlap with organizational learning characteristics) on effectiveness. For example, Birdi et al. (2008) examine the impact of psychologically based practices of empowerment, extensive training, and teamwork on organizational productivity. In a study of productivity of 308 companies over a 22-year period, the researchers found evidence that performance enhancements from empowerment, extensive training, and teamwork were higher than for the incorporation of operational practices such as quality management and "just-in-time" systems.

There have also been some studies of the specific practice of employee suggestion systems and organizational performance. For example, Arthur and Aiman-Smith (2001) analyzed employee suggestions submitted over the first four years of a gain-sharing plan and found that changes in the content of the suggestions changed over time in a way consistent with organizational learning processes. In particular, they found that initial suggestions indicated "first order learning" (i.e., single loop—routine and incremental change suggestions such as work orders that maintains existing systems), while later suggestions (while lower in total volume) were more congruent with "second order learning" (i.e., double loop or exploration of alternative routines, goals, assumptions). In a follow-up study, Arthur and Huntley (2005) found that the cumulated number of implemented employee suggestions significantly contributed to lower production costs. They viewed this result as attributable to the cumulative effects of increasing knowledge at the employee level, with the gain-sharing program over time supporting an organizational learning perspective.

While these studies point to the importance of learning within organizations and learning by organizations, there have been few studies that have directly examined the effectiveness of large-scale systems change efforts to become a learning organization (see knowledge management literature reviewed by Argote in chapter 28 of this handbook for examples of studies on this topic). In addition, there are few empirical studies that directly test propositions and hypotheses drawn from the conceptual frameworks developed for understanding organizational learning. We do have some case studies that attempt to examine conceptual issues, such as the exploitation and exploration of learning (Dixon, Meyer, & Day, 2007), the structural and cultural facets of organizational learning (Popper & Lipschitz, 2000), the barriers to implementing a learning organization (Tan & Heracleous, 2001), and the development of interorganizational network learning (Knight, 2002; Knight & Pye, 2005). For example, Dixon et al. (2007) used a cross-case analysis of four oil companies to explain the relationship of exploration and exploitation learning on organizational absorptive capacity and operational efficiency and strategic flexibility. They described changes over a 10-year period and interpreted the changes in terms of these concepts. Similarly, Popper and Lipschitz (2000) presented a case study of an internal medicine ward and through semistructured interviews and observations, concluded that organizational learning mechanisms (structural and cultural changes) were critical to the success of the change effort.

RESEARCH NEEDS

Empirical research that directly tests propositions from conceptual frameworks on organizational learning is fairly sparse, given the attention that the concept has received. One key conceptual limitation is the levels of analysis framework. While there is an acknowledgment of levels issues and the need to study cross-level phenomena in the work cited here, there has been limited attempt to develop a truly multilevel model (Kozlowski et al., 2010). Rather, the current work on organizational

learning takes a similar perspective to that of Weick (1991), who concluded that individual learning and organizational learning are fundamentally different, non-interchangeable conceptualizations. As noted by Kozlowski and Klein (2000), though, organizational systems are in essence multilevel systems. They note that "individual level processes can be manifest as a group, subunit, and organizational phenomenon and need to be explicitly incorporated into meaningful models of organizational behavior" (p. 11). We will return to the levels issue in the next section.

As a whole, the conceptual and empirical work on organizational learning is weak when it comes to explicitly developing and testing hypotheses and in defining a testable future research agenda. In addition, the literature has fallen short of specifying innovative methodologies to study the complex and dynamic phenomenon of organizational learning. Rather than a detailed discussion of specific methodologies and practices that can lead to studying the concepts and interrelationships in the conceptual models, what we typically get are a laundry list of general research questions (e.g., Crossan et al., 1999, provide nine questions, such as "Do individuals have the motivation, capability, and opportunity to interpret their environment?"). Researchers are encouraged to pursue questions of organizational learning from a dynamic perspective without any discussion of how to incorporate time and causality issues into organizational learning research. Research propositions such as "transformational leadership will have a positive impact on feed forward learning" is suggested (Vera & Crossan, 2004) without any suggestions on how to study these types of hypotheses. Lawrence et al. (2005) note the need for more finely grained conceptualizations of organizational learning without any discussion of what this means for improving the measurement of organizational learning concepts. Operational issues for producing reliable and valid measures, such as psychological safety, are avoided, or the complexities underlying operational issues are minimized. Lipschitz et al. (2002) bemoan the lack of progress in the field to integrate diverse literatures and the lack of development of knowledge that is helpful to the practitioner. Our perspective is that attempts to develop conceptual frameworks without any similar sustained effort to detail methodological and measurement issues to test the conceptual frameworks are bound to fail. Broad statements such as the need for the accumulation of research across multiple, thick description case studies (Popper & Lipschitz,

1998) provide little direction of how such methods can help us to better understand organizational learning or help to validate the frameworks that have been proposed.

A step in the right direction is a recent chapter that takes a multilevel approach to understanding organizational learning (Kozlowski et al., 2010). The authors build a model that explicitly identifies structural and enabling processes across and within micro-, meso- and macro-levels. They also discuss composition and compilation emergence issues relevant to organizational learning.

Insights and Research Needs

OD is a broad and expanding domain of research and practice. The field has "matured" into a host of strategies, concepts, theories, and consulting models relevant to change and organizational effectiveness. While any review cannot hope to be comprehensive, we have attempted to provide a focus on what changes have occurred within the field in terms of research, what theories have been developed to help us understand change, and what concepts have emerged to drive research and practice.

In this section, we have provided a review of three key concepts that have emerged that provide different lenses for understanding the factors impacting the effectiveness of planned change efforts. Table 29.1 describes the insights gained from these three research domains as well as summarizing future research needs in each area. The research needs in all three areas focus on the importance of building multilevel models of readiness, change capacity, and learning, as well as developing

Table 29.1 Key Change Concepts: Insights and Future Research Needs

Key Concept/Theme	Insight	Future Research Needs
Readiness for Change	• While there is much agreement that readiness is a critical component of the change process, the three main approaches to studying readiness (manifest, developmental, and conceptual) conceptualize and measure readiness in different ways. • Readiness for change has primarily been conceptualized as an individual-level phenomenon that includes beliefs about the discrepancy, appropriateness, and valence of the proposed changes and their or their organization's efficacy to pursue these changes. • Readiness for change has an important time component. Readiness beliefs can change and dynamically influence employee behavior throughout the duration of a change project.	• Under what organizational and change conditions are a manifest, developmental, and conceptual approaches to readiness most effective? • What is a multilevel conceptual model for readiness that includes antecedents and components at the individual, team/unit, and organizational level? • What is a dynamic, time dependent model of readiness for change? What are the critical components of readiness at different stages of a change endeavor? • What are the most effective interventions for fostering readiness components at each levels of analysis?
Change Capability	• Research is emerging that examines the absorptive capability of organizational units to value, assimilate, and use new knowledge including best practices. • An organization's capacity to identify, assimilate and apply knowledge is a function of the collaborative processes that members develop over time. • Social network theory provides a conceptual framework for understanding factors impacting change capability. • Change capacity research has tended to focus on understanding unit-level factors and not to address levels issues.	• What are the mechanisms and processes that promote the integration of new evidence-based ideas and knowledge? • How are collaborative processes developed over time, and what factors facilitate or hinder the implementation of innovative strategies? • What does a multilevel model of change capability look like, and how do we understand how this collective phenomenon emerges under different constraints and patterns of interaction?

(Continued)

Table 29.1 (Continued)

Key Concept/Theme	Insight	Future Research Needs
Organizational Learning	• There are multiple frameworks and models of organizational learning that differ in their emphasis on understanding how learning is embedded within and across systems, processes, and procedures within an organization. • Evidence for the value of taking a learning perspective has typically been in the form of case analyses. • There are limited validated measures of organizational learning processes and learning outcomes	• What does a comprehensive multilevel model of organizational learning look like that is tied to testable research propositions? • How can we better incorporate time and causality issues into organizational learning research? • How can we better link our conceptual variables of interest at each level of analysis with reliable and valid measures of learning processes and outcomes?

more dynamic, time-dependent models of change. The issues of multilevel modeling and time require taking a more comprehensive, systems perspective to understanding organizational change. In addition, there is a need to better integrate the concepts of readiness, change capacity, and learning into frameworks for change. The next section describes the progress that is being made in incorporating a more comprehensive systems perspective to change from both a conceptual and methodological perspective. The systems perspective has the potential to facilitate the integration of these key concepts and frameworks of change.

Organizational Change as Systems Change

The field of OD has moved from its initial issues of "who are we" to a mature profession (Mirvis, 1988). A set of techniques, methods, frameworks, and theories has been developed to build on our understanding of change. There is a body of research studies that have examined "what works." For example, Porras and Robertson (1991) summarized 63 methodologically sound studies (strong research designs) from 1975 to 1987 to examine the impact of structural (e.g., task forces, quality circles), social (e.g., team building), and technology (e.g., job redesign) interventions on a variety of individual and organizational outcomes. They reported that many interventions had a least some positive impact on organizational and individual outcomes. We have had critiques of the traditional approaches to the science of prediction and testing, leading some researchers to contend that the search for single intervention cause-effect relationships

overlooked the systemic nature of organizations (Beer & Walton, 1987). Others have noted how the focus on precision and quantification was leading to results not rooted in the context experienced by the change participants and called for the combination of qualitative and quantitative approaches to studying change (e.g., Argyris, 1985; Woodman, 1989). These calls ushered in a constructivist perspective to looking at the whole, which cautioned against taking a reductionist (positivist) perspective to research. Since this movement, there has been much research in OD on understanding change from a sense-making perspective and studying change concepts such as organizational learning based on thick, case-oriented qualitative studies.

Regardless of the changes in the field of OD, or whether one approaches understanding change from a positivist or constructivist perspective, one constant has been the embrace of taking a systems approach to change (Katz & Kahn, 1978). As noted by Lewin (1951), you cannot understand a system until you try to change it! Yet, historically, systems thinking has been discussed more as a metaphor, rather than as a distinct research area of study. We think that the future of OD has great potential by reaffirming its focus on putting the "system" back into systems change (Foster-Fishman, Nowell, & Yang, 2007). Fortunately, there are various attempts from multiple disciplines that are attempting to put systems at the forefront in understanding change processes. This section provides a historical perspective to systems thinking, identifies recent conceptual approaches to taking seriously a systems perspective to understanding change, and describes some recent methodological advances. The chapter concludes with thoughts on the sustainability of change and better linking OD research and practice from a systems perspective.

Systems Thinking

Significant advances have been made in how to both conceptualize and model these system processes. Within the systems thinking arena, there are numerous theories upon which to draw (e.g., Checkland, 1991; Olson & Eoyang, 2001; Senge, 1990; Stacey, 2003), and these theories make very different assumptions about how systems operate. They also provide diverse perspectives on how to define, understand, assess, and change a system like an organization. In addition, the methods used by these different approaches illuminate very different dynamics and elements within the targeted system. For these reasons, it is important for organizational change scholars to understand the different orientations to systems work, in order to ensure that the frameworks selected fit the targeted organization and the selected research methods and intervention strategies.

To inform this selection process, we review several of the key theories that have emerged as valuable tools within the organizational change field. This summary is not meant to be exhaustive; others have done considerable work in describing these approaches (e.g., Midgley, 2000; Olson & Eoyang, 2001; Senge, 1990). Instead, the review below is designed to highlight the assumptions and primary approaches guiding each of these theories.

SYSTEM DYNAMICS THINKING

System dynamics was started by Jay Forrester (Forrester, 1969) and has grown into perhaps one of the most popular approaches to systems thinking. Overall, this approach seeks to explain system behavior by understanding the patterns of cause-and-effect relationships within a system (Forrester, 1969; Jackson, 2003; Senge, 1990). Importantly, system dynamics theorists emphasize that the typical linear cause-effect models used to explain organizational behavior are inadequate. Instead, they note the need to create more complex modeling tools for capturing the complexities and patterns within systems. Particular attention is given to understanding the root causes of problems, system interactions, the role of feedback, the implications of delays between actions and consequences, and how unexpected consequences from actions can create new conditions or problems. Often, system behavior is displayed through multiple, interconnected causal-feedback loops. One powerful tool that has emerged from this field is the use of simulation models to explain the complex interactions across organizational processes and how change emerges over time. Simulation modeling is particularly powerful in that it allows the researcher to alter organizational conditions or the strength of specific variables or relationships and to understand the implications of these different states on organizational performance and change. For example, to understand how organizations implement innovations, Repenning (2002) modeled the process of organizational members collectively deciding to adopt new innovations. Sastry (1997) examined the process of punctuated organizational change by modeling how organizational change is a function of organization-environment fit and the trial-reorientation processes. Lant and Mezias (1992) demonstrated in their simulation model that an organizational learning model of change can create patterns of punctuated equilibrium in organizations. Hirsch, Levine, and Miller (2007) used system dynamics modeling to explain the factors facilitating and constraining educational reform.

It is also important to note that system dynamics theorists pay close attention to variables or constructs when attempting to model organizational behavior (e.g., Anderson, 1999); this is in contrast to the foci of other systems approaches that are described below. In addition, system dynamics assumes that organizational behavior, while complex, can be explained—hence the emphasis on the creation of dynamic models that can predict outcomes and organizational behavior.

Overall, since Senge introduced these principles to a broader audience in 1990 and applied them to organizational change, system dynamics has become an increasingly popular tool within the field of organizational change. Of particular note are the system archetypes that Senge highlighted in his book and reiterated in his second edition (Senge, 2006). He used causal-loop diagrams and feedback processes to illustrate and explain several dilemmas and dynamics commonly found in organizations, which have significant implications for organizational performance; the *tragedy of the commons* is one such archetype. The tragedy of the commons describes a situation in which what may be right for each part of a system is not appropriate for the sustainability of the whole. The causal model specifies how individual activity for each individual can lead to net gains for each person, which is reinforcing, but the total activity levels meet resource limits that decrease the effectiveness of these individual actions over time for the organization as a whole. In addition, while Senge promoted the use of system dynamics modeling to understand organizational behavior, he also paid considerable attention to the role of mental models in shaping behavior and facilitating/hindering change, the importance of building a shared vision to transform systems, and the role of personal mastery in effective change implementation (Senge, 1990).

Overall, system dynamics helps change researchers to understand the "why" of organizational behavior and to identify levers for promoting the change that is needed. While many theorists and researchers in this area rely on complex mathematical models and simulations, it is also possible to use system dynamics ideas without the computer expertise that these methods require. For example, some change researchers have described how they combine soft systems discourse processes with system dynamics concepts to illustrate organizational and/or community system dynamics (e.g., Foster-Fishman et al., 2007). Such an approach is particularly valuable when one hopes to create an understanding within members of the setting regarding the interactions and feedback processes that maintain the status quo and provide resistance to change.

System dynamics theory is most useful for change agents who aim to explain organizational behavior by understanding the complex interactions and patterns that emerge, over time, across system characteristics (variables). Through this process, change agents are able to identify: the forces facilitating and constraining change, potential levers for change, feedback processes that could be added or modified, and causal delays that could be avoided to promote the desired behavior.

COMPLEX ADAPTIVE SYSTEMS

While system dynamics theorists assume that organizational behavior can be explained through complex cause-effect modeling of variables and constructs, complex adaptive systems theorists assume that system behavior is more unpredictable (Hodge & Coronado, 2007; Price, 2004). Therefore, the key to understanding organizational behavior and change is an assessment of the interactions across organizational agents, including individuals, groups, units, or divisions within an organizations (Anderson, 1999). In fact, complexity theory suggests that the most powerful levers for change within an organization occur in the relationships

and simple rules that emerge through the interactions across individuals and other agents (Olson & Eoyang, 2001). It is through these interactions that self-organization and new structures and patterns emerge.

Complexity theorists seek to understand these patterns by assessing three key factors that define interactions across agents: boundaries, differences, and exchanges. Boundaries or containers define which agents interact with each other, and for what reason, providing the space for patterns to emerge. Containers can include departments or units within an organization, geographic locations of offices, organizational functions, and even policies or procedures. Understanding which containers exist—and which ones emerge over time—provides insight into how organizations organize their work, who is included and excluded in these processes, and where opportunities for self-organization may emerge. The degree to which similarities and differences across agents exist within an organization or container is perhaps one of the most powerful forces shaping behavior and patterns within organizations. Similarities and differences emerge along numerous dimensions, including demographic characteristics (e.g., gender, race, educational background), power differentials, resource diversity, and role and expertise disparities (Ng, 2003; Stacey, 2003). By understanding the content, alignment, and extent of these differences, change agents can gain tremendous insight in how and why certain behaviors and patterns have emerged and the extent of organizational coherence and rigidity. Of particular importance are those differences that are hidden within a system, extreme differences that hinder progression, and extreme similarities that stifle creativity. Finally, exchanges concern the resources (e.g., ideas, information, money) that are shared across agents and how that process affects the sender and recipients in this resource exchange. Complexity theorists are particularly interested in the manner in which resources are exchanged, who is included/excluded in these exchanges, the transformations that happen through these exchanges, and how those transformations, in turn, affect other agents. Together, containers, differences/similarities, and exchanges determine how interactions proceed across agents within an organization and, thus, define the patterns that drive organizational performance and behavior.

Complex adaptive theory is particularly useful for understanding how adaptive an organization can become when faced with changing contextual conditions. This approach is also an effective framework when conditions are ripe for self-organization. For example, when organizations are facing particularly chaotic or dynamic institutional or environmental conditions, self-organization may be a highly adaptive response to this ambiguity. Change agents and scholars should attend to if and how self-organization occurs, the containers created during this self-organization, the differences highlighted and diminished during this process, and if and how exchanges alter to accommodate this self-organization

SOFT SYSTEMS METHODOLOGIES

Soft systems methodologies (SSM) emphasize yet another set of dynamics within organizational life: the diverse perspectives within the system and the parameters of the system's boundaries. Overall, SSM challenges the notion that organizational and other human activity systems operate and thus should be assessed from the same functional objectivity approach used in understanding systems in the natural/physical world. Instead, Checkland and Scholes (1990) argued that human activity systems and their functions (e.g., purpose, problem definitions, system boundaries) are actually subjective phenomena, subject to the eye of the beholder. Thus, according to soft systems methodologists, the system and its functions may be experienced and understood differently by different stakeholders (Flaspohler et al., 2003).

SSM focuses on understanding these different worldviews by engaging multiple stakeholders in developing "rich pictures" (Checkland & Scholes, 1990) of a problem situation and desired state. The purpose of this process is to find ways for system members to accommodate these different perspectives, not form a consensus. For these reasons, soft system methodologist pay significant attention to where the boundaries of the system are drawn, since these boundaries determine whose perspective is included or excluded in problem-identification and solution-generation processes. Embedded in these decisions are explicit and implicit value judgments that, if ignored, can promote the marginalization of ideas and critical stakeholders (Churchman, 1970). Overall, change agents—in partnership with setting members—should strive to draw the boundary broadly enough to incorporate critical perspectives and dimensions of the targeted problem, yet narrowly enough to allow for a feasible process and scale for intervention (Midgley, 2006).

For change agents, SSM emphasizes the importance of avoiding purely structural or mechanistic frameworks and highlights the value of attending to the social construction of organizational realities, including the consideration of social, cultural, and political elements. Overall, SSM puts emphasis on the subjective nature of systems analysis and requires change agents and scholars to gain insight into the different stakeholder interpretations of the problem situation. Thus, it highlights that problem understanding and problem resolution are dependent upon the diversity of perspectives selected (Checkland & Scholes, 1990). In addition, SSM recognizes that the process of changing an organization is iterative, with the process as important as reaching the end state (e.g., Midgley, 2000). In fact, for some soft system methodologists, the most important component of a change effort is the drawing or redrawing of the systems boundaries and the critique of how these different boundaries are drawn, since this establishes the range of perspectives that will be considered, highlights those that will be excluded, and illuminates what is valued within the system (Midgley, 2006). Finally, soft system methodologists attend to both the experienced realities of system life and the desired state, with the goal of identifying gaps between the two so that levers for needed change can be identified.

SSM is particularly useful when change scholars and practitioners are faced with an organization whose members have divergent understandings of the problem and these different understandings are impeding the design or selection of a solution or system-wide support of a change endeavor. SSM is also a powerful strategy when the targeted problem could be more fully understood if organizational outsiders, including customers, clients, and key interorganizational partners, are engaged in problem understanding and analysis. For example, Midgley illustrates how SSM can be a useful tool for promoting change within the human service delivery sector (Midgley, 2000) and for designing effective interventions for homeless youth (Midgley, 2006).

INTEGRATION OF DIVERSE SYSTEM THEORIES

While past approaches to systems thinking and change have treated the above systems theories as inherently incompatible, in that they make distinct and sometimes contrary assumptions about systems, more recent developments in the systems world have suggested that their integration can promote more robust understandings of complex systems because they illuminate different system components and dynamics (Best et al., 2003; Foster-Fishman, Nowell, & Yang, 2007; Midgley, 2006). Both Best and colleagues (Best et al., 2003) and Foster-Fishman, Nowell, and Yang (2007) have presented frameworks that integrate these different systemic approaches. For example, Foster-Fishman and her colleagues describe how, in their organizational and community change projects, they apply soft systems approaches to engage diverse stakeholders in defining a system's boundary, to reveal different system understandings, and to develop a shared vision of the ideal system state. They then apply system dynamics approaches to assess system functioning, identify system components that are compatible and incompatible with the ideal system state, and identify patterns, systemic levers, and feedback loops for leveraging desired change. In addition, critical systems thinking (Flood & Jackson, 1991) and systemic intervention (Midgley, 2006) are both organizational and systems change approaches that integrate the hard (system dynamics thinking) and soft (soft systems methodologies) systems approaches in a manner similar to that used by Foster-Fishman and her colleagues. Most of these integrative approaches emphasize similar elements found within the above theories, including boundary critique, root-cause analysis, and attention to feedback processes. In addition, these integrative frameworks emphasize the importance of methodological pluralism and the engagement of multiple stakeholders in understanding, assessing, and changing complex organizational systems.

Studying Systems and Organizational Change

Action research is perhaps one of the most popular methodologies used by organizational researchers to engage employees in the research and change process. It involves a cycle of inquiry in which researchers and members of the setting join together to address an underlying issue or problem within a setting by pursuing an ongoing process of problem identification, action, and analysis (Heron & Reason, 1997; Stringer, 2007). To date, action research has been used to address a variety of organizational and interorganizational concerns, including improving intergroup relationships (McDonagh & Coghlan, 2001), interorganizational operations (Adler, Shani, & Styhre, 2004; Coghlan & Brannick, 2001), expanding health care services (Bellman, 2003; Bellman, Bywood, & Dale, 2003; Stringer & Genat, 2004), guiding education and

curriculum changes (Meyers & Rust, 2003; Mills, 2003; Sagor, 2000), and enhancing local government (Bell, 2008). Recent efforts have sought to expand the action research paradigm of inclusion and engagement of people in the change effort in order to understand change processes more fully and to drive the sustainability of change efforts.

SYSTEMIC ACTION RESEARCH

While action research has primarily targeted issues at the group or organizational level, some researchers have started to link action research methodologies to systems thinking ideas, particularly soft system theory, in order to target systems-level change within organizations, service delivery systems, and even communities (Burns, 2007). For example, Foth (2006) recommended that multiple, simultaneous action research processes within an organization can be linked together to create a "networked community of practice" that would promote broader systemic change within an organizational setting. Burns (2007), expanding on Foth's (2006) approach, developed systemic action research, a methodology that involves two processes. First, multiple, "parallel and interacting" action research processes at different locations and levels within a system are pursued to understand the diverse perspectives and multiple problems that exist within a setting. This phase of the systemic action research endeavor serves to promote widespread support of organizational change, while illuminating the organizational system's patterns, networks, and potential leverage points for change. Second, as these projects unfold and insights about the organizational system emerge, the researcher works to promote a broader understanding of organizational life and eventually merges these diverse efforts into a unified, broader effort that aims to promote change to the larger organizational system.

While systemic action research is a recent development and thus few examples exist in the literature, there is some evidence to suggest that it can be a powerful tool for engaging multiple stakeholders within an organization, interorganization, and community setting in a systems change effort. For example, systemic action research has successfully facilitated transformative agriculture and rural community development (Luckett, Ngubane, & Memela, 2001; Packham & Sriskandarajah, 2005) and systemic change within a psychiatric care facility (Burns, 2007). Given the increased interest in systemic approaches to organizational change and the role of learning in promoting innovation and change, systemic action research appears to be a promising method for inquiry and action within organizational change scholarship and practice.

MULTILEVEL MODELING

Many frameworks that have been developed to understand change have implicitly taken a multilevels perspective. For example, Burke-Litwin's (1994) model of change specifies macro-level constructs, such as mission, strategy, leadership, culture, structure, and policies, and links them through work unit climate to individual-level factors of motivation, individual skill/abilities, and individual needs and values to impact individual and organizational level performance. Porras and Robertson (1991) provide a model in which work setting issues, such as the vision, organizing arrangements, social factors, technology, and physical setting, impact individual cognition and on-the-job behaviors, which in turn impact individual development and organizational performance.

Multilevel modeling provides a powerful tool for examining change processes that have not been fully realized. To build multilevel research models of change processes, several steps need to be taken. First, the systems being studied must be decomposed into subsystems or levels (e.g., individual, group, organization). Second, the conceptual variables of interest (e.g., readiness for change) must be identified at each level of analysis. Third, operational measures (readiness for change as an individual-level variable, a group-level variable, and an organization-level variable) must be specified. Research can then be conducted to examine within-level and cross-level relationships. A key level of analysis idea is that of isomorphism and composition models (Kozlowski & Klein, 2000). In developing a conceptual model from a levels perspective, one must consider the functional similarities that exist across levels and particularly across adjacent levels (e.g., see Von Bertalanffy, 1968). The development of a composition model focuses on the concept of isomorphism and the shared and convergent processes within and the generalizability of a construct (e.g., readiness) across levels. This means that to build a levels model, the constructs of interest (say, the four processes noted by Crossan et al.. 1999, of intuiting, interpreting, integrating, and institutionalizing) must be conceptualized as having similar meanings across levels (i.e., a construct at one level is, therefore, related to another form of the construct at a different level; e.g., see James, 1982; Klein & Kozlowski, 2000). A complete multilevel

perspective to a concept such as readiness must also identify a compilation model (Kozlowski et al., 2010). A compilation model attempts to identify how higher level constructs (team readiness) emerge through divergent processes at the individual level (different expectations for change), which come together to form meaningful patterns that can be studied at the higher level. A levels perspective also acknowledges that there is vertical differentiation of levels, as time processes at any given level differ from those at other levels. Higher levels are said to have slower time scales than lower levels do. For example, absorption rates for best practices may take less time to be adopted on the ground level within a particular group within an organization and may take longer to be adopted at the higher levels to diffuse across an organization.

Kozlowski and Klein (2000) emphasize that taking a levels approach presents both conceptual and statistical challenges. It also necessitates a research design that samples multiple teams/units as well as multiple organizations to study higher level effects. Then, the interpretation of the results must be at the appropriate level of analysis. In particular, one must distinguish between levels of analysis and levels of measurement. Level of analysis refers to the level at which data are assigned for hypothesis testing and statistical analysis. Level of measurement refers to the level at which data are assigned meaning (e.g., are we measuring readiness at the individual level and then aggregating to a team-level construct?). Failure to acknowledge this distinction can lead to misspecification errors, aggregation bias, and cross-level facilities (Kozlowski & Klein, 2000). Composition and compilation models of key change constructs, such as readiness, capability, and learning, are needed to better understand how change emerges from a bottom-up process as well as a top-down process.

There have been some notable recent efforts to incorporate multilevel research in the study of organizational change in the field of organizational psychology. Caldwell, Herold, and Fedor (2004) conceptualized a number of change process variables as group-level phenomena (consequence of change, extent of change, change fairness, and management support), as well as a variables at the individual level (demands-ability fit, value-congruence fit, individual job impact, and mastery orientation), to examine individual reactions to a change effort. They examined whether various scales were valid as group-level measures (computed agreement among group members reporting on the same change, as well as intraclass coefficients to examine the extent to which group membership accounted for member's ratings). They examined 34 groups across 21 change initiatives. Because the data were multilevel, they used hierarchical linear modeling to assess the relationship between the predictor–group level constructs and the individual-level dependent variables. Results indicated that organizational changes were associated with changes in person-job fit indices as well as person-organization fit indices. Herold, Fedor, and Caldwell (2007) used a similar multilevel design and analysis strategy to investigate the relationship of organizational context, individual differences, and attitudes toward the change efforts. They found that the turbulence of the change setting interacted with individual differences in change efficacy to affect individual-level change outcomes such as commitment to the organization.

The efforts to understand organizational change from a multilevel perspective can be enhanced by future research that takes a more ecological approach to change. A multilevel framework has the potential to emphasize the important of context in change. For example, in the community psychology field, Shinn and Toohey (2003) and others have adopted an ecological perspective that makes context a central organizational concept for both community-oriented research and intervention. They suggest that psychologists have traditionally committed "context minimization error" by ignoring the enduring influences of contexts on human behavior. Trickett (2009) recently reviewed the research on high-impact social contexts and their effects on individual well-being and organizational effectiveness. For example, Dupere and Perkins (2007) used multilevel models for nested data (residents within blocks) to study the impact of environmental stressors and resident participation on mental health outcomes. The nesting of individuals within different contexts of change is a fruitful line for future research.

Another direction for multilevel change research would be to go beyond additive models of group composition (in which group constructs are the summation of lower level variables) or referent shift models (in which lower level variables are conceptually distinct from the group level) to what has been termed *dispersion models* (Chan, 1998). With dispersion models, the meaning of a group level construct is determined by the variance of the lower level variables. For example, climate strength has been operationalized as a within-group variability in climate perceptions, with the assumption that the less within-group variability, the stronger the climate (Schneider, Salvaggio, & Subirats, 2002). Organizational change concepts such as readiness for change could be examined from this dispersion perspective. In this way, we could examine the strength of the readiness for change across different groups and across different time periods in the change process. One could then ask why some groups seem more ready for change than others early in a change process, as well as asking why there are within-group changes in readiness as a change process unfolds. Similarly, one could also examine issues such as capacity building and organizational learning in a similar way.

Table 29.2 presents some insights that have emerged from this recent emphasis on systems thinking and organizational change. The insights focus on making systems thinking more than a metaphor for change and instead making it a framework that drives theory, research, and change methodology. While we are encouraged by this transformation to taking systems seriously, Table 29.2 also highlights research needs to expand our understanding of systems thinking. Theseresearch directions include better understanding of the different systems thinking frameworks that are most effective for understanding and changing organizations, and the need to expand upon systemic action research methodologies. These efforts will help us be in a better position to enhance organizational effectiveness and sustainability.

Sustainability

While the process of change is never-ending and is clearly not linear (e.g., see Crossan, Cunha, Vera, & Cunha, 2005; Gersick, 1991; Wheatley, 1992), one lens for examining change is in terms of distinct phases or stages (Berger, Sikora, & Berger, 1993; French & Bell, 1999; Rothwell, McLean, & Sullivan, 1995; Serverance & Passino, 2002). From this perspective, by dividing up "time" by stages, one distributes the flow of the change process into meaningful segments to study. The typical model of change consists of stages such as exploration of change strategies, commitment to a vision for change, planning to meet the vision, implementation of the plan to achieve the change and monitoring/revising change goals in order to adapt to the change effort (Ford, 2007). The ultimate criterion of success of the change effort has typically been defined as sustainability.

Sustainability is focused on meeting the goals of a change effort through adaptation and continuous change. Sustainability focuses on change as more of

Table 29.2 Systems Thinking: Insights and Future Research Needs

Key Concept/Theme	Insight	Future Research Needs
Systems Thinking	• The influence of systems thinking has been primarily at the metaphorical level. • There are numerous systems thinking theories to draw upon, and each one makes different assumptions about how systems operate and how to define, understand, assess, and change a system. • New approaches are emerging that reaffirm a focus on understanding the systemic nature of change e.g., system dynamics help us more clearly examine interactions and patterns that emerge across system characteristics; complex adaptive approaches identify simple rules (boundaries, differences, and exchanges) that emerge through organizational interactions; soft system methodology emphasizes the subjective nature (what and who are valued) of systemic experience and analysis. • Systemic action research involves parallel and interacting action research processes at different locations and levels within a system. It illuminates the organizational system's patterns, networks, and leverage points for change, and has the capacity to merge the diverse efforts into a unified, broader organizational change effort.	• Under what conditions are the different systems thinking frameworks most effective for understanding and changing organizations? • What are the organizational factors that facilitate self-organization? What types of change efforts are most responsive to self-organization? • What are the characteristics of a powerful lever for change? How do these characteristics shift across organizational type, change conditions, and change pursuit? • What are the implications of system boundary contraction and expansion for the success of a change endeavor? • What are the conditions most conducive to systemic action research as an organizational change methodology? What are the limits of this approach?

a continual process than as having a specific endpoint. From this perspective, organizations are in a state of constant flux and never reach a state of equilibrium. Change is viewed not as a single event but as inherent in the process of sense making and organizing (Clegg, Kornberger, & Rhodes, 2005; Sackmann, Eggenhofer-Rehart, & Friesl, 2009). Thus, continual change models such as Brown and Eisenhardt (1997) are more consistent with this criterion. The focus on sustainability is also consistent with Bartunek and Moch's (1987) models of second and third order change—where schemata are changed to meet ongoing realities.

As noted by Buchanan et al. (2005), sustainability is multidimensional and contingent. Rather, as stated by Senge et al. (1999), we need to appreciate the "dance of change"—the interplay of growth processes and limiting processes—by examining links and changes over time in relationships among key constructs. Sustainability also relates to the notion of "built to change" in which organizational members' perceptions change as to the importance, frequency, ease, and desirability of change (Lawler & Worley, 2006). Non-permanent structures, systems, and processes are continually changing while

maintaining high levels of efficiency and effectiveness. Thus, sustainability can be thought of as an outcome of a change effort or as a process that leads to the institutionalization of new practices, patterns, and beliefs.

As organizational researchers and consultants, we rely on our existing knowledge bank of organizational perspectives and change theories and seek frameworks to help us better understand organizational change processes. We work to understand the local "theories in use" (Schon, 1983)—insiders' explanation for why problems exist or why change is needed. However, we have found that it is the combination of emic (the knowledge of insiders such as employees) and etic (the knowledge of outsiders such as consultants) knowledge (e.g., Morris, Leung, Ames, & Lickel, 1999) that creates the most powerful tool for understanding an organizational system, understanding change processes, and identifying appropriate change activities. This perspective is consistent with an early review on organizational development by Friedlander and Brown (1974). They stressed that a theory of planned change must be a theory of practice that emerges from data within context.

The knowledge of insiders revolves around what the vision for the change process is and how best to achieve the goals of the change effort. For example, police personnel interested in a change to community policing are in the best position to articulate the vision for the change around issues of building a stronger linkage with community members to improve the delivery of police services. They are also in the best position to identify the key drivers and barriers to success and to develop plans to meet the vision and monitor its progress (Ford, 2002). The knowledge of outsiders can help an organization like a police department consider less tangible or visible change issues such as readiness, capacity building, learning, and systems thinking. During the planning phase, for example, readiness can be enhanced so as to increase the likelihood that change will be sustainable. It is this linkage of the tangible (what to change) and the less tangible (how to change) that has the greatest potential for facilitating change efforts.

Concluding Comments

In this chapter, we have examined advances in our understanding of organizational change and development. We then focused on emerging key concepts and frameworks that can further advance our understanding of change and development. In examining these advances, we have integrated research in organizational psychology, community psychology, organizational behavior, and other related disciplines that have direct relevance to understanding the dynamics of change. This integration of fields shows that, as change researchers, we are engaged in similar challenges, examining similar concepts such as readiness, change capacity, learning, and systems thinking, and employing complementary methodologies across private, non-profit, and public sectors.

We are encouraged by the strength seen in the field based on advances in understanding that have come from fields relevant to theory development, rigorous empirical studies, and sound methodologies. While not providing a straightforward road map for enacting change in organizations, this review hopefully provides a window for looking into the issues critical to the success of change efforts. It is the process of making the less tangible and less straightforward aspects of change more visible and open to discussion for organizational researchers, leaders, and members that will ultimately impact organizational effectiveness and sustainability.

References

Adler, N. B., Shani, A. B., & Styhre, A. (Eds.). (2004). *Collaborative research in organizations: Foundations for learning, change, and theoretical development.* Thousand Oaks, CA: Sage.

Agarwal, R., & Prasad, J. (1997). The role of innovation characteristics and perceived voluntariness in the acceptance of information technologies. *Decision Sciences, 28*(3), 557–582.

Alderfer, C. P. (1977). Organizational development. *Annual Review of Psychology, 28,* 197–223.

Amis, J., Slack, T., & Hinings, C. R. (2004). The pace, sequence, and linearity of radical change. *Academy of Management Journal, 47,* 15–39.

Anderson, P. (1999). Complexity theory and organizational science. *Organizational Science, 10,* 216–232.

Argyris, C. (1957). *Personality and organizations.* New York: Harper.

Argyris, C. (1973). Personality and organization theory revisited. *Administrative Science Quarterly, 18,* 141–167.

Argyris, C. (1976). Single-loop and double-loop models in research on decision making. *Administrative Science Quarterly, 21,* 363–382.

Argyris, C. (1985). *Strategy, change and defensive routines.* Boston, MA: Pitman.

Argyris, C. (1990). *Overcoming organizational defenses.* Needham, MA: Allyn-Bacon.

Argyris, C., & Schon, D. A. (1974). *Theory in practice.* San Francisco: Jossy-Bass.

Argyris, C., & Schon, D. A. (1978). *Organizational learning.* Reading, MA: Addison-Wesley.

Argyris, C., & Schon, D. A. (1996). *Organizational learning II: Theory, method, and practice.* Reading, MA: Blackwell.

Armenakis, A. A., Harris, S. G., & Feild, H. S. (1999). Making change permanent: A model for institutionalizing change interventions. *Research in Organizational Change and Development, 12,* 97–128.

Armenakis, A. A., Harris, S. G., & Mossholder, K. W. (1993). Creating readiness for organizational change. *Human Relations, 46,* 685–703.

Arthur, J., & Aiman-Smith, L. (2001). Gainsharing and organizational learning: An analysis of employee suggestions over time. *Academy of Management Journal, 44,* 737–754.

Arthur, J. B., & Huntley, C. L. (2005). Ramping up the organizational learning curve: Assessing the impact of deliberate learning on plant performance under gainsharing. *Academy of Management Journal, 48,* 1159–1170.

Austin, J., & Bartunek, J. (2003). Theories and practices of organizational development. In W. C. Borman, D. R. Ilgen, & R. Klimoski (Eds.), *Handbook of psychology* (Vol. 12, pp. 309–332). New York: Wiley.

Bandura, A. (1986). *Social foundations of thought and action: A social cognitive theory.* Englewood Cliffs, NJ: Prentice-Hall.

Bartunek, J., & Moch, M. (1987). First, second, and third order change and organizational development interventions: A cognitive approach. *Journal of Applied Behavioral Science, 23,* 483–500.

Beer, M., & Nohria, N. (2000). Cracking the code of change. *Harvard Business Review* (May-June), 133–141.

Beer, M., & Walton, A. E. (1987). Organizational change and development. *Annual Review of Psychology, 38,* 339–367.

Belasco, J. A. (1990). *Teaching the elephant to dance.* New York: Crown Publishing.

Bell, S. (2008). Systemic approaches to managing across the gap in the public sector: Results of an action research programme. *Systemic Practice and Action Research, 21,* 227–240.

Bellman, L. (2003). *Nurse led change and development in clinical practice.* London: Whurr Publishers.

Bellman, L., Bywood, C., & Dale, S. (2003). Advancing working and learning through critical action research: Creativity and constraints. *Nurse Education in Practice, 3,* 186–194.

Berger, L. A., Sikora, M. J., & Berger, D. R. (1993). *The change management handbook.* New York: McGraw-Hill.

Best, A., Moor, B. A., Holmes, B., Clark, P. I., Bruce, T., Leischow, S., Buchholz, K., & Krajnak, J. (2003). Systems thinking: towards an integrative model. *American Journal of Health Behavior, 27*(3), 206–216.

Birdi, K., Clegg, C., Patterson, M., Robinson, A., Stride, C. B., Wall, T. D., & Wood, S. J. (2008). The impact of human resource and operational management practices on company productivity: A longitudinal study. *Personnel Psychology, 61*(3), 467–501.

Brown, S. L., & Eisenhardt, K. M. (1997). The art of continuous change: Linking complexity theory and time paced evolution in relentlessly shifting organizations. *Administrative Science Quarterly, 42,* 1–34.

Bryk, A. S., & Schneider, B. (2002). *Trust in schools: A core resource for improvement.* New York: Russell Sage Foundation.

Buchanan, D., Fitzgerald, L., Ketley, D., Gollop, R., Jones, J. L, Lamont, S. S., Neath, A., & Whitby, E. (2005). No going back: A review of the literature on sustaining organizational change. *International Review of Management Reviews, 7,* 189–205.

Bunker, B. B., & Alban, B. T. (1997). *Large group interventions: Engaging the whole system for rapid change.* San Francisco: Jossey-Bass.

Burke, W. W. (1994). *Organizational development* (2nd ed.). Reading, MA: Addison-Wesley.

Burnes, B. (2009). Reflections: Ethics and organizational change: Time for a return to Lewinian values. *Journal of Change Management, 9,* 359–381.

Burnes, B., & James, H. (1995). Culture, cognitive dissonance, and the management of change. *International Journal of Operations and Production Management, 15,* 14–33.

Burns, D. (2007). *Systemic action research.* University of Bristol: The Policy Press.

Caldwell, S. D., Herold, D. M., & Fedor, D. B. (2004). Toward and understanding of the relationship between organizational change, individual differences, and changes in person-environmental fit: A cross-level study. *Journal of Applied Psychology, 89,* 868–882.

Cameron, K. S., & Quinn, R. E. (1999). *Diagnosing and changing organizational culture.* Reading, MA: Addison Wesley.

Cangelosi, V., & Dill, W. (1965). Organizational learning: Observations towards a theory. *Administrative Science Quarterly, 10,* 175–203.

Chan, D. (1998). Functional relations among constructs in the same content domain at different levels of analysis: A typology of composition models. *Journal of Applied Psychology, 83,* 234–246.

Checkland, P. (1991). *Systems thinking, systems practice.* Chichester, UK: John Wiley.

Checkland, P., & Scholes, J. (1990). *Soft systems methodology in action.* New York: John Wiley.

Churchman, C. W. (1970). Operations research as a profession. *Management Science, 17,* 37–53.

Clegg, S. R., Kornberger, M., & Rhodes, C. (2005). Learning/becoming/organizing. *Organization, 12,* 147–167.

Coch, L., & French, J. R. P. (1948). Overcoming resistance to change. *Human Relations, 1,* 512–532.

Coghlan, D., & Brannick, T. (2001). *Doing research in your own organization.* London: Sage.

Cohen, W. M., & Levinthal, D. A. (1990). Absorptive capacity: A new perspective on learning and innovation. *Administrative Science Quarterly, 35,* 128–152.

Cohen, M. D., & Sproull, L. S. (1996). *Organizational learning.* Thousand Oaks, CA: Sage.

Confessore, S. J., & Kops, W. J. (1998). Self-directed learning and the learning organization: Examining the connection between the individual and the learning environment. *Human Resource Development Quarterly, 9,* 365–375.

Cooperrider, D. L., & Srivastva, S. (1987). Appreciative inquiry into organizational life. In R. W. Woodman & W. A. Pasmore (Eds.), *Research in organizational change and development* (Vol. 1, pp. 126–169). Greeenwich, CT: JAI Press.

Crossan, M., Cunha, V., Vera, D., & Cunha, M. (2005). Time and organizational improvisation. *Academy of Management Review, 30,* 129–145.

Crossan, M. M., Lane, H. W., & White, R. E. (1999). An organizational learning framework: From intuition to institution. *Academy of Management Review, 24,* 522–537.

Cummings, T. G., & Worley, C. G. (2005). *Organization development and change.* Madison, WI: Thomson South-Western.

Cunningham, C. E., Woodward, C. A., Shannon, H. S., MacIntosh, J., Lendrum, B., Rosenbloom, D., et al. (2002). Readiness for organizational change: A longitudinal study of workplace, psychological, and behavioral correlates. *Journal of Occupational and Organizational Psychology, 75,* 377–392.

Cuther-Gershenfeld, J., & Ford, J. K. (2005). *Valuable disconnects in organizational learning.* New York: Oxford University Press.

Cyert, R. M., & March, J. G. (1963). *A behavioral theory of the firm.* Englewood Cliffs, NJ: Prentice-Hall.

Davenport, T. H., Eccles, R. G., & Prusak, L. (1992). Learning and governance. *Sloan Management Review, 34,* 53–65.

Dixon, S. E. A., Meyer, K. E., & Day, M. (2007). Exploitation and exploration learning and the development of organizational capabilities: A cross-case analysis of the Russian oil industry. *Human Relations, 60*(10), 1493–1523.

Drazin, R., Glynn, M. A., & Kazanjian, R. K. (2004). Dynamics of structural change. In M. S. Poole & A. H. Van de Ven (Eds.), *Handbook of organizational change and innovation* (pp. 161–188). New York: Oxford University Press.

Dupere, V., & Perkins, D. D. (2007). Block types and mental health: An ecological study of local environmental stress and coping. *American Journal of Community Psychology, 35,* 563–581.

Dyer, J. H., & Singh, H. (1998). The relational view: Cooperative strategy and sources of interorganizational competitive advantage. *Academy of Management Review, 23,* 660–679.

Eby, L. T., Adams, D. M., Russell, J. E. A., & Gaby, S. H. (2000). Perceptions of organizational readiness for change: Factors related to employees' reactions to the implementation of team-based selling. *Human Relations, 53*(3), 419–442.

Edwards, R. W., Jumper-Thurman, P., Plested, B. A., Oetting, E. R., & Swanson, L. (2000). Community readiness: Research to practice. *Journal of Community Psychology, 28,* 291–307.

Engstrom, M., Jason, L. A., Townsend, S. M., Pokorny, S. B., & Curie, C. J. (2002). Community readiness for prevention:

Applying stage theory to multi-community interventions. *Journal of Prevention & Intervention in the Community, 24*, 29–46.

Faucheux, C., Amado, G., & Laurent, A. (1982). Organizational development and change. *Annual Review of Psychology, 33*, 343–370.

Feighery, E., & Rogers, T. (1990). *How-to guide on building and maintaining effective coalitions.* Palo Alto, CA: Stanford Center for Research in Disease Prevention, Health Promotion Resource Center.

Fiol, C. M., & Lyles, M. A. (1985). Organizational learning. *Academy of Management Review, 10*, 803–813.

Flaspohler, P., Wandersman, A., Keener, D., Maxwell, K. N., Ace, A., Andrews, A. B., & Holmes, B. (2003). Promoting program success and fulfilling accountability requirements in a statewide community-based initiative: Challenges, progress, and lessons learned. *Journal of Prevention and Intervention in the Community, 26*, 37–52.

Flood R. L., & Jackson, M. C. (1991). *Creative problem solving: Total systems intervention.* Chichester, UK: John Wiley.

Ford, J. K. (2002). Organizational change and development: Fundamental principles, core dilemmas and leadership challenges in the move to community policing. In M. Morash & J. K. Ford (Eds.), *The move to community policing: Making change happen* (pp. 126–154). Thousand Oaks, CA: Sage.

Ford, J. K. (2007). Building capability throughout a change effort. *American Journal of Community Psychology, 39*, 321–334.

Forrester, J. (1969). *Urban dynamics.* Cambridge, MA: The MIT Press.

Foster-Fishman, P.G., Berkowitz, S. L, Lounsbury, D. W., Jacobson, S., & Allen, N. A. (2001). Building collaborative capacity in community coalitions: A review and integrative framework. *American Journal of Community Psychology, 29*, 241–261.

Foster-Fishman, P. G., Cantillon, D., Pierce, S. J., & Van Egeren, L. A. (2007). Building an active citizenry: The role of neighborhood problems, readiness, and capacity for change. *American Journal of Community Psychology, 39*, 91–106.

Foster-Fishman, P. G., Fitzgerald, K., Brandell, C., Nowell, B., Chavis, D. M., & Van Egeren, L. (2006). Building a community of possibility: The role of small wins and community organizing. *American Journal of Community Psychology, 38*, 143–152.

Foster-Fishman, P. G., Nowell, B., & Yang, E. (2007). Putting the system back into systems change: A framework for understanding and changing organizational and community systems. *American Journal of Community Psychology, 39*, 191–196.

Foth, G. (2006). Network action research. *Action Research, 4*(2), 205–226.

Frank, K. A., Krause, A., & Penuel, W. R. (March, 2009). *Knowledge flow and organizational change.* Invited presentation. Chicago: University of Chicago, Sociology Department.

Frank, K. A., Zhao, Y., & Borman, K. (2004). Social capital and the diffusion of innovations within organizations: The case of computer technology. *Sociology of Education, 7*, 148–171.

French, W. L, & Bell, C. H. (1973). *Organizational development: Behavioral science interventions for organizational improvement.* Englewood Cliffs, NJ: Prentice-Hall.

French, W. L., & Bell, C. H. (1995). *Organizational development* (5th ed.). Upper Saddle River, NJ: Prentice-Hall.

French, W. L., & Bell, C. H. (1999). *Organizational development* (6th ed.). Upper Saddle River, NJ: Prentice-Hall.

Friedlander, F., & Brown, L. D. (1974). Organizational development. *Annual Review of Psychology, 23*, 313–341.

Garud, R., & Nayyar, P. R. (1994). Transformative capacity: Continual structuring by intertemporal technology transfer. *Strategic Management Journal, 15*, 365–385.

Gersick, C. J. G. (1991). Revolutionary change theories: A multilevel exploration of the punctuated equilibrium paradigm. *Academy of Management Review, 32*, 274–309.

Goldman, K. D. (1994). Perceptions of innovations as predictors of implementation levels: The diffusion of a nation wide health education campaign. *Health Education and Behavior, 21*, 433–445.

Goldstein, I. L., & Ford, J. K. (2002). *Training in organizations: Needs assessment, development, and evaluation* (4th ed.). Belmont, CA: Wadsworth.

Goodman, R. M., Wandersman, A., Chinman, M. J., Imm, P. S., & Morrissey, E. (1996). An ecological assessment of community coalitions: Approaches to measuring community based interventions for prevention and health promotion. American Journal of Community Psychology, 24, 33–61.

Guzzo, R. A., Jette, R. D., & Katzell, R. A. (1983). The effects of psychologically based intervention programs on worker productivity: A meta-analysis. *Personnel Psychology, 38*, 275–291.

Hannaway, J. (1989). *Managers managing: The workings of an administrative system.* New York: Oxford University Press.

Hanpachern, C. (1997). *The extension of the theory of margin: A framework for assessing readiness for change.* Unpublished Ph.D. dissertation. Denver: Colorado State University.

Hanpachern, C., Morgan, G. A., & Griego, O. V. (1998). An extension of the theory of margin: A framework for assessing readiness for change. *Human Resource Development Quarterly, 9*, 339–350.

Hedberg, B. (1981). How organizations learn and unlearn. In P. C. Nystrom & W. H. Starbuck (Eds.), *Handbook of organizational design* (Vol. 1, pp. 3–27). New York: Oxford University Press.

Henderson, R. (1994). The evolution of integrative capability: Innovation in cardiovascular drug discovery. *Industrial and Corporate Culture, 3*, 607–630.

Herold, D. M., Fedor, D. B., & Caldwell, S. D. (2007). Beyond change management: A multilevel investigation of contextual personal influences on employees' commitment to change. *Journal of Applied Psychology, 92*, 942–951.

Heron, J., & Reason, P. (1997). A participatory inquiry paradigm. *Qualitative Inquiry, 3*, 274–294.

Highhouse, S. (2002). A history of the T-group and its early applications in management development. *Group Dynamics: Theory, Research, and Practice, 6*, 277–290.

Hirsch, G. B., Levine, R., & Miller, R. L. (2007). Using system dynamics modeling to understand the impact of social change initiatives. *American Journal of Community Psychology, 39*, 239–253.

Hodge, B., & Coronado, G. (2007). Understanding change in organizations in a far from equilibrium world. *Emergence: Complexity & Organization, 9*, 3–15.

Holt, D. T., Armenakis, A. A., Feild, H. S., & Harris, S. G. (2007). Readiness for organizational change: The systematic development of a scale. *The Journal of Applied Behavioral Science, 43*(2), 232–255.

Holt, D. T., Armenakis, A. A., Harris, S. G., & Feild, H. S. (2006). Toward a comprehensive definition of readiness for change: A review of research and instrumentation. In

W. A. Pasmore & R. W. Woodman (Eds.), *Research in organizational change and development, 16,* 289–336. Oxford: Elsevier.

Honig, M. I. (2003). Building policy from the practice: District central office administrators' roles and capacity for implementing collaborative education policy. *Education Administration Quarterly, 39,* 292–338.

Honig, M. I., & Coburn, C. (2008). Evidence-based decision making in school district central offices: Toward a policy and research agenda. *Educational Policy, 22,* 578–608.

Huber, G. P. (1991). Organizational learning: Contributing processes and the literatures. *Organization Science, 2,* 88–115.

Humphris, D., Littlejohns, P., Victor, C., O'Halloran, P., & Peacock, J. (2000). Implementing evidence-based practice: Factors that influence the use of research evidence by occupational therapists. *The British Journal of Occupational Therapy, 63,* 516–522.

Huy, Q. (2001). Time, temporal capability, and planned change. *Academy of Management Review, 26,* 601–623.

Jackson, M. C. (2003). *Systems thinking: Creative holism for managers.* New York: Wiley.

Jacobs, R. W. (1994). *Real time strategic change: How to involve an entire organization in fast and far-reaching change.* San Francisco: Berrett-Koehler.

Jacobson, E. H. (April, 1957). *The effect of changing industrial methods and automation on personnel.* Paper presented at the Symposium on Preventive and Social Psychology, Washington, DC.

James, L.R. (1982). Organizational climate: A review of theory and research. *Psychological Bulletin, 81,* 1096–1112.

Jason, L. A., Pokorny, S. B., Kunz, C., & Adams, M. (2004). Maintenance of community change: Enforcing youth access to tobacco laws. *Journal of Drug Education, 34,* 105–119.

Jones, R. A., Jimmieson, N. L., & Griffiths, A. (2005). The impact of organizational culture and reshaping capabilities on change implementation success: The mediating role of readiness for change. *Journal of Management Studies, 42,* 361–386.

Kahn, R. L. (1974). Organizational development: Some problems and proposals. *Journal of Applied Behavioral Science, 10,* 485–502.

Katz, D., & Kahn, R. L. (1978). *The social psychology of organizations* (2nd ed.). New York: John Wiley.

Katzell, R. A., & Guzzo, R. A. (1983). Psychological approaches to productivity improvement. *American Psychologist, 38,* 468–472.

Klein, K. J., & Kozlowski, S.W. J. (2000). *Multilevel theory, research, and methods in organizations.* San Francisco: Jossey-Bass.

Knight, L. (2002). Network learning: Exploring learning by interorganizational networks. *Human Relations, 55,* 427–454.

Knight, L., & Pye, A. (2005). Network learning: An empirically derived model of learning by groups of organizations. *Human Relations, 58,* 369–392.

Koza, M. P., & Lewin, A. Y. (1998). The co-evolution of strategic alliances. *Organization Science, 9,* 255–264.

Kozlowski, S. W. J., Chao, G. T., & Jensen, J. M. (2010). Building an infrastructure for organizational learning: A multilevel approach. In S. W. J. Kozlowski & E. Salas (Eds.), *Learning, training, and development in organizations* (pp. 361–400). New York: Routledge Academic.

Kozlowski, S. W. J., & Klein, K. J. (2000). A multilevel approach to theory and research in organizations: Contextual, temporal, and emergent processes. In K. J. Klein & S. W. J. Kozlowski (Eds.), *Multilevel theory, research, and methods in organizations* (pp. 3–90). San Francisco: Jossey-Bass.

Lane, P. J., Koka, B. R., & Pathak, S. (2006). The reification of absorptive capacity: A critical review and rejuvination of the construct. *Academy of Management Review, 80,* 833–863.

Lane, P. J., & Lubatkin, M. (1998). Relative absorptive capacity and interorganizational learning. *Strategic Management Journal, 19,* 461–477.

Lant, T. K., & Mezias, S. J. (1992). An organizational learning model of convergence and reorientation. *Organization Science, 3,* 47–71.

Lasker, R. D., & Weiss, E. S. (2003). Broadening participation in community problem solving: A multidisciplinary model to support collaborative practice and research. *Journal of Urban Health: Bulletin of the New York Academy of Medicine, 80,* 14–60.

Lawler, E. E. (1992). *The ultimate advantage: Creating the high-involvement organization.* San Francisco: Jossey-Bass.

Lawler, E. E., & Worley, C. G. (2006) *Built to change: How to achieve sustained organizational effectiveness.* San Francisco: Jossey-Bass.

Lawrence, T. B., Mauws, M. K., Dyck, B., & Kleysen, R. F. (2005). The politics of organizational learning: Integrating power into the 4I framework. *Academy of Management Review, 30,* 180–191.

Lewin, K. (1947). Frontiers in group dynamics. *Human Relations, 1,* 5–41.

Lewin, K. (1951). *Field theory in social science.* New York: Harper and Row.

Liao, K., Lu, J., & Yi, Y. (2007). Research on humanized web-based learning model. International *Journal of Innovation and Learning, 4,* 186–196.

Likert, R. (1961). *New patterns in management.* New York: McGraw-Hill.

Likert, R. (1967). *The human organization: Its management and value.* New York: McGraw-Hill.

Lipschitz, R., Popper, M., & Friedman, V. J. (2002). A multifacet model of organizational learning. *Journal of Applied Behavioral Science, 38,* 78–98.

Luckett, S., Ngubane, S., & Memela, B. (2001). Designing a management system for rural community development organization using a systemic action research process. *Journal of Systemic Practice and Action Research, 14*(4), 517–542.

Macy, B. A., Farias, G. F., Rosa, J. F., & Moore, C. (2007). Built to change: High performance work systems and self directed work teams—A longitudinal quasi-experimental field study. *Research in Organizational Change and Development, 16,* 337–416.

Macy, B. A., & Izumi, H. (1993). Organizational change, design, and work innovation: A meta-analysis of 131 North American field studies, 1961–1991. In R. W. Woodman & W. A. Pasmore (Eds.), *Research in organizational change and development* (Vol. 7, pp. 35–313). Greenwich, CT: JAI Press.

Macy, M. W. (1991). Chains of cooperation: Threshold effects in collective action. *American Sociological Review, 56,* 730–747.

Madsen, S. R., Miller, D., & John, C. R., (2005). Readiness for organizational change: Do organizational commitment and social relationships in the workplace make a difference? *Human Resource Development Quarterly, 16,* 213–233.

Manning, M. R., & Binzagr, F. (1996). Methods, values, and assumptions underlying large group interventions intended to change whole systems. *International Journal of Organizational Analysis, 4,* 268–284.

March, J. G. (1991). Exploration and exploitation in organizational learning. *Organization Science, 2,* 58–70.

March, J. G., & Olsen, J. P. (1975). The uncertainty of the past: Organizational learning under ambiguity. *European Journal of Political Research, 3*(2), 147–171.

March, J. G., & Simon, H. A. (1958). *Organizations.* New York: Wiley.

McDonagh, J., & Coghlan, D. (2001). The art of technical inquiry in IT-enabled change. In P. Reason & H. Bradbury (Eds.), *Handbook of action research* (pp. 172–178). London: Sage.

McGregor, D. M. (1960). *The human side of enterprise.* New York: McGraw-Hill.

McNabb, D. E., & Sepic, F. T. (1995). Culture, climate, and total quality management: Measuring readiness for change. *Public Productivity and Management Review, 18,* 369–385.

Meyers, E., & Rust, F. O. (Eds.). (2003). *Taking action with teacher research.* Portsmouth, NH: Heinemann.

Michael, D. N. (1973). *On learning to plan and planning to learn.* San Francisco: Jossey-Bass.

Midgley, G. (2000). *Systemic intervention: Philosophy, methodology, and practice.* New York: Kluwer.

Midgley, G. (2006). Systems thinking for evaluation. In B. Williams & I. Imam (Eds.), *Systems concepts in evaluation* (pp. 11–34). Fairhaven, MA: American Evaluation Association.

Miller, V. D., Johnson, J. R., & Grau, J. (1994). Antecedents to willingness to participate in planned organizational change. *Journal of Applied Communications Research, 22,* 59–60.

Mills, G. (2003). *Action research: A guide for the teacher researcher* (2nd ed.). Upper Saddle River, NJ: Merrill/Prentice Hall.

Mirvis, P. (1988). Organizational development: An evolutionary perspective. *Research in Organizational Change and Development, 2,* 1–57.

Moore, G. C., & Benbasat, I. (1991). Development of an instrument to measure the perceptions of adopting an information technology innovation. *Information Systems Research, 2,* 192–222.

Morris M., Leung K., Ames D., & Lickel, B. (1999). Incorporating perspectives from inside and outside synergy between emic and etic research on culture and justice. *Academy of Management Review,* 24, 781–796.

Ng, D. (2003). The social structure of organizational change and performance. *Emergence, 5*(1), 99–119.

Olson, E. E., & Eoyang, G. H. (2001). *Facilitating organization change: Lessons from complexity science.* San Francisco: Jossey-Bass.

Packham, R., & Sriskandarajah, N. (2005) Systemic action research for postgraduate education in agricultures and rural development. *Systems Research and Behavioral Science, 22*(2), 119–130.

Penuel, W. R., Riel, M., Krause, A. E., & Frank, K. A. (2009). Analyzing teachers' professional interactions in a school as social capital: A social network approach. *Teachers College Record, 111*(1), 124–163.

Pettigrew, A. M., Woodman, A. W., & Cameron, K. S. (2001). Studying organizational change and development: Challenges for future research. *Academy of Management Journal, 44,* 697–713.

Popper, M., & Lipschitz, R. (1998). Organizational learning mechanisms. *Journal of Applied Behavioral Science, 34,* 161–179.

Popper, M., & Lipschitz, R. (2000). Organizational learning: Mechanisms, culture, and feasibility. *Management Learning, 31,* 181–196.

Porras, J. I., (1987). *Stream analysis: A powerful new way to diagnose and manage change.* Reading, MA: Addison Wesley.

Porras, J. I., & Robertson, P. (1991). Organization development: Theory, research, and practice. In M. D. Dunnette (Ed.), *Handbook of industrial and organizational psychology* (pp. 719–822). Chicago: Rand McNally.

Porras, J. I., & Silvers, R. C. (1991). Organizational development and transformation. *Annual Review of Psychology, 42,* 51–78.

Price, I. (2004). Complexity, complicatedness and complexity: A new science behind organizational interventions? *Emergence, 6,* 40–48.

Prochaska, J. O., Norcross, J. C., & DiClemente, C. C. (1994). *Changing for good.* New York: Morrow.

Prochaska, J. O., Redding, C. A., & Evers, K. (1997). The transtheoretical model of change. In K. Glanz, F. M. Lewis, & B. K. Rimer (Eds.), *Health behavior and health education: Theory, research, and practice* (pp. 60–84). San Francisco: Jossey-Bass.

Pugh, D. S., Hickson, D. J., & Hinings, C. R. (1969). An empirical taxonomy of structures of work organizations. *Administrative Science Quarterly, 14,* 115–126.

Repenning, N. P. (2002). A simulation-based approach to understanding the dynamics of innovation implementation. *Organization Science, 13,* 107–127.

Retsas, A. (2000). Barriers to using research evidence in nursing practice. *Journal of Advanced Nursing, 31,* 599–606.

Rogers, E. M. (2003). *Diffusion of innovations* (5th ed.). New York: Free Press.

Rothwell, W. J., McLean, G. N., & Sullivan, R. (1995). *Practicing organizational development: A guide for consultants.* San Fransisco: Jossey-Bass.

Rousseau, D. M. (1997). Organizational behavior in the new organizational era. *Annual Review of Psychology, 48,* 515–546.

Roussos, S. T., & Fawcett, S. B. (2000). A review of collaborative partnerships as a strategy for improving community health. *Annual Review of Public Health, 21,* 369–402.

Sackmann, S. A., Eggenhofer-Rehart, P. M., & Friesl, M. (2009). Sustainable change: Long-term efforts toward developing a learning organization. *Journal of Applied Behavioral Science, 45,* 521–549.

Sagor, R. (2000). *Guiding school improvement with action research.* Alexandria, VA: Association for Supervision and Curriculum Development.

Sastry, M. A. (1997). Problems and paradoxes in a model of punctuated organizational change. *Administrative Science Quarterly, 42,* 237–275.

Schein, E. H. (1987). *Process consultation: Lessons for managers and consultants.* Reading, MA: Addison-Wesley.

Schein, E. H. (1999). *Process consultation revisited: Building the helping relationship.* Reading, MA: Addison-Wesley.

Schein, E. H. (2009). *The corporate culture survival guide.* San Francisco: Jossey-Bass

Schilling, J., & Kluge, A. (2009). Barriers to organizational learning: An integration of theory and research. *International Journal of Management Reviews, 11*(3), 337–360.

Schneider, B., Salvaggio, A. N., & Subirats, M. (2002). Service climate: A new direction for climate research. *Journal of Applied Psychology, 87,* 220–229.

Schon, D. (1983) *The reflective practitioner.* New York: Basic Books.

Senge, P. M. (1990). *The fifth discipline.* New York: Doubleday/Currency.

Senge, P. M. (2006). *The fifth discipline* (2nd ed.). New York: Doubleday/Currency.

Senge, P. M., Kleiner, A., Roberts, C., Roth, G., Ross, R., & Smith, B. (1999). *The dance of change: The challenges to sustaining momentum in learning organizations.* New York: Doubleday/Currency.

Serverance, D., & Passino, J. (2002). *Making I/T work: An executive's guide to implementing information technology systems.* San Francisco: Jossey-Bass.

Shani, A. B., & Elliott, O. (1989). Sociotechnical system design in transition. In W. Sikes, A. Drexler, & J. Gant (Eds.), *The emerging practice of organizational development* (pp. 187–189). Alexandria, VA: NTL Institute and University Associates.

Shinn, M., & Toohey, S. M. (2003). Community contexts of human welfare. *Annual Review of Psychology, 54,* 427–259.

Simon, H. A. (1991). Bounded rationality and organizational learning. *Organization Science, 2,* 125–134.

Spillane, J. P. (1998). State policy and the non-monolithic nature of the local school district: Organizational and professional considerations. *American Educational Research Journal, 35,* 33–63.

Spillane, J. P. (2000). Cognition and policy implementation: District policy-makers and the reform of mathematics education. *Cognition and Instruction, 18,* 141–179.

Spillane, J. P. (2002). Local theories of teacher change: The pedagogy of district policies and programs. *Teachers College Record, 104,* 377–420.

Spillane, J. P., Reiser, B. J., & Reimer, T. (2002). Policy implementation and cognition: Reframing and refocusing implementation research. *Review of Educational Research, 72,* 387–431.

Spillane, J. P., & Thompson, C. L. (1997). Reconstructing concepts of local capacity: The local education agency's capacity for ambitious instructional reform. *Educational Evaluation and Policy Analysis, 19,* 185–203.

Stacey, R. D. (2003). *Complexity and group processes: A radically social understanding of individuals.* New York: Brumner-Routledge, Taylor & Francis.

Starbuck, W. H. (1976). Organizations and their environments. In M. D. Dunnette (Eds.), *Handbook of industrial and organizational psychology* (pp. 1069–1123). Chicago: Rand McNally.

Starbuck, W. H., & Hedberg, B. (1977). Saving an organization from a stagnating environment. In H. B. Thorelli (Ed.), *Strategy and structure = performance* (pp. 249–258). Bloomington: Indiana University Press.

Stringer, E. (2007). *Action research* (3rd ed.). Los Angeles: Sage.

Stringer, E., & Genat, W. J. (2004). *Action research in health.* Upper Saddle River, NJ: Pearson.

Strong, B., Davenport, T., & Prusak, L. (2008). Organizational governance of knowledge and learning. *Knowledge and Process Management, 15,* 150–157.

Swan, J., & Scarbrough, H. (2001), Knowledge management: Concepts and controversies. *Journal of Management Studies, 38,* 913–921.

Szulanski, G. (1996). Exploring internal stickiness: Impediments to the transfer of best practice within the firm. *Strategic Management Journal, 17,* 27–43.

Tan, T. K., & Heracleous, L. (2001). Teaching old dogs new tricks: Implementing organizational learning at a Asian national police force. *Journal of Applied Behavioral Science, 37,* 361–380.

Tannenbaum, S. I. (1997). Enhancing continuous learning: Diagnostic findings from multiple companies. *Human Resource Management, 36,* 437–452.

Thietart, R. A., & Forgues, B. (1995). Chaos theory and organizations. *Organization Science, 6,* 19–31.

Thompson, J. D. (1967). *Organizations in action.* New York: McGraw-Hill.

Todorova, G., & Durisin, B. (2007). Absorptive capacity: Valuing a reconceptualization. *Academy of Management Review, 32,* 774–786.

Trickett, E. J. (2009). Community psychology: Individuals and interventions in community context. *Annual Review of Psychology, 60,* 395–419.

Trist, E. L., & Bamforth, K.W. (1951). Some social and psychological consequences of the long-wall method of coal-getting. *Human Relations, 4,* 3–38.

Turner, D., & Crawford, M. (1998). *Change power: Capabilities that drive corporate renewal.* Warriewood, NSW: Business and Professional Publishing.

Tushman, M., & Romanelli, E. (1985) Organizational evolution: A metamorphosis model of convergence and reorientation. In L. L. Cummings & B. M. Staw (Eds.), *Research in organizational behavior* (Vol. 7, pp.171–222). Greenwich, CT: JAI Press.

Van de Ven, A. H., & Poole, M. S. (1995). Explaining development and change in organizations. *Academy of Management Review, 20,* 510–540.

Van Slyke, C., Lou, H., & Day, J. (2002). The impact of perceived innovation characteristics on intention to use groupware. *Information Resource Management Journal, 15,* 5–12.

Vera, D., & Crossan, M. (2004). Strategic leadership and organizational learning. *Academy of Management Review, 29,* 222–240.

Von Bertalanffy, L. (1968). *General systems theory.* New York: Braziller.

Wandersman, A., Goodman, R., & Butterfoss, F. (1997). Understanding coalitions and how they operate. In M. Minkler (Ed.), *Community organizing and community building for health* (pp. 261–284). New Brunswick, NJ: Rutgers University Press.

Weber, P. S., & Weber, J. E. (2001). Changes in employee perceptions during organizational change. *Leadership and Organization Development Journal, 22,* 291–300.

Weeks, W. A., Roberts, J., Chonko, L. B., & Jones, E. (2004). Organizational readiness for change, individual fear of change, and sales manager performance: An empirical investigation. *Journal of Personal Selling & Sales Management, 24,* 7–18.

Weick, K. (1991). The nontraditional quality of organizational learning. *Organization Science, 2,* 116–124.

Weick, K. E., & Quinn, R. E. (1999). Organizational change and development. *Annual Review of Psychology, 50,* 361–386.

Wenger, E. (1999). *Communities of practice: Learning, meaning and identity.* Cambridge: Cambridge University Press.

Wenger, E., McDermoot, R., & Snyder, W. (2002). *Cultivating communities of practice: A guide to managing knowledge.* Cambridge, MA: Harvard Business School Press.

Wheatley, M. J. (1992). *Leadership and the new science.* San Francisco: Berrett-Koehler.

Winder, C. (2000). Integrating OHS, environmental, and quality management standards. *Quality Assurance, 8,* 105–135.

Wischnowski, M. W., & McCollum, J. A. (1995). Managing conflict on local interagency coordinating councils. *Topics in Early Childhood Special Education, 15,* 281–295.

Wittenbaum, G. M., & Bowman, J. M. (2005). Member status and information exchange in decision-making groups. *Research on Managing Groups and Teams, 7,* 143–168.

Woodman, R. W. (1989). Organizational change and development: New arenas for inquiry and action. *Journal of Management, 15,* 205–228.

Worley, C. G., & Feyerherm, A. E. (2003). Reflections on the future of organizational development. *Journal of Applied Behavioral Science, 39,* 97–115.

Zahra, S. A., & George, G. (2002). Absorptive capacity: A review, reconceptualization, and extension. *Academy of Management Review, 27,* 185–203.

Zollo, M., & Winter, S. G. (2002). Deliberate learning and the evolution of dynamic capabilities. *Organization Science, 13,* 339–351.

Strategic Human Resource Management

Charles C. Snow *and* Scott A. Snell

Abstract

The essence of strategic human resource management (SHRM) is a systemic view of the management of a firm's human resources, as well as an orientation toward the future. The management of human resources must be linked to the organization's total management system, and human resource professionals must work to ensure that the organization anticipates its future human resource needs and is prepared to address them. Our chapter examines two perspectives on the strategic management of human resources. The first perspective is that of *systemic fit,* which characterizes much of the early SHRM research. This perspective focuses on planned human resource deployments and activities that achieve continuity over time, as well as consistency with other management decisions and actions. The other perspective, *strategic resources and capabilities,* characterizes much of the more recent SHRM research. This perspective focuses on the future and helps the organization to identify opportunities to use strategic human resource management to its competitive advantage. We review the empirical evidence related to both the systemic fit and strategic resources/capabilities perspectives, and we suggest future research directions for scholars in SHRM.

Key Words: Strategic HRM, strategic HR planning, strategic HR systems, SHRM

The construct *strategic human resource management* (SHRM) first appeared in the organization sciences literature in the early 1980s (Devanna, Fombrun, & Tichy, 1981; Tichy, Fombrun, & Devanna, 1982). At the time, the U.S. economy had been performing poorly for several years, and American firms were being criticized in the business press for their declining competitiveness compared to foreign firms, particularly Japanese firms. Indeed, the researchers who originated the SHRM construct quoted Akio Morita, then chairman of Sony Corporation, who said: "The trouble with a large segment of American management is attributable to two misguided attitudes: American managers are too worried about short-term profits and too little concerned about their workers" (*New York Times Magazine,* January 3, 1981). The researchers

went on to say that few American corporations had a strong, proactive human resource (HR) function, and they called for the development of organizational and managerial approaches that place a high priority on human resources while simultaneously serving the strategic goals of the organization. Over the past three decades, SHRM has evolved into a research field that focuses on the HR strategies and practices that firms use to "compete through people" and how those approaches affect firm performance (e.g., Delery & Doty, 1996).

Where does the theory of strategic human resource management stand today, and how should it develop in the future? This is the overall question that we address in this chapter. Our discussion covers the historical development of the core constructs and relationships that constitute SHRM theory, the empirical evidence on which the theory rests, current theoretical issues in this evolving research area, and our recommendations for further research. In the first section, we describe early SHRM theory, arguing that much of it revolves around what can be called a *systemic fit* perspective. In the second section, we discuss more recent SHRM theory, showing how it is evolving from a *strategic resources and capabilities* perspective. The third section contains our recommendations for further research, and the final section presents our conclusions.

Early SHRM Theory

SHRM theory began to develop in earnest soon after DeVanna et al. (1981) and Tichy et al. (1982) called for increased professionalism on the part of HR specialists, as well as their active participation in the firm's strategic decision-making processes.[1] For example, Miles and Snow (1984a) were invited by Canadian Pacific's corporate HR group to help it develop HR "packages" (selection, training, career planning, pay, benefits, etc.) that would be appropriate for each of the company's 80-plus business units. This internal study was launched by CP's board of directors in 1982 when they asked the corporate HR group a single question: Is the company's human resource management system suitable for the year 2000? This question caused unprecedented thinking and activity within the HR group. Not only were CP's HR professionals being asked to develop alternative—and distant—future scenarios, but they were also expected to think contingently about each of the company's businesses and to strategize with line executives about how to strengthen the connections among people, financial, and operating processes. Strategic thinking—that which is future-oriented, systemic, and proactive—began to be recommended for all corporate HR groups, especially those that were part of large multinational companies where strategic thinking was most obviously needed.

The adoption of strategic thinking resulted in a number of changes within many HR groups and their parent firms. One of those changes, part of a trend in the 1980s to increase the use of market forces inside firms (Halal, Geranmayeh, & Pourdehnad, 1993), was to convert the HR department from a support function to a business unit. For example, in the early 1990s, IBM transformed its corporate HR group into an independent business called Workforce Solutions, Inc. Within a year, Workforce Solutions was not only selling its HR services to IBM business units but to other firms as well. HR departments at AT&T and several other large companies also sold their HR services on the open market.

When an HR group becomes a business with profit and loss responsibility, it quickly discovers that it cannot be all things to all people—it needs to have a clearly defined business strategy of its own. This means offering particular HR services to targeted customer groups, developing the capabilities to deliver services to those internal and/or external customers, and applying HR methods such as planning, recruiting, and staffing to the HR function itself. In the early 1990s, for example, the HR group at the Wellcome Foundation (now GlaxoSmithKline) committed to becoming the best in the world at facilitating the formation and development of multinational R&D teams (Snow, Snell, Davison, & Hambrick, 1996). To carry out its commitment, the HR group had to define the capabilities that it wished to develop, hire more than 50 master's-level organization development specialists, and build a business model that would be regarded as valuable by the organizational units that purchased its team-building services. That model ultimately became an HR business strategy focused on team-based change and development.

Systemic Fit Perspective

Within a decade of the introduction of the SHRM concept, there were numerous examples of firms and their HR groups working together to successfully implement business strategies. Simultaneously, the theoretical framework that guided and evaluated those efforts was also developing. For example, the idea of external fit in HR referred to the alignment of HR practices with the strategic needs of the business. Noting that firms in various industries typically pursued certain types of competitive strategies (Miles & Snow, 1978; Porter, 1980), researchers began to use a contingency perspective in analyzing HR strategies (e.g., Wright, Smart, & McMahan, 1995). Much of the early work on HR strategies focused on matching HR practices with commonly used or "generic" business strategies (e.g., Olian & Rynes, 1984; Wright & Snell, 1991). Miles and Snow (1978), in particular, are notable in that they were the first to develop a typology of competitive strategies (prospector, defender, and analyzer) and then extend their model to include sets of HR practices that were appropriate under each strategic orientation (Miles & Snow, 1984a). Subsequently, other contingency variables, such as desired employee contributions, HR philosophy, and person-environment fit, were added to the contingency framework (Lepak, Marrone, & Takeuchi, 2004; Werbel & DeMarie, 2005). Lastly, the contingency and fit approaches were tested in a series of studies whose samples were newly formed organizations, thereby extending the relevance of SHRM theory beyond the large mature organizations in which it began (Andrews & Welbourne, 2000; Cyr, Johnson, & Welbourne, 2000; Welbourne & Andrews, 1996; Welbourne & Cyr, 1999).

The theoretical logic of external fit and contingency approaches to HR strategy is compelling. Different companies compete in different ways and, therefore, need to manage people in a manner that reinforces those strategic priorities. Innovation-oriented firms, for example, are likely to emphasize HR approaches that encourage and reward creative and experimental behavior. Cost- and efficiency-oriented firms, on the other hand, are likely to emphasize HR approaches that minimize errors and reinforce standard operating routines. Despite the intuitive appeal of the external fit concept, the empirical research of the time did not provide a great deal of support for it (Delery, 1998; Wright & Sherman, 1999). Nevertheless, the field of SHRM seems to have accepted the basic notion that variation in how firms interact with their environments should and does produce variation in HR strategies, policies, and practices.

In concert with the notion of external fit, the concept of internal fit in HR strategy emphasized the importance of coordination among various HR practices in order for them to be mutually reinforcing. Beer, Spector, Lawrence, Mills, and Walton (1985) were among the first to propose a systems approach to HR strategy that exemplifies the notion of internal fit, and they argued that general managers should be aware of how HR practices can help their firms to be more competitive. Schuler (1992) described the main components of an HR system that need to be organized into a workable model (philosophy, policies, programs, practices, and processes), and other researchers extended the scope of HR activities to international companies (Milliman, von Glinow, & Nathan, 1991; Schuler, Dowling, & DeCieri, 1993) and to members of the firm's value chain, including customers (Lengnick-Hall & Lengnick-Hall, 1999; Schuler & MacMillan, 1984). Arthur (1994), Dyer and Reeves (1995), Huselid (1995), MacDuffie (1995), and others used the concept of internal fit to show how "bundles" of HR practices are used in firms in much the same way that bundles of resources are assembled and applied by firms to compete in the marketplace (Penrose, 1959, 1995). Recently, Kepes and Delery (2007) further expanded the concept of internal fit by proposing four types based upon a multilevel conceptualization of HR systems. All of these studies reflected a trend at the time toward synergistic views of HR (Doty & Glick, 1994; Lado & Wilson, 1994), and they paralleled the "configuration" approaches found in the strategic management literature (Miller, 1986, 1996; Miller & Mintzberg, 1983).

Empirical Studies of HR Practices

During the first decade and a half of SHRM research, theorists identified a set of internally consistent bundles of HR practices that they variously refer to as *high involvement* (Lawler, 1986, 1992), *high commitment* (Arthur, 1994), or *high performance work systems* (Huselid, 1995; Lawler, Mohrman, & Ledford, 1995). Such HR practices are purported to lead to desirable organization-wide outcomes such as high productivity, low costs, and profitability (e.g., Way, 2002). High-performance work systems (HPWS), according to Pfeffer (1998), include: (a) employment security; (b) selective hiring of new personnel; (c) self-managed teams and decentralized decision making as the basic principles of organizational design; (d) comparatively high compensation that is contingent on performance; (e) extensive training; (f) reduced status distinctions and barriers; and (g) sharing of financial and operating performance information throughout the organization.

Pfeffer (1998, p. 33) described the path by which HPWS lead to desired organizational outcomes:

1. People work harder, because of the increased involvement and commitment that comes from having more control over and say in their work.

2. People work smarter; high performance work practices encourage the building of skills and competence and, as importantly, facilitate the efforts of people in actually applying their wisdom and energy to enhancing organizational performance.

3. High commitment management practices, by placing more responsibility in the hands of people farther down in the organization, save on administrative overhead as well as other costs associated with having an alienated work force in an adversarial relationship with management.

According to this framework, people work harder because they are able to make their own decisions within self-managed teams and are well compensated for strong performance. They work smarter because they are being trained continuously and operate in an information-rich environment. And the organization benefits because it invests in building people's knowledge and capabilities rather than spending money on unneeded administrative tasks, perquisites, and other items that tend to hinder performance or waste resources. Reflecting years of research on human resource management, HPWS contribute to a stylized high-performing organization that should be viable in all circumstances.

The value of HPWS—and SHRM in general—is demonstrated by research that examines the impact of HRM on firm performance. A recent meta-analysis conducted by Combs, Liu, Hall, and Ketchen (2006) sheds considerable light on the practical significance of SHRM. In their review of 92 studies involving more than 19,000 organizations, the researchers reached four broad conclusions across the various studies. First, HRM makes a significant difference in organizational performance. In a companion paper (Liu, Combs, Ketchen, & Ireland, 2007), the authors point out a major practical implication of this finding: high-performance work practices have a larger influence on organizational performance than other well-established governance mechanisms, such as the independence of a firm's board of directors (Dalton, Daily, Ellstrand, & Johnson, 1998) or CEO incentive compensation (Tosi, Werner, Katz, & Gomez-Mejia, 2000).

Second, high-performance work practices have a larger impact on organizational performance when they are bundled and used as a management system than when they are implemented individually. Combs et al. (2006) surmise that bundling may have both additive and synergistic effects, and Liu et al. (2007) argue that skilled HR professionals can literally double the effect on firm performance by combining multiple work practices so that they reinforce each other. More generally, the desirability of developing and maintaining an alignment or fit among management actions as part of a holistic management approach is a long-established notion in both strategic management (e.g., Miles & Snow, 1984b) and SHRM research (e.g., Baird & Meshoulam, 1988; MacDuffie, 1995; Wright & Boswell, 2002).

Third, human resource work practices have a significant effect on organizational performance no matter whether performance is measured in operational terms or financial terms. Although this finding was not expected by the authors, it does serve to validate the main finding of their meta-analysis—that is, a well-aligned high-performance HRM system has a significant impact on organizational performance, according to both operational and financial measures.

Lastly, high-performance work practices have a larger influence on performance in manufacturing organizations than they do in service organizations. Combs et al. (2006) offer several possible explanations for this finding, and they suggest that future research should explore high-performance work systems that are specifically suited to service organizations and investigate the work system–performance relationship using fine-grained measures appropriate for the service environment.

From a strategic perspective, the Combs et al. (2006) meta-analysis suggests that strategic decision makers should invest in high-performance work practices as a means of improving the performance of their firms. Such a universal conclusion, however, is not yet fully supported by the data. Indeed, the field of SHRM is still struggling to sort out the explanatory power of the universalistic, contingency, and configurational approaches and their implications for HR strategies and practices (Martín-Alcázar, Romero-Fernández, & Sánchez-Gardey, 2005).

Flexibility-Agility Trade-off

Having essentially agreed on the importance of attaining overall or systemic fit in organizations (Jackson, Schuler, & Rivero, 1989; Milliman et al. 1991), researchers began a process of reconciling the presumed trade-off between fit and flexibility in HR systems. In industries characterized by change and volatility, strategic advantage often hinges on a firm's ability to respond rapidly to perceived opportunities and threats. Lengnick-Hall and Lengnick-Hall (1988), for example, pointed out that where adaptation and flexibility are required, the development of a tight fit between HR practices and firm strategy might be ill advised. "Fit can be counterproductive from a competitive perspective because it may inhibit innovativeness and constrain the firm's repertoire of skills" (p. 457). Schneider (1987) raised a similar concern in his framework of organizational attraction-selection-attrition (ASA) cycles. When organizations attract and retain a homogenous group of members, particularly with regard to their values and personalities, it can result in organizations that have unique structures, processes, and cultures. In the short term, this can be beneficial as regards organizational fit and resource inimitability. Over time, however, homogeneity may constrain the variety of interests and perspectives needed to generate new ideas. A tightly fitted ASA cycle may thus work against the organization's ability to adapt quickly and effectively to dynamic environmental conditions.

HR systems themselves may also inhibit flexibility. Snell and Dean (1992) noted that, once in place, administrative systems (including HR practices) tend to be intractable. Because they are held in place by numerous factors, such as written records, organizational traditions, corporate policies, and employee expectations about fairness and justice, they may create inertia that hinders or even prevents desired organizational and managerial changes.

To address the issue of the fit-flexibility trade-off, Wright and Snell (1998) developed a framework that balances the respective needs of fit and flexibility. Rather than viewing fit and flexibility as opposite ends of a continuum, these researchers conceptualized the two as complementary dimensions. In their formulation, fit is a static element seen at a point in time, whereas flexibility is viewed as the capacity for change and adaptation over time. This distinction raises the possibility that HR systems, as well as workforce characteristics, can be both flexible and fitted to the needs of the organization.

Dyer and Shafer (1999) provide perhaps the most comprehensive treatment of fit and flexibility in the context of HR strategy. Building on the innovation and organizational change literatures, they view organizational adaptation not as a one-time or even periodic event but as a continuous process requiring organizational "agility" (Brown & Eisenhardt, 1997). In agile organizations, the role of HR strategy is multifaceted; it is designed to help forge a stable core of shared values, vision, and common performance metrics. But around this core, HR strategy plays an instrumental role in developing the competencies of an agile workforce that embraces change and learning. HR strategy also comprises an infrastructure that can be reconfigured rapidly to facilitate adaptation.

Summary

During the period when the systemic fit perspective held sway, much of the SHRM research cast HR in the role of strategy implementer rather than strategy formulator. While researchers such as Dyer (1983) and Buller (1988) identified instances in which strategic planning and HR planning had a reciprocal relationship, most often there was a one-way contingent relationship in which business strategies determined HR strategies and their implementation. During this same period, however, the emerging discipline of SHRM developed a broader view of how administrative systems facilitated strategy implementation and, in the process, began to transform the way in which it viewed the design of HR systems. Using concepts such as fit and flexibility, SHRM began to investigate how sets of practices worked in concert to elicit and reinforce patterns of behavior that benefited the firm as well as the individual. As a result, HR in the most progressive firms began to take its place alongside the other functional areas in helping to formulate as well as implement business strategies. The core studies associated with the systemic fit perspective and their contributions to the SHRM literature are summarized in Table 30.1.

Recent SHRM Theory

Around the turn of this century, SHRM theory increasingly began to reflect the way that firms participate in the global economy. The prototypical model of today's large firm is one that is international if not global in its market reach, uses a multifirm supply chain to operate its global business, and is constantly learning and improving by adopting new technologies and using "best-practices" management. The modern organizational model requires new answers to the usual questions faced by HR such as: Who will be the firm's partners and suppliers, and where will the firm strategically locate its activities? How will work be organized? What is the composition of the workforce that can best perform this kind of work? The HR challenges posed by such questions began to push both line executives and HR professionals to take a "capabilities" perspective of competitive strategy and organizational design—to ask, in effect, what are the organizational capabilities needed by our firm to pursue business strategies in a dynamic global environment? What investments does our firm need to make in order to have the resources and capabilities available when they are needed?

Strategic Resources and Capabilities Perspective

The resource-based view of the firm (Barney, 1991; Wernerfelt, 1984), which has long dominated the field of strategic management, now includes the concept of organizational capabilities (Teece, Pisano, & Shuen, 1997). Eisenhardt and Martin (2000) define a firm's capabilities as a set

Table 30.1 The Systemic Fit Perspective: Core Studies and Contributions

Study	Contribution
Devanna, Fombrun, & Tichy (1981) Tichy, Fombrun, & Devanna (1982)	Introduced the SHRM construct and advocated increased participation of HR professionals in the firm's strategic decision-making process
Miles & Snow (1984a)	Argued for a contingent approach in which particular HR practices are fitted to a firm's business strategies
Beer, Spector, Lawrence, Mills, & Walton (1985)	Advocated a systems approach to HRM in which the various components of an HR system reinforce each other
Baird & Meshoulam (1988)	Applied the concepts of internal and external fit to HR system components
Milliman, von Glinow, & Nathan (1991) Schuler, Dowling, & DeCieri (1993)	Provided theoretical frameworks for the analysis of strategic international human resource management
Wright & Snell (1998)	Developed a framework that resolved the trade-off between HR system fit and flexibility
Dyer & Shafer (1999)	Added a dynamic dimension to the process of achieving fit

of specific and identifiable processes, such as product development and commercialization, customer relationship management, or lean manufacturing, which are crucial to the firm's success. The effective formulation and execution of competitive strategy require that firms understand their core capabilities, and that they systematically develop and leverage them (Miles, Miles, & Snow, 2005a; Ulrich & Smallwood, 2004). Simply having resources is not sufficient for organizational effectiveness. The firm must have strategically appropriate capabilities to organize and use those resources.

A number of studies have noted important differences among segments of the workforce in a single firm, implying that HR must develop the capability to recruit, select, place, and reward various types of employee groups. For example, Osterman (1984) argued that industrial, salaried, craft, and secondary workforces frequently are found in the same firm. Baron, Davis-Blake, and Bielby (1986) found that multiple internal labor markets exist within firms according to firm-specific skills, occupational differentiation, and technology. Other researchers have identified a variety of specific employment relationships that coexist within firms (Matusik & Hill, 1998; Rousseau, 1995), each of which has its own particular set of processes and outcomes (Tsui, Pearce, Porter, & Tripoli, 1997).

HR system complexity increases when its domain is extended beyond the boundaries of the firm to include members of the value chain (Schuler & MacMillan, 1984), alliance partners (Gardner, 2005), and even customers (Lengnick-Hall & Lengnick-Hall, 1999). By extending its focus, HR may be able to help the firm reap larger returns. For example, a 2008 survey of 600 companies by PricewaterhouseCoopers found that virtually all of them were seeking to gain more cost leverage from their international supply chains. The major initiatives fell into four main areas: (a) forecasting product demand to avoid supply chain disruptions; (b) seeking cost effectiveness in inventory management, transportation, fuel purchases, etc.; (c) working closely with suppliers to ensure long-term relationships; and (d) talent management—recruiting, developing, and maintaining top supply chain professionals. The survey found that the stock market was quick to punish companies, by 9 percent on average, that reported major supply chain problems. Thus, by focusing its efforts on cross-firm programs, HR can have a direct and significant impact on a key measure of firm performance.

Despite the increasing complexity evidenced in most firms' workforces, Lepak and Snell (1999) noted that researchers tend to aggregate, both conceptually and empirically, all of a firm's employees into one homogeneous workforce that is studied as though it were managed with a single (or at least dominant) set of HR practices. These researchers pointed out that a capabilities perspective suggests that different groups of employees contribute in different ways to the development of a firm's capabilities and, as a consequence, need to be managed differently. They called for studies of HR "architecture" that map the different talent pools of organizations and investigate the ways in which different cohorts are managed.

The Lepak-Snell (1999) framework proposed two key dimensions of firm-specific human capital: strategic value and uniqueness. Juxtaposing these two dimensions results in a matrix with four cells that represent different employee cohorts, all or some of which may coexist within the same firm. Follow-up research indicated that these cohorts differ in terms of employment modes, the psychological contracts that exist between employees and their organizations, the bundles of HR practices used to manage employees in the different employment modes, and the leadership styles associated with each employment mode (Lepak & Snell, 2002; Liu, Lepak, Takeuchi, & Sims, 2003). Furthermore, empirical evidence indicated that using a combination of different cohorts, managed in different but coordinated ways, is related to higher firm performance (Lepak, Takeuchi, & Snell, 2003). Subsequently, Kulkarni and Ramamoorthy (2005) expanded the number of employment modes in the Lepak-Snell framework from four to eight.

While the findings on HR architectures are consistent with the value of taking a resources/capabilities perspective, some observers caution against the wholesale outsourcing of talent. Mangum, Mayall, and Nelson (1985, p. 599), for example, noted that "many employers carefully select a core group of employees, invest in them, and take elaborate measures to reduce their turnover and maintain their attachment to the firm. Many of these same employers, however, also maintain a peripheral group of employees from whom they prefer to remain relatively detached, even at the cost of high turnover, and to whom they make few commitments."

Kaplan and Norton (2003) take a balanced approach that incorporates capabilities into their model of strategy "mapping." The strategy mapping model begins with a planning process that asks managers to identify key business processes and capabilities that drive value to customers, stockholders, and other stakeholders. Managers identify the various talent pools and job families required for these capabilities and then develop HR strategies to build the skill base, reinforce desired employee behaviors, and manage different employee groups in an integrated value chain. Thus, a firm's strategic capabilities comprise not just the skills of knowledge workers but also those of traditional employees, as well as contract workers and supply chain partners. Contemporary research in HR strategy highlights the fact that how the workforce is composed is a matter of strategic choice, and it is the particular configuration of people and their abilities, combined with the HR management system, that produces value.

The most recent focus of HR research is on knowledge management. Arguably, the most valuable resource to firms is knowledge that enables them to achieve a competitive advantage (Grant, 1996; Kogut & Zander, 1992; Spender, 1996). While knowledge is embedded in organizations in a variety of ways, such as in routines and technologies, people-embodied knowledge is the foundation of a firm's capabilities and is fundamental to the development of value creation. Dierickx and Cool (1989) note that a firm's accumulated skills, expertise, and wisdom can be viewed as knowledge stocks. In contrast, the streams of new knowledge that are created, transferred, and integrated to enrich and change a firm's knowledge stocks are its knowledge flows. Knowledge flows include exchanging new knowledge across organizational boundaries, as well as transferring underutilized yet potentially valuable knowledge within the organization (Argote & Ingram, 2000). While knowledge stocks provide the foundation for a firm's capabilities, knowledge flows are necessary for facilitating organizational learning by enabling a firm to expand, refine, and modify its knowledge stocks. The distinction between knowledge stocks and flows is important because, as Leonard-Barton (1995) pointed out, without continual knowledge flows to enhance and renew their strategic value, knowledge stocks can sometimes cause organizational rigidity. This implies that while managing current knowledge stocks is important for HRM, managing knowledge flows may be equally, if not more, important (Kang, Morris, & Snell, 2007).

Leana and Van Buren (1999) emphasized the potential role that HR strategies can play in nurturing and developing organizational social capital, the knowledge embedded in and available through professional networks within and across organizations. Similarly, Collins and Clark (2003) showed a connection among network-building HR practices, the development of internal and external social networks of top management teams, and firm performance. More recently, Collins and Smith (2006) found that HR practices affect the organizational social climate that facilitates knowledge exchange and integration, which, in turn, has an impact on firm performance. Tying social capital to human capital and the architectural view of HR strategy, Lepak, Taylor, Tekleab, Marrone, and Cohen (2007) found that while talent cohorts playing a support role may not be direct contributors to knowledge creation within a firm, their role is vital to indirectly facilitating innovation. These and other studies reinforce the notion that HR strategies must continue to evolve to support new organizational processes that focus on knowledge development and innovation.

SHRM Metrics and Outcomes

We have described how SHRM research made great strides over the past three decades by, first, fitting traditional HR practices to business strategy in a coherent, flexible organizational system and, more recently, by adopting an orientation toward the future and showing how resources and capabilities can be developed and managed to create economic value. As a field, has SHRM contributed significantly to lasting improvements in firm performance?

The answer to this question is not clear. On one hand, meta-analytical studies such as that of Combs et al. (2006) indicate that SHRM can have a significant impact on a firm's operational and financial performance. On the other hand, other researchers maintain that HR professionals still focus mostly on administrative and support activities, not on strategic decisions. For example, Boudreau and Ramstad (2007) argue that SHRM needs a "decision science," one that is similar to those found in finance or marketing. They propose a science of "talentship," which is concerned with improving decisions about the talents of people and how they organize and interact (Boudreau & Ramstad, 2009).

Such a decision science, relying on appropriate HR metrics to test its validity, is likely to use the standard measurement methods of industrial and organizational psychology. In their recent review of the SHRM literature, Lengnick-Hall et al. (2009) highlighted the main theoretical and measurement issues associated with empirical research in this area: (a) developing and using valid measures of all variables and outcomes; (b) identifying key outcomes using a stakeholder approach (e.g., measuring outcomes that benefit both the firm and its employees); (c) establishing the boundary conditions of any particular theoretical model; and (d) incorporating time, causality, and multilevel analysis into theoretical models as appropriate. Our own view is that the

SHRM literature could not have realistically started to address these measurement issues until recently. Now, however, the literature has accumulated to the point at which large-scale model testing can occur.

Summary

The resources and capabilities approach to HR strategy reflects three main changes from previous conceptualizations. First, it requires an explicit focus on the development of human, social, and organizational capital as a means of value creation, not just a focus on HR practices and their static combinations. Second, it requires managers to recognize that different kinds of employees need to be managed in different ways. If people are an organization's most important asset, then it stands to reason that a "one-size-fits-all" approach may not be appropriate. In this respect, an architectural view captures the complexity of HR strategy and practices, as well as the substantial challenge of developing a strategically differentiated workforce in a global marketplace. Third, the resources/capabilities approach to HR strategy extends beyond the firm's boundaries to include key stakeholders such as supply chain partners. Modern firms compete globally by using sophisticated organizational and managerial approaches, and HR's theoretical models are, for the most part, keeping pace with these developments.

The strategic resources and capabilities perspective of SHRM puts the HR function squarely in position to help the firm determine its various business models and to develop the organizational capabilities needed to operate them. The current competitive equation in the global economy places a premium on knowledge-intensive assets and the processes that underlie learning, innovation, and multiparty collaboration. This evolving paradigm is a marked contrast to previous HR strategy approaches. Rather than viewing HRM as a derivative of the business planning process, it is increasingly viewed as driving strategic planning via investments in organizational capabilities and a diverse workforce. The core studies associated with the strategic resources and capabilities perspective, and their contributions to the SHRM literature, are summarized in Table 30.2.

Future Research Directions

We believe that HR professionals can play an even stronger role in their firms' strategy formulation and implementation processes than they currently do—helping their firms to anticipate

Table 30.2 The Strategic Resources and Capabilities Perspective: Core Studies and Contributions

Study	Contribution
Teece, Pisano, & Shuen (1997)	Introduced the capabilities perspective to the strategic management literature
Baron, Davis-Blake, & Bielby (1986) Tsui, Pearce, Porter, & Tripoli (1997)	Demonstrated the importance of configuring multiple employee groups to fit strategic objectives
Lepak & Snell (1999)	Developed the concept of HR architecture to reflect increasingly complex workforce arrangements
Kogut & Zander (1992) Dierickx & Cool (1989) Leana & Van Buren (1999)	Recognized knowledge as the most important resource to be managed and leveraged, and developed theoretical frameworks for knowledge management as the basis of organizational learning and innovation
Boudreau & Ramstad (2007)	Called for the development of a full complement of HR metrics to measure SHRM processes and outcomes

the future business landscape, strategizing about the business models and organizational designs that will be needed, and determining the human resource investments that their firms must make in order to be prepared for the future. For HR to be able to play such a role moving forward, SHRM theory should continue to develop in three particular areas: (a) the composition and management of global workforces, especially those used in global supply chains; (b) knowledge management as the primary means of value creation; and (c) the anticipation of new organizational forms and their implications for HR strategies and investments.

Global Workforces

Although a considerable amount of research has been done on international HR strategy and management, much of it has focused on comparative systems or micro-level policy and practice distinctions (e.g., Bae & Lawler, 2000; Fey & Bjorkman, 2001). In the future, research on HR strategy also needs to address the practical and sometimes controversial issues related to the global sourcing of talent. Apart from contemporary dilemmas about outsourcing and off-shoring, multinational companies also need to devise strategies for managing the heterogeneity of geographically dispersed workforces.

McWilliams, Van Fleet, and Wright (2001) argued that, in an international context, a more diverse pool of employees represents a unique source of advantage in comparison to domestic labor pools in terms of value, rarity, inimitability, and nonsubstitutability (VRIN). They note that firms often derive two principal competitive advantages from a global workforce: (a) capitalizing on a more heterogeneous labor pool; and (b) leveraging the cultural synergies of a diverse workforce.

First, because global workforces are potentially more heterogeneous, the labor/talent pool may provide better access to human capital. When firms can draw from different labor pools to match the unique or local needs of particular markets, there may be better alignment between the demand for labor and the supply available within the firm (Bartlett & Ghoshal, 1989). This is not simply an argument for wage arbitrage in developing economies. Particular labor markets may have workers who, on average, have higher technical ability or greater access to education and training. For example, international firms increasingly look to India for skills in information technology, not just for low wages. With global access to human capital, firms can potentially draw from the highest quality labor pools for those functions that require particular abilities, education, and training (McWilliams et al., 2001).

Second, when firms draw from multiple labor pools, they have the potential to build competitive advantages due to cultural synergies. A diverse and flexible cadre of managers may enable firms to bring more varied perspectives to key decisions than a management group composed solely from the parent country (Ricks, 1993). Although the coordination requirements may increase, resource heterogeneity enables managers to be flexible in applying their skills throughout the different parts of the firm (Wright & Snell, 1998).

While McWilliams et al. (2001) highlighted the benefits of utilizing heterogeneous human resources, they also pointed out the difficulty in transferring and integrating such resources into multinational firms. One of the realities of global business is that resources are often immobile because of geographic, cultural, economic, and legislative boundaries. Those limitations represent mobility barriers for most firms and advantages for those firms that overcome them (Morris, Snell, & Wright, 2006). Researchers have begun to examine the methods by which firms transfer and integrate their global talent pools (Sparrow, Brewster, & Harris, 2004), sometimes through rotational assignments and expatriation, and increasingly through social networks, virtual teams, and knowledge management practices (Caligiuri & Tarique, 2006; Maznevski & Chudoba, 2000; Sparrow, 2006).

Recognizing the increasing use of global workforces, researchers have begun to examine more macro-level HR functional and structural issues. They have noted the underlying tension between the needs for local responsiveness and the requirements of global integration (e.g., Fey & Bjorkman, 2001). Local responsiveness and the value derived from customization imply variation (heterogeneity) within the firm. Global efficiency, on the other hand, requires integration across business units. Schuler, Dowling, and DeCieri (1993) modeled these trade-offs by framing the relationships between internal operations and interunit linkages. Each international subsidiary must operate as effectively as possible relative to its competitive imperative within the total firm. The need for integration, however, highlights the need for local responsiveness, owing to the advantages obtained from recognizing and developing HR practices that are appropriate for local markets, employment laws, cultural traditions, and the like.

The multinational firm must also establish interunit linkages to gain efficiencies of scale and scope across multiple countries. A basic premise of global commerce is that, without this form of integration, the global firm offers no incremental value beyond market returns. As Morris et al. (2006) noted, while overseas affiliates can generate advantages locally, the substantial advantages gained from integrated HR must also be managed. Each is important and carries with it a different set of organizational requirements. These requirements point directly to issues relevant for HRM. To encourage future research and practice, Taylor, Beechler, and Napier (1996) described how international firms can develop an integrative approach to HRM in which best practices from all parts of the firm are shared in order to create a global management system. They noted that while allowances can be made for local differentiation, the focus of an integrative approach is on substantial global integration. However, researchers have noted that coordination is not always easily achieved in this context (Stiles & Trevor, 2006). The exact features that provide operational advantages locally may complicate integration globally. Once in place, local practices are often difficult to modify, even when potentially better alternatives exist. The result is that heterogeneous local practices and policies, while justified in many cases, work against a firm's ability to leverage efficiencies of scope and scale on a global level.

The challenge for HR researchers is to continue studying the ways in which firms can manage their global workforces to take advantage of both local opportunities and circumstances, while capitalizing on the advantages of global reach. At the present stage of theory development, we believe that a series of in-depth case studies would be most useful. The first set of case studies might examine the HR philosophies and practices of the leading multinational corporations in a single global industry. Such studies would be able to highlight the role of the firm's business strategies and management philosophies on HRM while allowing national culture and institutions to vary. Those studies could then be followed by research that has a similar HR focus but utilizes samples of different global industries which are both manufacturing and service oriented.

Knowledge Management and Value Creation

As noted earlier, both strategy and HR researchers now emphasize the knowledge-based view of strategy and its implications for capability development as the primary means of value creation in organizations (Boxall & Purcell, 2000; Grant, 1996; Spender, 1996; Wright, Dunford, & Snell, 2001). In today's highly competitive global economy, which places a premium on the management of knowledge-intensive assets, HR researchers can help to create high-performance workforces by focusing their research efforts on the HR architecture of three types of value configurations: chains, shops, and networks (Stabell & Fjeldstad, 1998).

The most familiar value configuration is the value chain which shows how a firm can align its activities sequentially in order to convert raw materials into finished products and deliver them to buyers (Porter,

1985). The concept of the value chain works well for firms that produce and sell products through a process involving multiple stages of production, and it is in product-based firms that most of the HR literature has been developed. The value chain concept, however, does not offer much guidance to service-oriented firms, such as hospitals, consulting firms, telecommunications companies, financial services firms, airlines, or hotels. Those types of firms have different economics that underpin their value and performance, and therefore they require different HR architectures in order to be successful in the marketplace.

The value shop, perhaps best exemplified by a consulting firm or hospital, uses knowledge and mobilizes resources to solve problems for clients. The value shop is an effective problem solver—a mechanism for understanding customers' problems and organizing the resources necessary to solve them. Value creation in these types of organizations consists of activities related to: (a) problem diagnosis; (b) development, testing, and choice of alternative solutions; and (c) implementation and evaluation. In a value shop, value is created on a case-by-case basis by identifying a particular customer's problem and then designing a customized solution for it.

The relationship between business strategy and HR architecture is different in a value shop as compared to a value chain (Fjeldstad & Andersen, 2003). A value shop creates valuable human resources by means of specialized hiring and training and by choosing projects that develop the experience base of particular kinds of human resources. Continuous training, for example, constitutes a large portion of the premier consulting companies' HR practices. It is closely coordinated with on-the-job development of people, with junior professionals supporting the higher value activities of senior professionals while developing through a planned succession of roles (Kinnie et al., 2006). As people become more valuable, the cost of using them on client projects increases, requiring HR strategies to maximally leverage human capital (Hitt, Bierman, Shimizu, & Kochhar, 2001). Strategically, the assessment of what projects the firm will take on is guided by the learning opportunities they represent, by the impact they will have on the reputation of the firm, and operationally by the billing ratios they offer for different categories of available personnel. In value shops, strategic goals are tied to long-term capability development more than particular types of engagements and markets (Fjeldstad & Andersen, 2003). In this regard, Snow and Snell (1993) described how

staffing considerations can propel business strategy, rather than the other way around.

In the third type of value configuration, the value network, value is created by helping customers who are or wish to be interdependent to exchange goods, information, and/or capital. Representative firms in this category include banks, financial services firms, telecommunications companies, airlines, credit card companies, logistics and other transportation companies, and social media firms. Many dot-com companies are also value networks (Fjeldstad & Andersen, 2003). Telecommunications providers, banks, parcel services, and stock exchanges collectively organize and assist their customers in exchanging goods, information, cash, or ownership. Just like value chains and value shops, they have primary and secondary activity categories (Porter, 1985). In a value network, these activities are organized similar to a club. That is, promotion and contract management recruits members and manages contracts that determine member privileges and obligations (e.g., the size of credit lines or bandwidth and the cost associated with its use). Service provisioning assists customers in making the exchange, be it of money, information, or goods. Infrastructure operations maintains access points and basic operating capacity. In contrast to value chains and value shops, there is no sequence between these activities; they are developed and performed in parallel. Therefore, in terms of the HR architecture, value networks must be populated with people who understand and can interact with external stakeholders such as customers and partners. Such individuals must have a "mediating proclivity" (Obstfeld, 2005) that allows them to act as "bridge builders" among the firm's employees and its external stakeholders in order to effectively facilitate inter-customer relationships.

Future research in the area of knowledge management and value creation should pay particular attention to sample design. The key theoretical dimension along which variation should be sought is the type of value configuration. Therefore, the sample must include firms classified according to the three configurations of value chain, shop, and network. Surveys could be administered to firms within each of these value categories to determine the relationships between key knowledge management and HR practices.

New Organizational Forms

Virtually every generation of managers experiments with one or more major new business models and the organizational forms needed to support them. For example, the well-known business model that is focused on diversification into related markets succeeds primarily in those firms that are able to design and effectively operate a multidivisional organization structure. Similarly, business models linked to rapid product development based on new technologies succeed primarily in those firms that are able to effectively form and utilize small collaborative innovation teams. Each of these examples suggests the need to design effective linkages among organization structure, core capabilities, and HR strategies and practices.

Penrose (1959) argued that a firm grows and diversifies when its existing organization is unable to fully exploit its current stock of resources. For example, she focused on "excess managerial capacity" as the underutilized resource of the time that was a frequent cause of firm growth. Today, the most underutilized resource among firms in advanced economies is knowledge. The drive to turn knowledge and other underutilized resources into economic wealth is what pushes managers to experiment with new ways of reconfiguring strategies, structures, and processes to make their firms more effective and valuable. Certainly, managers would be aided in their efforts by organizational theories that not only describe and explain but also predict and prescribe (Weick, 1989, 1999). As a firm pushes against the limits of effectiveness of its existing organizational form, it would like to be able to anticipate the new form that it needs and to make the investments and other preparations required to operate that new form.

Much of the current experimentation with new business and organizational models is linked to technological and product/service innovation in knowledge-intensive industries, such as biotechnology (Powell, 1996; Powell, Koput, & Smith-Doerr, 1996), computer software (Chesbrough, 2006, 2007), nanotechnology, and medical devices. To obtain the full benefit of using knowledge as a resource, many existing organizations will have to be redesigned to increase their capability to create as well as acquire knowledge, transfer and share it both internally and externally, and integrate it with existing routines and processes. Knowledge creation and utilization require the ability to collaborate, both within and across firms, and the concept that appears to be taking hold in a growing number of firms in knowledge-intensive industries is collaborative innovation and entrepreneurship (Miles, Miles, & Snow, 2005b). The ability to engage in multifirm collaboration requires sophisticated actor-oriented

organizational designs and facilitative rather than directive management philosophies and processes (Fjeldstad et al., 2012).

The exploration of new business models and their supporting organizational and managerial systems will challenge both the imagination and the values of those who design or adopt them. HR professionals who want to contribute significantly to this process must have knowledge not only of traditional hierarchical organizational forms, such as functional, divisional, and matrix organizations, but also newer forms, such as collaborative communities of firms (Snow et al., 2011). HR professionals, guided by cutting-edge SHRM theory, can play a valuable role in designing (and redesigning) their organizations by helping to articulate and develop appropriate linkages across their firms' strategies, structures, and management processes.

Perhaps the highest priority item on the research agenda concerning new organizational forms should be studies that focus on the limits of existing organizational forms. This is because the next-generation organizational form will be one that relieves constraints on the efficiency and effectiveness associated with current forms. As discussed above, the newest organizational form that is being used in knowledge-intensive sectors is the collaborative community of firms. Research needs to explore HR strategies and practices in the multifirm collaborative context, particularly how the HR function can be designed to support a group of independent firms that work together temporarily on innovation projects (Bøllingtoft et al., 2012).

Conclusion

Throughout its evolution, SHRM theory has tended to follow developments in the strategic management literature. As SHRM now approaches its fourth decade, it is becoming more mature, much like its parent discipline. Should SHRM continue to follow in strategy's footsteps? We believe that this question is worth serious consideration by HR scholars. For example, one prominent contributor to the strategy literature recently bemoaned its "debilitating fragmentation," as the "wild proliferation" of theories developed over the past 40 to 50 years has failed to cumulate into a coherent body of knowledge that is useful to practitioners (Hambrick, 2004). That strategy scholar called for a consolidation of the field's gains before moving forward. The development of SHRM theory seems to be on the same trajectory as that of strategic management. Of course, this is not a problem for an emerging field. As SHRM matures, however, its theorists and researchers might consider engaging in a period of reflection and consolidation during which existing theoretical frameworks in SHRM are evaluated and debated. Moving forward, the most promising of those frameworks can then be pursued in a more systematic fashion.

Note

1. Kaufman (2001) discusses how the intellectual roots of SHRM can be traced to the practices used by some U.S. firms in the 1920s. "Progressive companies in the 1920s intentionally formulated and adopted innovative HR practices that represented a strategic approach to the management of labor" (Lengnick-Hall, Lengnick-Hall, Andrade, & Drake, 2009, p. 1). Our chapter discusses theoretical developments since the term *strategic* was first applied to human resource management in the early 1980s.

References

Andrews, A. O., & Welbourne, T. M. (2000). The people/performance balance in IPO firms: The effect of the Chief Executive Officer's financial orientation. *Entrepreneurship: Theory & Practice, 25*, 94–107.

Argote, L., & Ingram, P. (2000). Knowledge transfer: A basis for competitive advantage in firms. *Organizational Behavior and Human Decision Processes, 82*, 150–169.

Arthur, J. B. (1994). Effects of human resource systems on manufacturing performance and turnover. *Academy of Management Journal, 37*, 670–687.

Bae, J., & Lawler, J. J. (2000). Organizational and HRM strategies in Korea: Impact on firm performance in an emerging economy. *Academy of Management Journal, 43*, 502–517.

Baird, L., & Meshoulam, I. (1988). Managing two fits of strategic human resource management. *Academy of Management Review, 13*, 116–128.

Barney, J. B. (1991). Firm resources and sustained competitive advantage. *Journal of Management, 17*, 99–120.

Baron, J. N., Davis-Blake, A., & Bielby, W. T. (1986). The structure of opportunity: How promotion ladders vary within and among organizations. *Administrative Science Quarterly, 31*, 248–273.

Bartlett, C. A., & Ghoshal, S. (1989). *Managing across borders: The transnational solution.* Boston: Harvard Business School Press.

Beer, M., Spector, B., Lawrence, P. R., Mills, D. Q., & Walton, R. E. (1985). *Human resource management.* New York: Free Press.

Bøllingtoft, A., Müller, S., Ulhøi, J.P., & Snow, C.C. (2012). Collaborative innovation communities: Role of the shared services provider. In A. Bøllingtoft, L. Donaldson, G. Huber, D.D. Håkansson, & C.C. Snow (Eds.), *Collaborative communities: Purpose, process, and design* (pp. 89–104). New York: Springer.

Boudreau, J. W., & Ramstad, P. M. (2007). *Beyond HR: The new science of human capital.* Boston: Harvard Business School Press.

Boudreau, J. W., & Ramstad, P. M. (2009). Beyond HR: Extending the paradigm through a talent decision science. In J. Storey, P. Wright, & D. Ulrich (Eds.), *The Routledge companion to SHRM* (pp. 17–39). London: Taylor & Francis.

Boxall, P., & Purcell, J. (2000). Strategic human resource management: Where have we come from and where should we

be going? *International Journal of Management Reviews, 2*, 183–203.

Brown, S. L., & Eisenhardt, K. M. (1997). The art of continuous change: Linking complexity theory and time-paced evolution in relentlessly shifting organizations. *Administrative Science Quarterly, 42*, 1–34.

Buller, P. F. (1988). Successful partnerships: HR and strategic planning at eight top firms. *Organizational Dynamics, 17*, 27–44.

Caligiuri, P., & Tarique, I. (2006). International assigned selection and cross-culture training and development. In G. K. Stahl & I. Bjorkman (Eds.), *Handbook of research in international human resource management* (pp. 302–321). Cheltenham, UK: Edward Elgar Publishing.

Chesbrough, H. W. (2006). *Open innovation: The new imperative for creating and profiting from technology.* Boston: Harvard Business School Press.

Chesbrough, H. W. (2007). Why companies should have open business models. *M.I.T. Sloan Management Review, 48*, 22–28.

Collins, C. J., & Clark, K. D. (2003). Strategic human resource practices, top management team social networks, and firm performance: The role of human resource practices in creating organizational competitive advantage. *Academy of Management Journal, 46*, 740–751.

Collins, C. J., & Smith, K. G. (2006). Knowledge exchange and combination: The role of human resource practices in the performance of high technology firms. *Academy of Management Journal, 49*, 544–560.

Combs, J., Liu, Y., Hall, A., & Ketchen, D. (2006). How much do high-performance work practices matter? A meta-analysis of their effects on organizational performance. *Personnel Psychology, 59*, 501–528.

Cyr, L., Johnson, D., & Welbourne, T. M. (2000). Human resources in initial public offering firms: Do venture capitalists make a difference? *Entrepreneurship: Theory & Practice, 25*, 77–91.

Dalton, D. R., Daily, C. M., Ellstrand, A. E., & Johnson, J. L. (1998). Meta-analytic review of board composition, leadership structure, and financial performance. *Strategic Management Journal, 19*, 269–290.

Delery, J. D. (1998). Issues of fit in strategic human resource management: Implications for research. *Human Resource Management Review, 8*, 289–309.

Delery, J. E., & Doty, D. H. (1996). Modes of theorizing in strategic human resource management: Tests of universalistic, contingency, and configurational performance predictions. *Academy of Management Journal, 39*, 802–835.

Devanna, M. A., Fombrun, C. J., & Tichy, N. M. (1981). Human resource management: A strategic approach. *Organizational Dynamics, 8*, 51–67.

Dierickx, I., & Cool, K. (1989). Asset stock accumulation and sustainability of competitive advantage. *Management Science, 35*, 1504–1513.

Doty, D. H., & Glick, W. H. (1994). Typologies as a unique form of theory building: Toward improved understanding and modeling. *Academy of Management Review, 19*, 230–251.

Dyer, L. (1983). Bringing human resources into the strategy formulation process. *Human Resource Management, 22*, 257–271.

Dyer, L., & Reeves, T. (1995). Human resource strategies and firm performance: What do we know and where do we need to go? *International Journal of Human Resource Management, 6*, 656–670.

Dyer, L., & Shafer, R. A. (1999). From human resource strategy to organizational effectiveness: Lessons from research on organizational agility. In G. R. Ferris (Ed.), *Research in personnel and human resources management* (pp. 145–174). Supplement 4. Greenwich, CT: JAI Press.

Eisenhardt, K. M., & Martin, J. A. (2000). Dynamic capabilities: What are they? *Strategic Management Journal (Special Issue), 21*, 1105–1121.

Fjeldstad, Ø. D., & Andersen, E. (2003). Casting off the chains. *European Business Forum, 14*, 47–53.

Fjeldstad, Ø. D., Snow, C. C., Miles, R. E., & Lettl, C. (2012). The architecture of collaboration: Organizing resources among large sets of actors. *Strategic Management Journal (Special Issue), 33*, xx.

Fey, C. F., & Bjorkman, I. (2001). The effect of human resource management practices on MNC subsidiary performance in Russia. *Journal of International Business Studies, 32*, 59–75.

Gardner, T. (2005). Human resource alliances: Defining the construct and exploring the antecedents. *International Journal of Human Resource Management, 16*, 1049–1066.

Grant, R. M. (1996). Toward a knowledge-based theory of the firm. *Strategic Management Journal, 17*, 108–122.

Halal, W., Geranmayeh, A., & Pourdehnad, J. (Eds.). (1993). *Internal markets: Bringing the power of free enterprise inside your organization.* New York: Wiley.

Hambrick, D. C. (2004). The disintegration of strategic management: It's time to consolidate our gains. *Strategic Organization, 2*, 91–98.

Hitt, M. A., Bierman, L., Shimizu, K., & Kochhar, R. (2001). Direct and moderating effects of human capital on strategy and performance in professional service firms: A resource-based perspective. *Academy of Management Journal, 44*, 13–28.

Huselid, M. A. (1995). The impact of human resource management practices on turnover, productivity and corporate financial performance. *Academy of Management Journal, 38*, 635–672.

Jackson, S. E., Schuler, R., & Rivero, J. C. (1989). Organizational characteristics as predictors of personnel practices. *Personnel Psychology, 42*, 727–786.

Kang, S.-C., Morris, S. S., & Snell, S. A. (2007). Relational archetypes, organizational learning, and value creation: Extending the human resource architecture. *Academy of Management Review, 32*, 236–256.

Kaplan, R. S., & Norton, D. P. (2003). *Strategy maps: Converting intangible assets into tangible outcomes.* Boston: Harvard Business School Press.

Kaufman, B. (2001). The theory and practice of strategic HRM and participative management. *Human Resource Management Review, 11*, 505–533.

Kepes, S., & Delery, J. E. (2007). HRM systems and the problem of internal fit. In P. Boxall, J. Purcell, & P. M. Wright (Eds.), *The handbook of human resource management* (pp. 385–404). Oxford: Oxford University Press.

Kinnie, N., Swart, J., Lund, M., Morris, S., Snell, S., & Kang, S. (2006). *Managing people and knowledge in professional service firms.* London: Chartered Institute of Personnel and Development.

Kogut, B., & Zander, U. (1992). Knowledge of the firm, combinative capabilities and the replication of technology. *Organization Science, 3*, 387–397.

Kulkarni, S. P., & Ramamoorthy, N. (2005). Commitment, flexibility and the choice of employment contracts. *Human Relations, 58*, 741–761.

Lado, A. A., & Wilson, M. C. (1994). Human resource systems and sustained competitive advantage: A competency-based perspective. *Academy of Management Review, 19*, 699–727.

Lawler, E. E., III. (1986). *High-involvement management.* San Francisco: Jossey-Bass.

Lawler, E. E., III. (1992). *The ultimate advantage: Creating the high-involvement organization.* San Francisco: Jossey-Bass.

Lawler, E. E., III., Mohrman, S. A., & Ledford, G. E. (1995). *Creating high-performance organizations: Practices and results of employee involvement and total quality management in Fortune 1000 companies.* San Francisco: Jossey-Bass.

Leana, C. R., & Van Buren, H. J. (1999). Organizational social capital and employment practices. *Academy of Management Review, 24*, 538–555.

Lengnick-Hall, C. A., & Lengnick-Hall, M. L. (1988). Strategic human resources management: A review of the literature and a proposed typology. *Academy of Management Review, 13*, 454–470.

Lengnick-Hall, C. A., & Lengnick-Hall, M. L. (1999). Expanding customer orientation in the HR function. *Human Resource Management, 38*, 201–214.

Lengnick-Hall, M. L., Lengnick-Hall, C. A., Andrade, L. S., & Drake, B. (2009). Strategic human resource management: The evolution of the field. *Human Resource Management Review, 19*, 64–85.

Leonard-Barton, D. (1995). *Wellsprings of knowledge.* Boston: Harvard Business School Press.

Lepak, D. P., Marrone, J. A., & Takeuchi, R. (2004). The relativity of human HR systems: Conceptualizing the impact of desired employee contributions and HR philosophy. *International Journal of Technology Management, 27*, 639–655.

Lepak, D. P., & Snell, S. A. (1999). The human resource architecture: Toward a theory of human capital allocation and development. *Academy of Management Review, 24*, 31–48.

Lepak, D. P., & Snell, S. A. (2002). Examining the human resource architecture: The relationships among human capital, employment, and human resource configurations. *Journal of Management, 28*, 517–543.

Lepak, D. P., Takeuchi, R., & Snell, S. A. (2003). Employment flexibility and firm performance: Examining the moderating effects of employment mode, environmental dynamism, and technological intensity. *Journal of Management, 29*, 681–705.

Lepak, D. P., Taylor, M. S., Tekleab, A. G., Marrone, J. A., & Cohen, D. J. (2007). An examination of the use of high-investment human resource systems for core and support employees. *Human Resource Management, 46*, 223–246.

Liu, Y., Combs, J. G., Ketchen, D. J., Jr., & Ireland, R. D. (2007). The value of human resource management for organizational performance. *Business Horizons, 50*, 503–511.

Liu, Y., Lepak, D. P., Takeuchi, R., & Sims, H. P., Jr. (2003). Matching leadership styles with employment modes: Strategic human resource management perspective. *Human Resource Management Review, 13*, 127–152.

MacDuffie, J. P. (1995). Human resource bundles and manufacturing performance – Organizational logic and flexible production systems in the world auto industry. *Academy of Management Journal, 48*, 197–221.

Mangum, G., Mayall, D., & Nelson, K. (1985). The utilization of contingent work, knowledge creation, and competitive advantage. *Academy of Management Review, 23*, 680–697.

Martín-Alcázar, F., Romero-Fernández, P., & Sánchez-Gardey, G. (2005). Strategic human resource management: Integrating the universalistic, contingent, configurational and contextual perspectives. *International Journal of Human Resource Management, 16,* 633–659.

Matusik, S. F., & Hill, C. W. I. (1998). The utilization of contingent work, knowledge creation, and competitive advantage. *Academy of Management Review, 23,* 680–697.

Maznevski, M. L. & Chudoba, K. M. (2000). Bridging space over time: Global virtual team dynamics and effectiveness. *Organization Science, 11,* 473–492.

McWilliams, A., Van Fleet, D. D., & Wright, P. M. (2001). Strategic management of human resources for global competitive advantage. *Journal of Business Strategies, 18,* 1–23.

Miles, R. E., Miles, G., & Snow, C. C. (2005a). Creating the capability for collaborative entrepreneurship: HR's role in the development of a new organizational form. In M. Losey, S. Meisinger, & D. Ulrich (Eds.), *The future of human resource management: 64 thought leaders explore the critical HR issues of today and tomorrow* (pp. 242–247). New York: Wiley.

Miles, R. E., Miles, G., & Snow, C. C. (2005b). *Collaborative entrepreneurship: How communities of networked firms use continuous innovation to create economic value.* Stanford, CA: Stanford University Press.

Miles, R. E., & Snow, C. C. (1978). *Organizational strategy, structure, and process.* New York: McGraw-Hill.

Miles, R. E., & Snow, C. C. (1984a). Designing strategic human resource systems. *Organizational Dynamics, 11,* 36–52.

Miles, R. E., & Snow, C. C. (1984b). Fit, failure, and the hall of fame. *California Management Review, 26,* 10–28.

Miller, D. (1986). Configurations of strategy and structure: Towards a synthesis. *Strategic Management Journal, 7,* 233–249.

Miller, D. (1996). Configurations revisited. *Strategic Management Journal, 17,* 505–512.

Miller, D., & Mintzberg, H. (1983). The case for configuration. In G. Morgan (Ed.), *Beyond method: Strategies for social research* (pp. 57–73). Newbury Park, CA: Sage.

Milliman, J., von Glinow, M. A., & Nathan, M. (1991). Organizational life cycles and strategic international human resource management in multinational companies: Implications for congruence theory. *Academy of Management Review, 16,* 318–339.

Morris, S., Snell, S. A., & Wright, P. M. (2006). A resource-based view of international human resources: Toward a framework of integrative and creative capabilities. In G. K. Stahl & I. Bjorkman (Eds.), *Handbook of research in international human resource management* (pp. 433–444). Cheltenham, UK: Edward Elgar Publishing.

Obstfeld, D. (2005). Social networks, the *tertius iungens* orientation, and involvement in innovation. *Administrative Science Quarterly, 50,* 100–130.

Olian, J. D, & Rynes, S. L. (1984). Organizational staffing: Integrating practice with strategy. *Industrial Relations, 23,* 170–181.

Osterman, P. (1984). *Internal labor markets.* Cambridge, MA: M.I.T. Press.

Penrose, E. A. (1959). *The theory of the growth of the firm.* London: Basil Blackwell.

Penrose, E. A. (1995). *The theory of the growth of the firm* (Rev. ed.). London: Basil Blackwell.

Pfeffer, J. (1998). *The human equation: Building profits by putting people first.* Boston: Harvard Business School Press.

Porter, M. E. (1980). *Competitive strategy.* New York: Free Press.

Porter, M. E. (1985). *Competitive advantage.* New York: Free Press.

Powell, W. W. (1996). Inter-organizational collaboration in the biotechnology industry. *Journal of Institutional and Theoretical Economics, 151,* 197–215.

Powell, W. W., Koput, K. W., & Smith-Doerr, L. (1996). Interorganizational collaboration and the locus of innovation: Networks of learning in biotechnology. *Administrative Science Quarterly, 41,* 116–145.

Ricks, D. (1993). *Blunders in international business.* Cambridge, UK: Blackwell Business.

Rousseau, D. M. (1995). *Psychological contracts in organizations: Understanding written and unwritten agreements.* Thousand Oaks, CA: Sage.

Schneider, B. (1987). The people make the place. *Personnel Psychology, 40,* 437–454.

Schuler, R. S. (1992). Strategic human resources management: Linking the people with the strategic needs of the business. *Organizational Dynamics, 21,* 18–32.

Schuler, R. S., Dowling, P. J., & DeCieri, H. (1993). An integrative framework of strategic international human resource management. *International Journal of Human Resource Management, 4,* 717–764.

Schuler, R. S., & MacMillan, I. C. (1984). Gaining competitive advantage through human resource management practices. *Human Resource Management, 23,* 241–256.

Snell, S. A., & Dean, J. W. (1992) Integrated manufacturing and human resource management: A human capital perspective. *Academy of Management Journal, 35,* 467–504.

Snow, C. C., Fjeldstad, Ø. D., Lettl, C., & Miles, R. E. (2011). Organizing continuous product development and commercialization: The collaborative community of firms model. *Journal of Product Innovation Management, 28,* 3–16.

Snow, C. C., & Snell, S. A. (1993). Staffing as strategy. In N. Schmitt, W. C. Borman, & Associates (Eds.), *Personnel selection in organizations* (pp. 448–478). San Francisco: Jossey-Bass.

Snow, C. C., Snell, S. A., Davison, S. C., & Hambrick, D. C. (1996). Use transnational teams to globalize your company. *Organizational Dynamics, 23,* 50–67.

Sparrow, P. (2006). Global knowledge management and HRM. In G. K. Stahl & I. Bjorkman (Eds.), *Handbook of research in international human resource* management (pp. 113–139). Cheltenham, UK: Edward Elgar Publishing.

Sparrow, P., Brewster, C., & Harris, H. (2004). *Globalizing human resource management.* London: Routledge Press.

Spender, J. C. (1996). Making knowledge the basis of a dynamic theory of the firm. *Strategic Management Journal, 17,* 45–62.

Stabell, C. B., & Fjeldstad, Ø. D. (1998). Configuring value for competitive advantage: On chains, shops, and networks. *Strategic Management Journal, 19,* 413–437.

Stiles, P., & Trevor, J. (2006). The human resource department: Roles, coordination, and influence. In G. K. Stahl & I. Bjorkman (Eds.), *Handbook of research in international human resource management* (pp. 49–67). Cheltenham, UK: Edward Elgar Publishing.

Taylor, S., Beechler, S., & Napier, N. (1996). Toward an integrative model of strategic international human resource management. *Academy of Management Review, 21,* 959–985.

Teece, D. J., Pisano, G., & Shuen, A. (1997). Dynamic capabilities and strategic management. *Strategic Management Journal, 18,* 509–533.

Tichy, N. M., Fombrun, C. J., & Devanna, M. A. (1982). Strategic human resource management. *Sloan Management Review, 23*, 47–61.

Tosi, H. L., Werner, S., Katz, J. P., & Gomez-Mejia, L. R. (2000). How much does performance matter? A meta-analysis of CEO pay studies. *Journal of Management, 26*, 301–339.

Tsui, A. S., Pearce, J. L., Porter, L. W., & Tripoli, A. M. (1997). Alternative approaches to the employee-organization relationship: Does investment in employees pay off? *Academy of Management Journal, 40*, 1089–1121.

Ulrich, D., & Smallwood, N. (2004). Capitalizing on capabilities. *Harvard Business Review, 82*, 119–128.

Way, S. A. (2002). High performance work systems and intermediate indicators of firm performance within the U.S. small business sector. *Journal of Management, 28*, 765–785.

Weick, K. E. (1989). Theory construction as disciplined imagination. *Academy of Management Review, 14*, 516–531.

Weick, K. E. (1999). That's moving: Theories that matter. *Journal of Management Inquiry, 8*, 134–142.

Welbourne, T. M., & Andrews, A. O. (1996). Predicting the performance of initial public offerings: Should human resource management be in the equation? *Academy of Management Journal, 39*, 891–919.

Welbourne, T. M., & Cyr, L. (1999). The human resource executive effect in initial public offering firms. *Academy of Management Journal, 42*, 616–629.

Werbel, J. D., & DeMarie, S. M. (2005). Aligning strategic human resource management and person-environment fit. *Human Resource Management Review, 15*, 247–262.

Wernerfelt, B. (1984). A resource-based view of the firm. *Strategic Management Journal, 5*, 171–180.

Wright, P. M., & Boswell, W. (2002). Desegregating HRM: A review and synthesis of micro and macro human resource management research. *Journal of Management, 28*, 247–276.

Wright, P. M., Dunford, B., & Snell, S. A. (2001). Human resources and the resource-based view of the firm. *Journal of Management, 27*, 701–721.

Wright, P. M., & Sherman, S. (1999). Failing to find fit in strategic human resource management: Theoretical and empirical problems. In P. M. Wright, L. Dyer, J. Boudreau, & G. Milkovich (Eds.), *Research in personnel and human resource management* (pp. 53–74). Greenwich, CT: JAI Press.

Wright, P. M., Smart, D., & McMahan, G. C. (1995). On the integration of strategy and human resources: An investigation of the match between human resources and strategy among NCAA basketball teams. *Academy of Management Journal, 38*, 1052–1074.

Wright, P. M., & Snell, S.A. (1991). Toward an integrative view of strategic human resource management. *Human Resource Management Review, 1*, 203–225.

Wright, P. M., & Snell, S. A. (1998). Toward a unifying framework for exploring fit and flexibility in strategic human resource management. *Academy of Management Review, 23*, 756–772.

PART 8

Managing Differences Within and Across Organizations

Managing Diversity

Quinetta M. Roberson

Abstract

As we hear time and time again in the scholarly literature and business press, workforces have become more diverse. As such, there is a substantial body of research that investigates the concept of diversity, its effects, and the processes that underlie these effects. Interestingly, the findings from this body of research and subsequent conclusions that can be drawn are not very straightforward. This chapter summarizes the findings of research focused on the conceptualization of diversity, theoretical perspectives on the effects of diversity, such effects across levels of analysis, and the evolution of diversity management. In addition, challenges, unanswered questions, and other gaps in the diversity literature are highlighted, and directions for future research in this area are suggested.

Key Words: Diversity, demography, differences, diversity management, intergroup relations, in-group/out-group, majority/minority, similarity, dissimilarity, diversity management inclusion, business case

As predicted by Workforce 2000 (Johnson & Packer, 1987), a report by the Hudson Institute which predicted that the labor force would become characterized by greater diversity, the twenty-first-century workforce is characterized by more women and employees with diverse ethnic backgrounds, alternative lifestyles, and intergenerational differences than in the past (Langdon, McMenamin, & Krolik, 2002). At present, over 20 years since the report, business trends continue to make workforce diversity an important concern for organizations. First, with the increased globalization of both customer and labor markets, there is an increasing need to understand more about cultural diversity, which is more entrenched than workforce demography. Second, as economies transitioned from manufacturing to knowledge work, organizations experienced greater variability in job requirements and, subsequently, skill inventories. Third, in response to increased foreign competition, renewed interest in the quality of work life, and changing

task requirements and technologies, firms have moved toward flatter organizational structures featuring groups and teams during this same time (Kozlowski & Bell, 2003). Overall, while workforces continue to be characterized by gender, ethnic, and age diversity, such differences are spread throughout organizations—from line employees and lower level staff positions to the manager and executive levels. In addition, workforces are now far more diverse along a variety of diversity attributes, including skilled versus unskilled workers, exempt versus non-exempt employees, and home-country versus foreign-born nationals.

While current business trends have brought about more diverse workforces, they have also dismantled barriers that influence the nature and amount of interaction among employees. For example, employees may be required to work in geographically dispersed teams with people from different cultural backgrounds. Or, employees across functional areas may be required to collaborate on special project teams. Overall, effective interaction within diverse workforces is critical to smooth organizational functioning (Jackson & Ruderman, 1995). Interestingly, however, numerous observers have noted that diversity has both positive and negative effects on group and firm performance (Jackson, Joshi, & Erhardt, 2003; Kochan et al., 2003; Mannix & Neale, 2005). Thus, organizations are tasked with finding ways to maximize the potential benefits, and to minimize the potential disadvantages, of diversity.

To address the challenges of workforce diversity, employers have worked to develop internal environments where diversity is effectively valued and managed. Accordingly, programmatic initiatives, such as diversity training, recruiting, and mentoring, have become part of organizations' human resource strategies. In addition, organizations are increasingly relying upon diversity strategies and systemic organizational change processes to proactively manage diversity and to leverage its effects for organizational performance. Still, the ways in which organizations define and manage workforce diversity are still evolving.

To keep pace with the changing business environment, research has considered what diversity means and how it impacts group and organizational functioning. As such, there is a substantial body of research that investigates the concept of diversity, its effects, and the processes that underlie these effects (for reviews, see Mannix & Neale, 2005; Milliken & Martins, 1996; van Knippenberg & Schippers, 2007; Williams & O'Reilly, 1998). However, the findings from this body of research and subsequent conclusions that can be drawn are not very straightforward. A number of questions regarding the what, why, and when of diversity still remain. This chapter reviews the current literature and assesses the state of the field to highlight fruitful areas of development for diversity research. More specifically, the findings of research focused on the conceptualization of diversity, theoretical perspectives on the effects of diversity, such effects across levels of analysis, and the evolution of diversity management are summarized. Further, using this summary as a springboard, challenges, unanswered questions, and other gaps in the diversity literature and suggested directions for future research in this area are highlighted.

Conceptualization of Diversity

In principle, diversity refers to any difference between people that may lead them to perceive that another person is similar to, or different from, self (Jackson, 1992). Accordingly, diversity can indicate demographic attributes, such as gender and age, or non-demographic attributes, such as educational background and personality. As researchers have attempted to explore and understand the effects of diversity, several conceptualizations of diversity have emerged. These typologies of diversity are discussed below.

One approach to viewing diversity is as a characteristic of the individual that facilitates identity distinctions between people. Termed the *factor approach* by Mannix and Neale (2005), this conceptualization of diversity concentrates on a focal person's differences relative to others, based on specific types of diversity. Tsui and Gutek (1999) highlight a similar approach to the study of diversity—specifically, the categorical approach, which treats diversity as personal attributes of an individual and explores the effects of such attributes on individual-level outcomes. Using a factor/category lens, individuals may be separated into subgroups based on any number of attributes, such as gender, physical ability, expertise, cultural background, cognitive style, tenure, or socioeconomic status. However, given the range of attributes on which individuals may differ, researchers have attempted to categorize different types of diversity. For example, in a narrative review of diversity research by Jackson and her colleagues (1995), they differentiated between diversity attributes based on the degree to which they are visible or readily detected. Observable differences include such characteristics as gender, rage, age, and physical ability. Accordingly, observable diversity primarily encompasses biological or innate characteristics, many of which are legally protected from discrimination in the United States and other countries. In contrast, non-observable diversity is represented by personal characteristics, such as ability, education, knowledge, tenure, and background. Also labeled *diversity in underlying attributes* (Jackson, May, & Whitney, 1995), this category encapsulates less salient markers of diversity in organizational contexts. Other researchers have made similar distinctions between dimensions of diversity—in particular, differentiating between types of diversity based on their perceptibility or visual salience (see Milliken & Martins, 1996).

Research has also distinguished between types of diversity based on their relationship to work group performance. Pelled (1996) conceptualized another bifurcated classification of diversity in which diversity dimensions were separated according to job-relatedness, or the degree to which each dimension captures the knowledge, skills, and abilities relevant to the performance of cognitive tasks. Differences that are highly job-related are believed to facilitate effective group performance, while those that are less job-related are not seen as directly related to task-related group processes and performance (Simons, Pelled, & Smith, 1999). For example, diversity characteristics such as education or functional background are seen as engendering experiences and perspectives important to tasks performed by most work groups, thereby influencing group output. In contrast, characteristics such as gender and ethnicity, while influential to group members' experiences and perspectives, are considered to be less relevant to the technical work of groups. Instead, these more visible diversity characteristics are likely to impact member relations and attitudes (Pelled, 1996; Pelled, Eisenhardt, & Xin, 1999).

Harrison and colleagues (Harrison, Price, & Bell, 1998; Harrison, Price, Gavin, & Florey, 2002) built upon the two-factor conceptualization of diversity and distinguished between surface-level and deep-level diversity characteristics. Diversity at a surface level is described as innate differences among group members that are typically reflected in members' physical features (Harrison et al., 1998). Consistent with Jackson et al.'s (1995) typology, these characteristics, such as gender, age, and ethnicity, are observable or readily detected. However, Harrison et al. (1998) also note that such diversity in groups is easily measured. Deep-level diversity is described as acquired attributes that are task-relevant, yet not easily measured, such as education and functional expertise. Diversity at a deep level reflects differences in members' values, beliefs, and attitudes, and is revealed through interactions among group members (Harrison et al., 1998, 2002).

Other research has utilized a two-pronged categorization of diversity. Termed the *proportional approach* by Mannix and Neale (2005), researchers utilizing this view of diversity have focused on the amount of diversity within groups as the variable of interest. Similarly, Tsui and Gutek (1999) refer to the *compositional approach*, which views diversity as a structural property of groups, organizations, and other collectives, and examines its effects on outcomes across levels of analysis. Inspired by Blau's (1977) and Kanter's (1977) work on the influence of proportions on interactions between demographically dissimilar groups, the central premise of such research is that the percentage of any minority within a group will influence the quality of relations between group members. In other words, proportional/compositional approaches

to diversity separate differences based on group members' majority/minority or in-group/out-group status. Organizational demography research has explored gender, age, race, tenure, and background proportions in diverse work settings and has highlighted subsequent effects on group processes and functioning (see Williams & O'Reilly, 1998). Thus, a focus on relative differences, or the distribution of differences within groups, has also been a useful conceptualization of diversity.

Recently, Harrison and Klein (2007) put forth a model that also conceptualizes diversity as a structural characteristic of organizational work units. Similar to the proportional/compositional approaches described above, they describe diversity as "the distribution of differences among the members of a unit with respect to a common attribute" (p. 1200). However, Harrison and Klein (2007) propose that the distribution of differences within a group may take one of three forms—separation, variety, or disparity—based on the type of differences. Separation illustrates differences in values, beliefs, and attitudes, and signals perceptual disagreement between unit members. In contrast, variety focuses on differences in the knowledge, networks, and experiences of unit members, and reflects unique or distinctive sources of information within the unit. Also referred to as *informational diversity* by some scholars (e.g., Jehn, Northcraft, & Neale, 1999; Williams & O'Reilly, 1998), diversity as variety expands a collective's cognitive and behavioral resources. Thus, Harrison and Klein (2007) further distinguish between types of deep-level diversity (Harrison et al., 1998, 2002) or between the job-relatedness of diversity attributes (Pelled, 1996; Pelled et al, 1999). Beyond personal attributes, Harrison and Klein (2007) also conceptualize diversity as disparity, or differences in access to, or ownership of, valued resources such as privilege, status positions, and pay. Similar to research on status and power hierarchies (see Thye, 2000), the form of diversity as disparity focuses on inequality or the relative concentration of desired resources. Overall, Harrison and Klein (2007) offered a broader conceptualization of diversity intended to clarify its meaning and measurement.

Although the aforementioned approaches to diversity provide researchers with the means to examine a broad array of attributes, there is a key limitation to these approaches in that they focus only on a single attribute at one time. In other words, although a study may explore the effects of a number of diversity characteristics, such categorical conceptualizations of diversity do not allow a consideration of the interactions between the characteristics. Thus, Lau and Murnighan (1998) proposed a multifaceted conceptualization of diversity that reconciles and integrates the different categorical approaches. With a consistent focus on diversity as a structural property of groups and organizations, Lau and Murnighan (1998) offered their theory of group faultlines, which examines the effects of member characteristics in combination. According to the theory, faultlines are assumed lines of demarcation based on group member attributes that divide the group into smaller, identity subgroups. Further, fault line strength is dependent upon the number of observable attributes and the relationship between these attributes. Specifically, more attributes and high correlations between the attributes will cause group members to identify more strongly with their subgroups than with the larger groups. For example, a project team consisting of three males under the age of 30 with marketing backgrounds and three females over the age of 30 with operations backgrounds will experience strong faultlines, as members are likely to perceive greater similarity to others with whom they share demographic characteristics. Further, such divisions are likely to result in status differences, which negatively impact group processes and functioning (Lau & Murnighan, 1998).

In an effort to understand the effects of diversity, researchers have proposed a number of typologies. While many of these categorizations adopt a bifurcated view of diversity based on the extent to which a diversity attribute is observable or job-related, more recent research suggests that alternative approaches to diversity may provide greater insight into diversity's effects. First, multi-attribute conceptualizations of diversity may more accurately represent complex interactions between diversity attributes in groups. Second, matching diversity constructs to their underlying theoretical assumptions may allow more appropriate tests of the effects of heterogeneity in groups. Thus, even as current typologies establish a stronger link between diversity attributes and related theoretical perspectives, more methodological rigor in operationalizing diversity and investigating processes stimulated by diversity is needed.

Theoretical Perspectives on the Effects of Diversity

Beyond variability in the conceptualization of diversity, researchers have relied upon different theoretical approaches to observing the effects of diversity in organizations. Some approaches discuss diversity from an identity perspective, considering the social outcomes of individuals' cognitions about themselves and others. Other approaches study diversity with the group as a focal construct. Following these perspectives, researchers consider the processes underlying intergroup relations. More recent research approaches diversity from an organization-level perspective, with an eye toward the ways in which heterogeneity in the workforce enhances organizational functioning and competitiveness. All of these theoretical perspectives are reviewed below.

A considerable amount of diversity research has been framed within the ideas offered by social-psychological theories of intergroup relations, such as social identity and social categorization theories (Tajfel, 1978; Turner, 1985). These theories articulate processes through which individuals make sense of, and locate themselves within, their social environments (Turner, 1987), and therefore are useful for exploring the processes underlying diversity in groups. Social identity theory (Tajfel, 1978) argues that individuals are motivated to enhance their self-concept by seeking a positively valued distinctiveness for their in-groups. By engaging in social comparisons, people differentiate between their in-groups and relevant out-groups, and are able to evaluate their social identities (Tajfel & Turner, 1979). Self-categorization theory (Turner, 1985) proposes that as certain social categories become salient, there is a qualitative shift in social perception such that people come to view themselves (and others) more in terms of their group memberships than in terms of their personal identities (Turner, Hogg, Oakes, Reicher, & Wetherell, 1987). Accordingly, this categorization process accentuates similarities among individuals sharing group memberships and differences among individuals belonging to different identity groups (Turner, 1985).

Research suggests that group identification is a key determinant of individuals' proclivity for defining themselves as members of social groups and engaging in intergroup behavior (Tajfel, 1978; Turner, 1987). Specifically, group identification motivates individuals to maximize the distinction between their in-groups and other social groups and to create a positive group identity (Turner, 1985, 1987). In so doing, individuals tend to depersonalize their identity and, subsequently, to stereotype themselves and others as representatives of social categories rather than as unique individuals (Turner, 1987). Intergroup differentiation becomes more pronounced as perceived similarity to in-group members and dissimilarity to out-group members is amplified (Turner, 1987). Further, people tend to exhibit higher levels of trust for, and affective reactions to, members of their in-groups, thereby resulting in a bias in favor of members of one's in-groups and against members of one's out-groups (Tajfel & Turner, 1986; Turner et al., 1987).

Given that social categorization processes are primarily influenced by contextual factors that accentuate specific group identities (Oakes, 1987), this perspective provides theoretical insight into the effects of diversity. Research suggests that observable demographic attributes, such as gender and race, are likely to be salient in group contexts (Kanter, 1977), and influence feelings of group identification (Tsui, Egan, & O'Reilly, 1992). As such, demographic attributes are a likely basis for intergroup differentiation (Nelson & Klutas, 2000). Such differentiation is likely to impair social processes, such as communication and cohesion, within groups (Williams & O'Reilly, 1998).

A similar theoretical foundation for the effects of diversity derives from the similarity-attraction paradigm (Byrne, 1971). According to the paradigm, people are more attracted to those whom they perceive to have similar beliefs, values, and attitudes (Berscheid & Walster, 1978). Consistent with the predictions of social identity and categorization theories, such attraction is likely to produce in-group/out-group distinctions and to influence intergroup relations (Byrne, 1971; Clore & Byrne, 1974). Research has shown that demographic similarity also influences attraction (Berscheid, 1985) and social integration with groups (e.g., Jehn et al., 1997; Tsui, Ashford, St. Clair, & Xin, 1995). Thus, the similarity-attraction paradigm may also help to explain how diversity influences individual-level and group-level outcomes.

Other theories consider the ways in which diversity impacts intergroup relations, although their predictions for the effects of diversity on group functioning differ. For example, Blau's (1977) theory of intergroup relations suggests that group functioning is influenced by the opportunity for, and quality of, social interaction among diverse individuals. Based on the logic of the social-contact hypothesis, which suggests that interaction among individuals will increase attraction, liking, and understanding (Pettigrew, 1982), the theory suggests that diversity in groups will result in increased contact among dissimilar individuals. However, the proportional representation of different demographic groups will influence the quality of such interactions (Blau, 1977; Kanter, 1977). Groups with skewed proportions of demographic attributes will have qualitatively worse interactions, and consequently lower group functioning, due to the marginalization of minority members (Kanter, 1977). In contrast, greater demographic balance will result in increased intergroup contact, which will positively impact the quality of interpersonal relations and cooperation among diverse individuals. Competition theories (Blalock, 1967) assume a parallel perspective on the study of diversity, although the predictions are in the opposite direction. These theories suggest that intergroup relations are influenced by the perceived scarcity of available resources and the potential for loss of valued resources to other groups. More specifically, out-group members are perceived to present a challenge to the economic, political, and/or social resources of in-groups. Because the loss of resources may negatively affect a group's collective interests and identity (Bobo, 1983), groups are likely to develop defensive ideologies and strategies against competing groups (Bonacich, 1972). Subsequently, the balanced representation of in-groups and out-groups is likely to induce hostility, coalition formation, competition, and discrimination among diverse individuals (Levine & Campbell, 1972). Overall, these theories, which are congruent with proportional conceptualizations of diversity, focus on the relational effects of demographic similarity/dissimilarity in groups.

Another theoretical perspective on the effects of diversity is the *value-in-diversity* hypothesis (Cox, Lobel, & McLeod, 1991), which suggests that diversity enhances group decision making. More specifically, this perspective establishes that diversity can create value and benefit for groups because individuals in heterogeneous groups have a broader range of knowledge, skills, and abilities than homogeneous groups (Hoffman, 1959; Hoffman & Maier, 1961). With this larger pool of cognitive resources, diverse groups are assumed to have greater access to a variety of task-relevant information and expertise. Further, diversity in groups may provide access to a larger and more varied social network from which to draw additional resources (Ancona & Caldwell, 1992). Research suggests that such diversity in informational resources may also enhance group problem solving, as different opinions, approaches, and perspectives give rise to task conflict and dissent (Jehn et al., 1999; Pelled et al., 1999). Further, exposure to minority viewpoints may expose, and may motivate the consideration of, more creative alternatives and solutions (Ancona & Caldwell, 1992; Nemeth, 1986). Thus, the value-in-diversity perspective predicts that dissimilarity will enhance decision-making quality in groups and organizations.

Recently, researchers have started to view the effects of diversity from a macro standpoint. From a strategic human resource management perspective, a firm's human capital, or the combined knowledge, skills, and abilities in its workforce, may be a strategic resource (Wright & McMahan, 1992). Given that the specific demography of an organization cannot be perfectly duplicated by competitors and can facilitate competencies that develop from complex social relationships (Barney, 1991), diversity may serve as a source of sustained competitive advantage. Cox and Blake (1991) propose the ways through which such advantages could accrue from diversity in organizations, including the ability to understand the needs and demands of diverse consumer markets, to recruit the best talent, to adapt products or services to market needs, and to reduce costs associated with turnover, absenteeism, and lack of productivity. Similar to the value-in-diversity hypothesis (Cox et al., 1991), this perspective predicts that diversity will enhance problem-solving and decision-making processes. However, the effects of diversity are primarily through the economic value created by such demographic differences in organizations.

Overall, researchers have relied upon a number of perspectives to articulate the processes underlying diversity. These perspectives sort out the potential effects of a range of diversity characteristics—both demographic attributes and more latent individual differences. In addition, they allow an understanding of the constructive and destructive outcomes of distinctiveness and difference in groups and organizations. Although diversity research may benefit from more conceptual integration, these theoretical perspectives provide insight into individuals' capacities to work effectively together.

Diversity Effects Across Levels of Analysis

Several scholars have provided reviews of diversity research to assess the effects of diversity on teams and organizations (cf. Jackson et al., 2003; Mannix & Neale, 2005; Milliken & Martins, 1996; van Knippenberg & Schippers, 2007). Generally, such research shows that diversity influences various types of outcomes (e.g., affect, behavioral processes, performance) and at different levels of analysis (i.e., individual, group, organization). These outcomes, both within and across levels, are discussed below.

Individual Effects

Relational demography research, or research focusing on the proportional representation of differences in groups, has examined the effects of diversity on individual outcomes (Harrison & Klein, 2007). Based on the tenets of social identity and categorization (Tajfel, 1978; Turner, 1985), such research assumes that demographic similarity/dissimilarity will activate in-group/out-group distinctions. Another assumption is that these distinctions will influence liking for, or attraction to, members of the group (Byrne, 1971). Thus, with dyads or groups as the focal unit of analysis, researchers have explored the effects of group categorizations on member work-related attitudes and behavior.

Overall, the preponderance of the empirical evidence supports a link between demographic similarity, perceived similarity or attraction, and individual outcomes (see Williams & O'Reilly, 1998, for a review). Investigating a range of demographic characteristics, including gender, race, age, education, and tenure, such relational research demonstrates that greater diversity in groups is related to lower attachment and personal liking for dissimilar members (Tsui et al., 1992; Tsui & O'Reilly, 1989). Further, these similarity-attraction outcomes negatively impact several factors related to group functioning, such as member commitment, absenteeism, turnover, and, ultimately, performance (Tsui et al., 1992).

Based on the results of research highlighting the impact of group demographic composition on individuals, Williams and O'Reilly (1998) concluded that diversity in groups decreases the likelihood that member needs will be met by group membership. Further, they suggested that similarity-attraction outcomes will negatively impact member relations and their ability to work together effectively over time. While the results of research on the individual effects of diversity do evoke a pessimistic view of dissimilarity in groups, studies at the group level of analysis provide insight into both the destructive and constructive consequences of diversity in groups. This work is reviewed in the next section.

Group Effects

Much of the research on diversity's effects has focused on group processes and performance, although the findings provide support for different theoretical perspectives (Mannix & Neale, 2005; Milliken & Martins, 1996; Williams & O'Reilly, 1998). Following a social categorization perspective, researchers have explored the proposition that diversity weakens social processes. Accordingly, the findings of such research have shown diversity (in different forms) to be negatively associated to relational variables, such as group cohesion and communication (O'Reilly, Caldwell, & Barnett, 1989; Zenger & Lawrence, 1989). However, some studies have provided results contrary to the "pessimistic" predictions of social-psychological theories of intergroup relationships. For example, Smith et al. (1994) studied the effects of functional diversity in top management teams and found no significant relationship with intragroup social processes, such as social integration or communication. Similarly, research has also shown tenure and background diversity to be positively related to communication within groups (Ancona & Caldwell, 1992; O'Reilly, Snyder, & Boothe, 1993).

Given insufficient empirical support for the proposition that diversity impairs group functioning given weakened social processes, researchers have proposed boundary conditions for these relationships. One proposition is that group processes are dependent upon the type(s) of diversity in groups (see Jackson et al., 1995; Milliken & Martin, 1996). However, the findings of a meta-analysis by Webber and Donahue (2001), in which the authors explored the differential impact of social category diversity and informational diversity on group cohesion, did not provide support for this proposition. Distinguishing between the types of diversity in terms of their level of job-relatedness, the results revealed no significant relationships between either type of diversity and cohesion and, therefore, no differential impact across diversity types. A more recent study by Lau and Murnighan (2005) took a different perspective of the role of diversity type and explored the effects of demographic faultlines, or multi-attribute indices of diversity, on group communications. The results showed that the convergence of gender and ethnicity within groups increased the salience of demographic subgroups, resulting in suboptimal communication. Overall, current research suggests that the interaction between different types of diversity in groups (rather than the actual types of diversity) influence member identification and attachment, and, subsequently, member interactions.

Researchers have also explored the role of time in the social processes of diverse groups. For example, Watson, Kumar, and Michaelsen (1993) compared interaction processes of demographically homogeneous and heterogeneous groups over a 17-week period. While the less diverse groups initially had higher ratings of process effectiveness, the results showed that process ratings converged over time. Using a different diversity categorization scheme, Harrison and colleagues (1998) examined the impact of demographic (i.e., surface-level) versus attitudinal (i.e., deep-level) diversity on group social integration over time. The results showed that the negative effects of surface-level diversity weakened, and the positive effects of deep-level diversity strengthened, the longer group members worked together. As time may suppress the potentially negative effects of diversity in groups, given that members have increased opportunity to interact with and understand each other, these studies highlight time as a moderator to the relationship between diversity and group social processes.

Considering the established effects of conflict as a focal process in group functioning (De Dreu & Weingart, 2003), scholars have also investigated the impact of diversity on conflict. In doing so, they distinguish between two types of conflict—task conflict, or disagreements over ideas and opinions related to the task, and relationship conflict, or disagreements about non-work-related issues among members (Jehn, 1995, 1997), which are shown to be differentially related to group functioning. Some research proposes that task conflict stimulates the consideration of alternative points of view and solutions, which leads to improved group problem solving and decision making (Jehn, 1997). In contrast, research also proposes that relationship conflict detracts from group functioning, given the focus on individual differences and interpersonal issues (Jehn, 1995). Following this reasoning, diversity researchers have proposed that diversity will differentially relate to these two types of conflict. Given that social categorization processes may encourage intergroup differentiation, which subsequently influences social integration processes, research suggests that visible demographic characteristics, or surface-level diversity, will give rise to relationship conflict (Pelled, 1996). At the same time, less visible, or deep-level, diversity is argued to be associated with task conflict, given that this type of diversity brings about differences in opinions, perspectives, and approaches to problem solving (Pelled, 1996).

Research provides empirical evidence of the differential effects of diversity types on task and relationship conflict in groups. For example, using a three-category typology of diversity, Jehn et al. (1999) examined whether social category, informational, and value diversity differentially influenced group processes leading to specific types of conflict. The results showed that informational diversity increased task conflict within groups, while social category diversity brought about higher levels of relationship conflict. Interestingly, value diversity was associated with both types of conflict. In a similar study, Pelled and her colleagues (1999) categorized diversity characteristics based on visibility and job relevance, and examined the effects of gender, race, age, tenure, and functional diversity on task and relationship (termed *emotional*) conflict within teams. Consistent with the study's predictions, racial diversity, which is highly visible but low in job-relatedness, was found to influence higher levels of emotional conflict, while functional diversity, which has low visibility but is high in job-relatedness, was positively associated with task conflict. Interestingly, tenure diversity, which is argued to be high on both visibility and job-relatedness (Pelled, 1996), was shown to be linked to task, but not emotional conflict.

Although research has provided support for the differential effects of diversity on conflict in groups, the results of a study by Pelled et al. (1999) suggest that the relationships may not be as straightforward as predicted. The authors explored the role of group longevity (i.e., time) in the proposed relationships, and found evidence of moderating effects. Specifically, time interacted with race, tenure, and functional diversity such that the impact of these types of diversity on conflict was lessened as groups worked together for a longer period of time. Thus, as suggested by the authors, while time may give members of work groups the opportunity to develop a better interpersonal understanding of one another, it may give them the ability to learn and anticipate members' perspectives, which may facilitate less opposition to alternative opinions and ideas. This study also considered the effects of task routineness on group processes, although the pattern of results was quite complex. The positive association between racial and tenure diversity on emotional conflict was reduced for groups working on relatively routine tasks, while the relationship between functional diversity and task conflict was strengthened under such conditions. In addition to the interaction between diversity and task characteristics, Pelled et al. (1999) considered the combined effects of diversity dimensions included in the study. The findings showed that gender and age diversity interacted to produce a more negative effect on emotional conflict, while the interaction between age and tenure diversity lessened emotional conflict. Further, age and functional diversity facilitated higher levels of task conflict. Overall, these results highlight the complexities in the relationship between diversity and conflict in groups.

Given the demonstrated effects of diversity on group processes, research has also explored diversity's impact on group performance. Some research provides evidence of the indirect effects of diversity on performance through group conflict outcomes. For example, in Jehn, Chadwick, and Thatcher's (1997) study, demographic and value diversity were shown to increase relationship conflict, which subsequently lowered group functioning. In contrast, informational diversity, which increased task conflict, was positively related to ratings of group performance. While other research has demonstrated similar effects (Pelled et al., 1999), scholars have also examined a direct relationship between diversity and group performance. Research in this area has found both a positive association (Cox et. al., 1991; Jackson et al., 2003; Jehn et al., 1999) and a negative relationship (Jackson et al., 1991; Pelled et al., 1999) between diversity and performance or innovation. Thus, to tease out the true effects of diversity and explore different theoretical explanations for such effects, researchers have also explored the impact of specific types of diversity on performance. Similar to the results regarding the effects of diversity on group processes, studies have shown positive effects of informational dimensions of diversity, such as functional or occupational diversity, on performance (Jehn & Bezrukova, 2004; Pelled et al., 1999) and negative effects of racial diversity on performance (Jackson et al., 2003; Leonard, Levine, & Joshi, 2004). Research distinguishing between broader categories of diversity based on visibility or job-relatedness highlights similar patterns of performance effects (see Jehn et al., 1999).

Despite the findings of studies comparing the effects of demographic versus informational diversity on performance, recent meta-analyses provide mixed support for the moderating role of diversity type. Studies by Bowers, Pharmer, and Salas (2000) and by Webber and Donahue (2001) did not find significant relationships between observable or underlying diversity attributes and performance. However, in a meta-analysis by Horwitz and Horwitz (2007), task-related diversity was shown to be associated with the quantity and quality of team performance, although no significant relationship between demographic diversity and performance was found. Given the lack of strong support for neither the effects of social category diversity on group performance nor the value-in-diversity hypothesis (Cox et al., 1991), researchers have suggested that the existence of diversity in groups may be insufficient for influencing group functioning (van Knippenberg, De Dreu, & Homan, 2004). Instead, they suggest that groups must be able to recognize such diversity, reduce its potentially negative effects on group processes, and leverage its benefits for improved problem solving and decision making (Mannix & Neale, 2005; Williams & O'Reilly, 1998).

Researchers have also begun to identify the conditions under which different types of diversity have constructive or destructive effects on group performance. A number of studies have highlighted the importance of task characteristics as moderators of diversity effects (for a review, see Jackson, 1992). In addition, research provides evidence of temporal (Watson et al., 1993; Jehn & Mannix, 2001) and cultural (Chatman, Polzer, Barsade, & Neale, 1998; Chatman & Spataro, 2005) influences on the performance effects of diversity. A recent meta-analysis by Joshi and Roh (2009) examined the role of contextual factors across different levels of analysis on performance outcomes of task- and relationship-oriented diversity. The findings revealed few direct relationships between the diversity dimensions included in the study and performance. Social category dimensions of diversity, such as gender, race, and age, had small, negative relationships with team performance. In contrast, dimensions of informational diversity were positively related to team performance, although the effects of functional diversity were considerably larger than were those for educational and tenure diversity. Interestingly, these relationships were significantly larger after accounting for team, industry, and occupational moderators. Overall, these findings highlight context as an important determinant for how diversity is recognized and utilized in group contexts.

Organization Effects

Research within the strategic management literature has also examined the effects of diversity in groups—specifically, in top management teams. However, based on a different theoretical framework than is used in micro-research, this body of research has considered diversity's effects on organizational performance. Drawing upon upper echelons theory (Hambrick & Mason, 1984), which suggests that leaders will make decisions that are consistent with their executive orientation, researchers have posited that demographic characteristics are associated with executive orientation and thus influence strategic choices and decisions (Finkelstein & Hambrick,

1996). Accordingly, they predict that top management team demography will impact organizational performance. Studies that have tested this prediction have found mixed results, as both surface- and deep-level diversity characteristics were related to both positive and negative performance outcomes (for a review, see Milliken & Martins, 1996). To reconcile these results, researchers have investigated top management team decision-making processes. Similar to the findings of other research on diversity's effects on group processes, strategy research highlights a link between top management team demography and member interaction quality (cf. Knight et al., 1999).

While research demonstrates both direct and indirect links between executive diversity and firm performance, these inquires have primarily focused on the performance effects of skill and cognitive diversity. However, a recent study by Roberson and Park (2007) that examined the effects of racial diversity in leadership (operationalized as the 25 top-paid positions in a firm, given low representation of racial minorities on top management teams) on organizational performance is an exception. Using longitudinal data, the findings of this study offered support for a curvilinear relationship between leader racial diversity and several measures of firm financial performance, with the point of inflection occurring at between 20–25% minority representation on firm top management teams. Although few studies have considered the effects of demographic (other than age) diversity in top management teams, research has examined how gender and cultural diversity in management influences firm performance. In general, evidence of a positive relationship between female representation in management and firm returns exists (Shrader, Blackburn, & Iles, 1997). However, other studies suggest that this relationship is more complicated. For example, the findings of a study that assessed gender diversity among bank officials and managers showed that effects were conditioned upon the firm's strategic orientation, organizational culture, and the interaction among these variables (Dwyer, Richard, & Chadwick, 2003). In a similar study that included measures of both gender and racial diversity in management (Richard, Barnett, Dwyer & Chadwick, 2004), the results revealed additional complexities in the diversity-performance relationship. While the authors hypothesized a non-linear relationship, the results did not support their prediction. Instead, the authors found that a firm's entrepreneurial orientation moderated the U-shaped relationships, such that in firms with highly innovative strategic postures, both low and high racial diversity in management were associated with higher productivity than was moderate diversity. Overall, the results of studies on demographic diversity in leadership, while relatively inconclusive, suggest that diversity's effects can be either positive or negative, depending on a firm's strategic or cultural context.

Research has also examined the effects of workforce diversity on organizational performance. Similar to studies on diversity in management, the results of such research highlight the role of contextual moderators as determinants of the impact of diversity. For example, in a study of the diversity-performance relationship among financial institutions, Richard (2000) found no direct association between racial diversity in workforces and financial performance. Instead, the results highlighted the moderating influence of business strategy, as firms with greater diversity and a growth strategy were shown to experience higher return on equity than were firms with the same diversity and a no-growth or downsizing strategy. Similarly, Richard, McMillan, Chadwick, and Dwyer (2003) found that the performance effects of workforce racial diversity were contingent on firms' level of innovation, such that racial diversity enhanced performance for organizations pursuing an innovation strategy, whereas for banks low in innovation, performance declined. Frink and his colleagues (2003) considered the organizational performance effects stemming from the gender composition of workforces. Consistent with their predictions, the findings provided support for a curvilinear (i.e., inverted U) relationship between gender diversity and organizational performance, with the point of inflection occurring around the midpoint, or equal proportions of male and female employees. However, the results also showed an industry effect, as the pattern of results only held for the service/wholesale/retail industry sector.

Kochan and his colleagues (2003) undertook a series of field research projects to examine the relationships between race and gender diversity and business performance. While the results showed few direct effects of diversity on performance, they did reveal effects based on other demographic variables, such as manager characteristics and tenure diversity. In addition, the studies demonstrated positive effects of gender diversity on group bonuses in business units with people-oriented cultures, diversity-focused HR practices, and customer-oriented business strategies. The authors also found a negative relationship between racial diversity and performance in business units with competitive cultures, growth-oriented business strategies, and training-focused human resource practices. However, racial diversity was also found to have positive effects on performance in units that used diversity as a resource for innovation and learning. Similar to research on the effects of diversity in leadership, the results of Kochan et al. (2003) suggest that the organizational effects of diversity are contextually dependent.

Overall, the body of evidence regarding the effects of diversity highlights various ways that groups and organizations may be impacted by differences among people. Accordingly, conclusions about whether diversity and the context in which it occurs have important effects are relatively straightforward (see Table 31.1). What is not as clear is how to deal with such differences so that the perceptions and processes that can impair group functioning

Table 31.1 Summary of Diversity Effects Across Levels of Analysis

Level	Outcomes	Contextual Moderators
Individual	Similarity and attraction; e.g., attachment and personal liking Attitudes and behavior; e.g., commitment, absenteeism, turnover, performance	
Group	Relational variables; e.g., social integration, cohesion, communication, conflict (task and relationship) Performance (quantity and quality)	Time, task routineness, organizational culture, industry, occupation
Organization	Top management team variables; e.g., interaction quality and performance Firm productivity Firm financial performance	Business strategy, firm strategic orientation, industry, organizational culture, types of human resource practices

are constrained and the potential benefits of diversity are realized. To address this issue, organizations have designed and implemented human resource programs and initiatives. Accordingly, research has explored organizational approaches to diversity, the types of practices employed, and employees' experiences with, or reactions to, such practices. This research is reviewed in the following section.

Evolution of Diversity Management

Diversity management emerged from federal programs and initiatives designed to address employment discrimination in organizations. In the 1960s, the civil rights movement spawned employment legislation, such as Title VII of the Civil Rights Act, which made discrimination unlawful and required organizations to design programs to engender equal opportunity in the workplace. Equal employment opportunity and affirmative action (EEO/AA) initiatives soon developed into diversity management, as the result of a report describing anticipated changes in the business environment and the subsequent Workforce 2000 (Johnson & Packer, 1987). The report put forth that due to the globalization of markets and demographic shifts in the labor force, minorities and immigrants, women would become more largely represented in workforces. Accordingly, the authors predicted that organizations would be challenged to reconcile the work and family needs of women and to integrate ethnic minorities fully into the labor market (Johnson & Packer, 1987). Thus, by the late 1980s, organizations began recasting EEO/AA programs as part of efforts to manage increased diversity in organizations.

In organizations, managers distinguished diversity management from EEO/AA by emphasizing the business case for diversity, which suggests that there is value in the unique composition of a firm's workforce. Scholars have made a similar distinction, drawing from the resource-based view of the firm (Barney, 1991), which suggests that a firm's human capital, or the combined knowledge, skills, and abilities in its workforce, is a strategic resource. Specifically, because the specific combination of capabilities within, and social capital generated by, a firm's workforce cannot be duplicated or substituted by competitors (Barney, 1991), its workforce may serve as a source of sustained competitive advantage. Following this logic, the unique experiences, perspectives, and networks associated with demographic diversity in the workforce may also be beneficial to organizations. Such benefits are assumed to derive from an enhanced ability to understand and market

to diverse customer bases, to acquire more diverse talent pools, to procure resources, and to effectively respond to changes in the business environment (Cox & Blake, 1991). Konrad (2003) also suggests that demographic diversity brings about creativity, innovation, and enhanced problem solving, which will increase organizational competitiveness.

To realize these benefits, managers have adopted different approaches to diversity management. Accordingly, researchers have attempted to categorize the approaches. For example, Cox (1991) proposed a typology of organizations based on the degree of acculturation, structural and informal integration, lack of cultural bias, organizational identification, and intergroup conflict, which are considered to be conditions that influence whether organizations can fully realize the value in diversity. More specifically, Cox (1991) suggests that organizations can be characterized as monolithic, plural, or multicultural, based on the level of structural and cultural inclusion of employees across varying group memberships. Thus, while plural organizations may be characterized by a focus on employment profiles (i.e., workforce composition) and fair treatment, multicultural organizations may be characterized by policies and practices that facilitate the full utilization of human resources and enhance employees' abilities to contribute to their maximum potential.

Thomas and Ely (1996) also proposed a typology of organizational approaches to diversity that can be distinguished based on the degree to which diversity is considered as the varied knowledge and perspectives that members of different identity groups bring and is incorporated into the organization's strategies, operations, and practices. More specifically, Thomas and Ely (1996) identify the discrimination-and-fairness paradigm, which involves a focus on equal opportunity, fair treatment, recruitment and compliance, and the access-and-legitimacy paradigm, which focuses on matching workforce demographics with those of key consumer groups to expand and better serve specialized market segments, as the most common approaches to diversity management. However, they also highlight an emergent approach—the learning-and-effectiveness paradigm—which links diversity to organizational strategy, markets, processes, and culture. Following this approach, employee perspectives and work styles are incorporated into business processes to leverage the benefits of diversity for organizational learning and growth. Ely and Thomas (2001) found support for their proposed paradigms and subsequent effects on work group functioning in a qualitative study of three professional services organizations.

Given research which suggests that individuals from diverse social and cultural groups are often excluded from networks of information and opportunity in organizations (Ibarra, 1993), scholars have also identified the creation and maintenance of inclusive organizations as an approach to diversity management. Inclusion is defined as the extent to which individuals can access information and resources, are involved in work groups, and have the ability to influence decision-making processes (Mor Barak, & Cherin, 1998). Rather than emphasizing difference as an organizational commodity that has value in terms of economic performance, inclusion is focused on the degree to which individuals feel like full contributors in critical organizational processes (Mor Barak & Cherin, 1998). Although little empirical research to date has explored the concept of inclusion, a recent study by Roberson (2006) assessed the meanings of, and attributes for, diversity and inclusion in organizations. The results highlight the distinction between the two concepts, as well as the attributes that support each in organizations. However, due to overlap in the practices for managing diversity and those for facilitating inclusion, the results also suggest that the management of diversity is more complex than is currently articulated in both practitioner and scholarly research.

In a more fine-grained approach to the study of diversity management, researchers have identified specific practices to increase workforce diversity and manage differences among employees. Such practices include targeted recruitment initiatives, education and training, career development, and mentoring programs (Cox, 1991; Morrison, 1992). Researchers have also highlighted diversity initiatives to promote employee participation, communication, and community relations (Wentling & Palma-Rivas, 2000), which emphasize the removal of barriers that block employees from using the full range of their skills and competencies in organizations.

Konrad and Linnehan (1995) studied formalized human resource management structures, developed with the goal of improving the employment status of protected groups in organizations. In doing so, they propose two categories of structures—those that intentionally incorporate demographic identity into human resource decisions and those that do not. They distinguish between identity-blind structures, or formalized human resource management practices designed to ensure that decision-making processes are the same for each individual regardless of group identity, and identity-conscious structures, which are formalized human resource management practices that take both demographic group identity and individual merit into consideration. Thus, while the objective of both structures is to ensure that human resource decisions are based on individual merit, the method of achieving this objective differs for the two categories. Although research shows that identity-conscious practices are positively related to the employment status of protected groups in organizations (Konrad & Linnehan, 1995), research has also highlighted backlash against such practices and diversity management programs in general (see Linnehan & Konrad, 1999). In fact, members of both the majority group and protected groups in the United States have been shown to favor identity-blind over identity-conscious structures (Konrad & Linnehan, 1995). Thus, given negative reactions to identity-conscious structures, the authors suggest that organizations may be retreating from practices that focus on the specific and unique concerns of historically excluded groups in favor of more identity-blind structures that are responsive to the fears of exclusion and displacement among members of privileged groups (Konrad, 2003; Linnehan & Konrad, 1999).

A recent study examined the effectiveness of commonly implemented diversity programs that are designed to increase promote diversity in organizations (Kalev, Dobbin, & Kelly, 2006). Focusing on three sets of practices—those to establish organizational responsibility for diversity, those to reduce bias through education and feedback, and those to reduce the isolation of women and minority employees—the authors examined their subsequent effects on managerial diversity. The results showed that affirmative action plans, diversity committees and taskforces, and diversity managers (i.e., responsibility structures) were significantly related to increases in managerial diversity, while the effects of networking and mentoring programs (i.e., isolation reduction structures) were more modest. Diversity training and diversity evaluations for managers (i.e., bias reduction structures) were found to have no significant impact on managerial workforce composition. Interestingly, both isolation and bias reduction structures were found to be more effective when organizations had responsibility structures in place.

In addition to studying practices for managing diversity in organizations, researchers have also investigated how employees experience diversity and diversity management. A small body of research has examined diversity climates, or individual perceptions of the value for diversity in organizations as well as their organization's approach to diversity (Kossek & Zonia, 1993; Mor Barak, Cherin, & Berkman, 1998). Studies in this area have considered the dimensions of diversity climate and its role in explaining racial differences in employee outcomes (McKay, Avery, & Morris, 2008; McKay et al., 2007). Building upon diversity climate research, Roberson and Stevens (2006) examined the processes by which differences in employee diversity perceptions emerge. Using employees' recollections of diversity-related incidents at work, the authors assessed the types of incidents recalled, the language used to describe the incidents, and the salience of fairness issues within their descriptions to gain an understanding of diversity sense-making processes. In general, this study provides insight into how employees interpret their diversity-related experiences at work.

Overall, research on the evolution and execution of diversity management has established the importance of programs and initiatives to ensure that organizations create and maintain diversity workforces. This body of work also suggests the need for, and impact of, practices to manage similarities and differences between employees. Further, it highlights the potential for leveraging employees' unique skills and perspectives to improve organizational performance. While the findings in this area link research to practice and can inform organizations about the effective management of diversity, several unanswered questions still remain. These gaps, along with other opportunities for advancing the study of diversity and its effects, are discussed below.

State of the Field

As shown above, a large body of research has explored the meaning, import, and effects of diversity. Accordingly, we have a reasonable understanding of the cognitive and behavioral processes that are activated by differences—either actual or perceived—among members of organizational workgroups. In addition, the research allows some insight into how and under what conditions such processes impact group and organizational performance. Despite this progress within the field of diversity, much is still unclear about the operation and impact of diversity. These areas of development within the diversity literature are highlighted in the following section.

Limited View of Diversity

Although diversity research has considered the effects of a wide range of demographic characteristics and personal attributes, it has generally adopted a limited view of diversity. In their reviews of the literature, scholars have concluded that much of the research has primarily focused on readily-detected dimensions of diversity, such as gender, race/ethnicity, and age (Jackson et al., 2003). While top management team research has incorporated a broader focus on less visible characteristics, such as tenure and educational and functional background (Milliken & Martins, 1996), relatively less attention has been given to the compositional influences of such characteristics in work teams and organizational workforces. There may be several explanations for this focus on surface-level diversity. First, given that such demographic characteristics are observable, they are more easily measured (Harrison & Klein, 2007). Researchers can straightforwardly assess the spread of members across different categories, typically utilizing Blau's index (1977), which is the most commonly used indicator of demography or group composition (e.g., Bunderson & Sutcliffe, 2002). Thus, while other operationalizations of diversity or dispersion may more accurately reflect within-unit differences or meaningful relationships between variability in such differences and outcome variables (Harrison & Klein, 2007; Roberson, Sturman, & Simons, 2007), the measurement of diversity may have constrained the consideration of a broader range of diversity attributes.

Second, although researchers have begun conceptualizing and studying the effects of diversity as a multi-attribute construct (cf., Lau & Murnighan, 1998, 2005; Li & Hambrick, 2005; Thatcher, Jehn, & Zanutto, 2003), most research has focused on traditional categorizations of diversity attributes. Specifically, diversity continues to primarily be conceptualized as the degree to which individuals differ in terms of one demographic characteristic. Few studies have explored the interactive effects of different types of diversity within a group. Further, those studies that have adopted a multidimensional approach to diversity still concentrate on the confluence of readily detected attributes. Consequently, we have limited insight into whether the effects of observable diversity characteristics on group functioning are dependent upon the presence or absence of deeper level characteristics.

Finally, while scholars have highlighted the globalization of business as motivation for studying diversity in organizations, research has for the most part approached diversity from a U.S. perspective. As previously discussed, diversity management initiatives are an outpouring of equal employment opportunity and affirmative action laws and regulations, which generally prohibit discrimination based on certain protected categories. While the law makes treating people less favorably based on nationality, ethnicity, or accent illegal, little research has examined the effects of national origin diversity. More important, however, scant diversity research has given attention to the influence of culture. Generally, culture is defined as the "collective programming of the mind which distinguishes the members of one group or category of people from those of another" (Hofstede, 1994, p. 4). Engendering the values and beliefs that are widely shared within a specific society, culture influences how people think and behave (Schwartz, 1992). With globalization, companies are challenged to adjust their operating practices to accommodate the cultural styles, norms, and preferences of the regions of the world in which they operate. Some scholars and practitioners assert that U.S. diversity policies are built upon a national culture, which overlays a variety of subcultures and therefore may be applicable across a variety of contexts (Egan & Bendick, 2003). However, because other continents are amalgamations of countries, which give rise to different cultures, norms, and languages, conceptualizations of diversity must incorporate these differences.

Research-driven Measurement

Most existing studies have used experimental manipulations and survey measures designed by researchers to study organizational phenomena. Although useful for generating observations consistent with researchers' conceptions of those phenomena, these methodologies offer little insight into how employees themselves interpret their experiences or their relative sensitivity to various facets of those experiences. Further, it is difficult to gauge the salience of diversity concerns when survey questions cue respondents to consider such issues and on preselected dimensions. Thus, diversity research should utilize methodologies that ensure that people's responses are not altered by features or artifacts of the observational setting. Roberson and Stevens (2006) provide a useful example of employing an alternative methodology for the study of diversity. Adopting a sense-making perspective to analyze employees' recollections of diversity-related incidents in the workplace, the authors examined written accounts that employees had designated as

positive or negative examples of diversity incidents. By allowing respondents to describe in their own words the diversity incidents they had observed, Roberson and Stevens (2006) were able to explore the richness of people's natural language accounts of diversity-related experiences at work. The use of similar methodologies may allow researchers to study diversity-related processes that spontaneously occur in relatively unobservable settings.

Based on the assumption that demographic attributes are reasonable proxies for, and predictors of, deep-level differences, diversity research has also primarily relied on the measurement of observable characteristics. Although such characteristics may be easily measured, a critical concern is whether it is methodologically appropriate to link surface- and deep-level diversity characteristics (Mannix & Neale, 2005). Diversity research provides weak support for such a link (Lawrence, 1997). The findings of identity research also fail to support this proxy-driven approach by highlighting the extent to which one's self-views and appraisals by others can be misaligned (Swann, 1987). Thus, research that measures the relationship between demographic attributes and underlying psychological constructs is needed. Further, research should assess people's cognitions of themselves and/or identification with demographic groups for a better understanding of how diversity influences collective attitudes, experiences, and outcomes.

Fragmented Theory Development

To understand diversity in organizations, researchers have drawn upon a variety of theoretical perspectives. While such conceptual foundations have provided insight into the construct of diversity and its consequences, much of the research has largely developed in disconnected research traditions (van Knippenberg et al., 2004). For example, micro-diversity research focuses on how people experience diversity—in particular, their perceptions of others who belong to different social groups and the subsequent impact on intragroup dynamics. Accordingly, researchers have primarily worked within the traditions of social identity and self-categorization theories and the similarity-attraction paradigm. Other work has examined category-based perception from a cognitive rather than relational perspective. For example, research has explored the automaticity of categorizations, including stereotyping (Fiske & Taylor, 2008) and implicit bias (Banaji & Greenwald, 1995). Although such research has considered the effects of such processes on individual attitudes, behaviors, and career outcomes, few links have been made to intergroup relations and diversity management in organizations.

Diversity researchers have also explored diversity as a collective construct and its effects on intergroup dynamics. Focusing on the group as a unit of analysis, such work has examined proportional representation along specified demographic dimensions and consequent effects on group processes and performance. To study diversity from this perspective, researchers have primarily relied upon theories of intergroup relations. Within sociological traditions, however, a meso-level approach, which considers social interaction processes both within and between groups, has also been utilized. Because membership in various social groups is also associated with systematic differences in power, status, and access to resources (Ridgeway & Berger, 1986), such research has explored how such differences impact member social influence and other interaction processes. While this approach provides a more dynamic view of the effects of heterogeneity in groups, little research has considered the effects on group decision making and performance.

Macro-level diversity research has examined the effects of workforce diversity on organizational performance. Employing a strategic human resource management framework, organization-level diversity research has examined whether heterogeneity among employees as an organizational asset creates value that is manifested in firm financial performance. While the findings of such research support a diversity-performance linkage, the true value of diversity within organizations in relatively unknown. One key assumption is that greater workforce diversity will broaden and enhance problem solving and decision making within organizations. Another assumption is that matching the demographics of organizational workforces with that of consumers will help firms to gain access to, and legitimacy in, diverse markets (Thomas & Ely, 1996). However, few studies have explored the ways in which diversity translates into firm performance. Further, scant attention has been given to how and the extent to which diversity management practices implemented by organizations impact employees' diversity-related experiences and intergroup relations.

Limited Focus on Process

Most studies examining the effects of demographic diversity in teams either implicitly on explicitly propose an input-process-output (IPO) model (Jackson et al., 2003; Kochan et al., 2003;

Williams & O'Reilly, 1998). That is, the effects of diversity on group performance are generally explained by the effects of diversity on a range of cognitive (e.g., information processing), behavioral (e.g., conflict), and affective (e.g., liking, cohesion) group processes (Kozlowski & Bell, 2003). Jackson et al. (2003) note that relatively few studies have examined the effects of diversity on group processes alone or have examined these processes as mediators of the proposed diversity-to-performance relationship. When these linkages have been examined, the effects of demographic diversity on group processes, much like the effects on group performance, have often been mixed (Jackson et al., 2003; Williams & O'Reilly, 1998). Further, most studies have failed to support the argument that the effects of diversity on performance are mediated by group processes. In fact, there has been little empirical substantiation of the social categorization and informational processes through which diversity is theorized to operate (van Knippenberg & Schippers, 2007). In light of this finding, several researchers have suggested that the effects of diversity on group processes occur somewhat independently of the effects of diversity on performance (Jackson et al., 2003; Kochan et al., 2003). Overall, Mannix and Neale (2005, p. 43) conclude, "...the actual evidence for the input-process-output linkage is not as strong as one might like."

It has been suggested that to better understand these linkages, future research needs to focus greater attention on the underlying mechanisms that account for diversity's effects. Lawrence (1997), for example, has argued that demographic effects stem from a "black box" logic in which the social-psychological mechanisms of diversity have not been well explicated. While Williams and O'Reilly (1998) suggest that Lawrence's (1997) argument is "forced," they agree that "we need more explicit tests of the underlying theories which permit us to understand how and when demographic diversity will be associated with different outcomes" (p. 117). Mannix and Neale (2005) suggest that diversity research should also assess individual-level underlying constructs that are assumed to be driving group-level processes, such as the lack of social integration or conflict, which ultimately result in poor performance.

To better understand the diversity-performance link in organizations, research is needed to explore the mechanisms through which diversity creates value in organizations. While there has been some identification and examination of diversity practices implemented by organizations (e.g., diversity recruitment, mentoring, diversity education), there is little published research assessing the effectiveness of these practices or their impact on organizational outcomes. In addition, little attention has been given to the extent to which workforce diversity improves firm capabilities and business processes (e.g., procurement, manufacturing, marketing), or firm competitiveness. Accordingly, research is needed to investigate the usefulness of human resource interventions and initiatives in assisting work groups in understanding and utilizing the different knowledge, perspectives and skills represented in diverse workforces. Research is also needed to examine the impact of diversity and related interventions on organizations' complete diversity agendas.

The Bounded Role of Context

Theoretical perspectives on the effects of diversity provide some insight into how similarities and differences between people influence intergroup relations, group functioning, and organizational performance. Note, however, that research has also demonstrated that contradictory predictions of diversity's effects can be made, depending on the theoretical perspective that is emphasized. For instance, research on workgroup diversity suggests that while demographic diversity may stimulate destructive group processes, such effects are reduced over time. Similarly, organization-level diversity research suggests that racial workforce diversity may either increase or decrease organizational performance, based on firm strategy or culture. While researchers have identified context as an important determinant of the direction and strength of relationships between diversity and group or organizational outcomes, empirical investigations of the nature and magnitude of specific features of contexts have been limited.

One striking feature of research on diversity in groups is the tendency to decontextualize workgroups, or not account for idiosyncratic influences of environments in which individuals and groups operate. Jackson and her colleagues (2003) draw attention to this curious lack of information about the contexts in which diversity research is conducted. Although the features of experimental or field contexts might be described in diversity studies, little consideration is given to whether and how such features might amplify or diminish the effects of diversity. Of course, it is infeasible to think that all contextual characteristics of diversity research can measured and/or controlled. However, researchers should attempt to assess those characteristics that

have been shown to have an effect on how diversity relates to group and organizational outcomes. Further, researchers should both illustrate the contexts in which diversity studies are conducted and provide some discussion of how the contexts described may have influenced their study results (Jackson et al., 2003).

The limited attention to context within the diversity literature has also occurred regarding antecedents to diversity-related psychological processes and intergroup dynamics. As noted by Weick (1995), context influences what information becomes salient and how cues will be interpreted. Accordingly, without identifying context, we have a narrow understanding of the activation of social identity and categorization processes that facilitate the effects of diversity in groups. Further, the interactive effects of individuals' cognitive processes and organizational diversity interventions are relatively unknown. Therefore, research is needed to explore how contextual factors stimulate cross-level diversity processes and outcomes.

Gap Between Research and Practice

Scholars have articulated the "business case" for diversity by identifying the ways in which differences among employees can increase organizational competitiveness (Cox & Blake, 1991). In addition, research provides some support for this business case by highlighting a link between diversity and organizational performance (Dwyer et al., 2003; Frink et al., 2003; Kochan et al., 2003; Richard, 2000; Richard et al., 2003; Roberson & Park, 2007; Shrader et al., 1997). While these findings demonstrate the practical value for diversity in organizations, conclusions that can be drawn from this research are somewhat limited, given that there are numerous internal factors (e.g., strategy, leadership, culture, etc.) and external factors (e.g., economic conditions, culture, industry dynamics, etc.) that may influence firm performance. Research has, however, explored the interaction between diversity and context, and has highlighted conditions under which diversity is more likely to positively impact firm financial performance. Based on the findings of this research, practitioners may extrapolate that the alignment of diversity with strategic orientation and/ or organizational culture influences the strategy's or culture's effectiveness. However, because most organization-level research does not allow insight into how diversity impacts firms' strategic capabilities and value-creating activities, practitioners have little guidance on how to manage or leverage diversity to positively impact organizational strategy, culture, and, ultimately, performance.

Research has examined the effectiveness of specific diversity practices (for a review, see Kulik & Roberson, 2008). Accordingly, research in this area can be useful for understanding how to better design diversity programs in organizations to enhance applicant attraction, employee skill and career development, and retention. A key limitation of this research, however, is a narrow focus on a single diversity practice area (e.g., recruitment, training, or mentoring). Given that organizations typically enact human resource systems rather than unitary practices, a practice-based approach to studying diversity management and its effects limits the practical value of such research. Some strategic human resource management researchers have argued for the use of human resource bundles as a means of achieving competitive advantage (Huselid, 1995). While there is variation in the practice bundles studied within the human resource management literature, diversity practices have been relatively absent from such research.

Some research has adopted a system perspective to the study of diversity management. For example, Konrad and Linnehan (1995) explored the outcomes of identity-conscious versus identity-blind human resource management structures, and found that identity-conscious practices were related to the employment status of members of protected demographic categories. Perry-Smith and Blum (2000) argued for the inclusion of bundles of work-family policies, including flexible work schedules, dependent care service, and information/referral service, in best practice research and explored the effects of such policies on organizational performance. The authors suggested that work-family policies can signal to potential and current employees that an organization values employee membership and sympathizes with the multitude of demands placed on today's employee. In return, employees may reciprocate by embracing the goals and putting forth additional effort on behalf of the organization. Thus, consistent with their predictions, the authors found that organizations with more extensive work-family policies experienced higher levels of financial performance. Overall, these findings establish the importance of giving research consideration to the interplay between diversity practices in research to provide managers with guidance for creating consistent diversity management systems that positively impact organizational functioning and performance.

Future Directions

In my review of the state of the diversity field, I identified a number of "gaps" where lingering questions still remain. As shown by an analysis of the findings of research to date, there are many possibilities and questions that could be theoretically developed more fully and empirically tested. Although in the previous section I drew attention to specific areas where more research is needed, here I pose several questions intended to open the door to future research that will disentangle current findings on diversity and better explain its effects.

How might we evolve the conceptualization of diversity to be generalizable across a variety of cultures?

Given the increased globalization of work and labor forces, researchers need to deconstruct diversity to understand its definition from a broader perspective. More specifically, current conceptualizations of diversity need to "open up" to allow for the consideration of a wider range of differences among employees in organizations. By focusing on easily measured diversity attributes or attributes that tend to be salient within a U.S. context, the study of diversity largely ignores the composition of global workforces and the resulting dynamics and consequences. Further, by disregarding cultural differences and the germane assumptions (e.g., values, norms, etc.) that might be present within research contexts, there are inherent boundary conditions to the findings of diversity research. Thus, diversity typologies that incorporate culture and related attributes (e.g., geographic location, language, religion) are needed.

Some current conceptualizations of diversity may easily accommodate a broader range of attributes. For example, cultural values may be subsumed under the categories of non-observable diversity (Jackson et al., 1995) or deep-level diversity (Harrison et al., 1998, 2002). However, such categorizations would limit our understanding of the extent to which and how cultural values influence group processes and performance. Multifaceted conceptualizations of diversity may be more useful for studying cultural diversity and its effects in organizations. Given that multiple cultural identities are combined and interact in different ways, Chao and Moon (2005) suggest a framework for identifying demographic, geographic, and associative features underlying culture. Specifically, they highlight physical, nature, and relational categories of culture that may be used to describe individuals, and they examine the impact of culture on group dynamics and functioning.

Thus, future diversity research may benefit from a cultural mosaic perspective. Given research which shows that individuals from diverse social and cultural groups are often excluded from networks of information and opportunity in organizations (Ibarra, 1993; Pettigrew & Martin, 1989), an inclusion perspective to the study of diversity might also be useful. Described as the degree to which an individual can fully and effectively contribute to a group or organization (Pelled et al., 1999), the concept of inclusion incorporates any differences that are used to limit a person's acceptance by others, access to resources, and participation and influence in decision-making processes (Mor Barak & Cherin, 1998). Accordingly, future research on individual similarities and differences may also benefit from an inclusion perspective.

What causal mechanisms are responsible for diversity's effects within groups and organizations?

Although most studies examining the effects of demographic diversity assume an input-process-output (IPO) framework, Jackson et al. (2003) note that relatively few studies have examined the effects of diversity on group processes. However, as shown in this review, an increasing number of studies give attention to the effects of diversity on affective-motivational constructs, such as cohesion and conflict. While such studies provide insight into the effects of diversity on intergroup relations, our understanding of concurrent effects on group behavioral processes, such as communication, cooperation, and coordination, is limited. Some research has examined the relationship between team diversity and the amount of communication among members (e.g., Ancona & Caldwell, 1992; Smith et al., 1994; Zenger & Lawrence, 1989). Still, additional research is needed to explore how diversity influences the qualitative nature of communications among diverse employees. In addition, future research should consider diversity's impact on activities required to manage interdependencies within organizational workflows, as well as factors that may prevent uncooperative tendencies and instead induce collaboration. Given that most studies on the effects of diversity only implicitly propose rather than examine an input-process-output (IPO) model, future research should also explore process mechanisms related to group effectiveness. That is, research should explore the extent to which diversity's effects can be explained by affective, cognitive, and behavioral outcomes.

Although research on diversity in teams highlights the effects of composition on group and organizational effectiveness, teams research highlights other design factors and external conditions that may impact team outcomes (Kozlowski & Bell, 2003). More specifically, features of the task, group, and organization may create conditions that facilitate or hinder effective performance. Research is needed to identify such conditions and their subsequent effects on diversity processes and outcomes. For example, given that task characteristics, such as team type or the level of interdependence, have been shown to influence communication in teams (Bettenhausen, 1991), the effects of diversity on communication outcomes may be exacerbated under certain conditions (e.g., heterogeneity may matter more for teams engaged in more creative work). Similarly, heterogeneity and practices to manage differences among employees may be more strongly related to firm performance under specific industry conditions (e.g., service or retail industries). Overall, more attention to what and how contextual features influence the outcomes of diversity is needed.

How can diversity be leveraged to enhance organizational functioning and performance?

Prior diversity research has suggested that the effects of diversity on organizational performance depend on strategic orientation (e.g., Richard, 2000), but strategy encompasses a wide range of actions designed and coordinated to exploit a firm's capabilities and gain a competitive advantage. Strategic capabilities represent a firm's ability to coordinate diverse operational skills and resources, link value-creating activities, and leverage infrastructures for collective learning and productivity (Prahalad & Hamel, 1990). As such capabilities are often developed through a firm's resources, including interaction and knowledge sharing among employees (Wright & McMahan, 1992), diversity may impact a firm's strategic capabilities. Research suggests that diversity can enhance organizational competitiveness in a variety of areas including resource acquisition, marketing, and organizational flexibility (Cox & Blake, 1991). For example, diversity may lead to a broader range of multicultural competencies and multilingual skills that allow workforces to better understand the needs of customers and that help to distinguish the firm among its competitors. Thus, research should focus on how diversity contributes to the development of a firm's strategic capabilities that impact organizational functioning and performance.

Researchers should also expand their operationalization of organizational performance. In most firm-level diversity research, performance has been indicated by financial measures, such as revenues/

sales, net income, returns, and productivity per employee. However, because such performance indices are influenced by a variety of internal and external factors, it is difficult to isolate the effects of diversity on firm performance. Although longitudinal research may be useful for examining diversity's long-term or cumulative effects, research should explore its effects on unit-level measures, human capital outcomes, or other measures of organizational effectiveness. For example, future research examining relationships between diversity and customer perceptions, such as diversity reputation and customer service, may provide insight into whether diversity enhances a firm's access and legitimacy in diverse markets. Similarly, research to assess how firms' skill inventories move with changes in the composition of organizational workforces may provide insight into the value for diversity in organizations.

What is the interplay of diversity processes at the individual, group, and organization levels of analysis?

Research highlights individual, group, and organizational effects of diversity although studies have primarily been concentrated at the group level of analysis. Jackson et al. (2003) notes this trend by highlighting that in their review of workplace diversity research published between 1997 and 2002, 79% focused on team and organizational outcomes and only 13% were at the organizational level. While a large body of research within the field of psychology has examined individual effects of diversity, research on diversity at higher levels of analysis has not considered the influence of individual-level processes. Thus, research that views and investigates diversity as a multilevel phenomenon may offer novel insights into the operation and consequences of diversity in organizations. For example, future research should explore how identity-related cognitions, such as categorization and implicit bias, and their affective or behavioral manifestations influence group-level interactions. Similarly, organization-level diversity research would be strengthened by examining the role of group-level processes like communication and conflict in the diversity-performance relationship.

Beyond these cross-level effects, research should incorporate a greater focus on dyadic interactions. Given that diversity has been viewed as an individual characteristic that facilitates identity distinctions among people, the dyadic level of analysis may expose researchers to other diversity-related processes in group contexts and therefore may capture a fuller spectrum of effects in groups and organizations. Further, a focus on dyads may allow researchers to isolate or manipulate the type and flow of information among individuals, thus providing additional insight into influence and identity negotiation, which may subsequently impact intergroup relations.

How might theories, concepts, and methodologies from other literatures or social science disciplines be used to inform and enhance our understanding of diversity?

Because most existing studies have relied upon more traditional methodologies, diversity research should seek to employ more innovative methods that allow exploration into the complexities of the diversity phenomena. The Implicit Association Test (IAT; Greenwald, McGhee, & Schwartz, 1998) is one example. Given the automaticity and immediacy of subtle biases, such cognitions are difficult to assess using survey methodologies. Thus, the IAT is a response-latency measure that assesses implicit bias. To tap into more latent and recurring patterns of cognition and behavior, diversity research may also benefit from the use of qualitative data and analysis techniques. In particular, the use of such methods may allow researchers to explore interrelationships among multifaceted dimensions of group interactions and to reveal qualities of group experiences in a way that quantitative methods cannot, while accounting for context.

Taking cues from network research, network methodologies might also be useful for examining interactions between groups. Network research has highlighted the value in access to unique information, and has shown that interorganizational networks provide access to diverse perspectives and information (Burt, 1992). For example, the findings of a study by Reagans and Zuckerman (2001) showed that interactions and collaboration among scientists with different contacts beyond the boundaries of their team improved productivity. Specifically, ties to others outside the team gave individuals access to distinct and diverse knowledge and information, which resulted in greater creativity and innovation, and, subsequently, productivity (Cross & Cummings, 2004). Likewise, network range has been linked to improved access to financial resources and financial information (Burt, 1992). Thus, ties to wide range of organizations may be associated with greater access to resources and information that may positively affect the focal firm's financial value.

Conclusion

As highlighted by this review, diversity has both negative and positive effects on group and organizational effectiveness. Similarly, the study of diversity has yielded both negative and positive outcomes for the field of I/O psychology. On the negative side, there is still much that we do not know about diversity. On the positive side, there is still much that we do not know about diversity. That is, there is both the threat that diversity research may remain stagnant by continuing along similar paths of investigation, and there is the opportunity to advance our understanding of the effects of similarities and differences among people. So, under what conditions can we avoid the potential threats of diversity research, yet capitalize on the opportunities? While it is somewhat a cliché to call for greater theoretical development and more empirical exploration, greater attention to the what, why, when, and how of diversity may provide insight into the complexities of the diversity phenomenon. Greater diversity in our conceptualizations, theoretical approaches, and methodologies may reveal more and varied information and expertise about diversity, as well as ways in which researchers can collaborate across disciplines. Such diversity in our research resources may subsequently enhance our problem solving around diversity research questions and may stimulate even more creative ways of exploring diversity-related phenomena. Thus, the "value" in diversity research may also be found in diversity.

References

Ancona, D. G., & Caldwell, D. F. (1992). Demography and design: Predictors of new product design team performance. *Organizational Science, 3*, 321–339.

Banaji, M. R., & Greenwald, A. G. (1995). Implicit gender stereotyping in judgments of fame. *Journal of Personality and Social Psychology, 68*, 181–198.

Barney, J. B. (1991). Firm resources and sustained competitive advantage. *Journal of Management, 17*, 99–120.

Berscheid, E. (1985). Interpersonal attraction. In G. Lindzey & E. Aronson (Eds.), *Handbook of social psychology* (Vol. 2, pp. 413–484). New York: Random House.

Berscheid, E., & Walster, E. H. (1978). *Interpersonal attraction.* Reading, MA: Addison-Wesley.

Bettenhausen, K. L. (1991). Five years of groups research: What we have learned and what needs to be addressed. *Journal of Management, 17*, 345–381.

Blalock, H. M., Jr. (1967). *Toward a theory of minority group relations.* New York: Wiley.

Blau, P. M. (1977) *Inequality and heterogeneity.* New York: Free Press.

Bobo, L. (1983). Whites' opposition to busing: Symbolic racism or realistic group conflict? *Journal of Personality and Social Psychology, 45*, 1196–1210.

Bonacich, E. (1972). A theory of ethnic antagonism: The split labor market. *American Sociological Review, 37*, 547–559.

Bowers, C., Pharmer, J., & Salas, E. (2000). When member homogeneity is needed in work teams: A meta-analysis. *Small Group Research, 31*, 305–327.

Bunderson, J. S., & Sutcliffe, K. M. (2002). Comparing alternative conceptualizations of functional diversity in management teams: Process and performance effects. *Academy of Management Journal, 45*, 875–893.

Burt, R. (1992). *Structural holes: The social structure of competition.* Cambridge, MA: Harvard University Press.

Byrne, D. (1971). *The attraction paradigm.* New York: Academic.

Chao, G. T., & Moon, H. (2005). The cultural mosaic: A meta-theory for understanding the complexity of culture. *Journal of Applied Psychology, 90*, 1128–1140.

Chatman, J. A., Polzer, J. T., Barsade, S. G., & Neale, M. A. (1998). Being different yet feeling similar: The influence of demographic composition and organizational culture on work processes and outcomes. *Administrative Science Quarterly, 43*, 749–780.

Chatman, J. A., & Spataro, S. E. (2005). Using self-categorization theory to understand relational demography-based variations in people's responsiveness to organizational culture. *Academy of Management Journal, 48*, 321–331.

Clore, G. L., & Byrne, D. (1974). A reinforcement-affect model of attraction. In T. L. Huston (Ed.), *Foundations of interpersonal attraction* (pp. 143–170). New York: Academic Press.

Cox, T. H., Jr. (1991). The multicultural organization. *Academy of Management Executive, 5*, 34–47.

Cox, T. H., Jr., & Blake, S. (1991). Managing cultural diversity: Implications for organizational competitiveness. *Academy of Management Executive, 5*, 45–56.

Cox, T. H., Lobel, S., & McLeod, P. (1991). Effects of ethnic group cultural differences on cooperative and competitive behavior on a group task. *Academy of Management Journal, 34*, 827–847.

Cross, R., & Cummings, J. N. (2004). Tie and network correlates of individual performance in knowledge-intensive work. *Academy of Management Journal, 47*, 928–937.

De Dreu, C. K. W., & Weingart, L. R. (2003). Task versus relationship conflict, team performance, and team member satisfaction: A meta-analysis. *Journal of Applied Psychology, 88*, 741–749.

Dwyer, S., Richard, O. C., & Chadwick, K. (2003). Gender diversity in management and firm performance: The influence of growth orientation and organizational culture. *Journal of Business Research, 56*, 1009–1019.

Egan, M. L., & Bendick, M., Jr. (2003, November/December). Workforce diversity initiatives of U.S. multinational corporations in Europe. *Thunderbird International Business Review, 45*, 701–715.

Ely, R. J., & Thomas, D. A. (2001). Cultural diversity at work: The effects of diversity perspectives on work group processes and outcomes. *Administrative Science Quarterly, 46*, 229–273.

Finkelstein, S., & Hambrick, D. C. (1996). *Strategic leadership: Top executives and their effects on organizations.* St. Paul, MN: West.

Fiske, S. T., & Taylor, S. E. (2008). *Social cognition: From brains to culture* (2nd ed.). New York: McGraw-Hill.

Frink, D. D., Robinson, R. K., Reithel, B., Arthur, M. M., Ammeter, A. P., Ferris, G. R., Kaplan, D. M., & Morrisette,

H. S. (2003). Gender demography and organizational performance. *Group & Organization Management, 28*, 127–147.

Greenwald, A. G., McGhee, D. E., & Schwartz, J. L. K. (1998). Measuring individual differences in implicit cognition: The Implicit Association Test. *Journal of Personality and Social Psychology, 74*, 1464–1480.

Hambrick, D. C., & Mason, P. A. (1984). Upper echelons: The organization as a reflection of its top managers. *Academy of Management Review, 9*, 193–206.

Harrison, D. A., & Klein, K. J. (2007). What's the difference? Diversity constructs as separation, variety, or disparity in organizations. *Academy of Management Review, 32*, 1199–1228.

Harrison, D. A., Price, K. H., & Bell, M. P. (1998). Beyond relational demography: Time and the effects of surface- and deep-level diversity on work group cohesion. *Academy of Management Journal, 41*, 96–107.

Harrison, D. A., Price, K. H., Gavin, J. H, & Florey, A. T. (2002). Time, teams, and task performance: Changing effects of surface- and deep-level diversity on group functioning. *Academy of Management Journal, 45*, 1029–1045.

Hoffman, L. R. (1959). Homogeneity of member personality and its effects on group problem solving. *Journal of Abnormal and Social Psychology, 58*, 27–32.

Hoffman, L. R., & Maier, N. R. F. (1961). Quality and acceptance of problem solutions by members of homogeneous and heterogeneous groups. *Journal of Abnormal and Social Psychology, 62*, 401–407.

Hofstede, G. (1994). Management scientists are human. *Management Science, 40*, 4–13.

Horwitz, S. K., & Horwitz, I. B. (2007). The effects of team diversity on team outcomes: A meta-analytic review of team demography. *Journal of Management, 33*, 987–1015.

Huselid, M. A. (1995). The impact of human resource management practices on turnover, productivity, and corporate. *Academy of Management Journal, 38*, 635–672

Ibarra, H. (1993). Personal networks of women and minorities in management: A conceptual framework. *Academy of Management Review, 18*, 56–87.

Jackson, S. E. (1992). Team composition in organizational settings: Issues in managing an increasingly diverse workforce. In S. Worchel, W. Wood, & J. A., Simpson (Eds.), *Group process and productivity* (pp. 138–141). Newbury Park, CA: Sage.

Jackson, S., Brett, J., Sessa, V., Cooper, D., Julin, J., Peyronnin, K. (1991). Some differences make a difference: Individual dissimilarity and group heterogeneity as correlates of recruitment, promotions, and turnover. *Journal of Applied Psychology, 76*, 675–689.

Jackson, S. E., Joshi, A., & Erhardt, N. L. (2003). Recent research on team and organizational diversity: SWOT analysis and implications. *Journal of Management, 29*, 801–830.

Jackson, S. E., May, K. A., & Whitney, K. (1995). Understanding the dynamics of diversity in decision making teams. In R. A. Guzzo & E. Salas (Eds.), *Team decision making effectiveness in organizations* (pp. 204–261). San Francisco: Jossey-Bass.

Jackson, S. E., & Ruderman, M. N. (1995). *Diversity in work teams*. Washington, DC: APA.

Jehn, K. A. (1995). A multi-method examination of the benefits and detriments of intragroup conflicts. *Administrative Science Quarterly, 40*, 256–282.

Jehn, K. A. (1997). Qualitative analysis of conflict types and dimensions in organizational groups. *Administrative Science Quarterly, 42*, 530–557.

Jehn, K. A., & Bezrukova, K. (2004). A field study of group diversity, workgroup context, and performance. *Journal of Organizational Behavior, 25*, 703–729.

Jehn, K. A., Chadwick, C., & Thatcher, S. (1997). To agree or not to agree: The effects of value congruence, member diversity, and conflict on workgroup outcomes. *International Journal of Conflict Management, 8*, 287–305.

Jehn, K. A., & Mannix, E. A. (2001). The dynamic nature of conflict: A longitudinal study of intergroup conflict and group performance. *Academy of Management Journal, 44*, 238–251.

Jehn, K. A., Northcraft, G. B., & Neale, M. A. (1999). Why differences make a difference: A field study of diversity, conflict and performance in workgroups. *Administrative Science Quarterly, 44*, 741–763.

Johnson, W. B., & Packer, A. E. (1987). *Workforce 2000: Work and workers for the 21st century*. Indianapolis: Hudson Institute.

Joshi, A., & Roh, H. (2009). The role of context in work team diversity research: A meta-analytic review. *Academy of Management Journal, 52*, 599–627.

Kalev, A., Dobbin, F., & Kelly, E. (2006). Best practices or best guesses? Diversity management and the reduction of inequality. *American Sociological Review, 71*, 589–617.

Kanter, R. (1977). *Men and women of the organization*. New York: Basic Books.

Knight, D., Pearce, C. L., Smith, K. G., Olian, J. D., Sims, H. P., Jr., Smith, K. A., & Flood, P. (1999). Top management team diversity, group process, and strategic consensus. *Strategic Management Journal, 20*, 445–465.

Kochan, T., Bezrukova, K., Ely, R., Jackson, S., Joshi, A., Jehn, K., Leonard, J., Levine, D., & Thomas, D. (2003). The effects of diversity on business performance: Report of the diversity research network. *Human Resource Management, 42*, 3–21.

Konrad, A. (2003). Defining the domain of workplace diversity scholarship. *Group & Organization Management, 28*, 4–17.

Konrad, A. M., & Linnehan, F. (1995). Formalized HRM structures: Coordinating equal employment opportunity or concealing organizational practices? *Academy of Management Journal, 38*, 787–820.

Kossek, E. E., & Zonia, S. C. (1993). Assessing diversity climate: A field study of reactions to employer efforts to promote diversity. *Journal of Organizational Behavior, 14*, 61–81.

Kozlowski, S. W. J., & Bell, B. S. (2003). Work groups and teams in organizations. In W. C. Borman, D. R. Ilgen, & R. J. Klimoski (Eds.), *Handbook of psychology*, Volume 12, *Industrial and organizational psychology* (pp. 333–375). London: Wiley.

Kulik, C. T., & Roberson, L. (2008). Diversity initiative effectiveness: What organizations can (and cannot) expect from diversity recruitment, diversity training, and formal mentoring programs. In A. P. Brief (Ed.), *Diversity at work* (pp. 265–317). Cambridge: Cambridge University Press.

Langdon, D. S., McMenamin, T. M., & Krolik, T. J. (2002). U.S. labor market in 2001: Economy enters a recession. *Monthly Labor Review, 125*, 3–33.

Lau, D. C., & Murnighan, J. K. (1998). Demographic diversity and faultlines: The compositional dynamics of organizational groups. *Academy of Management Review, 23*, 325–340.

Lau, D., & Murnighan, J. K. (2005). Interactions with groups and subgroups: The effects of demographic faultlines. *Academy of Management Journal, 48*, 645–659.

Lawrence, B. S. (1997). The black box of organizational demography. *Organization Science, 8*, 1–22.

Leonard, J., Levine, D., & Joshi A. (2004). Do birds of a feather shop together? The effects on performance of employees' similarity with one another and with customers. *Journal of Organizational Behavior, 25*, 731–754.

Levine, R. A., & Campbell, D. T. (1972). *Ethnocentrism: Theories of conflict, ethnic attitudes and group behavior*. New York: Wiley.

Li, J., & Hambrick, D. C. (2005). Factional groups: A new vantage on demographic faultlines, conflict, and disintegration in work teams. *Academy of Management Journal, 48*, 794–813.

Linnehan, F., & Konrad, A. M. (1999). Diluting diversity: Implications for intergroup inequality in organizations. *Journal of Management Inquiry, 8*, 399–414.

Mannix, E., & Neale, M. A. (2005). What differences make a difference? The promise and reality of diverse teams in organizations. *Psychological Science in the Public Interest, 6*, 31–55.

McKay, P. F., Avery, D. R., & Morris, M. A. (2008). Mean racial-ethnic differences in work performance: The moderating role of diversity climate. *Personnel Psychology, 61*, 349–374.

McKay, P. F., Avery, D. R., Tonidandel, S., Morris, M. A, Hernandez, M., & Hebl, M. (2007). Racial differences in employee retention: Are diversity climate perceptions the key? *Personnel Psychology, 60*, 35–62.

Milliken, F., & Martins, L. (1996). Searching for common threads: Understanding the multiple effects of diversity in organizational groups. *Academy of Management Review, 21*, 402–433.

Mor Barak, M. E., & Cherin, D. (1998). A tool to expand organizational understanding of workforce diversity. *Administrative in Social Work, 22*, 47–64.

Mor Barak, M. E., Cherin, D. A., & Berkman, S. (1998). Organizational and personal dimensions in diversity climate. *Journal of Applied Behavioral Science, 34*, 82–104.

Morrison, A. M. (1992). *The new leaders: Guidelines on leadership diversity in America*. San Francisco: Jossey-Bass.

Nelson, L. J., & Klutas, K. (2000). The distinctiveness effect in social interaction: Creation of a self-fulfilling prophecy. *Personality and Social Psychology Bulletin, 26*, 126–135.

Nemeth, C. (1986). Differential contributions of majority and minority influence. *Psychological Review, 93*, 23–32.

Oakes, P. J. (1987). The salience of social categories. In J. C. Turner, M. A. Hogg, P. J. Oakes, S. D. Reicher, & M. S. Wetherell (Eds.), *Rediscovering the social group: A self-categorization theory* (pp. 117–141). Oxford and New York: Basil Blackwell.

O'Reilly, C., Caldwell, D., & Barnett, W. (1989). Work group demography, social integration, and turnover. *Administrative Science Quarterly, 34*, 21–37.

O'Reilly, C. A., Snyder, R. C., & Boothe, J. N. (1993). Effects of organizational demography on organizational change. In G. P. Huber and W. H. Glick (Eds.), *Organizational change and redesign* (pp. 147–175). New York: Oxford University Press.

Pelled, L. (1996). Demographic diversity, conflict, and work group outcomes: An intervening process theory. *Organization Science, 7*, 615–631.

Pelled, L. H., Eisenhardt, K. M., & Xin, K. R. (1999). Exploring the black box: An analysis of work group diversity, conflict and performance. *Administrative Science Quarterly, 44*, 1–28.

Perry-Smith, J. E., & Blum, T. C. (2000). Work-family human resource bundles and perceived organizational performance. *Academy of Management Journal, 43*, 1107–1117.

Pettigrew, T. (1982). *Prejudice*. Cambridge, MA: Belknap Press.

Pettigrew, T. F., & Martin, J. (1989). Organizational inclusion of minority groups: A social psychological analysis. In J. P. Van Oudenhoven & T. M. Willemsen (Eds.), *Ethnic minorities: Social psychological perspectives* (pp. 169–200). Berwyn, PA: Swets North America.

Prahalad, C. K., & Hamel, G. (1990). The core competence of the corporation. *Harvard Business Review, 68*, 79–91.

Reagans, R. E., & Zuckerman, E. W. (2001). Networks, diversity and performance: The social capital of R&D teams. *Organization Science, 12*, 502–518.

Richard, O. C. (2000). Racial diversity, business strategy, and firm performance: A resource-based view. *Academy of Management Journal, 43*, 164–177.

Richard, O. C., Barnett, T., Dwyer, S., & Chadwick, K. (2004). Cultural diversity in management, firm performance, and the moderating role of entrepreneurial orientation dimensions. *Academy of Management Journal, 47*, 255–266.

Richard, O., McMillan, A., Chadwick, K., & Dwyer, S. (2003). Employing an innovation strategy in racially diverse workforces. *Group & Organization Management, 28*, 107–126.

Ridgeway, C. L., & Berger, J. (1986). Expectations, legitimation and dominance behavior in task groups. *American Sociological Review, 51*, 603–617.

Roberson, Q. M. (2006). Disentangling the meanings of diversity and inclusion in organizations. *Group & Organization Management, 31*, 212–236.

Roberson, Q. M., & Park, H. J. (2007). Examining the link between diversity and firm performance: The effects of diversity reputation and leader racial diversity. *Group & Organization Management, 32*, 548–568.

Roberson, Q. M., & Stevens, C. K. (2006). Making sense of diversity in the workplace: Organizational justice and language abstraction in employees' accounts of diversity-related incidents. *Journal of Applied Psychology, 91*, 379–391.

Roberson, Q. M., Sturman, M. C., & Simons, T. L. (2007). Does the measure of dispersion matter in multilevel research? A comparison of the relative performance of dispersion indices. *Organizational Research Methods, 10*, 564–588.

Schwartz, S. H. (1992). Universals in the content and structure of values: Theoretical advances and empirical tests in 20 countries. In M. P. Zanna (Ed.), *Advances in experimental social psychology* (pp. 1–65). San Diego, CA: Academic Press.

Shrader, C. B., Blackburn, V. B., & Iles, P. (1997). Women in management and firm financial performance: An exploratory study. *Journal of Managerial Issues, 9*, 355–372.

Simons, T., Pelled, L. H., & Smith, K. A. (1999). Making use of difference: Diversity, debate, and decision comprehensiveness in top management teams. *Academy of Management Journal, 42*, 662–673.

Smith, K. G., Smith, K. A., Olian, J. D., Sims, H. P., Jr., O'Bannon, D. P., & Scully, J. A. (1994). Top management team demography and process: The role of social integration and communication. *Administrative Science Quarterly, 39*, 412–438.

Swann, W. B., Jr. (1987). Identity negotiation: Where two roads meet. *Journal of Personality and Social Psychology, 53*, 1038–1051.

Tajfel, H. (1978). *Differentiation between social groups*. London: Academic Press.

Tajfel, H., & Turner, J. C. (1979). An integrative theory of intergroup conflict. In S. Worchel & W. G. Austin (Eds.), *The social psychology of intergroup relations* (pp. 33–47). Monterey, CA: Brooks/Cole.

Tajfel, H., & Turner, J. C. (1986). The social identity theory of intergroup behavior. In S. Worchel & W. G. Austin (Eds.), *The psychology of intergroup relations* (pp. 7–24). Chicago: Nelson-Hall.

Thatcher, S. M. B., Jehn, K. A., & Zanutto, E. (2003). Cracks in diversity research: The effects of diversity faultlines on conflict and performance. *Group Decision and Negotiation, 12,* 217–241.

Thomas, D. A., & Ely, R. J. (1996). Making differences matter: A new paradigm for managing diversity. *Harvard Business Review, 74,* 79–90.

Thye, S. R. (2000). A status value theory of power in exchange relations. *American Sociological Review, 63,* 407–432.

Tsui, A., Ashford, S., St. Clair, L., & Xin, K. (1995). Dealing With discrepant expectations: Response strategies and managerial effectiveness. *Academy of Management Journal, 38,* 1515–1543.

Tsui, A. S., Egan, T. D., & O'Reilly, C. A. (1992). Being different: Relational demography and organizational attachment. *Administrative Science Quarterly, 37,* 549–579.

Tsui, A. S., & Gutek, B. A. (1999). *Demographic differences in organizations: Current research and future directions.* New York: Lexington Press.

Tsui, A. S., & O'Reilly, C. A. (1989). Beyond simple demographic effects: The importance of relational demography in superior-subordinate dyads. *Academy of Management Journal, 32,* 402–423.

Turner, J. C. (1985). Social categorization and the self-concept: A social cognitive theory of group behavior. In E. E. Lawler, III. (Ed.), *Advances in group processes* (Vol. 2, pp. 77–121). Greenwich, CT: JAI Press.

Turner, J. C. (1987). A self-categorization theory. In J. C. Turner, M. A. Hogg, P. J. Oakes, S. D. Reicher, & M. S. Wetherell (Eds.), *Rediscovering the social group: A self-categorization theory* (pp. 42–67). Oxford: Blackwell Publishers.

Turner, J. C., Hogg, M. A., Oakes, P. J., Reicher, S. D., & Wetherell, M. S. (1987). *Rediscovering the social group: A self-categorization theory.* Oxford: Blackwell.

van Knippenberg, D., De Dreu, C. K. W., & Homan, A. C. (2004). Work group diversity and group performance: An integrative model and research agenda. *Journal of Applied Psychology, 89,* 1008–1022.

van Knippenberg, D., & Schippers, M. C. (2007). Work group diversity. *Annual Review of Psychology, 58,* 515–541.

Watson, W., Kumar, K., & Michaelsen, L. K. (1993). Cultural diversity's impact on interaction process and performance: Comparing homogeneous and diverse task groups. *Academy of Management Journal, 36,* 590–602.

Webber, S. S., & Donahue, L. M. (2001). Impact of highly and less job-related diversity on work group cohesion and performance: A meta-analysis. *Journal of Management, 27,* 141–162.

Weick, K. E. (1995). *Sensemaking in organizations.* Thousand Oaks, CA: Sage.

Wentling, R. M., & Palma-Rivas, N. (2000). Current status of diversity initiatives in selected multinational corporations. *Human Resource Development Quarterly, 11,* 35–60.

Williams, K., & O'Reilly, C. (1998). The complexity of diversity: A review of forty years of research. In D. Gruenfeld & M. Neale (Eds.), *Research on managing in groups and teams* (Vol. 20, pp. 77–140). Greenwich, CT: JAI Press.

Wright, P. M., & McMahan, G. C. (1992). Theoretical perspectives for strategic human resource management. *Journal of Management, 18,* 295–320.

Zenger, T., & Lawrence, B. (1989). Organizational demography: The differential effects of age and tenure distributions on technical communications. *Academy of Management Journal, 32,* 353–376.

Employment Discrimination

Adrienne J. Colella, Patrick F. McKay, Shanna R. Daniels *and* Sloane M. Signal

Abstract

This chapter reviews the literature on employment discrimination. The review is organized around targets (e.g., sex, race, religion), causes (e.g., cognitive, in-group favoritism), forms (e.g., harassment, adverse impact), and results of discrimination (e.g., costs, stress). Primarily, literature from the field of industrial and organizational psychology is considered. However, research in other disciplines is also included. The paper concludes with suggestions for future research directions for this rich and diverse area of research: integration across disciplines, integration across levels of theory and analysis, and integration with practice.

Key Words: employment discrimination, racism, sexism, adverse impact, stereotypes, harassment

Employment discrimination has been an issue extensively addressed by industrial and organizational (I/O) psychologists both in research and in practice. A search of PsychInfo abstracts between 1965 and December 2009 yielded 1,757 articles for "employment discrimination," 218 articles for "adverse impact and selection," and 610 articles for "sexual harassment and work." This is just research appearing in psychology journals and does not cover the plethora of research published in other fields, such as law, labor economics, business, and sociology. In terms of practice, I/O psychologists deal with discrimination in a variety of contexts such as serving as expert witnesses in discrimination lawsuits, devising selection procedures that avoid adverse impact, and helping to change organization cultures in which discrimination has been a problem.

The task of reviewing the literature in this area is daunting, given the size, multidisciplinary nature, and fragmentation of this literature. Not only have I/O psychologists written a great a deal about employment discrimination, but so have social

psychologists, labor economists, legal scholars, sociologists, scholars in women's studies and ethnic/racial studies, scholars in gerontology and disability, and statisticians, to name just a few. Thus, the field of employment discrimination is one that is truly multidisciplinary. However, research in I/O psychology primarily relies on social psychology and legal concerns as its guides, with social psychology providing the theoretical groundwork and legal concerns driving the topics studied. Finally, the literature is fragmented by target of discrimination (e.g., race, gender, age, disability), type of discrimination (e.g., adverse impact, sexual harassment, unfair evaluations), conceptual underpinnings or reasons for discrimination (e.g., stereotyping, power dynamics), and the results of discrimination (e.g., stress, poor performance, lawsuits). Rather than provide an exhaustive review of the employment discrimination literature, we intend to integrate it into a coherent framework so that we can present a picture of where research in I/O psychology stands on employment discrimination, and where it needs to go from here. We do not intend (and would be unable, given the limitations of space) to review every article and idea on the topic.

Table 32.1 depicts the organization of our review. First we focus on target characteristics, aspects of individuals or group membership that are likely targets of discrimination. We cover both those characteristics covered by federal law (race, gender, color, ethnicity, national origin, religion, disability, and age), as well as some characteristics that are not covered by federal law but have been the focus of discrimination research (weight, sexual orientation). Next, we address research that focuses on why discrimination occurs, or the causes of discrimination. This research focuses on cognitive factors, individual differences, in-group favoritism, system justification, tokenism, group threat dynamics, and compliance. Next we move to the different forms that discrimination may take. Employees may experience discrimination in a number of ways, ranging from being a victim of unintentional adverse impact to being harassed because of group membership. We limit our discussion to five forms that have received the most research attention in the I/O literature: adverse impact, harassment, unfair evaluations, pay discrimination, and subtle discrimination. The fifth section concerns perceptions of discrimination and their aftermath. We could have chosen to focus on many outcomes of discrimination, occurring at organization and societal levels; however, given the psychological nature of this chapter, we focus on the reactions of targets. In our conclusion, we tie together this model and make suggestions for where research on employment discrimination needs to move from here—both in terms of understanding the phenomenon better and providing research that can inform practitioners. We do not focus specifically

on legal aspects because an excellent recent review (Goldman, Gutek, Stein, & Lewis, 2006) and book (Landy, 2005) have recently done so.

Before proceeding, a working definition of *workplace discrimination* is in order. Scholars vary in how they define discrimination (cf. Quillian, 2006). Most definitions in the social sciences emphasize unequal treatment of a group; however, the breadth with which discrimination is defined varies by author. The National Research Council of the National Academies defines racial discrimination as follows (National Research Council, 2004, p. 39): (a) *differential treatment on the basis of race* that disadvantages a racial group, and (b) *treatment on the basis of inadequately justified factors other than race* that disadvantages a racial group (differential effect).

We generalize this definition beyond race and adopt Dipboye and Colella's (2005, p. 2) definition of *discrimination* as the unfair behavioral biases demonstrated against members of groups to *which one does not belong*. Four features of this definition are important. First, discrimination concerns *behaviors*. For discrimination to take place, an act or decision must be conducted toward the target. Cognitive, attitudinal, and emotional biases, such as prejudice and stereotypes, all play a role in behavioral discrimination. However, we focus on discriminatory actions, often resulting from these cognitions. Second, the word *against* implies that either future or present harm for the target individual or group occurs because of the discrimination. Third, the behavior is an *unfair* bias, meaning that it occurs because of the target's perceived group membership, rather than a justifiable reason such as job performance, seniority, or random selection. Fourth, the discrimination occurs because of *group membership*

Table 32.1 Outline of the chapter.

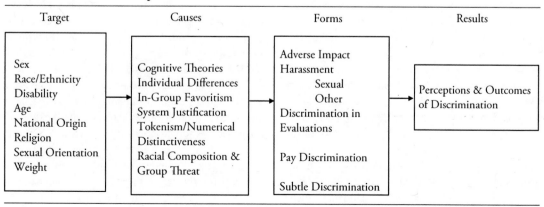

Target	Causes	Forms	Results

Sex
Race/Ethnicity
Disability
Age
National Origin
Religion
Sexual Orientation
Weight
	Cognitive Theories
	Individual Differences
	In-Group Favoritism
	System Justification
	Tokenism/Numerical
	Distinctiveness
	Racial Composition &
	Group Threat
		Adverse Impact
		Harassment
		  Sexual
		  Other
		Discrimination in
		Evaluations
		
		Pay Discrimination
		
		Subtle Discrimination
			Perceptions & Outcomes
			of Discrimination

(or perceived group membership), indicating that discrimination targets a class of persons rather than a person for individual reasons. For example, one may fail to promote a coworker with whom one has had a personal falling out. This may be unfair treatment; however, it is aimed at the target for individual reasons and is not based on group membership. The specification that the group be one to which the perpetrator does not belong is in italics because it references the usual case. However, as discussed later, there is evidence that shows that people do discriminate against members of their own group (Jost & Banaji, 1994).

The U.S. Equal Employment Opportunity Commission (EEOC, 2009a) provides a list of discriminatory employment practices when based on federal legally protected characteristics (e.g., race, sex, disability, age). These include: hiring and firing, compensation, classification of employees, job advertisements, recruitment, testing, use of company facilities, training and apprenticeship programs, fringe benefits, pay, retirement plans, disability leave, and harassment.

The measurement of discrimination is a tricky issue, and methodologies differ depending on the purpose of the study and discipline. Conceptually, discrimination is present when there is a difference between outcomes for a target of a given social group and the treatment they would receive if they were not members of that group (Quillian, 2006). Assessing whether discrimination has truly occurred can be difficult because other reasons for unequal treatment (such as unequal qualifications) must be ruled out. A National Research Council (2004) report provides an in-depth review of the measurement of racial discrimination.

Several types of evidence are used in the I/O psychology literature to determine if discrimination exists. One such type of evidence is the controlled experiment whereby the treatment of people who fall into a targeted group are compared to a control group of people who represent the majority, or non-targeted group. The scope of this research comprises thousands of studies examining discrimination against various target groups. For (a simplified) example, respondents view videotaped interviews of a black job applicant and a white applicant, holding qualifications constant. Respondents role play as hiring managers and their hiring recommendations for the black and white candidate are compared. Most of this research takes place in a laboratory setting using student respondents evaluating "paper people" (e.g., Colella, DeNisi, & Varma, 1998; Heilman, Wallen,

Fuchs, & Tamkins, 2004; Marlow, Schneider, & Nelson, 1996; Martell, 1991).

This type of research allows for control and manipulation of variables that would be impossible to study in an actual setting. For example, Brief, Dietz, Cohen, Pugh, and Vaslow (2000) examined the impact organizational climate for racial bias on hiring recommendations for a position of vice president. This was manipulated by exposing respondents to a statement from their boss which pointed out that the majority of the workforce in the company was white, and therefore, it was important to hire a white person for the VP job. Those in the control condition did not receive this justification for discrimination. Hiring recommendations for white and black target applicants were compared. It would be unthinkable to conduct this type of experiment in the field for legal and ethical reasons. Thus, on the one hand, the controlled laboratory experiment allows one to examine phenomena that would be virtually impossible to study in a natural setting, while having internal validity. On the other hand, there is an ongoing debate about the extent to which the results of these types of studies generalize to actual organizational settings (see the December 2008 issue of *Industrial Organizational Psychology*). We discuss this debate in more detail later in the chapter.

It is possible to conduct experiments in the field. One such design is the audit study, whereby confederate targets enter an actual employment situation (e.g., applying for a job). The group membership (e.g., race, sexual orientation, disability) of the confederates is varied, while an attempt is made to keep all other factors (e.g., qualifications, attractiveness) constant. The reactions of people who truly believe they are interacting with the target in a real setting are examined (e.g., Hebl, Foster, Mannix, & Dovidio, 2002; Johnson & Heal, 1976). Audit studies are relatively uncommon in the field of I/O psychology; however, there is a growing body of literature coming from a variety of fields (see Pager, 2007, for a review). The majority of discrimination audit studies concern housing discrimination (National Research Council, 2004).

While audit studies are a desirable way to obtain discrimination data (Quillian, 2006), they have also been criticized on several grounds. First, they are expensive and cumbersome to conduct. Second, they can only be used to study initial contact phenomena (e.g., applying for a job, resume screening, job interviews), rather than phenomena that occur after some time in the organization (e.g., performance appraisal, pay). Finally, there are also internal validity concerns, resulting from the fact that confederates are not blind to the experimental condition to which they have been assigned (for an exception, see Hebl et al., 2002). Confederates in different conditions may behave differently, making it difficult to infer the cause of any differences in treatment (National Research Council, 2004).

Rarer than audit interviews are true, natural quasi-experiments conducted in the field. Economists have used natural experiments in the labor market to determine the impact of antidiscrimination laws (Holzer & Ludwig, 2003). To draw inferences about the degree of discrimination reduction due to a change in law, employment rates are compared before and after its enactment. One frequently cited study was able to uncover discrimination at the organizational level. Goldin and Rouse (2000) examined the effects of gender discrimination on the selection of musicians into orchestras. During the 1970s and 1980s, orchestras began to hide auditioning musicians from the selection committee, in order to disguise the sex of the musician. When orchestras began doing this, women were hired at a much greater extent than they had been previously. Goldin and Rouse (2000) studied nine orchestras over a period of years, during which some used a screen and others did not. They were able to control for important factors such as the musicians' proficiencies. They found that women were much more likely to be hired when the judges did not know the sex of the musician, thus concluding that the screen had reduced discrimination against women. The Goldin and Rouse (2000) study offers compelling evidence of sex discrimination in hiring, and ideally, more studies of this type should be conducted. It also should be noted that this study was published in an economics journal.

Another method commonly used for obtaining evidence of discrimination is the self-reports of targets (e.g., Fitzgerald, Drasgow, Hulin, Gelfand, & Magley, 1997; Ragins & Cornwell, 2001). While this method allows for potentially rich data, there may be concern over the extent to which perceptions of discrimination actually reflect reality. Having a history as a target of discrimination and sensitivity to legal issues may lead to overreporting, while experiencing more subtle, non-obvious forms of discrimination may lead to underreporting (National Research Council, 2004; Quillian, 2006). Research that has compared self-reports of discrimination to objective indicators has generally found self-reports to be valid and reliable (Bobo & Suh,

2000). Another concern with this type of research is that the manner in which the question is asked can influence the likelihood of reporting discrimination. This has been a particular problem in the sexual harassment literature (Gutek, Murphy, & Douma, 2004), as well as in the courts (*EEOC v. Dial Corporation*, November 12, 2002. Ill, No. 99 C 3356).

Finally, there are studies that statistically analyze observational data to determine discrimination. One type of research that falls into this category is labor economic studies (e.g., Jacobs & Steinberg, 1990; O'Neill, 2003), which use regression analyses to determine the impact of group status (usually race or sex) on employment-related outcomes (e.g., employment rate, pay). This research first attempts to explain outcome disparities in terms of statistical controls (e.g., education, age), and then concludes that the discrimination effect is the residual unexplained variance in the remaining outcome disparity. Research in the I/O psychology literature that comes closest to this methodology is the correlational field study, whereby employment outcomes (e.g., performance ratings, job satisfaction) are regressed on group characteristics, after controlling for other possible explanatory variables (e.g., Colella & Varma, 2001; Lyness & Heilman, 2006). The major problem with this type of study is that it is difficult to infer causality between group status and outcome differentials. There is always a missing variable problem (National Research Council, 2004; Quillian, 2006); that is, the possibility that differential outcomes are due to a third factor unrelated to group membership.

In summary, there is no "perfect" way to measure and study discrimination. It is an elusive construct that perpetrators are unlikely to admit and can often be attributed (correctly or incorrectly) to factors other than group membership. Future work on employment discrimination should focus on triangulation of effects across different methodologies (cf. Leslie, King, Bradley, & Hebl, 2008). We concur with the National Research Council (2004), which concluded after their exhaustive review of measurement issues:

> No single approach to measuring racial discrimination *(or any other type of discrimination)* allows researchers to address all the important measurement issues or to answer all the questions of interest. Consistent patterns of results across studies and different approaches tend to provide the strongest argument. Public and private

agencies…and the research community should embrace a multidisciplinary, multimethod approach to the measurement of racial discrimination and seek improvements in all major methods employed. (pp. 88–89, italics added)

Targets of Discrimination

Any person can be the target of unfair treatment based on any personal characteristic not associated with relevant job requirements, performance, or accepted policies for making personnel decisions. There is a large body of literature concerning the stigmatization of individuals and their respective groups, indicating what personal characteristics are likely to be the source of systematic discrimination (cf. Major & O'Brien, 2005). Goffman's (1963) seminal work in this area states that stigmatizing attributes are based on blemishes of individual character, abominations of the body, and tribal membership. Furthermore, what constitutes a stigma is dependent on social and cultural context at a given time (Crocker, Major, & Steele, 1998). For example, after the 9/11 disaster, Arab Americans became stigmatized to a much greater degree than they had been previously (Esses, Dovidio, & Hodson, 2002).

The focus of work and concern over employment discrimination is aimed at examining discrimination toward members of groups that historically have been discriminated against and that suffer disadvantages in the labor market. One way of determining who is stigmatized in U.S. society is to examine which attributes are protected by Federal law, since such mandates are enacted in response to a history of discrimination.

Federal law Title VII of the Civil Rights Act of 1964, Civil Rights Act of 1991, Equal Pay Act (EPA) of 1963, Age Discrimination in Employment Act (ADEA) of 1967, and Title I and V of the Americans with Disabilities Act (ADA) of 1990 protect individuals on the basis of their race, color, religion, sex, national origin, and age (40 years old and over), as well as qualified individuals with disabilities in the private sector. The Pregnancy Discrimination Act (PDA) is an amendment to Title VII which makes it unlawful to discriminate on the basis of pregnancy, childbirth, or a related medical condition.

There are more stringent laws applied to federal employees and applicants, including the Civil Service Reform Act of 1978 (CSRA), which, in addition to the above characteristics, also protects individuals based on sexual orientation, whistle blowing, and exercising grievance and appeal rights (EEOC, 2009a). Because whistle-blowing and exercising appeals are individual acts, and discrimination is not targeted toward a group, we do not review this literature. Furthermore, specific state laws protect individuals based on other attributes such as sexual orientation, age (even under 40 years old), and marital status. We also examine discrimination against people based on weight, because this type of discrimination has garnered significant research attention and has been the focus of lawsuits. Next, we present evidence that various groups are disadvantaged in the U.S. labor market. Physical attractiveness is another attribute that has received significant attention in the I/O psychology discrimination literature (Dipboye, 2005), but is not discussed in this section because there are no large-scale data demonstrating labor market discrimination. The issue is brought up later in the chapter.

Sex

Discrimination based on sex and gender is one of the most studied types of discrimination. Labor statistics show that women are disadvantaged in the labor market compared to men, despite the fact that in 2008, women had a lower unemployment rate (5.3%) than men (6.2%). Women earn less than men, although there has been an increase in the male-female earnings ratio. In 2007, women who were full-time wage and salary workers had median weekly earnings ($614) of about 80% of the earnings of their male counterparts ($766). This ratio is up from 62% in 1979. Women's-to-men's earnings ratio, among 35- to 44-year-olds, rose from 58% in 1979 to 77% in 2007, and the ratio for 45- to 54-year-olds increased from 57% to 75% (Department of Labor, 2008b). The wage gap is smaller for black and Hispanic women, who earn about 90% of black and Hispanic men, respectively. The wage gap remains when other possible explanatory factors are considered (e.g., occupation, qualifications, training, experience; Budig, 2002; Jacobs & Steinberg, 1990; O'Neill, 2003).

Another issue facing female workers is that of sex segregation of jobs (Reskin & Bielby, 2005; Reskin & McBrier, 2000). Although women are far more concentrated in administrative support jobs, relatively few work in construction, production, or transportation occupations (Department of Labor, 2008a). Women are more likely than men to work in professional occupations. However, they also are more likely to work in less well-paying jobs than men in this category. For example, only 9% of female professionals were employed in the high-paying engineering fields and computer fields, compared to 43% of men. Sixty-seven percent of professional women worked in low-paying educational and health care fields, compared to only 30% of men (Department of Labor, 2008a).

Evidence of sex discrimination also comes from the number of discrimination charges filed with the EEOC, and ensuing monetary settlements to successful plaintiffs. In 2008, the EEOC received 28,372 charges of sex-based discrimination and resolved 24,018 sex discrimination charges, recovering $109.3 million in monetary benefits for charging parties and other aggrieved individuals (EEOC, 2009a). In that same year, there were 6,285 charges of pregnancy-based discrimination (EEOC, 2009c) and 13,867 charges of sexual harassment (about 16% by males; EEOC, 2009d), resulting in monetary recoveries of $12.2 million and $47.4 million, respectively.

Race and Ethnicity

Along with sex discrimination, racial-ethnic discrimination has received the most attention in all literatures, specifically racism against blacks or African Americans. Table 32.2 depicts U.S. national 2007 labor statistics for whites, blacks/African Americans, Asians, and Hispanics/Latinos (Department of Labor, 2008b). As can be seen in Table 32.2, there are labor outcome disparities, where by all indicators, whites and Asians are advantaged relative to blacks and Hispanics. The unemployment rate for blacks is about twice as high as it is for whites, and it takes black men looking for work longer to become employed (Department of Labor, 2008b).

In contrast, Asians had the lowest unemployment rate of all racial-ethnic subgroups. The wage gaps for black and Hispanic full-time workers, compared to whites, are about 80% and 70%, respectively, whereas Asians earn 116% of whites' salaries. These wage disparities hold across all occupational levels such that black and Hispanic professional or managerial workers only earn 74% and 81% of their white counterparts' salaries, respectively, while comparatively, Asians garner about 111% of whites' earnings.

There is also evidence of racial and ethnic segregation by occupation (Huffman & Cohen, 2004; Semyonov & Herring, 2007). Almost half of all Asians hold managerial or professional jobs, compared to less than 20% of Hispanics. Black and Hispanic workers are overrepresented in service, production, transportation, and moving occupations (Department of Labor, 2008b). Further evidence for racial-ethnic discrimination comes from EEOC charges. Goldman et al. (2006) present detailed statistical breakdowns of discrimination charges filed with the EEOC and found that 33% of charges were for racial-ethnic discrimination under Title VII. In 2008, there were 33,937 charges of race discrimination, and plaintiffs recovered $79.3 million in monetary benefits (EEOC, 2009e).

While racial and ethnic disparities are clear for black/African American and Hispanic/Latino workers, an examination of the general labor statistics for Asians indicates that they have the best labor outcomes of any group. Statistics such as these have led Asian Americans to be referred to as the "model minority." Interestingly, in a 2005 Gallup poll, 31%

Table 32.2 2007 Labor Statistics for White, Black, or African American, Asian, and Hispanic or Latino Workers

	White	Black/African American	Asian	Hispanic/Latino
Proportion of population employed	63.6%	58.4%	64.3%	64.9%
Unemployment rate	4.1%	8.3%	3.2%	5.6%
Median full-time weekly wage	$716	$569	$830	$503
Management, professional, and related occupations median weekly wage	$1,211	$899	$1,342	$985
Percentage of each group in the following occupations: management, professional service production, transportation, and moving	36.1% 15.5% 12.0%	27.1% 23.3% 16.5%	48.1% 16.0% 9.6%	17.8% 24.1% 17.6%

of Asians reported experiencing incidents of discrimination. This was the highest level of reported racial-ethnic discrimination of any racial-ethnic subgroup, followed by African Americans, of whom 26% expressed that they had been victims of discrimination (EEOC, 2008a). This is troubling in light of the fact that only 2% of private sector discrimination charges were filed by Asian Americans or Pacific Islanders (EEOC, 2008a). The EEOC commissioned a work group to study employment discrimination against Asian Americans and Pacific Islanders, which concluded that a "bamboo ceiling" exists. Although almost half of Asians hold managerial or professional jobs, they have an unduly difficult time breaking into the senior ranks of those positions (EEOC, 2008a).

Disability

Title 1 of the ADA pertaining to employment is different from other civil rights legislation in two major respects. First, not everyone is protected. Only qualified workers with a disability are protected; thus, defining who is "disabled" has become a legal and research concern. Second, the ADA specifies that the organization must make reasonable accommodations for employees with disabilities. Failure to do so constitutes discrimination. The ADA (1990) defines disability as (with respect to an individual): (a) a physical or mental impairment that substantially limits one or more of the major life activities of the individual; (b) having a record of such disability; or (c) being regarded as having a disability (EEOC, 1992; EEOC, 2002a). There is no specific listing of names of ADA-eligible impairments; however, the effect of such impairment on the life of a person defines the presence of a disability (EEOC, 1992). To be formally defined as a disability, a physical or mental impairment must also meet the "substantially limits" test. For example, someone with a learning disability affecting visual perception might have difficulty reading the print on memos with 12-point fonts, and, thus, be unable to read regular office communications. To further complicate matters, disability is defined differently for other purposes, such as medical considerations, public policy, or economic concerns. The reader is referred to Colella and Bruyère (2011) and Livermore and She (2007) for a more thorough treatment of the issue.

Accommodations are modifications in the job, work environment, work process, or conditions of work (e.g., allowing spaces for a wheelchair to pass through work areas, providing larger font print

media for vision-impaired personnel) that reduce physical and social barriers so that people with disabilities experience equal opportunity in a competitive work environment (EEOC, 1992). For an in-depth review of I/O psychology-related literature on disability accommodation, readers should consult Colella and Bruyère (2011). Reasonable accommodations are those that do not cause undue hardship, which is defined as causing significant expense or difficulty to implement (Knapp, Faley, & Long, 2006). Contrary to early expectations, monetary costs of accommodations are usually minimal (Braddock & Bachelder, 1994; Schartz, Hendricks, & Blanck, 2006). Yet, lawsuits over the failure to provide accommodations to disabled employees constitute approximately 25% of ADA discrimination charges (Bjelland, Bruyère, Houtenville, Ruiz-Quintanilla, & Webber, 2008). In 2008, the EEOC received 19,453 charges of disability discrimination, overall, and recovered $57.2 million in benefits for charging parties (EEOC, 2009f).

Labor statistics illustrate that people with disabilities have a more difficult time finding employment than people without disabilities. The 2006 American Community Survey (Rehabilitation Research and Training Center on Disability Demographics and Statistics, 2007) indicated that only 37.7% of disabled people are employed overall, compared to 79.7% of the general population, and that only 87.1% of those who report that they are able to work actually do so, compared 95.0% of the general population. Results from the Current Population Survey show that in 2005, people with disabilities had an unemployment rate of 10.5% compared to 4.7% in the general population (McMenamin, Miller, & Polivka, 2006). Disabled individuals also appear to be at a disadvantage in terms of promotions. A large-scale study of disability employment in the federal government (EEOC, 2008b) revealed that, between fiscal years 2002 and 2006, the number and rate of promotions decreased by 25.2% for disabled workers, compared to a decrease of 3.99% for non-disabled federal employees.

Age

There is a growing amount of research on age discrimination and age issues in general in the I/O psychology literature, which is being fueled by the aging of the U.S. workforce (Hedge, Borman, & Lammlein, 2006). Not only have discrimination claims based on age increased from 15,785 EEOC charges in 1997 to 24,582 in 2008 (EEOC, 2009h), but employers also desire to keep older workers in their jobs longer (Posthuma & Campion, 2009). Simultaneously, however, there is concern that layoffs will disproportionately affect older workers (Shore & Goldberg, 2005).

The issue of age discrimination also overlaps with the issue of disability discrimination (cf. Colella & Bruyère, 2011). The U.S. Census Bureau projects that the 45- to 54-year-old and 55- to 64-year-old populations in the United States will grow by nearly 44.2 million (17%) and 35 million (39%), respectively, between 2000 and 2010 (U.S. Census Bureau, 2004). By the year 2010, this group will account for nearly half (44%) of the working age population (20–64), and the number of people with disabilities between the ages of 50 and 65 will almost double (Weathers, 2006). One issue that this brings to mind, which has not received any research attention, is the role of employment accommodations for older workers.

National Origin/Immigration Status

There has not been much research in the I/O literature on discrimination against foreign-born workers. Furthermore, much of the research that has been conducted in other disciplines on immigrants in the labor force has taken place outside the United States. This is somewhat surprising, given that in 2008, foreign-born workers composed 15.6% of the U.S. workforce (U.S. Bureau of Labor Statistics, 2009). Forty-nine percent of the foreign-born U.S. workforce is Hispanic, while Asians make up 22.4%.

Although the unemployment rate is approximately the same for foreign- and native-born workers (U.S. Bureau of Labor Statistics, 2009), there is evidence of occupational segregation, with foreign-born workers more likely to be employed in lower level and lower paying occupations. Foreign-born workers are much more likely to work in service occupations (23.2%) than their native-born counterparts (15.6%), and much less apt to work in managerial and professional occupations (28.2%) compared to native-born workers (37.8%; U.S. Bureau of Labor Statistics, 2009). Overall, foreign-born personnel's earnings constitute about 80% of those earned by native-born employees.

One can attribute the differences in occupation level and pay to differences in educational attainment, which is generally lower for foreign-born workers. However, there is evidence for what has been called "skill discounting" (Esses, Dietz, & Bhardway, 2006). Skill discounting refers to the tendency to undervalue foreign education, training, and experience. Both economic and experimental evidence has been found for this effect (see Esses et al., 2006) in Canadian samples, which appears to extend to U.S. work contexts as well.

Religion

There is very little research addressing religious discrimination in employment settings, particularly in the United States. Because the U.S. Census Bureau and Bureau of Labor Statistics does not collect information on religion, workforce outcomes cannot be easily compared across religions. Furthermore, religious discrimination charges account for only about 3% of total EEOC charges (Goldman et al., 2006). In 2008, the EEOC received 3,273 charges of religious discrimination and recovered $7.5 million for charging parties (EEOC, 2009g); however, such charges continue to grow (Henle & Hogler, 2004; Kelly, 2008). This has been particularly true in the aftermath of the 9/11 attacks, when reports of religious discrimination from Muslim employees nearly doubled (EEOC 2002b; Henle & Hogler, 2004), prompting the EEOC to disseminate a special report on religious discrimination for employers. Increasing religious diversity in the United States might be another precipitating factor in the rise of religious discrimination claims. While Christianity is still the majority faith in the United States, the number of Muslims, Buddhists, and Hindus are rising (Henle & Hogler, 2004; Kelly, 2008). Kelly (2008) even argues that because the U.S. workforce is aging, and because people become more religious as they grow older, the expression of religion at work will continue to be an important workplace issue.

Religious discrimination is unique, relative to other forms of discrimination, for two reasons. First, employers are required to accommodate workers' religious beliefs. The EEOC states that "Employers must reasonably accommodate employees' sincerely held religious practices unless doing so would impose an undue hardship on the employer. A reasonable religious accommodation is any adjustment to the work environment that will allow the employee to practice his religion" (EEOC, 2009g). The three most common types of accommodations requested are those for religious observances or practices (e.g., not working on the Sabbath), allowing exceptions to grooming and dress code requirements (e.g., being allowed to wear a hijab when it is not part of the work uniform), and acknowledging conscientious objections to assigned work that violates religious beliefs (e.g., a Catholic pharmacist refusing to sell birth control pills; Kelly, 2008).

While a fair amount of I/O psychology research has examined the accommodation of disabilities in the workplace (see Colella, 2001; Colella & Bruyère, 2011; Colella, Paetzold, & Belliveau, 2004), essentially none has explored religious accommodation. Note that the EEOC's definition of accommodation states that it must be for "sincerely held" religious beliefs, which brings to light a second issue: defining religious beliefs.

The EEOC Compliance Manual, section 12 states:

> Title VII defines "religion" to include "all aspects of religious observance and practice as well as belief." Religion includes not only traditional, organized religions such as Christianity, Judaism, Islam, Hinduism, and Buddhism, but also religious beliefs that are new, uncommon, not part of a formal church or sect, only subscribed to by a small number of people, or that seem illogical or unreasonable to others. Further, a person's religious beliefs "need not be confined in either source or content to traditional or parochial concepts of religion." A belief is "religious" for Title VII purposes if it is "'religious' in the person's own scheme of things," *i.e.*, it is "a sincere and meaningful belief that occupies in the life of its possessor a place parallel to that filled by . . . God." An employee's belief or practice can be "religious" under Title VII even if the employee is affiliated with a religious group that does not espouse or recognize that individual's belief or practice, or if few—or no—other people adhere to it.
> Religious beliefs include theistic beliefs as well as non-theistic "moral" or ethical beliefs as to what is right and wrong which are sincerely held with the strength of traditional religious views . . . beliefs are not protected merely because they are strongly held. Rather, religion typically concerns "ultimate ideas" about life, purpose, and death. . . .
> (*EEOC*, 2009j, Section 12–1 A.1)

Clearly, Federal law takes a very broad view of religious beliefs. For research purposes, it would be useful to know how people determine what constitutes religious belief, how they categorize others according to religious beliefs, and what psychological mechanisms underlie discrimination based on religion. As with disability, religious beliefs are defined differently for different purposes, posing both challenges and opportunities alike for researchers.

Sexual Orientation

Badgett, Lau, Sears, and Ho (2007) recently reviewed the literature examining discrimination against gay, lesbian, bisexual, and transgender (GLBT) people. They summarized 15 self-report survey studies of GLBT people conducted since 1990, and found that 15% (Diaz, Ayala, Bein, Henne, & Marin, 2001) to 43% (Mays & Cochran, 2001; Seattle Office of Civil Rights, 2006) had reported being the victims of workplace discrimination. Surveys of heterosexual coworkers revealed that 12% to 30% reported witnessing antigay discrimination at work (Badgett et al., 2007).

There is recent national (U.S. Census) and General Social Survey data on the wage gap for gay and lesbian workers, compared to their heterosexual counterparts. Gay men earn 9% (Arabshebani, Marin, & Wadsworth, 2007) to 32% (Blandford, 2003) less than similarly qualified heterosexual men. Differences in estimates derive in part from how being gay is defined. Definitions range from various measures of sexual behavior, to the percentage of one's sex partners who are the same sex over a period of time, to self-categorization as GLBT. In contrast, findings of studies concerning the wage differential between lesbian women and heterosexual women are less conclusive. While none of the nine studies in Badgett et al.'s (2007) review showed that lesbian women were penalized, there were inconsistencies in whether or not lesbians were granted a wage premium. Estimates ranged from no differences (Badgett, 2001; Klawitter & Flatt, 1998) to a 30% premium (Berg & Lien, 2002) earned by lesbian women. Again, studies varied drastically in how they defined *lesbian*, which may account for the wide range of results.

Currently, 21 states have laws prohibiting discrimination based on sexual orientation. Data from these states show that the number of people filing discrimination suits based on sexual orientation is low (Badgett et al., 2007); however, because only a small portion of the population is GLBT, these rates are comparable, proportionally, to those filed for sex discrimination in these states (Badgett et al., 2007).

Weight

During the past 35 years, there has been a fair amount of research on employment discrimination due to being overweight or obese (Fikkan & Rothblum, 2005; Roehling, 1999; Rudolph, Wells, Weller, & Baltes, 2009). Legally, there are no federal laws protecting against weight discrimination—per se, yet, a handful of states (Michigan and District of Columbia) and municipalities have specific laws protecting against weight and appearance discrimination. In most cases, people who file discrimination claims based on weight often sue unsuccessfully under other federal laws (see Theran, 2005, for a review). For example, most courts have ruled against obesity alone as a disability under the ADA (1990), with the exception of some cases involving morbid obesity (100% or 100 pounds overweight). Courts have consistently ruled, under Title VII, that organizations (mostly airlines) cannot utilize differential weight standards for men and women (e.g., *Frank v. United Airlines, Inc.*, 9th Cir., 2000).

Based on self-reports, it appears that weight discrimination is increasing, beyond what would be expected by the increase in obesity in the U.S. population. In 1995–1996, one large-scale survey study (MacArthur Foundation National Survey of Midlife Development in the United States [MIDUS]) found that 4% of men and 10% of women reported being discriminated against due to weight. These values increased to 8% and 15.5%, respectively, in 2004–2006 (Andreyeva, Puhl, & Brownell, 2008). Roehling, Roehling, and Pichler (2007) provided more detailed analyses on a larger sample from the MIDUS survey, and showed that approximately twice the percentage of overweight or obese women reported weight-based discrimination, compared to overweight or obese men. Reports of discrimination increased monotonically from normal weight (.7%) to overweight (body mass index or BMI 25–29.9; 2.7%), to obese (BMI 30–34.9; 6.6%), to very obese (BMI of 40 or higher; 22.4%). The very obese were more likely than anyone in the entire sample to report being discriminated against for any reason, thus suggesting the stigmatizing nature of obesity. By comparison, the second-highest category of reported discrimination was due to gender (8.7%).

Additional evidence of discrimination against overweight or obese people, particularly women, comes from compensation research. Fikkan and Rothblum (2005) reviewed studies assessing pay differentials for overweight and obese individuals, relative to those of normal weight, and concluded that men do not receive much of a penalty for being severely obese. In contrast, overweight/obese women earn 7% to 30% less than their normal weight counterparts. Furthermore, these disparities were even larger for white women than for Hispanic and black women, as well as for highly versus less well-educated women.

Like disability and sexual orientation, weight discrimination research must face thorny definitional issues. The research cited here used the BMI, which is a person's weight in kilograms divided by his or her height in meters squared. The National Institutes of Health (NIH) guidelines are then used to determine in which weight category an individual falls. While seemingly an objective index, the BMI for athletic or muscular people will often indicate that they are overweight. Moreover, there is cultural variation in the extent to which people classify others as being overweight (Hebl & Heatherton, 1998), and individual differences in perceptions of one's own body weight. Such issues should be reconciled by scholars undertaking weight discrimination research.

In summary, the above discussion demonstrates that labor inequities still exist based on various group memberships. What these data do not tell us is why these inequalities exist. In the next section, we address causes of discrimination most relevant to the I/O psychology literature.

Why Does Discrimination Occur? Theories of Why People Discriminate

Research in the field of I/O psychology tends to not explicitly examine the underlying dynamics of discrimination—rather, it focuses on the occurrence of discrimination, conditions under which it occurs, and mitigating factors (for a recent exception see Rosette, Leonardelli & Phillips, 2008). Theoretical perspectives on the causes of discrimination that drive the I/O literature come from both social psychology and sociology. While theories of discrimination abound, we focus on those most utilized in the I/O psychology literature: cognitive theories, individual difference explanations, and group favoritism theories. We also briefly discuss several other theories that have been somewhat neglected in this literature, but are useful for future research.

Cognitive Theories of Discrimination

These theories suggest that people discriminate because of prejudices that they hold about certain groups of others. Allport first defined prejudice as "an antipathy based upon faulty and inflexible generalizations" ([1954] 1979, p. 9). Others have expounded on this definition in light of more recent research to point out that prejudices are not always *negative* attitudes (Eagly & Diekman, 2005; Rudman, 2005), nor are they always inflexible, but often depend on the social context (Eagly & Diekman, 2005), and that they are not always *innocently* irrational, but are often driven by rational, political, and self-interested motives (Jackman, 2005).

Since Allport's (1954) seminal work on prejudice, a plethora of research and theory has been generated examining the underlying cognitive mechanisms of prejudice and, consequently, discrimination. It is beyond the scope of this chapter to review that literature (see Dovidio, Glick, & Rudman, 2005; Fiske, 1998; Macrae & Bodenhausen, 2000; Major & O'Brien, 2005; Nelson, 2009; Uleman, Saribay, & Gonzalez, 2008 for reviews). Rather, we review developments that most directly bear on employment discrimination. Most of the work focuses on how we cognitively categorize groups of individuals, and the resulting stereotypical beliefs. It has been demonstrated that stereotypes: (a) direct attention to certain aspects of target stimuli; (b) guide the interpretation of that information; (c) influence memory and recall of the information; (d) act as working hypotheses, which we try hard to support; and (e) drive judgment and actions (Fiske, 1998; Jost & Hamilton, 2005; Macrae & Bodenhausen, 2000).

One area of research that has received a great deal of recent attention is that on the content of stereotypes. Research on stereotype content had taken a back seat to that on stereotype processes over the last 20 years. Recently, however, Cuddy, Fiske, Glick and their colleagues (Cuddy, Fiske, & Glick, 2007; Cuddy et al., 2009; Fiske, Cuddy, & Glick, 2006; Fiske, Cuddy, Glick, & Xu, 2002) developed a model of stereotype content derived to generalize across groups. Previously when considering stereotypes, each group was characterized by a unique set of traits. Furthermore, stereotypes were not always negative, as exemplified by ambivalent sexism whereby people hold both positive (e.g., nurturing, caring) and negative stereotypes (e.g., overly emotional, irrational) of women (Glick & Fiske, 1996). The Cuddy, Fiske, and Glick model also accounts for ambivalence in stereotypes. The model states that stereotypes fall along two dimensions: warmth and competence. Stereotypes characterized by high warmth and high competence lead to admiration and high-status perceptions. This is the stereotype most likely applied to housewives, Christians, Irish, middle class, Americans, and black professionals. Stereotypes characterized by high warmth and low competence lead to paternalistic prejudices and perceptions of low status, noncompetitiveness, and pity (Fiske et al., 2006). These stereotypes are applied to the elderly, blind people, and retarded individuals (Fiske et al., 2006). Low warmth and low competence stereotypes lead to contemptuous prejudice, perceptions of low status, contempt, disgust, anger, and resentment. These stereotypes are applied to Turks, Arabs, feminists,

poor blacks, and welfare recipients (Fiske et al., 2006). Finally, low warmth and high competence stereotypes lead to envious prejudice, perceptions of high status, envy, and jealousy. These stereotypes are applied to Asians, businesswomen, Jewish people, Northerners, and rich people (Fiske et al., 2006; Fiske et al. 2002) Cuddy et al. (2007) developed the BIAS map to locate (usually through cluster analysis) where various groups fall on dimensions of warmth and competence. The model has also been shown to generalize across national cultures (Cuddy et al., 2007).

Currently, this model has not received much attention in the I/O psychology literature (for recent exceptions, see Heilman & Okimoto, 2008, and Lai, 2008). However, it has a great deal of potential to have an impact on applied discrimination work. Cuddy et al. (2007) linked the BIAS map (where various groups fall on the stereotype grid) to emotions and behaviors. As stated above, stereotype content was associated with the emotions of pity (high warmth, low competence), admiration (high warmth, high competence), contempt (low warmth, low competence), and envy (low warmth and high competence). These emotions, in turn, predicted behavioral tendencies toward targets. Pity leads to both active facilitation (helping) and passive harm (neglecting). Admiration leads to both passive facilitation (associating) and active facilitation. Contempt was associated with both active harm (harassing) and passive harm. Envy was associated with passive facilitation and active harm.

The research allows for more specific predictions about how discrimination may play out in organizational settings, because it allows for ambivalent or mixed stereotypes (high warmth and low competence; low warmth and high competence). To date, most research has just assumed that discrimination will occur as active harm (i.e., bad ratings, harassment, and unfair treatment) due to the assumption of negative stereotypes. This classification system allows for more precise predictions on what forms discrimination may take and may be used to explain some of the more mixed findings found in the literature on discriminatory treatment in organizations (discussed later in this chapter). For example, the disability literature has been riddled by mixed findings about discrimination toward people with disabilities (Colella & Stone, 2005; Stone & Colella, 1996). A recent meta-analysis of experimental studies examining disability effects (Ren, Paetzold, & Colella, 2008) reported that the magnitude and direction of discriminatory behavior depended on the type of disability in question. Also, certain personnel decisions were subject to bias (predictions about future performance), whereas others were not. The Cuddy, Fiske, and Glick model can be used to conceptually explain these findings. For example, people who are paraplegic may be classified as high warmth/low competence, whereas people with depression may be classified as low warmth/low competence, leading to different stereotypes and different treatment (e.g. paternalism versus hostility).

Another area of cognitive research that has guided the I/O literature in examining discrimination is that on stereotypical fit (Dipboye, 1985; Heilman, 1983). In general, the stereotype-fit model states that observers possess stereotypes of targets based on their group membership and also stereotypes of the ideal incumbent for a particular job. Based on the congruence between target stereotype content and job stereotype content, observers form expectations about how a particular person will perform or "fit" in a particular job. A related line of research examines how group stereotypes coincide with particular roles, such as leader or manager. Most notable in this line of research is Eagly and colleagues' role congruity theory of prejudice (Eagly, 1987; Eagly & Karau, 2002; Eagly, Wood, & Diekman, 2000). Eagly and her colleagues argue that we hold both descriptive gender role stereotypes, that is, inferences about how men and women typically behave and their ensuing qualities, and injunctive gender role stereotypes, which prescribe how men and women should behave and be. Role incongruity exists when gender role stereotypes do not fit with the stereotypes, prototypes, or expectations that people have toward a certain role, specifically leadership roles. Men and leaders are characterized as agentic (competitive, aggressive, self-confident, ambitious, objective), in contrast to women, who are characterized as communal, nurturing, and relationship-oriented (Schein, 1973, 1975). Two types of prejudice and discrimination can occur. The first is a less favorable perception of the potential (i.e., future expectation) of women as leaders (Eagly & Karau, 2002). The second is a more negative evaluation of women as leaders when they behave more agentically, due to injunctive stereotype incongruity (Eagly & Karau, 2002).

Most research conducted in the area of stereotype fit and social role congruence has concerned gender stereotyping (e.g., Duehr & Bono, 2006; Heilman, Block, Martell, & Simon, 1989; Heilman & Haynes, 2005). Davison and Burke (2000) conducted a meta-analysis of 15 "simulated employment context" studies examining the lack of fit effect for sex and sex-typed jobs. Females were rated higher on female-typed jobs (mean corrected $r = -.13$) and males were rated more highly on male-typed jobs (mean corrected $r = .17$, $z = 5.94$, $p < .01$). Stereotypic fit, or "non-fit" effects, have also been found for race (e.g., Rosette et al., 2008), disability (Colella et al., 1998; Colella & Varma, 1999), age (e.g., Finkelstein, Burke, & Raju, 1995; Perry & Finkelstein, 1999), and motherhood status (e.g., Heilman & Okimoto, 2008; King, 2008) as well. While this research has been fruitful in helping to explain when discrimination will occur, there are several issues yet to be resolved.

First, ambiguity exists regarding the extent to which stereotype content about groups and about jobs changes over time and context. While this issue is relevant for all groups, we focus on gender because the changing stereotypes of women as managers or leaders have garnered the most research attention. Stereotypes about gender have been studied for decades, allowing for detection of changes in content (Lueptow, Garovich-Szabo, & Lueptow, 2001). This research points to differing results. Lueptow et al. (2001) concluded that gender stereotypes did not change between the 1970s and 1990s, whereas others (Diekman & Eagly, 2000, Twenge, 1997) suggested that stereotypes about women were becoming more agentic or masculine. Duehr and Bono (2006) examined this issue in a managerial context, using Schein's (1973) descriptive index. In this research paradigm, respondents are asked to rate a variety of groups (e.g., women in general, female managers, men, male managers, successful middle managers) on agentic characteristics (e.g., aggressive, analytical, assertive) and communal characteristics (e.g., aware of other's feelings, creative, helpful, kind). They also make ratings based on task-oriented leadership (e.g., competent, decisive, intelligent) and relationship-oriented leadership (e.g., intuitive, sociable, tactful). Duehr and Bono (2006) also added items reflecting transformational leadership qualities. The adjective scales for each group are then correlated with each other to determine how closely the stereotypes of each group are matched.

Schein (1973), Brenner, Tomkiewicz, Schein (1989), and Heilman et al. (1989) all used this same methodology and had male and female managers make ratings. Thus, a comparison was possible about how the results have changed over time. Interestingly, when male managers responded, these three studies found nonsignificant correlations (.06, −.01, −.25, respectively) between ratings for women and managers, indicating that there was no overlap between the description of women in general and managers. However, the 2006 study found that there was a correlation of .63 ($p < .001$), indicating that women and managers were described in similar terms. When female managers responded, the previous studies found significant correlations of .30 (Schein, 1973) and .52 (Brenner et al., 1989). Duehr and Bono (2006) found a correlation of .70 ($p < .001$). The results for all four studies did not differ so much when men in general were compared with male managers, as correlations for male manager respondents ranged from .62 (Schein, 1973) to .72 (Brenner et al., 1989). Correlations obtained from female manager respondents ranged from .49 (Duehr & Bono, 2006) to .59 (Brenner et al., 1989). By examining specific adjective comparisons, they were able to conclude that women were assigned more agentic adjectives. Another interesting conclusion is that female managers in the 2006 study demonstrated same-sex bias, rating women as more similar to managers than men.

The Duehr and Bono (2006) study points to the importance of the impact of the changing workplace demographics on the forms that discrimination may take. As workplaces become more diverse, stereotype content—at least in a work context—may change. While this is only a single study, it is suggestive because it indicates that we may not be able to assume stereotype content and dynamics in any given situation. Stereotype content may not change only over time, but also by context. For example, Ely (1995) found that female lawyers' stereotypes of sex roles varied as a function of the demography in their law firm. As the proportion of women in upper echelons decreased, sex role stereotypes became more feminine. Because most stereotype research is conducted in laboratory settings, future research needs to explore the generalizability of stereotype content over time and across contexts. This brings us to the next issue within stereotype literature: that of generalizing from research conducted in "simulated employment settings" to the "real world."

The December 2008 issue of *Industrial and Organizational Psychology* contained a series of articles summing up the debate concerning whether we can make generalizations from stereotype research conducted in artificial settings and using strangers to what actually happens on the job. Landy (2008), in the lead article, argued that it is questionable whether effects in the real world are as powerful as those found in laboratory settings using a "stranger-to stranger" paradigm (Copus,

2005). A major point in his argument is that typical stereotype research does not present individuating information (see also Copus, 2005; Dipboye, 1985). Respondents have little information on which to base their judgments (e.g., performance ratings, hiring decisions), other than that provided by the experimenter. He contrasts this to real life, where managers have a work history with the ratee, know the ratee as a person, and have a great deal of information about the person who is being evaluated. Since research has shown that stereotypes can quickly dissipate when evaluators are provided with more information or when the ratee is not a stranger (e.g., Fiske & Neuberg, 1990), he argues that stereotype effects will be weaker in real life.

Even though this is not a new issue, it is still a hot one, as evidenced by responses to Landy's (2008) article. Heilman and Eagly (2008) faulted this argument because it: (a) does not accurately portray current consensus on stereotype research (also see Ashburn-Nardo, 2008), particularly that focusing on ambivalent stereotypes (e.g., Eagly & Karau, 2002, described above) and prescriptive stereotypes (see also, Leslie et al., 2008); (b) presents a biased view of research by ignoring research conducted in real-world settings, such as audit research (e.g., Hebl et al., 2002; also see Pager, 2007 for a review); and (c) assumes that we know what characteristics affect the generalizability of this research and focuses only on the amount of information available (see also Hanges & Ziegert, 2008). Furthermore, Leslie et al. (2008) pointed out that research across different methods (e.g., laboratories, audit studies, and labor economic studies) often arrive at the same conclusions (e.g., Colella & Varma, 2001). Researchers (including the present authors) do agree that more research needs to focus on those conditions that mitigate or exasperate discrimination in real-world settings, and move from there to determine how generalizable results from laboratory studies actually are.

A third development for cognitive explanations for discrimination, particularly racial discrimination, is the relatively recent work on implicit social cognition (Dasgupta, 2009; Greenwald & Banaji, 1995; Greenwald et al., 2002; Uleman et al., 2008). This literature states that we form implicit attitudes (prejudice) about members of racial groups and beliefs about them (stereotypes) based on past associations, and that individuals are not always aware of these associations (Quillian, 2006), nor can we control them. Not only has this research received heavy scholarly attention in the last 10 years, it has also received popular press (Gladwell, 2005) and legal attention (Blanton & Jaccard, 2008; Greenwald & Krieger, 2006). It is also controversial.

Greenwald and Banaji (1995) define implicit attitudes (prejudice) and stereotypes as follows:

Implicit attitudes are introspectively unidentified (or inaccurately identified) traces of past experience that mediate favorable or unfavorable feeling, thought, or action toward social objects.

(p. 8)

Implicit stereotypes are the introspectively unidentified (or inaccurately identified) traces of past experience that mediate attributions of qualities to members of a social category.

(p. 15)

According to implicit cognition theories, prejudice consists of both controlled and automatic cognitive components (Devine, 1989). Research suggests that even people who are motivated not to be prejudiced or to consciously hold stereotypes about other racial groups, do indeed, through automatic processing, even though they may not be aware of it. This phenomenon cannot be assessed with typical introspective measures (e.g., racism questionnaires). Instead, it is studied through two primary techniques: priming and response latencies.

Fazio, Jackson, Dunton, and Williams (1995) provide an often-cited example of a priming study. They had student respondents indicate if adjectives flashed on a computer screen were "good" or "bad." In a later phase of the study, they had respondents complete the same task; however, this time the adjectives were presented with a photograph of either a white, black, or Asian face. The measure of the implicit attitude was the "facilitation score," the difference between the time it took to respond to the adjective without the prime and with the prime. White participants were much quicker to respond to negative adjectives paired with a black photograph than they were to respond to positive adjectives paired with black photographs, while this tendency was not observed for white photographs. Black subjects demonstrated the opposite pattern of results for black and white photographs. Interestingly, the unobtrusive facilitation score did not correlate with questionnaire assessments of racism (the Modern Racism Scale), but did correlate with how friendly subjects were with a black experimenter.

Another methodology for assessing individuals' automatic stereotypes and prejudice is the Implicit Association Test (IAT; Greenwald, McGhee, & Schwartz, 1998). Essentially, the IAT unobtrusively measures racist attitudes by the speed and accuracy with which respondents can categorize words. First, they categorize names as either black or white. Next, they categorize words as either pleasant or unpleasant. The measure is taken when these steps are combined and respondents are asked to categorize words as white-pleasant, white-unpleasant, black-pleasant, or black-unpleasant. Speed (response latency) and error rate in categorizing words are used as implicit attitude measures. Ziegert and Hanges (2005) found that scores on the IAT interacted with climate for racial discrimination to predict discrimination in hiring recommendations in a simulated work environment. For those respondents who displayed less racism on the IAT measure, the impact of organizational climate did not affect their likelihood of discriminating against black applicants. Those who had scores indicating racism were much more likely to discriminate when there was a climate for bias, as opposed to equality.

Although at the time of this writing, only one paper (Ziegert & Hanges, 2005) employing the IAT has appeared in the mainstream I/O psychology literature, there has been a great deal of controversy surrounding it (e.g., Blanton & Jaccard, 2008; Blanton et al., 2009; Landy, 2008). Criticisms include questions about the construct validity of the IAT, criterion validity; that is, whether it actually predicts discriminatory behavior, and the extent to which research conducted in the laboratory generalizes to real-world situations (Blanton et al., 2009; Landy, 2008). In an effort to address the second issue, Blanton et al. (2009) reanalyzed the results from Ziegert and Hanges (2005) and McConnell & Leibold (2001), two of eight studies they located that connected the IAT to discriminatory behavior. They were unable to obtain raw data from the others in time for publication. Using more sophisticated statistics, controlling for outliers, and reexamining the data transformations conducted in the original studies, they concluded that there was a pro-black bias in the McConnell and Leibold (2001) study, and that the original results from the Ziegert and Hanges (2005) study were sensitive to rater reliabilities, outliers, and statistical specifications. Given the applied attention given to this phenomenon, we expect this debate to continue to drive research in the field into the near future.

Individual Difference Explanations

Allport (1954) argued that some individuals were more prone than others to be prejudiced and, consequently, to engage in discrimination. This argument was based on the early work by Adorno, Frenkel-Brunswik, Levinson, and Stanford (1950) on the authoritarian personality. The focus on personality and prejudice waned in the early 1960s, to be replaced by research on the role of social and group factors on prejudice. The late 1970s saw a shift in focus to examining cognitive reasons for stereotypes (Sibley & Duckitt, 2008). However, as with other areas (e.g., selection), there has been somewhat of a resurgence of examining personality as a factor motivating prejudice and discrimination due to the development of the "Big Five" personality model (Costa & McCrae, 1992), social dominance theory (Sidanius & Pratto, 1999), and the constructs of modern racism (McConahay, 1986) and aversive racism (Dovidio & Gaertner, 2004; Gaertner & Dovidio, 1986).

Two individual difference constructs have received the most attention in terms of influencing prejudice: the authoritarian personality (Adorno et al., 1950; Altemeyer, 1981) and social dominance orientation (SDO; Pratto, Sidanius, Stallworth, & Malle, 1994; Sidanius & Pratto, 1999). The more modern measure of right wing authoritarianism (RWA; Altemeyer, 1981) measures conventionalism, authoritarian aggression, and authoritarian submission. SDO is described as a "general attitudinal orientation toward intergroup relations, reflecting whether one generally prefers such relations to be equal, versus hierarchical…the extent to which one desires that one's in-group dominate and be superior to out-groups" (Pratto et al., 1994, p. 742). Research has shown several findings regarding both the RWA and the SDO:

• RWA and SDO are weakly correlated with correlations around .20 (Altemeyer, 1998, p. 87; Sidanius & Pratto, 1999, p. 74; Whitley, 1999, p. 129). RWA is conceived as submission to authority and passive deference, whereas SDO is conceived as a more aggressive motive to derogate out-group members and maintain superiority of one's social group (Altemeyer, 1998; Jost, Glaser, Kruglanski, & Sulloway, 2003).
• RWA and SDO contribute incremental validity in predicting prejudice (e.g., anti-black racism, sexism, cultural elitism, attitudes unsupportive of women's rights, racial equality, affirmative action, and gay and lesbian rights; Altemeyer, 1998, Jost & Thompson, 2000; Pratto et al., 1994). They predict attitudes better than they predict behavior (Duriez & Van Hiel, 2002; Saucier, 2000).

• They predict attitudes and behaviors toward groups in general (e.g., women, Hispanics, and people with disabilities), rather than toward a specific group (e.g., Puerto Ricans) with whom the person has had contact (Sibley & Duckitt, 2008).
• Both RWA and SDO are better thought of as basic dimensions of social attitudes and values, rather than personality traits (Duckitt, 2001; Pratto et al., 1994; Sibley & Duckitt, 2008). They mediate the relationship between personality traits and prejudice.
• SDO has been found in a meta-analysis by Sibley and Duckitt (2008) to be moderately negatively associated with the Big Five trait of *agreeableness* (meta-analytic r ranged from −.26 to −.38, depending on Big Five scale) and weakly negatively associated with *openness to experience* (meta-analytic r ranged from −.11 to −.35, depending on Big Five scale). RWA was weakly positively associated with *conscientiousness* (meta-analytic r ranged from −.10 to −.19, depending on Big Five scale) and moderately negatively associated with *openness to experience* (meta-analytic r ranged from −.26 to −.49, depending on Big Five scale).

Recently, RWA and SDO have been examined in several studies in the I/O literature. Umphress, Smith-Crowe, Brief, Dietz, and Watkins (2007) and McKay and Avery (2006) examined the role SDO that plays in applicant attraction to organizations. Umphress et al. (2007) conducted three laboratory studies in which students rated the attractiveness of a potential employer. The status composition of the organization was varied by the names used in the recruiting letter (male-female or black-white). According to the similarity attraction paradigm (Byrne, 1971) and the attraction-selection-attrition model (Schneider, 1987), people should prefer to work in organizations where the demography of the workforce is similar to their own. Umphress et al. (2007) hypothesized and found that SDO moderated this relationship. They found that: (a) as the high-status group's (white males') SDO increased, so did their attraction for less diverse organizations composed of mostly other high-status individuals (white males); and (b) as SDO increased for low-status groups (women), their attraction for the organization composed of white males (high-status group) increased, despite the fact that they would be a minority in this organization. One conclusion drawn from this is that members of low-status groups who are high on SDO denigrate their own groups and prefer to associate with high-status groups. In a similar vein, McKay and Avery (2006) proposed that the relationship between actual diversity integration in an organization and diversity climate perceptions would be weak for racial-ethnic minority job candidates who were high on SDO. In other words, those who were high on SDO would not be as positively influenced during recruiting site visits by the diversity of composition and integration in an organization as those low on SDO.

Several studies have found that SDO and authoritarianism interact with discrimination "climate" in influencing hiring recommendations for out-group members. In a laboratory team performance simulation task study, Umphress, Simmons, Boswell, and Triana (2008) found that when team leaders told team members to select others based on qualifications, participant SDO had no impact on the selection of black team members. However, when such instructions were absent, SDO was positively related to discrimination. Petersen and Dietz (2000), in a laboratory in-basket study, found West German student participants were more likely to discriminate in hiring East German job applicants when instructed to do so, only if they were high on RWA. They replicated this pattern of findings using a scenario study with East German teachers as participants, who were more likely to discriminate in hiring West German teachers, when it was in compliance with the supervisor's wishes, as their authoritarianism score became higher.

Another individual difference that has garnered attention in the I/O psychology literature on discrimination is political conservatism. *Political conservatism* has been defined as "the resistance to change and the tendency to prefer safe, traditional and conventional forms of institutions and behaviour" (Wilson, 1973, p. 4). Jost et al. (2003) describe *political conservatism* as "a motivated social cognition" in which political ideologies are adopted because they satisfy psychological needs, such as fear and anxiety reduction or the enhancement of self-esteem. In their model, political conservatism is considered partially as a stable disposition, but one that is influenced by situational conditions such as threat. Jost et al. (2003), after an in-depth review and meta-analysis of correlates of political conservatism, state that there are two underlying dimensions: fear of change and acceptance of inequality.

Most of the work on the effects of conservatism on discrimination in the I/O psychology literature has focused on its relationship to attitudes toward affirmative action. Harrison, Kravitz, Mayer, Leslie, and Lev-Arey (2006) conducted a meta-analysis of the relationship between conservatism and attitudes toward affirmative action. In a sample of 23 studies, they found a mean correlation of −.284 (95% confidence interval: −.350 to −.218). This relationship was moderated by the justification given for the affirmative action plan. As the explicit statement of the plan became more oriented toward strong preferential treatment (and less toward merit and opportunity), the effects of conservatism became weaker. The strongest effect was found when respondents were not given any description of the affirmative action plan ($k = 8$, mean $r = -.487$, 95% confidence interval: −.541 to −.334). Note that when no justification is given for an affirmative action plan, respondents tend to rely on their tacit beliefs about affirmative action (Arriola & Cole, 2001; Golden, Hinkle, & Crosby, 2001).

While social dominance orientation, conservatism, and right wing authoritarianism may be directly related to explicit, "old-fashioned" forms of discrimination and prejudice (Dovidio & Hebl, 2005), more recent work, particularly in social psychology, has focused on more subtle forms of racism such as modern racism (McConahay, 1986) and aversive racism (Dovidio & Gaertner, 2004; Gaertner & Dovidio, 1986). Both of these types of racism are based on the notion that in modern U.S. society, there are strong norms against explicitly demonstrating racial prejudice and discrimination, yet people still harbor negative, prejudiced attitudes. Thus, people are torn between egalitarian goals (such as being non-prejudiced) and negative affect toward other racial groups (either conscious or unconscious). As a result, rather than taking explicit forms, such as racial harassment, racial discrimination will take more subtle forms.

Theory states that those high in modern racism will simply change the expression of their prejudice. Rather than discriminate outright, they will endorse and act upon beliefs that are stated as fact. McConahay (1986) presents four such beliefs:

(1) Discrimination is a thing of the past because Blacks now have the freedom to compete in the marketplace and to enjoy those things they can afford. (2) Blacks are pushing too hard, too fast and into places where they are not wanted. (3) These tactics and demands are unfair. (4) Therefore, recent gains are undeserved and the prestige granting institutions of society are giving Blacks more attention and the concomitant status than they deserve.
(p. 92)

Modern racism is usually measured with the Modern Racism Scale (McConahay, 1986), which contains items such as "Over the past few years, the government and news media have shown more respect to racial minorities than they deserve," and "It is easy to understand the anger of racial minorities in America." A similar construct is measured with the Symbolic Racism Scale (Henry & Sears, 2002). Although most research on modern racism has concerned U.S. white people's attitudes toward U.S. blacks, the notion and scale have been developed with respect to other groups (e.g., Asians: Son Hing, Li, & Zanna, 2002; Arabs: Echebarria-Echabe & Guede, 2007; women: Swim, Aikin, Hall, & Hunter, 1995).

Gaertner and Dovidio (1986) state that aversive racism "represents a particular type of ambivalence in which the conflict is between feelings and beliefs associated with a sincerely egalitarian value system and unacknowledged negative feelings and beliefs about blacks" (p. 62). Because aversive racism stems from an actual desire to hold egalitarian beliefs, aversive racists feel discomfort, unease, and fear toward members of other racial groups, rather than outright hostility. Furthermore, because of the nature of aversive racism, it cannot be directly measured. Rather, it is indicated by scoring low on explicit measures of racism and high on implicit measures (e.g., the IAT; Son Hing, Chung-Yan, Hamilton, & Zanna, 2008).

Both modern racism and aversive racism are proposed to lead to the attributional ambiguity effect (Son Hing et al., 2008; for a similar argument concerning persons with disabilities, see Katz & Glass, 1979). Because neither modern racists nor aversive racists wish to appear prejudicial against minorities, they should only discriminate when there is a reason, other than prejudice, to justify such discrimination. Thus, when there is attributional ambiguity about the cause for a behavior, discrimination should occur. However, when no such cause is present, modern racism and aversive racism should be unrelated to discrimination. Attributional ambiguity has been manipulated in several ways in laboratory studies. Brief et al. (2000) found that when respondents were given permission by authorities (high attributional-ambiguity condition), higher levels of modern racism were associated with lower hiring recommendations of a black target. Dovidio and Gaertner (2000) manipulated ambiguity by the strength of the qualifications for a fictional job candidate. Only in those conditions where the qualifications were ambiguous (as opposed to clearly high

or low) did respondents discriminate against black candidates. Son Hing et al. (2008) and McConahay (1983) found analogous results with a similar manipulation.

Although there are several exceptions, modern racism and aversive racism have not received the large amount of attention in the I/O literature that they have in the social psychology domain. Most work in this area has been conducted in laboratory settings using student respondents. The concepts of modern racism and aversive racism have important implications for understanding workplace discrimination since they suggest that discrimination may be more subtle than is usually conceptualized. We address the issue of subtle discrimination in the conclusion section of this chapter.

In-Group Favoritism Theories

In-group–favoritism theories are based on Byrne's (1971) similarity-attraction paradigm, which states that we are attracted to those who we perceive to be similar to ourselves, leading to more positive affect toward, trust of, and evaluations of similar others, compared to those whom we deem dissimilar. We focus on three frequently cited theoretical frameworks: social identity theory (Tajfel & Turner, 1979), relational demography (Riordan, 2000; Tsui, Egan, & O'Reilly, 1992; Tsui & O'Reilly, 1989), and the attraction-selection-attrition paradigm (ASA; Schneider, 1987). For a more in-depth discussion of other group theories of why discrimination occurs in organizations, see Thomas and Chrobot-Mason (2005). This group of theories is usually used to explain diversity effects within organizations. However, they do have implications as causes of discriminatory behavior (Riordan, Schaffer, & Stewart, 2005).

Social identity theory (Tajfel & Turner, 1986), and relatedly, self-categorization theory (Turner, 1985) state that people categorize themselves and others along salient social and demographic dimensions such as race, age, sex, class, and so on. Those who are classified as similar to oneself are viewed as in-group members, while those classified as dissimilar are out-group members. Social identity is defined as "that part of an individual's self-concept which derives from his knowledge of his membership of a social group...together with the value and emotional significance attached to that membership" (Tajfel, 1981, p. 255). The results of this categorization are minimizing within-group differences, maximizing intergroup differences, displaying favoritism and trust toward those in the in-group, and stereotyping out-group members (Brewer, 2007). These effects have been well documented (Brewer, 2007; Jetten, Spears, & Postmes, 2004). What is debated is the assumption that social identity categorization processes necessarily lead to the derogation of out-group members (Brewer, 2007).

Social identity theory is based on the idea that in-group bias results from a desire for positive distinctiveness for in-group members in terms of status and value, relative to out-group members (Turner, 1975). This has been termed the *self-esteem hypothesis* (Turner & Reynolds, 2001); that is, we favor the in-group to make ourselves feel better and to derive self-enhancement. This implies that we will derogate (or discriminate against) out-group members for self-enhancement purposes, as well as favoring in-group members. Brewer (2007) argues that the basis for in-group preferences is not self-enhancement, but rather the desire for security, group inclusion, and trust. Brewer's (1991) theory of optimal differentiation argues that there are competing social motives: the need for inclusion and the need for differentiation from others. Hostility toward the out-group will only occur when the out-group is seen as a threat to the survival and security of the in-group, and/or when an individual feels that he or she is a peripheral group member and seeks to enhance feelings of inclusion. Thus, favoritism toward the in-group does not always imply hostility toward the out-group.

Social identity theory is often cited as a theoretical basis for research on discrimination in the I/O literature. However, it is rarely ever directly tested. Nor is the notion that differences in treatment may be due to in-group favoritism, rather than derogation of the out-group tested. While either motive can lead to discriminatory behavior, it is important to know the reason why. We now turn to a line of research in which social identity theory has played a major role, which has received a great deal of empirical attention: relational demography.

The relational demography literature is based on the assumption that individuals compare themselves in terms of visible, salient demographic characteristics to the demographic makeup of their work units. Dissimilarity is usually thought to lead to negative work outcomes, such as less organizational attachment, commitment, poor group dynamics, and greater conflict (Riordan et al., 2005). Riordan et al. (2005) conducted a qualitative review of 145 studies and concluded that 54% of these studies found support for the relational demography hypothesis that dissimilarity is related to negative

outcomes, 32% found non-significant effects, and 14% found significant effects in the opposite direction. Most research is conducted in a diversity context, and does not concern discrimination per se. Common dependent variables are the effects of similarity on group performance, withdrawal behaviors, attitudes toward the organization and job, role ambiguity, and group process variables (e.g., cohesion, communication, cooperation; Riordan et al., 2005). Investigations that have examined outcomes relevant to discrimination report contradictory or weak results. For example, in support of relational demography predictions, Buckley, Jackson, Bolino, Veres, and Feild (2007) found that four-person job interview panels varied in their ratings of white and black candidates depending on the racial-ethnic makeup of the panel. All white panels gave higher ratings to white candidates, and all black panels assigned higher ratings to black candidates. Mixed groups tended to give higher ratings to white candidates. However, the effect size of panel racial-ethnic composition was small ($d = .29$). Contrary to these predictions, Goldberg (2005), in a study of recruiter applicant sex similarity on selction decisions, found dissimilarity effects. However, this was due to male recruiters preferring female applicants. Again, the effect size was small ($R^2 = .01$).

Two recent issues have emerged within the relational demography literature. The first concerns the frequently reported empirical finding (e.g., Bacharach & Bamberger, 2004; Pelled, Eisenhardt, & Xin, 1999; Tsui et al., 1992) of asymmetrical effects, where dissimilarity has a stronger negative effect on white or male respondents than it does on racial-ethnic minority respondents and women. These findings run counter to earlier theorizing that demographic dissimilarity should be the same for all groups (Tsui & O'Reilly, 1989). Several justifications have been given for this effect, and several have been given for the opposite effect whereby dissimilarity should be more problematic for minorities and women (see Tonidandel, Avery, Bucholtz, & McKay, 2008, for a review). However, recently, Tonidandel et al. (2008) demonstrated, using a Monte Carlo simulation, that asymmetrical effects are a statistical artifact of using a Euclidean distance measure (*D-scores*) to measure dissimilarity and of having one group underrepresented in the total sample (as is often the case when comparing majority groups to minority groups), which results in reduced variability. They suggested alternatives to this problem, such as using correction formulas for range restriction, using the proportion of people dissimilar, rather than D-scores, as a measure of dissimilarity, and/or using multilevel statistical approaches, but conclude that none of these approaches is without drawbacks.

The second issue that has emerged in the relational demography literature also concerns how one measures dissimilarity. Three measures are commonly used to measure dissimilarity: D-scores, interaction terms, and a perceptual measure. Riordan and Wayne (2008) illustrate that the three measures are driven by different theoretical concerns, often resulting in discrepant effects, and are prone to varying problems. In summary, the authors provide guidelines for employing perceptual measures and interaction term measures, and recommend that researchers no longer use D-scores to measure dissimilarity.

In conclusion, the relational demography literature has led to conflicting results regarding the impact of demographic dissimilarity on how individuals react to their organizations and those in it. However, the recent work above suggests that much of this confusion may be due to methodological artifacts. Future research in this area may lead to more insightful conclusions, given the recent focus on improving methodology. Furthermore, Brewer's (1991) theory of differential optimization may be applied to determine under what conditions demographic dissimilarity will lead to discrimination and when it will not. To our knowledge, no work has been done that examines relational demography effects under threat conditions (e.g., layoffs) and non-threatening conditions.

Another framework that relies on social identity theory and frequently appears in the I/O literature is the attraction-selection-attrition (ASA) paradigm. The ASA framework (Schneider, 1987) argues that the interrelated processes of attraction, selection, and attrition determine what types of people compose an organization, and that the types of people in an organization determine the prevailing forms of organizational structures, policies, and culture. Schneider (1987) argues that organizations tend toward homogeneity, because people are attracted to organizations composed of similar people, organizations tend to select people who are similar to those who are already members, and people who are dissimilar, yet do enter the organization, tend to leave. Later, Schneider, Goldstein, and Smith (1995) clarified that the dimensions of similarity of importance are attitudes, values, and personality (in contrast to demographic characteristics). Related to discrimination, one of the most relevant

implications of the ASA framework is the homogeneity hypothesis, which states that over time, due to the attraction-selection-attrition processes, organizations will become more homogeneous with respect to the types of people working in them. Indirect support has been found for the homogeneity hypothesis (Schneider et al., 1995). To the extent that attitudes, values, and personality covary with group status (for an argument that this is the case, see Pfeffer, 1983), then the ASA process works to exclude certain groups from organizational membership. As of yet, there have been no empirical studies linking ASA dynamics to discrimination.

In conclusion, in-group favoritism theories provide a conceptual background for explaining discrimination. Yet, as Brewer's (1991) work points out, the application of this reasoning to explain discrimination may be more complicated than it is usually depicted in the I/O literature. This is perhaps why empirical research based directly on this line of reasoning (i.e., relational demography research) yields mixed results. Future work in this area needs to take a more complex view of social identity dynamics to move this line of research forward.

Other Discrimination Theories
SYSTEM JUSTIFICATION THEORY

System Justification Theory (Jost & Banaji, 1994; Jost, Banaji, & Nosek, 2004) argues that people have three justification motives that can explain reactions to those in other groups. Ego justification is the desire to develop and maintain a positive self-image and to feel valued. Group justification concerns the desire to maintain a positive depiction of one's own group and its members. Social identity theory addresses both of these motives. Where system justification system differs from other theories is that it contends that people also have a motive to justify the system, that is, to maintain the status quo of status difference that exists in one's society. This theory has been used extensively to explain why members of disadvantaged or low-status groups often show favoritism toward higher status outgroups, particularly when reactions are measured using implicit measures (see Jost et al., 2004 for a review). The theory results in hypotheses similar to other theories (e.g., social identity theory, social dominance theory) with respect to reactions of dominant, high-status groups toward disadvantaged or low-status groups.

One finding from this literature that is particularly relevant to employment discrimination concerns the notion of depressed entitlement (Jost et al., 2004).

Depressed entitlement occurs when members of low-status groups undervalue their own contributions and deserved rewards, which is supposedly a sign of undervaluing their own worth relative to high-status groups. This explains why women may be more satisfied with lower pay for equal work compared to men (Major, 1994), and, thus, perpetuate a system in which women are underpaid. Jost (1997) conducted a study where he found that female Yale college students, supposedly in a feminist environment, paid themselves 18% less than men for the same work.

Although system justification theory is not frequently addressed in the I/O psychology literature, it clearly has implications that can take research on workplace discrimination in new directions. As cited above, it can be used to predict acceptance of unfair wages and other outcomes. Furthermore, the theory may provide insight into what type of organizational cultures are most likely to promote system justification motives on the part of both dominant group members and lower-status group members.

TOKENISM AND NUMERICAL DISTINCTIVENESS

McGuire and colleagues' (McGuire & McGuire, 1981; McGuire, McGuire, Child, & Fujioka, 1978; McGuire, McGuire, & Winton, 1979; McGuire & Padawer-Singer, 1976) numerical distinctiveness theory and Kanter's (1977) seminal work on women managers advanced the notion that the number of one's group within the organization influences how one is perceived. This line of research garnered quite a bit of attention in the 1980s. Kanter (1977) argued that token status within an organization leads to *token dynamics,* consisting of: increased visibility of the token; contrast, whereby tokens and other members focus on differences among themselves; and increased stereotyping of the token. However, subsequent research, while being generally supportive of Kanter's (1977) theory (see Goldman et al., 2006, for a review), has found that these dynamics only occur when the token is a member of a low-status or traditionally disadvantaged group (Zimmer, 1988). Most of the research resulting from Kanter's (1977) work has focused on sex discrimination.

While Kanter's (1977) work has seemed to be replaced by relational demography (Riordan et al., 2005), research has strayed away from examining the underlying effects of small numbers (i.e., visibility, contrast, and increased stereotyping) and focusing on final outcomes such as performance evaluations of women in traditionally male jobs (Sackett, DuBois, & Noe, 1991) and standards used

to determine promotions for women in traditionally male jobs (Lyness & Heilman, 2006). Perhaps future research on workplace discrimination would benefit from revisiting Kanter's (1977) original work by focusing on workplace dynamics and generalizing token dynamics across other groups.

RACIAL COMPOSITION OF THE COMMUNITY AND GROUP THREAT

Sociologists and economists have given a great deal of attention to the impact that the racial composition of an organization's community has on attitudes and prejudice (Reskin, 1998; Reskin, McBrier, & Kmec, 1999; Taylor, 1998). Generally, whites' prejudice against blacks, as evidenced by such indicators as traditional prejudice scales, attitudes toward non-discrimination policies, and housing, education, and income disparities, increases as the percentage of blacks in the local community rises (Taylor, 1998). These findings are explained by a series of theories which posit that antagonism arises between racial groups because they are in competition for resources. Thus, as the number of blacks in a community rises, so does white prejudice and discrimination as an attempt to protect their own welfare and resources in view of a real or perceived threat regarding economic standing, political power, and/or status. Blumer (1958) first made this argument by stating that racial antagonism derives from a group's defense of its own position in society. Later, Levine and Campbell (1972) put forth "realistic group conflict theory," which states that antagonism between groups is due to competition for scarce resources. Finally, Giles and Evans's (1986) "power theory" describes ethnic groups as means for the pursuit of self-interest, leading to in-group identification and perceptions of threat from outgroups.

Taylor (1998) reviewed the literature on race composition effects and conducted another large-scale study using 1990 General Social Survey (GSS) data. She found support for the increasing racial composition-discrimination effect, but only for whites' attitudes toward blacks. However, this effect was not found for whites' prejudice against Asian Americans and Latinos. The finding that racial composition only affects whites' prejudice toward blacks suggests that the group threat hypothesis may be more complicated than currently stated.

Recently, the impact of racial composition of the community has found its way into the I/O psychology literature (see Brief, Butz, & Deitch, 2005, for a discussion). Pugh, Dietz, Brief, and Wiley

(2008), in a study of bank employees, found that racial composition of the community moderated the relationship between diversity climate perceptions and workforce racial composition (percentage of minority employees in each business unit). When community racial composition was low (i.e., few minorities lived in the community), the relationship between workforce composition and diversity climate perceptions was stronger than when the community racial composition was high. They argued that under conditions of low racial composition, workforce composition would have a stronger signaling effect than when there were a large number of blacks in the community.

Beyond examining the effects of community racial composition on workplace discrimination (something that has not been done in our literature and at an individual or team level), there are other implications of this literature for future research directions. The notion of threat runs through several theories of discrimination, yet, this seems to be an ignored dynamic in our literature. Future research should consider what organizational culture characteristics and policies lead to perceptions of threat and link these situational cues to discriminatory behavior.

DISCRIMINATION AS COMPLIANCE

Recently, there has been a series of studies that have examined workplace discrimination as a function of compliance with authority's wishes (Brief et al., 2000; Petersen & Dietz, 2000, 2008). This research is based on the voluminous social psychology literature on obedience to authority (Hamilton & Sanders, 1992; Kelman & Hamilton, 1989; Milgram, 1974). According to this literature, employees adopt organizational roles that include complying with requests from legitimate authority figures within the organization (Brief, Buttram, & Dukerich, 2001). Willingness to comply with illegal or unethical directives derives from employees' transferring responsibility for their actions to the organization and the authorities issuing directives. Using an in-basket paradigm that involved selecting racial and ethnic minority employees, this research has demonstrated that respondents are much more likely to discriminate against racial or ethnic minority applicants when given "legitimate business reasons" to do so by a legitimate authority figure (Brief et al., 2000; Petersen & Dietz, 2000, 2008). It was also found that this tendency was greater for those who held strong modern racist beliefs (Brief et al., 2000), were high on authoritarianism (Petersen &

Dietz, 2000), and had high affective commitment to the organization (Petersen & Dietz, 2008).

This perspective on workplace discrimination deserves more attention in the I/O psychology literature than it has currently received. It calls attention to those organizational practices and policies, implicit or explicit, which may be sending the message that discrimination is necessary for the betterment of the business. Rather than focusing on how individuals process information (as in the cognitive approach), it focuses on what information individuals are receiving about the organization's views on discrimination. Examining organizational causes for discrimination has been largely neglected in our literature (Gelfand, Nishii, Raver, & Schneider, 2005), beyond the impact of certain human resource management procedures.

In summary, research on employment discrimination does not suffer from a lack of theoretical underpinnings. While cognitive, individual difference, and group favoritism theories have engendered a great deal of research, other theories that are relevant have been somewhat ignored. Expanding the lens from which we examine the process of organizational discrimination and empirically exploring frameworks that span across the societal, organizational, group, and individual levels should be the directions of future research.

Forms of Discrimination

Discrimination can take many forms in an organization. We focus on those that have received the most research attention in the I/O psychology literature: adverse impact, harassment, evaluation disparities, and pay disparities. We also address subtle discrimination, which has received less attention in the I/O literature.

Adverse Impact

Compared to adverse treatment, which concerns intentional discrimination against members of certain demographic groups, adverse impact (AI) refers to negative outcomes that befall members of groups protected by Title VII of the Civil Rights Act of 1964 (e.g., racial-ethnic minorities, women, religious minorities) when particular personnel procedures (e.g., employment tests/assessments, performance appraisals) are used in human resource decision making. The Uniform Guidelines on Employee Selection Procedures (1978) defines adverse impact formally using the four-fifths rule, stating that AI has occurred when the selection ratio (SR; i.e., number of applicants hired/total number of job applicants) for protected group members is less than 80% of the SR for the majority group (e.g., whites, men). As an example, if 20% (e.g., $SR = 20/100$) of white job applicants are hired for a position, at least 16% of the minority job seekers (e.g., $SR = 8/50$) must be selected to conclude an absence of AI. The use of a personnel procedure that has AI will result in lower selection rates for members of groups who earn lower scores on the procedure. Importantly, AI constitutes a prima facie case of discrimination; therefore, if a personnel procedure that causes AI is challenged in court, employers must demonstrate the validity of the procedure for eventual job performance, in terms of the job-relevance and/or business necessity of the knowledge, skills, abilities, and other characteristics (KSAOs) measured (Uniform Guidelines, 1978). Accordingly, we recommend that employers validate all methods used to make personnel decisions.

In sections to follow, we present the existing evidence on the extent of AI on selection measures and performance criteria. It should be noted that we do not endeavor to provide an exhaustive review of all literature on AI, but to provide a summary of general trends. We focus our attention primarily upon meta-analytic studies that have examined the extent of AI for various selection measures and performance criteria. Meta-analyses are useful because they summarize research conclusions across a number of studies while often controlling for the confounding effects of methodological and/or statistical artifacts (e.g., predictor and criterion unreliability, and restriction in range on the scores derived from tests/assessments and/or job performance criteria) inherent in individual primary studies (Hunter & Schmidt, 2004). Subsequently, we describe various strategies for reducing AI and, where appropriate, highlight primary studies that are informative in this regard.

ADVERSE IMPACT OF SELECTION MEASURES

AI of selection measures has implications for the likelihood that members of protected groups will be hired into organizations. Top-down selection decisions, wherein job applicants with top scores on selection methods are selected in a descending fashion until all job openings are filled, provides the greatest utility for selection systems in terms of subsequent job performance (Schmidt & Hunter, 1998). Research in this area has focused sharply on subgroup mean differences in scores on various selection procedures because these have direct bearing on the magnitude of AI for these methods

(Ployhart & Holtz, 2008). In reporting subgroup differences on the selection methods of interest, we will focus on the standardized mean difference, or Cohen's d, which reports score disparities in standard deviation units that are comparable across studies and procedures. Positive d values mean that members of the majority group (e.g., whites) earn higher scores, on average, than members of the minority group, whereas negative values denote a score difference favoring the minority group. In certain instances, we reversed the signs of effect sizes reported in reviewed studies to coincide with the above interpretation of the directions of subgroup mean differences. We also provide k values, which denote the number of studies analyzed to derive a given effect size (d) value, and N to identify the total sample sizes associated with effect size estimates. Readers should use caution in interpreting effect sizes based upon fewer than 10 studies.

Typically, analyses of subgroup differences in selection measure scores have contrasted whites with members of minority groups, as these have evidenced some of the starkest disparities, particularly for cognitive ability tests (CATs; Bobko, Roth, & Potosky, 1999; Roth, BeVier, Bobko, Switzer, & Tyler, 2001). Much of this empirical attention has been directed toward discovering alternative selection methods that reduce or mitigate the AI associated with CATs. Several of the most commonly studied alternative methods will be reviewed, including personality tests, integrity tests, interviews, work samples, situational judgment tests (SJTs), biodata forms, and assessment centers (ACs). In contrast, sex mean differences in selection test/assessment performance are generally smaller, with the exception of physical ability tests (PATs; Hogan, 1991; Sackett & Wilk, 1994). Similarly, age differences on selection measures are small (Hough, Oswald, & Ployhart, 2001), therefore, we do not address this topic.

Race-ethnicity. *Cognitive ability tests* (CATs) are designed to measure a person's general intellectual capabilities. General intelligence (g) is conceptualized as the apex of a mental ability hierarchy, with lower levels comprising more specific verbal, mathematical, perceptual speed, spatial, and memory-based abilities (Carroll, 1993; Jensen, 1998). CATs have been reported as one of the best predictors of job performance across all jobs, with a mean validity coefficient (r) of .51 (Hunter & Hunter, 1984; Schmidt & Hunter, 1998). Hunter's (1983) theory of job performance explains the general relevance of cognitive ability for job performance as follows. Cognitive ability relates to job performance through its influence on the acquisition of job knowledge. Workers who are higher in cognitive ability will learn job requirements more quickly and thoroughly, with beneficial effects on subsequent job performance. Moreover, this process should be amplified for complex jobs since these positions tend to have higher knowledge requirements. CAT scores have high AI against blacks ($d = 1.10$, $k = 105$, $N = 6,246,729$) and Hispanics ($d = .72$, $k = 39$, $N = 5,696,519$), indicating that members of these minority subgroups earn markedly lower CAT scores than their white counterparts (Roth et al., 2001). Furthermore, white-black mean differences were somewhat smaller for job incumbents ($d = .90$, $k = 13$, $N = 50,799$) than for job applicants ($d = 1.00$, $k = 11$, $N = 375,307$). Therefore, it is apparent that the use of CATs to make selection decisions will reduce substantially the proportion of black and Hispanic job applicants selected for available job openings.

The high validity and AI associated with the use of CATs present a quandary, aptly labeled "the diversity-validity dilemma" (Pyburn, Ployhart, & Kravitz, 2008), for organizations wishing to simultaneously maximize job performance and employee demographic diversity. Several authors have been critical of overly *g*-loaded selection batteries, since a wide range of KSAOs are necessary for effective job performance (Goldstein, Zedeck, & Goldstein, 2002; Murphy, 1996). For instance, Borman and Motowidlo (1993) broadened the performance (or criterion) domain to include both *task performance*, consisting of the core duties and tasks that constitute a job, and *contextual performance*, which refers to discretionary, pro-social work behaviors designed to assist individual employees and the organizational as a whole (e.g., working late to finish a project, helping a coworker with work-related tasks, following company rules and regulations, etc.). Research has shown that task performance is best predicted by cognitive ability, while contextual performance is forecasted well by dispositional variables such as personality constructs (Hattrup, O'Connell, & Wingate, 1998; Johnson, 2001).

From these expanded theories of job performance, it is apparent that cognitive ability is one of several constructs that have relevance for job performance. Consequently, a number of alternative predictors have been examined. The expectation is that the use of more non-cognitive selection tools (i.e., measures with low cognitive loadings or share low correlations with CAT scores) will reduce adverse

impact against minorities, thus increasing their probabilities of hire. In addition, to the extent that these alternative methods are (a) uncorrelated with cognitive ability and (b) valid predictors of performance, including them in selection batteries with CATs will improve the prediction of job performance (Goldstein et al., 2002; Schmidt & Hunter, 1998).

Beginning with *personality measures*, the "Big Five" personality theory (Goldberg, 1993) states that normal personality comprises five broad factors: emotional stability (i.e., the extent that one is secure, non-anxious, and relaxed); extraversion (i.e., the degree that a person is outgoing, sociable, and assertive); openness to experience (i.e., how curious, imaginative, and intellectual a person is); agreeableness (i.e. the degree that an individual is warm, friendly, and trusting); and conscientiousness (i.e., the extent that a person is dependable, responsible, and motivated). Prevailing meta-analytic evidence (Hurtz & Donovan, 2000) has shown that conscientiousness predicts performance across all jobs (p [true-score population estimate] = .22, $k = 45$, $N = 8,083$), and useful validities have been obtained for emotional stability ($p = .14$, $k = 37$, $N = 5,671$) and agreeableness as well ($p = .13$, $k = 40$, $N = 6,447$). Extraversion emerged as a valid predictor of sales performance ($p = .16$, $k = 8$, $N = 1,044$) and training performance ($p = .19$, $k = 2$, $N = 644$), with the latter criterion also exhibiting a meaningful relationship with openness to experience ($p = .14$, $k = 1$, $N = 644$). In addition to being a valid predictor of job performance, conscientiousness is virtually uncorrelated with cognitive ability (Bobko et al., 1999) and, consequently, this construct (captured at the broad, construct level) results in very little AI against minorities. Standardized racial-ethnic mean differences on conscientiousness range from .07 ($k = 67$, $N = 180,478$) for white-black contrasts to .25 for white–Native American comparisons ($k = 11$, $N = 13,139$; Foldes, Duehr, & Ones, 2008).

Integrity tests are employed by organizations concerned about their employees' honesty and trustworthiness (e.g., retailers, banks). Usually, these measures come in one of two forms: (a) overt (or clear purpose) integrity tests, which contain items that explicitly measure a respondent's level of honesty (e.g., "If I noticed a coworker stealing company merchandise, I would report him/her"; Likert scales, 1 = strongly disagree to 5 = strongly agree); and (b) personality-based (or disguised-purpose) integrity tests that assess personality attributes relevant to honesty, such as conscientiousness (Sackett, Burris, & Callahan, 1989).

Meta-analytic research has underscored the following conclusions regarding integrity tests. First, from a construct validation standpoint, integrity tests are most strongly correlated (in descending order) with the conscientiousness, agreeableness, and emotional stability factors of the "Big Five" personality model (Ones, Viswesvaran, & Dilchert, 2005). Second, integrity test scores display near-zero correlations with cognitive ability, and the use of them results in substantial incremental validity beyond CATs scores (Ones, Viswesvaran, & Schmidt, 1993; Schmidt & Hunter, 1998). Third, across the two test types, integrity tests have a mean true validity of .41 ($k = 23$, $N = 7,550$) in predicting supervisory ratings of overall job performance (Ones et al., 1993). Fourth, Ones et al. (1993) found that integrity tests exhibited even higher validities for predicting counterproductive work behaviors such as theft, absenteeism, tardiness, and violence ($p = .47$, $k = 443$, $N = 507,688$). Integrity test type further moderated these results, with overt measures ($p = .55$, $k = 305$, $N = 349,623$) showing higher validity than personality-based tests ($p = .32$, $k = 138$, $N = 158,065$; Ones et al., 1993). Finally, meta-analyses of mean subgroup differences in overt integrity test scores indicate effect sizes ranging from $-.05$ ($k = 4$, $N = 541,314$) for the white-Hispanic contrast to $-.16$ ($k = 4$, $N = 680,675$) for the male-female comparison (Ones & Viswesvaran, 1998). Thus, the use of overt integrity tests—and likely personality-based tests as well, given the low AI reported for personality measures above—results in little AI against protected groups.

The next series of selection procedures, interviews, work samples, situational judgment tests, biodata forms, and assessment centers are most accurately considered measurement methods. These procedures do not measure a distinct construct, but instead can be designed to measure myriad constructs such as cognitive ability, job knowledge, personality, integrity, and so on (Hough et al., 2001; Huffcutt, Conway, Roth, & Stone, 2001; McDaniel, Morgeson, Finnegan, Campion, & Braverman, 2001). Starting with *interviews*, these are one of the most widely used selection procedures (Heneman & Judge, 2009). Interviews vary typically with in regard to the level of structure with which they are constructed and administered. Unstructured interviews are not designed to measure KSAOs identified during job analyses; therefore, interview questions are not formulated to measure job applicants'

standings on job-relevant attributes. Associated features of unstructured interviews include (a) the use of non-standardized questions, and (b) lack of a standard scoring system. In contrast, structured interviews are based upon job analyses, ask applicants a standard set of job-relevant questions, and contain standard scoring schemes to compute interview scores. Differences between unstructured and structured interview construction result in reliability differences in scores (favoring structured interviews) and proneness to ratings bias (disfavoring unstructured interviews); accordingly, structured interviews ($p = .31$, $k = 106$, $N = 12,847$) predict subsequent job performance better than unstructured interviews ($p = .23$, $k = 39$, $N = 9330$; McDaniel, Whetzel, Schmidt, & Maurer, 1994).

Despite the finding that interviews are moderately correlated with cognitive ability ($p = .40$, $k = 49$, $N = 12,037$; Huffcutt, Roth, & McDaniel, 1996), these measures result in markedly lower AI than CATs (white-black $d = .25$, $k = 31$, 10,476; white-Hispanic $d = .26$, $k = 15$, $N = 4,902$; Huffcutt & Roth, 1998). Racial-ethnic mean effect sizes are moderated by interview structure, with larger disparities observed for low structure (white-black $d = .32$, $k = 10$, $N = 1,659$; white-Hispanic $d = .71$, $k = 3$, $N = 667$) than high structure interviews (white-black $d = .23$, $k = 21$, $N = 8,817$; white-Hispanic $d = .17$, $k = 12$, $N = 4,235$; Huffcutt & Roth, 1998).

Roth, Van Iddekinge, Huffcutt, Edison, and Bobko (2002) warned that prior meta-analytic estimates of racial-ethnic mean differences in interview scores may be underestimated due to range restriction owing to: (a) direct sources, as when effect sizes are computed only for those who have been selected using a particular selection tool; (b) indirect sources as when a multiple-hurdle selection system is employed wherein applicants are prescreened on other (valid) predictors before being interviewed; and (c) the use of job incumbent versus job applicant samples. Supporting this reasoning, Roth et al. (2002) found a white-black (corrected) mean effect size of .46 in scores on a structured, behavioral interview, a figure two times larger than the .23 meta-analytic estimate reported by Huffcutt and Roth (1998). Therefore, in summary, it appears that while structured interviews are associated with lower AI against blacks and Hispanics, these measures can result in sizable racial-ethnic mean differences in scores within applicant samples.

Work samples are designed to measure applicants' (and job incumbents', in certain instances) job-relevant KSAOs, using tests/assessments methods (e.g., simulations, in-basket tests, role-plays, etc.) that simulate actual work procedures to various degrees (Hough et al., 2001). These measures are most appropriately used for assessing individuals who have some level of prior work experience and associated job knowledge. High-fidelity simulations closely approximate the tasks performed on the job, whereas low-fidelity simulations measure psychological processes necessary for performing job duties effectively (Motowidlo, Dunnette, & Carter, 1990). Because work samples are closely aligned to actual job performance relative to other selection procedures, they are highly valid predictors of job performance (Hunter & Hunter, 1984; Roth, Bobko, & McFarland, 2005; Schmitt, Clause, & Pulakos, 1996). Meta-analytic studies report that work sample true validities range from .39 (Roth et al., 2005) to .54 (Hunter & Hunter, 1984). In addition to favorable validity evidence, work samples tend to display lower AI against blacks and Hispanics than CATs, with effect size values ranging from .00 for white-Hispanic contrasts (k = 20, N = 7,848; Schmitt et al., 1996) to .73 for white-black comparisons (k = 21, N = 2,476; Roth, Bobko, McFarland, & Buster, 2008).

Notably, work samples have been utilized as both predictors and criteria, and this has strong implications for effect size estimates. Roth et al. (2008) raised the concern that restriction-in-range on work sample performance among job incumbents may result in underestimation of racial-ethnic standardized mean differences in scores, compared to those derived from applicant samples. Findings from their recent meta-analysis confirmed this assumption, as white-black mean differences in work sample performance were larger among applicant samples (d = .73, k = 21, N = 2,476) than job incumbents (d = .36, k = 19, N = 5,611). Not surprisingly, these latter values were similar to those reported by McKay and McDaniel (2006) when comparing whites and blacks (d = .44, k = 7, N = 576) and Roth, Huffcutt, and Bobko (2003) for estimates of white-black and white-Hispanic mean effect sizes (d = .52, k = 10, N = 3,651 and d = .45, k = 4, N = 1,197, respectively). The McKay and McDaniel (2006) and Roth et al. (2003) meta-analyses included mostly concurrent validation studies involving current employees.

Among applicants, work samples have rather large racial-ethnic mean differences relative to other alternative selection procedures. Roth et al. (2005) found that work sample performance is cognitively loaded since scores on these measures were correlated .32 (k = 43, N = 17,563) with CAT scores. Furthermore, Roth et al. (2008) showed that white-black mean differences in work sample scores among applicants were moderated by the construct measured. Effect sizes were largest for work samples that measured cognitive ability and job knowledge (d = .80, k = 13, N = 785) and written skills (d = .70, k = 12, N = 675), and were smallest for those that assessed relatively non-cognitive constructs such as oral communication and interpersonal skills (d = .27, k = 14, N = 1,275) and leadership and persuasion (d = .27, k = 14, N = 1,301). In sum, work samples result in comparably high AI among alternative selection procedures, but the magnitude racial-ethnic mean differences vary by the constructs measured, and the sample from which effect sizes are derived (i.e., job applicants versus job incumbents).

Situational judgment tests (SJTs) measure job applicants' decision making and judgment in response to various work-related situations (McDaniel et al., 2001). Usually, these tests pose various job-relevant scenarios, and test takers are asked to select the best response to the scenario from a series of response options. A classic example of this method comes from the retail industry, where applicants for sales positions may be asked how they would react to an irate customer. SJTs are viewed as a viable alternative selection procedure to CATs because of their (a) greater sampling of job-relevant content and, correspondingly, expected criterion-related validity, (b) flexibility in measuring a variety of work-related constructs (e.g., job knowledge, problem-solving), and (c) potentially lower AI relative to CATs. McDaniel et al.'s (2001) meta-analysis examined the predictive validity of SJTs and found that they correlated .34 (k = 102, N = 10,640) with job performance. Furthermore, McDaniel et al. (2001) reported that SJTs displayed sizable correlations with CAT scores (p = .39, k = 80, N = 22,580), thus indicating that these measures are cognitively loaded.

A recent meta-analysis by Whetzel, McDaniel, and Nguyen (2008) examined subgroup differences associated with SJTs and found that effect sizes were largest for the white-black comparison (d = .38, k = 62, N = 42,178), followed by the white-Asian (d = .29, k = 25, N = 16,515), white-Hispanic (d = .24, k = 43, N = 15,195), and male-female contrasts (d = .11, k = 63, N = 37,829). Moreover, further analyses revealed that racial-ethnic mean effect sizes where slightly larger (ranging from .03 to .12 larger) for SJTs that used knowledge response instructions (i.e., "Select the most effective response to the scenario") than for those with behavioral tendency response instructions (i.e., "Select the response option that best reflects your typical response to the scenario"). Corresponding to a cognitive-loading explanation of these results, SJTs with knowledge-based instructions were more strongly correlated with cognitive ability (correlations ranged from .32 to .36) than those with behavioral tendency (correlations ranged from .14 to .17). Overall, SJTs are associated with lower AI than CATs, particularly those administered with behavioral tendency instructions.

Biodata forms are administered to gather information about applicants' personal history, interests, and accomplishments (Heneman & Judge, 2009). Job applicant responses to various background items are presumed to be *signs* of their likely future behavior on the job. Because biodata forms are a method of selection, they too can be designed to measure a variety of constructs such as cognitive ability, personality, integrity, emotional adjustment, and so on (Hough et al., 2001). Potosky, Bobko, and Roth (2005) report that biodata forms are valid predictors of job performance (corrected mean r = .32, k = 5, N = 11,332) and are moderately correlated with cognitive ability (corrected mean r = .37, k = 2, N = 5,475). Owing to this level of cognitive loading, the use of biodata forms results in relatively large white-black mean differences in scores (d = .57, k = 2, N = 6,115) compared to other alternative selection procedures (Potosky et al., 2005). We offer the caveat, however, that AI evidence regarding biodata forms is based upon a small number of studies; therefore, additional research work is needed to provide better footing upon which to interpret the AI associated with these measures.

Assessment centers (ACs) are used to gauge job incumbents' managerial potential as input for making subsequent employee advancement decisions (Gaugler, Rosenthal, Thorton, & Bentson, 1987; Klimoski, 1993). Usually, ACs utilize multiple exercises, such as in-basket tests, leaderless group discussions, role-plays, personality tests, and so on, formulated to measure a number of predictor constructs or dimensions (e.g., oral communication, planning, and decision making; Heneman & Judge, 2009). Each exercise is scored by a trained rater (or set of raters). Normally, test users compute AC scores (overall assessment scores or OARs) by averaging ratings earned across multiple dimensions. In their meta-analysis, Woehr and Arthur (2003) found that ACs typically measure an average of 10.60 dimensions (ranging from 3 to 25 dimensions).

An early meta-analytic investigation of AC validity reported a true-score validity estimate of .37 (k = 107, N = 12,235; Gaugler et al., 1987); however, it should be noted that this validity estimate was based upon OARs. Subsequently, Arthur, Day, McNelly, and Edens (2003) summarized AC dimension ratings using a seven-factor taxonomy consisting of communication, consideration/awareness of others, drive, influencing others, organizing and planning, problem solving, and tolerance for stress/uncertainty, in order to examine their criterion validities. Excluding tolerance for stress (due to conceptual definition concerns), they found validity evidence for individual AC dimensions (ps ranged from .25 for consideration/awareness of others [k = 37, N = 5,699] to .39 for problem solving [k = 52, N = 17,581]).

Research examining subgroup differences in AC scores is in its infancy. In a meta-analytic study, Dean, Roth, and Bobko (2008) obtained white-black, Hispanic-white, and male-female mean effect sizes of .52 (k = 17, N = 8,210), .28 (k = 9, N = 40,591), and -.19 (k = 18, N = 12,128) for OAR scores. These results indicate relatively high, moderate, and low AI against blacks, Hispanics, and *men*, respectively. Meriac, Hoffman, Woehr, and Fleisher's (2008) meta-analysis found that all seven AC dimensions were meaningfully correlated with cognitive ability test scores (corrected mean rs range from .22 for consideration/awareness of others [k = 21, N = 6,599] to .36 for organizing and planning [k = 15, N = 11,683]), which might explain why ACs have considerable AI against blacks and Hispanics.

Job knowledge tests (JKTs) are used to determine whether job applicants possess a body of information requisite for effective job performance (Hunter, 1983, 1986). JKTs are most appropriate for experienced job candidates who have had sufficient opportunity to develop work-related knowledge. These measures have been used as predictors (Hunter, 1986), work performance criteria (Gael, Grant, & Ritchie, 1975), and training proficiency criteria (Kriska, 1984) for jobs as diverse as police officer, firefighter, administrative assistant, and service representative. Generally, JKTs are power tests containing relatively difficult questions, most commonly presented in a multiple-choice format. Given these characteristics of JKTs, it is unsurprising that JKT scores are strongly correlated with CAT performance (corrected mean r = .46, k = 4, N = 1,474; Schmidt, Hunter, & Outerbridge, 1986). These authors found that JKTs are valid predictors of supervisory ratings of job performance (corrected mean $r = .42$, $k = 4$, $N = 1,474$) and work sample performance (corrected mean $r = .80$, $k = 4$, $N = 1,474$).

Consequently, two recent meta-analyses of subgroup mean differences in work performance (McKay & McDaniel, 2006; Roth et al., 2003) uncovered sizable white-black and white-Hispanic mean differences in JKT scores. McKay and McDaniel (2006) reported a white-black mean effect size of .53 ($k = 9$, $N = 2,216$), while Roth et al. (2003) estimated white-black and white-Hispanic mean effect sizes of .48 ($k = 12$, $N = 2,460$) and .47 ($k = 3$, $N = 977$), respectively. The white-black standardized mean difference derived by Roth et al. (2003) notwithstanding, current estimates of JKT AI against minorities groups, while sizable, is based upon relatively few effect sizes. Additional meta-analyses containing a greater number of studies that employ JKTs are necessary to provide firmer conclusions regarding AI.

Sex. Extant research indicates physical ability tests as a source of adverse impact against female job applicants (and Hispanics to a lesser extent). *Physical ability tests* (PATs) are used to assess job applicants' physical capabilities, such as muscular strength, cardiovascular endurance (i.e., aerobic conditioning), and movement quality (e.g., coordination and flexibility) as necessary for effective performance in physically demanding jobs such as police work, firefighting, and the construction trades (Biddle & Sill, 1999). Blakley, Quiñones, Crawford, and Jago (1994) examined the validity of isometric strength tests, which measure "the force exerted by a muscle group without requiring movement" (p. 251). As an example, the *shoulder lift test* of the Jackson Evaluation System requires examinees to stand up with their palms down and pull up on a bar (as in a dead lift motion), and records electronically the force applied to the bar. Across seven physically demanding jobs (e.g., law enforcement officer, firefighter, pipefitter, and utility worker), Blakley et al. (1994) found the true validities of the isometric strength composite (including five subtests) to be .28 for supervisor ratings of physical ability and .55 for composite performance on a physical ability work simulation ($k = 7$, $N = 1,364$).

Interpolating from results presented in Cooper (n.d.) and Hogan (1991), Hough et al. (2001) reported male-female mean differences in muscular strength, cardiovascular endurance, and movement quality of 1.66 ($k = 42$, $N = 69,058$), 1.09 ($k = 34,090$), and .20 ($k = 21$, $N = 34,118$),

respectively. Blakley et al. (1994) Study 2 provided means and standard deviations of composite isometric strength scores for male ($N = 12,199$), female ($N = 196$), white ($N = 6,785$), black ($N = 1,622$), and Hispanic job applicants ($N = 3,760$) for various jobs in a large, multinational civil engineering and construction firm. We used these values to further examine the subgroup mean differences associated with composite isometric strength test scores. These results revealed that test score differences were extremely large for the male-female comparison ($d = 1.81$), sizable for the white-Hispanic contrast ($d = .47$), and minimal when whites and blacks were compared ($d = -.01$). In sum, PATs result in considerable AI against women, and Hispanics to a lesser extent.

Summary. Overall, extant meta-analytic research chronicles a wide range of subgroup mean differences in scores on the most commonly studied selection procedures. It is encouraging, however, that all of the selection devices reviewed display useful criterion-related validities for predicting job performance; thus, these instruments can be defended on the basis of job-relevance if they are found to result in AI in a particular selection context. Most investigations show considerable racial-ethnic differences in test/assessment scores, whereas male-female and age-related disparities are minimal. The only exception to this general conclusion is the finding that PATs are associated with large male-female differences in scores disadvantageous to women. CATs, JKTs, work samples, ACs, and biodata forms result in substantial white-black, and to a lesser extent, white-Hispanic mean differences in scores disfavoring members of minority groups. The use of these devices in selection contexts will result in sizable AI against black and Hispanic job applicants. In contrast, SJTs, interviews, personality tests, and integrity tests evidence moderate to negligible racial-ethnic mean differences. Employing these selection instruments, therefore, will lessen AI against blacks and Hispanics, thereby increasing their probabilities of hire.

The primary factor that appears to underlie the magnitudes of racial-ethnic mean disparities on selection measures is their cognitive loadings. Selection devices that have relatively high correlations with cognitive ability (i.e., JKTs, work samples, and ACs) result in greater racial-ethnic differences in scores than those with weaker relationships with cognitive ability (i.e., personality tests and integrity tests). Moreover, structured interviews tend toward lower white-black and white-Hispanic mean differences in scores, and the use of SJTs with behavioral tendency instructions lead to reduced racial-ethnic score disparities than those that employ knowledge response instructions. The summary implication of our review is that, to the extent that racial-ethnic diversity of the workforce is a strategic concern, selection practitioners must take care in choosing the tests/assessments to be included in their selection batteries. Those that include CATs or other highly cognitively loaded devices will perpetuate considerable AI against blacks and Hispanics.

ADVERSE IMPACT OF WORK PERFORMANCE CRITERIA

Literature examining the AI of work performance criteria is less voluminous than investigations focused on the AI of selection procedures; therefore, our review of this research will be brief. The magnitudes of subgroup mean differences in work performance have considerable ramifications for potential disparities in career mobility and advancement opportunities in firms. Male-female and age-related mean disparities in work performance are minimal (Bowen, Swim, & Jacobs, 2000; McEvoy & Cascio, 1989), with the exception that older workers engage in relatively fewer counterproductive work behaviors (e.g., tardiness and absenteeism) than their younger counterparts (Ng & Feldman, 2008). Thus, we focus our review primarily upon racial-ethnic mean disparities in supervisory ratings of job performance, the most common form of work performance criteria. We now address in this topic in greater detail.

Race-ethnicity. Two recent studies have reported substantially lower racial-ethnic mean differences in work performance than typically found for CATs (McKay & McDaniel, 2006; Roth et al., 2003). Specifically, Roth et al. (2003) derived white-black and white-Hispanic mean disparities of .27 ($k = 37$, $N = 84,295$) and .04 ($k = 11$, $N = 46,530$), respectively, whereas McKay and McDaniel (2006) also obtained an overall white-black mean disparity of .27 ($k = 572$, $N = 109,974$). Although these overall estimates of racial-ethnic mean differences in work performance are informative, they mask several factors that considerably moderate the magnitudes of obtained effects. These moderators include criterion type, the cognitive loading of criteria, measurement level, and data source.

Criterion type refers to the nature of a work performance measure (e.g., productivity, job knowledge, and task performance and contextual performance). Various meta-analyses have shown sharp disparities

in the extent of racial-ethnic effects on work performance across different criterion measures (e.g., Ford, Kraiger, & Schechtman, 1986; Hauenstein, Sinclair, Robson, Quintella, & Donovan, 2003; McKay & McDaniel, 2006; Roth et al., 2003). A common finding across these studies is that effect sizes are larger for criteria with high versus low cognitive loadings. Using correlated vectors analysis, which assessed the extent to which several moderators related to the magnitudes of white-black mean effect sizes, criterion cognitive loading was shown to be strongly and positively correlated with effect sizes ($R = .34$, $k = 291$). Criterion type displayed a similar pattern and level of relationship with effect sizes ($R = .40$, $k = 572$), and, not surprisingly, the criterion type and cognitive loading vectors were strongly correlated ($r = .60$, weighted by k). In analyses involving studies that provided personality test scores, McKay and McDaniel (2006) also assessed how the personality loading of criteria related to effect sizes estimates. The vectors of personality constructs (e.g., conscientiousness, emotional stability, and agreeableness) were negatively related to white-black mean effect sizes, ranging from $-.46$ (conscientiousness) to $-.06$ (agreeableness). In short, these findings suggest that cognitively loaded work criteria will result in substantial AI against blacks, whereas personality-loaded performance measures will lead to sharply diminished AI against them.

Additionally, McKay and McDaniel's (2006) correlated vectors analyses uncovered data source ($R = .30$) and measurement level ($R = .28$) as meaningful moderators of black-white mean differences in work performance. Overall, larger magnitude effect sizes were obtained from unpublished sources of data such as conference papers ($d = .38$, $k = 16$, $N = 2,330$) and technical reports ($d = .24$, $k = 394$, $N = 34,219$) than published journal articles ($d = .17$, $k = 118$, $N = 32,026$) and doctoral dissertations ($d = .12$, $k = 36$, $N = 6,291$). Effect sizes also varied by measurement level, such that white-black mean performance differences were twice as large for presumably more reliable (multi-item) scale-level criteria ($d = .33$, $k = 385$, $N = 73,035$) than single-item performance measures ($d = .15$, $k = 187$, $N = 36,939$). Thus, to obtain sound meta-analytic estimates of racial-ethnic mean differences in work performance, investigators are advised to gather data from both published and unpublished sources, and to focus data collection efforts upon more reliable, scale-level measures of performance.

A series of recent primary studies underscore the influence of the work context on subgroup differences in work performance (Avery, McKay, Wilson, & Tonidandel, 2007; Joshi, Liao, & Jackson, 2006; McKay, Avery, & Morris, 2008; Zatzick, Elvira, & Cohen, 2003). Generally, disparities are reduced in settings where members of protected groups predominate because, according to the similarity-attraction paradigm, perceived similarity between individuals fosters cohesion and a sense of shared history. In addition, social identity theory (SIT; Tajfel & Turner, 1986) suggests that members of the same social group (e.g., blacks, women) have a sense of "shared fate" such that group success (or failure) has implications for self-esteem. In turn, these individuals will be motivated to secure beneficial outcomes for members of their group. Members of higher-status groups (e.g., men, whites) experience less group-based threat due to their privileged position in society (Chattopadhyay, Tluchowska, & George, 2004). Corroborating prior theory, Zatzick et al. (2003) found that minority representation exhibited a negative relationship with turnover. In addition, non-linear effects emerged such that the above tendency was amplified in work groups with few minorities, as opposed to those with a greater share of minority personnel. Likewise, Joshi et al. (2006) reported that female sales associates who worked in sales units with higher proportions of female managers earned $2,976 greater annual salaries, and achieved 14% higher percentage of their sales targets than those in sales units with a low proportion of women in management (i.e., 108% and 94%, respectively). In contrast, male representation in management had little effect on male associates' sales performance.

Diversity climate refers to the workers' perceptions of the extent that a work environment is fair and socially integrates members of underrepresented groups (McKay et al., 2008). Previous studies demonstrate how, compared to whites and men, respectively, minorities and women value diversity to a greater extent (Mor Barak, Cherin, & Berkman, 1998), presumably, as a means of mitigating discrimination at work. Accordingly, individual-level and aggregate-level studies have shown that diversity climate moderates racial-ethnic group differences in work outcomes such as absenteeism (Avery et al., 2007) and sales performance (McKay et al., 2008). For instance, using a national probability sample of working adults, Avery et al. (2007) found that white-black mean differences in absenteeism were moderated by perceived organizational value for diversity (an individual-level measure of diversity climate). Greater disparities in absences occurred when value for diversity was perceived as low than when it was viewed as high. A three-way interaction between employee race, value for diversity, and supervisor race emerged, such that blacks were absent more (less) often when perceived value for diversity was low (high) and their supervisors were black. The authors explained these findings are a function of the mixed signals associated with having a black supervisor (signaling a high value for diversity) and working in an environment characterized as low in value for diversity.

McKay et al. (2008) examined the moderating effects of store-level diversity climate on white-black and white-Hispanic mean differences in employee sales per hour, in sample of 6,130 sales associates working in 730 stores of a large U.S. retailer. Results indicated that black-white mean differences in sales per hour ($8.90), favoring whites, were larger in stores perceived as less pro-diversity in nature than those thought of as highly supportive of diversity (which advantaged black personnel by $7.41 per hour). Stronger moderation effects were evident for the white-Hispanic contrast as mean differences in sales per hour (disparaging the former group) were substantial in less pro-diversity store units ($23.40), and minimal in stores perceived as fostering highly pro-diversity work climates ($1.21). Stores with greater pro-diversity climates were associated with increments in sales per hour of $20.00 and $26.00 for black and Hispanic sales associates, respectively. These increases in sales per hour translated into estimated annual gains in sales performance of $20,800 and $27,040, per employee (assuming a work schedule of 20 hours per week), for black and Hispanic sales personnel, respectively.

Summary. In sum, meta-analytic research indicates notably smaller racial-ethnic mean differences in work performance compared to corresponding disparities in CAT performance. While encouraging, these conclusions must be tempered, since a number of moderators influence the observed magnitudes of racial-ethnic mean disparities in performance. Criterion type and the cognitive loading of criteria are strongly related, and, in tandem, these moderators have considerable implications for the AI of work performance measures against blacks and Hispanics. The use of highly cognitively loaded criteria (e.g., JKTs, work samples, and task performance, to a lesser extent) will result in substantial AI against members of these groups compared to less cognitively loaded measures such as contextual performance, personality-applied social skills, and absenteeism-lost time. Importantly, the current literature (and related findings) suggests that the work dimensions emphasized in a company's performance management systems could have substantial impact on the upward mobility of their black and Hispanic personnel, which correspondingly might pose retention and legal difficulties as well.

A relatively recent body of work has underscored the role of the work context on the magnitudes of subgroup differences in performance. Findings in this area suggest that environments with greater proportions of female or minority coworkers (and managers) and those with more strongly pro-diversity work climates are associated with reduced mean white-black, white-Hispanic, and male-female disparities in work performance (depending on the criterion examined). This preliminary work points to potential means for minimizing AI in organizations by improving workforce diversity and fostering supportive diversity climates.

STRATEGIES FOR REDUCING ADVERSE IMPACT OF SELECTION PROCEDURES

Ployhart and Holtz (2008) aptly summarized the literature devoted to strategies for reducing AI in selection. These authors found that *Category I* strategies, which use predictors with smaller subgroup differences, and *Category II* strategies, which combine and manipulate scores, have the greatest promise for mitigating the AI of selection procedures against blacks and Hispanics. There are a number of selection procedures with criterion-related validities that approximate values derived for CATs such as work samples, integrity tests, SJTs, structured interviews, and ACs, which are also associated with reduced mean racial-ethnic disparities in scores. Assessing a broad range of predictor constructs is warranted by recent societal trends wherein jobs are becoming more service-oriented and team-based, suggesting the increased relevance of dispositional variables to effective job performance (Goldstein et al., 2002). To the extent warranted by job-analytic evidence, selection professionals should determine the relative importance of task performance and contextual performance criteria, and should fashion selection batteries to include tests/assessments that predict both forms of criteria. Overreliance on task-based criteria, which tend to be more cognitively loaded than contextual performance measures, will result in higher degrees of AI (Hauenstein et al., 2003; McKay & McDaniel, 2006). Moreover, adding non-cognitive tests/assessments to predictor batteries will result in incremental validity for predicting job performance beyond CATs, to the extent that

these measures are valid and relatively uncorrelated with cognitive ability (Goldstein et al., 2002; Schmidt & Hunter, 1998). Practitioners are cautioned to consider the relative trade-offs in terms of test/assessment administration costs, validities, extent of AI reduction, and expected mean job performance when alternative predictor constructs are used to select job applicants.

Harassment

The EEOC (2009i) defines harassment as "unwelcome conduct that is based on race, color, sex, religion, national origin, disability, and/or age. Harassment becomes unlawful where (a) enduring the offensive conduct becomes a condition of continued employment, or (b) the conduct is severe or pervasive enough to create a work environment that a reasonable person would consider intimidating, hostile, or abusive." While harassment can occur against any group, sexual harassment has received the most research attention. The sexual harassment (SH) literature has recently been reviewed by O'Leary-Kelly, Bowes-Sperry, Bates, and Lean (2009), and we draw heavily upon their thorough review. Our discussion of SH focuses on the scenario in which men harass women, because this is the scenario considered in most research, and it is the most common form of reported SH (as opposed to women harassing men, or same-sex harassment; Berdahl & Moore, 2006). Furthermore, extending the literature beyond that of SH, we review literature on harassment based upon other characteristics.

Sexual Harassment

PERCEPTIONS OF SEXUAL HARASSMENT

One of the earliest problems facing researchers trying to understand sexual harassment (SH) was the definition of the phenomenon itself (Lengnick-Hall, 1995). As of now, there are four accepted definitions of SH (O'Leary-Kelly et al., 2009). The *legal definition* of sexual harassment addresses two types of harassment: quid pro quo and hostile work environment. Quid pro quo refers to employment decision threats based on compliance with sexual favors. Hostile work environment SH refers to "unwelcome sexual advances, requests for sexual favors, and other verbal or physical conduct of a sexual nature constitute sexual harassment when this conduct explicitly or implicitly affects an individual's employment, unreasonably interferes with an individual's work performance, or creates an intimidating, hostile, or offensive work environment" (29 C.F.R. §1604.11 [a] [3]). The *psychological definition* of SH states that an individual has experienced SH if he or she feels harassed, whether or not the behavior is illegal (O'Leary-Kelly et al., 2009). The *sex-based perspective* (Berdahl, 2007a, p. 644) defines sex-based harassment as behavior that "derogates, demeans, or humiliates an individual based on that individual's sex." The behavioral-based perspective (Bowes-Sperry & Tata, 1999; Fitzgerald, Gelfand, & Drasgow, 1995; Fitzgerald, Magley, Drasgow & Waldo, 1999) states that SH can be objectively defined by specific behaviors, whether or not they are illegal or cause psychological harm. Fitzgerald et al. (1995, 1999) categorize these behaviors as sexual hostility, sexist hostility (insulting non-sexual behaviors based on gender), and sexual coercion (similar to the legal quid pro quo definition). Relatedly, Rotundo, Nguyen, and Sackett (2001) advanced a taxonomy of seven behavioral categories of SH: impersonal derogatory attitudes (e.g., dirty jokes), personal derogatory attitudes (e.g., sexual comments aimed at the target), unwanted dating pressure, sexual propositions, physical sexual contact (e.g., kissing the target), physical non-sexual contact (e.g., congratulatory hugging the target), and sexual coercion.

As noted above, two of the above definitions of SH (legal hostile environment and psychological) depend on whether or not a person perceives a behavior to be harassment. Consequently, a great deal of research has been conducted on what influences observers and targets' perceptions of SH. The most studied factor has been the sex of the target or observer. Rotundo et al. (2001) conducted a meta-analysis examining the role that gender played in the perception of SH. They found that, overall, women were more likely to perceive a given behavior as sexual harassment ($d = .30$, $k = 66$, $N = 33,164$). This effect was moderated by the type of harassment, with men and women agreeing to a greater extent on quid pro quo SH ($d = .18$, $k = 16$, $N = 9,646$) than hostile environment SH ($d = .33$, $k = 45$, $N = 27,354$). Type of behavior also moderated the sex differences in perceptions of SH, with perceptions of derogatory impersonal attitudes, derogatory personal attitudes, pressure for dates, and sexual physical contact having the most disagreement ($d = .34, .33, .28$, and .36 respectively) compared to sexual propositions, physical non-sexual contact, and coercion ($d = .14$, .18, and .14, respectively). It appears that gender differences in perceptions narrow when behavior is relatively benign (physical non-sexual contact) and very blatant (coercion). Finally, harasser status had a large impact on gender differences, with smaller

disparities observed when the harasser had no formal authority ($d = .42$, $k = 6$, $N = 1,259$) compared to when he had formal authority ($d = .26$, $k = 14$, $N = 4,616$).

Many factors related to observers' perceptions of SH have received less systematic attention than gender, and thus have not been incorporated into published meta-analyses (see O'Leary-Kelly et al., 2009, for a thorough review). One such factor is the impact of SH programs on the labeling of SH behaviors. Antecol and Cobb-Clark (2003) found that SH awareness training did render employees, especially men, more likely to label sex-related behavior as SH, than those who did not receive training. Wilkerson (1999) found that SH training only affected perceptions of coercion, but not other sex-related behaviors. Clearly, we need to learn more about how to effectively design and evaluate SH awareness programs.

FACTORS RELATED TO THE OCCURRENCE OF SEXUAL HARASSMENT

Another issue that has garnered a great deal of attention is: Why does sexual harassment occur in organizations? Fitzgerald, Hulin, and Drasgow (1994; see also Fitzgerald et al., 1997) presented an influential guiding model for this line of research, which conceptualizes SH as a form of workplace stress. They articulate that the most dominant cause of SH occurs at the organizational level in terms of organization climate (does the organization communicate a tolerance for SH?) and the job gender context (e.g., male-female ratio, traditional job gender stereotype). In a study of 357 female utility employees, Fitzgerald et al. (1997) found that organizational tolerance for SH and gender type of job (measured by gender ratio of work group, sex of supervisor, and whether the respondent was one of the first women in her job) were strongly related to self-reports of SH.

Subsequently, in the next 10 years, a great deal of research examined these two factors as antecedents of SH. Most investigations used the Organizational Tolerance for Sexual Harassment (OTSH) inventory (Hulin, Fitzgerald, & Drasgow, 1996) to assess climate. The OTSH asks respondents to evaluate six scenarios involving sexual behavior in terms of the likely outcomes to the harasser, to the complainant, and the degree to which the complaint will be taken seriously. Job gender context is usually operationalized as the proportion of the women in the work group (Willness, Steel, & Lee, 2007). Willness et al. (2007) conducted a meta-analysis of this research and found that climate for SH had an extremely large effect on reports of SH ($r_c = .332$, $k = 21$, $N = 50,509$). Job gender context also had a significant effect ($r_c = -.192$, $k = 13$, $N = 48,165$). Military setting moderated the effect of job gender status, such that the effect was much stronger in non-military samples ($r_c = -.266$, $k = 6$, $N = 2,905$) versus military samples ($r_c = -.157$, $k = 6$, $N = 27,425$), probably reflecting the likelihood that non-military jobs are more likely to have a heterogeneous sex composition than those in the military (Willness et al., 2007).

Another series of studies conducted through the Department of Defense and the U.S. Merit Systems Protection Board (USMSPB; 1988) also found support for the heavy influence of situational factors, using a methodology different from the OTSH. In this case, supervisors' or commanding officers' tolerance for SH were expected to predict the number of reports of SH (see Pryor, Giedd, & Williams, 1995, for a review). For example, in one USMSPB survey (1988), it was reported that *men's* ratings of management's tolerance for SH and the number of impersonal sex-related behavior (e.g., nude calendars, sexual entertainment at office parties) in their office predicted 22% of the variance in women's reports of SH.

While climate seems to be the best single predictor of the occurrence of SH in organizations (Willness et al., 2007), more explanatory power can be derived by also considering individual differences in the likelihood to sexually harass coworkers. Pryor and his colleagues (Pryor, 1992; Pryor et al., 1995) formulated a model of sexual harassment which states that perpetrators' dispositions to harass interact with the organizational climate, such that dispositions only result in harassment when the organizational climate is tolerant of such behavior. Pryor (1987) developed the Likelihood to Sexually Harass (LSH) scale to overcome problems with directly asking men if they would be likely to commit sexual harassment. This methodology involves respondents reacting to a set of scenarios in which the man has some power over a woman, and then indicating the degree to which they would engage in various SH-related behaviors, if they could with impunity. The LSH scale has been found to be reliable and valid (Craig, Kelly, & Driscoll, 2001; Pryor et al., 1995). The LSH has been used to develop a profile of men who are likely to sexually harass female coworkers (see O'Leary-Kelly et al., 2009, for a thorough review). For example, men who score high on the LSH scale are prone to sexual violence

(e.g., Bargh, Raymond, Pryor, & Strack, 1995), hold traditional male sex role stereotypes (e.g., Driscoll, Kelly, & Henderson, 1998) and hostile attitudes toward women (Begany & Milburn, 2002), and are high in authoritarianism (Lee, Gizzarone, & Ashton, 2003).

O'Leary-Kelly, Paetzold, and Griffin (2000) developed an alternative approach to studying perpetrator characteristics based on the rationale that SH should be viewed as a goal-directed behavior aimed at achieving a specific purpose. Research supporting this proposition has shown that men are more likely to harass women when they were exposed to gender identity threats (e.g., having their masculinity questioned; Dall'Ara & Maas, 1999; Maass, Cadinu, Guarnieri, & Grasselli, 2003). However, a person-situation interaction was also evident in this research because LSH, gender identification, and SDO interacted with gender threat, such that men low on these characteristics did not perpetrate SH under threat conditions.

In addition to organizational climate and norms, and the disposition of the harasser, target characteristics have also received some research attention as potential antecedents of SH. Several studies have found evidence for SH as a means of "punishment" for women who go against traditional gender norms (Berdahl, 2007a). Evidence for this comes from investigations demonstrating that women in traditionally male blue collar jobs (Jackson & Newman, 2004) and women with more "masculine" personalities (Berdahl, 2007b) are much more likely to experience SH than those in more traditional female jobs and with more stereotypically feminine personalities. Correspondingly, Berdahl (2007b) refers to SH as a punishment for "uppity women." Another target characteristic that has been given more than passing consideration is race-ethnicity. Several studies have found that being a racial-ethnic minority is related to higher incidences of SH (Berdahl & Moore, 2006; Gettman & Gelfand, 2007).

RESPONSES TO SEXUAL HARASSMENT

Many studies have assessed how targets respond to SH (see O'Leary-Kelly et al., 2009 for a review). Targets' responses to SH are important to understand because the manner in which a person responds moderates the relationship between SH and negative employee outcomes such as stress (Fitzgerald et al., 1995). Early research (Knapp, Faley, Ekeberg, & DuBois, 1997; Malamut & Offerman, 2001) proposed and found that coping behaviors fall into four categories: (a) *advocacy seeking* (gaining support from authorities); (b) *social coping* (obtaining help and emotional support from trusted others); (c) *avoidance/denial* (avoiding the harassing situation by physically removing oneself from the situation, or by cognitively denying the situation); and (d) *confrontation/negotiation* (directly insisting that the SH behavior cease). Similarly, Wasti and Cortina (2002) found a five-type structure: (a) *advocacy-seeking behaviors,* (b) *social coping,* (c) *negotiation,* (d) *denial,* and (e) *avoidance.*

Cortina and Wasti (2005) conducted a thorough and integrative study by performing cluster analyses on responses to the 14-item Coping with Harassment Questionnaire (CHQ, Fitzgerald, 1990) within four samples which varied by nationality, ethnicity, and employment status (working-class and professional). Their results showed three strong clusters of coping behaviors: *avoidant-negotiating* (196/528 respondents), *support-seeking* (164/528 respondents), and *detached* (168/528 respondents). The avoidant-negotiating cluster engaged in denial and avoidance, but at the same time attempted to negotiate with the harasser to try to make the behavior stop. The support-seeking group also tried to avoid the situation and to negotiate, but also sought to gain social support. Professional women in this group also tried to gain support from authorities (advocacy seeking). Finally, the detached group engaged in very few coping behaviors and denied the severity of the situation. They also found that type of coping pattern was related to the severity of the SH (the more severe the behavior, the more coping strategies were used). This is in line with what other researchers have found (Bergman, Langhout, Palmieri, Cortina, & Fitzgerald, 2002; Lee, Heilmann, & Near, 2004; Malamut & Offerman, 2001). Cortina and Wasti (2005) also reported that climate for tolerance of SH (high tolerance led to more avoidant negotiating for the working class respondents and support seeking for the professional respondents), and ethnicity (U.S. Anglos were more likely to be detached than U.S. Hispanics and Turkish respondents) influenced coping responses.

Much more research is needed that examines how people respond to SH. The Cortina and Wasti (2005) classification scheme can further this line of research by providing a taxonomy of response types. Furthermore, additional work is necessary to explore the predictors of response patterns, in addition to the impact of severity, along with consideration of the role that these responses play in moderating the outcomes of SH.

OUTCOMES OF SEXUAL HARASSMENT

Based on Fitzgerald and colleagues' (Fitzgerald et al., 1997; Fitzgerald et al., 1994) model of SH as a stressor, Willness et al. (2007) meta-analyzed the results of 41 studies to determine the job-related and health-related outcomes of SH. They found that SH negatively impacted coworker satisfaction ($r_c = -.316$, $k = 25$, $N = 34,221$), supervisor satisfaction ($r_c = -.285$, $k = 26$, $N = 34,450$), work satisfaction ($r_c = -.241$, $k = 23$, $N = 33,486$), global job satisfaction ($r_c = -.245$, $k = 12$, $N = 14,455$), organizational commitment ($r_c = -.249$, $k = 16$, $N = 31,194$), job withdrawal ($r_c = .161$, $k = 16$, $N = 6,201$), work withdrawal ($r_c = .299$, $k = 12$, $N = 4,940$), work group productivity ($r_c = -.221$, $k = 6$, $N = 27,425$), mental health ($r_c = -.273$, $k = 29$, $N = 48,880$), physical health ($r_c = -.247$, $k = 16$, $N = 32,121$), post-traumatic stress disorder ($r_c = .247$, $k = 9$, $N = 4,076$), and life satisfaction ($r_c = -.119$, $k = 11$, $N = 4545$). Chan, Lam, Chow, and Chung (2008) also performed a meta-analysis using most of the same studies, and obtained very similar results. In addition, they observed that sex of the victim did not moderate the SH-outcome relationship. Men and women experienced negative effects to an equal degree. They also found that age moderated these relationships such that they were stronger for younger targets (under 40 years old) compared to older targets (over 40 years old). Given that Willness et al. (2007) and Chan et al. (2008) were only able to examine a few conceptual moderators, there is room for further systematic study of the factors which mitigate and amplify the negative outcomes of SH.

Harassment, Other Than Sexual Harassment

The literature on SH is vast compared to the literature examining harassment based upon other characteristics. Existing work in the I/O literature has mostly concerned racial-ethnic harassment. As stated above, the legal definition of harassment includes any unwelcome behavior that either becomes a condition of employment or creates a hostile working environment. Like sexual harassment, early research suffered from definitional issues, mainly discerning harassment from discrimination. In one of the first published studies to explicitly address this issue, Schneider, Hitlan, and Radhakrishnan (2000) made the following distinction between harassment as "threatening verbal conduct or exclusionary behavior that has an ethnic component and is directed at a target because of his or her ethnicity. The construct is composed of behaviors that may be encountered on a daily basis and may contribute to a hostile environment, particularly for ethnic minorities" (p. 3). They define discrimination as unequal job treatment or lack of positive opportunities because of one's race-ethnicity.

Bergman, Palmieri, Drasgow, and Ormerod (2007) studied the definitional issue from a measurement perspective, using 5,000 randomly drawn respondents from a Defense Manpower Data Center (DMDC) survey, administered to examine perceptions of fair treatment and equal employment opportunity. Fourteen items constituted comprised the Racial-ethnic Harassment (REH) scale and 26 items formed the Racial-ethnic Discrimination (RED) scale. The REH was similar to the Sexual Experiences Questionnaire, also developed for the military (Fitzgerald et al., 1999). The authors found that the REH and RED were distinct and that the REH consisted of two factors: derogatory and exclusionary behaviors and physical confrontation and assault. They also observed that the factor structure of these scales generalized across five racial-ethnic groups. This is an important study in the discrimination literature because it points out that reports of harassment and discrimination vary by group because they experience different levels of unfair treatment, as opposed to perceiving the measurement instrument differently.

Bergman et al. (2007) also compared the incidence of both types of harassment between racial-ethnic groups. With respect to derogatory and exclusionary behaviors, Asian/Pacific Islander (d = .27), black (d = .49), Hispanic (d = .42), and Native American respondents (d = .38) all reported significantly more harassment than whites. While effect sizes were much smaller with respect to physical confrontation and assault, Asian/Pacific Islanders (d = .03), black respondents (d = .06), Hispanic respondents (d = .06), and Native Americans (d = .06) all expressed significantly more harassment than whites. In terms of the RED scale, blacks and Native Americans reported more discrimination than did Hispanics, who, in turn, recounted more discrimination than Asians and whites.

Antecol and Cobb-Clark (2008), using the full sample from the DMDC survey (n = 18,035) and econometric analyses, found that 61% of whites, 75% of blacks, 78% of Hispanics, and 67.5% of Asians expressed experiencing at least one incidence of offensive harassment (this is almost the same scale as the derogatory and exclusionary behavior scale of the REH mentioned above). Eight percent

of whites, 13% of blacks, 11% of Hispanics, and 15% of Asians reported experiencing at least one incidence of threat behaviors in the past 12 months. This scale is similar to the physical confrontation and assault scale of the REH. Finally, 7.6% of whites, 29.1% of blacks, 20.1% of Hispanics, and 16.3% of Asians stated that they experienced career discrimination (similar to the RED scale) in the past 12 months. Bergman et al. (2007) concluded that the fairly large d-statistics for minority groups with respect to derogatory behaviors is in contrast to other researchers (e.g., Dovidio & Gaertner, 2000), who state that modern racism and prejudice is likely to be subtle. We concur with Bergman et al. (2007).

Schneider et al. (2000) found similar measurement results using another scale, the seven item Ethnic Harassment Experiences (EHE) scale, also modeled on the SEQ (Fitzgerald et al., 1988). They compared four samples (two undergraduate, school district employees, and graduate students) of Hispanic and Anglo respondents, and obtained a two-factor structure for harassment: verbal ethnic harassment and exclusionary harassment. In contrast to Bergman et al. (2007), they did not find significant differences between Anglos' and Hispanics' reports of harassment. One possibility for this finding is that the Anglos were the numerical minority group in the settings where the respondents worked or studied. Fifty-two percent and 67.4% of the undergraduate samples reported experiencing at least one incidence of harassment during the past 24 months, while 40.2% and 60.1% of employees and graduate students reported harassment. Of those who expressed being harassed, across the four samples, between 27% and 54% of respondents reported verbal harassment, between 7% and 29% encountered both verbal and exclusionary harassment, and between 2% and 5% endured only exclusionary harassment. They also found that verbal and exclusionary harassment interacted to influence life satisfaction and health condition, such that the effects of high exclusion were *worse* when there was little verbal harassment. The authors suggested that exclusionary behaviors, without accompanying verbal harassment, are more harmful because the situation leads to confusion regarding why such harassment occurs.

Apart from documenting incidences of racial-ethnic harassment and establishing valid measures, a few other studies have examined within-group variation of perceptions of harassment. Like SH, racial-ethnic harassment is often ambiguous and can be influenced by various harasser, target, and situational characteristics (Chrobot-Mason & Hepworth, 2005; McClelland & Hunter, 1992; Smeltzer & Leap, 1988). One factor which has garnered attention is the ethnic/racial identity of either the target or the bystander. Chrobot-Mason and Hepworth (2005) conducted a laboratory study in which student participants reacted to scenarios in which racial harassment was either ambiguous (coworkers tell offensive racial jokes) or unambiguous (coworkers makes threats, vandalize property, and use racially offensive symbols). They also varied management's response to the incidents by suspending the harasser; reprimanding the harasser with no further action; reframing, in which the victim was told that the harasser was only joking; and denial, in which the victim is told that she/he is being overly sensitive and that the problem does not exist. Results showed that for minorities, racial identification moderated the effect of type of harassment on perceived severity of the offense such that high identification only led to higher perceptions of severity for the *unambiguous* scenario, contrary to predictions. Also, there was no interaction found for likelihood of reporting the incident. Interestingly, for white participants, attitudes toward race interacted with the type of scenarios. Individuals who were low in blindness to privilege and high in awareness of racial issues rated the ambiguous scenario as much more severe than those with lower standings on these qualities. In contrast, little difference was found for the unambiguous scenario. It appears from this study that minority racial identity had less influence on how minorities perceived racial harassment, whereas whites' attitudes toward race affected their perceptions of racial harassment.

In contrast to Chrobot-Mason and Hepworth's (2005) findings, economists Antecol and Cobb-Clark (2008), using the DMDC data, operationalized identity by several factors, including interracial friendships, ease that the respondent felt in dealing with others of a different race-ethnicity, native status, English as first language, and similarity of supervisor and coworkers. Overall, they observed that this complex set of identity factors influenced reports of harassment beyond the influence of race-ethnicity alone, particularly whether the respondent was foreign-born, spoke English as a first language, and shared the same race with colleagues and supervisor. One distinction between this study and Chrobot-Mason and Hepworth (2005) is that the former examined "bystander perceptions," while the latter examined actual accounts with an instrument found valid across racial groups (Bergman et al., 2007) . The issue of identity influences and other factors on perceptions of harassment deserves much further study.

In summary, we know much less about racial-ethnic harassment than SH. While a burgeoning trend in the discrimination literature is to study subtle racism, these recent studies suggest that we should not avoid investigating more blatant forms as well. Moreover, I/O psychology researchers essentially have ignored harassment based on sexual orientation, religion, or weight, despite ample anecdotal and survey evidence indicating that it exists.

Discrimination in Performance Evaluations and Pay

The I/O psychology literature has focused extensively on discrimination in selection and performance evaluation ratings, and virtually has left the issue of pay discrimination to economists, labor studies scholars, and sociologists. Earlier, we indicated that discrimination in promotion is likely to exist; however, this literature has been extensively reviewed recently by Avery (2011), so we touch briefly on promotion when relevant. Accordingly, we review this literature with a focus on discrimination issues or bias in lieu of discussing the extent of subgroup of differences. Specifically, existing group differences in evaluations and pay are insufficient bases for concluding that discrimination is in operation. Alternatively, disparities could be due to other factors, such as corresponding differences in educational attainment, actual performance, and tenure. We do not refer to this type of discrimination as adverse treatment because this suggests that it is intentional, and most research has not been designed to address this. Therefore, we emphasis research that presents evidence of bias exists after other non-biased explanations have been taken into account. Bear in mind, however, that many seemingly "performance-related" explanations also can result from unfair bias due to group membership. As Ely and Padavic (2007) pointed out in relation to gender bias, many studies that explain gender differences in performance evaluations as a function of factors such as self-confidence ignore the influence of gender bias on one's self-confidence.

Discrimination in Performance Evaluations

A great deal of literature has been conducted on group biases in all types of performance evaluations. For the purpose of this review, we discuss two types of ratings: ratings of past performance (performance appraisal), and ratings that have an aspect of expectations for future performance (e.g., assessment center ratings, interview ratings, ratings of potential). We also focus mainly on meta-analysis results, which are plentiful for this line of research.

RACE-ETHNICITY

Table 32.3 presents the results of six meta-analyses examining evaluation differences between white and black ratees. Although all analyses show that white ratees are evaluated more positively than black ratees (with the exception of Kraiger and Ford's, 1985, results for black raters), there is no direct evidence that these disparities are due to rating bias because the analyses did not differentiate studies that held performance levels constant across racial-ethnic groups. Kraiger and Ford (1985) did examine the moderating role of field versus laboratory studies, where it can be presumed that actual performance was more likely to be controlled in the laboratory. They found that rating differences were

larger in the field ($k = 64$, $N = 16,149$, $r_c = .16$) than in the laboratory ($k = 10$, $N = 1,010$, $r_c = .031$).

Several authors have examined the effects of measurement method (i.e., whether performance is measured subjectively, which is prone to bias, or objectively by way of mechanical, judgment-free processes) on racial-ethnic mean disparities in performance evaluations (Chung-Yan & Cronshaw, 2002; Ford et al., 1986; McKay & McDaniel, 2006; Roth et al., 2003). The results of these meta-analyses fail to provide consistent evidence for ratings bias. For instance, Ford et al. (1986) found little effect of measurement method moderation since similar (uncorrected) white-black effect size estimates were obtained for objective ($d = .21$, $k = 53$, $N = 10,222$) and subjective criteria ($d = .20$, $k = 53$, $N = 9,443$), while Chung-Yan and Cronshaw (2002) found larger mean white-black mean differences for subjective ($d = .30$, $k = 57$, N not reported) versus objective criteria ($d = .12$, $k = 30$, N not reported). Roth et al. (2003), in contrast, reported larger (uncorrected) white-black mean effect sizes for objective measures

Table 32.3 Summary of Meta-analyses Examining the Relationship Between Race/Ethnicity and Performance Evaluations

Study	Dependent Variable	K	Mean n	Effect Size	Moderators & Notes
White-Black Comparisons (higher score: Whites evaluated more favorably)					
Kraiger & Ford 1985	Performance Ratings White Raters Black Raters	74 14	17,159 2428	d = .37 d = −.45	Effect sizes were larger for field studies.
Ford, Kraiger, & Schechtman 1986	Performance Ratings Subjective Objective	20 20	3122 3260	r_c = .221 r_c = .159	Subjective and objective correlations were significantly different.
Sackett & DuBois 1991	Performance Ratings Civilian Sample White Rater Black Rater Technical Skill & Job Effort Military Sample White Rater Black Rater		17,994 1771 24,039 12,091	d = .43 d = .16 d = .35 d = .14	Found a significant race interaction for rater x ratee race.
Roth, Huffcutt, & Bobko 2003	Overall Performance Ratings Promotion Ratings Quality Ratings Quantity Ratings Job Knowledge Absenteeism	37 7 15 8 12 10	84,295 1404 3613 1218 2460 2376	d = .35 d = .38 d = .25 d = .26 d = .54 d = .18	Objective vs. subjective ratings did not moderate quality and quantity; d for objective knowledge (.75) was much higher than for subjective (.05).

(Continued)

Table 32.3 (Continued)

Study	Dependent Variable	K	Mean n	Effect Size	Moderators & Notes
Huffcutt & Roth 1998	Interview Ratings	31	10,476	$d = .25$	Effects size reduced by structure, situational, & behavioral interview., Increasing job complexity and mental ability were not highly addressed, and the ratio of blacks in the labor pool was low.
Dean, Roth, & Bobko 2008	Assessment Center Ratings	17	8210	$d = .52$	Effects size larger for applicants (.56) than incumbents (.32).
McKay & McDaniel 2006	Overall Performance	302	58,808	$d = .46$	Measurement level, method, data source, criterion type, and cognitive loading all moderated effects.
	Task Performance	93	15,868	$d = .35$	
	Contextual Performance	31	3333	$d = .21$	
	Promotion	7	1422	$d = .34$	
	Subjective Ratings	510	94,555	$d = .40$	
	Objective Ratings	62	15,419	$d = .27$	

of quantity ($d = .32$, $k = 3$, $N = 774$), job knowledge ($d = .55$, $k = 10$, $N = 2,027$), and absenteeism ($d = .23$, $k = 8$, $N = 1,413$) than subjective measures of these criteria (quantity $d = .09$, $k = 5$, $N = 495$; job knowledge $d = .15$, $k = 4$, $N = 1,231$; absenteeism $d = .13$, $k = 4$, $N = 642$). Effect sizes for quality criteria did not vary by measurement method. Finally, McKay and McDaniel (2006) reported similar magnitude uncorrected effect sizes for subjective ($d = .28$, $k = 510$, $N = 94,555$) and objective criteria overall ($d = .22$, $k = 62$, $N = 15,419$). Further correlated vector analyses, which estimate the strengths of several proposed moderators simultaneously, revealed a multiple correlation of only .10 ($k = 572$) between measurement method and black-white mean performance effect sizes. Thus, measurement method accounted for merely one percent of the variance in effect sizes.

Another indirect way in which the question of bias has been addressed is to compare the results of black and white raters' ratings of white and black job incumbents. Kraiger and Ford (1985) presented results which supported the hypothesis that there is in-group favoritism and out-group bias in ratings, as white raters rated white applicants higher than black applicants, while the opposite tendency was observed for black raters (see Table 32.3). Sackett and DuBois (1991) reanalyzed these results, along with data from large-scale civilian and military

samples. They reported a significant rater x ratee race interaction across the three samples; however, unlike Kraiger and Ford (1985), they failed to find that black raters assigned more favorable ratings to Black ratees. Instead, they reported that *both* black and white raters rated whites more positively than blacks, but this disparity was much larger for white raters. The point of the Sackett and DuBois (1991) paper was that raters (specifically black raters) do not rate members of their own racial-ethnic group more favorably.

More recently, Stauffer and Buckley (2005) revisited the Sackett and DuBois (1991) study dataset to illustrate that bias may be more of a problem in performance ratings than previously believed (e.g., Landy, Shankster-Crawley, & Kohler Moran, 1995). For both the civilian and military data, Stauffer and Buckley (2005) observed, in within-study designs, that black raters rated both black and white ratees very similarly (mean corrected $d = .044$ and .053, respectively), such that white ratees received slightly higher ratings. By comparison, this difference was much larger for white raters, who rated white incumbents markedly higher than blacks (mean corrected $d = .398$ and .359 for civilians and the military, respectively). These findings indicate that when both white and black raters rated the same people, they rated white workers very similarly ($d = .035$ for civilian, $d = -.034$ for military, where a negative d means that black raters provided a higher rating), whereas when black workers were rated, white raters assigned much lower ratings than did their black counterparts ($d = -.319$ for civilian, $d = -.347$ for military). The authors concluded that these results strongly suggest that racial-ethnic disparities in ratings are due to bias rather than actual performance differences.

Conceptually, it has been argued (e.g., Colella, 1996) that evaluation bias should be stronger in those situations that require projections about future performance, such as hiring decisions, promotion decisions, and judgments about potential. The more clear-cut information and standards that a rater possesses about performance, the less likely that bias will enter into the evaluation (e.g., Arthur & Doverspike, 2005; Latham & Wexley, 1994; Tosi & Einbender, 1985). When raters are asked to make predictions about future performance, however, this clarity and structure is lacking, and thus, evaluations may be driven more by prescriptive stereotypes (Eagly, 1987; Eagly & Karau, 2002; Eagly, Wood, & Diekman, 2000). Examination of Table 32.3 shows that this proposition is not entirely supported. Roth et al. (2003) found that the mean corrected effect size for performance evaluations ($d = .35$, $k = 37$, $N = 84,295$) was only slightly smaller that that for promotion ratings ($d = .38$, $k = 7$, $N = 1,404$). McKay and McDaniel (2006), in their much larger meta-analysis, observed that the corrected effect size for overall performance evaluations ($d = .46$, $k = 302$, $N = 58,808$) was higher than that for promotion evaluations ($d = .34$, $k = 7$, $N = 1,422$). Huffcutt and Roth (1998) found a roughly equivalent effect size for unstructured interviews ($d = .32$, $k = 10$, $N = 1,659$). In contrast, Dean et al. (2008) found much larger effect sizes for black applicants on assessment center ratings ($d = .56$, $k = 17$, $N = 8,210$).

After 30 years of research and numerous meta-analyses, we are still in debate over the presence and extent of racial-ethnic bias in performance evaluations. Rotundo and Sackett (1999; p. 816) stated "there is no current method of establishing whether there is bias in performance ratings," and over ten years later, this still seems to be the case. Future research needs to address this issue by developing more creative methods for assessing the source of subjective rating differences. McKay and McDaniel (2006) found that white-black mean, work performance effect sizes were moderated by a variety of methodological issues (measurement level [i.e., whether performance was measured with one item

vs. multi-item scales], source of publication, measurement method [i.e., subjectively or objectively measured criteria], and data source), indicating that any future research should attend to these concerns. Furthermore, the search for moderators of racial-ethnic mean differences in performance evaluations should be theory-driven. One particularly interesting finding (Huffcutt & Roth, 1998) was that the ratio of blacks in the applicant pool moderated the difference in interview ratings of white and black applicants, such that the effect size was much higher ($d = .41$) when the ratio of blacks was high rather than low ($d = .15$). This finding corroborates threat theories of discrimination—a discrimination cause which has received scant attention in this literature, thus making it a potential fruitful area for future research.

SEX

A plethora of studies have explored the extent of gender bias in performance evaluations, primarily during the 1980s and 1990s. Yet, work in this area is far less voluminous than meta-analyses devoted to racial-ethnic differences in performance evaluations. Swim, Borgida, Maruyama, and Myers (1989) performed a meta-analysis of gender-effects in the evaluation of hypothetical targets on various forms of performance. Findings showed an extremely small effect size ($d = -.07$, $k = 119$, N not reported) indicating that women were rated slightly lower than men. Supplemental moderator analyses of sex of author, year of study, age of subjects, quality of journal, amount of information, and type of stimulus material failed to yield any meaningful effects. This coincides with an early meta-analysis by Olian, Schwab, and Haberfeld (1988), who also observed a very small gender effect on hiring decisions. A more recent meta-analysis of experimental studies in simulated work environments (Davison & Burke, 2000), in which actual performance levels were controlled, revealed that women were assigned higher selection ratings than men in female sex-typed jobs ($d = -.13$, $k = 8$, $N = 553$; negative ratings mean that females were rated higher), while men were received higher ratings in male sex-typed jobs ($d = .17$, $k = 13$, $N = 1,061$). Contrary to predictions, the authors found that both sexes rated men higher than women, and this trend was unaffected by the amount of information provided. Notably, these meta-analyses each relied on laboratory ratings of hypothetical targets.

In order to determine if sex bias exists outside the laboratory, Bowen et al. (2000) meta-analyzed 22 studies of actual performance evaluations in real work settings, after controlling for several potential confounding variables (e.g., performance, tenure, qualifications). Overall, results suggested a very slight bias in favor of women ($d = -.05$, $k = 22$, N not reported); however, these findings were moderated by several factors. For instance, male raters demonstrated bias against women ($d = .32$, $k = 5$), yet in contrast to theory and other meta-analyses (Davison & Burke, 2000; Eagly, Makhijani, & Klonsky, 1992), sex stereotype of the job failed to moderate sex bias in ratings. Morever, the Bowen et al. (2000) meta-analysis provided a more exacting test of the stereotypical fit hypothesis in that it explored the sex stereotypes of specific performance rating dimensions. For those evaluations concerning male-typed performance dimensions (e.g., leadership, planning), there was greater bias against women ($d = .13$, $k = 48$), whereas a pro-female bias was observed for more female-typed performance dimensions (e.g., interpersonal sensitivity, communication; $d = -.26$, $k = 35$).

Recently, Lyness and Heilman (2006) studied the performance evaluation-promotion relationship among nearly 500 male and female managers. This study is unique in that it actually uncovered a direct linkage between evaluation bias and likelihood of being promoted. Moreover, the authors reported a gender x job type interaction wherein men were rated higher than women for line jobs (male sex-typed), whereas women received higher ratings than men in staff jobs (female sex-typed). Of perhaps most interest was their finding that women's performance evaluations were more closely tied to promotion decisions than were men's, which indicated that promotion standards were more flexible for men. Likewise, Ford et al. (1986) proposed a positivity bias relevant to rater-ratee similarity effects on ratings that operates not through downwardly biased ratings of out-group subordinates, but instead as a function of upwardly biased ratings of subordinates from one's in-group. Interestingly, among men and women who were promoted, results revealed that women received significantly higher performance evaluations than men ($Ms = 23.89$ and 22.31, respectively on a 27-point scale).

In conclusion, the role congruence or lack of fit model seems to explain gender discrimination in performance evaluations. There is also some evidence of social identity or in-group favoritism effects, whereby men are demonstrate greater gender bias in evaluations than women. Additional research, in the vein of Lyness and Heilman's (2006) work, is necessary to further elucidate the linkages between actual performance evaluations and pivotal career outcomes.

DISABILITY

Research on evaluations and disability did not proliferate until after the passage of the ADA in 1990. Ren et al. (2008) conducted a meta-analysis on personnel evaluations and disabilities across 31 studies, which used a control group of non-disabled people. Contrary to predictions, they found a positive effect for disability on performance evaluations ($d = .25$, $k = 13$, $N = 1,154$). Colella and Bruyère (2011) reviewed additional literature and concluded that there was little evidence of negative bias in the performance evaluations of disabled workers. One explanation for these positive findings is the "norm to be kind hypothesis," which states that there is a social norm to be kind to disabled individuals (Hastorf, Northcraft, & Piciotto, 1979; Katz & Glass, 1979; Weinberg, 1983). Another explanation is that people have extremely low performance expectations for people with disabilities, and when they perform well, they are overrated because the initial standard was low (Czajka & DeNisi, 1988; Hastorf et al., 1979; Stone & Colella, 1996). Finally, research has shown that people act paternalistically toward disabled people (see Colella & Stone, 2005), which may lead them to kindly assign overly positive ratings.

Ren et al.'s (2008) findings supported the hypothesis that people make lower evaluations of people with disabilities when they are based on expectations about future performance, rather than direct observation of past performance. Overall disability was negatively related to performance expectations ($d = -.14$, $k = 14$, $N = 1,073$) and hiring decisions ($d = -.09$, $k = 37$, $N = 5,023$). Notably, the 95% confidence intervals for both these effects did not contain zero. Furthermore, these results were moderated by the type of disability. On the one hand, the effects of physical disability were non-significant for performance expectations and slightly negative for hiring recommendations ($d = -.08$, $k = 28$, $N = 4581$). On the other hand, the effect sizes for mental disabilities on performance expectations ($d = -.33$, $k = 4$, $N = 227$) and hiring recommendations ($d = -.58$, $k = 6$, $N = 298$) were more negative. The finding that discrimination is greater against people with mental as compared to physical disabilities corroborates both theory (Stone & Colella, 1996) and reviews of employers' attitudes (Ainspan, 2006; Unger, 2002). Correspondingly, health psychology research findings indicate greater stigma against individuals with mental versus physical disabilities (Alonso et al., 2009).

In conclusion, there appears to be little evidence for negative bias in performance evaluations among people with disabilities (Colella & Bruyère, 2011); however, in terms of hiring recommendations and expectations about future performance, negative bias is evident, particularly toward those with mental disabilities. Caution is warranted, given the lack of negative findings for physical disabilities, because most of the studies in the Ren et al. (2008) meta-analysis were conducted in artificial laboratory settings, wherein physical disability was manipulated by having a non-disabled confederate in a wheelchair.

AGE

Research on age bias in evaluations has a long history (e.g., Tuckman & Lorge, 1952) and has been the subject of many reviews (Arvey, 1979; Nelson, 2002; Shore & Goldberg, 2005). An early meta-analysis by Waldman and Avolio (1986) demonstrated that older workers actually exhibited higher performance when performance was measured by objective productivity indices ($r = .27$, $k = 15$). In contrast, they were rated lower than younger employees when performance was measured subjectively via supervisory ratings ($r = .-14$, $k = 18$). This bias was magnified for non-professionals compared to professionals. Therefore, we surmise that when older employees receive lower ratings, it is probably due to supervisory bias, as opposed to decrements in actual, objective performance, especially in the case of non-professionals.

One limitation of the research analyzed by Waldman and Avolio (1986) was that one must infer that objective performance for older employees and younger employees was, in fact, equivalent. In light of this concern, Finkelstein et al.'s (1995) meta-analysis included studies conducted in simulated employment settings wherein performance levels were controlled. Overall, they observed that younger workers discriminated against older workers in terms of job qualifications ($\rho = -.22$, $k = 17$, $N = 1,607$) and ratings of potential ($\rho = -.38$, $k = 13$, $N = 1,577$). Older workers, in contrast, did not discriminate against younger workers, thus, contradicting the in-group favoritism hypothesis. Moreover, the authors noted that the discrimination effect was larger for job qualification and potential ratings when no information was provided ($\rho = -.28$, $k = 12$, $N = 741$ and $\rho = -.81$, $k = 5$, $N = 445$, respectively). Age discrimination was still evident, yet attenuated, when respondents were provided with positive information ($\rho = -.19$, $k = 10$, $N = 765$ for job qualifications—no studies examined potential). Further, the salience of age impacted the extent of age bias such that it was stronger when older workers were compared to younger workers in a within-subjects design.

A more recent meta-analysis (Gordon & Arvey, 2004) incorporated studies included in the Finkelstein et al.'s (1995) and Kite and Johnson's (1988) meta-analyses, as well as additional field studies. The major goal of this analysis, in addition to updating the review, was to assess the generalizability of laboratory findings to those obtained in the field. Thus, they examined methodological moderators that addressed the external validity of prior findings. Overall, Gordon and Arvey (2004) found that younger targets received more positive ratings in terms of overall evaluations ($d = .10$, $k = 45$) and potential for development ($d = .45$, $k = 17$), whereas older targets received more positive stability ratings ($d = -.67$, $k = 9$). In contrast to Finkelstein et al. (1995), Gordon and Arvey (2004) reported that bias was greater against older targets in between-subjects ($d = .31$, $k = 15$) than in within-subjects designs ($d = .10$, $k = 34$). Specifically, the average effect size derived in the field ($d = .10$, $k = 8$) was nearly half of that obtained from laboratory settings ($d = .19$, $k = 33$), indicating that bias against older targets is stronger in laboratory settings. Furthermore, as aspects of the study became more ecologically valid (i.e., real applicants vs. paper people, more information about the target, more information about the job, and supervisor vs. student raters), the effects size for age bias diminished. Based on these findings, Gordon and Arvey (2004) concluded that there is minimal bias in the evaluations of older employees in actual work settings.

Another recent meta-analysis (Kite, Stockdale, Whitley, & Johnson, 2005) included 232 effect sizes gathered from studies evaluating general attitudes and stereotypes about older people. Although they did not specifically single out investigations concerning performance or hiring evaluations, they reported separate effects for studies including judgments of competence. Overall, they found that younger people were rated as more competent than older individuals ($d = .33$, $k = 75$). In correspondence with Gordon and Arvey's (2004) results, Kite et al. (2005) observed that as greater information was provided, the bias against older targets weakened. Unlike Gordon and Arvey (2004), however, bias was not reduced in ratings gathered from the general population, as compared to students. In addition, within-designs were associated with greater, not lesser bias than between-designs. Interestingly, they also found that middle-aged adults displayed the most bias in competence ratings of older adults ($d = .50$, $k = 11$) relative to young ($d = .35$, $k = 59$), and older adults ($d = .26$, $k = 10$). Again, these studies did not focus upon working relationships, but notably, students do not appear to always exhibit more bias than older (middle-aged) adults, or individuals from the general population.

In summary, meta-analytic evidence suggests a low level of age bias in the evaluations of older workers; however, this bias is markedly larger for ratings of potential than ratings of qualifications, and when there is ample information about performance.

OBESITY AND ATTRACTIVENESS

Sufficient research has addressed discrimination based upon weight and appearance to warrant recent meta-analyses of these literatures. Rudolph et al. (2009) examined the effect of weight-based bias on hiring, performance, and promotion outcomes. Overall, results revealed a larger discrimination effect than any other meta-analyses of discrimination on a particular characteristic ($d = -.52$, $k = 42$). Furthermore, this negative effect was larger for sales jobs ($d = -.72$, $k = 10$) and managerial jobs ($d = -.62$, $k = 7$), and discrimination was greater for hiring evaluations ($d = -.76$, $k = 17$) and suitability ratings ($d = -.65$, $k = 14$) than for performance evaluations ($d = -.24$, $k = 4$); however, the effect of attractiveness bias on promotion evaluations was non-significant. Rudolph et al. (2009) argued that the stronger effect for hiring evaluations was a function of raters possessing less information about applicants than those who made evaluations based upon observed performance.

Over the past several decades, voluminous research investigated physical attractiveness bias, culminating in several meta-analyses of such bias (Dion, Berscheid, & Walster, 1972; Eagly, Ashmore, Makhijani, & Longo, 1991; Feingold, 1992; Jackson, Hunter, & Hodge, 1995). Bias in favor of attractive people, relative to those considered unattractive, is predicted based upon implicit personality theory (Ashmore, 1981). This theory states that people have cognitive structures (stereotypes) that contain inferential relationships among personal characteristics. Physical attractiveness is associated with positive qualities, whereas unattractiveness is linked with negative qualities (Dion et al., 1972) For example, Feingold (1992) found

that intelligence and attractiveness were inferentially associated.

In the sole meta-analysis to address work-related evaluations, Hosoda, Stone-Romero, and Coats (2003) reported that attractive people received higher evaluations ($d = .37$, $k = 62$, $N = 3,207$). Moreover, they noted that effect sizes were stronger in within-subjects study designs compared to between-subjects designs, and that biasing effects decreased from 1,975 to 1,999. Interestingly, Hosoda et al. (2003) failed to find that the magnitude of bias varied between students in laboratory studies in contrast to workers in field settings, situations in which more rather than less information was provided, and between male and female targets. They further tested Heilman's (1983) lack-of-fit model predictions by considering the interaction of the sex-type of the job and target sex, which were not corroborated. Finally, effect sizes were higher for hiring decision, suitability, and potential evaluations ($d = .39$, $.42$, and $.44$, respectively) than those derived for actual performance evaluations ($d = .16$).

SUMMARY

A vast amount of research on bias and discrimination in work-related evaluations has been undertaken, as evidenced above by the numerous meta-analyses reported; however, much of this work remains quite inconclusive. The issue of racial-ethnic discrimination has been most extensively studied and meta-analyzed, yet there is still disagreement about the extent of racial-ethnic bias in evaluations. What is clear is that effect sizes across groups are relatively small, with the largest ($d = -.52$) for bias against overweight people. Effect sizes also are larger when individuals are asked to make evaluations concerning future performance (i.e., hiring recommendations, promotion evaluations) than for actual, observed performance.

Meta-analysis is a powerful research tool, but it cannot overcome methodological problems inherent in the original research. The methodological issues with discrimination research on evaluations has been discussed thoroughly elsewhere (e.g., Dipboye, 1985, Goldman et al., 2006; Landy, 2008; Stone, Hosoda, Lukaszewski, & Phillips, 2008; Tosi & Einbender, 1985). The principal criticisms include a lack of reality in the experimental settings, obtrusive measures which lead to socially desirable responding, overreliance on student subjects, lack of individuating information, and the possibility that differences are due to actual performance differences instead of bias, which is problematic in correlational studies.

Perhaps, dissatisfaction with primary study methodologies is why most authors of the meta-analyses discussed above strongly considered methodological moderators. Unfortunately, the patterns of findings provide little clarity regarding their effects on evaluative bias, other than that providing greater information about a target tends to attenuate the extent of bias due to the characteristic under study. Yet, Hosoda et al. (2003) report a null effect for amount of information on attractiveness bias. Therefore, there is uncertainty as to whether laboratory study findings are generalizable to the field. Various meta-analyses demonstrate that either effects are stronger in the laboratory (e.g., Gordon & Arvey, 2004, for age), have no effect (e.g., Hosoda et al., 2003, for attractiveness), or that stronger impact is evident in the field (e.g., Ren et al., 2008 for disability). Perhaps one issue plaguing this line of investigation is that field studies lack internal validity, and thus it is inappropriate to contrast them with laboratory studies. Another problem is that meta-analysis cannot elucidate the exact nature of methodological factors. For example, the quality as well as quantity of additional information about targets may vary, and their potentially differing impacts on evaluation bias must be disentangled. The solution to this problem is to conduct higher quality original studies for which many guidelines exist.

A second issue that warrants attention in future research is greater systematic consideration of theoretical moderators. The only such moderator that was examined sufficiently to include in meta-analyses (and lends itself to post hoc coding) is the lack of fit hypothesis (Heilman, 1983)—which was generally supported in terms of gender, age, and weight. For instance, we should not expect gender bias to occur universally since its incidence is affected by the gender stereotype associated with the job in question. Earlier, we reviewed the findings of Huffcutt and Roth (1998), which suggested that realistic group threat may act as a moderator, as white-black mean differences in effect sizes diminished with greater proportions of blacks in the samples analyzed. The point here is that in order to develop methods of overcoming bias at work, I/O scholars must investigate factors that operate in the real world contexts.

In addition, future researchers should extend studies of evaluative bias to other groups and personal characteristics. Essentially, no empirical work (with a few exceptions) has considered the extent of evaluation bias based upon religion, national origin, races and ethnicities other than blacks versus whites, and sexual orientation. Furthermore, the nature of stereotypes differ by groups, as well as discrimination dynamics (e.g., the "norm to be kind" to people with disabilities, which does not exist for people who are overweight). Generalizing or discriminating (no pun intended) among biases held against various stigmatized groups is a realistic goal for future research (see Cuddy et al., 2007, and Fiske et al., 2002, for examples), with practical implications rectifying these forms of discrimination.

A final concern that warrants further study is to specify how evaluation bias impacts a person's career. Most of the research examined here has been cross-sectional in nature; thus, it only provides one-time snapshots of performance evaluations; however, the longitudinal impact of performance evaluations on subsequent ones remains unclear. For instance, does future information decrease bias or is it ignored? Do evaluations at one career stage influence evaluations at later stages? As noted above, Lyness and Heilman (2006) demonstrated how gender bias in evaluations had implications for career outcomes such as promotion. More research of this type is needed. A recent sociological study (Castilla, 2008) illustrated that while performance evaluations may not reflect bias, the linkage between evaluations and rewards (i.e., promotions and pay) may be biased against women and minorities in the workplace. Accordingly, we now turn our focus to pay discrimination, while we direct readers to Avery (2011) who provides a current and very thorough review of discrimination in promotions.

Pay Discrimination

As indicated earlier in this chapter, economic data show pay differentials for a variety of stigmatized groups. Literally thousands of studies have addressed this issue, and most of them derive from the economics, social psychology, sociology, and labor relations disciplines (for reviews see Jarrell & Stanley, 2004; Marini, 1989; Stanley & Jarrell, 1998). We must note that pay differentials between groups do not necessarily indicate discrimination because such disparities may be a function of job-relevant, compensable factors (e.g., education, job level, work experience, industry). Typically, it is the purview of economists to determine what proportion of existing pay differentials is due to non-discriminatory factors (e.g., Holzer & Neumark, 2000), then any residual, unexplained variance is interpreted operatively as discrimination (Belliveau, 2005). For example, Blau and Kahn (2006, 2007) reported a 20.3% wage disparity between men and women, based on a large-scale, national sample.

After controlling for educational attainment, labor force experience, race-ethnicity, occupational category, industry category, and union status, 41.1% of the variance in the wage differential remained unexplained. In one of the most comprehensive investigations of explanatory factors, Keaveny, Inderreiden, and Toumanoff (2007), using two samples of new MBA graduates ($N = 2,054$ and $5,790$), uncovered overall pay differentials of 17.4% and 16.2% favoring men to women, with 8.6% and 4.6% unexplained variance. Their analyses controlled for human capital variables (i.e., college major, labor force experience, gaps in employment and length of service with current employer), job characteristics (i.e., hours worked, number of persons supervised, budgetary responsibilities, job training, and gender density of occupation), employer characteristics (i.e., industry and size), cognitive skills (i.e., verbal and quantitative skills), and demographic characteristics (i.e., marital status, age, race, children and gender). Another way of assessing the degree of potential discrimination within one organization is to regress pay on a variety of compensable factors (e.g., tenure, number of subordinates, job level), and then add group status (e.g., sex, race) to the equation to determine how much additional variance is accounted for group status alone (see Alkadry & Tower, 2006, for an example regarding gender discrepancies). Of interest to I/O psychology discrimination researchers, such analyses isolate the extent of remaining variance due to group membership.

Two noteworthy points follow from this body of research. First, it is possible that gender discrimination is not the only operative factor at play, as other, non-discriminatory, unmeasured factors could explain some of this variance (e.g., work interruption, skill level). Second, explanatory characteristics, which on the surface may seem non-discriminatory, themselves can be influenced by discrimination (Ely & Padavic, 2007). For example, by controlling for industry or job type, one might ignore prejudicial practices that cluster women into certain occupations, and then assign lesser value to that work (Bergmann, 1974; Fields & Wolff, 1991; Pfeffer & Davis-Blake, 1987; Reskin, 1993; Sorensen, 1990).

Reviewing the entire literature on pay discrimination, especially with respect to sex and race, is beyond the scope of this chapter. Rather, we explore several hypotheses that have been examined in the I/O psychology and related literatures, and provide illustrative examples of such work. Furthermore, the studies reviewed below focus primarily on sex differentials in pay because most of the psychologically based research has addressed this topic. Finally, we exclude literature that provides non-discriminatory justifications for existing gender differences, such as the argument that women are more accepting of lower pay than men (e.g., Witt & Nye, 1992).

One frequently given explanation for pay discrimination is that stereotyping and lowered performance expectations diminish the perceived value of contributions (e.g., Ostroff & Atwater, 2003) by either influencing individual pay decisions, or reflecting institutionalized norms and policies (Pfeffer & Davis-Blake, 1987). As germane to such arguments, stereotypes can operate in several ways. First, there is the impact of injunctive or prescriptive stereotypes (Eagly & Karau, 2002), which contain information about how certain groups will and should behave. Many of these stereotypes perpetuate an undermining of human capital (i.e., they cause others to believe that certain people will be less productive in the future than others). For example, older individuals, the disabled, and women are stereotyped as being less willing to learn new skills (Cuddy, Norton & Fiske, 2005; Posthuma & Campion, 2009), more likely to be absent (Stone & Colella, 1996), and less committed to their work (Graddy & Pistaferri, 2000), respectively, despite existing evidence to the contrary for all of these groups (Bielby & Bielby, 1998; Colella & Bruyère, 2011; Lyness & Judiesch, 2001; Posthuma & Campion, 2009). With respect to gender discrimination, motherhood seems to exacerbate these stereotypes (Anderson, Binder, & Krause, 2002; Budig & England, 2001; Crosby, Williams, & Biernat, 2004).

Another way in which stereotypes can affect pay decisions is through their influence on the value of a group's work. Most investigations on this topic concern gender discrimination. For example, it is well documented that as the proportion of women (and minorities) in an occupation or a job increases, pay diminishes (e.g., England, Farkas, Kilbourne, & Dou, 1988; Pfeffer & Davis-Blake, 1987). Reasons abound for this trend (for a thorough discussion, see Pfeffer & Davis-Blake, 1987), however, empirical data suggests that stereotypes and gender norms play a substantial role in devaluing work performed by most women (Pfeffer & Davis-Blake, 1987).

Finally, Heilman and her colleagues' (Heilman, Block, & Lucas, 1992; Heilman, Block, & Stathatos, 1997; Heilman & Haynes, 2005) work has uncovered what they call the "stigma of incompetence." In essence, individuals assume that women and minorities are hired due to sex- or race-based preferential hiring, rather than for their work qualifications, unless they are provided strong information to the contrary. Thus, women and minorities are accorded less prospective value to an organization relative to members of other, non-stigmatized groups. This phenomenon might explain prevailing differences in starting salaries (Graddy & Pistaferri, 2000; Keaveny et al., 2007).

Gerhart (1990) discovered that as much as 34% of the wage differences between men and women could be explained by initial salary disparities, and according to Babcock and Laschever (2003), such differentials accrue over time. Apart from the consequences of stereotyping and prejudice, which are generally inferred from prevailing wage discrepancies, an organized body of research has explored how gender effects on salary negotiations affect subsequent gaps in starting salaries. By and large, researchers consistently that find women, relative to men, tend to negotiate lower starting salaries, or are more reluctant to initiate negotiations (Babcock & Laschever, 2003; Gerhart & Rynes, 1991; Stuhlmacher & Walters, 1999). For example, in a sample of graduating MBA students, Babcock, Gelfand, Small, and Stayn (2006), demonstrated that 51.9% of men negotiated their job offer, compared to only 12.9% of women. As a result, women received average annual starting salaries that were 8.5% lower than men. Further supporting this pattern of gender differences in negotiation propensities, Stuhlmacher and Walters's (1999) meta-analysis of gender effects on negotiation settlements showed that women received slightly, although significantly, lower salaries than men ($d = .10$, $k = 21$, $N = 3,496$).

A primary reason for such effects is that negative stereotypes are applied to women's work (Stuhlmacher & Walters, 1999) as noted above. Moreover, an additional argument is that women negotiate less because they feel less entitled than men, a tendency that has been explained in three ways (see Major, 1987). First, women and racial minorities may value different rewards from those valued by white men (e.g., Avery, 2003). Second, women and minorities potentially have fewer entitlement concerns than men because they utilize different frames of references to evaluate acceptable pay levels. The social network literature demonstrates that when women and minorities maintain less powerful social networks, they receive less information or perceive that pay is lower than those who occupy more powerful social networks (Belliveau, 2005; Brass, 1985; Ibarra, 1995a,b; Ibarra & Andrews, 1993; Seidel, Polzer, & Stewart, 2000).

For example, Belliveau (2005), in a study of elite college students entering the labor market, found that the heterophily (i.e., gender diversity) of female students' social networks was positively related to starting salary offers, after controlling for college major and human capital. These findings suggest that women receive higher pay when more men are in their social networks. Baskerville Watkins et al. (2006) reporting similar findings for promotions. What this suggests is that women and minorities obtain comparatively lower reference figures than white males and, therefore, negotiate and accept less advantageous career outcomes; however, this tendency dissipates when women and minorities have equivalent social comparative information to use in judging what are deemed acceptable outcomes by others (Major, McFarlin, & Gagnon, 1984; Seidel et al., 2000). Third, women's and minorities' contributions are less valued relative to white men's (e.g., Esses et al., 2006; Heilman & Okimoto, 2008). Finally, the concept of depressed entitlement, as described by system justification theory, indicates that members of low-status groups devalue their own contributions due to lessened feelings of self-worth (Jost et al., 2004). As an example, several scholars have shown that women devalue their own contributions (Jackson, Gardner, & Sullivan, 1992; Major & Deaux, 1982; Major & Konar, 1984), in line with depressed entitlement predictions.

Recently, organizational scholars have considered additional factors that precipitate the gender wage gap. Judge and Livingston (2008), in a longitudinal study (lasting nearly 30 years) of nearly 7,600 people, found a significant gender orientation–earnings relationship, which was moderated by gender. For men, traditional gender role orientation was positively related to earnings, and negatively related among women. Notably, women with egalitarian gender role orientations earned about 93% of the salaries received by egalitarian men. Traditional women earned only 57% of the salaries of traditional men. Occupational segregation only partially explained these results. Another recent investigation, involving a series of experiments using adult respondents (Bowles, Babcock, & Lai, 2007), revealed that women incur greater social costs from engaging in salary negotiations and exhibit reluctance to do so for fear of these costs.

From sociological and economic perspectives, Petersen and Saporta (2004) categorize causes of wage discrimination into three types. "Allocative discrimination" occurs due to the clustering of women and minorities into certain low-paying occupations, industries, or organizations. "Within-job discrimination" is evident when women or minorities are paid lower than white men holding the same job, in the same establishment. This topic has received a great deal of attention. The third mechanism for discrimination is "valuative discrimination," in which "female-dominated occupations are paid lower wages than male-dominated ones, although skill requirements and other wage-relevant factors are equivalent. It is the issue addressed by comparable worth initiatives" (p. 853).

Using this taxonomy for causes of discrimination, Petersen and Saporta (2004) examined the careers of over 7,000 managerial, administrative, and professional workers through company personnel records. Employees were followed from the time of entry over an eight-year period. Findings showed that discrimination was most probable at the initial hiring point, where disparities of half a job level and 15% of wages, favoring men, were discovered. Gender gaps in job level and salary narrowed significantly with increasing seniority, mainly because women were promoted at a faster rate than men. In contrast to other explanations of wage discrimination, which tend to focus on cognitive factors involved in the discrimination process, Petersen and Saporta (2004) argued that discrimination at the time of hire was more prevalent because the opportunity to discriminate is greatest during this period. They further elaborated that the opportunity to discriminate depends on: (a) the ease with which information documenting discrimination can be assembled; (b) the ambiguity of information concerning discrimination; and (c) the willingness or ability of discrimination targets to file charges or complaints.

The Petersen and Saporta (2004) study is somewhat unique since it uncovered the factors that perpetuate discrimination in organizations, and examined these processes longitudinally. Subsequent studies utilized longitudinal research designs (e.g., Lyness & Heilman, 2006) or examined the impact of certain practices on subsequent subgroup disparities (e.g., Castilla, 2008, found that merit pay systems increased the gender and race gap in pay). Research of this nature, while very recent, is advancing our understanding of how discrimination works in organizations, and the measures useful for reducing it.

Beyond following the lead of the studies mentioned above, future wage discrimination research should extend its focus to a few additional areas on interest. First, as with performance evaluation research, most work has addressed wage gaps based upon gender and, to a lesser extent, race; however, wage disparities are evident in terms of ethnicity, sexual orientation, disability, motherhood status, and weight, as well. Additionally, I/O psychology scholars should direct further study toward uncovering the mechanisms underlying pay discrimination. Furthermore, it is questionable whether we can apply existing knowledge on the gender wage gap, and develop a theoretical model that generalizes across all disparaged groups. Second, the wage discrimination literature is highly fragmented; therefore, explanations for prevailing wage disparities still tend to focus on either micro versus macrofactors, and organization versus labor market issues. Potentially, greater insights into the mechanisms underlying the operation of wage discrimination will come from integrating these perspectives.

Subtle Discrimination

With the advent of modern racism and aversive racism in the social psychology literature, more attention has been devoted to subtle discrimination. Scholars who study this topic claim that since there are social norms against perpetrating overt discrimination (e.g., harassment, lower ratings), presently, discrimination is manifested in more covert ways (Crosby, Bromley, & Saxe, 1980; Deitch et al., 2003; Dovidio & Gaertner, 1986; Gaertner & Dovidio, 1986; McConahay, 1983). Primarily, I/O scholars who examine discrimination tend to emphasize rare and major events, such as negative performance ratings, sexual harassment, or unfair selection instruments (Deitch et al., 2003), yet discrimination is often experienced in minor ways on a daily basis (Cleveland, Vescio, & Barnes-Farrell, 2005; Essed, 1991). One can be discriminated against and not even attribute the unpleasant behavior to her or his group membership (Deitch et al., 2003). Other terms, such as *interpersonal discrimination* (Hebl et al., 2002; King, Shapiro, Hebl, Singletary, & Turner, 2006), *everyday discrimination* (Deitch et al., 2003), or *microaggressions* (Pettigrew & Martin, 1987), have been used in our literature to label subtle discrimination. A key limitation of such work is that there is no strong conceptual definition of subtle discrimination, and its operationalizations vary greatly across studies.

Social psychologists have measured subtle prejudice and discrimination using unobtrusive measures such as the IAT (Greenwald et al., 1998), social distance (Word, Zanna, & Cooper, 1974), facial expressions (Ruscher, 2001), and smiling (Biernat

& Vescio, 2002). Such measures are less feasible in an employment context. A few studies in the I/O psychology literature have attempted to empirically assess subtle discrimination. Deitch et al. (2003) conducted one of the first investigations, to our knowledge, in the I/O psychology and management domains to explicitly examine subtle, everyday racism. Specifically, the authors compared various samples of black and white civilian and military employees' responses to two instruments that simply asked about general mistreatment experienced at work. Items included rating the extent to which others "set you up for failure," "gave others privileges you didn't get," "treated you as if you didn't exist," "damaged your personal property," or "made insulting jokes or comments." It should be noted that the researchers did not ask respondents to indicate if the mistreatment was due to their race-ethnicity, since it is assumed that everyday discrimination is often attributionally ambiguous. Findings indicated that blacks experienced more mistreatment than whites, and this mistreatment further mediated racial disparities in job satisfaction, emotional well-being, and physical well-being.

The attributional ambiguity paradigm is yet another way in which subtle discrimination has been investigated. In these studies, respondents must interact or evaluate a target group member under conditions where it would be obvious that they were reacting negatively to the person or in conditions wherein their behavior can be attributed to some external, non-prejudicial factor. In the I/O psychology literature, Brief et al. (2000) showed that respondents exhibited a greater propensity to discriminate against a black job applicant when their behavior could be attributed to non-prejudicial factors (i.e., directives from an authority).

Interestingly, some I/O scholars have directly compared individuals' likelihoods to engage in formal versus informal forms of discrimination (Hebl et al., 2002; King et al., 2006). As an illustration of such work, Hebl et al. (2002; also see King et al., 2006) showed, in an audit study, that hiring managers did not formally discriminate against gay job applicants (e.g., deny them the opportunity to apply for a position), but evidenced "interpersonal" discrimination by engaging in shorter interactions with them. Notably, the authors took great strides to record the applicant-manager interactions, the former of which was actually a research confederate. Similarly, Frazer and Wiersma's (2001) laboratory study of students rating black and white hypothetical job candidates revealed no evidence of discrimination in actual ratings; however, when questioned one week later, participants recalled, stereotypically, that the answers given by black applicants were significantly less intelligent than those provided by white applicants.

Colella and Stone (2005) further discussed paternalism as an additional subtle form of discrimination aimed at people with disabilities. Paternalism can result in disadvantageous outcomes because targets are not given realistic feedback, or are not challenged sufficiently so that they may improve their work performance. Evidence of such discrimination has come from studies whereby respondents provide people with disabilities unrealistically positive performance feedback (Czajka & DeNisi, 1988; Hastorf et al., 1979). Currently, Colella and her colleagues are developing a measure of paternalism to directly examine its merit as a form of subtle gender, race-ethnicity, and disability discrimination (Colella & Garcia, 2004; Daniels, Colella, & Nishii, 2010; Garcia, Colella, Triana, Smith, & Baskerville Watkins, under review).

Subtle discrimination also may be manifested in the manner by which performance standards are constructed, how work is evaluated, and in establishing definitions of success (Cleveland & Colella, 2011; Cleveland et al., 2005). Particularly, standards may vary and/or be interpreted differently across subgroups. For example, Heilman and Okimoto (2007) showed, across a series of three laboratory experiments, that successful female CEOs were rated as less likable, more hostile, and less desirable as a boss than male CEOs. Thus, given identical performance information about a man and woman in a male-gendered job, women were penalized; however, these effects were ameliorated when respondents were provided with information suggesting that the successful female manager was also caring, sensitive, and supportive. In other words, women had to perform differently, and in more gender stereotypical ways, from men to receive the same evaluations.

In summary, the examination of subtle discrimination in organizational environments is in its infancy. We predict that this will be a popular area for future research, as it should be. However, before such research can move forward, more work is necessary to develop the subtle discrimination construct, and to devise a coherent framework for measuring it. Most importantly, several concerns pose difficulties for advancing the subtle discrimination framework. First of all, subtle discrimination can be attributionally ambiguous, meaning that targets may not perceive the maltreatment as discrimination, even though, subsequently, it can have negative consequences (see Deitch et al., 2003, for a discussion). Second, since subtle discrimination involves minor, everyday incidents, which may not cause immediate harm, yet over time can have negative effects on performance, career, and well-being outcomes (Cleveland et al., 2005; Pettigrew & Martin, 1987), it should be studied longitudinally; yet, current discrimination research has focused upon single, major discriminatory events (e.g., hiring decisions, compensation decisions). Finally, traditional unobtrusive measures of implicit prejudice used in the social psychology field may not be appropriate in real work settings (e.g., Blanton & Jaccard, 2008; Blanton et al., 2009; Landy, 2008).

Perceived Discrimination and Its Outcomes

Although a large body of work has chronicled the presence of discrimination in work-related outcomes against members of stigmatized groups (e.g., Colella & Varma, 2001; Finkelstein et al., 1995; Hebl et al., 2002; Martell, 2006; Roehling, 1999; Stauffer & Buckley, 2005), much less research has considered targets' reactions to perceptions of being discriminated against. Over the past 20 years, however, scholars from varied disciplines, including health psychology, sociology, and organizational behavior/human resource management, have turned their attention to exploring the implications of perceived discrimination for work outcomes such as job satisfaction (i.e., the degree of pleasure derived from one's job), job involvement (i.e., the relative importance of work in one's life), organizational commitment (i.e., workers' emotional attachment to organizations), organizational citizenship behaviors (OCBs; i.e., the extent to which an employee performs beneficial discretionary work behaviors), distributive justice (i.e., the fairness of disseminating work-related rewards), procedural justice (i.e., the fairness of procedures and work policies), productivity, and turnover intentions, as well as psychological and physical health (e.g., depression, anxiety, sick days, blood pressure, self-reported health).

In our non-exhaustive review of this literature, we focus upon perceived discrimination, defined as individuals' subjective perceptions that they have received differential treatment in regard to various outcomes (e.g., hiring, firing, job promotions, service quality, interpersonal treatment, medical care, police harassment, etc.) because of their race-ethnicity, gender, age, sexual orientation, and disability status. Perceived religious discrimination is not covered due to a dearth of organizational

research on this topic. We attend to perceived discrimination, as opposed to more objective forms of discrimination such as disparities in job promotions unexplained by differences in work qualifications (e.g., Baldi & McBrier, 1997), as individuals must acknowledge that they have been discriminated against in order to react to it (Branscombe, Schmitt, & Harvey, 1999; Davidson & Friedman, 1998).

Perceived Racial Discrimination

Various forms of perceived racial discrimination (e.g., everyday discrimination, lifetime discrimination) have been linked to negative effects on work-related attitudes and behaviors, and diminished mental and physical health. Myriad organizational researchers have found that perceived racial-ethnic discrimination is related to lower job satisfaction (Ensher, Grant-Vallone, & Donaldson, 2001; Foley, Kidder, & Powell, 2002; Holder & Vaux, 1998; Moyes, Williams, & Quigley, 2000; Sanchez & Brock, 1996), organizational commitment (Ensher et al., 2001; Sanchez & Brock, 1996), performance of OCBs (Ensher et al., 2001), perceptions of career prospects (Foley et al., 2002), distributive justice (Foley et al., 2002), work tension (Sanchez & Brock, 1996), heightened perceptions of "glass ceiling" (advancement) barriers (Foley et al., 2002), and turnover intentions (Foley et al., 2002). This body of work further reveals more disparate effects of perceived racial-ethnic discrimination on foreign-born individuals (Sanchez & Brock, 1996) and those who are members of the predominant ethnic group in a particular geographic location (Sanchez & Brock, 1996). These findings are a function of the lower assimilation of foreign-born people into U.S. culture, thus increasing proneness to discrimination, and membership in large ethnic groups provides greater social support to mitigate the negative effects of discrimination, respectively.

Similarly, perceived racial-ethnic discrimination has negative effects on mental and physical health, especially among members of racial-ethnic minority groups (i.e., blacks, Hispanics, and Asians). These studies show that greater reports of discrimination are linked to lower psychological well-being (Gee, 2002; James, Lovato, & Khoo, 1994; Williams, Yu, Jackson, & Anderson, 1997), self-reported health (James et al., 1994; Williams et al., 1997), a higher number of poor mental health days (Roberts, Swanson, & Murphy, 2004), and elevated blood pressure (James et al., 1994). In contrast, Kessler, Mickelson, and Williams (1999) found that although perceived discrimination was associated with greater odds for experiencing depression, generalized anxiety, and psychological distress, these likelihoods did not vary across race. Likewise, in a meta-analytic study of the impact of perceived discrimination on mental and physical health, stress response, and health behaviors, Pascoe and Smart Richman (2009) failed to find evidence that race-ethnicity moderated the perceived discrimination–mental health and perceived discrimination–health behaviors relationships, which were negative ($r = -.16$ and $-.18$, respectively) for the overall samples of studies ($k = 150$ and 13, respectively). Insufficient sample sizes for minority groups precluded analysis of race-ethnicity moderation of the perceived discrimination–physical health and perceived discrimination–stress responses linkages.

The above pattern of findings with respect to the mental and physical health outcomes of perceived discrimination might follow from Branscombe et al.'s (1999) rejection-identification model, which proposes that discrimination can have, simultaneously, negative effects on psychological well-being, as a form of rejection by the dominant group, and positive impact on well-being through fostering increased in-group identification. Therefore, losses in mental well-being (and perhaps physical well-being as well) due to discrimination might be offset by gains in in-group identification fostered by exposure to discrimination.

Perceived Gender (or Sex) Discrimination

Consistently, research has shown that perceived gender discrimination negatively affects women's work-related attitudes and behaviors and psychological and physical health. Higher perceived sex discrimination is associated with lower job satisfaction (Foley, Hang-Yue, & Wong, 2005; Settles, Cortina, Malley, & Stewart, 2006), job involvement (Gutek, Cohen, & Tsui, 1996), organizational commitment (Foley et al., 2005), procedural justice (Foley et al., 2005), distributive justice (Foley et al., 2005), productivity (Settles et al., 2006), likelihood of choosing the same profession (Gutek et al., 1996), power and prestige of one's job (Gutek et al., 1996), and increased work conflict (Gutek et al., 1996) and turnover intentions (Cunningham & Sagas, 2007; Gutek et al., 1996). Interestingly, Cunningham and Sagas (2007) showed that compared to their female counterparts, male coaches of National College Athletics Association (NCAA) women's sports teams reacted more negatively to treatment discrimination due to sex. The authors explained these results as indicative of men's relative lack of experience with

gender discrimination; therefore, they possess fewer resources to cope with it effectively.

In the mental and physical health domains, perceived gender discrimination has been linked with lower mental and physical well-being. Extant literature provides evidence of positive relations with menstrual, depressive, somatic, obsessive compulsive, and anxiety symptoms (Fischer & Holtz, 2007; Landrine, Klonoff, Gibbs, Manning, & Lund, 1995), physical mobility limitations at work (Pavalko, Mossakowski, & Hamilton, 2003), emotional distress (Pavalko et al., 2003), and reduced participation in healthy behaviors (Pascoe & Smart Richman, 2009). Importantly, Fischer and Holtz (2007) showed that perceived gender discrimination's negative effects on mental health were partially mediated by its debilitating influences on public collective self-esteem (i.e., how others view women as a group), private collective self-esteem (i.e., how one personally views women as a group), and personal self-esteem. Moreover, Landrine et al. (1995) found that perceived gender discrimination–mental (and physical) health associations persisted beyond controls for variance due to general life stressors, highlighting how women experience perceived sex discrimination as a unique form of stress.

Perceived Age Discrimination

In contrast to work on the impact of perceived racial-ethnic and gender discrimination on work outcomes, much less work has examined perceived age discrimination's work-related and mental and physical health consequences. We should note that age discrimination can occur against both younger and older subgroups because they are not members of the higher status, prime, middle-aged group (i.e., 35–50 years of age; Finkelstein et al., 1995; Garstka, Schmitt, Branscombe, & Hummert, 2004; Loretto, Duncan, & White, 2000; Shore, Cleveland, & Goldberg, 2003). A recent study by Redman and Snape (2006) is suggestive of perceived age discrimination's negative connotations for work outcomes. Within a sample of 402 British police officers, results showed that perceived age discrimination was negatively related to job satisfaction, power and prestige of one's job, job involvement, affective commitment, normative commitment (i.e., an employee's perceived obligation to stay with an organization), and continuance commitment (i.e., the extent of commitment due to potential loss of work-related rewards and resources), and was positively associated with withdrawal cognitions. Furthermore, relations with job satisfaction and normative commitment were moderated by non-work social support, such that these negative age discrimination–outcome relationships were attenuated when respondents reported higher degrees of social support from friends and family.

We uncovered a larger number of studies examining perceived age discrimination's effects on mental and physical health, which were consistently negative in nature. These investigations show that perceived age discrimination is associated with psychological well-being (Garstka et al., 2004), life satisfaction (Garstka et al., 2004; Redman & Snape, 2006), and positive well-being (Vogt Yuan, 2007), and is positively related to psychological distress (Vogt Yuan, 2007) and mortality risk (Barnes et al., 2008). Barnes et al. (2008) found that perceived discrimination was associated with a hazard ratio (HR) of 1.05 ($p < .05$) in their overall sample, meaning that each one-point increment in discrimination scores resulted in a 5% increase in mortality risk. These effects were heightened among white compared to black survey respondents ($HR = 1.12$ and 1.03, respectively, $p < .05$). The authors explained this trend as a function of whites' fewer lifetime experiences with discrimination than blacks; thus they have relatively lower coping resources to mitigate its effects.

The Garstka et al. (2004) study further proposed differential effects of age discrimination for younger and older adults, reasoning that the former, but not the latter, could move into the prime age category through aging. Accordingly, the negative perceived age discrimination–psychological well-being relationship was significant only among older adults. In addition, the effects of perceived age discrimination on psychological health were mediated by age group identification (for older adults; Garstka et al., 2004) and sense of control and social support (Vogt Yuan, 2007). Finally, Redman and Snape (2006) reported attenuated relations between perceived age discrimination and life satisfaction for respondents who indicated high levels of non-work social support.

Perceived Sexual Orientation Discrimination

Compared to other stigmatized groups (e.g., minorities, women), much less research has considered the work-related and mental and physical health consequences of discrimination on the basis of sexual orientation. Gay, lesbian, bisexual, and transgendered (GBLT) identity differs from other stigmatized identities due to its hidden or invisible nature. In this regard, one's choice to openly express a GBLT identity has ramifications for the extent that one will likely experience discrimination due to sexual orientation. Accordingly, existing research suggests that heterosexism, or "negative attitudes toward gay men and lesbians" (Waldo, 1999, p. 218), has negative effects on work attitudes and behaviors, as well as psychological well-being and physical health among those who experience it.

Organizational research has shown consistently that perceived discrimination based on sexual orientation is related to reduced job satisfaction (Button, 2001; Ragins & Cornwell, 2001; Waldo, 1999), organizational commitment (Button, 2001; Ragins & Cornwell, 2001; Waldo, 1999), career commitment (Ragins & Cornwell, 2001), compensation (Ragins & Cornwell, 2001), opportunities for promotion (Ragins & Cornwell, 2001), disclosure of sexual orientation (Button, 2001; Ragins & Cornwell, 2001), and organization-based self-esteem (i.e., "the degree that employees can satisfy their needs by participating in roles within the context of an organization"; Pierce, Gardner, Cummings, & Dunham, 1989, p. 625), and increased work withdrawal (i.e., desire to leave one's immediate work environment without quitting; Waldo, 1999) and turnover intentions (Ragins & Cornwell, 2001). A significant feature of the Button (2001) investigation was the assessment of how identification with one's sexual orientation moderated perceived treatment discrimination–work attitudes (job satisfaction and commitment) relationships. Results showed that stronger identification with gays/lesbians as a group amplified the negative discrimination–job satisfaction association, suggesting more debilitating effects of discrimination on work attitudes among gays/lesbians when sexual orientation is a central portion of the self-concept.

The extant literature on the mental and physical health ramifications of perceived sexual orientation discrimination underscores its robustly negative consequences. Perceived heterosexism is related to an increased number of health conditions (Waldo, 1999) and psychological distress (Waldo, 1999), after statistical control of general job stress. Mays and Cochran (2001) investigated the effects of perceived discrimination on mental and physical health outcomes. Compared to heterosexuals, gay, lesbian, and bisexual respondents had significantly greater odds of experiencing 11 lifetime discriminatory behaviors (e.g., not hired for a job, hassled by police; $OR = 1.82$, $p < .05$) and nine day-to-day discriminatory behaviors (e.g., treated as if not as good as others, verbal insults, threats and harassment;

$OR = 2.42$, $p < .05$). Furthermore, sexual orientation (1 = gay, lesbian, or bisexual) was significantly related to greater likelihoods of having any psychiatric disorder ($OR = 2.18$, $p < .05$), "poor" self-ratings of current mental health ($OR = 1.90$, $p < .05$), and high psychological distress ($OR = 1.56$, $p < .05$), showing that gay, lesbian, and bisexual respondents were more likely to report negative psychiatric conditions; however, these effects were attenuated to non-significance upon controlling for experiences of lifetime and day-to-day discrimination.

Huebner, Rebchook, and Kegeles (2004) investigated the relations between experiences of verbal harassment, perceived discrimination (e.g., in employment, housing, etc.), and physical violence and mental health outcomes (i.e., self-esteem and suicidal ideation), and reported higher perceived discrimination was related to reduced self-esteem and increased frequency of suicidal thoughts during the past two months. Additional results indicated that human immunodeficiency virus (HIV) status was significantly correlated with perceived discrimination ($OR = 2.59$, $p < .05$) and physical violence ($OR = 3.67$, $p < .05$), such that HIV-positive gay and bisexual men reported greater incidences of discrimination and physical violence than those who where HIV-negative. Moreover, gay and bisexual men who were "out" (i.e., openly expressed their sexual orientation to others) to more than half of the people they knew expressed higher incidences of verbal harassment ($OR = 1.45$, $p < .05$) and perceived discrimination ($OR = 1.73$, $p < .05$) than those who were "out" to only half or fewer of their acquaintances. Likewise, Waldo (1999) found that gay/lesbians who were more "out" experienced comparatively more overt forms of heterosexism than those were less "out" at work.

Perceived Disability-Based Discrimination

There is a virtual dearth of research addressing perceived disability-based discrimination in the organizational literature. The existing work presents a mixed picture of discrimination's effects on work outcomes among disabled individuals. Perry, Hendricks, and Broadbent (2000) examined the effects of disability status (0 = non-disability, 1 = some form of disability such as wheelchair bound, motor control deficits, visual and hearing deficits), perceived treatment discrimination (i.e., adequacy of medical, retirement, vacation, and sick leave benefits) and access discrimination (i.e., difficulties finding a job after graduation from college, a job related to one's chosen field, and the ability to

work as much as desired) on job satisfaction among recent college graduates. Disability status was positively related to access discrimination, especially for individuals with wheelchair and visual disabilities, while disability status was meaningfully correlated with access discrimination only for those with visual deficits compared to all other survey respondents. Most notably, access discrimination was negatively associated with job satisfaction, although disability status was associated with marginally higher job satisfaction, controlling for current health, ability to work, and other relevant control variables. These results suggest that since the disabled encounter many barriers to employment, any access to paid work is deemed satisfactory. A side effect of this tendency, however, is that employers underpay disabled workers for their work, and place them in lower-status jobs than their non-disabled colleagues (Schur, Kruse, Blasi, & Blanck, 2009).

Access discrimination has been highlighted as a work-related barrier amid people living with HIV/acquired immunodeficiency syndrome (AIDS). Martin, Brooks, Ortiz, and Veniegas (2003) showed that compared to those who continued to work after an HIV diagnosis, those who stopped working after contracting HIV communicated greater concerns about benefits losses, work-related health, discrimination, personal health care, and workplace accommodations. Greater HIV acuity level (i.e., the severity of HIV symptoms in ascending order from HIV asymptomatic, HIV symptomatic, and AIDS) was associated with more apprehension about work-related health and workplace accommodations.

Few studies have investigated the effects of perceived discrimination against the disabled on mental and physical health outcomes. The available work in this area has emphasized the stigmatizing effect of having a mental and/or physical disability, and has sought to delineate the result of such subordinate status on victims' well-being. As an illustrative study, Sanders Thompson, Noel, and Campbell (2004) studied the influence of perceived discrimination, in regard to a series of statuses (e.g., mental disability, physical disability, age, gender, race, religion, sexual orientation, etc.), on psychiatric symptoms (e.g., depression, anxiety, psychosis, or the extent to which one experiences hallucinations, hears voices, and feels paranoid) and perceived social rejection in a sample of 1,827 adults receiving mental health services. Findings revealed that respondents who reported discrimination based upon mental disabilities alone (i.e., major depression, bipolar, anxiety, or psychotic disorders), compared to those who encountered other forms of discrimination (e.g., race, gender, sexual orientation), also expressed lower feelings of social acceptance. In addition, mental disability discrimination, in combination with other discrimination bases, had even stronger negative effects on social acceptance, psychosis, and depression and anxiety, in contrast to respondents who experienced discrimination for reasons other than mental disability.

More recently, Alonso et al. (2009) assessed the associations between perceived stigma, defined as embarrassment and discriminatory treatment encountered due to one's mental illness, and mental and physical health outcomes (i.e., mental and physical quality of life, work limitations, social limitations, and help-seeking) in a sample of 8,796 non-institutionalized respondents from Belgium, France, Germany, Italy, the Netherlands, and Spain. Results showed that higher perceived stigma was correlated with lower poor physical health, and higher magnitudes of social and work limitations. Additionally, findings indicated that respondents with mental disorders had a greater likelihood of reporting perceived stigma than individuals with chronic physical disabilities ($OR = 3.80$, $p < .05$), thus illustrating the relatively greater stigma associated with mental versus physical disabilities. Correspondingly, using data collected across 17 countries including the Americas (e.g., the U.S. and Mexico), Asia (e.g., Japan and Israel), Oceania (New Zealand), Europe (e.g., Germany and France), and Africa (Nigeria), Alonso et al. (2008) found that those with physical and mental disabilities (e.g., anxiety and mood disorders combined) were significantly more likely to report perceiving stigma ($OR = 1.30$ and 3.40, $p < .05$) than individuals without disabilities.

Considering a broader array of health-related conditions, Van Brakel (2006) considered the effects of stigma associated with chronic health conditions such as HIV/AIDS, leprosy, tuberculosis, mental illness, disability, epilepsy, and other conditions on affected individuals. Reviewing research from around the world, the author concluded that stigma associated with these conditions has a number of negative effects on individuals including increased emotional stress and anxiety, increased psychiatric and psychological morbidity (incidence), reduced empowerment, and poorer (health) prognoses.

Summary

The availability evidence suggests that perceived discrimination based upon race-ethnicity, gender, age, sexual orientation, and disability status is associated with negative work attitudes and behaviors, and reductions in mental and physical health. The strongest available evidence exists for race-ethnicity and gender, while additional research examining the outcomes of perceived discrimination due to age, sexual orientation, and disability status are recommended. Pivotally, the reported findings have strong implications for organizations as the deterioration of organizational attitudes and pro-organizational behaviors resulting from discriminatory treatment can negatively impact employee retention (Hom, Roberson, & Ellis, 2008) and job performance (Griffeth & Hom, 2001), which, in turn, can compromise overall firm effectiveness (Gilbert & Ivancevich, 2000). Furthermore, employees who are victims of perceived discrimination may be compelled to file employment discrimination claims (Goldman et al., 2006; James & Wooten, 2006), which can be costly for organizations in terms of punitive damages awarded to successful plaintiffs, tarnished firm reputation (Roberson & Park, 2007), and reduced market share (Wright, Ferris, Hiller, & Kroll, 1995).

Conclusion

We began this chapter by stating that the research on employment discrimination is vast and fragmented. After writing this review, we still hold this opinion. While we know quite a bit about some topics, such as adverse impact, other areas remain virtually unexplored. This is summarized in Table 32.4. To conclude this chapter, we revisit the four issues examined (targets, causes, forms, and outcomes) and summarize where we think future research is needed.

Targets of Discrimination

Obviously, most research on discrimination has focused on racial-ethnic discrimination (primarily against blacks/African Americans) and women, with substantial, yet less, research focusing on age and disability discrimination. There are many reasons for this, including long histories of subjugation for these groups in the United States, legal concerns, and political awareness and activism by these group members. Although these are all important factors in stimulating research, we should not neglect other groups with traditionally shorter histories of discrimination in the United States (e.g., Arabs), that are not protected by federal law (e.g., overweight persons, GLBT persons), or that do not have the

Table 32.4 Summary of Research on Discrimination in the I/O Literature: Where We've Been and Directions for the Future

Research Area	Where We Have Been	Future Directions
Targets	Most research has concerned race (primarily African American) and sex/gender. A substantial body of literature is being built on age and disability discrimination. Also research on weight discrimination has become more popular.	Discrimination target characteristics needing more study include immigrant status, sexual orientation, religion, and other racial/ethnic groups. Research needs to focus on the extent to which different categories interact to influence the form and severity of discrimination. Models need to be developed that inform us of the extent to which we can generalize discrimination knowledge across different groups. Research needs to be done on generalizing discrimination theory across cultures. We need to study how context (e.g., history, law, population diversity) influences who becomes a target of discrimination and the form of that discrimination.
Causes of Discrimination	Much research focuses on cognitive processes (e.g., stereotyping) and social identity theory as the cause of discrimination. There is substantial research on individual differences as causes, although these are often treated as a moderator. Much of the research specifically addressing causes has been conducted in laboratory settings using students as respondents.	Research examining the generalizability of laboratory results to real organizational settings is needed. Longitudinal research is needed to connect causes of discrimination to actual discriminatory behavior. A more complex view of the causes of motivation needs to be taken that incorporates more macro and structural causes to develop multilevel framework.
Forms of Discrimination	A great deal of research in I/O has been done on adverse impact and methods to reduce it. There is a growing body of research on sexual harassment. A great deal of research has also been done on evaluation disparities, especially with regards to sex and race. However, this research is somewhat inconclusive. Pay and promotion discrimination have been given a great deal of attention in other fields, but relatively little attention in the I/O literature.	Systematic work needs to be conducted to examine the extent to which laboratory results generalize to the field. Systematic research needs to be conducted on specific moderators that influence when and in what form discrimination will occur. Most lines of research only focus on one group (e.g., AI: black vs. white, pay discrimination: female vs. male). Research needs to be done on other groups (e.g. religious harassment). More research needs to be done on subtle discrimination in organizational settings, harassment for reasons other than sex, and the I/O related causes of pay and promotion disparities. New research needs to be conducted on the interactive and long-term effects of various forms of discrimination.

(Continued)

Table 32.4 (Continued)

Research Area	Where We Have Been	Future Directions
Perceived Discrimination and Outcomes	A great deal of research has been conducted on perceived discrimination and its outcomes in terms of work attitudes, work behaviors (e.g. organizational citizenship behavior), and psychological and physical outcomes.	Research needs to continue on focusing on what leads to perceptions of discrimination. Future research needs to focus more heavily on the prevention of negative outcomes due to discrimination. Research needs to continue examining how people effectively cope with various forms of discrimination. Most of this research is currently being done in the area of sexual harassment. Research on perceptions of discrimination and outcomes need to extend to groups and characteristics that have received little attention in the literature (e.g., religion, sexual orientation).

activist contingents which serve to fuel both public and scholarly concern (e.g., new immigrants). Questions remain as to whether we can generalize what we have learned about racial-ethnic and sex discrimination to other stigmatized groups. At the very least, different stereotypes prevail about various groups, leading to particularly unique emotions and behavioral tendencies (Cuddy, Fiske, & Glick, 2007; Cuddy et al., 2009; Fiske, Cuddy, & Glick, 2006; Fiske, Cuddy, Glick, & Xu, 2002). Furthermore, assorted groups experience distinctive issues and have particular histories that may impact the form of discrimination they encounter. For example, workplace accommodation is legally required for religion and disability, which perpetuate forms of resentment and retaliation by non-beneficiaries, issues that are less relevant for other disparaged groups (Colella, 2001; Colella, Paetzold, & Belliveau, 2004).

A further concern regarding targets of discrimination is that the stigmatized groups and characteristics that are stigmatized vary across cultures. For instance, white-black differences are very important in the United States, whereas skin color is a weaker basis for stigmatization in many Latin American countries. Although discrimination research in the I/O literature is sometimes undertaken in other cultures (recall that most investigations of immigrants are performed outside the U.S.), there is very little discussion of how discrimination against various groups generalizes across national cultures.

An additional limitation of discrimination research lies in the relative neglect of context in determining who will be targeted for discrimination, with two exceptions. One exception to this trend is the literature on stereotypical fit, which primarily concerns women and the gender-role stereotype of the job (Heilman, 1983); however, as noted earlier, this phenomenon generalizes across age, disability, weight. Another exception is the work on numerical distinctiveness and tokenism, which states that treatment (and potentially discrimination) is a function of the proportional representation of one's group in the job, hierarchical level, and the organization as a whole. Moreover, there are other contextual factors such as the threat posed by a new group (e.g., immigrants entering a new market), occupation, and even location of the organization (e.g., are gay and lesbian people treated differently in municipalities where it is illegal to discriminate based on sexual orientation, compared to where there are no such laws?; Ragins & Cornwell, 2001). The economics, legal, sociological, and industrial relations literatures can offer myriad insights about what contextual factors may matter, and thus we recommend that these domains be better integrated into the extant I/O psychology discrimination literature.

Causes of Discrimination

Of the four major topics addressed in our review, the richest knowledge base has been culminated in regard to the causes of discrimination. A number of theoretical perspectives, including the cognitive, individual differences, social identity, and other bases of discrimination, have been quite informative in explaining why it occurs; however, several methodological issues plague work in these areas, potentially limiting their applicability to applied, work settings. First, as stated previously, most of these investigations have taken place in artificial, laboratory settings, thus raising concerns about the generalizability of observed findings.

Second, scholarship on the causes of discrimination has been largely cross-sectional; therefore, the I/O literature offers little knowledge regarding the true "causes" of discrimination. More accurately, the extant research is more informative with respect to "correlates" of discrimination. To provide stronger conclusions about causation, additional longitudinal research is necessary to determine predictor variables, measured at Time 1, predicting discrimination measures collected at Time 2 and beyond. Essentially, there is no work of this nature in the I/O psychology domain, particularly as related to organization-level causes of discrimination (Gelfand et al., 2005).

A final issue with regard to causes of discrimination is the relative neglect of mediating factors linking "causes" and "discrimination." More specifically, in organizational work, virtually no research has assessed the mechanisms through which various antecedents relate to discrimination. Research on demography (e.g., racial-ethnic or gender representation) suffers in this regard, as typically scholars provide little empirical insight concerning the mechanisms (e.g., work attitudes and behaviors) through which a given level of demography relates to disparate outcomes (e.g., Joshi et al., 2006; McKay et al., 2008; Zatzick et al., 2003).

Forms of Discrimination

Most of the I/O psychology research has focused on either adverse impact or bias in evaluations (including hiring, performance appraisal, and interviews). On the one hand, a good deal of recent study has been devoted to sexual harassment and the determinants of sex differentials in pay. These are the most probable forms of discrimination to precipitate lawsuits, and thus it is not surprising that they garner the bulk of research attention. On the other hand, there are other forms of discrimination that potentially may be the foundations for civil actions, yet that receive scant research consideration. These include discrimination in job assignments, termination, training and apprenticeship programs, classification of employees, and recruitment. In addition to these more major types of discrimination, we discussed subtle discrimination research, which is still in its infancy in the I/O

psychology literature. Future research that addresses these issues is sorely needed.

A second concern regarding forms of discrimination is a methodological one. It pertains to the generalizability of research conducted in the laboratory, and in artificial work contexts, to real life, organizational settings. This topic was covered early in this chapter, and therefore, we will not repeat those points here (see the December 2008 issue of *Industrial and Organizational Psychology*). However, we should note that meta-analyses of evaluation discrimination have reported mixed results, with some finding discriminatory effects slightly stronger in the field (race: Kraiger & Ford, 1985; disability: Ren et al., 2008), no difference between laboratory and field settings (attractiveness: Hosoda et al., 2003), or weaker relations in the field than in the laboratory (age: Gordon & Arvey, 2004). Thus, clear conclusions about the extent to which laboratory findings regarding evaluation can be generalized to the field remain elusive. Accordingly, additional theory-based investigation is necessary to better delineate the contextual factors that perpetuate the likelihood of discrimination (Heilman & Eagly, 2008).

An additional limitation of research on forms of discrimination is that such work tends to be "decontextualized," that is, the survey data are collected across, rather than within, organizations. The typical designs of such studies (e.g., Avery, McKay, & Wilson, 2008; Pavalko et al., 2003; Perry et al., 2000; Ragins & Cornwell, 2001; Sanchez & Brock, 1996) is to administer a survey (via mail, by hand, or the Internet) to individuals employed in a variety of organizations, and to examine relations between factors such as organizational policies and procedures, racial-ethnic and/or gender representation, self-reports of perceived discrimination, and various forms of work attitudes and behaviors. Such designs, however, are problematic because it is unclear whether there is consensus that a given set of organizational policies exist within a particular firm, since the data has been collected from *individuals across firms*. Yet, organizational climate work suggests that, at a unit or organizational level, consensual views of policies give rise to distinct unit/organizational climates (Bowen & Ostroff, 2004; Reichers & Schneider, 1990). Thus, it would be more appropriate to explore policy-based antecedents of discrimination using multilevel designs because employees are nested within organizations, and firm contextual features affect employees' perceptions (Chan, 1998; Kozlowski & Klein, 2000). Moreover, aggregating workers' perceptions of policies to the unit- or firm-level would require analysis of within-group agreement, to ensure that there is sufficient consistency in employees' reports of organizational policies, in line with climate-based research. Importantly, aggregate-level policy perceptions might have unique effects on employees' reports of discrimination above and beyond individual-level reports, an area yet to be explored in the I/O psychology domain.

Generally, discrimination research also has failed to incorporate multilevel theorizing regarding potential moderators of discrimination-outcome relationships. For instance, recent work on diversity climate shows that, at the aggregate, unit-level, racial-ethnic disparities in work performance are mitigated by supportive climates (McKay et al., 2008). Similarly, Gonzalez and DeNisi (2009) found that diversity climate interacted with employee race-ethnicity, such that climate exhibited stronger relations with work attitudes among minorities than their white counterparts. Given such findings, future discrimination work should incorporate multilevel theorizing about how constructs such as diversity climate moderate perceived discrimination's relationships with work attitudes, and job performance, as well as psychological and physical health.

Finally, various forms of discrimination usually are discussed and examined independently. Specifically, work in this area has failed to address the interactive effects and long-term effects of various types of discrimination. For example, uncertainty remains concerning the extent to which harassment influences performance expectations. In other words, bias in performance expectations may not be due to bias per se, but may result from poor performance resulting from other forms of discrimination, in this case harassment. Furthermore, Murphy and Cleveland (1995) proposed that a job incumbent's performance history may affect ratings of his or her future performance; thus, such reasoning could be usefully applied to work on evaluation bias. By and large, time-based perspectives on the operation of evaluative bias are lacking in the I/O psychology, despite the presence of suggestive research in this regard (Reb & Cropanzano, 2007).

Perceived Discrimination and Outcomes

As our review illustrated, a great deal of research has been conducted on perceived discrimination and its outcomes. Research in this area needs to move in a direction that focuses on how organizations can prevent discrimination and perceptions of discrimination. I/O psychologists have devoted a great deal of effort to understanding and ameliorating adverse impact in selection, recruiting, and other personnel decisions. The focus has been on discrimination during organizational entry. Scholarly work needs to be done that focuses on the prevention of more subtle forms of discrimination and discrimination that occurs every day.

In pursuit of this goal, some scholars have focused attention on what factors influence perceptions of discrimination. Harris, Lievens, and Van Hoye (2004) developed a model of the antecedents to perceived discrimination. Central to their model is the fairness heuristic that individuals form concerning decisions made about them. Rather than considering all information, they focus on information that is easily available and presented first. Other research has shown that organizational justice is an important determinant of how individuals react to actual employment discrimination (Foley et al., 2002; Goldman, 2001, 2003). More research along these lines would lead to prescriptions about how organizations can actually address perceived discrimination.

The diversity literature, which has grown exponentially over the past 15 years, should also be integrated with the discrimination literature (Smith, Brief, & Colella, 2010). Research has shown us that perceptions of diversity climate moderate the effects of perceived discrimination (Triana, Garcia, & Colella, 2010), but there is little scholarly work on how those perceptions are formed and what organizations can do to develop positive diversity climate perceptions. Again, this calls for multilevel theorizing and empirical examination.

Conclusion

The topic of employment discrimination has been given ample attention, yet there still remains much ground to cover. We know little about discrimination against groups other than sex and race; explanations for discrimination remain mostly cognitive; most research has focused on adverse impact, sexual harassment, and discrimination in evaluations; and there has been little research on how organizations can manage perceptions of discrimination. It is time for the I/O psychology literature on discrimination to move in three general directions. The first is to integrate research across disciplines (in addition to social psychology). Sociology, economics, and legal theory offer directions that have remained essentially ignored in our literature, such as the role of threat in fostering discrimination. The second direction is to take a multilevel view of discrimination. For example, research on sexual harassment has found that climate is the primary driver of harassment, with individual differences playing a secondary role. Most of our research focuses on individual-level, micro–variables, or organizational climate variables—we need to integrate these lines of research. Finally, we need to aim research on issues that can help inform organizations and the legal system on how to remedy employment discrimination. Much of research focuses on demonstrating that discrimination exists, but little focuses on how to get rid of it (one exception is the literature on adverse impact). Theory exists to guide this research, but I/O psychologists are uniquely placed to turn this theory into practice and then to assess the value of that practice.

References

Adorno, T. W., Frenkel-Brunswik, E., Levinson, D. J., & Stanford, R. N. (1950). *The authoritarian personality*. New York: Harper.

Age Discrimination in Employment Act. (1967). Pub. L. No. 90–202, 81 Stat. 602.

Ainspan, N. D. (2006). *Employers' opinions and attitudes of employing people with disabilities*. Paper presented at the annual meeting of the Society for Industrial and Organizational Psychology, Dallas, TX.

Alkadry, M. G., & Tower, L. E. (2006). Unequal pay: The role of gender. *Public Administration Review, 66*, 888–898.

Allport, G. (1954). *The nature of prejudice*. Reading, MA: Addison-Wesley.

Alonso, J., Buron, A., Bruffaerts, R., He, Y., Posada-Villa, J., Lepine, J. P., et al. (2008). Association of perceived stigma and mood and anxiety disorders: Results from the World Mental Health Surveys. *Acta Psychiatrica Scandinavia, 118*, 305–314.

Alonso, J., Buron, A., Rojas-Farreras, S., de Graaf, R., Haro, J. M., de Girolamo, G., et al. (2009). Perceived stigma among individuals with common mental disorders. *Journal of Affective Disorders, 118*, 180–186.

Altemeyer, R. A. (Ed.). (1981). *Right-wing authoritarianism*. Winnipeg: University of Manitoba Press.

Altemeyer, R. A. (1998). The other "authoritarian personality." In M. P. Zanna (Ed.), *Advances in experimental social psychology* (Vol. 30, pp. 47–91). New York: Academic Press.

Americans with Disabilities Act (ADA). (1990). Pub. L. No. 101–336, § 2, 104 Stat. 328.

Anderson, B. J., Binder, M., & Krause, K. (2002). The motherhood wage penalty revisited: Experience, heterogeneity, work effort, and work-schedule flexibility. *Industrial and Labor Relations Review, 56*(2), 273–294.

Andreyeva, T., Puhl, R. M., & Brownell, K. D. (2008). Changes in perceived weight discrimination among Americans. *Obesity, 16*, 1129–1134.

Antecol, H., & Cobb-Clark, D. (2003). Does sexual harassment training change attitudes? A view from the federal level. *Social Science Quarterly, 84*(4), 826–842.

Antecol, H., & Cobb-Clark, D. A. (2008). Identity and racial harassment. *Journal of Economic Behavior and Organization, 66*, 529–557.

Arabshebani, G. R., Marin, A., & Wadsworth, J. (2007). Variations in gay pay in the USA and the UK. In M. V. L. Badgett & J. Frank (Eds.), *Sexual orientation discrimination: An international perspective* (pp. 44–61). London: Routledge.

Arriola, K. R., & Cole, E. R. (2001). Framing the affirmative action debate: Attitudes toward out-group members and white identity. *Journal of Applied Social Psychology, 31*, 2462–2483.

Arthur, W., Jr., Day, E. A., McNelly, T. L., & Edens, P. S. (2003). A meta-analysis of the criterion-related validity of assessment center dimensions. *Personnel Psychology, 56*, 125–154.

Arthur, W., Jr., & Doverspike, D. (2005). Achieving diversity and reducing discrimination in the workplace through human resource management practices: Implications of research and theory for staffing, training, and rewarding performance. In R. L. Dipboye & A. Colella (Eds.), *Discrimination at work: The psychological and organizational bases* (pp. 305–327). San Francisco: Jossey-Bass.

Arvey, R. D. (1979). *Fairness in selecting employees*. Reading, MA: Addison-Wesley.

Ashburn-Nardo, L. (2008). Fairly representing the stereotype literature? *Industrial and Organizational Psychology, 1*, 412–414.

Ashmore, R. D. (1981). Sex stereotypes and implicit personality theory. In D. L. Hamilton (Ed.), *Cognitive processes in stereotyping and intergroup behavior* (pp. 37–81). Hillsdale, NJ: Erlbaum.

Avery, D. R. (2003). Racial differences in perceptions of starting salaries: How failing to discriminate can perpetuate discrimination. *Journal of Business and Psychology, 17*(4), 439–450.

Avery, D. R. (2011). Why the playing field remains uneven: Impediments to promotions in organizations. In S. Zedeck (Ed.), *APA Handbook of industrial and organizational psychology* (Vol. 3, pp. 577–613). Washington, DC: American Psychological Association.

Avery, D., McKay, P., & Wilson, D. (2008). What are the odds? How demographic similarity affects the prevalence of perceived employment discrimination. *Journal of Applied Psychology, 93*(2), 235–249.

Avery, D. R., McKay, P. F., Wilson, D. C., & Tonidandel, S. (2007). Unequal attendance: The relationships between race, organizational diversity cues, and absenteeism. *Personnel Psychology, 60*, 875–902.

Babcock, L., Gelfand, M. J., Small, D., & Stayn, H. (2006). Gender differences in the propensity to initiate negotiations. In D. D. Crèmer, M. Zeelenberg, & J. K. Murnighan (Eds.), *Social psychology and economics* (pp. 239–259). Mahwah, NJ: Erlbaum.

Babcock, L., & Laschever, S. (2003). *Women don't ask: Negotiation and the gender divide*. Princeton, NJ: Princeton University Press.

Bacharach, S., & Bamberger, P. (2004). Diversity and the union: The effect of demographic dissimilarity on members' union attachment. *Group & Organization Management, 29*(3), 385–418.

Badgett, M. V. L. (2001). *Money, myths and change: The economic lives of lesbians and gay men*. Chicago: University of Chicago Press.

Badgett, M. V. L., Lau, H., Sears, B., & Ho, D. (2007). *Bias in the workplace: Consistent evidence of sexual orientation and gender identity discrimination*. Los Angeles: University of California, The Williams Institute.

Baldi, S., & McBrier, D. B. (1997). Do the determinants of promotion differ for blacks and whites? *Work and Occupations, 24*(4), 478–497.

Bargh, J. A., Raymond, P., Pryor, J. B., & Strack, F. (1995). Attractiveness of the underling: An automatic power-sex association and its consequences for sexual harassment and aggression. *Journal of Personality and Social Psychology, 68,* 768–781.

Barnes, L. L., Mendes de Leon, C. F., Lewis, T. T., Bienias, J. L., Wilson, R. S., & Evans, D. A. (2008). Perceived discrimination and mortality in a population-based study of older adults. *American Journal of Public Health, 98,* 1241–1247.

Baskerville Watkins, M., Kaplan, S., Brief, A. P., Shull, A., Dietz, J., Mansfield, M.-T., & Cohen, R. (2006). Does it pay to be a sexist? The relationship between modern sexism and career outcomes. *Journal of Vocational Behavior, 69*(3), 524–537.

Begany, J. J., & Milburn, M. A. (2002). Psychological predictors of sexual harassment: Authoritarianism, hostile sexism, and rape myths. *Psychology of Men and Masculinity, 3,* 119–126.

Belliveau, M. A. (2005). Blind ambition? The effects of social networks and institutional sex composition on the job search outcomes of elite coeducational and women's college graduates. *Organization Science, 16*(2), 134–150.

Berdahl, J. L. (2007a). Harassment based on sex: Protecting social status in the context of gender hierarchy. *Academy of Management Review, 32,* 641–658.

Berdahl, J. L. (2007b). The sexual harassment of uppity women. *Journal of Applied Psychology, 92,* 425–437.

Berdahl, J. L., & Moore, C. (2006). Workplace harassment: Double jeopardy for minority women. *Journal of Applied Psychology, 91*(2), 426–436.

Berg, N., & Lien, D. (2002). Measuring the effect of sexual orientation on income: Evidence of discrimination? *Contemporary Economic Policy, 20*(4), 394–414.

Bergman, M. E., Langhout, R. D., Palmieri, P. A., Cortina, L. M., & Fitzgerald, L. F. (2002). The (un)reasonableness of reporting: Antecedents and consequences of reporting sexual harassment. *Journal of Applied Psychology, 87*(2), 230–242.

Bergman, M. E., Palmieri, P. A., Drasgow, F., & Ormerod, A. J. (2007). Racial and ethnic harassment and discrimination: In the eye of the beholder? *Journal of Organizational Health Psychology, 12,* 144–160.

Bergmann, B. R. (1974). Occupational segregation, wages and profits when employers discriminate by race or sex. *Eastern Economic Journal, 1*(2), 103–110.

Biddle, D., & Sill, N. S. (1999). Protective services physical ability tests: Establishing pass/fail, ranking, and banding procedures. *Public Personnel Management, 28,* 217–225.

Bielby, D., & Bielby, W. (1998). She works hard for the money: Household responsibilities and the allocation of work effort. *American Journal of Sociology, 93,* 1031–1059.

Biernat, M., & Vescio, T. K. (2002). She swings, she hits, she's great, she's benched: Implications of gender-based shifting standards for judgment and behavior. *Personality and Social Psychology Bulletin, 28,* 66–77.

Bjelland, M. B., Bruyère, S. M., Houtenville, A. J., Ruiz-Quintanilla, S. A., & Webber, D. A. (2008). Trends in disability employment discrimination claims: Implications for rehabilitation counseling practice, administration, training, and research (Working paper). Ithaca, NY.

Blakley, B. R., Quiñones, M. A., Crawford, M. S., & Jago, I. A. (1994). The validity of isometric tests. *Personnel Psychology, 47,* 247–274.

Blandford, J. M. (2003). The nexus of sexual orientation and gender in the determination of earnings. *Industrial and Labor Relations Review, 56*(4), 622–642.

Blanton, H., & Jaccard, J. (2008). Unconscious racism: A concept in pursuit of a measure. *Annual Review of Sociology, 34,* 277–297.

Blanton, H., Jaccard, J., Klick, J., Mellers, B., Mitchell, G., & Tetlock, P. E. (2009). Strong claims and weak evidence: Reassessing the predictive validity of the IAT. *Journal of Applied Psychology, 94,* 567–582.

Blau, F. D., & Kahn, L. M. (2006). The U.S. gender pay gap in the 1990s: Slowing convergence. *Industrial & Labor Relations Review, 60,* 45–66.

Blau, F. D., & Kahn, L. M. (2007). The gender pay gap: Have women gone as far as they can go? *Academy of Management Perspectives, 21*(1), 7–23.

Blumer, H. (1958). Race prejudice as a sense of group position. *Pacific Sociological Review, 23,* 3–7.

Bobko, P., Roth, P. L., & Potosky, D. (1999). Derivation and implications of a meta-analytic matrix incorporating cognitive ability, alternative predictors, and job performance. *Personnel Psychology, 52,* 561–589.

Bobo, L. D., & Suh, S. A. (2000). Surveying racial discrimination: Analyses from a multiethnic labor market. In L. D. Bobo, M. L. Oliver, J. J. H. Johnson, & J. A. Valenzuela (Eds.), *Prismatic metropolis: Inequality in Los Angeles* (pp. 523–560). New York: Russell Sage Foundation.

Borman, W. C., & Motowidlo, S. J. (1993). Expanding the criterion domain to include elements of contextual performance. In N. Schmitt & W. C. Borman (Eds.), *Personnel selection in organizations* (pp. 71–98). San Francisco: Jossey-Bass.

Bowen, D. E., & Ostroff, C. (2004). Understanding HRM-firm performance linkages: The role of the "strength" of the HRM system. *Academy of Management Review, 29,* 203–221.

Bowen, C. C., Swim, J. K., & Jacobs, R. R. (2000). Evaluating gender biases on actual job performance of real people: A meta-analysis. *Journal of Applied Social Psychology, 30,* 2194–2215.

Bowes-Sperry, L., & Tata, J. (1999). A multiperspective framework of sexual harassment: Reviewing two decades of research. In G. N. Powell (Ed.), *Handbook of gender and work* (pp. 263–280). Thousand Oaks, CA: Sage.

Bowles, H. J., Babcock, L., & Lai, L. (2007). Social incentives for gender differences in the propensity to initiate negotiations: Sometimes it does hurt to ask. *Organizational Behavior and Human Decision Processes, 103,* 84–103.

Braddock, D., & Bachelder, L. (1994). *The glass ceiling and persons with disabilities.* Washington, DC: U.S. Department of Labor, The Glass Ceiling Commission.

Branscombe, N., Schmitt, M., & Harvey, R. (1999). Perceiving pervasive discrimination among African Americans: Implications for group identification and well-being. *Journal of Personality and Social Psychology, 77*(1), 135–149.

Brass, D. (1985). Men's and women's networks: A study of interaction patterns and influence in an organization. *Academy of Management Journal, 28,* 327–343.

Brenner, O. C., Tomkiewicz, J., & Schein, V. E. (1989). The relationships between sex role stereotypes and requisite management characteristics revisited. *The Academy of Management Journal, 32,* 662–669.

Brewer, M. B. (1991). The social self: On being the same and different at the same time. *Personality and Social Psychology Bulletin, 17,* 475–482.

Brewer, M. B. (2007). The importance of being we: Human nature and intergroup relations. *American Psychologist, 62*, 738–751.

Brief, A. P., Buttram, R. T., & Dukerich, J. M. (2001). Collective corruption in the corporate world: Toward a process model. In M. E. Turner (Ed.), *Groups at work: Advances in theory and research* (pp. 471–499). Hillsdale, NJ: Erlbaum.

Brief, A. P., Butz, R. M., & Deitch, E. A. (2005). Organizations as reflections of their environments: The case of race composition. In R. L. Dipboye & A. Colella (Eds.), *Discrimination at work: The psychological and organizational bases* (pp. 119–148). Mahwah, NJ: Erlbaum.

Brief, A. P., Dietz, J., Cohen, R. R., Pugh, S. D., & Vaslow, J. B. (2000). Just doing business: Modern racism and obedience to authority as explanations for employment discrimination. *Organizational Behavior and Human Decision Processes, 81*, 72–97.

Buckley, M. R., Jackson, K. A., Bolino, M. C., Veres, J. G., III., & Feild, H. S. (2007). The influence of relational demography on panel interview ratings: A field experiment. *Personnel Psychology, 60*, 627–646.

Budig, M. J. (2002). Male advantage and the gender composition of jobs: Who rides the glass escalator? *Social Problems, 66*, 204–225.

Budig, M., & England, P. (2001). The wage penalty for motherhood. *American Sociological Review, 66*, 204–225.

Button, S. B. (2001). Organizational efforts to affirm sexual diversity: A cross-level examination. *Journal of Applied Psychology, 86*, 17–28.

Byrne, D. (1971). *The attraction paradigm*. New York: Academic Press.

Carroll, J. B. (1993). *Human cognitive abilities: A survey of factor-analytic studies*. New York: Cambridge University Press.

Castilla, E. (2008). Gender, race, and meritocracy in organizational careers. *American Journal of Sociology, 113*(6), 1479–1526.

Chan, D. (1998). Functional relations among constructs in the same content domain at different levels of analysis: A typology of compositional models. *Journal of Applied Psychology, 83*, 234–246.

Chan, D. K-S., Lam, C. B., Chow, S. Y., & Chung, S. F. (2008). Examining the job-related, psychological, and physical outcomes of workplace sexual harassment: A meta-analytic review. *Psychology of Women Quarterly, 32*, 362–376.

Chattopadhyay, P., Tluchowska, M., & George, E. (2004). Identifying the ingroup: A closer look at the influence of demographic dissimilarity on employee social identity. *Academy of Management Review, 29*, 180–202.

Chrobot-Mason, D., & Hepworth, W. K. (2005). Examining perceptions of ambiguous and unambiguous threats of racial harassment and managerial response strategies. *Journal of Applied Social Psychology, 35*, 2215–2261.

Chung-Yan, G., & Cronshaw, S. (2002). A critical re-examination and analysis of cognitive ability tests using the Thorndike model of fairness. *Journal of Occupational and Organizational Psychology, 75*(4), 489–509.

Civil Rights Act of 1964, P. L. 88–353, 78 Stat. 241 (1964).

Civil Rights Act of 1991. P. L.192–1066, 105 Stat. (1991).

Cleveland, J. N., & Colella, A. (2010). Who defines performance, contribution, and value? In J. L. Farr & N. T. Tippins (Eds.), *Handbook of employee selection*. London: Routledge Academic.

Cleveland, J. N., Vescio, T. K., & Barnes-Farrell, J. L. (2005). Gender discrimination in organizations. In R. L. Dipboye & A. Colella (Eds.), *Discrimination at work: The psychological and organizational bases* (pp. 149–176). Mahwah, NJ: Erlbaum.

Colella, A. (1996). The organizational socialization of employees with disabilities: Theory and research. In G. R. Ferris (Ed.), *Research in personnel and human resources management* (Vol. 14, pp. 351–417). Greenwich, CT: JAI Press.

Colella, A. (2001). Coworker distributive fairness judgments of the workplace accommodation of employees with disabilities. *Academy of Management Review, 26*, 100–116.

Colella, A., & Bruyère, S. M. (2011). Disability and employment: New directions for industrial/organizational psychology. In S. Zedeck (Ed.), *APA Handbook of industrial and organizational psychology* (Vol. 2, pp. 473–504). Washington, DC: American Psychological Association.

Colella, A., DeNisi, A. S., & Varma, A. (1998). The impact of ratee's disability on performance judgments and choice as partner: The role of disability-job fit stereotypes and interdependence of rewards. *Journal of Applied Psychology, 83*, 102–111.

Colella, A., & Garcia, M. F. (2004, August). *Paternalism: Hidden discrimination?* Paper presented at the meeting of the Academy of Management, New Orleans.

Colella, A., Paetzold, R., & Belliveau, M. A. (2004). Factors affecting coworkers' procedural justice inferences of the workplace accommodations of employees with disabilities. *Personnel Psychology, 57*(1), 1–23.

Colella, A., & Stone, D. (2005). Disability discrimination. In R. L. Dipboye & A. Colella (Eds.), *Discrimination at work: The psychological and organizational bases* (pp. 227–254). Mahwah, NJ: Erlbaum.

Colella, A., & Varma, A. (1999). Disability-job fit stereotypes and the evaluation of persons with disabilities at work. *Journal of Occupational Rehabilitation, 9*, 79–95.

Colella, A., & Varma, A. (2001). The impact of subordinate disability on leader-member exchange dynamics. *Academy of Management Journal, 44*, 304–315.

Copus, D. (2005). A lawyer's view: Avoiding junk science. In F. J. Landy (Ed.), *Employment discrimination litigation: Behavioral, quantitative, and legal perspectives* (pp. 450–462). San Francisco: Jossey-Bass.

Cortina, L. M., & Wasti, S. A. (2005). Profiles in coping: Responses to sexual harassment across persons, organizations, and cultures. *Journal of Applied Psychology, 90*(1), 182–192.

Costa, P. T., & McCrae, R. R. (1992). *The NEO Personality Inventory* (Rev. ed.). Odessa, FL: Psychological Assessment Resources.

Craig, T., Kelly, J., & Driscoll, D. (2001). Participant perceptions of potential employers. *Sex Roles, 44*(7–8), 389–400.

Crocker, J., Major, B., & Steele, C. (1998). Social stigma. In D. M. Gilbert, S. T. Fiske, & G. Lindzey (Eds.), *The handbook of social psychology* (pp. 540–553). New York: McGraw Hill.

Crosby, F. J., Bromley, S., & Saxe, L. (1980). Recent unobtrusive studies of black and white discrimination and prejudice: A literature review. *Psychological Bulletin, 87*, 546–563.

Crosby, F. J., Williams, J. C., & Biernat, M. (2004). The maternal wall. *Journal of Social Issues, 60*(4), 675–682.

Cuddy, A. J. C., Fiske, S. T., & Glick, P. (2007). The BIAS map: Behaviors from intergroup stereotypes. *Journal of Personality and Social Psychology, 92*, 631–648.

Cuddy, A. J. C., Fiske, S. T., Kwan, V. S. Y., Glick, P., Demoulin, S., Leyens, J.-P., et al. (2009). Stereotype content model across cultures: Towards universal similarities and some differences. *British Journal of Social Psychology, 48*, 1–33.

Cuddy, A., Norton, M., & Fiske, S. (2005). This old stereotype: The pervasiveness and persistence of the elderly stereotype. *Journal of Social Issues, 61*(2), 267–285.

Cunningham, G. B., & Sagas, M. (2007). Examining potential differences between men and women in the impact of treatment discrimination. *Journal of Applied Social Psychology, 37*, 3010–3024.

Czajka, J. M., & DeNisi, A. S. (1988). Effects of emotional disability and clear performance standards on performance ratings. *Academy of Management Journal, 31*, 394–404.

Dall'Ara, E., & Maas, A. (1999). Studying sexual harassment in the laboratory: Are egalitarian women at higher risk? *Sex Roles, 41*, 681–704.

Daniels, S. R., Colella, A., & Nishii, L. (2010, August). *Minority status and paternalism: Examining the influence on employee work experiences and turnover.* Paper presented at the annual meeting of the Academy of Management, Montreal.

Dasgupta, N. (2009). Mechanisms underlying the malleability of implicit prejudice and stereotypes: The role of automaticity and cognitive control. In T. D. Nelson (Ed.), *Handbook of prejudice, stereotyping, and discrimination* (pp. 267–284). New York: Psychology Press.

Davidson, M., & Friedman, R. A. (1998). When excuses don't work: The persistent injustice effect among black managers. *Administrative Science Quarterly, 43*, 154–183.

Davison, H. K., & Burke, M. J. (2000). Sex discrimination in simulated employment contexts: A meta-analytic investigation. *Journal of Vocational Behavior, 56*, 225–248.

Dean, M. A., Roth, P. L., & Bobko, P. (2008). Ethnic and gender subgroup differences in assessment center ratings: A meta-analysis. *Journal of Applied Psychology, 93*, 685–691.

Deitch, E. A., Barsky, A., Butz, R. M., Chan, S., Brief, A. P., & Bradley, J. (2003). Subtle yet significant: The existence and impact of everyday racial discrimination in the workplace. *Human Relations, 56*, 1299–1324.

Devine, P. G. (1989). Stereotypes and prejudice: Their automatic and controlled components. *Journal of Personality and Social Psychology, 56*, 5–18.

Diaz, R. M., Ayala, G., Bein, E., Henne, J., & Marin, B. V. (2001). The impact of homophobia, poverty, and racism on the mental health of gay and bisexual Latino men: Findings from 3 U.S. cities. *American Journal of Public Health, 91*(6), 927–932.

Diekman, A. B., & Eagly, A. H. (2000). Stereotypes as dynamic constructs: Women and men of the past, present, and future. *Personality and Social Psychology Bulletin, 10*, 1171–1188.

Dion, K., Berscheid, E., & Walster, E. (1972). What is beautiful is good. *Journal of Personality and Social Psychology, 24*, 285–290.

Dipboye, R. L. (1985). Some neglected variables in research on discrimination in appraisals. *Academy of Management Review, 10*, 116–127.

Dipboye, R. L. (2005). Looking the part: Bias against the physically unattractive as a discrimination issue. In R. L. Dipboye & A. Colella (Eds.), *Discrimination at work: The psychological and organizational bases* (pp. 281–301). Mahwah, NJ: Erlbaum.

Dipboye, R. L., & Colella, A. (2005). An introduction. In R. L. Dipboye & A. Colella (Eds.), *Discrimination at work: The psychological and organizational bases* (pp. 1–8). Mahwah, NJ: Erlbaum.

Dovidio, J. F., & Gaertner, S. L. (Eds.). (1986). *Prejudice, discrimination, and racism.* Orlando, FL: Academic Press.

Dovidio, J. F., & Gaertner, S. L. (2000). Aversive racism and selection decisions: 1989 and 1999. *Psychological Science, 11*(4), 315–319.

Dovidio, J. F., & Gaertner, S. L. (2004). Aversive racism. In M. P. Zanna (Ed.), *Advances in experimental social psychology* (Vol. 36, pp. 1–52). Thousand Oaks, CA: Sage.

Dovidio, J., Glick, P., & Rudman, L. (2005). *On the nature of prejudice: Fifty years after Allport.* Malden: Blackwell Publishing.

Dovidio, J. F., & Hebl, M. R. (2005). Discrimination at the level of the individual: Cognitive and affective factors. In R. L. Dipboye & A. Colella (Eds.), *Discrimination at work: The psychological and organizational bases* (pp. 11–36). Mahwah, NJ: Erlbaum.

Driscoll, D. M., Kelly, J. R., & Henderson, W. L. (1998). Can perceivers identify likelihood to sexually harass? *Sex Roles, 38*(7–8), 557–588.

Duckitt, J. (2001). A dual-process cognitive-motivational theory of ideology and prejudice. In M. P. Zanna (Ed.), *Advances in experimental social psychology* (Vol. 33, pp. 41–113). San Diego: Academic Press.

Duehr, E. E., & Bono, J. E. (2006). Men, women, and managers: Are stereotypes finally changing? *Personnel Psychology, 59*, 815–846.

Duriez, B., & Van Hiel, A. (2002). The march of modern fascism: A comparison of social dominance orientation and authoritarianism. *Personality and Individual Differences, 32*, 1199–1213.

Eagly, A. H. (1987). Reporting sex differences. *American Psychologist, 42*(7), 756–757.

Eagly, A. H., Ashmore, R. D., Makhijani, M. G., & Longo, L. C. (1991). What is beautiful is good, but…: A meta-analytic review of research on the physical attractiveness stereotype. *Psychological Bulletin, 110*, 109–128.

Eagly, A. H., & Diekman, A. B. (2005). What is the problem? Prejudice as an attitude-in-context. In J. F. Dovidio, P. Glick, & L. A. Rudman (Eds.), *On the nature of prejudice: Fifty years after Allport* (pp. 19–35). Oxford: Blackwell Publishing.

Eagly, A. H., & Karau, S. J. (2002). Role congruity theory of prejudice toward female leaders. *Psychological Review, 109*(3), 573–598.

Eagly, A. H., Makhijani, M. G., & Klonsky, B. G. (1992). Gender and the evaluation of leaders: A meta-analysis. *Psychological Bulletin, 111*, 2–33.

Eagly, A. H., Wood, W., & Diekman, A. (2000). Social role theory of sex differences and similarities: A current appraisal. *The developmental social psychology of gender* (pp. 123–174). Mahwah, NJ: Erlbaum.

Echebarria-Echabe, A., & Guede, E. F. (2007). A new measure of anti-Arab prejudice: Reliability and validity evidence. *Journal of Applied Social Psychology, 37*, 1077–1091.

Ely, R., & Padavic, I. (2007). A feminist analysis of organizational research on sex differences. *Academy of Management Review, 32*(4), 1121–1143.

Ely, R. J. (1995). The power of demography: Women's social constructions of gender identity at work. *Academy of Management Journal, 38*, 589–634.

England, P., Farkas, G., Kilbourne, B., & Dou, T. (1988). Explaining occupational sex segregation and wages: Findings from a model with fixed effects. *American Sociological Review, 53*, 544–558.

Ensher, E. A., Grant-Vallone, E. J., & Donaldson, S. I. (2001). Effects of perceived discrimination on job satisfaction, organizational commitment, organizational citizenship behavior, and grievances. *Human Resource Development Quarterly, 12*(1), 53–72.

Equal Pay Act. (1963). Pub. L. No. 88–38, 77 Stat. 56 (codified as amended at 29 U.S.C. § 206(d)).

Essed, P. (1991). *Understanding everyday racism.* Newbury Park, CA: Sage.

Esses, V. M., Dietz, J., & Bhardway, A. (2006). The role of prejudice in the discounting of immigrant skills. In R. Mahalingam (Ed.), *Cultural psychology of immigrants* (pp. 113–130). Mahwah, NJ: Erlbaum.

Esses, V. M., Dovidio, J. F., & Hodson, G. (2002). Public attitudes toward immigration in the United States and Canada in response to the September 11, 2001 'Attack on America.' *Analysis of Social Issues and Public Policy, 2*(1), 69–85.

Fazio, R. H., Jackson, J. R., Dunton, B. C., & Williams, C. J. (1995). Variability in automatic activation as an unobtrusive measure of racial attitudes: A bona fide pipeline. *Journal of Personality and Social Psychology, 69*, 1013–1027.

Feingold, A. (1992). Good-looking people are not what we think. *Psychological Bulletin, 111*, 304–341.

Fields, J., & Wolff, E. N. (1991). The decline of sex segregation and the wage gap, 1970–80. *Journal of Human Resources, 26*(4), 608–621.

Fikkan, J., & Rothblum, E. (2005). Weight bias in employment. In K. D. Brownell, R. M. Puhl, M. B. Schwartz, & L. Rudd (Eds.), *Weight bias: Nature, consequences, and remedies* (pp. 15–28). New York: The Guilford Press.

Finkelstein, L. M., Burke, M. J., & Raju, N. S. (1995). Age discrimination in simulated employment contexts: An integrative analysis. *Journal of Applied Psychology, 80*, 652–663.

Fischer, A. R., & Holtz, K. B. (2007). Perceived discrimination and women's psychological distress: The roles of collective and personal self-esteem. *Journal of Counseling Psychology, 54*(2), 154–164.

Fiske, S. T. (1998). Stereotyping, prejudice, and discrimination. In S. T. Fiske, D. T. Gilbert, & G. Lindsey (Eds.), *The handbook of social psychology* (Vol. 2, pp. 357–411). New York: McGraw-Hill.

Fiske, S. T., Cuddy, A. J. C., & Glick, P. (2006). Universal dimensions of social cognition: Warmth and competence. *Trends in Cognitive Science, 11*, 77–83.

Fiske, S. T., Cuddy, A. J. C., Glick, P., & Xu, J. (2002). A model of (often mixed) stereotype content: Competence and warmth respectively follow from perceived competence and competition. *Journal of Personality and Social Psychology, 82*, 878–902.

Fiske, S. T., & Neuberg, S. L. (1990). A continuum of impression formation from category-based to individuating processes: Influences of information and motivation on attention and interpretation. In M. P. Zanna (Ed.), *Advances in experimental social psychology* (Vol. 23, pp. 1–74). New York: Academic Press.

Fitzgerald, L. F. (1990, March). *Assessing strategies for coping with harassment: A theoretical/empirical approach.* Paper presented at the midwinter conference of the Association of Women in Psychology, Tempe, AZ.

Fitzgerald, L. F., Drasgow, F., Hulin, C. L., Gelfand, M. J., & Magley, V. J. (1997). Antecedents and consequences of sexual harassment in organizations. *Journal of Applied Psychology, 82*, 578–589.

Fitzgerald, L. F., Gelfand, M. J., & Drasgow, F. (1995). Measuring sexual harassment: Theoretical and psychometric advances. *Basic and Applied Social Psychology, 17*, 425–445.

Fitzgerald, L. F., Hulin, C. L., & Drasgow, F. (1994). The antecedents and consequences of sexual harassment in organizations: An integrated model. In G. P. Keita & J. J. Hurrell (Eds.), *Job stress in a changing workforce: Investigating gender, diversity, and family* (pp. 55–73). Washington, DC: American Psychological Association.

Fitzgerald, L. F., Magley, V. J., Drasgow, F., & Waldo, C. R. (1999). Measuring sexual harassment in the military: The Sexual Experiences Questionnaire (SEQ-DoD). *Military Psychology, 11*(3), 243–263.

Fitzgerald, L. F., Shullman, S. L., Bailey, N., Richards, M., Swecker, J., Gold, A., Ormerod, A. J., & Weitzman, L. (1988). The incidence and dimensions of sexual harassment in academia and the workplace. *Journal of Vocational Behavior, 32*, 152–175.

Foldes, H., Duehr, E., & Ones, D. (2008). Group differences in personality: Meta-analyses comparing five U.S. racial groups. *Personnel Psychology, 61*(3), 579–616.

Foley, S., Hang-Yue, N., & Wong, A. (2005). Perceptions of discrimination and justice: Are there gender differences in outcomes? *Group & Organization Management, 30*, 421–450.

Foley, S., Kidder, D. L., & Powell, G. N. (2002). The perceived glass ceiling and justice perceptions: An investigation of Hispanic law associates. *Journal of Management, 28*, 471–496.

Ford, J. K., Kraiger, K., & Schechtman, S. L. (1986). Study of race effects in objective indices and subjective evaluations of performance: A meta-analysis of performance criteria. *Psychological Bulletin, 99*, 330–337.

Frazer, R. A., & Wiersma, U. J. (2001). Prejudice versus discrimination in the employment interview: We may hire equally, but our memories harbour prejudice. *Human Relations, 54*(2), 173–191.

Gael, S., Grant, D. L., & Ritchie, R. J. (1975). Employment test validation for minority and nonminority clerks with work sample criteria. *Journal of Applied Psychology, 60*, 420–426.

Gaertner, S. L., & Dovidio, J. F. (1986). The aversive form of racism. In J. F. Dovidio & S. L. Gaertner (Eds.), *Prejudice, discrimination, and racism* (pp. 61–89). San Diego: Academic Press.

Garcia, M. F., Colella, A., Triana, M. D. C., Smith, A., & Baskerville Watkins, M. (under review). Perceptions of supervisor paternalism: A scale development and validation.

Garstka, T. A., Schmitt, M. T., Branscombe, N. R., & Hummert, M. L. (2004). How young and older adults differ in their responses to perceived age discrimination. *Psychology and Aging, 19*, 326–335.

Gaugler, B. B., Rosenthal, D. B., Thorton, G. C., III., & Bentson, C. (1987). Meta-analysis of assessment center validity [Monograph]. *Journal of Applied Psychology, 72*, 493–511.

Gee, G. C. (2002). A multilevel analysis of the relationship between institutional and individual racial discrimination and health status. *American Journal of Public Health, 92*, 615–623.

Gelfand, M. J., Nishii, L. H., Raver, J. L., & Schneider, B. (2005). Discrimination in organizations: An organizational-level systems perspective. In R. L. Dipboye & A. Colella (Eds.), *Discrimination at work: The psychological and organizational processes* (pp. 119–148). Mahwah, NJ: Erlbaum.

Gerhart, B. (1990). Voluntary turnover and alternative job opportunities. *Journal of Applied Psychology, 75*(5), 467–476.

Gerhart, B., & Rynes, S. (1991). Determinants and consequences of salary negotiations by male and female MBA graduates. *Journal of Applied Psychology, 76*(2), 256–262.

Gettman, H. J., & Gelfand, M. J. (2007). When the customer shouldn't be king: Antecedents and consequences of sexual harassment by clients and customers. *Journal of Applied Psychology, 92*(3), 757–770.

Gilbert, J. A., & Ivancevich, J. M. (2000). Valuing diversity: A tale of two organizations. *Academy of Management Executive, 14*, 93–105.

Giles, M. W., & Evans, A. S. (1986). The power approach to intergroup hostility. *Journal of Conflict Resolution, 30*, 469–486.

Gladwell, M. (2005). *Blink: The power of thinking without thinking.* New York: Little Brown.

Glick, P., & Fiske, S. (1996). The ambivalent sexism inventory: Differentiating hostile and benevolent sexism. *Journal of Personality and Social Psychology, 70*(3), 491–512

Goffman, E. (1963). *Stigma: Notes on the management of spoiled identity.* Englewood Cliffs, NJ: Prentice-Hall.

Goldberg, C. B. (2005). Relational demography and similarity-attraction in interview assessments and subsequent offer decisions. *Group and Organization Management, 30*, 597–624.

Goldberg, L. R. (1993). The structure of phenotypic traits. *American Psychologist, 48*, 26–34.

Golden, H., Hinkle, S., & Crosby, F. J. (2001). Reactions to affirmative action: Substance and semantics. *Journal of Applied Social Psychology, 31*, 73–88.

Goldin, C., & Rouse, C. (2000). Orchestrating impartiality: The impact of "blind" auditions on female musicians. *American Economic Review, 90*(4), 715–741.

Goldman, B. M. (2001). Toward an understanding of employment discrimination claiming: An integration of organizational justice and social information processing. *Personnel Psychology, 54*, 361–387.

Goldman, B. M. (2003). The application of referent cognitions theory to legal-claiming by terminated workers: The role of organizational justice and anger. *Journal of Management, 29*, 705–728.

Goldman, B. M., Gutek, B. A., Stein, J. H., & Lewis, K. (2006). Employment discrimination in organizations: Antecedents and consequences. *Journal of Management, 32*(6), 786.

Goldstein, H. W., Zedeck, S., & Goldstein, I. L. (2002). G: Is this your final answer? *Human Performance, 15*, 123–142.

Gonzalez, J. A., & DeNisi, A. S. (2009). Cross-level effects of demography and diversity climate on organizational attachment and firm effectiveness. *Journal of Organizational Behavior, 30*, 21–40.

Gordon, R. A., & Arvey, R. D. (2004). Age bias in laboratory and field settings: A meta-analytic investigation. *Journal of Applied Psychology, 34*, 468–492.

Graddy, K., & Pistaferri, L. (2000). Wage differences by gender: Evidence from recently graduated MBAs. *Oxford Bulletin of Economics and Statistics, 62*, 837–854.

Greenwald, A. G., & Banaji, M. R. (1995). Implicit social cognition: Attitudes, self-esteem, and stereotypes. *Psychological Review, 102*, 4–27.

Greenwald, A. G., Banaji, M. R., Rudman, L. A., Farnham, S. D., Nosek, B. A., & Mellott, D. S. (2002). A unified theory of implicit attitudes, stereotypes, self-esteem, and self-concept. *Psychological Review, 109*, 3–25.

Greenwald, A. G., & Krieger, L. H. (2006). Implicit bias: Scientific foundations. *California Law Review, 94*, 945–967.

Greenwald, A. G., McGhee, D. E., & Schwartz, J. L. K. (1998). Measuring individual differences in cognition: The Implicit Association Test. *Journal of Personality and Social Psychology, 85*, 197–216.

Griffeth, R. W., & Hom, P. W. (2001). *Retaining valued employees.* Thousand Oaks, CA: Sage.

Gutek, B. A., Cohen, A. G., & Tsui, A. (1996). Reactions to perceived sex discrimination. *Human Relations, 49*, 791–813.

Gutek, B. A., Murphy, R. O., & Douma, B. (2004). A review and critique of the Sexual Experiences Questionnaire (SEQ). *Law and Human Behavior, 28*, 457–482.

Hamilton, V. L., & Sanders, J. (1992). Responsibility and risk in organizational crimes of obedience. In B. M. Staw & L. L. Cummings (Eds.), *Research in organizational behavior* (Vol. 14, pp. 49–90). Greenwich, CT: JAI Press.

Hanges, P. L., & Ziegert, J. C. (2008). Stereotypes about stereotype research. *Industrial and Organizational Psychology, 1*, 436–438.

Harris, M., Lievens, F., & Van Hoye, G. (2004). 'I think they discriminated against me': Using prototype theory and organizational justice theory for understanding perceived discrimination in selection and promotion situations. *International Journal of Selection and Assessment, 12*(1–2), 54–65.

Harrison, D. A., Kravitz, D. A., Mayer, D. M., Leslie, L. M., & Lev-Arey, D. (2006). Understanding attitudes towards affirmative action programs in employment: Summary and meta-analysis of 35 years of research. *Journal of Applied Psychology, 91*, 1013–1036.

Hastorf, A. H., Northcraft, G. B., & Piciotto, S. R. (1979). Helping the handicapped: How realistic is the performance feedback received by the physically handicapped. *Personality and Social Psychology Bulletin, 5*, 373–376.

Hattrup, K., O'Connell, M. S., & Wingate, P. H. (1998). Prediction of multidimensional criteria: Distinguishing task and contextual performance. *Human Performance, 11*, 305–319.

Hauenstein, N. M. A., Sinclair, A. L., Robson, V., Quintella, Y., & Donovan, J. J. (2003, April). *Performance dimensionality and the occurrence of ratee race effects.* Paper presented at the 18th Annual Conference of the Society for Industrial and Organizational Psychology, Orlando, FL.

Hebl, M. R., Foster, J. B., Mannix, L. M., & Dovidio, J. F. (2002). Formal and interpersonal discrimination: A field study of bias towards homosexual applicants. *Personality and Social Psychology Bulletin, 28*, 815–825.

Hebl, M. R., & Heatherton, T. F. (1998). The stigma of obesity in women: The difference is black and white. *Personality and Social Psychology Bulletin, 24*, 417–426.

Hedge, J., Borman, W., & Lammlein, S. (2006). *The aging workforce: Realities, myths, and implications for organizations* (pp. 7–25). Washington, DC: American Psychological Association.

Heilman, M. E. (1983). Sex bias in work settings: The lack of fit model. *Research in Organizational Behavior, 5*, 269–298.

Heilman, M. E., Block, C. J., & Lucas, J. (1992). Presumed incompetent? Stigmatization and affirmative action efforts. *Journal of Applied Psychology, 77*, 536–544.

Heilman, M. E., Block, C. J., Martell, R. F., & Simon, M. C. (1989). Has anything changed? Current characterizations of men, women, and managers. *Journal of Applied Psychology, 74*(6), 935–942.

Heilman, M. E., Block, C. J., & Stathatos, P. (1997). The affirmative action stigma of incompetence: Effects of performance information ambiguity. *Academy of Management Journal, 40,* 603–625.

Heilman, M. E., & Eagly, A. H. (2008). Gender stereotypes are alive, well, and busy producing discrimination. *Industrial and Organizational Psychology, 1,* 393–398.

Heilman, M. E., & Haynes, M. C. (2005). No credit where credit is due: Attributional rationalization of women's success in male-female teams. *Journal of Applied Psychology, 90*(5), 905–916.

Heilman, M. E., & Okimoto, T. G. (2008). Motherhood: A potential source of bias in employment decisions. *Journal of Applied Psychology, 93*(1), 189–198.

Heilman, M., & Okimoto, T.G. (2007). Why are women penalized for success at male tasks?: The implied communality deficit. *Journal of Applied Psychology, 92,* 81–92.

Heilman, M. E., Wallen, A. S., Fuchs, D., & Tamkins, M. M. (2004). Penalties for success: Reactions to women who succeed at male gender typed tasks. *Journal of Applied Psychology, 89,* 416–427.

Heneman, H. G., III, & Judge, T. A. (2009). *Staffing organizations* (6th ed.). Middleton, WI: Mendota House.

Henle, C. A., & Hogler, R. (2004). The duty of accommodation and the Workplace Religious Freedom Act of 2003: From bad policy to worse law. *Labor Law Journal, 55,* 155–165.

Henry, P., & Sears, D. (2002). The symbolic racism 2000 scale. *Political Psychology, 23*(2), 253–283.

Hogan, J. C. (1991). Physical abilities. In M. D. Dunnette & L. M. Hough (Eds.), *Handbook of industrial and organizational psychology* (2nd ed., Vol. 2, pp. 753–831). Palo Alto, CA: Consulting Psychologists Press.

Holder, J. C., & Vaux, A. (1998). African American professionals: Coping with occupational stress in predominately white work environments. *Journal of Vocational Behavior, 53,* 315–333.

Holzer, H. J., & Ludwig, J. (2003). Measuring discrimination in education: Are methodologies from labor and housing markets useful? *Teachers College Record, 105,* 1147–1178.

Holzer, H. J., & Neumark, D. (2000). Assessing affirmative action. *Journal of Economic Literature, 38,* 483–568.

Hom, P. W., Roberson, L., & Ellis, A. D. (2008). Challenging conventional wisdom about who quits: Revelations from corporate America. *Journal of Applied Psychology, 93,* 1–34.

Hosoda, M., Stone-Romero, E., & Coats, G. (2003). The effects of physical attractiveness on job-related outcomes: A meta-analysis of experimental studies. *Personnel Psychology, 56*(2), 431–462.

Hough, L. M., Oswald, F. L., & Ployhart, R. E. (2001). Determinants, detection and amelioration of adverse impact in personnel selection procedures: Issues, evidence and lessons learned. *International Journal of Selection and Assessment, 9,* 152–194.

Huebner, D. M., Rebchook, G. M., & Kegeles, S. M. (2004). Experiences of harassment, discrimination, and physical violence among young gay and bisexual men. *American Journal of Public Health, 94,* 1200–1203.

Huffcutt, A. I., Conway, J. M., Roth, P. L., & Stone, N. J. (2001). Identification and meta-analytic assessment of psychological constructs measured in employment interviews. *Journal of Applied Psychology, 86,* 897–913.

Huffcutt, A. I., & Roth, P. L. (1998). Racial group differences in employment interview evaluations. *Journal of Applied Psychology, 83,* 179–189.

Huffcutt, A. I., Roth, P. L., & McDaniel, M. A. (1996). A meta-analytic investigation of cognitive ability in employment interview evaluations: Moderating characteristics and implications for incremental validity. *Journal of Applied Psychology, 81,* 459–473.

Huffman, M. L., & Cohen, P. N. (2004). Racial wage inequality: Job segregation and devaluation across U.S. labor markets. *American Journal of Sociology, 109,* 902–936.

Hulin, C. L., Fitzgerald, L. F., & Drasgow, F. (1996). Organizational influences on sexual harassment. In M. S. Stockdale (Ed.), *Sexual harassment in the workplace* (Vol. 5, pp. 127–150). Thousand Oaks, CA: Sage.

Hunter, J. E. (1983). A causal analysis of cognitive ability, job knowledge, job performance, and supervisory ratings. In F. Landy, S. Zedeck, & J. Cleveland (Eds.), *Performance measurement and theory* (pp. 257–266). Hillsdale, NJ: Erlbaum.

Hunter, J. E. (1986). Cognitive ability, cognitive aptitudes, job knowledge, and job performance. *Journal of Vocational Behavior, 29,* 340–362.

Hunter, J. E., & Hunter, R. F. (1984). Validity and utility of alternative predictors of job performance. *Psychological Bulletin, 96,* 72–98.

Hunter, J. E., & Schmidt, F. L. (2004). *Methods of meta-analysis: Correcting error and bias in research findings* (2nd ed.). Newbury Park, CA: Sage.

Hurtz, G. M., & Donovan, J. J. (2000). Personality and job performance: The big five revisited. *Journal of Applied Psychology, 85,* 869–879.

Ibarra, H. (1995a). Personal networks of women and minorities in management. *Academy of Management Review, 18,* 56–87.

Ibarra, H. (1995b). Race, opportunity, and diversity of social circles in managerial networks. *Academy of Management Journal, 38,* 673–703.

Ibarra, H., & Andrews, S. (1993). Power, social influence, and sense making: Effects of network centrality and proximity on employee perceptions. *Administrative Science Quarterly, 38*(2), 277–303.

Jackman, M. R. (2005). Rejection or inclusion of outgroups. In J. F. Dovidio, P. Glick, & L. A. Rudman (Eds.), *On the nature of prejudice: Fifty years after Allport* (pp. 89–105). Oxford: Blackwell Publishing.

Jackson, L. A., Gardner, P. D., & Sullivan, L. A. (1992). Explaining gender differences in self-pay expectations: Social comparison standards and perceptions of fair pay. *Journal of Applied Psychology, 77*(5), 651–663.

Jackson, L. A., Hunter, J. E., & Hodge, C. N. (1995). Physical attractiveness and intellectual competence: A meta-analytic review. *Social Psychology Quarterly, 58,* 108–122.

Jackson, R. A., & Newman, M. A. (2004). Sexual harassment in the federal workplace revisited: Influences on sexual harassment by gender. *Public Administration Review, 64,* 705–717.

Jacobs, J., & Steinberg, R. (1990). Compensating differentials and the male-female wage gap: Evidence from the New York State comparable worth study. *Social Forces, 69*(2), 439–468.

James, E. H., & Wooten, L. P. (2006). Diversity crises: How firms manage discrimination lawsuits. *Academy of Management Journal, 49,* 1103–1118.

James, K., Lovato, C., & Khoo, G. (1994). Social identity correlates of minority workers' health. *Academy of Management Journal, 37,* 383–396.

Jarrell, S. B., & Stanley, T. D. (2004). Declining bias and gender wage discrimination? A meta-regression analysis. *The Journal of Human Resources, 39,* 828–838.

Jensen, A. R. (1998). *The g factor: The science of mental ability.* Westport, CT: Praeger.

Jetten, J., Spears, R., & Postmes, T. (2004). Intergroup distinctiveness and differentiation: A meta-analytic integration. *Journal of Personality and Social Psychology, 86*, 862–879.

Johnson, J. W. (2001). The relative importance of task and contextual performance dimensions to supervisor judgments of overall performance. *Journal of Applied Psychology, 86*, 984–996.

Johnson, R., & Heal, L. W. (1976). Private employment agency responses to the physically handicapped applicant in a wheelchair. *Journal of Applied Rehabilitation Counseling, 7*, 12–21.

Joshi, A., Liao, H., & Jackson, S. E. (2006). Cross-level effects of workplace diversity on sales performance and pay. *Academy of Management Journal, 49*, 459–481.

Jost, J. T. (1997). An experimental replication of the depressed entitlement effect among women. *Psychology of Women Quarterly, 21*, 387–393.

Jost, J. T., & Banaji, M. R. (1994). The role of stereotyping in system justification and the production of false consciousness. *British Journal of Social Psychology, 33*, 1–27.

Jost, J. T., Banaji, M. R., & Nosek, B. A. (2004). A decade of system justification theory: Accumulated evidence of conscious and unconscious bolstering of the status quo. *Political Psychology, 25*, 881–919.

Jost, J. T., Glaser, J., Kruglanski, A. W., & Sulloway, F. J. (2003). Political conservatism as motivated social cognition. *Psychological Bulletin, 129*, 339–375.

Jost, J. T., & Hamilton, D. L. (2005). Stereotypes in our culture. In J. F. Dovidio, P. P. Glick, & L. A. Rudman (Eds.), *On the nature of prejudice: Fifty years after Allport* (pp. 208–224). Oxford: Blackwell Publishing.

Jost, J. T., & Thompson, E. P. (2000). Group-based dominance and opposition to equality as independent predictors of self-esteem, ethnocentrism, and social policy attitudes among African Americans and European Americans. *Journal of Experimental Social Psychology, 36*, 209–232.

Judge, T., & Livingston, B. A. (2008). Is the gap more than gender? A longitudinal analysis of gender, gender role orientation, and earnings. *Journal of Applied Psychology, 93*(5), 994–1012.

Kanter, R. M. (1977). Some effects of proportions on group life: Skewed sex ratios and responses to token women. *American Journal of Sociology, 829*(5), 965–990.

Katz, I., & Glass, D. C. (1979). An ambivalence amplification theory of behavior toward the stigmatized. In W. Austin & S. Worchel (Eds.), *The social psychology of intergroup relations* (pp. 55–70). Monterey, CA: Brooks/Cole.

Keaveny, T. J., Inderrieden, E. J., & Toumanoff, P. G. (2007). Gender differences of pay in young managers in the United States: A comprehensive view. *Journal of Labor Research, 28*, 327–346.

Kelly, E. P. (2008). Accommodating religious expression in the workplace. *Employee Rights and Responsibilities Journal, 20*, 45–56.

Kelman, H. C., & Hamilton, V. L. (1989). *Crimes of obedience.* New Haven, CT: Yale University Press.

Kessler, R. C., Mickelson, K. D., & Williams, D. R. (1999). The prevalence, distribution, and mental health correlates of perceived discrimination in the United States. *Journal of Health and Social Behavior, 40*, 208–230.

King, E. B. (2008). The effect of bias on the advancement of working mothers: Disentangling legitimate concerns from inaccurate stereotypes as predictors of advancement in academe. *Human Relations, 61*, 1677–1711.

King, E. B., Shapiro, J., Hebl, M., Singletary, S., & Turner, S. (2006). The stigma of obesity in customer service: A mechanism for remediation and bottom-line consequences of interpersonal discrimination. *Journal of Applied Psychology, 91*(3), 579–593.

Kite, M. E., & Johnson, B. T. (1988). Attitudes toward older and younger adults: A meta-analysis. *Psychology and Aging, 3*, 233–244.

Kite, M. E., Stockdale, G. D., Whitley, B. E., & Johnson, B. T. (2005). Attitudes toward younger and older adults: An updated meta-analytic review. *Journal of Social Issues, 61*, 241–266.

Klawitter, M. M., & Flatt, V. (1998). The effects of state and local antidiscrimination policies on earnings for gays and lesbians. *Journal of Policy Analysis and Management, 17*(4), 658–686.

Klimoski, R. J. (1993). Predictor constructs and their measurement. In N. Schmitt & W. C. Borman (Eds.), *Personnel selection in organizations* (pp. 99–134). San Francisco: Jossey-Bass.

Knapp, D. E., Faley, R. H., Ekeberg, S. E., & DuBois, C. L. Z. (1997). Determinants of target responses to sexual harassment: A conceptual framework. *Academy of Management Review, 22*, 687–729.

Knapp, D. E., Faley, R. H., & Long, L. K. (2006). The Americans with Disabilities Act: A review and synthesis of the legal literature with implications for practitioners. *Equal Opportunities International, 5*, 354–372.

Kozlowski, S. W. J., & Klein, K. J. (2000). A multilevel approach to theory and research in organizations: Contextual, temporal, and emergent processes. In K. J. Klein & S. W. J. Kozlowski (Eds.), *Multilevel theory, research, and methods in organizations* (pp. 3–90). San Francisco: Jossey-Bass.

Kraiger, K., & Ford, J. K. (1985). A meta-analysis of ratee race effects in performance ratings. *Journal of Applied Psychology, 70*, 56–65.

Kriska, S. D. (1984). *Firefighter selection test validation study for the city of Columbus.* Columbus, OH: Civil Service Commission.

Lai, L. (2008). The glass ceiling for Asian Americans: How perceptions of competence and social skills explain hiring differentials. Unpublished Ph.D. dissertation. Pittsburgh, PA: Carnegie Mellon University.

Landrine, H., Klonoff, E. A., Gibbs, J., Manning, V., & Lund, M. (1995). Physical and psychiatric correlates of gender discrimination: An application of the schedule of sexist events. *Psychology of Women Quarterly, 19*, 473–492.

Landy, F. J. (Ed.). (2005). *Employment discrimination litigation: Behavioral, quantitative, and legal perspectives.* San Francisco: Jossey-Bass.

Landy, F. J. (2008). Stereotypes, bias, and personnel decisions: Strange and stranger. *Industrial and Organizational Psychology, 1*, 379–392.

Landy, F. J., Shankster-Crawley, L., & Kohler Moran, S. (1995). Advancing personnel selection and placement methods. In A. Howard (ed.), *The changing nature of work* (pp. 252–289). San Francisco: Jossey-Bass.

Latham, G. P., & Wexley, K. N. (1994). *Increasing productivity through performance appraisal.* Reading, MA: Addison-Wesley.

Lee, J.-Y., Heilmann, S. G., & Near, J. P. (2004). Blowing the whistle on sexual harassment: Test of a model of predictors and outcomes. *Human Relations, 57*, 297–322.

Lee, K., Gizzarone, M., & Ashton, M. C. (2003). Personality and the likelihood to sexually harass. *Sex Roles, 49*, 59–69.

Lengnick-Hall, M. (1995). Sexual harassment research: A methodological critique. *Personnel Psychology, 48*(4), 841–864.

Leslie, L. M., King, E. B., Bradley, J. C., & Hebl, M. R. (2008). Triangulation across methodologies: All signs point to persistent stereotyping and discrimination in organizations. *Industrial and Organizational Psychology, 1*, 399–404.

Levine, R. A., & Campbell, D. T. (1972). *Ethnocentrism: Theories of conflict, ethnic attitudes, and group behavior.* New York: Wiley.

Livermore, G., & She, P. (2007). *Limitations in the National Disability Data System.* Ithaca, NY: Cornell University.

Loretto, W., Duncan, C., & White, P. (2000). Ageism and employment: controversies, ambiguities and younger people's perceptions. *Ageing and Society, 20*(3), 279–302.

Lueptow, L. B., Garovich-Szabo, L., & Lueptow, M. B. (2001). Social change and the persistence of sex typing: 1974–1997. *Social Forces, 80*, 1–35.

Lyness, K. S., & Heilman, M. E. (2006). When fit is fundamental: Performance evaluations and promotions of upper-level female and male managers. *Journal of Applied Psychology, 91*, 777–785.

Lyness, K. S., & Judiesch, M. K. (2001). Are female managers quitters? The relationships of gender, promotions, and family leaves of absence to voluntary turnover. *Journal of Applied Psychology, 86*, 1167–1178.

Maass, A., Cadinu, M., Guarnieri, G., & Grasselli, A. (2003). Sexual harassment under identity threat: The computer harassment paradigm. *Journal of Personality and Social Psychology, 85*(5), 853–870.

Macrae, C. N., & Bodenhausen, G. V. (2000). Social cognition: Thinking categorically about others. *Annual Review of Psychology, 51*, 93–120.

Major, B. (1987). Gender, justice, and the psychology of entitlement. In P. Shaver & C. Hendrick (Eds.), *Review of personality and social psychology: Sex and gender* (Vol. 7, pp. 124–148). Newbury Park, CA: Sage.

Major, B. (1994). From social inequality to personal entitlement: The role of social comparisons, legitimacy appraisals, and group memberships. *Advances in Experimental Social Psychology, 26*, 293–355.

Major, B., & Deaux, K. (1982). Individual differences in justice behavior. In J. Greenberg & R. I. Cohen (Eds.), *Equity and justice in social behavior* (pp. 43–76). New York: Academic Press.

Major, B., & Konar, E. (1984). An investigation of sex differences in pay expectations and their possible causes. *Academy of Management Journal, 27*(4), 777–792.

Major, B., McFarlin, D. B., & Gagnon, D. (1984). Overworked and underpaid: On the nature of gender differences in personal entitlement. *Journal of Personality and Social Psychology, 47*(6), 1399–1412.

Major, B., & O'Brien, L. T. (2005). The social psychology of stigma. *Annual Review of Psychology, 56*, 393–421.

Malamut, A. B., & Offerman, L. R. (2001). Coping with sexual harassment: Personal, environmental, and cognitive determinants. *Journal of Applied Psychology, 86*, 1152–1166.

Marini, M. M. (1989). Sex differences in earnings in the United States. *Annual Review of Sociology, 15*, 343–380.

Marlow, C. M., Schneider, S. L., & Nelson, C. E. (1996). Gender and attractiveness biases in hiring decisions: Are more experienced managers less biased? *Journal of Applied Psychology, 81*, 11–21.

Martell, R. F. (1991). Sex bias at work: The effects of attentional and memory demands on performance ratings of men and women. *Journal of Applied and Social Psychology, 21*, 1939–1960.

Martell, R. F. (2006). Sex bias at work: The effects of attentional and memory demands on performance ratings of men and women. *Journal of Applied Social Psychology, 21*, 1939–1960.

Martin, D. J., Brooks, R. A., Ortiz, D. J., & Veniegas, R. C. (2003). Perceived employment barriers and their relation to workforce-entry intent among people with HIV/AIDS. *Journal of Occupational Health Psychology, 8*, 181–194.

Mays, V., & Cochran, S. (2001). Mental health correlates of perceived discrimination among lesbian, gay, and bisexual adults in the United States. *American Journal of Public Health, 91*, 1869–1876.

McClelland, K., & Hunter, C. (1992). The perceived seriousness of racial harassment. *Social Problems, 39*, 92–107.

McConahay, J. B. (1983). Modern racism and modern discrimination: The effects of race, racial attitudes, and context on simulated hiring decisions. *Personality and Social Psychology Bulletin, 9*, 551–558.

McConahay, J. B. (1986). Modern racism, ambivalence, and the modern racism scale. In J. D. Dovidio & S. L. Gaertner (Eds.), *Prejudice, discrimination, and racism* (pp. 91–125). San Diego: Academic Press.

McConnell, A. R., & Leibold, J. M. (2001). Relations among the Implicit Association Test, discriminatory behavior, and explicit measures of racial attitudes. *Journal of Experimental Social Psychology, 37*, 435–442.

McDaniel, M. A., Morgeson, F. P., Finnegan, E. B., Campion, M. A., & Braverman, E. P. (2001). Use of situational judgment tests to predict job performance: A clarification of the literature. *Journal of Applied Psychology, 86*, 730–740.

McDaniel, M. A., Whetzel, D. L., Schmidt, F. L., & Maurer, S. D. (1994). The validity of employment interviews: A comprehensive review and meta-analysis. *Journal of Applied Psychology, 79*, 599–616.

McEvoy, G. M., & Cascio, W. F. (1989). Cumulative evidence of the relationship between employee age and job performance. *Journal of Applied Psychology, 74*, 11–17.

McGuire, W. J., & McGuire, C. V. (1981). The spontaneous self-concept as affected by personal distinctiveness. In K. Gergen, M. D. Lynch, & A. A. Norem-Hebeisen (Eds.), *Self-concept: Advances in theory and research* (pp. 147–171). New York: Ballinger.

McGuire, W. J., McGuire, C. V., Child, P., & Fujioka, T. (1978). Salience of ethnicity in the self-concept as a function of one's ethnic distinctiveness in the social environment. *Journal of Personality and Social Psychology, 36*, 511–520.

McGuire, W. J., McGuire, C. V., & Winton, W. (1979). Effects of household sex composition on the salience of one's gender in the spontaneous self-concept. *Journal of Experimental Social Psychology, 1*, 77–90.

McGuire, W. J., & Padawer-Singer, A. (1976). Trait salience in the spontaneous self-concept. *Journal of Personality and Social Psychology, 33*, 743–754.

McKay, P. F., & Avery, D. R. (2006). What has race got to do with it? Unraveling the role of racioethnicity in job seekers' reactions to site visits. *Personnel Psychology, 59*, 395–429.

McKay, P. F., Avery, D. R., & Morris, M. A. (2008). Mean racial differences in employee sales performance: The moderating role of diversity climate. *Personnel Psychology, 61*, 349–374.

McKay, P. F., & McDaniel, M. A. (2006). A reexamination of black-white mean differences in work performance: More data, more moderators. *Journal of Applied Psychology, 91*, 538–554.

McMenamin, T., Miller, S. M., & Polivka, A. E. (2006). *Discussion and presentation of the disability test results from the current population survey* (Working paper). Washington, DC: Bureau of Labor Statistics.

Meriac, J. P., Hoffman, B. J., Woehr, D. J., & Fleisher, M. S. (2008). Further evidence for the validity of assessment center dimensions: A meta-analysis of the incremental criterion-related validity of dimension ratings. *Journal of Applied Psychology, 93*, 1042–1052.

Milgram, S. (1974). *Obedience to authority: An experimental view.* New York: Harper & Row.

Mor Barak, M. E., Cherin, D. A., & Berkman, S. (1998). Organizational and personal dimensions in diversity climate: Ethnic and gender differences in employee perceptions. *Journal of Applied Behavioral Science, 34*, 82–104.

Motowidlo, S. J., Dunnette, M. D., & Carter, G. W. (1990). An alternative selection procedure: The low-fidelity simulation. *Journal of Applied Psychology, 75*, 640–647.

Moyes, G. D., Williams, P. A., & Quigley, B. Z. (2000). The relation between perceived treatment discrimination and job satisfaction among African-American accounting professionals. *Accounting Horizons, 14*, 21–48.

Murphy, K. R. (1996). Individual differences and behavior in organizations: Much more than g. In K. R. Murphy (Ed.), *Individual differences and behavior in organizations* (pp. 3–30). San Francisco: Jossey-Bass.

Murphy, K. R., & Cleveland, J. N. (1995). *Understanding performance appraisal: Social, organizational and goal-based perspectives.* Thousand Oaks, CA: Sage.

National Research Council. (2004). *Measuring racial discrimination.* Panel on Methods for Assessing Discrimination. Rebecca M. Blank, Marilyn Dabady, and Constance F. Citro (Eds.). Committee on National Statistics, Division of Behavioral and Social Sciences and Education. Washington, DC: The National Academies Press.

Nelson, T. D. (2002). *Ageism: Stereotyping and prejudice against older persons.* Cambridge, MA: MIT Press.

Nelson, T. D. (2009). *Handbook of prejudice, stereotyping, and discrimination.* New York: Psychology Press.

Ng, T. W. H., & Feldman, D. C. (2008). The relationship of age to ten dimensions of job performance. *Journal of Applied Psychology, 93*, 392–423.

O'Leary-Kelly, A. M., Bowes-Sperry, L., Bates, C. A., & Lean, E. R. (2009). Sexual harassment at work: A decade (plus) of progress. *Journal of Management, 35*, 503–536.

O'Leary-Kelly, A. M., Paetzold, R. L., & Griffin, R. W. (2000). Sexual harassment as aggressive behavior: An actor based perspective. *Academy of Management Review, 25*, 372–388.

Olian, J. D., Schwab, D. P., & Haberfeld, Y. (1988). The impact of applicant gender compared to qualifications on hiring recommendations: A meta-analysis of experimental studies. *Organizational Behavior and Human Decision Processes, 41*(2), 180–195.

O'Neill, J. (2003). The gender gap in wages, circa 2000. *The American Economic Review, 93*, 309–314.

Ones, D., & Viswesvaran, C. (1998). Gender, age, and race differences on overt integrity tests: Results across four large-scale job applicant datasets. *Journal of Applied Psychology, 83*(1), 35–42.

Ones, D. S., Viswesvaran, C., & Dilchert, S. (2005). Personality at work: Raising awareness and correcting misconceptions. *Human Performance, 18*, 389–404.

Ones, D. S., Viswesvaran, C., & Schmidt, F. L. (1993). Comprehensive meta-analysis of integrity test validities: Findings and implications for personnel selection and theories of job performance [Monograph]. *Journal of Applied Psychology, 78*, 679–703.

Ostroff, C., & Atwater, L. E. (2003). Does whom you work with matter? Effects of referent group gender and age composition on managers' compensation. *Journal of Applied Psychology, 88*, 725–740.

Pager, D. (2007). The use of field experiments for studies of employment discrimination: Contributions, critiques, and directions for the future. *Annals of the American Academy of Political and Social Science, 609*, 104–133.

Pascoe, E. A., & Smart Richman, L. (2009). Perceived discrimination and health: A meta-analytic review. *Psychological Bulletin, 135*, 531–554.

Pavalko, E. K., Mossakowski, K. N., & Hamilton, V. J. (2003). Does perceived discrimination affect health? Longitudinal relationships between work discrimination and women's physical and emotional health. *Journal of Health and Social Behavior, 44*, 18–33.

Pelled, L., Eisenhardt, K., & Xin, K. (1999). Exploring the black box: An analysis of work group diversity, conflict, and performance. *Administrative Science Quarterly, 44*(1), 1–28.

Perry, E., & Finkelstein, L. (1999). Toward a broader view of age discrimination in employment-related decisions: A joint consideration of organizational factors and cognitive processes. *Human Resource Management Review, 9*(1), 21–49.

Perry, E. L., Hendricks, W., & Broadbent, E. (2000). An exploration of access and treatment discrimination and job satisfaction among college graduates with and without physical disabilities. *Human Relations, 53*, 923–955.

Petersen, L. E., & Dietz, J. (2000). Social discrimination in a personnel selection context: The effects of an authority's instruction to discriminate and followers' authoritarianism. *Journal of Applied Social Psychology, 30*, 206–220.

Petersen, L. E., & Dietz, J. (2008). Employment discrimination: Authority figures' demographic preferences and followers' affective organizational commitment. *Journal of Applied Psychology, 93*, 1287–1300.

Petersen, T., & Saporta, I. (2004). The opportunity structure for discrimination. *American Journal of Sociology, 109*(4), 852–901.

Pettigrew, T. F., & Martin, J. (1987). Shaping the organizational context for Black American inclusion. *Journal of Social Issues, 43*, 41–78.

Pfeffer, J. (1983). Organizational demography. In L. L. Cummings & B. M. Staw (Eds.), *Research in organizational behavior* (Vol. 5, pp. 295–357). Greenwich, CT: JAI Press.

Pfeffer, J., & Davis-Blake, A. (1987). The effect of the proportion of women on salaries: The case of college administrators. *Administrative Science Quarterly, 32*, 1–24.

Pierce, J. L., Gardner, D. G., Cummings, L. L., & Dunham, R. B. (1989). Organization-based self-esteem: Construct definition, measurement, and validation. *Academy of Management Journal, 32*, 622–648.

Ployhart, R. E., & Holtz, B. C. (2008). The diversity-validity dilemma: Strategies for reducing racioethnic and sex subgroup differences and adverse impact in selection. *Personnel Psychology, 61*, 153–172.

Posthuma, R., & Campion, M. (2009). Age stereotypes in the workplace: Common stereotypes, moderators, and future research directions. *Journal of Management, 35*(1), 158–188.

Potosky, D., Bobko, P., & Roth, P. L. (2005). Forming composites of cognitive ability and alternative measures to predict job performance and reduce adverse impact: Corrected estimates and realistic expectations. *International Journal of Selection and Assessment, 13*, 304–315.

Pratto, F., Sidanius, J., Stallworth, L. M., & Malle, B. F. (1994). Social dominance orientation: A personality variable predicting social and political attitudes. *Journal of Personality and Social Psychology, 67*, 741–763.

Pryor, J. B. (1987). Sexual harassment proclivities in men. *Sex Roles, 17*, 269–290.

Pryor, J. B. (1992). The social psychology of sexual harassment: Person and situation factors which give rise to sexual harassment. In Northwest Women's Law Center, *Sex and power issues in the workplace: An interdisciplinary approach to understanding, preventing, and resolving harassment: Conference Proceedings* (pp. 89–105). Seattle: Northwest Women's Law Center.

Pryor, J. B., Giedd, J. L., & Williams, K. B. (1995). A social psychological model for predicting sexual harassment. *Journal of Social Issues, 51*(1), 69–84.

Pugh, S. D., Dietz, J., Brief, A. P., & Wiley, J. W. (2008). Looking inside and out: The impact of employee and community demographic composition on organizational diversity climate. *Journal of Applied Psychology, 93*, 1422–1428.

Pyburn, K. M., Jr., Ployhart, R. E., & Kravitz, D. A. (2008). The diversity-validity dilemma: An overview and legal context. *Personnel Psychology, 61*, 143–151.

Quillian, L. (2006). New approaches to understanding racial prejudice and discrimination. *Annual Review of Sociology, 32*, 299–328.

Ragins, B. R., & Cornwell, J. M. (2001). Pink triangles: Antecedents and consequences of perceived workplace discrimination against gay and lesbian employees. *Journal of Applied Psychology, 86*(6), 1244–1261.

Reb, J., & Cropanzano, R. (2007). Evaluating dynamic performance: The influence of salient Gestalt characteristics on performance ratings. *Journal of Applied Psychology, 92*, 490–499.

Redman, T., & Snape, E. (2006). The consequences of perceived age discrimination amongst older police officers: Is social support a buffer? *British Journal of Management, 17*(2), 167–175.

Rehabilitation Research and Training Center on Disability Demographics and Statistics (StatsRRTC). (2007). *2006 Disability Status Report*. Ithaca, NY: Cornell University.

Reichers, A. E., & Schneider, B. (1990). Climate and culture: An evolution of constructs. In B. Schneider (Ed.), *Organizational climate and culture* (pp. 5–39). San Francisco: Jossey-Bass.

Ren, L., Paetzold, R., & Colella, A. (2008). A meta-analysis of experimental studies on the effects of disability on human resource judgments. *Human Resource Management Review, 18*(3), 191–203.

Reskin, B. (1993). Sex segregation in the workplace. *Annual Review of Sociology, 19*, 241–270.

Reskin, B. F. (1998). *The realities of affirmative action in employment*. Washington, DC: American Sociological Association.

Reskin, B. F., & Bielby, D. D. (2005). A sociological perspective on gender and career outcomes. *Journal of Economic Perspectives, 19*, 71–86.

Reskin, B. F., & McBrier, D. B. (2000). Why not ascription? Organization's employment of male and female managers. *American Sociological Review, 65*, 210–233.

Reskin, B., McBrier, D. B., & Kmec, J. (1999). The determinants and consequences of workplace sex and race composition. *Annual Review of Sociology, 25*, 335–361.

Riordan, C. M. (2000). Relational demography within groups: Past developments, contradictions, and new directions. *Research in Personnel and Human Resources Management, 19*, 131–173.

Riordan, C. M., Schaffer, B. S., & Stewart, M. M. (2005). Relational demography within groups: Through the lens of discrimination. In R. L. Dipboye & A. Colella (Eds.), *Discrimination at work: The psychological and organizational processes* (pp. 37–61). Mahwah, NJ: Erlbaum.

Riordan, C. M., & Wayne, J. H. (2008). A review and examination of demographic similarity measures used to assess relational demography within groups. *Organizational Research Methods, 11*(3), 562–592.

Roberson, Q. M., & Park, H. J. (2007). Examining the link between diversity and firm performance: The effects of diversity reputation and leader racial diversity. *Group & Organization Management, 32*, 548–568.

Roberts, R. K., Swanson, N. G., & Murphy, L. R. (2004). Discrimination and occupational mental health. *Journal of Mental Health, 13*(2), 129–142.

Roehling, M. V. (1999). Weight-based discrimination in employment: Psychological and legal aspects. *Personnel Psychology, 52*, 969–1016.

Roehling, M. V., Roehling, P. V., & Pichler, S. (2007). The relationship between body weight and perceived weight-related employment discrimination: The role of sex and race. *Journal of Vocational Behavior, 71*, 300–318.

Rosette, A. S., Leonardelli, G. J., & Phillips, K. W. (2008). The white standard: Racial bias in leader categorization. *Journal of Applied Psychology, 93*(4), 758–777.

Roth, P. L., BeVier, C. A., Bobko, P., Switzer, F. S., III, & Tyler, P. (2001). Ethnic group differences in cognitive ability in employment and educational settings: A meta-analysis. *Personnel Psychology, 54*, 297–330.

Roth, P. L., Bobko, P., & McFarland, L. A. (2005). A meta-analysis of work sample test validity: Updating and integrating some classic literature. *Personnel Psychology, 58*, 1009–1037.

Roth, P. L., Bobko, P., McFarland, L. A., & Buster, M. (2008). Work sample tests in personnel selection: A meta-analysis of black-white differences in overall and exercise scores. *Personnel Psychology, 61*, 637–662.

Roth, P. L., Huffcutt, A. I., & Bobko, P. (2003). Ethnic group differences in measures of job performance: A new meta-analysis. *Journal of Applied Psychology, 88*, 694–706.

Roth, P. L., Van Iddekinge, C. H., Huffcutt, A. I., Edison, C. E., Jr., & Bobko, P. (2002). Corrections for range restriction in structured interview ethnic group differences: The values may be larger than researchers thought. *Journal of Applied Psychology, 87*, 369–376.

Rotundo, M., Nguyen, D. H., & Sackett, P. R. (2001). A meta-analytic review of gender differences in perceptions of sexual harassment. *Journal of Applied Psychology, 86*, 914–922.

Rotundo, M., & Sackett, P. (1999). Effect of rater race on conclusions regarding differential prediction in cognitive ability tests. *Journal of Applied Psychology, 84*(5), 815–822.

Rudman, L. A. (2005). Rejection of women? Beyond prejudice as antipathy. In J. F. Dovidio, P. Glick, & L. A. Rudman (Eds.), *On the nature of prejudice: Fifty years after Allport* (pp. 106–120). Oxford: Blackwell Publishing.

Rudolph, C., Wells, C., Weller, M., & Baltes, B. (2009). A meta-analysis of empirical studies of weight-based bias in the workplace. *Journal of Vocational Behavior, 74*(1), 1–10.

Ruscher, J. B. (2001). *Prejudiced communication: A social psychological perspective.* New York: Guilford Press.

Sackett, P. R., Burris, L. R., & Callahan, C. (1989). Integrity testing for personnel selection: An update. *Personnel Psychology, 42,* 491–529.

Sackett, P. R., & DuBois, C. L. (1991). Rater-ratee race effects on performance evaluation: Challenging meta-analytic conclusions. *Journal of Applied Psychology, 76*(6), 873–877.

Sackett, P. R., DuBois, C. L., & Noe, A. W. (1991). Tokenism in performance evaluation: The effects of work group representation on male-female and white-black differences in performance ratings. *Journal of Applied Psychology, 76,* 263–267.

Sackett, P. R., & Wilk, S. L. (1994). Within-group norming and other forms of adjustment in preemployment testing. *American Psychologist, 11,* 929–954.

Sanchez, J. I., & Brock, P. (1996). Outcomes of perceived discrimination among Hispanic employees: Is diversity management a luxury of a necessity? *Academy of Management Journal, 39,* 704–719.

Sanders Thompson, V. L., Noel, J. G., & Campbell, J. (2004). Stigmatization, discrimination, and mental health: The impact of multiple identity status. *American Journal of Orthopsychiatry, 74,* 529–544.

Saucier, G. (2000). Isms and the structure of social attitudes. *Journal of Personality and Social Psychology, 78,* 366–385.

Schartz. H., Hendricks, D. J., & Blanck, P. (2006). Workplace accommodations: Evidence-based outcomes. *Work, 27,* 345–354.

Schein, V. E. (1973). The relationship between sex role stereotypes and requisite management characteristics. *Journal of Applied Psychology, 57,* 95–100.

Schein, V. E. (1975). Relationships between sex role stereotypes and requisite management characteristics among female managers. *Journal of Applied Psychology, 60*(3), 340–344.

Schmidt, F. L., & Hunter, J. E. (1998). The validity and utility of selection methods in personnel psychology: Practical and theoretical implications of 85 years of research findings. *Psychological Bulletin, 124,* 262–274.

Schmidt, F. L., Hunter, J. E., & Outerbridge, A. N. (1986). Impact of job experience and ability on job knowledge, work sample performance, and supervisory ratings of job performance. *Journal of Applied Psychology, 71,* 432–439.

Schmitt, N., Clause, C. S., & Pulakos, E. D. (1996). Subgroup differences associated with different measures of some common job-relevant constructs. In C. L. Cooper & I. T. Robertson (Eds.), *International review of industrial and organizational psychology* (Vol. 11, pp. 115–139). New York: Wiley.

Schneider, B. (1987). The people make the place. *Personnel Psychology, 40,* 437–453.

Schneider, B., Goldstein, H., & Smith, D. (1995). The ASA framework: An update. *Personnel Psychology, 48*(4), 747–773.

Schneider, K. T., Hitlan, R. T., & Radhakrishnan, P. (2000). An examination of the nature and correlates of ethnic harassment experiences in multiple contexts. *Journal of Applied Psychology, 85,* 3–12.

Schur, L., Kruse, D., Blasi, J., & Blanck, P. (2009). Is disability disabling in all workplaces? Workplace disparities and corporate culture. *Industrial Relations, 48,* 381–410.

Seattle Office of Civil Rights. (2006). *Opinion survey of a small sample of participants at Pride 2006.* Retrieved May 30, 2009, from http://www.seattle.gov/scsm/documents/Pride06SexualOrient_Opinion_Survey_Final.doc.

Seidel, M. L., Polzer, J. T., Stewart, K. J. (2000). Friends in high places: The effect of social networks on discrimination in salary negotiations. *Administrative Science Quarterly, 45,* 1–24.

Semyonov, M., & Herring, C. (2007). Segregated jobs or ethnic niches?: The impact of racialized employment on earnings inequality. *Research in Social Stratification and Mobility, 25,* 245–257.

Settles, I. H., Cortina, L. M., Malley, J., & Stewart, A. J. (2006). The climate for women in academic science: The good, the bad, and the changeable. *Psychology of Women Quarterly, 30*(1), 47–58.

Shore, L., Cleveland, J. N., & Goldberg, C. B. (2003). Work attitudes and decisions as a function of manager age and employee age. *Journal of Applied Psychology, 88*(3), 529–537.

Shore, L. M., & Goldberg, C. B. (2005). Age discrimination in the workplace. In R. L. Dipboye & A. Colella (Eds.), *Discrimination at work: The psychological and organizational processes* (pp. 203–225). Mahwah, NJ: Erlbaum.

Sibley, C. G., & Duckitt, J. (2008). Personality and prejudice: A meta-analysis and theoretical review. *Personality and Social Psychology Review, 12,* 248–279.

Sidanius, J., & Pratto, F. (1999). *Social dominance: An intergroup theory of social hierarchy and oppression.* New York: Cambridge University Press.

Smith, A. N., Brief, A. P., & Colella, A. (2010). Bias in organizations. In J. F. Dovidio, M. Hewstone, P. Glick, & V. M. Esses (Eds.), *The Sage handbook of prejudice, stereotyping, and discrimination* (pp. 441–456). Los Angeles, CA: Sage.

Smeltzer, L. R., & Leap, T. L. (1988). An analysis of individual reactions to potentially offensive jokes in work settings. *Human Relations, 41,* 295–304.

Son Hing, L. S., Chung-Yan, G., Hamilton, L., & Zanna, M. P. (2008). A two-dimensional model that employs explicit and implicit attitudes to characterize prejudice. *Journal of Personality and Social Psychology, 94*(6), 971–987.

Son Hing, L. S., Li, W., & Zanna, M. P. (2002). Inducing hypocrisy to reduce prejudicial responses among aversive racists. *Journal of Experimental Social Psychology, 38,* 71–78.

Sorensen, E. (1990). The crowding hypothesis and comparable worth issue: A survey and new results. *Journal of Human Resources, 25*(1), 55–89.

Stanley, T., & Jarrell, S. (1998). Gender wage discrimination bias? A meta-regression analysis. *Journal of Human Resources, 33,* 947–973.

Stauffer, J., & Buckley, M. (2005). The existence and nature of racial bias in supervisory ratings. *Journal of Applied Psychology, 90*(3), 586–591.

Stone, D. L., & Colella, A. (1996). A framework for studying the effects of disability on work experiences. *Academy of Management Review, 21*(2), 352–401.

Stone, D. L., Hosoda, M., Lukaszewski, K. M., & Phillips, T. N. (2008). Methodological problems associated with research on unfair discrimination against racial minorities. *Human Resource Management Review, 18,* 243–258.

Stuhlmacher, A. F., & Walters, A. E. (1999). Gender differences in negotiation outcome: A meta-analysis. *Personnel Psychology, 52*(3), 653–677.

Swim, J. K., Aikin, K. J., Hall, W. S., & Hunter, B. A. (1995). Sexism and racism: Old-fashioned and modern prejudices. *Journal of Personality and Social Psychology, 68*, 199–214.

Swim, J. K., Borgida, E., Maruyama, G., & Myers, D. G. (1989). Joan McKay versus John McKay: Do gender stereotypes bias evaluations? *Psychological Bulletin, 105*, 409–429.

Tajfel, H. (1981). *Human groups and social categories.* Cambridge, UK: Cambridge University Press.

Tajfel, H., & Turner, J. C. (1979). An integrative theory of social conflict. In W. Austin & S. Worchel (Eds.). *The social psychology of inter-group relations* (pp. 33–47). Monterey, CA: Brooks/Cole.

Tajfel, H., & Turner, J. C. (1986). The social identity theory of intergroup behavior. In S. Worchel & W. G. Austin (Eds.), *Psychology of intergroup relations* (2nd ed., pp. 7–24). Chicago, IL: Nelson-Hall.

Taylor, M. C. (1998). How white attitudes vary with the racial composition of local populations: Numbers count. *American Sociological Review, 63*, 512–535.

Theran, E. (2005). Legal theory on weight discrimination. In K. D. Brownell, R. M. Puhl, M. B. Schwartz, & L. Rudd (Eds.), *Weight bias: Nature, consequences, and remedies* (pp. 195–211). New York: Guilford Publications.

Thomas, K. M., & Chrobot-Mason, D. (2005). Demographic group based discrimination: Theories and conclusions. In R. L. Dipboye & A. Colella (Eds.), *Discrimination at work: The psychological and organizational bases* (pp. 63–88). Mahwah, NJ: Erlbaum.

Tonidandel, S., Avery, D., Bucholtz, B., & McKay, P. (2008). An alternative explanation for the asymmetrical effects in relational demography research. *Personnel Psychology, 61*(3), 617–633.

Tosi, H. L., & Einbender, S. W. (1985). The effects of the type and amount of information in sex discrimination research: A meta-analysis. *Academy of Management Journal, 28*, 712–723.

Triana, M. D. C., Garcia. M. F., & Colella, A. (2010). Managing diversity: How organizational efforts to support diversity enhance affective commitment for employees who perceive discrimination at work. *Personnel Psychology, 63*, 817–843.

Tsui, A., Egan, T., & O'Reilly, C., III. (1992). Being different: Relational demography and organizational attachment. *Administrative Science Quarterly, 37*(4), 549–579.

Tsui, A., & O'Reilly, C., III. (1989). Beyond simple demographic effects: The importance of relational demography in superior-subordinate dyads. *Academy of Management Journal, 32*(2), 402–423.

Turner, J. C. (1975). Social comparison and social identity: Some prospects for intergroup behaviour. *European Journal of Social Psychology, 5*, 5–34.

Turner, J. C. (1985). Social categorization and the self-concept: A social cognitive theory of group behavior. In E. J. Lawler (Ed.), *Advances in group processes: Theory and research* (Vol. 2, pp. 77–122). Greenwich, CT: JAI Press.

Turner, J. C., & Reynolds, K. (2001). The social identity perspective in intergroup relations: Theories, themes, and controversies. In R. Brown & S. Gaertner (Eds.), *Blackwell handbook of social psychology. Intergroup processes* (pp. 133–152). Oxford, UK: Blackwell.

Tuckman, J., & Lorge, I. (1952). Experts' biases about the older worker. *Science, 115*, 685–681.

Twenge, J. M. (1997). Changes in masculine and feminine traits over time: A meta-analysis. *Sex Roles, 36*, 305–325.

Uleman, J. S., Saribay, S. A., & Gonzalez, C. M. (2008). Spontaneous inferences, implicit impressions, and implicit theories. *Annual Review of Psychology, 59*, 329–360.

Umphress, E. E., Simmons, A. L., Boswell, W. R., & Triana, M. D. C. (2008). Managing discrimination in selection: The influence of directives from an authority and social dominance orientation. *Journal of Applied Psychology, 93*, 982–993.

Umphress, E. E., Smith-Crowe, K., Brief, A. P., Dietz, J., & Watkins, M. B. (2007). When birds of a feather flock together and when they do not: Status composition, social dominance orientation and organizational attractiveness. *Journal of Applied Psychology, 92*, 396–409.

Unger, D. (2002). Employers' attitudes toward persons with disabilities in the workforce: Myths or realities? *Focus on Autism & Other Developmental Disabilities, 17*(1), 2.

Uniform guidelines on employee selection procedure (1978). *Federal Register, 43*, 38290–38309.

U.S. Bureau of Labor Statistics. (2009). *Foreign-born workers: Labor force characteristics in 2008.* Washington, DC: Author.

U.S. Census Bureau. (2004). *U.S. Census Bureau population projects.* Retrieved May 30, 2009, from http://www.census.gov/ipc/www/usinterimproj/.

U.S. Department of Labor. (2008a). *Highlights of women's earnings in 2007* (Department of Labor Statistics Report #1008). Retrieved May 30, 2009, from http://www.bls.gov/cps/cps-wom2007.pdf.

U.S. Department of Labor. (2008b). *Labor force characteristics by race and ethnicity, 2007* (Department of Labor Statistics Report #1005). Retrieved May 30, 2009, from http://www.bls.gov/cps/cpsrace2007.pdf.

U.S. Equal Employment Opportunity Commission. (1992). *A technical assistance manual on the employment provisions (Title I) of the American with Disabilities Act.* Washington, DC: Author.

U.S. Equal Employment Opportunity Commission. (2002a). *ADA Technical Assistance Manual Addendum* Retrieved September 20, 2008, from http://www.eeoc.gov/policy/docs/adamanual_add.html.

U.S. Equal Employment Opportunity Commission. (2002b). *Questions and answers about the workplace rights of Muslims, Arabs, South Asians, and Sikhs under equal employment opportunity laws.* Retrieved May 30, 2009, from http://www.eeoc.gov/facts/backlash-employee.html.

U.S. Equal Employment Opportunity Commission. (2008a). *Asian American and Pacific Islander work group report to the chair of the equal employment opportunity commission.* Retrieved May 30, 2009, from http://www.eeoc.gov/federal/report/aapi.html.

U.S. Equal Employment Opportunity Commission. (2008b). *Improving the participation rate of people with targeted disabilities in the federal work force.* Retrieved May 30, 2009, from http://www.eeoc.gov/federal/report/pwtd.html.

U.S. Equal Employment Opportunity Commission. (2009a). *Federal Equal Employment Opportunity (EEO) laws.* Retrieved January 30, 2009, from http://archive.eeoc.gov/abouteeo/overview_laws.html.

U.S. Equal Employment Opportunity Commission. (2009b). *Sex-based discrimination.* Retrieved May 30, 2009, from http://archive.eeoc.gov/types/sex.html.

U.S. Equal Employment Opportunity Commission. (2009c). Pregnancy discrimination. Retrieved May 30, 2009, from http://archive.eeoc.gov/types/pregnancy.html.

U.S. Equal Employment Opportunity Commission. (2009d). *Sexual harassment.* Retrieved May 30, 2009, from http://archive.eeoc.gov/types/sexual_harassment.html.

U.S. Equal Employment Opportunity Commission. (2009e). *Race/color discrimination.* Retrieved May 30, 2009, from http://archive.eeoc.gov/types/race.html.

U.S. Equal Employment Opportunity Commission. (2009f). *Disability discrimination.* Retrieved May 30, 2009, from http://archive.eeoc.gov/types/ada.html.

U.S. Equal Employment Opportunity Commission. (2009g). *Religious discrimination.* Retrieved May 30, 2009, from http://archive.eeoc.gov/types/religion.html.

U.S. Equal Employment Opportunity Commission. (2009h). *Age discrimination in employment act (ADEA)charges FY 1997-FY 2008.* Retrieved May 30, 2009, from http://archive.eeoc.gov/stats/adea.html.

U.S. Equal Employment Opportunity Commission. (2009i). *Harassment.* Retrieved May 30, 2009, from http://archive.eeoc.gov/types/harassment.html.

U.S. Equal Employment Opportunity Commission. (2009j). *Compliance manual section 12 – Religious discrimination.* Retrieved May 30, 2009, from http://archive.eeoc.gov/policy/docs/religion.html#_Toc203359487.

U.S. Merit Systems Protection Board. (1988). *Sexual harassment in the federal workplace: An update.* Washington, DC: U.S. Government Printing Office.

Van Brakel, W. H. (2006). Measuring health-related stigma: A literature review. *Psychology, Health, & Medicine, 11,* 307–334.

Vogt Yuan, A. S. (2007). Perceived age discrimination and mental health. *Social Forces, 86,* 291–311.

Waldman, D. A., & Avolio, B. J. (1986). A meta-analysis of age differences in job performance. *Journal of Applied Psychology, 71,* 33–38.

Waldo, C. R. (1999). Working in a majority context: A structural model of heterosexism as minority stress in the workplace. *Journal of Counseling Psychology, 46*(2), 218–232.

Wasti, S. A., & Cortina, L. M. (2002). Coping in context: Sociocultural determinants of responses to sexual harassment. *Journal of Personality and Social Psychology, 83,* 394–405.

Weathers, R. R., II. (2006). *Disability prevalence rates for an aging workforce.* Ithaca, NY: Cornell University.

Weinberg, N. (1983). Social equity and the physically disabled. *Social Work, 28*(5), 365–369.

Whetzel, D. L., McDaniel, M. A., & Nguyen, N. T. (2008). Subgroup differences in situational judgment test performance: A meta-analysis. *Human Performance, 21,* 291–309.

Whitley, B. E., Jr. (1999). Right-wing authoritarianism, social dominance orientation, and prejudice. *Journal of Personality and Social Psychology, 77,* 126–134.

Wilkerson, J. (1999). The impact of job level and prior training on sexual harassment labeling and remedy choice. *Journal of Applied Social Psychology, 29*(8), 1605–1623.

Williams, D. R., Yu, Y., Jackson, J. S., & Anderson, N. B. (1997). Racial differences in physical and mental health: Socio-economic status, stress, and discrimination. *Journal of Health Psychology, 2,* 335–351.

Willness, C. R., Steel, P., & Lee, K. (2007). A meta-analysis of the antecedents and consequences of workplace sexual harassment. *Personnel Psychology, 60*(1), 127–162.

Wilson, G. D. (1973). *The psychology of conservatism.* Oxford: London Academic Press.

Witt, L. A., & Nye, L. G. (1992). Gender and the relationship between perceived fairness of pay or promotion and job satisfaction. *Journal of Applied Psychology, 77*(6), 910–917.

Woehr, D. J., & Arthur, W., Jr. (2003). The construct-related validity of assessment center ratings: A review and meta-analysis of the role of methodological factors. *Journal of Management, 29,* 231–258.

Word, C. O., Zanna, M. P., & Cooper, J. (1974). The nonverbal mediation of self-fulfilling prophecies in interracial interaction. *Journal of Experimental Social Psychology, 10*(2), 109–120.

Wright, P., Ferris, S. P., Hiller, J. S., & Kroll, M. (1995). Competitiveness through management of diversity: Effects on stock price valuation. *Academy of Management Journal, 38,* 272–287.

Zatzick, C. D., Elvira, M. M., & Cohen, L. M. (2003). When more is better? The effects of racial composition on voluntary turnover. *Organization Science, 14,* 483–496.

Ziegert, J. C., & Hanges, P. J. (2005). Employment discrimination: The role of implicit attitudes, motivation, and a climate for racial bias. *Journal of Applied Psychology, 90,* 553–562.

Zimmer, L. (1988). Tokenism and women in the workplace: The limits of gender-neutral theory. *Social Problems, 35,* 64–76.

Cross-Cultural Organizational Psychology

Zeynep Aycan *and* Michele J. Gelfand

Abstract

The chapter presents an overview of the cross-cultural organizational psychology literature with three specific aims: to provide future research direction based on a historical projection of the development of the field; to summarize the state-of-the-art literature in substansive areas, including recruitment and selection, nature of jobs, criteria for performance, work motivation, job attitudes, teamwork, leadership, conflict and negotiation; and to discuss challenges faced by cross-cultural researchers (e.g., level of analysis, interaction between cultural and organizational contingencies). Our review indicates that individualism-collectivism attracts the most research attention and accounts for substantial variation in organizational behavior across cultures. Our review also points out that the impact of cultural values on organizational phenomena vary depending on organizational and task-related contingencies. The need is identified to expand the cross-cultural industrial and organizational (I/O) psychology literature to include more research on cross-cultural interactions and culture-specific enactments of organizational behavior.

Key Words: culture, motivation, leadership, teamwork, negotiation, organizational attitudes, HRM practices, levels of analysis, cross-cultural interfaces.

Introduction

Organizational psychology has a long past and a short history. Although the founding of the discipline can be traced to the early twentieth century (Koppes, 2007), in fact, the importance of understanding human behavior at work can be found in ancient Chinese, Greek, and Egyptian writings. Predating modern selection theories by thousands of years, the Chinese were known use ability testing to match individuals to jobs (Bowman, 1989), as well as tests to detect faking. Likewise, Greek philosophers discussed the importance of matching individuals to their abilities (e.g., Plato's *The Republic*; Williamson, 2008). Even religious texts focused on modern-day organizational psychological questions—discussions of what constitutes a virtuous organization can be found in the Old Testament (Wright & Goodstein, 2007), and the characteristics of an effective leader are discussed widely in the Qur'an (Mohsen, 2007) and in later texts such as Sun Tzu's *The Art of War* (Ko, 2003). Undoubtedly, as these examples attest, understanding the psychology of work behavior is a universal concern. Yet, despite the fact that questions regarding the psychology of work transcend history and cultures, the science of organizational psychology has only recently started to become more global in its scope.

The purpose of this chapter is to provide an overview of the field of cross-cultural organizational psychology. Below, we first provide a historical overview of how culture research has evolved in the field. We then discuss the functions of culture research in organizational psychology, what it can and should do for the field, and critical definitional and levels of analysis issues. We then review selected topics on culture and organizational psychology. We start with *culture and organizational entry*, covering such topics as cultural influences on selection practices, the nature of jobs, and criteria for performance. We then move to *culture and individual behavior* in organizations, covering such topics as cultural influences on work motivation, job attitudes, and organizational justice. We then consider *culture and the social animal in organizations*, covering topics such as culture and teams, culture and leadership, and culture and negotiation. We conclude the chapter with frontiers of research in cross-cultural organizational psychology (for other reviews on this topic, see Aguinis & Henle, 2003; Earley & Erez, 1997; Gelfand, Erez, & Aycan, 2007; Gelfand, Leslie, & Fehr, 2008; Hofstede, 2001; Hofstede & Hofstede, 2005; Kirkman, Lowe, & Gibson, 2006; Leung, Bhagat, Buchan, Erez, & Gibson, 2005; Sparrow, 2006; Taras, Kirkman, & Steel, 2010; Tsui, Nifadkar, & Ou, 2007).

History of Cross-Cultural Organizational Psychology

Like many topics in science, the evolution of cross-cultural research in organizational psychology has been shaped by the societal context in which the field evolved and by key people and events (Kashima & Gelfand, 2012). Organizational psychology, born on American soil, paid very little attention to culture in the early and mid-twentieth century. With its focus on scientific management and standardized approach to management (Taylor, 1911), with its involvement in U.S. Army efforts in the selection and placement of American soldiers in both World War I and II, and with its later work emanating from such American events such as the civil rights movement, the field of organizational psychology remained largely *culture bound* (i.e., tested its theories only on American samples) and *culture blind* (i.e., did not consider culture as an important factor in organizational research; Bond & Smith, 1996). The fact that the United States as a society has supported a "melting pot" view of cultural differences also likely contributed to the lack of attention to culture in organizational psychology.

Later, in 1976, an important paper that began to put cross-cultural research on the industrial and organizational (I/O) psychology "map," albeit far from its center, was Barrett and Bass's (1976) chapter on "Cross-cultural Industrial and Organizational Psychology," published in Dunette's first *Handbook of Industrial and Organizational Psychology*. Barrett and Bass (1976) provided one of the first systematic reviews of cross-cultural research, and made (at least) two astute observations: first, cross-cultural research that was done was generally atheoretical, descriptive, and plagued with methodological problems. Second, they lamented that culture was largely ignored in mainstream organizational psychology, arguing that "most research in industrial and organizational psychology is done within one cultural context. This context puts constraints upon both our theories and our practical solutions to the organizational problems. Since we are seldom faced with a range and variation of our variables which adequately reflect the possibilities of human behavior, we tend to take a limited view of the field" (p. 1675).

Later, in the 1980s, attention to national culture began to steadily increase, both as a response to empirical and international developments. With the landmark publication of Hofstede's (1980) study of national culture and advancement of scores on multiple cultural dimensions, the field now had a solid theoretical backbone to build upon. At the same time, research began to uncover the cultural boundaries of some Western organizational psychology models, which in some cases were not as applicable to the Far East. Likewise, Japanese models, such as quality control circles, were not successfully adopted in the West (Erez & Earley, 1993). Nonetheless, during this time period, cross-cultural research in organizational psychology was still more often the exception than the norm and was largely separate from mainstream research. It was, in essence, *tolerated* but was not particularly influential or widespread.

Now, almost a full century after the founding of the field, we are entering an era when culture research is beginning to gain momentum as an important and critical area of scholarly inquiry. On an optimistic note, a perusal of our journals illustrates that the field is considerably broadening its focus to use new taxonomies of cultural values (House, Hanges, Javidan, Dorfman, & Gupta, 2004, Schwartz, 1994, Smith, Dugan, & Trompenaars, 1996), beliefs (Bond, Leung, Au, Tong, & Chemonges-Nielson, 2004), norms (Gelfand, Nishii, & Raver, 2006), and sophisticated ways of combining *emic* (or culture-specific) with *etic* (or universal) perspectives on cultural differences (Farh, Earley, & Lin, 1997). The literature has considerably broadened its focus to include topics that span the scholarly discipline, from micro-studies of culture and motivation and attitudes; to more meso-topics such as leadership, conflict, negotiation, and teams; and to attention to culture at the macro-level, including organizational culture, human resource management (HRM) practices, and joint ventures. It is also broadening its methodological toolbox to include sophisticated ways of establishing equivalence, testing multilevel models, and utilizing meta-analyses to examine trends across diverse literatures. There are also other more subtle indices of progress, including greater representation of non-Western scholars on editorial boards (Rynes, 2005) and increases in new journals devoted to cross-cultural issues (e.g., *International Journal of Cross-Cultural Management; Management and Organizational Review*). Recent reviews have also shown that top tier outlets for organizational psychologists (*Journal of Applied Psychology; Personnel Psychology; Academy of Management Journal;* and *Organizational Behavior and Human Decision Processes*) are increasingly becoming more global in their scope, with fully 35.7% of articles having a non-U.S. coauthor and 28.7% of empirical articles having a non-U.S. sample (Ryan & Gelfand, 2011).

However, while there is cause for optimism, the empirical "facts" still suggest that the cross-cultural revolution in the field is in a nascent state. Ryan and Gelfand's (2011) review, for example, illustrates that only 6.4% of articles in the field's top tier journals focus on cross-cultural issues explicitly. This is consistent with Arnett's (2008) recent *American Psychologist* article "The Neglected 95%: Why American Psychology Needs to Become Less American," which illustrates that only 5% of articles on average are devoted to cross-cultural issues across a wide range of APA journals in psychology. Cross-cultural research that is done is largely done by Western authors. Among the 93 studies in Tsui, Nifadkar, and Ou's (2007) recent literature review of cross-cultural organizational science, a full 86% of the studies' first authors are from Western countries. Ten of the remaining 13 articles' first authors are from East Asia, leaving only three papers with first authors from Latin America, Africa, or the Middle East. Remarkably, a full 100% of the 69 unique first authors from Tsui et al. (2007) are from countries characterized by the HDI as having "high human development" (Gelfand, Leslie, & Fehr, 2008). Thus, even within a field specifically developed to combat the problems associated with Western hegemony, an implicit Western bias appears to be pervasive. Other analyses of the focus of cross-cultural issues at national conferences illustrate that attention to

culture still remains low. For example, Ryan and Gelfand (2011) show that only a small percentage of symposia (7.7%) and posters (5.7%) on culture are typically presented at the Society for Industrial and Organizational Psychology annual conference. Ryan and Gelfand (2011) also note that attention to culture in graduate and undergraduate training in the field is sorely lacking, with textbooks not giving in-depth attention to cultural issues, and syllabi devoting only minimal attention to cross-cultural research articles (3%). Other reviews also question whether the questions that are being asked, the constructs and theories that are being developed, and ultimately the knowledge that is being gleaned in cross-cultural organizational psychology are fundamentally infused with Western values and assumptions about the psychology of work (Gelfand et al., 2008). In all, while there is certainly a gradual global shift in the field, it can be characterized as reflecting small but steady incremental changes rather than catastrophic shifts. We return to ways to further globalize the field in the last section of this chapter.

With this historical backdrop in mind, we next turn to the value that cross-cultural research brings to the science and practice of organizational psychology.

Functions of Cross-Cultural Research in Organizational Psychology

Cross-cultural research has much to offer the science of organizational psychology. Below, we briefly discuss four specific ways that culture enhances the field (Triandis, 1994). Cross-cultural research expands the range of organizational behavior that we study; it enables us to test the universality of our theories; it illuminates emic or culture-specific organizational phenomena; and it helps to reduce ethnocentrism and to increase the effectiveness of intercultural interactions.

Expanding the Range of Organizational Behavior

One important benefit of cross-cultural research in organizational behavior (OB) is that it can *expand the range of variation* on the phenomena that we study. As Berry (1980) pointed out, "Only when all variation is present can its underlying structure be detected; for with limited data, only partial structures may be discovered" (Berry, 1980, p. 5). In doing cross-cultural research, scholars may find that theories once thought to be comprehensive are in need of expansion in order to capture the diversity of human cultures. For example, research has illustrated that while the five-factor model of personality does replicate in a number of cultures (e.g., Israel, Germany, Japan, Portugal, China, and Korea; Smith & Bond, 1999), there are also other dimensions of personality in other cultures that have not been found in the United States. For example, the dimension of *pakikisama*, or one's involvement in one's in-group, has been found to be an important component of personality in the Philippines (Smith & Bond, 1999). Along the same lines, in their study of organizational citizenship behavior (OCB) in China, Farh et al. (1997) found that while some dimensions of OCBs in China were similar to those found in the United States (e.g., civic virtue, altruism, conscientiousness), other dimensions found in the United States were not relevant in China (e.g., sportsmanship and courtesy) and at least one dimension found in China was not yet identified in the United States (interpersonal harmony, protecting company resources). At a more macro-level, Bond and the Chinese Culture Connection (1987) illuminated an additional cultural dimension of values—namely Confucian dynamism—that had not been discovered in previous research by Hofstede (1980), which originated in the West. This dimension, formerly unknown in the study of values, ultimately proved to be greatest predictor of gross national growth (GNG) ($r = .70, p < .001$) across 22 Asian nations. Sometimes "going global" with our constructs can also identify neglected dimensions that are critical in a Western context. For example, Ramesh and Gelfand (2010) showed that *family embeddedness*—a construct that is critical for predicting actual turnover in India—is also an important predictor of turnover in the United States. In all, it is critical to broaden the construct space to capture non-Western voices, not only so that constructs are global in their comprehensiveness, but because neglected dimensions may be critical in predicting behavior in other cultures.

Expanding the range of variation also serves another important function in research, namely the ability to "unconfound variables." In some cultures, two variables are so highly correlated (or confounded) that it is impossible to determine the independent influence of each variable on a third criterion variable. However, by doing cross-cultural research, one may be able to find cultures in which such variables are not correlated (are unconfounded), enabling one to assess each variable's effect on other variables. An interesting example of this is found in the area of clinical psychology in understanding the Oedipal complex (Triandis, 1994). Freud's theory

originally proposed that at certain ages, boys will have animosity toward their father, as a result of their jealousy of the father's role as their mother's lover. Although the phenomenon of animosity has not been challenged, the cause of it has been subject to debate. Specifically, Malinowski, an anthropologist, argued that such animosity stems from the fact that the father is the disciplinarian, not as a result of his role as the mother's lover. Unfortunately, in Austria (where most of Freud's work was conducted), fathers serve in *both* roles, and it is impossible to determine the locus of the animosity (and thus the explanations are confounded). However, in the Trobriand Islands, where Malinowski did his research, the variables are unconfounded: uncles serve as disciplinarians, whereas fathers retain their role as mother's lover. The natural question, then, is: Where is animosity directed in the Trobriand Islands? Malinowski's research illustrated that it was directed at uncles—not fathers, as Freud's theory had proposed. Although this example is not drawn from organizational research, and it remains controversial, it nevertheless illustrates that by extending the range of variation, cross-cultural research can expand (and correct, as in this case) our theories.

Testing the Universality of Organizational Theories

An important advantage of doing cultural research in OB is that it can help to illuminate what is *universal*, or *etic*, and what is *culture-specific*, or *emic*, in organizational phenomena.

There is already evidence that some of our theories, once assumed to be universal, are in fact, culturally contingent. For example, much research on procedural justice has illustrated that voice greatly enhances perceptions of fairness in organizations (Lind & Tyler, 1988). This line of inquiry has not only been highly productive in building theory on the role of justice in organizations, but has also been highly influential in the practice of management. Challenging this Western hegemony, Brockner and colleagues (2001) demonstrated that the benefits of voice were only found in cultures that had low power distance between supervisors and employees (i.e., the U.S.), as compared to high power distance cultures (i.e., China, Mexico, and Hong Kong; see Gelfand, et al., 2007 for reviews of the culture and justice literature). Similarly, research has shown that empowerment results in *lower* performance (Eylon & Au, 1999) and satisfaction (Robert, Probst, Martocchio, Drasgow, & Lawler, 2000) among individuals from high distance cultures. This illustrates how cross-cultural research not only identified boundary conditions for classic organizational theories, but also helped to illuminate reasons that voice and empowerment is so important in the United States (i.e., power distance beliefs).

As another example, much negotiation research has shown that when negotiators are accountable to constituents, they become highly competitive and reach suboptimal outcomes (Benton & Druckman, 1974). Gelfand & Realo (1999) argued that accountability is a norm-enforcement mechanism and would produce behavior that is normative in any particular cultural context. Consistent with this, they showed that accountability produced cooperative behavior among collectivists but competitive behavior among individualists. Moreover, unaccountability (when individuals are released from norms) produced cooperative behavior among individualists but competitive behavior among collectivists (see also Liu, Friedman, & Hong, 2012). This illustrates how cross-cultural research can help to show when findings are not universal, and moreover, how cross-cultural research can add new insight into why certain patterns are found within Western contexts. Whether it the impact of job characteristics such as autonomy on psychological states (Roe, Zinovieva, Dienes, & Ten Horn, 2000), what is considered a just and an appropriate contribution (Hundley & Kim, 1997), what is perceived as effective leadership (House et al., 2004), or how to develop trust (Branzei, Vertinsky, & Camp, 2007; Yuki, Maddux, Brewer, Takemura, 2005), core assumptions of our theories need to be tested for their universality in order to build a global science of organizational psychology.

To date, much of the work that is done in the field still makes the implicit assumption that the phenomena we study are universal (or *etic*), or that there is an underlying common ("true") nature to all human beings (Adamopoulos & Lonner, 1994). A perusal through the major texts or journals in organizational psychology reveals that it is rare when a theory or a finding is qualified by the notion that "we need to examine whether the theory applies to other cultural contexts." In this respect, we argue that the challenge for organizational science is not only in the low base-rates of cross-cultural research, but also in the *assumption* of universality of our theories. This often-unquestioned assumption limits the ultimate goal of our science: to be able to make generalizations to organizations and humankind.

Some might ask, why not begin with an assumption that our theories are universal? Along with others (Pepitone & Triandis, 1987; Wilson, 1980), we would argue that although universals exist, starting with this assumption is not logically tenable. An assumption of universality can only be credible to the extent that the variables that we study are influenced by factors that are common to all human beings. This includes, for example, variables that are closely related to *biological factors* that are shared among humans. It could also include variables that are linked to common *ecological pressures* or exposure to *similar social structures* (Pepitone & Triandis, 1987). However, given that many of the variables studied in the field are not of this nature, it is not safe to assume that theories and research generalize across cultures. Along the same lines, using an interesting metaphor, Wilson (1980) compared the issue of universality to the notion of behaviors being on "leashes" (as cited in Lonner & Malpass, 1994). Behaviors such as eating or sleeping are on "short and tight leashes," since human biological and physical characteristics do not allow for much variability in behaviors. Other behaviors such as decision-making or choice of activities are on "long and flexible leashes" that allow for greater variability in behaviors. From this perspective, the role of culture should increase as behavior shifts from a physiological basis, to that which is grounded in perceptual, cognitive, or personality bases, and should increase even more as one examines behavior in social and organizational contexts (Lonner & Malpass, 1994; Poortinga, Kop, & van de Vijver, 1990). We would caution readers, however, that even basic physiologically based behaviors can be subject to wide cultural variation, as recent evidence in cultural neuroscience attests (Chiao, 2009). In sum, while there may be some universals in organizational psychology, the assumption of universality in the field is not easily defensible on logical grounds.

Illuminating Emic *Phenomena*

Another way in which cross-cultural research can expand organizational psychology is by illuminating *emic*, or culture-specific phenomena. As we will discuss throughout this chapter, it is possible that a construct that is found to be universal may be manifested differently in different cultures. For example, dating back to the Ohio State studies on leadership, researchers have consistently found two dimensions of leader behavior: initiating structure (task-oriented), and consideration (relationally oriented). Cross-cultural research has revealed that these general distinctions are found in other cultures (e.g., Misumi, 1985). However, the specific behaviors that are associated with these dimensions vary considerably across cultures (Peterson, Smith, Bond, & Misumi, 1990). For example, talking about one's subordinate behind his or her back is seen as considerate in Japan, yet is seen as inconsiderate in the United States (Smith, Misumi, Tayeb, Peterson, & Bond, 1989). Such findings not only help to expand organizational theory, but also have wide practical implications for intercultural interactions.

By studying a particular culture in depth, cross-cultural research may reveal phenomena that are highly emic and that are not found in other cultures. Indeed, a number of emically derived variables have been discussed in the organizational literature. Many of these research programs illustrate the importance of relational constructs as central to organizational life. For example, Kashima and Callan (1994) argue that in Japan, motivation is regulated through an *amae-on-giri* exchange between supervisors and subordinates. Within this system, subordinates seek to be accepted by and dependent upon their superiors, which is referred to as *amae* (Doi, 1973). When superiors fulfill *amae,* this produces obligations (*giri*) among subordinates to repay such favors (*on*) through hard work and high performance. Thus, motivation is highly relational, and is constructed through particular culture-specific scripts in the Japanese context. Kim (1999) notes, for instance, how indigenous Korean constructs such as *kye* involve a strong focus on helping other people achieve their goals and needs. Likewise, *simpatia*, or "a general orientation among Hispanics toward establishing and maintaining harmony in interpersonal relations" (Rosenfeld & Culbertson, 1992, p. 221), has critical implications for leadership, negotiation, and group dynamics throughout Latin America. Metaphors for the family in organizational contexts abound in non-Western cultures. For example, Iranian scholars have noted that "employees view their managers as sympathetic brothers and sisters or compassionate fathers and mothers who [are] frequently involved in their employees' private lives and family matters" (Namazie & Tayeb, 2006, p. 29). (Davila & Elvira, 2005) (2005) similarly note that "family" is the metaphor used by management for leading Latin American firms. The concept of paternalistic leadership is similarly common in non-Western countries, where "the role of the superior is to provide care, protection, and guidance to the subordinate both in work and non-work domains" (Aycan, 2000, p. 446; see also Gibson & Zellmer-Bruhn, 2001, for metaphors for teamwork across cultures). The importance of the role of religion in organizational life is yet another example.

In many Islamic countries, the religious practice of *shura* requires managers to consult employees before making decisions (Mellahi, 2006). In Ghana, spiritual traditions affect forgiveness processes in organizations (Debrah, 2001). In Latin America, religious images, altars, and sculptures are commonplace in the workplace, and employees "expect freedom to express their faith in public" (Davila & Elvira, 2005, p. 10; Gelfand et al., 2008). Thus, whereas Western research generally treats religion as a private matter, and thus generally not relevant to organizational phenomena, religion has a major impact on organizational processes in some cultures. In sum, illuminating culture-specific phenomena is an important endeavor as we globalize our science.

Reducing Ethnocentrism and Improving Intercultural Interactions

All humans are ethnocentric (Triandis, 1994), which is to say that humans use their own cultural standards to judge what is right versus wrong, moral versus immoral, and so on. Such standards are imposed on others because they seem natural and because they are functional—in other words, they are adaptive in particular sociocultural contexts.

Shweder and colleagues provide a clear illustration that ethnocentric perspectives are found across cultures. Specifically, in his study of morality, Shweder asked people in both the United States and India about their judgments regarding a number of behaviors, including widows eating fish (Shweder, Mahapatra, & Miller, 1990). This included questions such as: Is this behavior a sin? Would it be better if all widows in the world did this? Would other countries that allow widows to eat fish be better off if they didn't? What if people in your country wanted to change the rule about widows eating fish? Would you agree? Across both student and adult samples, he illustrated that individuals in India consistently believed that it was a sin for widows to eat fish; that other countries would be better off if widows were not allowed to eat fish; and that the rule should certainly not be changed within India. Likewise, in the United States, individuals thought it was not at all a sin, and that widows around the world should be allowed to eat fish. Changing the rule in the United States, according to these samples, was also wrong.

Thus, both Americans and Indians had ethnocentric views of the same behaviors. Importantly, these beliefs are adaptive in that they are based on enduring cultural practices in both cultures. Specifically, in India, such beliefs are supportive of cultural collectivism. In this cultural context, the bond between husband and wife is eternal and sacred. Yet experience also illustrates that fish can be sexually arousing, and thus could ultimately tempt a widow to break such bonds—which would violate important cultural standards. In contrast, the beliefs among Americans about widows reflect the importance of individualism and the natural right to choice. Among this group, legislating food choices would also violate important cultural standards.

While it is a natural process, ethnocentrism can be reduced through cultural knowledge and perspective taking. In organizational psychology, cross-cultural research is needed to help design training programs to help managers understand the nature of other cultural systems, including how people from other cultures view leadership, negotiation, conflict, motivation, and so on. By illuminating why such beliefs vary—in other words, how they link to dominant cultural meaning systems—will help managers gain perspective about cultural differences, reduce ethnocentrism, and, ultimately, make intercultural interactions more effective.

A Counterpoint: Does Globalization Inevitably Yield Cultural Similarity?

One may ask, however, whether cross-cultural perspectives in organizational psychology are becoming less important because of the homogenization of world cultures. In other words, globalization is causing more cultural similarity, rendering the issue of universality in organizational psychology a fait acompli. This counterargument often rests upon the notion that developments in technology and the globalization of business have resulted (or will result) in the widespread adaptation of American culture throughout the world. Indeed, already skeptics will argue that youth in many countries—from the United States to Japan to Zimbabwe—are all eating Big Macs, drinking Coca-Cola, and wearing jeans, which is causing a homogenization of world culture (Huntington, 1996). Within this perspective, the lack of attention to cultural factors in organizational psychology becomes not only unimportant, but justified.

As noted by Huntington (1996), however, this argument is missing the essence of culture—which includes, at the most basic level, deeply rooted assumptions, beliefs, and values (Triandis, 1972)—and not superficial culinary or clothing choices. Put simply, the "essence of Western civilization is the Magna Carta, not the Magna Mac. The fact that non-Westerners may bite into the later has no implications for their accepting of the former"

(Huntington, 1996, p. 58). Indeed, research on cultural values first pioneered by Hofstede (1980), later refined in Schwartz (1994), and more recently replicated among the GLOBE research team (House et al., 2004) attests to the fact that variability in cultural values is alive and well. Furthermore, some have even argued that an emphasis on cultural identity is actually on the rise (Huntington, 1996) with the end of the superpower divide and the consequent emergence of age-old animosities and emerging cultural divides. As noted by Huntington (1996), "non-western societies can modernize and have modernized without abandoning their own cultures and adopting wholesale Western values, institutions, and practices" (p. 78). In sum, the argument that cultural differences are no longer important (or will cease to be important) in organizational psychology is not easily tenable.

In the remaining part of the chapter, we discuss extant research on culture and organizational psychology, from culture and organizational entry, to culture and individual behavior in organization, to culture and the social animal in organizations. Before we turn to these topics, we first consider critical distinctions and levels of analysis issues in the study of culture and organizations.

Developing Cross-Cultural Reseach Questions: Key Distinctions and Levels of Analysis

The definition of *culture* has long been a source of debate among anthropologists and cross-cultural psychologists (see Jahoda, 1984; Rohner 1984; Segall, 1984). Indeed, over 160 definitions of *culture* have been identified (Kroeber & Kluckhohn, 1952). Perhaps not surprisingly, definitions tend to reflect scholars' training and experience. For instance, Geertz (1973), an anthropologist, defined culture as a "historically transmitted pattern of meanings embodied in symbols, a system of inherited conceptions expressed in symbolic forms by means of which people communicate, perpetuate, and develop knowledge about attitudes toward life." Kluckhohn (1954) defined culture as consisting of "patterned ways of thinking, feeling and reacting, acquired and transmitted mainly by symbols, constituting the distinctive achievements of human groups." Skinner (1981), a behaviorist, argued that "culture is a set of schedules of reinforcements." Hofstede (1980), a psychologist, asserted that culture consists of "a set of mental programs that control an individual's responses in a given context." Definitions also vary in their scope. Shweder and LeVine (1984) argued that culture is a "set of shared meaning systems." Herskovits (1955), alternatively, provided a very broad definition of culture in arguing that culture is "the human-made part of the environment." Triandis (1972) further differentiated aspects of this definition by distinguishing between objective elements (i.e. housing, roads, tools), and subjective elements, or a "group's characteristic way of perceiving its social environment" (Triandis, 1972, p.3).

Although there is no one "right" definition of culture, the level at which culture is defined and operationalized should be determined theoretically and made explicit in research. Below, we draw upon Chan's (1998) terminology for understanding levels of analysis and illustrate the diversity at which culture can be theorized and assessed at different levels of analysis (Gelfand et al., 2008). We explicitly use different terminology at different levels in order to help reduce confusion and inconsistency regarding the level of culture.

Individual Measures of Subjective Culture

At the individual level of analysis, one can differentiate a number of conceptualizations of culture. *Psychological culture* refers to individuals' personal values, attitudes, or beliefs making the individual, not the culture, the referent (e.g., *I* value X). In this conceptualization, culture is treated as an individual-level construct, and is not aggregated to a higher level. This conception of culture is particularly relevant for research that is examining individuals who vary in their values, attitudes, or beliefs within a particular group, and, moreover, when values are not necessarily shared within subgroups of the sample (cf. Chao & Moon, 2005, on the notion of cultural mosaics). *Subjective cultural press* is another individual-level conceptualization of culture, which is defined as individual differences in perceptions of cultural values, attitudes, and/or norms (Gelfand et al. 2008). Like personal values, subjective cultural press is an individual-level definition of culture. Unlike personal values, however, subjective cultural press is measured using the culture as the referent (e.g., *people in this culture* value X; see Shytenberg, Gelfand, & Kim, 2009; Zou, 2009, and Chiu, Gelfand, Yamagishi, Shteynberg, & Wan, 2010 for reviews). This measure of culture is particularly relevant for assessing culture for researchers who theorize that perceptions of the society serve as a motivational force, but that this varies by individuals. For example, individuals high on need for closure may be more attuned to the environment and therefore have more accurate knowledge of the culture. *Implicit measures of cultures* are subconscious differences in attitudes, values, beliefs, or norms across cultural groups that can reflect psychological culture or subjective cultural press. Implicit culture, by definition, is assessed through non-explicit means, such as the Implicit Association Test (Greenwald, McGhee, & Schwartz, 1998) or other unobtrusive methods. Given that researchers have argued that culture is best described as tacit knowledge, rather than explicit knowledge (cf. Kitayama & Uchida, 2005), this is a promising conceptualization and measure of culture (see Kim, Sarason, & Sarason, 2006). Finally, *cultural frog ponds* (Klein, Dansereau, & Hall, 1994) are also potential individual-level conceptualizations of culture, wherein individual values, attitudes, and beliefs are seen in comparison to the mean levels of such constructs in the members of the culture. Such effects are particularly relevant when one is interested in whether the congruence of one's own values with the dominant values predicts organizational phenomena. For example, Van Vianen, Feij, Krausz, and Taris (2004) found that Schwartz's cultural value of self-transcendence predicted work adjustment and interaction adjustment when operationalized as the congruence between an expatriate's values and the perceived normative values of the host country (see Gelfand et al., 2008, for further discussion).

Unit-Level Measures of Subjective Culture

At a higher level of analysis, one can view culture through an additive model of personal values, which are assessed by measuring individual values (e.g., *I* value X) and calculating the value average across members of a given culture. In additive models of culture, the mean of personal values is taken as an adequate representation of unit-level culture, regardless of the degree of variation in individual values within that culture. Many additive models of culture have been advanced (Bond et al., 2004; Hofstede, 1980; Schwartz, 1992). *Consensus culture,* which is based on the direct consensus compositional model described by Chan (1998), in contrast, conceptualizes culture as an aggregate of individuals in cultures where values are *shared*. Like additive culture, consensus culture is measured by assessing individual values (e.g., *I* value X) and aggregating them to the unit level, though in this case, aggregation statistics are typically utilized to justify that constructs are shared (e.g., r_{wg}). Another type of unit-level culture is *cultural descriptive norms*, which fit the referent-shift compositional model described by Chan (1998). Descriptive norm models differ from additive and consensus models by using the culture, instead of the individual, as a referent when measuring values (e.g., *people in this culture* value X). Specifically, descriptive norms are measured by assessing individual perceptions of what is valued in the culture in general (i.e., subjective cultural press), and then averaging perceptions across members of a single culture. Like consensus models of culture, descriptive norm models of culture assume that perceptions of what is valued in a given society must be shared among members of that society in order for culture to be meaningful. Descriptive norm models are also comparatively rare, although the GLOBE study provides a notable exception (e.g., House et al., 1999). Finally, consistent with Chan's (1998) compositional model terminology, one might examine *dispersion* in subjective culture at the unit level as a meaningful conceptualization of culture. Culture as dispersion departs from the three other forms of unit-level culture in that dispersion models define culture as variance instead of central tendency. Dispersion models of culture can be grounded in either personal values (e.g., *I* value X) or subjective cultural press (e.g., *people in this culture* value X) and can be measured as the variance or standard deviation of the individual variable of interest. Cross-cultural researchers generally have not taken a dispersion approach to culture, though this is a promising area for research (Gelfand, et al., 2006).

Unit Measures of Objective Culture

Conceptualizations of culture need not be subjective in nature, as previously discussed, but rely on objective data that does not require explicit reports of values and/or norms. One alternative to subjective cultural ratings is *global culture*, which include objective artifacts, cultural practices, and behavioral patterns (e.g., Kozlowski & Klein, 2000; Triandis, 1972). Because they represent the culture in its entirety, these measures are unit-level definitions of culture. For example, Miyamoto, Nisbett, and Masuda (2006) coded street scenes from the United States and Japan in order to study cultural differences. Likewise, Levine and Norenzayan (1999) used walking speed, the speed at which postal workers complete a task, and the accuracy of public clocks to assess pace of life across cultures. One major advantage of objective measures of culture is that they are not grounded in the perceptions of individuals. Thus, factors that may bias response on surveys that measure cultural values (e.g., halo or central tendency rating biases) are less problematic. On the other hand, measures of objective culture

are not free from human biases, and a given artifact may have more than one cultural interpretation.

In summary, we have discussed definition of culture as both objective and subjective, implicit and explicit, and a property of both individuals and units. While we do not advocate one "right" definition of culture, or suggest that all scholars agree upon the most appropriate level for defining the construct of culture, we believe that it is critical to carefully consider different options for defining culture, to use the definition that is most appropriate given the context of a research study, and to provide an explicit rationale for why culture is defined at a particular level of analysis in any organizational research. Such careful attention to defining culture at the appropriate level of analysis will not only increase our ability to compare similar findings across studies, but will also contribute to achieving a truly global organizational science by building a deeper understanding of where culture operates.

Modeling Cultural Effects in Organizational Psychology

With these distinctions in mind, we now turn to developing models of how culture affects organizational phenomena. As in the former discussion, we advocate that research is explicit in the model that is being tested in cross-cultural research, and, in particular, whether it is a single-level model, a cross-level direct model, or a cross-level moderator model (see Gelfand, Leslie, & Shteynberg, 2007; Gelfand et al., 2008; Kozlowski & Klein, 2000).

Figure 33.1 shows numerous kinds of cross-research questions that might be tested in organizational psychology, as per Gelfand et al, 2007. As depicted in the figure, Linkages A and B in Figure 33.1 reflect examples of *single level* models that examine the macro antecedents and consequences of national culture. For example, one might examine how factors such as temperature, natural resources, population density, economic structure, or history of conflict between nations affect societal values, norms, or beliefs, or how societal values, norms, or beliefs affect societal crime rates, conformity, or innovation (see Gelfand et al., 2011). Although not reflected in the figure, likewise one might examine single-level models of culture at the individual level, using the psychological definitions of culture discussed above.

Linkages C–E reflect *cross-level direct effect* models that examine the direct effect of societal culture on organizations and individuals. For example, Linkage C reflects cross-level research that examines

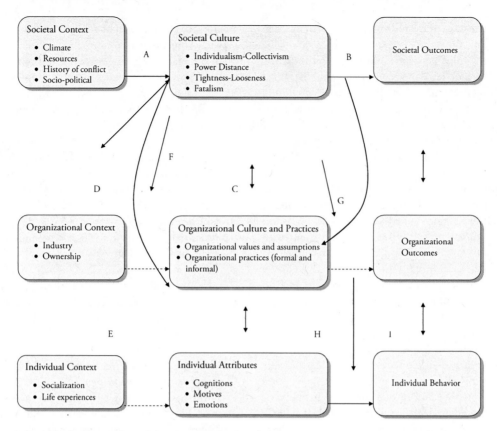

Figure 33.1 Levels of Analysis in Cross-Cultural Research
**Note: Examples given in each box are not exhaustive. From Gelfand, Leslie, & Shteynberg (2007)

the influence of societal culture on organizational culture (see the GLOBE research project; House et al., 2004). Other research at this level of analysis might examine how societal culture affects human resource practices—selection and job analysis techniques, performance appraisal methods, and/or training methods—that are implemented in organizations, as we will discuss extensively below. Research might also examine the indirect effect of societal culture on organizational outcomes, as mediated by cross-cultural differences in organizational culture and practices. For example, Gelfand et al. (2006) argued that organizations in tight societies would be better at implementation, whereas organizations in loose societies might be better at innovation, as mediated by differences in organizational cultures in constraint versus latitude. Linkage D in Figure 33.1 represents research that examines how societal culture has a cross-level direct effect on the institutional context of organizations. For example, it is possible that the prevalence of certain industries or ownership structures (e.g., private versus public) varies across societies.

While Linkages C and D represent societal cross-level effects on organizations, Linkage E represents research that examines how societal culture affects individual-level phenomena, such as cognitions, motives, or emotions. As reviewed below, research in organizational psychology, for example, has examined how societal culture affects employees' achievement motivation, self-efficacy, job attitudes, and perceptions of effective leadership. Alternatively, one might be interested in the indirect effect of societal culture on individual behavior, as mediated by individual perceptions, motives, or emotions. For example, research might examine whether there are cross-cultural differences in attitudes toward team-work, perceptions of justice, or organizational citizenship, as mediated by cross-cultural differences in individuals' perceptions, attitudes, and/or motives.

As seen in Figure 33.1, other research question might examine *cross-level moderator effect* models, wherein societal culture is expected to moderate relationships at the organizational and individual levels. Linkage F represents cross-level research that examines how societal culture interacts with features of the organizational context (e.g., industry, technology) to predict organizational culture and practices. For example, one might be interested in whether organizational cultures are more similar across societies within some industries (e.g., manufacturing) as compared to others (e.g., service). Linkage G illustrates that the relationship between organizational culture and practices and organizational outcomes can be moderated by societal culture. For example, research might address whether diversity in organizations is beneficial for organizational performance and how this relationship varies across societies. At lower levels of analysis, Linkage H represents research on how societal culture moderates the impact of organizational practices on individual cognitions, motives, or emotions. Research might address, for example, whether giving voice (an organizational justice practice) has similar effects on satisfaction in different societal cultures, or whether working in teams similarly affects motivation across cultures. Finally, Linkage I illustrates that societal culture might moderate the relationship between psychological states and behavior. For example, research might examine whether societal culture moderates the strength of attitudes as a predictor of behavior, or whether needs (e.g., need for closure) differentially affect behavior across cultures.

Figure 33.1 represents a heuristic for thinking about the kinds of research models that are tested in cross-cultural organizational psychology and the complexity of levels of analysis in cross-cultural research. Figure 33.1 does not represent all possible multilevel linkages that pertain to societal culture, yet it highlights the importance of making explicit the level and questions being addressed. What is not well represented in the figure are the numerous methodological challenges and judgment calls that are involved, once research questions have been developed. We refer the reader to a number of sources that deal with issues in sampling, translations, response biases, among other methodological concerns that are inherent to cross-cultural research (see, Gelfand, Raver, & Ehrhart, 2002; Van de Vijver & Leung, 1997, and van de Vijver, van Hemert, & Poortinga, Y. H. (2010) for other reviews; see also Berry, 1969; Brett, Tinsley, Janssens, Barsness, & Lytle, 1997; Cheung, & Rensvold, 2000; Peng, Nisbett, & Wong, 1997).

With these distinctions in mind, we now turn to a selective review of research on cross-cultural organizational psychology. We first consider cultural differences at the stage of organizational entry, asking questions such as: How does culture influence

selection practices? How does culture influences the nature of jobs and criteria for performance in organizations? While these issues of organizational entry have long been studied in organizational psychology, they have only recently received cross-cultural attention.

Culture and Organizational Entry
Culture and Staffing: Recruitment and Selection

One of the critical steps in organizational entry is staffing that involves recruitment and selection. Research over the last few decades has illustrated that culture influences the process of selection and recruitment in numerous ways, including the purpose of recruitment, the types of methods used to recruit and select employees, the criteria that are used to make recruitment and selection and decisions, and the perceived fairness and appropriateness of methods used to recruit and select employees, all of which are reviewed in turn below.

Recruitment in the Western literature is often depicted as a process of attracting the right number of applicants with the right level of qualification to the organization. Hence it is a process that should follow a careful HR planning and job analysis. Organizations in North America typically adopt this model, wherein the purpose of recruitment and selection is to differentiate among candidates and to maximize individual performance and ultimately organizational profit. Yet these recruitment and selection goals are not necessarily universal. For example, in India and Eastern Europe, organizations hire more employees than needed in order to combat poverty and unemployment (Herriot & Anderson, 1997; Sinha, 1997). Asian organizations, valuing benevolence and paternalism, adopt practices such as long-term employment to benefit and protect the individual more than the organization. Similarly, in former socialist economies, the duty of government and organizations was to provide employment for life. In such sociocultural contexts, organizations are expected to meet societal needs. Hence, the recruitment practices do not necessarily emphasize the number and qualifications of applicants that are right for the organizations' strategic needs.

Culture also influences methods used to recruit employees. Organizations striving to find the best-qualified applicants typically use widespread recruitment channels (e.g., online recruitment services, career fairs, newspaper ads), and these methods tend to be found in performance-oriented and individualistic cultures (Aycan, 2005). In contrast, organizations striving to maintain interpersonal harmony prefer to use close social networks and word of mouth to announce job openings, as compared to widespread announcements, and these methods tend to be found in collectivistic cultures where there is in-group favoritism, and in high power distant and uncertainty avoiding cultures (Aycan, 2005). Using social networks for recruitment in such cultures is perceived according to different criteria from individual performance per se. For example, employees recruited through personal contacts are perceived to be more likely to stay loyal and committed to the organization (cf. Bian & Ang, 1997; Wasti, 2000). The use of social networks is also useful for assessing the perceived "personal" fit with the organization. For example, some Korean high-level executives personally conduct campus visits to universities of which they are the alumni, and call on their former professors to solicit recommendations for good candidates (Hak-Chong, 1998). For those organizations, good interpersonal relationships, ascribed status and sociopolitical connections are more important than individual merit and credentials (Budhwar & Khatri, 2001; see also Ma & Allen, 2009, who argued that cultural values can moderate the relationship between recruitment practices and recruitment outcomes).

Culture also influences the relative preference that organizations have for internal and external recruitment for managerial positions. According to the findings of Cranet research, (Parry, Tyson, & Brough, 2006), there are differences in the use of internal recruitment to fill middle-level managerial vacancies among European countries (lowest was Bulgaria: 54% of organizations using internal recruitment; highest was Czech Republic: 85%). However, the difference in using internal recruitment is even larger to fill senior-level managerial vacancies (lowest was 27.4% of organizations in Denmark; highest was Czech Republic: 68%). Internal recruitment and promotions may be preferred to ensure *and* reward loyalty to the organization in cultures that are high in collectivism and power distance (e.g., Björkman & Lu, 1999a; Budhwar & Khatri, 2001). It is difficult for externally recruited employees to enter into strong social networks in collectivistic cultures and to cope with the resentment and resistance caused by their appointment, especially if an internal candidate has been supported for a managerial position.

There is also a wide variation in the type of questions directed to job applicants in application forms. In individualistic cultures, personal questions that are not job-related are not asked; they are perceived as violation of privacy and are not permitted on legal (e.g., equal employment opportunity law) and/or ethical grounds. However, in collectivistic cultures, job applicants are primarily evaluated on the basis of how well they will fit into the social and cultural context of the organization. Accordingly, personal questions to predict that aspect are freely asked in the application forms, such as marital status, religious affiliation, ethnic and cultural background, city or region of birth, family background (e.g., spouse's, father's and mother's occupation; number of siblings), socioeconomic status indicators (e.g., type of car driven, ownership of property), leisure time activities, and so on.

In sum, recruitment methods are not necessarily universal. At the same time, it is clear that differences across cultures in recruitment methods follow their own "cultural logic"—in other words, they are used to serve specific organizational goals, which themselves vary considerably across cultures.

Culture also influences the specific criteria being used in recruitment and selection. For example, in the United States, selection criteria are perceived to be relevant to the job as well as predictive of future performance. Some of the most commonly cited criteria for selection include education, past work experience, personality traits, and cognitive skills. Because of the equal employment opportunity laws in the United States, selection criteria should not discriminate against any particular ethnic, gender, or age group. In contrast, criteria for selection in collectivistic cultures are geared toward competence in interpersonal relationships more than competence in job-related areas (e.g., technical knowledge, skills, and abilities). Criteria used in employee selection include, for example: in Japan, team members' favorable opinions about the candidate (Huo & Von Glinow, 1995) and right temperament and personality (Evans, 1993); in Islamic Arab countries, agreeableness, good interpersonal relations and trustworthiness (Ali, 1989); in India, belonging to the same in-group as the manager (e.g., the same family or homeland; Sinha, 1997); in Latin America, positive attitudes toward family life (cf. Barrett & Bass, 1976). Ryan and colleagues found that in cultures fostering interdependent self, selection tools that focus on job-related competencies are perceived to constrain the candidate's ability to express his or her unique self vis-à-vis situational contingencies (Ryan et al., 2009). Others have indeed found that some of the criteria that successfully predict future performance in the United

States may fail to do so elsewhere. For example, the knowledge and skills that are acquired from formal education may not be the best predictors of performance in countries where the quality of formal education is low (e.g., Ingmar & Yuan, 1999; Rousseau & Tinsley, 1997)

Other research illustrates the notion that selection criteria match some important "cultural criterion" in the society in which organizations are embedded. In high power distant cultures, for example, selection criteria reflect the social order in the society. Organizations in high power distance cultures might feel pressure to recruit people who have a close relationship with influential government officers (Björkman & Lu, 1999a,b). Korean's *yon-go* system (a special social relationship or special connection) puts emphasis on the applicants' socioeconomic background, including family ties, school, and birthplace (Hak-Chong, 1998); applicants having "proper" family background are clearly favored. Age and gender are also criteria that are emphasized in culture of high power distance. For example, in Korea, there is age restriction at the entry level to prevent potential conflicts between subordinates and superiors (Hak-Chong, 1998). Because age-based hierarchy and status is prevalent in Korea, it is assumed that if subordinates are older than their superiors, it is more likely that they will be disrespectful to their superiors or that superiors will have difficulty establishing their authority. With respect to gender, there is clear male preference in societies with salient gender role stereotypes (cf. Adler & Izraeli, 1994; Davidson & Burke, 2004).

Consistent with the above discussion, the "Best Practices Project" (Von Glinow, Drost, & Teagarden, 2002) found wide cultural variability in the use of different selection criteria (Huo, Huang, & Napier, 2002). For instance, applicant's ability to perform the technical requirements of the job is an important selection criterion in Australia, Canada, and the United States, whereas it is much less important in Japan. Wide variation was found in the selection criteria of "having the right connections" (e.g., school, family, friends), with the most consideration given to these factors in Mexico and the least in Australia. Von Glinow and colleagues (2002) indicated that selection practices were remarkably similar among the Anglo countries, and that technical skill and work experience were the most important selection criteria. Selection criteria were also similar among Asian countries of Japan, Korea, and Taiwan, in which proven work experience was deemphasized. As a point of convergence, authors concluded that "getting along with others" and "fitting well with the corporate values" were criteria that became as important as technical competence in the majority of countries included in the study.

Culture also influences the methods of employee selection. In some European countries, such as Italy, France, Sweden, and Portugal, the issue of testing (e.g., standardized tests of cognitive ability) has a negative connotation, because it is perceived as an invasion of privacy, a violation of an individual's rights to control his or her own career, and a barrier to the holistic representation of oneself (Dany & Torchy, 1994; Levy-Leboyer, 1994; Ryan, McFarland, Baron, & Page, 1999; Shackleton & Newell, 1997; Shimmin, 1989; Sparrow & Hiltrop, 1994). Steiner and Gilliland (1996) found that French applicants, compared to American applicants, perceived written ability tests to be less impersonal and personality tests to be more offensive and more of a violation of their privacy. The authors argue that perceived fairness and appropriateness of a selection method by applicants is as important as its ability to predict future performance, and they refer to it as "social validity" (see also, Anderson & Witvliet, 2008). European countries also perceive selection as a process that maximizes the benefits of both employers and employees, and meets the needs of multiple stakeholders (e.g., employers, employees, labor unions, professional organizations) (e.g., Roe & Van den Berg, 2003).

As discussed above, organizations in collectivistic cultures attempt to ensure that the applicant fits the organization's social and cultural environment. Meeting with the candidate and developing a subjective impression about the fit between the organization and the candidate is very important. Accordingly, it is perhaps not surprising that collectivistic countries in Europe are more likely to use one-on-one interviews to select employees (e.g., in Spain 92%, in Portugal 91%, in Italy 77%, in Greece 74% of organizations), as compared to less collectivistic cultures (e.g., in Norway 21.4%, in Denmark 30.6%, in UK 43% of organizations; Parry et al., 2006). In Korea several executives participate in the interviews to personally assess applicants' personality with respect to working in harmony, having a sound moral character, and possessing the potential to become part of the team (Hak-Chong, 1998).

References or recommendations are used commonly in the majority of countries for different reasons and in varying degrees. For instance, in the United Kingdom, the United States, and Australia, recommendations are used as a final check, whereas they are heavily relied upon in southeastern European countries and in India (Sinha, 1997; Triandis & Vassiliou, 1972). Countries relying on references use it as a tool to favor in-group members and to discriminate against out-group members (see, Khatri, Tsang, & Begley, 2006, for an excellent discussion on cronyism).

Utility of the standardized selection tests and inventories developed in the United States (e.g., cognitive ability tests, personality inventories) in different cultural contexts has also been seriously questioned (e.g., Bartram, 2005; Greenfield, 1997; Sternberg, 2004), and reviews of the utility of certain assessment techniques has revealed significant variations across cultures (e.g., Bartram & Coyne, 1998; Oakland, 2004; Roe & Van den Berg, 2003). For example, Björkman and Lu (1999b) found that analytical problem-solving tests screen only a small portion of Chinese applicants because of their highly developed analytical thinking ability. To minimize such cultural misfits, there is a growing literature to guide international test users in the process of cultural adaptation and standardization for U.S.-based ability tests and personality inventories (e.g., McCrae & Costa, 1997; International Test Commission, 2000; Van Hemert, van de Vijver, Poortinga, & Georgas, 2002).

Assessment center techniques (AC) are another popular tool in North America, but because cultural context determines the "success criteria," their cross-cultural validity and utility are restricted (e.g., Briscoe, 1997; Dean, Roth, & Bobko, 2008). Depending on the cultural context, AC performance criteria and test contents must be modified. For instance, leaderless group discussion is less likely to work in high power distant cultures. Other situational exercises based on "what would you do if" scenarios are difficult to analyze for Chinese applicants, who are not used to thinking in hypothetical terms (Björkman & Lu, 1999a). Finally, while interviews are common in most cultural contexts (e.g., Ryan et al., 1999; Von Glinow et al., 2002), the way in which they are conducted (structured vs. unstructured) may be culture-specific (Huo et al., 2002).

In summary, this review makes clear that although recruitment and selection are universal processes, their purpose, methods, criteria, and implementation can be highly culture-specific.

Culture and Nature of Jobs and Performance Criteria

At organizational entry, employees must know about role requirements and criteria for high performance in their jobs. The process of defining job requirements, key performance indicators, and worker characteristics is generally referred to as job analysis. The ways in which cultural context influences job analysis, job design, performance criteria, and performance evaluation are discussed below.

First, culture influences the way in which jobs are defined, which is at the bedrock of all functions of job analysis, criteria, and evaluation (see Erez, 2010, for a review). For example, in highly individualistic cultures, jobs are defined in specific terms to highlight the unique characteristics of each job and the individual accountabilities of each job incumbent. In collectivistic cultures, jobs are defined for teams or work groups: individual accountabilities are blurred, and emphasis is placed on within-job activities among team members (e.g., Kashima & Callan, 1994; Sanchez & Levine, 1999). In high uncertainty avoiding cultures, jobs are defined in specific rather than broad terms to reduce role ambiguities (Wong & Birnbaum-More, 1994). Moreover, in cultures that avoid uncertainties, risks, and change, job definitions are detailed, narrow, and fixed, while in cultures that promote flexibility and change, job definitions are broad, flexible, and dynamic (Aycan, 2005). In diffuse, rather than specific cultural contexts, job boundaries are more likely to be permeable (Aycan, 2005). By contrast, in high power distance cultures, jobs are defined in broader terms, so that superiors have more latitude to ask employees to perform a variety of different tasks not included in their job descriptions. In high power distant cultures, there is heavy reliance on supervisory guidance in performing jobs and this may reduce the necessity to have specific job descriptions. As previously discussed, in collectivistic and high power distant cultures, in-group favoritism is common in recruitment and selection. This may imply that jobs are created and defined for particular individuals, rather than individuals being selected on the basis of specific job descriptions. This leads to greater flexibility in job descriptions and specifications to "accommodate" new recruits joining the organization through social networks.

Culture not only influences job descriptions but the design of work schedules, such as part-time work, shift work, temporary work, and telework. Raghuram, London, and Larsen (2001) conducted a cross-cultural study comparing work schedules of selected European countries that differ significantly on Hofstede's four cultural dimensions. Results revealed that shift work and contract work were related to high uncertainty avoidance, high power distance and high collectivism. They propose that shift work is preferred over telework, part-time work, or temporary work in high uncertainty avoidance cultures, because employers seek structured and predictable work arrangements to control the worker output. On the other hand, the flexible nature of telework, part-time work, or temporary work requires tolerance for ambiguities and uncertainties. It is easier to maintain the authority structure and monitor the workers closely in shift work, compared to part-time work or telework, where worker autonomy and discretion are high. Hence, shift work is common in high power distant cultures, whereas flexible work arrangements are common in low power distant cultures. Because shift-work and contract work reinforce solidarity among work groups, it is preferred more in collectivistic rather than individualistic cultures. Work group cohesiveness is not strong in part-time or temporary work arrangements, which are appealing to employees in individualistic cultures. Finally, it was found that temporary work, telework, and part-time work are more common among countries scoring high on femininity rather than masculinity, because workers prefer to have work flexibility to be able to spend time with their families and to socialize with their acquaintances.

Employees must know not only the key requirements and work schedules of their jobs, but also the criteria that will be used to evaluate performance. The criterion problem (cf., Campbell, Gasser, & Oswald, 1996) is exacerbated at the cross-cultural level, because what constitutes "good performance" is culture-bound. In individualistic cultures, for example, emphasis is placed on the individual and the work outcomes, rather than the group and team outcomes. Performance appraisal has the purpose of identifying individual differences, and individuals are held accountable for work outcomes (e.g., Milliman, Nason, Zhu, & De Cieri, 2002). In a recent multinational study, Chiang and Birtch (2010) found that uncertainty avoidance and in-group collectivism were negatively associated with the use of performance appraisal as a formal way to evaluate employees. In such cultures, the primary purpose of performance appraisal is to provide feedback to employees to facilitate development.

Performance criteria in individualistic cultures tend to be objective, quantifiable, and observable, such as meeting objectives, productivity, timeliness, quality of output, and job-specific knowledge and proficiency (Harris & Moran, 1996). In collectivist cultures, individual differences are downplayed,

and the primary purpose of performance evaluation is to justify decisions of compensation and promotion (e.g., Arthur, Woehr, Akande, & Strong, 1995; Triandis & Bhawuk, 1997). Employee loyalty to the in-group carries heavier weight than productivity in performance appraisal. In fact, high-performing employees who stand out in the group are disliked because this may disturb group harmony and invoke jealousy (Kovach, 1995; Vallance, 1999). Work outcomes are important, but social and relational criteria are weighted more heavily in evaluating employees. Such criteria include good human nature, harmony in interpersonal relations, trustworthiness, respectful attitude, loyalty and deference toward superiors, effort and willingness to work, awareness of duties and obligations, gratitude, organizational citizenship, conformity, and contribution to team maintenance (e.g., Blunt & Popoola, 1985; Kim, Park, & Suzuki, 1990; Negandhi, 1984; Singh, 1981; Sinha, 1990; Triandis, 1994; Tung, 1984). Seddon (1987) reports that in some African countries, employees' off-the-job behaviors are also included in the appraisal process to protect the company image in public.

Collectivism involves strong in-group and out-group differentiation in employee treatment. This inevitably leads to favoritism. In countries where favoritism is common, performance criteria are not spelled out specifically, so that differential criteria can be used to evaluate employees (cf., Vallance, 1999). For example, low performers are protected and tolerated so long as they are favored by power holders. In Hong Kong, performance appraisal is perceived to be a way of legitimizing rewards to favored employees, whereas in the United Kingdom, it is considered as a crucial process in determining training and development needs, in assessing future potential, and in career planning (Snape, Thompson, Yan, & Redman, 1998).

In fatalistic and uncertainty avoiding cultures, performance criteria are not specifically articulated. In fatalistic cultures, it is believed that work outcomes are beyond the control of the employee, who cannot be penalized for failing to meet objectives (e.g., Aycan, 2005). In this context, employees are usually evaluated on the basis of the effort and willingness to perform, rather than the outcomes of the goal-directed behavior (Kovach, 1995; Tung, 1984).

Uncertainty avoiding cultures also refrain from specifying performance criteria (e.g., setting specific objectives), because employees feel nervous about the uncertainty of what would happen to them if they could not meet performance criteria. For example, Russian managers avoid making plans and setting specific objectives, because if plans are not realized, they take it as a personal defeat (Michailova & Anisimova, 1999). There is also a danger of punishment by superiors. Therefore, failure to meet objectives carries personal risks for managers' psychological well-being (e.g., loss of face and self-esteem) as well as career development. In countries with volatile socioeconomic and political environment, setting specific performance goals is not only a challenge but also a factor that could demotivate employees (e.g., Davila & Elvira, 2005). "Performance criteria in Chinese organizations tend to be generic, broad, and focus on effort and behavior instead of/as much as outcome" (Cooke, 2008, p. 205). This holds true even in subsidiaries of U.S. multinational corporations (MNCs), which are supposed to be able to set specific performance goals and deploy them to all units. In a recent study, employees in U.S. subsidiaries in Taiwan reported to have lower clarity in performance goals and evaluation standards, compared to their counterparts in the parent company (Sauers, Lin, Kennedy, & Schrenkler, 2009).

In addition to cultural differences in criteria for performance, there is wide variation in the methods of performance evaluation and how individuals are given feedback about their performance (e.g., Peretz & Fried, 2011). In high power distant cultures, performance is usually evaluated by superiors only (immediate supervisor, manager and/or several levels up; Chiang & Birtch, 2010; Davis, 1998; Harris & Moran, 1996), and performance appraisal serves the purpose of reinforcing the authority structure and loyalty (Sinha, 1994). Performance criteria are not defined in specific terms, so that power holders have discretion to evaluate employees in a way that they see fit. Employees experience a tension between satisfying their superiors' demands on the one hand and meeting the performance standards set by the organization on the other (Davila & Elvira, 2005). Performance criteria and ratings may be highly subjective and biased, reflecting the nature of the relationship between the rater and ratee (e.g., Sharma, Budhwar & Varma, 2008).

Organizations also indicate, implicitly or explicitly, promotion criteria to their employees when they enter the organization. Evans (1993) reports that "seniority" is the most important promotion criterion followed by performance in Japanese enterprises. This not only reflects the collectivistic nature of the Japanese culture (i.e., honoring and rewarding the commitment to the organization—in-group—for many years). However, Japanese organizations face the tension between seniority and merit in promotion decisions (Shadur, Rodwell, & Bamber, 1995). In China the most important promotion criteria are loyalty to the Party (or the government or the organization), good interpersonal relationships, hard working, and good moral practices (Easterby-Smith, Malina, & Yuan, 1995). In an excellent analysis of employee categorization and promotion likelihood in Chinese organizations, Cheng (1999) described the process in which promotion decisions are made. The first criterion is the "relationship" of the candidate to the top manager (whether or not an in-group or an out-group member, based on kinship or other salient factors); next comes the "loyalty" criterion; this is followed by the "competence" criterion. According to this categorization, an employee even with high competence and high loyalty is not able to make it to the top if he or she is not related to the person at the top.

Schaubroeck and Lam (2002) found that similarity in personality and good relationships with *peers* was a significant predictor of the promotion decision in individualistic cultures, while similarity in personality and good relationships with *superiors* was a significant predictor of the promotion decision in collectivistic cultures. The authors reasoned that in individualistic cultures, peer integration is less likely and less naturally occurring than it is in collectivistic cultures. When it occurs, it is an important and positive indicator of the person's potential for a managerial position. On the other hand, in collectivistic cultures, superiors favor those employees who are similar to them with respect to personality, and who maintain good interpersonal relationships with them, for promotions. Such candidates are perceived as "in-group" members who are likely to remain loyal and deferent to their superiors when promoted.

Cross-cultural differences not only impact the nature of criteria (i.e., type of criteria and level of specificity in their definition), but also the interpretation of the same criteria. The same performance criteria may be interpreted differently by evaluators in diverse subsidiaries of MNCs. For example, organizational commitment may imply years in the organization in Japan, or expansion of extra effort in Singapore; leadership may imply cooperation and teamwork in Asia, or assertiveness and independence in the United States (Caligiuri, 2006). The same challenge is evident in culturally diverse organizations; that is, managers from diverse cultural backgrounds use different interpretations of performance criteria in evaluating employees (DeCieri & Sheehan, 2008).

We next turn to culture and individual behavior in organizations, asking such questions as: What directs and sustains goal-directed behavior in organizations and how does this vary across cultures? How does culture influence organizational attitudes, such as job satisfaction and organizational commitment?

Culture and Individual Behavior in Organizations
Culture and Motivation

Theories of work motivation can generally be grouped into content and process theories. Content theories attempt to answer the question of "what motivates people at work," whereas process theories attempt to answer the question of "how people are motivated." To preface the review below, research on culture and motivation suggests that the applicability of American theories in other cultural contexts is limited, because these theories are based on the following assumptions: (a) employees are primarily motivated by rewards and practices that satisfy and enhance their *individual self*; (b) it is the *individual* whose effort is important for high performance; (c) the individual has control of events in life—it is therefore *up to* him or her to meet high performance standards; and (d) the individual rationally evaluates the likelihood of achieving performance goals and *chooses* the ones that will be worth spending the effort. These assumptions reflect the cultural value orientations of individualism, low power distance, masculinity, uncertainty tolerance, and self determination. However, such assumptions underlying motivational theories are not as valid in cultures characterized by collectivism, power distance, fatalism, uncertainty avoidance, or femininity.

As a general principle, motivational practices that are congruent with the nature of the self that is emphasized in particular cultural contexts lead to greater goal-directed behavior in organizations (Erez & Earley, 1993). For example, in individualistic cultures, such as the United States, independent self-construals become highly developed (Markus & Kitayama, 1991; Triandis, 1989), and the self is defined in terms of specific accomplishments, attitudes, and abilities and is perceived as detached from collectives. The cultural ideal is to be separate from others, to express one's uniqueness, and to feel "good" about oneself (Markus & Kitayama, 1991). In such cultural systems, the self

is conceived to be a free agent (i.e., is entitled to do what one wishes) and there is a strong emphasis on values of self-determination, self-actualization, freedom, and *individual* responsibility (Triandis, 1989). In contrast, in collectivistic cultures, the self is represented as the interdependent self, guided by the desire to achieve goals of the social group (e.g., family, organization) and to fulfill obligations to the group to which one belongs (Markus & Kitayama, 1991). For the interdependent self, achievement in one's job means getting the approval and recognition of the esteemed and beloved people in one's life (e.g., family members, the employer), fulfilling their expectations, and not losing one's own "face" or that of others (Markus & Kitayama, 1991). Self-enhancement and self-promotion are perceived highly negatively in collectivistic cultures (e.g., Gelfand et al., 2002; Heine, Lehman, Markus, & Kitayama, 1999; Yoshida, Kojo, & Kaku, 1982). In such cultural systems, there is a strong emphasis on values of harmony, conformity, and *collective* responsibility (Triandis 1989). Motivational practices (e.g., sense of achievement, individual-based rewards, job enrichment) that would *primarily* enhance the individual's own self have limited utility to motivate employees, if not backfire, in collectivistic cultures. These themes become evident in much of the research on culture and motivation below.

CONTENT THEORIES OF MOTIVATION

One of the most highly cited content theories of motivation is *Maslow's theory of hierarchy of needs*. Maslow's theory was developed in the context of the Cold War, when the essence of American culture emphasized individualism and individual achievement (Cooke, Mills, & Kelley, 2005). Although by now many Western authors have also critiqued various theoretical and psychometric aspects of his theory, it is worth also noting that the theory has also received mixed support beyond Western borders. For example, earlier studies demonstrated similar but not identical ordering of needs in countries such as India (Jaggi, 1979), Libya (Buera & Glueck, 1979), and Peru (Stephens, Kedia, & Ezell, 1979), and in the Middle East (Badawy, 1980). However, as early as 1966, Haire and colleagues found that while *need satisfaction* (i.e., safety was the most satisfied need and self-actualization was the least) followed the hierarchy proposed by Maslow in the majority of countries, rankings of *need importance* did not. Social needs were more important for employees in cultures valuing maintenance of good interpersonal relationships and quality of life (i.e., collectivistic or feminine cultures) than those in cultures valuing achievement and accumulation of wealth (i.e., individualistic or masculine cultures; cf. Adler, 1991). As well, having a sense of belonging to the organization that is perceived as an extended family and the sense of contribution to society have been found to be more important needs than the sense of personal accomplishment for African managers (Jackson, 2004).

Others have taken *emic* perspectives to hierarchies of needs that are unique to particular cultural contexts (Nevis, 1983). Assumptions underlying individualistic (mainly the United States) management concepts endorse self-determination (i.e., mastery of individual of his or her fate), freedom of thought and expression, individual right to excel and independence; assumptions underlying collectivistic (mainly Chinese) management concepts include the priority of nation and loyalty to it, consideration for the family, respect for age and wisdom, respect for traditional ways, and importance of communal property over private possessions. Based on these differences, Nevis (1983) proposed a hierarchy of needs applicable for Chinese employees. In this model, belonging (social needs) are the most basic needs at the bottom of the hierarchy, followed by physiological needs and safety needs. At the top, there is *self-actualization in the service of society*, which is defined as the "highest order of attainment of individual competence for reasons related to superordinate goals" (Nevis, 1983, p. 261). Nevis did not include "self-esteem need" in his model because individualism is de-emphasized and the self is defined in terms of group (Gambrel & Cianci, 2003).

Others have also illustrated that Maslow's original theory was laden with cultural values. For example, Hofstede (1983) argued that Maslow's hierarchy also reflects low uncertainty avoidance. In cultures with high uncertainty avoidance, employees are more strongly motivated by satisfying safety and security needs than self-actualization needs. For example, Blunt and Jones (1992) observed that African managers placed higher importance on security other than higher order needs. Adigun and Stephenson (1992) also found that Nigerian workers were motivated by satisfaction of lower order needs (e.g., pay, fringe benefits, working conditions), whereas British workers were motivated by satisfaction of higher order need (e.g., achievement, interesting work, recognition).

The needs in Maslow's hierarchy do not necessarily predict behavior in similar ways across cultures.

For example, Huang and Van de Vliert (2003) found that satisfying higher order needs exerted different effects across 49 nations. Job characteristics that satisfy higher order needs (e.g., autonomy, challenge) are associated with high job satisfaction only in economically developed countries with a strong social security system and low power distance. In another recent study, Russians were found to be motivated more than Swedes when their salary increased (Fey, 2005). Russia is a country where the social security system functions poorly and earnings are shared with aging parents; thus increased salary is the key to satisfy survival and safety needs for employees.

Schwartz's typology of motivational domains of values (Schwartz & Bilsky, 1990) draws parallel to Maslow's classification of needs. The security domain of values (e.g., safety, stability, harmony) corresponds to Maslow's physiological and safety needs; the achievement domain of values (e.g., competence, achievement) corresponds to Maslow's esteem need; the pro-social value domain (e.g., altruism, benevolence, kindness) corresponds to Maslow's need for affiliation; and the maturity domain (e.g., learning, growth, attainment of goals) corresponds to Maslow's self-actualization need category (Gambrel & Cianci, 2003). It would be possible to predict cross-cultural differences in work motivation using Schwartz's framework, and this would be a fruitful avenue for future research.

Another content theory is *Herzberg's motivation-hygiene theory*. Factors related to the job content (e.g., autonomy, challenge, opportunity to learn and grow) are generally referred to as "intrinsic factors" and are associated with high motivation and job satisfaction. Factors related to the job-context (e.g., safe work environment, pay, compensation package, supervision), which are generally referred to as "extrinsic factors" or hygiene factors, are those taken for granted, and are generally unrelated to motivation and job satisfaction. Hygiene factors (i.e., extrinsic factors) largely correspond to Maslow's lower order needs, whereas motivators (i.e., intrinsic factors) correspond to higher order needs. Although some have found support for components of the theory cross-culturally (Brislin and colleagues, 2005), based on the parallels between this theory and Maslow's, one can predict that Herzberg's theory has similar limitations in cross-cultural settings.

More recent research has examined the factors that promote intrinsic motivation across cultures. In the West, freedom and autonomy in one's job are considered to be critical intrinsic factors motivating employees. However, Iyengar and Lepper (1999) showed that Asian Americans' intrinsic motivation and performance were highest when valued and trusted in-group members made choices for them. In contrast, Anglo Americans had the highest intrinsic motivation when they had the autonomy to make choices themselves. Moneta (2004) found that Chinese experienced the highest level of intrinsic motivation in conditions requiring low challenge and high skill level, rather than high challenge and high skill level. The author attributes this to the endorsement of Taoism in the Chinese cultural system emphasizing prudence, interconnectedness, and emotional moderation. More generally, exploration, curiosity, and variety are associated less with intrinsic motivation in collectivistic cultures where conformity to the norm is valued (Kim & Drolet, 2003; Kim & Markus, 1999).

Research has also shown that the relative importance of intrinsic versus extrinsic motivation in prediction motivation varies across cultures. Furnham and colleagues (1994) reported cross-cultural variations in 41 countries in the factors that were considered to be extrinsically or intrinsically motivating. Participants from the Americas (e.g., Argentina, Mexico, Chile, the United States) placed high importance on mastery, hard work, and savings, whereas those from Asian/Eastern countries (e.g., Bangladesh, China, India, Israel) placed high importance on competitiveness and money. The authors explain these differences by culture as well as level of economic development of countries (see also Adigun & Stephenson, 1992). Huang and Van de Vliert (2003) found that in collectivistic and high power distant cultures, intrinsic job characteristics (e.g., challenge, recognition, autonomy, feedback) were less closely related to job satisfaction than were extrinsic job characteristics (e.g., pay, job security, working conditions). However, other studies reported the importance of *both* intrinsic and extrinsic factors for work motivation and job satisfaction (e.g., Aycan & Fikret-Pasa, 2003).

DeVoe and Iyengar (2004) examined the relationship between managerial perceptions of employee motivation and their evaluation of employee performance. North American managers assigned high performance evaluation scores to those employees who they believed to be intrinsically motivated, whereas Asian managers assigned high scores to those who they believed to be both intrinsically and extrinsically motivated. North American managers

positively evaluated those who stand out for their uniqueness (i.e., working mainly for intrinsic reasons), whereas Asian managers valued conformity to the norm and did not punish employees who were like others (i.e., working for extrinsic reasons).

Another content theory focusing on needs is *McClleland's typology of needs.* McClelland (1985) suggested that among the three motives (i.e., achievement, affiliation, power), achievement motivation had the strongest association with performance. An early study provided supporting evidence to the theory in New Zealand (Hines, 1973). This is not surprising. Hofstede argued that need for achievement implied a willingness to take risks (i.e., low uncertainty avoidance) and a desire to achieve a visible success (i.e., masculinity). The countries at the junction of low uncertainty avoidance and masculinity in Hofstede's study were all English-speaking Anglo-Saxon countries, plus a number of their former colonies (1983, p. 67). Sagie, Elizur, and Yamauchi (1996) investigated achievement orientation in five countries, the United States, the Netherlands, Israel, Hungary, and Japan. They found similarities regarding the structure of achievement motivation but differences regarding the strength of it. People with more individualistic orientations had higher achievement motivation tendencies. The findings of the study, however, suggested two types of achievement motivation: personal and collective. The individualistic perspective to achievement motivation emphasizes the need for personal success, whereas the collectivistic perspective emphasizes the need for group success, which cannot be achieved without teamwork (see also Stewart, Carland, Carland, Watson & Sweo, 2003).

Other work illustrates that the very meaning of *achievement* carries different connotations across cultures. Yu and Yang (1994) reviewed studies examining different meanings of success and failure and reported that for Thais, for example, success was closely related to respect for others and tradition, and for Americans it was related to free will and realism. Early studies in Japan also showed that continuity in family tradition was more highly praised than attainment of individual achievements (DeVos, 1973). Chinese emphasize the importance of contribution to the social group and fulfilling the expectations of the family and social group when explaining achievement motivation (Wilson & Pusey, 1982). Yu and Yang (1994) proposed a new term, *social-oriented achievement motivation,* and developed a scale to measure it that contained items such as "the major goal in my life is to work hard to achieve something which will make my parents proud of me."

PROCESS THEORIES OF MOTIVATION

Equity theory is one of the few process theories of motivation that has been subjected to extensive cross-cultural replications. Early studies asserted that equity principle in distributing rewards had limited motivating utility in non-U.S. contexts (e.g., Gergen, Morse & Gergen, 1980), and that employees had a tendency to prefer equality and need principles more than they did equity principle (e.g., Chen, 1995). However, studies in recent years yielded mixed results. A meta-analysis by Sama and Papamarcos (2000) suggested that equity was preferred by employees in individualistic cultures, whereas equality was preferred by those in collectivistic cultures, especially toward in-group members. However, the meta-analysis by Fischer and Smith (2003) demonstrated that individualism and collectivism were not related to reward allocation preference. These contradictory findings may be explained by the contextual factors (e.g., see, Chen, Meindl, & Hui, 1998). For example, Leung (1997) found that when the reward allocator was also a recipient of rewards, there was a preference for equality in collectivistic cultures, whereas if the reward allocator was not a recipient of rewards (e.g., an external agent), equity was preferred in both individualistic and collectivistic cultures.

Power distance was shown to be more important than individualism-collectivism to predict individuals' preferences of equity over equality (Fey, 2005; Fischer & Smith, 2003). Equity is preferred in high power distance cultures, whereas equality is preferred in low power distance cultures. Fischer and Smith (2003) also found that Hofstede's masculinity dimension was correlated strongly with the preference of equity, while femininity was correlated strongly with the preference for equality.

Only a few studies focused on need as a distribution criterion. Fischer (2004) reported cross-cultural differences in the need-based allocation of rewards and resources. People had a preference for need-based distribution in conditions of high unemployment and high collectivism. Giacobbe-Miller, Miller, and Victorov (1998) used a scenario approach to assess the importance placed on need: Russian subjects were much more likely to state that need should be the sole criterion, as compared to Americans.

There are important cross-cultural differences in the ways in which people consider what constitutes inputs, outputs, and referent groups. Seniority and education are emphasized more than performance as important inputs in Korea (Hundley & Kim, 1997). Gómez, Kirkman, and Shapiro (2000) found that collectivistic cultures value employee's behaviors that contribute to the maintenance of harmony and enhancement of team environment more than individualistic cultures do. Accordingly, behaviors geared toward helping others and maintaining good interpersonal relationships are inputs that are more important than job performance in collectivistic cultures (Bolino & Turnley, 2008). In high power distance cultures, seniority, age, and social class are considered as inputs that deserve valued organizational outcomes (e.g., promotion). Loyalty, respect, and adherence to social norms are also considered to be inputs in the exchange relationship (Fadil, Williams, Limpaphayom, & Smatt, 2005).

In collectivistic cultures, valued outcomes include long-term employment, and respect and recognition from the supervisor, and good interpersonal relationships (Fadil et al., 2005). In high power distance cultures, people expect to earn status symbols (e.g., a bigger office, company car, job title) in exchange for inputs (e.g., hard work or loyalty).

According to Bolino and Turnley (2008), cross-cultural variations in referent group preferences can be summarized in three ways. First, in high power distant cultures, employees are unlikely to compare themselves with high-level managers because it is acceptable that those managers have privileges due to their high status. Second, in individualistic cultures, the referent group is made up of employees who are holding similar jobs and others with whom they share the most similarity. In collectivistic cultures, employees are also concerned with the fair treatment of their in-groups (e.g., the team members in the work unit), and may be involved in comparisons between their groups and other groups in or outside the organization.

Compared to individualistic cultures, people in collectivistic cultures are more concerned with restoring equity to save the relationship (Allen, Takeda, & White, 2005; Fok, Hartman, Villere, & Freibert, 1996; Westman, Park, & Lee, 2007; Wheeler, 2002). It is also possible that in collectivistic cultures, people may resort to cognitive restoration of equity (i.e., thinking that the outcome must have been deserved for reasons that are not apparent to the individual), rather than taking an action to actually correct it, especially if there is a concern that taking any action would harm the relationship (Bolino & Turnley, 2008). Fatalistic beliefs in a culture would lead to accepting the inequities as they are (Bolino & Turnley, 2008), and expecting that equity will be established one day, if not in the short run (Weick, Bougan, & Maruyama, 1976).

Another process theory of motivation, *expectancy theory*, holds that employees are motivated when they believe that their behavior will enhance the probability of desired outcomes. The magnitude of motivation is determined by the product of the expectancy, instrumentality, and valence. An early test of the theory showed that the motivational force score predicted by the theory was associated with effort and performance outcomes of sales personnel in both the United States and Japan (Matsui & Terai, 1975). However, more recent research shed doubt about the cross-cultural validity of the original theory and its three elements.

For example, Geiger and colleagues (1998) tested components of expectancy theory in ten cultures: Australia, Canada, Hong Kong, India, Indonesia, Malaysia, Mexico, Oman, Singapore, and the United States. They found that individualism and long-term orientation (i.e., importance of planning) were positively associated with expectancy beliefs, whereas power distance and uncertainty avoidance orientation were negatively associated with expectancy beliefs. Emery and Oertel (2006) found that there was a strong correlation between German employees' belief that it was possible to perform well if they exerted effort (i.e., expectancy) and if they work closely with their supervisor. German employees, coming from a high power distant culture, believe that effort would lead to performance when they had close working relationships with their supervisors.

Culture also plays a key role in the *instrumentality* component of the theory. Research showed that performance-reward contingency is low in cultures that are high in power distance and high in fatalism (Aycan et al., 2000). As discussed earlier, in high power distance cultures, reward allocation is based on criteria other than performance, such as seniority or good relationships with top management (e.g., Brown & Reich, 1997; Hui & Luk, 1997; Leung, 1997; Smith & Bond, 1993). Schuler and Rogovsky (1998) also found that seniority-based compensation systems were preferred in countries with high levels of uncertainty avoidance, because such practices emphasize predictability and certainty, whereas performance and skill-based compensation systems were preferred in countries with low uncertainty avoidance. Pay-for-performance schemes are used widely in individualistic cultures, whereas group-based rewards are preferred in collectivistic cultures

(Gluskinos, 1988). More generally, individual differences are downplayed in collectivistic cultures and the "equality" principle in compensation and reward system reflects that. Wage differentials are narrow, even among the lowest and highest ranking officials in collectivistic cultures, whereas they are very high in individualistic and performance-oriented cultures (Easterby-Smith et al., 1995; Huo & Von Glinow, 1995).

Cross-cultural variations in what are considered to be *valued outcomes* (i.e., the "valence" component in the expectancy theory) are well-documented in the literature (e.g., Erez, 1997; Gelfand et al., 200, 2007; Kim et al., 1990; Mendonca & Kanungo, 1994; Miller, Hom, & Gomez-Mejia, 2001) and were discussed above in content theories of motivation. For example, promotion is usually considered to be an important outcome of good performance. However, promotion of an individual to a higher position may mean separating the individual from his or her work team, increasing the jealousies of others who did not get the promotion, having extra responsibilities, and therefore working longer hours and taking risks in one's job. Thus, "promotion" can have negative connotations for employees in collectivistic, high power distant, or uncertainty avoidant cultures (Adler, 1991). Corney and Richards (2005) reported that promotion was the most preferred reward for American students, while good pay and bonuses were the most preferred rewards for Chilean and Chinese students.

Goal-setting theory, which also received cross-cultural research attention, postulates that employees are motivated when they have clearly set goals that are *specific, challenging*, and *acceptable*. Compared to the "do your best" condition, goals are found to increase performance in a variety of countries such as the Caribbean, Australia, Israel, and Sri Lanka (cf. Punnett, 2004). As a general principle, people who have strong achievement needs are more likely to be motivated by specific and challenging goals. However, people with strong affiliation needs (e.g., as is found in many collectivistic cultures) are less likely to be motivated by specific and challenging goals because such goals have the potential to increase competition in the workplace as well as the possibility of failure, which will cause embarrassment and loss of face. People in collectivistic cultures may also resent individually set goals, as they may surface individual differences and give people individual accountabilities. Indeed, Kurman (2001) found that in collectivistic and high power distance cultures, ensuring high performance by setting goals with moderate difficulty was more motivating than setting goals that are challenging. Hard and specific goals may also be less motivating in cultures high on fatalism. Punnett (2004) argued that "where people feel that they have little control over their environment, the idea of setting a specific target may seem foolish at best and possibly thought of as going against God's will" (p. 150).

In a recent study, Grouzet and colleagues (2005) compared the *types of goals* that were preferred among employees in 15 different countries. The goals were classified in four categories driven from the combination of two dimensions: intrinsic versus extrinsic dimension, and self-transcendence versus physical self-dimension. For example, in the category of self-transcendent and intrinsic goals, there are spirituality and service to community, whereas in the category of physical self and extrinsic goals, there is financial success. The structure of goal categorization was similar across cultures; however, the placement of goals was different. For instance, financial success as a goal in life was further from hedonism and closer to safety-physical health goals in poorer cultures than in the wealthier cultures. In another cross-cultural study comparing employees from Singapore, Malaysia, India, Thailand, Brunei, and Mongolia, Chatterjee and Pearson (2002) found that there were wide variations among Asian employees in their work goals (e.g., autonomy, variety, promotion, learning, salary). For example, having an interesting work and autonomy in decision making were important goals for all Asian countries except for Malaysia; job security was a valued goal in all Asian countries except Thailand. The findings suggested that cross-cultural variations within the Asian region should be taken into consideration in goal setting, especially in multinational corporations with a diverse workforce.

Research has also examined the question of whether participative goal setting motivates employees to a greater extent than assigned goals. Participative goal setting increases the motivation of people in egalitarian cultural contexts; however, in high power distance cultures, people do not have difficulty accepting and committing to assigned goals (Sue-Chan & Ong, 2002). A comparative study between Israeli and U.S. employees demonstrated that Israelis performed lower than Americans under the assigned, rather than participative goal setting condition (Erez & Earley, 1987). The authors replicated their findings with different samples and found that lack of participation in goal

setting led to a lower level of commitment among the Israelis than among Americans (Latham, Erez, & Locke, 1988). Overall, Americans were found to be committed to goals that were either assigned or participatively set, whereas Israelis were committed to goals only when they were participatively set. The authors argued that the difference between U.S. and Israeli workers was caused by the power distance experienced in these cultures. According to Hofstede's and GLOBE's data, Americans are higher than Israelis on power distance, and therefore find it easier than Israelis to commit to goals assigned by their supervisors.

According to another process theory of motivation, *job characteristics theory*, employees are motivated to the extent that their jobs are enriched. Job enrichment involves increasing autonomy, feedback, skill variety, task significance and task identity. Roe and colleagues (2000) discovered that characteristics of enriched jobs have differential impacts on psychological states and organizational attitudes of employees in Bulgaria, Hungary, and the Netherlands. For example, autonomy, feedback, and skill variety had positive impacts on psychological and work outcomes in the Netherlands (an individualistic culture), but had no or marginal impact in Bulgaria and Hungary (collectivistic cultures). Fey (2005) found that feedback had a marginally positive impact on employee performance in Russia but not in Sweden, probably due to the fact that feedback was considered to be a hygiene factor in Sweden but a motivator in Russia, where it was uncommon. Lee-Ross (2005) compared employees in Australia and Mauritius (an island in the Indian Ocean) and found that Australian employees feel empowered by the presence of all five characteristics of enriched jobs to a greater extent than those in Mauritius. Aycan and colleagues (2000) found that in fatalistic cultures, managers assumed that employees' nature could not change or improve. As a result, they did not provide enriched jobs to their employees. Managers in collectivistic cultures implemented job enrichment, because they considered it an obligation to their employees.

Compared to other job characteristics, feedback has attracted the most attention from cross-cultural researchers. Although feedback is very important to motivate employees, there are significant cross-cultural differences in the prevalence and method of giving and receiving feedback. For example, in collectivistic and high power distant cultures, there is reluctance to seek feedback (Morrison, Chen, & Salgado, 2004). The process is usually initiated by the superior, who is trusted for his or her expertise and wisdom (Huo & Von Glinow, 1995). In collectivistic cultures, feedback is indirect, non-confrontational, subtle, and private (Fletcher & Perry, 2001); face-to-face performance interviews are extremely rare (Elenkov, 1998). In individualistic cultures, self-efficacy beliefs are enhanced by feedback to the individual, whereas in collectivistic cultures, self-efficacy beliefs are enhanced by feedback to the group as well (Earley, Gibson, & Chen, 1999). In cultures where the distinction between life and work space is blurred (i.e., diffuse cultures; Trompenaars, 1993), negative feedback on one's job performance is perceived as attacking the person's personality. Therefore, there is a tendency to avoid giving negative feedback to save the employee from losing face (e.g., Seddon, 1987). Vallance (1999) reports that in some organizations in the Philippines, two forms are submitted, one to the HR department and the other to the employee—the latter has a more positive tone.

In collectivistic cultures, positive feedback on performance is not well-received, either. Positive feedback to individual performance could disturb group harmony, as it may induce jealousy and resentment among those who did not receive such feedback. Also, in collectivist cultures, positive feedback is expected to come from the outside. When a manager praises his or her own employees, it is perceived as self-serving (Triandis, 1994). Bailey, Chen, and Dou (1997) showed that Japanese and Chinese employees did not take any initiative to seek feedback on individual performance. Seeking feedback on individual performance was perceived as " . . . vulgar self-centeredness" (Bailey et al., 1997, p. 611). Feedback on *group* performance is more acceptable than that on individual performance. Moreover, in collectivist cultures, high-context communication patterns prevail (Gibson, 1997). Feedback on performance can be embedded in contextual cues. As such, contextual cues provide indirect, implicit and subtle messages about performance to prevent tension and conflicts that may arise as a result of direct and confrontational communication.

It is work mentioning that job enrichment for the group, rather than the individual employee enhances motivation in collectivistic cultures (Erez, 2000). The socio-technical system and autonomous work groups popular in northern Europe involve job enrichment at the group level by enhancing team autonomy, team responsibility, feedback on team performance, and task meaningfulness.

In sum, the above review illustrates that the factors that direct and sustain goal-directed behavior in organizations are highly culturally contingent. It is clear from this review that many, if not all, motivational theories have been developed in the West, making it critical to examine whether their underlying general principles hold across cultures. The above review also illustrates that the meaning of motivational concepts (e.g., achievement) can be highly culture-specific, making it critical to examine how affiliation, power, input, output, referent group, or autonomy are *defined* in different cultural contexts. There also might be culture-specific motivational practices or themes (e.g., needs, expectations) related to work motivation that await empirical investigation. For example, Murray (1938; cited in Markus & Kitayama, 1991) proposed a list of dominant needs in collectivistic cultures, including deference (the need to admire and willingly follow a superior), similance (the need to imitate and emulate others), affiliation (the need to form friendships and associations), nurturance (the need to nourish, aid, and protect), and avoidance of blame (the need to avoid blame and punishment; see also Lockwood, Marshall, & Sadler, 2005, for a discussion on the motivation to avoid failure among Asian-Canadians). In the Confucian tradition, the emphasis placed on morality is associated with "learning," rather than "achievement" motivation (Li, 2002; Stevenson, Hofer, & Randel, 2000). Self-improvement (awareness of weakness and desire to improve oneself) is a stronger motivator for employees in collectivistic cultures than self-enhancement (see Heine and his colleagues, 2001; Kitayama, Markus, Matsumoto, & Norasakkunkit, 1997). More generally, understanding the nature of goals, how they should be set, how one monitors progress, and how one adapts to discrepancies is a critical direction for culture and motivation research. As the above review attests, culture also plays a role in the relationship between motivational practices and organizational outcomes. For example, satisfying high-order needs was not found to increase job satisfaction and work performance in cultures with strong power hierarchies, such as China (Eylon & Au, 1999) and India (Robert et al., 2000). The above review also illustrates that research is sorely needed on dimensions in addition to individualism-collectivism and power distance. Cultural dimensions that are particularly meaningful in relation to work motivation are fatalism (Aycan et al., 2000), performance-orientation (House et al., 2004), and uncertainty avoidance (Hofstede, 1980).

ORGANIZATIONAL ATTITUDES

Job satisfaction is one of the most well researched topics in organizational psychology, perhaps due to the role that happiness takes in Western contexts more generally, where much of the theories and research on job satisfaction originate. Cross-cultural research on job satisfaction focuses on a number of questions, such as whether there are differences across cultures in levels of job satisfaction, whether there are similar predictors of job satisfaction, and whether there are similar consequences of job satisfactions across cultures.

For example, research has illustrated that job satisfaction is higher in Western and in capitalistic developed cultures, as compared to Eastern cultures and socialist developing cultures (Vecernik, 2003). An important question is whether the meaning of job satisfaction, however, is equivalent across cultures. Liu, Borg, and Spector (2004) showed that the meaning of job satisfaction is equivalent across countries speaking the same language and sharing similar cultural backgrounds, yet its equivalence decreases with increasing cultural distance (Liu et al., 2004).

There are some universal predictors of job satisfaction. For example, positive self-concepts and internal locus of control are related to job satisfaction across a wide range of cultures (Piccolo, Judge, Takahashi, Watanabe, & Locke, 2005; Spector et al., 2002). Sweeney and McFarlin (2004) found that making social comparisons is universally related to pay satisfaction across cultures. Yet the factors that contribute to satisfaction also vary across cultures. Extrinsic job characteristics tend to be positively related to job satisfaction across cultures, yet intrinsic job characteristics are more strongly associated with job satisfaction in rich countries dominated by individualistic and low power distance values (Huang & Van de Vliert, 2003; Hui, Lee, & Rousseau, 2004; see also So, West, & Dawson, 2011, for an analysis of job design and team strucgture on satisfaction across cultures). In a 42-nation study, Van de Vliert and Janssens (2002) also showed that satisfaction is highly correlated with self-referent motivation and negatively related to other-referent motivation, and these effects were pronounced in countries of high income levels, education, and life expectancy (Van de Vliert & Janssens, 2002). Contextual factors can also differentially affect job satisfaction across cultures. For example, a warm and congenial work group facilitates high satisfaction among collectivists but low satisfaction among individualists (Hui & Yee, 1999).

An interesting question is whether culture moderates the impact of job satisfaction on employee outcomes. Much of the impetus for job satisfaction research is tied to the fact that being satisfied (or dissatisfied) with one's job has important consequences, and there is widespread evidence that dissatisfaction leads to a host of withdrawal behaviors in organizations (Hulin, 1991). At the same time, research in cross-cultural psychology would suggest that individuals do not necessarily believe that attitudes and behavior are related across cultures (Kashima, Siegal, Tanaka, & Kashima, 1992). Work is perceived more as a "duty" than as "right" in collectivistic cultures (Ramesh & Gelfand, 2010), raising the possibility that job satisfaction exerts smaller effects than in individualistic cultures. Indeed, growing evidence shows that culture moderates the impact of job satisfaction on withdrawal behaviors; a stronger relationship exists in individualistic cultures, as compared to collectivistic cultures (Posthuma, Joplin, & Maetz, 2005; Thomas & Au, 2002; Thomas & Pekerti, 2003). Chiu & Kosinski (1999) similarly noted that while Chinese experienced less job satisfaction than did Westerners, they complained less about it and accepted the situation as it was.

While satisfaction drives many employee outcomes such as withdrawal in the West, factors other than satisfaction might be important for withdrawal in non-Western cultures. For example, Ramesh and Gelfand (2010) found that turnover in India was predicted by employees' links and their fit with the organization, whereas turnover in the United States was more highly predicted by one's perception that one's skills matched those of the job. Overall, the nature, antecedents, and consequences of job satisfaction can vary widely across cultures.

Research on other attitudes, such as organizational commitment, shows considerable cultural variation. For example, the meaning of organizational commitment can vary across cultures. Several studies have shown construct validity for existing measures of organizational commitment across a wide variety of countries (Gautam, van Dick, Wagner, Upadhyay, & Davis, 2005; Vandenberghe, 1996; Vandenberghe, Stinglhamber, Bentein, & Delhaise, 2001; Yousef, 2003). Yet others have questioned whether existing organizational commitment constructs and measures can simply be applied to other cultures. Cheng and Stockdale (2003) and Chen and Francesco (2003) found that the three-factor model of commitment (normative, affective, and continuance) was not optimal in Chinese samples, and others have questioned the validity of existing commitment scales in Korea (Ko, Price, & Mueller,

1997; Lee, Allen, Meyer, & Rhee, 2001. These differing conclusions raise the question of whether differences in factor validity are due to translation problems, or whether they are due to differences in the organizational commitment construct in other cultures (e.g., construct contamination or deficiency). On the one hand, Lee et al. (2001) argued that if one adopts general items that minimize differences in translation problems, factor structures are similar in Korea. Others, however, have shown that it is important to develop *emic*, or culture-specific, items for organizational commitment in the Turkish context (see Wasti, 1999). This research suggests caution in simply importing translated measures of existing organizational commitment across cultures.

Another central question examined in culture and organizational commitment (OC) research is whether demographic and situational predictors of commitment are similar across cultures. In a meta-analysis, Meyer, Stanley, Herscovitch, and Topolnytsky (2002) found that normative commitment was more strongly associated with perceived organizational support and less strongly associated with demographics (e.g., age and tenure) in studies outside versus inside the United States. By contrast, job-related factors such as role conflict and role ambiguity were stronger predictors of OC within the United States, particularly for affective commitment. These results are consistent with some more recent studies that examined how individual values moderate the impact of situational factors on organizational commitment. Wasti (2003) similarly found that satisfaction with work and promotions were the strongest predictors of organizational commitment among individualists, whereas satisfaction with supervisor was an important predictor of organizational commitment among collectivists. Andolsek and Stebe (2004) also found that material job values (e.g., job quality) were more predictive of organizational commitment in individualistic societies, whereas post-materialistic job values (e.g., helping others) were more predictive of organizational commitment in collectivistic societies. Other studies have shown the importance of examining *emic* predictors of commitment. In the Turkish context, Wasti (1999) found that *in-group opinions* about the organization were strongly linked to continuance commitment, particularly among individuals who emphasized collectivistic values (see also Abrams, Ando, & Hinkle, 1998, on the importance of subjective norms for commitment in Japan; Ramesh & Gelfand, 2010, on the importance of links and

fit for turnover in India; and Yousef, 2000, on the importance of the *Islamic work ethic* for commitment in Middle Eastern samples).

Cross-cultural research has also examined the consequences of organizational commitment. A meta-analysis by Jaramillo, Mulki, and Marshall (2005) found that organizational commitment is a more powerful predictor of job performance in nations scoring high on collectivism than those scoring high on individualism (but see Francesco & Chen, 2004, who found the opposite when examining values at the individual level in the Chinese context). Another meta-analysis (Meyer et al., 2002) found that affective commitment is a more powerful predictor of job outcomes (e.g., job satisfaction, withdrawal cognitions) in the United States. In contrast, normative commitment was more important for job outcomes (e.g., work withdrawal, performance, OCBs) in studies outside the United States. Finally, although the organization is the focus of cross-cultural research on commitment, there is emerging work that suggests that other foci of commitment, such as commitment to one's group and to one's supervisor, are influenced by cultural values. Clugston, Howell, and Dorfman (2000) found that individual-level measures of power distance were related to normative commitment across multiple foci (e.g., organization, supervisor, and workgroup), power distance was related to continuance commitment across all foci, and collectivism was related to work group commitment, suggesting the need to move beyond simply the organization as the foci commitment in studies across cultures.

Culture and the Social Animal in Organizations

In this section, we now turn to how culture affects social behavior in organizations. As many core theories in the field attest, individuals do not exist in isolation in organizations; rather they must manage and coordinate their interdependence with others. Below we consider how culture affects the process of teamwork, conflict and negotiation, and leadership.

Culture and Teams

Given the flattening of organizations and increased competition to produce valued goods and services, as compared to a century ago, many organizations rely on teams to work together to produce superior performance. Teams have been characterized as being composed of two or more individuals who interact adaptively and interdependently toward a common goal (Salas, Dickinson, Converse, & Tannenbaum, 1992). Questions abound regarding cultural influence on teams, including: (a) How do individuals react to team situations and does this vary across cultures? (b) Do teams organize and get work done in similar ways across cultures? (c) How does cultural diversity within a team affect team processes and outcomes? Each of these questions is reviewed in turn.

With respect to the first question, research has illustrated that there are cultural differences in *cognitive team processes* (Kozlowski & Bell, 2003). People across cultures have very different perceptions of what constitutes "teamwork." For example, Gibson and Zellmer-Bruhn (2001) found that employees construe teamwork through different metaphors (military, sports, community, family, and associates) across national cultures, which leads to divergent expectations of team roles, scope, membership, and team objectives. For example, participants from individualist cultures tended to describe teamwork with sports metaphors, which was associated where roles and objectives are explicitly defined, there is little expectation of hierarchy, membership is largely voluntary, and the scope of activity is narrow. Associate metaphors were also common in individualistic cultures, where the scope of activity was narrow, there was little role definition, and objectives were explicit. In contrast, participants from collectivistic cultures tended to conceptualize teamwork through family metaphors, wherein the scope of activity was broad, objectives were social in nature, and there was the expectation of a paternalistic hierarchy. They also tended to conceive of teamwork through community metaphors, wherein roles were shared and informal, and activities and objectives were broad in scope and ambiguous. Power distance, in contrast, was correlated with military metaphors, wherein there was a hierarchical structure, task-focused outcomes, and roles of a limited scope. Similar to this metaphorical analysis, Sanchez-Burks and colleagues have shown that schemas for what constitutes "successful" work groups also vary across cultures. For example, consistent with a family metaphor, Mexicans perceived that socio-emotional behaviors were important for group success, whereas consistent with a sports metaphor, Anglos perceived that high task orientation and low socio-emotional behaviors were important for group success (Sanchez-Burks, Nisbett, & Ybarra, 2000). Overall, Gibson and Zellmer-Bruhn (2001) and Sanchez-Burks et al. (2000) illustrate that the very definition of *teamwork* varies

considerably around the globe, with implications for how work is to be coordinated, accomplished, and evaluated for its success.

Culture also affects *motivational processes* in teams. A natural question that arises is whether individuals are motivated to work in teams more or less in different cultures. Earley (1989) demonstrated that social loafing occurred more in individualistic samples (Americans) as compared to collectivistic samples (Chinese). In a later study, Earley (1993) showed that social loafing was a function of both culture and situational conditions, particularly when people were working alone versus working with in-group members versus working with out-group members. Interestingly, individualists performed much better when working *alone* as compared to when they worked in groups (whether with in-groups or out-groups). In contrast, collectivists performed much worse when they worked alone or in out-groups, and performed the best when working with *in-group members*. These results were partially explained in terms of self- and group efficacy that individualists and collectivists had in these respective conditions. For example, collectivists had much greater efficacy in in-group conditions, whereas individualists had much greater efficacy in the individual condition, explaining their respective performance boosts in each condition. In a later study, Gibson (1999) found that when collectivism in teams was high, group efficacy was more strongly related to group effectiveness (see also Katz & Erez, 2005). Earley (1999) also showed that what contributes to efficacy judgments in teams can vary dramatically across cultures. For example, in high power distance cultures, group efficacy judgments were more strongly tied to higher rather than lower status group judgments, whereas in low power distance cultures, members contributed equally to collective efficacy judgments.

More recent work has also linked cultural values to resistance to team work. Consistent with Earley's (1989, 1993) results, Kirkman and Shapiro and colleagues have shown that values of individualism are associated with general resistance to teams (Kirkman & Shapiro, 1997, 2001a), and less support for team-based rewards (Kirkman & Shapiro, 2000). Similarly, Ramamoorthy and Flood (2004) linked individualism to lower team loyalty. Other cultural values have been shown to relate to resistance to other aspects of teamwork, particularly to self-managing teams. For example, values of high power distance, being-orientation, and determinism are related to resistance to self-management in teams (Kirkman & Shapiro, 1997, 2001a). Similarly, at the team level, Kirkman and Shapiro (2001b) found that collectivism and doing-orientation were related to lower resistance to teams and lower resistance to self-management, respectively, which in turn increased team effectiveness. However, it is also important to note that cultural influences on reactions to teams are highly dynamic, and situational conditions can moderate attitudes and efficacy related to teamwork. For example, Chen, Brockner, and Katz (1998) showed that Americans have particularly negative attitudes toward teams when they perform well individually but their teams perform poorly. Erez and Somach (1996) found that individualist samples performed quite poorly when only given a "do your best goal" for their team (perhaps suggesting a diffusion of responsibility), whereas collectivistic samples in Israel experienced fewer group performance losses regardless of the type of group goal. Individualists might also feel more obligated to teams when they feel they have high pay equity (pay related to individual performance), yet collectivists felt less obligated under these conditions (Ramamoorthy & Flood, 2002). Taiwanese had more negative attitudes when teams had a highly fluid, changing membership as compared to Australians, in part due to differences in the perceived importance of maintaining relationships in groups (Harrison, McKinnon, Wu, & Chow, 2000).

Given the importance of trust for teamwork, a critical question is whether the same conditions create trust in different cultures. The answer to this is decidedly no, as several authors have shown that different conditions create feelings of attraction and trust toward group members across cultures. For example, Yuki and his colleagues (Yuki, 2003; Yuki et al., 2005) showed that trust is developed through different relational bases across cultures: having indirect personal ties with other group members is an important basis for trust in Japan, whereas having a strong identification based on a shared category membership (e.g., being from the same school) is an important basis for trust in the United States. Branzei et al. (2007) showed that people rely on different signs when trusting others: individualists tend to trust based on their perception of a trustee's perceived ability and integrity, whereas collectivists tend to trust based on their perception of a trustee's benevolence. Situational conditions also differentially affect attraction in groups. Man and Lam (2003) found that job complexity and autonomy were much more important for group cohesiveness

in the United States than in Taiwan. Likewise, Tata (2000) similarly argued that high levels of autonomy are critical for teams in low versus high power distance and low versus high uncertainty avoidance cultures. At the same time, some conditions that have been argued to be empowering in the United States, such as task identity and flexibility, have been found to have negative effects on teams in high power distance groups (Drach-Zahavy, 2004).

Culture affects *behavioral team processes,* most notably cooperation. Eby and Dobbins (1997) found that teams with a high percentage of collectivistic members exhibited higher levels of cooperation, which in turn was related to higher performance (see also Oetzel, 1998). As with our former review, situational conditions likely affect cooperation in groups in different cultures. For example, Chen, Chen, and Meindl (1998) theorized that instrumental factors such as high goal interdependence, enhancement of personal identity, and cognitive-based trust foster cooperation in individualistic cultures, whereas in collectivistic cultures, socio-emotional factors such as goal sharing, enhancement of group identity, and affect-based trust foster cooperation in collectivistic cultures. Yamagishi (2003) also argued that cooperation is a function of mutual monitoring in cultures such as Japan and showed that teams with mutual monitoring are much more cooperative than those without monitoring in the Japanese context. Nguyen, Le, and Boles (2010) found that the relationship cooperation was much higher in collectivistic organizational cultures, yet this relationships was much stronger in individualistic cultures (e.g., the U.S.) than collectivistic cultures (e.g., Vietnam).

Culture also affects *social influence processes* in teams. In a meta-analysis, Bond and Smith (1996) found that national collectivism scores predicted rates of conformity in Asch-type influence experiments. Values at the individual level also affect influence processes. Ng and Van Dyne (2001) found that decision quality improved for individuals exposed to a minority perspective, yet this was particularly the case for targets that were high on horizontal individualism and low on horizontal collectivism. Influence targets with high vertical collectivism also demonstrated higher quality decisions, but only when the influence agent held a high status position in the group. An interesting question is whether culture affects *debate and dissent processes.* While some have been shown that debate results in higher productivity across Chinese, French, and U.S. cultural groups (Nemeth, Personnaz, Personnaz, & Goncalo, 2004; Tjosvold, Law, &

Sun, 2003), others have shown that high levels of debate may benefit U.S. but not Chinese groups (Nibler & Harris, 2003).

Finally, numerous studies have examined processes and performance associated with *multicultural teams*. Several authors have argued that multicultural teams (MCTs) can provide strategic advantages for organizations (Subramaniam & Venkatraman, 2001; see reviews by Earley & Gibson, 2002; Gibson & Cohen, 2003; Shapiro, Von Glinow, & Cheng, 2005). However, cultural differences, combined with other features of group work (e.g., virtuality) can produce a number of negative effects for teamwork. Numerous studies have shown that multicultural teams can be fraught with high levels of conflict (Ayoko & Härtel, 2003; Crampton & Hinds, 2005; Elron, 1997; Jehn & Weldon, 1997; Joshi, Labianca & Caligiuri, 2002; Li, Xin, & Pillutla, 2002; Von Glinow, Shapiro, & Brett, 2004), ethnocentrism (Crampton & Hinds, 2005), and in-group biases (Salk & Brannen, 2000). Very little work has been done to examine what might mitigate such effects (see Chao & Moon, 2005, for a theoretical analysis). Extant theorizing would suggest that leaders who are transformational in their approach can help diverse teams. Culturally heterogeneous teams can perform as or more effectively than homogeneous teams when leaders or other third parties provide directive advice (Gibson & Saxton, 2005), help to prevent communication breakdowns (Ayoko, Härtel, & Callan, 2002), and broker hidden knowledge between culturally diverse members (Baba, Gluesing, Ratner, & Wagner, 2004). Others have advocated implementing structural interventions, such as formal temporal coordinating mechanisms (Montoya-Weiss, Massey, & Song, 2001) and internal norms for meaningful participation (Janssens & Brett, 1997) to help multicultural teams. Other research suggests that helping to preserve yet respecting cultural differences (Janssens & Brett, 2006) as well as developing a strong team identity (Van Der Zee, Atsma, & Brodbeck, 2004) help to increase positive outcomes among multicultural teams. Time is also an important moderator of processes in multicultural teams. Although some research shows that culturally diverse teams generally have lower performance than homogeneous teams and take longer to make decisions (Punnett & Clemens, 1999; Thomas, 1999), culturally heterogeneous teams perform as well as homogeneous groups over time (Earley & Mosakowski, 2000; Watson, Johnson, Kumar, & Critelli, 1998; see also Watson, BarNir, & Pavur, 2005; Watson,

Johnson, & Merritt, 1998). Demographic composition of teams also moderates effects. For example, Earley and Mosakowski (2000) showed that highly heterogeneous teams also outperform moderately heterogeneous teams because they avert subgroup fractionalization and fault lines.

In conclusion, the above review of research on culture and teams also suggests that the applicability of the American theories in other cultural contexts may not always generalize to other cultures. Like research on motivation, individuals in the United States and other Western contexts tend to approach teamwork in ways that are consistent with values of individualism and low power distance, and tend to: (a) perceive teamwork through metaphors that are consistent with American and Western practices, including sports; (b) be resistant to teamwork and "loaf" in such contexts as compared to other cultures; and (c) be less cooperative and less subject to social influence in teams. Not surprisingly, such cultural differences make multicultural teamwork more difficult, though, as noted above, with the right situational interventions such teams can be as productive as homogenous teams.

Culture and Conflict/Negotiation

Organizational life is replete with negotiations. Negotiations are frequently conducted in formal arenas, such as industrial relations and joint ventures, as well as informal arenas, such as between supervisors and among peers (Pruitt & Carnevale, 1993). It also increasingly occurs very frequently across cultural borders, making it critical to understand how and when culture influences negotiation processes and outcomes.

Much research on negotiation over the last several decades has focused on negotiators' psychological processes, including negotiator cognition (how negotiators think and their deviations from rationality); motivation (what motivates negotiators and how this influences their strategic choices); and emotion (how emotions of both the self and others influence negotiation processes). Much of the *cognitive tradition* in negotiation is predicated upon the seminal work of March and Simon (1958) and the notion that decision makers have bounded rationality (Kahneman & Tversky, 1973, 1979) and fall victim to a wider range of decision biases, particularly related to the negotiation context. A wide range of classic information-processing biases, such as framing, anchoring, and availability, as well as social perception biases, such as competitive fixed-pie perceptions, attributional biases, and reactive devaluation, have been found among Western samples in negotiation (see Gelfand, Fulmer, & Severance, 2010, for a review). Research on culture and negotiation has shown cultural variability in a wide range of these biases.

For example, anchoring is a classic bias identified by Tversky and Kahneman (1974) wherein individuals rely on irrelevant values (i.e., an "anchor") and fail to adjust their evaluations sufficiently in subsequent decision making. Research has found that information provided prior to or at the beginning of negotiations has been found to influence negotiators' initial offers, aspiration levels, bottom lines, and estimates of opponent's bottom lines (Kristensen & Gärling, 1997; Whyte & Sebenius, 1997). As compared with previous research, research has found that *anchoring biases* are not necessarily universal. Instead of producing an anchoring effect, Adair, Weingart, and Brett (2007) found that opening offers facilitate information exchange and increase joint gains for Japanese negotiators. The authors attributed the cross-cultural differences to divergence in communication styles. The U.S. negotiators, accustomed to direct communication, see opening offers as a signal of the opponent's strong stance. In contrast, Japanese negotiators commonly use indirect methods of communication and see opening offers as a subtle way to engage in information exchange. At the same time, anchoring effects among Asian samples have also not been uniform. For example, Liu, Friedman, and Chi (2005) found that Chinese negotiators are more susceptible to the influence of others' first offers as compared to Americans.

A decision bias unique to the negotiation context is the phenomenon wherein negotiators assume negotiations to be a fixed-pie perception and zero-sum situation (Bazerman & Neale, 1983; Pruitt, 1981; Pruitt & Lewis, 1975; Schelling, 1960). The fixed-pie bias occurs when negotiators erroneously perceive the opponent's interests to be opposite to their own and, thus, underestimate the bargaining zone (Bazerman & Neale, 1983; Larrick & Wu, 2007; Thompson & Hastie, 1990). This perception is a result of the false consensus effect, in which people believe that others share the same views and desire the same things as themselves (Sherman, Judd, & Park, 1989). Again, as with other work, there is cross-cultural variability in this decision bias. Gelfand and Christakopoulou (1999) found that American negotiators had much more fixed-pie perceptions (were less accurate in reporting the priorities of their counterparts) as compared to their Greek counterparts, even after the same

priority information was exchanged within dyads. Americans, interestingly, were more (over)confident that they understood their counterparts' interests as compared to Greeks.

Research in the United States has shown that negotiators often make a fundamental attribution error, in that they attribute opponents' behaviors to internal factors as compared to situational factors. Morris, Larrick, and Su (1999), for example, found that negotiators tend to see others' actions as a result of their personality, such as disagreeableness and emotional instability, which can lead to a self-fulfilling prophecy in which negotiators' behaviors confirm responses from their opponents (Morris et al., 1999). Americans are more prone to the *fundamental attribution error* in negotiations; they tend to make more internal attributions to their counterparts' behavior than negotiators in other cultures, such as Korea and Hong Kong (Morris et al, 1999; Valenzuela, Srivastava, & Lee, 2005).

Other research on negotiator cognition has examined how negotiators' schemas, perceptual frames, and mental models can dramatically affect negotiation processes and outcomes. Because negotiators generally do not have complete information, they need to rely on their prior knowledge and perceptions of the situations. Klar, Bar-Tal, and Kruglanski (1987) stated that individuals develop conflict schemata from past experience and socialization, and use them to approach current conflicts. Culture is one source of experience on negotiator schemas. Using multidimensional scaling, Gelfand et al. (2001) showed that while individuals in both the United States and Japan viewed conflicts in terms of whether they were about mutual blame (cooperation) or unilateral blame (competition), there were culture-specific dimensions through which they perceived identical conflict episodes. For example, Americans perceived more findings to be about winning (with one party to blame) and Japanese perceived the identical conflicts to be more about compromise (with both parties to blame). Americans also perceived conflicts to be concerned with individual rights and autonomy, whereas Japanese perceived the same conflicts to be concerned with violations of duties and obligations (or *giri violations* in Japanese terminology). As with previous findings in the domain of teams, these findings suggest that the very definition of conflicts can vary dramatically across cultures, suggesting that people are playing a "different game" at the outset.

Culture also influences *motivation* in negotiation. Cai (1998) found that U.S. negotiators focused more on achieving short-term, instrumental goals, whereas Taiwanese focused on long-term, global goals. Other research has focused on motivational biases, such as the tendency to have self-serving biases in negotiation. In the United States, Thompson and Loewenstein (1992) found that negotiators had self-serving conceptions of fairness and that such biases were related to the length of strikes during simulated negotiations. Self-serving biases have been linked to impasses (Loewenstein, Issacharoff, Camerer, & Babcock, 1993), length of strikes (Babcock, Wang, & Loewenstein, 1996), and reduced problem solving and feelings of frustration (De Dreu, Nauta, & Van de Vliert, 1995). Gelfand et al. (2002) predicted that disputants' self-serving biases of fairness would be more prevalent in individualistic cultures, such as the United States, in which the self is served by focusing on one's positive attributes to "stand out" and be better than others, yet would be attenuated in collectivistic cultures, such as Japan, where the self is served by focusing on one's negative characteristics to "blend in" (cf. Heine et al., 1999). Results from numerous studies were consistent with this prediction. Americans associated themselves with fair behaviors and others with unfair behaviors to a much greater extent than Japanese. They also found, in the domain of conflict, that American disputants believed that an "objective third party" would judge their behavior as more fair, judge offers from the counterpart as unfair, and would reject these offers more, as compared to Japanese disputants. And consistent with our argument, they found that Americans had greater independent self-construals, and that these construals were related to greater egocentric bias and lower outcomes in a negotiation simulation. In sum, egocentric bias in judging fairness varies across cultures as a function of underlying differences in self-conception. More recent work also shows that self-enhancement among Americans promotes endowment effects (i.e., the tendency to overvalue objects that one owns) as compared to East Asians (Maddux et al., 2010).

A number of studies have begun to examine cultural influences on *emotions* in negotiation. Chinese negotiators reported more anxiety and uncertainty than Dutch negotiators, whereas Dutch negotiators reported more irritation and less friendliness than Chinese negotiators (Ulijn, Rutkowski, Kumar, & Zhu, 2005). Kopelman and Rosette (2008) found that compared to Israeli negotiators, East Asian negotiators are more likely to accept an offer from an opponent who displays positive emotion (e.g., smiling, nodding, and appearing cordial) and are less likely to accept an offer from an opponent who displays negative emotion (e.g., appearing intimidating and irritated). The researchers proposed that East Asians value positive emotional display more because of their cultural emphasis on "face" and respect. For the same reason, negative emotional display is more incongruent with East Asian culture values than Israeli cultural values. Adam, Shirako, and Maddux (2010) similarly found that Asians made much smaller concessions when negotiating with angry opponents as compared to Caucasians, and this was due to different cultural norms regarding the appropriateness of anger expressions in negotiations.

Moving beyond the individual level of analysis, research has shown that culture affects the dynamics of how parties *communicate* and sequence their actions when negotiating. A consistent finding is that information tends to be shared directly (e.g., through questions about preferences) in the individualistic, low context cultures, whereas it tends to be shared indirectly (through offer behavior) in high context, collectivistic cultures such as Japan, Russia, Hong Kong, and Brazil (Adair, Okumura, & Brett, 2001, Adair et al., 2004). Moreover, the path to obtaining joint gains in negotiation is culturally contingent. For example, U.S. negotiators achieve higher joint gains when they share information directly, whereas Japanese negotiators achieve higher joint gains when they share information indirectly (Adair et al., 2001). Culture also affects communication sequences. Negotiators from collectivistic cultures are better able to use both direct and indirect forms of information exchange, as compared to negotiators from individualistic cultures. In effect, collectivistic negotiators are shown to be more flexible in their use of different information exchange tactics, whereas individualistic negotiators are primarily skilled in direct information sharing (Adair & Brett, 2005; Adair et al., 2001).

Situational conditions can dramatically affect negotiation processes and outcomes. The relationship that one has with one's opponent is a case in point. Chan (1992) found that negotiators in collectivistic cultures (e.g., Hong Kong) were much more cooperative with friends and much more competitive with strangers, whereas individualists did not differentiate between strangers and friends as much (see also Chen & Li, 2005; Probst, Carnevale, & Triandis, 1999; Triandis et al., 2001; (see also Gunia, Brett, Nandkeolyar, & Kamdar, 2011, who found India negotiators had very low trust of strangers). Triandis et al. (2001) also found that collectivists were much more likely to engage in deception with out-groups in negotiations as compared to individualists. Cooperation and competition is also a function of external monitoring, as was discussed in the teams section above. For example, Gelfand and Realo (1999) argued that accountability is a norm enforcement mechanism, essentially amplifying whatever norm is salient in a particular cultural context. Because norms vary across cultures, accountability was theorized to have divergent cultural effects. Consistent with previous research that showed accountability related to competition, they found that accountability activated competitive construals and behaviors, and resulted in lower negotiation outcomes for individualistic samples. By contrast, among collectivists, accountability activated cooperative construals and behaviors, and resulted in higher negotiation outcomes. These effects were reversed in unaccountable negotiations, when, in effect, negotiators were released from normative pressures to do what is expected. In unaccountable conditions, collectivists were more competitive and achieved lower negotiation outcomes, as compared to individualists, who were more cooperative and achieved higher negotiation outcomes (see also Rosette, Brett, Barsness, & Lytle, 2006, who found that Hong Kong Chinese were more aggressive in lean media such as e-mail where there is less constraint, as compared to face-to-face negotiations). Overall, these results indicate that the same "objective" condition (e.g., relationships, accountability, and technology) can produce very different dynamics in negotiations in different cultures.

Situational factors also exacerbate cultural differences to the extent that they cause individuals to engage in automatic processing and rely on well learned cultural tendencies. For example, research has also shown that need for closure exacerbates base-line cultural tendencies (Fu et al., 2007, Morris & Fu, 2001). For example, America disputants who are high in NFC prefer relationally unconnected mediators, whereas Chinese disputants who are high in NFC tend to seek relationally connected mediators, illustrating a positive relationship of NFC with conformity to cultural norms (Fu et al., 2007). Similarly, cultural differences have been found to be exacerbated in situations of high ambiguity, which also tends to cause people to rely on automatic tendencies (Morris, Leung, & Iyengar, 2004).

As with other areas within organizational psychology, there has been little attention to negotiation at the cultural interface—in other words, the processes and outcomes, and situational conditions that affect *intercultural negotiations*. As with

multicultural teams, effects that are cited are quite negative—intercultural dyads have been found to be less cooperative (Graham, 1985) and to achieve lower joint profits, as compared to intracultural dyads (Brett & Okumura, 1998; Natlandsmyr & Rognes, 1995). In an insightful analysis, Brett and Okumura (1998) found that lower joint gains were lower in intercultural negotiations between U.S. and Japanese negotiators, based in part on less accuracy in understanding of others' priorities and conflicting styles of information exchange in intercultural negotiations (Adair et al., 2001).

Some emerging research suggests that socially shared cognition is lower in intercultural negotiations, causing resultant lower outcomes. Gelfand and McCusker (2002) argued that different metaphoric mappings of negotiation (e.g. sports in the United States and the Japanese *ie* metaphor in Japan) create different goals, scripts, and feelings in negotiation in intercultural contexts, making it difficult to organize social action (Weick, [1969] 1979) and arrive at a common understanding of the task. In a laboratory simulation, Gelfand, Nishii, Godfrey, and Raver (2003) found that metaphoric similarity in negotiation (i.e., agreement on the domain to which negotiation was mapped) was indeed an important predictor of joint gains. More recent evidence using network scaling has shown that negotiators in intercultural negotiations are much more likely to have different mental models of the negotiation at the start, and to have less convergence at the end of negotiations, as compared to intracultural negotiations (Liu, Friedman, Barry, Gelfand, & Zheng, under review). This was particularly the case for negotiators who had high need for closure, consistent with the evidence discussed above. Adair, Taylor, and Tinsley (2009) found that American and Japanese negotiation schemas were highly discrepant in intercultural negotiators and this was due to the fact that they were trying to adjust to their counterpart's assumptions and therefore overcompensated in their expectations of what was appropriate. Liu, Chua, and Stahl (2010) also found that quality of communication experience is much lower in intercultural negotiations as compared to intracultural negotiations. In all, these studies suggest that in intercultural negotiations, negotiators need to *negotiate the negotiation*—or come to a common metaphor about the task—prior to negotiating (see also George, Jones, & Gonzalez, 1998; Kumar, 1999).

Despite the practical need, there is little research on the factors that predict intercultural negotiation effectiveness. Imai and Gelfand (2010) showed that cultural intelligence, or a "person's capability for successful adaptation to new cultural settings" (Earley & Ang, 2003, p. 9) is a predictor of effective integrative bargaining sequences in intercultural negotiation. Cultural intelligence (CQ) also predicted processes and outcomes over and above other personality constructs (i.e., openness, extraversion), other forms of intelligence (e.g., IQ, emotional intelligence), and international travel and living experience. Interestingly, the minimum CQ score within the dyad was enough to predict behavioral sequences, showing that it takes only one, not two high-CQ negotiators in order to become in-sync.

In conclusion, the review of research on culture and negotiation again suggests that applicability of American theories in other cultural contexts needs to be questioned. Much research on negotiation in the United States rests on a number of individualistic assumptions, including that: (a) negotiators will be victim to competitive decision biases and construals and dispositional attributions in negotiation; (b) direct communication strategies and rational argumentation are the way to "get to yes"; (c) the same situational conditions (e.g., accountability) will exert similar effects across cultures. At a more meta-level, the negotiation literature focuses largely on economic capital and short-term agreements, as compared to relational capital and long-term agreements, which might be more important in non-Western cultures (Brett & Gelfand, 2006).

Culture and Leadership

Culture's consequences for leadership have been one of the most widely researched topics in cross-cultural organizational literature. This is evident from a number of reviews on the topic (e.g., Aycan, 2008; Ayman, 2004; Bass, 1997; Dickson, Den Hartog, & Mitchelson, 2003; Dorfman, 2004; House, Wright, & Aditya, 1997; Scandura & Dorfman, 2004; Smith & Peterson, 2002), including a special issue (Hunt & Peterson, 1997). Furthermore, one of the most ambitious projects in the cross-cultural I/O literature was conducted on leadership (Project GLOBE; House et al., 2004). We will use the main theoretical perspectives to leadership to summarize the cross-cultural literature.

In line with the *trait approach*, the majority of culture and leadership research has investigated cross-cultural differences in attributes of effective leaders. Robie, Johnson, Nilsen, & Hazucha (2001) compared the United States and seven European countries and found that intelligence, conscientiousness, and ability to motivate subordinates were

reported as characteristics of effective leaders in all countries, while less agreement was evident on other characteristics, such as ability to act with integrity and criticality. For Confucian Asian nations (e.g., Gupta, MacMillan, & Surie, 2004; Leung, 2005; Silverthorne, 2001), conscientiousness and agreeableness were attributes of effective leaders, whereas openness to new experiences was not. Geletkanycz (1997) found that strategic orientation as an attribute of effective leadership was associated with individualism, low uncertainty avoidance, low power distance, and short-term orientation. Perception of effectiveness has also been associated with different non-verbal cues in different cultures. For example, a strong voice with ups and downs was associated with the perception of enthusiasm in Latin American cultures, whereas a monotonous tone is a way to display respect and self-control in East Asian cultures (Den Hartog & Verburg, 1997). Charisma is one of the attributes of effective leaders. In individualistic cultures, leaders were perceived as charismatic when they fit the prototype of "good" and "effective" leader, whereas in collectivistic cultures they were perceived charismatic when they produced high performance outcomes (Ensari & Murphy, 2003; see also, Valikangas & Okumura, 1997).

One of the largest projects in the cross-cultural organizational literature investigated the effects of culture on the perceived attributes of effective leaders. The data for the GLOBE Project (House et al., 2004) were gathered from 17,000 middle-managers and employees from 62 cultural groups. The theoretical foundation of the project is rooted in the implicit leadership theory (Lord & Maher, 1990). The term *culturally endorsed implicit leadership theories* coined in this project denoted shared role schemes and prototypical attributes concerning leadership embedded in the cultural context. Two leadership attributes that were universally endorsed were charisma/value-based leadership and team orientation. Leadership attributes that were universally considered as representing ineffective leadership were asocial, non-cooperative, irritable, non-explicit, egocentric, ruthless, and dictatorial. The largest cross-cultural variations were detected in perceived effectiveness of participative, humane, autonomous, and narcissistic leadership.

Culturally endorsed leadership attributes were found to be associated with cultural values and practices at societal and organizational levels. For example, societal and organizational level collectivism was associated with preference for charismatic and team-oriented leadership; gender egalitarianism was associated with preference for participative leadership; power distance was associated with preference for self-protective leadership (Dorfman, Hanges, & Brodbeck, 2004). Den Hartog, House, and colleagues (1999) further reported variations in leadership prototypes according to the hierarchical position of the leader. For example, being innovative, visionary, persuasive, long-term oriented, diplomatic, and courageous were considered to be more important for higher compared to lower managerial positions. Attributes of lower level managers included attention to subordinates, team building, and participation. Using the GLOBE data, Resick, Hanges, Dickson, and Mitchelson (2006) found that aspects of ethical leadership were endorsed as important for effective leadership across 62 cultures, but cultures varied in the degree of endorsement of each of the ethical leadership dimensions. For example, the character/integrity dimension was highly endorsed by Nordic European society, leader altruism was highly endorsed by Southeast Asian societies, and collective motivation (e.g., communication, team building) was highly endorsed by Latin American and Anglo societies.

The *behavioral approach* to leadership asserts that the key to differentiating effective leaders from ineffective ones is the type of behaviors that they display. As early as 1966, comparative research by Haire et al., conducted in 13 countries in Europe, Asia, and Latin America, as well as the United States, showed that national differences accounted for almost one-third of the variance in leadership behaviors. The most highly cited two-dimensional model of leadership behavior (e.g., Fleishman, 1953), namely consideration versus initiating structure, has found cross-cultural research support (Ayman & Chemers, 1983; Bond & Hwang, 1986; Drost & Von Glinow, 1998; Misumi & Peterson, 1985; Shenkar, Ronen, Shefy, & Hau-Siu Chow, 1998). Additional behavioral dimensions other than consideration versus initiating structure, however, have been found to characterize effective leadership in China—most notably modeling a *moral* character (e.g., fairness to all employees, remaining within the law, and resisting the temptation for personal gain; Xu, 1987), and political behavior (Shenkar et al., 1998).

The effects of leaders' consideration and initiating structure behavior can vary across cultures. Lok and Crawford (2004) showed that consideration was more strongly related to commitment in collectivistic than individualistic cultures. Agarwal, DeCarlo, and Vyas (1999) found that task and social roles (i.e., initiating structure and consideration, respectively)

had different effects on employees' organizational attitudes. Organizational commitment of Indian employees was associated with leaders' consideration behavior, whereas that of U.S. employees was associated with both consideration and initiating structure. Smith et al. (1989) found that task and social roles were manifested in different ways, depending on the cultural context. For example, a culturally-specific item associated with task role in Japan described the supervisor as speaking about a subordinate's personal difficulties with others in his or her absence. In contrast, the item for the task role in the United States described the supervisor as being consultative and participative, and not dealing with the problem through written memos.

Research investigating cross-cultural differences in leadership behaviors, practices and roles revealed that differences outweigh similarities. The applicability of a commonly used measurement of leadership, the Leadership Behavioral Description Questionnaire (LBDQ), in non-Western cultural contexts was questioned by researchers reporting different factor structures (e.g., Littrell, 2002; Schneider, & Littrell, 2003). Zagorsek, Jaklic, and Stough (2004) compared leadership practices in the United States, Nigeria, and Slovenia using another popular measure, the Leadership Practices Inventory (LPI; Kousez & Posner, 1993), to find similarities except in "modeling the way" and "enabling others to act" dimensions. Scandura and Dorfman (2004) found that Mexican leaders scored lower than U.S. leaders on all five dimensions of LPI.

Another important behavioral approach to leadership examines the effect of participative leadership behavior on employee and organizational outcomes. The GLOBE Project has demonstrated that there are wide cross-cultural differences in the degree to which participative leadership was endorsed as an effective style. The cultural groups that highly endorse participative leadership are Germanic Europe, Nordic Europe, and Anglo clusters. This is followed by Latin American, Latin European, and Sub-Saharan African cultural groups. Those at the bottom of the list were Eastern European, Southern Asian, Confucian Asian, and Middle Eastern, in that order (House et al., 2004, p. 683). The data in this project also showed that endorsement of participative leadership was negatively associated with power distance, but positively associated with performance orientation and gender egalitarianism (House et al., 2004).

Other studies also found that power distance as a cultural characteristic was associated with non-participative leadership style. For example, Dorfman and Howell (1988) examined the effects of various leadership roles on employee job satisfaction, organizational commitment, and job performance. They found that directive leadership behavior (low participation and high close monitoring) was more effective in large power distance and collectivistic cultures. In a later study, Dorfman et al. (1997) found that directive leadership had a strong positive impact in Taiwan and Mexico on job performance, but had no impact in the United States, Japan, and South Korea. In a study conducted in Hong Kong, directive leadership was found to enhance employee performance, morale, and satisfaction in large, compared to small power distance contexts (Fellows, Liu, & Fong, 2003). Similarly, managers in collectivistic cultures used directive and supportive leadership more than those in individualistic cultures (Wendt, Euwema, & van Emmerik, 2009). Leader participative behaviors were found to be counterproductive in Russia, a large power distance culture (e.g., Welsh, Luthans, & Sommer, 1993). In a study including 176 work units of a large U.S.-based multinational operating in 18 European and Asian countries (including Australia, Belgium, Denmark, France, Turkey, Hong Kong, and Japan), Newman and Nollen (1996) found that participative leadership practices improved the profitability of work units in small power distance, but not in large power distance cultures. Lam, Chen, and Schaubroeck (2002) found that idiocentrism and allocentrism explained cultural differences in how participative decision making and efficacy perceptions interacted to predict employee performance.

Sagie and Aycan (2003) argued that power distance and individualism/collectivism were the two cultural dimensions related to how well participative decision making (PDM) behavior of leaders works in organizations. One of the reasons that participative behavior does not result in uniform employee reactions may be the way in which participation is construed in different cultures. For example, having asked employees' opinions, despite the fact that the final decision is contrary to the one provided by the employees, may be perceived as participative leadership in large power distance cultures, but as non-participative in small power distance cultures. There are three ways to explain the effects of power distance on PDM. First, in high power distant cultures, responsibility of and authority in decision making is vested in the hands of a few at the top, and delegation is avoided (Sagie & Koslowsky, 2000). Those higher in the hierarchy are assumed to be more knowledgeable and experienced than the rest of the people in the organization, and therefore must be respected and trusted to give the right decision (Miles, 1975). Second, in high power distance cultures, decision making is perceived as a privilege of management, and participation is considered as an infringement on management prerogatives. Finally, in high power distance cultures, the "inequality" belief creates not only dependency of subordinates on their superiors, but also fear of punishment if employees question, challenge, or disagree with their management's decisions.

According to Sagie and Aycan (2003), while power distance influences the level of employee participation, individualism and collectivism influence the person or group involved in making decisions. In collectivistic cultures, joint effort is perceived as the only feasible way to bring about change, whereas in individualistic cultures, it is believed that individuals have the potential and power to change things. As such, in individualistic cultures, participation is mostly relevant to individuals, whereas in collectivistic cultures, it is relevant to entire groups. Additionally, in collectivistic cultures, the entire group may be held responsible for the actions of its individual members. Therefore, no one is allowed to make decisions alone without the approval of the entire group. Conversely, as each member in an individualistic society is responsible for his or her actions, one's participation in decision making is not the business of everyone else.

The prevalence of participative and consultative leadership has been compared in different countries. In a recent study, Hong Kong Chinese managers were found to invite subordinates' participation in problem solving, whereas Australian managers were found to engage in consensus-checking before arriving at a final decision (Yeung, 2003). U.S. leaders scored higher on consensus-based leadership style compared to Turkish leaders, whereas Turkish leaders scored higher on autocratic leadership style compared to U.S. leaders (Marcoulides, Yavas, Bilgin and Gibson, 1998).

The Event Management Project (Smith, Peterson, & Schwartz, 2002) is among the most comprehensive investigations of leadership behaviors and practices in 47 countries. In this research, middle managers reported the ways in which they handled work events by using different sources of guidance. The events were: (a) when a vacancy arises that requires appointment of a new subordinate in your department; (b) when one of your subordinates does consistently good work; (c) when one of your subordinates does consistently poor work;

(d) when some of the equipment or machinery in your department seems to need replacement; (e) when another department does not provide the resources or support you require; (f) when there are differing opinions within your department; (g) when you see the need to introduce new work procedures into your department; and (h) when the time comes to evaluate the success of new work procedures. The eight sources of guidance were listed in turn and described as follows: (a) formal rules and procedures; (b) unwritten rules as to "how things are usually done around here"; (c) my subordinates; (d) specialists outside my department; (e) other people at my level; (f) my superior; (g) opinions based on my own experience and training; and (h) beliefs that are widely accepted in my country as to what is right. The findings confirmed that large power distance was the strongest predictor of reliance on vertical sources of guidance, that is, superiors and rules within organizations. Small power distance, on the other hand, predicted reliance on one's own experience and on subordinates to solve problems (Smith, Peterson, et al., 2005).

The power and influence approach to leadership suggests that leaders' effectiveness is influenced by the type of power source and influence tactics used. There is limited attention to the power and influence tactics used by leaders and their effectiveness in different cultural contexts. In an early study, US managers were found to rely on resource-based influence strategies (e.g., use of reward and punishment), whereas Japanese managers were found to rely on altruism and rational persuasion strategies (Hirokawa & Miyahara, 1986). Rahim and Magner (1995) found that the factor structure of Rahim's Leader Power Inventory was replicated in individualistic and collectivistic cultures (the U.S., Bangladesh, S. Korea), and that there was strong emphasis on coercive power in individualistic and expert power in collectivistic cultures (see also, Montesino, 2003). Another popular measure, the Profile of Organizational Influence (POIS; Kipnis & Schmidt, 1982) was administered to Japanese managers (Rao, Hashimoto & Rao, 1997) to find both commonalities with the U.S. findings in the use of some influence strategies (i.e., assertiveness, sanctions, and appeals to higher authority) as well as culture-specific strategies (i.e., socialization and personal development in Japan). In a 6-country comparison, Ralston and Pearson (2003) found that U.S. and Dutch managers favored "soft" influence tactics (e.g., rational persuasion, willingness to put in extra work), whereas Mexican and Hong Kong managers favored "hard" tactics (e.g., withholding information; see also Rahim, Antonioni, Krumov, & Ilieva, 2000). Fu and Liu (2008) proposed another type of power to the typology in the literature: relational power driving from the relationship between the agent and the target person (as in *guanxi*). The authors argue that this type of power is common and effective in Eastern Asian cultures.

Rahim et al. (2000) provided evidence for the differential effect of power types on employee effectiveness: effectiveness was associated with leaders' referent power in the United States and legitimate power in Bulgaria. Afza (2005) further demonstrated that in Indian performance-contingent reward, expert and referent power bases were strongly associated with employees' higher organizational commitment, higher job satisfaction, and lower turnover intention. Legitimate power base was effective to solicit compliance, but performance-contingent coercive power was ineffective in yielding positive employee attitudes. Fu et al. (2004) found that persuasive tactics were rated to be more effective by managers who endorsed the belief in reward for application, whereas assertive and relationship-based tactics were rated to be effective by those endorsing social cynicism, fate control, and religiosity.

Contingency theories of leadership assert that leaders are effective to the extent that they behave in accordance to mainly two types of contingencies: the task characteristics and follower characteristics. Interestingly, there are almost no studies directly testing the validity of any of the four key contingency theories (i.e., Fiedler's LPC, Vroom & Jago's normative decision theory, House's path-goal theory, and Graen's LMX) across cultures. This void must be filled in future cross-cultural research. Only a few studies focused on the effect of leader-member exchange (LMX) and showed that is was associated with positive employee attitudes in different cultural contexts. For example, LMX was correlated with positive evaluation of leadership in both India and the United States (Varma, Srinivas & Stroh, 2005). In another study, LMX was associated with job satisfaction in Columbia (Pillai, Scandura, & Williams, 1999).

In the leadership literature, few studies highlight the importance of follower characteristics, including value orientations (e.g., Ehrhart & Klein, 2001; Jung, Yammarino, & Lee, 2009; Parker, 1996), personality (e.g., Ehrhart & Klein, 2001; Ergin & Kozan, 2004), demographic characteristics (e.g., Yu & Miller, 2005), occupational grouping (e.g., Zander

& Romani, 2004), and motives (e.g., Valikangas & Okumura, 1997), as factors accounting for variance across as well as within cultures. The findings suggest that across-country variance accounts more in leadership preferences than within-country variance.

The final approach to leadership suggests that leadership effectiveness is associated with the extent to which leaders are transformational and charismatic. The universality of Bass's two dimensional structure of leadership—transformational and transactional—and the effectiveness of the former, compared to the latter, has been supported by much research (see Bass, 1997, for a review of international research; Dorfman, et al., 1997; Littrell & Valentin, 2005; Drost & Von Glinow, 1998; Shenkar et al., 1998; Walumbwa, Orwa, Wang, & Lawler, 2005). Other studies found culture-specific enactment of transformational leadership and proposed new dimensions of leadership (in addition to transactional and transformational) in non-Western cultures. For example, important aspects of transformational leadership included social integration in Egypt (Shahin & Wright, 2004); good moral character, belief in relationships, and a naturalistic approach in China (Wah, 2004); and *svadharma*-orientation (following one's own Dharma or duty) in India (Mehra & Krishnan, 2005; see also Ardichvili, 2001; Kuchinke, 1999; Sarros & Santora, 2001).

The combined effect of organizational structure (i.e., organic structure) and unit-level culture (i.e., collectivism) was found to be associated with emergence of charismatic leadership (Pillai & Meindl, 1998). Executives in Taiwan and Canada showed similarities in charismatic leadership, but the specific items on which they score highly were different (Javidan, & Carl, 2005; see also, Javidan & Carl, 2004 for questions about charismatic leadership manifestations in Iran).

Transformational leadership had a more positive influence on employees' organizational attitudes in high, rather than low levels of collectivism (e.g., Jung & Avolio, 1999; Jung et al., 2009; Spreitzer, Perttula, & Xin, 2005; Walumbwa & Lawler, 2003). However, contrary to the above research, Pillai et al. (1999) showed that transformational leadership was not associated with job satisfaction, but was associated with perception of justice in collectivistic countries in the Middle East, India, and Columbia. This was further elaborated by a recent research showing that followers with high power distance orientation perceived the decisions of transformational leaders as fair more so than those with low power distance orientation (Kirkman, Chen, Farh, Chen, & Lowe, 2009). Among other organizational outcomes, employees' innovation was facilitated by charisma, demonstration of confidence, idealized influence (dimensions of transformational leadership), as well as active and passive management by exception (dimensions of transactional leadership) in Russia, whereas it was facilitated by inspirational motivation and intellectual stimulation (Elenkov & Manev, 2005).

In recent years, paternalistic leadership started to attract the attention of researchers. Paternalistic leadership is common in cultures that are characterized by high power distance and high collectivism, including Asian, Latin American, Middle Eastern, and African nations (e.g., Aycan, Kanungo, et al., 2000; Farh & Cheng, 2000; Jackson, Amaeshi, & Yavuz, 2008; Ogbor & Williams, 2003; Rousseau, 1998; Saini & Budhwar, 2008; Sinha, 1997; Westwood, 1997). Aycan (2006) developed and validated the Paternalistic Leadership Questionnaire (PLQ) that included 21 items in five dimensions: creating a family atmosphere at work, establishing individualized relationships with subordinates, involving in subordinates' non-work lives (e.g., attending their weddings or funerals, acting as a mediator in family disputes), expecting loyalty from subordinates, and maintaining status hierarchy and authority in their relationship with subordinates. The first three dimensions outline the role prescriptions for paternalistic leaders (i.e., guidance and nurturance in subordinates' professional *and* professional lives), whereas the last two dimensions allude to leaders' expectations from subordinates (i.e., loyalty and deference). Pellegrini and Scandura (2008) concluded that the empirical research they conducted using the initial item pool of Aycan (2006) showed that paternalistic leadership was correlated positively with LMX, job satisfaction, and organizational commitment in both collectivistic (e.g., Turkey) and individualistic (e.g., the U.S.) countries (see also, Pellegrini, Scandura & Jayaraman, 2010). Similar findings have been reported by Chen and colleagues for Chinese employees (e.g., Cheng, Chou, Wu, Huang, & Farh, 2004).

LEADERSHIP IN MULTICULTURAL CONTEXT

Leadership in the context of expatriate-local interaction received research attention in the last decade. There were studies comparing leadership styles of expatriate and local managers (e.g., Deng & Gibson, 2009; Howell, Romero, Dorfman, Paul, & Bautista, 2003; Quang, Swierczek, Chi, 1998; Suutari, 1996; Suutari & Riusala, 2001;

Wilson, Callaghan, & Wright, 1996) as well as those investigating the extent to which expatriates change their leadership style to fit to the local context (e.g., Hui & Graen, 1997; Smith, Wang, & Leung, 1997; Suutari, 1996; Suutari, Raharjo, & Riikkila, 2002). Setting cooperative (rather than competitive) goals (Chen & Tjosvold, 2005), effective management of relationship (Bhawuk, 1997; Li & Tsui, 1999; Makilouko, 2004), and adopting a consultative style and team leadership (Darwish, 1998) were identified as factors fostering leadership effectiveness in cross-cultural interactions. Leader-follower match in ethnicity is positively associated with follower satisfaction, and commitment and trust toward the leader in multicultural work settings (Chong & Thomas, 1997; Testa, 2002).

Aycan (2008) recently proposed the Dynamic Model of Leader-Follower Interaction to study leadership effectiveness in contexts requiring cross-cultural interactions (e.g., expatriation). Borrowing from the LMX, the model acknowledges the importance of leaders' and followers' cultural backgrounds in their interaction. According to the model, leaders behave in accordance with their values, beliefs, and assumptions about the task and the nature of employees. Based on social cognitive information processing theory, followers observe and evaluate the leader's behaviors, and make attributions about the leader's behavior. Followers' attributions are also based on their own cultural values, beliefs, assumptions, and CLTs. In turn, followers react in particular ways towards the leader's behavior. If followers' behaviors or reactions reinforce the leader's initial values, beliefs, and assumptions, then there is a culture fit, which leads to leader acceptance and effectiveness. While the most important contingency in this model is "culture," the author also includes non-cultural contingencies that influence leader-member interaction (e.g., organizational contingencies and structural elements, individuals' demographic characteristics and competencies).

Frontiers of Research in Cross-Cultural Organizational Psychology

As can be seen from the review of the literature summarized in Table 33.1 cross-cultural research in I/O psychology is thriving and developing as a legitimate field of its own right. Thanks to the contributions of cross-cultural research, theories in I/O have been broader, more global, and

Table 33.1 Summary Findings

Recruitment and selection

- Cultural collectivism and/or power distance are positively associated with: (1) reliance on social networks and informal channels in recruitment, (2) focus on characteristics (e.g., personality, age, gender) and competencies leading to harmonious interpersonal relationships and loyalty as selection criteria. Cultural individualism, egalitarianism, and/or performance-orientation are positively associated with: (1) reliance on wide-spread recruitment channels, (2) focus on job-related technical and social competencies and their "objective" assessment (e.g., cognitive ability test, personality inventories) in selection.

Nature of jobs and performance criteria

- Cultural collectivism and power distance are positively associated with: (1) job definitions for teams or workgroups, rather than individuals, (2) broad and vague job descriptions allowing supervisors to exercise power to decide what needs to be done and how, (3) stronger preference for shift work in job design, compared to telework, part-time, or temporary work.
- Performance and promotion criteria in individualistic or performance-oriented cultures tend to be objective, quantifiable and observable (e.g., meeting task objectives, productivity, timeliness and quality of output, job-specific knowledge and proficiency). In collectivistic or high power distance cultures, performance criteria and ratings may be subjective and biased, reflecting the nature of the relationship between the rater and ratee. Social and relational criteria (e.g., good human nature, harmony in interpersonal relations, trustworthiness, respectful attitude, loyalty and deference toward superiors, effort and willingness to work, awareness of duties and obligations, organizational citizenship, conformity, and contribution to team maintenance) carry more weight in evaluating employees than objective work outcomes.
- Setting specific performance goals or criteria are avoided in fatalistic and uncertainty avoiding cultures, while it is preferred in goal- and performance-oriented cultures.

(Continued)

Table 33.1 (Continued)

Motivation

- Cultural individualism, low power distance, masculinity, uncertainty tolerance or self determination are positively associated with motivation techniques focusing on: (1) allocating rewards or designing practices (e.g., job enrichment) to satisfy and enhance the independent "self" (e.g., fulfill individual expectations and growth needs), (2) empowering individuals to exercise control on work outcomes (e.g., performance-reward contingency), and (3) enhancing rational decision making in setting performance goals and determining the ways to achieve them (e.g., participation in decisions, self-regulatory techniques).
- Cultural collectivism, high power distance, femininity or fatalism are associated with motivational techniques focusing on: (1) allocating rewards or designing practices to satisfy and enhance the interdependent "self" (e.g., achieve group goals, fulfill obligations to the family, organization or nation), (2) enhancing work-life integration, (3) fulfilling safety and security needs (e.g., guaranteed salary that is not contingent upon performance).

Teams

- Individualism and low power distance are associated with: (1) preference to work individually rather than in teams (especially when they perform well individually but their teams perform poorly), (2) explicit definition of roles and objectives in the team, (3) narrow scope of activity, (4) low level of hierarchy and high level of autonomy in team structure, (5) voluntary membership, (6) emphasis on task-related behavior as key to team success, and (7) goal interdependence, enhancement of personal identity, and cognitive-based trust as conditions fostering trust and cooperation.
- Collectivism and high power distance are associated with: (1) preference to and efficiency in working in teams consisting of a leader and in-group members, (2) broadly defined goals that are social in nature, (3) paternalistic hierarchy in team structure, (4) broadly defined scope of activities, (5) emphasis on socio-emotional behaviors as key to team success, and (6) goal sharing, enhancement of group identity, and affect-based trust as conditions fostering trust and cooperation.
- Culturally heterogeneous teams can outperform homogeneous teams when: (1) leaders provide close supervision to prevent communication breakdowns and surface hidden knowledge between culturally diverse members, (2) formal temporal coordinating mechanisms and internal norms for meaningful participation are formed, (3) strong team identity is fostered, and (4) sufficient time to overcome process loses are allowed.

Conflict and negotiation

- Individualism is associated with: (1) perception of conflict and negotiation as a way to enhance personal benefits, (2) a focus on short-term, instrumental goals in negotiations, (3) high likelihood of self-serving bias, (4) acceptance of negative emotions in negotiation (5) use of direct communication style in negotiation (i.e., information sharing in an open and direct way), (6) preference of relationally unconnected mediators.
- Collectivism is associated with: (1) perception of conflict and negotiation as a possible threat to group harmony unless benefits of both parties (esp. if the opposite party comprised in-group members) are enhanced, (2) a focus on long-term, holistic goals in negotiation, (3) display of positive emotions in negotiations, (4) use of both indirect and direct communication style in negotiation, (5) preference of relationally-connected mediators.

Leadership

- Collectivism increases the likelihood of preference for transformational/charismatic and team-oriented leaders and their effectiveness in producing work outcomes and enhancing positive employee attitudes. Collectivism is also associated with leader's use of expert, legitimate, and referent power.
- Confucianism is associated with endorsement of leaders with high moral character.
- Power distance is negatively associated with preference for participative leadership, whereas performance orientation is positively associated with it.
- Collectivism and power distance are associated with endorsement and effectiveness of paternalistic leadership.

less ethnocentric. Despite advancements in many areas (especially theory and methodology), some of the problems pointed out by Roberts (1970) still pervade. For example, there is still a paucity of research on culture beyond the individual level in organizations, there is a lack of integrated theory for understanding cultural effects, and therefore it can be difficult to draw firm conclusions in many areas of cross-cultural organizational research. In this section, we present some critical frontiers for cross-cultural organizational research in the coming decades.

The Role of Cultural Versus Contextual Influences

Organizations are complex systems that operate under multiple environmental forces that are both internal and external to the organization. The challenge for the cross-cultural researchers is to disentangle the contribution of culture (i.e., sociocultural context) vis-à-vis other contextual factors both internal and external to the organization (cf. Aycan, 2005). At the *national* level, contextual factors includes factors such as political, economic, legal, educational systems, climate, resources, level of technological advancement, and demographic composition; at the *organizational* level, contextual factors include industry, size, ownership, life stage, strategy, technology, workforce characteristics; at the *team* level, contextual factors include team structure and processes, team member composition, task characteristics; and at the *individual* level, include such factors as personality and demographics (Gelfand, Erez, & Aycan, 2007). Global context at the macro-level also influences organizational behavior across cultures. In the present state of cross-cultural research, we have passed beyond the point of questioning "whether or not" culture influences organizational phenomena; the more relevant questions now are "to what extent" and "in what ways" culture influences organizations and their practices.

Based on such theoretical foundations, future cross-cultural research should identify the "cultural" and "non-cultural" contextual forces influencing organizational behavior. Tayeb warns us against cultural reductionism by stating that "...socio-cultural context should not be viewed as a strait-jacket, stifling organizations' deviation and initiatives" (1995, p. 591). In designing and testing hypotheses on cross-cultural differences, researchers must pay attention to the factors other than the cultural context, so that the "external validity" of their findings is tested by considering a host of alternative explanations (cf. van de Vijver & Leung, 1997). For instance, organizations in collectivistic cultures may prefer internal (rather than external) recruitment. Suppose also that small (rather than large) size organizations prefer internal sources in recruitment (see, for example, Ryan et al., 2009, for the effect of interaction between culture and GDP on recruitment and selection practices). To focus on the impact of the cultural context, we may control organization size either in sampling or in conducting analysis (assigning size as a covariate). This way, it would be possible to study the "extent to which" cultural collectivism influences recruitment vis-à-vis size.

Alternatively, cross-cultural I/O researchers should study the *interaction* between the sociocultural context and other contextual factors to examine whether the sociocultural context is a main predictor of various organizational behavior and practices or a moderator in the relationship between the contextual factors and organizational behavior and practices. In the majority of research reviewed in this chapter, culture is treated as the main effect (Type I hypothesis; Lytle, Brett, Barsness, Tinsley, & Janssens, 1995). Culture is conceptualized as an antecedent predicting certain behavior or attitudes in a particular group. Researchers who adopt this perspective attribute differences in observed phenomena to cultural variations. This perspective has limitations, as it overlooks alternative hypotheses that may be based on differential interpretation, functioning, and/or structuring of constructs under study, and their relationships among one another. In the second approach, culture is treated as the moderator (Type II hypothesis). This approach acknowledges that constructs may be related in a non-uniform way across cultures. However, the assumption still remains that constructs mean and function in similar ways in different cultural groups. Type II research attributes differences in the strength and magnitude of relationships among constructs to cultural variations. Finally, in the third approach, culture is treated as the source of meaning (Type III hypothesis). This approach is very different from the others in that the research starts out by examining the culture-specific meanings of constructs. Conceptual, structural, and functional equivalences across cultures are not assumed but tested. Culture is not treated as external to the individual or to the practice; it is treated as *the* individual, *the* practice. Frontiers of cross-cultural organizational psychology should work on theory development in which conceptualization of culture (i.e., as a predictor, moderator, or source of meaning) is explicitly stated and justified.

Top-down and Bottom-up Influence Processes

Organizational phenomena emerge out of the reciprocal interaction between top-down and bottom-up influence processes (Kozlowski & Klein, 2000). Top-down process occurs when the higher level contextual factors (especially culture) influence the system at lower levels (e.g., organizations and employees). Bottom-up process, in contrast, emerges at lower levels (e.g., individuals, groups) and, through the interactions among individuals and groups, transforms into shared phenomenon at the higher, collective level (i.e., culture).

The literature reviewed in this chapter mainly focused on the top-down process, namely the impact of culture on various aspects of organizational behavior. Bottom-up processes can also emerge as a result of employees interacting with counterparts around the world and facilitating culture change. In the age of technology, it is impossible to keep people away from accessing information on practices in other organizations. Through business interactions with colleagues and customers, employees become aware of managerial practices and organizational dynamics, and may pressure their organizations to adopt them. In the long run, such practices may become commonplace and may lead to changes in cultural values, assumptions, and behavioral patterns. For example, the presence of multinational corporations in developing countries pressures local organizations to change their practices toward more participation and more professionalism. Transformations in organizational cultures may result in changes in sociocultural values, assumptions, and practices. Future research should also study bottom-up processes across various levels of analysis, and should pay special attention to changes in the sociocultural environment stimulated by individuals and organizations.

Levels of Analysis

"Culture is everywhere and always relevant in organizational life, but there is no obvious or natural level of analysis from which to observe it" (Van Maanen & Laurent, 1992, p. 23). The challenge for researchers at the frontiers of cross-cultural I/O psychology is to capture culture at the appropriate level of analysis. In the majority of research reviewed in this chapter, culture is captured at the national level. However, this approach has limitations. Most notably, it assumes that national cultures are homogenous, which is frequently challenged (e.g., Au, 2001). It also assumes that people in a national culture hold single cultural identities, whereas the most recent literature suggests that individuals may hold multiple cultural identities (Hong, Morris, Chiu, & Benet-Martinez, 2000; Brannen & Thomas, 2010). And it assumes that within-culture variability is

smaller than between-culture variability, but this may not apply to some countries whose national borders arbitrarily divide people of the same cultural heritage. Capturing culture at a higher level of analysis is also problematic because of the risk of falling into ecological fallacy (Hofstede, 1980). For example, the term *North American culture* wrongly assumes that the United States and Canada have similar cultural characteristics, or the term *developing country culture* wrongly assumes that homogeneity among these countries is larger than heterogeneity.

The frontiers should capture culture at the right level of analysis depending on the phenomenon under study. For example, research on teamwork or OCBs benefits from focusing on both national and *organizational* level of cultural contexts. Figure 33.1 represents the various cross-level effects that future research must also take into account.

Capturing Cultural Differences

Our review suggests that the literature is dominated by research examining cross-cultural differences mainly through cultural *values*. Among values, individualism-collectivism has received the most attention, despite the difficulty capturing it (e.g., Oyserman & Lee, 2008). Frontiers of cross-cultural I/O research should capture culture, a highly complex construct, by going beyond individualism and collectivism. For example, Aycan (2005) related a large number of cultural dimensions to variations in HRM practices, such as fatalism, paternalism, high (vs. low) context, universalism (vs. particularism), performance orientation, future orientation, and specificity (vs. diffuseness). Advances in the cross-cultural psychology literature enable us to include norms (Gelfand et al., 2006, 2011), roles (Peterson & Smith, 2000), and beliefs (Leung et al., 2005). The choice of constructs to capture culture should allow us to conduct analyses at and across individual, dyadic, team, unit, and organizational levels (Gelfand et al., 2007). For example, Robert and Wasti (2002) developed a measure to capture individualism and collectivism at the organizational level. Similarly, Aycan and Kabasakal (2006) described paternalism at societal, organizational, and dyadic levels (i.e., in leader-follower relationship).

Measurement of cultural constructs has been and still is a problem. Due to space limitations, we cannot discuss methodological pitfalls in cross-cultural research and recommendations to overcome them (See Gelfand, Raver, & Ehrhart, 2002). However, we would recommend that the field complement its current "tool kit," which consists mainly of measures of personal values to use additional innovative methodologies. Emerging evidence illustrates that descriptive norm measures of culture (e.g., what others do in the cultural context) can help to explain cultural differences (Chiu, Gelfand, Yamagishi, Shteynberg, & Wan, 2010; Fischer et al., 2009; Shteynberg, Gelfand, & Kim, 2009; Wan et al., 2007; Zou et al., 2009). Implicit measures of culture are also fruitful for understanding behavior in organizations. Qualitative measures are sorely needed in the field of cross-cultural organizational psychology. For example, one methodology to capture cultural differences could be "strangification"—that is, looking at the phenomenon from the outside:

> [S]trangification is a set of strategies having one point in common: transferring one (logical) system of propositions from their original context into another context and judging this system out of this context. Strangification is the central methodological proposal of Constructive Realism. Changing the context enables us to get new insights, perspectives and views in the system of the system of propositions. If we look at these contexts where the system of propositions gets absurd, we will notice the implicit assumptions and considerations of this system—i.e. we investigate its tacit knowledge.
> (*Wallner & Jandl*, 2006)

For example, expatriates have a unique perspective to narrate the cultural characteristics of their home culture, as they "take them out" from their context and test them.

Cross-cultural Interfaces

One of the most important mandates of cross-cultural I/O psychology research is to understand dynamics of cross-cultural *interactions* and produce scientific knowledge to guide practitioners to successfully manage them (Adler, 1991; Imai & Gelfand, 2010; Jackson & Aycan, 2006). Our review in this chapter suggests that the majority of research focuses on comparisons among cultural groups in organizational behavior and practices. Frontiers of cross-cultural organizational psychology research should pay much more attention to understanding the interfaces at the juncture where

cultures meet. The literature on expatriate management and on multicultural teams are one of the best examples of the research specifically focusing on cross-cultural interfaces. Similarly, a growing body of literature on HRM practices of multinational corporations examines how they deal with the challenge of balancing between global integration and local responsiveness in HRM practices (cf. Prahalad & Doz, 1987). Erez and Gati (2004) also advocate the study of cross-cultural interfaces in relation to the effects of globalization at the individual (e.g., formation of a sense of global identity), organizational (e.g., globalization vs. hybridization of organizational practices), and national levels (e.g., regulations and labor trends).

Jackson and Aycan (2006) advocated research on interfaces to advance theory in cross-cultural I/O psychology and proposed the following avenues for future research:

1. Cross-cultural interactions and interfaces at multiple levels including inter-continental, inter-national, inter-ethnic, inter-group, inter-organizational levels.

2. Interactions at the interface of cultural units at different levels of analysis, for example the relationship between a foreign company and a local community (e.g., the harm or contribution of multinationals to the local community in developing countries).

3. The products and processes of cultural convergence, divergence and crossvergence, including cultural fusion, adaptations and hybridization (e.g., hybridization of HRM practices in multinational corporations).

4. Power relations in the diffusion, interaction, fusion, adaptation and hybridization of cultures such as in post- and neo-colonialism, and the political, business or occupational dominance of one ethnic group over another (e.g., the dominance of white South-Africans over black workers in work settings, and the reversal of these relationships in the post-Apartheid period).

5. Cross-cultural analysis in the context of shifting and varying cultural units of analysis such as political realignment of ethnic allegiances, intermarrying across ethnic and cultural groups, urbanization and cosmopolitanization. Studies examining the effect of a countries' changing demographic structure (e.g., unity of West and East Germany

after the fall of the Berlin wall) on organizations is an example of research addressing this issue. (Jackson & Aycan 2006, p. 11)

Indigenous Perspectives

Frontiers of cross-cultural I/O research should focus on the meanings of organizational phenomena and the relationships among them within their own cultural context. As stated by Holden (2002): "Cross-cultural impacts cannot be anticipated or meaningfully analyzed solely by the application of cultural categories such as values, language differences, or Hofstedian mental programs *without* an appreciation of the peculiarities—even the idiosyncrasies—of contextual embedding" (p. 14). Our review reveals that a number of constructs indeed have culture-specific meanings, such as leadership, achievement, teamwork, OCB, and negotiation. Studying culture-specific or indigenous phenomena brings us closer to developing universal theories in three ways. First, because all behaviors exist in all cultural contexts to a varying degree, a dominant phenomenon (e.g., paternalistic leadership or *guanxi*) in a particular context may be a recessive phenomenon in another. Therefore, by studying culture-specific or indigenous phenomena, we will be able to capture the characteristics that are recessive to the culture of our own: " . . . By studying other societies where these features are dominant, they can develop concepts and theories that will eventually be useful for understanding their own" (Pruitt, 2004, xii). Second, by studying culture-specific or indigenous phenomena, we can capture the different enactment of the same constructs ("variform universals"; Bass, 1997) and the varying degree of relationships among them, depending on the cultural context ("variform functional universals"; Bass, 1997). Finally, as our reviews on motivation, teamwork, and negotiation have demonstrated, studying the same phenomena in other cultures enables us to discover the *assumptions* underlying theories driven from West. These assumptions provide the boundary conditions of theories and make them more universal.

It is worth noting that we believe every research on organizational behavior and practices is "indigenous" because it occurs in a specific cultural context. Therefore, we object to the naming of research as "indigenous" only when it is conducted in non-Western (or Anglo-Saxon) cultural contexts. We also object to journal reviewers asking for explanation of cultural context only when research is conducted in non-Western countries. To us, research in Western and Anglo-Saxon cultural contexts also reflects the indigenous cultural characteristics of the countries, which requires explanation in publications. Otherwise, it is implicitly assumed that findings from Western cultures are universal.

Conclusion

Cross-cultural organizational psychology has emerged as a field that has much to offer to building universal theories and guiding practice to manage cross-cultural relationships in the era of globalization. Our review of the cross-cultural literature points to a number of exciting directions to be taken by the next generation of cross-cultural I/O psychologists (cf. Gelfand, Erez, & Aycan, 2007): (a) cross-cultural interfaces in expatriation, teamwork, negotiation, and mergers and acquisitions; (b) interaction between cultural and contextual factors; (c) cultural values beyond individualism and collectivism captured at multiple levels; (d) multilevel analysis at theory, methodology, and data analysis; (e) top-down and bottom-up processes of cultural influence on organizational behavior and practices; and (f) culture-specific or indigenous constructs and culture-specific relationships among constructs. Some of the research directions are summarized in Table 33.2. The field of cross-cultural organizational psychology has come a long way over the last several decades, and it confirms what Herodotus—arguably the first cross-cultural psychologist—first noted thousands of years ago, namely, the marked human diversity that exists across the globe.

Acknowledgement

This research is based upon work supported by the Turkish Academy of Sciences and the U. S. Army Research Laboratory and the U. S. Army Research Office under grant number W911NF-08-1-0144. Many thanks to Steve Kozlowski, Marcy Schafer, and Rebecca Mohr for their helpful comments on the manuscript.

Table 33.2 Future Research Questions in Cross-Cultural Organizational Psychology

- *HRM.* How are HRM practices influenced by the *interplay* of cultural (e.g., values and assumptions) and institutional context (e.g., size, industry, ownership status)?

- *Motivation.* (1) What are the culture-specific construals of key elements in motivational theories, such as achievement, affiliation, power, input, output, referent group, or autonomy? (2) How does culture moderate the relationship between motivational practices (e.g., job enrichment) and organizational outcomes (e.g., performance, job satisfaction)? (3) What are the culture-specific motivation techniques effective to enhance individual and organizational outcomes?

- *Teams.* (1) How does the interaction between cultural and situational contexts (e.g., size of the team, task and membership structure, duration of teamwork) influence team performance (e.g., task performance and member satisfaction)? (2) What are the conditions under which culturally diverse teams perform as good as homogenous teams?

- *Conflict & negotiation.* (1) What role do salient cultural values in collectivistic and high power distance cultures, such as face, honor, and modesty, play in negotiations? (2) What are the causes and consequences of conflict in work contexts across cultures? (3) What factors amplify, reduce, or suppress cultural differences in conflict and negotiation? (4) How does negotiation vary in culturally diverse teams (i.e., intercultural negotiation) versus homogeneous teams, and what moderates such effects? (5) What are the individual (e.g., cultural intelligence) and situational characteristics (e.g., task structure, social support) enhancing success in intercultural negotiations?

- *Leadership.* (1) What are the contingencies (e.g., task and follower characteristics) under which different leadership approaches (e.g., participative, transformational, paternalistic) yield positive work and employee outcomes in different cultural contexts? (2) What are the culture-specific enactments of different leadership styles (e.g., how do participative leaders behave in high vs. low power distance cultures)? (3) What are the leadership competencies required to manage culturally diverse teams?

References

Abrams, D., Ando, K., & Hinkle, S. (1998). Psychological attachment to the group: Cross-cultural differences in organizational identification and subjective norms as predictors of workers' turnover intentions. *Personality and Social Psychology Bulletin, 24,* 1027–1039.

Adair, W. L., & Brett, J. (2005). The negotiation dance: Culture and behavioral sequence in negotiation. *Organizational Science, 16,* 33–51.

Adair, W. L., Brett, J., Lempereur, A., Okumura, T., Shikhirev, P., Tinsley, C., et al. (2004). Culture and negotiation strategy. *Negotiation Journal, January, 20,* 87–111.

Adair, W. L., Okumura, T., & Brett, J. (2001). Negotiation behavior when cultures collide. *Journal of Applied Psychology, 86,* 371–385.

Adair, W. L., Taylor, M. S., & Tinsley, C. H. (2009). Starting out on the right foot: Negotiation schemas when cultures collide. *Negotiation and conflict management research, 2,* 138–163.

Adair, W. L., Weingart, L. R., & Brett, J. M. (2007). The timing and function of offers in U.S. and Japanese negotiations. *Journal of Applied Psychology, 92*(4), 1056–1068.

Adam, H., Shirako, A., & Maddux, W. W. (2010). Cultural variance in the interpersonal effects of anger in negotiations. *Psychological Science, 21,* 882–889.

Adamopoulos, J., & Lonner, W. J. (1994). Absolutism, relativism, and universalism in the study of human behavior. In W. J. Lonner & R. Malpass (Eds.), *Psychology and culture* (pp. 129–134). Boston: Allyn & Bacon.

Adigun, I. O., & Stephenson, G. M. (1992). Sources of job motivation and satisfaction among British and Nigerian employees. *Journal of Social Psychology, 132,* 369–376.

Adler, N. J. (1991). *International dimensions of organizational behavior* (2nd Ed.). Boston: PWS-Kent.

Adler, N. J., & Izraeli, D. (Eds.). (1994). *Competitive frontiers: Women managers in a global economy.* Cambridge, UK: Blackwell.

Afza, M. (2005). Superior-subordinate relationships and satisfaction in Indian small business enterprises. *Vikalpa, 3,* 11–19.

Agarwal, S., DeCarlo, T. E., & Vyas, S. B. (1999). Leadership behavior and organizational commitment: A comparative study of American and Indian salesperson. *Journal of International Business Studies, 30,* 727–744.

Aguinis, H., & Henle, C. A. (2003). The search for universals in cross-cultural organizational behavior. In J. Greenberg (Ed.), *Organizational behavior: The state of the science* (2nd Ed., pp. 373–413). Mahwah, NJ: Erlbaum.

Ali, A. J. (1989). Decision style and work satisfaction of Arab Gulf executives: A cross-national study. *International Studies of Management & Organization, 2,* 22–37.

Allen, R. S., Takeda, M., & White, C. S. (2005). Cross-cultural equity sensitivity: A test of differences between the United States and Japan. *The Journal of Managerial Psychology, 20,* 641–662.

Anderson, N., & Witvliet, C. (2008). Fairness reactions to personnel selection methods: An international comparison between the Netherlands, the United States, France, Spain, Portugal, and Singapore. *International Journal of Selection and Assessment, 16,* 1–13.

Andolsek, D. M., & Stebe, J. (2004). Multinational perspectives on work values and commitment. *International Journal of Cross Cultural Management, 4,* 181–209.

Ardichvili, A. (2001). Leadership styles and work-related values of managers and employees of manufacturing enterprises in post-communist countries. *Human Resource Development Quarterly, 12*, 363–383.

Arnett, J. J. (2008). The neglected 95%: Why American psychology needs to become less American. *American Psychologist, 63*, 602–614.

Arthur, W., Jr., Woehr, D. J., Akande, D., & Strong, M. H. (1995). Human resource management in West Africa: Practices and perceptions. *The International Journal of Human Resource Management, 6*, 347–367.

Au, K. H. (2001, July/August). Culturally responsive instruction as a dimension of new literacies. Reading Online, 5(1). Available at: www.readingonline.org/newliteracies/lit_index.asp? HREF=/newliteracies/xu/index.htlm.

Aycan, Z. (Ed.). (2000). *Management, leadership and human resource practices in Turkey*. Ankara: Turkish Psychological Association Press.

Aycan, Z. (2005). The interface between cultural and institutional/structural contingencies in human resource management. *International Journal of Human Resource Management, 16*, 1083–1120.

Aycan, Z. (2006). Paternalism: Towards conceptual refinement and operationalization. In K. S. Yang, K. K. Hwang, & U. Kim (Eds.), *Scientific advances in indigenous psychologies: Empirical, philosophical, and cultural contributions* (pp. 445–466). Cambridge, UK: Cambridge University Press.

Aycan, Z. (2008). Cross-cultural perspectives to work-family conflict. In K. Korabik & D. Lero (Eds.), *Handbook of work-family conflict* (pp. 359–371). London: Cambridge University Press.

Aycan, Z., & Fikret-Pasa, S. (2003). Career choices, job selection criteria and leadership preferences in a transitional nation: The case of Turkey. *Journal of Career Development, 30*, 129–144.

Aycan, Z., & Kabasakal, H. (2006). Social contract and perceived justice of workplace practices to cope with financial crises. *Group and Organization Management, 31*, 469–503.

Aycan, Z., Kanungo, R. N., Mendonca, M., Yu, K., Deller, J., Stahl, G., & Kurshid, A. (2000). Impact of culture on human resource management practices: A 10-country comparison. *Applied Psychology, 49*, 192–222.

Ayman, R. (2004). Situational and contingency approaches to leadership. In J. Antonakis, A. T. Cianciolo, & R. J. Sternberg (Eds.), *The nature of leadership* (pp. 148–170). Thousand Oaks, CA: Sage.

Ayman, R., & Chemers, M. M. (1983). Relationship of supervisory behavior ratings to work group effectiveness and subordinate satisfaction among Iranian managers. *Journal of Applied Psychology, 68*, 338–341.

Ayoko, O. B., & Härtel, C. E. J. (2003). The role of space as both a conflict trigger and a conflict control mechanism in culturally heterogeneous workgroups. *Applied Psychology, 52*, 383–412.

Ayoko, O. B., Härtel, C. E. J., & Callan, V. (2002). Resolving the puzzle of productive and destructive conflict in culturally heterogeneous workgroups: A communication accommodation theory approach. *International Journal of Conflict Management, 13*, 165–185.

Baba, M. L., Gluesing, J., Ratner, H., & Wagner, K. H. (2004). The contexts of knowing: Natural history of a globally distributed team. *Journal of Organizational Behavior, 25*, 547–587.

Babcock, L. C., Wang, X., & Loewenstein, G. (1996). Choosing the wrong pond: Social comparisons in negotiations that reflect a self-serving bias. *The Quarterly Journal of Economics, 111*, 1–19.

Badawy, M. K. (1980). Styles of Mid-Eastern managers. *California Management Review, 22*, 51–58.

Bailey, J. R., Chen, C. C., & Dou, S. G. (1997). Conceptions of self and performance-related feedback in the U.S., Japan and China. *Journal of International Business Studies, 28*, 605–625.

Barrett, G. V., & Bass, B. M. (1976). Cross-cultural issues in industrial and organizational psychology. In M. D. Dunnette (Ed.), *Handbook of industrial and organizational psychology* (pp. 1639–1686). Chicago: Rand McNally College Publishing.

Bartram, D. (2005). The changing face of testing. *The Psychologist, 18*, 666–668.

Bartram, D., & Coyne, I. J. (1998). Variations in national patterns of testing and test use: The ITC/EFPPA international survey. *European Journal of Psychological Assessment, 14*, 249–260.

Bass, B. M. (1997). Does the transactional-transformational leadership paradigm transcend organizational and national boundaries? *American Psychologist, 52*, 130–139.

Bazerman, M. H., & Neale, M. A. (1983). Heuristics in negotiation: Limitations to dispute resolution effectiveness. In M. H. Bazerman & R. J. Lewicki (Eds.), *Negotiations in organizations* (pp. 51–67). Beverly Hills, CA: Sage.

Benton, A. A., & Druckman, D. (1974). Constituent's bargaining orientation and intergroup negotiations. *Journal of Applied Psychology, 4*, 141–150.

Berry, J. W. (1969). On cross-cultural comparability. *International Journal of Psychology, 4*, 119–128.

Berry, J. W. (1980). Social and cultural change. In H. C. Triandis & R. W. Brislin (Eds.), *Handbook of cross-cultural psychology: Social psychology* (Vol. 5, pp. 211–279). Boston: Allyn and Bacon.

Bhawuk, D. P. S. (1997). Leadership through relationship management: Using the theory of individualism and collectivism. In R. W. Brislin & K. Cushner (Eds.), *Improving intercultural interactions: Modules for cross-cultural training programs* (Vol. 2, pp. 40–56). Thousand Oaks, CA: Sage.

Bian, Y., & Ang, S. (1997). Guanxi networks and job mobility in China and Singapore. *Social Forces, 75*, 981–1005.

Björkman, I., & Lu, Y. (1999a). A corporate perspective on the management of human resources in China. *Journal of World Business, 34*, 16–25.

Björkman, I., & Lu, Y. (1999b). The management of human resources in Chinese-Western joint ventures. *Journal of World Business, 34*, 306–324.

Blunt, P., & Jones, M. (1992). *Managing organizations in Africa*. Berlin and New York: Walter de Gruyter.

Blunt, P., & Popoola, O. (1985). *Personnel management in Africa*. New York: Longman.

Bolino, M. C., & Turnley, W. H. (2008). Old faces, new places: Equity theory in cross-cultural contexts. *Journal of Organizational Behavior, 29*(1), 29–50.

Bond, M. (1987). Chinese values and the search for culture-free dimensions of culture. *Journal of Cross-Cultural Psychology, 18*, 143–164. (Author often quoted as Chinese Culture Connection).

Bond, M. H., & Hwang, K. (1986). The social psychology of Chinese people. In M. H. Bond (Ed.), *The psychology of the Chinese people* (pp. 213–266). New York: Oxford University Press.

Bond, M. H., Leung, K., Au, A., Tong, K. K., & Chemonges-Nielson, Z. (2004). Combining social axioms with values in predicting social behaviours. *European Journal of Personality, 18*, 177–191.

Bond, R. A., & Smith, P. B. (1996). Culture and conformity: A meta-analysis of studies using Asch's (1952b, 1956) line judgment task. *Psychological Bulletin, 119*, 111–137.

Bowman, P. J. (1989). Research perspectives on Black men: Role strain and adaptation across the adult life cycle. In R. L. Jones (Ed.), *Black adult development and aging* (pp. 117–150). Berkeley, CA: Cobbs & Henry.

Brannen, M. Y., & Thomas, D. C. (2010). Bicultural individuals in organizations: Implications and opportunity. *International Journal of Cross Cultural Management, 10*, 5–16.

Branzei, O., Vertinsky, I., & Camp, R. D., II. (2007). Culture-contingent signs of trust in emergent relationships. *Organizational Behavior and Human Decision Processes, 104*, 61–82.

Brett, J. M., & Gelfand, M. J. (2006). A cultural analysis of the underlying assumption of negotiation theory. In L. Thompson (Ed.), *Frontiers of negotiation research* (pp. 173–201). New York: Psychology Press.

Brett, J. M., & Okumura, T. (1998). Inter- and intracultural negotiations: US and Japanese negotiators. *Academy of Management Journal, 41*, 495–510.

Brett, J. M., Tinsley, C. H., Janssens, M., Barsness, Z. I., & Lytle, A. L. (1997). New approaches to the study of culture in I/O psychology. In P. C. Earley & M. Erez (Eds.), *New perspectives on international/industrial/organizational psychology* (pp. 75–129). San Francisco: Jossey-Bass.

Briscoe, D. R. (1997). Assesment centers: Cross-cultural and cross-national issues. *Journal of Social Behavior and Personality, 12*, 261–266.

Brislin, R. W., MacNab, B., Worthley, R., Kabigting, F., & Zukis, B. (2005). Evolving perceptions of Japanese workplace motivation: An employee-manager comparison. *International Journal of Cross-Cultural Management, 5*, 87–104.

Brockner, J., Ackerman, G., Greenberg, J., Gelfand, M. J., Francesco, A. M., Chen, Z. X., Leung, K., & Shapiro, D. (2001). Culture and procedural justice: The influence of power distance on reactions to voice. *Journal of Experimental Social Psychology, 37*, 300–315.

Brown, C., & Reich, M. (1997). *Company HR policies and compensation systems: Implications for income inequality.* (Working paper). Berkeley: University of California, Institute of Industrial Relations.

Budhwar, P. S., & Khatri, N. (2001). A comparative study of HR practices in Britain and India. *International Journal of Human Resource Management, 12*, 800–826.

Buera, A., & Glueck, W. F. (1979). The need satisfactions of managers in Libya. *Management International Review, 19*, 115.

Cai, D. A. (1998). Culture, plans, and the pursuit of negotiation goals. *Journal of Asian Pacific Communication, 8*, 103–123.

Caligiuri, P. (2006). Developing global leaders. *Human Resource Management Review, 16*, 219–228.

Campbell, J. P., Gasser, M. B., & Oswald, F. L. (1996). The substantive nature of job performance variability. In K. R. Murphy (Ed.), *Individual differences and behavior in organizations* (pp. 258–299). San Francisco: Jossey-Bass.

Chan, D. (1998). Functional relations among constructs in the same content domain at different levels of analysis: A typology of composition models. *Journal of Applied Psychology, 83*, 234–246.

Chan, J. (1992). *Policing in a multicultural society: A study of the New South Wales police.* Final report to the New South Wales, Australia Police Service.

Chao, G. T., & Moon, H. (2005). The cultural mosaic: A methatheory for understanding the complexity of culture. *Journal of Applied Psychology, 90*, 1128–1140.

Chatterjee, S. R., & Pearson, C. A. L. (2002). Work goals of Asian managers: Field evidence from Singapore, Malaysia, India, Thailand, Brunei and Mongolia. *International Journal of Cross-Cultural Management, 2*, 251–268.

Chen, C. C. (1995). New trends in rewards allocation preferences: A Sino-US comparison. *Academy of Management Journal, 38*, 408–428.

Chen, C. C., Chen, X., & Meindl, J. R. (1998). How can cooperation be fostered? The cultural effects of individualism-collectivism. *Academy of Management Review, 23*, 285–305.

Chen, C. C., Meindl, J. R., & Hui, H. (1998). Deciding on equity or parity: A test of situational, cultural, and individual factors. *Journal of Organizational Behavior, 19*, 115–129.

Chen, X. P., & Li, S. (2005). Cross-national differences in cooperative decision-making in mixed motive business contexts: The mediating effect of vertical and horizontal individualism. *Journal of International Business Studies, 36*, 622–636.

Chen, Y., Brockner, J., & Katz, T. (1998). Toward an explanation of cultural differences in in-group favoritism: The role of individual versus collective primacy. *Journal of Personality and Social Psychology, 75*, 1490–1502.

Chen, Y. F., & Tjosvold, D. (2005). Cross-cultural leadership: Goal interdependence and leader-member relations in foreign ventures in China. *Journal of International Management, 11*, 417–439.

Chen, Z. X., & Francesco, A. M. (2003). The relationship between the three components of commitment and employee performance in China. *Journal of Vocational Behavior, 62*, 490–510.

Cheng, B. (1999). Chinese chief executive officers' employee categorization and managerial behavior. In H. S. R. Kao, D. Sinha, & B. Wilpert (Eds.), *Management and cultural values: The indigenization of organizations in Asia* (pp. 233–252). London: Sage.

Cheng, B. S., Chou, L. F., Wu, T. Y., Huang, M. P., & Farh, J. L. (2004). Paternalistic leadership and subordinate responses: Establishing a leadership model in Chinese organizations. *Asian Journal of Social Psychology, 7*, 89–117.

Cheng, Y., & Stockdale, M. S. (2003). The validity of the three-component model of organizational commitment in a Chinese context. *Journal of Vocational Behavior, 62*, 465–489.

Cheung, G. W., & Rensvold, R. B. (2000). Assessing extreme and acquiescence response sets in cross-cultural research using structural equations modeling. *Journal of Cross-Cultural Psychology, 31*, 187–212.

Chiang, F. F. T., & Birtch, T. A. (2010). Appraising performance across borders: An empirical examination of the purposes and practices of performance appraisal in a multi-country context. *Journal of Management Studies, 47*, 1365–1393.

Chiao, J. (Ed.). (2009). Cultural neuroscience: Cultural influences on brain function. *Progress in Brain Research.* New York: Elsevier.

Chinese Culture Connection. (1987). Chinese values and the search for culture-free dimensions of culture. *Journal of Cross-Cultural Psychology, 18*, 143–164.

Chiu, C-Y., Gelfand, M. J., Yamagishi, T., Shteynberg, G., & Wan, G. (2010). Intersubjective culture: The role of inter-subjective perceptions in cross-cultural research. *International Journal of Psychology, 34*, 19–28.

Chiu, R. K., & Kosinski, F. A. (1999). The role of affective dis-position in job satisfaction and work strain: Comparing col-lectivist and individualist societies. *International Journal of Psychology, 34*, 19–28.

Clugston, M., Howell, J. P., & Dorfman, D. W. (2000). Does cultural socialization predicate multiple bases and foci of commitment. *Journal of Management, 26*, 5–30.

Chong, L. M., & Thomas, D. C. (1997). Leadership perceptions in cross-cultural context: Pakeha and Pakeha and Pacific islanders in New Zealand. *Leadership Quarterly, 8*, 275–293.

Cooke, B. (2008). If critical management studies is your prob-lem: A short comment. *Organization, 15*, 912–914.

Cooke, B., Mills, A. J., & Kelley, E. S. (2005). Situating Maslow in cold war America: A Recontextualization of management theory. *Group & Organization Management, 30*, 129–152.

Corney, W. J., & Richards, C. H. (2005).A comparative analy-sis of the desirability of work characteristics: Chile versus the United States. *International Journal of Management, 22*, 159–165.

Crampton, C. D., & Hinds, P. J. (2005). Subgroup dynamics in internationally distributed teams: Ethnocentrism or cross-national learning? *Research in Organizational Behavior, 26*, 231–263.

Dany, F., & Torchy, V. (1994). Recruitment and selection in Europe: Policies, practices and methods. In C. Brewster & A. Hegewisch (Eds.), *Policy and practices in European human resource management. The Price Waterhouse Cranfield Survey* (pp. 68–88). London: Routledge.

Darwish, A. (1998). Translation as a decision making process under contraints. Ph.D. dissertation, Queensland University of Technology.

Davidson, M. J., & Burke, R. J. (2004) (Eds.). *Women in man-agement worldwide: Facts, figures and analysis.* London, UK: Ashgate.

Davila, A., & Elvira, M. M. (2005). Culture and human resource management in Latin America. In M. M. Elvira & A. Davila (Eds.), *Managing human resources in Latin America: An agenda for international leaders* (pp. 3–24). Oxford: Routledge.

Davis, D. D. (1998). International performance measurement and management. In J. W. Smither (Ed.), *Performance appraisal* (pp. 95–131). San Francisco: Jossey-Bass.

Dean, M. A., Roth, P. L., & Bobko, P. (2008). Ethnic and gender subgroup differences in assessment center ratings: A meta-analysis. *Journal of Applied Psychology, 88*, 683–691.

Debrah, Y. A. (2001). Human resources management in Ghana. In P. S. Budhwar & Y. A. Debrah (Eds.), *Human resource management in developing countries* (pp. 190–208). London: Routledge.

DeCieri, H., & Sheehan, C. (2008). Performance management in Australia. In A. Varma, P. Budhwar, & A. DeNisi (Eds.), *Management performance management: A global perspective* (pp. 239–253). London: Routledge/Palgrave Macmillan.

De Dreu, C. K. W., Nauta, A., & Van de Vliert, E. (1995). Self-serving evaluations of conflict behavior and escalation of the dispute. *Journal of Applied Social Psychology, 25*, 2049–2066.

Deng, L., & Gibson, P. (2009). Mapping and modeling the capacities that underlie effective cross-cultural leadership: An interpretive study with practical outcomes. *Cross-Cultural Management: An International Journal, 16*, 347–366.

Den Hartog, D. N., House, R. J., Hanges, P. J., Ruiz-Quintanilla, S. A., & Dorfman, P. W. (1999). Culture-specific and cross-culturally generalizable implicit leadership theories: Are the attributes of charismatic/transformational leadership univer-sally endorsed? *Leadership Quarterly, 10*, 219–256.

Den Hartog, D. N., & Verburg, R. M. (1997). Cjaros and rhetoric: Communicative techniques of international busi-ness leaders. *Leadership Quarterly, 8*, 355–391.

DeVoe, S. E., & Iyengar, S. S. (2004). Managers' theories of subordinates: A cross-cultural examination of manager perceptions of motivation and appraisal of performance. *Organizational Behavior and Human Decision Processes, 93*, 47–61.

DeVos, G. (1973). *Socialization for achievement.* Berkeley: University of California.

Dickson, M. W., Den Hartog, D. N., & Mitchelson, J. K. (2003). Research on leadership in a cross-cultural context. Making progress and raising new questions. *Leadership Quarterly, 14*, 729–768.

Doi, L. T. (1973). *The anatomy of dependence* (J. Bester, Trans.). Tokyo: Kodansha International.

Dorfman, P. W. (2004). International and cross-cultural lead-ership research. In B. J. Punnett & O. Shenkar (Eds.), *Handbook for international management research* (2nd ed., pp. 265–355). Ann Arbor: University of Michigan.

Dorfman, P. W., Hanges, P. J., & Brodbeck, F. C. (2004). Leadership and cultural cariation: The identification cultur-ally endorsed leadership profiles. In R. J. House, P. J. Hanges, M. Javidan, P. Dorfman, & V. Gupta (Eds.), *Leadership, culture, and organizations: The GLOBE study of 62 societies* (pp. 667–718). Thousand Oaks, CA: Sage.

Dorfman, P. W., & Howell, J. P. (1988). Dimensions of national culture and effective leadership patterns: Hofstede revisited. In E. G. McGoun (Ed.), *Advances in international compara-tive management* (Vol. 3, pp. 127–149). Greenwich, CT: JAI Press.

Dorfman, P. W., Howell, J. P., Hibino, S., Lee, J. K., Tate, U., & Bautista, A. (1997). Leadership in Western and Asian coun-tries: Commonalities and differences in effective leadership processes. *Leadership Quarterly, 8*, 233–274.

Drach-Zahavy, A. (2004). The proficiency trap: How to balance enriched job designs and the team's need for support. *Journal of Organizational Behavior, 25*, 1–18.

Drost, E. A., & Von Glinow, M. A. (1998). Leadership behav-ior in Mexico: Etic philosophies, emic practices. *Research in International Business and International Relations: Leadership and Innovation in Emerging Markets, 7*, 3–28.

Earley, P. C. (1989). Social loafing and collectivism: A compari-son of the United States with the People's Republic of China. *Administrative Science Quarterly, 34*, 565–581.

Earley, P. C. (1993). East meets West meets Mideast: Further explorations of collectivistic and individualistic work groups. *Academy of Management Journal, 36*, 319–348.

Earley, P. C. (1999). Playing follow the leader: Status-determining traits in relation to collective efficacy across cul-tures. *Organizational Behavior and Human Decision Processes, 80*, 1–21.

Earley, P. C., & Ang, S. (2003). *Cultural intelligence: Individual interactions across culture.* Stanford, CA: Stanford University Press.

Earley, P. C., & Erez, M. (1997). *New perspectives in interna-tional industrial/organizational psychology.* San Francisco: Jossey-Bass.

Earley, P. C., & Gibson, C. B. (2002). *Multinational work teams: A new perspective.* Mahwah, NJ: Erlbaum.

Earley, P. C., Gibson, C. B., & Chen, C. C. (1999). How did I do versus how did we do? Intercultural contrasts of performance feedback search and self efficacy. *Journal of Cross-Cultural Psychology, 30,* 596–621.

Earley, P. C., & Mosakowski, E. (2000). Creating hybrid team cultures: An empirical test of international team functioning. *Academy of Management Journal, 43,* 26–49.

Easterby-Smith, M., Malina, D., & Yuan, L. (1995). How culture sensitive is HRM? A comparative analysis of Chinese and UK companies. *International Journal of Human Resource Management, 6*(1), 31–59.

Eby, L., & Dobbins, G. (1997). Collectivistic orientation in teams: An individual and group-level analysis. *Journal of Organizational Behaviour, 18,* 275–295.

Ehrhart, M. G., & Klein, K. J. (2001). Predicting followers' preferences for charismatic leadership: The influence of follower values and personality. *Leadership Quarterly, 12,* 153–179.

Elenkov, D. S. (1998). Can American management concepts work in Russia? *California Management Review, 40,* 133–157.

Elenkov, D. S., & Manev, I. M. (2005). Top management leadership and influence on innovation: The role of socio-cultural context. *Journal of Management, 31,* 381–402.

Elron, E. (1997). Top management teams within multinational corporations: Effects of cultural heterogeneity. *Leadership Quarterly, 8,* 393–412.

Emery, C. R., & Oertel, S. (2006). An examination of employees' culture-based perceptions as a predictor of motivation. *Journal of Organizational Culture, Communications, and Conflict, 10,* 13–30.

Ensari, N., & Murphy, S. E. (2003). Cross-cultural variation in leadership perceptions and attribution of charisma to the leader *Organizational Behavior and Human Decision Processes, 92,* 52–66.

Erez, M. (1997). A culture-based model of work motivation. In P. C. Earley & M. Erez (Eds.), *New perspectives on international industrial/organizational psychology* (pp. 193–242). San Francisco: Jossey-Bass.

Erez, M. (2000). Make management practice fit the national culture. In E. A. Locke (Ed.), *Basic principles of organizational behavior: A handbook* (pp. 418–434). New York: Blackwell.

Erez, M. (2010). Culture and job design. *Journal of Organizational Behavior, 31,* 389–400.

Erez, M., & Earley, P. C. (1987). Comparative analysis of goal-setting strategies across cultures. *Journal of Applied Psychology, 72,* 658–665.

Erez, M., & Earley, P. C. (1993). *Culture, self-identity, and work.* New York: Oxford University Press.

Erez, M., & Gati, E. (2004). A dynamic multi-level model of culture: From the micro-level of the individual to the macro level of a global culture. *Applied Psychology, 53,* 583–598.

Erez, M., & Somach, A. (1996). Group productivity loss – the rule or the exception? Effects of culture and group-based motivation. *Academy of Management Journal, 39,* 1513–1537.

Ergin, C., & Kozan, M. K. (2004). Subordinates' basic values and the appeal of transformational and transactional leadership in Turkey. *Turk Psikoloji Dergisi, 19,* 37–51.

Evans, S. (1993). Resolving conflicts with diverse groups. *Cultural Diversity at Work, 5,* 4–5.

Eylon, D., & Au, K. Y. (1999). Exploring empowerment cross-cultural differences along the power distance dimension. *International Journal of Intercultural Relations, 23,* 373–385.

Fadil, P. A., Williams, R. J., Limpaphayom, W. T., & Smatt, C. (2005). Equity or equality? A conceptual examination of the influence of individualism/collectivism on the cross-cultural application of equity theory. *Cross-Cultural Management: An International Journal, 12,* 17–35.

Farh, J. L., & Cheng, B. S. (2000). A cultural analysis of paternalistic leadership in Chinese organizations. In J. T. Li, A. S. Tsui, & E. Weldon (Eds.), *Management and organizations in the Chinese context* (pp. 84–127). London: MacMillian.

Farh, J. L., Earley, P. C., & Lin, S. C. (1997). Impetus for action: A cultural analysis of justice and organizational citizenship behavior in Chinese society. *Administrative Science Quarterly, 42,* 421–444.

Fellows, R., Liu, A., & Fong, C. M. (2003). Leadership style and power relations in quantity surveying in Hong Kong. *Construction management and economics, 21,* 809–818.

Fey, C. F. (2005). Opening the black box of motivation: A cross-cultural comparison of Sweden and Russia. *International Business Review, 14,* 345–367.

Fischer, R. (2004). Organizational justice and cultural values in Europe: Justice is in the eye of the beholder. In S. Schmid & A. Thomas (Eds.), *Impact of values and norms on intercultural training and education* (pp. 83–92). Vienna: IDM.

Fischer, R., Ferreira, M. C., Assmar, E., Redford, P., Harb, C., Glazer, S., . . . & Achoui, I. (2009). Individualism-collectivism as descriptive norms: Development of a subjective norm approach to culture measurement. *Journal of Cross-Cultural Psychology, 40,* 187–213.

Fischer, R., & Smith, P. B. (2003). Reward allocation and culture: A meta-analysis. *Journal of Cross-Cultural Psychology, 34,* 251–268.

Fleishman, E. A. (1953). The description of supervisory behavior. *Personnel Psychology, 37,* 1–6.

Fletcher, C., & Perry, E. L. (2001). Performance appraisal and feedback: A consideration of national culture and a review of contemporary research and future trends. In N. Anderson, D. S. Ones, K. Sinangil, & C. Viswesvaran (Eds.), *Handbook of industrial, work, and organizational psychology* (pp. 127–144). Thousand Oaks, CA: Sage.

Fok, L. Y., Hartman, S. J., Villere, M. F., & Freibert, R. C., III. (1996). A study of the impact of cross-cultural differences on perceptions of equity and organizational citizenship behavior. *International Journal of Management, 13,* 3–14.

Francesco, A. M., & Chen, Z. X. (2004). Collectivism in action: Its moderating effect on the relationship between organizational commitment and employee performance in China. *Group Organization Management, 29,* 425–441.

Fu, P. P., Kennedy, J., Tata, J., Yukl, G., Bond, M. H., et al. (2004). The impact of societal cultural values and individual social beliefs on the perceived effectiveness of managerial influence strategies: A meso approach. *Journal of International Business Studies, 35,* 284–305.

Fu, P. P., & Liu, J. (2008). Cross-cultural influence strategies and power sources. In P. B. Smith, M. F. Peterson, & D. C. Thomas (Eds.), *Handbook of cross-cultural management research* (pp. 239–252). Thousand Oaks, CA: Sage.

Fu, J., Morris, M. W., Lee, S., Chao, M., Chiu, C., & Hong, Y. (2007). Epistemic motives and cultural conformity: Need for closure, culture, and context as determinants of conflict judgments. *Journal of Personality and Social Psychology, 92*(2), 191–207.

Furnham, A., Kirkcaldi, B. D., & Lynn, R. (1994). National attitudes to competitiveness, money, and work among young people: First, second, and third world differences. *Human Relations, 47*, 119–132.

Gambrel, P. A., & Cianci, R. (2003). Maslow's Hierarchy of Needs: Does it apply in collectivist culture. *Journal of Applied Management and Entrepreneurship, 8*, 143–162.

Gautam, T., Van Dick, R., Wagner, U., Upadhyay, N., & Davis, A. J. (2005). Organizational citizenship behavior and organizational commitment in Nepal. *Asian Journal of Social Psychology, 8*, 336–345.

Geertz, C. (1973). *The interpretation of cultures*. New York: Basic.

Geiger, M. A., Cooper, E. A., Hussain, I., O'Connell, B. T., Power, J., Raghundandan, K…& Sanchez, G. (1998). Using expectancy theory to assess student motivation: An international replication. *Issues in Accounting Education, 13*, 139–156.

Geletkanycz, M. A. (1997). The salience of 'culture's consequences': The effects of cultural values on top executive commitment to the status quo. *Strategic Management Journal, 18*, 615–634.

Gelfand, M. J., & Christakopoulou, S. (1999). Culture and negotiator cognition: Judgment accuracy and negotiation processes in individualistic and collectivistic cultures. *Organizational Behavior and Human Decision Processes, 79*(3), 248–269.

Gelfand, M. J., Erez, M., & Aycan, Z. (2007). Cross-cultural organizational behavior. *Annual Review of Psychology, 58*, 479–514.

Gelfand, M. J., Fulmer, A., & Severance, L. (2010). The psychology of negotiation and mediation. In S. Zedeck (Ed.), *APA handbook of industrial and organizational psychology* (pp. 495–554). Washington, DC: American Psychological Association.

Gelfand, M. J., Higgins, M., Nishii, L. H., Raver, J. L., Dominguez, A., Murakami, F., Yamaguchi, S., & Toyama, M. (2002). Culture and egocentric perceptions of fairness in conflict and negotiation. *Journal of Applied Psychology, 87*(5), 833–845.

Gelfand, M. J., Leslie, L., & Fehr, R. (2008). In order to prosper, organizational psychology…should adopt a global perspective. *Journal of Organizational Behavior, 29*, 493–517.

Gelfand, M. J., Leslie, L., & Shteynberg, G. (2007). Cross-cultural theory/methods. In S. Rogelberg (Ed.), *Encyclopedia of industrial and organizational psychology* (Vol. 1, pp. 136–142). Mahwah, NJ: Erlbaum.

Gelfand, M. J., & McCusker, C. (2002). Metaphor and the cultural construction of negotiation: A paradigm for theory and research. In M. Gannon & K. L. Newman (Eds.), *Handbook of cross-cultural management* (pp. 292–314). New York: Blackwell.

Gelfand, M. J., Nishii, L. H., Godfrey, E., & Raver, J. (2003). Culture and metaphor in negotiation. In W. Adair (Chair), *Culture and negotiation*. Symposium presented at the annual conference of the Academy of Management, Seattle.

Gelfand, M. J., Nishii, L. H., Holcombe, K. M., Dyer, N., Ohbuchi, K., & Fukuno, M. (2001). Cultural influences on cognitive representations of conflict: Interpretations of conflict episodes in the United States and Japan. *Journal of Applied Psychology, 86*(6), 1059–1074.

Gelfand, M. J., Nishii, L., & Raver, J. (2006). On the nature and importance of cultural tightness-looseness. *Journal of Applied Psychology, 91*, 1225–1244.

Gelfand, M. J., Raver, J. L., & Ehrhart, K. (2002). Methodological issues in cross-cultural organizational research. In S. Rogelberg (Ed.), *Handbook of industrial and organizational psychology research methods* (pp. 216–241). New York: Blackwell.

Gelfand, M. J., Raver, J. L., Nishii, L., Leslie, L. M., Lun, J., & colleagues (2011). Differences between tight and loose cultures: A 33-nation study. *Science, 332*, 1100–1104.

Gelfand, M. J., & Realo, A. (1999). Individualism-collectivism and accountability in intergroup negotiations. *Journal of Applied Psychology, 84*, 721–736.

Gelfand, M. J., Smith Major, V., Raver, J. L., Nishii, L. H., & O'Brien, K. (2008). Negotiating relationally: The dynamics of the relational self in negotiations. *Academy of Management Review, 31*, 427–451.

George, J. M., Jones, G. R., & Gonzalez, J. A. (1998). The role of affect in cross-cultural negotiation. *Journal of International Business Studies, 29*, 749–772.

Gergen, K. J., Morse, S. J., & Gergen, M. (1980). Behavior exchange in cross-cultural perspective. In H. Triandis & R. W. Brislin (Eds.), *Handbook of cross-cultural psychology* (Vol. 5, pp. 121–153). New York: Allyn Bacon.

Giacobbe-Miller, J. K., Miller, D. J., & Victorov, V. I. (1998). A comparison of Russian and U.S. pay allocation decisions, distributive justice judgments, and productivity under different payment conditions. *Personnel Psychology, 51*, 137–163.

Gibson, C. B. (1997). Do you hear what I hear? A framework for reconciling intercultural communication difficulties arising from cognitive styles and cultural values. In P. C. Earley & M. Erez (Eds.), *New perspectives on international industrial and organizational psychology* (pp. 335–362). San Francisco: The New Lexington Press.

Gibson, C. B. (1999). Do they do what they think they can? Group-efficacy and group effectiveness across tasks and cultures. *Academy of Management Journal, 42*, 138–152.

Gibson, C. B., & Cohen, S. G. (2003). *Virtual teams that work: Creating conditions for virtual team effectiveness*. San Francisco: Jossey-Bass.

Gibson, C. B., & Saxton, T. (2005). Thinking outside the black box: Outcomes of team decisions with third party interventions. *Small Group Research, 36*, 208–236.

Gibson, C. B., & Zellmer-Bruhn, M. E. (2001). Metaphors and meaning: An intercultural analysis of teamwork. *Administrative Science Quarterly, 46*, 274–303.

Gibson, C. B., & Zellmer-Bruhn, M. E. (2002). Minding your metaphors: Applying the concept of teamwork metaphors to the management of teams in multicultural contexts. *Organizational Dynamics, 31*, 101–116.

Gluskinos, U. M. (1988). Cultural and political considerations in the introduction of Western technologies: The Mekorot project. *Journal of Management Development, 6*, 34–46.

Gómez, C., Kirkman, B. L., & Shapiro, D. L. (2000). The impact of collectivism and ingroup/outgroup membership on evaluation generosity. *Academy of Management Journal, 43*, 1097–2007.

Graham, J. (1985). The influence of culture on the process of business negotiations: An exploratory study. *Journal of International Business Studies, 16*, 81–96.

Greenfield, P. M. (1997). Culture as process: Empirical methods for cultural psychology. In J. W. Berry & Y. H. Poortinga (Eds.), *Handbook of cross-cultural psychology* (Vol. 1, pp. 301–346). London: Sage.

Greenwald, A. G., McGhee, D. E., & Schwartz, J. L. K. (1998). Measuring individual differences in implicit cognition: The implicit association test. *Journal of Personality and Social Psychology, 74,* 1464–1480.

Grouzet, F. M. E., Kasser, T., Ahuvia,A., Fernandez Dois, J. M., Kim, Y., Lau, S., & Sheldon, K. M. (2005). The structure of goal contents across 5 cultures. *Journal of Personality and Social Psychology, 89,* 800–816.

Gunia, B. C., Brett, J. M., Nandkeolyar, A. K., Kamdar, D. (2011). Paying a price: Culture, trust, and negotiation consequences. *Journal of Applied Psychology, 96(4),* 774–789.

Gupta, V., MacMillan, I., & Surie, G. (2004). Entrepreneurial leadership: Developing a cross-cultural construct. *Journal of Business Venturing, 19,* 241–260.

Haire, M., Ghiselli, E. E., & Porter, L. W. (1966). *Managerial thinking: An international study.* Chichester, UK: Wiley.

Hak-Chong, L. (1998). Transformation of employment practices in Korean businesses. *International Studies of Management and Organization, 28,* 112–145.

Harris, P. R., & Moran, R. T. (1996). *Managing cultural differences* (4th ed.). Houston: Gulf.

Harrison, G. L., McKinnon, J. L., Wu, A., & Chow, C. W. (2000). Cultural influences on adaptation to fluid workgroups and teams. *Journal of International Business Studies, 31,* 489–505.

Heine, S. J., Lehman, D. R., Markus, H. R., & Kitayama, S. (1999). Is there a universal need for positive self-regard? *Psychological Review, 106,* 766–794.

Heine, S. J., Kitayama, S., Lehman, D. R., Takata, T., Ide, E., Lueng, C., & Matsumoto, H. (2001). Divergent consequences of success and failure in Japan and North America: An investigation of self-improving motivations and malleable selves. *Journal of Personality and Social Psychology, 81,* 599–615.

Herriot, P., & Anderson, N. (1997). Selecting for change: How will personnel and selection psychology survive? In N. Anderson & P. Herriot (Eds.), *International handbook of selection and assessment* (pp. 1–38). Oxford, UK: Wiley.

Herskovits, M. J. (1955). *Cultural anthropology.* New York: Knopf.

Hines, G. H. (1973). The image of industrial psychologists in cross-cultural perspective. *Professional Psychology: Research & Practice, 4,* 64–71.

Hirokawa, R., & Miyahara, A. (1986). A comparison of influence strategies utilized by managers in American and Japanese organizations. *Communication Quarterly, 34,* 250–265.

Hofstede, G. (1980). Motivation, leadership and organization: Do American theories apply abroad? *Organizational Dynamics, 9,* 42–63.

Hofstede, G. (1983). Dimensions of national cultures in fifty countries and three regions. In J. B. Deregowski, S. Dziurawiec, & R. C. Annis (Eds.), *Expisications in cross-cultural psychology* (pp. 335–355). Lisse: Swets and Zeitlinger.

Hofstede, G. (2001). *Cultures' consequences: Comparing values, behaviors, institutions and organizations across nations* (2nd ed.). Thousand Oaks, CA: Sage.

Hofstede, G., & Hofstede, G. J. (2005). *Cultures and organizations: Software of the mind* (Rev. 2nd Ed.). New York: McGraw-Hill.

Holden, N. (2002). *Cross-cultural management: A knowledge management perspective.* Essex: Prentice Hall.

Hong, Y., Morris, M. W., Chiu, C., & Benet-Martinez, V. (2000). Multicultural minds: A dynamic constructivist approach to culture and cognition. *American Psychologist, 55,* 709–720.

House, R. J., Hanges, P. J., Javidan, M., Dorfman, P. W., & Gupta, V. (Eds.). (2004). *Culture, leadership, and organizations: The GLOBE study of 62 societies.* Thousand Oaks, CA: Sage.

House, R. J., Hanges, P. J., Ruiz-Quintanilla, S. A., Dorfman, P.W., Javidan, M., Dickson, M. W., et al. (1999). Cultural influences on leadership and organizations: Project GLOBE. In W. H. Mobley, M. J. Gessner, & V. Arnold. (Eds.), *Advances in global leadership* (Vol 1, pp.171–233). Greenwich, CT: JAI Press.

House, R. J., Wright, N. S., & Aditya, R. N. (1997). Cross-cultural research on organizational leadership: A critical analysis and a proposed theory. In P. C. Earley & M. Erez (Eds.), *New perspectives on international industrial/organizational psychology* (pp. 535–626). San Francisco: The New Lexington Press.

Howell, J. P., Romero, E. J., Dorfman, P. W., Paul, J., & Bautista, J. A. (2003). Effective leadership in the Mexican maquiladora: Challenging common expectations. *Journal of International Management, 9,* 51–73.

Huang, X., & Van de Vliert, E. (2003). Where intrinsic job satisfaction fails to work : National moderators of intrinsic motivation. *Journal of Organizational Behavior, 24,* 159–179.

Hui, C. H., & Graen, G. B. (1997). Guanxi and professional leadership in contemporary Sino-American joint ventures in mainland China. *LeadershipQuarterly, 8,* 451–465.

Hui, C. H., Lee, C., & Rousseau, D. M. (2004). Psychological contract and organizational citizenship behavior in China: Investigating generalizability and instrumentality. *Journal of Applied Psychology, 89,* 311–321.

Hui, C. H., & Luk, C. L. (1997). Industrial/organizational psychology. In J. W. Berry, Y. H. Poortinga, & J. Randey (Eds.), *Handbook of cross-cultural psychology.* Boston: Allyn and Bacon.

Hui, C. H., & Yee, C. (1999). The impact of psychological collectivism and workgroup atmosphere on Chinese employees' job satisfaction. *Applied Psychology International Review, 48,* 175–185.

Hulin, C. (1991). Adaptation, persistence, and commitment in organizations. In M. D. Dunnette & L. M. Hough (Eds.), *Handbook of industrial and organizational psychology* (2nd ed., Vol. 2, pp. 445–506). Palo Alto, CA: Consulting Psychologists Press.

Hundley, G., & Kim, J. (1997). National culture and the factors affecting perceptions of pay fairness in Korea and the United States. *International Journal of Organizational Analysis, 5,* 325–341.

Hunt, J. G., & Peterson, M. F. (1997). Two scholars' views of some nooks and crannies in cross-cultural leadership. *The Leadership Quarterly, 8,* 343–354.

Huntington, S. P. (1996). *The clash of civilations: Remaking of world order.* New York: Simon & Schuster.

Huo, Y. P., Huang, H. J., & Napier, N. K. (2002). Divergence or convergence: A cross-national comparison of personnel selection practices. *Human Resource Management, 41,* 31–44.

Huo, Y. P., & Von Glinow, M. A. (1995). On transplanting human resource practices to China: A culture-driven approach. *International Journal of Manpower, 16,* 3–11.

Imai, L., & Gelfand, M. J. (2010). The culturally intelligent negotiator: The impact of cultural intelligence (CQ) on negotiation sequences and outcomes. *Organizational Behavior and Human Decision Processes, 112*, 83–98.

Ingmar, B., & Yuan, L. (1999). The management of human resources in Chinese-Western joint ventures. *Journal of World Business, 34*, 306.

International Test Commission. (2000). *International guidelines for test use*. Louvain-la-Neuve, Belgium.

Iyengar, S. S., & Lepper, M. R. (1999). Rethinking the value of choice: A cultural perspective on intrinsic motivation. *Journal of Personality and Social Psychology, 76*, 349–366.

Jackson, T. (2004). *Management and change in Africa: A cross-cultural perspective*. London: Routledge.

Jackson, T., Amaeshi, K., & Yavuz, S. (2008). Untangling African indigenous management: Multiple influences on the success of SMEs in Kenya. *Journal of World Business, 43*, 400–416.

Jackson, T., & Aycan, Z. (2006). Editorial: From cultural values to cross-cultural interfaces. *International Journal of Cross-Cultural Management, 6*(1), 5–13.

Jaggi, B. (1979). Need importantance of Indian managers. *Management International Review, 19*, 107–113.

Jahoda, G. (1984). Do we need a concept of culture? *Journal of Cross-Cultural Psychology, 15*, 139–151.

Janssens, M., & Brett, J. M. (1997). Meaningful participation in transition teams. *European Journal of Work and Organizational Psychology, 6*, 153–158.

Janssens, M., & Brett, J. M. (2006). Cultural intelligence in global teams: A fusion model of collaboration. *Group and Organization Management, 31*(1), 124–153.

Jaramillo, F., Mulki, J. P., & Marshall, G. W. (2005). A meta-analysis of the relationship between organizational commitment and salesperson job performance. *Journal of Business Research, 58*, 705–714.

Javidan, M., & Carl, D. E. (2004). East meets West: A cross-cultural comparison of charismatic leadership among Canadian and Iranian executives. *The Journal of Management Studies, 41*, 665–691.

Javidan, M., & Carl, D. E. (2005). Leadership across cultures: A study of Canadian and Taiwanese executives. *Management International Review, 45*(1), 23–44.

Jehn, K., & Weldon, E. (1997). Managerial attitudes toward conflict: Cross-cultural differences in resolution styles. *Journal of International Management, 4*, 291–321.

Joshi, A., Labianca, G., & Caligiuri, P. M. (2002). Getting along long distance: Understanding conflict in a multinational team through network analysis. *Journal of World Business, 37*, 277–292.

Jung, D. I., & Avolio, B. J. (1999). Effects of leadership style and followers' cultural orientation on performance in groups and individual task conditions. *Academy of Management Journal, 47*, 208–218.

Jung, D. I., Yammarino, F. J., & Lee, J. K. (2009). Moderating role of subordinates' attitudes on transformational leadership and effectiveness: A multi-cultural and multi-level perspective. *The Leadership Quarterly, 20*, 586–603.

Kahneman, D., & Tversky, A. (1973) On the psychology of prediction. *Psychology Review, 80*, 237–251.

Kahneman, D., & Tversky, A. (1979). Prospect theory: An analysis of decision under risk. *Econometrica, 47*(2), 263–292.

Kashima, Y., & Callan, V. (1994). The Japanese work group. In H. C. Triandis, M. D. Dunnette, & L. M. Hough (Eds.), *Handbook of industrial/organizational psychology* (Vol. 4, pp. 610–646). Palo Alto, CA: Consulting Psychologists Press.

Kashima, Y., & Gelfand, M. J. (2012). A history of cultural in psychology. In W. Stroebe & A. W. Kruglanski (Eds.), *History of social psychology* (pp. 499–520). New York: Psychology Press.

Kashima, Y., Siegal, M., Tanaka, K., & Kashima, E. P. (1992). Do people believe behaviours are consistent with attitudes? Toward a cultural psychology of attribution processes. *British Journal of Social Psychology, 31*, 111–124.

Katz, T., & Erez, M. (2005). Collective- and self-efficacy in the context of high and low task interdependence. *Small Group Research, 36*, 437–465.

Khatri, N., Tsang, E. W. K., & Begley, T. (2006). Cronyism: A cross-cultural analysis. *Journal of International Business Studies, 37*, 61–75.

Kim, D., Sarason, B. R., & Sarason, I. G. (2006). Implicit social cognition and culture: Explicit and implicit psychological acculturation, and distress of Korean-American young adults. *Journal of Social and Clinical Psychology, 25*, 1–32.

Kim, H. S., & Drolet, A. (2003). Choice and self-expression: A cultural analysis of variety-seeking. *Journal of Personality and Social Psychology, 85*, 373–382.

Kim, H. S., & Markus, H. R. (1999). Deviance or uniqueness, harmony or conformity? A cultural analysis. *Journal of Personality and Social Psychology, 77*, 785–800.

Kim, K. I., Park, H-J., & Suzuki, N. (1990). Reward allocations in the United States, Japan, and Korea. *Academy of Management Journal, 33*, 188–199.

Kim, S. U. (1999). The truly familial work organization: Extending the organizational boundary to include employees' families in the Indian context. In H. S. R. Kao, D. Sinha, & B. Wilpert (Eds.), *Management and cultural values: The indigenization of organizations in Asia* (pp. 102–120). New Delhi, India: Sage.

Kipnis, D., & Schmidt, S. M. (1982). *Profiles of organizational influence strategies, Form M*. San Diego, CA: University Associates.

Kirkman, B. L., Chen, G., Farh, J-L., Chen, Z. X., & Lowe, K. B. (2009). Individual power distance orientation and follower reactions to transformational leaders: A cross-level, cross-cultural examination. *Academy of Management Journal, 52*, 744–764.

Kirkman, B. L., Lowe, K. B., & Gibson, C. B. (2006). A quarter century of Culture's Consequences: A review of empirical research incorporating Hofstede's cultural values framework. *Journal of International Business Studies, 36*, 285–320.

Kirkman, B. L., & Shapiro, D. L. (1997). The impact of cultural values on employee resistance to teams: Toward a model of globalized self-managing work team effectiveness. *Academy of Management Review, 22*, 730–757.

Kirkman, B. L., & Shapiro, D. L. (2000). Understanding why team members won't share: An examination of factors related to employee receptivity to team-based reqards. *Small Group Research, 31*, 175–200.

Kirkman, B. L., & Shapiro, D. L. (2001a). The impact of cultural values on job satisfaction and organizational commitment in self-managing work teams: The mediating role of employee resistance. *Academy of Management Journal, 44*, 557–569.

Kirkman, B. L., & Shapiro, D. L. (2001b). The impact of team members' cultural values on productivity, cooperation and empowerment in self-managing working teams. *Journal of Cross-Cultural of Psychology, 32*, 597–617.

Kitayama, S., Markus, H. R., Matsumoto, H., & Norasakkunkit, V. (1997). Individual and collective processes in the construction of the self: Self-enhancement in the United States and self-criticism in Japan. *Journal of Personality and Social Psychology, 72*, 1245–1267.

Kitayama, S., & Uchida, Y. (2005). Interdependent agency: An alternative system for action. In R. Sorrentino, D. Cohen, J. M. Ison, & M. P. Zanna (Eds.), *Culture and social behaviour: The Ontario symposium* (Vol. 10, pp. 165–198). Mahwah, NJ: Erlbaum.

Klar, Y., Bar-Tal, D., & Kruglanski, A. W. (1987). On the epistemology of conflicts: Toward a social cognitive analysis of conflict resolution. In W. Stroebe, A. W. Kruglanski, D. Bar-Tal, & M. Hewstone (Eds.), *Social psychology and intergroup and international conflict* (pp. 112–137). New York: Springer-Verlag.

Klein, K. J., Dansereau, F., & Hall, R. J. (1994). Levels issues in theory development, data collection, and analysis. *Academy of Management Review, 19*, 195–229.

Kluckhohn, C. (1954). Culture and behavior. In G. Lindzey (Ed.), *Handbook of social psychology* (Vol. 2, pp. 921–976). NJ: Wiley and Sons.

Ko, A. S. O. (2003). Can principles from Sun Tzu's *Art of War* be used to address the problems of consensus-seeking organizations? *Corporate Communications, 8*, 208–212.

Ko, J-W., Price, J. L., & Mueller, C. W. (1997). Assessment of Meyer and Allen's three-component model: Organizational commitment in South Korea. *Journal of Applied Psychology, 82*, 961–973.

Kopelman, S., & Rosette, A. (2008). Cultural variation in response to strategic display of emotion in negotiation. *Group Decision and Negotiation, 17*, 65–77.

Koppes, L. L. (Ed.). (2007). *Historical perspectives in industrial and organizational psychology*. Mahwah, NJ: Erlbaum.

Kousez, J. M., & Posner, B. Z. (1993). *Creditility*. San Francisco, Jossey-Bass.

Kovach, R. C., Jr. (1995). Matching assumptions to environment in the transfer of management practices. *International Studies of Management and Organization, 24*, 83–100.

Kozlowski, S. W. J., & Bell, B. S. (2003). Work groups and teams in organizations. In W. C. Borman, D. R. Ilgen, & R. J. Klimoski (Eds.), *Handbook of psychology: Industrial and organizational psychology* (Vol. 12, pp. 333–375). London: Wiley.

Kozlowski, S. W. J., & Klein, K. J. (2000). A multilevel approach in theory and research in organizations: Contextual, temporal and emergent processes. In K. J. Klein, & S. W. J. Kozlowski (Eds.), *Multilevel theory, research, and methods in organizations: Foundations, extensions, and new directions* (pp. 3–90). San Francisco: Jossey-Bass.

Kristensen, H., & Gärling, T. (1997). Determinants of buyers' aspiration and reservation price. *Journal of Economic Psychology, 18*(5), 487–503.

Kroeber, A., & Kluckhohn, C. (1952). *Culture*. New York: Meridian Books.

Kuchinke, K. P. (1999). Adult development towards what end? A philosophical analysis of the concept of human resource development. *Adult Education Quarterly, 49*, 148–162.

Kumar, R. (1999). A script theoretical analysis of international negotiating behavior. In R. J. Lewicki, R. Bies, & B. Sheppard (Eds.), *Research of negotiation and organizations* (pp. 285–311). Stamford, CT: JAI Press.

Kurman, J. (2001). Self-regulation strategies in achievement settings: Culture and gender differences. *Journal of Cross-Cultural Psychology, 32*, 491–503.

Lam, S. S. K., Chen, X. P., & Schaubroeck, J. (2002). Participative decision making and employee performance in different cultures: The moderating effects of allocentrism/idiocentrism and efficacy. *Academy of Management Journal, 45*, 905–914.

Larrick, R. P., & Wu, G. (2007). Claiming a large slice of a small pie: Asymmetric disconfirmation in negotiation. *Journal of Personality and Social Psychology, 93*(2), 212–233.

Latham, G. P., Erez, M., & Locke, E. A. (1988). Resolving scientific disputes by the joint design of crucial experiments: Application to the Erez-Latham dispute regarding participation in goal setting. (Monograph). *Journal of Applied Psychology, 73*, 753–777.

Lee, K., Allen, N. J., Meyer, J. P., & Rhee K. Y. (2001). The three-component commitment model of organization commitment: An approach to South Korea. *Applied Psychology: An International Review, 50*, 596–614.

Lee-Ross, D. (2005). Perceived job characteristics and internal work motivation: An exploratory cross-cultural analysis of the motivational antecedents of hotel workers in Mauritius and Australia. *Journal of Management Development, 24*, 253–266.

Leung, A. (2005). Emotional intelligence or emotional blackmail: A study of a Chinese professional-service firm. *International Journal of Cross-Cultural Management, 5*, 181–196.

Leung, K. (1997). Negotiation and reward allocations across cultures. In P. C. Earley & M. Erez (Eds.), *New perspectives on international industrial/organizational psychology* (pp. 640–675). San Francisco: The New Lexington Press.

Leung, K., Bhagat, R. S., Buchan, N. R., Erez, M., & Gibson, C. B. (2005). Culture and international business: Recent advances and their implications for future research. *Journal of International Business Studies, 36*(4), 357–378.

Levine, R. V., & Norenzayan, A. (1999). The pace of life in 31 countries. *Journal of Cross-Cultural Psychology, 30*, 178–205.

Levy-Leboyer, C. (1994). Selection and assessment in Europe. In H. C. Triandis, M. D. Dunnette & L. M. Hough (Eds.), *Handbook of industrial and organizational psychology* (2nd ed., Vol. 4, pp. 173–190). Palo Alto, CA: Consulting Psychologists Press.

Li, J. (2002). A cultural model of learning. *Journal of Cross-Cultural Psychology, 33*, 248–269.

Li, J., & Tsui, A. (1999). Building effective international joint venture leadership teams in China. *Journal of World Business, 34*, 52–68.

Li, J., Xin, K., & Pillutla, M. (2002). Who calls the shots in a joint venture? *International Journal of Human Resource Management, 13*, 320–337.

Lind, E. A., & Tyler, T. R. (1988). *The social psychology of procedural justice*. New York: Plenum Press.

Littrell, R. F. (2002). Desirable leadership behavior of multicultural managers in China. *Journal of Management Development, 21*, 5–74.

Littrell, R. F., & Valentin, L. N. (2005). Preferred leadership behaviors: Exploring results from Romania, Germany, and the UK. *The Journal of Management Development, 24*, 421–442.

Liu, C., Borg, I., & Spector, P. E. (2004). Measurement equivalence of the German Job Satisfaction Survey used in a multinational organization: Implications of Schwartz's culture model. *Journal of Applied Psychology, 89*, 1070–1082.

Liu, L. A., Chua, C. H., & Stahl, G. K. (2010). Quality of communication experience: Definition, measurement, and implications for intercultural negotiations. *Journal of Applied Psychology, 95*, 469–487.

Liu, L. A., Friedman, R. A., Barry, B., Gelfand, M. J., & Zheng, Z. (2010). Culture and shared mental models in negotiation. Manuscript under review.

Liu, L. A., Friedman, R. A., & Chi, S. (2005). "*Ren qing*" versus the "big five:" The role of culturally sensitive measures of individual difference in distributive negotiations. *Management & Organization Review, 1*, 225–247.

Liu, W., Friedman, R., & Hong, Y. (2012). Culture and Accountability in Negotiation: Recognizing the Importance of In-group Relations. *Organizational Behavior and Human Decision Processes, 117*, 221–234.

Lockwood, P., Marshall, T. C., & Sadler, P. (2005). Promoting success or preventing failure: Cultural differences in motivation by positive and negative role models. *Personality & Social Psychology Bulletin, 31*, 379–392.

Loewenstein, G., Issacharoff, S., Camerer, C., & Babcock, L. (1993). Self serving assessments of fairness and pretrial bargaining. *Journal of Legal Studies, 22*, 135–139.

Lok, P., & Crawford, J. (2004). The effect of organizational culture and leadership style on job satisfaction and organizational commitment: A cross-national comparison. *Journal of Management Development, 23*, 321–338.

Lonner, W., & Malpass, R. S. (1994). When psychology and culture meet: An introduction to cross-cultural psychology. In W. J. Lonner & R. S. Malpass (Eds.), *Psychology and culture* (pp. 1–12). Boston: Allyn & Bacon.

Lord, R. G., & Maher, K. J. (1990). Perceptions of leadership and their implications in organizations. In J. Carroll (Ed.), *Applied social psychology and organizational settings* (pp. 129–154). Hillsdale, NJ: Erlbaum.

Lytle, A. L., Brett, J. M., Barsness, Z., Tinsley, C. H., & Janssens, M., (1995). A paradigm for quantitative cross-cultural research in organizational behavior. In B. M. Staw & L. L. Cummings (Eds.), *Research in organizational behavior* (Vol. 17, pp. 167–214). Greenwich, CT: JAI Press.

Ma, R., & Allen, D. G. (2009). Recruiting across cultures: A value-based model of recruitment. *Human Resource Management Review, 19*, 334–346.

Maddux, W. W., Yang, H., Falk, C., Adam, H, Adair, W., Endo, Y…Heine, S. J. (2010). For whom is parting with possessions more painful? Cultural differences in the endowment effect. *Psychological Science, 21,* 1910–1917.

Makilouko, M. (2004). Coping with multi-cultural projects: The leadership style of Finnish project managers. *International Journal of Project Management, 22*, 387–396.

Man, D. C., & Lam, S. S. K. (2003). The effects of job complexity and autonomy on cohesiveness in collectivistic and individualistic work groups: A cross-cultural analysis. *Journal of Organizational Behavior, 24*, 979–1001.

March, J. G., & Simon, H. A. (1958). *Organizations.* New York: Wiley.

Marcoulides, G. A., Yavas, B. F., Bilgin, Z., & Gibson, C. B. (1998). Reconciling culturalist and rationalist approaches: Leadership in the United States and Turkey. *Thunderbird International Business Review, 40*, 563–584.

Markus, H. R., & Kitayama, S. (1991). Culture and the self: Implications for cognition, emotion, and motivation. *Psychological Review, 98*, 224–253.

Matsui, T., & Terai, T. (1975). A cross-cultural study of the validity of the expectancy theory of work motivation. *Journal of Applied Psychology, 60*, 263–265.

McClelland, D. C. (1985). *Human motivation.* Cambridge, UK: Cambridge University Press.

McCrae, R. R., & Costa, P. T. (1997). Personality trait structure as a human universal. *American Psychologist, 52*, 509–516.

Mehra, P., & Krishnan, V. R. (2005). Impact of svadharma-orientation on transformational leadership and followers' trust in leader. *Journal of Indian Psychology, 23*(1), 1–11.

Mellahi, K. (2006). Managing human resources in Saudi Arabia. In P. S. Budhwar & K. Mellahi (Eds.), *Managing human resources in the Middle East* (pp. 97–120). London: Routledge.

Mendonca, M., & Kanungo, R. N. (1994). Managing human resources: the issue of cultural fit. *Journal of Management Inquiry, 3*, 189–205.

Meyer, J. P., Stanley, D. J., Herscovitch, L., & Topolnytsky, L. (2002). Affective, continuance, and normative commitment to the organization: A meta-analysis of antecedents, correlates, and consequences. *Journal of Vocational Behavior, 61*, 20–52.

Michailova, S., & Anisimova, A. (1999). Russian voices from a Danish company. *Business Strategy Review, 10*, 65–78.

Miles, R. E. (1975). *Theories of management.* New York: McGraw-Hill.

Miller, J. S., Hom, P. W., & Gomez-Mejia, L. R. (2001).The high cost of low wages: Does Maquiladora compensation reduce turnover? *Journal of International Business Studies, 32*, 585–595.

Milliman, J., Nason, S., Zhu, C., & De Cieri, H. (2002). An exploratory assessment of the purpose of PA in North & Central America and the Pacific Rim. *Asia Pacific Journal of Human Resources, 40*, 87–107.

Misumi, J. (1985). *The behavioral science of leadership: An interdisciplinary Japanese research program.* Ann Arbor: University of Michigan Press.

Misumi, J., & Peterson, M. F. (1985). The performance-maintenance (PM) theory of leadership: Review of a Japanese research program. *Administrative Science Quarterly, 30*, 198–223.

Miyamoto, Y., Nisbett, R. E., & Masuda, T. (2006). Culture and the physical environment: Holistic versus analytic perceptual affordances. *Psychological Science, 17*, 113–119.

Mohsen, N. R. M. (2007). Leadership from the Qur'an relationship between taqwa, trust, and business leadership effectiveness. Ph.D. dissertation. Universiti Sains Malaysia.

Moneta, G. B. (2004). The flow experience across cultures. *Journal of Happiness Studies, 5*, 115–121.

Montesino, M. (2003). Leadership/followship similarities between people in a developed and a developing country: The case of Dominicans in NYC and Dominicans on the island. *Journal of Leadership and Organization Studies, 10*, 82–92.

Montoya-Weiss, M., Massey, A. P., & Song, M. (2001). Getting it together: Temporal coordination and conflict management in global virtual teams. *Academy of Management Journal, 44*, 1251–1263.

Morris, M. W., & Fu, H. (2001). How does culture influence conflict resolution? A dynamic constructionist analysis. *Social Cognition, 19*, 324–349.

Morris, M. W., Larrick, R. P., & Su, S. K. (1999). Misperceiving negotiation counterparts: When situationally determined bargaining behaviors are attributed to personality traits. *Journal of Personality and Social Psychology, 77*(1), 52–67.

Morris, M. W., Leung, K., & Iyengar, S. S. (2004). Person perception in the heat of conflict: Negative trait attributions affect procedural preferences and account for situational and cultural differences. *Asian Journal of Social Psychology, 7*, 127–147.

Morrison, E. W., Chen, Y., & Salgado, S. R. (2004). Cultural differences in newcomer feedback seeking: A comparison of the United States and Hong Kong. *Journal of Applied Psychology, 53*, 1–22.

Murray, H. A. (1938). *Explorations in personality.* New York: Oxford University Press.

Namazie, P., & Tayeb, M. (2006). Human resource management in Iran. In P. S. Budhwar & K. Mellahi (Eds.), *Managing human resources in the Middle East* (pp. 20–39). New York: Routledge.

Natlandsmyr, J., & Rognes, J. (1995). Culture, behavior, and negotiation outcomes: A comparative and cross-cultural study of Mexican and Norwegian negotiations. *International Journal of Conflict Management, 6*, 5–29.

Negandhi, A. R. (1984). Management in the third world. *Advances in International Comparative Management, 1*, 123–154.

Nemeth, C., Personnaz, M., Personnaz, B., & Goncalo, J. (2004). The liberating role of conflict in group creativity: A cross-cultural study. Submitted to European *Journal of Social Psychology, 34*, 365–374.

Nevis, B. C. (1983). Using an American perspective in understanding another culture: Toward a hierarchy of needs for the People's Republic of China. *Journal of Applied Behavioral Science, 19*(3), 249–264.

Newman, K. L., & Nollen, S. D. (1996). Culture and congruence: The fit between management practices and national culture. *Journal of International Business Studies, 27*, 753–779.

Ng, K. Y., & Van Dyne, L. (2001). Culture and minority influence: Effects on persuasion and originality. In C. W. K. De Dreu & N. K. De Vries (Eds.), *Group consensus and minority influence: Implications for innovation* (pp. 284–306). Oxford: Blackwell.

Nguyen, H-H. D., Le, H., & Boles, T. (2010). Individualism-collectivism and cooperation: A cross-society and cross-level examination. *Negotiation and Conflict Management Research, 3*(3), 179–204.

Nibler, R., & Harris, K. L. (2003). The effects of culture and cohesiveness on intragroup conflict and effectiveness. *Journal of Social Psychology, 143*(5), 613–631.

Oakland, T. (2004). Use of educational and psychological tests internationally. *Applied Psychology: An international Review, 53*, 157–172.

Oetzel, J. G. (1998). The effects of ethnicity and self-construals on self-reported conflict styles. *Communication Reports, 11*, 133–144.

Ogbor, J. O., & Williams, J. (2003). The cross-cultural transfer of management practices: The case for creative synthesis. *Cross Cultural Management, 10*(2), 3–23.

Oyserman, D., & Lee, W. S. (2008). Does culture influence what and how we think? Effects of priming individualism and collectivism. *Psychological Bulletin, 134*(2), 311–342.

Parker, P. S. (1996).Gender, culture, and leadership: Towards a culturally distinct model of African-American women and executives' leadership strategies. *Leadership Quarterly, 7*, 189–214.

Parry, E., Tyson, S., & Brough, S. (Eds.). (2006). *Cranet survey on comparative HRM: International executive report.* UK: Cranfield University Press.

Pellegrini, E. K., & Scandura, T. A. (2008). Paternalistic leadership: A review and agenda for future research. *Journal of Management, 34*, 566–593.

Pellegrini, E. K., Scandura, T. A., & Jayaraman, V. (2010). Cross-cultural generalizability of paternalistic leadership: An expansion of leader-member exchange theory. *Group & Organization Management, 35*, 391–420.

Peretz, H., & Fried, Y. (2011, October 31). National Cultures, Performance Appraisal Practices, and Organizational Absenteeism and Turnover: A Study Across 21 Countries. *Journal of Applied Psychology.* Advance online publication. doi: 10.1037/a0026011

Peng, K., Nisbett, R. E., & Wong, N. (1997). Validity problems of cross-cultural value comparison and possible solutions. *Psychological Methods, 2*, 329–341.

Pepitone, A., & Triandis, H. C. (1987). On the universality of social psychological theories. *Journal of Cross-Cultural Psychology, 18*, 471–499.

Peterson, M. F., & Smith, P. B. (2000). Meanings, organization and culture: Using sources of meaning to make sense of organizational events. In N. Ashkanasy, C. P. M. Wilderom, & M. F. Peterson (Eds.), *Handbook of organizational culture and climate* (pp. 101–116). Thousand Oaks, CA: Sage.

Peterson, M. F., Smith, P. B., Bond, M. H., & Misumi, J. (1990). Personal reliance on alternative event-management processes in four countries. *Group and Organization Studies*, 15, 75–91.

Piccolo, R. F., Judge, T. A., Takahashi, K., Watanabe, N., & Locke, E. A. (2005). Core self-evaluations in Japan: Relative effects on job satisfaction, life satisfaction, and happiness. *Journal of Organizational Behavior, 26*, 965–984.

Pillai, R., & Meindl, J. R. (1998). Context and charisma: A "meso" level examination of the relationship of organic structure, collectivism, and crises to charismatic leadership. *Journal of Management, 24*, 643–672.

Pillai, R., Scandura, T. A., & Williams, E. A. (1999). Leadership and organizational justice: Similarities and differences across cultures. *Journal of International Business Studies, 30*, 763–779.

Plato (Translated 1901). *The Republic.* Benjamin Jowett (Trans.). New York: The Colonial Press.

Poortinga, Y. H., Kop, P. F. M., & van de Vijver, F. J. R. (1990). Differences between psychological domains in the range of cross-cultural variation. In P. J. D. Drenth, J. A. Sergeant, & R. J. Tak (Eds.), *European perspectives in psychology* (pp. 355–376). New York: Wiley.

Posthuma, R. A., Joplin, J. R., & Maetz, C. P., Jr. (2005). Comparing the validity of turnover prediction in the United States and Mexico. *International Journal of Cross-Cultural Management, 5*, 165–180.

Prahalad, C. K., & Doz, Y. L. (1987). *The multinational mission, balancing global integration with local responsiveness.* New York: Free Press.

Probst, T., Carnevale, P. J., & Triandis, H. C. (1999). Cultural values in intergroup and singe group social dilemmas. *Organizational Behavior and Human Decision Processes, 77*, 171–191.

Pruitt, D. G. (1981). *Negotiation behavior.* New York: Academic Press.

Pruitt, D. G. (2004). Foreword. In M. J. Gelfand & J. Brett (Eds.), *The handbook of negotiation and culture* (pp. xi–xiii). Palo Alto, CA: Stanford University Press.

Pruitt, D. G., & Carnevale, P. J. (1993). *Negotiation in social conflict.* Pacific Grove, CA: Brooks/Cole Publishing.

Pruitt, D. G., & Lewis, S. A. (1975). Development of integrative solutions in bilateral negotiation. *Journal of Personality and Social Psychology, 31*(4), 621–633.

Punnett, B. J. (2004). *International perspectives on organizational behavior and human resource management.* London: M. E. Sharpe.

Punnett, B. J., & Clemens, J. (1999). Cross-national diversity: Implications for international expansion decisions. *Journal of World Business, 34,* 167–177.

Quang, T., Swierczek, F., & Chi, D. (1998). Effective leadership in joint ventures in Vietnam: A cross-cultural perspective. *Journal of Organisational Change Management, 11,* 357–372.

Raghuram, S., London, M., & Larsen, H. (2001). Flexible employment practices in Europe: Country versus culture. *The International Journal of Human Resource Management, 12,* 738–753.

Rahim, A., & Magner, N. R. (1995). Confirmatory factor analysis of the styles of handling interpersonal conflict: First-order factor model and its invariance across groups. *Journal of Applied Psychology, 80,* 122–132.

Rahim, M. A., Antonioni, D., Krumov, K., & Ilieva, S. (2000). Power, conflict, and effectiveness. A cross-cultural study in the United States and Bulgaria. *European Psychologist, 5,* 28–33.

Ralston, D. A., & Pearson, A. (2003). Measuring interpersonal political influence on organizations: The development of a cross-cultural instrument of upward influence strategies. *Southern Management Association Proceedings, 432–438.*

Ramamoorthy, N., & Flood, P. C. (2002). Employee attitudes and behavioural intentions: A test of the main and moderating effects of individualism-collectivism. *Human Relations, 55,* 1071–1096.

Ramamoorthy, N., & Flood, P. C. (2004). Individualism/collectivism, perceived task interdependence and teamwork attitudes among Irish blue collar employees: A test of the main and moderating effects. *Human Relations, 57,* 347–366.

Ramesh, A., & Gelfand, M. J. (2010). Should we stay or should we go: Job embeddedness in the US and India. *Journal of Applied Psychology, 95,* 807–823.

Rao, A., Hashimoto, K., & Rao, A. (1997). Universal and culturally specific aspects of managerial influence: A study of Japanese managers. *Leadership Quarterly, 8,* 295–312.

Resick, C. J., Hanges, P. J., Dickson, M. W., & Mitchelson, J. K. (2006). A cross-cultural examination of the endorsement of ethical leadership. *Journal of Business Ethics, 63,* 345–359.

Robert, C., Probst, T. M., Martocchio, J. J., Drasgow, F., & Lawler, J. J. (2000). Empowerment and continuous improvement in the United States, Mexico, Poland, and India: Predicting fit on the basis of the dimensions of power distance and individualism. *Journal of Applied Psychology, 85,* 643–658.

Robert, C., & Wasti, S. A. (2002). Organizational individualism and collectivism: Theoretical development and an empirical test of a measure. *Journal of Management, 28,* 544–566.

Roberts, K. H. (1970). On looking at an elephant: An evaluation of cross-cultural research related to organizations. *Psychological Bulletin, 74,* 327–350.

Robie, C., Johnson, K. M., Nilsen, D., & Hazucha, J. F. (2001). The right stuff: Understanding cultural differences in leadership performance. *Journal of Management Development, 20,* 639–649.

Roe, R. A., & Van den Berg, P. T. (2003). Selection in Europe: Context, developments and research agenda. *European Journal of Work and Organizational Psychology, 12,* 257–270.

Roe, R. A., Zinovieva, I. L., Dienes, E., & Ten Horn, L. (2000). A comparison of work motivation in Bulgaria, Hungary, and the Netherlands: Test of a model. *Applied Psychology: An International Review, 49*(4), 658–687.

Rohner, R. P. (1984). Toward a conception of culture for cross-cultural psychology. *Journal of Cross-Cultural Psychology, 15,* 111–138.

Rosenfeld, P., & Culbertson, A. L. (1992). Hispanics in the military. In S. B. Knouse, P. Rosenfeld, & A. L. Culbertson (Eds.), *Hispanics in the workplace* (pp. 211–230). Thousand Oaks, CA: Sage.

Rosette, A. S., Brett, J. M., Barsness, Z., & Lytle, A. L. (2006, December). When cultures clash electronically: The impact of e-mail and culture on negotiation behavior. Dispute Resolution Research Center Working Paper No. 302. Available at SSRN: http://ssrn. com/abstract=959034.

Rousseau, D. M. (1998). The 'problem' of the psychological contract considered. *Journal of Organizational Behavior, 19,* 665–671.

Rousseau, D. M., & Tinsley, K. (1997). Human resources are local: Society and social contracts in a global economy. In N. Anderson & P. Herriot (Eds.), *International handbook of selection and appraisal* (pp. 39–62). London: Wiley.

Ryan, A. M., Boyce, A. S., Ghumman, S., Jundt, D., Schmidt, G., Gibby, R. (2009). Going global: Cultural values and perceptions of selection procedures. *Aplied Psychology: An International Review, 58,* 520–556.

Ryan, A. M., & Gelfand, M. J. (in press). Going global: Internationalizing the organizational psychology curriculum. In F. T. L. Leong, W. E. Pickren, M. M. Leach, & A. J. Marsella (Eds.), *Internationalizing the psychology curriculum in the United States: Meeting the challenges of globalization.* New York: Springer.

Ryan, A. M., McFarland, L., Baron, H., & Page, R. (1999). An international look at selection practices: National and culture as explanations for variability in practice. *Personnel Psychology, 52,* 359–391.

Rynes, S. L. (2005). Taking stock and looking ahead. *Academy of Management Journal, 48,* 9–15.

Sagie, A., & Aycan, Z. (2003). A cross-cultural analysis of participative decision-making in organizations. *Human Relations, 56,* 453–473.

Sagie, A., Elizur, D., & Yamauchi, H. (1996). The structure and strength of achievement motivation: A cross-cultural comparison. *Journal of Organizational Behavior, 17,* 431–444.

Sagie, A., & Koslowsky, M. (2000). *Participation and empowerment in organizational settings: Modeling, effectiveness, and applications.* Thousand Oaks, CA: Sage.

Saini, D., & Budhwar, P. (2008). Managing the human resource in Indian SMEs: The role of indigenous realities in organizational working. *Journal of World Business, 43,* 417–434.

Salas, E., Dickinson, T. L., Converse, S. A., & Tannenbaum, S. I. (1992). Toward an understanding of team performance and training in teams. In R. W. Swezey & E. Salas (Eds.), *Teams: Their training and performance* (pp. 3–29). Norwood, NJ: Ablex.

Salk, J. E., & Brannen, M. Y. (2000). National culture, networks, and individual influence in a multinational management team. *Academy of Management Journal, 43*(2), 191–202.

Sama, L. M., & Papamarcos, S. D. (2000). Hofstede's I-C dimension as predictive of allocative behaviors: A meta-analysis. *International Journal of Value-Based Management, 13*, 173–188.

Sanchez, J. I., & Levine, E. L. (1999). Is job analysis dead, misunderstood, or both? New forms of work analysis and design. In A. I. Kraut, & A. K. Korman (Eds.), *Evolving practices in human resource management* (pp. 43–69). San Francisco: Jossey-Bass.

Sanchez-Burks, J., Nisbett, R. E., & Ybarra, O. (2000). Cultural styles, relational schemas and prejudice against outgroups. *Journal of Personality & Social Psychology, 79*, 174–189.

Sarros, J. C., & Santora, J. C. (2001). The transformational-transactional leadership model in practice. *Leadership & Organization Development Journal, 22*(8), 383–393.

Sauers, D. A., Lin, S. C. H., Kennedy, J., & Schrenkler, J. (2009). A comparison of the performance appraisal practices of US multinational subsidiaries with parent company and local Taiwanese practices. *Management Research News, 32*, 286–296.

Scandura, T. A., & Dorfman, P. (2004). Leadership research in a post-GLOBE world. *Leadership Quarterly, 15*, 277–307.

Schaubroeck, J., & Lam, S. S. K. (2002). How similarity to peers and supervisor influences organizational advancement in different cultures. *Academy of Management Journal, 45*, 1120–1136.

Schelling, T. C. (1960). *The strategy of conflict.* Cambridge, MA: Harvard University Press.

Schneider, J., & Littrell, R. F. (2003). Ideal leader perceptions in German and English managers. *The Journal of Management Development, 22*, 130–148.

Schuler, R. S., & Rogovsky, N. (1998). Understanding compensation practice variations across firms: The impact of national culture. *Journal of International Business Studies, 29*, 159–177.

Schwartz, S. (1992). Universals in the content and structures of values: Theoretical advances and empirical tests in 20 countries. *Advances in Experimental Social Psychology, 25*, 1–65.

Schwartz, S. (1994). Are there universal aspects in content and structure of values? *Journal of Social Issues, 50*, 19–45.

Schwartz, S. H., & Bilsky, W. (1990). Toward a theory of the universal content and structure of values: Extentions and cross-cultural replications. *Journal of Personality and Social Psychology, 58*, 878–891.

Seddon, J. (1987). Assumptions, culture and performance appraisal. *Journal of Management Development, 6*, 47–54.

Segall, M. H. (1984). More than we need to know about culture, but are afraid not to ask. *Journal of Cross-Cultural Psychology, 15*, 153–162.

Shackleton, N. J., & Newell, S. (1997). International assessment and selection. In N. Anderson & P. Herriot (Eds.), *International handbook of selection and assessment* (pp. 81–96). Chichester, UK: John Wiley & Sons.

Shadur, M. A., Rodwell, J. J., & Bamber, G. J. (1995). The adoption of international best practices in a western culture: East meets West. *International Journal of Human Resource Management, 6*, 735–757.

Shahin, A. I., & Wright, P. L. (2004). Leadership in the context of culture: An Egyptian perspective. *Leadership and Organization Development Journal, 25*, 499–511.

Shapiro, D. L., Von Glinow, M. A., & Cheng, J. L. (2005). *Managing multinational teams: Global perspectives.* London, UK: Elseview/JAI Press.

Sharma, T., Budhwar, P. S., & Varma, A. (2008). Performance management in India. In A. Varma, P. S. Budhwar, & A. DeNisi (Eds.), *Performance management systems: A global perspective* (pp. 180–192). London: Routledge.

Shenkar, O., Ronen, S., Shefy, E., & Hau-Siu Chow, I. (1998). The role structure of Chinese managers. *Human Relations, 51*, 51–72.

Sherman, S. J., Judd, C. M., & Park, B. (1989). Social cognition. In M. R. Rosenzweig & L. W. Porter (Eds.), *Annual review of psychology* (Vol. 40, pp. 281–326). Palo Alto, CA: Annual Reviews.

Shimmin, S. (1989). Selection in a European context. In N. Anderson & P. Herriot (Eds.), *Assessment and selection in organizations: Methods and practice for recruitment and appraisal* (109–118). Chichester: Wiley & Sons.

Shteynberg, G., Gelfand, M. J., & Kim, K. (2009). Peering into the 'magnum mysterium' of culture: The explanatory power of descriptive norms. *Journal of Cross-Cultural Psychology, 40*, 46, 69.

Shweder, R., & LeVine, R. (1984). *Culture theory: Essays on mind, self, and emotion.* London: Cambridge University Press.

Shweder, R. A., Mahapatra, M., & Miller, J. G. (1990). Culture and moral development. In J. W. Stigler, R. A. Shweder, & G. Herdt (Eds.), *Cultural psychology: Essays on comparative human development* (pp. 130–204). Cambridge: Cambridge University Press.

Silverthorne, C. (2001). Leadership effectiveness and personality: A cross-cultural evaluation. *Personality and Individual Differences, 30*, 303–309.

Singh, R. (1981). Prediction of performance from motivation and ability: An appraisal of the cultural difference hypothesis. In J. Pandey (Ed.), *Perspectives on experimental social psychology in India* (pp. 112–145). New Delhi: Concept.

Sinha, J. B. P. (1990). *Work culture in the Indian context.* New Delhi: Sage.

Sinha, J. B. P. (1994). Cultural embeddedness and the development role of industrial organizational psychology in India. In H. C. Triandis, M. D. Dunnette, and L. M. Hough (Eds.), *Handbook of industrial and organizational psychology* (2nd Ed., Vol. 4, pp. 727–764). Palo Alto, CA: Consulting Psychologists Press.

Sinha, J. B. P. (1997). A cultural perspective on organizational behavior in India. In P. C. Earley, & M. Erez (Eds.), *New perspectives on international industrial/organizational psychology* (pp. 53–75). San Francisco: The New Lexington Press.

Skinner, B. F. (1981). Selection by consequences. *Science, 213*, 501–504.

Smith, P. B., & Bond, M. H. (1993). *Social psychology across cultures.* New York: Harvester Wheatsheaf.

Smith, P. B., & Bond, M. H. (1999). *Social psychology across cultures.* Boston: Allyn & Bacon.

Smith, P. B., Dugan, S., & Trompenaars, F. (1996). National culture and the values of organizational employees: A dimensional analysis across 43 nations. *Journal of Cross-Cultural Psychology, 27*, 231–264.

Smith, P. B., Misumi, J., Tayeb, M. H., Peterson, M. F., & Bond, M. H. (1989). On the generality of leadership style measures across cultures. *Journal of Occupational Psychology, 62*, 97–109.

Smith, P. B., & Peterson, M. F. (2002). Cross-cultural leadership. In M. J. Gannon & K. L Newman (Eds.), *Handbook of cross-cultural management* (pp. 217–235). Oxford: Blackwell.

Smith, P. B., Peterson, M. F., & Schwartz, S. H. (2002). Cultural values, sources of guidance and their relevance to managerial behavior. *Journal of Cross-Cultural Psychology, 33*, 188–208.

Smith, P. B., Peterson, M. F., Ahmad, A. H., Akande, D., Andersen, J. A., Avestaran, S.,…Yanchuk, V. (2005). Demographic effects on the use of vertical sources of guidance by managers in widely different cultural contexts. *International Journal of Cross-Cultural Management, 5*, 1–26.

Smith, P. B., Peterson, M. F., & Schwartz, S. H. (2002). Cultural values, sources of guidance and their relevance to managerial behavior. *Journal of Cross-Cultural Psychology, 33*, 188–208.

Smith, P. B., Wang, Z. M., & Leung, K. (1997). Leadership, decision-making and cultural context: Event management within Chinese joint ventures. *Leadership Quarterly, 8*, 413–431.

Snape, E., Thompson, D., Yan, F. K., & Redman, T. (1998). Performance appraisal and culture: Practice and attitudes in Hong Kong and Great Britain. *International Journal of Human Resource Management, 9*, 841–861.

So, T., West, M., & Dawson, J. F. (2011). Team-based working and employee well-being: A cross-cultural comparison of United Kingdom and Hong Kong health services, *European Journal of Work and Organizational Psychology, 20*, 305–325.

Sparrow, P. R. (2006). International management: Some key challenges for industrial and organizational psychology. In G. P. Hodgkinson & J. K. Ford (Eds.), *International review of industrial and organizational psychology* (Vol. 21, pp. 189–265). Chichester, UK: Wiley.

Sparrow, P., & Hiltrop, J. M. (1994). *European human resource management in transition*. Hemel Hempstead: Prentice Hall.

Spector, P. E., Cooper, C. L., Sanchez, J. I., O'Driscoll, M., Sparks, K., Bernin, P.,…& Yu, S. (2002). Locual of control and well-being at work: How generalizable are Western findings. *Academy of Management Journal, 43*, 453–466.

Spreitzer, G. M., Perttula, K. H., & Xin, K. (2005). Traditionality matters: An examination of the effectiveness of transformational leadership in the United States and Taiwan. *Journal of Organizational Behavior, 26*, 5–27.

Steiner, D. D., & Gilliland, S. W. (1996). Fairness reactions to personnel selection techniques in France and the U.S. *Journal of Applied Psychology, 81*, 134–141.

Stephens, D., Kedia, B., & Ezell, D. (1979). Managerial need structures in U.S. and Peruvian industries. *Managerial International Review, 19*, 27–39.

Sternberg, R. J. (2004). Culture and intelligence. *American Psychologist, 59*, 325–338.

Stevenson, H. W., Hofer, B. K., & Randel, B. (2000). Mathematics achievement and attitudes about mathematics in China and the West. *Journal of Psychology Chinese Societies, 1*, 1–16.

Stewart, W. H., Carland, J. C., Carland, J. W., Watson, W. E., & Sweo, R. (2003). Entrepreneurial dispositions and goal orientations: A comparative exploration of United States and Russian entrepreneurs. *Journal of Small Business Management, 41*, 27–46.

Subramaniam, M., & Venkatraman, N. (2001). Determinants of transnational new product development capability: Testing the influence of transferring and deploying tacit overseas knowledge. *Strategic Management Journal, 22*, 359–378.

Sue-Chan, C., & Ong, M. (2002). Goal assignment and performance: Assessing the mediating roles of goal commitment and self-efficacy and the moderating role of power distance. *Organizational Behavior & Human Decision Processes, 89*, 1140–1161.

Suutari, V. (1996). Variation in the average leadership behavior of managers across countries: Finnish expatriates' experiences from Germany, Sweden, France and Great Britain. *International Journal of Human Resource Management, 7*, 677–707.

Suutari, V., Raharjo, K., & Riikkila, T. (2002). The challenge of cross-cultural leadership interaction: Finnish expatriates in Indonesia. *Career Development International, 7*, 415–429.

Suutari, V., & Riusala, K. (2001). Leadership styles in Central Eastern Europe: Experiences of Finnish expatriates in the Czech Republic, Hungary and Poland. *Scandinavian Journal of Management, 17*, 249–280.

Sweeney, P. D., & McFarlin, D. B. (2004). Social comparisons and income satisfaction: A cross-national examination. *Journal of Occupational and Organizational Psychology, 77*, 149–154.

Taras, V., Kirkman, B. L., & Steel, P. (2010). Examining the impact of *Culture's Consequences*: A three-decade, multi-level, meta-analytic review of Hofstede's cultural value dimensions. *Journal of Applied Psychology, 95*, 405–439.

Tata, J. (2000). Implicit theories of account-giving: Influence of culture and gender. *International Journal of Intercultural Relations, 24*, 437–454.

Tayeb, M. (1995). The competitive advantage of nations: the role of HRM and its socio-cultural context. *International Journal of Human Resource Management, 6*(3), 588–605.

Taylor, F. W. (1911). *The principles of scientific management*. New York: Norton.

Testa, M. R. (2002). Leadership dyads in the cruise industry: The impact of cultural congruency. *The International Journal of Hospitality Management, 21*, 425–441.

Thomas, D. C. (1999). Cultural diversity and work group effectiveness: An experimental study. *Journal of Cross-Cultural Psychology, 30*, 242–263.

Thomas, D. C., & Au, K. (2002). The effect of cultural differences on behavioral responses to low job satisfaction. *Journal of International Business Studies, 33*, 309–326.

Thomas, D. C., & Pekerti, A. A. (2003). Effect of culture on situational determinants of exchange behavior in organizations: A comparison of New Zealand and Indonesia. *Journal of Cross-Cultural Psychology, 34*, 269–281.

Thompson, L., & Hastie, R. (1990). Social perception in negotiation. *Organizational Behavior and Human Decision Processes, 47*(1), 98–123.

Thompson, L., & Loewenstein, G. (1992). Egocentric interpretations of fairness and interpersonal conflict. *Organizational Behavior and Human Decision Processes, 51*, 176–97.

Tjosvold, D., Law, K. S., & Sun, H. (2003). Collectivistic and individualistic values: Their effects on group dynamics and productivity in China. *Group Decision and Negotiation, 12*, 243–263.

Triandis, H. C. (1972). *The analysis of subjective culture*. New York: Wiley.

Triandis, H. C. (1989). The self and social behavior in differing cultural contexts. *Psychological Review, 96*, 506–520.

Triandis, H. C. (1994). Cross-cultural industrial and organizational psychology. In H. C. Triandis, M. D. Dunnette, & L. M. Hough (Eds.), *Handbook of industrial organizational psychology* (Vol. 4, pp 103–172). Palo Alto, CA: Consulting Psychologists Press.

Triandis, H. C., & Bhawuk, D. P. S. (1997). Culture theory and the meaning of relatedness. In P. C. Earley & M. Erez (Eds.),

New perspectives on international/industrial/organizational psychology (pp. 13–53). San Francisco: Jossey-Bass.

Triandis, H. C., Carnevale, P., Gelfand, M. J., Robert, C., Aruz Wasti, S., Probst, T.,...& Schmitz, P. (2001). Culture and deception in business negotiations: A multilevel analysis. *International Journal of Cross-Cultural Management, 1*, 73–90.

Triandis, H. C., & Vassiliou, V. (1972). Interpersonal influence and employee selection in two cultures. *Journal of Applied Psychology, 56*, 140–145.

Trompenaars, F. (1993). *Riding the waves of culture*. Avon, UK: The Economist Books.

Tsui, A. S., Nifadkar, S. S., & Ou, A. Y. (2007). Cross-national, cross-cultural organizational behavior research: Advances, gaps, and recommendations. *Journal of Management, 33*(3), 426–478.

Tung, R. L. (1984). Human resource planning in Japanese multinationalists: A model for US firms? *Journal of International Business Studies, 15*, 139–149.

Tversky, A., & Kahneman, D. 1974). Judgment under uncertainty: Heuristics and biases. *Science, 185*, 1124–1131.

Ulijn, J., Rutkowski, A. F., Kumar, R., & Zhu, Y. (2005). Patterns of feelings in face-to-face negotiation: A Sino-Dutch pilot study. *International Journal of Cross Cultural Management, 12*, 103–118.

Valenzuela, A., Srivastava, J., & Lee, S. (2005). The role of culture orientation in bargaining under incomplete information: Differences in causal attribution. *Organizational Behavior and Human Decision Processes, 96*, 72–88.

Valikangas, L., & Okumura, A. (1997). Why do people follow leaders? A study of a US and a Japanese change program. *Leadership Quarterly, 8*, 313–337.

Vallance, S. (1999). Performance appraisal in Singapore, Thailand and the Philippines: A cultural perspective. *Australian Journal of Public Administration, 58*, 78–86.

Vandenberghe, C. (1996). Assessing organizational commitment in a Belgian context: Evidence for the three-dimensional model. *Applied Psychology: An International Review, 45*, 371–386.

Vandenberghe, C., Stinglhamber, F., Bentein, K., & Delhaise, T. (2001). An examination of the cross-cultural validity of a multidimensional model of commitment in Europe. *Journal of Cross Cultural Psychology, 32*, 322–347.

Van Der Zee, K., Atsma, N., & Brodbeck, F. (2004). The influence of social identity and personality on outcomes of cultural diversity in teams. *Journal of Cross-Cultural Psychology, 35*, 283–303.

Van de Vijver, F., & Leung, K. (1997). *Methods and data analysis for cross-cultural research*. London: Sage.

Van de Vliert, E., & Janssens, O. (2002). Better than performance motives as roots of satisfaction across more and less developed countries. *Cross Cultural Psychology 33*, 380–397.

van de Vijver, F. J. R., van Hemert, D. A., & Poortinga, Y. H. (2010). *Multilevel analysis of individuals and cultures*. Mahwah, New Jersey: Psychology Press.

Van Hemert, D., van de Vijver, F., Poortinga, Y. H., & Georgas, J. (2002). Structural and functional equivalence of the Eysenck Personality Questionnaire within and between countries. *Personality and Individual Differences, 33*, 1229–1249.

Van Maanen, J., & Laurent, A. (1992). The flow of culture. In E. Westney & S. Ghoshal (Eds.), *Organization theory and the multinational cooperation* (pp. 275–312). London: Macmillan.

Van Vianen, A. E. M., Feij, J. A., Krausz, M., & Taris, R. (2004). Personality factors and adult attachment affecting job employability. *International Journal of Selection and Assessment, 11*, 253–264.

Varma, A., Srinivas, E. S., & Stroh, L. K. (2005). A comparative study of the impact of leader-member exchange in US and Indian samples. *Cross-Cultural Management, 12*(1), 84–95.

Vecernik, J. (2003). Skating on thin ice: A comparison of work values and job satisfaction in CEE and EU countries. *International Journal of Comparative Sociology, 44*(5), 444–471.

Von Glinow, M. A., & Drost, E. A., & Teagarden, M. B. (2002). Converging on IHRM best practices: Lessons learned from a globally distributed consortium on theory and practice. *Human Resource Management, 41*, 123–140.

Von Glinow, M. A., Shapiro, D. L., & Brett, J. M. (2004). Can we talk, and should we? Managing emotional conflict in multicultural teams. *Academy of Management Review, 29*, 578–592.

Wah, S. S. (2004). Entrepreneurial leaders in family business organizations. *Journal of Enterprising Culture, 12*, 1–34.

Wallner, F. G., & Jandl, M. J. (2006). The importance of constructive realism for the indigenious psychologies approach. In U. Kim, K. S. Yang, & K. K. Hwang (Eds.), *Indigenous and cultural psychology* (pp. 49–73). New York: Springer.

Walumbwa, F. O., & Lawler, J. J. (2003). Building effective organizations, transformational leadership, collectivist orientation, work-related attitudes and withdrawal behaviours in three emerging economies. *International Journal of Human Resource Management, 14*, 1083–1101.

Walumbwa, F. O., Orwa, B., Wang, P., & Lawler, J. J. (2005). Transformational leadership, organization commitment and job satisfaction: A comparative study of Kenyan and U.S. financial firms. *Human Resource Development Quarterly, 16*, 235–256.

Wan, C., Chiu, C-Y., Tam, K., Lee, V. S., Lau, I. Y., & Peng, S. (2007). Perceived cultural importance and actual self-importance of values in cultural identification. *Journal of Personality and Social Personality, 92*, 337–354.

Wasti, S. A. (1999). *A cultural analysis of organizational commitment and turnover intentions in a collectivist society*. Paper presented at the annual meetings of the Academy of Management, Chicago.

Wasti, S. A. (2000). Universal and cultural factors leading to organizational commitment. In Z. Aycan (Ed.), *Management, leadership and HRM practices in Turkey* (pp. 201–225). Istanbul: Turkish Psychological Association Press.

Wasti, S. A. (2003). The influence of cultural values on antecedents of organizational commitment: An individual-level analysis. *Applied Psychology International Review, 52*, 533–354.

Watson, W. E., BarNir, A., & Pavur, R. (2005). Cultural diversity and learning teams: The impact on desired academic team processes. *International Journal of Intercultural Relations, 29*, 449–467.

Watson, W. E., Johnson, L., Kumar, K., & Critelli, J. (1998). Process gain and process loss: Comparing interpersonal processes and performance of culturally diverse and nondiverse teams across time. *International Journal of Intercultural Relations, 22*, 409–430.

Watson, W. E., Johnson, L., & Merritt, D. (1998). Team orientation, self-orientation, and diversity in task groups. *Group and Organization Management, 23*, 161–188.

Weick, K. ([1969] 1979). *The social psychology of organizing.* Reading, MA: Addison-Wesley.

Weick, K. E., Bougan, M. G., & Maruyama, G. (1976). The equity context. *Organizational Behavior and Human Performance, 15,* 32–65.

Welsh, D. H. B., Luthans, F., & Sommer, S. M. (1993). Managing Russian factory workers: The impact of U.S.-based behavioral and participative techniques. *Academy of Management Journal, 36,* 58–79.

Wendt, H., Euwema, M. C., & van Emmerik, I. J. (2009). Leadership and team cohesiveness across cultures. *Leadership Quarterly, 20,* 358–370.Westman, C. Y., Park, H. S. & Lee, H. E. (2007). A test of equity theory in multi-dimensional friendship: A comparison of the United States and Korea. *Journal of Communication, 57,* 576–598.

Westwood, R. (1997). Harmony and patriarchy: The cultural basis for "paternalistic headship" among the overseas Chinese. *Organizational Studies, 18,* 445–480.

Wheeler, K. G. (2002). Cultural values in relation to equity sensitivity within and across cultures. *Journal of Managerial Psychology, 17,* 612–627.

Whyte, G., & Sebenius, J. K. (1997). The effect of multiple anchors on anchoring in individual and group judgment. *Organizational Behavior and Human Decision Processes, 69*(1), 75–85.

Williamson, T. (2008). The good society and the good soul: *Plato's Republic* on leadership. *Leadership Quarterly, 19,* 397–408.

Wilson, E. O. (1980). *Sociobiology.* Cambridge, MA: Belknap.

Wilson, H. J., Callaghan, C. A., & Wright, P. L. (1996). Observing differences in verbal communication: Filipino and British manager-subordinate interactions. *Journal of Managerial Psychology (UK), 11,* 43–55.

Wilson, R. W., & Pusey, A. W. (1982). Achievement motivation and small business relationship patterns in Chinese society. In S. L. Greenblatt, R. W. Wilson, & A. A. Wilson (Eds.), *Social interaction in Chinese society* (pp. 195–208). New York: Praeger.

Wong, G. Y. Y., & Birnbaum-More, P. H. (1994). Culture, context and structure: A test on Hong Kong banks. *Organization Studies, 15*(1), 99–124.

Wright, T. A., & Goodstein, J. (2007). Character is not "dead" in management research: A review of individual character and organizational-level virtue. *Journal of Management, 33,* 928–958.

Xu, L. C. (1987). A cross-cultural study on the leadership behaviour of Chinese and Japanese executives. *Asian Pacific Journal of Management, 4,* 203–209.

Yamagishi, T. (2003). Cross-societal experimentation on trust: A comparison of the United States and Japan. In E. Ostrom & J. Walker (Eds.), *Trust and reciprocity: Interdisciplinary lessons from experimental research* (pp. 352–367). New York: Russell Sage.

Yeung, L. (2003). Management discourse in Australian banking contexts: In search of an Australian model of participation as compared with that of Hong Kong Chinese. *Journal of Intercultural Studies, 24,* 47–63.

Yoshida, T., Kojo, K., & Kaku, H. (1982). A study on the development of self-presentation in children. *Japanese Journal of Educational Psychology, 30,* 120–127.

Yousef, D. A. (2000). Organizational commitment as a mediator of the relationship between Islamic work ethic and attitudes toward organizational change. *Human Relations, 53,* 513–537.

Yousef, D. A. (2003). Validating the dimensionality of Porter et al.'s measurement of organizational commitment in a non-Western culture setting. *International Journal of Human Resource Management, 14,* 1067–1079.

Yu, H. C., & Miller, P. (2005). Leadership style: The X generation and baby boomers compared in different cultural contexts. *Leadership & Organization Development Journal, 26,* 35–50.

Yu, A., & Yang, K. (1994). The nature of achievement motivation in collectivist societies. In U. Kim, H. Triandis, C. Kagitcibasi, S. Choi, & G. Yoon (Eds.), *Individualism and collectivism: Theory, method and applications* (pp. 239–250). London: Sage.

Yuki, M. (2003). Intergroup comparison versus intragroup relationships: A cross-cultural examination of social identity theory in North American and East Asian cultural contexts. *Social Psychology Quarterly, 66,* 166–183.

Yuki, M., Maddux, W. W., Brewer, M. B., & Takemura, K. (2005). Cross-cultural differences in relationship- and group-based trust. *Personality and Social Psychology Bulletin, 31*(1), 48–62.

Zagorsek, H., Jaklic, M., & Stough, S. J. (2004). Comparing leadership practices between the United States, Nigeria, and Slovenia: Does culture matter. *Cross-Cultural Management, 11,* 16–34.

Zander, L., & Romani, L. (2004). When nationality matters: A study of departmental, hierarchical, professional, gender and age-based employee groupings' leadership preferences across 15 countries. *International Journal of Cross-Cultural Management, 4,* 291–315.

Zou, X., Tam, K. P., Morris, M. W., Lee, S-L., Lau, I. Y-M., & Chiu, C-Y. (2009). Culture as common sense: Perceived consensus versus personal beliefs as mechanism of cultural influence. *Journal of Personality and Social Psychology, 97,* 579–597.

PART 9

The Interface of Work and Life

The Work and Family Interface

Tammy D. Allen

Abstract

Work and family constitute a contemporary topic within the field of industrial and organizational psychology that traverses disciplinary boundaries and has important implications for both individuals and organizations. As family structures have become more heterogeneous, interest in the topic has virtually exploded over the past several decades. The aim of this chapter is to review what we know about work and family interactions. The chapter is organized so that research is reviewed from various perspectives: individual, family, organization, and global. The chapter concludes with an agenda for future research.

Key Words: Work-family conflict, work-family balance, work-family interactions, dual-career couples, positive spillover

Introduction

The study of work and family has grown tremendously over the past several decades. Work-family research examines the intersection of employee work experiences and family lives. A burgeoning interest in the topic has been fueled by a variety of factors. A primary driver of the interest in studying work and family issues has been the increased heterogeneity in family structure. Traditional male-breadwinner families, in which the male pursues full-time work while the female pursues full-time homemaking, are the statistical minority. The majority of individuals today are involved in both paid employment and unpaid family work. According to the 2006 U.S. Census, 52% of all married couples are in a dual-earner marriage. The percentage climbs to 62.2% in married couples with children under the age of 18 and to 67.6% in couples with children aged 6–17 (but none younger; U.S. Bureau of Labor Statistics, 2007). In addition, data from the 2008 National Study of Employers indicates that an increasing percentage of employees have eldercare responsibilities (Galinsky, Bond, Sakai, Kim, & Giuntoli, 2008).

Another factor that has created interest in work and family is the changing expectations between employers and employees. Organizations no longer offer lifetime security, and employees are less willing to sacrifice family for career (Sullivan, 1999). In addition, although the average number of hours that Americans work each week has remained relatively stable, the number of Americans who work long hours (more than 50 hours a week) has been on the incline (Barnett, 2006). Technology has created more opportunities for individuals to devote more time to work anytime and anyplace (Olson-Buchanan & Boswell, 2006). Thus, the boundaries between work lives and family lives have become increasingly blurred (Fletcher & Bailyn, 1996).

Also contributing to the growth of work-family research is the fact that work-family balance is an issue that resonates beyond the halls of academia. Indeed, it is a "kitchen table" subject that has become part of the public vernacular. Columns on work-family balance are included in newspapers such as the *Wall Street Journal*. The topic is one that crosses the science-practice divide within industrial and organizational psychology. Balancing work and personal demands and aspirations may be one of the greatest challenges that individuals face in contemporary society (Halpern, 2004; Kossek & Lambert, 2005). Data from the 2002 National Study of the Changing Workforce indicated that 45% of the U.S. workforce reported experiencing interference between their job and their family life a lot/somewhat (Bond, Thompson, Galinsky, & Prottas, 2002). Integrating career, marriage, and family can affect career progression, marital satisfaction, and overall health and well-being. Given these changes and challenges, it is not surprising that industrial and organizational psychologists have made a concerted effort to increase our understanding of the work-family intersection.

Interest in the topic is demonstrated by the explosion of edited books that have been recently published with a focus on work and family (e.g., Bianchi, Casper, & King, 2005; Halpern & Murphy, 2005; Korabik, Lero, & Whitehead, 2008; Kossek & Lambert, 2005; Pitt-Catsouphes, Kossek, & Sweet, 2005; Poelmans, 2005b). Additionally, in recent years, there have been numerous special issues devoted to the topic in scholarly journals such as *American Behavioral Scientist* (Halpern, 2006), *Human Relations* (Kossek, Hammer, & Lewis, 2010) *Journal of Managerial Psychology* (Bakker, Westman, & van Emmerik, 2009; Heraty, Morley, & Cleveland, 2008), *Journal of Occupational and Organizational Behavior* (Greenhaus, 2008), *Journal of Organizational Behavior* (Brough & Kalliath, 2009), and *The Psychologist-Manager Journal* (Koppes & Swanberg, 2008). Finally, both qualitative and quantitative comprehensive reviews of the literature have appeared in recent years (Casper, Eby, Bordeaux, Lockwood, & Lambert 2007; Greenhaus & Allen, 2010; Ford, Heinen, & Langkamer 2007).

Historical Perspective/Key Events

The growth of the work and family field can be traced to several key works and events. While other authors have traced time lines of the work and family field in general (e.g., Pruitt & Rapoport, 2008), in the following section I outline key events that I believe sparked and have sustained scholarly interest in the topic within industrial and organizational psychology during the past several decades.

Women entered the workforce in record numbers in the 1970s, leading to the emergence of the dual-career couple. In their book entitled *Dual Career Families*, dual-career couple Rhona and Robert Rapoport brought attention to the roles of men and women living dual-career marriages (Rapoport & Rapoport, 1971). Kanter (1977) is often credited with shattering the myth of separate worlds between work and family. Kanter (1977) recognized that organizations acted as if employees' home lives did not exist and that all that mattered was their life at work. The 1977 Quality of Employment Survey (Quinn & Staines, 1979) provided data that formed the basis for a number of early studies examining conflict between work and family, including publications in *Journal of Applied Psychology* (Staines & Pleck, 1984).

In 1985, Greenhaus and Beutell published their seminal article that provided the theoretical underpinnings of work-family conflict. In this article, different types of work-family conflict, based on time, strain, and behavior, were delineated, shaping the field of work-family conflict research for the next several decades. A citation classic, this piece has been cited over 700 times according the SSI database. A watershed event that brought work-family issues widespread attention to industrial and organizational psychologists was Zedeck's 1987 Society for Industrial and Organizational Psychology (SIOP) presidential address. In his address, Zedeck (1987) called for industrial and organizational (I-O) psychologists to study the relationship between work and family roles. The groundbreaking publication of the I-O Frontiers Series edited volume entitled *Work, Family, and Organizations* (Zedeck, 1992) soon followed. Work and family issues rapidly became a recognized and growing area of focal study within the field of I-O psychology.

A decade later, in his 1998 SIOP presidential address, Kevin Murphy again raised the need to increase our understanding of work and family issues. Murphy's (1998) address bemoaned the lack of attention given by I/O psychologists to the relationship between careers and the rest of one's life. Murphy (1998) suggested that we should reconsider the definition of career success in light of the extent to which career conflicts with (or enhances) the family role. As president of the American Psychological Association in 2004, Diane Halpern also brought visibility to the topic by making work-family synthesis one of her presidential initiatives and developing a guide intended to help shape public policy (Halpern, 2004). The 1990s also witnessed dedicated financial support provided for the study of work and family. Since 1994, the Alfred P. Sloan Foundation has played a pivotal role in nurturing work-family scholarship through funding research projects and academic centers that focus on work-family issues, and through the development and financial support of a comprehensive online information resource (Sloan Work and Family Research Network; http://wfnetwork.bc.edu/).

Most recently, the need for work and family intervention research received recognition and a financial boost when the Work, Family and Health Network Initiative was funded through a cooperative agreement by the National Institutes of Health and the Centers for Disease Control and Prevention. The Network is composed of interdisciplinary research teams from multiple universities; it was developed to better understand the relationship between work stress and the health of workers, their children, and other dependents (http://www.kpchr.org/workplacenetwork/).

Chapter Overview

The intent of the current chapter is to review the state of knowledge within the work and family field and to present ideas designed to stimulate boundary-expanding research on the topic. Work and family researchers have mined from an extensive quarry of research questions and issues that are both micro and macro in scope. The literature base has become voluminous. A search in the Psychinfo database alone (as of December 2011), using the term *work-family*, produced 2,968 hits. Given the expansive nature of the literature, there are many different ways in which this chapter could be organized. The approach taken in the current chapter is to view the literature from the perspective of the worker, the family, the organization, and global. This organizing structure is not meant to imply that the constructs discussed necessarily reside at these given levels. Moreover, these perspectives are overlapping and interdependent. However, it is hoped that this framework will provide some shape to the vast array of topics to be covered. Given the breadth of knowledge that has accumulated on the topic, the review is broad in scope. The chapter concludes with an agenda for future research that highlights specific suggested areas of inquiry for moving the field forward.

Focus on the Worker
Theoretical Overview

The theoretical foundation for most conjecture regarding the blending of work and family roles began to emerge in the 1960s (MacDermid, 2005). Three competing mechanisms were posed to explain the linkage (or lack thereof) between work and family: segmentation, compensation, and spillover (Lambert, 1990; Edwards & Rothbard, 2000). The segmentation view refers to the notion that work and family are independent spheres that do not relate to each other (Blood & Wolfe, 1960). The compensation hypothesis suggests that individuals compensate for dissatisfaction in one role by increasing their involvement in the other role or by pursuing rewards in the other role (Dubin, 1967; Edwards & Rothbard, 2000). That is, there is an inverse relationship between work and family variables. In contrast, spillover suggests that experiences in one domain carry over into the other, such that changes in one domain (work or family) lead to similar changes in the other domain (e.g., Burke & Greenglass, 1987; Staines, 1980). The nature of spillover can be positive or negative (Piotrkowski, 1979). For example, positive or negative affect can be carried from work and can result in positive or negative affect, respectively, at home. Both spillover and compensation have been supported under different conditions, but the majority of research finds evidence for spillover (Staines, 1980).

A related line of theory focused on the impact of role accumulation. One perspective regarding role accumulation emphasizes the potential for role interference and strain among individuals who simultaneously participate in work and family roles. Goode (1960) developed what was termed the *scarcity hypothesis*. The scarcity hypothesis refers to the idea that individuals possess a finite amount of time, energy, and attention, and that greedy social organizations tend to demand the majority of those resources. It is presumed that the more roles that an individual accumulates, the greater the probability that he or she will face conflicting obligations and therefore will suffer role strain and distress. Kahn, Wolfe, Quinn, Snoek, and Rosenthal (1964) examined organizational stress that arose from role conflict and role ambiguity. The term *interrole conflict* was coined to describe a situation in which pressures in one role become incompatible with the pressures from another role.

An alternative point of view emerged at the time with regard to role accumulation that suggested that the advantages of multiple role engagement outweighed the disadvantages (Marks, 1977; Sieber, 1974). The *enhancement hypothesis* suggests that individuals' supply of energy is expandable and that multiple roles can increase psychological well-being (e.g., Barnett & Baruch, 1985; Thoits, 1983). Crouter (1984) used the term *positive spill-over* to describe circumstances in which activities in one role support, facilitate, or enhance activities in the other role. Although slow to gain traction, an impressive body of research is beginning to develop from this perspective.

Most recently, researchers have articulated theory regarding integrative rather than causal relationships between work and family that feature the construct of work-family balance (Carlson & Grzywacz, 2008; Greenhaus & Allen, 2010). Although definitions of work-family balance are continuing to be developed and refined, one theme that has emerged is that balance reflects an overall appraisal of and/or orientation toward work and family life.

In subsequent sections, a review of the literature that reflects the conflict, enhancement, and integrative perspectives is provided. The dominant approach to date has been to examine the negative aspects of combining work and family roles, chiefly by focusing on the work-family conflict construct.

The Role Conflict Perspective

By far, the greatest attention within the work-family literature has been on the issue of conflict between work and family roles. Work-family conflict (WFC) research is grounded in theories of role stress and interrole conflict. Greenhaus and Beutell (1985) extended Kahn et al.'s (1964) definition of interrole conflict to form a definition of WFC that has become the operative definition on which most research and measurement has been based. Specifically, WFC is defined as "a form of interrole conflict in which the role pressures from the work and family domains are mutually incompatible in some respect" (p. 77). WFC is the mechanism that links constructs within one domain, such as job demands, with constructs in other domains, such as family satisfaction (Frone, Russell, & Cooper, 1992).

Current research distinguishes the directionality of the conflict. Family interference with work (FIW) is viewed as a distinct construct from work interference with family (WIF). Each has unique antecedents and consequences (e.g., Carlson, 1999). As noted by Greenhaus and Powell (2003), work-family conflict itself involves simultaneous pressures from

the work and family roles. The directionality of the conflict only becomes apparent after the individual makes a decision regarding the resolution of the conflict. Those decisions generally appear to favor work over family. In terms of prevalence, mean rates of WIF are consistently higher than that of FIW (Bellavia & Frone, 2005). The family boundary is more permeable than is the work boundary.

DIMENSIONS

While researchers generally agree that there are two directions in which work-family interference flows (work interferes with family; family interferes with work), there is less consensus regarding the dimensions or type of conflict. The most recognized dimensional structure is that proposed by Greenhaus and Beutell (1985), which consists of time-based conflict, strain-based conflict, and behavior-based conflict. Time-based conflict occurs when time spent on activities in one role inhibits the fulfillment of responsibilities in another role. Strain-based conflict occurs when pressures from one role impede the fulfillment of requirements in another role. Lastly, behavior-based conflict occurs when behaviors necessary to fulfill one role are incompatible or incongruent with behavior patterns necessary in the other role. Of these three dimensions, greater emphasis has been placed on time and strain, often to the exclusion of the behavior dimension.

Greenhaus, Allen, and Spector (2006) proposed a modified typology that refined the strain-based aspect of WFC into that which is effort-based and emotion-based. van Steenbergen, Ellemers, and Mooijaart (2007) used a similar modified typology in recent work that examined strain, time, behavioral, and psychological WIF and FIW. Carlson and Frone (2003) proposed two dimensions, internal and external. *External interference* refers to interference generated by demands in one role that inhibit or preclude participation in the other role. *Internal interference* is represented by psychological preoccupation with one role that interferes with the ability to fully engage in the other role while present in the other role. They show that external WIF was primarily associated with work hours, while internal WIF was associated with psychological work involvement. However, there has been little subsequent research using this typology.

CAUSES

Different approaches have been taken to understand the occurrence of WFC. Early research tended to focus on demographic factors, viewing gender and family status as primary predictors of WFC (e.g., Gutek, Searle, & Klepa, 1991). Most predictor research has focused on characteristics associated with work and home, postulating that work-related factors are the primary predictors of WIF, and family-related factors are the primary predictors of FIW (Frone, 2003). More recent research has begun to identify dispositional variables that relate to WFC, suggesting that personality contributes incremental variance beyond situational factors in explaining WFC (e.g., Wayne, Musisca, & Fleeson, 2004). Brief reviews of findings are described below.

Demographic variables, such as gender and number of children, are thought to predict WFC through their association with work and family demands. With regard to gender, the direction of the interference is thought to matter. Because men tend to spend more time in the work domain than do women, men should experience more WIF than women. Because women tend to take primary responsibility for the home domain, women should experience greater FIW than men. Meta-analytic research is consistent with this notion, but the effect sizes are small. Specifically, Byron (2005) reported an average effect size of -.03 for WIF and .06 for FIW, suggesting that men were slightly more likely to report WIF than were women and that women were slightly more likely to report FIW than were men.

Number of children at home consistently relates to reports of both WIF and FIW (e.g., Bruck & Allen, 2003; Carlson, 1999; Hammer, Allen, & Grigsby, 1997; Kinnunen & Mauno, 1998). Parental responsibility generates more opportunities for conflicts between work and family roles to occur. In her study that included multiple demographic, situational, and dispositional predictors, Carlson found that the number of children living at home was one of the strongest and most consistent predictors of WFC. Importantly, Byron (2005) also found that parental status moderated the relationship between WFC and gender. Specifically, when samples included more parents, the gender difference in the experience of WIF and FIW widened such that women reported significantly more WIF and FIW than did fathers. Parenthood appears to increase both directions of interference for women.

Meta-analytic results show little difference in WIF or FIW by marital status (single versus married), but parental status again moderates this effect (Byron, 2005). Single parents report more WIF and FIW than do married parents, while married and single employees without children report similar levels of WIF and FIW (Byron, 2005). Marital type (single-earner versus dual-earner) has also been examined. Dual-earner couple members are thought to experience more WFC than their single-earner counterparts (e.g., Higgins & Duxbury, 1992), but meta-analytic research shows no difference (Byron, 2005).

The most widely studied work/family environment variables are role stressors, role involvement, and social support. These variables are theorized to best explain WFC when they are divided into the work and family domains and predict the conflict originating from that respective domain (e.g., work role stressors predict WIF; Frone, 2003).

Role stressors are chronic sources of stress that can originate in either the work or the family domain (e.g., Carlson, 1999; Frone et al., 1992). Repeated exposure to role stressors has been linked to WFC (e.g., Aryee, 1992; Carlson & Perrewe, 1999; Parasuraman, Greenhaus, & Granrose, 1992; Shamir, 1983). Role stressors may result in cognitive preoccupation or in reduced energy needed to fulfill multiple roles (Frone, 2003). Of all of the predictors examined, Byron (2005) found that job stress, family stress, and family conflict had the strongest meta-analytic effect sizes with both WIF and FIW.

The importance of work and family roles, or job involvement and family involvement, also relates to WFC (e.g., Adams, King, & King, 1996; Duxbury & Higgins, 1991; Hammer et al., 1997; Parasuraman, Purohit, Godshalk, & Beutell, 1996). The greater the extent of one's involvement in a role, the more likely it is that one will experience conflict originating within that role (Gutek et al., 1991). In addition, high levels of involvement in a role may create preoccupation with that role, resulting in difficulty fulfilling the other role (Frone et al., 1992). An objective indicator of work and family involvement is the number of hours spent engaged in paid work and family work. Kanter (1977) noted that occupational time demands are among the most obvious ways in which work life affects family life. Because time is a finite resource, time spent in paid work restricts the time available to participate in family activities. Byron (2005) found relatively small meta-analytic effect sizes associated with subjective and objective role involvement.

Existing models of work-family conflict (e.g., Frone, Russell & Cooper, 1997) for the most part do not take into account dispositional differences. However, there is a growing body of research that demonstrates linkages between personality and reports of WFC (Allen, Johnson, Saboe, Cho,

Dumani, & Evans, 2012). The dispositional variable that has received the most research attention is negative affect (NA). NA has been proposed to impact how individuals perceive their jobs and other life experiences and consistently has been associated with reports of stressors and strains (Spector, Zapf, Chen, & Frese, 2000). Thus, it is not surprising that multiple studies indicate individuals with greater NA also report greater WFC (Allen, et al., 2012; Bruck & Allen, 2003; Carlson, 1999; Stoeva, Chiu, & Greenhaus, 2002). Similarly, neuroticism has been linked to both WIF and FIW (Grzywacz & Marks, 2000; Wayne et al., 2004). Two studies have examined the "Big Five" variables in relation to WFC (Bruck & Allen, 2003; Wayne et al., 2004). Both studies found that agreeableness and conscientiousness relate to WFC. Less agreeable individuals are more likely to report WFC, while more conscientious individuals report less WFC (Bruck & Allen, 2003; Wayne et al., 2004). Personality also moderates relationships between WFC and outcomes. In a study of employed fathers, Kinnunen, Vermulst, Gerris, and Makikangas (2003) reported that emotionally stable fathers were protected from the negative effects of WIF on well-being, while agreeable fathers were protected from the negative effects of FIW on marital satisfaction.

OUTCOMES

Over the last several decades, a large body of research has demonstrated that work-family conflict (WFC) is associated with a variety of outcomes. Numerous quantitative and qualitative reviews of this literature exist (e.g., Allen, Herst, Bruck, & Sutton, 2000; Dorio, Bryant, & Allen, 2008; Greenhaus et al., 2006; Kossek & Ozeki, 1998). These reviews establish that both WIF and FIW are associated with work outcomes (e.g., job satisfaction, organizational commitment, intention to leave), family outcomes (e.g., marital and family satisfaction), and physical and psychological health outcomes (e.g., depression, physical health complaints, substance abuse disorders).

Of particular interest have been the links between work-family conflict and health and health behavior outcomes. Based on data from the National Institute of Mental Health's National Comorbidity Survey, Frone (2000) reported that individuals who reported WIF were significantly more at risk for mood, anxiety, and substance dependence disorders, compared with those who reported less WIF. The rate of psychiatric disorders was tenfold greater among those who reported WIF. There are a

growing number of studies revealing links between WFC and health-related behaviors associated with diet and exercise (e.g., Allen & Armstrong, 2006; Roos, Sarlio-Lahteenkorva, Lallukka, & Lahelma, 2007). Greater FIW has been associated with eating more high-fat foods and less physical activity (Allen & Armstrong, 2006). In addition, Allen and Armstrong (2006) reported that WIF was associated with eating fewer healthy foods. These findings have been attributed to perceptions of time scarcity. Food choices may be used as a way to cope with the competing time demands between work and family (Devine et al., 2006). Only 13% of parents reported maintaining health (eating right, exercising) as a strategy used to *help* meet the demands and expectations of work and home (Pitt-Catsouphes, Matz-Costa, & MacDermid, 2007). Poor diet and exercise contribute to overweight and obesity (Rosenbaum, Leibel, & Hirsch, 1997), which may help explain the finding of Grzywacz (2000), who reported a direct relationship between WIF and obesity. Frone and colleagues have amassed a considerable body of research showing that WFC is associated with alcohol problems (e.g., Frone et al., 1997; Grzywacz & Bass, 2003).

It is important to note that the vast majority of work-family research has been based on cross-sectional research designs. However, there are a growing number of longitudinal studies. While the findings are not consistent, longitudinal support of relationships between WFC and job satisfaction (Grandey, Cordeiro, & Crouter, 2005), hypertension (Frone et al., 1997), depression (Frone et al., 1997), and well-being (Grant-Vallone & Donaldson, 2001) have been reported. However, there have also been longitudinal studies suggesting alternative causal flows. Variables typically considered as outcomes of WFC, such as psychological well-being, have been found to act as precursors to WFC, rather than as outcomes (Kelloway, Gottlieb, & Barham, 1999; Kinnunen, Geurts, & Mauno, 2004).

On the basis of the longitudinal research conducted thus far, several conclusions can be drawn. The causal direction of WFC-outcome relationships is not well understood. The longitudinal studies to date have been based on different time lags and have included different dependent variables, making comparisons difficult. This is complicated by the fact that behavioral, psychological, and physiological symptoms of strain can be expected to have different patterns of development over the same time course (Semmer, Grebner, & Elfering, 2004). There is also evidence that temporal effects may differ across gender (Kinnunen et al., 2004), direction of conflict (WIF versus FIW; Kelloway et al., 1999), and type of conflict (time-based versus strain-based; van Hooff et al., 2005).

MEASUREMENT

Measurement issues have been a frequent topic of discussion within the work-family conflict literature. Despite efforts to develop psychometrically sound measures of WFC (e.g., Carlson, Kacmar, & Williams, 2000; Netemeyer, Boles, & McMurrian, 1996), problems remain. A major criticism is that the scale items from common measures often confound cause and effect (Bellavia & Frone, 2005). Strain is embedded in many of the items used to measure WFC. For example, one item commonly used to assess FIW is, "Because of the demands I face at home, I am tired at work." Because this item assesses fatigue during the workday, it is not surprising that it also correlates with strain. As a result of this construct overlap, relationships observed between WFC and strains such as anxiety and depression may be spurious or may be inflated. Moreover, subjective measures such as those currently used to assess WFC may be prone to distortion due to trait affect (Schaubroeck, 1999). This potential problem is underscored by recent studies linking NA/neuroticism to WFC (Bruck & Allen, 2003; Wayne et al., 2004).

A related issue is that most existing measures of WFC are based on the use of "strongly disagree" to "strongly agree" response anchors (Bellavia & Frone, 2005). Work-family conflict is manifested on a day-to-day basis (Williams & Alliger, 1994) yet current measurement systems do not capture this aspect of the construct. Another issue for consideration is the clarity with which the non-work side of the equation is specified (Huffman, Youngcourt, Payne, & Castro, 2008). For example, most scales refer to family (e.g., Netemeyer et al., 1996), but some use the term *home* (e.g., Grzywacz & Marks, 2000) instead. Still others refer to specific individuals in the family network as the referent for the conflict (e.g., work-spouse conflict; Aryee, 1992). Such differences make comparisons of results across studies difficult.

The Role Enhancement Perspective

Although the conflict approach to work and family has been dominant, in recent years the number of studies examining the positive side of the work-family interface has grown substantially. Several unique, but highly related concepts have been developed, including positive spillover (Hanson, Hammer, & Colton, 2006; Kirchmeyer, 1993; Small & Riley, 1990), work-family facilitation (Grzywacz & Bass, 2003; Wayne et al., 2004), and work-family enrichment (Carlson Kacmar, Wayne, & Grzywacz, 2006; Greenhaus & Powell, 2006).

Positive spillover is defined as the transfer of generative mood, skills, behaviors, and values from work to family or from family to work (Edwards & Rothbard, 2000; Hanson et al., 2006). Studies first began to investigate positive spillover between work and family in the early 1990s (Small & Riley, 1990). The measure of positive spillover developed by Hanson et al. (2006) captures three types of work-to-family positive spillover: affective, behavior-based instrumental, and values-based. Each of these types of spillover can occur from family to work, as well as from work to family.

Facilitation refers to the extent that engagement in one life domain provides gains that contribute to enhanced functions in another life domain (Wayne, Grzywacz, Carlson, & Kacmar, 2007). van Steenbergen et al. (2007) considered facilitation to be the conceptual counterpart of conflict. That is, while conflict deals with the extent that participation in one role is made more difficult by participation in the other role, facilitation refers to the extent that participation in one role is made easier by virtue of participation in the other role. They identified four types of facilitation similar to the types of conflict examined in the literature: energy-based, time-based, behavioral, and psychological. Grzywacz, Carlson, Kacmar, and Wayne (2007) suggested that the term *facilitation* be used to denote theory and research that pertains to system-level issues within the work-family interface. However, it is important to be aware that existing studies have used the term *facilitation* when conducting research investigating intraindividual across-domain experiences (e.g., Rotundo & Kincaid, 2008).

Enrichment is defined as the extent that experiences in one role improve the quality of life (performance and positive affect) in the other role through the transfer of resources or positive affect from one role to the other role (Greenhaus & Powell, 2006). Greenhaus and Powell (2006) specify two paths by which enrichment occurs. Resources generated in one role can be directly transferred to the other role. In addition, a resource generated in one role can generate positive affect within that role, which in turn produces high performance and positive affect in the other role. Greenhaus and Powell (2006) also identify five types of resources that can be role generated, including: skills and perspectives, psychological and physical resources, social-capital resources, flexibility, and material resources.

Carlson et al. (2006) suggested that the distinction between enrichment and spillover is that enrichment requires that resources not only be transferred but that they be applied in ways that result in improved performance or affect for the individual. Wayne et al. (2007) suggested that enrichment and facilitation can be distinguished by virtue of the idea that enrichment involves the within-individual transfer of resources from one domain to the other, while facilitation involves the positive influence of involvement in one domain on the functioning of the other system. An example of enrichment would be when skills learned in the workplace help make the individual a better parent. Facilitation would occur when the skills learned in the workplace help the individual improve the functioning of the family unit, such as through enhanced interpersonal communication. Thus, enrichment involves intraindividual cross-domain transfer, while facilitation involves individual to family system transfer.

Carlson et al. (2006) developed and validated a measure of work to family enrichment composed of three dimensions: developmental, affect, and capital. Their family to work enrichment measure included three dimensions entitled: development, affect, and efficiency. Developmental gains refer to the acquisition of skills, knowledge, values, or perspectives. Affective gains involve the alteration of moods, attitudes, and confidence. Capital gains involve the acquisition of economic, social, or health assets. Efficiency gains are enhanced focus or attention.

Although the distinctions between the various constructs are not always clear, all reflect the perspective that combining multiple roles can result in beneficial outcomes for the individual. Moreover, despite differences in definitions, the terms have been used interchangeably. In some cases, the same measure (the MIDUS scale) has been referred to as positive spillover in one study (Grzywacz & Marks, 2000) and as facilitation in another (Grzywacz & Butler, 2005). For the purposes of reviewing predictors and outcomes, the term *enhancement* is used in the following section as a generic way to denote research on the positive benefits of multiple role engagement. Like current research regarding WFC, work-family enhancement is typically studied in terms of direction. That is, positive benefits can flow from the work domain to the family domain (abbreviated hereafter as WFE), or from the family domain to the work domain (FWE).

PREDICTORS

The sets of variables that have been examined as predictors of work-family enhancement to date are limited. Greenhaus and Powell (2006) suggested that the antecedents of WFE/FWE would be resources acquired from the originating domain. Consistent with this line of thought, research to date suggests that family factors such as psychological involvement in the family and marital role commitment are predictors of FWE (e.g., Allis & O'Driscoll, 2008; Graves, Ohlott, & Ruderman, 2007). Similarly, work-related factors such as job involvement have been associated with WFE (Aryee, Srinivas, & Tan, 2005). Grzywacz and Butler (2005) found that characteristics of the job, such as greater decision latitude, variety, and complexity, were associated with greater WFE. Butler, Grzywacz, Bass, and Linney (2005) provided further support for this finding, based on a within-person daily diary design that linked skill level and control with WFE.

Research has also examined individual differences associated with enhancement. Higher levels of enhancement have been found for women than for men (Aryee et al., 2005; Roehling, Moen, & Batt, 2003; Rotundo & Kincaid, 2008; van Steenbergen et al., 2007). In addition, van Steenbergen et al. (2007) reported that enhancement differentially predicted the work and non-work outcomes of men and women. Several studies have shown that personality is associated with enhancement (e.g., Grzywacz & Butler, 2005; Grzywacz & Marks, 2000; Wayne et al., 2004). Findings suggest that greater extraversion relates to greater WFE, as well as to greater FWE. A secure attachment style has also been associated with greater enhancement in both directions (Sumer & Knight, 2001). Rotundo and Kincaid (2008) examined coping styles and found that a direct-action coping style was positively related to WFE but not to FEW. Advice seeking was positively associated with FWE, but not to WFE.

OUTCOMES

Enhancement shares many of the same outcomes as does work-family conflict, but opposite in effect. Outcomes examined include job-related attitudes, family outcomes, and health and well-being (McNall, Nicklin, & Masuda, 2010). Multiple studies have found that greater enhancement relates to greater job satisfaction and organizational commitment (e.g., Aryee et al., 2005; Boyar & Mosley, 2007; Carlson et al., 2006; Geurts, Taris, Kompier, Dikkers, van Hooff, & Kinnunen, 2005; Hanson et al., 2006). Similarly, greater enhancement has been associated with greater marital satisfaction and family satisfaction (Hill, 2005; Voydanoff, 2005). In terms of directional differences, there is some indication that WFE more highly correlates with job satisfaction, while FWE is more highly associated with family satisfaction (Carlson et al., 2006).

Enhancement has been associated with a variety of health and well-being outcomes, but the number of accumulated studies on any given single variable is small. One study has reported a positive relationship between FWE and sleep quality (Williams, Franche, Ibrahim, Mustard, & Layton, 2006). Research also documents that positive work-family interactions are associated with general well-being (e.g., Allis & O'Driscoll, 2008). One study has examined enhancement and depression longitudinally. Hammer, Cullen, Neal, Sinclair, and Shafiro (2005) found no significant bivariate relationship between either direction of enhancement with depression measured one year later.

Relationship Between Work-Family Conflict and Work-Family Enhancement

Most scholars agree that work-family conflict and work-family enhancement constructs are conceptually distinct (e.g., Hanson et al., 2006). One is not simply the absence of the other. Empirical evidence also supports the distinction between the two in that the two have been found to have unique antecedents and outcomes (e.g., Aryee et al., 2005). In addition, correlations between the two constructs tend to be low. Greenhaus and Powell (2006) reported an average correlation of .02 across 21 studies. It is also interesting to note prevalence differences across the two in terms of direction. Research consistently shows that work is more likely to interfere with family than family is likely to interfere with work, while family is more likely to enhance work than work is to enhance family (Greenhaus & Powell, 2006).

Work-Family Balance

The term *work-family balance* is frequently used in both the popular and scholarly press, but its definition has been nebulous. Unlike constructs such as work-family conflict and work-family enrichment, balance is not a linking mechanism between work and family because it does not specify how conditions or experiences in one role are causally related to conditions or experiences in the other role (Greenhaus, Collins, & Shaw, 2003). Rather, it reflects an interrole phenomenon. However, some scholars equate low or a lack of work-family conflict

with work-family balance (e.g., Duxbury & Higgins, 2001; Hill, Hawkins, Ferris, & Weitzman, 2001). Frone (2003) suggested that work-family balance is represented by a low level of work-family conflict, accompanied by a high level of work-family facilitation. Others refer to balance in terms of investments in multiple roles (e.g., Kirchmeyer, 2000; Marks & MacDermid, 1996).

Some scholars have linked balance with the "superwoman" myth, which suggests that all women can and should have an exciting career, handsome husband, and well-behaved children (Thompson & Beauvais, 2000). Rejecting the notion of balance, recent articles in the popular press have even encouraged individuals to "enjoy being unbalanced" (Beck, 2008).

Several recent efforts have been made to systematically review the balance construct and to offer precise definitions. Greenhaus and Allen (2010) define work-family balance as, "the extent to which an individual's effectiveness and satisfaction in work and family roles are compatible with the individual's life role priorities at a given point in time." Life role priority refers to the relative priority, focus, or emphasis placed on different life roles (Friedman & Greenhaus, 2000). Career-focused people and family-focused people place work and family, respectively, at the center of their lives and derive their strongest sense of identity from their higher priority role, while career-*and*-family-focused people place similar emphasis on both roles, and they derive their sense of self from their experiences in both roles.

Another recent perspective on balance is that it should be viewed as a social, rather than a psychological, construct. Grzywacz and Carlson (2007) argue that a decontextualized view of balance isolates individuals from their families and organizations. They define balance as "accomplishment of role-related expectations that are negotiated and shared between an individual and his or her role-related partners in the work and family domains" (p. 458).

There has been little empirical research on balance as an interrole concept. Greenhaus et al. (2003) investigated the impact of employees' relative involvement in work and family roles on life outcomes. They found that those highly involved in both work and family roles experienced a higher quality of life if they were more involved in family than in work than if they were equally involved in work and family. The concept of balance adds to the ways in which we view the intersection of work and family roles and is likely to be a major topic of future study.

Focus on the Family

As might be expected, industrial and organizational psychologists have tended to focus on the work-related side of the work-family equation. Limited attention has been given to outcomes that reside in the family domain (Eby, Casper, Lockwood, Bordeaux, & Brinley, 2005). In addition, there has been an overemphasis on individual effects. In their review of critical gaps in work-family research, Parasuraman and Greenhaus (2002) highlight that there has been limited investigation of couple-level work-family relationships and crossover effects from one partner to the other. This observation was echoed in Casper et al.'s (2007) review of methods used to study work-family issues. The authors reported that a mere 13% of the work and family studies published in industrial-organizational and organizational behavior journals examined crossover relationships and that only 5% used the couple as the level of analysis. Arguments for why employers need to be concerned with family-related outcomes such as child health have begun to emerge (Cleveland, 2005; Major, Allard, & Cardenas, 2004). The following section takes a closer look at work-family issues with a focus on the family. Specifically, research on dual-career couple issues, crossover, and child health is reviewed.

Dual-Career Couples

Rapoport and Rapoport (1969) first coined the term *dual-career families* to designate a type of family structure in which both heads of household—the husband and the wife—pursue active careers and family life. Breadwinning patterns among married couples have changed in several ways during the last three decades. From 1970 to 2001, wives' income relative to that of their husbands increased steadily. In addition, wives' employment hours have increased 23% within the same time period, while husbands' employment hours have remained relatively constant (Raley, Mattingly, & Bianchi, 2006).

The work and family lives of dual-career couples are interdependent. Each partner's work and family experiences and outcomes are impacted by his or her own set of circumstances, as well as by those of his or her partner (Parasuraman & Greenhaus, 2002). Research suggests that work and family roles within couples remains consistent with traditional gender roles in which men are career-primary and

women are family-primary. For example, 90% of the time when a child of a two-parent family is sick, the woman is the caretaker (Maccoby, 1998). Couples are often faced with decisions in which the career advancement of one member may come at the expense of the career advancement of the second member of the couple. The vast majority of trailing spouses in job relocations are female (Eby, 2001). Women are more likely than men to take parental leaves (Judiesch & Lyness, 1999). Even in Sweden, where there have been concerted governmental efforts to encourage male parental leave, fathers take a small proportion of paid leave available (Hass, Allard, & Hwang, 2002). As noted by Greenhaus (2003), a man's marital status generally does not influence his choice of career roles, while family responsibilities often interfere with female career success.

A major topic within the dual-career couple literature is division of labor. Decades of research continue to show that division of labor tends to be unequally divided between men and women. Specifically, based on time diary data, men tend to contribute more hours to the paid labor force, while women contribute more hours to home-related activities (Bianchi, Robinson, & Milkie, 2006). Employed mothers average five hours more per week than employed fathers in terms of total workload inside and outside the home. Other estimates suggests that women spend two to three times as many hours engaged in unpaid routine housework, relative to men (Coltrane, 2000). Several theoretical approaches are used to study household division of labor. The time availability approach asserts that household members will divide tasks according to the time they each have available (Arrighi & Maume, 2000). However, research shows little relationship between wife's employment and husband's time in housework, suggesting that marital partners do not allocate family work on the basis of time availability. The relative-resources approach is based on the premise that housework is distasteful and will be avoided. Hence, individuals within the marital dyad who have greater resources (e.g., more earning power) leverage those resources to avoid housework. Strong support for this perspective is lacking in that women do more housework than men even when they earn more than their spouses (e.g., Brines, 1994). The gender ideology framework poses that division of labor is based on attitudes regarding gender roles, with more egalitarian views reflecting a more equal division of labor. For example, Arrighi and Maume (2000) found that egalitarian men spend more time in housework than do men who espouse more traditional gender role values.

The unequal division holds in samples of men and women in high-status jobs. For example, based on a sample of academic physicians, Bergman, Ahmad, and Stewart (2008) found that men and women had the same total workload, but men spent more time in professional work than did women, while women spent more time in unpaid work and childcare activities than did men.

Male and female partners in dual-career marriages differ with regard to their views on how household responsibilities are shared. For example, Friedman and Greenhaus (2000) found that 62% of fathers reported that care of the children was fully shared between the partners, while only 47% of mothers reported equal sharing. In the 500 Family Study, both husbands and wives were asked to self-report their total number of hours spent in common household chores and to also report on their spouses. Spouses tended to agree on the amount of time that the wife spent on these activities. However, men tended to report a higher estimate of their own hours than that reported by their wives (Lee, 2005).

Some attempt has been made to tie the division of labor to workplace conditions. Arrighi and Maume (2000) found that men who faced masculinity challenges at work participated less in household work. Men avoid housework because it is thought of as women's work and therefore is inconsistent with their identities as men. Hochschild (1989) also concluded that a man's identity cannot be further threatened by engaging in women's work at home when it is otherwise threatened by work-related factors. More research linking workplace factors with how couples negotiate their work and family responsibilities would be a welcome addition to the literature.

Crossover Research

The strain that individuals face as a result of work-family demands and conflict can be contagious. That is, the experience can be shared with family members and/or with coworkers. This can result in what is referred to as *crossover*. Within the work-family and stress literature, crossover effects refer to a process whereby stresses and strains experienced by one individual affect the stresses and strains experienced by a partner in that individual's social system (Westman, 1991; Westman & Etzion, 1995; Westman & Vinokur, 1998).

Westman and Vinokur (1998) proposed that there are three mechanisms by which crossover occurs. Direct transmission occurs between partners who are closely related and have empathetic reactions for one another. Indirect crossover involves interpersonal exchange as a mediator. The experienced stress of one partner activates a negative interaction sequence, which results in conflictual interactions such as social undermining (Westman & Vinokur, 1998; Westman, Vinokur, Hamilton, & Roziner (2004). The third way in which crossover occurs in through common stressors (e.g., financial strain, threat of job loss). The shared environment of the partners results in the simultaneous increase of the strains of both partners, producing a spurious relationship between strains.

Westman (2006) charts several trends in crossover research over the past 30 years. The first wave of crossover studies, conducted in the 1980s, focused on the crossover of stress and strain from husbands to wives among men in high-stress jobs (e.g., police work). These studies viewed wives as the victims of their husband's job stress. With the advent of an increasing number of women in the workforce, the second wave of research, conducted in the 1990s, focused on wife-to-husband as well as husband-to-wife crossover. Researchers also began to expand the types of variables examined. Specifically, studies included those that examined the crossover of job stressors of the individual to the strain of the spouse, and some examined the crossover of strain of the individual to the strain of the spouse. Crossover effects have been found for psychological strains such as anxiety, burnout, depression, distress, and marital dissatisfaction (e.g., Jones & Fletcher, 1993; Pavett, 1986; Westman & Etzion, 1995; Westman et al., 2004).

Of particular interest to work-family researchers has been the crossover of WFC. Some studies examine the crossover of WFC from one partner to the other, showing a positive correlation between the self-reports of WFC of each spouse. For example, Hammer et al. (1997) reported that husbands' and wives' WFC explained unique variance in their partners' WFC beyond their partners' work salience, perceived flexibility, and family involvement. Westman and Etzion (2005) found that husbands' and wives' WIF explained unique variance in their partners' WIF beyond their partners' job stressors and family demands. Similarly, husbands' and wives' FIW explained unique variance in their partners' FIW beyond the same set of variables.

Other studies examine how the WFC of one partner relates to the strains of another partner. Many of these studies find asymmetric effects for wives and husbands. Husbands' FIW has been associated with wives' lateness to work (Hammer, Bauer, & Grandey, 2003). The same study found that wives' FIW predicted husbands' interruptions at work and absences. Grandey et al. (2005) found that husbands' WIF predicted wives' job satisfaction one year later. However, wives' WIF did not predict husbands' job satisfaction cross-sectionally or longitudinally. Hammer et al. (2005) found support for the crossover of a husband's WIF on his wife's depression. Matthews, Del Priore, Acitelli, and Barnes-Farrell (2006) found while wives' WIF was associated with *increased* relationship tension for their husbands, husbands' WIF was associated with *decreased* relationship tension for their wives.

There are several crossover topics just beginning to gain research attention (Westman, 2006). One topic ripe for research is positive crossover. Just as stressful demands have a negative impact on the partner's well-being, positive job events may also cross over to the partner and have a positive effect on his or her well-being. In addition, the crossover of FIW and family stressors into the workplace is in need of study. For example, individuals may bring stressors from home into the workplace, thereby creating strain in coworker relationships.

Child Outcomes

While family researchers have a history of examining the relationship between parents' work experiences and child outcomes (e.g., Crouter, MacDermid, McHale, & Perry-Jenkins, 1990), child outcomes have rarely been the focus of research by industrial and organizational psychologists. Recently, scholars have argued that children are unseen stakeholders at work and that child health should be considered a legitimate business concern (Friedman & Greenhaus, 2000; Major et al., 2004). Further, Cleveland (2005) noted that employer requirements, such as long hours and face time, can result in employees who are dysfunctional in their roles as spouses or parents.

There are several ways in which children are affected by their parents' working lives. Children sense and are aware of parental work stress. In her "ask the children" research, Galinsky (1999) found that what children most wish for is that their parents would be less stressed and less tired. Similarly, Sallinen, Ronka, Kinnunen, and Kokka (2007) investigated mother and father work experiences,

along with reports from their adolescent children. Their results were consistent with Galinsky's (1999) in that lack of parents' time due to work was less of a concern than was parents' fatigue and bad mood.

Parental work experiences relate to the quality of parent-child interactions, which in turn relate to child health and well-being outcomes (Crouter & Bumpus, 2001; Stewart & Barling, 1996). Sallinen et al. (2007) reported adolescents' perceptions of parents' negative spillover from work to home was connected to less autonomy-granting parental behaviors and to increased parent-adolescent conflict, which in turn was associated with adolescent depression.

Aspects of the work environment and work-family conflict can also impact family activities such as family dinners. Family routines and rituals contribute to the quality of family life and serve as a protective factor for children (Fiese et al., 2002). Research shows that what children remember most about their childhood are the everyday rituals and traditions that bring the family together (Galinsky, 1999). Allen, Shockley, and Poteat (2008) found that less family-supportive supervision was associated with fewer family dinners. This relationship was mediated by WIF. In addition, the availability of flexplace (i.e., telecommuting) was negatively associated with the frequency with which children ate fast food for dinner. These findings are important in that more frequent family dinners are associated with reduced risk for teen illegal drug use, drinking, smoking, and aggressive behaviors and with healthy food intake (CASA, 2005; Fulkerson et al., 2006; Gillman et al., 2000). Fast food intake is associated with poor dietary quality and places children at risk for obesity (Bowman, Gortmaker, Ebbeling, Pereira, & Ludwig, 2004). Based on a longitudinal study using daily surveys at both home and work, Ilies et al. (2007) found that employee social behaviors (e.g, going on family outings, eating meals together) as reported by spouses was predicted by employee WIF.

Just as engagement in multiple roles has advantages and disadvantages for individuals, the same may be said in terms of child outcomes. Crouter, Helms-Erikson, Updegraff, and McHale (1999) found that mothers working longer hours knew as much about the children's daily experiences as did mothers working fewer hours. However, husbands married to mothers working longer hours were better informed than were husbands married to mothers working fewer hours. Thus, children of mothers who work longer hours may benefit due to increased involvement of fathers. The time period during which work is performed appears to be an important factor. Children appear to be more at risk when parents work evenings or nights (Heymann, 2000; Presser, 2000). Non-standard shifts inhibit parents from participating in family dinners, helping with schoolwork, and reading bedtime stories (Crouter & McHale, 2005).

Why should employers care about child health? The business case for caring about child health is that child health affects employees' work lives (Major et al., 2004). In addition, child illnesses impact insurance claims and costs for the organization and increase employees' absenteeism. Employers have implemented a number of different policies designed to help individuals manage work and family life. Such policies are the focus of the following section.

Focus on the Organization
Overview

Considerable attention has been given to the role of the organization in helping individuals manage work and non-work responsibilities. For the purposes of this chapter, three different types of support are reviewed. The first is the formal resources that are available to employees, such as child care and flexible work arrangements. Such resources are commonly referred to as "family-friendly benefits." The second is the relational support provided by supervisors. The third type of support is based on the organization as a whole, which considers factors such as the norms regarding expected prioritization of work and family among employees.

Formal Resources
OVERVIEW

Family-supportive/friendly benefits, policies, and programs (FSB) are those that are designed to help employees be effective in both their work and their family lives. A wide variety benefits may be included under the rubric of FSB (Lobel & Kossek, 1996). Although there is no commonly accepted categorization system, FSB are often clustered into two categories, those that involve dependent care and those that involve the timing and location of work. A review of the most commonly discussed and researched FSB follow.

FLEXIBILITY

Flexibility has received a great deal of attention from both the practice and the research community. It has been cited as key to helping employees

manage work and non-work responsibilities, and there are a variety of initiatives in place to promote flexibility within the workplace (Galinsky & Backon, 2008).

Flexible work arrangements (FWA) are defined as "alternative work options that allow work to be accomplished outside of the traditional temporal and/or spatial boundaries of a standard workday" (Rau, 2003). FWA permit deviance from the traditional 9:00 A.M. to 5:00 P.M., Monday through Friday, 40-hour workweek by allowing work to be performed on a reduced hours basis, before or after normal working hours, and/or from remote locations. Flextime has been reported as the most frequently offered family-friendly benefit, followed by telework, within the United States and in Canada (Comfort, Johnson, & Wallace, 2003; SHRM Foundation, 2001). Flexible policies are assumed to facilitate the management of competing demands from work and non-work through increases in temporal flexibility (when work is done) and in spatial flexibility (where work is done; Rau, 2003). Individuals may choose to use FWA for a variety of reasons, including a decrease/elimination of commute time, ease in scheduling appointments or running errands, continuing education, child care needs, or productivity purposes (Sharpe, Hermsen, & Billings, 2002).

The two most popular forms of FWA are flextime and flexplace (SHRM Foundation, 2001). Flextime refers to flexibility in the timing of work. For instance, employees may be empowered to alter the start and stop times of work, though they are still required to be present during a set of specified core hours (e.g., 10:00 A.M. to 3:00 P.M.; Baltes, Briggs, Huff, Wright, & Neuman, 1999). Flexplace involves flexibility in the location where work is completed, often referring to work conducted at home (also known as *telework* or *telecommuting*). Flexplace arrangements may also involve flexibility in the timing of work, but this is not always so. For example, some organizations permit employees to work from home but require them to be electronically available and to work traditional hours, whereas other employers place no temporal restrictions on remote work. Thus, there is a considerable variation in the restrictions associated with flexplace policies.

A number of positive outcomes have been associated with FWA. Baltes et al. (1999) reported the effects of flexible and compressed work schedules on a variety of work outcomes and found that they related positively to productivity, job satisfaction, and work schedule satisfaction, and related negatively to absenteeism. Importantly, this meta-analytic review was limited to intervention studies. The availability of FWA has also been associated with greater organizational commitment (Grover & Crooker, 1995).

In their qualitative review of the research on FWA and WFC, Allen and Shockley (2009) suggest that the human case for FWA has been overshadowed by the business case. Specifically, although there is a robust relationship between FWA and organizational variables such as productivity and absenteeism, the evidence regarding WFC is considerably more mixed.

Demonstrating the heterogeneity of effects, two recent meta-analyses came to two different conclusions. Byron (2005) reported a meta-analytic effect size of -.30 between flexibility and WIF and of −.17 with FIW, while Mesmer-Magnus and Viswesvaran (2006) reported an effect size of .00 with WIF and .06 with FIW. More recently, Gajendran and Harrison (2007) reported a mean effect size of −.11 between telecommuting and WFC, suggesting a small but significant relationship.

One explanation for the heterogeneous results regarding FWA and work-family conflict is that some individuals benefit from flexibility more than others. Family responsibility appears to be a moderating factor. In her meta-analysis, Byron (2005) found that having a higher percentage of females in a sample was negatively related to the study effect size between schedule flexibility and WIF and FIW. Shockley and Allen (2007) found that family responsibility moderated the relationship between WFC and FWA availability such that the relationship was stronger for women with greater family responsibility than for women with less family responsibility. Thus, FWA may provide more of a protective benefit for women than for men by virtue of women's greater family responsibility. More specifically, women are still primarily responsible for tasks such as scheduling doctor appointments, meetings with teachers, and so on. The type of flexibility also makes a difference. Shockley and Allen (2007) reported FWA related more highly to WIF than to FIW, and flextime availability was more highly associated with WIF than was flexplace availability.

EXTENDING THE FLEXIBILITY CONCEPT

The concept of flexibility has been extended to include flexibility in the timing of work across the life span. This can be referred to as *career flexibility*; it involves the ability to reduce commitment to work during certain life cycles while maintaining the ability to opt back in when desired. Moen and Roehling (2005) argue that lockstep arrangements that force a pattern based on education, work, family, and then retirement are outdated. Research has shown that 37% of highly qualified women voluntarily leave their career for a period of time. The vast majority of women (93%) who take a break want to return to work (Hewlett, 2005). Organizations that acknowledge and accommodate such changes in pace over the career course make provisions for employees to slow their career progress while also avoiding permanent career derailment.

PAID LEAVE

Under the Family Leave and Medical Act (FLMA), companies with at least 50 employees are required to allow employees to take up to 12 weeks of unpaid leave a year to care for a newborn, a sick family member, or their own medical problem. However, some individual employers go beyond these requirements and provide paid leave. Leaves following the birth or adoption of a child generally demonstrate positive health benefits for mothers (Chatterji & Markowitz, 2004), but research that examines specific organizational paid leave policies and individual health and well-being outcomes is sparse. There is some data based on a review of the California paid leave program to suggest that offering extensive family and medical leave benefits helps reduce turnover, but the data cannot rule out the possibility that companies that offer more extensive leaves are better employers in general (Milkman & Appelbaum, 2004). Other studies have found that generous leaves, paid or unpaid, increase the likelihood that women will return to work following childbirth (Glass & Riley, 1995). On the other hand, taking a leave of absence has also been associated with negative career consequences for both men and women (Allen & Russell, 1999; Judiesch & Lyness, 1999).

DEPENDENT CARE SUPPORTS

The research regarding the efficacy of dependent care support is surprisingly sparse. Only a handful of studies have specifically examined the use of employer-supported child care centers. Goff, Mount, and Jamison (1990) found no relationship between child care center use and employee absenteeism or work-family conflict. However, satisfaction with child care arrangements was associated with less work-family conflict regardless of location. Kossek and Nichols (1992) found that parents who used an employer-sponsored onsite child care center reported fewer child care problems and more positive work-family attitudes than those who were on the waiting list. No relationship was found with performance or employee absenteeism. More recently, Hammer, Neal, Newsom, Brockwood, and Colton (2005) found that the use of dependent care supports (a variety of supports that included child and eldercare) were *positively* associated with WIF for dual-career women. Grover and Crooker (1995) found that the *availability* of child care was associated with attachment to the organization.

Mesmer-Magnus and Viswesvaran (2006) reported a meta-analytic effect size of -.14 for WFC and -.04 for WIF with dependent care availability and satisfaction. These effect sizes should be interpreted with caution because their research did not distinguish between child care arrangements provided by an employer versus those provided by another source (e.g., home care).

A large proportion of employees not only have responsibility for the care of children, but also for the care of parents (Neal & Hammer, 2007). Estimates indicate that 35% of workers provide care for an aging family member and that proportion is likely to increase (Bond et al., 2002). In response to this challenge, a greater percentage of employers are providing elder care resources to employees, with 35% providing such a benefit in 2005, based on data from the National Study of Employers (Bond, Galinsky, Kim & Brownfield, 2005). To my knowledge, research has yet to isolate the availability or use of eldercare benefits alone with employee outcomes.

Supervisor Support

The importance of the supervisor in determining how employees experience the workplace has been well documented. Employees who have positive relationships with their supervisors are more satisfied, more committed, and perform better (Gerstner & Day, 1997). Those with abusive supervisors have unfavorable job attitudes, more psychological strain, and lower family well-being (Tepper, 2007). Thus, it should not be surprising that supervisors also play a critical role regarding the extent that individuals are able to manage their work and family responsibilities.

Individuals who report that their supervisors are more family-supportive also report less WFC (e.g., Allen, 2001; Anderson, Coffey, & Byerly, 2002; Frone et al, 1997; Goff et al., 1990; Lapierre & Allen, 2006; Thomas & Ganster, 1995; Thompson,

Beauvais, & Lyness, 1999). Breaugh and Frye (2008) recently corroborated the relationship through other reports of WFC. That is, employee reports of supervisor support were associated with reports provided by significant others of employee WFC. Family-supportive supervision has also been positively associated with positive job attitudes and lower intentions to leave the organization (e.g., Allen, 2001; Anderson et al., 2002; Roehling, Roehling, & Moen, 2001).

Unsupportive supervisors may block or make it difficult for employees to access structural supports such as flexibility (Brewer, 2000; Glass & Fujimoto, 1995; Warren & Johnson, 1995), or may place demands on employees that make it challenging for them to be available to family members when needed (e.g., Allen et al., 2008; Galinsky & Stein 1990). Indeed, several studies have shown positive correlations between family-supportive policy use and family-supportive supervision (Allen, 2001; Breaugh & Frye, 2008; Thompson et al, 1999).

Hammer, Kossek, Zimmerman, and Daniels (2007) recently proposed that family-supportive supervisor behavior is composed of four dimensions. The dimensions include: emotional support, instrumental support, role model behaviors, and recognition of the strategic importance of the work-family issue. Hammer and colleagues (2007) also linked family-supportive supervision with health outcomes. Specifically, Hammer, Kossek, Yragui, Zimmerman, and Daniels (2008) found that family-supportive supervision was associated with workday systolic and diastolic blood pressure. Thus family-supportive supervision has the potential to be implicated as a cardiovascular risk factor. This is not surprising when considering that cardiovascular disease risk has been linked to a lack of social support in previous research (Uchino, Cacippo, & Kiecolt-Glaser, 1996).

Informal Organizational Support

It has been noted that, despite the implementation of specific family-supportive policies such as flextime, organizations have changed little in terms of overall structure and approach. That is, they continue to expect employees to put everything into their work, even at the sacrifice of family (Williams, 2000). The "ideal worker" is available 24/7 and takes little time off for childbearing or for caregiving. Such entrenched expectations can negate the usefulness of formal policies and can undermine employee efforts to achieve work-family balance.

Several related constructs and measures have been developed to assess informal organizational work-family support. Thompson and colleagues (1999) refer to work-family culture as "the shared assumptions, beliefs, and values regarding the extent to which an organization supports and values the integration of employees' work and family lives." (p. 394). Allen (2001) used the term *family-supportive organizational perceptions* (FSOP) to describe the global perceptions that employees form regarding the extent that the organization is family-supportive. Thompson et al. (1999) consider three dimensions of culture: career penalties, time demands, and managerial support. In contrast, Allen's (2001) conceptualization is unidimensional and is based on the notion that supervisor/manager support is a related, but distinct construct. Other dimensions that might be considered part of the domain of family-supportive organizations/cultures have also been proposed, such as face-time orientation (Shockley & Allen, 2010).

Employees who perceive their organizations as more family-supportive report less WFC than do those who perceive the organization to be less family-supportive (Allen, 2001; Behson, 2005; Shockley & Allen, 2007; Thompson et al., 1999). These findings have been supported in studies conducted outside the United States (Lapierre, Spector, Allen, Poelmans et al., 2008; Mauno, Kinnunen, & Pyykko, 2005; O'Driscoll, Poelmans, Spector, Kalliath et al., 2003). In addition, stronger perceptions that the organization is family-supportive have been associated with less intent to leave the organization (Allen, 2001; Thompson et al., 1999), greater job satisfaction (Allen, 2001; Lapierre et al., 2008), and greater family and life satisfaction (Lapierre et al., 2008).

Thompson, Andreassi, and Prottas (2005) identified the structural factors thought to serve as antecedents of work-family culture. They include: market focus (e.g., product life cycle), job demands (e.g., 24/7 service orientation), job characteristics (e.g., measurability of job performance), characteristics of the organization (product technology), and work group characteristics (group cohesiveness).

Summary

Because there have been few studies based on large representative samples of the working population and even fewer based on experimental designs, it is difficult at this point to present firm prescriptive recommendations for what organizations should and should not do in terms of specific policies, benefits, and practices. A quote from Urie Bronfenbrenner that is often repeated is that, "If you want to understand something, try to change it" (Bronfenbrenner, 1979, p. 291). Change-driven research is sorely lacking within the work-family literature (see Rapoport, Bailyn, Fletcher, & Pruitt, 2002, for an exception). Our knowledge of effective workplace practices is hampered by a limited number of intervention studies. For example, we know surprising little regarding how the implementation of flexible work policies relate to *changes* in employee WFC. This may change over the next few years as research from the Work, Family and Health Network Initiative begins to emerge.

Focus on the Globe

Overview

Dual-earner families are common in developed nations around the world (Caligiuri & Givelekian, 2008). Thus, it is no surprise that a concerted effort has been made in recent years to expand work and family research across the globe. International research, particularly from Europe and Asia, has proliferated (e.g., (Aryee, Luk, Leung, & Lo, 1999; Aryee et al., 2005; Cousins & Tang, 2004; Janssen, Peeters, de Jonge, Houkes, & Tummers, 2004). In examining issues from a global perspective, it is also important to consider societal level issues that influence work-family interactions. Accordingly, in this section, research is considered that focuses on work-family issues across societies, as well as the influence that societies have on how individuals experience their work and family lives.

International and Multicultural Research

International comparative studies of work-family issues remain relatively rare. Given the expanding global economy, this is a critical gap in the literature. Comparative studies that do exist have been limited in theoretical scope, focusing primarily on individualism-collectivism to explain cross-national differences in work-family conflict relations with other variables (Lu & Gilmour, 2005; Spector, Allen, Poelmans, Lapierre, et al., 2007; Spector, Cooper, Poelmans, Allen, et al, 2004; Yang, 2005; Yang, Chen, Choi, & Zou, 2000). These studies generally demonstrate that the relations between work-family conflict and predictors such as work demands and outcomes such as job satisfaction are weaker in collectivist societies than in individualist societies (e.g., Spector et al., 2007; Spector et al., 2004). This is attributed to the notion that in collectivist cultures, work hours are viewed as a contribution made to the family, while in individualistic societies, work hours are viewed as something that the individual does for his or her own career gain. Not all studies show differences. In a 48-country study, Hill, Yang, Hawkins and Ferris (2004) demonstrated that a model that linked work demands to WIF and job attitudes held universally across four country clusters. However, all of the participants in the study were employees of IBM. Hence one possible explanation for the findings was that the IBM culture was stronger than the country culture.

Other research suggests that work-family experiences may not be similar across all cultures. Grzywacz, Arcury, et al. (2007) found no association between WFC and health among a sample of immigrant Latino low-wage workers after controlling for job characteristics. However, these findings differed across gender in that there was a relationship between WIF and greater anxiety and depressive symptoms for women but not for men. Research by Lyness and Kropf (2005) also points to the potentially important role of gender and gender role ideology in examining work-family across cultures. In a study of European managers from 20 different countries, national gender equality was related to perceived work-family culture and the availability of flexible work arrangements, which in turn was related to work-family balance (Lyness & Kropf, 2005).

The prevalence of work-family conflict itself may differ across countries/cultures. Grzywacz, Arcury, et al. (2007) found that the degree of conflict reported by the immigrant workers in their study was infrequent compared to findings based on the typical American professional sample. In a comparison of 18 different countries with regard to work-family pressures, Spector et al. (2005) found significant mean differences in the level of work-family pressure reported by participants, with individuals from Taiwan and Hong Kong reporting the highest and individuals from the United Kingdom and Australia reporting the lowest.

Country-Level Social Policy

Social policies or government-level supports for work and family vary enormously across the world (Heymann, Earle, & Hayes, 2007; Waldfogel, 2001). For example, countries differ in terms of the existence or availability of paid leave for childbirth and adoption, affordable child care, and early education programs.

The welfare regime typology has been used as an organizing framework for understanding variation in social policy across countries (Esping-Andersen, 1990). The welfare regime typology represents the way in which the state, the market, and the family shape different backgrounds for understanding the work-family interface (den Dulk, 2005). The three distinct regimes are referred to as liberal, conservative, and social democratic. *Liberal* regimes are characterized as market-dominated (Eikemo & Bambra, 2008). In such regimes, state provision of welfare is minimal. Government interventions and regulation for work-family supports are limited and are left to market forces. The ideology of the liberal welfare regime centers on free-market capitalism with minimal state interference (Esping-Andersen, 1990). Working parents are encouraged to rely on their own resources for managing work and family, and the adoption of work-family arrangements within organizations is framed as a business case (den Dulk, 2005). Government aid that is provided is primarily means-based. *Conservative* regimes are characterized as state-dominated and occupationally related. Benefits are typically related to earnings and are administered through employers (Eikemo, & Bambra, 2008). In such regimes, the state and organizations are viewed as active participants who both should contribute to the development of work-family policy. The state provides services, but simultaneously retains social status differences. In *social democratic* regimes, the state dominates and the focus is on egalitarianism. Government takes responsibility for a wide array of social issues, including work-family arrangements such as child care and parental leave. Full employment of all citizens is encouraged.

As a liberal regime nation, it is often noted that the United States lags behind other industrialized nations in terms of social policies that help individuals manage work and family. For example, Heymann et al. (2007) reported that 169 of the 173 countries they studied offered guaranteed leave with income to women in connection with childbirth, and 98 of those countries offer 14 or more weeks of paid leave. In contrast, the United States has no federal guaranteed paid leave for mothers. In the United States, parents rely on tax credits to help with child care expenses, while child care assistance in Europe is usually provided through publicly funded programs (Waldfogel, 2001).

Greater family-related government social supports are often called for in the United States (e.g., Gornick & Meyers, 2003; Neal & Hammer, 2007).

Welfare regime research indicates that individual health tends to be best in social democratic welfare states (e.g., Chung & Muntaner, 2007; Coburn, 2004). However, there is little research linking social policy with individual outcomes such as work-family conflict. It is also worth noting that within the United States, several individual states have enacted paid family leave laws. Signed into law in 2002, California was the first state to create a paid leave program (Milkman & Appelbaum, 2004). Workers who participate in the State Disability Insurance Program are eligible for up to six weeks of partial pay each year for the purposes of bonding with a newborn or adopted child or to care for an ill family member. This program is funded by the state, not the employer. Washington approved a law in 2007 that provides up to five weeks of paid family leave due to the birth or adoption of a child. Most recently, New Jersey passed a law based on the California model. Other states are currently considering their own versions of paid leave. Research tracking the outcomes associated with these changes in policy for working parents would be informative.

An Agenda for Future Research
Overview

As underscored at the beginning of this chapter, there has been a tremendous amount of research conducted on work and family issues in the past five years alone. However, much remains to be learned. Greenhaus (2008) made the call for work-family researchers to ask new and theoretically meaningful questions with more innovative methods. Below, I describe five areas thought to be worthy of concerted research attention over the next five years.

Multilevel Models and Approaches

As the organizing structure of the review portion of this chapter illustrates, work-family interactions can naturally be viewed from several different levels of analysis. Although work-family relationships inherently involve multilevel phenomena, and researchers recognize this fact, the research itself has been primarily based on individual-level perceptions (Casper et al., 2007). For example, constructs that naturally reside at higher levels of the organization, such as culture and climate, have been studied from primarily an individual perspective (e.g., Kossek, Colquitt, & Noe, 2001; Thompson et al., 1999). Moreover, Bronfenbrenner's (1979) multilevel ecological model of human development increasingly has been used in recent years as a theoretical platform for work-family studies, but the data collected

and analyzed have been solely at the individual level (e.g., Grzywacz & Marks, 2000). Individual perceptions are important to study and are often what most influences individual behavior. However, by focusing almost entirely on individual perceptions, we are likely limiting our understanding of work-family issues.

Kozlowski and Klein (2000) describe multilevel models as those that link phenomena at one level with phenomena at another level through both bottom-up processes (e.g., from the individual to the organization) as well as top-down processes (e.g., from the organization to individuals). There have been several recent attempts to develop multilevel models that describe different aspects of the work-family interface. Most of these models address issues related to family-supportive policies. Poelmans and Sahibzada (2004) presented a multilevel framework intended to illuminate the macro- and meso-level factors thought to influence individual perceptions and the adoption of work-family policies. For example, it is proposed that companies in countries that have more extensive family-supportive policies (e.g., paid maternity leave) will be more likely to adopt organizational level family-supportive policies. Along the same lines, Poelmans and Beham (2008) developed a multilevel model of the processes involved in work-family policy allowance decisions of managers. Swody and Powell (2007) proposed a multilevel model intended to explain employee participation in family-friendly programs. Finally, Van Dyne, Kossek, and Lobel (2007) developed a cross-level model designed to examine how the individual use of flexibility influences group-level processes and outcomes. In total, these models provide a rich array of research propositions that remain to be tested.

Empirical research at multiple levels of analysis is rare. Several notable exceptions have appeared in the literature, which help demonstrate the potential fruitfulness of further study. Kopelman, Prottas, Thompson, and Jahn (2006) found that at both the individual and the work-unit levels, offering more work-family practices was associated with greater perceived organizational family support and affective commitment. In contrast, the number of programs offered was not associated with FIW or with WIF at either level. The authors also found that results were stronger at the work-unit level than at the individual level, giving credence to the notion that shared climates result in an emergent social system that relates to individuals' overall affective reactions. Major, Fletcher, Davis, and Germano (2008) examined cross-level relationships between work-family culture, leader-member exchange (LMX), coworker support, and WIF among employees from 10 different organizations who worked in the IT industry. They found that employees do form shared perceptions of the organization's work-family culture and that these perceptions indirectly relate to individual WIF through its influence on LMX and coworker support. Hammer et al. (2005) examined the use of workplace family supports (e.g., flexibility, child care) at both the couple and individual level of analysis. Findings revealed no significant longitudinal couple-use effects on WIF or job satisfaction.

There are many multilevel questions that need to be answered. Such research involves several challenges (Kozlowski & Klein, 2000). Measures designed to captured system-level constructs need to be developed. Samples that consist of multiple organizations and multiple family units will be required. The family as a unit, in particular, has rarely been examined. In addition to testing the propositions developed from the multilevel frameworks of researchers as noted above, below are several additional ideas:

- How do organization-level policies interact with government-level support to impact individual-level work-family conflict?
- Do organizations possess micro-level climates of family supportiveness in addition to organizational cultures of family support?
- How do the aggregate job demands of dual-career couples as a unit influence individual child health and behavior outcomes?
- How does aggregate family support relate to individual job performance?
- How do work group norms relate to individual experiences of work-family conflict and work-family enhancement?
- How does individual WFC relate to group-level performance?
- Can constructs such as balance be studied from the couple and/or family level?

Less Reliance on Self-Reports

Methodological limitations associated with work-family research are well documented (Casper et al., 2007). The work-family literature has been dominated by studies in which both the independent and dependent variables are based on self-report. Studies based on such designs are relatively easy and inexpensive to conduct and often serve the important function of establishing initial support for relationships prior to conducting more complex, costly, and time-consuming studies. Moreover, this is a criticism that is not necessarily unique to work-family research, as it applies to many areas of study within industrial and organizational psychology. However, it is particularly vexing for the area of work and family.

The ability to offer sound, evidence-based suggestions for organizational practice are hampered because of the limited inferences that can be drawn from such research designs. For example, relationships between variables such as WFC and health may be overstated because of statistical artifacts such as consistency effects. Several potential directions for future research that can help remedy this limitation seem particularly fruitful.

OUTCOMES

As discussed previously, work-family conflict has been an issue of particular concern because of its association with health and well-being. However, the vast majority of this work has been based on self-reported health outcomes. The inclusion of objectively measured health indicators can help lead to more firm conclusions regarding the relationship between WFC and health. Moreover, this type of evidence can provide compelling evidence to organizations and policy makers regarding the need to take action to address work-family issues.

Physiological systems have their own characteristics, which differ from those captured through self-reports of health. As noted by Sonnentag and Fritz (2006), self-reports and physiological measures do not substitute for each other, but likely reflect different underlying processes or aspects of stress responses. Indicators of health such as cortisol levels, catecholamines, and blood pressure can add to our understanding of the health effects associated with simultaneous pressures from work and family roles.

Cortisol is a stress hormone that is sensitive to socio-emotional demands at work (Lundberg, Granqvist, Hansson, Magnusson & Wallin, 1989). It can be measured relatively non-invasively, such as through saliva samples. Cortisol stimulates the mobilization of energy in demanding situations. Sustained levels of cortisol have been associated with an assortment of negative health effects, ranging from depression and immune suppression to cardiovascular disease (e.g., Bergman et al., 2008; Ganster, Fox, & Dwyer, 2001). Cortisol patterns can reflect the demands that individuals face in their work and family lives. Bergman et al. (2008) found that there is a combined effect of sex and home responsibility that contributes to cortisol release over the day. The more perceived responsibility at home, the higher the cortisol level in the evening. This finding held for both men and women. Goldstein, Shapiro, Chicz-DeMet, and Guthrie (1999) observed that married women had higher cortisol levels at night than did unmarried women.

Catecholamines such as epinephrine (adrenaline) and norepinephrine (noradrenaline) reflect the sympathetic nervous system's reaction to stress. Their levels, too, appear to be patterned based on the challenges of meeting work and family demands. Goldstein et al. (1999) showed that unmarried women experienced significant decreases in norepinephrine on off days as compared to workdays, whereas married women had similar levels of norepinephrine on off days and workdays. Frankenhaeuser, Lundberg, Fredrikson, and Melin (1989) reported that male managers' catecholamine output dropped sharply at 5 P.M., whereas female managers' norepinephrine secretion increased after work. Similarly, Lundberg and Frankenhaeuser (1999) found that the elevation of norepinephrine after work was significantly greater for women than for men, especially for women with children.

Elevated blood pressure is a significant marker for cardiovascular risk. Frankenhaeuser et al. (1989) found that male managers' blood pressure fell after work, whereas female managers' blood pressure remained high. Extensive family responsibilities, in conjunction with high job strain, were associated with high levels of systolic and diastolic blood pressure among white-collar women holding a university degree (Brisson, Laflamme, & Moisan, 1999). Similarly, Goldstein et al. (1999) found that decreases in heart rate from day to evening were significantly greater for women without children than for women with children. As mentioned previously, there is also research indicating that family-supportive supervisor behavior is associated with blood pressure (Hammer et al., 2008). Relatively inexpensive portable blood pressure monitors designed to record multiple readings throughout the day make the incorporation of blood pressure assessments more feasible than in the past.

Most of the research to date provides indirect evidence that the combination of work and family demands results in detrimental physiological responses. Research is needed that directly assesses and links reports of work-family conflict with physiological assessments. In addition, the potential positive effects of multiple role engagement should also be examined. For example, it may be useful to investigate what type of after-work family activities serve to reduce cortisol and blood pressure from day to evening. Finally, while it is important to incorporate physiological measures, it should also be noted that physiological measures are not without their own limitations (Semmer et al., 2004). For example, single readings of blood pressure are known to be unreliable. Cortisol reading levels have been found to vary across laboratories.

PREDICTORS

As mentioned earlier, the primary predictors of WIF are thought to reside in the workplace. Here again, workplace factors are often limited to self-reports. Most research linking organizational characteristics with constructs such as work-family conflict has been based on employee reports. One way to more objectively assess occupational conditions is to assess variables such as job complexity using the O*Net. Developed by the Department of Labor, O*Net is a continuously updated online database that has extensive information regarding U.S. jobs (http://online.onetcenter.org). Crouter, Lanza, Pirretti, Goodman and Neebe (2006) provide a primer on how the O*Net may be used by work-family researchers. Researchers must collect data in sufficient detail regarding occupations so that it can be further coded. For example, an occupation such as "teacher" is too vague in that O*Net has over 70 different codes for teacher. This approach can shed new light with regard to the occupational conditions that give rise to both work-family conflict and work-family enhancement.

A similar, occupationally focused approach was taken in recent research. Dierdorff and Ellington (2008) used O*Net information to capture behavior-based antecedents of work-family conflict. The authors concluded that the occupation in which someone works accounts for significant variation in WFC (based on a single item bidirectional measure). Specifically, individuals working in occupations that required greater interdependence and responsibility for others (e.g., police detectives, firefighters) reported greater WFC than did those working in occupations that required less interdependence and responsibility for others (e.g., taxi drivers, tellers).

Again, this type of methodology is not without its limitations. The use of occupational codes such as that provided by the O*Net treats all jobs from the same classification as identical, which misses potential differences in individual job design (Morgeson, & Campion, 1997). Thus, such approaches may be considered as complements rather than replacements of self-reports. Nevertheless, including alternative assessments of workplace factors is important to those interested in organizational policies and work-family cultures because this measurement approach can better clarify the role of environmental factors that induce WFC and related health outcomes (Dohrenwend, Dohrenwend, Dodson, & Shrout, 1984). Although individuals' perceptions and feelings regarding work experiences are helpful to study, it is primarily so when one's purpose is to try to change those perceptions. When the interest is to contribute to job design and/or develop interventions that address a specific need, it is more helpful to understand objective stress exposure (Frese & Zapf, 1999). Organizational work-family interventions typically are not designed to change people's perceptions of WFC. Interventions are focused on changing the conditions of the work environment that create the opportunity for WFC to occur; thus an objective standard is needed from which to evaluate the success of such interventions. Accordingly, more objective assessments of the work environment should be considered a welcome addition to the work-family literature.

Affect, Emotion, and Self-regulation

It is becoming clear that affect plays an important role in both positive and negative work-family experiences. As described previously, trait negative affect has been strongly associated with work-family conflict (e.g., Bruck & Allen, 2003). Recent work using experience sampling indicated that the affective states experienced at work continued at home after controlling for stable individual differences and work conditions (Ilies et al., 2007). Affect is a key variable in Greenhaus and Powell's (2006) theory of work-family enrichment, as well as in theories of positive spillover (e.g., Hanson et al., 2006). Still, our understanding of the role that affect and self-regulatory strategies play in work-family experiences is at a nascent stage. Programmatic research with systematic integration of affect within the work-family literature is needed. There are several existing bodies of literature from which work-family researchers may draw inspiration for such efforts.

George and Brief's (1996) theory concerning motivational agendas provides one foundation for developing a theory of affect in work-family relationships. As noted by George and Brief (1996), people have motivational agendas involving many possible selves that cross both work and non-work domains. Possible selves refer to what people want to become. Individuals are not singularly directed, but rather they strive to become many things. For example, individuals strive to be accomplished professionals, caring parents, and loving spouses. However, individuals do not have the capacity to focus motivationally on all possible selves simultaneously. Feelings serve as a cue as to which of the motivational selves require attention. That is, feelings serve as a source of information used to direct motivational attention (Schwarz, 1990). For example, a sick child can shift the motivational attention of an individual away from the self as high job performer to the self as caring parent.

One feeling that is part of the popular discourse regarding work and family, but that has received little scholarly attention, is guilt. Guilt has long been linked with working parents, especially mothers. Current thinking is that guilt can be understood as a response to threats to interpersonal attachments (Baumeister, Stillwell, & Heatherton, 1994). When faced with a work-family conflict, guilt may occur if/when an individual perceives that he/she had a choice in the matter (e.g., a parent chooses to work on Saturday rather than attend a child's soccer game), the individual cannot fully justify the decision (working Saturday was not required by the employer), the employee's values about balancing work and family life are violated (the employee believes weekends should be reserved for the family), and the individual perceived that the action was foreseeable/preventable (e.g., the employee knew about the child's soccer game; Kubany et al., 1996; McElwain & Korabik, 2005).

Guilt typically has a negative connotation, but it can motivate reparative behavior, such as confessing, apologizing, undoing, or repairing (Tangney, 1990). That is, it can serve as a signal that a motivational self needs attention. In the example used above, the parent may apologize to the child and provide the child with his or her undivided attention all day Sunday in an effort to restore his "caring parent" motivational self. Guilt can also be a tool used by role senders (a mother expresses her unhappiness with her son for not calling home more often). Individuals induce guilt in their relationship partners as a behavioral change tactic (e.g., as a way to get one partner to spend more time with the other). Investigating such dynamics sets the stage for new insights into understanding work-family experiences.

Another affective-laden topic that could inform the work-family literature is rumination. Rumination is defined as "the process of thinking perseveratively about one's feelings and problems rather than in terms of the specific content of thoughts" (Nolen-Hoeksema, Wisco, & Lyubomirsky, 2008, p. 400). Self-regulation theories regard rumination as initiated by perceived discrepancies between one's current state or situation and a goal or desired state (e.g., Carver & Scheier, 1998; Martin & Tesser, 1996). For example, if an individual has the goal of maintaining a loving marriage and a fulfilling career but is frequently required to be out of town for work-related travel, she is likely to focus on the discrepancy between her goal (devoted wife) and her current state (absentee wife). Self-regulation theory proposes that rumination can be adaptive or maladaptive. In this case, the result may be adaptive if the woman takes action to resolve the discrepancy (finds another job that does not require travel) or she modifies her goal (she quits work and abandons the goal of pursuing a fulfilling career) or be maladaptive (she perseverates regarding the amount of travel needed to advance her career and lack of time with spouse).

Perseverating on self-discrepancies results in negative affect (Pyszczynski & Greenberg, 1987). Rumination has also been found to predict depression, binge eating, and binge drinking (Nolen-Hoeksema et al., 2008). In addition, chronic rumination can result in the loss of social support, as friends and family members become frustrated with the ruminator's need to continue to discuss his or her problems (Nolen-Hoeksema & Davis, 1999). Rumination should be examined as a response to work-family conflict, as it may be one of the mechanisms that explain the relationship between work-family conflict and negative outcomes such as depression and health behaviors. Moreover, incorporating rumination into work-family research could reveal new ways in which men and women differ in response to WFC. For example, women are more likely to use rumination to regulate their negative moods, while men are more likely to medicate with alcohol (Nolen-Hoeksema & Corte, 2004).

Another focal point that involves attentional resources for further study is distractions. Distractions play a key role in the experience of work and family conflict. Individuals commonly find themselves participating in one role while simultaneously feeling preoccupied by thoughts, emotions, or demands associated with another role (Ashforth, Kreiner, & Fugate, 2000; Cardenas, Major, & Bernas, 2004). For example, consider the parent who is thinking about work while his or her child is relating a problem in school that day. Such distractions can erode role quality and can result

in negative performance outcomes. Self-regulation involves the exertion of control over the self by the self (Muraven & Baumeister, 2000). Self-regulatory skills enable individuals to maintain focus in a given domain, particularly when demands in the other domain are high.

Work-family research has primarily focused on externally generated conflict from role senders, as opposed to internally generated preoccupation or distraction. Cardenas et al. (2004) investigated the total number of hours per week that women felt distracted by family while working and total number of hours they felt distracted by work while with family. Participants reported more work distractions at home ($M = 9.30$) than family distractions at work ($M = 5.54$), despite spending more hours at work than at home. This suggests that individuals have a more difficult time regulating their focus on their family role than on their work role and is consistent with research suggesting that the family role boundary is more permeable than is the work role boundary (Eagle, Miles, & Icenogle, 1997). A related line of research is that of psychological detachment. Psychological detachment from work involves not participating in work-related activities or thoughts when away from the workplace. The inability to detach from one's job has been associated with indicators of poor well-being, such as fatigue and sleep complaints (e.g., Grebner, Semmer, & Elfering, 2005). Sonnentag, Mojza, Binnewies, and Scholl (2008) found that individuals who detached from the job during the week reported a positive affective state at the end of the workweek. The inability to focus psychological attention on members within the social system who share our physical location may ultimately be damaging to both the individual and his or her relationship partners.

Research on distraction and detachment may be further expanded by considering the growing body of literature regarding the concept of *mindfulness*. Mindfulness has been defined as "intentionally paying attention to present-moment experience (physical sensations, perceptions, affective states, thoughts and imagery) in a nonjudgmental way, thereby cultivating a stable and nonreactive awareness" (Carmody, Reed, Kristeller, & Merriam, 2008, p. 394). It has been lamented that the fast-paced, technology-overloaded nature of today's society has eroded opportunities for deep focus, awareness, and reflection (Jackson, 2008). Cultivating a mindful awareness can be a valuable self-regulatory behavior that gives individuals a greater sense of control (Carmody et al., 2008). It is consistent with self-determination theory, which promotes the individual's ability to choose behaviors consistent with one's needs, values, and life interests (Kostanski & Hassed, 2008; Ryan & Deci, 2000). Being aware of moods and thoughts should enable individuals to fully attend to others within the moment, as well as to identify which motivational self needs to be called into attention.

Therapeutic interventions have been developed intended to help cultivate "everyday mindfulness." Such interventions have been associated with improvement in depression, social functioning, and anxiety (Grossman, Niemann, Schmidt, & Walach, 2004). Recently, a work-site mindfulness-based intervention was investigated (Klatt, Buckworth, & Malarkey, 2009), with results that showed the intervention resulted in reduced stress among a group of working adults. The two critical components to mindfulness are: (a) self-regulation of attention, and (b) the adoption of an orientation toward one's experiences in the present moment; thus it has the potential to serve as a means to help individuals cope with the management of work and non-work boundaries. It would be particularly interesting to examine the connection between the ability to practice mindfulness and work-family balance.

Finally, work-family researchers may also be informed by neuroscience research. There may be a neurobiological basis to an individual's ability to manage high demands between work and family. The prefrontal cortex (PFC) is important for attentional control, and when people are stressed, their PFC does not function optimally. The PFC is critical to the regulation of behavior, attention, and affect (Brennan & Arnsten, 2008). Neuroscience research is beginning to elucidate the cognitive changes that occur in response to stressors. Specifically, the amygdala may be turned on while the PFC, which is the higher cognitive center, is turned off (Arnsten, 1998). This is important in that the PFC inhibits distractions, permitting individuals to plan and organize effectively. In addition, inhibition of the PFC impairs the ability to multitask (Diamond, Campbell, Park, Halonen, & Zoladz, 2007). Thus, the PFC plays a key role in the skills and abilities that are important to the effective management of work and non-work. Moreover, during stress, the amygdala induces catecholamine release in the prefrontal cortex, which results in cognitive dysfunction. The PFC functions optimally under conditions of moderate catecholamine release. PFC working-memory functions are impaired under conditions of high catecholamine release. Fatigue can result in underproduction of catecholamines, and stress can result in overproduction. This is important in that, as reviewed earlier, catecholamine release has been associated with patterns of work-family demands (e.g., Lundberg & Frankenhaeuser, 1999).

In short, neuroscience research may be able to help us understand the brain processes involved in the ability to self-regulate work and family roles.

Understanding the Role of Individual Differences

There has been some tension within the work-family literature regarding placing the onus for the management of work and family on the individual versus the organization. One point of view is that organizational barriers and constraints are the primary drivers of work-family conflict and that the degree to which an individual experiences work-family conflict is largely driven by his or her work and/or family situation (e.g., Lewis, Gambles, & Rapoport, 2007). Recommendations for managing work and family often focus on organization- or government-level policy (Neal & Hammer, 2007). Employer-centered solutions and workplace redesign are thought to be the needed solutions (Eby et al., 2005). As noted previously, existing models of key constructs within the work-family literature, such as work-family conflict, do not take into account dispositional differences. It has been argued that viewing concepts such as work-life balance from the individual perspective is akin to "blaming the victim" (Grzywacz & Carlson, 2007). Lewis et al. (2007) further suggest that there are numerous constraints to personal choice in contemporary contexts. For example, high commitment management practices are viewed as manipulative maneuvers designed to encourage workers to increase efforts and work harder to improve performance.

Such a focus seemingly gives the individual little direct control over his or her work-family situation. Individuals are free agents who make a series of daily life decisions that impact the opportunity for work and family to conflict and/or harmonize with each other (Poelmans, 2005a). Because attention has been focused primarily on organizational benefits and systems, less research has focused on what individuals can do to actively balance their work and family lives. Person-situation debates are not uncommon in organizational research. However, most of the field of industrial and organizational psychology has accepted the notion that dispositional differences can be a significant determinant of how individuals experience and perform within the workplace (e.g., Judge & Locke, 1993; Staw & Ross, 1985). Moreover, a substantial body of research has shown that personal characteristics can influence the subjective experience and appraisal of a situation (see Thompson, Poelmans, Allen, & Andreassi, 2007, for a review of the work-family and coping literature).

Research concerning the personal characteristics, strategies, and decisions made by individuals is needed to garner a more comprehensive understanding of work-family experiences (Greenhaus, 2008; Parasuraman & Greenhaus, 2002). The evidence for individual differences does not negate the need for, nor the potential efficacy of, organizational interventions designed to help individuals be successful in both their work and their family roles. Rather, it potentially broadens our repertoire of possible solutions to individual work-family dilemmas. Two specific suggestions for focus are described below.

INTEGRATION/SEGMENTATION

One individual difference that has recently been examined is a person's preference for segmenting his or her work and family lives versus integrating them. Segmentation/integration preferences are based on boundary theory (Ashforth et al., 2000; Nippert-Eng, 1996). Boundary role theory suggests that individuals develop boundaries to attempt to manage their work and family roles (Ashforth et al., 2000). Segmenters prefer the two domains to be kept apart, while integrators prefer to remove boundaries and blend work and family together. Current conceptualizations place integration and segmentation at opposite ends of the same continuum (Kreiner, 2006). It been proposed that there are costs and benefits to either extreme on the continuum (Ashforth et al., 2000). Role segmentation allows for less role blurring of role boundaries, but makes transitions between role boundaries more difficult. Effective boundary management is thought to facilitate role performance in both work and family domains (Edwards & Rothbard, 1999).

There have been only a handful of studies to date that have directly tested segmentation/integration preferences. Kreiner (2006) found no relationship between segmentation/integration and WIF. The items used in Kreiner (2006) all refer to preferences with regard to keeping work separate from home (e.g., "I don't like to think about work when I am at home."). Shockley and Allen (2010) used the same measure and found no relationship with WIF and a slightly higher, but non-significant ($r = .13$)

relationship with FIW in the direction of suggesting that a stronger segmentation preference was associated with more FIW. Shockley and Allen (2010) also reported that a stronger segmentation preference was associated with less use of flextime and flexplace. In contrast to Shockley and Allen (2010), Kossek, Lautsch, and Eaton (2006) reported that those who preferred integration telecommuted less. Their findings also indicated that individuals who preferred integration reported more FIW than those who preferred segmentation; however, the correlation was small ($r = .16$). No relationship with WIF was detected. It is interesting to note that the items developed by Kossek et al. (2006) are more reflective of keeping family out of the workplace ("I prefer to not talk about my family issues with most people I work with"), while others do not specify direction ("I actively strive to keep my family and work-life separate").

The findings to date suggest several directions for future research. First, the direction of the preference may matter. That is, individuals may vary in terms of the extent that they prefer to keep work out of the home versus home out of work. In addition, by placing segmentation and integration on a continuum, the extent that individuals may engage in dual strategies is lost. Finally, it seems important to separate preferences from behaviors or strategies. The measure developed by Kossek et al. (2006) gets closer to assessment of the active strategies that individuals may choose to use versus their stated preferences. It seems important to develop measures that tap into the actual strategies that individuals use to manage their work and non-work boundaries and to recognize that those strategies may vary both within and across domains. Moreover, discrepancies between preferences and required strategies may be interesting to examine. A wide range of outcomes should be examined, such as work-family enhancement and work-family balance. For example, it may be that integration increases conflict, but also increases work-family enhancement. Finally, mediating processes that may be involved should also be examined. For example, integration strategies may result in what Allport (1933) referred to as *partial inclusion*. Partial inclusion theory recognizes that individuals are members of multiple social systems and have multiple competing roles, both physically and psychologically. For example, individuals who bring family to work-related events such as professional conferences may find themselves unable to fully engage in either role, thus decreasing their satisfaction in both.

DECISION-MAKING PERSPECTIVE

Decisions that involve work and family roles occur on a daily basis. Choices are made, such as whether to allocate time to work or to family, to accept or decline a promotion requiring relocation and the loss of a spouse's job, and whether to help a spouse with the dishes or to read a report in preparation for a work meeting the next day. Such decisions make up the fabric of everyday working lives.

Work-family decisions are important to examine from both an individual- and a couple-level perspective. Research is emerging that examines the decisions that individuals make with regard to their work and family lives (Poelmans, 2005a; Greenhaus & Powell, 2003; Powell & Greenhaus, 2006). For example, Greenhaus and Powell (2003) used an experimental vignette study to investigate the factors that influence an individual's decision in participate in a conflicting work versus family activity. The relative salience of work and family roles had the strongest influence on the decision. However, the decision was also influenced by external pressure received from role senders (managers and spouses). This study was followed by a critical incidents study in which participants were asked to describe a time when they faced a difficult choice between participation in a work activity and participation in a family activity (Powell & Greenhaus, 2006). This study illustrates how, when confronted with difficult choices, individuals may try to find solutions that prevent a decrement in performance in either role (e.g, mobilize support from others). Further study is needed to examine the long-term effects on the self and on others of various decisions and decision-making strategies.

The specific ways that dual career couples negotiate and make decisions regarding their work and family roles is not well understood. As noted by Parasuraman and Greenhaus (2002), it would be instructive to investigate how dual-earner couples make decisions about the relative priority of each partner's career and family. There have been several attempts to classify couples based on how they share involvement in home and career. Hall and Hall (1980) described four types of couples. *Accommodating* couples are those in which each party is highly involved in a different domain (e.g., husband is highly involved in work and wife is highly involved in home). *Allied* couples have members who are both involved in the same sphere, and neither is concerned with perfection in the other. *Adversarial* couples are those in which both members are highly involved in work and each want

the other member to do more home tasks. Finally, *acrobats* are couples in which both members are highly involved in both home and work. Gilbert (1993) used the term *participant dual-career families* to designate couples in which parenting is shared but household duties are primarily the wife's. *Role-sharing relationships* are those in which both members of the couple share responsibility for parenting and household duties.

Such classification systems are helpful in a descriptive sense but do not provide information regarding the processes that occur by which couples evolve to form a particular type of lifestyle. For example, many couples may begin as egalitarian earners in which they are both career and family focused but then shift into a male career-dominant, female family-dominant pattern as children enter the picture. What are the within-couple negotiations and processes that unfold over time and underlie such shifts? Research that attempts to assess decisions at the couple level of analysis, as well as subsequent health and well-being outcomes for both the individual and the couple, is needed.

Capturing Change Dynamics and Time

The issue of time has long played a central role in the study of work and family experiences. Time scarcity is a prominent element in the development of theory concerning multiple role engagement. Time-based conflict is a key dimension of work-family conflict research. Zimbardo (2002) notes that we are a nation that is perpetually trapped in a time crunch. Individuals opine that if they only had more time, they could better balance their work and family life. "Take Back Your Time" is an initiative intended to challenge overwork (de Graaf, 2003). Many organizational policy initiatives are based on trying to help individuals manage time. For example, workplace flexibility is thought to be important because it gives individuals more control over the temporal elements of their work life. However, we also know that time spent in a role does not completely capture the subjective experiences that contribute to reports of WFC (Cardenas et al., 2004).

A more nuanced approach to the way that we think about time and use the time construct may reveal new insights into work-family interactions. Organizational behavior theorists have argued that time should play a more important role in theory and theory building (George & Jones, 2000; Mitchell & James, 2001; Roe, 2008). Individuals' state of existence in the present is closely connected to their past and to their future (George & Jones, 2000). For example, in attempting to make a work-family decision (Should I take a promotion that involves relocation and will it result in my spouse leaving a job she loves?), individuals may look to the past (I relocated for my spouse last time), as well as to the future (this will be the last time we relocate). As noted by Greenhaus and Allen (2010) in thinking about work-life balance, individuals may reflect on their past, present, and current situations.

Incorporating the psychological construct of *time perspective* may help researchers begin to understand ways in which time plays a role in work-family experiences beyond quantifying objective units of hours allocated to the work and to the family domains. Time perspective refers to an individual's way of relating to the psychological concepts of past, present, and future (Boniwell & Zimbardo, 2004). Time perspectives can be "balanced." Optimally balanced time perspectives blend, past, present, and future components and can be engaged in a flexible manner that best fits the situation's demands and individual needs and values. Boniwell and Zimbardo (2004) argue that a time-balanced individual is capable of operating within a temporal mode that is appropriate to the situation. When with families and friends, the individual is truly with them. When working, the individual is fully engaged in the work role. This ties in with the concept of mindfulness described previously. For those with a strong future orientation, enjoyment of the moment can be sacrificed in order to achieve work-related goals.

CHANGE DYNAMICS

An often-repeated anecdote in reference to seeking work-family balance is, "No one on their deathbed ever said, 'I wish I spent more time at work.'" Contrary to this popular homily, meta-analytic research regarding the content of regret shows that individuals are more likely to express regrets regarding career than they are about family (Roese & Summerville, 2005). This apparent discrepancy helps to illustrate the importance of furthering our understanding of work-family decisions and dynamics from a long-term, life course perspective. The vast majority of work-family studies have been cross-sectional (Casper et al., 2007). Calls for more longitudinal research have occurred for many years within the work-family literature (Christensen & Staines, 1990). While longitudinal studies are beginning to emerge with greater frequency (e.g., Hammer, Neal, et al., 2005), few studies to date

capture long-term change or even long-term retrospective approaches in family circumstances and dynamics. Career and family priorities can shift across the life course, often in response to major life transitions (Sweet & Moen, 2006). Moreover, long-term study designs are also important because the dependent variables that are often of interest to work-family researchers have varying time lags (Frese & Zapf, 1988; Semmer et al., 2004).

Moen and colleagues have enriched the work-family field by incorporating a life course perspective into work-family research (Moen, 2003; Sweet & Moen, 2006). The Cornell Couples and Careers Study examined dual career couples in seven life stages. Life stages were operationalized based on primarily on family stage. That is, seven groups were created, based on parental status and age of children (Roehling et al., 2003). Results revealed that FIW varied significantly across life stage for both men and women. FIW was highest for parents with preschool children and was lower among groups as children grew older. Interestingly, WIF was highest for younger couples without children. With regard to work-family enhancement, FWE varied across life stages for women but not for men. Mothers with young children reported less FWE than did women who were yet to have children. FWE was again higher among women with older children. WFE did not vary across life stage for men or women. These findings begin to elucidate the potential ways in which work-family relationships may differ across the life course; however, they are based on cross-sectional data. Moreover, the sample was restricted to middle-age, middle-class professionals.

Long-term studies that incorporate life-span development issues represent an important future direction for work-family researchers. Career development researchers have long incorporated developmental models into their understanding of how careers unfold across the life span (e.g., see Greenhaus, Callanan, & Godshalk, 2000 for a review). Baltes and Dickson (2001) have suggested that life-span models, such as selective organization and compensation (SOC), can be used help understand individual differences in work-family conflict, and subsequent research has shown that the use of SOC behaviors relates to less WIF and FIW (Baltes & Heydens-Gahir, 2003). However, the data again are cross-sectional.

In sum, there is a need to understand the role that time plays in work-family dynamics in more complex ways. As noted by Mitchell and James (2001) in their excellent review of time in organizational theory, "Nonlinear relationships over time are possible, as are cyclical and oscillating ones. Change can be incremental or discontinuous. Cycles can spiral up or down, and the intensity can change. Various relationships can have rhythms or patterns over time" (p. 532). Thinking about work-family dynamics with these time complexities in mind offers rich fodder for future research.

Conclusion

With training that focuses on the well-being of both individuals and organizations, industrial and organizational psychologists are ideally suited for conducting research on the intersection of work and family roles. The dynamics at the center of the work-family intersection will continue to evolve such that new issues, concerns, and benefits can be expected to consistently arise. The continued development of the field will depend on innovative research that transcends any single culture, discipline, or level of analysis. It is hoped that this chapter provides a foundation and springboard for many future such studies.

References

Adams, G. A., King, L. A., & King, D. W. (1996). Relationships of job and family involvement, family social support, and work-family conflict with job and life satisfaction. *Journal of Applied Psychology, 81*, 411–420.

Allen, T. D. (2001). Family-supportive work environments: The role of organizational perceptions. *Journal of Vocational Behavior, 58*, 414–435.

Allen, T. D., & Armstrong, J. (2006). Further examination of the link between work-family conflict and physical health: The role of health-related behaviors. *American Behavioral Scientist, 49*, 1204–1221.

Allen, T. D., Herst, D. E. L., Bruck, C. S., & Sutton, M. (2000). Consequences associated with work-to-family conflict: A review and agenda for future research. *Journal of Occupational Health Psychology, 5*, 278–308.

Allen, T. D., Johnson, R., Saboe, K., Cho, E., Dumani, S., & Evans, S. (2012). Dispositional variables and work-family conflict: A meta-analysis. *Journal of Vocational Behavior, 80*, 17–26.

Allen, T. D., & Russell, J. E. A. (1999). Parental leave of absence: Some not so family friendly implications. *Journal of Applied Social Psychology, 29*, 166–191.

Allen, T. D., & Shockley, K. (2009). Flexible work arrangements: Help or hype? In D. R. Crane & E. J. Hill (Eds). *Handbook of families and work: Interdisciplinary perspectives* (pp. 265–284). Lanham, MD: University Press of America.

Allen, T. D., Shockley, K. M., & Poteat, L. F. (2008). Workplace factors associated with family dinner behaviors. *Journal of Vocational Behavior, 73*, 336–342.

Allis P., & O'Driscoll, M. (2008). Positive effects of nonwork-to-work facilitation on well-being in work, family and personal domains. *Journal of Managerial Psychology, 23*, 273–291.

Allport, F. H. (1933). *Institutional behavior*. Chapel Hill: University of North Carolina Press.

Anderson, S. E., Coffey B. S., & Byerly, R. T. (2002). Formal organizational initiatives and informal workplace practices: Links to work-family conflict and job-related outcomes. *Journal of Management, 28*, 787–810.

Arnsten, A. F. T. (1998). The biology of being frazzled. *Science, 280*, 1711–1712.

Arrighi, B. A., & Maume, D. J. (2000). Workplace subordination and men's avoidance of housework. *Journal of Family Issues, 21*, 464–487.

Aryee, S. (1992). Antecedents and outcomes of work-family conflicts among married professional women: Evidence from Singapore. *Human Relations, 45*, 813–837.

Aryee, S., Luk, V., Leung, A., & Lo, S. (1999). Role stressors, interrole conflict, and well-being: The moderating influence of spousal support and coping behaviors among employed parents in Hong Kong. *Journal of Vocational Behavior, 54*, 259–278.

Aryee, S., Srinivas, E. S., & Tan, H. H. (2005). Rhythms of life: Antecedents and outcomes of work-family balance in employed parents. *Journal of Applied Psychology, 90*, 132–146.

Ashforth, B. E., Kreiner, G. E., & Fugate, M. (2000). All in a day's work: Boundaries and micro role transitions. *Academy of Management Review, 25*, 472–491.

Bakker, A. B., Westman, M., van Emmerik, I. J. H. (2009). Advancements in crossover theory. *Journal of Managerial Psychology, 24*, 206–219.

Baltes, B. B., Briggs, T. E., Huff, J. W., Wright, J. A., & Neuman G. A. (1999). Flexible and compressed workweek schedules: A meta-analysis of their effects on work-related criteria. *Journal of Applied Psychology, 84*(4), 496–513.

Baltes, B. B., & Dickson, M. W. (2001). Using life-span models in industrial-organizational psychology: The theory of selective optimization with compensation. *Applied Developmental, 5*, 51–62.

Baltes, B. B., & Heydens-Gahir, H. A. (2003). Reduction of work-family conflict through the use of selection, optimization, and compensation behaviors. *Journal of Applied Psychology, 88*, 1005–1018.

Barnett, R. C. (2006). Relationship of the number and distribution of work hours to health and quality-of-life (QOL) outcomes. In P. L. Perrewe & D. C. Ganster (Eds.). *Research in occupational stress and well being* (Vol. 5, pp. 99–138). Oxford: Elsevier.

Barnett, R. C., & Baruch, G. K. (1985). Women's involvement in multiple roles and psychological distress. *Journal of Personality and Social Psychology, 49*, 135–145.

Baumeister, R. G., Stillwell, A. M., & Heatherton, T. F. (1994). Guilt: An interpersonal approach. *Psychological Bulletin, 115*, 243–267.

Beck, M. (2008). Enjoy being unbalanced, urges expert. http://www.cnn.com/2008/LIVING/worklife/05/21/o.balance/index.html. Accessed August 22, 2009.

Behson, S. J. (2005). The relative contribution of formal and informal organizational work-family support. *Journal of Vocational Behavior, 66*, 487–500.

Bellavia, G., & Frone, M. R. (2005). Work-family conflict. In J. Barling, E. K. Kelloway, & M. R. Frone (Eds.), *Handbook of work stress* (pp. 113–147). Thousand Oaks, CA: Sage.

Bergman, B., Ahmad, F., & Stewart, D. E. (2008). Work family balance, stress, and salivary cortisol in men and women academic physicians. *International Journal of Behavioral Medicine, 15,* 54–61.

Bianchi, S. M., Casper, L. M., & King, R. B. (2005). *Work, family, health, and well-being.* Mahwah, NJ: Erlbaum.

Bianchi, S. M., Robinson, J. P., & Milkie, M. A. (2006). *Changing rhythms of American family life.* ASA Rose Series. New York: Sage.

Blood, R. O., & Wolfe, D. M. (1960). *Husbands and wives.* New York: McMillan.

Bond, T., Galinsky, E., Kim, S., & Brownfield, E. (2005). *National study of employers.* New York: Families and Work Institute.

Bond, T., Thompson, C., Galinsky, E., & Prottas, D. (2002). *Highlights of the national study of the changing workforce.* New York: Families and Work Institute.

Boniwell, I., & Zimbardo, P. G. (2004). Balancing one's time perspective in pursuit of optimal functioning. In P. A. Linley & S. Joseph (Eds.), *Positive psychology in practice* (pp. 165–178). Hoboken, NJ: John Wiley & Sons.

Bowman, S. A., Gortmaker, S. L., Ebbeling, C. B., Pereira, M. A., & Ludwig, D. S. (2004). Effects of fast-food consumption on energy intake and diet quality among children in a national household survey. *Pediatrics, 113,* 112–118.

Boyar, S. L., & Mosley, D. C. (2007). The relationship between core self-evaluations and work and family satisfaction: The mediating role of work-family conflict and facilitation. *Journal of Vocational Behavior, 71,* 265–281.

Breaugh, J. A., & Frye, N. K. (2008). Work-family conflict: The importance of family-friendly employment practices and family-supportive supervisors. *Journal of Business and Psychology, 22,* 345–353.

Brennan, A. R., & Arnsten, A. F. T. (2008). Neuronal mechanisms underlying attention deficit hyperactivity disorder: The influence of arousal on prefrontal cortical function. *Annals of the New York Academy of Sciences, 1129,* 236–245.

Brewer, A. M. (2000). Work design for flexible work scheduling: Barriers and gender implications. *Gender, Work, and Organization, 7,* 33–44.

Brines, J. (1994). Economic dependency, gender, and the division of labor at home. *American Journal of Sociology, 100,* 652–688.

Brisson, C., Laflamme, N., & Moisan, J. (1999). Effect of family responsibilities and job strain on ambulatory blood pressure among white-collar women. *Psychosomatic Medicine, 61,* 205–213.

Bronfenbrenner, U. (1979). *The ecology of human development.* Cambridge, MA: Harvard University Press.

Brough, P., & Kalliath, T. (2009). Work-family balance: Theoretical and empirical advancements. *Journal of Organizational Behavior, 30,* 581–585.

Bruck, C. S., & Allen, T. D. (2003). The relationship between big five traits, negative affectivity, type A behavior, and work-family conflict. *Journal of Personality Vocational Behavior, 63,* 457–472.

Burke, R. J., & Greenglass, E. R. (1987). Work and family. In C. L. Cooper & I. T. Robertson (Eds.), *International review of industrial and organizational psychology* (pp. 273–320). New York: Wiley.

Butler, A. B., Grzywacz, J. G., Bass, B. L., & Linney, K. D. (2005). Extending the demands-control model: A daily diary study of job characteristics, work-family conflict and work-family facilitation. *Journal of Occupational and Organizational Psychology, 78,* 155–169.

Byron, K. (2005). A meta-analytic review of work-family conflict and its antecedents. *Journal of Vocational Behavior, 62,* 169–198.

Caligiuri, P., & Givelekian, N. (2008). Strategic human resources and work-life balance. In S. A. Y. Poelmans & P. Caligiuri (Eds.), *Harmonizing work, family, and personal life* (pp. 19–38). Cambridge: Cambridge University Press.

Cardenas, R. A., Major, D. A., & Bernas, K. H. (2004). Exploring work and family distractions: Antecedents and outcomes. *International Journal of Stress Management, 11,* 346–365.

Carlson, D. S. (1999). Personality and role variables as predictors of three forms of work-family conflict. *Journal of Vocational Behavior, 55,* 236–253.

Carlson, D. S., & Frone, M. R. (2003). Relation of behavioral and psychological involvement to a new four-factor conceptualization of the work–family interference. *Journal of Business and Psychology, 17,* 515–535.

Carlson, D. S., & Grzywacz, J. G. (2008). Reflections and future directions on measurement in work-family research. In K. Korabik, D. Lero, & D. Whitehead (Eds.), *Handbook of work-family integration* (pp. 57–73). Amsterdam: Academic Press.

Carlson, D. S., Kacmar, K. M., Wayne, J. H., & Grzywacz, J. G. (2006). Measuring the positive side of the work-family interface: Development and validation of a work-family enrichment scale. *Journal of Vocational Behavior, 68,* 131–164.

Carlson, D. S., Kacmar, K. M., & Williams, L. J. (2000). Construction and initial validation of a multidimensional measure of work-family conflict. *Journal of Vocational Behavior, 56,* 249–276.

Carlson, D. S., & Perrewe, P. L. (1999). The role of social support in the stressor-strain relationship: An examination of work-family conflict. *Journal of Management, 25,* 513–540.

Carmody, J., Reed, R., Kristeller, J., & Merriam, P. (2008). Mindfulness, spirituality, and health-related symptoms. *Journal of Psychosomatic Research, 64,* 393–403.

Carver, C. S., & Scheier, M. F. (1998). *On the self-regulation of behavior.* Cambridge: Cambridge University Press.

CASA (2005, September). *The importance of family dinners II.* The National Center on Addiction and Substance Abuse at Columbia University.

Casper, W. J., Eby, L. T., Bordeaux, C., Lockwood, A., & Lambert, D. (2007). A review of research methods in IO/OB work-family research. *Journal of Applied Psychology, 92,* 28–43.

Chatterji, P., & Markowitz, S. (2004). *Does the length of maternity leave affect maternal health?* NBER Working Paper No. W10206. Cambridge, MA.

Christensen, K. E., & Staines, G. L. (1990). Flextime: A viable solution to work/family conflict? *Journal of Family Issues, 11*(4), 455–476.

Chung, H., & Muntaner, C. (2007). Welfare state matters: A typological multilevel analysis of wealthy countries. *Health Policy, 80,* 328–339.

Cleveland, J. B. (2005). What is success? Who defines it? Perspectives on the criterion problem as it relates to work and family. In E. E. Kossek & S. J. Lambert (Eds.), *Work and life integration: Organizational, cultural, and individual perspectives* (pp. 319–345). Mahwah, NJ: Lawrence Erlbaum Associates.

Coburn, D. (2004). Beyond the income inequity hypothesis: Class, neo-liberalism, and health inequalities. *Social Science Medicine, 58,* 41–56.

Coltrane, S. (2000). Research on household labor: Modeling and measuring the social embeddedness of routine family work. *Journal of Marriage the Family, 62*, 1208–1233.

Comfort, D., Johnson, K., & Wallace, D. (2003). *Part-time work and family-friendly practices in Canadian workplaces* (The Evolving Workplace Series, No. 71–584-MIE No. 6). Ottawa: Statistics Canada/Human Resources Development Canada.

Cousins, C. R., & Tang, N. (2004). Working time and work and family conflict in the Netherlands, Sweden and the UK. *Work, Employment & Society, 18*, 531–549.

Crouter, A. C. (1984). Spillover from family to work: The neglected side of the work-family interface. *Human Relations, 37*, 425–442.

Crouter, A. C., & Bumpus, M. F. (2001). Linking parents' work stress to child and adolescent psychological adjustment. *Current Directions in Psychological Science, 10*, 156–159.

Crouter, A. C., Helms-Erikson, H., Updegraff, K., & McHale, S. M. (1999). Conditions underlying parents' knowledge about children's daily lives in middle childhood: Between- and within-family comparisons. *Child Development, 70*, 246–259.

Crouter, A. C., Lanza, S. T., Pirretti, A., Goodman, W. B., & Neebe, E. (2006). The O*Net jobs classification system: A primer for family researchers. *Family Relations, 55*, 461–472.

Crouter, A. C., MacDermid, S., McHale, S. M., & Perry-Jenkins, M. (1990). Parental monitoring and perceptions of children's school performance and conduct in dual- and single-earner families. *Developmental Psychology, 26*, 649–657.

Crouter, A. C., & McHale, S. M. (2005). Work, family, and children's time: Implications for youth. In S. Bianchi, L. Casper, & R. B. King (Eds.), *Work, family, health, and well-being*. Mahwah, NJ: Lawrence Erlbaum Associates.

de Graaf, J. (2003). *Take back your time: Fighting overwork & time poverty in America*. San Francisco: Berrett-Koehler.

den Dulk, L. (2005). Workplace work-family arrangements: A study and explanatory framework of differences between organizational provisions in different welfare states. In S. A. Y. Poelmans (Ed.), *Work and family: An international research perspective* (pp. 211–238). Mahwah, NJ: Lawrence Erlbaum Associates.

Devine, C. M., Jastran, M., Jabs, J., Wethington, E., Farell, T. J., Bisogni, C. A. (2006). "A lot of sacrifices:" Work-family spillover and the food choice coping strategies of low-wage employed parents. *Social Science & Medicine, 63*, 2591–2603.

Diamond, D. M., Campbell, A. M., Park, C. R., Halonen, J., & Zoladz, P. R. (2007). The temporal dynamics model of emotional memory processing: A synthesis on the neurobiological basis of stress-induced amnesia, flashbulb and traumatic memories, and the Yerkes-Dodson law. *Neural Plasticity, 2007*, 1–33.

Dierdorff, E. C., & Ellington, J. K. (2008). It's the nature of the work: Examining behavior-based sources of work-family conflict across occupations. *Journal of Applied Psychology, 93*, 883–892.

Dohrenwend, B. S., Dohrenwend, B. P., Dodson, M., & Shrout, P. E. (1984). Symptoms, hassles, social supports, and life events: Problem of confounded measures. *Journal of Abnormal Psychology, 93*, 222–230.

Dorio, J. M., Bryant, R. H., & Allen, T. D. (2008). Work-related outcomes of the work-family interface: Why organizations should care. In K. Korabik, D. Lero, & D. Whitehead (Eds.), *Handbook of work-family integration* (pp. 157–176). Amsterdam: Academic Press.

Dubin, R. (1967). Industrial workers' worlds: A study of the central life interests of industrial workers. In E. Smigel (Eds.), *Work and leisure* (pp. 153–174). New Haven, CT: College and University Press.

Duxbury, L. E., & Higgins, C. A. (1991). Gender differences in work-family conflict. *Journal of Applied Psychology, 76*, 60–74.

Duxbury, L., & Higgins, C. (2001). *Work-life balance in the new millennium: Where are we? Where do we need to go?* CPRN Discussion Paper No. W/12. Ottawa: Canadian Policy Research Networks.

Eagle, B. W., Miles, E. W., & Icenogle, M. L. (1997). Interrole conflicts and the permeability of work and family domains: Are there gender differences? *Journal of Vocational Behavior, 50*, 168–184.

Eby, L. T. (2001). The boundaryless career experiences of mobile spouses in dual-earner marriages. *Group and Organization Management, 26*, 343–368.

Eby, L. T., Casper, W. J., Lockwood, A., Bordeaux, C., & Brinley, A. (2005). Work and family research in IO/OB: Content analysis and review of the literature (1980–2002). *Journal of Vocational Behavior, 66*, 124–197.

Edwards, J. R., & Rothbard, N. P. (1999). Work and family stress and well-being: An examination of person-environment fit in the work and family domains. *Organizational Behavior & Human Decision Processes, 77*, 85–129.

Edwards, J. R., & Rothbard, N. P. (2000). Mechanisms linking work and family: Clarifying the relationship between work and family constructs. *Academy of Management Review, 25*, 179–199.

Eikemo, T. A., & Bambra, C. (2008). The welfare state: A glossary for public health. *Journal of Epidemiology and Community Health, 62*, 3–6.

Esping-Andersen, G. (1990). *The three worlds of welfare capitalism*. London: Polity.

Fiese, B. H., Tomcho, T. J., Douglas, M., Josephs, K., Poltrock, S., & Baker, T. (2002). A review of 50 years of research on naturally occurring family routines and rituals: Cause for celebration? *Journal of Family Psychology, 16*, 381–390.

Fletcher, J. K., & Bailyn, L. (1996). Challenging the last boundary: Reconnecting work and family. In M. B. Arthur & D. Rousseau (Eds.), *The boundaryless career: A new employment principle for a new organizational era* (pp. 256–267). New York: Oxford University Press.

Ford, M. T., Heinen, B. A., & Langkamer, C. L. (2007). Work and family satisfaction and conflict: A meta-analysis of cross-domain relations. *Journal of Applied Psychology, 92*, 57–80.

Frankenhaeuser, M., Lundberg, U., Fredrikson, M., & Melin, B. (1989). Stress on and off the job as related to sex and occupational status in white-collar workers. *Journal of Organizational Behavior, 10*, 321–346.

Frese, M., & Zapf, D. (1988). Methodological issues in the study of work and stress: Objective versus subjective measurement of stress at work and the question of longitudinal studies. In C. L. Cooper & R. Payne (Eds.), *Causes, coping, and consequences of stress and work* (pp. 375–411). Chichester, UK: Wiley.

Frese, M., & Zapf, D. (1999). On the importance of the objective environment in stress and attribution theory: Counterpoint to Perrewe and Zellars. *Journal of Organizational Behavior, 20*, 761–765.

Friedman, S. D., & Greenhaus, J. H. (2000). *Work and Family: Allies or Enemies?* New York: Oxford University Press.

Frone, M. R. (2000). Work-family conflict and employee psychiatric disorders: The national comorbidity survey. *Journal of Applied Psychology, 85*, 888–895.

Frone, M. R. (2003). Work-family balance. In J. C. Quick & L. E. Tetrick (Eds.), *Handbook of occupational health psychology* (pp. 143–162). Washington, DC: American Psychological Association.

Frone, M. R., Russell, M., & Cooper, M. L. (1992). Antecedents and outcomes of work-family conflict: Testing a model of the work-family interface. *Journal of Applied Psychology, 77*(1), 65–78.

Frone, M. R., Russell, M., & Cooper, M. L. (1997). Relation of work-family conflict to health outcomes: A four-year longitudinal study of employed parents. *Journal of Occupational and Organizational Psychology, 70*, 325–335.

Fulkerson, J. A., Story, M., Mellin, A., Leffert, N., Neumark-Sztainer, D., & French, S. A. (2006). Family dinner meal frequency and adolescent development: Relationships with developmental assets and high-risk behaviors. *Journal of Adolescent Health, 39*, 337–345.

Gajendran, R. S., & Harrison, D. A. (2007). The good, the bad, and the unknown about telecommuting: Meta-analysis of psychological mediators and individual consequences. *Journal of Applied Psychology, 92*, 1524–1541.

Galinsky, E. (1999). *Ask the children: What America's children really think about working parents.* New York: HarperCollins.

Galinsky, E., & Backon, L. (2008). *2008 Guide to bold new ideas for making work work.* New York: Families and Work Institute.

Galinsky, E., Bond, J. T., Sakai, K., Kim, S. S., & Giuntoli, N. (2008). *2008 National study of employers.* New York: Families and Work Institute.

Galinsky, E., & Stein, P. J. (1990). The impact of human resource policies on employees. *Journal of Family Issues, 11*(4), 368–383.

Ganster, D. C., Fox, M. L., & Dwyer, D. J. (2001). Explaining employees' health care costs: A prospective examination of stressful job demands, personal control, and physiological reactivity. *Journal of Applied Psychology, 86*, 954–964.

George, J. M., & Brief, A. P. (1996). Motivational agendas in the workplace: The effects of feelings on focus of attention and work motivation. In B. M. Staw & E. E. Cummings (Eds.), *Research in organizational behavior* (pp. 75–109). Greenwich, CT: JAI Press.

George, J. M., & Jones, G. R. (2000). The role of time in theory and theory building. *Journal of Management, 26*, 657–684.

Gerstner, C. R., & Day, D. V. (1997). Meta-analytic review of leader-member exchange theory: Correlates and construct issues. *Journal of Applied Psychology, 82*, 824–844.

Geurts, S. A. E., Taris, T. W., Kompier, M. A. J., Dikkers, J. S. E., van Hooff, M. L. M., & Kinnunen, U. M. (2005). Work-home interaction from a work psychological perspective: Development and validation of a new questionnaire, the SWING. *Work and Stress, 19*, 319–339.

Gilbert, L. A. (1993). *Two careers/one family.* Newbury Park, CA: Sage.

Gillman, M. W., Rifas-Shiman, S. L., Frazier, A. L., Rockett, H. R., Camargo, C. A., Field, A. E., Berkey, C. S., & Colditz, G. A. (2000). Family dinner and diet quality among older children and adolescents. *Archives of Family Medicine, 9*, 235–240.

Glass, J. L., & Fujimoto, T. (1995). Employer characteristics and the provision of family responsive policies. *Work and Occupations, 22*(4), 380–411.

Glass, J. L., & Riley, L. (1995). Family responsive policies and employee retention following childbirth. *Social Forces, 76*, 1401–1435.

Goff, S. J., Mount, M. K., & Jamison, R. L. (1990). Employer supported child care, work-family, and absenteeism: A field study. *Personnel Psychology, 43*, 793–809.

Goldstein, I. B., Shapiro, D., Chicz-DeMet, A., & Guthrie, D. (1999). Ambulatory blood pressure, heart rate, and neuroendocrine responses in women nurses during work and off work days. *Psychosomatic Medicine, 61*, 387–296.

Goode, W. J. (1960). A theory of role strain. *American Sociological Review, 25*, 483–496.

Gornick, J. C., & Meyers, M. (2003). *Families that work: Policies for reconciling parenthood and employment.* New York: Russell Sage Foundation.

Grandey, A. A., Cordeiro, B. L., & Crouter, A. C. (2005). A longitudinal and multi-source test of the work-family conflict and job satisfaction relationship. *Journal of Occupational and Organizational Psychology, 78*, 305–323.

Grant-Vallone, E. J., & Donaldson, S. I. (2001). Consequences of work-family conflict on employee well-being over time. *Work & Stress, 15*, 214–226.

Graves, L. M., Ohlott, P. J., & Ruderman, M. N. (2007). Commitment to family roles: Effects on managers' attitudes and performance. *Journal of Applied Psychology, 92*, 44–56.

Grebner, S., Semmer, N. K., & Elfering, A. (2005). Working conditions and three types of well-being: A longitudinal study with self-report and rating data. *Journal of Occupational Health Psychology, 10*, 31–43.

Greenhaus, J. H. (2003). Career dynamics. In W. C. Borman, D. R. Ilgen, & R. J. Klimoski (Eds.), *Handbook of psychology: Industrial and organizational psychology* (Vol. 12, pp. 519–540). New York: Wiley.

Greenhaus, J. H. (2008, August). *Decision making and work-family balance: A boundaryless career perspective.* Everett Cherrington Hughes Award talk presented at the annual meeting of the Academy of Management, Anaheim, CA.

Greenhaus, G. H., & Allen, T. D. (2010). Work-family balance: A review and extension of the literature. In L. Tetrick & J. C. Quick (Eds.), *Handbook of occupational health psychology* (2nd ed.). Washington, DC: American Psychological Association.

Greenhaus, J. H., Allen, T. D., & Spector, P. E. (2006). Health consequences of work-family conflict: The dark side of the work-family interface. In P. L. Perrewe & D. C. Ganster (Eds.), *Research in occupational stress and well being* (Vol. 5, pp. 61–99). Oxford: JAI Press/Elsevier.

Greenhaus, J. H., & Beutell, N. J. (1985). Sources and conflict between work and family roles. *Academy of Management Review, 10*, 76–88.

Greenhaus, J. H., Callanan, G. A., & Godshalk, V. M. (2000). *Career management.* Fort Worth, TX: The Dryden Press.

Greenhaus, J. H., Collins, K. M., & Shaw, J. D. (2003). The relation between work-family balance and quality of life. *Journal of Vocational Behavior, 63*, 510–531.

Greenhaus, J. H., & Powell, G. N. (2003). When work and family collide: Deciding between competing demands. *Organizational Behavior and Human Decision Processes, 90*, 291–303.

Greenhaus, J. H., & Powell, G. N. (2006). When work and family are allies: A theory of work-family enrichment. *Academy of Management Review, 31*, 72–92.

Grossman, P., Niemann, L., Schmidt, S., & Walach, H. (2004). Mindfulness-based stress reduction and health benefits. *Journal of Psychomatic Research, 57*, 35–43.

Grover, S. L., & Crooker, K. (1995). Who appreciates family-responsive human resource policies: The impact of family-friendly policies on the organizational attachment of parents and non-parents. *Personnel Psychology, 48*, 271–288.

Grzywacz, J. G. (2000). Work-family spillover and health during midlife: Is managing conflict everything? *American Journal of Health Promotion, 14*, 236–243.

Grzywacz, J. G., Arcury, T. A., Marint, A., Carrillo, L., Burke, B., Coates, M. L., & Quandt, S. A. (2007). Work-family conflict: Experiences and health implications among immigrant Latinos. *Journal of Applied Psychology, 92*, 1119–1130.

Grzywacz, J. G., & Bass, B. L. (2003). Work, family, and mental health: Testing different models of work-family fit. *Journal of Marriage and the Family, 65*(1), 248–261.

Grzywacz, J. G., & Butler, A. B. (2005). The impact of job characteristics on work-to-family facilitation: Testing a theory and distinguishing a construct. *Journal of Occupational Health Psychology, 10*, 97–109.

Grzywacz, J. G., & Carlson, D. S. (2007). Conceptualizing work-family balance: Implications for practice and research. *Advances in Developing Human Resources, 9*, 455–471.

Grzywacz, J. G., Carlson, D. S., Kacmar, K. M., & Wayne, J. H. (2007). A multi-level perspective on the synergies between work and family. *Journal of Occupational & Organizational Psychology, 80*, 559–574.

Grzywacz, J. G., & Marks, N. F. (2000). Reconceptualizing the work-family interface: An ecological perspective on the correlates of positive and negative spillover between work and family. *Journal of Occupational Health Psychology, 5*, 111–126.

Gutek, B. A., Searle, S., & Klepa, L. (1991). Rational versus gender role explanations for work family conflict. *Journal of Applied Psychology, 7*, 560–568.

Hass, L., Allard, K., & Hwang, P. (2002). The impact of organizational culture on men's use of parental leave in Sweden. *Community, Work & Family, 5*, 319–342.

Hall, D. T., & Hall, F. S. (1980). Stress and the two-career couples. In C. L. Cooper & R. Payne (Eds.), *Current concerns in occupational stress* (pp. 243–266). London: Wiley.

Halpern, D. F. (2004). *Public policy, work, and families: The report of the APA presidential initiative on work and families*. Washington, DC: American Psychological Association. Available online at: http://www.apa.org/work-family/

Halpern, D. F. (2006). Introduction: How organizations can alleviate the traffic jam at the intersection of work and family. *American Behavioral Scientist, 49*, 1147–1151.

Halpern, D. F., & Murphy, S. E. (2005). *From work-family balance to work-family interaction: Changing the metaphor*. Mahwah, NJ: Lawrence Erlbaum Associates.

Hammer, L. B., Allen, E., & Grigsby, T. D. (1997). Work-family conflict in dual-earner couples: Within-individual and cross-over effects of work and family. *Journal of Vocational Behavior, 50*, 185–203.

Hammer, L. B., Bauer, T. N., & Grandey, A. A. (2003). Work-family conflict and work-related withdrawal behaviors. *Journal of Business and Psychology, 17*, 419–426.

Hammer, L. B., Cullen, J. C., Neal, M. B., Sinclair, R. R., & Shafiro, M. V. (2005). The longitudinal effects of work-family conflict and positive spillover on depressive symptoms among dual-earner couples. *Journal of Occupational Health Psychology, 10*, 138–154.

Hammer, L. B., Kossek, E. E., Zimmerman, K., & Daniels, R. (2007). Clarifying the construct of family-supportive supervisory behaviors (FSSB): A multilevel perspective. In P. L. Perrewe & D. C. Ganster (Eds.), *Exploring the work and non-work interface: Research in occupational stress and well being* (Vol. 6, pp. 165–204). Oxford: Elsevier.

Hammer, L. B., Kossek, E. E., Yragui, N., Zimmerman, K., & Daniels, R. (2008). *Family supportive supervisor behaviors and cardiovascular disesase*. Paper presented at the 23rd Annual Conference of the Society for Industrial and Organizational Psychology, San Francisco, CA.

Hammer, L. B., Neal, M. B., Newsom, J. T., Brockwood, K. J., & Colton, C. L. (2005). A longitudinal study of the effects of dual-earner couples' utilization of family-friendly workplace supports on work and family outcomes. *Journal of Applied Psychology, 90*, 799–810.

Hanson, G. C., Hammer, L. B., & Colton, C. L. (2006). Development and validation of a multidimensional scale of perceived work-family positive spillover. *Journal of Occupational Health Psychology, 11*, 249–265.

Hass, L., Allard, K., & Hwang, P. (2002). The impact of organizational culture on men's use of parental leave in Sweden. *Community, Work & Family, 5*, 319–342.

Heraty, N., Morley, M. J., & Cleveland, J. (2008). Introduction: Complexities and challenges in the work-family interface. *Journal of Managerial Psychology, 23*, 209–214.

Hewlett, S. (2005). *Creating a life*. New York: Hyperion.

Heymann, J. (2000). *The widening gap: Why American's working families are in jeopardy—and what can be done about it*. New York: Basic Books.

Heymann, J., Earle, A., & Hayes, J. (2007). *The work, family, and equity index: How does the United States measure up?* Boston/Montreal: Project on Global Working Families. Available online at: http://www.mcgill.ca/files/ihsp/WFEIFinal2007.pdf.

Higgins, C. A., & Duxbury, L. W. (1992). Work-family conflict: A comparison of dual-career and traditional-career men. *Journal of Organizational Behavior, 13*, 389–411.

Hill, E. J. (2005). Working fathers and mothers, work-family stressors and support. *Journal of Family Issues, 26*, 793–819.

Hill, E. J., Hawkins, A. J., Ferris, M., & Weitzman, M. (2001). Finding an extra day a week: The positive influence of perceived job flexibility on work and family life balance. *Family Relations, 50*, 49–58.

Hill, E. J., Yang, C., Hawkins, A. J., & Ferris, M. (2004). A cross-cultural test of the work-family interface in 48 countries. *Journal of Marriage and Family, 66*, 1300–1316.

Hochschild, A. (1989). *The second shift*. New York: Penguin Books.

Huffman, A. H., Youngcourt, S. S., Payne, S. C., & Castro, C. A. (2008). The importance of construct breadth when examining interrole conflict. *Educational and Psychological Measurement, 68*, 515–530.

Ilies, R., Schwind, K., Wagner, D. T., Johnson, M., DeRue, D. S., & Ilgen, D. R. (2007). When can employees have a family life? The effects of daily workload and affect on work-family conflict and social activities at home. *Journal of Applied Psychology, 92*, 1368–1379.

Jackson, M. (2008). *Distracted: The erosion of attention and the coming dark age*. Amherst, NY: Prometheus Books.

Janssen, P. P. M., Peeters, M. C. W., de Jonge, J., Houkes, I., & Tummers, G. E. R. (2004). Specific relationships between job demands, job resources and psychological outcomes and the mediating role of negative work-home interference. *Journal of Vocational Behavior, 65*, 411–429.

Jones, E., & Fletcher, B. (1993). An empirical study of occupational stress transmission in working couples. *Human Relations, 46*, 881–902.

Judge, T. A., & Locke, E. A. (1993). Effect of dysfunctional thought processes on subjective well-being and job satisfaction. *Journal of Applied Psychology, 78*, 475–490.

Judiesch, M. K., & Lyness, K. S. (1999). Left behind? The impact of leaves of absence on managers' career success. *Academy of Management Journal, 42*, 641–651.

Kahn, R. L., Wolfe, D. M., Quinn, R., Snoek, J. D., & Rosenthal, R. A. (1964). *Organizational stress*. New York: Wiley.

Kanter, R. M. (1977). *Work and family in the United States: A critical review and agenda for research and policy*. New York: Russell Sage Foundation.

Kelloway, E. K., Gottlieb, B. H., & Barham, L. (1999). The source, nature and direction of work and family conflict: A longitudinal investigation. *Journal of Occupational Health Psychology, 43*, 37–346.

Kinnunen, U., & Geurts, S. A. E., & Mauno, S. (2004). Work-to-family conflict and its relationship with well-being: A one-year longitudinal study. *Work & Stress, 18*, 1–22.

Kinnunen, U., & Mauno, S. (1998). Antecedents and outcomes of work-family conflict among employed women and men in Finland. *Human Relations, 51*, 157–175.

Kinnunen, U., Vermulst, A., Gerris, J., & Makikangas, A. (2003). Work-family conflict and its relations to well-being: The role of personality as a moderating factor. *Personality and Individual Differences, 35*, 1669–1683.

Kirchmeyer, C. (1993). Nonwork-to-work spillover: A more balanced view of the experiences and coping of professional women and men. *Sex Roles, 28*, 531–552.

Kirchmeyer, C. (2000). Work-life initiatives: Greed or benevolence regarding workers' time? In C. L. Cooper & D. M. Rousseau (Eds.), *Trends in organizational behavior* (Vol. 7, pp. 79–93). West Sussex, UK: John Wiley & Sons.

Klatt, M., Buckworth, J., & Malarkey, W. B. (2009). Effects of low-dose mindfulness-based stress reduction on working adults. *Health Education & Behavior, 36*, 601–614.

Kopelman, R. E., Prottas, D. J., Thompson, C. A., & Jahn, E. W. (2006). A multilevel examination of work-life practices: Is more always better? *Journal of Managerial Issues, 18*, 232–253.

Koppes, L. L., & Swanberg, J. (2008). Work-life effectiveness: Implications for organizations. *The Psychologist-Manager Journal, 11*, 1–4.

Korabik, K., Lero, D. S., & Whitehead, D. L. (2008). *Handbook of work-family integration: Research, theory, and best practices*. London: Elsevier.

Kossek, E. E., Colquitt, J., & Noe, R. A. (2001). Caregiving decisions, well-being and performance: The effects of place and provider as a function of dependent type and work-family climates. *Academy of Management Journal, 44*, 29–44.

Kossek, E. E., Hammer, L. B., & Lewis, S. (2010). Special issue: Work-life initiatives and organizational change. *Human Relations, 63*(1).

Kossek, E. E., & Lambert, S. J. (2005). *Work and life integration: Organizational, cultural, and individual perspectives*. Mahwah, NJ: Lawrence Erlbaum Associates.

Kossek, E. E., Lautsch, B. A., & Eaton, S. C. (2006). Telecommuting, control, and boundary management: Correlates of policy use and practice, job control, and work-family effectiveness. *Journal of Vocational Behavior, 68*, 347–367.

Kossek, E. E., & Nichol, V. (1992). The effects of on-site childcare on employee attitudes and performance. *Personnel Psychology, 45*, 485–509.

Kossek, E. E., & Ozeki, C. (1998). Work-family conflict, policies, and the job-life satisfaction relationship: A review and directions for organizational behavior human resources research. *Journal of Applied Psychology, 83*, 139–149.

Kostanski, M., & Hassed, C. (2008). Mindfulness as a concept and a process. *Australian Psychologist, 43*, 15–21.

Kozlowski, S. W. J., & Klein, K. J. (2000). A multilevel approach to theory and research in organizations: Contextual, temporal, and emergent processes. In K. J. Klein & S. W. J. Kozlowski (Eds.), *Multilevel theory, research and methods in organizations: Foundations, extensions, and new directions* (pp. 3–90). San Francisco: Jossey-Bass.

Kreiner, G. E. (2006). Consequences of work-home segmentation or integration: A person-environment fit perspective. *Journal of Organizational Behavior, 27*, 485–507.

Kubany, E. S., Haynes, S. N., Abueg, F. R, Manke, F. P., Brennan, J. M., & Starhura, C. (1996). Development and validation of the Trauma-Related Guilt Inventory (TRGI). *Psychological Assessment, 5*, 428–444.

Lambert, S. J. (1990). Processes linking work and family: A critical review and research agenda. *Human Relations, 43*, 239–257.

Lapierre, L. M., & Allen, T. D. (2006). Work-supportive family, family-supportive supervision, use of organizational benefits, and problem-focused coping: Implications for work-family conflict and employee well-being. *Journal of Occupational Health Psychology, 11*, 169–181.

Lapierre, L. M., Spector, P. E., Allen, T. D., Poelmans, S., et al. (2008). Family-supportive organization perceptions, multiple dimensions of work-family conflict, and employee satisfaction: A test of model across five samples. *Journal of Vocational Behavior, 73*, 92–106.

Lee, Y.-S. (2005). Measuring the gender gap in household labor: Accurately estimating wives' and husbands' contributions. In B. Schneider & L. J. Waite (Eds.), *Being together, working apart: Dual-career families and the work-life balance* (pp. 229–247). Cambridge: Cambridge University Press.

Lewis, S., Gambles, R., & Rapoport, R. (2007). The constraints of a 'work-life balance' approach: An international perspective. *International Journal of Human Resource Management, 18*, 360–373.

Lobel, S., & Kossek, E. E. (1996). Human resource strategies to support diversity in work and personal lifestyles: Beyond the "family friendly" organization. In E. E. Kossek & S. Lobel (Eds.), *Managing diversity: Human resource strategies for transforming the workplace* (pp. 221–244). Oxford: Blackwell.

Lu, L., & Gilmour, R. (2005). A cross-cultural study of work/family demands, work/family conflict and wellbeing: The Taiwanese vs. British. *Career Development International, 11*, 9–27.

Lundberg, U., & Frankenhaeuser, M. (1999). Stress and workload of men and women in high-ranking positions. *Journal of Occupational Health Psychology, 4,* 142–151.

Lundberg, U., Granqvist, M., Hansson, T., Magnusson, M., & Wallin, L. (1989). Psychological and physiological stress responses during repetitive work on an assembly line. *Work & Stress, 3,* 143–153.

Lyness, K. S., & Kropf, M. B. (2005). The relationships of national gender equality and organizational support with work-family balance: A study of European managers. *Human Relations, 58,* 33–60.

Maccoby, E. (1998). *Two sexes: Growing up apart, coming together.* Cambridge, MA: Belknap Press.

MacDermid, S. M. (2005). (Re)considering conflict between work and family. In E. E. Kossek & S. J. Lambert (Eds.), *Work and life integration* (pp. 19–40). Mahwah, NJ: Lawrence Erlbaum Associates.

Major, D. A., Allard, C. B., & Cardenas, R. A. (2004). Child health: A legitimate business concern. *Journal of Occupational Health Psychology, 9,* 306–321.

Major, D. A., Fletcher, T. D., Davis, D. D., & Germano, L. M. (2008). The influence of work-family culture and workplace relationships on work interference with family: A multilevel model. *Journal of Organizational Behavior, 29,* 881–897.

Marks, S. (1977). Multiple roles and role strain: Some notes on human energy, time, and commitment. *American Sociological Review, 42,* 921–936.

Marks, S. R., & MacDermid, S. M. (1996). Multiple roles and the self: A theory of role balance. *Journal of Marriage and the Family, 58,* 417–432.

Martin, L. L., & Tesser, A. (1996). Some ruminative thoughts. In R. S. Wyer, Jr. (Ed.), *Ruminative thoughts* (pp. 1–47). Mahwah, NJ: Lawrence Erlbaum Associates.

Matthews, R. A., Del Priore, R., Acitelli, L., & Barnes-Farrell, J. L. (2006). Work-to-relationship conflict at the systems level: A study of crossover effects in dual-earner couples. *Journal of Occupational Health Psychology, 11,* 228–240.

Mauno, S., Kinnunen, U., & Pyykko, M. (2005). Does work-family conflict mediate the relationship between work-family culture and self-reported distress? Evidence from five Finnish organizations. *Journal of Occupational and Organizational Psychology, 78,* 509–530.

McElwain, A. K., & Korabik, K. (2005). *Work-family guilt.* Sloan Work and Family Research Network Encyclopedia, http://wfnetwork.bc.edu/encyclopedia_template.php?id=270.

McNall, L. A., Nicklin, J. M., & Masuda, A. D. (2010). A meta-analytic review of the consequences associated with work–family enrichment. *Journal of Business & Psychology, 25,* 381–396.

Mesmer-Magnus, J. R., & Viswesvaran, C. (2006). How family-friendly work environments affect work/family conflict: A meta-analytic examination. *Journal of Labor Research, 27,* 555–574.

Milkman, R., & Appelbaum, E. (2004). Paid family leave in California: New research findings. *The State of California Labor, 4,* 45–67.

Mitchell, T., & James, L. R. (2001). Building better theory: Time and the specification of when things happen. *Academy of Management Review, 26,* 530–547.

Moen, P. (2003). *It's about time: Couples and careers.* Ithaca, NY: Cornell University Press.

Moen, P., & Roehling, P. (2005). *The career mystique: Cracks in the American dream.* Lanham, MD: Rowman & Littlefield.

Morgeson, F. P., & Campion, M. A. (1997). Social and cognitive sources of potential inaccuracy in job analysis. *Journal of Applied Psychology, 82,* 627–655.

Muraven, M., & Baumeister, R. F. (2000). Self-regulation and depletion of limited resource: Does self-control resemble a muscle? *Psychological Bulletin, 126,* 247–259.

Murphy, K. (1998). *In search of success: Everyone's criterion problem.* Presidential address presented at the 30th annual Society for Industrial and Organizational Psychology conference, Dallas, TX.

Neal, M. B., & Hammer, L. B. (2007). *Working couples caring for children and aging parents: Effects on work and well-being.* Mahwah, NJ: Lawrence Erlbaum Associates.

Netemeyer, R. G., Boles, J. S., & McMurrian, R. (1996). Development and validation of work-family conflict and family-work conflict scales. *Journal of Applied Psychology, 81,* 400–410.

Nippert-Eng, C. (1996). *Home and work: Negotiating boundaries through everyday life.* Chicago: University of Chicago Press.

Nolen-Hoeksema, S., & Corte, C. (2004). Gender and self-regulation. In R. F. Baumeister & K. Vohs (Eds.), *Handbook of self-regulation: Research, theory, and applications* (pp. 411–421). New York: Guilford Press.

Nolen-Hoeksema, S., & Davis, C. G. (1999). "Thanks for sharing that": Ruminators and their social support networks. *Journal of Personality and Social Psychology, 77,* 801–814.

Nolen-Hoeksema, S., Wisco, B. E., & Lyubomirsky, S. (2008). Rethinking rumination. *Perspectives on Psychological Science, 3,* 400–424.

O'Driscoll, M. P., Poelmans, S. A. Y., Spector, P. E., Kalliath, T., Allen, T. D., Cooper, C. L., & Sanchez, J. I. (2003). Family-responsive interventions, perceived organizational and supervisor support, work-family conflict, and psychological strain. *International Journal of Stress Management, 10,* 326–344.

Olson-Buchanan, J. B., & Boswell, W. R. (2006). Blurring boundaries: Correlates of integration and segmentation between work and nonwork. *Journal of Vocational Behavior, 68,* 432–445.

Parasuraman, S., & Greenhaus, J. H. (2002). Toward reducing some critical gaps in work-family research. *Human Resource Management Review, 12,* 299–312.

Parasuraman, S., Greenhaus, J. H., & Granrose, C. S. (1992). Role stressors, social support, and well-being among two-career couples. *Journal of Organizational Behavior, 13,* 339–356.

Parasuraman, S., Purohit, Y. S., Godshalk, V. M., & Beutell, N. J. (1996). Work and family variables, entrepreneurial career success, and psychological well-being. *Journal of Vocational Behavior, 48,* 275–300.

Pavett, C. M. (1986). High-stress professions: Satisfaction, stress, and well-being of spouses of professionals. *Human Relations, 39,* 1141–1154.

Piotrkowski, C. (1979). *Work and the family system.* New York: The Free Press.

Pitt-Catsouphes, M., Kossek, E. E., & Sweet, S. (2005). *The work and family handbook: Multi-disciplinary perspectives and approaches.* Mahwah, NJ: Lawrence Erlbaum Associates.

Pitt-Catsouphes, M., Matz-Costa, C., MacDermid, S. M. (2007). HRD responses to work family stressors. *Advances in Developing Human Resources, 9,* 527–543.

Poelmans, S. A. Y. (2005a). The decision process theory of work and family. In E. E. Kossek & S. J. Lambert (Eds.), *Work* and life integration (pp. 263–286). Mahwah, NJ: Lawrence Erlbaum Associates.

Poelmans, S. A. Y. (2005b). *Work and family: An international research perspective*. Mahwah, NJ: Lawrence Erlbaum Associates.

Poelmans, S. A. Y., & Beham, B. (2008). The moment of truth: Conceptualizing managerial work-life policy allowance decisions. *Journal of Organizational and Occupational Psychology, 81*, 393–410.

Poelmans, S. A. Y., & Sahibzada, K. (2004). A multi-level model for studying the context and impact of work-family policies and culture in organizations. *Human Resource Management Review, 14*, 409–431.

Powell, G. N., & Greenhaus, J. H. (2006). Managing incidents of work-family conflict: A decision-making perspective. *Human Relations, 59*, 1179–1212.

Presser, H. (2000). Nonstandard work schedules and marital instability. *Journal of Marriage and Family, 62*, 93–110.

Pruitt, B. H., & Rapoport, R. (2008). *Looking backwards to go forward: A timeline of the work-family field in the United States since World War II*. Boston: Boston College, Sloan Work and Family Resource Center.

Pyszczynski, T., & Greenberg, J. (1987). Self-regulatory perseveration and the depressive self-focusing style: A self-awareness theory of reactive depression. *Psychological Bulletin, 102*, 122–138.

Quinn, R. P., & Staines, G. L. (1979). *The 1977 quality of employment survey*. Ann Arbor: University of Michigan, Institute for Social Research.

Raley, S. B., Mattingly, M. J., & Bianchi, S. M (2006). How dual are dual-income couples? Documenting change from 1970 to 2001. *Journal of Marriage and Family, 68*(1), 11–28.

Rapoport, R., & Rapoport, R. (1969). The dual career family. *Human Relations, 22*, 3–30.

Rapoport, R., & Rapoport, R. (1971). *Dual-career families*. Baltimore, MD: Penguin Books.

Rapoport, R., Bailyn, L., Fletcher, J. K., & Pruitt, B. H. (2002). *Beyond work-family balance: Advancing gender equity and workplace performance*. San Francisco: Jossey-Bass.

Rau, B. L. (2003). Flexible work arrangements. *Sloan Online Work and Family Encyclopedia*, http://wfnetwork.bc.edu/encyclopedia_entry.php?id=240&area=All.

Roe, R. A. (2008). The study of "what happens" rather than "what is." *European Psychologist, 13*, 37–52.

Roos, E., Sarlio-Lahteenkorva, S., Lallukka, T., & Lahelma, E. (2007). Associations of work-family conflicts with food habits and physical activity. *Public Health Nutrition, 10*, 222–229.

Roese, N. J., & Summerville, A. (2005). What we regret most…and why. *Personality and Social Psychology Bulletin, 31*, 1273–1285.

Roehling, P. V., Moen, P., & Batt, R. M. (2003). Spillover. In P. Moen (Ed.), *It's about time* (pp. 101–121). Ithaca, NY: Cornell University Press.

Roehling, P. V., Roehling, M. V., & Moen, P. (2001). The relationship between work-life policies and practices and employee loyalty: A life course perspective. *Journal of Family and Economic Issues, 22*, 141–170.

Rosenbaum, M., Leibel, R., & Hirsch, J. (1997). Obesity. *New England Journal of Medicine, 337*, 396–407.

Rotundo, D. M., & Kincaid, J. F. (2008). Conflict, facilitation, and individual coping styles across the work and family domains. *Journal of Managerial Psychology, 23*, 484–506.

Ryan, R. M., & Deci, E. L. (2000). Self-determination theory and the facilitation of intrinsic motivation, social development, and well-being. *American Psychologist, 55*, 68–78.

Sallinen, M., Ronka, A., Kinnunen, U., & Kokka, K. (2007). Trajectories of depressive mood in adolescents: Does parental work or parent-adolescent relationship matter? A follow-up study through junior high school in Finland. *International Journal of Behavioral Development, 31*, 181–190.

Schaubroeck, J. (1999). Should the subjective be the objective? On studying mental processes, coping behavior, and actual exposures in organizational stress research. *Journal of Organizational Behavior, 20*, 753–760.

Schwarz, N. (1990). Feelings as information. In E. T. Higgins & R. M. Sorrentino (Eds.), *Handbook of motivation and cognition: Foundations of social behavior* (Vol. 2, pp. 527–561). New York: Guilford Press.

Semmer, N. K., Grebner, S., & Elfering, A. (2004). Beyond self-report: Using observational, physiological, and event-based measures in occupational stress. In P. L. Perrewe & D. C. Ganster (Eds.), *Research in occupational stress and well-being* (Vol. 3, pp. 205–263). Amsterdam: Elsevier.

Shamir, B. (1983). Some antecedents of work-family conflict. *Journal of Vocational Behavior, 23*, 98–111.

Sharpe, D. L., Hermsen, J. M., & Billings, J. (2002). Factors associated with having flextime: A focus on married workers. *Journal of Family and Economic Issues, 23*, 51–72.

Shockley, K. M., & Allen, T. D. (2007). When flexibility helps: Another look at the availability of flexible work arrangements and work-family conflict. *Journal of Vocational Behavior, 71*, 479–493.

Shockley, K., & Allen, T. D. (2010). Investigating the missing link in flexible work arrangement utilization: An individual difference perspective. *Journal of Vocational Behavior, 76*, 131–142.

SHRM Foundation. (2001). *SHRM 2001 benefits survey*. Alexandria, VA: Society for Human Resource Management.

Sieber, S. D. (1974). Toward a theory of role accumulation. *American Sociological Review, 39*, 567–578.

Sloan Work and Family Research Network. Online at http://wfnetwork.bc.edu/ Accessed December, 2011.

Small, S. A., & Riley, D. (1990). Toward a multidimensional assessment of work spillover into family life. *Journal of Marriage and the Family, 52*, 51–61.

Sonnentag, S., & Fritz, C. (2006). Endocrinological processes associated with job stress: Catecholamine and cortisol responses to acute and chronic stressors. In P. L. Perrewé & D. C. Ganster (Eds.), *Research in organizational stress and well-being: Employee health, coping, and methodologies* (pp. 1–59). Amsterdam: Elsevier.

Sonnentag, S., Mojza, E. J., Binnewies, C., & Scholl, A. (2008). Being engaged at work and detached at home: A week-level study on work engagement, psychological detachment and affect. *Work & Stress, 22*, 257–276.

Spector, P. E., Allen, T. D., Poelmans, S., Lapierre, L. M., Cooper, C. L., O'Driscoll, M., Sanchez, J. I., Abarca, N., Alexandrova, M., Beham, B., Brough, P., Ferreiro, P., Fraile, G., Lu, C. Q., Lu, L., et al. (2007). Cross-national differences in relationships of work demands, job satisfaction and turnover intentions with work-family conflict. *Personnel Psychology, 60*, 805–835.

Spector, P. E., Allen, T. D., Poelmans, S., Cooper, C. L., et al. (2005). An international comparative study of work-family stress and occupational strain. In S. A. Y. Poelmans

(Ed.), *Work and family: An international research perspective* (pp. 71–86). Mahwah, NJ: Lawrence Erlbaum Associates.

Spector, P. E., Cooper, C. L., Poelmans, S., Allen, T. D., O'Driscoll, M., Sanchez, J. I., Siu, O. L., Dewe, P., Hart, P., Lu, L., de Moraes, L. F. R., Ostrognay, G. M., Sparks, K., Wong, P., & Yu, S. (2004). A cross-national comparative study of work/family stressors, working hours, and well-being: China and Latin America vs. the Anglo world. *Personnel Psychology, 57*, 119–142.

Spector, P. E., Zapf, D., Chen, P. Y., & Frese, M. (2000). Why negative affectivity should not be controlled in job stress research: Don't throw out the baby with the bath water. *Journal of Organizational Behavior, 21*, 79–95.

Staines, G. L. (1980). Spillover versus compensation: A review of the literature on the relationship between work and non-work. Human Relations, *33*(2), 111–129.

Staines, G. L., & Pleck, J. H. (1984). Nonstandard work schedules and family life. *Journal of Applied Psychology, 69*, 515–523.

Staw, B. M., & Ross, J. (1985). Stability in the midst of change: A dispositional approach to job attitudes. *Journal of Applied Psychology, 70*, 469–480.

Stewart, W., & Barling, J. (1996). Fathers' work experiences effect children's behaviors via job-related affect and parenting behaviors. *Journal of Organizational Behavior, 17*, 221–232.

Stoeva, A. Z., Chiu, R. K., & Greenhaus, J. H. (2002). Negative affectivity, role stress, and work-family conflict. *Journal of Vocational Behavior, 60*, 1–16.

Sullivan, S. (1999). The changing nature of careers: A review and research agenda. *Journal of Management, 25*, 457–484.

Sumer, H. C., & Knight, P. A. (2001). How do people with different attachment styles balance work and family? A personality perspective on work-family linkage. *Journal of Applied Psychology, 86*, 653–663.

Sweet, S., & Moen, P. (2006). Advancing a career focus on work and family: Insights from the life course perspective. In M. Pitt-Catsouphes, E. E. Kossek, & S. Sweet (Eds.), *Work-family handbook: Multi-disciplinary perspectives and approaches* (pp. 189–208). Mahwah, NJ: Lawrence Erlbaum Associates.

Swody, C. A., & Powell, G. N. (2007). Determinants of employee participation in organizations' family-friendly programs: A multi-level approach. *Journal of Business Psychology, 22*, 111–122.

Tangney, J. P. (1990). Assessing individual differences in proneness to shame and guilt: Development of the self-conscious affect and attribution inventory. *Journal of Personality and Social Psychology, 59*, 102–111.

Tepper, B. J. (2007). Abusive supervision in work organizations: Review, synthesis, and research agenda. *Journal of Management, 33*, 261–289.

Thoits, P. (1983). Multiple identities and psychological wellbeing: A reformulation and test of social isolation hypothesis. *American Sociological Review, 48*, 174–187.

Thomas, L. T., & Ganster, D. C. (1995). Impact of family-supportive work variables on work-family conflict and strain: A control perspective. *Journal of Applied Psychology, 80*, 6–15.

Thompson, C. A., Andreassi, J., & Prottas, D. (2005). Work-family culture: Key to reducing workforce-workplace mismatch? In S. M. Bianchi, L. M. Casper, & R. Berkowitz King, (Eds.), *Workforce/workplace mismatch? Work, family, health and well-being* (pp. 117–132). Mahwah, NJ: Lawrence Erlbaum Associates.

Thompson, C. A., & Beauvais L. L., (2000). Balancing work/life. In D. M. Smith (Ed.), *Women at work: Leadership for the next century* (pp. 162–189). Upper Saddle River, NJ: Prentice-Hall.

Thompson, C. A., Beauvais L. L., & Lyness, K. S. (1999). When work-family benefits are not enough: The influence of work-family culture on benefit utilization, organizational attachment, and work-family conflict. *Journal of Vocational Behavior, 54*, 392–415.

Thompson, C., Poelmans, S. E. A., Allen, T. D., & Andreassi, J. (2007). On the importance of coping: A model and new directions for research on work and family. In P. L. Perrewe & D. C. Ganster (Eds.). *Research in occupational stress and well being* (Vol. 6, pp 73–113). Oxford: JAI Press/Elsevier.

Uchino, B. N., Cacippo, J. T., & Kiecolt-Glaser, J. K. (1996). The relationship between social support and physiological processes: A review with emphasis on underlying mechanisms and implications for health. *Psychological Bulletin, 119*, 488–531.

U.S. Bureau of Labor Statistics. (2007). Table 4. Families with own children: Employment status of parents by age of youngest child and family type, 2006–2007 annual averages. Washington, DC: retrieved from http://www.bls.gov/news. release/famee.t04.htm.

U.S. Census. (2006). *Married couple family groups, by labor force status of both spouses, and race and Hispanic origin of the reference person: 2006 Table FG1*. Washington, DC: U.S. Census Bureau.

Van Dyne, L., Kossek, E. E., & Lobel, S. (2007). Less need to be there: Cross-level effects of work practices that support work-life flexibility and enhance group processes and group-level OCB. *Human Relations, 60*, 1123–1154.

van Hooff, M. L. M., Geurts, S. A. E., Taris, T. W., Kompier, M. A. J., Dikkers, J. S. E., Houtman, I. L. D., & Van Den Heuvel, F. M. M. (2005). Disentangling the causal relationships between work-home interference and employee health. *Scandinavian Journal of Work & Environmental Health, 31*, 15–29.

van Steenbergen, E. F., Ellemers, N., & Mooijaart, A. (2007). How work and family can facilitate each other: Distinct types of work-family facilitation and outcomes for women and men. *Journal of Occupational Health Psychology, 12*, 279–300.

Voydanoff, P. (2005). Social integration, work-family conflict and facilitation, and job and marital quality. *Journal of Marriage and Family, 67*, 666–679.

Waldfogel, J. (2001). International policies toward parental leave and child care. *The Future of Children, 11*, 99–111.

Warren, J. A., & Johnson, P. J. (1995). The impact of workplace support on work-family role strain. *Family Relations, 44*, 163–169.

Wayne, J. H., Grzywacz, J. G., Carlson, D. S., & Kacmar, K. M. (2007). Work-family facilitation: A theoretical explanation and model of primary antecedents and consequences. *Human Resource Management Review, 17*, 63–76.

Wayne, J. H., Musisca N., & Fleeson, W. (2004). Considering the role of personality in the work-family experience: Relationships of the big five to work-family conflict and facilitation. *Journal of Vocational Behavior, 64*, 108–130.

Westman, M. (1991). Stress and strain crossover. *Human Relations, 54*, 717–751.

Westman, M. (2006). Crossover of stress and strain in the work-family context. In F. Jones, R. J. Burke, &

M. Westman (Eds.), *Work-life balance: A psychological perspective* (pp. 163–184). New York: Psychology Press.

Westman, M., & Etzion, D. (1995). Crossover of stress, strain and resources from one spouse to another. *Journal of Organizational Behavior, 16*, 169–181.

Westman, M., & Etzion, D. (2005). The crossover of work-family conflict from one spouse to another. *Journal of Applied Social Psychology, 35*, 1936–1957.

Westman, M., & Vinokur, A. D. (1998). Unraveling the relationship of distress levels within couples: Common stressors, empathic reactions, or crossover via social interaction? *Human Relations, 51*, 137–156.

Westman, M., Vinokur A. D., Hamilton V. L., & Roziner I. (2004). Crossover of marital dissatisfaction during military downsizing among Russian army officers and their spouses. *Journal of Applied Psychology, 89*, 769–779.

Williams, J. (2000). *Unbending gender: Why family and work conflict and what to do about it.* New York: Oxford University Press.

Williams, K., & Alliger, G. M. (1994). Role stressors, mood spillover, and perceptions of work-family conflict in employed parents. *Academy of Management Journal, 37*, 837–868.

Williams, A., Franche, R.-L., Ibrahim, S., Mustard, C. A., & Layton, F. R. (2006). Examining the relationship between work-family spillover and sleep quality. *Journal of Occupational Health Psychology, 11*, 27–37.

Yang, N. (2005). Individualism-collectivism and work-family interfaces: A sino-U.S. comparison. In S. A. Y. Poelmans (Ed.), *Work and family an international research perspective* (pp. 287–318). Mahwah, NJ: Lawrence Erlbaum Associates.

Yang, N., Chen, C. C., Choi, J., & Zou, Y. (2000). Sources of work-family conflict: A sino-U.S. comparison of the effects of work and family demands. *Academy of Management Journal, 41*, 113–123.

Zedeck S. (1987, October). Work, family, and organizations: An untapped research triangle. Paper iirwps-010-87. *Institute for Research on Labor and Employment Working Paper Series.* Online at http://www.escholarship.org/uc/item/47v559vj. Accessed December, 2011.

Zedeck, S. (1992). Introduction: Exploring the domain of work and family concerns. In S. Zedeck (Ed.), *Work, families and organizations* (pp.1–32). San Francisco: Jossey-Bass.

Zimbardo, P. G. (2002). Time to take our time. *Psychology Today*, March/April, 62.

Lifelong Learning

Manuel London

Abstract

This chapter examines lifelong learning from the standpoint of organizational needs and expectations, the importance of learning and development for career growth, individual differences in propensity for continuous learning, and support and reinforcement for development. The chapter starts by examining alternative definitions of lifelong learning for skill development, discovery, and innovation. Trends driving continuous learning include pressures to maintain competitiveness and readiness to meet future needs. Learning is then viewed in relation to life stage and ongoing generativity. Foundational learning theories focus on individual differences affecting learning motivation, life stage models of development, and explanations for how people learn. Support for learning includes the corporate environment and culture, the emergence of learning organizations, empowerment for self-development, and formal and informal methods of development. Technological advances in development include online multisource feedback surveys, just-in-time coaching, and web-based training. The chapter concludes with an agenda for future research and practice, including new modes of education throughout the life cycle, assessments of learning outcomes, ways to meet individual and organizational needs for adaptive, generative, and transformative learning, and forces for future research and practice.

Key Words: Learning, development, career growth, support for learning, learning outcomes assessment

The illiterate of the 21st century will not be those who cannot read and write but those who cannot learn, unlearn and relearn.
—*Alvin Toffler* (futurist)

Lifelong, or continuous, learning has become the hallmark of career and employee development during the last 30 years. In prior years, people prepared for careers and for the most part stayed in them unless they confronted a major problem, such a debilitating illness or another event that caused a major dislocation (a national economic disaster such as the Great Depression, forced immigration, or fleeing oppression). People acquired professions and positions, or at least jobs. For those who were not self-employed, their employers ensured their job security. If employers wanted them to acquire new knowledge or skills, the employers would provide training in the form of printed job aids, on-the-job training delivered by supervisors, or courses and workshops in corporate training centers or local universities.

Today, corporate dislocations, advancing technologies, shifting world economies, increased competition, and a host of other factors have drastically affected learning and development from individual and organizational perspectives. Individuals need to take responsibility for their own career development. Their employer may or may not provide training when it is needed. Moreover, individuals need to be concerned about their own competitiveness for jobs with their employer or with other organizations. Companies will downsize or adjust their staffs, depending on their financial condition and their strategic direction. An organization that did business domestically may decide to "go global," creating the need for employees with considerably different skills and experiences. The organization will fire or transfer current employees and will hire a new batch of employees, rather than take the time to develop current employees.

Many people change careers once, twice, or even more times throughout their lives to maintain their job security or to satisfy changing interests or career goals. When they shift jobs and careers, they need considerable retraining. Some people have a drive for learning, perhaps as a result of natural tendencies or role models. This serves them well, since we all face an abundance of new ideas and ready access to a wealth of information via the Internet and associated technologies and databases. Continuous learning is becoming a mainstay of many people's lives today. People pursue learning opportunities in connection with vocational interests and volunteer work, sometimes turning hobbies into new career directions or part-time jobs after retirement. Living longer with a high quality of life and an abundance of learning resources, often available at no or lost cost, gives people a wide array of developmental opportunities.

Hall (2004, 1976; Hall & Mirvis, , 1995, 1996) coined the term *protean career* to reflect continuous learning and multiple career changes. Organizational restructuring, decentralization, and globalization have meant that organizations no longer take parental control over employees' careers. Instead, individuals take responsibility for their own careers. The organization provides the opportunities and developmental resources, but the individual cannot count on the organization for job security and continued promotion. People's core values drive their career decisions, and they form their own definition of career success that may not include continued upward advancement and income. Indeed, people may reshape and redirect their careers, not just within a single profession, but by embarking on entirely new professions, sometimes turning hobbies into money-making jobs or becoming entrepreneurs (e.g., the college professor becoming a realtor; the police sergeant becoming a lawyer), often with the intensity of a calling. This self-based and self-paced career development and the rapid pace of technological and organizational change mean that people need to learn how to learn. These are "meta-skills" that prepare people to adapt and to change their identities (Hall & Mirvis, 1995), thus creating ongoing cycles of learning stages or continuous learning.

This chapter presents definitions of lifelong learning and indicates trends influencing the need for lifelong learning. The chapter reviews theories that help explain motivation for lifelong learning and theory-based methods that organizations and instructional technologists use to support employees' lifelong learning. The chapter concludes with directions for policies and research to guide and improve opportunities for lifelong learning in the future.

Definitions of Lifelong Learning

Lifelong learning implies development and continuity. Development is learning that builds on prior learning, expanding knowledge and skills in depth and breadth. Marsick (1987, p. 4) defined workplace learning as "...the way in which individuals or groups acquire, interpret, reorganize, change or assimilate a related cluster of information, skills, and feelings. It is also primary to the way in which people construct meaning in their personal and shared organizational lives" (as quoted in Matthews, 1999, p. 19). Workplace learning is task focused, collaborative, often stems from problem-solving experiences, and occurs in a political and economic environment of behavior expectations and consequences (Matthews, 1999). Of course, people learn unwittingly from all their experiences. Lifelong learning refers to people's acquisition of knowledge and skills throughout their lives.

People seek learning for a variety of reasons. Some learn for personal edification, and any practical application occurs serendipitously. People also learn to retrain and to start new careers—for instance, a physicist college professor becoming a realtor. They learn to expand avocational interests (e.g., travel, sports, history, etc.), improve their job performance, meet professional credentialing requirements, or prepare for future career advancement (e.g., taking an MBA degree in mid-career).

Formal learning during childhood, adolescence, and young adulthood gives people a foundation and presumably skills for gainful employment. However, learning does not stop with formal education:

> The basic premise of lifelong learning is that it is not feasible to equip learners at school, college or university with all the knowledge and skills they need to prosper throughout their lifetimes. Therefore, people will need continually to enhance their knowledge and skills, in order to address immediate problems and to participate in a process of continuous vocational and professional development. The new educational imperative is to empower people to manage their own learning in a variety of contexts throughout their lifetimes.
>
> (*Sharples*, 2000, p. 178; see also Bentley, 1998)

A simple definition of lifelong learning is "development after formal education: the continuing development of knowledge and skills that people experience after formal education and throughout their lives" (Encarta, 2008). It can be viewed from an individual, group, organizational, and even national perspective. From an individual perspective, lifelong learning is self-directed. Learners seek and are open to new ideas and knowledge, whether about one's professional interests, interpersonal relationships, or oneself. Lifelong learning can be viewed even more expansively to include (Ehrlich, 2008):

- the ability to accept oneself as well as others;
- spontaneous but ethical behavior;
- a strong focus on problems outside oneself;
- the ability to capitalize on the qualities of detachment and solitude;
- independent stability in the face of hard knocks;
- freshness of appreciation;
- deep feelings of identification, sympathy, and affection for humankind;
- profound interpersonal relationships;
- a democratic character structure;
- strong ethics with definite moral standards;
- philosophical, non-hostile sense of humor;
- a special kind of creativity;
- the ability to function independently as a part of the growing tip of humanity.

Lifelong learning is "the acquisition of knowledge and skills in social interaction, with a focus on the interplay of society, organizational, and individual processes that enhance or inhibit the ability to learn to live a life" (Hake, 1999, p. 79).

Maurer (2002) distinguished between *learning* as "an increase or change in knowledge or skill that occurs as a result of some experience" and *development* as "an on-going, longer-term change or evolution that occurs through many learning experiences" (p. 14). Kegan and Lahey (2001) distinguished between *information learning,* which changes *what* we know, and *transformation learning,* which changes *how* we know. Baltes (1987) defined life-span development as "...constancy and change in behavior throughout the life course.... The goal [of developmental psychology] is to obtain knowledge about general principles of lifelong development, about interindividual differences and similarities in development, as well as about the degree and conditions of individual plasticity or modifiability of development" (p. 611). No age period is more important than another in regulating the nature of development. Rather, development entails continuous (cumulative) and discontinuous (innovative) processes that are different over time. Life-span development is multidirectional, with different foci at different times in a person's life or developing in different ways at one time. People vary in their range of adaptability and changeability, depending on their own abilities and personality as well as the constraints they face and the resources available to them, in addition to the historical and cultural conditions under which they live. Fischer (2000) focused on the mindset required for lifelong learning:

> Lifelong learning is more than adult education and/or training—it is a mindset and a habit for people to acquire. Lifelong learning creates the challenge to understand, explore, and support new essential dimensions of learning such as self-directed learning, learning on demand, collaborative learning, and organizational learning. These approaches need new media and innovative technologies to be adequately supported.... In the emerging knowledge society, an educated person will be someone who is willing to consider learning as a lifelong process.
>
> (*Fischer*, 2000, p. 265)

Lifelong learning is collaborative rather than competitive. Also, people belong to multiple communities that encourage learning and provide resources (e.g., employers, professional organizations, governments, religious organizations, athletic groups, etc.; Sharples, 2000).

Sessa and London (2006) defined continuous learning of employees as a deepening and broadening of organizational capabilities in (re)structuring to meet changing conditions, adding new skills and knowledge, and (re)creating into a more and more sophisticated system through reflection on the individual's actions and consequences.

Career-Related Continuous Learning

Career-related continuous learning is a pattern of formal and informal activities that people sustain over time for the benefit of their career development (London & Smither, 1999a). Acquiring new knowledge is self-initiated, discretionary, planned, and proactive. Individuals first recognize the need for learning, they then engage in activities to acquire new skills and knowledge and monitor their learning. They apply the learning—using, evaluating, and achieving the benefits of their newfound knowledge and skills. Career-related continuous learning is not just a continuous accumulation of new information and knowledge. Also, it is not learning for its own sake, that is, only for a sense of personal growth or self-satisfaction (not that this isn't important). Career-related continuous learning benefits career growth, performance improvement, and/or readiness for more responsible positions or transitions in different career directions. An organization that supports employees' career-related continuous learning is likely to become a learning organization that is able to form new interactions and work routines quickly to meet changing needs or at least to increase the core competencies available in the organization to meet changing work demands (Senge, 1990).

Consider several examples of people engaged in career-related continuous learning (from London and Smither, 1999a, p. 84):

• The director of international human resources for a telecommunications company travels the world to observe ("benchmark") the operations of other firms, actively works on learning new languages, acquires information about different cultures (their economies, values, educational programs, religious practices, and behavioral norms such as modes of negotiation and conflict resolution), and uses the information to shape the company's management practices as it establishes new operations and ventures.

• The manufacturing worker on the shop floor becomes fascinated by the firm's continuous quality initiatives, identifies skill and knowledge gaps (e.g., difficulty working with control charts, statistics, and process flow diagrams) by proactively seeking feedback from coworkers, attends evening courses at a community college to acquire the needed skills and knowledge, volunteers for cross-functional

teams (hoping to learn more by working with people from other areas), tries new manufacturing techniques, and is continuously on the lookout for bookstores for new ideas.

Maurer, Pierce, and Shore (2002) provided examples of different career-related continuous learning opportunities. These include:

• Job-related challenging activities: most learning comes about through job-related activities that are challenging or difficult (Maurer, Pierce, & Shore, 2002; McCall, Lombardo, & Morrison, 1988);
• Job-related courses or programs that enhance current job performance;
• Community projects that are challenging, interesting, and not required (i.e., done on a volunteer basis); the activities are likely to be unrelated to job or organizationally valued competencies;
• An undesired but challenging and important role;
• A task force addressing a challenging or difficult issue (probably requires being absent from the department for a time, costing the supervisor);
• Developing skill or knowledge specific to the organization to help the supervisor or organization, even though the skill or knowledge will probably not be useful in other organizations if the employee wants to change jobs;
• Continuing education courses required to maintain professional accreditation.

Career-related continuous learning is driven by a combination of individual and situational conditions. People are pressured by changes in their profession and organization, as well as their personal desires to learn. Consider, for instance, the software developer who must continuously be on the lookout for advances in the field, must learn them, and must apply them in developing new products (London & Smither, 1999b).

Learning is affected by an individual's relationship to the environment, including coworkers, work expectations, and support for learning. These include the following conditions proposed by Holliday (1994; cited in Matthews, 1999):

• Self—the need for positive feelings about oneself;
• Personal meaning—how one's self-perceptions are affected by learning;

- Action—one's ability to develop, apply, and measure ones own and other's ideas and to learn from experience;
- Collegiality—one's capacity to learn with and from colleagues directly and indirectly;
- Empowerment—one's ability to feel a sense of ownership, autonomy, and self-direction over the processes and outcomes of learning.

Trends Driving Continuous Learning

Organizations have moved from a paternalistic culture of company-directed development typical of organizations post–World War II (delivering training to meet immediate organizational needs) to a self-regulatory philosophy with organizations providing the resources to enable individual's self-initiated learning. Corporate mergers, buyouts, and downsizings starting in the 1980s and continuing today force mid- and late-career employees into premature retirement. For some, this will become a period of prolonged unemployment. However, older workers are often highly motivated to overcome career barriers (London, 1996). The need for labor and competition for talent pressure companies to build, sustain, and effectively use continuous learning systems (Marsick & Watkins, 1999). The need for learning is driven by changing economic conditions, global competition, the increased complexity of work and life demands (Johnson, 1997), technological developments, and organizational restructuring. Employers, policy makers (governments), and individuals have recognized the importance of developing human capital to promote economic prosperity and social inclusion (Jenkins, Vignoles, Wolf, & Galindo-Rueda, 2003). Lifelong learning, particularly the continuous development of skills and knowledge, is necessary to meet the expanding needs of employers.

Jenkins et al. (2003) used data from a longitudinal panel of people in the United Kingdom to identify who undertakes lifelong learning and why, as well as the economic benefits of lifelong learning. They found that learning leads to more learning. Specifically, acquiring more learning when in school increases the likelihood of participating in academic and vocationally related learning later in life. Also, participating in adult learning at least once increased the likelihood of participating in further learning. However, they did not find wage effects from lifelong learning, although adult education increased the wages of the least educated workers. They highlighted the importance of knowing more about who is motivated to engage in continuous education and why, as well as who pays for it, in order to understand the economic outcomes that one might expect from lifelong learning.

People who engage in learning for its own sake or for non-economic and non-job related reasons should not expect the learning to lead to high wages. However, there may be non-economic benefits (e.g., personal gratification, expanded social interactions), intellectual growth (which may have indirect effects on career advancement), and deepening of interests. Increased qualifications may be a signal of individuals' potential for performance and career achievement. However, adult education later in life may not send the same signal to employers. For instance, the experienced manager who undertakes a law degree may be seen as preparing for a second career or a part-time job or hobby after retirement (Jenkins et al., 2003).

Trend Toward Contract Employees

Job insecurity is an increasing problem, which suggests the need for people to guard their own career interests. An employment trend is toward increased use of contract employees. These may be freelancers who are hired to complete specific projects. Another insecure employment arrangement is call "permalancers." These are people who work full-time for several years with duties, hours, and responsibilities very similar to those of regular employees (Kamenetz, 2007). However, they are classified as temporary employees or independent contractors. As a result, they do not receive the same benefits (e.g., health care, retirement, entitlement to severance). Employers are unlikely to invest in these employees' development. Permalancers are hired to do a job, and are let go when no longer needed. They reduce employers' labor costs and provide employers with maximum staffing flexibility. If employers need people with different skills and talents, they will hire them on a temporary basis. The disadvantage is that employers give up having a dedicated workforce with valuable experience and history about how the organization operates. Even if most employees are still full-time, permanent staff, the temporary presence of independent contractors is likely to undermine the loyalty of permanent employees. From the contract employee's standpoint, the arrangement provides employment opportunities that might not be available otherwise. They may be gaining experience that makes them competitive for regular employment at this firm or elsewhere. However, unless they invest in their own training and development, their skills and experiences may be limited to their current position requirements. Recognizing these disadvantages and the growing number of contract employees, the Freelancers Union (2008) provides options for mutual support and advocacy. There is no cost for joining, and members can pay for insurance and educational events on a variety of business topics.

Increased Job and Organizational Complexity

Challenges to learning stem from information overload, the advent of high-functioning systems, and a climate of rapid technological change (Fischer, 2000). New learning methods are needed to circumvent the difficult problems of trying to teach people everything they may need to know in the future (coverage) with trying to predict what specific knowledge a person will need or not need in the future (obsolescence).

Ilgen and Pulakos (1999) examined seven key changes in the nature of work—changes in technology, job design, type of workforce, training methodology, external control, leadership, and work structure—as variables that affect job performance and learning requirements. London and Smither (1999a) listed factors in the environment that prompt employees, managers, and professionals to engage in career-related continuous learning. These include: technological change; deregulation and increased competition; contingent (temporary) employment contracts; reengineering and quality improvement efforts that demand change; reorganizations that decentralize departments (giving people more responsibility and control over their work) and empower individuals (employees have more freedom to act); and organizational changes such as global expansion, downsizing, and mergers and acquisitions.

London and Maurer (2004) outlined job and organizational changes as drivers of leadership development, including organizations needing on-going transformation and transaction capabilities from leaders; leaders wanting customized, business-oriented, time efficient development; organizations providing resources that enable development and create cultures that support continuous learning; technology allowing customized, self-administered developmental resources; and leaders taking personal responsibility for their own career development in light of organizational dislocations resulting from changing economic conditions, downsizing, restructuring, and crises of ethics and finance.

Organizational factors driving development include the following (London & Maurer, 2004):

• Changing nature of work resulting from: flatter organizational structures requiring increased communications between leaders and subordinates about organizational direction and monitoring and controlling performance; matrix management imposing interdependencies; virtual organizations and geographically dispersed work team creating looser confederations of employees and the need for cultural understanding and sensitivity; and temporary organizational structures that require increased understanding of organizational purpose and performance goals while valuing others' input, welcoming newcomers, and being flexible; prevalence of teams to accomplish work (project teams and task forces) requiring increased communication, coordination, and cooperation; and continuous quality improvement demanding attention to customer needs and customer-supplier relationships.

• New ventures requiring employees to learn as they go, monitoring the environment, maintaining high energy, garnering resources, seeking new ideas, seeking feedback, and taking risks. E-commerce requires creative thinking, knowledge of an ever-changing (highly competitive and uncertain) marketplace, and continuous tracking of operations, customers, and outcomes. Similarly, mergers and joint ventures require managing and learning from change as conflicts are resolved, different cultures clash, and new shared missions emerge. Such dynamic environments provide little time for experimentation. Decisions need to be made on the spot and actions taken immediately. Employees in this context are continuously learning about emerging technologies, trying to stay ahead of the competition, compared to employees in more stable organizations who learn continuously to increase their performance.

Continuous Learning as Core Competence

Continuous learning has come to be viewed as a core competency for employees at all career stages (Hall & Mirvis, 1995). This was evident in a survey of 400 human resource managers who were asked to rate the importance of 29 employee qualities. The following were among the top 15: "flexible in doing different tasks"; "will participate in training programs"; "try new approaches"; "up-to-date skills"; "learn new technology"; and "comfortable with new technology" (AARP, 2000). Businesses based on emerging technologies (the dot coms, for instance) face fast-paced, competitive, global pressures that depend on employees with energy, vision, and the ability to learn continuously (Kanter, 2001). These organizations—for example, research and development labs, business incubators, and other organizations that place a premium on design and constant improvement of their products—encourage and reward experimentation and innovation (London & Maurer, 2004). People in rapidly evolving disciplines such as medicine, engineering, and the sciences face pressures to maintain, expand, and apply their knowledge and skills (Kozlowski & Hults, 1987).

Employers view lifelong learning as a key to maintaining the capability of its workforce. For instance, Ohio's Office of Training and Development offers training courses to its state employees in an online brochure entitled "Blueprint for Lifelong Learning: A Guide for Your Continuous Improvement and Professional Development" (2008). The department's goal is "to maximize public employees' potential through training and educational opportunities."

Societal Goals

"Lifelong learning is an essential challenge for inventing the future of our societies; it is a necessity rather than a possibility or a luxury to be considered" (Fischer, 2000, p. 265). Forces for lifelong learning include the prevalence of high-technology jobs that require support for learning on demand, state requirements to maintain professional licenses, the inevitability of change in the course of a professional lifetime as disciplines evolve, and the deepening division between opportunities available to the educated and the uneducated. Lifelong learning is necessary for survival in late modernity and is necessary for globalization and competitiveness (Hake, 1999). Lifelong learning is the result of a complex interplay among three societal goals: economic development, personal development, and social inclusion (Aspin & Chapman, 2000). These goals contribute to the development of a highly skilled workforce and democratic policies and institutions.

Lifelong learning is viewed by some national governments as a key to ongoing economic prosperity. For instance, the government of Scotland offers a web site that explains the government's vision for lifelong learning. The goal is "the best possible match between the learning opportunities open to people and the skills, knowledge, attitudes and behaviours which will strengthen Scotland's economy and society" (Scotland, 2003). The site outlines five people-centered goals to realize this vision: (a) people have the confidence, enterprise, knowledge, creativity, and skills they need to participate in economic, social, and civic life; (b) people demand and providers deliver a high-quality learning experience; (c) people's knowledge and skills are recognized, used, and developed to best effect in their workplace; (d) people are given the information, guidance, and support they need to make effective learning decisions and transitions; and (e) people have the chance to learn, irrespective of their background or current personal circumstances. The site explains that lifelong learning is about "personal fulfilment and enterprise; employability and adaptability; active citizenship and social inclusion.... Lifelong learning encompasses the whole range of learning: formal and informal learning, workplace learning, and the skills, knowledge, attitudes and behaviours that people acquire in day-to-day experiences." Economic development is only one benefit of lifelong learning. More broadly, it contributes to "the development of society through the achievement of other social goals such as civic participation, sustainable development, improved health and wellbeing, reduced crime and greater social cohesion."

National policies can fund continuous learning opportunities. The United Kingdom's Open University (OU) is a good example. It was established about 40 years ago to provide distant learning opportunities to people of all ages. With regional centers throughout Great Britain, the university awards undergraduate and postgraduate degrees, diplomas, and certificates. It offers part-time and distance learning courses and encourages training and education for disabled people. There are no entry requirements, other than the ability to study at an appropriate level. Postgraduate courses require evidence of previous study or equivalent life experience. Students register for individual courses or modules that in turn are linked to degree programs. About 70% of the students are full-time. Teaching methods include written and audio materials, the Internet, disc-based software, and programs on DVD.

MIT's Open Courseware is a good example of a university recognizing the societal value of knowledge and "giving learning away." Available on the web to anyone, course materials include videotaped lectures, Powerpoint presentations, and readings. Although the courses do not lead to degrees, they serve as an archive of knowledge and learning, available to anyone with a computer and access to the Internet.

Theoretical Foundation for Lifelong Learning

Theories of learning and development focus on the interaction among environmental conditions and forces, individual differences, task demands, educational technology, and career opportunities to produce learning across the life span. Individual differences encompass traits and motivation, stage of life, and models of how people learn. There is considerable support for this individual/environment interaction. Colquitt, LePine, and Noe (2000) conducted a meta-analytic path analysis of 20 years of research on factors that predict training motivation and outcomes, such as declarative knowledge, skill acquisition, and transfer. Significant predictors included individual characteristics (e.g., locus of control, conscientiousness, anxiety, age, cognitive ability, self-efficacy, valence, job involvement) and situational characteristics (e.g., climate). In addition, they found that motivation to engage in training predicted outcomes beyond the effects of cognitive ability.

Models of Lifelong Learning

Kozlowski and Farr (1988) developed and tested an interactionist framework to predict employee participation in updating skills. Innovation, adaptation to innovative change, and effective performance require up-to-date technical skills and knowledge obtained through participation in professional activities, continuing education, and new work assignments. Individual characteristics (e.g., technical curiosity and interest, readiness to participate in professional and continuing education activities) and contextual features (e.g., support for continued training, work characteristics that allow autonomy, and on-the-job support for learning, including feedback, the need to work with others, having a range of job functions, encountering novel problems, and uncertainty of outcomes) jointly affect individuals' perceptions and interpretation of pressures for learning, which in turn relate to participation in updating. Training motivation is an important antecedent to participation in training.

Matthews (1999) developed a holistic view of workplace learning that included environmental influences, such as market competition, product change, technological development, economic conditions, political stability, societal values, and educational standards. Individual differences that affect motivation to learn include needs, desires, interests, self-esteem, and self-worth. Conditions for learning, such as encouragement and support, also affect involvement in learning. Learning outcomes include better competencies, higher qualification, improved productivity, and higher qualifications, as well as increased potential, rewards (e.g., promotion), and increased commitment to learning. Development requires opportunities to learn, the ability and will to learn (a combination of motivation, personal orientation, and skills), and organizational support for development, including contextual factors such as feedback, coaching, and rewards for development (McCauley, 2001).

London and Maurer (2004), focusing on leaders, presented a model to assess continuous learning needs, processes, and outcomes. Organizational conditions and employee characteristics determine learning needs. Conditions of the organization and its situation include challenges and demands faced by the organization, the behaviors and performance expected of employees, and the organization's development strategy and competency requirements related to each position. These variables determine the goals for development and methods and processes for learning in the organization. Employee characteristics include the individual's readiness to change, learning and development orientation (proclivity to engage in learning), goals to achieve mastery or specific levels of performance, beliefs that he or she can learn and apply the learning for performance improvement (learning self-efficacy), as well as standards, conscientiousness, expansiveness, and learning style. These individual difference variables also influence development goals and methods. The congruence of individual and organizational characteristics is important to effective learning outcomes. For instance, the organization's and a given employee's development goals may coincide, perhaps for different reasons. The employee may want to learn to attain a promotion or to maintain job security. The organization may want to retain talented, innovative employees. If the individual and organizational goals are not congruent, developmental efforts and investments on the part of the individual or the organization would be wasted, or at least limited.

Learning methods can be customized to meet each employee's specific needs. The learning process depends on the methods used, the organization's support for learning (e.g., feedback), and the employee's self-affirming, developmental behaviors, such as seeking and using feedback from a variety of sources. Individual difference variables, such as the desire to learn for its own sake (mastery learning), and support at the organizational level (e.g., coaching) "boost" or enhance the effectiveness of the development process.

Next we will consider individual differences that affect continuous learning motivation, development across the life span, and learning theories.

Individual Differences Affecting Motivation to Learn

SELF-DIRECTION

Self-directed learning requires that individuals have acquired broad self-management competencies, are familiar with the subject matter, and have a sense of their competence to learn (self-learning efficacy). Self-direction in learning involves: (1) personal autonomy; (2) willingness and ability to manage one's overall learning efforts; (3) independent pursuit of learning without formal institutional support or affiliation; and (4) learner-control of instruction (Candy, 1991).

EMPLOYEE LEARNING AND DEVELOPMENT ORIENTATION

Maurer (2002) defined *learning and development orientation* as the tendency to feel favorably about learning experiences and to be continually and persistently involved in such experiences in the pursuit of one's own development. These individuals believe that they are constantly changing and evolving. Dweck and Leggett (1988) called this subscribing to an implicit *incremental theory of traits*—a belief that, indeed, they can change. They are mastery learners who acquire skills and knowledge for their own sake, not for any immediate benefits they might bring. They have a conception of what they might become (Wurf & Markus, 1991). People who subscribe to an *entity theory of traits* believe that their personal characteristics are fixed. They are motivated to avoid failure or to use their abilities to maximize their performance.

EXPANSIVENESS

London and Diamante (2002; Diamante & London, 2002) suggested that individuals need to be expansive to be successful in high-technology work environments. They conceptualized expansiveness as demonstrating self-directed energy, showing a continuous quest to learn and generate new ideas, and having a desire to apply newly acquired knowledge and novel ideas. Expansive individuals sustain a deep focus on their area of expertise while they simultaneously challenge conventional thought and understanding. They are driven to be successful and to strive for continuous growth and innovation (Kaplan, Drath, & Kofodimos, 1991; MacDonald, Gagnier, & Friedman, 2000). They engage in learning both for its own sake and for how it can be used for personal and organizational gain.

CAREER MOTIVATION

London (1983, 1985, 2002; London & Noe, 1997) conceptualized three domains of career motivation. *Career insight* is the motivational spark. It consists of awareness of one's own strengths and weaknesses as well as the resources, opportunities, and barriers in the environment. *Career identity* is the direction of one's motivation. It is an awareness of the potential rewards in the environment, as well as possible losses. *Career resilience* consists of the self-oriented personality characteristics that provide strength for overcoming career barriers. Resilience encompasses self-efficacy, the feeling of internal control, self-regulation, and self-esteem (cf., Greenberg, 2008).

Career resilience sets the stage for gaining career insight and establishing a meaningful and realistic career identity. Supervisors and others in the individual's environment can affect all three components. However, career resilience is more difficult to change. It is fairly well established early in life and changes as an individual receives a stream of reinforcement (or criticism) at formative and transitional stages in his or her life. Career insight and identity stem from information in the environment. Supervisors provide employees with performance feedback and information about performance expectations and career opportunities. Employees who are high in career resilience are able to take advantage of this information—for instance, absorbing and applying critical feedback to improve their performance. Employees who are low in career resilience are less likely to use such information productively, and are likely to ignore or withdraw from situations that offer criticism and to seek only self-affirming information.

Career motivation is an important factor in older workers' response to career barriers. Organizational transitions can cause severe stress, including long-term unemployment and premature retirements for those who lose their jobs, and resentment and insecurity for those who remain (London, 1996). Although such major dislocations are times of discouragement and self-doubt, they can help people to be more resilient and more receptive to new insights about themselves and their environment. Wolf, London, Casey, and Pufahl (1995) studied 72 displaced engineers who were participating in a semester-long career retraining program in technology management. For participants who were high in career motivation, prior successful career experiences in technology management were positively related to their engaging in productive training behaviors during the program. For participants who were low in career motivation, prior career experiences were negatively related to productive behavior during the program. The more these individuals had experience with technology management, the less they were able to absorb new information and ideas. They had difficulty overcoming their disappointment and believing that they could bring about renewed opportunities for themselves.

Building on the concept of career motivation, London and Maurer (2004) identified four groups of individual characteristics that affect lifelong learning: (1) self-insight, recognizing the need for change, setting learning goals, and evaluating progress; (2) being ready to change one's behavior in relation to changing organizational needs; (3) stage of cognitive/emotional development; and (4) self-monitoring and self-regulation. Self-insight is understanding one's own strengths and weaknesses, recognizing organizational needs (including behaviors needed for improved job performance and shifting goals at the departmental, organizational, and industry level), and using this insight to set development goals (London, 2002; London & Noe, 1997). Insight and reflection are critical to the process of development. Continuous learning in the workplace requires "reflective practice" (Marsick & Watkins, 1992). This entails viewing experiences as potential learning and reexamining assumptions values, methods, policies, and practices. Steps for continuous learning are: clarify thinking; be open to questions; notice context; test hunches; investigate; name and rename the problems; uncover what underlies thinking; and experiment (Marsick & Watkins, 1992).

FEEDBACK ORIENTATION

London and Smither (2002) conceptualized *feedback orientation* as "an individual's overall receptivity to feedback and the extent to which the individual welcomes guidance and coaching" (pp. 82–83). People who are high in feedback orientation have positive feelings about feedback and a low level of apprehension about being evaluated. They believe that feedback provides useful information to

direct ways to improve their performance. So they have a propensity to seek feedback and process it consciously and conscientiously. They are sensitive to, and care about, others' perceptions and reactions to their performance. Moreover, they feel accountable for use of the feedback. Such individuals have a general desire to learn about themselves, to verify their self-image, and to enhance their self-esteem (Baumeister, 1999). They are open to new experiences (Barrick & Mount, 1991) and are ready to take action to change (Prochaska, Prochaska, & Levesque, 2001). Even when feedback is not forthcoming, people who are high in feedback orientation seek feedback from supervisors and other coworkers. The also seek objective data about task progress and accomplishment (Brink, 2002).

MASTERY LEARNERS AND SELF-REGULATION

Mastery learners diagnose their own abilities and gaps in knowledge and skills, observe their own performance, and evaluate what they need to do to achieve their goals (Bandura, 1986). Mastery learners focus less on comparing themselves to others or to external standards and more on their ongoing learning (Dweck, 1986). Nevertheless, their motivation rests on setting specific, challenging, and realistic goals (Locke & Latham, 1990) and perceiving a gap between current levels of skills, knowledge, and performance, and potential levels of skills, knowledge, and performance (Carver & Scheier, 1990; Scherbaum & Vancouver, 2002).

Individual differences (cognitive abilities, skills, dispositions, and motives) and the elements of training (its design, how information is presented, use of technology) produce learning outcomes and performance improvement through active, self-regulatory processes, such as engaging in practice, self-monitoring, and self-evaluation (Bell & Kozlowski, 2009; Kozlowski et al., 2001). Metacognition is the exertion of control over learning processes, which helps learners to engage actively in their learning, rather than being passive recipients of instruction (cf., Bell & Kozlowski, 2009; Cannon-Bowers, Rhodenizer, Salas, & Bowers, 1998; Keith & Frese, 2005). Training that incorporates active learning involves: exploration, experimentation, and inductive learning; inductions to motivate mastery learning; and support for processing feedback and controlling emotions in dealing with, and making appropriate attributions for, errors. Self-regulatory processes, such as metacognition, mental models, goal orientation, self-efficacy, and emotion, produce learning outcomes, especially when individuals have the requisite cognitive ability, openness to experience, conscientiousness, and traits that help them cope with anxiety and focus on mastery, rather than possible positive consequences from performance improvement or negative consequences from making mistakes (Bell & Kozlowski, 2009).

EXPECTANCY-VALUE COGNITIONS

Expectancy-value cognitions that participation in learning experiences will produce positive outcomes are strongly related to the intention to participate in future employee development activities (Birdi, Allan, & Warr, 1997; Facteau, Dobbins, Russell, Ladd, & Kudisch, 1995; Fishbein & Stasson, 1990; Garofano & Salas, 2005; Hurtz & Williams, 2009; Maurer &Tarulli, 1994; Noe & Wilk, 1993). Hurtz and Williams (2009) conceptualized one aspect of the intention to participate as a felt responsibility or obligation to develop oneself as an employee. They suggested that the feeling of obligation to help the organization realize beneficial outcomes, regardless of (or in addition to) any personal benefits or costs that the employee would expect from participation, plays a key role in predicting intentions and participation in training and development.

Additional theoretical work differentiated variables predicting participation in continuous learning, including: (a) learning motivation, or a desire to continue learning; (b) the anticipation of career development outcomes, such as promotions, improved work assignments, and intrinsic feelings of achievement; and (c) psychosocial development, for instance, increased self-confidence and making new friends (cf. Maurer & Tarulli, 1994; Noe & Wilk, 1993; Nordhaug, 1989; Tharenou, 2001).

Life-Span Development

London and Sessa (2006) summarized how career development progresses throughout the life cycle from initial career-related learning, to becoming and being an adult, and then reflecting on adulthood. Career development is both external (outward signs of career success, stagnation, or failure) and internal (self-satisfaction from meeting challenges, for instance). Table 35.1 recognizes that inner-life elements beyond one's career are also important, such as autonomy, self-worth, and commitment to primary relationships.

Lifelong learning needs to be understood across a lifetime because professional activity has become knowledge-intensive and fluid. There is no longer the traditional divide: education followed by work (Fischer, 2000). Moreover, learning is not an individual activity but a collaborative effort among colleagues. Intelligence includes the ability to learn and the ability to adapt to meet the demands of the environment effectively, and people may develop different aspects of intelligence throughout their lives (Sternberg, 1997a).

People develop multiple elements of their being—physical, emotional, cognitive, social, and so on. Intelligence is not a unitary construct but a multiple one (Sternberg, 1997a, 1997b). Gardner (1983, 1993, 1999) identified eight relatively independent multiple intelligences: linguistic, logical-mathematical, spatial, musical, bodily-kinesthetic, interpersonal, intrapersonal, and naturalist intelligence, and considered the possibility of two more: spiritual and existential. Lifelong learning applies to all these types of intelligence.

The nature of learning may change as people age, and what is needed for learning and functioning may change at different times in an individual's life span. As some abilities decline with age, people learn to compensate for the abilities they lose by optimizing the abilities that remain. This is the mechanism of *selective optimization with compensation* (cf., Baltes, Dittman-Kohli, & Dixon, 1984, cited in Sternberg, 1997a). The meaning of loss and gain will depend on the resulting consequences and the individual's adaptive capacity (Baltes, 1987). People learn to adapt to and shape their environmental contexts as they select and to some extent create the environment in which they feel most comfortable. This environment may change over time relative to people's abilities, sometimes motivating a career or job change.

COGNITIVE PROCESSING

The ability to process information and knowledge is likely to affect learning competence and motivation. Bloom's (1956) classic typology of multilevel thinking skills includes: (a) knowledge and comprehension, including reading, memorizing, and repeating information in one's own words; (b) transfer and application of knowledge and use of information in new and different ways; (c) analyzing complex information and breaking it into sub-elements; (d) synthesizing discrete pieces of knowledge and information to produce new concepts and ideas; and (e) evaluating information, judging newly synthesized concepts, and placing a value on the results. This taxonomy of educational objectives suggests that all learners can achieve the five levels. Krathwohl (2002) revised the taxonomy to encompass factual knowledge (knowledge of terminology,

Table 35.1 Adult Development Through Life Stages as Related to Career and Inner Life

	20–30 Leave home and enter the adult world	30–40 Develop and extend roots	40–50 Midlife	50–60 Stabilization	60–70 Late maturity and retirement	70–Death Life review and termination issues
	Identify self as an adult		Becoming and being an adult		Time for reflection	
Career: External	Find a job and begin paying own bills. Job exploration, training/education, and trial entry. Commit to specific work area or continue career exploration.	Commit to set career pattern and strive for vertical movement (play the corporate game). Commit to a function or profession. Enter or leave due to children (women especially).	Focus on making one's mark, legacy. Enter period of peak work commitment, achievement and recognition. Take on supervisory, managing and mentoring responsibilities. Feel that corporate games are less important than they were. Possibly face midlife career change to meet changing values or changing opportunities—e.g., lose corporate job in downsizing and start own business.	Culminate career. Act as mentor/advisor. Evaluate retirement security. Face increasing age-related employment problems (unskilled especially).	Retire from full-time work. Detach from formal work role. Become interested in hobbies again and learn for learning's sake instead of learning on the job. Increase community service. Fulfill honorific and sage roles.	Cultivate leisure activities and new outlets for skill development and use. Continue to fulfillment of honorific and sage roles (though may be quietly amused at any recognition received).
Career: Internal	Establish specific work identity. Commit to generativity (ongoing learning and professional and personal growth) or productivity with push toward a "dream."	Readjust career goals to realign with changing expectations of self and significant other. Seeking mastery, promotion, recognition, credentials, and confidence	Redefine work roles/goals in light of changing values, priorities, and possibilities.	Begin to disengage, or postpone and ignore upcoming retirement. Evaluate and review work accomplishments.	Redirect energy into "non-work" activities and life maintenance routines.	

Inner life					
Establish self as an adult. Develop autonomy and competence. Develop sense of personal worth and identity. Establish and commit to primary relationships. Increase self-knowledge. Establish personal worldview, values, beliefs, priorities, and goals. Detach from parents and siblings; start own family.	Commit to generativity and striving for productivity. Integrate and prioritize multiple commitments and responsibilities to work, family, mate, friends, community. Compromise and adjust goals to reality—life's demands. Begin to feel concern about own and parents' aging.	Begin midlife review—face contradictions, and adjust. Feel midlife shift in time perspective (look forward and backward).	Increase personalization of death and consciousness of own vulnerability. Stabilize support systems again. Consolidate resources in response to recognition of increasing vulnerability. Deal with aging parents/death of parents.	Detach personal identity from work role. Develop leisure orientation and life enrichment. Adapt to increased distance from mainstream—accept "subculture" status. Adapt to decreasing vigor. Begin to conserve one's energy.	Conduct life review and reminisce. Consolidate symbolic belief system. Feel that one's life had meaning and was well spent. Accept aid from children. Face increasing social separation; bury friends and family. Deal with physical frailty. Deal with aloneness or loss of privacy.

Note. Adapted from Wortley & Amatea (1982) and Jackson (1996) by Sessa & London (2006). Reprinted from Sessa & London (2006, pp. 44–45) with permission.

specific details, and elements), conceptual (knowledge of classifications, theories, models, principles, and generalizations), procedural (skills, techniques, and criteria for applying different methods of analysis), and metacognitive knowledge (strategic knowledge, knowledge about context and condition, and self-knowledge). Baltes (cf. Baltes & Smith, 2008) developed a family of four metacriteria of knowledge, which together characterize wisdom. These are: factual and strategic knowledge about the fundamental pragmatics of life; knowledge that considers the relativism of values and life goals; knowledge about context and how these change over time; and knowledge about fundamental uncertainties of life and ways to manage. Together they form wisdom, a system of exceptional knowledge and expertise that motivates an individual to further expansion of learning.

Adults progress toward wisdom but rarely achieve it. The question is whether the environment supports higher level cognitive processing or focuses mainly on factual knowledge, comprehension, and adaptive applications rather then transformative syntheses. The latter are needed for novel uses of emerging technologies, going beyond accumulation and reactive adaptations to discover, experiment (test), and apply creative uses of technologies to generate new methods and processes.

ZONE OF PROXIMAL DEVELOPMENT

Vygotsky (1978) extended the idea of an individual's level of development by contrasting the person's current level of ability and accomplishment with the person's potential level. The difference is the *zone of proximal development*. This refers to the functions that are in the process of maturation. Learning creates the zone of proximal development by stimulating an awareness of potential in the individual and awakening more mature, internal development processes. People learn how to learn in a more complex way that requires increased cognitive complexity and exposure to richer ways of thinking and learning.

ORDERS OF MIND

Kegan's model of life-span development recognizes the importance of self-awareness in relation to understanding organizational and interpersonal conditions (Kegan, 1982, 1994; Kegan & Lahey, 2001; described by London & Maurer, 2004, and Day, 2002). Development is a transformation to more complex ways of thinking and feeling. An individual moves to increasingly complex "orders of mind" and deeper levels of self-understanding and an awareness of how others see the world, which were previously taken for granted or hidden from consciousness. These stages of mind represent qualitatively different levels of social construction.

The first stage represents the cognitive processes of a young child. The second represents older children, teens, and some adults. It centers on others' feelings in which one's own feelings are inseparable from those of others. These individuals operate with a schema of fixed role behaviors. The third stage, "traditionalism," is again represented in teens and many adults. They distinguish between their own and others' viewpoints. However, they feel responsible for others' feelings. They are excellent team players who share a sense of identity, which, in adulthood, is tied to their profession. More than half of all adults do not proceed beyond the third stage. The fourth stage, "modernism," is having a sense of self that is separate from a connection to others. These individuals are autonomous and self-driven. Individuals who reach this fourth stage are self-governing and principled, but yet do not quite comprehend the limits of self-governing systems. Even fewer people reach the "postmodern," fifth stage. If they do achieve this stage of cognitive development, it does not happen before midlife. These individuals recognize the limits of their own system of principles. An individual's movement through these stages is a function of his or her experiences.

Kegan's (1994) model has implications for how organizations can construct experiences that promote cognitive learning and development. Such experiences recognize how people interpret events and deal with challenges that require a higher level of cognitive and emotional functioning. Experiences that enhance cognitive and emotional development include work that requires dedication and commitment, opportunities for inventions and experimentation, being self-evaluative and self-correcting, creating and being guided by one's own vision, taking responsibility for one's own actions and outcomes, achieving a level of mastery, and recognizing how others see the organization (Kegan, 1994). Since most people are third order thinkers, consider how they react to challenging situations. They recognize diverse perspectives and others' viewpoints. However, they do not have a sense of self-ownership. Situations that challenge third order individuals are ill-defined roles, conflicting demands from work and family, and being in a minority position (Van Velsor, 2002). Fourth order thinkers see themselves as role models who are able to argue for a minority perspective. They see challenge of conveying a vision and motivating others to work collaboratively.

CAREER GROWTH CURVE

Hall (1976) suggested a simple model of career growth throughout the life cycle. He called it the "career growth curve." It consists of several distinct stages: exploration and trial (age 15–30); establishment and advancement (age 30–45); and continued growth and maintenance, or decline and disengagement (after age 45).

LIFE CYCLE MODELS

Levinson (1979, 1986, 1997) formulated a life cycle model consisting of a sequence of eras, each characterized by biopsychosocial development. Major changes occur between eras. A cross-era transition, which lasts about five years, ends the previous era and begins the new. The age ranges have been found consistently in research. *Preadulthood,* from birth to about age 22, is the formative period, as the individual defines and develops relationships and gains a sense of inedependence. The *early adult transition* ranges from ages 17 to 22. The individual modifies his or her relationships and develops a new sense of individuation, establishing a place in the adult world. *Early adulthood* is from ages 17 to 45. It starts with the *early adult transition*, which is often a period of contradiction and stress. These are the peak years biologically, and it is the time of passionate pursuit of youthful ambitions, establishing a niche in society, and raising a family. It can be a time of rich satisfaction from career advancement, creativitiy, and realization of major goals. However, for some, it is marked by disappointment and stress, with overwhelming financial obligations, marital problems, and difficulties of parenthood. The *midlife transition* is roughly from 40 to 45 years of age. This is the end of early adulthood and the beginning of middle adulthood. This is a developmental period during which the character of living changes appreciably. The individual in this stage can gain a new sense of individuation and contentment, becoming more compassionate, reflective, and judicious. Without this transition, life could become trivial or stagnant. During *middle adulthood,* from ages 40 to 65, biological capacity diminishes, but the individual has sufficient energy for a personally and socially satisfying life, unless life was hampered in some way during the forties or fifties. Middle adulthood can be a time of mentoring the younger generation. *Late adult transition* ranges from ages 60 to 65, moving into *late adulthood*. This can be a time for continued generative and reflective development, but it may also be a time of physical or mental decline. Current heath care technology extends this age into retirement, and, for some, continued career progress or transitions into new career-related directions, perhaps part-time work or experimenting with new endeavors.

Cognitive ability usually decreases with age. However, this is not just a function of an inevitable decline in brain power. Individual differences in intellectual functioning in old age are related to sensory functioning. In a study of old and very old individuals (mean age = 85 years), age-related declines in cognitive abilities (speed, reasoning, memory, knowledge, and fluency) are mediated by differences in visual and auditory acuity (Lindenberger, 1994). A further study of more than 600 people ranging in age from 15 to 103 years found that visual and auditory acuity accounted for larger proportions of variance in intelligence as people aged (Baltes & Lindenberger, 1997). In particular, sensory acuity accounted for 11% of variance in intelligence in adulthood (25 to 69 years) to 31% in older age people. These studies suggest the importance of maintaining individuals' sight and hearing through regular exams and medical advances and treatments that maintain and in some cases improve these functions (e.g., cataract and laser surgery).

Theories About How People Learn

Kolb (1984) distinguished between reflective/passive learners, who learn by watching and listening, and experiential/active learners, who learn by doing. Experiential learning entails concrete experience, reflective observations, conceptualization, and active experimentation (Boyatzis & Kolb, 1991; Kolb, 1984; Mainemelis, Boyatzis, & Kolb, 2002). Experiential learning on the job is a powerful vehicle for continuous development. People often learn most from events and assignments that are unexpected and pose challenges. These may be tough assignments, failures, mistakes, disappointment (being passed over for a promotion), difficult personnel issues (overcoming subordinates' performance problems), or simply new responsibilities and functions. Executives learn most from assignments that are start-ups, turnarounds, changes in job scope, reassignments from line to staff or vice versa, and being a member of a cross-functional, geographically dispersed team (Lindsey, Homes, & McCall, 1987). Also, executives learn by modeling others who have exceptional skills or faults.

Kolb (1984; Boyatzis & Kolb, 1991; Mainemelis et al., 2002) suggested that learning styles depend on individuals' orientations or preferences for types of experiences, as well as transforming those experiences. Learning styles are a function of mode of experience and mode of transforming experience. Both modes can be expressed as doing or thinking. One mode of experience is *apprehension*—a preference for concrete experiences (doing) and real feelings and sensing rather than thinking. People who are high in apprehension orientation are open-minded and want to understand the uniqueness and complexity of situations, rather than forming theories that generalize across situations. Another mode of experience is *comprehension*—a preference for abstract conceptualizations and focusing on thinking (using logic, ideas, and concepts) rather than feelings to understand information. People who are high in comprehension value precision, rigor, quantitative analysis, and analyzing ideas. One mode of transforming experience is *extension*—a preference for active experimentation and practical applications rather than reflective understanding. People who are high in extension are open to new experiences and understanding how things work. Another mode of transformation experience is *intension*—a preference for reflective observation and understanding the meaning of ideas and situations through careful observation and impartial description. People who are high in intention focus on understanding rather than practical application. These form four learning styles:

Convergent: preference for abstract conceptualization (comprehension) and transforming experience through active experimentation (extension); strength in problem solving, decision making, and the practical application of ideas. Convergent learners prefer to deal with tasks and problems rather than social and interpersonal issues.

Divergent: preference for concrete experience (apprehension) and transforming experience through reflective observation (intention); strength in imagination and awareness of meaning and values. Divergent learners understand events from different perspectives and organize them into a *gestalt*; they learn by generating alternative ideas and exploring their implications.

Assimilation: preference for abstract conceptualization (comprehension) and transforming experience by reflective observation (intention); strength in inductive reasoning and the ability to create theoretical models. They learn by forming abstract ideas and concepts that are sound theories but not necessarily worthwhile applications.

Accommodation: preference for concrete experience (apprehension) and transformation of experience through active experimentation (extension); strength in doing things, carrying out plans and tasks, and getting involved in new experiences. People who learn using accommodation solve problems in intuitive trial-and-error ways.

Another taxonomy of learning identified four learning tactics (Van Velsor & Guthrie, 1998): thinking; taking action; asking others; and dealing with one's feelings, for instance, overcoming a fear of failure or the anxiety of trying new behaviors. People usually prefer one learning style, but may use two or more during a given learning process. Unless constrained by a structured learning task, they will likely start learning using their preferred style and continue in that mode unless that fails to work. "Blocked" learners keep trying one approach without changing it (Bunker & Webb, 1992). Effective learners are able to alter their style and tactic of learning to meet the needs of the situation. Training professionals need to recognize that adults use a variety of learning styles, but they do have preferences. As such, learning experiences (whether formal training programs, informal on-the-job assignments, or online training) should provide an opportunity for people to apply different styles, perhaps choosing different ways of learning the same constructs. For example, a training program could give learners the option of reading about and discussing concepts and ideas, collecting and interpreting data, trying new modes of behavior and receiving feedback, and participating in unstructured problem-solving tasks. Engaging in a variety of learning styles will help individuals be less dependent on one style and will help them learn how to learn in different ways (Van Velsor & Guthrie, 1998).

ADAPTIVE, GENERATIVE, AND TRANSFORMATIVE LEARNING

Sessa and London (2006; London & Sessa, 2006; 2007) conceptualized three ways in which people change and learn: adaptive, generative, and transformative learning. Adaptive learning is an almost automatic reaction to shifts in the environment. This learning stems from behavioral learning theories (Guthrie, 1952; Thorndike, 1932; Tolman, 1932; Watson, 1924). Stimuli in the environment, including reinforcements (or sometimes punishments or withholding positive or negative reinforcement), indicate the need for individuals to alter their behavior from habitual patterns. Adaptations occur without much thought, as the individual encounters unexpected demands and non-routine situations (Berry & Dienes, 1993; Reber, 1993). This is a reactive learning process. People may not even realize what they are learning, at least not until they have time to reflect on events. They do something that "works" (has positive outcomes) and so they repeat it.

In contrast, generative learning is proactive. Individuals challenge themselves to become masters of a field or discipline. It is intentionally learning new behaviors, skills, and knowledge (Senge, 1990). The concept of generative learning arose from cognitive learning theorists (Ausubel, 1968; Bruner, 1960; Gagné, 1978). Generative learners strive toward mastery, not learning for its instrumental value (Bunderson & Sutcliffe, 2003; Dweck, 1986; VandeWalle, 1997). They believe themselves able to change and learn. That is, they are high in self-efficacy and the ability to learn from others (social learning; Bandura, 1997). They recognize that they are responsible for their own learning (concept of *andragogy*; Knowles, 1975). As people try new behaviors, they discover new, constructive ways to work with others and to accomplish tasks (Kasl, Marsick, & Dechant, 1997; Lawrence, Mauws, Dyck, & Kleysen, 2005; Senge, 1990).

People who learn generatively are likely to be prepared for current and future challenges. They do not resist change or adapt to it in minor ways, but seek and embrace learning and change through continuous explorations, questioning, challenging assumptions, seeking different viewpoints, evaluating alternatives, and thinking about outcomes (Van der Vegt & Bunderson, 2005). They use feedback to revise their self-perceptions. Generative learners actually learn how to be better generative learners in the future. Generative learners seek the knowledge they need when they need it and before they need it. They are constantly on the lookout for new ideas and information, as well as opportunities to acquire new skills and knowledge. Then they are creative in applying this learning, taking initiative rather than waiting for events to make the knowledge useful.

Transformative learning goes beyond generative learning. Transformative learners reconstruct meaning and alter the ways that they operate in fundamental and sometimes dramatic ways. This stems from constructivist theories of learning (Dewey, 1933/1986; Mezirow, 1991, 1994; Rogoff, 1990; von Glaserfeld, 1996; Vygotsky, 1978). They use language to change the way that they conceptualize and communicate their vision of the world (Anderson, 1997). They learn by interchanging and evolving ideas with others, formulating new visions and modes of transactions with others that are then used when unexpected events occur (Gergen, 1991; Wenger, 1999). Sometimes people are forced into transformational change, but in doing so, they recognize the need, take the initiative to create change (getting a jump start and taking control, rather than waiting to be controlled), and establishing a transformation. This starts with what is likely to be an uncomfortable process of critical reflection that upsets the status quo (Langer, 2000). Assessment is an important part of learning. People who engage in reflection and self-assessment gain an understanding of their own capabilities (Krechevsky & Seidel, 1998; Sternberg, 1997b). Moreover, assessments can monitor growth over time. People give up old behaviors, create new patterns of acting and interacting with others, evaluating and revising these behaviors as they go. It is a process of reinvention and experimentation. People who learn transformatively may have some trepidation, but basically they are excited by the process of self-reflection, discovery, and re-creation.

Transformational learning mixes Kolb's (1984) learning styles with transformation of experience through active experimentation (extension) and reflective observation (intention). Critical reflection is a central ingredient, challenging the validity of our suppositions in prior learning and allowing us to evaluate our actions, others' reactions, and alternative responses, taking our own and others' values, ideals, feelings, and moral decisions into account (Mezirow, 1991). This is the avenue by which we change our assumptions about what we thought we knew. We become open to new ideas (inclusivity), comprehend fine points (discrimination), and identify interactions and linkages that were previously transparent to us (integrative).

READINESS TO LEARN

Readiness to change requires being open to new ideas and experiences (Barrick & Mount, 1991). London and Smither (1999a) identified a number of personal characteristics that influence an individual's tendency to be involved in career-related continuous learning. These include self-efficacy and internal locus of control, extraversion, mastery learning orientation, cognitive ability, conscientiousness, self-monitoring, feedback seeking, openness to new experiences, and public self-consciousness.

Individual difference characteristics predispose people to learn in these different ways. Sessa and London (2006; London & Sessa, 2006, 2007) suggested that whether people are adaptive, generative, and/or transformational learners depends on their readiness to learn. Those who are high in variables that foster readiness to learn are likely to be generative and transformative learners, especially when the situation is also high in pressure to change and learn. Those who are low in readiness are likely to ignore stimuli that encourage or require learning, or may adapt their behavior to the situation but may not learn or apply new knowledge and skills in new and different ways. Readiness is a function of the resilience and insight components of career motivation (London, 1985). These include self-awareness, awareness of environmental opportunities and pressures, self-esteem, self-efficacy, and self-regulation. That is, people are going to be more willing to change and learn when they have high regard for themselves, see themselves as able to change and be effective, and believe that they are able to control situations to bring about positive outcomes.

Self-monitoring is also important. People who are high in self-monitoring are responsive to social and interpersonal cues, including role expectations and situationally appropriate behavior (Gangestad & Snyder, 2000; Snyder, 1974). High self-monitors constantly compare and adjust their behavior to their perceptions of what others expect of them or others' reactions to them. People who are low in self-monitoring have fairly stable behavior related to their personal characteristics. A good example is cultural sensitivity (Albert, 1996; Dunbar, 1996). Culturally sensitive expatriates are able to learn the host country's customs, values, and perspectives more readily than those who are not as culturally sensitive. A related concept is emotional or interpersonal intelligence (Gardner, 1993; Salovey & Mayer, 1990), which includes self-awareness (accurately recognizing one's own feelings), managing emotions (discovering how to cope with stress, fears, and anxiety), self-motivation (self-regulation of emotions to accomplish goals), empathy (sensitivity to others' feeling), and human relationships (social competence and social skills). People who are generative learners are self-driven. Knowles (1975) called this concept *andragogy*. This captures the idea that adults are responsible for their own decisions and learning. They are problem- and task-centered and are ready to learn those things that they need in order to cope with life's challenges. They learn best when they understand why they need to know something. Although they have a rich base of knowledge

and experience already, they have habits and biases that sometimes limit their learning. Also, internal motivation is more potent than external rewards or pressures for learning.

In summary, individual differences, a life-span perspective, and learning theories provide a foundation for understanding lifelong learning. Next, we will consider organizational factors that support learning and methods for delivering on-going education.

Support for Lifelong Learning

Support for lifelong learning entails: understanding the organization's environment and corporate culture; understanding how empowered individual learning contributes to, and is supported by, the creation of learning organizations, and formal and informal learning opportunities; and establishing clear learning objectives and assessing learning outcomes.

Environment and Culture for Learning

Hall (2001) articulated a model of how the organization's environment and culture influence lifelong learning. Components of an environment that supports learning include: a culture of discussing performance requirements, assessing performance, and providing in-the-moment coaching and feedback about performance in specific tasks and events (e.g., discussing how well a presentation went and how it could be improved the next time). Another component is a learning culture, one that includes training resources, whether in the form of online material and/or in-person training. The available training resources are tied to the needs of the organizations. For instance, companies that want to encourage supervisors to pay attention to subordinates' development needs may offer workshops on "the supervisor as coach and developer" and include "support for subordinates' development" as a dimension of the annual performance review.

Social support and social networks are important for lifelong learning (Molloy & Noe, 2009). Social networks vary in size, diversity, and strength of relationships (Higgins & Kram, 2001) in generative and transformative environments (Sessa & London, 2006). For instance, diverse, strong ties produce entrepreneurial relationships, especially when combined with opportunities; pressures for career change, coupled with enabling resources, produce high involvement in continuous learning. Diverse weak relationships, combined with an environment that supports the acquisition and application of new knowledge, can also produce high involvement in continuous learning.

Corporate philosophy is another element of support for development. Some organizations have the philosophy of hiring talented people when they are needed. Others have the philosophy of developing their current employees to meet changing needs. This maintains employees' loyalty and commitment, as well as their experience and expertise, while broadening their capabilities and value to the organization. So a company that is "going global" may provide training in cultural sensitivity and managing diversity. Some employers provide training only when it is needed to enhance performance to meet immediate corporate goals. Others provide opportunities for managers' and employees' ongoing development, simply to make them more competitive and valuable to the organization, under the assumption that the investment in learning will pay off in unforeseeable ways, for instance, in new products and services, new markets, and attracting talented employees who want to work for an organization that appreciates and support their continuous growth.

Some organizations focus on developing younger people, promoting those who show promise early in their careers and showing the door to those who do not. Other organizations provide developmental opportunities for employees of all ages, recognizing differences in capabilities, career goals, and life priorities as people age. Employees may make different contributions at different career stages and at different levels of the organization. Some mid-level managers whose careers have plateaued may be challenged by new assignments, perhaps moving from line to staff or into different job functions. Older managers may make excellent coaches and trainers. Still others are as ambitious as ever, seek increased responsibilities, and want to continue their career advancement.

London and Smither (1999a) described organizational practices and characteristics of organizational culture that promote involvement in career-related continuous learning. These include the availability of feedback (from the supervisor and/or survey feedback data, such as 360-degree feedback), learning resources, rewards for learning (e.g., increased pay), and supervisors evaluating employees' participation in development as part of the annual performance appraisal.

London (1996, p. 76; also see London, 1990) suggested how organizations support the career motivation of older workers as follows:

To build career resilience:

• Reward older workers for mentoring younger employees (enhancing the mentor's sense of accomplishment and personal value);
• Make organizational structures flatter to give all managers more responsibility (giving individuals more control over their work and generating new opportunities for achievement);
• Provide stress coping workshops that focus on the needs of older workers (reducing their vulnerability in the face of major changes, and increasing their understanding of the job search process and ways to react constructively).

To build career insight:

• Provide self-assessment methods and workbooks to guide older workers' thinking about their career objectives in relation to other life concerns;
• Join a consortium with other firms and/or government agencies to hold job fairs targeted to older workers (enhancing insight by informing retirees and older workers about the range of job possibilities open to them);
• Transfer older workers between departments (helping them to learn new skills and maintaining their job interest by offering a new job setting and new challenges);
• Provide older workers with training to enhance their marketability outside, as well as inside, the firm in anticipation of organizational change or in preparation for retirement;
• Offer guidance for career-end management (recognizing diminished capabilities and/or interests). Retirement workshops and counseling can suggest ideas for expanding identification outside work and shifting motivation to non-work pursuits (e.g., by identifying employees who are ready for retirement planning and pairing successfully retired individuals with employees who are planning retirement).

To build career identity:

• Rehire retirees for temporary full- or part-time work;
• Look to older workers to be sources of quality control and ideas for quality improvement;
• Offer retirement planning workshops;

- Offer financial incentives to encourage retirement or job change;
- Phase retirement jobs (encouraging incremental change in career identity without the stress and self-doubt that accompanies a sudden and forced change).

Creating Empowering Learning Organizations

According to Marsick and Watkins (1996), learning organizations support learning at three levels: (a) individual, through continuous opportunities, inquiry, and dialogue; (b) team, through action learning and collaboration; and (c) organization, through systems that capture learning, empower participants, and link to the environment. Feedback promotes learning when it provides information about behaviors without threatening self-image or character (DiNisi & Kluger, 2000).

Marsick, Cederholm, Turner, and Pearson (1992, p. 298) defined a learning organization as "one in which learning is a continuous, strategically used process—integrated with, and running parallel to, work—that may yield changes in individual and collectively held perceptions, thinking, behaviors, attitudes, values, beliefs, mental models, systems, strategies, policies and procedures." In learning organizations, people continually expand their capacity, develop expansive patterns of thinking, and continuously learn how to learn together (Senge, 1990).

Kozlowski, Chao, and Jensen (2009) proposed a multilevel and cross-level model of organizational system alignment for organizational learning. They suggest that the degree of alignment between elements of the techno-structure and formal and informal enabling processes produce organizational learning outcomes at and between levels. At the micro-level, requisite task and teamwork knowledge, skills, and abilities align with opportunities for acquiring technical and process knowledge through informal means, such as implicit learning, socialization, and mentoring, and formal means, such as workshops, courses, and on-the-job training, to increase employees' task-relevant knowledge. At the meso-level, unit technology and work-flow structures align with opportunities to share and distribute knowledge through team learning and development leader training to produce shared mental models, transactive memory, and the production and distribution of a knowledge pool. At the macro-level, the organization's mission, strategies, technologies, and structure align with a climate for learning and leadership training to produce vertical transfer of knowledge.

EMPOWERED SELF-DEVELOPMENT

Environments that provide learning resources but leave it to individuals to use them or not are likely to increase self-detrermination for individuals who are high in learning orientation (Deci & Ryan, 1991; Dweck & Leggett, 1988). London and Smither (1999b) called this *empowered self-development*. Elements of empowered self-development include: non-threatening performance feedback, ensuring behavioral choices for learning, encouraging feedback seeking, and rewarding participation in learning activities, whether formal or informal. For instance, supervisors can be encouraged to support and reward employees who "(1) anticipate learning requirements, by, for instance, identifying areas for future job requirements and implications for needed skill updates, (2) set development goals that reflect needed knowledge and skill structures, (3) participate in learning activities, (4) ask for feedback to test goal relevance, and (5) track progress" (London & Smither, 1999b, p. 11).

London and Smither (1999b) summarized the ingredients of environments that support empowered self-development. The organization and supervisors provide employees with information feedback in a way that is not threatening or controlling. The feedback focuses on behaviors that can be improved, not on personal characteristics that make a person defensive and weaken self-esteem. The company is likely to have a 360-degree feedback process and perhaps an assessment center that gives participants a chance to get feedback from a variety of different perspectives. The organization may pay to have a professional coach provide the feedback to ensure that the individual understands it and spends time thinking about what it means for development. Another element of support is information about organizational goals, directions, and implications for future performance. If the organization is changing strategy, supervisors should be prepared to provide that information and to discuss the implications for the talent and competencies that employees will need to be effective in the changing environment. Supervisors can help employees evaluate their talents relative to these changing goals, determine training gaps, and find ways for the employees to acquire the experiences and skills they need for future success with the company or, if not with this company, then other jobs or career paths that may be more satisfying and productive for them. Employees are provided with resources for assessment and development and are given choices and resources for development, as well as the freedom to make decisions about their own development. The company may offer a tool kit of self-paced assessment and training methods. Online technology gives a wide array of options, some publicly available, and others that are proprietary and available for a fee. Even assessment centers are available online, with employees participating in simulations, sometimes talking to real people (role players) on the phone or through instant messaging to demonstrate their communications, interpersonal, and problem-solving capabilities, receiving immediate feedback from observers who "tune in" to the interactions.

In general, self-development is more likely in an open, participation-oriented work climate (London & Smither, 1999b). This is an environment in which employees can interact with each other freely, regardless of level, function, or department. People set objectives for themselves in relation to organizational goals. Individuals and teams are accountable for the decisions they make. Employees are encouraged by their supervisors to learn and use new skills and knowledge on the job. Managers are expected to be coaches, advocates, and developers of employees. Managers and employees are held accountable for their own and employees' continuous learning. Indeed, they are measured on the time spent on development (holding developmental discussions, attending workshops and conferences, etc.). Ultimately, this is an environment in which employees are responsible for recognizing their own developmental needs. They assume responsibility for their own learning. For instance, they actively seek performance feedback, compare their self-assessments to current and future skill requirements, investigate opportunities for development, and set development goals, evaluate their progress, and adjust their goals (London & Smither, 1999b).

Maurer, Mitchell, and Barbeite (2002) studied managers' attitudes toward 360-degree feedback and their subsequent involvement in on- and off-the-job development activities. There were few significant relationships between feedback results and later involvement in development. However, participation in development was the belief by feedback recipients that people in general can improve their skills (an incremental implicit theory of skill malleability) and that they themselves could improve (self-efficacy for development). Also, development was higher for managers who perceived that the work environment included people who supported their development (social support). The results indicate that specific feedback results may be as or even less important to predicting participation in development as believing that one can improve and that the organization encourages and rewards development.

Maurer, Pierce, and Shore (2002) presented a model of employees' decisions to participate in learning and development activities, depending on personal values, leader-members exchange, perceived organizational support, self-efficacy for development, and credibility of information source. Self-development requires employees to sacrifice their time, energy, and other resources on and possibly off the job. As such, it is pro-social behavior (Maurer, Pierce, & Shore, 2002). In some cases, the individual alone benefits. However, in many cases, there are other beneficiaries, such as peers, the supervisor, subordinates, and the organization as a whole. Perceived organizational support for development represents a social exchange between the organization and the employee. Employees are motivated to participate in development to benefit others or their organization when they believe that there is mutual support, for instance, that the supervisor values and rewards development or, more generally, that the supervisor appreciates and cares about the employee's job performance, satisfaction with the job, and career success. Similarly, the employee will be more inclined to participate in development activities when there are opportunities to use newly learned behaviors, development is expected and appreciated, and career advancement opportunities are forthcoming.

In summary, employer-provided training and development programs maximize employees' value to the organization, increase retention, match individual capabilities to organizational needs, and promote innovation. Employees' voluntary participation in training enhances their value to the organization, prepares them for promotions, helps them remain competitive for jobs, and/or prepares them for job or career change. Organizations vary in their development philosophy. Some companies develop talent within a functional or technical department/discipline, and others develop generalists and managers/leaders. Organizations are likely to have a mix of these developmental strategies. Some employers take responsibility for their employees' development, whereas others delegate the responsibility to the employees themselves, retaining the responsibility of providing developmental resources, such as assessment, feedback, and training opportunities. Some organizations provide these resources while using them to make decisions about people (for instance, collecting feedback data and then using it to make promotion decisions). Other organizations provide such information solely for the employees' development so that the feedback will be given and received in an objective way without instrumental purpose (what it might "get me" in return or how it might affect the ratee negatively). Companies offer development to employees of all ages, often in recognition of competition for talent and the need to retain and motivate valued employees.

Formal and Informal Development Methods

Lifelong learning is supported by a wide array of formal and informal tools. They include:

• Learning from experiences and challenges (life and career transition points, successes, failures, changes, and disruptions, learning something totally new, job transfers, exposure to different cultures, visible and difficult job assignments) and training methods (didactic/lectures or experiential, relating to individual learning style as well as age/life stage);
• Training delivery options, including classroom/in-person training and distance/e-learning, just-in-time on-the-job training, web-based training delivery, methods that blend web with in-person training and formal training with informal, on-the-job learning experiences;
• Measurement and feedback methods, including assessment centers that can be delivered in person and now online;
• Training needs analysis: methods to assess employees' development needs, such as feedback surveys with data aggregated across all employees in a department; such information provides data on training gaps and needs for courses or other developmental experiences;
• 360-degree (multisource) feedback surveys administered online, with managers selecting the items that are of interest to them and asking for feedback when they want it and will be most likely to value it;
• Social learning opportunities, including observing coworkers, role models, mentors, coaching (executive coaches, supervisor feedback and in-the-moment coaching), providing information about career opportunities and organizational skill needs;
• Incentives for learning (expectations of positive and negative outcomes from learning and resulting behavior change).

Johnson (1997) explained the difference between informal and formal learning. Informal learning can occur at any time and place. The natural environment is a meaningful context in which to learn and test new skills. It usually includes interaction with coworkers, some of whom are more experienced and others of whom are also learning. Skills are acquired as coworkers cooperate, collaborate, observe, share, and give each other feedback. The experience is task- or project-oriented. Learning is sought when it is needed, that is, when the participants realize that they need more information, knowledge, or skills to accomplish the task. They are motivated to learn because the learning is self-initiated and self-directed. It may involve games, competition, and imagination. Of course, facilitators (supervisors, instructors) may guide informal learning, but there is usually little or no external control.

Informal learning is (a) learner-directed and self-guided, not controlled by a supervisor, trainer, or the organization; (b) motivated by an intention for learning or improvement; (c) entails action or doing (i.e., not just treading or attending a program); and (d) does not occur in a formal setting such as a classroom or online (Tannenbaum, Beard, McNall, & Salas, 2009). In addition to self-guided intent and active learning, informal learning entails receiving feedback and engaging in reflection to understand one's experiences. Experience, feedback, action, and reflection are influenced by the dynamic interchange of organizational/situational characteristics (e.g., learning opportunities and support for learning) and individual characteristics (motivation, self-awareness, feedback orientation). Together, they produce both individual outcomes (e.g., learning, performance improvement, self-efficacy) and organizational outcomes (learning culture, agility, capacity for performance, and readiness to support learning in the future; Tannenbaum et al., 2009).

Formal learning methods teach new behavior, cognitive understanding, and skills and knowledge, with practice and feedback in a non-threatening environment. Methods may include coaching, simulations, and personal growth challenges (e.g., Outward Bound wilderness events). Also developmental experiences occur naturally in work settings, for instance, assignments that require making transitions, handling new experiences, building relationships, and facing barriers (McCauley, 2001). These experiences require setting agendas, managing relationships, showing basic values, including sensitivity to others, and becoming more aware of one's own strengths and weaknesses. People learn by participating in new, unfamiliar tasks and uncertain decision-making situations. Challenging assignments include creating change, handling high levels of responsibility, influencing others, and managing diversity (Maurer, 2002; McCall, Lombardo, & Morrison, 1988; McCauley, Ruderman, Ohlott, & Morrow, 1994).

Formal learning emphasizes individual work and assessment (Johnson, 1997). Study groups may be encouraged, but individual work is assessed, and joint work may be viewed as cheating. The content is taught in standardized ways, meaning that students are given the same tasks and time frames for completion, regardless of their ability levels and prior experience. Formal learning is structured and inflexible. There is a structured curriculum that outlines learning objectives and required competencies for entry. It is directed by the instructor and generally draws on the concept of transmitted or transferring knowledge. There is usually more emphasis on thought than action and experience.

Johnson and Thomas (1994) offered six principles for designing instructional methods to enhance cognitive learning:

(1) Reduce the load on limited working memory (e.g., focus attention through graphic cues, help learners organize their memory into chunks with techniques such as mapping and mnemonic devices).

(2) Activate the learner's existing knowledge structures (e.g., ask through providing and probing question; use analogies; remind learners of what they know already).

(3) Support encoding and representation of new knowledge (e.g., establish a purpose for what is to be learned; highlight distinctive features of new information; contrast similarities and differences).

(4) Facilitate deep thinking (e.g., encourage learners to think about their actions and beliefs; facilitate interaction among learners; challenge learners though dialectic dialogue; encourage learners to generate questions, explanations, and summaries).

(5) Enhance cognitive control processes (e.g., encourage learners to think aloud while problem solving to make their thought processes explicit).

(6) Support the use of transfer of knowledge and skills (e.g., plan ways to apply learning to real problems, provide opportunities to practice).

Johnson (1997) suggested that formal learning would be more effective if it incorporated elements of informal learning. In particular:

(1) Formal learning should adopt a rich learning environment with authentic problems and realistic situations with expertise created by interaction with the environment, not isolation from it.

(2) Formal learning should be peer-based, with cognitive activity socially defined, interpreted, and supported through interactions, mentoring, observation, and tutoring.

(3) Formal learning should incorporate activity-based practice. Knowing and doing should be integrated to gain a rich understanding of how to function in a complex, continuously changing environment. This can be accomplished through discovery, project-based learning, including structure-on-the-job training, internships, project-based or problem-based tasks, goal-based tasks, and action learning, all of which emphasize learning from experience.

(4) Formal learning should include reflective practice. People need to think about their experiences in order to learn. This is easier said than done, since people shy away from self-evaluation. It often requires feedback, coaching, and facilitation to encourage seeking and using feedback. People need to be encouraged and rewarded for reviewing their strengths and weaknesses, recognizing gaps in abilities and performance, setting goals for improvement, taking actions to learn and apply this learning, and evaluating their improvement in an ongoing cycle. Reflective practice is needed for continuous learning for continuous improvement (Marsick & Watkins, 1992, 2001).

Employees now recognize that they are responsible for their own job security. They need to monitor opportunities and recognize the skills and knowledge that they need to meet and exceed performance expectations today and to be competitive for jobs in the future. London (1996) provided examples of programs that provide support for older workers' learning, in particular, helping mid- and late career employees who lost their jobs as a result of organizational downsizing and restructuring. University or community college–based programs can help displaced employees review their skills, prepare resumes, overcome depression and frustration, and learn marketable job skills. One such program at the State University of New York at Stony Brook ran a government-funded retraining program for displaced engineers from the defense industry. The participants took courses in a learning community—an eight-hour-a-day program during a semester. Students engaged in career planning, resume writing, role playing in simulations and problem-solving exercises, and using new business software. They chose tracks for in-depth study in such areas as management of manufacturing, information systems, environment, or materials. They formed teams to work on real problems posed by companies that were invited to participate. Some of these firms hired the team members after the program. Other participants found new employment elsewhere. Some started their own businesses, building on their newly acquired knowledge of entrepreneurship.

Establishing Learning Objectives and Assessing Learning Outcomes

Increasingly, professionals in the area of training and development as well as faculty in educational institutions at all levels, are being held accountable for providing training that works—that is, education that leads to expected and needed outcomes. Learning objectives are stated in behavioral terms, not what people need to know, but what they can do. For instance, the following are general skills that are needed by employees in many work settings in business, government, and not-for-profit sectors. Educational programs and experiences would help individuals acquire and maintain these generic skills.

- *Critical thinking, problem solving and decision making*: analyze a complex issue and identify realistic solutions, communicating the findings in a written case with appropriate supporting material (e.g., demonstrate the ability to analyze data, use charts and figures and understand financial statements).
- *Ethics and corporate social responsibility*: analyze an issue from legal, ethical, and socially responsible perspectives and recommend appropriate actions for a practical situation.
- *Leadership and team interaction:* create a vision and communicate that vision in a way that would generate commitment, and structure teams for goal achievement. Participate actively and collaboratively in a project team, present their contribution to the team project in a project report or presentation, and describe how you contributed to team interaction based on principles of group dynamics and team building.
- *Innovative practices:* demonstrate knowledge of innovative practices, processes, technologies and methods through a case analysis, project, simulation or workshop.

- *Cross-cultural understanding:* participate in a study abroad program or in a group project with people from different cultural backgrounds domestically and internationally and apply knowledge of an international environment.
- *Value creation*: produce a plan that shows the creation of value through the production and marketing of goods and services.

Similar competencies can be developed for specific functions (say, accounting, finance, marketing, human resources, etc.) at more sophisticated levels of complexity.

Agenda for the Future

Longworth and Davies (1996) called the twenty-first century the "learning century." They proposed new roles for education, government, business organizations, and societies in the development process. They proposed encouraging the development of lifelong learning in elementary through adult education across the globe by mobilizing schools, the workplace, and communities.

Field (2000) explored the increase in interest in lifelong learning among policy makers in Great Britain and elsewhere. He described lifelong learning as a design for the future, achieving a global policy consensus on lifelong learning. Lifelong learning creates a "reflexive modernization" and a learning economy that would support changing the skill mix and creating learning organizations. Workers would be economic nomads, self-directed, learning to work and learning from work. Policy makers must avoid leaving groups behind due to social exclusion and redundancy of the poor and legitimating equalities. He called for a new social order that included education in the meaning of a learning society, widening participation, investments in social capital, and pursuing the search for meaning.

Goodyear (2002) challenged educational technologists to move beyond the design of instructional tasks in developing training programs to become "architects and creators of virtual learning environments reflective of real world activities" (p. 1). They need to remove barriers in content and structure for learning to occur, to increase learner autonomy, and to move away from the idea of a compliant learner, taking advantage of technology's ability to merge the real and the virtual world.

Sharples (2000) outlined a theory of lifelong learning mediated by technology. In particular, he suggested requirements for the software, hardware, communications and design interfaces for handheld learning resources that provide support for learning from anywhere. In the future, learners will not be tied to particular locations. They will be able to study anywhere at any time, interacting with people and databases to acquire and apply knowledge and skills. Technologies for lifelong learning need to be portable, adaptable to individual needs, unobstrusive, available anywhere, transferable as technology advances so that earlier information and uses will not be lost, useful for everyday needs, and usable with no prior experience (intuitive). Technologies need to be personal, user-centered, mobile, networked, ubiquitous, and durable to mach lifelong learning requirements.

Sharples's (2000) model of lifelong learning proposes that technology needs to support meta-learning (learning how to learn) through reflection and action. Technology provides computer-based teachers, tutors, and mentors, who may be people, software systems, or a combination. Software for teaching and problem solving may be virtual learning environments, problem-solving tools, and simulations. Software for reflection (idea generation, creativity, and knowledge sharing) that promotes collaborative learning may be synchronous and asynchronous communication tools, search engineers, and systems for sharing knowledge. Software for meta-learning (learning to learn and organizing knowledge) may be concept maps, timelines, and notes networks. Software and hardware will allow people to develop personal area networks that support communication (similar to social networking internet sites). Technology will integrate pen, keyboard, and speech while combining handheld units, peripherals (e.g., miniature cameras, microphones, and earpieces), will allow a mix of direct manipulation and voice, and will provide secure and efficient information storage of multimedia over time. Research is needed to match systems and software interfaces to learners' cognitive and social capabilities, to manage and support resources that will be transferable across time and technology development, to take advantage of expanding bandwidths to distribute resources, to support easy and unobtrusive capturing of data and events, and to foster collaboration between mobile learners (Sharples, 2000).

Ten Forces Driving Research and Practice for the Future

In conclusion, a number of forces will drive future directions for lifelong learning. I offer with ten:

1. The fast pace of technological and economic advancement will continue to demand learning.

2. Technology makes education accessible for people of all ages and socioeconomic conditions. There will be continued developments in new ways to blend technologies and to deliver them when they are needed inexpensively across the globe.

3. Economic forces and globalization will give rise to changing career opportunities. This creates challenges (e.g., managing global work teams in virtual environments) and competencies (the need for cultural knowledge and sensitivity, not to mention language training).

4. New theories or theory extensions will integrate cognitive, emotional, and behavioral domains across the life span.

5. Theories will recognize multiple levels of analysis, focusing on individual, group, and organizational learning, and the ways in which learning at one level contributes to learning at another.

6. Training and development will mesh with developing groups and creating learning organizations. There will be a need to help individuals, groups, and organizations become adaptive, generative, and transformative learners as people move between work teams, learn new patterns of interaction, and contribute to innovation.

7. Research methods will include a variety of techniques, with different methods for examining complex phenomena (triangulation). For instance, research will use qualitative and quantitative methods, multitrait/multimethod measures, longitudinal designs, and technology for tracking development and career movement within and across organizations.

8. Organizations will expect training professionals to set learning objectives and assess outcomes to demonstrate their value, accept accountability for outcomes, and provide feedback to improve learning.

9. Living longer, people will want to work later in life, perhaps working part-time and at home. They will expect continued learning opportunities, and organizations will need to provide them in order to attract and retain talented people.

10. Work environments will facilitate individuals' and groups' readiness to learn, as well as supporting their continuous learning. That is, organizations will encourage and reward openness to new ideas, highlight changes (opportunities and demands) that make people sensitive to the need

for learning, and reward people for participating in development. People will learn to envision a future for themselves and the organization, recognizing trends, discussing the implications of these trends for skills and knowledge that they will need in the future, and taking responsibility for their own lifelong learning.

References

AARP. (2000). *American business and older employees survey.* Washington, DC: American Association of Retired Persons.

Albert, R. D. (1996). A framework and model for understanding Latin American and Latino/Hispanic cultural patterns. In D. Landis & R. S. Bhagat (Eds.), *Handbook of intercultural training* (2nd ed., pp. 327–348). Thousand Oaks, CA: Sage.

Anderson, W. T. (1997). *The future of self: Inventing the postmodern person.* New York: Putnam.

Aspin, D. N., & Chapman, J. D. (2000). Lifelong learning: Concepts and conceptions. *International Journal of Lifelong Education, 19,* 2–19.

Ausubel, D. P. (1968). *Educational psychology: A cognitive view.* New York: Holt, Rinehart & Winston.

Baltes, P. B. (1987). Theoretical propositions of life-span developmental psychology: On the dynamics between growth and decline. *Developmental Psychology, 23,* 611–626.

Baltes, P. B., Dittman-Kohli, F., & Dixon, R. A. (1984). New perspectives on the development of intelligence in adulthood: Toward a dual-process conception and a model of selective optimization with compensation. In P. B. Baltes & O. G. Brim, Jr. (Eds.), *Life-span development and behavior* (Vol. 6, pp. 33–76). New York: Academic Press.

Baltes, P. B., & Lindenberger, U. (1997). Emergence of a powerful connection between sensory and cognitive functions across the adult life span: A new window to the study of cognitive aging? *Psychology and Aging, 12,* 1–21.

Baltes, P. D., & Smith, J. (2008). The fascination of wisdom: Its nature, ontogeny, and function. *Perspectives on Psychological Science, 3,* 56–64.

Bandura, A. (1986). *Social foundations of thought and action: A social cognitive theory.* Englewood Cliffs, NJ: Prentice-Hall.

Bandura, A. (1997). *Self-efficacy: The exercise of control.* New York: W. H. Freeman.

Barrick, M. R., & Mount, M. K. (1991). The big five personality dimensions and job performance: A meta-analysis. *Personnel Psychology, 44*(1), 1–26.

Baumeister, R. F. (1999). The nature and structure of the self: An overview. In R. F. Baumeister (Ed.), *The self in social psychology* (pp. 1–20). Philadelphia: Psychology Press.

Bell, B. S., & Kozlowski, S. W. J. (2009). Toward a theory of learner centered training design: An integrative framework of active learning. In S. W. J. Kozlowski, & E. Salas (Eds.), *Learning, training, and development in organizations* (pp. 263–301). New York: Routledge Academic.

Bentley, T. (1998). *Learning beyond the classroom: Education for a changing world.* London: Routledge.

Berry, D. C., & Dienes, Z. (1993). *Implicit learning: Theoretical and empirical issues.* Hove, UK: Erlbaum.

Birdi, K., Allan, C., & Warr, P. (1997). Correlates and perceived outcomes of four types of employee development activity. *Journal of Applied Psychology, 82,* 845–857.

Bloom, B. S. (1956). *Taxonomy of educational objectives. Handbook I: The cognitive domain.* New York: David McKay.

Blueprint for lifelong learning: A guide for your continuous improvement and professional development. (2008). State of Ohio, Columbus, OH: http://das.ohio.gov/hrd/Training/pdf/BlueprintCourseCatalogpackage.pdf.

Boyatzis, R. E., & Kolb, D. A. (1991). Assessing individuality in learning: The learning skills profile. *Educational Psychology, 11,* 279–295.

Brink, K. E., (2002, April). *Self-efficacy and goal change in the absence of external feedback. Predicting executive performance with multi-rater surveys: Who you ask matters.* Paper presented at the 17th Annual Meeting of the Society for Industrial and Organizational Psychology, Toronto.

Bruner, J. S. (1960). *The process of education.* New York: Vintage.

Bunderson, J. S., & Sutcliffe, K. M. (2003). Management team learning orientation and business unit performance. *Journal of Applied Psychology, 88*(3), 552–560.

Bunker, K. A., & Webb, A. D. (1992). *Learning how to learn from experience: Impact on stress and coping* (Report No. 154). Greensboro, NC: Center for Creative Leadership.

Candy, P. D. (1991). *Self-direction for lifelong learning: A comprehensive guide to theory and practice.* San Francisco: Jossey-Bass.

Cannon-Bowers, J. A., Rhodenizer, L., Salas, E., & Bowers, C. A. (1998). A framework for understanding pre-practice conditions and their impact on learning. *Personnel Psychology, 51,* 291–320.

Carver, C. S., & Scheier, M. F. (1990). Origins and functions of positive and negative affect: A control-process view. *Psychological Review, 97,* 19–35.

Colquitt, J. A., LePine J. A., & Noe, R. A. (2000). Toward an integration theory of training motivation: A meta-analytic path analysis of 20 years of research. *Journal of Applied Psychology, 85,* 678–707.

Day, D. V. (2002, April). *Social constructivist perspectives on leadership development.* Paper presented at the 17th Annual Meeting of the Society for Industrial and Organizational Psychology, Toronto.

Deci, E., & Ryan, R. (1991). Intrinsic motivation and self-determination in human behavior. In R. Steers & L. Porter (Eds.), *Motivation and work behavior* (pp. 44–58). New York: McGraw-Hill.

DeNisi, A. S., & Kluger, A. N. (2000). Feedback effectiveness: Can 360-degree appraisals be improved. *Academy of Management Executive, 14*(1), 129–139.

Dewey, J. (1933/1986). *How we think: A restatement of the relation of reflective thinking to the educative process.* Boston: Heath.

Diamante, T., & London, M. (2002). Expansive leadership in the age of digital technology. *Journal of Management Development, 21*(6), 404–416.

Dunbar, E. (1996). Sociocultural and contextual challenges of organizational life in Eastern Europe. In D. Landis & R. S. Bhagat (Eds.), *Handbook of intercultural training* (2nd ed., pp. 349–365). Thousand Oaks, CA: Sage.

Dweck, C. S. (1986). Motivational processes affecting learning. *American Psychologist, 41,* 1040–1048.

Dweck, C., & Leggett, E. (1988). A social cognitive approach to motivation and personality. *Psychological Review, 95,* 256–273.

Ehrlich, D. (2008). Northeastern Illinois University. http://www.neiu.edu/~dbehrlic/hrd408/glossary.htm#l. Accessed December 15, 2008.

Encarta (2008). http://encarta.msn.com/dictionary_561547417/lifelong_learning.html. Accessed October 9, 2008.

Facteau, J. D., Dobbins, G. H., Russell, J. E. A., Ladd, R. T., & Kudisch, J. D. (1995). The influence of general perceptions of the training environment on pretraining motivation and perceived training transfer. *Journal of Management, 21*, 1–25.

Field, J. (2000). *Lifelong learning and the new educational order*. London: Trentham Books.

Fischer, G. (2000). Lifelong learning: More than training. *Journal of Interactive Learning Research, 11*, 265–294.

Fishbein, M., & Stasson, M. (1990). The role of desire, self-prediction, and perceived control in the prediction of training session attendance. *Journal of Applied Social Psychology, 20*, 173–198.

Freelancers Union (2008). http://www.freelancersunion.org/. Accessed December 3, 2008.

Gagné, N. L. (1978). *The scientific basis of the art of teaching*. New York: Teachers College Press.

Gangestad, S. W., & Snyder, M. (2000). Self-monitoring: Appraisal and reappraisal. *Psychological Bulletin, 126*, 530–555.

Gardner, H. (1983). *Frames of mind: The theory of multiple intelligences*. New York: Basic Books.

Gardner, H. (1993). *Multiple intelligences: The theory in practice*. New York: Basic Books.

Gardner, H. (1999) *Intelligence reframed: Multiple intelligences for the 21st century*. New York: Basic Books

Garofano, C. M., & Salas, E. (2005). What influences continuous employee development decisions? *Human Resource Management Review, 15*, 281–304.

Gergen, J. J. (1991). *The saturated self: Dilemmas of identity in contemporary life*. New York: Basic Books.

Goodyear, P. (2002). Environments for lifelong learning: Ergonomics, architecture, and educational design. In J. M. Spector & T. M. Anderson (Eds.), *Integrated and holistic perspectives on learning, instruction, and technology: Understanding complexity* (pp. 1–18). Dordrecht, Netherlands: Kluwer.

Greenberg, J. (2008). Understanding the vital human quest for self-esteem. *Perspectives on Psychological Science, 3*, 48–55.

Guthrie, E. R. (1952). *The psychology of learning* (Rev. ed.). New York: Harper & Brothers.

Hake, B. J. (1999). Lifelong learning in late modernity: The challenges to society, organizations, and individuals. *Adult Education Quarterly, 49*, 79–90.

Hall, D. T. (1976). *Careers in organizations*. Pacific Palisades, CA: Goodyear.

Hall, D. T. (2001). *Careers in and out of organizations*. Thousand Oaks, CA: Sage.

Hall, D. T. (2004). The protean career: A quarter-century journey. *Journal of Vocational Behavior, 65*, 1–13.

Hall, D. T., & Mirvis, P. H. (1995). The new career contract: Developing the whole person at midlife and beyond. *Journal of Vocational behavior, 47*, 269–289

Hall, D. T., & Mirvis, P. H. (1996) Psychological success and the boundaryless career. In M. B. Arthur & D. M. Rousseau (Eds.), *The boundaryless career: A new employment principle for a new organizational era* (pp. 1237–1255). New York: Oxford University Press.

Higgins, M., & Kram, K. E. (2001). Reconceptualizing mentoring at work: A developmental network perspective. *Academy of Management Review, 26*, 264–289.

Holliday, R. R. (1994). Teachers as learners: A case study of conditions that promote teachers' professional learning. Ph.D. dissertation, University of New England, Australia.

Hurtz, G. M., & Williams, K. J. (2009). Attitudinal and motivational antecedents of participation in voluntary employee development activities. *Journal of Applied Psychology, 94*, 635–653.

Ilgen, D. R., & Pulakos, E. D. (1999). Introduction: Employee performance in today's organizations. In D. R. Ilgen, & E. D. Pulakos (Eds.), *The changing nature of performance: Implications for staffing, motivation, and development* (pp. 1–20). San Francisco: Jossey-Bass.

Jackson, W.H. (1996). Androgogical stages of development. [On-line]. Available:http://internet.cybermesa.com/~bjackson/Papers/AndroStage.htm. Accessed January 20, 2012.

Jenkins, A., Vignoles, A., Wolf, A., & Galindo-Rueda, F. (2003). The determinants of labour market effects of lifelong learning. *Applied Economics, 35*, 1711–1721.

Johnson, S. D. (1997). Learning technological concepts and developing intellectual skills. *International Journal of Technology and Design Education, 7*, 161–180.

Johnson, S. D., & Thomas, R. G. (1994). Implications of cognitive science for instructional design in technology education. *The Journal of Technology Studies, 20*, 33–45.

Kamenetz, A. (2007). Permalancers, Unite! *The Nation*, December 13 (http://www.thenation.com/doc/20071231/kamenetz).

Kanter, R. M. (2001). *E-volve!: Succeeding in the digital culture of tomorrow*. Boston: Harvard Business School Press.

Kaplan, R. E., Drath, W. H., & Kofodimos, J. R. (1991). *Beyond ambition: How driven managers can lead better and live better*. San Francisco: Jossey-Bass.

Kasl, E., Marsick, V. J., & Dechant, K. (1997). Team as learners: A research-based model of team learning. *Journal of Applied Behavioral Science, 33*, 227–246.

Kegan, R. (1982). *The evolving self: Problem and process in human development*. Cambridge, MA: Harvard University Press.

Kegan, R. (1994). *In over our heads: The mental demands of modern life*. Cambridge, MA: Harvard University Press.

Kegan, R., & Lahey, L. L. (2001). *How the way we talk can change the way we work: Seven languages for transformation*. San Francisco: Jossey-Bass.

Keith, N., & Frese, M. (2005). Self-regulation in error management training: Emotion control and metacognition as mediators of performance effects. *Journal of Applied Psychology, 90*, 677–691.

Knowles, M. S. (1975). *Self-directed learning*. River Grove, IL: Follett.

Kolb, D. A. (1984). *Experiential learning: Experience as a source of learning and development*. Englewood Cliffs, NJ: Prentice Hall.

Kozlowski, S. W. J., Chao, G. T., & Jensen, J. M. (2009). Building an infrastructure for organizational learning: A multilevel approach. In S. W. J. Kozlowski, & E. Salas (Eds.), *Learning, training, and development in organizations* (pp. 363–404). New York: Routledge Academic.

Kozlowski, S. W. J., & Farr, J. L. (1988). An integrative model of updating and performance. *Human Performance, 1*, 5–29.

Kozlowski, S. W. J., & Hults, B. M. (1987). An exploration of climates for technical updating and performance. *Personnel Psychology, 40*(3), 539–563.

Kozlowski, S. W. J., Toney, R. J., Mullins, M. E., Weissbein, D. A., Brown, K. G., & Bell, B. S. (2001). Developing adaptability: A theory for the design of integrated-embedded training systems. In E. Salas (Ed.), *Advances in human performance and cognitive engineering research* (Vol. 1, pp. 59–123). Amsterdam: JAI/Elsevier Science.

Krathwohl, D. R. (2002). A revision of Bloom's Taxonomy: An overview. *Theory into Practice, 41*, 212–218.

Krechevsky, M., & Seidel, S. (1998). Minds at work: Applying multiple intelligences in the classroom. In R. J. Sternberg & W. M. Williams (Eds.), *Intelligence, instruction, and assessment* (pp. 17–24). Mahwah, NJ: Erlbaum.

Langer, E. J. (2000). Mindful learning. *Current directions in psychological science, 9*, 220–223.

Lawrence, T. B., Mauws, M. K., Dyck, B., & Kleysen, R. F. (2005). The politics of organizational learning: Integrating power into the 4I framework. *Academy of Management Review, 30*, 180–192.

Levinson, D. J. (1979). *The seasons of a man's life*. New York: Random House.

Levinson, D. J. (1986). A conception of adult development. *American Psychologist, 41*, 3–13.

Levinson, D. J. (1997). *The seasons of a woman's life*. New York: Random House.

Lindenberger, U. (1994). Sensory functioning and intelligence in old age: A strong connection. *Psychology and Aging, 9*, 339–355.

Lindsey, E. H., Homes, V., & McCall, M. W. (1987). *Key events in executives' lives*. Greensboro, NC: Center for Creative Leadership.

Locke, E. A., & Latham, G. P. (1990). *A theory of goal setting and task performance*. Englewood Cliffs, NJ: Prentice Hall.

London, M. (1983). Toward a theory of career motivation. *Academy of Management Review, 8*, 620–630.

London, M. (1985). *Developing managers*. San Francisco: Jossey-Bass.

London, M. (1990). Enhancing career motivation in late career. *Journal of Organizational Change Management, 3*, 58–71.

London, M. (1996). Redeployment and continuous learning in the 21st century: Hard lessons and positive examples from the downsizing era. *Academy of Management Executive, 10*, 67–79.

London, M. (2002). *Leadership development: Paths to self-insight and professional growth*. Mahwah, NJ: Erlbaum.

London, M., & Diamante, T. (2002). Technology-focused expansive professionals: Developing continuous learning in the high tech sector. *Human Resource Development Review, 1*(4), 500–524.

London, M., & Maurer, T. J. (2004). Leadership development: A diagnostic model for continuous learning in dynamic organizations. In J. Antonakis, A. T. Cianciolo, & R. J. Sternberg (Eds.), *The nature of leadership* (pp. 222–246). Thousand Oaks, CA: Sage.

London, M., & Noe, R. A. (1997). London's career motivation theory: An update on measurement and research. *Journal of Career Assessment, 5*(1), 61–80.

London, M., & Sessa, V. I. (2006). Continuous learning in organizations: A living systems analysis of individual, group, and organization learning. In F. J. Yammarino & F. Dansereau (Eds.), *Research in multi-level issues* (Vol. 5, pp.123–172). Oxford: Elsevier Science.

London, M., & Sessa, V. I. (2007). How groups learn, continuously. *Human Resource Management Journal, 46*, 651–669.

London, M., & Smither, J. W. (1999a). Career-related continuous learning: Defining the construct and mapping the process. In G. R. Ferris (Ed.), *Research in human resources management* (Vol. 17, pp. 81–121). Greenwich, CT: JAI Press.

London, M., & Smither, J. W. (1999b). Empowered self-development and continuous learning. *Journal of Human Resource Management, 38*(1), 3–16.

London, M., & Smither, J. W. (2002). Feedback orientation, feedback culture, and the longitudinal performance management process. *Human Resource Management Review, 12*(1), 81–100.

Longworth, N., & Davies, W. K. (1996). *Lifelong learning: New vision, new implications, new roles for people, organizations, nations and communities in the 21st Century*. London: Kogan Page.

MacDonald, D. A., Gagnier, J. J., & Friedman, H. L. (2000). The self-expansiveness level form: Examination of its validity and relation to the NEO Personality Inventory—Revise. *Psychological Reports, 86*(3, Pt. 1), 707–726.

Mainemelis, C., Boyatzis, R. E., & Kolb, D. A. (2002). Learning styles and adaptive flexibility: Testing experiential learning theory. *Management Learning, 33*, 5–33.

Marsick, V. J. (1987). New paradigms for learning in the workplace. In V. J. Marsick (Ed.), *Learning in the workplace* (pp. 11–30). London: Croom Helm.

Marsick, V. J., Cederholm L., Turner, E., & Pearson, T. (1992). Action-reflection learning. *Training and Development, 46*, 63–66.

Marsick, V. J., & Watkins, K. E. (1992). Continuous learning in the workplace. *Adult Learning, 3*, 9–12.

Marsick, V. J., & Watkins, K. E. (1996). Adult educators and the challenge of the learning organization. *Adult Learning, 7*, 18–20.

Marsick, V. J., & Watkins, K. E. (1999). *Facilitating learning organizations: Making learning count*. Brookfield, VT: Ashgate.

Marsick, V. J., & Watkins, K. E. (2001). Informal and incidental learning. *New Directions for Adult and Continuing Education, 89*, 25–34.

Matthews, P. (1999). Workplace learning: Developing an holistic model. *The Learning Organization, 6*, 18–29.

Maurer, T. J. (2002). Employee learning and development orientation: Toward an integrative model of involvement in continuous learning. *Human Resource Development Review, 1*, 9–44.

Maurer, T. J., Mitchell, D. R. D., & Barbeite, F. G. (2002). Predictors of attitudes toward a 360-degree feedback system and involvement in post-feedback management development activity. *Journal of Occupational and Organizational Psychology, 75*, 87–107.

Maurer, T. J., Pierce, H. R., & Shore, L. M. (2002). Perceived beneficiary of employee development activity: A three dimensional social exchange model. *Academy of Management Review, 27*, 432–444.

Maurer, T. J., & Tarulli, B. A. (1994). Investigation of perceived environment, perceived outcome and person variables in relationship to voluntary development activity by employees. *Journal of Applied Psychology, 74*, 3–14.

McCall, M. W., Jr., Lombardo, M. M., & Morrison, A. M. (1988). *The lessons of experience: How successful executives develop on the job*. San Francisco: New Lexington Press.

McCauley, C. D. (2001). Leader training and development. In S. J. Zaccaro & R. J. Klimoski (Eds.), *The nature of organizational leadership* (pp. 347–383). San Francisco: Jossey-Bass.

McCauley, C. D., Ruderman, M. N., Ohlott, P. J., & Morrow, J. E. (1994). Assessing the developmental components of managerial jobs. *Journal of Applied Psychology, 79*, 544–560.

Mezirow, J. (1991). *Tranformative dimensions of adult learning.* San Francisco: Jossey-Bass.

Mezirow, J. (1994). Understanding transformation theory. *Adult Education Quarterly, 444*, 222–232.

Molloy, J. C., & Noe, R. A. (2009). "Learning" a living: Continuous learning for survival in today's talent market. In S. W. J. Kozlowski & E. Salas (Eds.), *Learning, training, and development in organizations* (pp. 333–362). New York: Routledge Academic.

Noe, R. A., & Wilk, S. L. (1993). Investigation of the factors that influence employee participation in development activities. *Journal of Applied Psychology, 78*, 291–302.

Nordhaug, O. (1989). Reward functions of personnel training. *Human Relations, 42*, 373–388.

Prochaska, J. M., Prochaska, J. O., & Levesque, D. A. (2001). A transtheoretical approach to changing organizations. *Administration and Policy in Mental Health, 28*(4), 247–261.

Reber, A. S. (1993). *Implicit learning and tacit knowledge.* Oxford: Oxford University Press.

Rogoff, B. (1990). *Apprenticeship in thinking: Cognitive development in the social context.* New York: Oxford University Press.

Salovey, P., & Mayer, J. D. (1990). Emotional intelligence. *Imagination, Cognition, and Personality, 9*, 185–211.

Scherbaum, C. A., & Vancouver, J. B. (2002, April). *Testing two explanations for goal-setting effects: A persistent question.* Paper presented at the 17th Annual Meeting of the Society for Industrial and Organizational Psychology, Toronto.

Scotland. (2003). http://www.scotland.gov.uk/Publications/2003/02/16308/17752. Accessed December 4, 2008.

Senge, P. M. (1990). *The fifth discipline: The art and practice of the learning organization.* New York: Doubleday.

Sessa, V., & London, M. (2006). *Continuous learning: Directions for individual and organization development.* Mahwah, NJ: Erlbaum.

Sharples, M. (2000). The design of personal mobile technologies for lifelong leaning. *Computers & Education, 34*, 177–193.

Snyder, M. (1974). Self-monitoring of expressive behavior. *Journal of Personality and Social Psychology, 30*, 526–527.

Sternberg, R. J. (1997a). The concept of intelligence and its role in lifelong learning and success. *American Psychologist, 52*, 1030–1037.

Sternberg, R. J. (1997b). Intelligence and lifelong learning. *American Psychologist, 52*, 1134–1139.

Tannenbaum, S. I., Beard, R. L., McNall, L. A., & Salas, E. (2009). Informal learning and development in organizations. In S. W. J. Kozlowski & E. Salas (Eds.), *Learning, training, and development in organizations* (pp. 303–332). New York: Routledge Academic.

Tharenou, P. (2001). The relationship of training motivation to participation in training and development. *Journal of Occupational and Organizational Psychology, 74*, 599–621.

Thorndike, E. L. (1932). *The fundamentals of learning.* New York: Teachers College Press.

Tolman, E. C. (1932). *Purposive behavior in animals and men.* New York: Appleton-Century-Crofts.

Van der Vegt, G. S., & Bunderson, J. S. (2005). Learning and performance in multidisciplinary teams: The importance of collective team identification. *Academy of Management Journal, 48*, 532–547.

Van Velsor, E. (2002, April). *Reflective leadership conversations.* Paper presented at the 17th Annual Meeting of the Society for Industrial and Organizational Psychology, Toronto.

Van Velsor, E., & Guthrie, V. A. (1998). Enhancing the ability to learn from experience. In C. D. McCauley, R. S. Moxley, & E. Van Velsor (Eds.), *The Center for Creative Leadership handbook of leadership development* (pp. 242–261). San Francisco: Jossey-Bass.

VandeWalle, D. (1997). Development and validation of a work domain goal orientation instrument. *Educational and Psychological Measurement, 57*, 995–1015.

von Glaserfeld, E. (1996). Introduction: Aspects of constructivism. In C. Fosnot (Ed.), *Constructivism: Theory, perspectives, and practice* (pp. 3–7). New York: Teachers College Press.

Vygotsky, L. (1978). *Mind in society: The development of higher psychological process.* Cambridge, MA: Harvard University Press.

Watson, J. B. (1924). *Behaviorism.* New York: Norton.

Wenger, E. (1999). *Communities of practice: Learning, meaning, and identity.* Cambridge, UK: Cambridge University Press.

Wolf, G., London, M., Casey, J., & Pufahl, J. (1995). Career experience and motivation as predictors of training behaviors and outcomes for displaced engineers. *Journal of Vocational Behavior, 47*, 316–331.

Wortley, D.B. & Amatea, E.S. (April, 1982). Mapping adult life changes: A conceptual framework for organizing adult development theory. *Personnel and Guidance Journal,* 476–482.

Wurf, E., & Markus, H. (1991). Possible selves and the psychology of personal growth. *Perspectives in Personality, 3*, 39–62.

Occupational Safety and Health

Lois E. Tetrick *and* José M. Peiró

Abstract

Occupational health and safety reflects the effect of the work environment on employees, groups and work units in organizations, and organizations as a whole. This chapter provides an overview of the research on workplace safety and specifically discusses safety training, regulatory focus, safety climate, leadership, and job design as they relate to safety. Additionally, the literature on occupational health, drawing heavily on the occupational stress literature, discusses the employee-employer relationship from a psychological contract perspective, including climate for sexual harassment, collective burnout and its contagion, recovery, and organizational wellness programs. Particular attention is given to primary interventions to enhance safety, health, and well-being of employees and to eliminate the harmful effects that may arise through individual characteristics, group/work unit factors, and aspects of the organization.

Key Words: Safety, health, occupational health psychology, accident proneness, leadership

Introduction

Industrial and organizational psychology has incorporated a concern for health and safety from its outset as a field within psychology, although some have suggested that in the early days of industrial and organizational psychology, the emphasis was more on efficiency than on worker well-being (Zickar, 2003). Many factors have brought a more balanced approach between well-being and efficiency over the past couple of decades, but one factor that we suggest for this shift is the global emergence of occupational health psychology (OHP) in the mid-1990s as a distinct field. OHP applies psychological theory and research for the purpose of improving the quality of work life for workers and to protecting and promoting the safety, health, and well-being of workers. According to the *Journal of Occupational Health Psychology*, there are three major domains of OHP: the work environment; the individual; and the interface between work and non-work relative to employees' safety, health, and well-being. OHP takes a primary prevention perspective, focusing on the elimination of risks to employees' safety and health (Quick & Tetrick, 2003) and, more recently, countervailing interventions that, rather than aiming to prevent illness and injury, seek to enhance development and to promote growth and positive experiences (Kelloway, Hurrell, & Day, 2008). Thus the major emphasis of OHP is on the development of a safe and healthy work environment, recognizing that individual differences may interact with an individual employee's specific context to enhance or worsen the individual's safety and well-being. We will take an OHP perspective in this chapter on occupational safety and health.

Health and Well-being

Before proceeding, it is important to briefly consider the ultimate criterion for OHP—that is, what is meant by *health and well-being*. Consistent with the World Health Organization's definition of *health*, OHP has adopted a definition of *health* to mean more than simply the absence of illness. *Health* refers to optimal functioning (Hofmann & Tetrick, 2003; Tetrick, 2002; Tetrick, Quick, & Quick, 2005). Taking this approach, OHP has extended beyond the medical model of health to include not only the physical and mental health model from an "ill-health" perspective but from a positive health perspective. As such, OHP should not be limited to protecting workers from illness and accidents or to restoring health, but also should deal with the promotion of health, well-being, and flourishing (Hofmann & Tetrick, 2003; Macik-Frey, Quick, & Nelson, 2007; Schaufeli, 2004). Second, it should explicitly consider and promote healthy workplaces as contexts where people may use their talents and gifts to "achieve high performance, high satisfaction, and well-being" (Quick, 1999, p. 82). Third, an individual approach must be complemented by the collective one, paying attention to promote healthy organizations and to analyze cross-level interactions (Peiró, 2008). Fourth, time perspective needs to be considered in a more comprehensive manner, combining short- versus long-term goals and outcomes (Hofmann & Tetrick, 2003), and a proactive and anticipatory approach is needed to enhance prevention (Peiró, 2008); further, close consideration of the dynamics of risk prevention and health promotion is required. Fifth, there needs to be explicit attention to work phenomena outside the work place (such as unemployment, work-family issues, cultural context, etc.) and, finally, the broader societal context, including legislation, policies, juridical issues, and the role of social agents, deserves attention (Brotherton, 2003). This is a more comprehensive approach to health and well-being than is often considered in research on safety and health.

The Origins of OHP

Given the recent development of OHP as a field, it may be helpful to provide a brief history of OHP. One might argue that the health and well-being of workers has been of concern to industrial and organizational psychologists since the studies carried out at the Western Electric Company at Hawthorne (Mayo, 1933; Roethlisberger & Dickson, 1939) or Taylor's (1911) work; however, these early works were primarily focused on productivity, performance, and efficiency and were not explicitly concerned with workers' health and well-being. Perhaps as a result of the findings of the Hawthorne studies, researchers and theorists in both the United States

and Europe began to expand the focus on employee behavior from a relatively myopic, short-term perspective on performance to a more holistic perspective of human potential that includes a long-term perspective.

These developments are reflected in Maslow's (1943) conceptualization of self-actualization and the explicit recognition of the importance of considering the psychological well-being of employees in the design of jobs (Trist & Bamforth, 1951). During the 1960s and 1970s, additional theoretical perspectives of the role of the work environment in workers' well-being emerged, including the job characteristics model (Hackman & Oldham, 1980), the job demands and control model of occupational stress (Karasek, 1979), and the recognition of the role of the psychosocial work environment in understanding worker health (Levi, 1971). During the last decades, the European Union and its country members, as well as the United States, established institutes for the specific purpose of advancing healthy and safe work environments for employees. The National Institute of Occupational Safety and Health was established in the United States in 1970; in Europe, the European Foundation for the Improvement of Living and Working Conditions was created in 1975 and the European Agency for Safety and Health at Work in 1996. European countries also have established institutes such as the Finnish Institute of Occupational Health. In addition, a number of research centers have been initiated, such as the Karolinska Institute in Sweden, and the Institute of Work, Health & Organisations at the University of Nottingham (for a more complete history of OHP, see Barling & Griffiths, 2003). These institutes and affiliated universities have supported research and theoretical development toward understanding the link between work and employee well-being. Additionally, they have trained professionals in occupational medicine, occupational nursing, industrial hygiene, safety engineering, occupational health psychology, and other disciplines, primarily from a public health perspective. Raymond, Wood, and Patrick (1990) are generally recognized as the first to apply the term *occupational health psychology* to the study of work environment factors contributing to employee health and well-being from this multidisciplinary perspective. Since then, the scientific community in the discipline has been growing and institutionalizing. Specialized journals in the field, such as *Work and Stress* and the *Journal of Occupational Health Psychology*, are well established. Scientific associations have been created in the last decade (the European Academy of Occupational Health Psychology and the Society for Occupational Health Psychology), and specialized conferences are organized by these associations biannually on both sides of the Atlantic.

This history and developments in OHP help to explain the body of knowledge that has been drawn upon in understanding workers' safety, health, and well-being, with much of the theorizing and empirical research in OHP focusing on safety, stress, and, more recently, the interface between work and non-work, with the work-family interface receiving the most attention to date. The remainder of this chapter will be organized around safety and health (readers are referred to chapter 34 on work-family issues in this handbook). Within each of these substantive areas, it has been recognized that contextual effects within the work environment exhibit multilevel influences on employees' health and well-being. Therefore, we will specifically discuss individual, group/work unit, and organizational factors influencing safety and stress.

Safety

As mentioned above, much of the early industrial and organizational psychology literature, such as Taylor's (1911) principles of scientific management, took a short-term perspective on workers' immediate performance and productivity. This may explain, at least in part, why much of the safety literature has focused on physical safety and, more specifically, accidents and acute injuries, rather than cumulative injuries and occupational illnesses arising from long-term exposure to toxins and pathogens. The literature on safety has a decidedly human factors orientation, incorporating a concern for the human-machine interface, a focus on physical work environment hazards, and the protection of workers from these physical hazards. OHP has advanced this approach to safety by extending the conceptualization of safety to include psychosocial factors in the work environment that facilitate safe behavior or discourage or create barriers to safe behavior.

Much of the safety literature has taken the perspective that a safe work environment is the responsibility of the employer. In fact, the United States' Occupational Safety and Health Act of 1970 explicitly indicated that organizations are responsible for providing a safe and healthy workplace. The European Framework Directive (Council Directive 89/391) established similar responsibilities that have been conveyed through specific legislation in every member state. The legislation in the United States and Europe recognized that workers frequently are exposed to hazards in the workplace involuntarily and may not even be aware of the risks to which they are exposed.

In reviewing the safety literature, three broad perspectives emerge. These roughly parallel the level of analysis, with perspectives that focus on the individual, those that focus on the unit and immediate supervisor, and those that focus on organizational factors. There have been relatively few examinations of both the group and organizational levels within studies; therefore, for the purpose of this chapter, group/unit and organizational levels are considered jointly.

Individual Factors in Safety

The first broad perspective on safety, which one might call the industrial psychology approach, traditionally sought to identify accident-prone individuals and then to prevent accidents and injuries by not selecting accident-prone individuals for jobs where there are identifiable hazards. This approach resulted in considerable research attempting to relate individual characteristics, especially personality characteristics as reflected by stable traits, to accident involvement, thus reflecting accident proneness. As Hansen in his 1988 review of the literature suggested, there were differences in how accident proneness was defined, but generally the definitions implied that accident proneness was a unitary trait, which was innate and stable over time. This trait "caused" individuals to be involved in accidents, and these individuals therefore would have repeated accidents. However, Hansen (1988) concluded that the research findings did not support these conditions of accident proneness.

Based on an examination of the literature from the early 1970s to late 1980s, Hansen (1988) concluded that there was evidence of certain personality and individual characteristics that were associated with accident involvement. These included external locus of control, extroversion, aggression, social maladjustment, general neurosis, anxiety, depression, and impulsivity. Based on the evidence that discredited accident proneness theory, Hansen (1988) did conclude that a differential accident liability approach might be useful, recognizing that there are individual differences that may be related to accidents, but that these individual differences are not necessarily stable over time. Additionally, there are other characteristics such as "intellectual capabilities and aptitudes, perceptual-motor abilities, physical capabilities such as strength and endurance, current health status, susceptibilities to disease..." that contribute to accident involvement (Smith, Karsh, Carayon, & Conway, 2003, p. 39). This differential accident liability approach posits that the few people who are involved in accidents are actually a shifting population; therefore, selection decisions made on the notion of accident proneness become less useful over time.

Interestingly, the debate continues about the existence of accident proneness as a construct that is descriptive of individuals and can predict accident involvement over time. A recent meta-analysis (Visser, Pijl, Stolk, Neeleman, & Rosmalen, 2007) found that, despite the differences in operationalizations of accident proneness, the number of individuals involved in repeated accidents is higher than what would be expected by chance, compared to the distribution of the number of individuals in the population involved in accidents. This at least provides some suggestion that there are individual differences operating. However, the differences in operationalizations of accident proneness and the differences in populations and organizational settings—only a small number of the studies included in Visser et al.'s (2007) meta-analysis involved work settings—definitely constrain any firm conclusions about our ability to select "out" people who are accident prone. A more fruitful approach might be to focus on malleable individual differences, such as knowledge, skills and abilities.

In fact, there is a large literature examining interventions to improve safety performance at the individual level. These individual behavior-based interventions for improving the safety performance of individuals have focused on changing individuals' behavior through the identification of critical safety behavior, feedback and reinforcement, goal setting, and communication among employees and supervisors. These interventions rely directly on major motivation theories, such as reinforcement, feedback, and goal theory. However, for the most part, they have not engaged self-regulatory theories and instead have drawn heavily on leadership as a mechanism for directing these behaviors (Ford & Tetrick, 2008). In this section, we will focus on training and regulatory focus theory as two individual-level safety interventions; training because it is a widely used safety intervention, and regulatory focus theory because this relatively recent motivational theory promises to inform safety interventions.

Training

Safety training is considered by many managers to be an important, if not the most important, activity for improving workplace safety (Huang, Leamon, Courtney, Chen, & DeArmond, 2007). Whether this is because managers believe that engineering solutions have been exhausted, whether they recognize that most workplace accidents have a human error component (Reason, 1990), or whether the managers are committing the fundamental attribution error is not clear, and perhaps it is not even relevant. There is evidence that safety training can improve workplace safety (e.g., Burke, Sarpy, et al. 2006; Colligan & Cohen, 2004) in a variety of settings and occupational groups, such as restaurant wait staff (Scherrer & Wilder, 2008), agricultural workers (Anger et al., 2006), and older workers (Wallen & Mulloy, 2006). Safety training programs, to date, have relied heavily on reinforcement theory, social learning and action regulation theory, and stage theories of learning.

Burke, Sarpy, et al. (2006) concluded, based on their meta-analysis, that safety training programs that engaged participants more were more effective. Burke, Scheuer, and Meredith (2007) and Burke, Holman, and Birdi (2006) argued that typical behavioral modeling and practice fall short. They suggest that applying a dialogic learning perspective to the development of safety skills and behaviors enhances safety training. The dialogic learning perspective includes structured interpersonal dialogue and intrapersonal dialogue (i.e., reflection) and leads to greater understanding. This dialogue thus can increase the effectiveness of safety training. Empirical tests of Burke and colleagues' propositions relative to the usefulness of dialogic learning theory are needed to more clearly demonstrate the mechanism(s) by which dialogue may increase training effectiveness, as well as the effect size of dialogue on training effectiveness relative to other components of safety training.

Regulatory Focus Theory

Apparent in much of the safety literature is the implicit, if not explicit, assumption that employee motivation is important for safety behavior. In fact, this is the underpinning of much of the safety training literature. A recent theoretical development not covered by Burke et al. (2007) is Higgins's (1997, 2002, 2006) regulatory focus theory. Regulatory focus theory posits that individuals can take a prevention or promotion perspective relative to a given goal (see Tetrick & Ford, 2008, for a review).

A prevention focus is characterized as seeking to avoid pain and loss, with individuals taking a vigilance orientation. A promotion focus, on the other hand, is characterized as seeking gains and approaching a task eagerly. Initially, Higgins (1997) proposed regulatory focus as a malleable characteristic reflecting a state in which individuals' strategies are prevention or promotion focused. In fact, he suggested that the two foci are independent such that one could be pursuing a promotion focus and a prevention focus simultaneously. Subsequently, Higgins (2002, 2006) proposed that, in addition to the state regulatory focus, individuals have a chronic regulatory focus in which they tend to approach goals or adopt strategies for achieving goals with a prevention focus or promotion focus.

Regulatory focus theory has been studied almost exclusively in laboratory settings and has only recently been extended to explaining safety behavior. In one of the few applied studies examining the relation of regulatory focus and safety, Wallace and Chen (2006) found that safety climate was positively related to a prevention regulatory focus and negatively related to a promotion regulatory focus, and a prevention regulatory focus was positively related to safety performance. These results suggest that it is possible to activate a prevention regulatory focus to enhance safe behaviors. In laboratory studies, this activation has been accomplished by framing the task or, as implied in Wallace and Chen (2006), by creating a strong safety climate (the latter intervention would be more of a group-level intervention; see section on safety climate below).

There have not been many empirical investigations of regulatory focus conducted in the field, and most of the studies that have been conducted in the field have tended to focus on chronic regulatory focus rather than state regulatory focus. Chronic regulatory focus is a more stable characteristic, and one might argue that it is not malleable, as it is a relatively enduring characteristic of individuals. The literature on regulatory focus suggests, however, that a match between an individual's chronic regulatory focus and the situationally invoked regulatory focus may result in an enhanced effect of either chronic or state regulatory focus alone (Higgins, Idson, Freitas, Spiegel, & Molden, 2003). Therefore, a match on prevention focus would be expected to enhance the effectiveness of safety training, and a mismatch might lessen the effectiveness of safety training. To date, this aspect of regulatory focus theory has not been empirically examined with respect to safety training.

Group, Unit, and Organizational Factors

As stated earlier, safety behavior is a function of individual factors, but it is also a function of group, unit, and organizational factors. In the safety literature, one approach for enhancing safety that clearly takes a group, work unit, or organization-level approach is that of engineering solutions. This approach seeks to first remove hazards; if this is not possible, then block access to hazards; if this is not possible, then change the physical work environment, especially the tools and/or equipment used; if this still does not block injuries, then warn employees of hazards; and, as a course of last resort, train employees on how to avoid hazards. Indeed, this engineering approach to safety has been widely adopted and has reduced accidents and injuries. For example, the redesign of injection needles used in medical settings, including needleless systems, guarded fistula needles, and safety syringes, have effectively removed the risk of accidental sticking by medical personnel (Tuma & Sepkowitz, 2006). However, it is not always possible to remove the hazard or to shield employees from hazards by an engineering solution. In these cases, employees need to have the knowledge and skills to perform their work safely, and they need to have the motivation to adhere to safety guidelines and to actually perform safely (Ford & Tetrick, 2008).

The engineering approach to safety focuses primarily on the physical environment. There is a growing recognition that organizations and work units' psychosocial environments also have an impact on workers' safety. Recognizing that group and/or work units comprise individuals sharing the same perceptions of the policies, procedures, and practices relative to safety (i.e., climate for safety), working for the same supervisor, and performing the same or similar jobs, we have chosen to include safety climate, leadership, and job design as three group/organization-level factors affecting safety.

Safety Climate

Zohar (1980) pioneered research on safety climate by arguing that employees develop a shared sense of the relative importance of safety in the work environment. This seminal work identified the perceived importance of safety training programs as one of the dimensions of safety climate, although Zohar (1980) concluded that the most important dimension of safety climate was management's attitude toward safety. Subsequent research on safety climate has converged to demonstrate that safety climate does predict safety behavior and accident experience (Johnson, 2007), and management's attitude toward safety is the key driver of safety climate, although safety training also has been demonstrated to be one of the major aspects of safety climate (Evans, Glendon, & Creed, 2007; Huang, Ho, Smith, & Chen, 2006; Lu & Tsai, 2008; Wu, Liu, & Lu, 2007).

A recent meta-analysis of the relationship between safety climate and safety performance (Clarke, 2006) found that a positive safety climate was related to safety compliance, defined as adherence to safety rules and regulations, and also with safety participation, defined as engaging in safety behaviors that went beyond simple adherence to safety procedures, such as helping coworkers and promoting the safety program. The results of this meta-analysis found that a positive safety climate was more strongly related to safety participation behaviors than with the compliance behaviors. In addition, Clarke (2006) found that the relation between a positive safety climate and fewer accidents overall was weak. However, study design was found to moderate this relation such that when the assessment of safety climate preceded the measurement of accidents, the link between a positive safety climate and a reduction in accidents was stronger.

Clarke (2006) suggests that there may be additional moderators of the relations found between safety climate and safety performance. One moderator that Clarke (2006) proposed was whether safety climate was assessed at the individual level (psychological climate) or at the group/unit or organization level. She posited that specific leadership practices and priorities, group processes, and strength of the safety climate may moderate the relation between safety climate and safety performance; however, there were insufficient numbers of studies to examine these potential moderators. More research in these areas may enhance our understanding of the mechanism by which safety climate affects accidents.

With the relation between safety climate and safety performance established, research has turned to other outcomes of safety climate. For example, Tucker, Chmiel, Turner, Hershcovis, and Stride (2008) examined one component of safety participation as defined by Clarke (2006)—that of employee safety voice, which was defined as speaking out against unsafe working conditions. Rather than focusing on safety climate per se, Tucker et al. (2008) posited that perceived organizational support was related to safety participation, based on social exchange theory. They found that coworker support for safety was an important social influence on speaking out about safety issues, with coworker support for safety mediating the relation between perceived organizational support for safety and voice. This supports Clarke's (2006) suggestion that group processes may impact the effect of organization-level safety climate and further demonstrates the importance of social influences on safety performance.

Researchers are beginning to examine more macro-aspects of safety climate. For instance, Probst, Brubaker, and Barsotti (2008) examined organization-level safety climate's effect on the underreporting of organizational injury rate. Safety climate data were obtained from employees of the participating construction companies and were related to Occupational Safety and Health Administration logs. They found that organizations with poorer safety climates had substantially higher rates of underreporting of occupational injuries. Therefore, safety climate appears to affect organizations' "behavior" as well as individual employees' behavior and may reflect an organizational culture in which safety of employees may or may not be valued.

Leadership

The role of the leader in safety behavior has been examined in numerous studies (see Hofmann & Morgeson, 2004, for a review). Leader behavior is a core aspect of safety climate, as management (organizational leadership) is a core dimension of safety climate (Zohar, 1980). Kelloway, Mullen, and Francis (2006) examined the relation of safety-specific transformational and passive leadership to safety climate. They found that transformational leadership was positively related to safety climate and safety consciousness (i.e., safety knowledge and safety behavior), and passive leadership was negatively related to both safety climate and safety consciousness. But leadership and safety consciousness did not have a direct effect on safety performance, whereas safety climate did have a direct effect on safety performance, reducing the number of negative safety events and injuries. Similarly, Zohar and Tenne-Gazit (2008) found that transformational leadership was positively related to safety climate strength and the extent of agreement among employees within the unit. However, based on social network analysis, they found that the density of the group communication network mediated the relation between transformational leadership and the strength of the safety climate. This supports the importance not only of leadership per se but also the role of coworkers in safety.

Taking a more behavioral approach, Luria, Zohar, and Erev (2008) investigated the effect of leader visibility on safety performance. In this intervention study, it was found that the more visible the supervisor (leader) was, the greater the interaction between the supervisor and the employees on safety-related behaviors and, subsequently, the greater safety performance. Perhaps more important, department-level effects were found such that in departments where supervisors were more visible, there were more safety-related exchanges between supervisors and employees and higher levels of safety performance.

Although most of the empirical research has examined the effects of leadership and safety climate at the individual level of analysis, support is accumulating for group/unit- and organization-level effects of leadership on safety performance (Hofmann & Stetzer, 1996; Zohar & Tenne-Gazit, 2008). The empirical evidence supports the role of leadership in creating a climate for safety, as well as having direct effects on employees' safety performance. These effects can arise from leaders' values, practices, and priorities. However, the literature also indicates that coworkers and social networks may be critical. There have been only a few studies of social networks and coworker support for safety in conjunction with leadership support for safety, so it is still underdetermined whether the group effects fully mediate the effects of the leader or complement the effects of the leader. Future research integrating the effects of leaders and coworkers on safety climate, climate strength, and safety performance is needed.

Job Design

There is a long history of the importance of job design in accidents and injuries. The human factors, ergonomics, and industrial engineering literatures are replete with examples and principles of design intended to simplify tasks within jobs to reduce cognitive interference in safely performing the required tasks. As stated above, much of this literature has taken the approach of attempting to design out hazards from the job by taking into consideration the person-machine interface with respect to physical characteristics and principles of memory and learning. For example, standardization of the locations for brakes and accelerator pedals on motorized vehicles serves to prevent negative transfer when moving from operating one vehicle to another. Over the past decade or so, there has been a growing recognition that we need to take a more integrative,

multidisciplinary approach to work design to integrate the mechanistic models with the psychosocial aspects of work design (Genaidy, Salem, Karwowski, Paez, & Tuncel, 2007; Parker & Wall, 1998; Sauter, Murphy, & Hurrell, 1990).

A recent meta-analysis by Humphrey, Nahrgang and Morgeson (2007) reviewed several motivational characteristics, social characteristics, and work contexts and their effects on behavioral outcomes, attitudes, role perceptions, and well-being outcomes. Unfortunately, they did not specifically include safety outcomes. Nevertheless, this meta-analysis did find that work context (physical demands, working conditions, and ergonomics) was negatively related to well-being and role perceptions. This relation was primarily due to working conditions and physical demands. Further, work context did predict stress and burnout beyond that accounted for by motivational characteristics and social characteristics. The results of this meta-analysis, although not directly assessing safety performance, are consistent with the conclusions drawn about safety climate and leadership. Work context may play a part in safety, but psychosocial factors may enhance or offset the effects of the physical work environment.

There are two specific aspects of job design that seem to be especially relevant in today's employment context. These are shift work and musculoskeletal injuries. Both are reflective of the increased use of technology and the movement to a 24-hour society, as well as the globalization of work. Working night shifts has been associated with increased occupational injuries and, to some extent, occupational illness (Smith, Folkard, Tucker, & Evans, 2011). Shift work may be especially difficult for older workers and although older workers do not experience as many accidents and injuries on the job, when they are injured it takes longer for them to recover. Folkard (2008) expresses a concern about our lack of knowledge of the impact of shift work on older individuals, especially given the aging population and the trend toward people continuing to work longer. This is a significant gap in the literature.

Accompanying the increasing age of the working population, the increasing use of technology, especially computers and other devices that require workers to interact with equipment over long periods of time, appears to be associated with the rising incidence of musculokeletal injuries. This has been accompanied by increasingly sedentary jobs, especially in the information age. The combination of longer periods of work with little physical activity is expected to result in negative health consequences.

Jobs may need to be redesigned to actually increase physical activity (Straker & Mathiassen, 2009), contrary to prior attempts to design physical risks out of jobs by reducing physical work load. Increasing physical activity as long as it does not increase the risk of accidents and injuries may enhance well-being. Alternatively, physical activity may need to be enhanced through non-job-related activities, such as engagement in health promotion programs. The empirical literature is relatively silent, however, as to how much physical activity, under what circumstances, is optimal for employees' health and well-being.

Health

Employee health typically has been viewed from the medical model perspective, focusing on ill-health or occupational illnesses. Indeed, there is a literature that links exposure to elements in the work environment to the development of illnesses such as cancer, pulmonary diseases, and cardiovascular diseases, for example (e.g., Belkic, Landsbergis, Schnall, & Baker, 2004). These elements historically were focused on physical toxins, but in the last few decades there has been an increasing recognition that psychosocial toxins also exist in the work environment that result in ill-health. The underlying mechanism for many of the effects of work environment factors on employees' health has been based on theories of occupational stress. In fact, occupational stress has been one of the core mechanisms, if not "the" core mechanism, by which the work environment has been understood to negatively affect workers' health and well-being. Certainly, many of the early contributors to OHP were researchers who demonstrated a link between work, stress, and health (e.g., Robert Karasek, Lennart Levi). Despite the fact that Selye (1976) described stress as being both positive and negative (e.g., eustress and distress, respectively), the occupational stress literature has more frequently examined employee ill-health as indicated by anxiety, depression, and psychosomatic complaints than considering positive health (e.g., optimal functioning and flourishing).

The occupational stress literature has generated a vast literature on the antecedents and consequences of occupational stress. A search of PSYCINFO using the keywords *job stress, occupational stress*, and *burnout* resulted in over 15,000 references. Clearly, an exhaustive review of this literature is beyond the limits of this chapter, but it is possible to summarize the major findings. Before considering the antecedents of occupational stress from a multilevel perspective, it is important to review the literature on the consequences of occupational stress.

Consequences of Occupational Stress

Perhaps one of the first reviews of the consequences of occupational stress appeared in *Personnel Psychology* (Beehr & Newman, 1978). This literature review, based on theory and empirical work, concluded that occupational stress resulted in the following consequences on individuals' health: anxiety, tension, depression, dissatisfaction, boredom, somatic complaints, psychological fatigue, feelings of futility, inadequacy, low self-esteem, cardiovascular disease, gastrointestinal disorders, dispensary visits, and drug use and abuse (including alcohol, caffeine, and nicotine). In addition, Beehr and Newman's (1978) framework and review also suggested that occupational stress resulted in feelings of alienation, psychoses, anger, repression, suppression of feelings and ideas, loss of concentration, respiratory problems, cancer, arthritis, headaches, bodily injuries, skin disorders, physical/physiological fatigue or strain, death, over- or under-eating, nervous gesturing, pacing, risky behavior (e.g., reckless driving, gambling, aggression, vandalism, stealing), poor interpersonal relations (with friends, family, coworkers), and suicide or attempted suicide, although at the time there had not been empirical evidence to support these consequences. Similarly, the work-related consequences that had been empirically demonstrated at the time that Beehr and Newman (1978) were writing their review were changes in quantity of work, decreases in the quality of job performance, and increases or decreases in withdrawal behaviors (absenteeism, turnover, and early retirement). Other organizational consequences that they suggested, based on their theoretical analysis (although lacking empirical evidence at the time), were changes in profits, sales, earnings, changes in ability to recruit and retain quality employees, changes in ability to obtain raw materials, increase or decrease in control over environment, changes in innovation and creativity, changes in quality of work life, increase or decrease in employee strikes, changes in level of influence of supervisors, and grievances. Beehr and Newman (1978) did note that the empirical studies that did examine the link between job stress and consequences had serious methodological concerns, such as reliance on self-report and cross-sectional designs, that restrict the ability to make causal inferences.

In the almost four decades since Beehr and Newman's (1978) article was published, empirical research has filled in the gaps for many of these consequences of job stress, although some still have little or no empirical evidence to support them as being the consequences of job stress. In some instances, the association between job stress and some of the consequences mentioned by Beehr and Newman (1978) have become better understood. For example, a recent meta-analysis by Darr and Johns (2008) found that there was a weak positive association between stress and absence. They found support for this association being mediated by physical and psychological symptoms such that stress was positively related to physical and psychological symptoms, which were in turn related to absence. Another example is the demonstrated link between stress and sleep disturbances. Armon, Shirom, Shapira, and Melamed (2008), for example, found in a prospective study that burnout predicted new cases of insomnia over an 18-month period.

In some instances, new research has tended to question some of the outcomes included in Beehr and Newman's (1978) framework. For example, under the category of gastrointestinal disorders, ulcers have been identified as being the result of a virus, although perhaps there may still be some more distal link to stress. Therefore, while progress may have been slow, many of the employee and organizational outcomes of occupational stress included in Beehr and Newman (1978) have received some empirical support. The prior limitations of the study designs continue to exist, with an overemphasis on cross-sectional, self-report methodologies, but the quality of the study designs has been improving, with more intervention studies being reported and new methodologies such as experience sampling (Sonnentag & Zijlstra, 2006) becoming more prevalent.

Antecedents of Occupational Stress

Kelloway and Day (2005), in a special issue of the *Canadian Journal of Behavioural Science* on building healthy workplaces, summarize what we know empirically that is unhealthy. They suggest that there are six categories of stressors in the work environment that are related to ill-health of employees: work overload and too great a work pace; role stressors including role conflict, role ambiguity, and interrole conflict; career concerns such as job insecurity, fear of job obsolescence, under- and over-promotion, and lack of career development; timing of work to include rotating shifts and night shifts; poor interpersonal relationships including lack of support from supervisor and peers, workplace aggression, bullying, and incivility; and jobs

whose content is too narrow or individuals have too little control and autonomy. As was the case with safety, there are individual- and group-level factors influencing employees' experience of stress and the subsequent ill-health outcomes.

Individual-Level Stressors

There have been a number of individual differences that have been identified as relevant to the experience of stress, such as resilience, tolerance for ambiguity, and perceptions of control (Parkes, 1994). Some individual differences appear to have direct effects on the experience of work stress (Ferris, Sinclair, & Kline, 2005), and others have been found to moderate the relation between stressors and the experience of stress or the relation between the experience of stress and the negative consequences of this experience of stress (Xie, Schaubroeck, & Lam, 2008). In addition to specific individual differences, there is a large literature on person-environment fit that recognizes the interaction between individual characteristics, such as values, attitudes, preferences, and abilities, and characteristics of the work environment (Edwards & Rothbard, 2005). A lack of fit, according to the person-environment fit model, or a mismatch between chronic regulatory focus and state regulatory focus (Higgins et al., 2003), as mentioned above, can result in stress.

Rather than review the literature on individual differences and person-environment fit, however, two more recent advances in our understanding of occupational stress and employee health—recovery and organizational wellness programs are discussed in this section. These two lines of inquiry take a somewhat more positive approach to employee well-being in the workplace.

RECOVERY

Much of the literature on occupational stress, as indicated above, focused on the negative effects of stressors on employees' health and well-being. Recently, a line of research has emerged positing that there is a need for recovery from the demands of work. The concept of need for recovery from the demands of work recognizes that work expends individuals' physiological and psychological resources and that these resources need to be replenished after work in order for individuals to be able to return to work the following day (Sonnentag & Fritz, 2007; Sonnentag & Zijlstra, 2006). Failure to recover to pre-stressor levels prior to returning to work results in fatigue and a reduction in well-being. The recovery experiences of psychological detachment from work, relaxation, mastery experiences, and freedom from non-work stress (Fritz & Sonnentag, 2006; Sonnentag, Binnewies, & Mojza, 2008) have been shown to be related to enhanced sleep quality, positive activation rather than negative activation, serenity, reduced fatigue, and well-being. These effects have been observed for evening recovery experiences as well as vacation effects. Therefore, recovery experiences have been related to employees' well-being as a function of on-the-job effects and off-the-job activities.

This emerging literature suggests potential stress interventions at the individual level to alleviate the negative effects of work, but also may provide the theoretical underpinning for an intervention to enhance the positive experiences of work. Additionally, the emerging literature on recovery recognizes that the interaction between work and non-work is important for employees' health and well-being, along similar lines to the work-family literature, reinforcing the notion that the lines between work and non-work are porous, at least with respect to health and well-being. Further research integrating the literature on recovery with the work-family literature may be a useful pursuit in understanding positive and negative effects of work, family, and the interface between the two domains.

ORGANIZATIONAL WELLNESS PROGRAMS

Organizational wellness programs are included as an individual-level factor that seeks to improve employees' health because they typically are based on individual participation and focus on the individual. It could be argued, however, that they are actually an organization-level phenomenon in that they are typically offered to all employees and reflect organizational policies and practices. Organizational wellness programs have been in existence since the 1970s, and it has been argued that one of the major incentives to organizations was to reduce expenditures on employee health care costs by encouraging individuals to change modifiable health risk factors associated with their lifestyles (Rothstein, 1983). Organizational wellness programs are not monolithic, but typically they focus on fitness, nutrition and weight management, smoking cessation, health education, and stress management. These programs are believed to increase productivity, enhance morale, and reduce absenteeism (Parks & Steelman, 2008; Shurtz, 2005).

Surprisingly, empirical evidence of the effects of organizational wellness programs on employees' health is still somewhat limited, but Shurtz (2005)

suggested that the return on investment of organizational wellness programs based on health care expenditures ranged from $1.49 to $4.91. Parks and Steelman's (2008) meta-analysis found that participation in an organizational wellness program was positively related to job satisfaction and negatively related to absenteeism. They did not directly examine the relation of participation in an organizational wellness program and health per se; however, job satisfaction has been treated as a lack of strain in the occupational stress literature, and absence can be indicative of ill-health and strain. Some of the challenges in determining the effectiveness of organizational wellness programs are getting employees to participate in the programs, especially the employees who are most in need of the programs being offered, as well as the complexities of conducting evaluation research in organizations (Parks & Steelman, 2008). More evidence of the impact of organizational wellness programs, based on strong intervention evaluation designs, is needed.

Group and Organization-Level Stressors

To the extent that organizational policies and practices and employer-employee relationships are a source of stress, then one can conceptualize an organization-level effect on employees' experience of stress and subsequent health. For example, based on Kelloway and Day's (2005) review, there appear to be several potential organization-level or group-level stressors, and these stressors tend to affect all employees or groups of employees, at least under the assumption that the policies apply equally to all employees. Poor organizational financial health may signal job insecurity to employees; poor job design can result in overload, time pressure, and under-utilization, and the literature has shown that job insecurity, overload, time pressure, and under-utilization can contribute to individual employees' stress levels (Barling, Kelloway, & Frone, 2004; Quick & Tetrick, 2003, 2011). Shiftwork, especially rotating shiftwork, has been long recognized to be a source of stress and ill-health (Smith, Folkard, & Fuller, 2003). However, most of the research examining the relation of these stressors and employees' health has been conducted at the individual level of analysis only and has neglected the cross-level effects of either work group or organization. Admittedly, policies and practices espoused at the organizational and group levels do not necessarily indicate the enacted policies and practices that individual workers may experience (Schein, 1992), and thus individual-level effects should not be automatically ignored.

Recently, occupational stress researchers have specifically posited group-level phenomena; three of these concepts are: the employee-employment relationship in the form of psychological contracts, climate for sexual harassment, and burnout contagion.

Employee-Employer Relationships

Stress has been often conceptualized from the perspective of (mis)fit between demands and control, or demands and resources of the individual. An outstanding theoretical model in this tradition is the demands-control model (Karasek, 1979). However, alternative views have been derived from the exchange theory (Blau, 1964; Rupp & Cropanzano, 2002), in which concepts such as fairness, reciprocity, and justice play an important role. This approach is especially relevant when we aim to analyze employer-employee relationships, organizational support, and human resources practices as potential significant source of stress. All these phenomena may have negative health effects when an imbalance in the exchange between employer and employee occurs (Siegrist 1996). In many instances, the interpretations that employees make about this type of exchange are influenced by the promises they have received from their employer and by the breaches and violations of those promises that they perceive.

There is evidence showing that violation experiences are followed by employees' negative emotional reactions, such as disappointment, frustration, and distress or strain, together with feelings of anger, resentment, bitterness, indignation, and outrage. These feelings may deteriorate well-being and health (Gakovic & Tetrick, 2003). Recently, a large cross-national study carried out by the Psycones International Research team has evaluated the relations between psychological contract and well-being and health in a sample of 5,288 employees in six European countries (Sweden, Spain, UK, Germany, Belgium and the Netherlands) and Israel (Guest, Isaksson, & De Witte, 2010). It was found that all seven dimensions of the psychological contract considered (content, fulfillment, violation, trust, and fairness relative to employers' obligations perceived by the employees, plus content and fulfilment concerning employees' obligations to their employers as perceived by themselves) had a significant association with one or more of a broad array of outcomes considered (occupational self-efficacy, positive work-life influence, anxiety, depression, irritation, sick leave, sick presence, accidents, harassment and violence, job satisfaction, organizational commitment, intention to quit, perceived performance, general health, and life satisfaction). Interestingly enough, violation of the psychological contract was the feature that showed the strongest association with most of the outcomes (Guest & Clinton, i2010).

Given that perceptions of psychological contract were obtained from both employers and employees, mutuality and reciprocity in psychological contracts were also explicitly incorporated in the study. Mutuality refers to agreement on the promises and commitments shaping the content of the psychological contract, while reciprocity is defined as agreement on the fulfillment of the mutual commitments. Mutuality and reciprocity both had a significant influence on the outcomes mentioned above, after controlling for country sector and a broad array of organizational, individual, and work-related variables. However, when three fairness measures (HRM practices, a direct measure of fairness perception, and violation of the contract) were included in the analyses, mutuality and reciprocity often were not significant. These results points out the "need to be cautious in interpreting existing studies of mutuality and reciprocity if they do not take account of perceptions of fairness.... It is the state of the psychological contract, reflected in the quality of the relationship in terms of perceptions of fairness of treatment that has the major influence on outcomes" (Isaksson, Gracia, Caballer, & Peiró, 2010, p. 183). Violation of the psychological contract had important effects on health and well-being at work and in general. In sum, the employee-employer relationship, as viewed from psychological contract theory, plays a significant role in employees' health and well-being. Future research needs to consider the physiological and psychological mechanisms that account for these effects.

Climate for Sexual Harassment

Fitzgerald, Drasgow, Hulin, Gelfand, and Magley (1997) proposed that sexual harassment in organizations was a result of organizational characteristics that formed a climate for sexual harassment. A test of this model supported the claim that climate for sexual harassment is an antecedent of sexual harassment and the subsequent negative effects associated with sexual harassment. This model was extended by Bergman and Henning (2008), in which gender and ethnicity were considered as moderators of the effects of climate for sexual harassment on sexual harassment and of the effects of sexual harassment on health. Support was found for the proposed moderating effects of gender on the relation between climate for sexual harassment and sexual harassment, with the relation being stronger for women than men, but ethnicity was not a moderator; additionally, neither gender nor ethnicity moderated the relation between the experience of sexual harassment and health outcomes.

These two studies provide evidence that organizational climate may impact employees' health and well-being either directly or indirectly. Bergman and Henning (2008) also suggested that the climate for sexual harassment may be extended to climates for bullying and workplace violence and, in fact, Kessler, Spector, Chang, and Parr (2008) have provided support for the concept of an organizational climate for violence. This is clearly an emerging area of research, and more work remains to be done. To date, the analytic approach taken has primarily remained at the individual level of analysis, relying on perceptions of climate, rather than a multilevel approach. Taking a multilevel approach is needed to strengthen the support for linking an organizational climate for sexual harassment or violence and effects on employees' health and well-being.

Collective Burnout and Burnout Contagion

Another recent development that acknowledges the embeddedness of individuals within their work organization are the concepts of collective burnout (Moliner, Martinez-Tur, Peiró, Ramos, & Cropanzano, 2005) and burnout contagion (Bakker & Schaufeli, 2000). Individuals may work in organizations or work units where burnout experiences are generalized among their members, thus becoming a collective phenomenon. This contextual factor posits individuals working in it to be at higher risk of burnout, essentially through a social comparison process (Buunk, Zurriaga, & Peiró, 2009; Carmona, Buunk, Peiró, Rodriguez, & Bravo, 2006). In one of the first investigations of burnout contagion, Bakker and Schaufeli (2000) found that perceived burnout complaints of coworkers were the most important predictor of both individual- and unit-level burnout, supporting their hypothesis that burnout is contagious. In two subsequent studies with different professional groups, additional support has been obtained, suggesting that emotional contagion from one colleague to another can account for individual levels of burnout as well as group levels of burnout (Bakker, Le Blanc, & Schaufeli, 2005; Bakker, Schaufeli, Sixma, & Bosveld, 2001). Therefore, evidence is accumulating that it is not only the objective characteristics of organizations and units (e.g., policies, procedures, and practices) within

organizations that have negative consequences for employees' health, but there are psychosocial factors and group processes (i.e., social climates) operating as well.

Research Evidence from Evaluations of Interventions

Not only is there a need for more evaluation research of organizational wellness programs as indicated above, there is a paucity of research on interventions to reduce the negative effects of the work environment or to enhance the positive effects of the work environment on employees' health and well-being. Much of the literature on occupational safety and health continues to rely on cross-sectional, mono-method, correlational research designs. However, we are seeing an increase in experiments and quasi-experiments. Plus, field studies and case studies are increasingly being accumulated using meta-analytic and systematic review techniques, which help to summarize findings, although these techniques cannot correct for the weaknesses in the research designs per se.

An empirical investigation carried out by Kompier, De Gier, Smulders, and Draaisma (1994) offered a perspective of the situation during the late 1980s and early 1990s about the practices concerning interventions to prevent work stress in five European countries. Out of this research, the authors found differences across countries in terms of the attention paid to work stress and to its prevention and/or correction. The practices used, when they existed, were characterized as focusing on the individual rather than on the organization as the main target, being concentrated disproportionally on reducing the effects of stressors rather than reducing the presence of stressors at work, and were mostly oriented to the management of stress.

One decade later, Van der Klink, Blonk, Schene, and Van Dijk (2001) reviewed 48 experimental studies seeking to determine the effectiveness of the occupational stress-reducing interventions; 43 were focused on individuals, while only 5 were organization based. In these studies, a moderate effect was found for cognitive-behavioral interventions and for multimodal interventions on the outcome criteria, including several strain indicators such as complaints or quality of work life. A significant but small effect was shown for relaxation. No significant effect was found for organizational interventions.

Subsequently, Semmer (2003) reviewed job stress interventions and organization of work factors, paying attention to task and technical interventions, changes in working conditions (such as ergonomics, time, and workload), improvements in role clarity, and social relationships. He also included interventions with multiple changes. Results were complex, not only because of the wide variety of interventions and contextual contingencies but because the diversity of outcome criteria, and measures were more or less distant from the immediate intervention in a chain that aims, first, to identify if they change the intended workers' experiences (e.g., more autonomy), and second, if they do or do not affect measures of health and well-being. In any case, "it is not very reasonable to expect all indicators of well-being and health to show changes in means after a specific time following intervention" (p. 341). Semmer (2003) also pointed out that "trade-offs" in the process of improving working conditions need to be taken into account when changes are introduced. In some cases, even after acknowledging the value of the new system, the preference may be for the old one because the costs of the improvement to be implemented are too high. Semmer (2003) concludes that "the state of the affairs seems less pessimistic than it appears at first.... There are many positive findings, many null effects but not very many negative ones—although intervening in a complex system will always run the risk of negative effects" (Semmer, 2003, p. 345). However, he suggested several methodological improvements for the evaluation of interventions (Semmer, 2006). Semmer (2003, 2006) points out that attention should not only focus on the design of the interventions, but also on the process. Careful documentation of the process during the intervention is needed, followed by subgroup analyses to better understand the situation and conditions of the different individuals within an intervention's targeted group.

More recently, additional meta-analyses offer empirical evidence about the effects of occupational stress interventions and wellness programs. Richardson and Rothstein (2008) reported significant medium to large effects of interventions on psychological rather than on physiological or organizational outcomes. Again, cognitive-behavioral programs produced larger effects than relaxation or organizational interventions. However, when other interventions were included (e.g., multimodal), the cognitive-behavioral interventions effect was reduced. Parks and Steelman (2008), as mentioned above, found that participating in organizational wellness programs was related to decreased absenteeism and increased job satisfaction.

There are some areas where interventions have been less frequent than in others, and evaluation of the efficacy of these interventions is more difficult. More empirical evidence is needed for interventions at the organizational level, especially relative to the interface between external and organizational realities influencing occupational health, safety, and well-being (Schaufeli, 2004). Moreover, methodologies need to be improved to obtain more rigorous data and results of the evaluations and their external validity.

Professional interventions in psychosocial risk prevention and health promotion imply designing and developing models, strategies, and tools based on research and theory. Organizational development and organizational design provide a rich armamentarium that may help in health protection and promotion. Moreover, the implementation of changes requires the incorporation of theories of organizational change and change management. In fact, professionals who want to contribute to risk prevention and health promotion (Tetrick, 2008) need to be competent in change planning and management as well as in program evaluation. In this context, it is especially important that they pay attention to the human and social side of organizational change (psychosocial dynamics, synergies, and resistance to change) and to the analysis of stakeholders, agents, and relevant audiences. The dynamics of change deserve important attention, balancing both short- and long-term perspectives about maintaining the process, as well as assessing substantive outcomes.

Summary and Future Directions

The empirical evidence is clear that workplace factors are directly related to the health and safety of employees. These factors may be physical attributes of the work environment, such as working conditions and activities such as repetitive movements required by individuals to do their jobs, but there are also numerous psychosocial factors that can either result in lack of safety and ill-health, or actual safety and positive health. These psychosocial factors include such factors as climate for safety, climate for sexual harassment, interpersonal relations, coworker support, and leadership. In the discussion above, we have identified some gaps in the literature and have made suggestions for areas in need of continued or new investigations. In closing, we would like to offer some additional, perhaps more future directions to enhance the safety, health and well-being of employees.

Much of the theorizing and research on occupational safety and health has actually focused on lack of safety and ill-health. Additionally, much of this work has been conducted in workplaces that are far different from today's dynamic, global, service/knowledge-oriented occupations. We recommend that future work on occupational safety and health should: (a) incorporate the realities of today's work environments, and (b) integrate a positive approach with countervailing interventions (Kelloway et al., 2006), so as not to just focus on prevention but also on enhancement and development of workers, the work environment, and the interaction between workers and the environment. Such an orientation would expand our understanding of occupational demands and the experience of those demands as either positive stress or distress.

Taking a positive approach to occupational health and safety will require more complete conceptualizations of positive health. There is general agreement that positive health is not just the absence of illness, but beyond this there does not appear to be consensus. Health is viewed as optimal functioning, although the exact operationalization of this is not clear. Further, the literature is not clear regarding the relation between health and safety. It has been recognized that ill-health can be related to lack of safety, and one logically might argue that if one is not safe, it might result in ill-health. However, the literature has not directly addressed these relations (either in the negative health realm or the positive health realm) and definitely has not sought to examine these empirically.

The literature on occupational safety and health has primarily focused on explanatory studies, which is important in theory development. However, the accumulated evidence is such that it is now time to focus more on the design and implementation of interventions and on the evaluation of the effectiveness of these interventions to enhance and maintain occupational safety and health. Intervention design (based on theory and empirical evidence), implementation, and evaluation are challenging in the field, and often the strongest designs must be modified to meet organizational constraints. Nevertheless, intervention studies are critical in actually creating safe and healthy work environments that can be adopted in organizations.

Innovations in research design, such as experience sampling methods, can provide us with much richer and more complete pictures of the experience of employees. Additionally, reliance on self-report measures has limited the strength of much of the research on occupational safety and health. Future research adopting observational and physiological measures promises to advance our understanding of occupational safety and health.

References

Anger, W. K., Stupfel, J., Ammerman, T., Tamulinas, A., Bodner, T., & Rohlman, D. S. (2006). The suitability of computer-based training for workers with limited formal education: A case from the U.S. agricultural sector. *International Journal of Training and Development, 10*, 269–284.

Armon, G., Shirom, A., Shapira, I., & Melamed, S. (2008). On the nature of burnout-insomnia relationships: A prospective study of employed adults. *Journal of Psychosomatic Research, 65*, 5–12.

Bakker, A. G., Le Blanc, P. M., & Schaufeli, W. B. (2005). Burnout contagion among intensive care nurses. *Journal of Advanced Nursing, 51*, 276–287.

Bakker, A. B., & Schaufeli, W. G. (2000). Burnout contagion processes among teachers. *Journal of Applied Social Psychology, 30*, 2289–2308.

Bakker, A. G., Schaufeli, W. B., Sixma, H. J., Bosveld, W. (2001). Burnout contagion among general practitioners. *Journal of Social and Clinical Psychology, 20*, 82–98.

Barling, J., & Griffiths, A. (2003). A history of occupational health psychology. In J. C. Quick & L. E. Tetrick (Eds.), *Handbook of occupational health psychology* (pp. 19–34). Washington, DC: APA Books.

Barling, J., Kelloway, E. K., & Frone, M. R. (2004). *Handbook of work stress.* Thousand Oaks, CA: Sage.

Beehr, T. A., & Newman, J. E. (1978). Job stress, employee health, and organizational effectiveness: A facet analysis, model, and literature review. *Personnel Psychology, 31*, 665–699.

Belkic, K. L., Landsbergis, P. A., Schnall, P. L., & Baker, D. (2004). Is job strain a major source of cardiovascular disease risk? *Scandinavian Journal of Work, Environment & Health, 30*, 85–128.

Bergman, M. E., & Henning, J. B. (2008). Sex and ethnicity as moderators in the sexual harassment phenomenon: A revision and test of Fitzgerald et al. (1994). *Journal of Occupational Health Psychology, 13*, 152–167.

Blau, P. (1964). *Exchange and power in social life.* New York: Wiley.

Brotherton, C. (2003). The role of external policies in shaping organizational health and safety. In D. A. Hofmann & L. E Tetrick (Eds.), *Health and safety in organizations* (pp. 372–396). San Francisco: Jossey Bass.

Burke, M. J., Holman, D., & Birdi, K. (2006). A walk on the safe side: The implications of learning theory for developing effective safety and health training. In G. P. Hodgkinson & J. K. Ford (Eds.), *International review of industrial and organizational psychology* (pp. 1–44). London: John Wiley & Sons.

Burke, M. J., Sarpy, S. A., Smith-Crowe, K., Chan-Serafin, S., Islam, G., & Salvador, R. (2006). The relative effectiveness of worker safety and health training methods. *American Journal of Public Health, 96*, 315–324.

Burke, M. J., Scheuer, J. L., & Meredith, R. J. (2007). A dialogical approach to skill development: The case of safety skills. *Human Resource Management Review, 17*, 235–250.

Buunk, A. P., Zurriaga, R., & Peiró, J. M. (2009). Social comparison as a predictor of changes in burnout among nurses. *Anxiety, Stress and Coping, 22*, 1–14.

Carmona, C., Buunk, A. P., Peiró, J. M., Rodriguez, I., & Bravo, M. J. (2006). Do social comparison and coping styles play a role in the development of burnout? Cross-sectional and longitudinal findings. *Journal of Occupational and Organizational Psychology, 79*, 85–99.

Clarke, S. (2006). The relationship between safety climate and safety performance: A meta-analytic review. *Journal of Occupational Health Psychology, 11*, 315–327.

Colligan, M., & Cohen, A. (2004). The role of training in promoting workplace safety and health. In J. Barling & M. R. Frone (Eds.), *The psychology of workplace safety* (pp. 223–248). Washington, DC: American Psychological Association.

Darr, W., & Johns, G. (2008). Work strain, health, and absenteeism: A meta-analysis. *Journal of Occupational Health Psychology, 13*, 293–318.

Edwards, J. R., & Rothbard, N. P. (2005). Work and family stress and well-being: An integrative model of person-environment fit within and between the work and family domains. In E. E. Kossek & S. J. Lambert (Eds.), *Work and life integration: Organizational, cultural, and individual perspectives* (pp. 211–242). Mahwah, NJ: Erlbaum.

Evans, B., Glendon, A. I., & Creed, P. A. (2007). Development and initial validation of an Aviation Safety Climate Scale. *Journal of Safety Research, 38*, 675–682.

Ferris, P. A., Sinclair, C., & Kline, T. J. (2005). It takes two to tango: Personal and organizational resilience as predictors of strain and cardiovascular disease risk in a work sample. *Journal of Occupational Health Psychology, 10*, 225–238.

Fitzgerald, L. F., Drasgow, F., Hulin, C. L., Gelfand, M. J., & Magley, V. J. (1997). Antecedents and consequences of sexual harassment in organizations: A test of an integrated model. *Journal of Applied Psychology, 82*, 578–589.

Folkard, S. (2008). Shiftwork, safety and ageing. *Chronobiology International, 25*, 183–198.

Ford, M. E., & Tetrick, L. E. (2008). Safety motivation and human resource management in North America. *The International Journal of Human Resource Management.19*, 1472–1485.

Friedman, H. S., & Cohen Silver, R. (Eds.). (2007). *Foundations of health psychology.* New York: Oxford University Press.

Fritz, C., & Sonnentag, S. (2006). Recovery, well-being, and performance-related outcomes: The role of workload and vacation experiences. *Journal of Applied Psychology, 91*, 936–945.

Gakovic, A., & Tetrick, L. E. (2003). Psychological contract breach as a source of strain for employees. *Journal of Business and Psychology, 18*, 235–246.

Genaidy, A., Salem, S., Karwowski, W., Paez, O., & Tuncel, S. (2007). The work compatibility improvement framework: An integrated perspective of the human-at-work system. *Ergonomics, 50*, 3–25.

Guest, D. E., & Clinton, M. (2010). Causes and consequences of the Psychological Contract. In D. E. Guest, K. Isaksson, & H. De Witte (Eds.), *Employment contracts, psychological contracts and employee well-being: An international study* (pp. 121–160). Oxford: Oxford University Press.

Guest, D. E., Isaksson, K., & De Witte, H. (Eds.). (2010). *Employment contracts, psychological contracts and employee well-being: An international study.* Oxford: Oxford University Press.

Hackman, J. R., & Oldham, G. R. (1980). *Work redesign.* Reading, MA: Addison-Wesley.

Hansen, C. P. (1988). Personality characteristics of the accident-involved individual. *Journal of Business and Psychology, 2*, 346–365.

Higgins, E. T. (1997). Beyond pleasure and pain. *American Psychologist, 52*, 1280–1300.

Higgins, E. T. (2002). How self-regulation creates distinct values: The case of promotion and prevention decision making. *Journal of Consumer Psychology, 12*, 177–191.

Higgins, E. T. (2006). Value from hedonic experience and engagement. *Psychological Review, 113*, 439–460.

Higgins, E. T., Idson, L. C., Freitas, A. L., Spiegel, S., & Molden, D. C. (2003). Transfer of value from fit. *Journal of Personality and Social Psychology, 84*, 1140–1153.

Hofmann, D. A., & Morgeson, F. P. (2004). The role of leadership in safety. In J. Barling & M. R. Frone (Eds.), *The psychology of workplace safety* (pp. 159–180). Washington, DC: American Psychological Association.

Hofmann, D. A., & Stetzer, A. (1996). A cross-level investigation of factors influencing unsafe behaviors and accidents. *Personnel Psychology, 49*, 207–339.

Hofmann, D. A., & Tetrick, L. E. (2003). On the etiology of health: Implications for "organizing" individual and organizational health. In D. A. Hofmann & L. E. Tetrick (Eds.), *Health and safety in organizations: A multilevel perspective* (pp. 1–26). San Francisco: Jossey-Bass.

Huang, Y. H., Ho, M., Smith, G. S., & Chen, P. Y. (2006). Safety climate and self-reported injury: Assessing the mediating role of employee safety control. *Accident Analysis & Prevention, 38*, 425–433.

Huang, Y. H., Leamon, T. G., Courtney, T. K., Chen, P. Y., & DeArmond, S. (2007). Corporate financial decision-makers' perceptions of workplace safety. *Accident Analysis & Prevention, 39*, 767–775.

Humphrey, S. E., Nahrgang, J. D., & Morgeson, F. P. (2007). Integrating motivational, social and contextual work design features: A meta-analytic summary and theoretical extension of the work design literature. *Journal of Applied Psychology, 92*, 1332–1356.

Isaksson, K., Gracia, F., Caballer, A., & Peiró, J. M. (2010). Mutuality and reciprocity in the psychological contracts of temporary and permanent workers. In D. E. Guest, K. Isaksson & H. De Witte (Eds.), *Employment contracts, psychological contracts and employee well-being: An international study* (pp. 161–184). Oxford: Oxford University Press.

Johnson, S. E. (2007). The predictive validity of safety climate. *Journal of Safety Research, 38*, 511–521.

Karasek, R. A. (1979). Job demands, job decision latitude, and mental strain: Implications for job redesign. *Administrative Science Quarterly, 24*, 285–308.

Kelloway, E. K., & Day, A. L. (2005). Building healthy workplaces: What we know so far. *Canadian Journal of Behavioural Science, 37*, 223–235.

Kelloway, E. K., Hurrell, J. J., Jr., & Day, A. (2008). Workplace interventions for occupational stress. In K. Näswall, J. Hellgren, & M. Sverke (Eds.), *The individual in the changing working life* (pp. 419–441). Cambridge: Cambridge University Press.

Kelloway, E. K., Mullen, J., & Francis, L. (2006). Divergent effects of transformational and passive leadership on employee safety. *Journal of Occupational Health Psychology, 11*, 76–86.

Kessler, S. R., Spector, P. E., Chang, C., & Parr, A. D. (2008). Organizational violence and aggression: Development of the three-factor violence climate survey. *Work & Stress, 22*, 108–124.

Kompier, M., De Gier, E., Smulders, P., & Draaisma, D. (1994). Regulations, policies and practices concerning work stress in five European countries. *Work and Stress, 8*, 296–318.

Levi, L. (1971). *Society, stress and disease.* Oxford: Oxford University Press.

Lu, C. S., & Tsai, C. L. (2008). The effects of safety climate on vessel accidents in the container shipping context. *Accident Analysis & Prevention, 40*, 594–601.

Luria, G., Zohar, D., & Erev, I. (2008). The effect of workers' visibility on effectiveness of intervention programs: Supervisory-based safety interventions. *Journal of Safety Research, 39*, 273–280.

Macik-Frey, M., Quick, J. C., & Nelson, D. L. (2007) Advances in occupational health: From a stressful beginning to a positive future. *Journal of Management, 33*, 809–840.

Maslow, A. H. (1943). A theory of human motivation. *Psychological Review, 50*, 370–396.

Mayo, E. (1933). *The human problems of an industrial civilization.* New York: MacMillan.

Moliner, C., Martinez-Tur, V., Peiró, J. M., Ramos, J., & Cropanzano, R. (2005). Relationships between organizational justice and burnout at the work-unit level. *International Journal of Stress Management, 12*, 99–116.

Parker, S. K., & Wall, T. D. (1998). *Job and work design: Organizing work to promote well-being and effectiveness.* Thousand Oaks, CA: Sage.

Parkes, K. R. (1994). Personality and coping as moderators of work stress processes: Models, methods and measures. *Work & Stress, 8*, 110–129.

Parks, K. M., & Steelman, L. A. (2008). Organizational wellness programs: A meta-analysis. *Journal of Occupational Health Psychology, 13*, 58–68.

Peiró, J. M. (2008). Stress and coping at work: New research trends and their implications for practice. In K. Näswall, J. Hellgren, & M. Sverke (Eds.), *The individual in the changing working life* (pp. 284–310). Cambridge: Cambridge University Press.

Probst, T. M., Brubaker, T. L., & Barsotti, A. (2008). Organizational injury rate underreporting: The moderating effect of organizational safety climate. *Journal of Applied Psychology, 93*, 1147–1154.

Quick, J. C. (1999) Occupational health psychology: Historical roots and future directions. *Health Psychology, 18*, 82–88.

Quick, J. C., & Tetrick, L. E. (Eds.). (2003). *Handbook of occupational health psychology.* Washington, DC: APA Books.

Quick, J. C., & Tetrick, L. E. (Eds.). (2011). *Handbook of occupational health psychology* (2nd ed.). Washington, DC: APA Books.

Raymond, J. S., Wood, W., & Patrick, W. K. (1990). Psychology doctoral training in work and health. *American Psychologist, 45*, 1159–1161.

Reason, J. (1990). *Human error.* New York: Cambridge University Press.

Reason, J. (2003). Human error: Models and management. *British Medical Journal, 320*, 768–770.

Richardson, K. M., & Rothstein, H. R. (2008). Effects of occupational stress management intervention programs: A meta-analysis. *Journal of Occupational Health Psychology, 13*, 69–93.

Roethlisberger, F. J., & Dickson, W. J. (1939). Management and the worker. Cambridge, MA: Harvard University, Graduate School of Business Administration.

Rothstein, M. A. (1983). *Occupational safety and health law.* St. Paul, MN: West Group.

Rupp, D., & Cropanzano, R. (2002). The mediating effect of social exchange relationships in predicting workplace outcomes from multifoci organizational justice. *Organizational Behaviour and Human Decision Processes, 89*, 925–946.

Sauter, S. L., Murphy, L. R., & Hurrell, J. J. (1990). Prevention of work-related psychological disorders: A national strategy proposed by the National Institute for Occupational Safety and Health (NIOSH). *American Psychologist, 45*, 1146–1158.

Schabracq, M. J., Winnubst, J. A. M., & Cooper, C. L. (Eds.). (2003). *Handbook of work and health psychology* (2nd ed.). Chichester, UK: John Wiley & Sons.

Schaufeli, W. B. (2004). The future of occupational health psychology. *Applied Psychology: An International Review, 53*, 502–517.

Scherrer, M. D., & Wilder, D. A. (2008). Training to increase safe tray carrying among cocktail servers. *Journal of Applied Behavior Analysis, 41*, 131–135.

Schein, E. (1992). *Organizational culture and leadership* (2nd ed.). San Francisco: Jossey-Bass.

Selye, H. (1976). *Stress in health and disease.* Boston: Butterworths.

Semmer, N. (2003), Job stress interventions and organization of work. In J. C. Quick & L. E. Tetrick (Eds.), *Handbook of occupational health psychology* (pp. 51–86). Washington DC: American Psychological Association.

Semmer, N. (2006) Job stress interventions and the organization of work. *Scandinavian Journal of Work Environment and Health, 32*, 515–527.

Shurtz, R. D. (2005). Reining health care costs with wellness programs: Frequently overlooked legal issues. *Benefits Law Journal, 18*, 31–60.

Siegrist, J. (1996). Adverse health effects of high-effort/low-reward conditions. *Journal of Occupational Health Psychology, 1*, 27–41.

Smith, C. S., Folkard, S., & Fuller, J. A. (2003). Shiftwork and working hours. In J. C. Quick & L. E. Tetrick, (Eds.), *Handbook of occupational health psychology* (pp. 163–184). Washington, DC: APA Books.

Smith, C. S., Folkard, S., Tucker, P., & Evans, M. S. (2011). Work schedules, health and safety. In J. C. Quick & L. E. Tetrick (Eds.), *Handbook of occupational health psychology* (2nd ed.) (pp. 185–204). Washington, DC: APA Books.

Smith, M. J., Karsh, B., Carayon, P., & Conway, F. T. (2003). Controlling occupational safety and health hazards. In J. C. Quick & L. E. Tetrick (Eds.), *Handbook of occupational health psychology* (pp. 35–68). Washington, DC: APA Books.

Sonnentag, S., Binnewies, C., & Mojza, E. J. (2008). "Did you have a nice evening?" A day-level study on recovery experiences, sleep, and affect. *Journal of Applied Psychology, 93*, 674–684.

Sonnentag, S., & Fritz, C. (2007). The recovery experience questionnaire: Development and validation of a measure for assessing recuperation and unwinding from work. *Journal of Occupational Health Psychology, 12*, 204–221.

Sonnentag, S., & Zijlstra, F. R. H. (2006). Job characteristics and off-job activities as predictors of need for recovery, well-being, and fatigue. *Journal of Applied Psychology, 91*, 330–350.

Straker, L., & Mathiassen, S. E. (2009). Increased physical work loads in modern work: A necessity for better health and performance. *Ergonomics, 52,* 1215–1225.

Taylor, F. W. (1911). *The principles of scientific management.* New York: Harper & Brothers.

Tetrick, L. E. (2002). Individual and organizational health. In P. Perrewé & D. Ganster (Eds.), *Research in occupational stress and well-being* (Vol. 2, pp. 117–141). Stamford, CT: JAI Press.

Tetrick, L. E. (2008). Prevention: Integrating health protection and health promotion perspectives. In M. Sverke, K. Näswall, & J. Hellgren (Eds.), *The individual in the changing work life* (pp. 403–418). Cambridge: Cambridge University Press.

Tetrick, L. E., & Ford, M. T. (2008). Health protection and promotion: A review and application of value and regulatory focus theory. In G. P. Hodgkinson & J. K. Ford (Eds.), *2008 International Review of I/O Psychology* (pp. 239–260). Chichester, UK: Wiley.

Tetrick, L. E., Quick, J. C., & Quick, J. D. (2005). Prevention perspectives in occupational health psychology. In A. G. Antoniou & C. L. Cooper (Eds.), *Research companion to organizational health psychology* (pp. 209–217). Cheltenham, UK: Edward Elgar.

Trist, E. L., & Bamforth, K. W. (1951). Some social and psychological consequences of the longwall method of coal-getting. *Human Relations, 14,* 3–38.

Tucker, S., Chmiel, N., Turner, N., Hershcovis, M. S., & Stride, C. B. (2008). Perceived organizational support for safety and employee safety voice: The mediating role of coworker support for safety. *Journal of Occupational Health Psychology, 13,* 319–330.

Tuma, S., & Sepkowitz, K. A. (2006). Efficacy of safety-engineered device implementation in the prevention of percutaneous injuries: A review of published studies. *Clinical Infectious Diseases, 42,* 1159–1170.

Van der Klink, J. J. L., Blonk, R. W. B., Schene, A. H., & Van Dijk, F. J. H. (2001). The benefits of interventions for work-related stress. *American Journal of Public Health, 91,* 270–276.

Visser, E., Pijl, Y. J., Stolk, R. P., Neeleman, J., & Rosmalen, J. G. M. (2007). Accident proneness, does it exist? A review and meta-analysis. *Accident Analysis & Prevention, 39,* 556–564.

Wallace, C., & Chen, G., (2006). A multilevel integration of personality, climate, self-regulation and performance. *Personnel Psychology, 59,* 529–557.

Wallen, E. S., & Mulloy, K. B. (2006). Computer-based training for safety: Comparing methods with older and younger workers. *Journal of Safety Research, 37,* 461–467.

Wu, T. C., Liu, C. W., & Lu, M. C. (2007). Safety climate in university and college laboratories: Impact of organizational and individual factors. *Journal of Safety Research, 38,* 91–102.

Xie, J. L., Schaubroeck, J., & Lam, S. S. K. (2008). Theories of job stress and the role of traditional values: A longitudinal study in China. *Journal of Applied Psychology, 93,* 831–848.

Zickar, M. J. (2003). Remembering Arthur Kornhauser: Industrial psychology's advocate for worker well-being. *Journal of Applied Psychology, 88,* 363–369.

Zohar, D. (1980). Safety climate in industrial organizations: Theoretical and applied implications. *Journal of Applied Psychology, 65,* 96–102.

Zohar, D., & Tenne-Gazit, O. (2008). Transformational leadership and group interaction as climate antecedents: A social network analysis. *Journal of Applied Psychology, 93,* 744–757.

Work and Aging

Jerry W. Hedge *and* Walter C. Borman

Abstract

Global aging of the workforce means that the human resource management landscape of tomorrow will be vastly different and more challenging than it is today. This chapter examines the aging workforce from an individual worker, organization, and societal perspective. It includes the latest thinking and research on physical attributes, cognitive abilities, knowledge, personality traits, and motivation, as they relate to aging. In addition, we discuss organizational norms and culture, age stereotyping, and age discrimination, as well as strategies for recruiting and hiring older workers, and job design and redesign to accommodate the effects of aging. The chapter also examines strategies for: training throughout the career life cycle; flexible work alternatives; developing employee benefit programs in ways that are attractive to older workers; and linking employee retention programs directly to knowledge retention tactics. A longer term human resource (HR) perspective for an aging workforce is also included by examining career planning and career management, succession planning, long-range workforce planning, and retirement planning. The chapter concludes with an agenda for where research and application should be directed in the future to address issues of an aging workforce.

Key Words: Global aging, aging workforce, cognitive and non-cognitive abilities, job performance, age bias, flexible work alternatives, career management, retirement

Introduction

The global aging of the workforce will bring significant changes to almost every aspect of public and private life. Changing retirement patterns, changing occupational trends fueled by ever-evolving technological innovations, and changing motivations and capabilities of workers as they age mean that the human resource management (HRM) landscape of tomorrow will be vastly different and more challenging than it is today. This chapter examines the aging workforce from individual worker, organizational, and societal perspectives. It begins with a broad look at the problems and potential of an aging global population, and how this trend will shape the workplace and the workforce of tomorrow. The chapter examines the latest thinking and

research on physical attributes, cognitive abilities, knowledge, personality traits, and motivation as they relate to aging, as well as how age bias can lead to misperceptions and problematic decision making.

Changes in demographics and retirement trends point to a need to develop strategies that better allow for successful integration of older workers into the workforce, including strategies for recruiting and hiring older workers, and job design and redesign to accommodate the effects of aging as well as to make jobs more appealing to older workers. We also examine strategies for: keeping skills fresh by training throughout the career life cycle; flexible work alternatives; rethinking/reorganizing employee benefits in ways that are attractive to older workers;

and linking employee retention programs directly to knowledge retention tactics. A section on human resource management perspectives for an aging workforce includes discussion of long-range workforce planning; career management and planning, and retirement planning. The chapter concludes with a brief examination of the work-to-retirement transition.

Demographic Perspectives on Work and Aging

The world's population is aging, but historically, the elderly have comprised only a small percentage of that total. The most rapid acceleration in aging will occur after 2010, when the post–World War II cohorts begin to reach age 65. Among the world's regions, Europe has the highest proportion of men and women 65 and older; however, other regions will begin to age much more rapidly in coming decades. For example, Asia, Latin America and the Caribbean, and the Near East/North Africa will more than triple their 65+ population by 2050 (National Academy of Sciences, 2001).

In one sense, global aging epitomizes a triumph of medical, social, and economic advances. Not only are people living longer, disability rates are declining among the older population in the United States, Japan, and a number of countries in Europe (AARP, 2003). Still, population aging will also have a dramatic impact on labor supply and social entitlement programs, and may demand new fiscal approaches to accommodate a changing world (Li & Iadarola, 2007).

The Foundation of Changing Demographics

A number of factors influence population demographics. Principal among these are mortality, fertility, and immigration.

MORTALITY

Projections of mortality are based on the average number of years that a child born in a given year can expect to live. Life expectancy is increasing, with most countries showing a steady increase in longevity. In fact, global life expectancy has grown more in the last 50 years than over the previous 5,000 (Peterson, 1999). People age 85+ are the fastest growing portion of many national populations. As Li and Iadarola (2007) noted, the 85+ population is projected to increase over 150% globally between 2005 and 2030, and the 65+ population will increase just over 100%, while the under age 65 population increases just over 20%.

FERTILITY

Of the factors affecting population growth, the fertility rate probably has the most significant impact on *long-term* growth. The fertility rate is the average total number of children that would be born to a woman over her lifetime. In terms of population aging, a decline in the number of births means fewer young people and proportionally more people at older ages. The world population growth is slowing markedly, and total world population now is expected to peak at 8 to 9 billion persons between 2040 and 2050, and then begin to decline. More than 20 countries are expected to face population declines in the next several decades. For example, Russia's population is expected to drop by 18 million between 2006 and 2030, while Japan, Ukraine, South Africa, Germany, Italy, Poland, Romania, Bulgaria, and Spain will likely watch their populations shrink by at least one million people during the same time period (Li & Iadarola, 2007).

IMMIGRATION

Immigration refers to the movement of individuals from one country to another, and of all the *assumptions* about future population growth, assumptions about migration affect its size and composition the most. In addition, because immigration rates can be greatly affected by public policy, such assumptions are the most uncertain (Toossi, 2007). While there is much current political debate about immigration—both economic and security-related—generally, immigrants are motivated by economic opportunity and therefore will likely have higher average labor force participation rates than the resident population (Franklin, 2007). In addition, they tend to have higher fertility rates.

The Demographics of Work, Retirement, and Financial Security

As Kinsella and Phillips (2005) astutely observed, nothing has galvanized public discussion about aging more than issues surrounding work, retirement, and economic security in old age. The foundations of changing demographics were discussed previously because they hold significant implications for governments, employers, and individuals. Within the next decade, organizations will begin to lose the services of millions of highly skilled and experienced workers, as the so-called baby boom cohort begins to retire. This problem is exacerbated by the drop in fertility rates following the baby boom, creating the potential for both labor shortages and the loss of significant institutional knowledge and expertise

(Penner, Perun, & Steuerle, 2002). In addition, as people live longer, they will likely have more time in retirement; thus growing numbers of retirees may be dependent on a shrinking working population to support them. In Japan, for example, by 2025 there will be roughly one person 65+ for every two persons ages 15–64 (Muhleisen & Faruqee, 2001). The combination of decreasing fertility rates and increasing mortality rates have a powerful effect on the "age dependency ratio"—the retirement-age population (65+) as a percentage of those in their working years (15–64). Changes in the old age dependency ratio can challenge society's ability to fund pensions and social programs associated with retirement and health care (Charman, Feinsod, & Arthurs, 2007).

Since the 1950s, governments and organizations have adopted a wide range of approaches to providing old age security, and workers have had a wide array of routes to retirement. For example, Germany, France, and Italy have long promoted early retirement, with state subsidies and regulations that included options to receive pension benefits before legal retirement. As a result, retirement ages have decreased over time to just above 60 years of age in Germany and Italy, and just under age 60 in France.

Some form of public, old-age pension plans now cover a large percentage of the labor force in most industrialized countries. With such plans, governments are responsible for financing, implementing, and insuring public pensions, and benefits are financed by payroll taxes. These "pay-as-you-go" systems tax working adults to finance the pension payments of retirees.

Initially, many of these programs involved a small number of retirees relative to a large number of workers, and often promised generous benefits. Unfortunately, over the last 50 years, the ratios of pensioners to contributors has grown, and in some countries these programs have become difficult to sustain (Kinsella & Phillips, 2005). As the old-age dependency ratio has continued to grow, governments and organizations have been forced to identify new strategies to grapple with this problem, including the development of private pension systems to complement public systems, increasing worker contribution rates, restructuring or reducing benefits, increasing the number of women in the workforce, encouraging population growth via immigration or higher birth rates, and increasing the labor force participation of workers approaching retirement eligibility (Charman et al., 2007).

Increasing the number of older people in the workplace holds promise for having a positive near-term impact. Greater labor force participation is an area in which policy makers can make changes quickly, in contrast to the alternatives of immigration or an increased fertility rate. Certainly, the challenges from country to country vary, based on current demographics, labor force participation, immigration, and birth rates.

Summary
Global aging will bring significant changes to almost every aspect of public and private life. Patterns of work and retirement are changing. Shrinking ratios of workers to retirees increasingly strain existing health and pension systems, especially when these retirees are spending a larger portion of their lives in retirement. Family structures are changing. As life expectancies increase, including the numbers of the most elderly, four-generation families become more common. As a result, many working adults may feel the financial and emotional pressures of juggling multiple responsibilities—including the possibility of supporting children, older parents, and even grandparents simultaneously (Li & Iadarola, 2007).

Growing life expectancy and better health at later ages represent a significant opportunity to extend the working lives of many members of today's workforce. However, some "retirement-eligible" workers who want to (or need to) continue working encounter financial, policy, or cultural barriers to doing so (Geipel, 2003). This can change if the right incentives can be put in place and the current barriers eliminated, but what is necessary is a careful balancing act between allowing those who want to retire to do so without feeling pressured, while not preventing those who are able and want to continue working from pursuing that path. The changing work landscape underscores the need to examine, revise, and reshape employment and retirement policies to better meet the needs of older workers and their employers in the twenty-first century.

Age Bias and Age Discrimination at Work
The aging of the population will pose social, economic, and public policy challenges over the next few decades, one of which is fostering longer work lives in the face of slowing labor force growth in many countries. If older workers are to remain in the workforce later in life, as some wish and others need to, appropriate jobs must be available and

employers must be willing to hire and retain them. Workers should get and keep jobs based on their ability, not age, yet older workers face a variety of barriers in their efforts to remain employed or to find new employment (Neumark, 2008). The workplace reflects the stereotypes and biases that define our social environment, and they are often detrimental to individual and organizational productivity. Regardless of whether age bias is accidental or intentional, subtle or blatant, it can lead to age discrimination when it negatively affects workplace decisions about employment, training, promotion, termination, benefits, or retirement (Dennis & Thomas, 2007).

Over the last several decades, there has been a considerable amount of research and theorizing about age bias in society, as well as age bias in the work environment. What follows is a representative sampling of research on age stereotyping, age-norming, and age discrimination. In addition, we briefly describe the current legal environment related to age discrimination.

A Research Perspective
AGE STEREOTYPING

Stereotypes are learned ways of perceiving and organizing the world, and they provide us with information that guides our interactions with others. They are affected by cultural, economic, and social factors; peer pressure; and even firsthand observations. Age stereotyping in a work context refers to implicit ideas that people have about the relationship between age and worker characteristics, and it can have a profound impact on decision making in areas such as hiring, training allocation, and performance management (Hedge, Borman, & Lammlein, 2006).

Popular writings and research offer stereotypical descriptions of older people, applicants, and employees that include: being less productive, flexible, creative, ambitious, serious, innovative; being less capable of working under pressure or of learning quickly; possessing less stamina; being harder to train; being more opinionated, conservative, traditional, and moral; possessing a better work ethic; being better able to get along with coworkers; and being more forgetful, absent-minded, and slower (e.g., Bassili & Reil, 1981; Craft, Doctors, Shkop, & Benecki, 1979; Doering, Rhodes, & Schuster, 1983; Forte & Hansvick, 1999, Heckhausen, Dixon, & Baltes, 1989; Johnson, 2007; Kulik, Perry, & Bourhis, 2000; Mauer, 2007; Rosen & Jerdee, 1976a, 1976b; Sonnenfeld, 1988).

Although there is not sufficient space in this chapter to discuss the large volume of studies in this area in detail, suffice it to say that such stereotyping can lead to misinformed decision making. Rosen and Jerdee (1985) suggested that to the extent to which age stereotypes influence managerial decisions, there are potentially serious consequences for older employees, including lowered performance evaluations, reduced motivation, career stagnation, and job loss. Because of age stereotyping, for example, managers may make much less effort to give older persons feedback about needed changes in performance, provide limited organizational support for their career development and retraining, or limit their promotion opportunities. A study by Simon (1996) found that 55- to 64-year-olds received training opportunities only a third as often as 35- to 44-year-olds. Wren and Mauer (2004) concluded that beliefs about the decline of abilities are associated with older workers' waning inclination to participate in developmental activities.

Maurer, Wrenn, and Weiss (2003) suggested that stereotypes might also influence older workers' perceptions of what is appropriate or possible for individuals in their age group, through a self-fulfilling prophecy. For example, Miller et al. (1993) found that older employees who believed that a perception exists that older workers' performance deteriorates with age experienced low levels of job involvement and more alienation from the job. Hassell and Perrewe (1993) found that older workers who believed that age discrimination existed in their own organization had lower levels of self-esteem and satisfaction with growth opportunities than those who did not perceive the presence of age discrimination. Greller and Stroh (1995) suggested that stereotypes might influence workers' concepts of appropriate aging behavior, leading them to conform more closely to others' expectations. Posthuma and Campion (2009) identified and reviewed the most prevalent age stereotypes that occur in work settings, and provided research evidence to refute them.

AGE-NORMING

When beliefs about older workers are shared by an organization's members, they help establish age norms for that organization, and reinforce age-related patterns of behavior. These norms, in turn, often have a direct and adverse impact on managerial behavior toward the older employee. Lawrence (1988) suggested that the age distribution of old and young workers in a particular job helps to dictate an age-based timetable for that job. Because speed and extent of progression up a career ladder vary by job, some jobs have a wider distribution of typical ages than others, as do organizations and industries. According to Lawrence (1987, 1988, 1996), society has expectations concerning the levels of success that should be reached by certain ages. Thus, people develop perceptions of what age milestones mark those who are on schedule, ahead of schedule, or behind schedule in their careers. Young people in "older" jobs acquire high status and power as a result of their age, whereas old people in "young" jobs tend to acquire low status and power labels. In sum, age-norming of jobs and organizational contexts represents implicit correlations between jobs or other organizational variables and the typical age of persons with whom these variables are associated.

Gordon and Arvey (1986) examined the idea of occupational age norms. They asked study participants to estimate the average age of workers in 59 occupations, and then compared these estimates with the actual average ages. They found that individuals were relatively accurate at age-typing different occupations. Cleveland, Festa, and Montgomery (1988) discovered that when a job applicant pool became more heavily composed of older applicants, the age stereotype of the target job began to increase as well, thus, suggesting that job-age stereotypes themselves may be fluid, and are capable of being influenced by the demographics of the people in the applicant pool. Similarly, Cleveland and Hollman (1990) found that as the proportion of older workers in a job increased, so, too, would the rating of a job as appropriate for older adults. Perry, Kulik, and Bourhis (1996) concluded that the nature of the job affects the extent to which biased raters penalized older applicants.

Specifically, the older applicant was evaluated less favorably than the younger applicant when the rater was generally biased, and the applicant applied for a young-typed job. However, when the older applicant applied for an older-type job, he or she was evaluated more favorably than the younger applicant. Similarly, Greller (2000) studied beliefs about age appropriateness across a variety of work-related domains (e.g., career advancement, forming new relationships, developing new skills, health, mentoring), and suggested that the policies, procedures, and practices of the organization might foster the shared beliefs by members of that organization. Thus, as Shore and Goldberg (2004) concluded, it is clear that being older than others, whether relative to the immediate manager, the work group, or job

level, works to the disadvantage of individuals for most employment opportunities.

AGE DISCRIMINATION

In real work situations, age discrimination is often inferred—by the length of time it takes older workers to find employment, the wage loss so many older workers experience upon reemployment, or the size of awards to victims of discrimination (Rix, 2004). However, this is much more difficult to demonstrate empirically, so much of the research that has focused on age discrimination tends to do so in a simulated environment. But, as Morgeson, Reider, Campion, and Bull (2008) found, in a review of age discrimination research on the employment interview, studies conducted in field settings tended to show less overall age discrimination effects than studies conducted in laboratory settings; and they cautioned others not to necessarily infer a direct link between stereotypes and interviewer behavior. Obviously, much research is still needed. To that end, several researchers have attempted to more clearly summarize research findings or to point out new directions for research, particularly in recent years.

For example, Finkelstein, Burke, and Raju (1995) examined age discrimination in simulated employment settings. Their meta-analysis found that *younger respondents* judged: (a) younger workers to have higher job qualifications, developmental potential, and qualifications for physically demanding jobs; and (b) older workers as more dependable, careful, and stable than younger workers. In contrast, *older respondents* perceived no differences in job qualifications between younger and older workers.

Gordon and Arvey (2004) meta-analyzed laboratory and field studies of age discrimination. They found a small overall bias against older applicants/workers when the studies used overall evaluations (e.g., hiring recommendations, promotions, salary increases) or potential for development as dependent measures. No significant differences were found between young and old in terms of interpersonal skills, while older workers were evaluated more positively in terms of reliability/stability.

Posthuma and Campion (2009) reviewed the age stereotyping literature, and provided recommendations for practice and future research. These included a focus on: (a) more *complex relationships* with age stereotypes (e.g., moderators/mediators, recursive effects, non-linear effects, and multiple dimensions of stereotypes, employee performance, and outcomes); (b) *managerial practices* that will create a more age-friendly work environment; (c) examining whether *awareness training* reduces the effects of age stereotyping; (d) investigating the relationship between national cultures and age stereotypes; and (e) use of *research designs* that emphasize objective methodologies that are not biased toward validating age stereotyping, as well as more use of longitudinal methods.

Shore and Goldberg's (2004) review of the literature led to the development of a model of age discrimination that suggests: (a) age derives meaning from the work group context; (b) the resulting age comparisons influence employment opportunities; and (c) employment opportunities for older workers are influenced by forces both inside and outside the organization. The authors also developed a model that characterized the age-norming process as involving: (a) selection of the age comparison standards (e.g., occupational, organizational, industry, work group, and societal norms; (b) target-standard comparisons (e.g., if a hiring manager makes comparisons using work group norms, then age and its associated meaning becomes one component used in the comparison process); and (c) information evaluation (e. g., the hiring manager may decide that the applicant is a poor fit with the job because of the age-position mismatch).

Finkelstein and Farrell (2007) suggested using a "broader lens" to examine age biases and to categorize age bias (both work and non-work) research. They did so by applying a tripartite view of attitudes framework (i.e., cognitive, behavioral, affective; see for example, Fiske, 2004). Within this framework, the *cognitive* component comprises beliefs and expectations about a social object as a result of membership in a particular group (e.g., age stereotyping). The *behavioral* component of an attitude involves a tendency to treat others in a particular manner due to their social category membership (e.g., age discrimination). There is also an *affective* component of a biased attitude (e.g., age prejudice). In summary, then, they suggested that age bias at work can involve some thoughts, beliefs, feelings, evaluations, and treatment of older workers in routine interactions and important employment decisions. Finally, as Finkelstein and Farrell (2007) noted, it is good news that reviews have begun to appear more frequently, with updates on what the research suggests about major issues and with new insights on conceptual frameworks for understanding age discrimination. Clearly, despite the extensive literature, many unanswered questions remain.

A Legal Perspective

For many years, the United States was the only country to have a law specifically banning age discrimination in employment. The Age Discrimination in Employment Act (ADEA) is the primary federal statute in the United States for dealing with age discrimination complaints. Enacted in 1967, then amended in 1974 (to cover government employees), and in 1978 (to abolish mandatory retirement for federal employees), the ADEA was designed to protect individuals age 40 and older from employment discrimination based on age, and to promote opportunities for older workers capable of meeting job requirements. The ADEA binds every employer with 20 or more employees that is covered by federal labor laws, and covers employment agencies and labor organizations, the federal government, and state and local governments. The intent of the ADEA is to: (a) promote employment of older persons based on their ability; (b) prohibit arbitrary age discrimination in employment; and (c) help employers and workers find ways to overcome problems arising from the impact of age on employment (ADEA, 2004).

There are several important exceptions to the ADEA's general prohibitions. All have figured prominently in court cases since the ADEA's enactment because if an employer can prove that an exception applies, the employer's activities do not violate the ADEA. The law recognizes that age may sometimes be a "bona fide occupational qualification" (BFOQ) reasonably necessary to the normal operation of the business. It also allows adverse personnel action if the action is based on "reasonable factors other than age," ranging from lack of basic job skills to broad, organization-wide problems. A "good cause" exception also allows the employer to discharge or discipline an employee, even though he or she is part of a protected class, if it can be shown that age is not a determining factor in the decision. The last exception, associated with an organization's seniority system, allows differentiation based on age when the employer is abiding by the terms of a bona fide seniority system or any bona fide employee benefit plan, such as retirement, pension, or insurance plan, as long as the plan was not designed as a means of evading the purposes of the ADEA.

There are two basic ways in which a plaintiff can establish a showing of discrimination: disparate treatment and disparate impact. The disparate treatment model requires proof that an employee was specifically and intentionally discriminated against; that is, the plaintiff must show proof of an employer motive to act in ways that lead to less favorable employment consequences for older workers. The disparate impact model focuses on establishing that a specific employment practice adversely affects all employees within a protected group, and to prove disparate impact, it is only necessary to show that the employment practice under scrutiny had a differential effect on older workers, regardless of the motivation (see Sterns, Doverspike, & Lax, 2005, for a review of the ADEA).

The ADEA in the United States was followed by laws in a number of other countries, including Australia, New Zealand, Finland, Ireland, and Canada. In 2000, the European Union (EU) adopted a Framework Directive for Equal Treatment in Employment and Occupation, which outlawed a number of discriminatory grounds for employment decisions, including age. The directive required member states to implement legislation, since most did not have any existing laws prohibiting age discrimination in employment at that time. According to McCann (2003), the Employment Directive is not as forceful in condemning age discrimination as the ADEA, and allows member states to continue mandatory retirement practices and to provide differences of treatment on grounds of age if they are objectively and reasonably justified (see also Monseau, 2005).

In the United Kingdom, the Employment Equality (Age) Regulations (2006) were implemented to comply with the legislative requirements for age discrimination of the EU Directive. These regulations establish a national default retirement age of 65 and the rights of employees to work beyond that age. Employers are prohibited from directly or indirectly discriminating against employees on the basis of age, unless the discrimination can be objectively justified by the employer. Other member states have taken similar steps to comply with the directive.

Also, as noted by Berkowitz and Jackson (2008), Japan and China have recently amended their laws to address employment discrimination. Japan's Employment Promotion Law—effective as of October 1, 2007—addresses employment discrimination based on age in recruiting and hiring (and covers young and old employees, both foreign and domestic). China's Employment Promotion Law—effective as of January 1, 2008—addresses employment discrimination based on ethnicity, race, gender, disability, and religious belief (and gives employees, for the first time, the right to sue employers for discrimination).

Obviously, many of these countries will require some time before they will be able to gauge the effectiveness of their recently implemented legislation. Other countries have yet to implement legislation specifically covering age discrimination. In sum, Charters (2008) has suggested that, while future legislation may be influenced by international efforts (as the Age Regulations in the United Kingdom were influenced by the European Union's Framework Directive for Equal Treatment in Employment and Occupation of 2000), most legislation will likely continue to develop independently by country.

The United States, with the earliest legislation, still notes high numbers of registered cases of age discrimination, and is seeing the number of cases increase (McCann, 2006). Historically, enforcement of the ADEA has focused on *termination* more than on *hiring*. However, in a recent review of the ADEA, Neumark (2008) concluded that as the number of older workers increases, by sheer volume alone, increasing numbers will join the ranks of displaced workers seeking employment. In addition, many of these workers may leave their long-term career employment and seek part-time or shorter term jobs. As a result, ADEA enforcement efforts on terminations might not be such a dominant focus going forward. Instead, it may become more important to determine how to ensure that age discrimination does not deter the hiring of older adults after seeking employment.

JOB LOSS AND REEMPLOYMENT

It will be interesting to see if ADEA enforcement begins to emphasize discriminatory hiring, and if legislative/judicial activity will follow this shift in focus. Some of the literature in this area suggests that older workers remain unemployed longer than younger workers (e.g., Hanisch, 1999; Kanfer, Wanberg, & Kantrowitz, 2001; Valetta, 1991). As noted by McKee-Ryan, Song, Wanberg, and Kinicki (2005), there are likely elements of discrimination at play, but there may also be age-related differences in the activities and expectations of unemployed workers which influence opportunities. In addition, the literature suggests that experiencing job loss and unemployment can have profound effects on people's lives (e.g., Wanberg, 1997). Both psychological and physical well-being seems to be lower for individuals with longer lengths of unemployment. Thus, the impact of displacement may be more severe for older workers (McKee-Ryan et al., 2005).

In addition, Chan and Stevens (1999, 2001) examined employment, earnings, and wealth changes following involuntary job loss among workers aged 50 and over, and found significant disparities (between originally displaced and non-displaced workers) in employment rates two, four, and six years after job loss. In addition, the earnings of those individuals (50 years of age or older) who return to work following job loss were also dramatically affected, dropping initially to only two-thirds of their expected value had the job loss not occurred. Consistent with this study, Haider and Stephens (2001) found not only large earnings losses following displacement, but significant losses in pension wealth and health insurance. Thus, the long spells of non-employment, large earnings reductions, and perhaps some reductions in pension and non-pension wealth point to significant costs of job loss for workers in their fifties and sixties. Even if these workers were prepared for retirement prior to a job loss, changes in earnings and wealth associated with displacement may significantly reduce the private resources available to them during retirement.

Summary

Myths of aging are found in a work organization's culture, often reinforced by its policies and procedures. These myths influence the attitudes of others toward "older people." Unfortunately, older persons' perceptions of aging and expectations of being old are also shaped by these myths, potentially becoming a self-fulfilling prophecy. Such stereotyping may likely result in an underutilization of human resources, to say nothing of the potential adverse impact to an individual's self-esteem or career progression. Moreover, stereotyping may lead to illegal differential treatment of particular employee groups. Age discrimination continues to be pervasive in the workplace. Strict adherence to the law is necessary to avoid costly lawsuits, but while legislation can mandate particular organizational policies, it cannot dictate attitudes or behaviors (Hedge et al., 2006).

Changing long-held stereotypes is not an easy process. In part, it requires changing the perspectives and mechanisms on which age norms are based and age stereotypes operate. Shea (1991) suggested that managers at all organizational levels may struggle when dealing with age issues because they lack clear information on the laws related to age discrimination and the application of these laws in the workplace. These problems are often exacerbated by misunderstandings of the nature of the relationship between age and work performance. Hedge (2008) suggested that training can also be an important tool for combating stereotypes and age norms, and recommended both: (a) training aimed at creating a better understanding of the aging process and the workplace, and (b) knowledge of legal issues relevant to older workers. In the next section, we explore in greater detail what is known about older worker capabilities and the aging process.

The Aging Worker

Overall, research on aging suggests that physical and cognitive abilities do decline in older age. However, these declines may not always generalize to deficits in performance (e.g., Salthouse, 1990; Salthouse & Maurer, 1996). In fact, older workers generally seem to adapt well and to compensate for declining abilities by adjusting their approach to the job (e.g., the selection, optimization, and compensation model; Baltes & Baltes, 1990).

Apparently, being successful in work and non-work situations is a function not only of an individual's knowledge, skills, and abilities, but also of certain non-cognitive attributes. Therefore, in this section we also discuss: (a) relationships between age and job satisfaction, job involvement, and organizational commitment; (b) the role of personality in older people and, indeed, across the entire adult life span; and (c) various coping strategies that older workers might use to ensure personal and occupational well-being.

Physical Capabilities

Some of our physical and sensory capabilities tend to decline with age; however, general statements about such decline mask considerable individual variation in physical aging. Physical capabilities are a product of both genetics and environment, and variation in both areas across persons produces dramatic variation in observed physical and sensory capabilities as the process of aging unfolds (Sheppard & Rix, 1977).

Aging is generally associated with both functional loss and declining homeostasis (McDonald, 1988). *Functional loss* refers to some functions of the body operating at a reduced capacity, including muscle strength, aerobic capacity, cardiac function, and sensory perception. The *decline in homeostasis* refers to the reduced ability of the body to maintain normal operation across environments and a slowing of the process of returning to normal after some environmental change. For example, older persons recover more slowly from altered sleep patterns than do younger people and thus may develop more shift work intolerance. They are also more susceptible to stress, are less able to ward off illness, take longer to recover from injury, and are thus more susceptible to disease and chronic health conditions (Hansson, DeKoekkoek, Neece, & Patterson, 1997).

A decline in physical strength with age has been well-documented (e.g., A. A. Sterns, Sterns & Hollis, 1996; Warr, 1994). This loss of strength occurs relative to both muscle tone and muscle mass decline. Psychomotor ability also shows decline with age (Forteza & Prieto, 1994). Older individuals take longer to react to stimuli, require more time to carry out movements, and show decreased performance at tasks requiring speeded and coordinated response.

Changes in the two most important sensory functions, sight and hearing, occur with age (Forteza & Prieto, 1994). Visual acuity starts to decline between ages 40 and 50, leading to increased difficulty seeing distant objects and requiring more light to see them. Visual accommodation declines, making it more difficult to focus on close objects. With regard to hearing, older individuals first lose some sensitivity to high-pitched sounds and later to low-pitched ones; lose some ability to distinguish between concurrent sounds, often observed in increasing difficulty understanding conversations; find it more difficult to locate the sources of sounds; and experience more interference from background noise.

It does not automatically follow that these declines result in lower work performance. In fact, the declines are generally quite gradual and frequently do not impact work performance in the majority of jobs. Second, it is possible to compensate for many of these declines through, for example, corrective eyeglasses, change in work strategies, and job redesign. As a result of their experience, older persons often move to jobs that are less dependent on physical capacity (Hale, 1990; Warr, 1994). Finally, some of the declines can be slowed through environmental intervention. Wellness programs, for example, can increase functional capacity, improve mental outlook, reduce health care costs, and reduce lost work time (Hale, 1990; McDonald, 1988).

Cognitive Abilities

Perhaps the most comprehensive research program on cognitive abilities and aging has been conducted by K. Warner Schaie (Schaie, 1983, 1993, 1994). Schaie and colleagues have followed several cohorts of adults from age 25 through 88 and beyond. The design of the study has been to test in a laboratory setting a new cohort of adults every seven years, beginning in 1956 and extending through 1998. Starting in 1963, attempts were also made to test all previously tested cohorts. So, in 1963, for example, a new group of 997 persons was tested, but the first cohort was also contacted to return for testing (average age by then being 32 years old), and 303 of the original 500 participated. In 1970, Schaie and colleagues tested a new cohort of 705, and the two earlier cohorts (Ns = 162 and 420, respectively, with average ages of 39 and 32). Regarding the samples, Schaie (1994) estimates that only the bottom 25% of the socioeconomic range was not represented. Sample members have included a reasonably wide range of white- and blue-collar occupations.

The test battery administered has included measures of verbal, spatial, reasoning, numerical, and work fluency abilities. Beginning with the 1984 cycle, the primary mental abilities of verbal comprehension, verbal memory, spatial orientation, inductive reasoning, numerical ability, and perceptual speed were measured at the latent construct level (i.e., with multiple marker tests).

Results of the longitudinal data suggest, first, that except for perceptual speed, which begins declining between ages 25 and 32, all abilities show modest increases from age 25 until about age 46, when they level off or begin to decline slightly. Ability × gender interactions were also identified, with women performing better in the areas of verbal comprehension and inductive reasoning, and men better in the areas of spatial orientation and numerical ability. Gender differences also occur in ability declines: when abilities are categorized as *fluid* (i.e., abilities in reasoning and related higher mental processes) versus *crystallized* (i.e., abilities related to already acquired knowledge), women decline earlier in fluid ability, men earlier in crystallized ability.

In general, four of the six mental abilities that Schaie and colleagues studied reached an asymptote (peaked and then leveled off) in early middle age and then declined modestly after that (Schaie, 1994). As mentioned, perceptual speed began declining by age 25; numerical ability reached an asymptote earlier, with fairly steep declines beginning about age 60. Regarding the older age ranges, comparing age 25 and 88, there was virtually no decline in verbal ability, with declines of 0.5 standard deviation for inductive reasoning and verbal memory, 1.0 standard deviation for spatial orientation, and 1.5 standard deviations for numerical ability and perceptual speed.

More recent work largely supports these findings for declines in cognitive ability. For example, McArdle, Ferrer-Caja, Hamagami, and Woodcock (2002) found that fluid intelligence declined among older adults, whereas crystallized intelligence did not (see Kanfer & Ackerman, 2004). Similarly, Finkel, Reynolds, McArdle, Gatz, and Pedersen (2003), found across a six-year period that crystallized intelligence remained stable among older adults, and most other abilities declined linearly. An exception was cognitive abilities with a speed component, which showed accelerating declines after age 65. However, Allen, Lien, Murphy, Sanders, and McCann (2002) found that older adults can multitask as well as younger adults, albeit at a slower speed.

Another cognitive-related domain where older adults are hypothesized to perform more poorly is in computer-related tasks. There is some support for this hypothesis. Czaja and Sharit (1998) asked women ages 25 to 70 years to perform three simulated computer-interactive tasks. Results showed that age had a significant impact on task performance, with older subjects having longer response times and greater numbers of errors.

Thus, Schaie's and others' work demonstrates that, on average, most cognitive abilities are at least gradually declining as people reach their late fifties. This is especially true for perceptual speed and numerical ability. The emphasis here, however, should be on *average*; there are large individual differences in when and how much these mental abilities decline among older persons. In fact, Schaie (1994), Warr (1998), and Reynolds, Finkel, Gatz, and Pedersen (2002), among others, have observed that the standard deviations in abilities increase with older study participants.

FACTORS ASSOCIATED WITH COGNITIVE ABILITY AND AGING

A central factor affecting individual functioning in older adults is declining health, including cardiovascular and other debilitating diseases (e.g., Hertzog, Schaie, & Gribbin, 1978). Barnes, Yaffe, Satariano, and Tager (2003) showed a relationship between poorer cardiovascular fitness in older adults age 59–88 and declines in all cognitive abilities tested six years later. The direction of causation has not been well established, and it is possible that lifestyle variables led to both the onset of such diseases and intellectual decline (Schaie, 1994).

A second factor seems to be involvement in complex, intellectually stimulating activities, such as a job requiring considerable intellectual activity. These kinds of activities are associated with lower rates of decline in older workers. For example, Masunaga and Horn (2001) found that older people with high levels of expertise on a complex job showed very little decline in deductive and fluid reasoning, short-term memory, and cognitive speed. And, Bosma, van Boxtel, Ponds, Houx, and Jolles (2003), using data from the Maastricht Aging Study, found that seniors with higher educational level showed less decline in information-processing speed and general cognitive functioning than their less-educated counterparts. It is important to note that these differences were lower when the lower education group had relatively high levels of work-related mental challenge.

Leisure activities like reading and participation in continuing education also can contribute to the maintenance of cognitive abilities (Gribbin, Schaie, & Parham, 1980). In fact, Bosma et al. (2002) found that participation in mental, social, and physical activities mitigated the decline in cognitive ability over a three-year period. Similarly, Schaie (1983) suggested that older adults having a more "engaged" lifestyle are more likely to maintain levels of cognitive functioning. It is interesting that in the Bosma et al. (2002) study, seniors with relatively high levels of cognitive ability at initial testing were more likely to increase the amount of these activities, suggesting a reciprocal relationship between cognitive ability and participation in such activities.

A related factor is having a history of involvement in intellectually stimulating activities and, even more broadly, a history of living in a favorable environment, including having been well-educated and having had access to money (Gribbin et al., 1980). Yet another correlate of avoiding cognitive decline as an older adult is living with someone (especially a spouse) who has a high level of cognitive functioning (e.g., Gruber & Schaie, 1986).

Are declines in abilities among older people reversible, or, said another way, can training improve seniors' abilities? This and related questions have been addressed as part of Schaie and colleagues' research program. In particular, Schaie and Willis (1986) and Willis and Schaie (1986) focused on educational interventions related to spatial orientation and inductive reasoning. For the sample, they identified people 65 years of age or older who scored low in the last two testing periods (a total of 14 years) in one or both of these abilities.

The initial training intervention consisted of five one-hour sessions for each of the abilities. The design was pre-test–intervention–post-test, with each training group (i.e., spatial orientation or inductive reasoning) serving as the control for the other group. Results showed that about two-thirds of participants significantly improved after the interventions, and 40% actually improved to levels attained before the 14-year decline. These findings are encouraging and suggest that engaging in activities related to an ability helps to maintain that ability or at least slow its decline.

Methodological Observations

A few methodological observations should be made about research comparing the cognitive abilities of persons at different times in their life spans. First, longitudinal studies are almost always better than cross-sectional studies. This is primarily because of potential cohort effects that confound age differences in cross-sectional research. The best way to estimate these cohort effects is to test multiple cohorts at the same ages and examine mean differences in test scores for the different cohorts. The Seattle Longitudinal Study did just that for cohorts born around 1900 all the way to 1966, testing them every seven years.

Results show large cohort differences for many of the abilities examined in the study. For example, inductive reasoning and verbal memory increased nearly linearly by 1.5 standard deviations from the earliest to the latest cohort (averaging across all of the testing periods for each cohort). Another pattern was increases in average ability for the early cohorts, followed by a leveling in the middle cohorts, and then a decline in the latest cohorts. This was noted for numerical ability, perceptual speed, and verbal ability. Substantive reasons for these differences are unclear except that the improving abilities may be a function of increasing educational levels and better nutrition in later cohorts. However, the main point here is a methodological one. Increasing levels of an ability mean that in cross-sectional research, decline in the ability with age are underestimated. More generally, any cohort differences render across-age comparisons inaccurate.

A second methodological observation is that even longitudinal studies have a potential problem interpreting across-age ability levels, especially as the sample members reach advanced age. This is because as the cohort being followed reaches older age, those who drop out of the sample may have done so because of dementia or even death. In fact, the Scottish Mental Survey results provide a rather direct estimate of this bias. In 1932 and again in 1947, practically every 11-year-old in school in Scotland was tested (Ns = 89,498 and 70,805) using the Morey House Tests (Scottish Council for Research in Education, 1933). These tests, although not directly measuring general cognitive ability, were shown to correlate .80 with a commonly used test of cognitive ability, the Stanford-Binet (Deary, Whiteman, Starr, Whalley, & Fox, 2004). The 1932 and 1947 cohorts were followed up to identify deaths and various debilitating illnesses among cohort members. Using psychometric cognitive ability at age 11 as the independent variable, differences were tested between those deceased and those alive at age 76.

Large differences were found, with higher ability being associated with considerably lower mortality rates (Whalley & Deary, 2001). Similarly, higher ability was associated with lower levels of cancer, cardiovascular disease, and hospital stays (Deary, Whalley, & Starr, 2003). Thus, longitudinal studies may on balance underestimate average declines in ability because the more able members of the cohort are likely to remain in the sample.

Finally, as will be discussed in a subsequent section in relation to individual studies on links between age and personality, sophisticated approaches for tracking *individuals'* different trajectories in personality changes have been applied in aging research (e.g., Bergeman & Wallace, 2006; Ferraro & Kelley-Moore, 2003; Hertzog & Nesselroade, 2003; Nesselroade, 2006). Structural equation modeling, hierarchical linear modeling, and latent curve analysis are examples of analytical techniques that have been used in this context. Similar techniques have been employed in studying changes in intellectual abilities (e.g., Ferrer, Salthouse, McArdle, Stewart, & Schwartz, 2005; McArdle & Hamagami, 2006).

Job Performance

Although the consensus is that adults older than about age 55 show declines in several abilities, research correlating age with job performance generally finds almost no correlation between the two. For example, in an early review, Rhodes (1983) concluded that there was evidence for at least four different age-job performance relations: weak positive, weak negative, an inverted U, and non-significant. In their meta-analysis investigating this relationship, McEvoy and Cascio (1989) found a correlation of .06 between age and job performance. Sturman (2003) also conducted a meta-analysis and found some evidence for an inverted U relation, although the mean effect size was only .03. Finally, Waldman and Avolio (1986) conducted a meta-analysis and found an overall mean correlation of near zero between age and job performance, but they also identified a moderator of this relationship. When performance measures were objective, the relation was positive; when ratings were used as the performance measure, the mean correlation was negative (see also H. L. Sterns & Alexander, 1987). The authors noted that one possible reason for the latter finding is rater bias against older workers.

Another moderator that has been studied is job type. Waldman and Avolio (1986) found a more positive correlation between age and job performance for professional jobs compared to non-professional jobs. Yet another potential moderator is the dimension of job performance. For example, Gilbert, Collins, and Valenzi (1993) examined performance ratings on different dimensions for workers ages 25 to over 50. For the dimensions of technical competence and job commitment, the highest ratings were associated with 25- to 30-year-olds; the lowest ratings were given to those over 50. For the dimension of work relations, the pattern was the opposite, with workers over age 50 receiving the highest performance ratings. On the other hand, Schappe (1998) and Williams and Shaw (1999) both found virtually no correlation between age and citizenship performance (see also Cleveland and Lim, 2004), although Ng and Feldman (2008) observed a low positive relationship. Finally, Ng and Feldman's (2008) meta-analysis found negative correlations between age and both counterproductive work behavior and absences and no correlation between age and creativity.

Although not exactly a dimension of job performance, another dependent variable studied in relation to age is on-the-job injuries or accidents. The incidence of injuries is actually lower for older workers (e.g., Ng & Feldman, 2008; H. L. Sterns, Barrett & Alexander, 1985); however, once injured, they generally take longer to heal and get back to work.

Several explanations have been offered for the low correlation between age and job performance. Park (1994) suggested that older workers often have jobs that are very familiar, and they often have considerable practice and experience with their job tasks, thus allowing for successful performance even if broader cognitive functioning has declined. As an example, Artistico, Cervone, and Pezzuti (2003) found that older employees were actually better than their younger counterparts when working on problems that they have already encountered on the job. Moreover, older workers may have developed complex detailed knowledge structures (i.e., expertise) that compensate for any loss in general skills or abilities. Support for this contention comes from Thornton and Dumke (2005), who noted that professional expertise gained during a long career can often overcome deterioration in certain abilities. In a somewhat different vein, Kanfer and Ackerman (2004) observed that general declines in fluid intellectual abilities with age are often accompanied by increases in crystallized intellectual capabilities, and they suggest that a good strategy for older employees is to gravitate to jobs that emphasize the latter abilities, such as those with requirements for managerial and interpersonal skills. Finally, senior workers may often have more access to coworker support to help them with their tasks.

Schooler, Caplan, and Oates (1998) suggested the following reasons for smaller or no age differences in job performance compared with the age differences in cognitive abilities found in laboratory settings: (a) expertise and experience may help make up for declines in cognitive functioning; (b) lab tasks tend to push people to their cognitive limits, whereas actual jobs usually do not; and (c) older people with large declines in cognitive abilities have often left the workplace.

Age-Job Attitude Relationships

In cross-sectional studies, there appears to be a small positive correlation between chronological age and job satisfaction. Whereas Warr (1994) estimated the relationship to be relatively modest (between .10 and .20), others have posited a more complex relationship, with job satisfaction relatively high very early in a career (e.g., early twenties), lower between the mid-twenties to early thirties, and then rising through the forites and beyond (see Warr, 1994). If this is the case, the age-job satisfaction relation for individuals in their early thirties and beyond is likely to be stronger than it is for those in their twenties. Kacmar and Ferris (1989) made the excellent methodological point that studies of the age-job satisfaction correlation should control for tenure. In their study, they controlled for organizational tenure, job tenure, and tenure working with present supervisor. They also examined multiple facets of job satisfaction, using the Job Descriptive Index (a multifaceted measure of job satisfaction; Smith, Kendall, & Hulin, 1969). Results showed that for four of the five facets (supervision, coworkers, pay, and promotions), a U-shaped relationship emerged; with the work itself facet, the correlation was positive and linear. So this well-controlled study reported results reasonably similar to the more complex relationship suggested earlier.

There are several possible explanations for this changing relationship across different age groups. The first is the model of workers moving from job to job until they find one they like and then staying in that job. One way to at least partially test for this is to control for job level. This kind of analysis, however, generally does not reduce the age-job satisfaction correlation (Birdi, Warr, & Oswald, 1995; Clark & Oswald, 1996).

A second possible explanation for this relationship is cohort differences in levels of job satisfaction. This argument is that cohorts of older workers have always been more satisfied with their jobs, even when they were younger. The argument against this explanation is that average job satisfaction levels over time suggest that job satisfaction is actually reasonably high for some of the younger cohorts as well (Warr, 1998).

A third explanation is that as employees become older, their expectations about what a job should offer are reduced (e.g., Brandstädter & Rothermund, 1994). A fourth is that broader mental health, which may on average be higher for older workers, "causes" the higher levels of job satisfaction (Warr, 1998). However, when life satisfaction, at least as indexed by the admittedly somewhat superficial variables of marital status and number of dependents, is controlled for, the age-job satisfaction relationship is not affected. Clearly, more research is needed on this explanation.

The last potential explanation for the age-satisfaction relationship is the same as with earlier discussions about the age-job performance relationship. That is, older people who had low levels of job satisfaction may have already left the workforce. It is certainly the case that a significantly larger percentage of older people are not working, typically through retirement, than younger people (e.g., Ellison, Melville, & Gutman, 1996). To the extent that older persons who leave the workforce are those less satisfied with their job—a plausible hypothesis—the positive relationship between age and job satisfaction will tend to be overestimated. On balance, each of these explanations likely has some merit. However, in each case the empirical evidence is somewhat mixed, and it is not clear to what extent the relative contribution to the age-job satisfaction correlation is influenced by each of these explanations (Warr, 1998).

It appears that older workers also tend to report higher levels of job involvement and organizational commitment (Warr, 1994). Explanations for these relationships may partially parallel the explanations just discussed in connection with job satisfaction, especially the birth cohort effect rationale. The cohorts of older workers are typically thought of as standing higher on the Protestant work ethic (Schooler et al., 1998), and this could account for higher levels of job involvement and organizational commitment. Another possible explanation is that job autonomy and organizational rewards tend to be higher on average for older workers, and this could in turn account for higher involvement/commitment (Schooler et al., 1998).

Two organizational outcome variables often related to job satisfaction and involvement, as well as organizational commitment, are turnover and absenteeism (Borman, 1991). These variables have also been studied in relation to age. Research suggests a negative correlation between age and turnover, in the range of −.20 to −.25 (e.g., Beehr & Bowling, 2002). Warr (1994) offered two possible explanations for this relationship. First, older workers stay in their jobs because they do not believe that other employers are likely to hire someone at their career stage. And second, older workers are likely to be more satisfied because they occupy relatively high-paying jobs and thus tend not to seek employment elsewhere. A "sunk costs model" (i.e., the notion that time and effort have already been expended on this job) has also been suggested as a reason for lower turnover among older employees (Arkes & Blumer, 1985).

A similar negative correlation is found between age and avoidable absences (i.e., absences under the employee's control; Rhodes, 1983; Thompson, Griffiths, & Davison, 2000). However, for unavoidable absences, the correlation with age is positive, presumably because older workers are more likely to have health problems that result in absences.

Overall, the picture for job attitudes and related outcomes related to the older worker is quite positive for both employers and employees. Older employees are on average more satisfied, show greater commitment and involvement with their jobs and the organization, and tend to stay with the organization longer than younger workers. From a management perspective, older employees are likely to be easier to manage. These results are also favorable for older workers themselves. There is some evidence that employees can look forward to relatively satisfying experiences with work toward the end of their career. The cross-sectional nature of most research in this area renders the conclusion somewhat tentative but certainly suggestive. We now turn to a discussion of the relationship between age and personality.

Age and Personality

A central question related to personality and age is, how coherent and consistent is personality across time? An important aspect of any close examination of this age-personality question is the analytical techniques used. Most researchers on personality changes across time use correlational analysis to compare trait scores at different points in time or examine mean trait differences over time by using a repeated measures analysis of variance (ANOVA) statistical technique. It turns out that research using a correlational strategy shows reasonably high correlations, indicating considerable consistency across the life span, especially in adulthood (e.g., Block, 1971; Costa & McCrae, 1980; Moss & Susman, 1980). Researchers using the ANOVA technique tend to find only small changes in adult personality, indicating stability in these scores over time (e.g., Haan, Milsap, & Hartka, 1986).

Research that examines the stability of personality over time has been useful and informative. However, there are certain limitations with these two methods. Correlational analysis ignores possible shifts in mean levels across time. ANOVA results that find no differences could reflect either no change for everyone in the sample or different patterns of change for individuals in the sample, with these changes essentially canceling each other out and thus resulting in small mean differences (but considerable change for individuals). Recent advances in statistical theory and computing (as mentioned earlier) have enabled researchers to address some of these issues. We now review three recent studies that used methods more conducive to focusing on change in personality and on the nature of those changes.

An important study was conducted by Helson, Jones, and Kwan (2002) using the California Psychological Inventory (CPI; Gough, 1996) and a sophisticated analytical technique known as hierarchical linear modeling (HLM). This study examined three longitudinal samples tested as many as five times between ages 21 and 75. HLM allows the researcher to separate individual and group effects as well as to examine relationships other than linear, or straight-line, relationships between variables (Bryk & Raudenbush, 1987).

Helson et al. (2002) found that for both men and women, there were increases with age in several norm-adherence dimensions (e.g., self-control). They also found decreases over time for all of the social vitality dimensions of the CPI (e.g., sociability and social presence). Finally, their results, along with earlier cross-sectional studies, suggest that personality changes with age are very similar across culture, cohort, and gender. However, the HLM results gave evidence in several cases of non-linear change patterns. These findings cast some doubt on the maturational hypothesis (McCrae et al., 1999, 2000), which posits that the vast majority of personality changes occur before age 30, with considerable stability after that. This is because there is evidence that personality changes occur throughout the life span for most of the traits, with for the most part curvilinear trajectories. We should add, however, that Terracciano, McCrae, Brant, and Costa (2005), although finding the same general trends across age in a large-scale longitudinal study (the Baltimore Study of Aging) using hierarchical modeling, estimated that the changes are only about 0.1 standard deviation (SD) on average per decade (see also a recent exchange: Costa & McCrae, 2006; Roberts, Walton, & Viechtbauer, 2006a, 2006b).

There is also impressive evidence for environmental, event-related change in personality. For example, there is a curvilinear change in dominance and independence, with peaks in middle age when most people attained their maximum power and status at work. Thus, work experiences and the work-related environment do influence this personality change. Also suggestive are the curvilinear results for responsibility, with a temporary drop from approximately 1960 to 1980, even though the cohorts were born almost 20 years apart. A plausible explanation is that this period witnessed the height of individualism, with an emphasis on private and interpersonal experience and a de-emphasis on formal roles and social commitments. Apparently cultural or environmental events do affect personality change (Helson et al., 2002).

Jones and Meredith (1996) conducted longitudinal research on stability and change in personality over a 30- to 40-year period. Similar to Helson et al. (2002), they were most interested in exploring personality change over time. They employed a complex analytical technique known as *latent curve analysis*, a method that allows a view of individuals' unique patterns of change over time (Meredith & Tisak, 1990). It is similar to HLM but has more flexibility. Personality data were available for a sample of approximately 100–200 men and women tested at intervals of about 10 years from age 20 through age 60. The target personality variables were self-confidence, assertiveness, cognitive commitment (e.g., values intellect, is introspective), outgoingness, dependability, and warmth.

Most people gained in self-confidence between ages 30 and 50, leveling off after 50. Assertiveness showed considerable consistency, with men scoring higher across the entire life span. Cognitive commitment increased from ages 18 to 30, remained steady from ages 30 to 50, and then decreased somewhat from ages 50 to 60. The main finding for outgoingness was that women showed consistently higher scores and that both men and women increased their scores over time. Dependability showed an increase from age 18 to 30 and then stabilized across the rest of the life span. For warmth, the individual differences in across-time trajectories varied so greatly that no group pattern could be determined.

In addition, analyses with the latent curve method indicated individual differences in the amount and direction of change over time. For example, regarding self-confidence, for one of the two cohort groups studied, 32% significantly increased, 2% significantly decreased, and 66% remained the same across the life span studied. Overall, the results suggest adult developmental effects in self-confidence, cognitive commitment, outgoingness, and dependability. Assertiveness appears more consistent across time. Finally, the merit of examining individual differences with the latent curve strategy was convincingly demonstrated. Most notably with warmth, a more traditional analytic method of analysis (ANOVA) would likely have shown little change longitudinally; this would have been highly misleading, masking the wide variation in trajectories for individuals in the sample.

An intriguing basic question about personality and work is: Do the job and the workplace bring about change in personality, or is the effect in the opposite direction, with personality leading to choices of jobs and work settings? One theoretical framework, the attraction-selection-attrition (ASA) formulation proposed by Schneider (e.g., Schneider, Smith, Taylor, & Fleenor, 1998), suggests the latter. People gravitate to jobs and organizations that fit with their values, interests, and personalities, and provided the fit is good, they tend to stay in those jobs and organizations. There is some evidence for the validity of the ASA model (Schneider, Goldstein, & Smith, 1995; Schneider et al., 1998).

However, recently some evidence emerged for the former possibility. Roberts, Caspi, and Moffitt (2003) studied a sample of 18-year-olds, relatively new to the workforce, and then tracked this group,

conducting a second data gathering when they were age 26. A personality inventory was administered at Time 1 and then again at Time 2. The authors found that work experiences during their early career years were associated with personality changes. Furthermore, the traits that had a role in selecting members of the sample into the organization at Time 1 tended to be the traits that showed the most positive change across the eight years. An interpretation of this finding is that work experiences will deepen and elaborate traits that we already have, rather than bring out traits that are not as evident in us.

The implication of these results for older workers is that the effects of work experiences on personality are likely to be even larger because of their longer time in the workforce compared to this sample. Accordingly, although there is considerable coherence and stability in personality across older persons' lives, there are predictable changes in personality as well, and as suggested by this study, some of those changes are likely a result of cumulative work experience.

Erikson's (1959) concept of generativity in developmental theory suggests that during midlife, individuals typically move beyond concerns about the self and identity and the interpersonal focus on intimacy to concerns for others, including family and younger colleagues. The generativity concept has received attention again more recently (McAdams, 2001; McAdams & de St. Aubin, 1998). An interesting feature about generativity is that it falls outside the usual trait domain (for example, the Big Five or the CPI dimensions). Thus, although there is considerable evidence for stability and coherence in many of the typically targeted personality constructs, change is more evident from this developmental perspective.

In sum, although there is evidence for stability of personality, particularly during the adult life span, recent research has found reliable shifts in some traits for certain periods of life. Evidence has also emerged for substantial individual differences in trajectories on several traits, with increases, decreases, and stability evident for different people.

First, at the Big Five level, neuroticism, extraversion, and openness to experience tend to decline with age, and agreeableness and conscientiousness have upward trajectories across the adult life span. Declines in neuroticism derive primarily from reduced impulsiveness later in life. Likewise, increases in conscientiousness seem largely a result of increased self-control, dutifulness, and other norm-adherence-related constructs. Regarding extraversion, the declines with age seem primarily due to reduced social vitality, including lower sociability, social presence, and excitement seeking. For agreeableness, there appear to be gradual increases across the life span, including modestly higher standing on trust, straightforwardness, and compliance. Finally, lower scores for older adults on openness seem to be associated with lower behavioral flexibility. The declines in openness also likely tie in with the cognitive literature that shows deficits in speed-related abilities and fluid intelligence (e.g., Schaie, 1994).

With the possible exception of the openness findings, the personality change results support the role of older workers in the workplace because they are likely to be less impulsive and more conscientious in carrying out their tasks. The higher level of agreeableness also means that they should get along more smoothly with supervisors, coworkers, and customers, compared with younger workers. From a management perspective, this is highly desirable. Dependability and, to a lesser extent, agreeableness have been linked to organizational citizenship (e.g., Organ, 1997) or citizenship performance (Borman & Motowidlo, 1993; Borman, Penner, Allen, & Motowidlo, 2001). Citizenship performance has in turn been found to relate to individuals' overall performance and, more broadly, to organizational effectiveness. Thus, it appears that personality characteristics likely to be on average higher for older workers are correlated with positive individual and organizational performance outcomes.

To reinforce this point, conscientiousness has been found, consistently across all types of occupations and criteria, to be a good predictor of overall performance (Barrick, Mount, & Judge, 2001). Moreover, emotional stability (the inverse of neuroticism) predicts overall job performance and some specific criteria (e.g., teamwork). Finally, agreeableness was found to predict teamwork-related criteria (Barrick et al., 2001). These relationships are also favorable for older workers. For all three of these Big Five personality traits, older workers score higher than younger workers.

Another important result is that salient environmental influences associated with the job or with cultural events may cause personality changes. Roberts et al. (2003) demonstrated that work experiences were associated with personality changes, especially on those traits important for the hiring decision in the first place. Thus, traits that were useful for successful job performance actually had a positive change trajectory. Also, certain important societal effects, such as the women's movement (Roberts, Helson, & Klohnen, 2002) and the individualism phenomenon (Helson et al., 2002), appeared to have at least temporarily affected adult personality patterns.

Summary

On balance, older workers often perform on jobs as effectively as their younger counterparts. This is especially true when they: (a) avoid suffering the physical and cognitive declines usually evident in their age cohort; (b) have a relatively high degree of experience and expertise in their job; (c) have some flexibility in how to approach and accomplish their job; (d) retain a high amount of motivation to succeed on the job, (e) have a job that does not involve a lot of change; (f) receive management and coworker support at work; and (g) get the appropriate job training in an environment that meets the special needs of older workers.

Much of the research reviewed in this section supports the proposition that older workers have the capacity to be successful on the job and, more broadly, to maintain job and life satisfaction well into older age. Positive correlations between age and job attitudes mean that older employees are likely to be more satisfied, committed, and involved in their jobs, and, for the most part, easier to manage than younger employees because of their generally more tempered attitudes and more effective behaviors (e.g., citizenship; Borman, 2004).

In the area of personality, there are also reasons to be positive about the potential contributions of older workers. Research suggests that, on average, older people are higher on traits desirable in work settings, such as conscientiousness and dependability, emotional stability, and agreeableness. The only negative finding in this regard is that older people are likely to be lower than younger people in openness to new experiences and behavioral flexibility; overall, however, the scorecard is favorable for senior workers.

Organizational Strategies for an Older Workforce

The aging workforce presents organizations with numerous challenges and opportunities. As the large post–World War II cohort moves toward retirement eligibility, late-career workers will make up a larger and larger share of the labor pool. In addition, many of today's older workers may delay retirement, or work well into it. As these changes begin to shape the world of work, it will be more important than ever for employers to recognize and address this evolution in their workforce.

The availability of creative career management practices may be particularly important to members of the baby-boom generation who are now beginning to be classified as older workers. Surveys have suggested (e.g., Feinsod, Davenport, & Arthurs, 2005) that these workers, as they move into the latter stages of their careers, are often less focused solely on hierarchical advancement in the organization. Rather, they seem more oriented toward utilizing their potential, developing new skill sets, and being challenged in their job assignments and responsibilities.

These challenges will affect employer policies and practices, especially as they relate to recruiting, hiring, training, and retaining older workers. If organizations are to adapt successfully to these changing workforce dynamics, they will need to ensure that their organizational policies and actions are designed in ways that will encourage and promote continued investment in older employees.

Recruitment

In a recent review of the employee recruitment literature, Breaugh (2008) noted that over the last 40 years, research has increased dramatically, with considerable emphasis on topics such as recruitment methods and recruiter characteristics/behavior. Unfortunately, little research within the recruitment domain has focused on the older worker. Nevertheless, as the workforce ages and labor pools shrink, companies must consider more focused approaches to attracting key talent among older workers.

Dychtwald, Erickson, and Morison (2004) suggested a number of ways in which organizations might target recruiting efforts and market their company to older workers. These included: (a) conducting information seminars focusing on issues tailored to the older community, such as retirement, financial planning, and health and fitness; (b) holding or attending open houses and career fairs targeting older adults; (c) being creative with job postings, including posting notices at universities, research centers, and government retraining agencies to tap into an already motivated segment of the older population; and (d) creating a recruitment message that emphasizes the intangible values of the job, such as variety and independence, instead of focusing solely on the financial gains, which may not be a concern for many older workers. In general, their message

concerning recruitment is to "know your target market."

A recent Government Accountability Office (GAO) report noted the importance of recognizing that employers cannot exclusively rely on the same recruiting techniques if they want to reach older workers (U.S. GAO, 2007). They suggested that traditional recruiting mechanisms (e.g., job boards and newspapers) only find workers who are actively looking for work. They also recommended that organizations could enhance their recruiting efforts by partnering with other organizations to help advertise themselves as employers of older workers (e.g., working with the National Council on Aging or AARP to recruit older workers). For example, an employer that works with one of these types of organizations to hold a job fair for seniors is likely to convey that it is genuinely interested in hiring them. Knowing this, seniors may be more likely to submit applications and go through the selection process.

In his review, Breaugh (2008) suggested that, although research on the topic of targeted recruitment is rare, it is basic to the recruitment process and increased attention is warranted. This would seem to be particularly true for work with an aging workforce. Targeted recruitment refers to explicit recruitment efforts directed at a specific group of individuals for purposes of increasing employment of those group members, as opposed to increasing the general applicant pool. While such research is the exception, Rau and Adams (2005) noted that older adults are likely to have objectives and motivation for participating in the labor force that are different from their younger counterparts, and suggested that a better understanding of the factors that influence their attraction may help organizations become more successful at targeting older workers in recruitment. They investigated the degree to which work hours, staffing policy, and work design influence older workers, and found that scheduling flexibility and a targeted equal employment opportunity (EEO) statement positively influenced older workers' attraction to an organization, whereas opportunities to transfer knowledge had little impact. They also underscored the notion that particular policy combinations may be attractive to older workers, and should be explored further. Some confirmation of this speculation comes from a recent study by Armstrong-Stassen (2008), who found that people in post-retirement jobs are drawn to organizations that explicitly value older workers and signal this through HR practices that accommodate the needs of older workers.

Taylor, Shultz, and Doverspike (2005) cautioned that targeted recruitment should not ignore the reality that, although baby boomers have some characteristics in common, they constitute a diverse group, and an analysis of the cohort reveals wide diversity relative to background and needs. For example, older boomers tend to be wealthier than younger boomers, while women and African Americans are much more likely to be financially disadvantaged than Caucasians across baby boomer groups. They suggested that organizations should also consider other characteristics of work, including the social climate, the challenge of the job, and the opportunity to contribute to the community when crafting their recruitment message.

Companies are slowly adjusting to the prospect of hiring retirees—either their own retirees or those from other employers—as part of an expanded candidate mix. Hedge et al. (2006) noted that a relatively recent innovation has been the creation of job banks for older workers, providing them with a variety of part-time employment opportunities. As described by Menchin (2000), these job banks can provide not only part-time work but also a diversity of assignments. Some companies refer to these temporary work pools as "skills banks" to note that they include high-responsibility positions requiring advanced engineering and technical skills. Job and skill banks help to offset the loss of valuable expertise that results from retirements and downsizing.

Job banks are often established by companies as internal recruitment facilities for purposes of implementing flexible work arrangements for retirees and other experienced workers. In terms of rehiring retirees, Dychtwald et al. (2004) noted that recruitment and placement costs would be close to zero because the organization is already in contact with these workers, and training costs should be minimal. One additional benefit of such a program is that it would help to retain institutional knowledge.

Selection

Any effort to select workers properly begins with a careful consideration of the challenges they must meet on the job. With the physical and psychological changes that occur with age, and especially with the *variability* of such changes, it is imperative to analyze jobs and compare them with the functional capacities of *individual* older workers (e.g., Sterns & Miklos, 1995; Warr, 1994). Sterns, Sterns, and Hollis (1996) advocate using job analytic techniques to identify the specific levels of task performance that are required on a job, so that those levels

can be compared to individual capabilities. Because the performance of older workers is characterized by complexity (e.g., they can compensate for age-related declines in certain capacities), a layer of challenge is added to task-analytic techniques and selection. For example, older workers develop work strategies that can compensate for their loss of information-processing efficiency (cf. Fisk & Rogers, 2000; Schooler et al., 1998). Consequently, Hoyer (1998) recommended the use of high-fidelity job simulations wherever possible in selection, as such measures allow compensating mechanisms to influence test performance. In addition, Farr, Tesluk, & Klein (1998) suggested that knowledge be emphasized in selection/placement decisions, given the demonstrated association between job knowledge and job performance.

There is a need to learn more about the impact of age on the mean levels and validities of personnel selection measures. Based on earlier discussions, we might expect older persons to be at a disadvantage where tests are highly speeded, and the use of these measures should only be considered if the job requires such speed. On measures that are not speeded, older persons typically perform as well as their younger counterparts (Sonnenfeld, 1988); indeed, on measures such as job knowledge or other experiential assessments, older experienced persons may be at an advantage (Warr, 2001).

Likewise, measures of physical ability may put older workers at a disadvantage, but again it will be important to match carefully the physical ability level sought to the level required in the job, as the existence of an age-related decline does not necessarily mean that the extent of decline places a person below the threshold necessary for job performance (Schooler et al., 1998). Also, selection measures that require human judgment in the scoring processes (e.g., structured interviews, assessment exercises, etc.) are susceptible to the age-stereotyping and age-norming effects mentioned earlier. It is therefore important that evaluators be properly trained.

Flexible Work Alternatives

Beyond basic pay and compensation benefits derived from working, it is often noted that in midlife, workers also begin to place emphasis on intrinsic rewards from work, such as a feeling of accomplishment, of learning and experiencing new things, and of doing something worthwhile (Penner et al., 2002). Sterns and Huyck (2001) suggested that older workers often go through a period of self-assessment that may lead them to place more emphasis on leisure and other non-work pursuits, as well as to question the sacrifices that they make to stress in the workplace. The result is that they often want to continue working, but with a somewhat different perspective—one geared toward more flexible work arrangements, fewer hours, and jobs and work environments that are more responsive to their needs (Barth, McNaught, & Rizzi, 1995; Greller & Stroh, 2003; Shultz, 2003).

A variety of human resource management strategies have been suggested that offer older workers opportunities for flexible work scheduling, developing new knowledge and skills or utilizing their current skills and abilities differently, and work environments tailored to their needs and preferences. A number of these strategies are discussed next (see also Eyster, Johnson, & Toder, 2008).

FLEXIBLE WORK SCHEDULING

Work schedule adjustments may be a relatively simple method of keeping older workers motivated and productive (Sparks, Faragher, & Cooper, 2001). Many work-schedule innovations have already been used to address the needs of younger workers, especially related to child care issues. Given the steady increase in the proportion of the elderly, it is likely that the number of working adults attempting to balance careers and eldercare responsibilities will become a bigger issue in the future (e.g., Baltes & Young, 2007). Establishing such practices to respond to the wishes or needs of older workers may involve small additional monetary costs relative to the payoffs. In addition, innovative thinking about the "packaging" of work may be beneficial. Flexible work arrangements have been linked to lower work-family conflict and increased work-family balance (e.g., Eby, Casper, Lockwood, Bordeaux, & Brinkley, 2005), job satisfaction, lower absenteeism, and greater employee productivity (e.g., Baltes, Briggs, Huff, Wright, & Neuman, 1999). In addition, Moen, Kelly, and Huang (2008) tested a life-course fit model and found, among other things, that employees in their thirties, forties, and fifties were more likely to have greater work time control than do employees in their twenties.

JOB SHARING

Job sharing usually involves the sharing of one full-time job by two (or more) part-time workers, with the work split in some agreed-upon way. Rix (1990) noted that job sharing allows different skills, abilities, and perspectives to be brought to jobs; makes it easier for organizations to retain valued employees; provides a means for skill transfer from older to younger workers; and provides staffing continuity, as those sharing a job can fill in for each other as necessary.

JOB TRANSFER AND SPECIAL ASSIGNMENTS

Job transfers (especially if they are lateral transfers) allow workers to gain some variety in work activities, to work with a different group of coworkers, and possibly even to reduce the stress of the work environment. These may include such schemes as job rotation, in which employees are allowed to move to different jobs with similar levels of responsibility. Some organizations use strategies in which older employees are given special assignments that require a high level of organization-specific knowledge that they have accumulated over the years. These job placement practices can be a useful way of utilizing older workers, because older employees can be given assignments that match their particular interests and talents. Beehr and Bowling (2002) noted that older workers may make excellent mentors for newer employees, and others have echoed this (e.g., Belous, 1990; Doeringer & Terkla, 1990; Marshall, 1998). Such an arrangement also provides critical organizational knowledge transfer.

PART-TIME WORK

Another alternative work arrangement for older employees is to allow them to have choices through part-time working arrangements (Stein, 2002). Penner et al. (2002) found that many of those who had left the workforce or found other jobs after their career employment said they would have stayed on with their career employer if they could have worked fewer hours (see also Barth et al., 1995, and Sterns and Sterns, 1995). However, Penner et al. (2002) also noted that relatively few employees have the option of working fewer hours, and when organizations offer such an alternative, it is usually on a case-by-case basis, rather than as a program available to the broader group of older employees (Doeringer & Terkla, 1990).

BRIDGE JOBS

Bridge employment is often part of the transitional process to retirement for older workers. Bridge jobs are jobs that can be pursued after career employment is over, to "bridge" the gap between a late-career job and retirement. Cahill, Giandrea, and Quinn (2006) found that a majority of older workers leaving full-time career employment moved first to bridge jobs rather than directly out of the workforce. They also found that moving to bridge jobs was more common among younger respondents, respondents without defined-benefit plans, and respondents at both the lower and upper ends of the wage scale. Generally, bridge jobs involve changes in occupation and industry, often with some losses in occupational status and pay (Christensen, 1990; Ruhm, 1990). Many bridge jobs are unskilled or entry-level, and are generally filled by younger workers, with unattractive job content, poor working conditions, and poor job security (Doeringer & Terkla, 1990). Not all bridge jobs are so undesirable (Shultz, 2003), however. There are higher quality bridge jobs that may be found in informal arrangements by some firms to keep valued workers beyond the normal retirement age. Because these jobs preserve the match between worker competencies and job demands, they tend to also provide the flexibility, economic benefits, and status that make bridge employment an attractive option (Shultz, 2003). Finally, Wang, Zhan, Liu, and Shultz (2008) found that retirees with better financial status, and who had experienced more job satisfaction and less job stress in their career jobs, tended to seek bridge employment within the career field over bridge employment in a different career field.

PHASED RETIREMENT

Phased retirement is typically used as an employment option for full-time employees who are several years away from retirement. The concept underlying the use of phased retirement is that workers can "phase" into retirement gradually, rather than work full-time until the day they retire (Paul, 1988). Penner et al. (2002) noted that phased retirement can be a very attractive option for older workers, although Greller and Stroh (2003) questioned whether such programs amount to anything more than a way to turn veteran employees into a contingent workforce.

Hutchens and Pappa (2004) found that employers appear to prefer informal over formal arrangements, often because they want to maintain control over which employees are offered the opportunity for phased retirement. In a recent review, Chen and Scott (2006) found that phased retirement tends to be more available to persons who are best able to cope with change—those who are better educated, better off financially, healthier, and in management positions. Phased retirement also appears more prevalent at the younger end of the older worker age span (in their sample, early fifties), reflecting its role as a transition stage to full retirement.

Training

Training can be another important component of an organization's portfolio of strategic human resource management policies for older workers. Robson (2001) noted that the pace of technological change and its effect on the workforce make training an important strategy for organizations contemplating an aging workforce. Changes in average education levels of aging workers may make this challenge easier to deal with than is often assumed, and older workers themselves represent a training resource that is often insufficiently tapped. For individuals who are already employed, the fast pace of change and the rate at which technology has rendered many jobs obsolete have made the need for lifelong learning obvious. In fact, Hall and Mirvis (1995), in discussing continuous learning as a developmental strategy for older workers, suggested that the focus of training should be on when the learning is demanded by the job.

Certainly, continuous learning and skill development by workers of all ages is becoming more important than ever before. Maurer (2001) noted that, although mid- and late-career stages were once viewed as periods of mastery and maintenance, with no real demand for learning new things, now all workers are increasingly being called upon to continuously learn and adapt. Indeed, new skills are required of workers at midlife and beyond, just to continue to perform their jobs, and those who fail to embrace the notion of continuous learning at work may find their careers cut short (Greller & Stroh, 1995).

TRAINING BARRIERS AND OPPORTUNITY

Keeping skills fresh through training throughout the career life cycle is critical, but some studies have suggested that older workers may be less likely to participate in training programs than younger workers, either because they may be more hesitant, or because employers may not encourage them to participate. In fact, as noted by Farr et al. (1998), the pace of change of the work environment may set off a negative spiral for older workers related to their self-efficacy around the development of new knowledge and skills, keeping pace with new work practices as they are implemented, developing new knowledge and skills, and subsequent job performance. One of the most persistent stereotypes about older workers is that they are not worth training (see Maurer, 2007). Studies have shown that older workers are persistently viewed as untrainable, not interested in training, and a poor place to invest training resources due to their attenuated careers (e.g., Novelli, 2002). As a result, older workers are more often denied training opportunities (Farr et al., 1998), their skills degrade and become obsolete, and, once again, the perception becomes self-fulfilling prophecy.

However, some surveys and studies show older employees to be quite interested in training (Hale, 1990), and Simpson, Greller, and Stroh (2001) reported a high level of training activity among older workers in response to recent competitive pressures in the labor market. Simpson et al. criticized studies showing a lower incidence of training among older employees, because such studies typically focus only on employer-provided training. They observed that older workers are actually more likely to participate in training off the job, a result reinforced by survey results cited by Peterson and Wendt (1995). Simpson et al. (2001) demonstrated in their study that younger workers are more likely to seek apprenticeships and training in basic skills. Older employees are more likely to invest in training that is directly job-related, including credentialing programs, targeted career and job-related courses, and on-the-job computer-based training. Similarly, Warr (2001) noted older workers' higher interest in training that is directly job-related. The low interest level of older workers for many in-house training programs may say more about the content of those programs, their job relevance, and the degree of comfort that older trainees perceive in this type of training than it does about older workers' general interest in training.

AGE AND TRAINING

A meta-analysis of training studies by Kubeck, Delp, Haslett, and McDaniel (1996) showed that older workers tend to show less mastery of training material, take longer to learn the tasks being trained, and take longer to complete training programs, compared to younger workers. Beier (2008) suggested that differences in performance between younger and older learners are likely associated with the person (changes in abilities, personality, and self-regulation associated with age) and the situation (the training intervention itself), and concluded that the same training intervention will not be equally effective for everyone, and must be adapted to individuals or to homogeneous groups of individuals to be maximally effective. In fact, Kubeck et al. (1996) pointed out that the post-training differences observed between older and younger trainees may be a function of pre-training levels and thus may not necessarily mean that older trainees receive less benefit from training experiences.

TRAINING PRINCIPLES FOR OLDER WORKERS

In reality, as noted by Schooler et al. (1998), training is rarely tailored to the learning skills or the interests of older adults. Indeed, typical organizational training environments are often poor learning environments for older adults. Effective training principles for older workers must recognize their unique situation. Their information-processing abilities may have declined, such that they are no longer able to learn new material as efficiently as they once did, and they are more susceptible to distraction (e.g., Sonnenfeld, 1988). However, older workers often have the benefits of more knowledge and experience with which to link new training (Warr, 2001). They may falsely attribute their training difficulties to an inability to retain information (Hansson et al., 1997) and thus lose confidence in their ability to profit from training (Warr, 1994). Their confidence may be further eroded by being overlooked for training and by past experiences with training that had been poorly designed for them (Farr et al., 1998). They may have more fear of failure in training and fear of embarrassment, especially in the presence of younger trainees, in part because their previous training experiences may have taken place some time ago.

A number of training strategies have been shown to be useful when designing training for older adults, including: (a) attend to motivation and confidence; (b) use clearly relevant training; (c) incorporate procedural performance where possible; (d) utilize active and open learning; (e) attend to the sensory and physical environment; and (f) ensure transfer and reinforcement on the job. These principles reflect what is known about cognitive and physical changes with aging, preferences of older workers, and the importance of individual factors such as self-efficacy related to training. In general, good instructional design depends on careful needs analysis; evaluation of training is essential as well. In addition, research has demonstrated that while these principles have been useful with older adults, they will also enhance younger adult performance; that is, better training for older adults is better training for all workers. The reader interested in a more detailed discussion of these principles and strategies is referred to Hedge et al. (2006) and Beier (2008).

As the world of work becomes increasingly influenced by technology and global concerns, the pace of change is accelerating. This has given rise to the concept of learning as a career-long process. The organization that adopts this learning and performance perspective for all its employees will have created a human resources management philosophy and practice in which older workers will be among those striving for skill updating and performance improvement. These training opportunities should include older workers, and they should be encouraged to participate. There has been surprisingly little empirical work on age and training, and research in this area has the potential to significantly impact both science and practice.

Flexible Compensation and Benefits

In addition to manipulating job responsibilities and assignments, or offering training opportunities, sometimes a rethinking of existing pay and benefits can make a big difference to older workers. Evidence indicates that older workers have different preferences, compared to younger workers, in the areas of compensation and benefits (Hale, 1990). Whereas many older workers may have a need for monetary compensation, benefits tend to become relatively more important to workers as they age (Belous, 1990). Older workers tend to choose different health care plans than younger workers, preferring fee-for-service plans over health maintenance organizations so that they have more flexibility in choosing providers (Barringer & Mitchell, 1993).

Although older people are healthier than in past eras, certain chronic conditions become more common with age. Consequently, some older employees may be particularly attracted to improved health insurance, or other medical benefits. In fact, they may want to work beyond normal retirement age in order to keep their health insurance coverage. The absence of such benefits for part-time workers will make part-time schedules and phased retirement unfeasible for some individuals. Where benefits are available, they support a company's ability to restructure work arrangements and responsibilities for workers with key skills and know-how so that they will stay on the job during a period of knowledge transfer and development of the necessary replacement talent. Extending health care benefits to part-time workers and those in other non-traditional arrangements will undoubtedly increase the cost of such plans. Consequently, organizations who seek older workers to fill part-time and consulting positions (which often do not come with health care benefits) may need to consider adding health care as a major incentive (Wellner, 2002).

In general, it appears that organizations that wish to attract and retain older workers will need to be more flexible with compensation and benefits, just as they must be with work arrangements (Barringer & Mitchell, 1993). Pension plans and health care benefits are large factors in the decisions of older employees to retire, remain on the job, or seek other employment. The specific needs and preferences of older workers must be addressed. While there are challenges to the establishment of such systems (see, for example, Penner, 2005, for a discussion of legal and regulatory difficulties in the U.S.), they are beneficial to both organizations and employees and are certainly worth considering.

Job Design

Although considerable individual variability exists, aging is associated with both functional loss and decline in homeostasis, as we noted earlier. Consequently, it makes sense to expect that job design will see increased use as the workforce ages. Areas for redesign suggested by the literature on aging may be as diverse as work location, job content, work pacing, autonomy for completing assigned tasks, the physical environment, tools and work aids, and so on (e.g., Hansson et al., 1997; Warr, 2001). The potential benefits for organizations include not only better utilization of older workers, but also increased productivity and satisfaction of workers, and safer jobs for all employees (Sterns & Miklos, 1995). Faley, Kleiman, and Lengnick-Hall (1984) also noted that job redesign may be critical in preventing legal action under the ADEA. Job redesign can be as idiosyncratic as jobs themselves and the people who occupy them. Some major categories of job redesign for older workers include the following:

PHYSICAL REDESIGN

Ergonomic workplace design can reduce the potential for strain and injury (Farr et al., 1998). Sterns et al. (1996) discussed custom workstation design to match older employees' changing body structures (e.g., size, strength, flexibility) and sensory capabilities, while Paul (1988) noted special supports for workers who must stand all day.

SENSORY REDESIGN

Jobs can be redesigned to compensate for losses of sensory skills, with improvements such as larger computer screens, larger print on warning signs, better lighting, use of easily discriminated colors, and sound amplification (see for example, Hansson et al., 1997; Sterns et al., 1996; Warr, 2001; Wegman & McGee, 2004).

INFORMATION-PROCESSING REDESIGN

Declines in information-processing ability make it more difficult for older persons to rely on internal representations of information (Warr, 1994). To accommodate this, jobs can be redesigned with decision-making aids (e.g., flowcharts, written procedures, lists, menus for action); or even task or equipment modifications that reduce the extent of age-related performance differences.

WORK FLOW AND PACE REDESIGN

Older workers may function better with a slower work pace, or a work pace over which they have some control (Beier, 2008; Levine, 1988), particularly as a means of avoiding fatigue (Czaja & Sharit, 1993; Hale, 1990).

REDESIGN FOR STRESS CONTROL

Sterns et al. (1996) noted the importance of removing stressors from work environments, as such stressors can be more distracting for older workers. These include factors such as information overload, noise, overcrowding, dirt, and poor air quality.

In summary, there are a wide variety of job design interventions that can support older workers' comfort and productivity. Any job redesign that focuses on improving physical comfort would likely be beneficial to older workers (Jex, Wang, & Zarubin, 2007).

Knowledge Retention

Regardless of economic conditions, or how successful recruitment or retention efforts aimed at older workers prove to be, it is a certainty that many experienced workers will be leaving their jobs in the next decade. Thus, the challenge facing many organizations is not only the loss of some of their most experienced employees, but also a knowledge shortage, as organizations lose technical, scientific, and managerial know-how at unprecedented rates. So the problem becomes one of retaining or replacing the sophisticated, context-dependent knowledge that resides with the employees who are leaving (DeLong, 2004).

Schetagne (2001) argued that of all the available HR strategies and practices, the most important should be those that favor the transfer of knowledge and skills between generations of workers. He suggested that only a small part of knowledge and skills are transmitted from older to younger workers before they leave the organization. So, whether they take the form of support for training or a mentoring program between an older worker near retirement and a younger worker, these strategies, policies, and practices should encourage the transfer of knowledge and acquired skills from older workers to their younger successors. Lowe (2006) suggested that the transfer of tacit knowledge possessed by retiring workers requires more than succession planning for senior management, because such knowledge is found at all organizational levels.

DeLong (2004) suggested that organizations need to be more systematic in their design of human resource management programs and tools if organizations are to retain organizational knowledge. These programs should include: (a) systems for evaluating skill/knowledge (a skills inventory that also includes where an organization is most at risk for lost knowledge); (b) career development/succession planning processes (a system to retain employees—or at least slow turnover—and build long-term workforce capabilities); (c) the development of a retention culture (to ensure that the organization's values, norms, and practices better support the retention of employees and their valuable knowledge); (d) phased retirement programs (as one method to extend the tenure of their most valuable veteran employees); and (e) knowledge-sharing practices (including interviews/videotaping, training, storytelling, mentoring, and communities of practice).

As Rappaport, Bancroft, and Okum (2003) suggested, knowledge is a competitive advantage, so documenting and transferring knowledge within the organization is vital. When important knowledge resides with older workers nearing retirement age—or with workers of any age who are susceptible to turnover and will be difficult to replace—an organization needs to take deliberate steps to record and disseminate that know-how.

Summary

Changing workforce demographics and dynamics offer both opportunities and challenges for organizations. In order to effectively engage older workers, new recruiting approaches, workplace flexibility, and the right mix of benefits and incentives will be required.

As Morris and Venkatesh (2000) have suggested, management strategies that treat the "workforce" as a monolithic entity, with no real appreciation of differences across age groups, are likely to fail. Organizations wishing to remain successful in the future must create a work environment that supports and includes the different styles that reflect today's workforce. Much has been written about organizational struggles with cross-generational conflicts, but scant research exists to support or refute such claims. This should become a particularly fruitful area for future research. Dychtwald, Erickson, and Morison (2006) suggested that organizations should adopt a broader *flexible work* perspective, which includes *flexible time* (flexible hours and shifts and compressed workweeks), *reduced time* (part-time and seasonal work, job sharing, reduced hours or days worked, and various less-than-full-time contract work), and *flexible place* (e.g., telecommuting, mobile work, and other forms of off-site work).

While some solid empirical research has been executed that has helped to establish a better understanding of effective HRM strategies for older workers, much of the work described in this section is based on surveys of worker/retiree preferences, and informed speculation, and therefore the field is "ripe" for scientific inquiry. Still, it seems clear that different approaches and different policies of work will be necessary to take full advantage of the talents of these workers moving into later career stages.

Strategic Planning for an Aging Workforce

Human resource planning is essential to ensure that the people and competencies are in place to meet an organization's needs. As the baby boom cohort moves rapidly toward retirement eligibility, a strategic human resource management challenge will be to create new and attractive opportunities that capture the desire of older workers to make significant organizational contributions. These opportunities may involve part-time work, job redesign, organizational retraining, and alternative career paths. In order to meet these challenges, organizations need to create structures, policies, and procedures that foster an environment supportive of older workers' performance, work attitudes and motivation, and physical and psychological well-being. Unfortunately, most organizations are ill-prepared to meet the challenges associated with older workers. In this section, we discuss several areas where strategic planning—by individuals and organizations—can bolster effective and efficient use of HRM practices. The topics highlighted are in no way meant to be exhaustive of all strategic planning activities, but underscore several that are particularly relevant to an aging workforce.

Workforce Planning

Most organizations engage in some form of workforce planning, but considerable variability exists in terms of its depth, breadth, and strategic value. Essentially, the goal is to help organizations align their workforce requirements with their business strategies. One aspect of this process, of particular relevance to our discussion, is gathering data that depict the organization's workforce profile, including its current age structure, and how that might impact various organizational policies and practices. For example, an organization might make very different decisions about its career development practices and succession planning activities for a relatively old workforce, compared to a relatively young workforce. However, as fundamental as this process would seem to be, all organizations do not routinely gather and analyze such data.

For example, a 2003 Conference Board survey of 150 HR executives revealed that 66% of those organizations responding did not have an age profile of their workforce (Munson, 2003). This makes it impossible to accurately predict where and when retirements are likely to occur, as well as when personnel and knowledge retention problems could arise. More recently, interviews conducted by Feinsod et al. (2005) showed that this may be changing, as an increasing number of companies are starting to analyze their workforce demographics to assist in targeting the recruitment and retention of older workers, and the retention of the knowledge of workers nearing retirement. Workforce planning is geared toward understanding the characteristics of the workforce, including such things as analyzing the demographics of the workforce, reviewing turnover statistics and retirement projections, and developing strategies to meet current and future needs. Next, we briefly describe four types of organizational audits that can inform strategic human resource management (SHRM) where an organization stands in terms of its aging workforce.

AGE AUDIT

Before identifying a direction to proceed or a plan of action to pursue, it is necessary to have a clear understanding of what an organization looks like. An age audit involves gathering and analyzing data relative to characteristics such as age, length of service, retirement opportunities, work location, and so forth (Montana, 1985). The focus of the age audit should be to (at the very least) analyze the current population by length of service, retirement opportunities, and work location for each key job category. Such information can then be used to see how many older workers there are overall, what departments and positions they occupy, who may retire early, who is likely to stay, and beyond that, who the organization might want to keep, and what inducements would support such efforts.

KNOWLEDGE AUDIT

Mapping the age profile of a workforce provides insight into one dimension of workforce planning. Another key dimension is experience, and a *knowledge audit* is a method that management can use in this diagnostic process to identify where the organization is most vulnerable to the loss of specialized expertise (DeLong, 2004). Knowledge audits can provide detailed information about the dynamics of knowledge use and reuse in an organization, as well as potentially uncovering critical knowledge sources. Lowe (2006) suggested that the more an organization has downsized and restructured, the more likely it is that only a small cluster of key senior managers and professionals have deep experience in their roles. This creates a serious risk of knowledge drain, so employers need to think of flexible retirement options and reemployment not only as ways to respond to the needs of employees, but also as a knowledge-transfer strategy.

HUMAN RESOURCE MANAGEMENT AUDIT

In addition to knowing workforce demographics, it is also critical to understand how the organization's policies and procedures promote or detract from worker productivity. This can be accomplished by examining an organization's policies and practices in recruitment, hiring, evaluation, training, promotion, and termination to check for age-neutral or age-friendly policies. An HRM audit can reveal how an organization's current policies and procedures align with what the available research suggests as key considerations by older workers in deciding whether to join or stay with an organization (Armstrong-Stassen, 2008; Armstrong-Stassen & Templer, 2005).

CULTURE AUDIT

While HR management systems can offer older workers the opportunity for challenging job responsibilities and can motivate them to pursue learning and self-development activities, these systems are influenced by an organization's norms and stereotypes toward older workers. In turn, an organization's culture affects its policies and practices. As we have discussed previously, age-related stereotypes still exist within organizations, and if these norms and stereotypes are a part of the general culture of the organization, they may influence decisions regarding pay, promotions, assignments, and training opportunities. So, another strategy would be to audit an organization's culture. This might be done by distributing voluntary employee surveys, which can reveal how employees of various ages feel about older workers. A culture audit can also be undertaken to identify things such as cultural barriers to improving knowledge sharing (DeLong, 2004).

SUMMARY

There are a variety of ways that one can gather useful information to inform decision making. Some large organizations have computerized HR inventories, in which case some of the data of interest might already be available. In addition, many organizations routinely survey their workforce concerning opinions and recommendations about a variety of issues, so aging workforce–relevant items could be included at that time. Also, discussions with older workers regarding their current retirement intentions, their desires for reduced work schedules, or their interest in possible new roles in late career stages can provide important inputs to a human resource inventory.

Career Planning and Progression

The current work environment is such that many organizations can no longer promise steady upward mobility or lifelong employment. Instead, these ever-changing work conditions require employees to continually adapt to the demands of novel situations and continually learning new knowledge and skills. This new type of career focus emphasizes a more flexible, mobile career course, rather than the more traditional notion of linear progression through a series of predictable, discrete career stages. Hall and Mirvis (1995) suggested that this shift has dictated a change in the nature of the contract between employer and employee, whereas primary responsibility for career planning and management lies with the individual. This new perspective, which they referred to as a *person-centered* or *protean career*, is characterized by variability, adjustment, and change. The protean career concept provides a new way of thinking about the relationship between the organization and the employee, with organizations merely providing a context in which individuals can pursue their personal aspirations.

A fundamental precept of the new type of psychological contract is that a worker's needs and career concerns change in dynamic ways over the course of a career. One of the keys, therefore, is whether and how workers in midlife can successfully adopt a continual learning and adaptation mode. If the older person is proficient at self-assessment, and can engage in a personal "needs analysis," then the chances are much better for successful mid-career transitions, and are a good match with the new work environment. Hall and Mirvis (1995) argued that careers will be increasingly driven by the changing skill demands of the fields in which a person works. When the life cycle of technologies and products is short, so too will be a worker's personal mastery cycles. According to Farr et al. (1998), careers of the future will involve periodic cycles of skill learning, mastery, and "reskilling" in order to transition into new positions, jobs, and assignments. This career planning process involves becoming aware of opportunities, constraints, choices, and consequences; identifying career-related goals; and engaging in work, education, and related developmental experiences aimed at attaining specific career goals.

Still, Sterns and Kaplan (2003) have suggested that older workers may not be as well-suited for embracing greater career self-management as are younger workers. After all, many older workers initially entered the workforce with a one career–one employer ideal, and transitioning from an organization-driven career to a protean career may be a daunting task. Many of the present 50- and 60-year-olds were hired at a time when they could choose among jobs, and they expected that they would have control over how long they worked and when they exited the workforce (Hedge et al., 2006).

Organizations can assist with the process by providing career management resources to all employees. Doing so provides workers with additional information and assistance that can be very beneficial in dealing with the rapidly changing employment market. From an organizational viewpoint, strategic career management programs based on careful HR planning can help organizations keep valued employees, including older ones; can fill positions that may be difficult to adequately fill from the external market due to the specialized training, knowledge, or expertise involved (Hale, 1990); and can reduce HR costs through retraining existing workers rather than hiring new ones (Rosen & Jerdee, 1985). This perspective relates to the activities of the organization that will effectively select and develop employees to meet future organizational needs. This organization-level career management is an ongoing process of preparing, implementing, and monitoring career plans undertaken by the individual, alone or in concert with the organization's career systems (Hall, 1986).

It seems quite reasonable, then, that employers should assume that workers of all ages would likely benefit from training programs, opportunities to take on challenging developmental assignments, and interventions aimed at organizational change. Hansson et al. (1997) have suggested that age-related changes should be viewed from an adaptation perspective, offering older workers numerous opportunities. Older workers, then, should think in terms of continued career aspirations and involvements, and training should focus on that unique potential.

Still, several decades of organizational downsizing and restructuring in the United States have forced workers of all ages to adapt to decreased job, career, and work environment security. Adaptation is difficult in an environment where older workers may feel the impact of age stereotyping, age discrimination, and pressure to retire. In such an environment, older workers may become convinced that their skills are becoming obsolete, that training is unavailable, and that much of their organizational value may not be particularly transferable (Hansson et al. (1997).

A variety of unique issues face mid-career and late-career workers, including their perspectives on their careers, possible job changes required to progress, work and family balance demands, and transitions toward retirement. Feldman (2002b) pointed out that researchers have increasingly begun to examine how the nature of traditional career paths, individual career management strategies, and organizational career management practices are changing in conjunction with increasing environmental complexity. He also suggested that career plans are shaped by previous work histories, current skills and interests, and long-term plans for the future; and these evolve over time. Shultz and Wang (2008) suggested, however, there is relatively little empirical and theoretical work on the unique career issues faced by workers in their mid- to late-career stages, and encouraged researchers to pay more attention to the differences among early mid-career, late mid-career, and late-career workers, as the motives for their careers as well as their career environment could be considerably different. As Feldman (2007) noted, being mindful and purposeful about managing one's own career is as important in late career as it is in early career.

Retirement Planning

Atchley (1981) succinctly described retirement planning as "concerned with easing the transition to retirement and with putting retirement on sound footing with respect to finances, health, and lifestyle" (p. 79). Retirement planning can play an important role in adjustment to retirement. Recently, Taylor and Doverspike (2003) reviewed the research literature, noting that retirement planning can be linked to lower anxiety and depression, better attitudes toward retirement, better post-retirement adjustment, and workforce exit at an earlier age. They suggested that these effects are primarily due to the formation of realistic expectations about retirement, both socially and financially. In addition, the planning process also facilitates the setting of goals for financial, physical, and social well-being after retirement, with the goals leading to more planning and preparatory activity.

Retirement planning occurs both formally, through participation in pre-retirement planning programs, and informally, as individuals develop strategies for dealing with life changes that accompany retirement. In general, as individuals move through midlife, they increase retirement preparation activities, especially informal retirement planning behaviors, such as reading about retirement and discussing plans with friends (Kim & Moen, 2001). Interestingly, research has suggested that those who are most likely to experience problems with the impending reality of retirement may be the least likely to plan for it, while those who do participate in planning may already be mindful and accepting of this new stage of life (Heidbreder, 1972; Kasschau, 1974).

While a significant number of organizations can attest to having retirement planning as part of their HR portfolio, the breadth, depth, and quality of the programs vary considerably. Over time, such programs have become more encompassing in scope, moving from primarily financial to covering more of the social and psychological issues of retirement (Sterns & Doverspike, 1988). Some of the issues being addressed in programs include financial planning, health and wellness issues, living arrangements, use of time, interpersonal relationships, caring for older parents, and substance abuse (Dennis, 1988; Forteza & Prieto, 1994). Retirement programs have also begun to deal with employment and career development topics, as employment during retirement is common and will become more common as labor force changes unfold in the future.

Dennis (1988) advocated that retirement planning programs emphasize role change; psychological and social impacts of leaving the workforce; and differential needs associated with health, socio-economic status, and gender and minority status. She also advocated offering retirement planning programs earlier, as suggested by many participants. Taylor and Doverspike (2003) suggested that retirement planning programs focus on: (a) building self-efficacy to meet the challenges and changes in retirement; (b) reducing the ambiguity and uncertainty of the retirement process; (c) the importance of physical well-being on subsequent adjustment; (d) financial planning for retirement; and (e) ensuring that retirees understand the importance of supportive social relationships.

For organizations looking to offer such programs, most advice suggests that a "one size fits all" approach to program development will be inadequate. Rather than assuming that the financial, health, and social aspects are equally important for all groups, these dimensions of planning may interact with retiree characteristics in determining the effectiveness of retirement planning programs as a means to enhance later adjustment. In sum, a needs assessment would be particularly useful as a way to identify the issues facing retirees, and around which to build a comprehensive planning seminar.

Retirement planning cannot be completely left to the organization, however. Self-management of retirement will become more important for the same reasons that self-management of career is becoming important (Sterns & Gray, 1999). Indeed, laws and economic forces have, for many, already put into self-management one important component of retirement planning—the accumulation and management of retirement funds. A fulfilling retirement will come to depend more on individuals planning other parts of their retirement experience, as well. In fact, research suggests that even those individuals who plan their own retirement without the benefit of formal planning seminars experience more positive levels of retirement satisfaction (Anderson & Weber, 1993).

Summary

Yeatts, Folts, and Knapp (2000) discussed two philosophical models representative of human resource management practices. They labeled these two approaches the *depreciation* model and the *conservation* model. The depreciation model implies that an individual's value to an organization peaks early in a career, levels off at mid-career, and steadily declines until retirement. The alternative approach is the conservation model, which views employees of all ages as renewable assets that will yield a high rate of return over long periods of time, if they are adequately educated, trained, and managed. Thus, an important component of strategic human capital management is to plan and manage these investments intelligently.

Retirement Transitions

Retirement is typically defined as later life withdrawal from the workforce, but it has become an increasingly "phased" phenomenon, involving multiple exits from and reentries into paid and unpaid work. This increasingly "blurred" definition speaks to both the complexity of the retirement decision and the concept itself. Exiting from one's career job is a key life change, transforming roles, relationships, and daily routines. Because healthy adults spend a large portion of their time and energy working, these work activities provide considerable structure to their lives; work activities draw on a fairly large portion of an individual's repertoire of aptitudes, skills, knowledge, competence, and creativity. In addition, a large portion of personal interactions occur in the work setting, and generally some measure of an individual's stature and influence is derived from work (Forteza & Prieto, 1994).

Consequently, any consideration related to retirement transitions, retirement planning, and postretirement reemployment must also be interpreted within the context of the meaning that work has for those who continue working, and for those who have stopped working. And, although retirement in many countries has become an almost universal transition, there are no clearly defined functions or behaviors for retirees (Kim & Moen, 2001). In fact, Ekerdt, Hackney, Kosloski, and DeViney (2001) suggested that while theories of retirement behavior might imply rational decision making regarding retirement preferences, plans, and strategies, both the expectations and actual transitions are characterized by considerable uncertainty.

Retirement Influences

Research has shown that midlife workers' decisions to exit the workforce on a permanent basis are based on a wide range of personal and family circumstances. Prior to retirement-friendly policies and pensions, poor health tended to be the primary differentiator between work and retirement. Currently, research suggests that the two most consistent predictors of retirement are health (e.g., Jex

et al., 2007), and wealth (e.g., pension eligibility and financial circumstances; Quinn & Burkhauser, 1990; Talaga & Beehr, 1995). They affect both retirement decisions and timing, and are particularly important because they likely mitigate the influence of other variables that might otherwise shape retirement transitions (Barnes-Farrell, 2003). Attitudes toward work also shape expected retirement age; dissatisfaction with one's job is related to a lower anticipated retirement age among both white and black retirees, regardless of gender (e.g., Richardson & Kilty, 1992). In addition, research findings suggest that individuals who have planned for their retirement are better prepared for it; are more likely to report earlier planned retirement ages; and are more likely to actually retire (Taylor & Doverspike, 2003).

Moen, Sweet, and Swisher (2005) also suggested that retirement planning is influenced by forces both at home and at work, with spouses and coworkers serving as important frames of reference. For example, Blau (1998), and Henretta, O'Rand, and Chan (1993) have shown that couples tend to synchronize their retirement exits. In addition, employees shape their plans for retirement timing in accordance with the timing patterns of the coworkers in particular work environments. Kim and Moen (2001) noted that this may suggest that organizations provide both a structural and cultural environment in which workers make decisions, including plans for retirement.

Retirement and Well-Being

A number of studies have investigated the circumstances related to post-retirement adjustment in terms of physical and psychological well-being. Income is important for adjusting to retirement, with both *perceptions* of having an inadequate income, as well as real inadequate income and financial problems being associated with dissatisfaction and maladjustment (Kim & Moen, 2001). In addition, research has demonstrated that social relationships (e.g., family, friendships, and group affiliations) promote retirement adjustment, or as Mutran et al. (1997) suggested, social support may buffer the uncertainty of retirement. In addition, van Solinge and Henkens (2005) found that social embeddedness was an important determinant of adjustment to retirement. However, they also suggested that while partners played an important role in decision making with regard to retirement, the actual adjustment to retirement was a highly individualized process experienced differently by each partner. Van Solinge and Henkens (2005, 2008) differentiated between satisfaction in retirement and adjustment to retirement, and suggested that examining the two as distinct constructs would help to establish a better understanding of the psychological processes that follow from retirement and its outcomes.

Personal resources (e.g., health, socioeconomic status, and self-concept) have also been shown to play an important role in retirement well-being. A substantial body of research has shown that better adjustment to retirement is related to better health (e.g., Schmitt, White, Coyle, & Rauschenberger, 1979). Having a higher education and a higher occupational prestige level in the pre-retirement job were also related to greater retirement satisfaction (Kim & Moen, 2001). For example, House (1998) noted that at higher socioeconomic levels, self-efficacy tends to decline modestly with age, especially around the period of retirement. Conversely, self-efficacy tends to increase with age at lower socioeconomic levels, again most notably in the post-retirement years. He suggested that these findings might reflect the different experience and meaning of retirement for people at different socioeconomic levels. For those at higher socioeconomic levels, retirement often results in the loss of a position that had allowed them to acquire esteem, autonomy, and self-direction, while at lower socioeconomic levels, retirement often means escaping from a role characterized by the absence of these positive attributes and experiencing new work opportunities, or leisure roles that are more conducive to a sense of self-efficacy.

Different Retirement Pathways

Szinovacz (2003) discussed the concept of pathways into retirement as a way to convey the notion that retirement decisions reflect long-term and sequential processes over the life course. This dynamic view of retirement processes suggests that transitions are imbedded in societal and organizational structures, and are tied to past and current experiences in individuals' lives. Thus, retirement decisions evolve not only from occupational and employment experiences but also from a variety of contextual influences and lifelong experiences in work and non-work realms. One challenge to retirement research is to untangle these dynamics and complexities, including those associated with changing retirement policies and cohort flow.

Most previous studies have focused on men's retirement, but research has continued to show that variables predicting retirement timing for men do not necessarily predict women's retirement timing (DeViney & O'Rand, 1988; Kim & Moen, 2002), and given that women are becoming an ever-increasing component of the workforce, an understanding of how this might impact retirement models is also important. As Taylor and Doverspike (2003) noted, specific predictors of retirement behaviors may interact with gender, and thus the very nature of retirement may differ. In addition, few studies have considered potential racial and ethnic differences in the retirement transition. This suggests that what is required is the development of more comprehensive models of retirement transitions that can promote understanding of the ways in which gender, ethnicity, and culture contribute to the retirement process.

Moreover, although most retirement research has focused on the retirement status of individuals, retirement is increasingly a coupled transition, with husbands and wives having to negotiate the timing and sequencing of both spouses' retirement. Available research suggests that the couple's joint retirement status matters for retirement satisfaction as well as post-retirement marital quality and psychological well-being (Kim & Moen, 2001).

Beehr and Bowling (2002) have suggested that an individual's perception of whether his or her retirement is voluntary or involuntary has both physical and psychological ramifications. For example, perceiving retirement as involuntary has been linked to problems with physical and emotional health, depression, and general life and retirement dissatisfaction. In addition, research examining the impact of downsizing demonstrated that psychological well-being and physical health were both adversely affected by the perception of forced retirement. Conversely, when retirement was perceived as voluntary, the result was greater satisfaction with health, finances, activities, life, marriage, and retirement.

Wang (2007) examined five waves of data from the Health and Retirement Study (HRS), and concluded that retirees do not follow a uniform pattern during the retirement process, suggesting that researchers should use a broad range of variables to profile retiree subgroups that correspond to different psychological well-being change patterns, and in so doing identify corresponding intervention programs that can be designed and tailored to improve their retirement quality. Moen et al. (2005) noted the dynamic nature of this process, and suggested that contemporary cohorts moving through midlife are also confronting a world in which the structure and culture of retirement is continually being recast, which may render prior research findings suspect in terms of broad generalizability.

Life After Retirement

Being retired in late midlife means, for many, the opportunity to pursue new directions; however, it does not necessarily mean extensive leisure time. For example, Maestas (2005), using the first five waves of the HRS data, showed that nearly half of retirees followed a retirement path that involved only partial retirement or unretirement, and those who "unretired" suggested that a return to work was largely planned and anticipated before retirement. In addition, Kim and Moen (2001) found a significant positive impact of post-retirement employment on psychological well-being.

A growing option for older workers is some form of part-time or bridge employment. The concept of bridge employment complicates the traditional view that older workers simply move from employment to retirement. In part, because of the growing popularity of bridge employment, it has become more difficult to distinguish between individuals who are retired and those who are not. Consequently, Feldman (1994) redefined retirement to emphasize exit from a position or career path after having spent a considerable length of time in a position, taken by a worker at middle age or beyond, so as to reduce his or her psychological commitment to work.

Weckerle and Schultz (1999) examined factors associated with retirement—continued full-time employment in the present job, bridge employment in the present type of work, or bridge employment in a different type of work—for workers 50 years of age or older who had been in their current job at least 10 years. They found that workers' perceptions of their current and expected financial situation were the most consistent factors that influenced their thoughts and actions. Those who were considering early retirement were more satisfied with their current financial situation; those who were less satisfied with their future financial prospects were considering continued full-time employment, and those whose average financial satisfaction fell between the other two groups were most likely to be considering some form of bridge employment.

A second possibility is unpaid work, whether as an informal volunteer or as an active participant in a community association. Volunteer participation in retirement may be either a continuation of activities begun earlier or a qualitative shift in relative emphasis from paid work to unpaid volunteer labor (Kim & Moen, 2001). Moen and Fields (2002) suggested that community participation in midlife may help to replace social networks lost when an individual exits the world of work.

Summary

As Beehr (1986) noted, retirement is a process that starts with planning and decision making some time before the actual end of one's working life and is not completed for years after the point of retirement. Retirement rarely occurs for one reason alone. Usually, a number of variables interact to influence the decision to retire, thus suggesting a need for more comprehensive models of the retirement process that examine a larger set of variables and their interactions. With an ever-growing contingent of older workers, many of whom expect to work past traditional retirement age, it becomes all the more important to develop a more thorough understanding of older workers, the nature of their interactions with work and the organizations for which they work, and the process of transitioning to retirement.

Conclusion

Global aging, technological advances, and financial pressures on health and pension systems are sure to influence future patterns of work and retirement, and this changing work landscape underscores the need to examine and reshape employment and retirement policies to better meet the needs of older workers and their employers in the coming years. Myths of aging are found in a work organization's culture, and are often reinforced by its policies and procedures. Changing long-held stereotypes is not an easy process. In part, it requires changing the perspectives and mechanisms on which age norms are based and age stereotypes operate. Much of the research reviewed in this chapter supports the proposition that older workers have the capacity to be successful on the job and, more broadly, to maintain job and life satisfaction well into older age; they are likely to be more satisfied, committed, and involved in their jobs; and tend to be higher on traits desirable in work settings, such as conscientiousness and dependability, emotional stability, and agreeableness than younger workers. Changing workforce demographics and dynamics offer both opportunities and challenges for organizations, but in order to effectively engage older workers, new approaches to recruiting, workplace flexibility, and the right mix of benefits and incentives will be needed. In addition, a better understanding of workforce profiles—age, retirement eligibility, and expertise—is necessary to allow organizations to gauge who is adding different kinds of value, who has the potential to add future value, and where to invest in workforce development, regardless of age. With an ever-growing contingent of older workers suggesting they will likely continue to work past traditional retirement age, it becomes all the more important that we increase our efforts to develop a more thorough understanding of older workers, the nature of their interactions with work and the organizations for which they work, and the process of transitioning to retirement.

Nininger and Scourtoudis (2003) observed that organizations have constructed extensive "scaffolding" for new employees designed to orient, integrate, and develop them, but suggested that almost no attention is given to the need to create similar scaffolding to support older employees entering the final phase of their careers. Certainly, there is a growing realization of the integral role that these workers will play in the labor force of the future. In addition, the decline in traditional career trajectories, technological advancements that, for example, encourage work from home, as well as evolving policies geared toward the increased use of older workers in the labor force render boundaries between work and other life spheres less well-defined and more variable than ever before.

Feldman (2002a) recently discussed research on work careers in terms of theory building and empirical research and made a number of insightful comments that are pertinent to the work and aging literature. He noted that, for a variety of reasons, practitioner advice on career development has often outstripped empirical research on the topic, and he encouraged theory building that leads to research that informs additional theorizing and research that leads to solid practical applications. Feldman (2002a) also encouraged a focus on midrange models that avoid theoretical frameworks and constructs that are so broad that it is nearly impossible to frame testable hypotheses, while also avoiding theories that can become too narrowly focused and context-specific. Many similarities exist in the work and aging domain. Looking toward the future, the dynamic nature of the work and the timeliness of the topic offer much promise for wide-ranging advances in theory and practice.

Future Directions

1. No set of issues has galvanized public discourse about aging more than those surrounding work, retirement, and economic security in old age. Changing demographics hold significant implications for governments, employers, and individuals. As people live longer, they can expect to have more time in retirement. At the same time, however, this means that growing numbers of retirees will be dependent on a shrinking working population to support them. Research that examines work and retirement issues must also take into account the influence of broader environmental factors as well.

2. Historically, enforcement of the ADEA has focused on *termination* more than on *hiring*. However, as the number of older workers increases, many may leave their long-term career employment and seek part-time or shorter term jobs, or may join the ranks of displaced workers seeking employment. As a result, ADEA enforcement efforts need to shift to recruitment and hiring to ensure that age discrimination does not deter the hiring of older adults seeking employment. Consequently, it will be important to closely monitor shifting enforcement policy and to renew efforts to contribute insights from the research as well.

3. In the area of cognitive ability and aging, more research is needed on training and related interventions to help older people maintain their abilities or even possibly reverse deficits. At a minimum, the goal of these interventions should be to slow some of the declines. There is hope in this area, with Willis and Schaie (1986) demonstrating impressive gains in spatial orientation and inductive reasoning for people 65 years or older. After a training intervention more than 60% of participants significantly improved in these abilities, with 40% improving to levels they had enjoyed before declines during the preceeding 14 years. We know that involvement in complex, intellectually stimulating activities, having a flexible personal lifestyle, living with someone who has a high level of cognitive functioning, and so on, all contribute to seniors' maintaining relatively high levels of cognitive ability; if training and related programmed experiences could be implemented to help older people avoid cognitive declines, this could have considerable impact on our older population, those working *and* those who are retired.

4. Relevant for the topic of personality change and aging, we need more longitudinal studies that employ advanced statistical methodologies such as hierarchical linear modeling and latent curve

analysis. The breakthrough with these technologies is that, in addition to mapping longitudinal changes regarding mean trait levels in personality for the entire sample, we can map changes in trait trajectories for *individuals* in the sample. This can lead to more interesting and potentially less misleading findings. For example, some traits have shown little longitudinal change at the mean trait level but considerable variation in trajectories for individuals, with some upward and other downward trajectories revealed.

5. Organizations wishing to remain successful in the future must create a work environment that supports and includes the different styles that reflect today's workforce. Much has been written about organizational struggles with cross-generational conflicts, but scant research exists to support or refute such claims. This should become a particularly fruitful area for future research.

6. Work-family balance and work-family conflict have developed a relatively large research base over the last decade or so. However, there is surprisingly little research on whether there are differences between older and younger workers in the ways that they experience and react to juggling the two domains of work and family. The increase in the number of elderly individuals in the industrialized societies and the need for families to care for them should increase the importance of researching this area in the future.

7. There is relatively little empirical and theoretical work on the unique career issues faced by workers in their mid- to late-career stages. In addition, researchers need to pay more attention to the differences among early mid-career, late mid-career, and late-career workers, as the motives for their careers as well as their career environment could be considerably different.

8. As the workforce continues to age, post-retirement employment will become increasingly important to both employers and retirees who want to return to work. The research challenge will be to examine post-retirement opportunities and HR practices, both individually and in tandem, to clarify which demonstrate value for older workers, and which do not.

References

AARP. (2003, April). *Global aging: Achieving its potential.* Washington, DC: AARP Policy and Research.

Adams, G. A., & Beehr, T. A. (Eds.). (2003). *Retirement: Reasons, processes, and results.* New York: Springer.

Age Discrimination in Employment Act of 1967, 29 U.S.C. § 621 *et seq.* (2004).

Allen, P. A., Lien, M., Murphy, M. D., Sanders, R. E., & McCann, R. S. (2002). Age differences in overlapping-task performance: Evidence for efficient parallel processes in older adults. *Psychology and Aging, 17,* 505–519.

Anderson, C. E., & Weber, J. A. (1993). Preretirement planning and perceptions of satisfaction among retirees. *Educational Gerontology, 19,* 397–406.

Arkes, H., & Blumer, C. (1985). The psychology of sunk cost. *Organisational Behaviour and Human Decision Processes, 35,* 124–140.

Armstrong-Stassen, M. (2008). Organizational practices and the postretirement employment experience of older workers. *Human Resource Management Journal, 18,* 36–53.

Armstrong-Stassen, M., & Templer, A. (2005). Adapting training for older employees: The Canadian response to an aging workforce. *The Journal of Management Development, 24,* 57–67.

Artistico, D., Cervone, D., & Pezzuti, L. (2003). Perceived self-efficacy and everyday problem solving among young and older adults. *Psychology and Aging, 18,* 68–79.

Atchley, R. C. (1981). What happened to retirement planning in the 1970s? In N. G. McCluskey & E. F. Borgatta (Eds.), *Aging and retirement: Prospects, planning, and policy* (pp. 79–87). Beverly Hills, CA: Sage.

Baltes, B. B., Briggs, T. E., Huff, J. W., Wright, J. A., & Neuman, G. A. (1999). Flexible and compressed workweek schedules: A meta-analysis of their effects on work-related criteria. *Journal of Applied Psychology, 84,* 496–513.

Baltes, B. B., & Young, L. M. (2007). Aging and work/family issues. In K. S. Schultz & G. A. Adams (Eds.), *Aging and work in the 21st century* (pp. 251–275). Mahwah, NJ: Erlbaum.

Baltes, P. B., & Baltes, M. M. (Eds.). (1990). *Successful aging: Perspectives from the behavioral sciences.* Cambridge, UK: Cambridge University Press.

Barnes, D. E., Yaffe, K., Satariano, W. A., & Tager, I. B. (2003). A longitudinal study of cardio-respiratory fitness and cognitive function in healthy older adults. *Journal of the American Geriatrics Society, 51,* 459–465.

Barnes-Farrell, J. L. (2003). Beyond health and wealth: Attitudinal and other influences on retirement decision-making. In G. A. Adams & T. A. Beehr (Eds.), *Retirement: Reasons, processes, and results* (pp. 159–187). New York: Springer Publishing.

Barrick, M. R., Mount, M. K., & Judge, T. A. (2001). Personality and performance at the beginning of the new millennium: What do we know and where do we go next? *International Journal of Selection and Assessment, 9,* 9–30.

Barringer, M. W., & Mitchell, O. S. (1993). Health insurance choice and the older worker. In O. S. Mitchell (Ed.), *As the workforce ages: Costs, benefits, and policy challenges* (pp. 125–146). Ithaca, NY: ILR Press.

Barth, M. C., McNaught, W., & Rizzi, P. (1995). Older Americans as workers. In S. A. Bass (Ed.), *Older and active: How Americans over 55 are contributing to society* (pp. 35–70). New Haven, CT: Yale University Press.

Bassili, J. N., & Reil, J. E. (1981). On the dominance of old age stereotypes. *Journal of Gerontology, 36,* 682–688.

Beehr, T. A. (1986). The process of retirement: A review and recommendations for future investigation. *Personnel Psychology, 39,* 31–55.

Beehr, T. A., & Bowling, N. A. (2002). Career issues facing older workers. In D. C. Feldman (Ed.), *Work careers: A developmental perspective* (pp. 214–244). San Francisco: Jossey-Bass.

Beier, M. E. (2008). Age and learning in organizations. In G. P. Hodgkinson & J. K. Ford (Eds.), *International review of industrial and organizational psychology* (Vol. 23, pp. 83–106). New York: John Wiley.

Belous, R. S. (1990). Flexible employment: The employer's point of view. In P. B. Doeringer (Ed.), *Bridges to retirement: Older workers in a changing labor market* (pp. 111–128). Ithaca, NY: ILR Press.

Bergeman, C. S., & Boker, S. M. (Eds.). (2006). *Methodological issues in aging research.* Mahwah, NJ: Erlbaum.

Bergeman, C. S., & Wallace, K. A. (2006). The theory-methods interface. In C. S. Bergeman & S. M. Boker (Eds.), *Methodological issues in aging research* (pp. 19–42). Mahwah, NJ: Erlbaum.

Berkowitz, P. M., & Jackson, R. M. (2008, April). *The implications of new overseas discrimination laws on multinational corporations.* Boston: Nixon Peabody LLP: Employment Law Alert.

Birdi, K. M., Warr, P. B., & Oswald, A. J. (1995). Age differences in three components of employee well-being. *Applied Psychology: An International Review, 44,* 345–373.

Blau, D. M. (1998). Labor force dynamics of older married couples. *Journal of Labor Economics, 16,* 595–629.

Block, J. (1971). *Lives through time.* Berkeley, CA: Bancroft Books.

Borman, W. C. (1991). Job behavior, performance, and effectiveness. In M. D. Dunnette & L. M. Hough (Eds.), *Handbook of industrial and organizational psychology* (pp. 271–326). Palo Alto, CA: Consulting Psychologists Press.

Borman, W. C. (2004). The concept of organizational citizenship. *Current Directions in Psychological Science, 13,* 238–241.

Borman, W. C., & Motowidlo, S. M. (1993). Expanding the criterion domain to include elements of contextual performance. In N. Schmitt & W. C. Borman (Eds.), *Personnel selection* (pp. 71–98). San Francisco: Jossey-Bass.

Borman, W. C., Penner, L. A., Allen, T. D., & Motowidlo, S. J. (2001). Personality predictors of citizenship performance. *International Journal of Selection and Assessment, 9,* 52–69.

Bosma, H., van Boxtel, M. P. J., Ponds, R. W. H. M., Houx, P. S. H., & Jolles, J. (2003). Education and age-related cognitive decline: The contribution of mental workload. *Educational Gerontology, 29,* 165–173.

Bosma, H., van Boxtel, M. P. J., Ponds, R. W. H. M., Jelicic, M., Houx, P. S. H., Metsemakers, J., & Jolles, J. (2002). Engaged lifestyle and cognitive function in middle and old-aged, non-demented persons: A reciprocal association? *Journal for the German Society of Gerontology and Geriatrics, 35,* 575–581.

Brandstädter, J., & Rothermund, K. (1994). Self-percepts of control in middle and later adulthood: Buffering losses by rescaling goals. *Psychology and Aging, 9,* 265–273.

Breaugh, J. A. (2008). Employee recruitment: Current knowledge and important areas for future research. *Human Resource Management Review, 18,* 103–118.

Bryk, A. S., & Raudenbush, S.W. (1987). Application of hierarchical linear models to assessing change. *Psychological Bulletin, 101,* 147–158.

Cahill, K. E., Giandrea, M. D., & Quinn, J. F. (2006). Retirement patterns from career employment. *The Gerontologist, 46,* 514–523.

Chan, S., & Stevens, A. H. (1999). Employment and retirement following a late-career job loss. *American Economic Review: Papers and Proceedings, 89,* 211–216

Chan, S., & Stevens, A. H. (2001). The effects of job loss on older workers: Employment, earnings, and wealth. In P. P. Budetti, R. V. Burkhauser, J. M. Gregory, & H. A. Hunt (Eds.), *Ensuring health and income security for an aging workforce* (pp. 189–211). Kalamazoo, MI: W. E. Upjohn Institute for Employment Research.

Charman, C., Feinsod, R., & Arthurs, R. (2007). *AARP profit from experience: Perspectives of employers, workers, and policymakers in the G7 countries on the new demographic realities.* Washington, DC: AARP International.

Charters, S. (2008, January). *Age related policies: A global review on age discrimination legislation.* Montréal QC, Canada: International Federation on Aging.

Chen, Y., & Scott, J. C. (2006, January). *Phased retirement: Who opts for it and toward what end?* (Report # 2006-01). Washington, DC: AARP Public Policy Institute.

Christensen, K. (1990). Bridges over troubled water: How older workers view the labor market. In P. B. Doeringer (Ed.), *Bridges to retirement: Older workers in a changing labor market* (pp. 175–207). Ithaca, NY: ILR Press.

Clark, A. E., & Oswald, A. J. (1996). Satisfaction and comparison income. *Journal of Public Economics, 61,* 359–381.

Cleveland, J. N., Festa, R. M., & Montgomery, L. (1988). Applicant pool composition and job perceptions: Impact on decisions regarding an older applicant. *Journal of Vocational Behavior, 32,* 112–125.

Cleveland, J. N., & Hollman, G. (1990). The effects of the age-type of tasks and incumbent age composition on job perceptions. *Journal of Vocational Behavior, 36,* 181–194.

Cleveland, J. N., & Lim, A. S. (2004). Employee age and performance in organizations. In K. S. Shultz & G. A. Adams (Eds.), *Aging and work in the 21st century* (pp. 109–137). Mahwah, NJ: Erlbaum.

Costa, P. T., Jr., & McCrae, R. R. (1980). Still stable after all these years: Personality as a key to some issues in adulthood and old age. In P. B. Baltes & O. G. Brim, Jr. (Eds.), *Life span development and behavior* (Vol. 3, pp. 65–102). New York: Academic Press.

Costa, P. T., Jr., & McCrae, R. R. (2006). Age changes in personality and their origins: Comment on Roberts, Walton, and Viechtbauer (2006). *Psychological Bulletin, 132,* 26–28.

Craft, J. A., Doctors, S. I., Shkop, Y. M., & Benecki, T. J. (1979). Simulated management perceptions, hiring decisions and age. *Aging and Work, 2,* 95–102.

Czaja, S. J., & Sharit, J. (1993). Age differences in the performance of computer-based work. *Psychology & Aging, 8*(1), 59–67.

Czaja, S. J., & Sharit, J. (1998). Ability-performance relationships as a function of age and task experience for a data entry task. *Journal of Experimental Psychology: Applied, 4,* 332–351.

Deary, I. J., Whalley, L. J., & Starr, J. M. (2003). IQ at age 11 and longevity: Results from a follow-up of the Scottish Mental Survey 1932. In C. Finch, J. M. Robine, & Y. Christen (Eds.), *Brain and longevity: Perspectives in longevity* (pp. 153–164). Berlin: Springer-Verlag.

Deary, I. J., Whiteman, M. C., Starr, J. M., Whalley, L. J., & Fox, H. (2004). The impact of childhood intelligence on later life: Following up the Scottish Mental Surveys of 1932 and 1947. *Journal of Personality and Social Psychology, 86,* 130–147.

DeLong, D. W. (2004). *Lost knowledge: Confronting the threat of an aging workforce.* Oxford: Oxford University Press.

Dennis, H. (1988). Retirement planning. In H. Dennis (Ed.), *Fourteen steps in managing an aging work force* (pp. 215–229). Lexington, MA: Lexington.

Dennis, H., & Thomas, K. (2007). Ageism in the workplace. *Generations, 31*, 84–89.

DeViney, S., & O'Rand, A. M. (1988). Gender cohort succession and retirement among older men and women, 1951–1984. *Sociological Quarterly, 29*, 525–540.

Doering, M., Rhodes, S. R., & Schuster, M. (1983). *The aging worker: Research and recommendations*. Beverly Hills, CA: Sage.

Doeringer, P. B., & Terkla, D. G. (1990). Business necessity, bridge jobs, and the nonbureaucratic firm. In P. B. Doeringer (Ed.), *Bridges to retirement: Older workers in a changing labor market* (pp. 146–171). Ithaca, NY: ILR Press.

Dychtwald, K., Erickson, T. J., & Morison, B. (2004). It's time to retire. *Harvard Business Review*, 48–57.

Dychtwald, K., Erickson, T. J., & Morison, R. (2006). *Workforce crisis: How to beat the coming shortage of skills and talent*. Boston, MA: Harvard Business School Press.

Eby, L. T., Casper, W. J., Lockwood, A., Bordeaux, C., & Brinkley, A. (2005). Work and family research in IO/OB: Content analysis and review of the literature (1980–2002). *Journal of Vocational Behavior, 66*, 124–197.

Ekerdt, D. J., Hackney, J., Kosloski, K., & DeViney, S. (2001). Eddies in the stream: The prevalence of uncertain plans for retirement. *Journal of Gerontology, 56*(3), S162-S170.

Ellison, R., Melville, D., & Gutman, R. (1996). British labour force projections: 1996–2006. *Labour Market Trends, 104*, 197–213.

Erikson, E. (1959). Identity and the life cycle. *Psychological Issues, 1*, 18–164.

Eyster, L., Johnson, R. W., & Toder, E. (2008, January). *Current strategies to employ and retain older workers*. Washington, DC: The Urban Institute.

Faley, R. H., Kleiman, L. S., & Lengnick-Hall, M. L. (1984). Age discrimination and personnel psychology: A review and synthesis of the legal literature with implications for future research. *Personnel Psychology, 37*, 327–350.

Farr, J. L., Tesluk, P. E., & Klein, S. R. (1998). Organizational structure of the workplace and the older worker. In K. Schaie & C. Schooler (Eds.), *Impact of work on older adults* (pp. 143–185). New York: Springer.

Feinsod, R., Davenport, T., & Arthurs, R. (2005). *The business case for workers age 50+: Planning for tomorrow's talent needs in today's competitive environment*. Washington, DC: AARP Knowledge Management.

Feldman, D. C. (1994). The decision to retire early: A review and conceptualization. *Academy of Management Review, 19*, 285–311.

Feldman, D. C. (2002a). Advancing research on work careers. In D. Feldman (Ed.), *Work careers: A developmental perspective* (pp. 346–371). San Francisco: Jossey-Bass.

Feldman, D. C. (2002b). Stability in the midst of change. In D. Feldman (Ed.), *Work careers: A developmental perspective* (pp. 3–26). San Francisco: Jossey-Bass.

Feldman, D. C. (2007). Career mobility and career stability among older workers. In K. S. Shultz & G. A. Adams (Eds.), *Aging and work in the 21st century* (pp. 179–197). Mahwah, NJ: Erlbaum.

Ferraro, K. F., & Kelley-Moore, J. A. (2003). A half-century of longitudinal methods in social gerontology: Evidence of change in the journal. *Journal of Gerontology, 58*B, S264-S270.

Ferrer, E., Salthouse, T. A., McArdle, J. J., Stewart, W. F., & Schwartz, B. S. (2005). Multivariate modeling of age and retest in longitudinal studies of cognitive abilities. *Psychology and Aging, 20*, 412–422.

Finkel, D., Reynolds, C. A., McArdle, J. J., Gatz, M., & Pedersen, N. L. (2003). Latent growth curve analyses of accelerating decline in cognitive abilities in adulthood. *Developmental Psychology, 39*, 535–550.

Finkelstein, L. M., Burke, M. J., & Raju, N. S. (1995). Age discrimination in simulated employment contexts: An integrative analysis. *Journal of Applied Psychology, 80*, 652–663.

Finkelstein, L. M., & Farrell, S. K. (2007). An expanded view of age bias in the workplace. In K. S. Shultz & G. A. Adams (Eds.), *Aging and work in the 21st century* (pp. 73–108). Mahwah, NJ: Erlbaum.

Fisk, A. D., & Rogers, W. A. (2000). Influence of training and experience on skill acquisition and maintenance in older adults. *Journal of Aging and Physical Activity, 8*, 373–378.

Fisk, A. D., & Rogers, W. A. (2002). Psychology and aging: Enhancing the lives of an aging population. *Current Directions in Psychological Science, 11*, 107–110.

Fiske, S. T. (2004). *Social beings: A core motives approach to social psychology*. New York: Wiley.

Forte, C. S., & Hansvick, C. L. (1999). Applicant age as a subjective employability factor: A study of workers over and under fifty. *Journal of Employment Counseling, 36*, 24–34.

Forteza, J. A., & Prieto, J. M. (1994). Aging and work behavior. In H. C. Triandis & M. D. Dunnette (Eds.), *Handbook of industrial and organizational psychology* (2nd ed., Vol. 4, pp. 447–483). Palo Alto, CA: Consulting Psychologists Press.

Franklin, J. C. (2007). An overview of BLS projections to 2016. *Monthly Labor Review, 130*, 3–12.

Geipel, G. L. (March 3, 2003). *Global aging and the global workforce*. Washington, DC: Hudson Institute.

Gilbert, G. R., Collins, R. W., & Valenzi, E. (1993). Relationship of age and job performance: From the eye of the supervisor. *Journal of Employee Assistance Research, 2*, 36–46.

Gordon, R. A., & Arvey, R. D. (1986). Perceived and actual ages of workers. *Journal of Vocational Behavior, 28*, 21–28.

Gordon, R. A., & Arvey, R. D. (2004). Age bias in laboratory and field settings: A meta-analytic investigation. *Journal of Applied Social Psychology, 34*, 468–492.

Gough, H. G. (1996). *CPI manual* (3rd ed.). Palo Alto, CA: Consulting Psychologists Press.

Greller, M. M. (2000). Age norms and career motivation. *International Journal of Aging and Human Development, 50*, 215–226.

Greller, M. M., & Stroh, L. K. (1995). Careers in midlife and beyond: A fallow field in need of sustenance. *Journal of Vocational Behavior, 47*, 232–247.

Greller, M. M., & Stroh, L. K. (2003). Extending working lives: Are current approaches tools or talismans? In. G. A. Adams & T. A. Beehr (Eds.), *Retirement: Reasons, processes and results* (pp. 115–135). New York: Springer.

Gribbin, K., Schaie, K. W., & Parham, I. A. (1980). Complexity of life style and maintenance of intellectual abilities. *Journal of Social Issues, 36*, 47–61.

Gruber, A. L., & Schaie, K. W. (1986, November). *Longitudinal-sequential studies of marital assortativity*. Paper presented at the annual meeting of the Gerontological Society of America, Chicago.

Haan, N., Milsap, R., & Hartka, E. (1986). As time goes by: Change and stability in personality over 50 years. *Psychology and Aging, 1,* 220–232.

Haider, S. J., & Stephens, M. (2001). *The impact of displacement on older workers* (DRU-2631-NIA). Santa Monica, CA: Rand Center for the Study of Aging.

Hale, N. (1990). *The older worker: Effective strategies for management and human resource development.* San Francisco: Jossey-Bass.

Hall, D. T. (1986). An overview of current career development, theory, research, and practice. In D. T. Hall (Ed.), *Career development in organizations* (pp. 1–20). San Francisco: Jossey-Bass.

Hall, D. T., & Mirvis, P. H. (1995). The new career contract: Developing the whole person at midlife and beyond. *Journal of Vocational Psychology, 47,* 269–289.

Hanisch, K. A. (1999). Job loss and unemployment research from 1994–1998: A review and recommendations for research and intervention. *Journal of Vocational Behavior, 55,* 188–220.

Hansson, R. O., DeKoekkoek, P. D., Neece, W. M., & Patterson, D. W. (1997). Successful aging at work: Annual Review, 1992–1996: The older worker and transitions to retirement. *Journal of Vocational Behavior, 51,* 202–233.

Hassell, B. L., & Perrewe, P.L. (1993). An examination of the relationship between older workers' perceptions of age discrimination and employee psychological states. *Journal of Management Issues, 5,* 109–120.

Heckhausen, J., Dixon, R. A., & Baltes, P. B. (1989). Gains and losses in development throughout adulthood as perceived by different age groups. *Developmental Psychology, 25,* 109–121.

Hedge, J. W. (2008). Strategic human resource management and the older worker. *Journal of Workplace Behavioral Health, 23,* 109–123.

Hedge, J. W., Borman, W. C., & Lammlein, S. L. (2006). *The aging workforce: Realities, myths, and implications for organizations.* Washington, DC: APA Books.

Heidbreder, E. M. (1972). Factors in retirement adjustment, white collar/blue collar experience. *Industrial Gerontology, 12,* 69–74.

Helson, R., Jones, C., & Kwan, V. S. Y. (2002). Personality change in adulthood: Hierarchical Linear Modeling analyses of two longitudinal samples. *Journal of Personality and Social Psychology, 83,* 752–766.

Henretta, J. C., O'Rand, A. M., & Chan, C. G. (1993). Joint role investments and synchronization of retirement: A sequential approach to couples' retirement timing. *Social Forces, 71,* 981–1000.

Hertzog, C., & Nesselroade, J. R. (2003). Assessing psychological change in adulthood: An overview of methodological issues. *Psychology and Aging, 18,* 639–657.

Hertzog, C., Schaie, K. W., & Gribbin, K. (1978). Cardiovascular disease and changes in intellectual functioning from middle to old age. *Journal of Gerontology, 33,* 872–883.

House, J. S. (1998). Commentary: Age, work, and well-being: Toward a broader view. In K. Schaie & C. Schooler (Eds.), *Impact of work on older adults* (pp. 297–303). New York: Springer.

Hoyer, W. J. (1998). Commentary: The older individual in a rapidly changing work context: Developmental and cognitive issues. In K. W. Schaie & C. Schooler (Eds.), *Impact of work on older adults* (pp. 28–44). New York: Springer.

Hutchens, R., & Pappa, K. L. (2004). *Developments in phased retirement* (PRC WP 2004–14). Philadelphia: University of Pennsylvania, Wharton School. Pension Research Council Working Paper.

Jex, S. M., Wang, M., & Zarubin, A. (2007). Aging and occupational health. In K. S. Shultz & G. A. Adams (Eds.), *Aging and work in the 21st century* (pp. 199–223). Mahwah, NJ: Erlbaum.

Johnson, R. W. (2007, September). *Managerial attitudes toward older workers: A review of the evidence* (Discussion paper 07-05). Washington, DC: The Urban Institute.

Jones, C. J., & Meredith, W. (1996). Patterns of personality change across the life span. *Psychology and Aging, 11,* 57–65.

Kacmar, K. M., & Ferris, G. R. (1989). Theoretical and methodological considerations in the age-job satisfaction relationship. *Journal of Applied Psychology, 74,* 201–207.

Kanfer, R., & Ackerman, P. L. (2004). Aging, adult development, and work motivation. *Academy of Management Review, 29,* 440–458.

Kanfer, R., Wanberg, C. R., & Kantrowitz, T. M. (2001). Job search and employment: A personality-motivational analysis and meta-analytic review. *Journal of Applied Psychology, 86,* 837–855.

Kasschau, P. L. (1974). Re-evaluating the need for retirement preparation programs. *Industrial Gerontology, 14,* 42–59.

Kim, J. E., & Moen, P. (2001). Moving into retirement: Preparation and transitions in late midlife. In M. E. Lachman (Ed.), *Handbook of midlife development* (pp. 487–527). New York: John Wiley.

Kim, J. E., & Moen, P. (2002). Retirement transitions, gender, and psychological well-being: A life-course, ecological model. *Journal of Gerontology, 57*B, P212–222.

Kinsella, K., & Phillips, D. R. (2005, March). *Global aging: The challenge of success* (Population Bulletin, Vol. 60, No. 1). Washington, DC: Population Reference Bureau.

Kubeck, J. E., Delp, N. D., Haslett, T. K., & McDaniel, M. A. (1996). Does job-related training performance decline with age? *Psychology and Aging, 11,* 92–107.

Kulik, C. T., Perry, E. L., & Bourhis, A. C. (2000). Ironic evaluation processes: Effects of thought suppression on evaluations of older job applicants. *Journal of Organizational Behavior, 21,* 689–711.

Lawrence, B. S. (1987). An organizational theory of age effects. *Research in the Sociology of Organizations, 5,* 37–71.

Lawrence, B. S. (1988). New wrinkles in the theory of age demography norms and performance ratings. *Academy of Management Journal, 31,* 309–337.

Lawrence, B. S. (1996). Interest and indifference: The role of age in the organizational sciences. In G. R. Ferris (Ed.), *Research in personnel and human resources management* (pp. 1–59). Greenwich, CT: JAI Press.

Levine, M. L. (1988). Age discrimination: The law and its underlying policy. In H. Dennis (Ed.), *Fourteen steps in managing an aging work force* (pp. 25–35). Lexington, MA: Lexington Books.

Li, R. M., & Iadarola, A. C. (2007, March). *Why population aging matters: A global perspective* (Publication No. 07–6134). Washington, DC: National Institute on Aging, National Institutes of Health.

Lowe, G. (February 27, 2006). Are you ready to tap older workers' talents? *Canadian HR Reporter,* on the Internet at http://www.hrreporter.com (accessed January 21, 2007).

Maestas, N. (2005, August). *Back to work: Expectations and realizations of work after retirement* (WR-196–1). Rand Labor and Population working paper.

Marshall, V. W. (1998). Commentary: The older worker and organizational restructuring: Beyond systems theory. In K. W. Schaie & C. Schooler (Eds.), *Impact of work on older adults* (pp. 195–206). New York: Springer.

Masunaga, H., & Horn, J. L. (2001). Expertise and age-related changes in components of intelligence. *Psychology and Aging, 16*, 293–331.

Maurer, T. J. (2001). Career-relevant learning and development, worker age, and beliefs about self-efficacy for development. *Journal of Management, 27*, 123–140.

Maurer, T. J. (2007). Employee development and training issues related to the aging workforce. In K. S. Shultz & G. A. Adams (Eds.), *Aging and work in the 21st century* (pp. 163–177). Mahwah, NJ: Erlbaum.

Maurer, T. J., Wrenn, K. A., & Weiss, E. M. (2003). Toward understanding and managing stereotypical beliefs about older workers' ability and desire for learning and development. In J. J. Martocchio & G. R. Ferris (Eds.), *Research in personnel and human resources management* (Vol. 22, pp. 253–285). Stamford, CT: JAI Press.

McAdams, D. P. (2001). Generativity in midlife. In M. E. Lachman (Ed.), *Handbook of midlife development* (pp. 395–446). New York: Wiley.

McAdams, D. P., & de St. Aubin, E. (1998). *Generativity and adult development: How and why we care for the next generation.* Washington, DC: American Psychological Association.

McArdle, J. J., Ferrer-Caja, E., Hamagami, F., & Woodcock, R. W. (2002). Comparative longitudinal structural analyses of the growth and decline of multiple intellectual abilities over the life span. *Developmental Psychology, 38*, 115–142.

McArdle, J. J., & Hamagami, F. (2006). Longitudinal tests of dynamic hypotheses on intellectual abilities measured over sixty years. In C. S. Bergeman & S. M. Boker (Eds.), *Methodological issues in aging research* (pp. 43–98). Mahwah, NJ: Erlbaum.

McCann, L. (2003). *Age discrimination law: The slow drag to 2006.* Washington, D C: AARP Policy Institute.

McCann, L. (2006). *Age discrimination: A historical and contemporary analysis.* Cambridge, MA: Cambridge University Press.

McCrae, R. R., Costa, P. T., Jr., de Lima, M. P., Simões, A., Ostendorf, F., Angleitner A., Marušić, I., Bratko, D., Caprara, G. V., Barbaranelli, C., Chae, J. H., & Piedmont, R. L. (1999). Age differences in personality across the adult lifespan: Parallels in five cultures. *Developmental Psychology, 35*, 466–477.

McCrae, R. R., Costa, P. T., Jr., Ostendorf, F., Angleitner, A., Hrebickova, M., Avia, M. D., et al. (2000). Nature over nurture: Temperament, personality, and life span development. *Journal of Personality and Social Psychology, 78*, 173–186.

McDonald, R. B. (1988). The physiological aspects of aging. In H. Dennis (Ed.), *Fourteen steps in managing an aging work force* (pp. 39–51). Lexington, MA: Lexington Books.

McEvoy, G. M., & Cascio, W. F. (1989). Cumulative evidence of the relationship between employee age and job performance. *Journal of Applied Psychology, 74*, 11–17.

McKee-Ryan, F. M., Song, Z., Wanberg, C. R., & Kinicki, A. J. (2005). Psychological and physical well-being during unemployment: A meta-analytic study. *Journal of Applied Psychology, 90*, 53–76.

Menchin, R. S. (2000). *New work opportunities for older Americans.* New York: toExcel.

Meredith, W., & Tisak, J. (1990). Latent curve analysis. *Psychometrika, 55*, 107–122.

Miller, D. M., Cox, S., Gieson, M., Bean, C., Adams-Price, C., Sanderson, P., & Topping, J. S. (1993). Further development and validation of an age-based equal opportunity measure for organizations: An operational definition of ecological dissonance. *Psychology: A Journal of Human Behavior, 30*, 32–37.

Moen, P., & Fields, V. (2002). Midcourse in the United States: Does unpaid community participation replace paid work? *Ageing International, 27*, 21–48.

Moen, P., Kelly, E., & Huang, Q. (2008). Work, family, and life-course fit: Does control over work time matter? *Journal of Vocational Behavior, 73*, 414–425.

Moen, P., Sweet, S., & Swisher, R. (2005). Embedded career clocks: The case of retirement planning. In R. MacMillan (Ed.), *The structure of the life course: Standardized? Individualized? Differentiated? Advances in life course research* (Vol. 9, pp. 237–265). New York: Elsevier.

Monseau, S. (2005). Too old to work? The U.K. government's policy and proposals on banning age discrimination in the workforce to comply with new European law. *International Business Law Review, 5*, 1–15.

Montana, P. J. (1985). *Retirement programs: How to develop and implement them.* Englewood Cliffs, NJ: Prentice-Hall.

Morgeson, F. P., Reider, M. H., Campion, M. A., & Bull, R. A. (2008). Review of age discrimination in the employment interview. *Journal of Business Psychology, 22*, 223–232.

Morris, M. G., & Venkatesh, V. (2000). Age differences in technology adoption decisions: Implications for a changing work force. *Personnel Psychology, 53*, 375–403.

Moss, H. A., & Susman, E. J. (1980). Constancy and change in personality development. In O. G. Brim & J. Kagan (Eds.), *Constancy and change in human development* (pp. 530–595). Cambridge, MA: Harvard University Press.

Muhleisen, M., & Faruqee, H. (2001, March). Japan: Population aging and the fiscal challenge. *Finance and Development, 38*, 1–7.

Munson, H. (2003, March). *Valuing experience: How to motivate and retain mature workers* (Report # 1329-03-RR). New York: The Conference Board.

Mutran, E. J., Reitzes, D. C., & Fernandez, M. E. (1997). Factors that influence attitudes toward retirement. *Research on Aging, 19*, 251–273.

National Academy of Sciences (2001). *Preparing for an aging world: The case for cross-national research.* Panel on a research agenda and new data for an aging world, Committee on Population, Committee on National Statistics, National Research Council. Washington, DC: National Academy Press.

Nesselroade, J. R. (2006). Quantitative modeling in adult development and aging: Reflections and projections. In C. S. Bergeman & S. M. Boker (Eds.), *Methodological issues in aging research* (pp. 1–17). Mahwah, NJ: Erlbaum.

Neumark, D. (2008, June). *Reassessing the age discrimination in employment act.* Washington, DC: AARP Public Policy Institute.

Ng, T. W. H., & Feldman, D. C. (2008). The relationship of age to ten dimensions of job performance. *Journal of Applied Psychology, 93*, 392–423.

Nininger, J. R., & Scourtoudis, L. (2003, April). *Moving beyond the workplace: Exploring life's journey.* Ottawa: Canadian Centre for Management Development.

Novelli, W. D. (2002, February). *How aging boomers will affect American business.* Paper presented at the meeting of the meeting of The Wisemen, New York.

Organ, D. W. (1997). Organizational citizenship behavior: It's construct clean-up time. *Human Performance, 10*, 85–97.

Park, D. C. (1994). Aging, cognition, and work. *Human Performance, 7*, 181–205.

Paul, C. E. (1988). Implementing alternative work arrangements for older workers. In H. Dennis (Ed.), *Fourteen steps in managing an aging work force* (pp. 113–119). Lexington, MA: Lexington Books.

Penner, R. G. (2005). Adapting pensions to demographic change. In M. A. Taylor & R. M. S. Visser (Eds.), *Thriving on an aging workforce* (pp. 145–151). Malabar, FL: Krieger Publishing.

Penner, R. G., Perun, P., & Steuerle, E. (2002). *Legal and institutional impediments to partial retirement and part-time work by older workers.* Washington, DC: The Urban Institute.

Perry, E. L., Kulik, C. T., & Bourhis, A. C. (1996). Moderating effects of personal and contextual factors in age discrimination. *Journal of Applied Psychology, 81*, 628–647.

Peterson, D. A., & Wendt, P. F. (1995). Training and education of older Americans as workers and volunteers. In S. A. Bass (Ed.), *Older and active* (pp. 217–236). New Haven: Yale University Press.

Peterson, P. G. (1999). Gray dawn: The global aging crisis. *Foreign Affairs, 78*, 42–55.

Posthuma, R. A., & Campion, M. A. (2009). Age stereotypes in the workplace: Common stereotypes, moderators, and future research. *Journal of Management, 35*, 158–188.

Quinn, J. F., & Burkhauser, R. V. (1990). Work and retirement. In R. Binstock & L. George (Eds.), *Handbook of aging and the social sciences* (3rd ed., pp. 308–327). San Diego, CA: Academic Press.

Rappaport, A., Bancroft, E., & Okum, L. (2003). The aging workforce raises new talent management issues for employers. *Journal of Organizational Excellence, 23*, 55–66.

Rau, B. L., & Adams, G. A. (2005). Attracting retirees to apply: Desired organizational characteristics of bridge employment. *Journal of Organizational Behavior, 26*, 649–660.

Reynolds, C. A., Finkel, D., Gatz, M., & Pedersen, N. L. (2002). Sources of influences on rate of cognitive change over time in Swedish twins: An application of latent growth models. *Experimental Aging Research, 28*, 407–433.

Rhodes, S. R. (1983). Age-related differences in work attitudes and behavior: A review and conceptual analysis. *Psychological Bulletin, 93*, 328–367.

Richardson, V., & Kilty, K. (1992). Retirement intentions among black professionals: Implications for practice with older black adults. *The Gerontologist, 32*, 7–16.

Rix, S. E. (1990). *Older workers.* Santa Barbara: ABC-CLIO.

Rix, S. E. (2004, February). *Aging and work: A view from the United States* (Report #2004-02). Washington, DC: AARP Public Policy Institute.

Roberts, B. W., Caspi, A., & Moffitt, T. E. (2003). Work experiences and personality development in young adulthood. *Journal of Personality and Social Psychology, 84*, 582–593.

Roberts, B. W., Helson, R., & Klohnen, E. (2002). Personality development and growth in women across 30 years: Three perspectives. *Journal of Personality, 70*, 79–102.

Roberts, B. W., Walton, K. E., & Viechtbauer, W. (2006a). Patterns of mean-level change in personality traits across the life course: A meta-analysis of longitudinal studies. *Psychological Bulletin, 132*, 1–25.

Roberts, B. W., Walton, K. E., & Viechtbauer, W. (2006b). Personality traits change in adulthood: Reply to Costa and McCrae (2006). *Psychological Bulletin, 132*, 29–32.

Robson, W. B. P. (2001, October). *Aging populations and the workforce: Challenges for employers.* Winnipeg, Manitoba: British-North American Committee.

Rosen, B., & Jerdee, T. H. (1976a). The influence of age stereotypes on managerial decisions. *Journal of Applied Psychology, 62*, 428–432.

Rosen, B., & Jerdee, T. H. (1976b). The nature of job-related age stereotypes. *Journal of Applied Psychology, 61*, 180–183.

Rosen, B., & Jerdee, T. H. (1985). *Older employees: New roles for valued resources.* Homewood, IL: Dow-Jones-Irwin.

Ruhm, C. J. (1990). Career jobs, bridge employment, and retirement. In P. B. Doeringer (Ed.), *Bridges to retirement: Older workers in a changing labor market* (pp. 92–107). Ithaca, NY: ILR Press.

Salthouse, T. A. (1990). Working memory as a processing resource in cognitive aging. *Developmental Review, 10*, 101–124.

Salthouse, T. A., & Maurer, J. J. (1996). Aging, job performance, and career development. In J. E. Birren & K. W. Schaie (Eds.), *Handbook of the psychology of aging* (4th ed., pp. 353–364). New York: Academic Press.

Schaie, K. W. (1983). The Seattle longitudinal study: A 21-year exploration of psychometric intelligence in adulthood. In K. W. Schaie (Ed.), *Longitudinal studies of adult psychological development* (pp. 31–44). New York: Springer.

Schaie, K. W. (1993). The Seattle longitudinal studies of adult intelligence. *Current Directions in Psychological Science, 2*, 171–175.

Schaie, K. W. (1994). The course of adult intellectual development. *American Psychologist, 49*, 304–313.

Schaie, K. W., & Willis, S. L. (1986). Can intellectual decline in the elderly be reversed? *Developmental Psychology, 22*, 223–232.

Schappe, S. P. (1998). The influence of job satisfaction, organizational commitment, and fairness perceptions on organizational citizenship behavior. *Journal of Psychology, 132*, 277–290.

Schetagne, S. (2001). *Building bridges across generations in the workplace: A response to aging of the workforce* (Report # 702). Vancouver, BC: Columbia Foundation.

Schmitt, N., White, J. K., Coyle, B. W., & Rauschenberger, J. (1979). Retirement and life satisfaction. *Academy of Management Journal, 22*, 282–291.

Schneider, B., Goldstein, H. W., & Smith, D. B. (1995). The ASA framework: An update. *Personnel Psychology, 40*, 747–773.

Schneider, B., Smith, D. B., Taylor, S., & Fleenor, J. (1998). Personality and organizations: A test of the homogeneity of personality hypothesis. *Journal of Applied Psychology, 83*, 462–470.

Schooler, C., Caplan, L., & Oates, G. (1998). Aging and work: An overview. In K. W. Schaie & C. Schooler (Eds.), *Impact of work on older adults* (pp. 1–19) New York: Springer.

Scottish Council for Research in Education (SCRE). (1933). *The intelligence of Scottish children: A national survey of an age-group.* London: University of London Press.

Shea, G. F. (1991). *Managing older employees.* San Francisco: Jossey-Bass.

Sheppard, H. L., & Rix, S. E. (1977). *The graying of working America: The coming crisis in retirement-age policy.* New York: Free Press.

Shore, L. M., & Goldberg, C. B. (2004). Age discrimination in the work place. In R. L. Dipboye and A. Colella (Eds.), *The psychological and organizational bases of discrimination at work* (pp. 203–225). Mahwah, NJ: Erlbaum.

Shultz, K. S. (2003). Bridge employment. In G. A. Adams & T. A. Beehr (Eds.), *Retirement: Reasons, processes, and results* (pp. 214–241). New York: Springer.

Shultz, K. S., & Adams, G. A. (Eds.). (2007). *Aging and work in the 21st century*. Mahwah, NJ: Erlbaum.

Shultz, K. S., & Wang, M. (2008). The changing nature of mid and late careers. In C. Wankel (Ed.), *The handbook of 21st century management* (pp. 130–138). Thousand Oaks, CA: Sage.

Simon, R. (1996, July). Too damn old. *Money, 25*(7), 118–126.

Simpson, P. A., Greller, M. M., & Stroh, L. K. (2001). Variations in human capital investment activity by age. *Journal of Vocational Behavior, 61*, 109–138.

Smith, P., Kendall, L., & Hulin, C. (1969). *The measurement of satisfaction of work and retirement*. Chicago: Rand McNally

Sonnenfeld, J. (1988). Continued work contributions in late career. In H. Dennis (Ed.), *Fourteen steps in managing an aging work force* (pp. 191–211). Lexington, MA: Lexington.

Sparks, K., Faragher, B., & Cooper, C. L. (2001). Well-being and occupational health in the 21st century. *Journal of Occupational and Organizational Psychology, 74*, 489–510.

Stein, A. W. (2002). The new face of the workforce. *HR Magazine, 47*, 1–6.

Sterns, A. A., Sterns, H. L., & Hollis, L. A. (1996). The productivity and functional limitation of older adult workers. In W. Crown (Ed.), *Handbook on employment and the elderly* (pp. 276–303). Westport, CT: Greenwood Press.

Sterns, H. L., & Alexander, R. A. (1987). Industrial gerontology: The aging individual and work. In K. Schaie (Ed.), *Annual review of gerontology and geriatrics* (pp. 93–113). New York: Springer.

Sterns, H. L., Barrett, G. V., & Alexander, R. A. (1985). Accidents and the aging individual. In J. E. Birrin & K. W. Schaie (Eds.), *Handbook of the psychology of aging* (pp. 703–724). New York: Van Nostrand Reinhold.

Sterns, H. L., & Doverspike, D. (1988). Training and developing the older worker: Implications for human resource management. In H. Dennis (Ed.), *Fourteen steps in managing an aging work force* (pp. 97–110). Lexington, MA: Lexington Books.

Sterns, H. L., Doverspike, D., & Lax, G. A. (2005). The age discrimination in employment act. In F. S. Landy (Eds.), *Employment discrimination litigation: Behavioral, quantitative, and legal perspectives* (pp. 256–293). San Francisco: Jossey-Bass.

Sterns, H. L., & Gray, J. H. (1999). Work, leisure, and retirement. In J. C. Cavanaugh & S. K. Whitbourne (Eds.), *Gerontology: An interdisciplinary perspective* (pp. 355–390). New York: Oxford University Press.

Sterns, H. L., & Huyck, M. H. (2001). The role of work in midlife. In M. E. Lachman (Ed.), *Handbook of midlife development* (pp. 447–486). New York: John Wiley.

Sterns, H. L., & Kaplan, J. (2003). Self-management of career and retirement. In G. A. Adams & T. A. Beehr (Eds.), *Retirement: Reasons, processes, and results* (pp. 188–213). New York: Springer.

Sterns, H. L., & Miklos, S. M. (1995). The aging worker in a changing environment: Organizational and individual issues. *Journal of Vocational Behavior, 47*, 248–268.

Sterns, H. L., & Sterns, A. A. (1995). Health and the employment capability of older Americans. In S. A. Bass (Ed.), *Older and active* (pp. 10–34). New Haven: Yale University Press.

Sturman, M. C. (2003). Searching for the inverted U-shaped relationship between time and performance: Meta-analyses of the experience/performance, tenure/performance, and age/performance relationships. *Journal of Management, 29*, 609–640.

Szinovacz, M. E. (2003). Contexts and pathways: Retirement as institution, process, and experience. In G. A. Adams & T. A. Beehr (Eds.), *Retirement: Reasons, processes, and results* (pp. 6–52). New York: Springer.

Talaga, J. A., & Beehr, T. A. (1995). Are there gender differences in predicting retirement? *Journal of Applied Psychology, 80*, 16–28.

Taylor, M. A., & Doverspike, D. (2003). Retirement planning and preparation. In G. A. Adams & T. A. Beehr (Eds.), *Retirement: Reasons, processes, and results* (pp. 53–82). New York: Springer.

Taylor, M. A., Shultz, K. S., & Doverspike, D. (2005). Academic perspectives on recruiting and retaining older workers. In M. A. Taylor & R. M. S. Visser (Eds.), *Thriving on an aging workforce* (pp. 43–50). Malabar, FL: Krieger Publishing.

Terracciano, A., McCrae, R. R., Brant, L. J., & Costa, P. T., Jr. (2005). Hierarchical linear modeling analyses of the NEO-PI-R scales in the Baltimore Longitudinal Study of Aging. *Psychology and Aging, 20*, 493–506.

Thompson, L., Griffiths, A., & Davison, S. (2000). Employee absence, age and tenure: A study of nonlinear effects and trivariate models. *Work and Stress, 14*, 16–34.

Thornton, W. J. L., & Dumke, H. A. (2005). Age differences in everyday problem-solving and decision-making effectiveness: A meta-analytic review. *Psychology and Aging, 20*, 85–99.

Toossi, M. (2007). Labor force projections to 2016: More workers in their golden years. *Monthly Labor Review, 130*, 33–52.

United States Government Accountability Office (2007, February). *Engaging and retaining older workers: Highlights of a GAO forum* (GAO-07-438SP). Washington, DC.

Valetta, R. (1991). Job tenure and joblessness of displaced workers. *Journal of Human Resources, 26*, 726–744.

Van Solinge, H., & Henkens, K. (2005). Couples' adjustment to retirement: A multi-actor panel study. *Journal of Gerontology Series B: Psychological and Social Sciences, 60*, S11-S20.

Van Solinge, H., & Henkens, K. (2008). Adjustment to and satisfaction with retirement: Two of a kind. *Psychology and Aging, 23*, 422–434.

Waldman, D. A., & Avolio, B. J. (1986). A meta-analysis of age differences in job performance. *Journal of Applied Psychology, 71*, 33–38.

Wanberg, C. R. (1997). Antecedents and outcomes of coping behaviors among unemployed and reemployed individuals. *Journal of Applied Psychology, 82*, 731–744.

Wang. M. (2007). Profiling retirees in the retirement transition and adjustment process: Examining the longitudinal change patterns of retirees' psychological well-being. *Journal of Applied Psychology, 92*, 455–474.

Wang, M., Zhan, Y., Liu, S., & Shultz, K. S. (2008). Antecedents of bridge employment: A longitudinal investigation. *Journal of Applied Psychology, 93*, 818–830.

Warr, P. (1994). Age and employment. In H. C. Triandis, M. D. Dunnette, & L. M. Hough (Eds.), *Handbook of industrial and organizational psychology* (2nd ed., Vol. 4, pp. 485–550). Palo Alto, CA: Consulting Psychologists Press.

Warr, P. (1998). Age, work, and mental health. In K. W. Schaie & C. Schooler (Eds.), *Impact of work on older adults* (pp. 252–303). New York: Springer.

Warr, P. (2001). Age and work behaviour: Physical attributes, cognitive abilities, knowledge, personality traits, and motives. *International Review of Industrial and Organizational Psychology, 16*, 1–36.

Weckerle, J. R., & Schultz, K. S. (1999). Influences on the bridge employment decision among older USA workers. *Journal of Occupational and Organizational Psychology, 72*, 317–329.

Wegman, D. H., & McGee, J. P. (Eds.). (2004). *Health and safety needs of older workers*. Washington, DC: National Academies Press.

Wellner, A. S. (2002, March). Tapping a silver mine. *HR Magazine, 47*, 26–32.

Whalley, L. J., & Deary, I. J. (2001). Longitudinal cohort study of childhood IQ and survival up to age 76. *British Medical Journal, 322*, 1–5.

Williams, S., & Shaw, W. T. (1999). Mood and organizational citizenship behavior: The effects of positive affect on employee organizational citizenship behavior intentions. *Journal of Psychology, 133*, 656–668.

Willis, S. L., & Schaie, K. W. (1986). Training the elderly on the ability factors of spatial orientation and inductive reasoning. *Psychology and Aging, 1*, 239–247.

Wren, K., & Mauer, T. (2004). Beliefs about older workers' learning and development behavior in relation to beliefs about malleability of skills, age-related decline, and control. *Journal of Applied Social Psychology, 34*, 223–242.

Yeatts, D. L., Folts, W. E., & Knapp, J. (2000). Older workers' adaptation to a changing workplace: Employment issues for the 21st century. *Educational Gerontology, 26*, 566–582.

PART 10

Technology, System Design, and Human Performance

An Overview of Human Factors Psychology

Alex Kirlik

Abstract

This chapter presents a contemporary overview of human factors psychology, including its origins, core problems, methodological approaches, and overviews of state-of-the-art research in three key areas likely to be relevant to industrial/organizational psychology. These include: human-automation interaction, or HAI; situation awareness, or SA; and distraction, multitasking, and interruption, or DMI. Each of these areas has arisen as a result of the increased challenges and opportunities provided by ever increasing levels of technological sophistication in the workplace. The chapter concludes by noting that human factors researchers are increasingly drawing on, and contributing to, social, in addition to cognitive, psychological research. This trend, motivated by both increasing levels of technological autonomy and opacity, as well as by the fact that social coordination and teamwork is increasingly mediated by information and communication technologies, bodes well for human factors and industrial/organizational psychology to have an even greater symbiotic and mutually informing relationship in the future.

Key Words: Human factors, human-technology interaction, applied cognition, representative design, human-automation interaction, situation awareness, distraction, multitasking, interruption

Over 50 years have passed since Paul Fitts wrote the inaugural article on "Engineering Psychology" for the *Annual Review of Psychology* (Fitts, 1958). In the eighth such article with the same title, Howell (1993) noted that the areas of psychology contributing to human factors had broadened well beyond applied experimental psychology to the point where engineering psychology "may well be disappearing as an identifiable specialty" (p. 232). Consistent with Howell's (1993) observation, in the most recent *Annual Review* article in this area, Proctor and Vu (2009) chose to use the term *human factors* rather than *engineering psychology* in order to "include the full range of psychological research relevant to designing for human use" (p. 4.2).

Proctor and Vu's (2009) decision to describe the discipline of human factors as psychological research relevant to design, however, remains fully consistent with the initial definition of the discipline provided by Fitts (1958). To delimit the territory covered in his own review article, Fitts (1958) wrote that he had excluded all psychological research that did "not involve machine or system design variables, or have implications for design problems" (p. 267). Accordingly, the focus of the current chapter remains true to this tradition and is thus restricted in scope to psychological research with design relevance and, more specifically, to those areas of human factors psychology most likely to be relevant to the concerns of industrial and organizational (I/O) psychology.

Proctor and Vu's (2009) choice to use the more inclusive term *human factors* is apt for other reasons as well. As discussed in the following chapters in this section of the handbook, on naturalistic decision making, cognition and technology, and system design, those concerned with psychological issues associated with the design of interactive technologies or technological work contexts today are just as likely to come from engineering, computer science (especially human-computer interaction; see Olson & Olson, 2003), informatics and other related disciplines as they are from psychology. Although few would doubt that research at the intersection of humans and technology design does not benefit by being informed by as many perspectives as possible, the large and rapidly growing multidisciplinary literature in this area can be confusing to those largely seeking to mine lessons learned from a psychological science perspective.

As such, it is useful to introduce a review of the human factors literature for a handbook such as this by attempting to describe the particular concerns shared and contributions made by those approaching this area from the perspective of human factors psychology. The purpose of the following section is to provide just such a focus, both as an orientation to, and a motivation for, the material to be covered in the remainder of the chapter. A second purpose of this section is to alert the reader to the fact that, while the first *Annual Review* article on design-relevant psychological research may have appeared as recently as 50 years ago, the intellectual and social issues at stake have a much longer history.

Human Factors Psychology and the Legacy of Thamus

Questions dealing with the consequences of inventions, tools, and technologies for human society, and for individual cognition and performance, have been the topic of concern and inquiry for millennia. In Plato's *Phaedrus*, Socrates tells us of the Egyptian king Thamus being regaled by the god Theuth, the originator of many wondrous inventions such as calculation, geometry, and writing. Among Theuth's urgings that these novelties should be made widely available to all the king's subjects, when Theuth came to the particular topic of writing he declared to Thamus:

> "Here is an accomplishment, my lord the King, which will improve both the wisdom and the memory of the Egyptians. I have discovered a sure receipt for memory and wisdom."
> (Plato, 1973, p. 96)

Thamus was having none of it. Of what he took to be the likely consequences of writing spreading broadly throughout his kingdom, he responded to Theuth:

> "Those who acquire it will cease to exercise their memory and become forgetful; they will rely on writing to bring things to their remembrance by external signs instead of their own internal resources. What you have discovered is a receipt for recollection, not memory. And as for wisdom, your pupils will have a reputation for it without the reality: they will receive a quantity of information without proper instruction, and in consequence be thought very knowledgeable when they are for the most part ignorant."
> (*Plato*, 1973, p. 96)

The logic of this dialogue continues to this day. No better proof is the media hubbub that arose in 2008 in response to Nicholas Carr's article "Is Google Making Us Stupid?" in the *Atlantic*. Carr's (2008) critique of Google, and his admission that his powers of concentration and sustained attention seemed to be slipping away as he made more and more use of the Internet, resonated with countless readers. While the debate continues, together with Plato's king Thamus, with this much, at least, we can all agree: "...the discoverer of an art is not the best judge of the good or harm which will accrue to those who practice it" (Plato, 1973, p. 96).

The rapid changes brought about by modern information and communication technologies and workplace automation should be of interest to the I/O psychologist because they bear directly on central, practical problems, such as job design, performance, training, selection, evaluation, teamwork, organizational design and learning, workplace safety and occupational health. It is also possible, if not likely, that research devoted to achieving a better understanding of the consequences of technology in the workplace may even contribute to fundamental issues of theory and method in I/O psychology. Perhaps the most obvious reason is that, unlike Plato's (1973) king Thamus, we all now recognize that these consequences are hardly simple, intuitive, or obvious, and hardly unequivocal as to their positive versus negative effects. Reflecting on the interchange between Thamus and Theuth in *Phaedrus*, the social critic and communications theorist Neil Postman noted that:

> Thamus' error is in his belief that writing will be a burden to society and nothing but a burden. For

all his wisdom, he fails to imagine what writing's benefits might be, which, as we know, have been considerable. We may learn from this that it is a mistake to suppose that any technological innovation has a one-sided effect. Every technology is both a blessing and a burden, not either-or, but this-and-that.

(*Postman*, 1993, pp. 4–5)

Postman (1993) notes correctly that every technology is likely to be both a blessing and a burden, and this observation helps us to understand how much of the research activity on the intersection of cognition and technology is organized today.

In large part, contemporary researchers and scholars working at the intersection of cognition and technology can be classified into those groups who focus their efforts largely on the good, versus those who focus largely on the harm, that accrues to those who either choose, or are required, to interact with environments of ever-increasing technological sophistication. Although some research in human-computer interaction (HCI), for example, is devoted to identifying the negative consequences of the widespread computerization of the workplace (e.g., Czerwinski, Horvitz, & Wilhite, 2004), much more attention in HCI is given to the conceptualization, design, and testing of novel, often profitable, and even entertaining information and communication technologies, as well as their associated "applications," such as software packages, videoconferencing systems, video games, and cell phone shareware.

Those engaged in the pursuit of such aims often give the appearance of viewing the benefits of technological advancement as wholly self-evident, and they typically display little explicit attention to anticipating any negative consequences of these creations for their intended users. Related comments apply to many engineers engaged in designing and deploying automation in industrial settings and in such contexts as transportation and service systems, including heath care and retail. For reasons that are beyond the scope of the current discussion, the onus today is typically squarely placed upon the advocate of existing levels of technology and automation to defend the status quo in the face of pressures coming from those urging increased levels of technological sophistication.

In human factors psychology, in contrast, the emphasis is largely reversed. Although some human factors researchers have indeed focused on describing and analyzing how tools and artifacts benefit cognition in terms of "cognitive amplification" (Nickerson, 2005), it is fair to say that the lion's share of human factors research conducted by experimental and cognitive psychologists nevertheless focuses much more heavily on identifying the (often unforeseen) negative consequences or side effects of increased levels of technology and automation.

It may be tempting to infer that many human factors psychologists have this orientation solely because engineers and technologists are typically not trained to consider the human factor (capabilities, limitations, preferences, etc.) in design, as rarely is a course in human factors a required component of an engineering education (Pew & Mavor, 2007). However, this is likely to be only half the story. In a thoughtful accounting, Klatzky (2009) notes that, after a long history of deep concern with practical problems (e.g., Munsterberg, Thorndike, Broadbent, etc.), psychological science today often speaks strongly of its devotion to everyday relevance, yet tends to offer not applications but instead "promissory notes" (p. 528). Of contemporary academic psychology, Klatzky writes, "Find me the apps!" (p. 524):

> Consider the contrast between psychology and other fields. Engineers and computer scientists perform and publish research, file for patents on the ensuing widgets and software, and perhaps spin off companies. Academic psychologists tend to stop at the perform-and-publish stage.
>
> (*Klatzky*, 2009, p. 527)

My own experience as a researcher with one foot set squarely in the engineering of human-technology systems, and the other in a recognition of the demand, and opportunity, to draw upon and even extend psychological theory in doing so, is largely consistent with Klatzky's (2009) observations. I have even heard of graduate students in various psychology programs counseled to avoid gaining a reputation as being interested in "applied" problems, as if this stigma would put a premature end to what would otherwise prove to be a successful academic career. And I know of very few degree programs at the undergraduate level in psychology that produce students capable of joining and immediately making much-needed contributions to industry in engineering and technology design.

Future such programs would require psychology curricula on psychological theory and method to be complemented with coursework (and even labs and studios) on technology and design. To fully appreciate the nature of Klatzky's (2009) lament that application is not taken more seriously in psychological science, especially in light of the many practically relevant contributions provided by specialized fields such as human factors and I/O psychology, it is informative to note that Klatzky (2009) considers these two specialties to be "whole applied fields" that were "spun off" from psychological science in the years since World War II (p. 522).

While both human factors psychologists and I/O psychologists may find it peculiar to see their disciplines described as spin-offs of psychological science, this view is not uncommon among scientists with the naïve view that applications appear only after the basic science has been done. In contrast, recent scholarship such as Stokes (1997) convincingly demonstrates that the belief that practically relevant applications arise solely from pure or basic science is both surprisingly recent, and also at odds with many historical facts. Clearly, my colleagues in engineering disciplines hardly ever understand or describe their fields to be spin-offs of basic science—putting a human being on the moon required enormous advances in engineering, coupled with some additional scientific advancements, in a simultaneous, mutually informing fashion. As such, it may be fair to characterize disciplines such as human factors, I/O psychology, and related areas such as human-computer interaction to be the heirs and champions of what Stokes (1997) described as "Use-Inspired Basic Research," in the spirit of Louis Pasteur, among the contemporary social and behavioral sciences. Pasteur is famous for not only inventing procedures and vaccines that have saved countless lives, but is one of the founders of the science of microbiology and the germ theory of disease.

So it is probably no wonder that the design of many current interactive systems and technological workplaces reflect a mix of excessive engineering exuberance and psychological naïveté. Although much is said of the value of inter- and multidisciplinary (or "translational") research and the gains made in this direction, in large measure these gains have yet to trickle down into similar enhancements to undergraduate degree programs in either engineering or psychology. In short, we may well be getting the technological products and services we deserve, given our current, highly disciplinary educational offerings.

At any rate, and as a proper overview of human factors psychology, the current chapter will follow suit with tradition and will focus on some of the most important problems occupying the attention of human factors psychologists, and the implications of their research for understanding and supporting human cognition and performance in technological workplaces. Complementary perspectives, that is, those that focus on design itself as a synthetic activity, rather than on the consequences of design, and on conceptual frameworks other than those central to psychological science for the analysis and support of cognitive work, can be found in the following chapters in this section of the handbook.

More specifically, the overview provided in the following is organized in terms of an introductory section on contemporary methodological issues in human factors psychology, followed by a review of research in three areas that have garnered a significant amount of attention from human factors psychologists in recent years. These areas are:

1. Human-automation interaction (HAI): Frameworks for understanding the psychological consequences of automation, the effects of imperfect automation on worker reliance and compliance, factors that moderate worker trust or distrust in automation, and ethical issues surrounding the use of automation in the workplace.

2. Situation awareness (SA): Frameworks for understanding the psychological consequences of technologically mediated (rather than direct) engagement with the objects of work, how the construct can be modeled and measured, and the nature of interventions to overcome the cognitive distancing associated with viewing work through a technological lens.

3. Distraction, multitasking, and interruption (DMI): Frameworks for understanding the psychological consequences of work environments in which technology either provides or requires a significant amount of time-shared or rapidly interleaved cognitive activity.

These three areas account for a significant amount of research performed by human factors psychologists in recent decades. Each is directly attributable to the rapidly increased availability or prevalence of information and communication technology and automation in the workplace over this period.

Contemporary Methodology in Human Factors Psychology

While human factors research today is characterized by a healthy and diverse reliance on a variety methods and approaches, the past decades have seen some general trends. First, although a few studies employ the largely correlational methods often used in the study of abilities, intelligence, personality, and individual differences more generally, human factors psychology remains largely an experimental science focused on identifying regularities in the cognition and behavior of humans as a species, or on average, within technological environments of various designs. While the importance of individual differences has been recognized (e.g., one of the 23 technical groups of the Human Factors and Ergonomics Society is devoted to this research area), this type of research has largely been the exception rather than the rule in human factors.

As such, while some other types of research central to I/O psychology focus on mapping various dimensions and spaces of individual differences of various kinds, human factors focuses more heavily on mapping the dimensions and spaces of "environmental differences" (Kirlik, 2005; Preiss & Sternberg, 2006). This is only natural, as the human factors practitioner's major leverage is design manipulation, rather than who will come to encounter the design. As such, human factors researchers largely seek main effects of design differences, such as different interface modalities, as key determinants of human learning and performance. As a result, individual differences are largely, if unfortunately, consigned to the error term.

Only very recently has a critical mass of human factors research begun to emerge that focuses on individual differences in relation to technology (Szalma, 2009). These studies include the use of molecular genetics to understand individual differences in selective attention, working memory and vigilance (Parasuraman, 2009), differences in vulnerability to task-induced stress and their possible ties to personality variables such as neuroticism (Mathews & Campbell, 2009), and differences with respect to preference for display modality (e.g., visual, auditory, or both) with implications for interface design (Baldwin, 2009).

Second, and as foreshadowed by the previously cited comment by Howell (1993) on the gradual disappearance of engineering psychology as an identifiable specialty, much human factors research remains grounded in experimental methods, but has found a need to supplement the traditional methods of experimental psychology with others to ensure a reliable degree of generalization of experimental findings to target (often called "operational") contexts or work environments. Human factors researchers have a relatively immediate obligation to ensure that design guidance based on experimentation transcends the context of scientific discovery and justification (i.e., the laboratory)—an obligation that may not so strongly characterize some other areas of academic psychology (the study of expertise is a notable exception: see Ericsson & Williams, 2007, on the need for representatively designed tasks to tap into expert knowledge and abilities, and Tuffiash, Roring, & Ericsson, 2007, for an elegant illustration in the context of elite and expert SCRABBLE players).

As such, contemporary human factors researchers are increasingly performing their experiments in conditions that closely resemble or represent the conditions to which they desire their findings to generalize (in high-fidelity simulations, "scaled worlds," "microworlds," and "synthetic task environments"; see Gray, 2002). This stands in contrast to the types of relatively more spartan experimental tasks (or laboratory paradigms) characteristic of the applied experimental psychology approach that dominated engineering psychology research of the 1960s–1980s. One lesson that has been slowly learned by human factors psychologists (not in the least because it is largely omitted in many standard psychology textbooks on experimental methodology) is that the types of inferential statistics, such as analysis of variance, or ANOVA (on which students are rigorously trained), were designed to guarantee statistical generalization from the experimental subjects (participants) studied to the larger population from which they were sampled, yet they provide no similar guarantee of generalization from the conditions studied to conditions other than those of the experiment.

This asymmetry, noted originally by Brunswik (1955, 1956; also see Dhami, Hertwig, & Hoffrage, 2004; Hammond & Stewart, 2001) has prompted many of those conducting research in human factors psychology to complement inferential techniques such as ANOVA (e.g., in testing various hypotheses about design or training interventions) with at least a gesture toward, if not full acceptance of, Brunswik's (1956) methodological program of representative design. This methodology was motivated, in part, to try to eliminate fruitless debates about the laboratory versus the "real world," and to reorient the focus of attention on the degree to which the context of research represents, in psychologically and behaviorally meaningful ways, the class of contexts to which the generalization of scientific findings is intended. Rogers (2008) put the matter in the following way in an editorial upon accepting editorship of the *Journal of Experimental Psychology: Applied*:

> Hallmarks of any good research are internal and external validity, and this may be especially important to consider in the context of applied research (see Shadish, Cook, & Campbell, 2002). One issue that is particularly important to the concept of external validity is representative design. Egon Brunswik is credited with delineating the importance of representative design for psychological research and developing the concept of ecological validity to describe the "trustworthiness" or predictive validity of environmental cues (for a review see Hammond & Stewart, 2001, *The Essential Brunswik*). Unfortunately, since the original work was published (e.g., Brunswik, 1949) those terms have somehow become merged in the psychologist's lexicon. In the interest of historical purity, if authors mean that their experimental context resembles the situation to which they wish to generalize, they should use the term "representative."
>
> A disturbingly frequent phrase that I have observed in submissions to *JEP: Applied* is "the real world" or "in real life." These expressions are empty. Hammond and Stewart (2001) said it best: "The real trouble with introducing the terms real world or real life and the reason that they should be abandoned is that they are simply low-grade escape mechanisms; their use makes it unnecessary to define the conditions toward which the generalization is intended. One need only assume (without evidence) that everyone knows what these terms entail" (pp. 7–8). Instead, authors should be specific about the situations to which they expect their results to generalize.
>
> (*Rogers*, 2008, pp. 1–2)

Those interested in additional lessons learned from human factors researchers who are striving to simultaneously inform psychological theory as well as achieve practical relevance beyond the context of scientific inquiry should see Rogers, Pak, and Fisk (2007) for an informative discussion of a variety of misconceptions that some psychologists appear to share about the relationship between basic and applied psychological research. Those interested in learning more about the methodology of representative design and how it has been employed in a diverse variety of human factors research contexts should see Goldstein (2006). The body of research discussed by Goldstein (2006) was conducted by those who explicitly and self-consciously framed their research in terms of Brunswik's methodology

of representative design in an attempt to simultaneously strive for a reasonable level of fidelity in representing central aspects of the contexts to which they intended their research to generalize, and an ability to test hypotheses to identify and verify cause-effect relations from empirical data.

Overviews of Contemporary Research Areas in Human Factors Psychology

I now turn to providing an overview of contemporary human factors research in three areas of increasing importance in today's workplace: (a) human-automation interaction (HAI); (b) situation awareness (SA); and (c) distraction, multitasking, and interruption (DMI). Prior to doing so, a few words are necessary to place contemporary research in these areas into their proper historical perspective. As has been already discussed, the past few decades have witnessed a general, though by no means complete, shift in human factors psychology from the study of tightly controlled experimental situations that sacrifice much of the complexity and structure representative of operational or natural work environments to experiments in higher fidelity simulations or tasks that represent more of this environmental complexity or structure.

It is important to note that this shift is largely a reflection of the changing nature of the environments of concern to human factors, and not in any way a repudiation of previous research conducted using more traditional engineering psychology methodology. Those methods were perfectly adequate for addressing human factors problems associated with achieving an efficient coupling between humans and their immediately available, proximal interfaces or physical workplaces. In addition, and as will be seen in the following, those methods remain largely adequate for performing research in at least one of the three topical areas to be reviewed below: distraction, multitasking, and interruption (DMI). Contemporary DMI research can largely be viewed as a continuation of human factors psychology's long-standing concern with selective, divided, and focused attention and time-sharing (Kramer, Wiegmann, & Kirlik, 2007; Moray, 1993; Wickens, 1980, 1989, 2004). However, even those currently performing DMI research have also found it useful, and in some cases necessary, to augment traditional hypothesis-testing methods with the use of higher fidelity simulations or task environments than were typical of earlier human factors research (e.g., Fisher & Pollatsek, 2007; Fisk & Rogers, 2007; Strayer & Drews, 2007; Wickens, McCarley, Alexander,

Thomas, Ambinder & Zheng, 2008). Often, this need arises in order to persuade corporate or public policy makers, funding agencies, or even lawmakers on matters of safety, or to better ensure the relevance of research findings to naturalistic situations such as the home, the highway, or aviation.

As such, it would be wrong to ignore the significant advances that have been made from an engineering psychology perspective, even if advances may still be needed in additional directions. For example, perhaps the best of what we now have along these lines is reflected in human factors textbooks such as Wickens, Lee, Liu, and Gordon-Becker (2003). This text is a particularly valuable resource for providing guidance on optimizing the efficiency and effectiveness of the relationship between a person and the information and actions made directly and immediately, that is, proximally, available from a system interface or a physical workplace (stimulus-response compatibility and Fitts's [1958] law are prime examples). Many of the products and devices that we use every day unfortunately still do not benefit from the tremendous amount of knowledge and guidance that texts such as these provide.

However, despite these important advances made by the engineering psychology approach, back in the mid-1980s it was becoming increasingly apparent that the (high) technology work environments that were increasingly requiring analysis and design were becoming so complex (some going by the name *socio-technical systems*—nuclear power plants, health care delivery, military command and control, to name a few) that the limitations of traditional engineering psychology methods were increasingly being felt in tangible ways, and from many different quarters (see chapter 41 in this handbook, on naturalistic decision making, and chapter 39, on cognitive engineering, for additional discussion). Work environments such as these have so many degrees of design freedom that it was becoming increasingly implausible to argue that every design decision having a psychological dimension could be decided empirically, via experimentation, or that these systems would be amenable to analysis and design in terms of the types of context-free (i.e., proximally oriented) design principles available in traditional human factors textbooks. Research sponsors were more frequently expressing dissatisfaction with what human factors had to offer. Human factors researchers were themselves becoming ever more frustrated with the inadequacy of their training, their methods, and their techniques for effectively engaging research problems in their full complexity.

A variety of human factors researchers wrote scholarly, often searching, pieces offering their own diagnoses of the situation, and sketching possible remedies and alternative futures. Jens Rasmussen (1986), who, along with Donald Norman (1982), championed the use of the term *cognitive engineering*, in an attempt to define a new discipline transcending solely the engineering psychology approach, offered a particularly cogent diagnosis of the situation, and pointed to an especially influential way forward. Rasmussen (1983) observed a variety of mismatches between both the theoretical and methodological tools available in the engineering psychology marketplace of the time and the pressing needs of contemporary human factors researchers and practitioners.

First, Rasmussen (1983), a control engineer working to ensure the safety of nuclear power plants and operations, observed that, in the crucially important area of interface design, semantics had overtaken syntax as the chief barrier to effective system control and problem diagnosis. It was not that system operators had great difficulty perceiving or attending to proximal displays, but rather in understanding what they meant.

Adopting a largely extensional semantics as a theory of meaning, Rasmussen (1983) cashed out meaning in terms of external reference. The operator's actual task, Rasmussen (1983) noted, is to control, diagnose, and so on, a plant "behind" the interface, so to speak, not to observe and manipulate the interface itself. In other words, the proximal interface must be functionally considered not as the true, end target of human interaction, but instead as a window to a (distal) plant or remote environment comprising the true target of work. Just as Bruner (1973) had characterized cognition as "going beyond the information given," Rasmussen (1983) described an operator's cognitive task in terms of exactly the same sort of going beyond, but in this case, going beyond the interface given. This characterization applies not solely to process control, but equally to modern "knowledge workers" (Zuboff, 1984) more generally, whose windows to the world of work increasingly consist of computer interfaces of one sort or another, and who thereby are rarely able to perceive and manipulate the objects of their work in a direct, unmediated fashion.

In 1983, Rasmussen published a seminal paper in which he presented a conceptual framework that both acknowledged the importance of the large body of engineering psychology research that had grown up around relatively simple technological contexts in which the primary goal was safe and efficient interaction with a proximal interface or workplace, yet nevertheless indicated a need for novel theory and method for better understanding the cognitive activities of knowledge workers. Rasmussen's (1983) observations have proven prescient: the research problems that occupy the lion's share of the attention of today's human factors psychologists are those in which technology is not viewed as the end target of human interaction, but rather as an intermediary through which humans interact with the actual objects of work (for additional discussion and elaboration, see Vicente, 1999).

In the three sections that follow, I provide an overview of this type of research in the contexts of human-automation interaction (HAI) and situation awareness (SA). Contemporary human factors research on distraction, multitasking and interruption (DMI) is presented last.

HAI research deals primarily with how humans cope with the mediational nature of automation. The review of human factors research on HAI will be presented in somewhat greater depth than the reviews of SA and DMI research because the encroachment of increased levels of automation into the workplace is likely to be the area with the greatest prospects for enhanced synergy between I/O and human factors psychology in coming decades.

SA research focuses on how humans cope with the mediational nature of technological interfaces through which the work environment is viewed and understood. DMI research primarily involves understanding the effects of the widespread encroachment of information, communication, and media technology into nearly all aspects of modern life. Human factors research concerning the cognitive challenges and disruptive effects associated with distraction, multitasking, and interruption once had implications solely for those with very attentionally demanding jobs, such as air traffic control or piloting a helicopter. Today, with the advent of e-mail, text messaging, chat, the Internet, and the smart phone (as both telephone and computer), much of modern life in both the home and workplace now offers, for better and worse, ample opportunities for all of us to experience these challenges and disruptive effects.

Human-Automation Interaction

As has been noted previously, Rasmussen (1983) was among the first to alert the human factors research community to the implications of the fact that increasingly high levels of technology and automation in industrial settings created a new agenda of research problems. Many of these problems are associated with how humans control and monitor remote or distal systems or processes on the basis of information and controls available from proximal interfaces.

While much of the impetus for Rasmussen's (1983, 1986) research came from his observations of power plant technicians engaged in troubleshooting tasks (see Vicente, 2001, for a detailed history and overview), Rasmussen was also influenced by the seminal research of Sheridan (1976), who was actively engaged in the problems of remote control and monitoring of distant vehicles, in contexts such as space and undersea exploration. Sheridan (1976) coined the term *supervisory control* to describe the situation in which the human is not in direct, manual control of a system or process, but instead, inputs commands to automated systems that themselves act directly on the distal system, process, or vehicle. Once the province solely of high technology systems, supervisory control is now commonplace. You are a supervisory controller when you set your iPod to shuffle mode, enter settings on a programmable thermostat, or engage and monitor cruise control in your car.

This initial, seminal research by Rasmussen (1983, 1986) and Sheridan (1976) has spawned dozens of studies by human factors psychologists over the past decades trying to characterize human-automation interaction (HAI) with models or taxonomies, to understand the consequences of introducing automation into systems or workplaces, to identify and describe human tendencies in dealing with those consequences, and to identify design principles, frameworks, and techniques to support human operators or workers in doing so.

Bainbridge (1983) was among the first to note a fundamental, hardly intuitive, irony associated with introducing increasingly higher levels of automation into systems and workplaces: "The more advanced a control system is, so the more crucial may be the contribution of the human operator" (p. 775). Bainbridge (1983) went on to note that the engineer or system designer often has a pessimistic view of human competence ("human error"), so he or she will likely attempt to eliminate or minimize the operator's role to solely the tasks that the designer cannot figure out how to automate. As such, the operator's role and tasks are not designed systematically in terms of what humans do well versus poorly, but rather arbitrarily, with the designer often paying little attention to providing support in carrying them out. Just one of many negative outcomes of this situation is that many of the operator's tasks shift from active engagement with a system or work environment to passive monitoring, with all manner of resulting problems associated with vigilance, mental underload, ineffective monitoring, and complacency (e.g., Moray, 1993; Parasuraman, Molloy, & Singh, 1993; Sheridan & Johannsen, 1976; Young & Stanton, 2002).

Although much that is currently known about the consequences of automation on human cognition and performance comes from experiments using tasks or simulations attempting to replicate many aspects of HAI work settings, Sheridan and Parasuraman (2005, p. 95) have noted that much of the impetus behind this research came from detailed analyses of HAI failures or breakdowns in operational or field settings, such as those following in the footsteps of a seminal study by Wiener and Curry (1980) on aviation incidents and accidents. Excellent examples are provided by Sarter and Woods (1995) on mode confusion (What is the flight management computer or autopilot doing?) and by Sarter, Woods, and Billings (1987) on "surprises" that opaquely designed, rather than transparent, automation can cause for system operators. This lack of transparency to the operator, rather than the underlying design of automation itself, has been claimed by Norman (1990) to be the main source of HAI problems, in his article "The problem with automation: Inappropriate feedback and interaction, not over-automation."

A landmark in the study of HAI came in 1997, when Parasuraman and Riley reviewed, organized, and summarized what had been learned through HAI research to that point on the basis of forensic, simulation-based, and laboratory research. The title of their article (Parasuraman & Riley, 1997) aptly summarizes the gist of their findings: "Humans and automation: Use, misuse, disuse, and abuse." These authors characterized their findings on the problems associated with HAI using the taxonomy of *use, misuse, disuse*, and *abuse* to mean the following:

Use refers to the voluntary activation and disengagement of automation by human operators. Trust, mental workload, and risk can influence automation use, but interaction between [these] factors and large individual differences make prediction of automation use difficult. Misuse refers to overreliance on automation, which can result in failures of monitoring and decision biases. Factors affecting the monitoring of automation include workload, automation reliability and consistency, and the saliency of automation state indicators. Disuse, or the neglect or underutilization of automation, is commonly caused by alarms that are activated falsely. This often occurs because the base rate of the condition to be detected is not considered in setting the trade-off between false alarms and omissions. Automation abuse, or the automation of functions by designers and implementation by managers without due regard for the consequences of human performance, tends to define the operator's roles as by-products of the automation. Automation abuse can also promote misuse and disuse of automation by human operators.

(p. 230)

Concrete examples of these phenomena are not hard to find. For example, in my collaboration with colleagues and students, I have found it nearly impossible to predict the level or amount of automation that others will activate or engage ("use") using a word processing tool such as Microsoft Word. These varying levels (automated style sheets, formatted bullets and lists, and so forth) can make collaboration on a document more problematic than it need be. Any case in which an unwanted word appears in a final document due to inappropriate overreliance on an autocorrect feature or function demonstrates "misuse." I may disable the "autocorrect as you type" or "check spelling as you type" features due to the numerous false alarms caused by authors' names and technical terms that are acceptable within one sphere of discourse but that do not appear in the electronic dictionary. Finally, automation "abuse" occurs each time I am required to update my software to a new version that may provide additional features yet may short-circuit the many automatized skills that I have acquired over years using the existing version.

Parasuraman and Riley (1997) implicated trust, a construct from social psychology, as an important mediator of HAI. Lee and his colleagues (e.g., Lee & Moray, 1992, 1994; Lee & See, 2004) have conducted a sustained series of investigations into human trust and lack of trust in automation, with the premise that automation often behaves with such a degree of autonomy that humans relate to automation socially. Lee and See (2004) introduced the notion of comparing the objective reliability or trustworthiness of automation with the degree of trust displayed by the automation user, to define concepts of overtrust, distrust (undertrust), and calibrated trust. In their conceptualization, trust is a dynamic process that rises and falls through HAI interactions of various types over time. Lee and See (2004) provided the following guidelines for fostering a calibrated level of user, worker, or operator trust in automation (p. 74):

- Design for appropriate trust, not greater trust.
- Show the past performance of the automation.
- Show the process and algorithms of the automation by revealing intermediate results in a way that is comprehensible to the operators.
- Simplify the algorithms and operation of the automation to make it more understandable.
- Show the purpose of the automation, design basis, and range of applications in a way that relates to the users' goals.
- Train operators regarding its expected reliability, the mechanisms governing its behavior, and its intended use.
- Carefully evaluate any anthropomorphizing of the automation, such as using speech to create a synthetic conversational partner, to ensure appropriate trust.

Current directions in the HAI literature include research on the relative roles of false alarms and misses in alerting automation on mediating trust (Dixon, Wickens, & McCarley, 2007; Meyer, 2004), and in expanding our understanding of the affective relationship between humans and automation beyond trust to include emotion and mood (Lee, 2007). Note that the rationale behind much of this research is the demonstrably realistic assumption that automation is rarely perfect. Parasuraman and Wickens (2008) have summed up the situation well in the title of the most recent review of the HAI human factors literature: "Humans: Still vital after all these years of automation" (p. 511).

Additionally, modeling HAI is another active area of research in human factors psychology. Parasuraman, Sheridan, and Wickens (2000) present a conceptual model or taxonomy of HAI in terms of various "stages" such as information acquisition, information analysis, decision making, and action, crossed with various "levels" indicating the relative autonomy of automation on a scale from low to high. This two-dimensional taxonomy defines the space of design possibilities for HAI, and also provides a classification scheme for organizing findings from the empirical literature.

Degani, Shafto, and Kirlik (1999) provide a taxonomy of modes in HAI, contrasting interface modes, functional modes, and supervisory modes,

noting that these contrasting types create different demands upon the operator in maintaining mode awareness and reducing mode error. Degani and Heymann (2002) present a technique to formally verify that a proximal system interface contains sufficient information for adequately specifying the underlying, distal mode in which automation is operating (also see Degani, 2004). Jamieson and Vicente (2005) provide a closed-loop, control theoretic perspective to the analysis and design of human-automation-plant interfaces.

Research on HAI devoted to improving the compatibility between human operators and automated alerting systems and decision aids has been provided by Pritchett and Bisantz (2006), Seong, Bisantz, and Gattie (2006), and Bass and Pritchett (2006), using modeling techniques largely based on correlative statistics. These statistical models have been useful, for example, to describe the degree of match and mismatch between a human's judgment strategy (cue weighting pattern) and the strategy used by alerting automation (Pritchett & Bisantz, 2006), to understand how feedback provided to humans by automation may lead to better judgments in cooperation with automation (Seong et al., 2006), and how the interpersonal learning paradigm (IPL) drawn from social psychology (Hammond, Wilkins, & Todd, 1966) can be extended to human-automation interaction in addition to human-human social interaction. Also taking a statistical approach, Casner (2006) presented an ambitious study combining naturalistic observation within commercial airline cockpits and modeling of the data collected there to demonstrate that cockpit automation often supports flight crews when they need it least, and leaves crews relatively unsupported when they need it most.

Finally, it should be noted that human factors psychologists studying HAI are indeed aware of the ethical issues surrounding the implementation of increasing levels of automation in the workplace. These ethical issues are also likely to be of concern to I/O psychologists working in technological work environments. Sheridan and Parasuraman (2005) discuss a number of factors that should be considered, and perhaps even managed, as additional types or levels of automation are introduced (pp. 122–123): (1) threatened or actual unemployment; (2) centralized management and loss of a worker's local control; (3) desocialization as the ratio of humans to autonomous agents decreases; (4) deskilling as workers are put out of the loop; (5) intimidation by greater power and responsibility associated with supervising increasingly powerful technology; (6) growing technological illiteracy as automation becomes increasingly difficult to understand; (7) mystification and misplaced trust in technology; (8) sense of not contributing; (9) abandonment of responsibility—"the computer did it."

Although human factors psychology has made many advances to both understand and support HAI in today's workplaces and technological systems, much research remains to be done to further understand how to trade off the inevitable and simultaneous "blessings and burdens," of technology, as the tensions that existed between Plato's Thamus and Theuth remain with us to this day.

Situation Awareness

Information technology and automation in many industrial systems, vehicles, and workplaces increasingly mediate the interaction between a human operator (or team) and a controlled system or the actual, distal objects of a work environment. The need for operators or workers to maintain adequate levels of situation awareness (SA) in these contexts is frequently cited as a key to effective and efficient performance and the reduction of error (e.g., Adams, Tenney, & Pew, 1995; Durso & Gronlund, 1999; Endsley & Garland, 2001). In human factors, one of the most influential perspectives on SA has been put forth by Endsley (1995a, 1995b) who has studied the phenomenon within the contexts of automation (Endsley, 1996), air traffic control (Endsley & Smolensky, 1998), and naturalistic decision making (Endsley, 1997). Endsley's definition of SA, which has been particularly influential in human factors psychology, is "the perception of the elements of the environment within a volume of time and space, the comprehension of their meaning, and the projection of their status in the near future" (Endsley, 1995a, p. 36).

Figure 38.1 provides a visual depiction of Endsley's model of SA, which can be seen to rely largely on information processing concepts and constructivist approaches to knowledge acquisition. Of particular interest is the assumption that SA occurs at three distinct, successive levels. Level 1

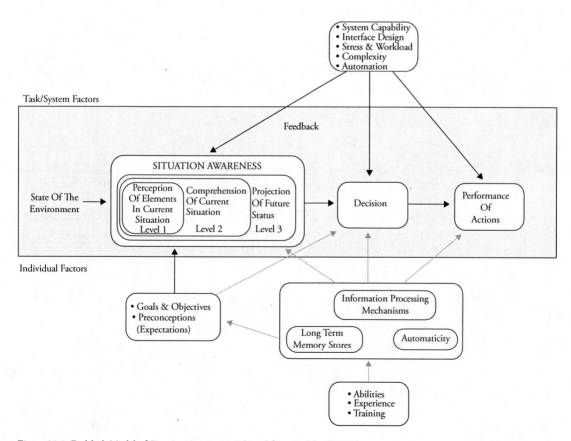

Figure 38.1 Endsley's Model of Situation Awareness, Adapted from Endsley (1995a)

concerns perception of the here and now as delivered by perception. Level 2 concerns the comprehension or understanding of the situation in light of experiential knowledge, expectations, and operator or worker goals. Level 3 consists of a prediction of how the current situation will evolve into the future, as either a point prediction or as a set of various possible futures. Note the bolded arrow from the "Situation Awareness" box to the box labeled "Decision," reflecting Endsley's assumption that the perception, comprehension, and prediction of current and future states of the world is the key foundation of decision making and action selection (cf. chapter 41 of this handbook on naturalistic decision making and the key role assumed to be played by situation assessment).

Supporting human operators and workers in intensively technologically mediated situations through interface design and training promises to be a growing concern in human factors. An especially challenging aspect of studying a psychological phenomenon as rich as how people maintain awareness of distal processes, objects, and events via proximal representations of those entities is that, in the environments of interest to human factors, these psychological activities can be expected to richly benefit from the products of experience and aspects of the concrete context in which that experience was gained (Kirlik & Bisantz, 1999). Although there are many dimensions to SA, and its functional role depends on the specifics of the environment and task, few would disagree that continued advances into understanding and supporting SA are sure to depend on advances in measurement. Salas, Prince, Baker, and Shrestha (1995) summed up the situation well: "a central problem in understanding situation awareness is the lack of well-developed measurement tools" (p. 131).

Whatever cognitive processes account for SA, by necessity its measurement must have its basis in observable variables. One category of existing measurement techniques relies on largely verbal, qualitative data gathered through case-study examinations of critical incidents (e.g., Klein, 1999). These methods rely on subjective reports of retrospective memory for actual, past incidents and process-tracing (think out-loud) protocols for an examination of simulated or ongoing incidents. Information is gathered on the environmental cues attended, active operator goals and expectations, and critical decision points. One primary focus is to identify any differences between novice and expert performers in how SA is achieved.

A second category of SA measurement techniques relies on subjectively reported measures of SA. One well-known example is the Situation Awareness Rating Technique, or SART (Taylor, 1990), although Pew (2000) has noted that the SART technique may confound SA measurement with workload measurement.

Perhaps the most popular and widely used SA measurement technique relies on probes or questions embedded within experimental or simulation studies in real-time, interactive contexts. In this technique, a task or dynamic situation is frozen at various times, and operators are presented queries about the state of the controlled system or task environment. The best example of this approach is the Situation Awareness Global Assessment Technique, or SAGAT (Endsley, 2000). SAGAT is used to design and administer queries pertaining to all three levels of SA described in Endsley's (1995a) model. The accuracy of these queries is then measured (percent correct) and aggregated to result in an overall or global metric of SA, and one that is considered to be direct: "This type of measure is a direct measure of SA—it taps into the operator's perceptions rather than infers them from behaviors that may be influenced by many other factors besides SA" (Endsley, 2000, p. 147). Endsley (2000) presents a comprehensive overview of the SAGAT technique, including discussions of sensitivity, reliability, validity, and implementation. Endsley (2004) provides a recent discussion of progress and directions in the study of SA in the context of the general framework depicted in Figure 38.1.

Another perspective on SA modeling and measurement in human factors has its origins in the psychology of judgment, and in particular, weather prediction. In their studies of experienced weather forecasters using technological displays of weather information (e.g., Doppler radar) to predict thunderstorm microbursts, Lusk, Stewart, Hammond, and Potts (1990) noted that two features of this task situation beyond the control of weather forecasters nevertheless contributed to their performance. These were the inherent uncertainty characterizing the meteorological environment and any departures from ideal performance in the technological sensors and information systems that provided the sources of information ultimately presented to forecasters on interface displays. As such, these researchers realized that a performance measure such as percent correct would not be suitable for characterizing the cognitive competence of forecasters because it would be confounded by these two sources of uncontrollable uncertainty. Therefore, they created a model of the entire weather-sensor-display-forecaster system as the object of scientific study, and analyzed its properties based on empirical data collected during potential microburst events.

This original, context-specific model was subsequently generalized beyond solely the context of weather prediction by Stewart and Lusk (1994). Figure 38.2 depicts their model, which is itself a generalization or extension of Brunswik's (1956) "lens model," representing an SA task in terms of a cascading flow of probabilistic information from the distal situation state (the atmosphere, shop floor, airspace, plant, etc.) to a human operator, worker, or forecaster.

Note that the left (of the "X") half of Stewart & Lusk's (1994) Extended Lens Model (ELM) represents the external situation and technological information processing, while the right half represents human information processing. The situational state (O) is the property or event that the human is attempting to judge (e.g., whether a microburst will occur, whether two aircraft will collide). The descriptors (T) are the technologically sensed variable values that are potentially informative about this state, to a greater or lesser degree depending on the context. The primary cues (X) are the perceptual judgments of the values of these variables made on the basis of their presentation on interface displays. Systematic differences between the perceived X cue values and their actual T values reflect errors of perceptual measurement or ability. The secondary cues U correspond to the qualitative (exists, does not exist) or quantitative (value of) concepts by which the human conceives of the domain, and these may be either perfectly or imperfectly inferred from the values of the cues X. Finally, the human makes a judgment Y on the basis of the secondary cues, such as that two aircraft will not collide, or that the fault lies in the fact that an electronic document is no longer readable by the most recent version of one's software application. Stewart and Lusk (1994) showed how overall judgment could be measured by the use of a Skill Score (SS) measure grounded in the mean square error of a set of judgments corrected for chance, and also how this molar measure of judgment performance could be decomposed, and thus localized to its various contributing factors, using the correlative measures depicted in Figure 38.3.

Stewart and Lusk's (1994) ELM model was applied to the study of SA in human factors by Kirlik and Strauss (2006) and Strauss and Kirlik (2006), in the context of a study of submarine stealth judgments made on the basis of tactical situation displays. Using the statistical decomposition depicted in Figure 38.3, these authors were able to localize particular types of SA performance decrements and increments to differences in both interface display design as well as to individual differences between experimental participants in the accuracy of their perceptual judgments (reliability of information acquisition in Figure 38.3) and in their ability to accurately combine base rate and case-specific information (conditional/regression bias in Figure 38.3).

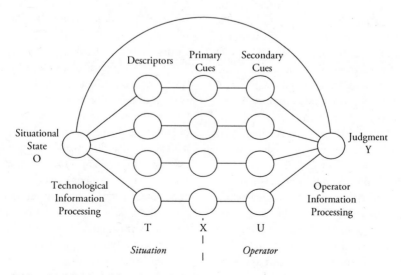

Figure 38.2 Extended Lens Model, Adapted from Stewart & Lusk (1994).

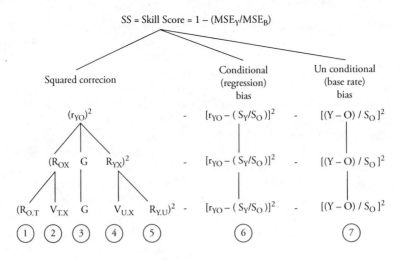

$$SS = \text{Skill Score} = 1 - (MSE_Y/MSE_B)$$

Squared correcion

Conditional (regression) bias

Un conditional (base rate) bias

$$(r_{YO})^2 \qquad - \qquad [r_{YO} - (S_Y/S_O)]^2 \qquad - \qquad [(Y - O)/S_O]^2$$

$$(R_{OX} \quad G \quad R_{YX})^2 \qquad - \qquad [r_{YO} - (S_Y/S_O)]^2 \qquad - \qquad [(Y - O)/S_O]^2$$

$$(R_{O.T} \quad V_{T.X} \quad G \quad V_{U.X} \quad R_{Y.U})^2 \quad - \qquad [r_{YO} - (S_Y/S_O)]^2 \qquad - \qquad [(Y - O)/S_O]^2$$

(1) (2) (3) (4) (5)   (6)   (7)

Components of skill:
1. Environmental predicability
2. Fideity of the information system
3. Match between environment and forecaster
4. Reliability of information acquisition
5. Reliability of information processing
6. Conditional/regression bias
7. Unconditional/base rate bias

Figure 38.3 Decomposition of SA Performance into its Constitutive Components from Stewart & Lusk (1994)

Distraction, Multitasking, and Interruption

Contemporary human factors research in the area of distraction, multitasking, and interruption is simultaneously adding increasing relevance and salience to much earlier human factors research on multitasking and timesharing (e.g., Wickens, 1989, 2004) as well as creating a relatively new research agenda in areas such as driver distraction (e.g., Strayer & Drews, 2007) and interruptions in the computerized workplace (Trafton & Monk, 2008). Although distraction has long been of interest to human factors researchers studying activities such as driving and flying, the proliferation of information and communication technologies such as cell phones and GPS navigational aids in automobiles has created a great deal of recent interest in the disruptive effects of these technologies. At the time of this writing, an increasing number of states in the United States are passing laws against the use of cell phones for voice conversation or text messaging while driving. While this progress has lagged behind the accumulating knowledge base of findings on the dangers of technology-induced driver distraction, human factors research can rightly claim at least partial, perhaps even significant, credit for these developments.

Less well-known are the huge costs to society associated with the consequences of information and communication technologies causing interruptions in the workplace. As noted by Trafton and Monk (2008), in their timely review of the rapidly growing interruption literature, workplace interruptions have been estimated by the information technology research firm Basex as costing over $500 billion a year in decreased worker productivity. Trafton and Monk (2008) discuss theoretical research on interruption, such as Monsell's (2003) theory of task switching, and computational cognitive models (e.g., see Byrne, 2003, for a general overview; see Altman, 2004, for an example in the context of interruptions).

For the present purposes, the focus here will be on some of the central empirical findings. In a field study including worker shadowing, interviewing, and observation, Gonzalez and Mark (2004) found that knowledge workers switched tasks approximately every three minutes. In a diary study, Czerwinski et al. (2004) found that knowledge workers were interrupted most frequently during cognitively demanding tasks, and not surprisingly, that performance on these effortful tasks were most severely impaired by interruption. The frequency of interruptions due to instant message users in the workplace has been found to be startlingly high: as noted by Trafton and Monk (2008), 92% of instant messages were responded to within five minutes, with half of these responses occurring within 15 seconds (Avrahami & Hudson, 2006).

Some researchers have taken up the challenge of trying to design new technologies to mitigate the effects of interruptions in the workplace. In a series of studies, Bailey and his coworkers (Adamczyk & Bailey, 2004; Bailey, Busbey, & Iqbal, 2007; Bailey & Konstan, 2006; Bailey, Konstan, & Carlis, 2000; Iqbal & Bailey, 2005; Iqbal, Zheng, & Bailey, 2004) have used techniques such as task modeling and methods such as workload measurements based on pupil size in order to schedule interruptions (e.g., text messages or software update notifications) at coarse breakpoints between tasks and at times of low workload.

Many people today have become so dependent on information and communication technologies in the home and workplace that it is commonplace to hear people boast of their ability to multitask. In closing this overview, and in keeping with the theme by which it began, it may be useful to ponder whether the many interruptions, sources of distraction, and opportunities for multitasking in our everyday lives are more of a blessing or more of a burden. Ophir, Nass, and Wagner (2009) recently reported the results of a study that begins to speak to this issue. These authors used a trait multitasking index to identify groups of participants who self-identified as either chronically high or chronically low multitaskers in their everyday lives. They then subjected these two groups of participants to a battery of cognitive tests, including those measuring the ability to filter out environmental distractors, the ability to filter out task-irrelevant representations in memory, and task-switching ability.

The results of this study were as striking as they were surprising to the investigators: chronically high multitasking participants scored significantly lower on all three measures of cognitive performance than did the chronically low multitaskers. Considering these findings, Ophir et al. (2009) concluded "breadth-based media consumption is indeed mirrored by breadth-based cognitive control" (p. 3). That is, those who frequently engage in multitasking appear to have their flow of cognitive activity driven more exogenously, and more shallowly, than those who rarely engage in multitasking. In the authors words, "...those who infrequently multitask are more effective at volitionally allocating their attention in the face of distractions" (p. 3).

Although this is among the first studies of its kind, and the directions of the causal arrows need to be established, these findings should at least give us pause about the consequences of living in a world of ever increasing information, media, and communication technologies. The jury may still be out on whether Google is "Making Us Stupid" (Carr, 2008). However, little doubt remains that "the discoverer of an art is not the best judge of the good or harm which will accrue to those who practice it" (Plato, 1973, p. 96).

Conclusion

The research agenda of human factors psychology continues to change rapidly to remain relevant to the equally rapid changes in the technological nature of the human ecology. This is a direct reflection of the fact that human factors research has come to recognize that little can be said about human behavior without a detailed understanding of the environment and task, and that even minor, often unforeseen, changes to the designed environment can significantly impact human performance. As such, human factors psychologists are increasingly studying these phenomena in contexts or simulations intended to represent the target contexts to which the generalization of scientific theories, models, and findings is desired.

A related trend can be seen in many of the research areas central to I/O psychology, such as personality, motivation, training, and abilities. The past decades have witnessed an increased concern among members of these research communities to ensure a defensible level of representativeness in the research contexts studied, and a desire to expand theory in the direction of better understanding the situational or contextual factors mediating the expression of individual differences in performance (e.g., Ackerman, 2007; Christiansen & Tett, 2008; Hattrup & Jackson, 1996; Hough & Oswald, 2008; Kanfer, 2009; Kozlowski & DeShon, 2004). As such, it is only natural to expect that, in the future, human factors and I/O psychologists will increasingly benefit from one another in pursuing their shared agenda of identifying and systematically describing the psychologically relevant dimensions, entities, and organization of the human ecology.

A second factor suggests that human factors and I/O psychology will become increasingly relevant and mutually informative in coming decades. I/O psychology wears its concern with social psychological issues on its sleeve. Historically, human factors psychology has had its core scientific basis in cognitive, rather than social, psychology, but a shift in emphasis is clearly underway. When selecting three areas of human factors research to review in this chapter, I selected human-automation interaction (HAI), situation awareness (SA), and distraction, multitasking, and interruption (DMI) on the basis of the fact that they are among the most active and rapidly growing areas in contemporary human factors research. However, by reflecting on these areas, one can see that they also are united by a shared concern with the social dimensions of human-technology interaction.

As illustrated in the review of HAI research, human factors is increasingly finding a need to draw on social psychological constructs, such as trust in, supervision of, and intimidation by, automation, as technology is perceived by its users to be increasingly autonomous (in reality, opaque and complex, thus unpredictable). And although this fact was not highlighted in the discussion of Stewart and Lusk's (1994) Extended Lens Model of technologically mediated SA, this model has its origins in social judgment theory developed by Hammond, Brehmer, Joyce and their coworkers (Brehmer & Joyce, 1988)—that is, a theory of how humans make judgments or attributions of covert states or dispositions of others, based on socially available information sources or cues. Finally, the review of DMI research revealed that much of the distraction, multitasking, and interruption now common in both everyday life and the modern workplace arises as a result of the use of information and communication technologies mediating their users' social behavior. As such, human factors is currently demonstrating an increasing need to embrace the social dimensions of technology design, and as such, is likely to increasingly resonate with the concerns of I/O psychology in coming decades.

In closing, note that many, if not most, of us today live and work in an ecology consisting of a variety of technological niches. Some researchers studying the intersection of technology and cognition, human factors psychologists, have assigned themselves the task of identifying and describing the often-unanticipated consequences of the juggernaut of technological change. In this manner, human factors psychologists participate in helping society understand which of these changes may be for the better, which may be for the worse, and for whom. Increasingly, these changes have a social

dimension, in addition to the cognitive dimension that provided the primary foundation for human factors in prior decades, boding well for enhanced opportunities for human factors and I/O psychologists to learn from one another in the future.

The importance of the tasks that lie before us should provide more than sufficient motivation for increased communication and collaboration across these lines. While law and public or corporate policy bearing on the design and use of technology are influenced by myriad forces and concerns, we now understand that these laws and policies do more than shape our behavior. Increasingly, they determine the world in which we work and live.

References

Ackerman, P. L. (2007). Outgoing editorial: Bridging science and application. *Journal of Experimental Psychology: Applied, 13*(4), 179–181.

Adams, M. J., Tenney, Y. J., & Pew, R. W. (1995). Situation awareness and cognitive management of complex systems. *Human Factors, 37*(1), 85–104.

Adamczyk, P. D., & Bailey, B. P. (2004). If not now, when? The effects of interruption at different moments within task execution. In *Human Factors in Computing Systems CHI'04* (pp. 271–278). New York: ACM Press.

Altman, E. M. (2004). The preparation effect in task switching: Carryover of SOA. *Memory and Cognition, 32*, 153–163.

Avrahami, D., & Hudson, S. E. (2006). Responsiveness in instant messaging. Predictive models supporting personal communication. In *Proceedings of Conference of Human Factors in Computing Systems, CHI '06* (pp. 731–740). New York: ACM Press.

Bailey, B. P., Busbey, C. W., & Iqbal, S. T. (2007). TAPRAV: An interactive analysis tool for exploring workload aligned to models of task execution. *Interacting with Computers, 19*(3), 314–329.

Bailey, B. P., & Konstan, J. A. (2006). On the need for attention-aware systems: Measuring effects of interruption on task performance, error rate, and affective state. *Computers in Human Behavior, 22*, 685–708.

Bailey, B. P., Konstan, J. A., & Carlis, J. V. (2000). Measuring the effects of interruptions on task performance in the user interface. *IEEE Conference on Systems, Man, and Cybernetics* (pp. 757–762). Los Alamitos, CA: IEEE Press.

Bainbridge, L. (1983). Ironies of automation. *Automatica, 19*(6), 775–779.

Baldwin, C. L. (2009). Individual differences in navigational strategy: Implications for display design. *Theoretical Issues in Ergonomics Science, 10*(5), 443–458.

Bass, E. J., & Pritchett, A. M. (2006). Human-automated judgment learning: Enhancing interaction with automated judgment systems. In A. Kirlik (Ed.), *Adaptive perspectives on human-technology interaction* (pp. 114–128). New York: Oxford University Press.

Brehmer, B., & Joyce, C. R. B. (1988). *Human judgment: The SJT view.* Amsterdam: North-Holland.

Bruner, J. (1973). *Going beyond the information given.* New York: Norton.

Byrne, M. D. (2003). Cognitive architecture. In J. Jacko & A. Sears (Eds.), *The human-computer interaction handbook* (pp. 97–117). Mahwah, NJ: Erlbaum.

Brunswik, E. (1949). Discussion: Remarks on functionalism in perception: *Journal of Personality, 18*, 56–65.

Brunswik, E. (1955). Representative design and probabilistic theory in a functional psychology. *Psychological Review, 62*, 193–217.

Brunswik, E. (1956). *Perception and the representative design of psychological experiments*. Berkeley: University of California Press.

Carr, N. (2008). Is Google making us stupid? *The Atlantic Monthly*, July/August. Retrieved (August 2009) from: http://www.theatlantic.com/doc/200807/google

Casner, S. (2006). Understanding the determinants of adaptive behavior in a modern airline cockpit. In A. Kirlik (Ed.), *Adaptive perspectives on human-technology interaction* (pp. 197–211). New York: Oxford University Press.

Christiansen, N. D., & Tett, R. P. (2008). Toward a better understanding of the role of situations in linking personality, work behavior, and job performance. *Industrial & Organizational Psychology, 1*, 312–316.

Czerwinski, M. P., Horvitz, E., & Wilhite, S. (2004). A diary study of task switching and interruptions. In *Human Factors in Computing Systems: Proceedings of CHI'04* (pp. 175–182). New York: Association for Computing Machinery Press.

Degani, A. (2004). *Taming HAL: Designing interfaces beyond 2001*. New York: Palmgrave Macmillan.

Degani, A., & Heymann, M. (2002). Formal verification of human-automation interaction. *Human Factors, 44*, 28–43.

Degani, A., Shafto, M., & Kirlik, A. (1999). Modes in human-machine systems: Review, classification, and application. *International Journal of Aviation Psychology, 9*, 125–138.

Dhami, M., Hertwig, R., & Hoffrage, U. (2004). The role of representative design in an ecological approach to cognition. *Psychological Bulletin, 130*, 959–988.

Dixon, S. R., Wickens, C. D., & McCarley, J. S. (2007). On the independence of compliance and reliance: Are automation false alarms worse than misses? *Human Factors, 49*(4), 564–572.

Durso, F. T., & Gronlund, S. (1999). Situation awareness. In F. T. Durso, R. Nickerson, R. W. Schvaneveldt, S. T. Dumais, D. S. Lindsay, & M. T. H. Chi (Eds.), *The handbook of applied cognition* (pp. 284–314). New York: Wiley.

Endsley, M. R. (1995a). Toward a theory of situation awareness in dynamic systems. *Human Factors, 37*(1), 32–64.

Endsley, M. R. (1995b). Measurement of situation awareness in dynamic systems. *Human Factors, 37*(1), 65–84.

Endsley, M. R. (1996). Automation and situation awareness. In R. Parasuraman & M. Mouloua (Eds.), *Automation and human performance: Theory and applications* (pp. 163–181). Mahwah, NJ: Erlbaum.

Endsley, M. R. (1997). The role of situation awareness in naturalistic decision making. In C. E. Zsambok & G. Klein (Eds.), *Naturalistic decision making* (pp. 269–283). Mahwah, NJ: Erlbaum.

Endsley, M. R. (2000). Direct measurement of situation awareness: Validity and use of SAGAT. In M. R. Endsley & D. J. Garland (Eds.), *Situation awareness analysis and measurement* (pp. 147–174). Mahwah, NJ: Erlbaum.

Endsley, M. R. (2004). Situation awareness: Progress and directions. In S. Banbury & S. Tremblay (Eds.), *A cognitive approach to situation awareness: Theory, measurement and application* (pp. 317–341). Aldershot, UK: Ashgate Publishing.

Endsley, M. R., & Garland, D. J. (Eds.). (2001). *Situation awareness: analysis and measurement*. Mahwah, NJ: Erlbaum.

Endsley, M. R., & Smolensky, M. W. (1998). Situation awareness is air traffic control: The picture. In M. W. Smolensky & E. S. Stein (Eds.), *Human factors in Air Traffic Control* (pp. 115–154). San Diego, CA: Academic Press.

Ericsson, K. A., & Williams, A. M. (2007). Capturing naturally occurring superior performance in the laboratory: Translational research on expert performance. *Journal of Experimental Psychology: Applied, 13*(3), 115–123.

Fisher, D. L., & Pollatsek, A. (2007). Novice driver crashes: Failure to divide attention or failure to recognize risks. In A. F. Kramer, D. A. Wiegmann, & A. Kirlik (Ed.), *Attention: From theory to practice* (pp. 134–156). New York: Oxford University Press.

Fisk, A. D., & Rogers, W. A. (2007). Attention goes home: Support for aging adults. In A. F. Kramer, D. A. Wiegmann, & A. Kirlik (Ed.), *Attention: From theory to practice* (pp. 157–169). New York: Oxford University Press.

Fitts, P. M. (1958). Engineering psychology. *Annual Review of Psychology, 9*, 267–294.

Goldstein, W. (2006). Introduction to Brunswikian theory and method. In A. Kirlik (Ed.), *Adaptive perspectives on human-technology interaction* (pp. 10–26). New York: Oxford University Press.

Gonzalez, V. M., & Mark, G. (2004). Constant, constant, multi-tasking craziness: Managing multiple working spheres. In *Human Factors in Computer Systems: Proceedings of CHI '04* (pp. 113–120). New York: ACM Press.

Gray, W. D. (2002). Simulated task environments: The role of high-fidelity simulations, scaled worlds, synthetic environments, and laboratory tasks in basic and applied cognitive research. *Cognitive Science Quarterly, 2*, 205–227.

Hammond, K. R., & Stewart, T. R. (2001). *The essential Brunswik*. New York: Oxford University Press.

Hammond, K. R., Wilkins, M., & Todd, F. J. (1966). A research paradigm for the study of interpersonal learning. *Psychological Bulletin, 65*, 221–232.

Hattrup, K., & Jackson, S. E. (1996). Learning about individual differences by taking situations seriously. In K. R. Murphy (Ed.), *Individual differences and behavior in organizations* (pp. 507–541). San Francisco: Jossey-Bass.

Hough, L. M., & Oswald, F. L. (2008). Personality testing and industrial-organizational psychology: Reflections, progress, and prospects. *Industrial and Organizational Psychology, 1*, 272–290.

Howell, W. C. (1993). Engineering psychology in a changing world. *Annual Review of Psychology, 44*, 231–263.

Iqbal, S. T., & Bailey, B. P. (2005). Investigating the effectiveness of mental workload as a predictor of opportune moments for interruption. In *Conference on Human Factors in Computing Systems, CHI '05* (pp. 1489–1492). New York: ACM Press.

Iqbal, S. T., Zheng, X. S., & Bailey, B. P. (2004). Task-evoked pupillary response to mental workload in human-computer interaction. In *Conference on Human Factors in Computing Systems, CHI '04* (pp. 1477–1480). New York: ACM Press.

Jamieson, G. A., & Vicente, K. J. (2005). Designing effective human-automation-plant interfaces: A control theoretic perspective. *Human Factors, 47*(1), 12–34.

Kanfer, R. (2009). Work motivation: Identifying use-inspired basic research directions. *Industrial and Organizational Psychology, 2*, 77–93.

Kirlik, A. (2005). Work in progress: Reinventing intelligence for a reinvented world. In R. J. Sternberg & D. D. Preiss (Eds.), *Intelligence and technology: The impact of tools and technologies on the nature and development of human abilities* (pp.105–134). Mahwah, NJ: Erlbaum.

Kirlik, A., & Bisantz, A. M. (1999). Cognition in human-machine systems: Experiential and environmental aspects of adaptation. In P. A. Hancock (Ed.), *Handbook of perception and cognition: Human performance and ergonomics* (pp. 47–68). New York: Academic Press.

Kirlik, A., & Strauss, R. (2006). Situation awareness as judgment. I: Statistical modeling and quantitative measurement. *International Journal of Industrial Ergonomics, 36*, 463–474.

Klatzky, R. (2009). Giving psychological science away: The role of applications courses. *Perspectives on Psychological Science, 4*(5), 522–530.

Klein, G. A. (1999). Applied decision making. In P. A. Hancock (Ed.), *Handbook of perception and cognition: Human performance and ergonomics* (pp. 87–108). New York: Academic Press.

Kozlowski, S. W. J., & DeShon, R. P. (2004). A psychological fidelity approach to simulation-based training: Theory, research, and principles. In E. Salas, L. R. Elliott, S. G. Schflett, & M. D. Coovert (Eds.), *Scaled worlds: Development, validation, and applications* (pp. 75–99). Burlington, VT: Ashgate Publishing.

Kramer, A. F., Wiegmann, D. A., & Kirlik, A. (2007). *Attention: From theory to practice.* New York: Oxford University Press.

Lee, J. D. (2007). Affect, attention, and automation. In A. F. Kramer, D. A. Wiegmann, & A. Kirlik (Ed.), *Attention: From theory to practice* (pp. 73–89). New York: Oxford University Press.

Lee, J. D., & Moray, N. (1992). Trust, control strategies, and allocation of function in human-machine systems. *Ergonomics, 35*, 1243–1270.

Lee, J. D., & Moray, N. (1994). Trust, self-confidence, and operators' adaptation to automation. *International Journal of Human-Computer Studies, 40*, 153–184.

Lee, J. D., & See, K. A. (2004). Trust in automation: Designing for appropriate reliance. *Human Factors, 46*(1), 50–80.

Lusk, C. M., Stewart, T. R., Hammond, K. R., & Potts, R. J. (1990). Judgment and decision making in dynamic tasks: The case of forecasting the microburst. *Weather and Forecasting, 5*(4), 627–639.

Mathews, G., & Campbell, S. E. (2009). Sustained performance under overload: Personality and individual differences in stress and coping. *Theoretical Issues in Ergonomics Science, 10*(5), 417–442.

Meyer, J. (2004). Conceptual issues in the study of dynamic hazard warnings. *Human Factors, 46*, 196–204.

Monsell, S. (2003). Task switching. *Trends in Cognitive Sciences, 7*, 137–140.

Moray, N. (1993). Designing for attention. In A. Baddeley & L. Weiskrantz (Eds.), *Attention, selection, awareness, and control* (pp. 111–134). Oxford: Oxford University Press.

Nickerson, R. S. (2005) Technology and cognitive amplification. In R. J. Sternberg & D. D. Preiss (Eds.), *Intelligence and technology: The impact of tools and technologies on the nature and development of human abilities* (pp. 3–25). Mahwah, NJ: Erlbaum.

Norman, D. A. (1982). Steps toward a cognitive engineering: Design rules based on analyses of human error. In J. A. Nichols & M. L. Schneider (Eds.), *Proceedings of the SIGCHI Conference on Human Factors in Computing Systems* (pp. 378–382). Gaithersburg, MD: Association for Computer Machinery.

Norman, D. A. (1990). The problem with automation: Inappropriate feedback and interaction, not over-automation. *Philosophical Transactions of the Royal Society of London, B3277*, No. 1241, 585–593.

Olson, G. M., & Olson, J. S. (2003). Human-computer interaction: Psychological aspects of the use of computing. *Annual Review of Psychology, 54*, 491–516.

Ophir, E., Nass, C., & Wagner, A. D. (2009). Cognitive control in media multitaskers. Proceedings of the National Academy of Sciences. Retrieved (August 2009) from: http://www.pnas.org_cgi_doi_10.1073_pnas.0903620106.

Parasuraman, R. (2009). Assaying individual differences in cognition with molecular genetics: theory and application. *Theoretical Issues in Ergonomics Science, 10*(5), 399–416.

Parasuraman, R., Molloy, R., & Singh, I. L. (1993). Performance consequences of automation-induced "complacency." *The International Journal of Aviation Psychology, 3*(1), 1–23.

Parasuraman, R., & Riley, V. (1997). Humans and automation use: Use, misuse, disuse, abuse. *Human Factors, 39*(2), 230–253.

Parasuraman, R., Sheridan, T. B., & Wickens, C. D. (2000). A model for types and levels of human interaction with automation. *IEEE Transactions on Systems, Man, and Cybernetics—Part A: Systems and Humans, 30*(3), 286–297.

Parasuraman, R., & Wickens, C. D. (2008). Humans: Still vital after all these years of automation. *Human Factors, 50*(3), 511–520.

Pew, R. W. (2000). The state of situation awareness measurement: Heading toward the next century. In M. R. Endsley & D. J. Garland (Eds.), *Situation awareness analysis and measurement* (pp. 33–50). Mahwah, NJ: Erlbaum.

Pew, R. W., & Mavor, A. S. (2007). *Human-system integration in the system development process: A new look.* Committee on Human-System Design Support for Changing Technology. Washington DC: National Academies Press.

Plato. ([n.d.] 1973). *Phaedrus and Letters VII and VIII.* New York: Penguin.

Preiss, D. D., & Sternberg, R. J. (2006). Effects of technology on verbal and visual-spatial abilities. *Cognitive Technology, 11*(1), 1–9.

Postman, N. (1993). *Technopoly: The surrender of culture to technology.* New York: Vintage Books.

Pritchett, A. R., & Bisantz, A. M. (2006). Measuring the fit between human judgments and alerting systems: A study of collision detection in aviation. In A. Kirlik (Ed.), *Adaptive perspectives on human-technology interaction* (pp. 91–104). New York: Oxford University Press.

Proctor, R. W., & Vu, K-P. L. (2009). Cummulative knowledge and progress in human factors. *Annual Review of Psychology, 51*, 623–651.

Rasmussen, J. (1983). Skills, rules, knowledge; signals, signs, and symbols, and other distinctions in human performance models. *IEEE Transactions on Systems, Man and Cybernetics, 13*, 257–266.

Rasmussen, J. (1986). *Information processing and human-machine interaction: An approach to cognitive engineering.* New York: North-Holland.

Rogers, W. A. (2008). Editorial. *Journal of Experimental Psychology: Applied, 14*(1), 1–4.

Rogers, W. A., Pak, R., & Fisk, A. D. (2007). Applied cognitive psychology in the context of everyday living. In F. T. Durso (Ed.), *Handbook of applied cognition* (2nd Ed.). (pp. 3–27). New York: Wiley.

Salas, E., Prince, C., Baker, D. P., & Shrestha, L. (1995). Situation awareness in team performance: Implications for measurement and training. *Human Factors, 37*(1), 123–136.

Sarter, N. B., & Woods, D. D. (1995). How in the world did we ever get into that mode? Mode error and awareness in supervisory control. *Human Factors, 37*, 1–19.

Sarter, N. B., Woods, D. D., & Billings, C. E. (1987). Automation surprises. In G. Salvendy (Ed.), *Handbook of human factors* (pp. 1409–1448). New York: Wiley.

Seong, Y., Bisantz, A. M., & Gattie, G. J. (2006). Trust, automation, and feedback: An integrated approach. In A. Kirlik (Ed.), *Adaptive perspectives on human-technology interaction* (pp. 105–113). New York: Oxford University Press.

Shadish, W. R., Cook, T. D., & Campbell, D. T. (2002). *Experimental and quasi-experimental designs for generalized causal inference.* New York: Wadsworth.

Sheridan, T. B. (1976). Toward a general model of supervisory control. In T. B. Sheridan & G. Johannsen (Eds.), *Monitoring behavior and supervisory control* (pp. 271–282). Elmsford, NY: Plenum.

Sheridan, T. B., & Johannsen, G. (1976). *Monitoring behavior and supervisory control.* New York: Plenum.

Sheridan, T. B., & Parasuraman, R. (2005). Human-automation interaction. In H. W. Hendrick (Ed.), *Reviews of human factors and ergonomics* (Vol. 1, pp. 89–129). Santa Monica, CA: Human Factors and Ergonomics Society.

Stewart, T. R., & Lusk, C. M. (1994). Seven components of judgmental forecasting skill: Implications for research and improvement of forecasts. *Journal of Forecasting, 13*, 579–599.

Stokes, D. E. (1997). *Pasteur's quadrant: Basic science and technological innovation.* Washington, DC: Brookings Institution Press.

Strauss, R., & Kirlik, A. (2006). Situation awareness as judgment. II: Experimental demonstration. *International Journal of Industrial Ergonomics, 36*, 475–484.

Strayer, D. L., & Drews, F. A. (2007). Multitasking in the automobile. In A. F. Kramer, D. A. Wiegmann, & A. Kirlik (Ed.), *Attention: From theory to practice* (pp. 121–133). New York: Oxford University Press.

Szalma, J. L. (2009). Individual differences in human-technology interaction: Incorporating human characteristics into human factors research and design. *Theoretical Issues in Ergonomics Science, 10*(5), 381–397.

Taylor, R. M. (1990). *Situational awareness rating technique (SART): The development of a tool for aircrew systems design.* Paper presented at the Situational Awareness in Aerospace Operations, Copenhagen, Denmark.

Trafton, J. G., & Monk, C. A. (2008). Task interruptions. In D. A. Boehm-Davis (Ed.), *Reviews of human factors and ergonomics* (Vol. 3, pp. 111–126). Santa Monica, CA: Human Factors & Ergonomics Society.

Tuffiash, M., Roring, R. W., & Ericsson, K. A. (2007). Expert performance in SCRABBLE: Implications for the study of the structure and acquisition of complex skills. *Journal of Experimental Psychology: Applied, 15*(3), 124–134.

Vicente, K. J. (1999). *Cognitive work analysis: Toward safe, productive, and healthy computer based work.* Mahwah, NJ: Erlbaum.

Vicente, K. J. (2001). Cognitive engineering research at Riso from 1962–1979. In E. Salas (Ed.), *Advances in human performance and cognitive engineering* research (Vol. 1, pp. 1–57). Oxford: Elsevier.

Wickens, C. D. (1980). The structure of attentional resources. In R. Nickerson (Ed.), *Attention and performance VIII* (pp. 239–257). Hillsdale, NJ: Erlbaum.

Wickens, C. D. (1989). Models of multitask situations. In G. McMillan, D. Beevis, E. Salas, M. H. Strub, R. Sutton, & L. Van Breda (Eds.), *Applications of human performance models to system design* (pp. 259–263). New York: Plenum Press.

Wickens, C. D. (2004). Multiple resource time sharing model. In N. A. Stanton, E. Salas, H. W. Hendrick, A. Hedge, & K. Brookhuis (Eds.), *Handbook of human factors and ergonomics methods* (pp. 40-1–40-7). London: Taylor & Francis.

Wickens, C. D., Lee, J. D., Liu, Y., & Gordon-Becker, S. (2003). *An introduction to human factors engineering* (2nd Ed.). Upper Saddle River, NJ: Prentice Hall.

Wickens, C. D., McCarley, J. S., Alexander, A., Thomas, L., Ambinder, M., & Zheng, S. (2008). Attention-situation awareness (ASA) model of pilot error. In D. Foyle & B. Hooey (Eds.), *Human performance modeling in aviation* (pp. 213–242). Boca Raton: CRC Press.

Wiener, E. L., & Curry, R. E. (1980). Flight-deck automation: Promises and problems. *Ergonomics, 23*, 995–1011.

Young, M. S., & Stanton, N. A. (2002). Attention and automation: New perspectives on mental underload and performance. *Theoretical Issues in Ergonomics Science, 3*(2), 178–194.

Zuboff, S. (1984). *In the age of the smart machine.* New York: Basic Books.

Cognition and Technology: Interdisciplinarity and the Impact of Cognitive Engineering Research on Organizational Productivity

Stephen M. Fiore

Abstract

In this chapter I describe the dynamic intersection of cognition and technology as it has emerged through the development of cognitive engineering research. This discipline has matured over the past several decades into an interdisciplinary approach, melding concepts and methods from cognitive psychology, computer science, and engineering with a holistic approach to understanding human-technology integration. I show how cognitive engineering has contributed to both a fundamental and practical understanding of human performance embedded in context, and I offer suggestions for developments in the field that may provide a more cohesive and unified approach to understanding and expanding human-systems integration.

Key Words: Cognitive engineering, human-system interaction, cognitive technology, problem solving, decision making, human performance

The twentieth century saw a tremendous increase in the integration of theory and methods with tools and technologies to support cognitive processing in individuals and in teams. Concomitant with this was a tremendous growth in the disciplines seeking to understand human cognition, and such research can now be found far beyond the halls of psychology departments. From this, we have seen important developments in which complex socio-technical systems are being built, based upon a sophisticated understanding of human cognition and human interaction with technology. Indeed, in recent writing on how such developments have helped to transform thought and society, we see articulated a simple, yet powerful statement—*the promise of cognitive psychology lies in the progress of cognitive technology* (Walker & Herrmann, 2005).

This chapter traces the development and evolution of aspects of *cognitive engineering*, a field driving the dynamic intersection of cognition and technology. For this chapter I specifically define *cognitive engineering* as a discipline that melds concepts and methods from cognitive psychology, computer science, and engineering with a holistic approach to understanding human-technology integration. Research in this area has addressed the unfolding of cognition in naturalistic and dynamic work environments, typically characterized by a multitude of human operators and, more recently, by automated technologies, all interacting collaboratively to accomplish their mission. The invariant emphasis of this research has been on improving the safety, quality, and efficiency of work systems for human operators through analysis of the interactions of the technology, the people, and the environment of operation, including the organization within which the humans operate.

Two interrelated threads of thinking—that of the tension between basic and applied research, and the need to understand cognition in complex environments—are used to show how this discipline has evolved into a truly interdisciplinary area of inquiry. In particular, cognitive engineering is a deeply interdisciplinary field drawing upon multiple disciplines—all to inform engineering and design. Framed within the context of debates in the history and philosophy of science and science policy, I use the notion of use-inspired basic research to show how this tension has led to a number of significant impacts on understanding and improving cognition during interactions with technology and as it unfolds in naturalistic settings.

In the first section of this chapter, I define what is meant by *use-inspired basic science* to set the stage for explaining the epistemological approach taken by cognitive engineering researchers. I also discuss research across disciplines and current thinking on interdisciplinary research to illustrate its relevance to cognitive engineering. In the second section, I discuss the history and primary developments in cognitive engineering. The history of cognitive engineering is tightly interconnected with applied psychology and, as such, any discussion of cognitive engineering must be understood within its applied contexts. I do this via juxtaposition of the somewhat parallel but intermingled developments in the United States in human factors research and in studies of cognitive work in both Europe and the Soviet Union. In the final section, I discuss important new developments in cognitive engineering and point to emerging directions of research that will shape organizational productivity in the twenty-first century.

Epistemological Approaches to Research and Development
Defining Use-Inspired Basic Science

By necessity, cognitive engineering is largely an applied science. It is driven by the "need" to remedy an existing organizational or system-based problem—a problem requiring one to examine the specific behavior, task, and technology. Although a seemingly obvious point, I bring this distinction to the forefront because cognitive engineering research, while being "need" based, has, nonetheless, been pursued with the curiosity inherent in basic science. As such, since its inception, cognitive engineering has bridged the divide between basic and applied science. By focusing on specific needs in particular contexts, yet pursuing a fundamental understanding of human cognition in these contexts, it has operated in a mode of research that can be described as "use-inspired" science (Stokes, 1997). The notion of use-inspired science was developed to illustrate the

problems arising from the standard dichotomy that categorizes research, that is, the split between basic research and applied science. Specifically, traditional views of science hold that basic research pursues a curiosity-driven increase in fundamental knowledge, whereas applied research considers a given need to develop technology, tools, or methods.

In his discussion of science policy for the twenty-first century, Stokes (1997) noted that the basic-applied dichotomy fails by not addressing research that exists both to advance scientific understanding and to produce a beneficial outcome. This form of research, what he labeled use-inspired basic science, captures the areas of inquiry where tremendous gains have been made when one considers fundamental questions while addressing particular needs. The groundbreaking research of Louis Pasteur illustrated Stokes's (1997) point in that Pasteur not only pursued innovative methods of disease prevention, he also contributed to a richer understanding of microbiology (Stokes, 1997). Stated most simply, use-inspired basic science addresses a particular need while simultaneously providing knowledge and understanding in a particular area, thus eliminating the misguided gap separating knowledge and use.

I suggest that *use-inspired science* illustrates the scientific considerations that set cognitive engineering research apart from so much of psychological science. More important, this concept of use-inspired science helps us to understand the history of this field (see also Fiore, 2008b), and I use this concept to contextualize key developments in the history of cognitive engineering research.

Research Across Disciplines

Not only has cognitive engineering effectively bridged the divide between basic and applied science, it has also played an important role in fostering interdisciplinary research. But *interdisciplinarity* as a term is often used without much consideration of its meaning. As such, it is useful to provide some definitional context for the terminology used to describe science across disciplines. My goal is to illustrate how cognitive engineering can truly be considered an interdisciplinary field and one that has, perhaps, been successful because of its focus on solving complex real-world problems.

At the simplest level, *cross-disciplinary research* merely involves researchers from different disciplines working together. What makes this rudimentary is that the nature of the interaction is not specified; as such, little if any collaboration must unfold. At a more complex level, *multidisciplinary research* is generally described as a more coordinated interaction among researchers from different disciplines. Further, these researchers are in pursuit of shared goals. Importantly, the contributions from the contributing disciplines are *complementary* and not *integrative*. This implies that methods and theories may be *adopted* but not necessarily *adapted* in innovative ways.

At the more complex level, we have *interdisciplinary research* in which the overarching goal is a systematic *integration* of ideas. This is distinguished from multidisciplinarity in research in that it involves developing a new approach to understanding. As such, interdisciplinarity demands more than just complementarity. It requires leading to design of *new types* of complex *empirical approaches,* along with *integrated analyses* combining the methods and concepts from participating disciplines (e.g., Klein, 1996; Pellmar & Eisenberg 2000). Indeed, this has been articulated by the National Academies of Science (2004), which states that it:

> integrates information, data, techniques, tools, perspectives, concepts, and/or theories from two or more disciplines or bodies of specialized knowledge to advance fundamental understanding or to solve problems whose solutions are beyond the scope of a single discipline or field of research practice (p. 26).

Essentially, interdisciplinary research must integrate a set of disciplines so as to create not only a unified outcome, but also something new, a new language, a new way of understanding and to do so in such a way that it is possible for a new discipline to evolve over time (cf. Barthes, 1977). In short, what emerges from this is a coordinated effort to synthesize concepts and methods from respective disciplines in such a way that a common, but much more complex, goal is met.

In other work (Fiore, 2008a), I have argued that interdisciplinary research is inherently a *team activity;* that is, it involves *action,* the act of connecting or *inter*acting among teams of researchers from differing disciplines. Given this, we can make a strong argument that cognitive engineering is an interdisciplinary field. It is an activity whereby researchers from different disciplines have focused on common goals arising from the shared need to solve complex problems. And, it has moved from the adoption of methods from psychology, computer science, and engineering, to the creation of new methods such as cognitive work analysis (e.g., Davies & Burns, 2008;

Roth, 2008; Vicente, 1999), and new theories such as Rasmussen's abstraction hierarchy (Rasmussen, 1985).

Use-Inspired Science and Interdisciplinary Research

In the remainder of this chapter, I weave together the two aforementioned themes—*problem focus* and *interdisciplinary* research—to illustrate the development of cognitive engineering. I do this because a *problem focus* has long been dismissed by universities as unworthy of academic research. Indeed, interdisciplinary research, which tends to be problem focused, was initially viewed as being too close to applied or industry research. In a review of the history of interdisciplinary research, Lynch (2006) noted that most articles discussing anything to do with research across disciplines seemed to focus on ways to come up with improved solutions to applied problems, and he noted that the idea is often expressed that "the need for interdisciplinarity is greatest in the applied arenas of intervention and policy change" (p. 1119). But this view has a long history—a history arguing that research seeking practical results to solve problems had its place in industry, and that research seeking fundamental answers to scientific questions belonged in academia. For example, Brozek and Keys (1944) noted, over 60 years ago, in one of the first articles to discuss interdisciplinarity, that many "problems of a fundamental theoretical character which require a cooperative approach are not likely to be studied by industrial laboratories, the very existence of which often depends upon immediate, practical results" (p. 509).

Despite this tension between basic/applied science and the complexity of interdisciplinary research, I use this distinction to illustrate the core thesis of this essay—that interdisciplinarity is most successful when it is problem focused. This point is a non-trivial one because problem-based research has typically been seen as only the purview of applied research. Although this view has merit, I suggest that it obscures a key issue. Specifically, as Stokes (1997) suggested, basic science often emerges most fruitfully out of attempts to understand very real problems. But my argument takes Stokes's (1997) point about "use-inspired science" to a new level. Whereas Stokes (1997) noted that one could do basic science in the consideration of real-world problems, I argue that a problem focus produces the most successful form of interdisciplinarity; that is, an activity of research that is robust enough to sustain itself over time such that a new discipline emerges. I suggest that, given the teamwork challenges associated with interdisciplinary research (see Fiore, 2008a), this focus on a problem unites a team of researchers from different disciplines, allowing them to develop a shared understanding of their problem context. Further, this shared understanding allows them to adapt theory and methods from their respective disciplines to the needs of this problem, thus increasing the likelihood of creating something new. I next discuss key developments in the history of applied science to illustrate how they formed an important foundation for cognitive engineering research and the solving of complex real-world problems while contributing to a fundamental understanding of particular phenomena.

A Brief History of Cognitive Engineering

Nearly a half century's worth of research related to cognitive engineering cogently illustrates the benefits of use-inspired science. But to understand the evolution of cognitive engineering we must examine the interdisciplinary efforts that constituted its beginnings. These exemplify how fields have long crossed disciplinary boundaries while adding to the body of knowledge and addressing complex real-world problems.

Early Applied Research and the Birth of Psychology

Much of the early research in human behavior focused on applied problems in particular contexts. Early pioneers in the study of human performance in applied settings include Bryan and Harter, Taylor, and Münsterberg. For example, in their investigations of telegraph operators, Bryan and Harter (1899) set the stage for experimental examination of industrial skills. Importantly, their methods included observation and interview of what would today be characterized as expert and novice telegraph operators and provided important insights into our understanding of learning and training motor skills. Further, they were some of the first researchers to develop notions of a learning curve and the influence of practice on skill development. Early human factors research can be traced to the methods of Frederick Taylor, who pioneered the development of "scientific management." Taylor, who was president of the American Society of Mechanical Engineers, took some of the first steps in integrating engineering with an understanding of human behavior. This work in time-and-motion studies was an early formulation of the systematic investigation of human behavior in the industrial process (Taylor, 1911).

The work of Hugo Münsterberg, though, is argued by some to represent some of the most important early contributions to what would become applied psychology as the twentieth century began to unfold (see Moskowitz, 1977). Münsterberg's (1908) research was clearly psychological in nature, moving studies of behavior from the motor to the mental. Further, he cogently illustrates my point about how problem-based research can both inform and drive theory development. In his studies of courtroom testimony, he was able to both explore and understand human behavior and biases within that context, marking a paradigm shift within the field of psychology. His work *On the Witness Stand* (1908) documents applied psychology's inherently interdisciplinary essence. He called for theoretical psychology to be adjusted to the problems in the world by the insights of multiple disciplines, stating, "The time for such Applied Psychology is surely near, and work has been started from most various sides. Those fields of practical life which come first in question may be said to be education, medicine, art, economics, and law" (Münsterberg, 1908, p. 9).

Setting the stage for philosophical arguments that continue to this day, his call to collaboration was met with a resistance still echoed in contemporary clashes between proponents of basic and applied psychology research. As such, the field of applied psychology has not emerged without challenges through the decades since Münsterberg. These challenges grew from divergent perspectives in the purpose and intention of science as psychology was maturing as a discipline. On one side of the debate, psychology's purists asserted that the mind must be studied for the sake of understanding the mind itself, whereas applied psychologists believed that the knowledge was not enough and should result in some practical end (Moskowitz, 1977). At the time, most of academia comprised traditional psychologists who were concerned with academic and scientific integrity, a valid imperative. Applied psychologists rebutted by providing real-world examples of psychological science's appositeness (see Hoffman & Deffenbacher 1992). But it was research and development during the world wars that helped to cement its place in the practice of science.

Though applied psychology had a strong foothold in Great Britain and the United States, the events of World War I would press it forward in unforeseeable contexts (Koppes, Thayer, Vinchur, & Salas, 2007). The very nature of this new form of large-scale war and industrialized complex combat machinery demanded new approaches to examining human behavior in the context of efficiency and productivity. World War I would elicit studies like those conducted by Watson and Dunlap on the effects of fatigue and oxygen deprivation on aviation operators (see Hoffman & Deffenbacher, 1992). The military had particular interest in the performance of this new combatant, the pilot, and consequently made efforts to understand and facilitate successful aviation performance. From this unavoidable element of modern battle, one of the earliest non-medical tests would come forth. Dunlap developed psychological tests to determine which individuals could function successfully under the effects of high-altitude stress (see Meister, 1999). Though this genre of research was driven by application, it would contribute to the field's body of theory as well. For example, Thorndike provided empirical research in cognitive bias of cadets and their trainers—research that led to the development of the "halo effect" theory (Thorndike, 1920).

The early twentieth century also saw the creation of Cambridge University's very influential psychology laboratories (Smith, 2007). These labs were founded by Samuel Myers, who published one of the early volumes on *industrial psychology*—the phrase he used to describe the study of human behavior in the workplace (Myers, 1929). Frederick Bartlett, known more for his studies of remembering, conducted early important work on pilot selection and training at these laboratories (Bartlett, 1937). This also led to the development of the "Cambridge Cockpit," which represented some of the first research on the use of simulations to inform both design and a deeper understanding of human behavior in complex contexts (Smith, 2007). As two world wars were informed and supported by the application of psychology, the field had become woven into the military's selection processes, training, and human factors (Driskell & Olmstead, 1989; Katzell & Austin, 1992).

This historical review brings the reader to a critical culminating observation: demand for practical, need-driven insight into human-technology interaction resulted in applied psychology connecting with other sciences. These productive collaborations improved human performance in high-stakes situations because of the diverse contributions from engineering, biology, and psychology (Katzell & Austin, 1992). Watson and Dunlap could not have

made the same contributions to aviation in a psychology vacuum; their work depended on collaboration with military medical officers and physiologists (see Meister, 1999). The expanded role of computers by the end of World War II only emphasized the demand for previously diametric fields, such as psychology and computer science, to contribute to shared research. The burgeoning study of human behavior in complex settings would welcome insight from any science that could illuminate the puzzles of human, system, and task—all setting the stage for acceptance of interdisciplinary research in what would evolve into cognitive engineering.

Growth of Human Factors and Applied Cognitive Research

System enhancement through design and training evolved as some of the primary arms of applied performance research (Katzell & Austin, 1992; Moray, 2008). The work of Paul Fitts pioneered the development of *engineering psychology* and elegantly illustrated interdisciplinary value by the introduction of mathematical modeling to the study of human behavior (Fitts, 1951). Norbert Wiener at MIT developed the term *cybernetics* in the 1940s to describe the increasing focus on the control of systems, and his work included some of the early use of concepts such as *input* and *output* (Wiener, 1948). Other developments around this time included signal detection theory, designed to understand the perceptual and cognitive processes involved in varying levels of signal and noise. Illustrating how problem-driven research can drive theory development, signal detection theory research arose out of the "need" to understand how to detect enemy aircraft via radar waves (see Green & Swets, 1966). Alphonse Chapanis similarly helped to bridge the basic-applied research gap in the development of the field of human factors and ergonomics. His research during World War II helped him to understand the importance of carefully controlled experimental studies to inform complex real-world problems (see Chapanis, 1967). But he also helped to articulate why system designers needed to carefully attend to both psychology and physiology as ever more complex machines were being integrated into the activity of human work (Chapanis, 1970). This era also saw the work of George Miller help define the field of cognitive psychology as its own discipline. While at Bell Labs, his work on language weakened the theoretical primacy of behaviorism, and his research on memory represented seminal thinking in information-processing theory (Miller, 1956). But it was his publication of *Plans and the Structure of Behavior* (Miller, Galanter, & Pribram, 1960) that helped to cement the computer metaphor for understanding human cognition via discussion of learning as encoding and retrieval.

In Europe and the Soviet Union, there were also important theoretical developments in the expansion of the role of context in the study of work. Soviet psychology began to develop a number of influential theories that brought attention to context more to the forefront and which today still make an impact on our understanding of complex cognition. Led by psychologists such as Vygotsky (1978), Luria (1979), and Leont'ev (1978), this group pioneered paradigms and frameworks for examining the relation between the individual and systemic work. The resulting activity theory provided conceptual tools for looking at the activity of a person simultaneously in macro- and micro-levels and while embedded in particular contexts (for a discussion, see Engeström, 2000; Nardi, 1996a).

Central to activity theory is *mediation by artifacts*, the connections between humans and their experiences in the world (Nardi, 1996a). Mediators may take many forms—signs, tools, language, machines, and so forth—but the defining factor is the cyclical role that they play as humans create their own experiences. Artifacts are intrinsically historical, anthropological, and sociological, and can be understood through lenses of traditionally hard and soft sciences. Activity theory displaced the imperative to distinguish applied science from pure science by employing multidisciplinary research so that context (internally and externally) would be considered at every turn.

Context became a meaningful concept, applied by activity theorists in a specific way. In this approach, the activity *is* the context. Context is not simply the space or time in which people behave. As Nardi describes:

> Context is both internal to people—involving specific objects and goals—and at the same time, external to people, involving artifacts, other people, specific settings. The crucial point is that in activity theory, external and internal are fused, unified ... context cannot be conceived as simply a set of external "resources" lying about. One's ability—and choice—to marshal and use resources is, rather, the result of specific historical and developmental processes in which a person is changed.
> (*Nardi*, 1996b, p. 38)

Therefore, internal cognitive processes cannot be understood if isolated from the numerous aspects of the external environment, an observation that would impact applied psychology.

Soviet activity theory would work its way into cognitive analysis of system designs throughout Europe and eventually North America during the following decades. To illustrate how this contextually grounded theoretical approach helped to both understand a particular phenomenon and solve complex real-world problems, consider the following example. Engeström (2000) applied activity theory to a work redesign at a children's medical facility in Finland. The complex activity of patient care, which involved a network of activity containing such components as computers with patient test results, primary and specialist physicians, paper charts, and families, helped Engeström (2000) articulate the dynamic interconnections of subjects, objects, instruments, rules, community, division of labor, and outcome. The longitudinal study disproved the theory that continuity in action could be fully credited to an internal script, directing the normal order for every task. He observed, "Activity systems realize and reproduce themselves by generating actions and operations" (Engeström, 2000). The distinction between static knowledge and evolving, networked, and collective activity became clear as deviations from a standard script inevitably arose. He observed that these *disturbances* typically indicated "developmentally significant systemic contradictions and change potentials within the activity" (p. 964).

With this we see the important iterative nature of this give-and-take between theory and problem. At one level, these organizational disturbances were shown to result in higher expenses and disrupted care. But, at another level, by identifying such problems, the researchers were able to conceptualize the nature of this work as evolving and collective. In conjunction, such work contributes to our theoretical understanding of dynamic collaborative work while making practical recommendations for improvement, thus solving real-world problems. It is unlikely that any analyses other than in-field could have brought the type of rich understanding that can contribute to building a theoretical understanding of this form of complex collaboration.

Of Tasks and Systems

The prior sections were designed to illustrate important early thinking that coupled psychology with computer science and engineering. This type of human-system integration helped to inform theory regarding contextual performance and simultaneously provided immediate application of said theories. The use-inspired nature of human-system integration and human-computer interaction helped to create accessible exemplars, and the attention to context provided the type of information that necessarily feeds training. But the term *cognitive engineering* itself did not emerge until the early 1980s (e.g., Woods & Roth, 1988) as researchers begin to more specifically emphasize how it was that both theory and method from cognitive psychology could be considered in the design of human-machine systems. The related discipline of *cognitive systems engineering* also emerged at this time, to call closer attention to phenomena that emerge at the intersection of technology and people in the workplace (Flach, 1998; Hollnagel & Woods, 1983; Rasmussen, Pejtersen, & Goodstein, 1994).

The nuclear power plant failures of the late twentieth century provided an important catalyst for acceptance of the need to understand complex work in context. The profound costs of nuclear system failures compelled researchers to examine the fundamental problems from the perspective of numerous fields, leading to advancements in computer-based cognitive aids, effective training, automation, and human-centered design (e.g., Hollnagel & Woods, 2005; Hollnagel, Woods, & Leveson, 2006; Moray & Huey, 1988). One critical component of complex work—context—became a focus for research and a foundational concept for developing multilevel theories of performance (Hoffman & Woods, 2000; Woods & Roth, 1988). Research on contextualized performance helped to understand how an operator can successfully resolve a crisis when, for example, controls are limited, or the environment shifts; just as significantly, it helped to better understand the avenues for system success when the operator is under stress (Moray & Huey, 1988). I next describe in more detail some of the problem-driven research that the field of cognitive engineering pursued as it matured into its own interdisciplinary field (for more detailed reviews, see Endsley, Hoffman, Kaber, & Roth, 2007; Hoffman, Klein, & Laughery, 2002; Moray, 2008).

From Task Analysis to Cognitive Task Analysis

The surfacing of new technologies and the creation of new work in the latter half of the last century would require research to consider topics that had either not existed or, at least, were the exception rather than the norm. After all, at no point in human history did the average worker have a personal computer at his or her desk until the 1980s. As an example of how "use" drives theory development, the commonplace infiltration of complex equipment into already complex environments (e.g., command centers, power plants) compelled reassessment of the theories and frameworks that traditional approaches had advanced. As the field became increasingly user-inspired, cognitive engineering followed the scientific trend and moved from a basic framework of task analysis to a more holistic and useful cognitive task analysis (see Hoffman & Militello, 2008).

Task analysis creates simple chains of activity in which steps in an activity follow each other linearly. In some contexts, this works effectively, as in the early task analysis found in Taylor's (1911) time-and-motion studies of coke shoveling. Here we have a quintessential example of how behavior was observed within a task context and was analyzed to identify inefficiencies and to recommend procedures for improvement. Essentially, a simplified version of task analysis allows one to slow down a process (which is most likely automatically carried out), break it into steps, and carefully coach one to mastery.

But this parsing obscured the overall nature of the task in that it completely ignored the mental aspects of the task—something particularly problematic in high-tech environments. As Hoffman et al. (2002) noted:

> The point is not that something is inherently wrong about the notion of a task as an expression of a particular goal, but that task analysis as it has been applied can sometimes be limiting. When regularly occurring sequences are regarded as invariant and therefore predefined, systems designed on this basis can run a substantial risk of being flawed. Specifically, you can expect them to lead to fragilities, hostilities, and automation surprises. In short, they might not be human-centered.
>
> (p. 73)

Using a more gestalt approach, it was argued that the decision-making process in a dynamic and complex system could be better informed by *cognitive task analysis* (Crandall, Klein, & Hoffman, 2006; Militello & Hutton, 1998; Rasmussen, 1986). Built on the tradition of applied psychology, *cognitive task analysis* (CTA) developed methodologies and means of practice that would emerge as particularly significant in the 1980s as technology integration rapidly grew. Knowledge elicitation, data analysis, and knowledge representation became the primary aspects of CTA (Crandall et al., 2006). It however, is not one tidy concept, as elements (which now are incorporated into CTA) developed simultaneously but independently in different parts of the world.

In application, the bulk of data gathered in CTA comes from in-depth observation and interviews with experts (Crandall et al., 2006; Klein & Militello, 2001; Militello & Hutton, 1998). Studying expert cognition in subjects ranging from firefighters to pilots has provided rich insight into the knowledge, skills, and cognitive flow necessary for optimal performance. Workers' narratives provide key data sources as to how they determine the best choice or what they were thinking when a given problem initiated. For example, a researcher may ask a probing question such as, "Can you think of a time when a decision you made had an important impact…or the outcome of a circumstance would have been different without you?" Or, if analyzing a particular system disturbance, "What were you noticing at that point?" (Crandall et al., 2006). The answers to these types of questions capture knowledge and reasoning; they present data on what makes a task work or what could make it work better in ways that basic research could not. By recognizing both the importance of the context of the task, and by considering the mental components of the work, this represented an important evolution of applied cognitive work that produced fruitful collaborations between psychology, engineering, and organizational science—all to improve the experience of work.

Indeed, it was this collaboration between psychology, engineering, and organizational science that influenced Jens Rasmussen, at RISØ National Laboratory in Denmark, to develop some of the early influential theories of cognitive task analysis. As ergonomics intrinsically seeks to fit people, work, and tools, it comes as no surprise that an engineer in ergonomics could contribute significantly to the evolution of cognitive task analysis. Perhaps more than any researcher, he eloquently argued that support for operators required analysis of the mental activities of decision making within tasks (Rasmussen, 1985). His goal was not to describe the information process so much as it was to analyze and identify requirements that were to be considered in making a decision. His cognitive task analysis offered three domains: the problem, the decision sequence, and the mental strategies and heuristics. Further, his development of the "abstraction hierarchy," where complex work was analyzed across multiple levels,

and through multiple perspectives, helped influence the design and understanding of complex cognitive work in domains such as nuclear power. Here one looks at the functional purpose of a task, but also considers abstract and generalized functions, along with physical functions and forms. From this, researchers were better able to illustrate how work analysis benefited from numerous perspectives (Crandall et al., 2006; Rasmussen, 1985).

Out of this research came more specific tools to support system design—tools that more fully blurred the distinctions between cognition and engineering. Vicente and Rasmussen (1990) proposed ecological interface design (EID) as a valuable approach to mediating perception and machine in complex work domains. EID is a theoretical framework that allows Rasmussen's means-end hierarchy to address the connate problems of cognitive engineering—problems such as dynamics, slow feedback, and high-stake situations (Vicente & Rasmussen, 1990). The principles of EID do not provide a "design cookbook" (p. 227) with step-by-step procedures, but guide designers in asking useful questions. Their theoretical tools provided an example of how applied cognitive psychology could be used to extrapolate the affordances of a work domain and to provide technical support in problem solving. Frameworks, such as EID, assist engineers in creating bridges from empirical and computational research to field study and more complex cognitive activity (Davies & Burns, 2008).

Cognitive Work Analysis and Understanding Humans In Situ

Rapid advances in computer applications, which tremendously increased the complexity of man-machine systems, led many to argue that theory was not keeping pace with many of the developments impinging on modern work (Hollnagel & Woods, 1999). Methods such as CTA and EID were not enough to address this growing complexity. Researchers such as Hollnagel (2002) were making inroads into modifications to standard human-system interaction models, and he presented a model of joint cognitive systems (JCS), arguing more eloquently for the importance of context in understanding human-machine interaction. He traced the philosophical lineage of the language that researchers have used to describe the function and structure of technologies and human cognition. He questioned the traditional premise of considering the machine isolated from the operator, viewed entirely as a tool, with human cognition viewed as an input-output model of the computation metaphor. Hollnagel (2002) argued that those narrow views moved human-machine systems research to focus on human limitations rather than on functional versatility and impeded designing intelligent dynamic systems that could work within multiple levels. He wrote:

> Cognitive Systems Engineering (CSE) has tried to overcome this limitation by shifting the focus from the internal functions of either human or machine to the external functions of the Joint Cognitive System (JCS). An important consequence of putting the focus on the JCS is that the boundaries must be explicitly defined, both those between the system and its environment or context, and those between the elements or parts of the system.
> (*Hollnagel*, 2002, p. 3)

That natural consequence of defining the boundaries allows researchers to begin examining systems within systems and to distinguish systemic components from environmental factors. Hollnagel (2002) uses the example of a pilot and a cockpit as one joint cognitive system, but one that is within a larger cognitive system that includes such components as company and aviation authority. The smaller JCS (pilot/cockpit) and the larger one (all components) are within the environment, which includes weather. Hollnagel (2002) says, "The boundary depends on the purpose of the analysis, hence on the function of the JCS rather than on its structure or composition" (p. 3). Hollnagel (2002) outlined a contextual control model to examine the functions needed to establish desired performance; its three constituents are: *competence, control,* and *constructs*. As actions take place on multiple levels, the spiraling nature of the JCS lends itself to a detailed extended control model, whose activity loops Hollnagel calls *tracking, regulating, monitoring,* and *targeting* (Hollnagel, 2002; see also Vicente, 1999; Woods, 1985). Further, illustrating the primacy of context, as noted by Roth (2008), what is required is "understanding both the domain characteristics and constraints that define cognitive requirements and challenges and the knowledge and strategies that underlie expert and error-vulnerable performance" (p. 478).

In short, not unlike multilevel theoretical views emerging in organizational psychology, Hollnagel and colleagues recognized the value of looking at a level above or below a given phenomenon to identify causal factors. In particular, multilevel theorizing integrates several levels of analysis (e.g., individuals, groups, and organizations) and articulates how constructs cut across levels (see Dansereau & Yammarino, 2002; Klein & Kozlowski, 2000a; 2000b). Considering these approaches in light of complex systems, the argument is that, without a multilevel theoretical approach, critical relationships might be missed, and designers and trainers might inaccurately specify the relations that they are attempting to address (cf. Mumford, Schultz, & Osburn, 2002; Hackman, 2003). Thus, by moving beyond the traditional input-throughput-output models and taking a more holistic view of work, such approaches were able to significantly contribute to theoretical developments of complex collaborative activity.

Summary

In sum, during the 1980s, independent and parallel groups of researchers from across the globe generated complimentary fields of study contributing to the growth of cognitive engineering as a discipline—these include cognitive systems engineering, European work analysis, instructional design, cognitive architectures (which would include computer simulation and human-computer interaction), workplace ethnography/cognitive anthropology, cognitive machines and AI, cognitive field research, and naturalistic decision making (Crandall et al., 2006). Further, many of these techniques have been developed, themselves, as a collaborative activity between practitioner and analyst, to uncover what experts know about their tasks in ways to inform and improve system design (Hoffman & Lintern, 2006; Roth, 2008). Though developing in different places and nuanced with distinct perspectives, cognitive engineering research began to converge to provide unprecedented epistemological insights.

Future Directions in Cognitive Engineering

Future advances in cognitive engineering will need to build upon the research foundations that have coalesced basic and applied approaches examining human, system, and task in context. However, the successful development of new technologies and methods for improving organizational productivity will only emerge from strategic integration of these interdisciplinary approaches (cf. Fiore & Salas, 2007). Strategic integration implies a shared and explicit expression of *how* to develop policy-level research projects aimed at addressing particular needs and voids in the current body of knowledge. From this, research in cognitive engineering can develop theoretically valid and applicable understanding of how technology supports the user in important new areas emerging in industry and the military. Fundamentally, this requires enhancing human and systems interaction, decreasing impairment of human performance and, all the while, ensuring that the role of the person is paramount.

I argue that the core of such an approach must continue to be the twin need of epistemology and ecology, the combination of which create the substructure of strategic human-centered engineering research and development. From this foundation, researchers can formulate not only the design issues, but also the processes of learning and performance involved in complex hybrid tasks where humans are now seamlessly blending with systems. In the following section, I describe interrelated research and provide examples to guide researchers in applying history to the future—learning from the past in hopes of intelligently shaping the direction of the field of cognitive engineering tomorrow. Two key areas that I present as examples of research that are changing the face of performance and productivity in complex environments are intelligent agent technology and augmented cognition.

Intelligent Agents and Human-Agent Collaboration

The idea of an *intelligent agent* was born from the intermingling concepts and theories from simulation, psychology, and computer science (e.g. Wooldridge & Jennings, 1995) and is now making inroads into cognitive engineering. Importantly, the potential for application is immense, as they have already demonstrated usefulness in a variety of contexts, including on-time decision support (Bul & Lee, 1999; Taylor, Stensrud, Eitelman, Dunham, & Harger, 2007) and simulations (Harbers, Bosch, & Meyer, 2008; Stacy, Freeman, Lackey, & Merket, 2004; Tambe et al., 1995). These examples show that intelligent agents can play a worthwhile role in training and support of humans in high-stress contexts (Petrox & Stoyen, 2000). But the question is, to what degree, and how specifically, can intelligent agents more seamlessly blend with organizational needs, and how can cognitive engineering help drive such research?

One promising area is that of examining human-agent teamwork. Over the past several decades, the prevalence of teams and teamwork in organizations has significantly increased. But, to a large degree, team members must still do all aspects of their task, from the simple to the complex, from the mundane to the intriguing. I submit that an important contribution to organizational productivity can be in the off-loading of the simple and/or mundane to agents as team members. Although not a ground-breaking idea, it is one that has, surprisingly, not gained a great deal of research attention. Technologies exist, and are currently in use, that need to be researched in the context of organizational teams. Information-gathering agents are increasingly being used to scour the Internet for data of interest to us, and scheduling agents are able to manage simple tasks such as identifying and filling travel requirements. Research needs to examine the applicability and extensibility of these capabilities to organizational teams. For example, a long line of research in team performance suggests that experienced teams develop a shared understanding or shared mental model utilized to coordinate behaviors by anticipating and predicting each other's needs and adapting to task demands (Cannon-Bowers, Salas, & Converse, 1993; Marks, Zaccaro, & Mathieu, 2000; Mathieu, Heffner, Goodwin, Salas, & Cannon-Bowers, 2000; Salas & Fiore, 2004).

Despite findings surrounding effective interaction and coordination for teams in general, little is known about what is important in effective *human-agent teams*. In order for such developments to reach broader acceptance, research must help us understand the communication and coordination processes arising from such interaction and the specific conditions affecting them. Human-agent team interaction introduces a number of issues with respect to both team and individual cognition that are distinct from traditional team interactions (Sycara & Lewis, 2004). For example, individuals operating in human-agent teams may have to deal with an increased level of abstraction that may place unique demands on their information processing (Fiore, Cuevas, Schooler, & Salas, 2005). Important questions in this regard include addressing the utility of intelligent agents reflecting or imitating human emotion or cognition to support collaboration efforts (Wooldridge & Jennings, 1995).

A significant challenge with these new technologically based "teammates" is to understand the intricacies of the interactions between humans with agents or even with robots (Goodrich & Schultz, 2007). This encompasses understanding basic phenomena such as how agents are able to contribute to, and manage, various forms of social engagement (Argall et al., 2009; Asada et al., 2009). Importantly, as the field moves forward, we will see the need for capabilities in natural social communication such as shared attention, and making and recognizing gestures turn taking (Elias et al., 2011;

Streater et al., 2011). This, in turn, will require an understanding of how to train or teach agents and robots the appropriate forms of interaction and interdependencies within teams (cf. Argall et al., 2009; Thomaz & Breazeal, 2008). Recent research in the use of advanced capabilities in simulation and training may enable this (Bockelman et al., 2011).

Given its human-centered approach, cognitive engineering is well-positioned to lead this charge. For example, one unifying component in seeking the answer to such questions is context, as both presentation and interaction with intelligent agents is largely governed by the context in which they are employed. In essence, cognitive engineering can begin to address context concerns before the technology is even developed or deployed. Such a direct approach to preparing organizations for the implementation of intelligent agents calls for research that crosses modalities and interacts in varied contexts. Researchers employing "man behind the curtain studies" (where full emulation is not necessary, as a researcher assumes the role of the agent in high-tech puppetry) can develop behavioral frameworks for the future when intelligent and emotional agents are implemented. This approach to research creates empirical authority with the future applications succinctly in mind, a future with artificial agents who will be sophisticated enough to not only reflect aspects of humanity, but to enhance human performance.

Augmented Cognition and the Brain-Computer Interface

Whereas intelligent agents provide cognitive assistants to support human performance, *augmented cognition* seeks to directly enhance the cognitive processes of humans. More specifically, it seeks to mitigate the limitations and boost the faculties of human cognition (St. John, Kobus, Morrison, & Schmorrow, 2004). From psychology, education, and neuroscience, we have gained an intimate understanding of human cognitive limitations—ranging from biases in decision making to limitations in memory capacity (e.g., Gabrieli, 1998; Simon, 1990). But, in complement, computer systems are advancing in ability and complexity every day. Augmented cognition seeks to bridge such theory with technology to truly meld human with system (Stanney et al., 2009). As such, it represents another important development on which the human-centered lens of cognitive engineering can focus.

Importantly, methods and theories from the study of cognition are developing enough to inform these approaches. In the context of cognitive engineering, the field of ergonomics has spawned a subdiscipline to examine the underlying neurology of operational tasks—referred to as *neuroergonomics* (e.g., Hancock & Szalma, 2003; Parasuraman, 2003). In line with cognitive engineering more generally, but quite fitting with developing systems for the brain-computer interface, neuroergonomics aims to combine findings from the cognitive sciences with knowledge of brain function to better design performance-support systems. For example, when an individual is unable (or unlikely) to attend to a cognitive task, a computer system may act as a cognitive prosthesis, not replacing the human, but enhancing (e.g., Pavel, Wang, & Li, 2003). Although primarily explored in defense applications (e.g., Stanney et al., 2009), the potential applications of augmented cognition are being explored for civilian settings, such as providing memory aids for impaired seniors (e.g., Adams & Gill, 2007).

Nonetheless, organizational scientists have yet to seriously consider these developments in their research. But consideration of such capabilities in organizations represents fertile ground for research that has a significant chance of expanding efficiencies and productivity. I submit that cognitive engineering research needs to explore augmentation at the intra- and interindividual level in order to address the needs to organizations. As an example of how to augment intraindividual cognition, consider that, although personal digital assistants (PDAs) are commonplace, we have yet to see research that seriously addresses their utility as a cognitive aid for either individuals or teams within organizations. Ubiquitous computing represents an important development out of computer science (e.g., Kawamura, Fukuhara, Takeda, Kono, & Kidode, 2006; Svanaes, 2001) that could be merged with research in augmented cognition and examined via the analytical lens of cognitive engineering in pursuit of organizational productivity. Computing is now ever present in the background of our lives, with powerful information-processing capabilities available through everyday devices such as PDAs and televisions, and soon through tabletops and walls. (Polsad, 2009). For example, information overlays, where handheld PDAs are linked to GPS devices or embedded sensors, will be capable of providing real-time, anywhere information to suit our needs. Rather than requiring a standard computer to do a search for us, such technology is capable of pushing that information our way based merely on location information.

We can also envision research on augmenting interindividual cognition. This is where the theoretical strengths of cognitive engineering and organizational science can truly complement each other. Training needs analyses, where one identifies the organizational, team, and individual-level needs, represents the kind of tool that could identify technology intervention targets. For example, if a needs analysis finds that backup behavior is an important component of teamwork (e.g., Marks, Mathieu, & Zaccaro, 2001), then research could consider how embedded prompts can be developed to ensure that teammates stay on top of each other's needs. Information sharing is another component of collaboration where technology can be explored. Although news feeds are commonplace, we have yet to see serious research in how to manage such information in a way that does not overwhelm users and/or deliver such information at the time of need. In short, these are the sorts of research issues that, when cognitive engineering is considered in light of organizational needs and the potential for augmented cognition, can be explored to support productivity in the workplace.

Indeed, much of this theorizing fits with developments in the cognitive sciences that relate the interaction of brain, body, and environment. Theorizing about extended or externalized cognition helps to explain how cognition emerges beyond the brain in highly situated contexts (see Clark, 2001; Hutchins, 1995; Rowlands, 1999). This notion has recently been used to explain team cognition in complex contexts whereby collaborating teams use each other, their environment, and tools to solve problems (Fiore et al., 2010a; 2010b). These approaches emphasize the practice of cognition "by which internal representations are incomplete contributors in a context-sensitive system rather than fixed determinants of output: and they too focus on the ongoing interactive dance between brain and world" (Sutton, 2006, p. 282). This research builds upon earlier work which has explored how externalized problem representations scaffold collaborative problem solving. These are viewed as "...knowledge and structure in the environment, as physical symbols, objects, or dimensions...and as external rules, constraints, or relations embedded in physical configurations" (Zhang, 1997, p. 180). Relevant to the integration of technologies for improving organizational productivity, research in the cognitive sciences suggests that problem features are often distributed across internal cognitive systems and the environment or technologies being used (Zhang & Norman, 1994; 1995) as well as between the environment and multiple individuals (Zhang, 1998). Others argue that "the degree the team-task requires the construction of a shared understanding, external representational tools can act as a scaffolding to facilitate the building of that shared representation" (Fiore & Schooler, 2004, p. 134). In this context, externalized cognition becomes "a concrete manifestation of the team's conceptualization of the problem...[noting that these] allow collaborators to visually articulate abstract concepts and manipulate these task artifacts as the problem solving process proceeds [and] act as a scaffolding with which the team can construct a truly shared, and concrete, depiction of the process problem" (p. 144). The value of external cognition to complex collaborative environments has been extensively researched in area like medical decision making (Nemeth et al., 2004; 2006) where schedules, lists and display boards inform distributed planning and "mediate collective work...as a way to maintain an overview of the total activity...[and] are products of various work activities that are distributed in time and location" (2006, p. 728). Thus, theorizing about externalized cognition in an important development arising from cognitive engineering and, now that it is becoming integrated with team research in the development of the notion of "macrocognition in teams" (Fiore et al., 2010a; 2010b; Kozlowski & Chao, 2012), it is likely to significantly influence organizational productivity.

Nonetheless, despite such advances, the pervasiveness of such technological power introduces as many challenges as it does opportunities for enhancing organizational productivity. As such, cognitive engineering must be ever mindful of its human-centered approach to technology development and ensure that new technologies are designed with users in mind, rather than being merely designed for use. As a science, it must consider the recognized frailties of humans and approach novel employment of augmented cognition technology to remove their impact in volatile circumstances, while concurrently using and amplifying the skills at which people excel.

Conclusions

I have worked to make a case that cognitive engineering has emerged as an important interdisciplinary field that has contributed to both a fundamental and practical understanding of human performance embedded in context. I conclude by suggesting that what is required is for the field to continue melding historically disparate fields but to do so, not organically, as it has done over the last several decades, but more strategically. A more cohesive science is required, that is, one reaching for more unified theories and methods to understand and expand human-systems integration. This would benefit cognitive engineering more generally and organizational science more specifically.

Understanding the nature of "work" requires cohesive integration of ecological relevance and epistemological validity across, within, and among contributing domains. Effective and expanded disciplinary syntrophy can lead to theories that guide the field in design, training, and selection for systematic advancement. But this type of cross-talk requires not only cognitive engineering reaching into organizations, it requires organizational psychology reaching out to cognitive engineering. Organizational research embraced the cognitive revolution during the 1980s, but I submit that, if they look even farther afield, the potential for tremendous gains are apparent. We must establish policies that encourage researchers and funders to work more closely and to plan for research portfolios that foster the necessary integration and understanding of theory, technology, and context. Such policies can create the bridges required to improve human performance through the intertwined fields of human psychology and technical engineering.

Understanding of brain-body-environment coherence presents a launching point for the multiple disciplines that cognitive engineering can bring to bear on organizational problems. For example, through a focus on intelligent agents facilitating human connection with a networked world, and with augmented cognition enhancing human capabilities through and within physical and networked realms, cognitive engineering can provide a cohesive integration of ecological relevance and epistemological validity to produce theory that supports organizational productivity. As noted at the start of this chapter, cognitive engineering dismissed the single domain approach, which examined systems in fragments. Rather than relying on a purely ergonomics approach that focused on physical limitations, or a purely cognitive approach that focused on information-processing inputs and outputs (Newell & Simon, 1972), the field chose to ignore these isolationist views, as they could not address the complexities of performance in modern work.

But cognitive engineering has not yet developed a broad enough theoretical framework capable of capturing and guiding further developments in efficiency and productivity. The brain-body-environment linkage becomes evident and significant as scientists consider the neurological and computational processes in task performance contexts. I submit that what is necessary is just such a comprehensive theoretical structure supporting the next evolution of cognitive engineering research. This requires taking approaches such as cognitive systems engineering the next level down—that is, to the neurobiological level—and more fully connecting it to the levels up. In this way, just as context and environment were wedded with understanding of task, by moving down a level, into the biological, we can then begin to see how technologies originating in research in areas such as augmented cognition can begin to be integrated into the workplace.

Promising theoretical developments can be found in cognitive science, such as Clark's notions of extended cognition (e.g., Clark, 1997, 2001). Such theorizing provides the type of epistemological and ecological grounding that cognitive engineering needs to take it to this next level. For example, Clark (1997, 2001) has articulated how cognition emanates and exists beyond the biological confines of the brain and is situated in specific contexts. The enmeshed concepts of *embodied, enactive,* and *embedded* cognition have moved the field from an information-processing model to a complex, yet more holistically accurate, framework (see Clark, 2001; Clark & Chalmers, 1998; Hutchins, 1995; Rowlands, 1999, 2003). Interwoven among embodied, enactive, and embedded cognition is the focus on the *practice* of cognition, "by which internal representations are incomplete contributors in a context sensitive system rather than fixed determinants of output: and they too focus on the ongoing interactive dance between brain and world" (Sutton, 2006, p. 282). Clark refers to the elaborate interdependence between body, brain, and world as a "continuous reciprocal causation." He states:

> Much of what matters about human intelligence is hidden not in the brain, nor in the technology, but in the complex and iterated interactions and collaborations between the two.... The study of these interaction spaces is not easy, and depends both on new multidisciplinary alliances and new forms of modeling and analysis. The pay-off, however, could be spectacular: nothing less than a new kind of cognitive scientific collaboration involving

neuroscience, physiology, and social, cultural, and technological studies in about equal measure. (*Clark*, 2001, p. 154)

Cognitive engineers desiring to improve organizational productivity have, within these developments, a taxonomy for not only classifying context, but also bridging it with multiple levels of performance. To examine embodied performance, one considers the cognitive and physical aspects, acknowledging cognition beyond the biological confines of the skull (e.g., Gallagher, 2005). To examine enactive performance, scientists look at motivations, values, and goals that impact decisions and emergent cognitive activity in the intimately linked body-brain-task context (e.g., Frose & Ziemke, 2009; Varela, Thompson, & Rosch, 1991). To examine embedded performance, researchers consider performance beyond body-brain-task, accepting that people act and interact within a world of societal and cultural influence which perpetually molds and reshapes cognitive processes (e.g., Clark, 2001). I suggest that cognitive engineering needs to apply and integrate these concepts in the hopes of leading to a richer understanding of organizational productivity—one with epistemological validity, ecological relevance, and consistency across disciplines.

Returning now to the importance of a guiding policy in the process of developing a more cohesive, purposeful, and productive understanding of organizational productivity, cognitive engineering provides the kind of effective merging of basic and applied science that can increase the practical and theoretical research results while addressing organizational needs. Above, I have briefly described components of what could become a unified theoretical approach to cognition and performance; what is also required, however, is support from the policy community. To that end, policy makers and scientists need to work more collaboratively to align ecological and societal importance of work in a more collaborative cognitive science. Stokes (1997) suggested that a "system for appraising scientific promise and social value at the project level should enlist the insight of the working scientist into the nature of the social goals on which his or her research bears" (p. 116). Hoffman and Deffenbacher (1993) propose a similar ascendant, arguing that it is up to the research community to encourage both epistemological and ecological direction. As these views apply to cognitive engineering and organizational performance, research policy needs to consider the theoretical and applied worth of a portfolio of research and direct funding appropriately.

In sum, cognitive engineering provides a pertinent example of the interdisciplinary approaches that hold the keys to enhancing organizational productivity. Whether drawing from examples of industry, medicine, power management, or defense, the subsequent observations are connected through research efforts seeking to improve the ways in which work is conducted. The growth of cognitive engineering has altered training, selection, and design, but the scientific and policy-making communities stand at a crossroad for future impact and direction in this field. As technology advances, complex tasks and situations will present new challenges, which can be addressed by looking back toward examples of various research contributions and forward through newer lenses and concepts being refined in both laboratory and field. By gleaning insight from lessons of the past, and merging them with developing theory, it will be possible for research to better meet the needs arising as technology and task merge in ever more complex ways.

These arguments serve to stress the significance of finding the harmonious blend of applied and basic research that values the insight and influence of a human-centered approach to technology and task. I have sought to emphasize the importance of new developments in cognitive science and to consider them within the field of cognitive engineering. All of these are founded on epistemologically and ecologically valid theories and represent the types of emerging pathways that can help shape research on organizational productivity in the future.

Acknowledgments
The writing of this paper was partially supported by Grant SES-0915602 from the National Science Foundation and Grant N0001408C0186 from the Office of Naval Research. I thank Patricia Bockelman and Davin Pavlas for assistance on literature reviews related to this manuscript. The views, opinions, and findings contained in this article are the author's and should not be construed as official or as reflecting the views of the University of Central Florida, the National Science Foundation, or the Department of Defense.

References
Adams, R., & Gill, S. (2007). Augmented cognition, universal access and social intelligence in the information society. In D. D. Schmorrow, L. M. Reeves (Eds.), *Augmented cognition* (pp. 231–240). Heidelberg: Spring-Verlag.

Asada, M., Hosoda, K., Kuniyoshi, Y., Ishiguro, H., Inui, T., Yoshikawa, Y., Ogino, M., & Yoshida, C. (2009). Cognitive Developmental Robotics: A Survey. *IEEE Transactions on Autonomous Mental Development, 1, 1,* 12–34.

Argall, B.D., Chernova, S., Veloso, M., & Browning, B. (2009). A Survey of Robot Learning from Demonstration. *Robotics and Autonomous Systems, 57, 5,* 469–483.

Barthes, R. (1977). *Image music text.* London: Harper Collins.

Bartlett, F. C. (1937). Psychology and the Royal Air Force: A general survey. *Royal Air Force Quarterly, 8,* 270–276.

Bockelman Morrow, P., Elias, J., Streater, J., Ososky, S., Phillips, E., Fiore, S. M., & Jentsch, F. (2011). Embodied Cognitive Fidelity and the Advancement of Human Robot Team Simulations. *Proceedings of 55th Annual Meeting of the Human Factors and Ergonomics Society* (pp. 1506–1510). Santa Monica, CA: Human Factors and Ergonomics Society.

Brozek, J., & Keys, A. (1944). General aspects of interdisciplinary research in experimental biology. *Science, 100,* 507–512.

Bryan, W. L., & Harter, N. (1899). Studies on the telegraphic language: The acquisition of a hierarchy of habits. *Psychology Review, 6,* 345–375.

Bul, T., & Lee, J. (1999). An agent-based framework for building decision support systems. *Decision Support Systems, 3,* 225–237.

Cannon-Bowers, J. A., Salas, E., & Converse, S. A. (1993). Shared mental models in expert team decision making. In N. J. Castellan, Jr. (Ed.), *Current issues in individual and group decision making* (pp. 221–246). Hillsdale, NJ: Erlbaum.

Chapanis, A. (1967). The relevance of laboratory studies to practical situations. *Ergonomics, 10,* 557–577.

Chapanis, A. (1970). Relevance of physiological and psychological criteria to man-machine systems. *Ergonomics, 13,* 337–346.

Clark, A. (1997). *Being there: Putting brain, body, and world together again.* Cambridge, MA: MIT Press.

Clark, A. (2001). *Mindware.* Oxford: Oxford University Press.

Clark, A., & Chalmers, D. (1998). The extended mind. *Analysis, 58,* 7–19.

Crandall, B., Klein, G., & Hoffman, R. R. (2006). *Working minds: A practitioner's guide to cognitive task analysis.* Cambridge, MA: MIT Press.

Dansereau, F., & Yammarino, F. (Eds.). (2002). *Research in multi-level issues.* Oxford: Elsevier.

Davies, C., & Burns, C. M. (2008). Advances in cognitive work analysis and the design of ecological visual and auditory displays. *Cognitive Technology, 13*(2), 17–23.

Driskell, J. E., & Olmstead, B. (1989). Psychology and the military: Research applications and trends. *American Psychologist, 44,* 43–54.

Elias, J., Bockelman Morrow, P., Streater, J., Gallaher, S., & Fiore, S. M. (2011). Towards Triadic Interactions in Autism and Beyond: Transitional Objects, Joint Attention, and Social Robotics. *Proceedings of 55th Annual Meeting of the Human Factors and Ergonomics Society* (pp. 1486–1490). Santa Monica, CA: Human Factors and Ergonomics Society.

Endsley, M. R., Hoffman, R., Kaber, D. B., & Roth, E. (2007). Cognitive engineering and decision making: An overview and future course. *Journal of Cognitive Engineering and Decision Making, 1*(1), 1–21.

Engeström, Y. (2000). Activity theory as a framework for analyzing and redesigning work. *Ergonomics, 43*(7), 960–974.

Fiore, S. M. (2008a). Interdisciplinarity as teamwork: How the science of teams can inform team science. *Small Group Research, 39,* 251–277.

Fiore, S. M. (2008b). Power and promise: Cognitive psychology and cognitive technology. *Cognitive Technology, 13*(1), 5–8.

Fiore, S. M., Cuevas, H. M., Schooler, J., & Salas, E. (2005). Understanding memory actions and memory failures in complex environments: Implications for distributed team performance. In C. A. Bowers, E. Salas, & F. Jentsch (Eds.), *Creating high-tech teams: Practical guidance on work performance and technology* (pp. 71–87). Washington, DC: American Psychological Association.

Fiore, S. M., Rosen, M. A., Smith-Jentsch, K. A., Salas, E., Letsky, M., & Warner, N. (2010a). Toward an understanding of macrocognition in teams: Predicting processes in complex collaborative contexts. *Human Factors, 52*(2), 203–224.

Fiore, S. M., & Salas, E. (2007). Problems and possibilities: Strategically pursuing a science of learning in distributed environments. In S. M. Fiore & E. Salas (Eds.), *Towards a science of distributed learning* (pp. 237–264). Washington, DC: American Psychological Association.

Fiore, S. M., & Schooler, J. W. (2004). Process mapping and shared cognition: Teamwork and the development of shared problem models. In E. Salas & S. M. Fiore (Eds.), *Team Cognition: Understanding the factors that drive process and performance* (pp. 133–152). Washington, DC: American Psychological Association.

Fiore, S. M., Smith-Jentsch, K. A., Salas, E., Warner, N., & Letsky, M. (2010b). Toward an understanding of macrocognition in teams: Developing and defining complex collaborative processes and products. *Theoretical Issues in Ergonomic Science, 11*(4), 250–271.

Fitts, P. M. (1951). Engineering psychology and equipment design. In S. S. Stevens (Ed.), *Handbook of experimental psychology* (pp. 1287–1340). New York: Wiley.

Flach, J. M. (1998). Cognitive systems engineering: Putting things in context. *Ergonomics, 41*(2), 163–168.

Frose, T., & Ziemke, T. (2009). Enactive artificial intelligence: Investigating the systemic organization of life and mind. *Artificial Intelligence, 173*(3–4), 466–500.

Gabrieli, J. D. (1998). Cognitive neuroscience of human memory. *Annual Review of Psychology, 49,* 87–115.

Gallagher, S. (2005). *How the body shapes the mind.* Oxford: Oxford University Press.

Goodrich, M. A. & Schultz, A. C. (2007). Human-robot interaction: A survey. *Foundations and Trends in Human–Computer Interaction, 1*(3), 203–275.

Green, D. M., & Swets J. A. (1966). *Signal detection theory and psychophysics.* New York: Wiley.

Hackman, J. R. (2003). Learning more from crossing levels: Evidence from airplanes, orchestras, and hospitals. *Journal of Organizational Behavior, 24,* 1–18.

Hancock, P. A., & Szalma, J. L. (2003). The future of ergonomics. *Theoretical Issues in Ergonomic Science, 44,* 238–249.

Harbers, M., Bosch, K. van den & Meyer, J-J.Ch. (2008). Self-explaining agents in virtual training. CEUR Workshop Proceedings of 3rd EC-TEL 2008 PROLEARN. Maastricht, Nederland.

Hoffman, R. R., & Deffenbacher, K. (1992). A brief history of applied cognitive psychology. *Applied Cognitive Psychology, 6,* 1–48.

Hoffman, R. R., & Deffenbacher, K. A. (1993). An analysis of the relations of basic and applied science. *Ecological Psychology, 5,* 315–352.

Hoffman, R. R., Klein, G., & Laughery, K. R. (2002). The state of cognitive systems engineering. *IEEE Intelligent Systems, 17*(1), 73–75.

Hoffman, R. R., & Lintern, G. (2006). Eliciting and representing the knowledge of experts. In K. A. Ericsson, N. Charness, P. Feltovich, & R. Hoffman (Eds.), *Cambridge handbook of expertise and expert performance* (pp. 203–222). New York: Cambridge University Press.

Hoffman, R. R., & Militello, L. (2008). *Perspectives on cognitive task analysis: Historical origins and modern communities of practice.* Boca Raton, FL: CRC Press/Taylor and Francis.

Hoffman, R. R., & Woods, D. D. (2000). Studying cognitive systems in context. *Human Factors, 42,* 1–7.

Hollnagel, E. (2002). Cognition as control: A pragmatic approach to the modeling of joint cognitive systems. *Theoretical Issues in Ergonomic Science, 2*(3), 309–315.

Hollnagel, E., & Woods, D. D. (1983). Cognitive systems engineering: New wine in new bottles. *International Journal of Man-Machine Studies, 18,* 583–600.

Hollnagel, E., & Woods, D. D. (1999). Cognitive systems engineering: New wine in new bottles. *International Journal of Human-Computer Studies, 51*(2), 339–356.

Hollnagel, E., Woods, D. D. (2005). *Joint cognitive systems: Foundations of cognitive systems engineering.* Boca Raton, FL: Talyor & Francis/CRC Press

Hollnagel, E., Woods, D. D., & Leveson, N. (Eds.). (2006). *Resilience engineering: Concepts and precepts.* Aldershot, UK: Ashgate.

Hutchins, E. (1995). *Cognition in the wild.* Cambridge, MA: MIT Press.

Katzell, R. A., & Austin, J. T. (1992). From then to now: The development of industrial-organizational psychology in the United States. *Journal of Applied Psychology, 77*(6), 803–835.

Kawamura, T., Fukuhara, T., Takeda, H., Kono, Y., & Kidode, M. (2006). Ubiquitous Memories: A memory externalization system using physical objects. *Journal Personal and Ubiquitous Computing, 6,* 1–12.

Klein, G., & Militello, L. (2001). Some guidelines for conducting a cognitive task analysis. *Advances in Human Performance and Cognitive Engineering Research, 1,* 161–199.

Klein, J. T. (1996). *Crossing boundaries: Knowledge, disciplinarities, and interdisciplinarities.* Charlottesville: University of Virginia Press.

Klein, K. J., & Kozlowski, S. W. J., (Eds.). (2000a). *Multilevel theory, research, and methods in organizations: Foundations, extensions, and new directions.* San Francisco: Jossey-Bass.

Klein, K. J., & Kozlowski, S. W. J. (2000b). From micro to meso: Critical steps in conceptualizing and conducting multilevel research. *Organizational Research Methods, 3,* 211–236.

Koppes, L. L., Thayer, P. W., Vinchur, A. J., & Salas, E. (2007). *Historical perspectives in industrial and organizational psychology.* London: Routledge.

Kozlowski, S. W. J., & Chao, G. T. (2012). Macrocognition, team learning, and team knowledge: Origins, emergence, and measurement. In E. Salas, S. Fiore, & M. P. Letsky (Eds.). *Theories of Team Cognition: Cross-Disciplinary Perspectives* (pp. 19–48). New York: Routledge Academic.

Leont'ev, A. N. (1978). *Activity, consciousness, and personality.* Englewood Cliffs, NJ: Prentice Hall.

Luria, A. R. (1979). *The making of mind.* Cambridge, MA: Harvard University Press.

Lynch, J. (2006). It's not easy being interdisciplinary. *International Journal of Epidemiology, 35,* 1119–1122.

Marks, M. A., Mathieu, J. E., & Zaccaro, S. J. (2001). A conceptual framework and taxonomy of team processes. *Academy of Management Review, 26,* 356–376.

Marks, M. A., Zaccaro, S. J., & Mathieu, J. E. (2000). Performance implications of leader briefings and team interaction training for team adaptation to novel environments. *Journal of Applied Psychology, 85,* 971–986.

Mathieu, J. E., Heffner, T. S., Goodwin, G. F., Salas, E., & Cannon-Bowers, J. A. (2000). The influence of shared mental models on team process and effectiveness. *Journal of Applied Psychology, 85,* 273–283.

Meister, D. (1999). *The history of human factors and ergonomics.* Mahwah, NJ: Erlbaum.

Militello, L. G., Hutton, R. J. B. (1998). Applied cognitive task analysis (ACTA): A practitioner's toolkit for understanding cognitive task demands. *Ergonomics, 41*(11), 1618–1641.

Miller, G. A. (1956). The magical number seven, plus or minus two: Some limits on our capacity for processing information. *Psychological Review, 63,* 81–97.

Miller, G., Galanter, E., & Pribram, K. (1960). *Plans and the structure of behavior.* New York: Holt, Rinehart and Winston.

Moray, N. (2008). The good, the bad, and the future: On the archaeology of ergonomics. *Human Factors, 50*(3), 411–417.

Moray, N., & Huey, B. (1988). *Human factors research and nuclear safety.* Washington, DC: National Academies Press.

Moskowitz, M. J. (1977). Hugo Münsterberg: A study in the history of applied psychology. *American Psychologist, 32,* 824–842.

Mumford, M. D., Schultz, R. A., & Osburn, H. K. (2002). Planning in organizations: Performance as a multi-level phenomenon. In F. J. Yammarino & F. Dansereau (Eds.), *Research in multi-level issues: The many faces of multi-level issues* (pp. 3–25). Oxford: Elsevier.

Münsterberg, H. (1908). *On the witness stand.* New York: Doubleday Page.

Myers, C. S. (1929). *Industrial psychology.* London: Home University.

Nardi, B. (1996a). Activity theory and human-computer interaction. In B. Nardi (Ed.), *Context and consciousness: Activity theory and human-computer interaction* (pp. 4–8). Cambridge, MA: MIT Press.

Nardi, B. (1996b). Studying context: A comparison of activity theory, situated action models, and distributed cognition. In B. Nardi (Ed.), *Context and consciousness: Activity theory and human-computer interaction* (pp. 35–52). Cambridge, MA: MIT Press.

National Academies of Science. (2004). *Committee on facilitating interdisciplinary research.* Washington, DC: National Academies Press.

Nemeth, C. P., Cook, R. I., O'Connor, M. F., & Klock, P. A. (2004). Using cognitive artifacts to understand distributed cognition. *IEEE Transactions on Systems, Man and Cybernetics—Part A: Systems and Humans, 34*(6), 726–735.

Nemeth, C. P., O'Connor, M. F., Klock, P. A., & Cook, R. I. (2006). Discovering healthcare cognition: the use of cognitive artifacts to reveal cognitive work. *Organization Studies, 27*(7), 1011–1035.

Newell, A., & Simon, H. A. (1972). *Human problem solving*. Englewood Cliffs, NJ: Prentice-Hall.

Parasuraman, R. (2003). Neuroergonomics: Research and practice. *Theoretical Issues in Ergonomic Science, 44*, 5–20.

Pavel, M, Wang, G., Li, K. (2003). Augmented cognition: Allocation of attention. *Proceedings of 36th Hawaii International Conference on System Sciences*, January 6–9, 2003, Big Island, HI, USA. IEEE Computer Society, 2003, ISBN 0-7695-1874-5.

Pellmar, T. C., & Eisenberg, L. (Eds.). (2000). *Bridging disciplines in the brain, behavioral, and clinical sciences*. Washington, DC: Institute of Medicine/National Academy Press.

Petrox, P. V., & Stoyen, A. D. (2000). An intelligent-agent based decision support system for a complex command and control application. *Proceedings of the Sixth IEEE International Conference on Engineering of Complex Computer Systems* (pp. 94–104).

Polsad, S. (2009). *Ubiquitous computing: Smart devices, environments and interactions export*. New York: Wiley.

Rasmussen, J. (1985). The role of hierarchical knowledge representation in decision-making and system management. *IEEE Transactions on Systems, Man and Cybernetics, 15*(2), 234–243.

Rasmussen, J. (1986). *Information processing and human-machine interaction: an approach to cognitive engineering*. New York: North-Holland.

Rasmussen, J., Pejtersen, A. M., & Goodstein, L. P. (1994). *Cognitive systems engineering*. New York: Wiley.

Roth, E. M. (2008). Uncovering the requirements of cognitive work. *Human Factors, 50*(3), 475–480.

Rowlands, M. (1999). *The body in mind: Understanding cognitive processes*. Cambridge: Cambridge University Press.

Rowlands, M. (2003). *Externalism: Putting mind and world back together again*. Chesham, UK: Acumen.

Salas, E., & Fiore, S. M. (Eds.). (2004). *Team cognition: Understanding the factors that drive process and performance*. Washington, DC: American Psychological Association.

Simon, H. A. (1990). Invariants of human behavior. *Annual Review of Psychology, 41*, 1–19.

Smith, D. J. (2007). Situation(al) awareness (SA) in effective command and control. www.smithsrisca.demon.co.uk/situational-awareness.html. Downloaded September 15, 2009.

St. John, M., Kobus, D. A., Morrison, J. G., & Schmorrow, D. (2004). Overview of the DARPA augmented cognition technical integration experiment. *International Journal of Human-Computer Interaction, 17*(2), 131–150.

Stacy, W., Freeman, J., Lackey, S., & Merket, D. (2004). Enhancing simulation-based training with performance measurement objects. *Proceedings of the Interservice/Industry Training, Simulation and Education Conference (I/ITSEC)*. Arlington, VA: NDIA.

Stanney, K. M., Schmorrow, D. D., Johnston, M., Fuchs, S., Jones, D., Hale, K. S., Ahmad, A., & Young, P. (2009). Augmented cognition: An overview. *Reviews of Human Factors and Ergonomics, 5*, 195–224.

Stokes, D. E. (1997). *Pasteur's quadrant: Basic science and technological innovation*. Washington, DC: Brookings Institution Press.

Streater, J., Elias, J., Bockelman Morrow, P., & Fiore, S. M. (2011). Towards an Interdisciplinary Understanding of Perspective for Human-Robot Teamwork. *Proceedings of 55th Annual Meeting of the Human Factors and Ergonomics Society* (pp. 1481–1485). Santa Monica, CA: Human Factors and Ergonomics Society.

Sutton, J. (2006) Introduction: Memory, embodied cognition, and the extended mind. *Philosophical Psychology, 19*(3), 281–289.

Svanaes, D. (2001). Context-aware technology: A phenomenological perspective. *Human-Computer Interaction, 16*(2), 379–400.

Sycara, K., & Lewis, M. (2004). Integrating intelligent agents into human teams. In E. Salas & S. M. Fiore (Eds.), *Team cognition: Understanding the factors driving process and performance* (pp. 203–231). Washington, DC: American Psychological Association.

Tambe, M., Johnson, W. L., Jones, R. M., Koss, F., Laird, J. E., Rosenbloom, P. S., & Schwamb, K. (1995). Intelligent agents for interactive simulation environments. *AI Magazine, 16*(1), 15–39.

Taylor, F. W. (1911). *Principles of scientific management*. New York and London: Harper & Brothers.

Taylor, G., Stensrud, B., Eitelman, S., Dunham, C., & Harger, E. (2007). Toward automating airspace management. *Computational Intelligence for Security and Defense Applications (CISDA)*. Honolulu, HI: IEEE Press.

Thomaz, A. L., & Breazeal, C. (2008). Teachable robots: Understanding human teaching behavior to build more effective robot learners. *Artificial Intelligence Journal, 172*, 716–737.

Thorndike, E. L. (1920). A constant error in psychological ratings. *Journal of Applied Psychology, 4*, 25–29.

Varela, F., Thompson, E., & Rosch, E. (1991). *The embodied mind*. Cambridge, MA: MIT Press.

Vicente, K. J. (1999). *Cognitive work analysis: Toward safe, productive, and healthy computer-based work*. Mahwah, NJ: Erlbaum.

Vicente, K. J., & Rasmussen, J. (1990). The ecology of human-machine systems. II: Mediating "direct perception" in complex work domains. *Ecological Psychology, 2*(3), 207–249.

Vygotsky, L. S. (1978). *Mind in society: The development of higher psychological processes*. Cambridge, MA: Harvard University Press.

Walker, W. R., & Herrmann, D. J. (Eds.). (2005). *Cognitive technology: Essays on the transformation of thought and society*. Jefferson, NC: McFarland.

Wiener, N. (1948). *Cybernetics or control and communication in the animal and the machine*. Cambridge, MA: Wiley.

Woods, D. D. (1985). Cognitive technologies: The design of joint human-machine cognitive systems. *AI Magazine, 6*(4), 86–91.

Woods, D. D., & Roth, E. M. (1988). Cognitive engineering: Human problem-solving with tools. *Human Factors, 30*, 415–430.

Wooldridge, M., & Jennings, N. (1995). Intelligent agents: Theory and practice. *The Knowledge Engineering Review, 10*(2), 115–152.

Zhang, J. (1997). The nature of external representations in problem solving. *Cognitive Science, 21*(2), 179–217.

Zhang, J. (1998). A distributed representation approach to group problem solving. *Journal of the American Society for Information Science, 49*(9), 801–809.

Zhang, J., & Norman, D. (1994). Representations in distributed cognitive tasks. *Cognitive Science, 18*, 87–122.

Zhang, J., & Norman, D. A. (1995). A representational analysis of numeration systems. *Cognition, 57*, 271–295.

Taxonomy and Theory in Computer Supported Cooperative Work

Jonathan Grudin *and* Steven Poltrock

Abstract

In the mid-1980s, when most hands-on computer use was still confined to one person and one computer, a group comprising social scientists and technologists began convening under the label Computer Supported Cooperative Work (CSCW) to discuss how technology could support groups, organizations, and communities. The resulting research, presented in annual conferences and journals, has had to adjust to the extraordinary growth of activity as the Internet and World Wide Web have transformed work. In this chapter, we examine the evolution of the participants and topics covered in CSCW, the frameworks and typologies that have been used, and we discuss the diverse if somewhat limited roles that theory has played in guiding CSCW research and application.

Key Words: Computer Supported Cooperative Work, CSCW, human-computer interaction, HCI, technology, typology, framework

Introduction

Computer Supported Cooperative Work (CSCW) is a community of behavioral researchers and system builders. They reside primarily in human-computer interaction (HCI) groups in computer science departments, information schools, and industry research laboratories. CSCW generally focuses on software developed for widely available platforms and directly used in end-to-end support of communication, collaboration, and coordination tasks.

Individual tool use may contribute indirectly to such tasks, but its study is left to other HCI disciplines. For example, a project management system in which every team member enters status information would be considered a CSCW system, whereas if one person collects and enters the data, it would not. Typically, CSCW software includes a representation of group participants or tasks. A typical database that strives to treat each user in isolation is not within the scope of CSCW; one that supports communication among its users could be.

Given its preference for platforms in widespread use, CSCW had a narrow but growing focus through the 1980s and 1990s. Inspiration was drawn from early writers and prototype builders who foresaw a future of discretionary computer use in group settings. A celebrated instance is Douglas Engelbart's public demonstration of e-mail, videoconferencing, and other novel hardware and software on December 9, 1968, in San Francisco.

Social science has always been part of CSCW, but the research has primarily resided in computer science departments and industry research labs that had the infrastructure support and technical skills to build experimental prototypes. A notable, if not ultimately successful, exception was work on electronic meeting rooms, central to *group decision support systems*, carried out in management schools. Product developers also contributed to early research. Recently, some CSCW research has migrated to information schools as they have become more open to system development as a facet of research.

In this chapter, our principal goal is to provide a guide to what is in the CSCW literature, what is not found there, and a sense of where CSCW research is headed. In the abstract, a broad span could be envisioned, but in reality CSCW is a research niche determined by forces that act on and around the contributing disciplines. Since 1990 we have given survey tutorials on CSCW at most major HCI and CSCW conferences, requiring continual examination of technology development and the research literature. Grudin and Poltrock (1997) and Grudin (1994, 2007) are sources for some of the history and participation discussed in this chapter.

The next section is a high-level view of CSCW technologies and social research, concluding with descriptions of two published analyses of the CSCW literature. Then CSCW precursors, its emergence in 1984–1986, and its subsequent evolution are detailed. A critical and often underemphasized aspect of the history is the dramatic change in the power and capability of the underlying hardware over the past 30 years. The instability resulting from technology change profoundly affects the prospects for developing useful theory in this field. Different paths taken by North American and European CSCW are also described. We then present framing models of technology development and use, followed by descriptions of many of the taxonomies and typologies found in the CSCW literature. These typically include a mix of technical, behavioral, and activity characteristics. We review uses of theory in CSCW research and practice. We conclude with a description of research issues and directions that we anticipate or encourage.

In this chapter we cite some journal articles and many conference papers. Curious readers from journal-oriented disciplines must understand that most North American computer science research is found in its final form in highly selective, widely accessible conference proceedings. This is the case for CSCW.

Overview of CSCW

In this section we describe the technologies spanned by CSCW research, closely following the outline of a recent handbook chapter by Gary and Judy Olson titled "Groupware and Computer-Supported Cooperative Work" (Olson & Olson, 2007). We then cover the potential and realized social science contributions, drawing on a 2003 book chapter by Robert Kraut. We finish by describing two analyses of the CSCW literature. A comprehensive view of CSCW origins is found in Ron Baecker's collection *Readings in Groupware and Computer-Supported Cooperative* Work (1993).

Technology Overview

Olson and Olson (2007) begin with a discussion of infrastructure requirements. This was once a core consideration, but with the near-universal presence of the Web and client-server architectures, it is now generally taken for granted. A 1999 volume with chapters by several leading CSCW researchers, now available online, has contributions titled "architectures for collaborative applications," "groupware toolkits for synchronous work," "group editors," and seven others (Beaudouin-Lafon, 1999).

When CSCW emerged in the mid-1980s communication tools were its first focus and have remained central. E-mail was first and is occasionally a topic of research today. Weblogs and microblogging sites such as Twitter are recent foci, as is the use of other social networking sites. Other topics have included voice, video, and text conferencing, coauthorship support, instant messaging, and text messaging. Studies of prototype desktop video systems have been prominent in CSCW, with waves of research in the late 1980s, mid-1990s, and early 2000s. If video communication finally blossoms, CSCW studies covering a range of social and interface issues, some quite complex, could contribute (Poltrock and Grudin, 2005).

Tools that support coordination include meeting support systems and group calendars, which were prevalent in the first decade. Awareness indicators became prominent in the second decade. Workflow management systems garnered attention despite a weak track record. Characteristic of the skeptical view of CSCW toward the relatively inflexible workflow approach is Bowers, Button, and Sharrock's (1995) nice description of problems that arose during a significant deployment of workflow technology in a large printing enterprise.

Computer supported cooperative learning is a conceptually relevant field predominantly published in other venues, but with a few papers in the CSCW literature. Artificial intelligence was briefly present at the origin of CSCW but is now represented mainly in work on recommender systems, which themselves are reported on more extensively in other venues such as the Intelligent User Interfaces conferences.

Information repositories are another technology focus. They range from document management systems to wikis. Today, Wikipedia is a mountain of freely accessible information with a complete edit history over which an army of graduate students swarms, analyzing it in different ways. Papers by CSCW researchers, published at CSCW conferences and related tracks at other conferences, include studies of conflict through history flow visualizations (Viégas, Wattenberg, & Dave, 2004), image contribution and editing (Viégas, 2007), Wikipedia administration (Bryant, Forte, & Bruckman, 2005; Burke & Kraut, 2008), and incentive systems (Kriplean, Beschastnikh & McDonald, 2008).

The creation of virtual spaces or places in which to interact has been a thread of CSCW research, beginning with the *media spaces* first explored at Xerox PARC in the early 1980s. Research into virtual environments, such as multiuser simulations and virtual worlds, has, like desktop video, waxed and waned in interest and representation. The most ambitious efforts are collaboratories developed to support large-scale multisite efforts, primarily in scientific research, engineering, and education. The Olsons and their colleagues have been at the heart of this work (Olson & Olson, 2007).

Social Research

In an excellent review 15 years after CSCW emerged, Kraut (2003) outlines how social psychology might contribute to the design and use of tools to support groups in novel ways or to enable novel forms of collaboration. Kraut (2003) notes the value of understanding factors that contribute to effective group processes and factors that lead to social loafing and process losses, and that these could differ for collocated versus distributed groups.

Kraut (2003) then explains why social psychology has not contributed much to this engineering discipline. Contextual and motivational factors that are typically abstracted away in experiments are crucial in the settings of interest to CSCW researchers. For example, the experiential and motivational heterogeneity of real-world groups can yield variability that swamps the experimental effects of studies conducted with small groups of psychology or MBA students.

CSCW formed precisely when research into group and team behaviors shifted from social psychology to organizational psychology. Circa 1985, emphasis on interpersonal interaction and performance gave way to research into what groups do and how they do it (Kozlowski & Bell, 2003). Social and organizational psychologists initially participated in CSCW, but the organizational psychologists who focused on technology use had alternative publication outlets and soon left. CSCW in North America only slowly recapitulated the progression noted by Kozlowski and Bell (2003). It took time for the allure of small-group solutions that might be independent of organizational context to yield to studies embedded in particular contexts. When it came, this evolution did not mark the return of organizational psychologists to CSCW, but resulted from the contributions of ethnographers studying technology use in industrial settings. These scholars were more academically marginalized and open to participation in CSCW. Some of these disciplinary shifts are described in surveys such as Grudin (2007). In addition to living through the changes, we have retrospectively analyzed participation on program committees and have conducted interviews of participants.

Sciences generally strive for frameworks that are independent of technology, which is consigned to engineering. With CSCW, engineering and other contextual factors cannot be extricated because they affect the frameworks that emerge from behavioral studies. For example, Kraut (2003) divides group size into these units: individual, dyad, small group/team, organization, and society. CSCW technologies do not readily span these group sizes. The limitation of viewing digital information on small displays and the early development of software tools to support large software development projects motivated different unit sizes. Desktop video software could only comfortably support three or four simultaneous participants, who do not need mechanisms for controlling who speaks, whereas other applications support larger groups who do need these control mechanisms. Quite different considerations arose in supporting units larger than a group but smaller than an organization.

Two Analyses of the CSCW Literature

The CSCW conference held in 2006 marked 20 years since the first open conference. Two papers marked this anniversary by analyzing and summarizing the conference papers published from 1986 to 2004 (North American conference only). Jacovi, Soroka, Gilboa-Freedman, Ur, Shahar, and Marmasse (2006) analyzed the citation graph of all 465 papers to identify the core and major clusters within the field. They identified eight clusters, of which the two largest correspond roughly to social science (83 papers) and computer science (82 papers). The social science cluster includes papers about theories and models, ethnography, and user studies. The next largest cluster (43 papers) comprises meeting/decision support, shared media spaces, and conferencing. A fourth cluster comprises 12 papers on instant messaging, social spaces, and presence. The fifth is seven papers on the use of computer tools such as e-mail in the workplace. The remaining clusters (each of five papers) were groupware design and workspace awareness; management of computing and information systems; and video-mediated communication and shared visual spaces. The computer science cluster was relatively stable over 20 years, but the others evolved considerably. The current social science cluster was a collection of much smaller clusters that coalesced. The 47 core papers identified by the authors are listed at http://en.wikipedia.org/wiki/CSCW.

Convertino, Kannampallil, and Councill (2006) categorized each paper by type of institutional affiliation, author's geographical location, its level of analysis (individual, group or organization), type of contribution (theory, design, or evaluation), and type of collaboration function investigated (communication, coordination, or cooperation). They reported that 60% of authors are from academia and 40% from industry, and although most are from North America, European and Asian participation has grown. About 80% of the papers are about small group collaboration, and nearly all of the rest have an organizational focus. The proportions of design (corresponding roughly to the computer science cluster of Jacovi et al., 2006) and evaluation (corresponding to the social science cluster) are about equal, although in any given year one or the other may dominate. At the first three conferences, about 30% of the papers offered a theoretical contribution, but with the flight of MIS researchers this subsequently declined to fewer than 10%. Throughout the history of the conference, the preponderance of research has focused on communication. In early years relatively few CSCW papers discussed coordination, but now about half the papers address this topic. Fewer than 20% of recent papers address cooperative work by their measure.

In the next section, we consider crucial historical forces, including one omitted from most accounts: technology change.

Historical Context and Evolution

In 1980, an era was ending. For 15 years, business computing had been dominated by huge, expensive mainframe computers sold by Burroughs, Control Data, IBM, Sperry, and others. Mainframes were acquired to support key organizational goals. The principal users were executives and managers, who read printed output. Few people interacted directly with the technology, which was generally too expensive to be used for interactive tasks such as e-mail or word processing.

The 1980s would see the rise and fall of minicomputers. Supplanted by PCs and largely forgotten today, minicomputers catapulted companies such as Data General, Digital Equipment Corporation, and Wang Laboratories into prominence. The PDP series, culminating in the VAX, made Digital the second-largest computer company in the world in the mid-1980s. Dr. Wang was briefly the fourth wealthiest American. Minicomputers changed the way that many people thought about computers and work. This included the research community, which embraced their use.

Minicomputers, a fraction of the size and price of a mainframe, were acquired by small businesses or to support departments and groups within large organizations. Minis ran productivity applications such as word processing, business graphics, spreadsheets, and e-mail. Use of these *office information systems* was hands-on and interactive. *Office automation* was an explicit goal and was included in the name of four conference series and symposia first held between 1980 and 1982, one affiliated with a large trade show.

In 1984, two office-automation researchers, Irene Greif of MIT and Paul Cashman of Digital Equipment Corporation, coined the acronym CSCW for an invited workshop of technologists and social scientists focused on supporting or understanding workplace collaboration. E-mail use was a major topic—at the time, e-mail was poorly designed, not interoperable across products, and bereft of social norms to govern use. An account of this workshop, titled "Computer Supported Cooperative Groups," was given at the 1985 Office Automation Conference (Greif, 1985). The first open CSCW conference was held the next year. By 1988, the minicomputer industry was collapsing, the office automation conferences had dissolved, but CSCW had seized the baton. Beginning that year, CSCW was sponsored by the Association for Computing Machinery Special Interest Group on Computer-Human Interaction (ACM SIGCHI), the psychologist-heavy enclave within the principal professional organization of computer scientists. The era of client-server PC networks was getting underway.

The term *computer mediated communication* was used prior to the arrival of computer supported cooperative work, and continued to be used by some researchers with that specific focus. *Groupware* was commonly used to describe the technologies by 1990, but lost currency a decade later, when group support features could appear in virtually any application.

The introduction of technology to support teams had several consequences. First, digital technology revealed and often left a persistent record of previously ephemeral group activity. This facilitated the study of group behavior. Second, designing, marketing, introducing, and using these technologies created new challenges for vendors and purchasers, focusing their attention on the activities to be supported (or automated). Third, over time, use of the technologies altered aspects of group work.

In theory, computer supported cooperative work could be broadly construed to cover any aspect of work in which digital technology plays a role. In practice, the CSCW research field is what it is, constrained by severe technological limitations in its early years, and by the shifting backgrounds and interests of the researchers who contribute to CSCW conferences, journals, and books. It includes some research that ranges broadly, emphasizing collaboration without computers. It includes useful methods that could be applied beyond group settings. It includes study of entertainment and play. In addition, research that conceptually fits under the label is not covered in the conferences or in CSCW surveys; it may be reported in other conferences and journals, or its absence may reflect different interpretations of the scope, such as how extensive the representation of groups or group processes should be in the software to be considered.

Technology Change

Work is the core noun in CSCW, revealing a strong commitment to a focus on behavior. The North American conference series typically has parallel tracks on technology use and technology design. However, the view of CSCW as a figure with one foot firmly planted on human nature and behavior and the other on digital technology is misleading. The two foundations differ dramatically in their stability.

Human nature and social organization change slowly—the management of pyramid builders and Roman legions may differ from that of shopping center construction and infantry battalions today, but perhaps not by much. In contrast, technology has been changing at a pace unparalleled in the history of tool-building.

The stability of human nature provides the time and incentive to build and test models or theories that govern individual, social, organizational, and cultural behavior. In contrast, the name *computer supported cooperative work* has been a constant, but the computer of 1985 has scant resemblance to the computer of today. A 10 megabyte memory drum cost several thousand dollars then. Today, 10 terabytes—a million-fold increase—is less expensive, smaller, faster, more reliable, and easier to install and use. On various dimensions, computer hardware capability increased two orders of magnitude each decade, giving rise to major new platforms and human-computer interaction research disciplines (see Figure 40.1).

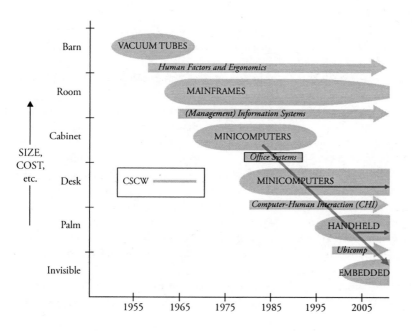

Figure 40.1 Hardware Platforms, HCI Research Fields, and CSCW. CSCW is represented by the branching arrows that start with and descend from Minicomputers

Successive waves of technology and falling prices enabled new applications, brought computation into new domains, and supported activities at ever finer granularities. It made geographically distributed teams and global organizations more manageable, affecting social behavior in workplaces.

The role of technology change is often overlooked. For example, in his 2003 survey, Kraut wrote that the CSCW research community coalesced out of dismay at the individual user focus of human-computer interaction research and development. But prior to 1985, technology at affordable prices was hard pressed to support a single user, much less a group. Many of the people involved early in CSCW were cognitive psychologists who realized that the single-user focus, although useful, was increasingly limiting. The telecommunications companies were an exception: with their focus on communication, often dyadic, they had from the outset hired social psychologists, including Kraut himself.

To see the impact of technology change on social research in CSCW, consider studies of the ongoing *awareness* that people have of the activities of distant collaborators. For many years, people were aware of what collaborators sent them, and little else. Passive awareness was technically difficult, and no papers with *awareness* in the title appeared in the first five CSCW conferences. At that point, local and wide-area networks were becoming robust, and from 1992 through 1995 there were three papers with *awareness* in the title. By 1995, the World Wide Web was taking hold, and *awareness* appeared in the titles of 12 papers from 1996 through 1999.

Equally interesting is a marked shift in the stances taken toward the phenomenon of remote awareness. The first paper, "Awareness and Coordination in Shared Workspaces" (Dourish & Bellotti, 1992) was a widely cited celebration of the achievement and potential utility of this new capability. Several years later, post-Web, the focus shifted in no small measure to risks of *too much* awareness, as in "Techniques for Addressing Fundamental Privacy and Disruption Tradeoffs in Awareness Support Systems" (Hudson & Smith, 1996). In 1992, early desktop video prototype builders could write in defense of allowing people to surreptitiously watch their colleagues: "One-way connections have advantages we are unwilling to give up. Glances allow us to maintain our awareness of colleagues without actually engaging in interaction with them....Video provides an excellent means to gain awareness unobtrusively; enforcing symmetry for the sake of privacy would undermine this functionality" (Gaver et al., 1992, pp. 29–30).

This view retreated slowly. A novel technology elicits efforts to maximize its use and tolerance for rough edges. A subsequent system provided an audible notification that one was being watched, but no indication of who was looking. Eventually, the desirability of invitation and reciprocity in collaboration among peers was established. Research also identified designs that worked or did not; for example, people reacted poorly to an intuitively simple feature of inviting someone to a video conference by dragging his or her icon into your office on a floor plan map.

Impact on Theory

Instability wrought by technology change undermines theory building. A researcher has no sooner staked out theoretical turf and started to farm it then a wave of innovation washes the shoots out to sea. This affects CSCW, but is a broader problem.

Researchers still alive once worked at packing information more efficiently on 80-column punchcards. In the early 1980s, command-line interfaces dominated interactive computer use. Cognitive psychologists at the forefront of HCI research worked on command naming as part of a theoretical framework that would enable us to design from principles. The commercial success of the graphical user interface (GUI) in 1985 rendered the project moot, to the dismay of those who expected their work to be a foundation for future research and development. Other theoreticians worked rigorously on effective representations of information on static, monochrome monitors. Color monitors and animation swept in, rendering that work irrelevant before it was complete.

Closer to social technologies is the case of language understanding, the holy grail of human-computer interaction. Billions of research dollars were spent developing computational models of linguistic theory. Careers were built on topics such as anaphoric reference. But it went slowly, and when technology made possible the rapid processing of huge text corpora, statistical approaches to language understanding largely supplanted linguistic theory. The researcher-editor of a special issue of *Communications of the ACM* on natural language understanding railed against changes underway, but then seemed resigned to the idea that "it would be bags of tricks and not theory that would advance computational linguistics in the future" (Wilks, 1996, p. 62).

Interpersonal messaging systems offer another example. Studies of e-mail conventions were prevalent in office automation and early CSCW research, but e-mail as a medium changed radically over time. Throughout the 1980s, memory was too expensive to save messages, so e-mail was initially an informal, ephemeral medium, in which spelling and grammar were not important. E-mail did not support attachments, so printed or typed documents were distributed. The business value of e-mail was uncertain: a 1992 CSCW paper argued from the perspective of organizational theory that e-mail undermined productivity (Pickering & King, 1992).

Then technology changed everything. Standards enabled the reliable exchange of documents, spreadsheets, and slide decks, and e-mail became mission-critical for managers. Memory costs fell, spelling checkers appeared, and archived e-mail became formal records. Early data and theory about e-mail use no longer applied at all; they were outdated soon after publication. Perhaps they could have had an afterlife when instant messaging (IM) spread in the early 2000s, lauded as the informal, ephemeral, attachment-free alternative to e-mail. But the lessons had not been learned. Corporate IM etiquette guides appeared; analysts counseled organizations that IM was a threat to productivity, and the cycle repeated.

Four examples follow of major research conclusions that ignored or were quickly reversed by dynamic changes in technology. In some cases, mainstream media picked up the original report but not the subsequent about-face. Some are by CSCW leaders and published in other venues. Others were published in *Communications of the ACM*, received by all ACM members, which evolved from being a journal to a serious professional magazine over these years.

Example 1. A well-executed study of Internet use suggested negative effects on social development (Kraut et al., 1998), whereas subsequent data suggested that changes in experience, technology, or the Internet itself had erased this effect (Kraut et al., 2002). Although data were carefully analyzed and speak for themselves, they were shifting sand, not a promising foundation for theory construction.

Example 2. The "productivity paradox" debate of the 1980s and 1990s was given prominence by a 1987 observation of Nobel laureate economist Robert Solow. Analyses indicated that organizations were not realizing benefits commensurate with IT investments. A decade later, new analyses appeared, claiming to refute this. For example, Brynjolfsson (1993) presented the paradox, and Brynjolfson and Hitt (1998) refuted it. There is evidence, though,

that IBM had recognized in the 1960s and 1970s that its customers were getting not productivity but prestige and a reputation for being forward-looking (Greenbaum, 1979). And, in fact, both sets of analyses could have been accurate—not discussed is the fact that decade after decade, many cost components dropped and capability increased sharply, especially in the 1990s. Hardware costs dropped, fewer companies had to develop all software internally, and with computer savvy rising among employees new and old, less training was required.

Example 3. Hoffman, Kalsbeek, and Novak (1996) reported that flawed sampling by Nielsen had created a 30% exaggeration in Internet participation. This was described as significant for market planning. But no one disputed that Internet participation was doubling annually, ergo a 30% exaggeration was insignificant—it was an *underestimate* by the time the study was reported. This example points to the lack of understanding of the implications of rapid change. In a similar misreading of supralinear growth, earlier studies that showed a high number of inactive Internet nodes were taken as a sign that Internet use might collapse. As long as the number of nodes doubled annually—and this did not stop—the rate of abandonment was inconsequential.

Example 4. The possibility of obsolescence always looms, threatening even results that seem established. Consider geographically distributed teams. Studies indicated that to perform effectively, they should initially and periodically meet face to face. But now consider the millions of multiplayer game enthusiasts. Game quests can require up to three dozen participants with different skills and roles, who must show up at a set time and execute well for an hour or more, or the beast will win. They do not meet face to face, disproving the truism. We do not know which factors might be critical, but we do know that those players enter the workforce in growing numbers and may establish different approaches to distributed team formation and motivation (Brown & Thomas, 2006; Reeves, Malone, & O'Driscoll, 2008).

Forays into theory are covered in a later section, but CSCW largely eschews theory building and experimental hypothesis testing. Many CSCW researchers are wary of fields such as information systems that dwell on such approaches. Many of them (including the authors of this chapter) were trained in experimental approaches, but moved to qualitative studies and the natural quasi-experiments that waves of technology deployment make feasible. A technology could be adopted by projects in different life-cycle phases, teams with different compositions and cultural norms, or organizations facing different external pressures. Temporal and contextual variables that are present in workplaces but not in controlled experiments can prove more important than factors that are feasibly manipulated. Widespread technology adoption enables patterns to emerge, or not, across organizations of diverse natures, rewarding qualitative study.

It is easy to underestimate the value of descriptive and other pre-theoretical contributions to science. Mendeleyev constructed the periodic table based on patterns in observed properties of elements. He had no theory, just as Linnaeus had no theory behind his classification of plants and animals or Brahe behind his organization of celestial observations. But their work was crucial to the theorists Bohr, Darwin, and Kepler. Theoreticians were active before these frameworks were constructed, but most were alchemists, theologians, and astrologers who retarded science more than they advanced it. Taxonomies and typologies that have been used in CSCW, despite being pre-theoretical in this sense, are addressed in a later section.

North America and Europe

Since 1988, CSCW conferences have alternated between ACM-sponsored conferences in North America and European conferences (ECSCW). The series began with different emphases, but participation overlaps and some differences attenuated over time.

North American CSCW began with participants from psychology, software engineering, sociology, anthropology, management information systems (MIS), organizational theory, and AI (artificial intelligence, in particular multi-agent systems; Greif, 1988). AI was riding high in 1984 with well-financed responses to the Japanese *Fifth Generation* effort, but by 1990 an *AI winter* had set in and AI disappeared from CSCW. The psychologists and software engineers were mostly CHI researchers expanding their focus from individuals to small groups. The relevant MIS and organizational theory research resulted from scaling down from an organizational focus to large groups that less expensive systems could support. Group decision support system research had begun in MIS departments in the early 1970s, continued through the 1980s, and in 1990 two start-ups and IBM brought them to market, albeit without much success.

In North America, and in Japanese and other Asian countries in the 1990s, CSCW comprised mainly young researchers and practitioners, the latter employed by large computer and software vendor companies. With the success of single-user applications such as word processors and spreadsheets in mind, these companies sought *killer apps* that supported groups. Powerful workstations emerged in the late 1980s that enabled CSCW research to extend beyond e-mail and computer-controlled analog video to applications such as collaborative writing and knowledge management.

In contrast, Europe lacked an intensely competitive software product industry. The IT focus was on computer use in government and industry. The European CSCW community had an organizational perspective, but in contrast to the managerial bias of MIS, it was political and focused on empowering workers. This provided common ground with the young North Americans focused on pleasing consumers, but significant differences in research orientations stemmed from organizational versus small-group foci.

Research method biases differed, at times sharply. Although North American researchers largely avoided experimental studies and social theory, they engaged in user studies to quickly identify probable flaws in interaction design. Many ECSCW researchers eschewed laboratory studies altogether due to the salience of contextual factors in organizational behavior. European research often supported long-term development: a system might take ten years to design, build, and deploy. Accordingly, a European paper might only describe requirements analysis or a theoretical justification for a system. With far shorter product development cycles as the norm for North American CSCW efforts, papers were expected to cut to the chase and include use data, for at least a prototype system. Participatory Design, an approach to development that originated in egalitarian Scandinavian settings, enlisted eventual users as active participants in the in-house organizational development that was the primary focus of European research. It did not transfer easily to the production of mass-market applications.

Until recently, neither CSCW nor ECSCW embraced quantitative approaches, sociological analysis, network analysis, or data mining. With participatory Design and small-scale user studies in the beginning and ethnography in later years, researchers favored specific or qualitative approaches. With the emergence of high volumes of accessible behavioral data on the Internet, Web, and other networks, this is changing. It is still rare to see work that employs both quantitative and qualitative methods, despite the likelihood that the future lies there.

An influential development in North America was ACM's decision in the early 1980s to archive conference proceedings. They were initially available by mail order after conferences as inexpensive hard copies, and later in a digital library. As U.S. conferences shifted from a community-building role to quality gatekeeping, rejection rates rose to 75%–85%. This, in turn, reduced the incentive to progress CSCW conference papers to journal publications.

Interviews indicate that the conference focus was a factor in driving MIS research out of CSCW. To write a paper that met the standards of an ACM conference required almost the effort of journal publication in a field that valued the latter more. In contrast, European conferences proceedings were not generally accessible after the conference. There the emphasis remained on journals, and the 1992 formation of a research journal *Computer Supported Cooperative Work* was an all-European effort. No U.S. journal followed. (Several of the ECSCW proceedings were published as expensive books by Kluwer, and they are now available online.)

Both branches of CSCW welcomed ethnographers. The design-oriented North Americans favored broad observations, and the Europeans leaned toward ethnomethodology and sociology. More Europeans embraced action research and overt political objectives; North Americans reaching for mass markets saw such considerations as tangential or unscientific.

Over time there was convergence, arguably mediated by researchers in the United Kingdom. In particular, Xerox established a CSCW-oriented basic research laboratory in the UK that interacted with its sibling Xerox PARC. Comprising a mix of ethnographers, sociologists, and technologists, it played strong roles in both conference series. Researchers came to appreciate different perspectives, at least more than they had previously.

Incoming waves of technology helped wash away differences by promoting fresh starts. In Europe, organizations that once built systems from the ground up and thus had insular perspectives increasingly relied upon commercial applications. In North America, the desire to support activities in ever finer detail pushed small-group researchers to greater consideration of organizational and community contexts.

Consequences of Technology Evolution

Between 1988 and 1996, ten or more books with "computer supported cooperative work" in their titles were published. The most significant technology-driven shift was the growth of the Internet and emergence of the Web around 1995. CSCW did not take the lead in research in these consumer-driven areas, and attention shifted. To our knowledge, for almost 15 years, no new essays examined CSCW as a field and Ackerman, Halverson, Erickson, and Kellogg (2008) was the only book published in English with CSCW in its title, other than conference proceedings.

A striking effect of the rapid advance of technology was that each of the terms in the CSCW acronym has lost applicability.

Computer. The computer was a sensible focus in the 1980s. Digital technology is now embedded in many relevant devices that are not called computers.

Supported. Twenty-five years ago, computation was brought in to support existing activities. Today much work is centered on digital information. Computation is in a focal role, not a support role.

Cooperative. This word reflected the small-group product focus that dominated in North America. Designers of a coauthorship system, for example, are happy if it succeeds with cooperative coauthors. This word displeased organizational behaviorists from the outset. In a CSCW 1988 conference panel, Rob Kling challenged the assumption of cooperation, noting that organizational behavior is more complex: "Why not computer supported conflictual work? Coercive work?" Other suggestions were collective, coordinated, or collaborative work, the latter marred by lingering associations to World War II collaborators.

Work. Well into the e-mail era, use of computation to support group activity was restricted to workplaces. The cost of sending a single e-mail message was greater than the price of a postage stamp (Panko, 1981). PCs and Macintoshes were difficult to network until around 1990. Today, the CSCW research community engages a full range of consumer activity, including play.

Reflecting this shift, in 2009 the Springer CSCW book series adopted the tagline *Collaboration, Sociality, Computation and the Web,* as did CSCW 2010.

Models of Technology Development and Use

Figure 40.2 depicts a model that we find useful. We begin at the top with people collaborating,

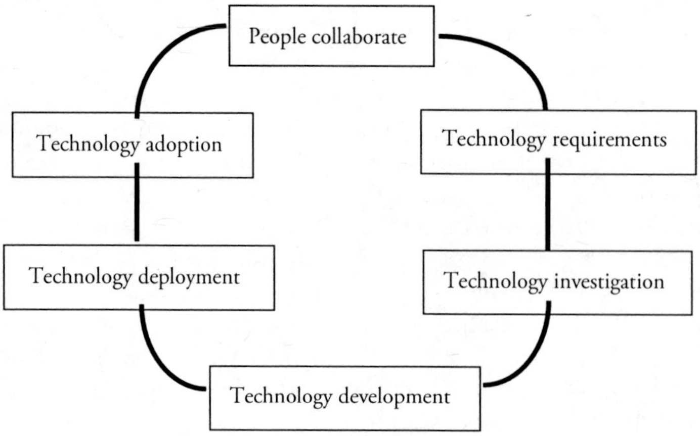

Figure 40.2 A Model of Collaboration and Technology Introduction

The diagram shows a clockwise cycle connecting: People collaborate → Technology requirements → Technology investigation → Technology development → Technology deployment → Technology adoption → (back to People collaborate).

perhaps with digital technology, perhaps not. That is the core issue. People collaborate. A fundamental premise in CSCW is that technology could help them do so more efficiently or effectively or enjoyably. This is not always true, but with advances in power and scope, digital technology can often support activities, and in ever finer-grained detail. Where does that technology come from? Following the diagram clockwise from the top, someone must determine the requirements for a technology that could help people collaborate. Second, research or investigation may be needed to find the technology if it exists, or to define a new technology and a process for making it. Third, the technology must be developed and made ready for people to actually use. Then one of two things must happen, depending on who has created the technology. If it is made by a company for its own internal use, it is deployed to the employees. If made for others to use, people must be persuaded to acquire it, and, therefore, it must be marketed. Finally, people must adopt it. They must decide to use it and figure out how to do so.

We are then again at the top of Figure 40.2. People may or may not use the technology as envisioned, and over time their use evolves as the technology is understood better or is used alongside other new technologies or processes. And then, in no small part because of the shifting price and power of digital technology, it may be time to begin the cycle again, by gaining a deeper understanding of current use and considering requirements all over.

Each step in Figure 40.2 constitutes a domain of human activity for which methods or theories have been developed or adapted. Social scientists in the CSCW community explore how people collaborate in various settings, define high-level requirements, and investigate adoption patterns. Computer scientists explore technology requirements and investigate and develop new technologies. Technology deployment or marketing have received relatively little attention within the CSCW community.

Maturation of Technology Use

In a field of invention and rapid maturation, not all design and assessment follows the same course. Figure 40.3 shows stages that often occur as a technology matures, with rows for the users of a technology, the priorities of the interaction models or user interfaces (UI), and typical research approaches at different points. A novel technology or application faces shifting considerations as it matures. Use begins with hobbyists and researchers, often moves to routine use in business where kinks are worked out, then to adoption by consumers delighted to be able to afford it, and finally to sophisticated use marked by a desire for personalization. Watches began with inventors, were later used by railroads, eventually reached broad markets with inexpensive identical Timex watches, and later came Swatches as fashion statements. This progression is seen in products from washing machines to word processors, although steps may be omitted or the progression may be more complex.

Consider the computer keyboard and monitor. Little consideration was given to their design or usability until businesses hired data entry personnel, such as airline reservation agents or telephone operators. Then keyboards were carefully optimized for efficiency. With consumers came the need to

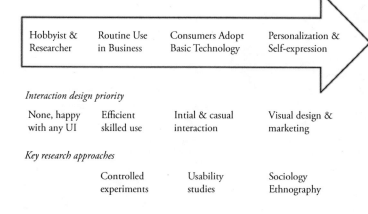

Figure 40.3 Adoption of New Technologies

Hobbyist & Researcher	Routine Use in Business	Consumers Adopt Basic Technology	Personalization & Self-expression

Interaction design priority

None, happy with any UI	Efficient skilled use	Intial & casual interaction	Visual design & marketing

Key research approaches

	Controlled experiments	Usability studies	Sociology Ethnography

support initial or casual use, leading to greater simplicity, such as dedicated function keys. Eventually, personalization arrived, with keyboards that differ in color, sleekness, and ergonomic considerations.

CSCW's focus on widely used platforms with minimal expectation of training means that progression from initial encounter and casual use to personalization can be relatively rapid. Students became early adopters who shaped technology use, despite lacking the money usually required, because government underwrote many expensive university computers. The technologies of interest to students were primarily those supporting communication and personal information management, such as e-mail and word processing, and not, for example, databases.

The flow of novelty means that at any point in time, different technologies are at different points of the Figure 40.3 progression. This affects research and application. E-mail had reached wide use when IM made its first inroads into business. Digital videoconferencing moved slowly from research into business, and is likely to become a successful consumer product. Products in mature technology areas, such as the Blackberry and the iPhone, compete through design.

Maturation of Technology Design

A technology can be disruptive or can represent an incremental change. For example, the first wiki introduced into an organization could represent a fundamentally different way of looking at collaboration. When anyone can enter information and edit others' contributions, issues of authority and accountability are raised. After these issues have been resolved, a new and improved wiki will

encounter different constraints on design, introduction, and use. In Figure 40.4, steps from Figure 40.2 are shown with bar heights as rough, schematic representations of the relative significance of steps in each context. For an innovation intended for use by hobbyists, early stages require attention; for a new version of a mature product, later stages get more attention. The key point is that the literature contains many descriptions of both mature and innovative system development and use that do not call attention to differences that lead to the use of different methods, frameworks, or emphases.

Figures 40.2 through 40.4 are intended to guide thinking about the frameworks and theories that follow and the CSCW literature in general. The application/conceptual frameworks, research methods, and development approaches differ greatly, according to phase of development and use. The link often is not spelled out in specific papers. In surveying the literature, readers are encouraged to give thought to when a paper was written, its author's field, the maturity of the technology, the context of intended or actual use, and the points in the collaboration and technology cycles that are under consideration.

Taxonomies and Typologies Used in CSCW

Taxonomies and typologies in CSCW are pretheoretical constructs that characterize cooperative work and identify the technologies that support different types of work. Especially in the early years, technical features were often explicitly tied to their position within one of the frameworks that we will describe.

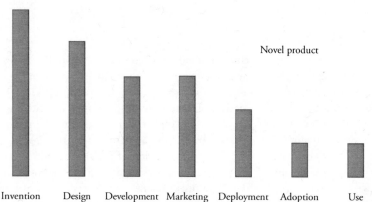

New version of mature product

Requirements · Design · Development · Marketing · Deployment · Adoption · Use

Novel product

Invention · Design · Development · Marketing · Deployment · Adoption · Use

Figure 40.4 Schematic Illustration of Relative Emphasis in Two Technology Categories

Johansen's Four-Square Map and a Nine-Square Extension

The simplest and most widely cited taxonomy is the Four-Square Map of Groupware Options proposed by Robert Johansen and his colleagues in the late 1980s (Figure 40.5a). It inspired researchers and developers to reflect on the dimensions that influence collaboration and different ways of supporting group activities.

Interaction can occur synchronously or asynchronously, and it can be co-located or distributed. Representative applications illustrate the different cells. People unfamiliar with CSCW technologies could quickly grasp this framework and apply it to their work environments. Indeed, it provides a convenient way to pigeonhole new technologies. Spatial and temporal differences translate into different technical requirements. Well into the 1990s, technology limitations often forced applications to focus on activity residing in only one cell, such as support of a real-time face-to-face meeting.

A subtle issue was the degree of predictability of a digitally mediated interaction. An activity can be carried out in a single place, in multiple locations known to the participants (e.g., e-mail exchanges), or in numerous places, not all of which are known (messages posted to a netnews group). Activity can be carried out in real time, asynchronously yet predictably or constrained, as with e-mail sent to a colleague, or at times that are highly unpredictable, as in open-ended collaborative writing projects. In 1991, we extended Johansen's framework by subdividing the *different place* and *different time* categories, shown in Figure 40.5b. Of course, a task type may not fit uniformly into a cell—for example, one collaborative writing project could take place in a single session, another could involve a large set of people assembling a major piece of documentation over time. And research was not uniformly extensive across cells; support for work shift handoffs and team rooms was of less concern.

Groupware Taxonomy Based on Organizational Research

MIS researchers who examined organizational support saw that the one-person-per-office assumptions of most distributed work experiments did not fit organizations, where distributed groups

(a)

Time \ Place	Same	Different
Same	Electronic meeting room	Application sharing
Different	Shift work, team rooms	E-mail, newsgroups

Figure 40.5 (a) Four-Square Map of Groupware Options, from Johansen et al. (1991). (b) Distinguishing Predictable and Unpredictable Differences in Time and Place, from Grudin and Poltrock (1991)

(b)

Time \ Place	Same	Different but predictable	Different and unpredictable
Same	Electronic meeting room	Desktop video-conferencing	Multicast events
Different but predictable	Work shifts	Electronic mail	Newsgroups
Different and unpredictable	Team rooms	Collaborative writing	Workflow

often involved multiple people at each location. Nunamaker, Dennis, Valacich, Vogel, and George (1991) proposed the taxonomy shown in Figure 40.6 that distinguishes a single co-located group, individual participants at different locations, and multiple co-located groups. In conformance with the constraints imposed by display size, they distinguish groups of up to seven from larger groups. Display technology has *not* changed rapidly. If a long-predicted breakthrough in displays materializes, another wave of innovation is likely.

A Developer's Taxonomy

Ellis and Wainer (1994) proposed a conceptual model to guide developers, which has seen some use. It integrated aspects of technology with basic characteristics of use. Its three components were: an ontology of groupware, the temporal coordination or organization of activities, and the user interface. The ontology covers the data structure supported by a groupware system and the operations that it supports. For example, a collaborative drawing program comprises objects such as polygons and operations for creating and modifying them. The coordination model describes how participants' interactions with the system are managed. A system could permit simultaneous interaction with the same object or permit only one person at a time to interact with it. The user interface model describes how actors interact through the system. Interaction may be achieved

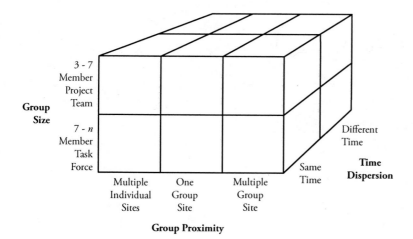

Figure 40.6 Taxonomy of Groupware, from Nunamaker et al (1991).

by displaying attributes of the objects manipulated by other participants, by displaying representations of other participants, or by displaying shared context, such as progress toward an objective.

Two Recent Activity-Based Taxonomies

In tutorials on CSCW and groupware over 15 years, we used many of the aforementioned taxonomies before settling on the framework shown in Figure 40.7a. It retains the temporal dimension, adds an activity dimension, and includes a social structure dimension that is hidden in the figure but emerges as overlays. The core activities are communicating, sharing information, and coordinating. Features of a technology can support any combination of these activities, performed synchronously or asynchronously. In practice, people collaborating face-to-face in real time, as in meetings, often have little interest in using technology to coordinate their contributions. Instead, they rely on formal or informal social protocols, such as Robert's Rules of Order or the lessons learned when playing together as children. Because the social protocols often rely on nonverbal information that is not communicated by a technology, support for real-time collaboration across distance, such as teleconferences or application sharing, requires features such as floor control and session management to facilitate coordination.

When people collaborate, it is generally in the context of: (a) small groups or teams, (b) organizations, or (c) large-scale communities. Communities in the online context only rarely have a geographic element. When groups of more than around seven work together, they generally establish subgroups and an organizational structure to coordinate the work. These different social structures rely upon different sets of cells of the Figure 40.7a framework. Small groups or teams are likely to work together in real time, communicate informally and share information, and they have minimal need for coordination technologies. Organizational collaboration involves the coordinated activity of different groups or teams to achieve common goals. Asynchronous collaboration is the dominant mode for large organizations, and information sharing and coordination are critical. Most communities have fewer explicit shared goals and thus do not require coordination

(a)

	Real time	Asynchronous
Communication	· AV conferencing · Telephone · Chat, messaging · Broadcast video	· E-mail · Voice mail · FAX
Information sharing	· Whiteboards · Application sharing · Meeting facilitation · MUDs and CVEs	· Document management · Threaded discussions · Hypertext · Team workspaces
Coordination	· Floor control · Session management	· Workflow management · Case tools · Project management · Calendar & scheduling

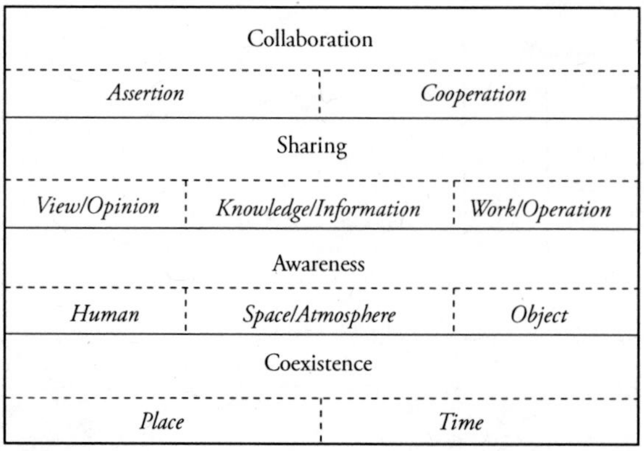

Figure 40.7 (a) Modes of Collaboration, from Poltrock & Grudin (1998). (b) A Hierarchical Collaboration Model, from Okada (2007).

(b)

Collaboration		
Assertion		Cooperation
Sharing		
View/Opinion	Knowledge/Information	Work/Operation
Awareness		
Human	Space/Atmosphere	Object
Coexistence		
Place		Time

technologies. Community members want to communicate and share information asynchronously with each other.

Okada (2007) proposed an ambitious, multilayered hierarchical framework, the result of a decade of analysis of experience with a range of systems (Figure 40.7b). This framework posits that the experience of collaboration is strongly influenced by the degrees of assertion and cooperation exhibited by participants. Low levels of both result in compromise, more assertion than cooperation results in collision, more cooperation than assertion results in concession, and high levels of both result in coordination. This collaboration layer is supported by sharing: sharing views and opinions through communication, sharing knowledge and information, and sharing work and operations. The sharing layer, in turn, is supported by awareness of other human participants, the environment in which the work occurs, and the objects and tools that are involved. Finally, awareness is affected by the temporal and spatial factors that were the focus of earlier taxonomies.

The DeSanctis and Gallupe Taxonomy

In 1987, MIS researchers DeSanctis and Gallupe proposed the first taxonomy, specifying three dimensions that they felt should drive the design of groupware (Figure 40.8). Physical location and group size were dimensions picked up by others, but we introduce this taxonomy here because their third dimension, task types, bridges to typologies that did not originate in CSCW but which have proved very useful in understanding CSCW research findings. Specifically, their task types were

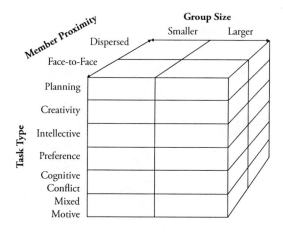

Figure 40.8 A Taxonomy Representing Group Size, Member Proximity, and Task Types, from DeSanctis & Gallupe (1987)

based on McGrath's framework (1984), which is discussed below and appears in Figure 40.9b.

Why was the focus on task types dropped from taxonomies that found favor over the next 20 years? The answer lies in the historical context outlined above. CSCW is an engineering discipline, driven by technology-producing companies and academic computer scientists with common interests. They sought lowest-common-denominator tools that would be useful in as many contexts as possible. E-mail was the quintessential success case, yet it had little representation of social context. CSCW researchers generally avoided special cases (such as *mixed motive*). When MIS researchers ceased participating in CSCW, pressure to consider such factors subsided. Perhaps this enabled more focus and progress in some directions, but overlooking these considerations slowed the recognition of some patterns that were emerging.

A more recently developed taxonomy (Bolstad & Endsley, 2003) includes elements of all the taxonomies above, including task types. Its dimensions include tool category (e.g., video conferencing, e-mail), collaboration characteristics (i.e., time, predictability, place, and interaction), tool characteristics (i.e., recordable, identifiable, and structured), information types (e.g., verbal, textual, video), and processes, which are similar to the task type dimension of DeSanctis and Gallupe (1987). The purpose of this taxonomy was to guide the development and selection of tools to support the military, not the common-denominator tools of interest to CSCW researchers and developers.

McGrath's Typologies of Team Behavior

We conclude this section with two social science typologies: Joseph McGrath on the functions and modes of activities in groups or teams, and Henry Mintzberg's analysis of the forces at work in different parts of organizations. Neither author focused on technology use, but the potential relevance of their work has become clear.

McGrath (1991) described team behavior in terms of three functions and four modes, shown in Figure 40.9a. This typology may seem evident, yet it can be a revelation, because studies of technology deployment and use focus almost exclusively on a single cell of this framework: performance, combining the production function and execution mode. The holy grail of *return on investment* translates into short-term measures of productivity (Grudin, 2004b). Even when a specialized technology focuses on another mode, such as a negotiation support

(a)

	Production	Group well-being	Member support
Inception	Production demand and opportunity	Interaction demand and opportunity	Inclusion demand and opportunity
Problem-solving	Technical problem solving	Role network definition	Position and status achievements
Conflict resolution	Policy resolution	Power and payoff distribution	Contribution and payoff distribution
Execution	Performance	Interaction	Participation

(b)

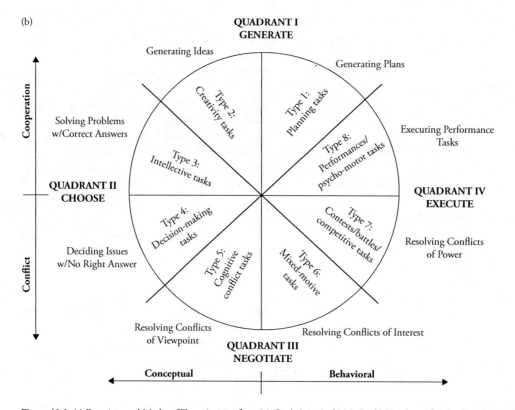

Figure 40.9 (a) Functions and Modes of Team Activity, from McGrath (1991). (b) McGrath's Typology of Tasks, from McGrath (1984).

system, policy resolution becomes the performance measure.

Activities that support group health and support group members are common in organizations, but they often occur without conscious consideration or are overlooked as tangential to the task at hand. This tendency to focus on the production function explains some apparent mysteries in the literature. Dennis and Reinicke (2004) found evidence that the absence of support for group and member well-being explains the lack of commercial success of group support systems with proven ability to increase performance. Anonymous brainstorming may work well in studies, but the identity of a speaker may be crucial in the workplace, and credit for their contributions may motivate participants. One participant in a meeting that was conducted using a group support system told us that it was the most unpleasant meeting he had experienced in his life, despite its success at accomplishing its stated objective. Video is a second example: decades of studies showed that it provided no performance advantage over audio, but more recently video had significant effects in problem-solving and conflict-resolution tasks (Veinott, Olson, Olson, & Fu, 2001; Williams, 1997).

McGrath's (1984) circumplex in Figure 40.9b has three task dimensions: conceptual versus behavioral; conflictual versus cooperative; and whether the focus is on generation, selection, negotiation, or execution. Once again, most CSCW research and application focuses on a single cell, executing performance tasks. Although this figure has impressed many CSCW researchers and students, the field's performance focus seems to hinder using it to advantage. The narrow focus can mean that users of resulting systems struggle to find ways to use them to support activities in other cells, or may abandon use altogether.

Mintzberg's Typology of Organizational Parts

A consistent finding in the CSCW literature, perhaps first appearing in Perin (1991) for e-mail, is that organizational stakeholders often have radically different responses to an application. Perin (1991) noted that in the mid-1980s e-mail solved problems for individual contributors and created them for managers. Subsequently, many studies have found differences consistent with Henry Mintzberg's elegant dissection of organizational parts (Figure 40.10). Executives (strategic apex), managers (middle line), individual contributors (operating core), the people formulating work processes (technostructure), and the support staff often have different approaches, constraints, opportunities for action, and competing priorities.

Individual contributors who make up the operating core are typically heavily engaged in communication; managers focus on sharing structured information in the form of documents, spreadsheets, and slide decks; and executives focus on coordinating activity of different groups. Note that these foci constitute one dimension of the Figure 40.7a framework. Executives' time is heavily scheduled with meetings, managers' less so, individual contributors' least. The ability to delegate work correlates with level in the organization, as does the sensitivity to public disclosure of one's work activities. The three groups have very different structures to their workdays, with major impact on tool use

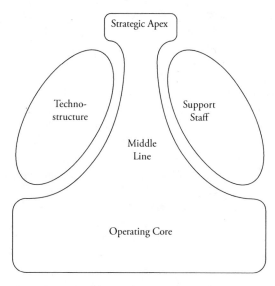

Figure 40.10 Central Parts of an Organization, from Mintzberg (1984).

for tools that they use (Grudin, 2004a). Within the support staff, IT professionals show yet another pattern of tool use. The technostructure role is less fully reported upon, but difficulties incorporating work processes in software in an effective way, notably in workflow systems, could be felt disproportionately there because they are often expected to deliver automated process systems.

A recent CSCW taxonomy of the capabilities of collaboration tools builds explicitly on the work of these social scientists. Weiseth, Munkvold, Tvedte, and Larsen's (2006) *wheel* is centered on models of content, content life cycle, and process integration, with 13 distinct activities in support of coordination, decision making, or production. Each is a potential focus of technology support. They identify physical workspace, digital devices, and portals as technological components that bear consideration.

Conclusions: Taxonomy Use and Evolution

It is noteworthy that the taxonomies proposed by social scientists made no reference to the temporal and spatial dimensions that were central in the taxonomies produced and used by the CSCW community. Digital technology greatly amplified the ability to interact across space, but created new challenges by filtering out contextual information. Asynchronous communication and exchange provided far finer granularity than travel and post had, and also created new temporal challenges. These challenges captured the attention of researchers and developers, but as problems were addressed, patterns emerged that confirm the relevance of some prior social science.

The new challenges were initially tackled one at a time. Rooms to support meetings were built as stand-alone systems, not networked to the outside world. Johansen et al. (1991) used such stand-alone systems, but noted that eventually we would need *anytime, anyplace* solutions. Today, software would not be taken seriously if it supported real-time face-to-face activity but did not allow easy importation of documents prepared earlier, participation by remote participants, and exporting the fruit of the activity digitally for subsequent use.

Spatial and temporal distinctions retain technical and behavioral implications, but as conventions for handling digital capabilities come into place, those distinctions are less central. The social behaviors that have governed groups and organizations for thousands of years again rise to prominence.

Theory in CSCW

We have noted that cognitive psychologists who focused on human-computer interaction initially had a mission of constructing a theoretical foundation for design. By the late 1980s, the pace of technology change had stilled these ambitions. CSCW also began with efforts to construct an encompassing conceptual base. These, too, lasted for only a few years. Beyond that, most invocation of social science theory is to broaden theories developed elsewhere, with little building or testing of conceptual constructs. The choices of theories are often governed by the phases of the development and technology use cycle in Figure 40.2.

We identify four distinct roles of theory in CSCW: (a) there is some traditional theory development through hypothesis-testing; (b) a theory's use as a referent can support efficient communication among people familiar with its terminology and constructs; (c) a theory can motivate or justify system architectures or development approaches; and (d) theory can serve as a guideline or checklist for researchers or systems developers.

Traditional Theory Construction

The engineering orientation of North American CSCW, defined by Greif (1988) as a research field focused on the role of the computer in group work, was immediately countered by European participants who attended in large numbers in 1988. These included Scandinavians influenced by the trade union movement and others who desired to develop a conceptual and theoretical framework.

The Scandinavians' political stance focused on worker empowerment. They cited philosophical approaches (e.g., Heidegger's) and especially the psychologically and culturally focused activity theory.

Liam Bannon, Kjeld Schmidt, and Mike Robinson led efforts to forge a unifying conceptual framework for CSCW. Bannon and Schmidt (1989) was a manifesto in the first European CSCW conference that cited the work of Robinson inter alia. The three formed the journal *CSCW*, with a revision of the 1989 paper as the first article (Schmidt & Bannon, 1992). The papers are worth reading 20 years later. They identify core issues that have not been resolved and they present a vision of the future of CSCW that did not materialize in illuminating ways.

Bannon and Schmidt (1989) took issue with Greif's (1988) notion that CSCW should focus on the group as a unit of analysis. They took even stronger issue with the notion that technology or groupware should be the focus. They argued for adopting an organizational focus, writing, "We need to develop a theoretical framework that will help us understand the complex interactions between the technical subsystem, the work organization, and the requirements of the task environments. To design CSCW systems designers must analyze the target organizations" (p. 369). and they identified a range of sensible issues for analysis.

Both articles focus on two core issues: (a) the underappreciated role in organizational work of secondary tasks (often invisible to management and system specification writers) that mediate, mesh, and adjust the work of individuals and groups in accordance with shifting circumstances; and (b) the tension between providing people with some control over self-disclosure and creating a common information space that includes details about individuals and their work, often needed for interaction but stripped away by the digital systems of the era. This boundary between disclosure and privacy is notoriously difficult for people to place and continues to be a problem in CSCW systems. The earlier article added a third core issue, nicely outlining the complex issues involved in the unplanned co-evolution of technologies and organizations. The authors concluded by decrying the absence of attention within CSCW to topics including computer-integrated manufacturing, computer-assisted design, and organizational information systems. They argued for including everything that fit a careful unpacking of *computer supported cooperative work.*

No serious effort to address their agenda materialized. Few, if any, continued to call for broad theory development. The reasons seem clear. Bannon and Schmidt's (1989) analysis showed that the task would be daunting, and CSCW was indeed primarily an engineering discipline. The North Americans remained focused on supporting groups and hoped to find solutions that were independent of organizational context, as they had with word processors, spreadsheets, and e-mail.

Finally, technology changed too rapidly to draw a theoretical bead on its development and use. The articles were written when large organizations developed software internally, the context in which the British socio-technical systems and Scandinavian design approaches appeared. As those days ended, technology acquisition and adaptation took on a different cast.

A few CSCW researchers worked to extend theory, most notably activity theory. Originally a theory of the development of intellectual, social, and cultural understanding in children, it was extended to include CSCW. Yuri Engestrom was a major theorist who made minor contributions to CSCW (Engestrom, Engestrom, & Saarelma, 1988). Kari Kuutti wrote of the potential of activity theory and explored case studies as tests of its elements, although in truth the elegant theory has a limited degree of falsifiability (e.g., Kuutti, 1991; Kuutti & Arvonen, 1992). Arne Raiethel's (1991) chapter was an ambitious effort by a theoretician who was active in the CSCW milieu. Jacob Bardram (1998) explicitly expanded the individual focus of activity theory to encompass collaboration. He wrote, "Theory within a design discipline, such as CSCW . . . is to be judged upon its contribution to a systematic expansion of possible actions within a particular practice" (p. 93). Not everyone sees CSCW as solely a design discipline subject to this utilitarian view, but arguably no adequate body of organized, stable observations exists on which to build useful high-level theory.

As the 1990s progressed, the drawbacks of a technology-centric focus were countered not by an influx of theory but by its opposite, an influx of ethnography, much of which eschewed efforts at generalization. Some used *grounded theory* to justify hypothesis-free exploration to theory-obsessed colleagues, but few of the grounded theory proponents in CSCW pursued theory building beyond the identification of patterns.

In 2008, an explicit effort to define what might constitute theory in CSCW and then build one was published (Ackerman et al., 2008). This edited collection of analyses, some dating from studies conducted in the early 1990s, undertook to build a small-scale theory of artifacts or resources "that would allow CSCW and adjacent fields to move forward in a more systematic and less hit-or-miss way" (p. 2). With contributions from leading CSCW researchers, they claimed progress on developing statements with "descriptive power" and "rhetorical power," but concluded that "years of research work and many dissertations" would be needed to achieve "inferential power" or "application."

Nevertheless, despite rarely being created, extended, tested, or discussed in a deep way in CSCW, a wide range of theories are invoked with no explication and little explanation, to the possible consternation of students and other readers. The rest of this section explores rationales for the invocations of theory.

Theory as Communicative Expedient

Invoking the common ground of a familiar theory is particularly useful in a conference-oriented field with short papers and a bias for empirical results. It is a shorthand way of communicating with those already familiar with the theory, and perhaps of impressing those who are not. For example, frequent allusions to media richness theory in the literature rarely explain it and never discuss prior results that appear to support or refute it. Activity theory is invoked with perhaps a paragraph of explanation, wholly inadequate as an explanation of this extensive, complex theory. Communication via theory can be a double-edged sword, as when a CSCW researcher confided to us that she was reframing her results around Goffman because she felt it would be more acceptable to reviewers than her original and preferred construction around the concepts of Durkheim.

Theory as Motivation or Justification for System Design or Experimental Methodology

Some successful CSCW papers primarily serve to introduce the CSCW audience to a theory developed in another field. For example, Fitzpatrick, Kaplan, and Tolone (1995) is divided evenly between a presentation of Strauss's (1993) theory of action and the description of a system comprising relatively familiar features assembled in a manner inspired by the theory. At CSCW'88, Bødker, Ehn, Knudsen, Kyng, and Madsen and Engestrom et al. described activity theory as an inspiration for their designs and analyses, but did not explain it to an audience that was almost entirely unacquainted with it.

Theory as Guideline or Checklist

The use of theoretical constructs and associated frameworks as a prompt to look for patterns in observations or data is often implicit in the justifications of theory use in design or in placing results in a theoretical structure. Researchers and system designers can draw on theoretical constructs to insure that they consider potentially relevant aspects of a situation. Actor-network theory and activity theory often appear to be used to direct attention and to expand views of a particular socio-technical setting, uncovering significant aspects that are at risk of being overlooked.

Discussion

We are now ready to reexamine the models and theoretical approaches with the phases of our model of collaboration and technology introduced in Figure 40.2. An example could give this abstract discussion some concreteness, so we first describe the CSCW literature citations of one theory.

Case Study: Citations of Media Richness Theory in CSCW

Media richness theory originated outside CSCW but is often invoked. We conducted an informal study by identifying all citations within the CSCW literature to a seminal work, Daft and Lengel (1986). Media richness theory states that richer communication media should be employed to support tasks that are more ambiguous and uncertain, and that task performance will suffer if the medium is insufficiently rich. This theory is unquestionably relevant to technological support for collaboration. Daft and Lengel's (1986) paper describing the theory has been referenced by 12 papers presented at CSCW conferences, three papers presented at ECSCW conferences, and three papers published in the CSCW journal. Only two of the 18 papers explicitly tested Media richness theory; both were coauthored by Robert Kraut, who also wrote the survey of social psychology discussed in the introduction. Kraut, Cool, Rice, and Fish (1994) found results consistent with the theory, and Galegher and Kraut (1992) disconfirmed it, finding that users adapted their work practices to available media with no impact on performance.

Half of the papers (Bietz, 2008; Dabbish & Kraut, 2006; DiMicco, Pandolfo, & Bender, 2004; Grinter & Palen, 2002; Karsten, 2003; Nardi, Whittaker, & Bradner, 2000; Setlock, Fussell, & Neuwirth, 2004; Weiseth et al., 2006; Yamauchi, Yokozawa, Shinohara, & Ishida, 2000) explore factors that influence preferences for media or the performance effects of using different media. These papers do not test media richness theory or even attempt to manipulate richness. They establish common ground by citing Daft and Lengel (1986) when noting that collaboration via media can be challenging. Another paper (Fish, Kraut, & Chalfonte, 1990) described differences between formal and informal communication and noted that these differences paralleled, to some extent, differences between impoverished and rich communication channels as described by Daft and Lengel (1986). These are examples of using a theory as a communicative expedient.

One paper (Hauber, Regenbrecht, Billinghurst, & Cockburn, 2006) cited media richness theory as the motivation for choosing a task that has a high level of uncertainty. We noted that researchers at times use theory to justify a system design choice; in this case, it justified a choice of experimental methodology.

The explicit use of theory or frameworks as guideline or checklist is more likely in a development project than in a research paper. The closest we saw to this was Huysman et al. (2003), who referenced Daft and Lengel (1986) without citing the paper or mentioning media richness theory at all, alerting the reader to the authors' familiarity with the theory.

Revisiting the Model

Each step depicted in Figure 40.2 constitutes a domain of human activity of potential relevance, but the principal CSCW focus is on four of them. For example, of 62 papers presented at the closely analyzed twentieth-anniversary CSCW 2006 conference, 24% aimed at understanding collaboration in a context, generally concluding with implications for technologies that might support this collaboration. Defining technology requirements was the primary focus of 11%. Innovative new technologies and comparisons of technological approaches were the principal focus of 29% of the papers. Nearly a third of the papers (32%) investigated the adoption of technologies and how it influenced collaboration.

At the top of Figure 40.2 is collaboration, with or without technology, a major focus of social science research. CSCW research rarely proceeds far without foregrounding technology. A partial exception is Malone's development of coordination theory (Malone & Crowston, 1990). Coordination theory reflects the interdisciplinary origins and ambitions of CSCW, building on the observation that similar fundamental questions about the coordination of activities are asked in eight disciplines, ranging from linguistics to computer science. Coordination theory considers the goals, activities, and actors in group or organizational contexts, and their interdependencies. It then works out the effects of technologies on the management of different kinds of interdependencies.

Malone and Crowston (1990) sought to define a general theory of coordination, but most CSCW research into collaboration employs ethnographic fieldwork in specific settings. CSCW 2006 included studies of collaboration in playing the online game World of Warcraft (Nardi & Harris, 2006), how pastors use technology to communicate with church attendees (Wyche, Hayes, Harvel, & Grinter, 2006), how elderly people manage their medications (Palen & Aaløkke, 2006), and how users of high-performance computing systems collaborate (Danis, 2006). Extracting general principles from ethnographies performed in such diverse settings is an unsolved challenge.

Some of this work had a long-term goal of informing technology requirements; requirements are often a principal research focus. For potentially novel technologies, this may take the form of ethnographic or ethnographically inspired research. For example, Nomura, Hutchins, and Holder (2006) employed ethnography to study the uses of paper in commercial airline flight operations as a foundation for future technology requirements, their methods shaped by a distributed cognition theoretical framework (Hollan, Hutchins, & Kirsh, 2000). Also within the air travel industry, Lucy Suchman (1993) employed ethnography to study complex collaborative airport ground operations and to make the findings accessible to system designers (Suchman, 1995). With more mature technologies, a requirements analysis may comprise a comparison of alternatives, such as an experimental study exploring the efficacy of alternative video camera views of remote tutors guiding a worker performing a complex physical task (Ranjan, Birnholtz, & Balakrishnan, 2006).

System developers engage in technology investigations when creating new capabilities. For example, Xia, Sun, Sun, Chen, and Shen (2004) and Li and Lu (2006) developed technology that allows people to collaborate using applications designed for individual use. Such investigations are rarely guided overtly by social science frameworks or theory.

Technology development itself can become the focus of research studies. It is a costly and collaborative activity, and CSCW researchers have sought to understand it and define requirements for tools to support it. For example, Gutwin, Penner, and Schneider (2004) studied how people maintain group awareness while contributing to an open source development project. They cited no theories but conducted qualitative field research.

CSCW research often spans multiple steps in the model, but the page limits of conference proceedings compel most researchers to focus on one at a time. Ackerman (1994) and McDonald (2001) are careful studies of organizational behavior that led directly to building systems for locating information or expertise. Thus, they took the work through the first three steps of the cycle.

At the bottom of the Figure 40.2 cycle is technology development. CSCW is a showcase for prototype systems. A subset of the HCI field, which emphasizes constant user testing and iterative design, CSCW accounts of prototype system building almost always include limited user tests to gather feedback. A team that has invested heavily in building a system invariably also conducts the test, which can inhibit candid feedback and imbue the report with an optimistic bias. Typical reports show some successes, some areas for improvement, and generally positive users. However, remarkably few of the prototype systems see extended use, even when such was the plan. This does not mean that nothing of value was learned, but it does mean that readers must reflect carefully and consider whether or not follow-ups have appeared.

Marketing often coexists uneasily with engineering. Despite its potential relevance, it is not studied or discussed in the CSCW community. Adoption, in contrast, is frequently studied, both to understand responses to new technologies and to identify direct and indirect influences on social interactions and work performance. Studies of technology adoption often serve as requirements analysis for the next version of a maturing application.

Two influential CSCW papers examined obstacles to adoption. Grudin (1988) surveyed a range of technologies and identified three factors affecting small-group collaboration support that were not present in individual productivity tools or organizational systems: (a) use of relatively inexpensive groupware tools was rarely mandated, so those that required more work from some group members who perceived no benefit often were not used, even when a collective benefit might exist; (b) decision makers with good intuition for individual applications often did not anticipate these problems; and (c) evaluation was much more difficult than for individual productivity tools.

Orlikowski (1992) examined a consulting company's adoption of Lotus Notes and reported that it was influenced by cognitive and structural elements of the organization itself, not just by features of the technology. In particular, the benefits of the system were most apparent to senior partners; the incentives for consultants did not support its intended collaborative use. Orlikowski's (1992) description of the co-evolution of technology and the organization is widely seen as an extension of Giddens's (1979) structuration theory, although the latter's work is not directly cited. The interplay of technology, organizational structure, and collaborative practices has been the focus of many studies of technology adoption. Grinter and Palen (2002) employed the concepts of structuration theory to describe how teenage children use instant messaging and how it affects other elements of their lives. Munkvold, Ellingsen, and Koksvik (2006) and Bossen (2006) described the adoption of electronic patient records in hospitals, leading to unanticipated collaboration changes with negative consequences.

A major thread of research on technology deployment in enterprise settings explores variants of the technology acceptance model (TAM) proposed by Davis (1989), which is rarely cited in CSCW but is heavily cited in the management information systems literature. CSCW focuses on discretionary use of tools, and thus refers to technology *adoption*, whereas for much of the past quarter century MIS has focused more on mandated enterprise use, hence *acceptance*.

Conclusion and Directions

CSCW is the principal locus within computer science for dialogue and collaboration among social scientists and technologists. It quickly became a major ACM conference series and spawned a European series and a journal. Submissions and publications have risen steadily over a quarter century. The conferences are very selective, comprising highly polished papers. CSCW conference papers are in the ACM Digital Library at http://portal. acm.org/dl.cfm. Abstracts are freely accessible. To obtain the full papers requires a membership, but most research universities have a site license.

ECSCW papers are accessible at http://www.ecscw. uni-siegen.de.

CSCW was conceived as a forum, and although not all of the early vendors and shoppers continue to visit, the marketplace attracts technologists, psychologists, sociologists, and ethnographers. There are CSCW courses but no CSCW departments, programs, degrees, handbooks, or professionals. HCI is a core component of the computer science curriculum, and CSCW is a component of HCI, but it is relatively distant from mainstream computer science. Being somewhat marginal there, CSCW is susceptible to flight, notably to information schools.

The high selectivity of the conferences redirects much of the submitted work to a host of closely related conferences and conference tracks. These include CollabTech, predominantly a showcase for Asian work; CollaborateCom, which emphasizes technology; Collaborative Technologies and Systems, a broad conference focused on government systems; WikiSym, International Conference on Weblogs and Social Media (ICWSM); and GROUP, the latter comparable to CSCW with perhaps more of an organizational focus. Tracks and minitracks of the Hawaii International Conference on Systems Sciences (HICSS) series have emphasized relevant MIS work, computer-medicated communication, and social computing. This proliferation yields high-energy specialized small conferences. The cost is that related work is scattered, at least until sophisticated search tools appear that can re-aggregate it.

The dispersal of effort is greatly accelerated by a consequence of recent technology advances. Communication and information sharing technologies such as Facebook, Twitter, and Wikipedia are of considerable influence to the academics and software companies that drive much North American research, but not to the Europeans, whose primary focus remains organizational uses of technology. This new wave of technology has returned the situation to that of the 1980s, and the two camps have moved apart. CSCW focuses heavily, though not exclusively, on social computing. ECSCW is delving more deeply into basic issues in supporting activity in different domains. It seems inevitable that the two will reconverge, as the same forces build that did in the 1990s. How long this will take and whether the convergence will come under the CSCW rubric remains to be seen.

This conflict has created considerably reflection, especially within the smaller ECSCW community whose members felt marginalized within CSCW.

After 15 quiet years, three substantial books by European authors emerged with CSCW in their title (Randall & Salembier, 2010; Borghoff & Schlichter, 2010; Schmidt, 2011). Schmidt in particular reassesses the direction of the field.

CSCW has produced a significant repository of grounded qualitative research on technology use and impact. Technical explorations of architectures for synchronized activity, backtracking ("group undo") in collaborative use, and other topics have formed a foundation on which systems are built. Studies of technology prototypes virtually always include a report on usage, albeit not often in neutral contexts. Some of the technical work has been rendered obsolete by advances in capabilities and the platforms and tools that are available. To progress from a research prototype to a commercial system now involves a major effort to engage with a complex federation of services and assumed capabilities.

At a 1988 panel discussion, CSCW founder Irene Greif predicted that what was then a niche interest in a world of individual productivity tools would come to embrace all of digital technology use—support for group activity would be part of all software. That has largely come to pass. Nevertheless, opportunities for social scientists expand. Technology is drawn upon to support our activities in finer-grained detail. Applications are shifting from general-purpose to domain-specific, extending attention from group behavior to organizational dynamics. And the allure of new technology requires that researchers understand the present context, the significant effects on organizations and society that unfold around the inventions that have succeeded.

Research Trajectories and Opportunities

Twenty-five years ago, there were no courses, a handful of researchers, and scattered product developers working on collaboration support. Few of the latter had any exposure to social science. Everyone knew one another, and research proceeded at a leisurely pace. Today, there are thousands of researchers and tens of thousands of fiercely competitive developers, many of them trained at universities and familiar with the literature. It once took many years to get any software into use; today, a Facebook application can be launched within minutes of completion. The gap between research involving system construction and development shrank.

Although much has changed, research from industrial and organizational psychology has made only a small impact, and there is a considerable opportunity here, both for CSCW researchers to learn from past work in the social sciences and for more social scientists to contribute to the understanding of emerging phenomena, working together with or independently from today's CSCW researchers.

CSCW research has only recently come to appreciate some of the simple frameworks developed by Mintzberg and McGrath in the 1980s, and has not done so in any depth. For example, the work of Van de Ven et al. (1976) and Mintzberg (1983) on modes of coordinating work activity has not been applied. One technology trajectory is to support work in ever finer detail, requiring an understanding of workflow at a finer granularity, as well as an understanding of how work differs across organizations and industries, to which this and work that has followed can contribute. Similarly, much has been done since McGrath on the nature of tasks engaged by work groups (e.g. Kozlowski & Ilgen, 2006), which will certainly be of use in guiding CSCW research and in understanding study results, and at the same time may itself need to be extended to account for emerging phenomena.

The hardware curve points to another opening frontier: embedded systems, networks of sensors and effectors that will be used to pick up, filter, and report huge amounts of contextual information. To date, research into computational analysis of contextual information has focused on supporting personal information management, but determining how to route, organize, and present contextual information to facilitate collaboration is a pressing challenge. Information visualization is a rapidly growing research area, and we are still in the infancy of the information explosion.

The reader may not be surprised to hear us endorse qualitative field research as an area with unlimited potential. As technology extends its reach in all directions, we have never looked closely at its deployment without finding phenomena of interest. In reporting our results, we have found that qualitative researchers often dismiss quantitative data, and some quantitative researchers consider it to ask people to explain what they have done. This creates great opportunities for a new generation of researchers and research teams that combine quantitative and qualitative expertise—that can follow the analysis of the vast flow of quantitative information available over networks to find patterns with qualitative research to discover what the patterns mean, and then to formulate the next round of quantitative analysis.

References

Ackerman, M. (1994). Augmenting the organizational memory: A field study of Answer Garden. *Proceedings CSCW'94*, 243–252.

Ackerman, M. S., Halverson, C. A., Erickson, T., & Kellogg, W. A. (2008). *Resources, co-evolution and artifacts: Theory in CSCW*. London: Springer.

Baecker, R. M. (1993). *Readings in groupware and computer-supported cooperative work*. San Mateo, CA: Morgan Kaufmann.

Bannon, L. J., & Schmidt, K. (1989). CSCW: Four characters in search of a context. *Proceedings EC-CSCW'89*, 358–372.

Bardram, J. (1998). Designing for the dynamics of cooperative work activities. *Proceedings CSCW'98*, 89–98.

Beaudouin-Lafon, M. (Ed.). (1999). *Computer supported co-operative work: Trends in software* (Vol. 7). Chichester, UK: Wiley.

Bietz, M. J. (2008). Effects of communication media on the interpretation of critical feedback. *Proceedings CSCW'08*, 467–476.

Bolstad, C. A., & Endsley, M. R. (2003). Tools for supporting team SA and collaboration in army operations. *Proceedings Collaborative Technology Alliances'03*. SA Technologies. http://www.satechnologies.com/Papers/pdf/Bolstad%20%282003%29%20Collab%20Tools%20CTAC.pdf

Borghoff, U. M. & Schlichter, J. H. (2010). Computer-supported cooperative work: Introduction to distributed applications. Berlin: Springer.

Bossen, C. (2006). Representations at work: a national standard for electronic health records. *Proceedings CSCW'06*, 69–78.

Bowers, J., Button, G., & Sharrock, W. (1995). Workflow from within and without. Technology and cooperative work on the print industry shopfloor. *Proceedings ECSCW'95*, 51–66.

Brown, J. S., & Thomas, D. (2006). You play World of Warcraft? You're hired! *Wired, 14,* 4.

Bryant, S. L., Forte, A., & Bruckman, A. (2005). Becoming Wikipedian: Transformation of participation in a collaborative online encyclopedia. *Proceedings Group'05*, 1–10.

Brynjolfsson, E. (1993). The productivity paradox of information technology. *Commun. ACM, 36*(12), 66–77.

Brynjolfsson, E., & Hitt, L. M. (1998). Beyond the productivity paradox. *Commun. ACM, 41*(8), 49–55.

Burke, M., & Kraut, R. (2008). Mopping up: Modeling Wikipedia promotion decisions. *Proceedings CSCW'08*, 27–36.

Bødker, S., Ehn, P., Knudsen, J., Kyng, M., & Madsen, K. (1988). Computer support for cooperative design. *Proceedings CSCW'88*, 377–394.

Convertino, G., Kannampallil, T. G., & Councill, I. (2006). Mapping the intellectual landscape of CSCW research. Poster presented at *CSCW'06*.

Dabbish, L. A., & Kraut, R. E. (2006). Email overload at work: An analysis of factors associated with email strain. *Proceedings CSCW'06*, 431–440.

Daft, R. L., & Lengel, R. H. (1986). Organizational information requirements, media richness and structural design. *Management Science, 32,* 554–571.

Davis, F. D. (1989). Perceived usefulness, perceived ease of use, and user acceptance of information technology. *MIS Quarterly, 13,* 319–340.

Danis, C. (2006). Forms of collaboration in high performance computing: Exploring implications for learning. *Proceedings CSCW 2006*, 501–504.

Dennis, A. R., & Reinicke, B. A. (2004). Beta versus VHS and the acceptance of electronic brainstorming technology. *MIS Quarterly, 28*(1), 1–20.

DeSanctis, G., & Gallupe, R. B. (1987). A foundation for the study of group decision support systems. *Management Science, 33*(5), 589–610.

DiMicco, J. M., Pandolfo, A., & Bender, W. (2004). Influencing group participation with a shared display. *Proceedings CSCW 2004*, 614–623.

Dourish, P., & Bellotti, V. (1992). Awareness and coordination in shared workspaces. *Proceedings CSCW'92*, 107–114.

Ellis, C., & Wainer, J. (1994). A conceptual model of groupware. *Proceedings CSCW'94*, 79–88.

Engestron, Y., Engestrom, R., & Saarelma, O. (1988). Computerized medical records, production pressure and compartmentalization in the work activity of health center physicians. *Proceedings CSCW'88*, 65–84.

Fish, R. S., Kraut, R. E., & Chalfonte, B. L. (1990). The VideoWindow system in informal communications. *Proceedings CSCW'90*, 1–11.

Fitzpatrick, G., Kaplan, S. M., & Tolone, W. J. (1995). Work, locales and distributed social worlds. *Proceedings ECSCW'95*, 1–16.

Galegher, J., & Kraut, R. E. (1992). Computer-mediated communication and collaborative writing: Media influence and adaptation to communication constraints. *Proceedings CSCW'92*, 155–162.

Gaver, W., Moran, T., MacLean, A., Lövstrand, L., Dourish, P., Carter, K., & Buxton, W. (1992). Realizing a video environment: EUROPARC's RAVE system. *Proceedings CHI'92*, 27–35.

Giddens, A. (1979). *Central problems of social theory*. Berkeley: University of California Press.

Greenbaum, J. (1979). *In the name of efficiency*. Philadelphia: Temple.

Greif, I. (1985). Computer-supported cooperative groups: What are the issues? *Proceedings AFIPS Office Automation Conference (OAC'85)*. Montvale, NJ: AFIPS Press.

Greif, I. (Ed.). (1988). *Computer-supported cooperative work: A book of readings*. San Mateo, CA: Morgan Kaufmann.

Grinter, R. E., & Palen, L. (2002). Instant messaging in teen life. *Proceedings CSCW'02*, 21–30.

Grudin, J. (1988). Why CSCW applications fail: Problems in the design and evaluation of organizational interfaces. *Proceedings CSCW'88*, 85–93.

Grudin, J. (1994). CSCW: History and focus. *IEEE Computer, 27*(5), 19–26.

Grudin, J. (2004a). Managerial use and emerging norms: Effects of activity patterns on software design and development. *Proceedings HICSS-37,* 10 pp. Digital Object Identifier 10.1109/HICSS.2004.1265111. IEEE.

Grudin, J. (2004b). Return on investment and organizational adoption. *Proceedings CSCW'04*, 274–277.

Grudin, J. (2007). A moving target: The evolution of human-computer interaction. In A. Sears & J. Jacko (Eds.), *Handbook of human-computer interaction* (pp. 1–24). Boca Raton, FL: CRC Press.

Grudin, J., & Poltrock, S. E. (1991). Computer-supported cooperative work and groupware. Tutorial Notes, *CHI'91 Conference on Human Factors in Computing Systems*.

Grudin, J., & Poltrock, S. E. (1997). Computer-supported cooperative work and groupware. In M. Zelkowitz (Ed.), *Advances in computers* (Vol. 45, pp. 269–320). San Diego: Academic Press.

Gutwin, C., Penner, R., & Schneider, K. (2004). Group awareness in distributed software development. *Proceedings CSCW'04*, 72–81.

Hauber, J., Regenbrecht, H., Billinghurst, M., & Cockburn, A. (2006). Spatiality in videoconferencing: Trade-offs between efficiency and social presence. *Proceedings CSCW'06*, 413–422.

Hoffman, D. L., Kalsbeek, W. D., & Novak, T. P. (1996). Internet and web use in the United States: Baselines for commercial development. *Commun. ACM, 39*(12), 36–46.

Hollan, J., Hutchins, E., & Kirsh, D. (2000). Distributed cognition: Toward a new foundation for human-computer Interaction. *ACM Transactions on Computer-Human Interaction, 7*(2), 174–196.

Hudson, S., & Smith, I. (1996). Techniques for addressing fundamental privacy and disruption tradeoffs in awareness support systems. *Proceedings CSCW'96*, 248–257.

Huysman, M., Steinfield, C., Jang, C., David, K., Veld, M. H., Poot, J., & Mulder, I. (2003). Virtual teams and the appropriation of communication technology: Exploring the concept of media stickiness. *Computer Supported Cooperative Work, 12*, 411–436.

Jacovi, M., Soroka, V., Gilboa-Freedman, G., Ur, S., Shahar, E., & Marmasse, N. (2006). The chasms of CSCW: A citation graph analysis of the CSCW conference. *Proceedings CSCW'06*, 289–298.

Johansen, R., Sibbet, D., Benson, S., Martin, A., Mittman, R., & Saffo, P. (1991). *Leading business teams.* Reading, MA: Addison-Wesley.

Karsten, H. (2003). Constructing interdependencies with collaborative information technology. *Computer Supported Cooperative Work, 12*, 437–464.

Kozlowski, S. W. J., & Bell, B. S. (2003). Work groups and teams in organizations. In W. C. Borman, D. R. Ilgen, & R. J. Klimoski (Eds.), *Handbook of psychology: Industrial and organizational psychology* (Vol. 12, pp. 333–375). London: Wiley.

Kozlowski, S. W. J. & Ilgen, D. R. (2006). Enhancing the effectiveness of work groups and teams. *Psychological Science in the Public Interest, 7*(8), 77–124.

Kraut, R. (2003). Applying social psychological theory to the problems of group work. In J. Carroll (Ed.), *HCI models, theories and frameworks: Toward a multi-disciplinary science* (pp. 325–356). San Mateo, CA: Morgan Kaufmann.

Kraut, R. E., Cool, C., Rice, R. E., & Fish, R. S. (1994). Life and death of new technology: Task, utility and social influences on the use of a communication medium. *Proceedings CSCW'94*, 13–21.

Kraut, R., Kiesler, S., Boneva, B., Cummings, J. N., Helgeson, V., & Crawford, A. M. (2002). Internet paradox revisited. *Journal of Social Issues, 58*(1), 49–74.

Kraut, R., Patterson, M., Lundmark, V., Kiesler, S., Mukhopadhyay, T., & Scherlis, W. (1998). Internet paradox: A social technology that reduces social involvement and psychological well-being? *American Psychologist, 53*(9), 1017–1031.

Kriplean, T., Beschastnikh, I., & McDonald, D. W. (2008). Articulations of wikiwork: Uncovering valued work in wikipedia through barnstars. *Proceedings CSCW'08*, 47–56.

Kuutti, K. (1991). The concept of activity as a basic unit of analysis for CSCW research. *Proceedings ECSCW'91*, 249–264.

Kuutti, K., & Arvonen, T. (1992). Identifying potential CSCW applications by means of activity theory concepts: A case example. *Proceedings CSCW'92*, 233–240.

Li, D., & Lu, J. (2006). A lightweight approach to transparent sharing of familiar single-user editors. *Proceedings CSCW'06*, 139–148.

Malone, T. W., & Crowston, K. (1990). What is Coordination Theory and how can it help design cooperative systems? *Proceedings CSCW'90*, 357–370.

McDonald, D. W. (2001). Evaluating expertise recommendations. *Proceedings GROUP'01*, 214–223.

McGrath, J. E. (1984). *Groups: Interaction and performance.* Englewood Cliffs, NJ: Prentice Hall.

McGrath, J. E. (1991). Time, interaction, and performance (TIP): A theory of groups. *Small Group Research, 22*(2), 147–174.

Mintzberg, H. (1983). *Structure in 5's: Designing effective organizations.* Englewood Cliffs, NJ: Prentice-Hall.

Mintzberg, H. (1984). A typology of organizational structure. In D. Miller & P. H. Friesen (Eds.), *Organizations: A quantum view* (pp. 68–86). Englewood Cliffs, NJ: Prentice-Hall. Reprinted in R. Baecker (Ed.). (1993). *Readings in groupware and computer-supported cooperative work.* San Mateo, CA: Morgan Kaufmann.

Munkvold, G., Ellingsen, G., & Koksvik, H. (2006). Formalizing work: Reallocating redundancy. *Proceedings CSCW'06*, 59–68.

Nardi, B., & Harris, J. (2006). Strangers and friends: Collaborative play in World of Warcraft. *Proceedings CSCW'06*, 149–158.

Nardi, B. A., Whittaker, S., & Bradner, E. (2000). Interaction and outeraction: Instant messaging in action. *Proceedings CSCW'00*, 79–88.

Nomura, S., Hutchins, E., & Holder, B. E. (2006). The uses of paper in commercial airline flight operations. *Proceedings CSCW'06*, 249–258.

Nunamaker, J. F., Dennis, A. R., Valacich, J. S., Vogel, D. R., & George, J. F. (1991). Electronic meeting systems to support group work. *Communications of the ACM, 34*(7), 40–61.

Okada, K. (2007). Collaboration support in the information sharing space. *IPSJ Magazine, 48*(2), 123–125.

Olson, G. M., & Olson, J. S. (2007). Groupware and computer-supported cooperative work. In A. Sears & J. Jacko (Eds.), *Handbook of human-computer interaction*, 2nd edition (5445–558). Boca Raton, FL: CRC Press. A revision "collaboration technologies," will appear in J. Jacko (Ed.), *Handbook of human-computer interaction*, 3rd edition, Boca Raton, FL: CRC Press, in press.

Orlikowski, W. (1992). Learning from notes: Organizational issues in groupware implementation. *Proceedings CSCW'92*, 362–369.

Palen, L., & Aaløkke, S. (2006). Of pill boxes and piano benches: "Home-made" methods for managing medications. *Proceedings CSCW'06*, 79–88.

Panko, R. R. (1981). The cost of EMS. *Computer Networks, 5*, 35–46.

Perin, C. (1991). Electronic social fields in bureaucracies. *Communications of the ACM, 12*, 74–82.

Pickering, J. M., & King, J. L. (1992). Hardwiring weak ties: Individual and institutional issues in computer mediated communication. *Proceedings CSCW'92*, 356–361.

Poltrock, S., & Grudin, J. (1998). Computer supported cooperative work and groupware. Tutorial notes. *CH'98 Conference on Human Factors in Computing Systems.*

Poltrock, S., & Grudin, J. (2005). Videoconferencing: Recent experiments and reassessment. *Proc. Hawaii International Conferences on Systems Sciences.* 10 pages. IEEE. http://www.computer.org/portal/web/csdl/doi/10.1109/HICSS.2005.672. Accessed December 23, 2011.

Raiethel, A. (1991). Activity Theory as a foundation for design. In C. Floyd, H. Züllighoven, R. Budde, & R. Keil-Slawik, (Eds.), *Software development and reality construction* (pp. 391–415). New York: Springer-Verlag.

Randall, D. & Salembier, P. (Eds.) (2010). *From CSCW to Web 2.0: European developments in collaborative design.* London: Springer.

Ranjan, A., Birnholtz, J. P., & Balakrishnan, R. (2006). An exploratory analysis of partner action and camera control in a video-mediated collaborative task. *Proceedings CSCW'06,* 403–412.

Reeves, B., Malone, T., & O'Driscoll, T. (2008). Leadership's online labs. *Harvard Business Review, 86,* 58–67.

Schmidt, K. (2011). *Cooperative work and coordinative practices: Contributions to the conceptual foundations of computer-supported cooperative work (CSCW).* London: Springer.

Schmidt, K., & Bannon, L. (1992). Taking CSCW seriously: Supporting articulation work. *Computer Supported Cooperative Work, 1,* 7–40.

Setlock, L. D., Fussell, S. R., & Neuwirth, C. (2004). Taking it out of context: Collaborating within and across cultures in face-to-face settings and via instant messaging. *Proceedings CSCW'04,* 604–613.

Strauss, A. (1993). *Continual permutations of action.* New York: Aldine de Gruyter.

Suchman, L. (1993). Technologies of accountability: On lizards and airplanes. In G. Button (Ed.), *Technology in working order* (pp. 113–126). London: Routledge.

Suchman, L. (1995). Making work visible. *Communications of the ACM, 38*(9), 56–64.

Van de Ven, A. H., Delbecq, A. L., & Koenig, R. (1976). Determinants of coordination modes within organizations. *American Sociological Review, 41,* 322–338.

Veinott, E. S., Olson, J., Olson, G. M., & Fu, X. (2001). Video helps remote work: Speakers who need to negotiate common ground benefit from seeing each other. *Proc. CHI'01,* 302–309.

Viégas, F. (2007). The visual side of Wikipedia. *Proceedings HICSS.* 10 pages. IEEE.

Viégas, F., Wattenberg, M., & Dave, K. (2004). Studying cooperation and conflict between authors with history flow visualizations. *Proceedings CHI'04,* 575–582.

Weiseth, P. E., Munkvold, B. E., Tvedte, B., & Larsen, S. (2006). The wheel of collaboration tools: A typology for analysis within a holistic framework. *Proceedings CSCW'06,* 239–248.

Wilks, Y. (1996). Natural language processing. (Introduction to special issue.) *Commun. ACM, 39*(1), 60–62.

Williams, G. (1997). Task conflict and language differences: Opportunities for videoconferencing? *Proceedings ECSCW'97,* 97–108.

Wyche, S. P., Hayes, G. R., Harvel, L. D., & Grinter, R. E. (2006). Technology in spiritual formation: An exploratory study of computer mediated religious communications. *Proceedings CSCW'06,* 199–208.

Xia, S., Sun, D., Sun, C., Chen, D., & Shen, H. (2004). Leveraging single-user applications for multi-user collaboration: The CoWord approach. *Proceedings CSCW'04,* 162–171.

Yamauchi, Y., Yokozawa, M., Shinohara, T., & Ishida, T. (2000). Collaboration with lean media: How open-source software succeeds. *Proceedings CSCW'00,* 329–338.

Decision Making in Naturalistic Environments

Eduardo Salas, Michael A. Rosen *and* Deborah DiazGranados

Abstract

Understanding how experts are able to manage the complexity of modern work environments can inform the strategies and tools used to develop and support effective performance. To that end, this chapter provides a comprehensive review of naturalistic decision making (NDM) research for industrial and organizational (I/O) psychologists. The community of NDM researchers focuses on understanding how experts use their experience to make good decisions in complex real-world situations characterized by stress and uncertainty. NDM and the study of expertise in real-world settings is a rich scientific and practically relevant research area that has yet to be integrated with the I/O field. This chapter is intended to facilitate this cross-fertilization of perspectives. In this chapter, six specific goals are addressed: (a) definitions of the core features of NDM as a field of inquiry as well as the fundamental issues in the domain are reviewed; (b) an introduction to the fundamental theoretical perspectives in NDM is provided; (c) perspectives on the methodological approaches employed in the process of understanding complex cognition in the real world are summarized; (d) NDM research findings are synthesized and presented as a set of performance mechanisms of expert individual and team decision making; (e) applications of NDM research to improving decision-making performance in organizations are reviewed with specific attention to training the expert decision maker; and (f) future directions for NDM as a field of inquiry are outlined.

Key Words: Decision making, naturalistic decision making, decision training, team decision making, individual decision making, recognition primed decisions, expert decision making.

> With good judgment, little else matters. Without good judgment, nothing else matters.
> *Noel M. Tichy* and *Warren G. Bennis* (2007)

Introduction

What do airline pilots, CEOs, explosive ordnance disposal technicians, nuclear power plant control room operators, military leaders (and followers), and emergency department physicians, nurses, and technicians share in common? On the surface, these people perform very different tasks in very different settings. However, all of these professionals must manage complexity, stress, high stakes, uncertainty, conflicting goals, and other factors characterizing "unkind" environments for human performance and decision making. In many organizations, it is the norm rather than the exception that people make highly consequential decisions under difficult conditions, conditions that tax the limits of human abilities such as perception and comprehension. Environments such as these do not provide the nearly limitless time or the completeness and accuracy of information necessary to make a classically defined rational decision, to generate a set of all possible solutions and select the best option available. The reality is that decision making in the real world is bounded both by the abilities of the decision maker (e.g., limited processing capacity) and the context of the decision-making environment (e.g., time pressure and inherent uncertainty in information). Despite these conditions and limitations, professionals in complex domains manage to make reliably good decisions on a regular basis.

This begs the question of how; by what means are people able to make good decisions in such environments? What enables experts within a domain to adapt to these "unkind" decision-making situations and to produce rapid and reliably effective performance when the assumptions of traditional rationality cannot be met? These questions have received a great deal of attention in the popular media in recent years (Gladwell, 2005; Groopman, 2007), and a community of researchers has been investigating the nature of expert decision making in complex real-world settings for decades. Research from this community, the naturalistic decision making (NDM) tradition, and related traditions have produced a literature base that affords many insights into the mechanisms of expert decision making. This understanding has been translated into training and socio-technical system design interventions to improve decision-making effectiveness in situations in which decision outcomes involve life and death, or large-scale loss of material property and wealth. However, these insights and the interventions they have fueled have largely been confined to the NDM community of practice.

Therefore, this chapter is intended to serve as an introduction and comprehensive overview to the field of NDM for industrial and organizational psychologists. To that end, we address six specific goals. First, we define the core features of NDM as a field of inquiry and practice and give an overview of key issues. Second, we provide a review of the fundamental theoretical perspectives resulting from and driving NDM research and application. Third, we discuss methodological approaches employed in the process of understanding complex cognition in the real world. Fourth, emerging themes in NDM research findings are presented in relation to individual and team decision making. Fifth, applications of

NDM research to improving decision-making performance in organizations will be reviewed. Sixth, future directions for NDM as a field of inquiry will be provided.

Naturalistic Decision Making: An Overview

The quote that opens this chapter expresses the sentiment that decision-making performance is at the heart of effectiveness. NDM, a relatively new research perspective that has emerged within the past 25 years, shares this sentiment. In its relatively short history, NDM has produced scientific advancements as well as practical impact within organizations by exploring the nature of decision-making performance in complex real-world situations. This section provides a high-level overview of the NDM perspective by exploring its historical origins, relation to other traditions of decision-making research, and core features as a field of inquiry.

The Roots of NDM

The origins of NDM can be traced back to a general inability of rational choice models of decision making to provide insight into how professionals in domains such as the military, health care, power generation, and aviation make decisions. Early work began in the 1980s with naturalistic observations of firefighters and intensive care unit nurses (Calderwood, Crandall, & Klein, 1987; Crandall & Calderwood, 1989). This tradition was amplified by the TADMUS (Tactical Decision Making Under Stress) project, which was initiated by the U.S. Congress after a tragic case of mistaken identity that resulted in Iran Air Flight 655 (a civilian flight) being shot down by the USS *Vincennes* over the Persian Gulf in 1988 (Cannon-Bowers & Salas, 1998). A complex web of technical, communication, and social issues contributed to this catastrophic decision-making outcome. The incident was a tragedy in human terms, and a strong depiction of the lack of theories available to explain what had happened, let alone to provide guidance on how to prevent the occurrence of this type of disaster in the future.

Consequently, NDM developed around the need to fill a theoretical void that left applied scientists with no real tools for understanding or improving decision-making in complex and stressful settings. Researchers working in many domains found themselves confronted with similar issues. From nuclear power generation to the oil industry, to health care and law enforcement, no substantive theory existed that could explain competent decision-making performance. Applied researchers in these areas began to self-organize through a series of conferences, the first in Dayton, Ohio, in 1989 (Klein, Orasanu, Calderwood, & Zsambok, 1993). These conferences still continue to date without a formal organization or professional society (e.g., Hoffman, 2007; Montgomery, Lipshitz, & Brehmer, 2005; Salas & Klein, 2001). This informal community of practice comprises researchers working in different application domains, and includes multidisciplinary perspectives. For a detailed account of the development of NDM as a community of practice, see Hoffman and Militello (2009).

The Relation of NDM to Traditional Decision-Making Research

Cohen (1993) categorized the extant decision-making research into three major paradigms: the formal-empiricist, the rationalist, and the naturalistic. The classical decision-making (CDM) approach rooted in Bernoulli's (1738) work is described as the formal-empiricist paradigm because it involves building mathematical models and testing them against actual behavioral data. Researchers in this paradigm used formal normative models of choice between concurrently available options. Lipshitz and colleagues (2001b) further describe this paradigm in terms of the need for comprehensive information search on the part of the decision maker, and the development of formal, abstract, and context-free models on the part of the researcher. Researchers tested their formal models against behavioral data and attempted to refine their models to account for the behavior of people in contrived tasks that were not representative of any real-world performance. This paradigm reached its zenith with the work of Savage (1954), who proposed the concept of subjective-expected utility. That is, decision makers have a preference structure, which can be expressed by a utility function. Decision makers try to maximize this expected utility by analyzing each possible option and choosing the one with the highest benefit to them.

The judgment and decision making (JDM) research tradition belongs to the rationalist paradigm (e.g., Kahneman, Slovic, & Tversky, 1982). This perspective focuses on the concept of errors due to bias in unaided decision making (Ross, Shafer, & Klein, 2006). Similar to the formal-empirical tradition, the rationalist approach involves developing formal models of choice between concurrently available options. However, contrary to the formal empiricist paradigm, which modified the model when discrepancies were found, the rationalist paradigm views these errors as fundamental flaws in the decision maker rather than the model. This approach led to cataloging a vast array of decision-making biases, those systematic ways in which people deviated from supposed optimal decisions based upon statistical models. The validity of these biases has come to be criticized, most notably from Gigerenzer (1996), who illustrated how these biases were tied to assumptions about the optimal statistical model chosen (i.e., there is no one optimal model), and presentation of information to research participants.

The NDM and organizational decision making (ODM) traditions belong to the naturalistic paradigm (Lipshitz, Klein, & Carroll, 2006). This approach does not begin with prescriptive models, as do the two preceding approaches. Instead, it begins with description of the processes that real decision makers use. It forgoes artificial decision-making tasks where people are often presented with multiple options and instead focuses on how people develop options for themselves. Additionally, NDM emphasizes the expertise of the decision maker and not general or domain-independent decision-making tasks (Lipshitz et al., 2001b). Comprehensive search and choice between concurrently available options are replaced by the development of rules that match situations to actions; the input-output focus of research is replaced with a process orientation; and, the domain-independent formal model is replaced by context-bound informal modeling (Lipshitz et al., 2001a, 2001b).

The Core Features of NDM Research

NDM focuses on "the way people use their experience to make decisions in field settings" (Zsambok, 1997, p. 4). The context of these field settings is of particular importance to NDM researchers. In general, the types of settings of interest in NDM can be described as having extreme time pressure, high stakes, ill-defined goals, and dynamic conditions (Orasanu & Connolly, 1993). Additionally, Cannon-Bowers and colleagues (1996) added task characteristics such as information quantity, decision complexity, and the level of expertise of the decision maker to the description of the environment of interest to NDM researchers. When these features are present, the traditional models of decision making are least likely to be applicable. While every NDM research project does not address every one of these environmental features, usually one (if not several) plays a major role in the task.

Key Theories and Perspectives in NDM Research

As described above, the recognition that traditional models of rationality were inadequate to understand decision making in complex organizations and environments started to spread in the mid-twentieth century (March & Simon, 1958); however, to date, no single unified theory has emerged to explain decision making across all contexts. This has been attributed to the inherent complexity of the phenomenon and the near limitless variations in types of contexts in which decision making can occur, and how these contextual variations interact with the abilities and limitations of decision makers (Doyle, 1999). For this reason, NDM emphasizes building context-sensitive models of decision making in a specific domain (Lipshitz et al., 2001a, 2001b). However, NDM is not entirely reliant upon "bottom-up" models of decision making (i.e., an understanding of decision-making performance that is created anew from pre-suppositionless observations in each domain explored). There are several theoretical perspectives that drive the development of more robust and contextual models. This section is intended to serve as an introduction to some of the key theoretical perspectives guiding NDM research.

First, we begin our review of theory by considering the scientific understanding of expertise. This is a large, diverse, and mature literature base. The NDM community both draws from and contributes to the theoretical understanding of decision making expertise (Ross et al., 2006; Salas, Rosen, Burke, Goodwin, & Fiore, 2006). Second, we discuss the recognition-primed decision (RPD) model (Klein, 1993), an exemplar NDM model that has been found to describe expert decision making in several domains, including firefighting, commercial aviation, army tank operations, navy command and control environments, nursing, and others (Klein, 1997, 1998). This model is general in nature and serves as a guiding framework for building more context-sensitive models of decision making within a given domain. Third, we discuss the ecological decision-making tradition. This approach is distinct from yet highly related to NDM work in that they share similar assumptions about the nature of decision making but differ methodologically (Todd & Gigerenzer, 2001). Fourth, we discuss the distributed cognition approach. This perspective shifts the unit of analysis away from an individual decision maker and emphasizes the role of the broader sociotechnical system, including people and physical artifacts in the decision-making process (Hutchins & Klausen, 1996). Sixth, we discuss shared mental model theory, a perspective developed in the NDM community to explain expert team decision making (Cannon-Bowers, Salas, & Converse, 1993). As real-world decisions frequently are made by teams rather than by isolated individuals, this perspective adds a needed dimension to understanding how decisions are made in field settings, and seventh, we discuss team adaptation.

Expertise

As described above, NDM researchers acknowledge the central role that expertise plays in real-world and complex decision making. Consequently, the study of decision making in naturalistic environments is informed by the science of expertise, the systematic study of the highest levels of performance within a given domain. There are many perspectives on the nature of expertise, including the historical-cultural (Engestrom & Middleton, 1998), computer science and artificial intelligence (i.e., expert systems; Buchanan, Davis, & Feigenbaum, 2006), sociological (Evetts, Mieg, & Felt, 2006), and social psychology perspectives (Mieg, 2001), to name but a few. Many of these perspectives provide unique insights into expert decision making; however, the approach emerging from cognitive psychology has been the most widely influential in the NDM community. Consequently, we focus primarily on this approach in the following sections, beginning with definitional issues, the process of acquisition, and a consideration of the nature of expertise in different types of task domains.

DEFINING EXPERTISE

The scientific understanding of expertise has progressed dramatically in recent decades, moving from the long-held notion of expertise being rooted in innate talent (e.g., Gardner, 1983) to an understanding of expertise as acquired skill. Initially, expertise was thought of as mastery of a set of general performance and problem-solving strategies, such as hill climbing and means-ends analysis (e.g., Newell & Simon, 1972). However, empirical evidence did not support this perspective. Early studies revealed the importance of domain-specific knowledge in expert performance. For example, chess champions achieved the highest levels of performance because of their large and well-organized knowledge base of chess positions, and not through more efficient application of general strategies (de Groot, 1946/1978). In fact, the performance of the novice is best characterized by the use of general performance and problem-solving strategies, not the expert (Dreyfus & Dreyfus, 1986). This finding has been replicated in numerous domains of expertise (Ericsson & Charness, 1994; Ericsson & Lehmann, 1996) and has been expanded beyond domain-specific knowledge alone. Experts develop domain-specific reasoning strategies, heuristics, memory skills, automaticity, and even physiological adaptations to the nature of their domain of expertise (see Bedard & Chi, 1992; Salas & Rosen, 2010). The nature of expertise therefore can be very different across domains. This domain specificity is one of the primary challenges to developing general theories of expertise (Ericsson & Smith, 1991) and closely parallels the challenges to developing a general theory of bounded rationality (Doyle, 1999). However, what has emerged across these domains is a prototype view of expertise (Holyoak, 1991; Sternberg, 1997); that is, there are a set of mechanisms that characterize expert performance in different domains, but the importance and specific nature of any one mechanism will depend on the nature of the task constraints associated with the domain of expertise. Figure 41.1 presents a summary framework of mechanisms of performance

and development underlying expertise. These mechanisms will be discussed throughout this chapter.

ACQUIRING EXPERTISE

The long-held notion that expertise is a product of innate talent or skill persists to some degree; however, it has largely been replaced with models of development that emphasize large amounts of experience within a given domain and focused practice. If expertise is acquired and not innate, what then determines who becomes an expert and who does not? The theory of deliberate practice (Ericsson, Krampe, & Tesch-Romer, 1993) proposes that expertise is acquired through a specific type of experience within a domain. More specifically, expertise is a function of time spent engaged in motivated and focused effort in highly structured practice activities. These activities are repetitive and are designed to be at the upper boundary of the learner's present skill level. Additionally, receiving immediate feedback on performance in these activities is critical for developing expertise. While this theory pertains most directly to domains characterized by long periods of rehearsal leading up to competitions or performances (e.g., sports and the performing arts), the central theme of focused experience in a

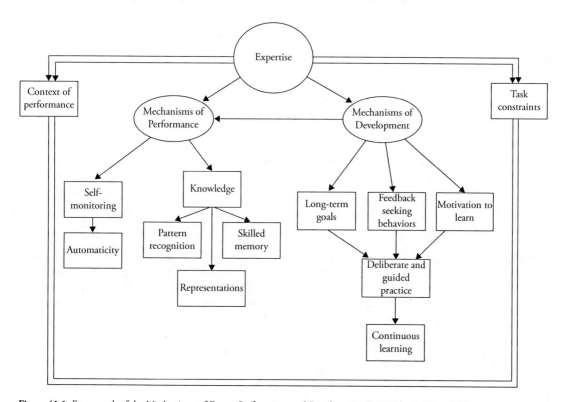

Figure 41.1 Framework of the Mechanisms of Expert Performance and Development From Salas & Rosen (2010).

task domain is broadly generalizable. Additionally, there is evidence suggesting that experts cannot maintain high levels of performance without engaging in continuous practice activities (Krampe & Ericsson, 1996). This suggests that expertise is a continuous process of building and maintaining performance capacities; therefore, a description of these developmental processes is integral to understanding expertise.

Although deliberate practice is likely the most widely accepted theory, there are alternative perspectives on the development of expertise. For example, Dreyfus and Dreyfus (1986) present a descriptive account of stages characterizing the development of expertise. Essentially, Dreyfus and Dreyfus (1986) propose that the process of developing from a novice to an expert begins with the use of discrete pieces of information in the environment and "context-free rules" (i.e., general rules that are adhered to rigidly). As someone gains experience in a domain, they begin to view information in the environment in a more holistic manner and use more nuanced rules adapted to specific situations (Benner, 2004). This model illustrates the general process of development, but it does not explain why everyone does not become an expert. To address this issue, Ericsson (1998, 2004) builds on a general stage model of skill acquisition proposed by Fitts and Posner (1967) and proposes that while most people within a domain reach a performance asymptote when they develop automaticity of skills, experts are able to continue learning and make performance improvements by seeking out opportunities to learn, while developing the ability to monitor and control their own performance processes. Automaticity has advantages in that it produces rapid and low effort performance (Moors & De Houwer, 2006), but it also makes the processes of performance inaccessible to the performer and rigid.

EXPERTISE IN WELL- AND ILL-STRUCTURED TASK DOMAINS

The expertise literature has been integral to the development of NDM perspectives; however, there are limitations to the generalizability of this literature to the types of environments studied by NDM researchers. For example, chess is probably the task most associated with expertise research. This task can be traced back to the game of *chaturanga*, which was used as a training tool for Indian military leaders; however, there are obvious differences between a chess master who is engaging in an abstraction of military conflict, and a military commander who is actually engaged in battle. Differences in complexity, uncertainty, dynamism, time pressure, stakes for errors, and interdependencies and social relations with others pose large obstacles for generalizing findings. In order to better understand expertise in different contexts, various organizations of task features have been proposed. As expertise is an adaptation to the constraints of the task environment, understanding the structure of the environment is a critical step for predicting the types of mechanisms that will be effective in a given task domain. Most broadly, researchers have identified task features in which expertise is most likely to develop in a reliable manner (Hammond, 1996; Hogarth, 2001; Shanteau, 1992). These features include relatively static stimuli, repetition, decomposable and predictable problems, and availability of feedback. Essentially, as commonly conceived, expertise is most readily developed in well-structured and stable domains. For example, Devine and Kozlowski (1995) found that experts (i.e., those with high levels of knowledge in a domain) were no better than novices when task features shifted from well to ill-structured. This has strong implications for understanding expert decision making in modern organizations, as discussed below.

There is an unfortunate implication of the idea that expertise is a function of adapting to a specific set of task constraints, an implication well supported by empirical studies: expertise can be fragile (Feltovich, Spiro, & Coulson, 1997; Sternberg & Frensch, 1991). It does not transfer to other domains, even highly related domains. The importance of this idea cannot be overstated for modern organizations, where the fundamental knowledge and task structure within a domain can change rapidly. While the rules and nature of the task for chess masters do not change, the same is not true for professionals in the software industry or in the modern military, for example. Most of the features defining "good domains" for the development of expertise are not present in many organizational settings; however, research into expertise in dynamic and ill-structured domains has shown that a different type of expertise can be developed (Canas, Antoli, Fajardo, & Salmeron, 2005; Cellier, Eyrolle, & Marine, 1997; Schunn, McGregor, & Saner, 2005). In efforts to understand how expertise may be maintained in domains with rapid rates of change, researchers have developed proposed notions of routine and adaptive expertise (Hatano & Inagaki, 1986). Routine expertise involves high levels of performance on a given set of tasks, but no real ability to adjust performance processes to variations in those tasks. Alternatively, adaptive expertise involves an ability to apply expertise to new variations within a domain. This adaptation is afforded by a deeper conceptual understanding of a domain. Additionally, proficiency with domain-general psychological support skills (e.g., mental imagery and rehearsal, goal-setting skills, emotion regulation, and planning and organizational skills) and abilities (e.g., capacity to sustain high levels of efficacy, motivation, and attention) enable rapid transfer of expertise across domains (Eccles & Feltovich, 2008). While there has been some initial work on applying this concept to organizations (e.g., Smith, Ford, & Kozlowski, 1997), further research is needed to more fully develop the concept of adaptive expertise and to translate that into effective training interventions.

The Recognition-Primed Decision-Making Model

The expertise literature discussed above has had a strong influence on the development of NDM theory. One specific NDM model that is strongly rooted in the expertise tradition is the recognition-primed decision (RPD) making model (Klein, 1993, 1998). The RPD model describes the decision-making process of experts, specifically the process by which these experts use their experience to understand and evaluate a situation, even a novel one, as prototypical and subsequently use this experience-driven understanding to determine the best way to respond. Moreover, in contrast to prescriptive models of decision making, which assume no real limits on time or information and suggest that decision makers generate and evaluate a large set of possible decision options, the RPD model describes a sequential process in which only one option at a time is generated and evaluated.

The RPD model describes decision making in terms of two core processes: pattern recognition and mental simulation. Decision makers analyze their situation and recall a course of action that was successful in a similar situation in the past. Subsequently, decision makers evaluate applicability of the recalled course of action in the present situation through mental simulation, conducting a walkthrough of the course of action. This type of decision making is succinctly characterized by Dreyfus and Dreyfus (1986) when they state that "experts don't make decisions, they do what normally works" (pp. 30–31). In the classical sense of a decision being a choice between multiple options, expert decision makers do not make decisions. They rely on their previous experiences and modify solutions that have been effective in the past to the uniqueness of their present situation. Experientially, this type of decision making can be affectively charged and described in terms of "gut feelings"; decision makers may know why one option is best without immediately knowing why that option is best. This has been termed *expertise-based intuition* (Salas, Rosen, & DiazGranados, 2010). We briefly elaborate on pattern recognition and mental simulation below—the primary mechanisms of how experts use intuitive abilities based in accumulated experience.

PATTERN RECOGNITION

As described above, situation assessment is a fundamental mechanism of expert performance, and it is the first stage of the RPD model. Here, decision makers scan the environment for cues and build an awareness of the present situation (Endsley, 1997). From this awareness, the decision maker matches important features of the environment to similar situations that he or she has encountered in the past. If the decision maker cannot readily match the situation to past experience, he or she continues gathering information and working to understand the present situation. Once an analogous situation has been found, the decision maker retrieves other information, along with the successful course of action. This can include goals for the situation, as well as important information that should be sought. It is important to realize that this assessment happens extremely quickly and automatically. This diagnosis of the situation and recall of a course of action is contrary to the traditional assumptions of decision making, which emphasize the multiattribute analysis of a decision.

MENTAL SIMULATION

Once the decision maker has retrieved a course of action that has been successful in similar past situations, he or she engages in mental simulation activities to evaluate the appropriateness of the retrieved course of action. The RPD model does recognize that the process of decision making will differ based on the situation. That is, a more recognizable situation may not require the mental simulation that is required of a more complex unrecognizable situation. The mental simulation helps to create scenarios from implementation to execution. It allows the decision maker to generate previews of events so that the decision maker can examine the course of action for any pitfalls. In the end, this evaluation allows us to determine if the course of action should be implemented or if another course of action should be considered. Mental simulations can result in the adoption of a recalled course of action without changes, a modification of the course of action so that it is more suitable to the given context, or a rejection of the course of action as inappropriate. If the course of action is rejected, the decision maker returns to information-gathering and pattern-matching activities.

Ecological Decision Making

The ecological decision-making tradition has a long history, with roots dating back to the psychology of Egon Brunswick (for a review see Hammond & Stewart, 2001) and Herbert Simon's notion of bounded rationality (1945). From this tradition, the idea of vicarious functioning (i.e., adaptive cognition stemming from the ability to interpret multiple uncertain cues as proximal indicators of distal features of the environment; Gigerenzer & Kurz, 2001; Tolman & Brunswik, 1935) has inspired a wealth of research that focuses on ways that decision makers make use of the information structure of the environment. This includes recognition processes that eliminate the need for broad search (i.e., the RPD model discussed above), heuristics for guiding the search for information, and simple decision rules. In a recent and influential incarnation of this tradition, the fast and frugal heuristics approach, work has focused on three core objects of inquiry (Gigerenzer & Selten, 2001; Gigerenzer, Todd, & The ABC Research Group, 1999). First, ecological decision making is concerned with the heuristics that people use to make decisions. By employing heuristics, people are able to make good decisions without exploring all possible options available. Second, ecological decision making seeks to understand the information structure in the environment. That is, researchers investigate the types of and relationships between information available for decision making. Third, ecological decision making seeks to understand the fit between the heuristics used by decision makers and the environment. The degree to which the heuristic "fits" the environment (i.e., affords good decisions) is described as the ecological rationality of the heuristic. Expert decision makers are those individuals who possesses an "adaptive toolbox" (Gigerenzer et al., 1999), a set of heuristics that are well matched to the information structure of the environment.

The core ideas of ecological decision making resonate with the expert performance approach as well as the RPD model. Additionally, ecological decision making provides a unique set of tools for understanding expert decision making. Specifically, researchers in the ecological decision-making tradition focus on building formal models of real-world expert decision makers through various statistical and computational models (Cooksey, 1996; Gigerenzer et al., 1999; Kirlik, 2006). However, these models are built upon data obtained from real-world decision making and are not based upon theoretical models of optimality.

Distributed Cognition

The distributed cognition approach emphasizes the physical, social, technological, and cultural embeddedness of task performance and acquisition of knowledge and skill (Salomon, 1993). Fundamentally, the distributed cognition perspective is rooted in the idea that the boundaries of a cognitive system can extend beyond the internal mental operations of an individual, as is classically viewed in the cognitive sciences (Hutchins, 1995). Essentially, a distributed cognitive system comprises the knowledge representations and processes performed on these representations that are internal to the individual as well as those representations and processes external to an individual (i.e., in artifacts or other individuals). These external representations dramatically impact the nature of performance by serving as memory aids, scaffolding processes, and performing other functions (Zhang, 1997; Zhang & Norman, 1994). The distributed cognition approach has been applied to such contexts as large ship navigation in the U.S. Navy (Hutchins, 1995), coordination in medical teams, and aviation crew performance (Hutchins, 1996; Hutchins & Klausen, 1996). It also serves as the basis for approaches to designing socio-technical systems to support expert performance (Hollan, Hutchins, & Kirsh, 1999; Perry, 2003).

Distributed cognition resonates with the notion that experts are coupled to their domains of expertise as well as their contexts of performance. The tools and structure (technical and social) used to perform a task are a critical part of defining a domain of expertise. Changes in the tools available to an expert can change the nature of performance in a domain, and the types of adaptations necessary for expert performance. Distributed cognition attends to these issues by broadening the view of the cognitive system performing a task.

SMM Theory and Team Cognition

Besides the distributed cognition approach that views groups as cognitive systems, the preceding discussion has focused exclusively on individual decision making. However, a large amount of decisions in naturalistic environments are made in the context of teams. Shared mental model (SMM) theory was developed to explain the nature of expert decision making in team settings (Cannon-Bowers et al., 1993). Shared mental models are organized knowledge structures that individuals in a team hold. These shared knowledge representations allow them to coordinate with one another and interact with their environment in a compatible or complimentary manner as they work toward a shared goal (Klimoski & Mohammed, 1994). On an individual level, mental models allow people to draw inferences, make predictions, and decide which actions to take (Johnson-Laird, 1983). By sharing or distributing these representations, team members are better able to anticipate the needs of their fellow team members because information from the environment is interpreted in a similar way. Stout, Cannon-Bowers, and Salas (1996) expanded the notion of SMMs by suggesting that the task which a team performs will dictate how the team utilizes SMMs. For example, a team which operates under an environment that is not time pressured has the time to strategize and plan their course of action. However, a team under great time constraints or high workload will rely more on their shared mental models to coordinate and execute a course of action because of their lack of opportunity to explicitly communicate and strategize (Mohammed & Dumville, 2001).

SMM theory has matured significantly since its inception. As initially proposed, it focuses on static knowledge structures of team members. Recent work has focused on viewing teams as information-processing units; that is, the team acts on knowledge representations with team-level cognitive processes manifested through communication (Cooke, Salas, Kiekel, & Bell, 2004; Hinsz, Tindale, & Vollrath, 1997; Salas & Fiore, 2004). Additionally, these perspectives continue to evolve in efforts to explain an increasingly broad range of phenomenon. Traditionally, SMM theory and team cognition have been used to explain how teams achieve behavioral coordination. Recent efforts have focused on explaining more complex cognitive phenomena in team settings, such as problem solving and planning (Letsky, Warner, Fiore, & Smith, 2008). This work, conducted under the umbrella

term of *macrocognition,* will be discussed in more detail at the end of this chapter.

Leadership

Undoubtedly, leaders are not all the same. They can differ by traits, leadership style, and even their focus as leaders. What most leaders do have in common is the task in which they operate. That is, leaders must often manage ill-structured problems, dynamic environments, ill-defined or competing goals, and situations that contain high stakes. The NDM approach offers managers a viable method of understanding how to successfully manage individuals, teams, and organizations, and how to make effective decisions. How do leaders make sense of the available information and make effective decisions?

Kozlowski, Gully, Nason, and Smith (1999) presented the team compilation model. They expand on the compilation process by stating that this process is an experience by teams at different levels (e.g., individual, dyad, or team) and times of their developmental continuum. More specifically, teams experience phases that are "characterized by a particular level of focus, a primary learning process and content domain, and a set of knowledge and performance outcomes that trigger compilation to the next level and phase" (p. 256). Kozlowski and colleagues have noted the leader's role in this compilation process is as an enhancer of this process (Kozlowski, 1998; see also Kozlowski, Gully, McHugh, Salas, & Cannon-Bowers, 1996; Kozlowski, Gully, Salas, & Cannon-Bowers, 1996). Specifically, the leader's primary role is to develop understanding—by sharing, aligning and creating compatibility—around the affect, knowledge, and skills that are directly related to team performance.

Hollenbeck, Ilgen, Sego, Hedlund, Major, and Phillips's (1995) multilevel theory of hierarchical team decision making and Brehmer and Hagafors (1986) model of staff decision making focus on the hierarchical nature of leader decision making. Judgments are made by subordinates based on the cues that they have available to them and the ultimate decision being made by a leader. The manner in which the leader develops his or her decision can be based on the same cues that the subordinates had access to, the judgments of the subordinates, or some combination of both.

Image theory (Beach & Mitchell, 1987), a highly cited theory in the decision making literature, states that decision makers have three images that guide or constrain their decisions (i.e., their beliefs and values, more specific goals to which the decision maker is striving, or specific operational plans for reaching the goals). Image theory posits that when a possible solution in decision making is incompatible with at least one of these images, then the decision maker will eliminate that potential solution. Therefore, the solution cannot be adopted unless it has been examined for compatibility with the decision maker's images. Tubbs and Eckeberg (1991) offer a clear illustration of image theory in their argument that the nature and role of intentions is critical to the process of decision making. They argue that this examination conducted by decision makers is critical in determining what actions need to be taken by the decision maker.

Research on organizational culture and image theory found that the acceptance of a leader's decision is based on the compatibility of a decision with the organization's culture (Beach 1993; Mitchell, Rediker, & Beach, 1986). That is, if a leader chooses a decision that is incompatible with the organization's culture, then the members of the organization will not endorse that decision. Rediker, Mitchell, Beach, and Beard (1993) examined leader decision making via a simulation in which a CEO had to determine which computer firm to acquire in order to diversify the company's services. Results indicated that the acceptability ratings that the CEO made were highly correlated to the violations of each computer firm in terms of the stated standards of the company. Thus, the CEO made the decision based on an evaluation of acceptability and the number of violations the firm had acquired. Therefore, this study supports the notion that for those making decisions, a rejection threshold does exist (see also, Beach, Smith, Lundell, & Mitchell, 1988; Beach & Strom, 1989; Potter & Beach, 1994).

Serfaty, MacMillan, Entin, and Entin (1997) presented a theoretical framework that was based on the premise of mental models and how these mental models are utilized to create appropriate action plans for a situation. Their framework was based on a series of interviews with military commanders (Serfaty, MacMillan, & Deckert, 1991; Serfaty & Michel, 1990) and an analysis of their experiences. The framework highlights how mental models are developed and used by an expert. Specifically, experts use a three-stage hourglass model that depicts the recognition-exploration-matching process.

During the stage of recognition, an expert organizes his or her knowledge, based on experience, in order to store a large amount of information, creating chunks of information that can be grouped together to develop patterns. The retrieval of information is based on a mental model that represents the current situation and the appropriate manner in which to react to the situation. Whether or not the initial manner to react to the situation is appropriate is yet to be determined. The stage of exploration is dedicated to exploring the details of the current situation and the plan being considered. The expert's mental model helps her to determine what kind of critical information is missing and what type of information needs to be acquired. The final stage consists of matching. That is, the plan that has been developed can be implemented and assessed for feasibility and effectiveness.

In the political science literature, poliheuristic theory is used to explain how foreign leaders make their decisions. Poliheuristic choice theory hypothesizes a two-stage process, which integrates elements from the cognitive psychology and rational choice approach to explaining decision making (Mintz, 2004). The first stage involves a non-compensatory and non-holistic search. In other words, during the first stage, the leader utilizes decision heuristics to understand the problem and to evaluate the problem on an attribute by attribute basis. Those alternatives that are unacceptable to the leader on a critical dimension are rejected. The second stage involves analytic processing of the remaining alternatives. The alternative that maximizes benefits and minimizes risks is chosen (Mintz, 1993, 2003). This stage corresponds most to the rational choice theory, which emphasizes utility maximization.

Research does support that a two-stage decision-making process exists in which non-compensatory, dimension-based processing is followed by more rational, alternative-based calculations (see Christensen & Redd, 2004; Dacey & Carlson, 2004). Keller and Yang (2008) expanded this two-stage process by arguing that poliheuristic theory fails to explain the potential variation in non-compensatory thresholds during the analysis and evaluation of the problem, as well as individual-level and contextual variables that might lead to variation in the screening dimensions and thresholds. Specifically, Keller and Yang (2008) found that situational context and leadership style affect both: (a) the "non-compensatory threshold" at which decision makers reject options as unacceptable, and (b) how much decision makers rely on others' views in making policy choices.

Team Adaptation

In a naturalistic decision-making setting, coordinated action is required. This coordinated action can be effectively executed by the utilization of shared mental models. However, under such extreme environments as those found in the context of NDM, team adaptation may be what determines the safe return of a firefighting team from fighting a fire or a military team from the front line of battle.

Many researchers have attempted to define adaptation. Cannon-Bowers, Tannenbaum, Salas, and Volpe (1995) defined *team adaptation* as the process by which a team is able to use information gathered from the task environment to adjust strategies through the use of compensatory behaviors and reallocation of intrateam resources. Kozlowski and colleagues couch their definitions of *adaptation* around novel and non-routine tasks—specifically, a team's capability to shift metamorphically in the short term to deal with performance demands of a non-routine task (Kozlowski, Gully, Nason, & Smith, 1999); adaptability is the generalization of trained knowledge and skills to new, more difficult, and more complex tasks (Kozlowski, Toney, Mullins, Weissbein, Brown, & Bell, 2001).

Fleming, Wood, Dudley, Bader, and Zaccaro (2003) presented their definition of *team adaptation* as the functional change in response to altered environmental contingencies and a higher order process that emerges from an integrated set of individual attributes. In the NDM literature, Klein and Pierce (2001) define *team adaptation* as the ability to make the necessary modifications in order to meet new challenges. Similarly, LePine (2003) defines adaptability as reactive and non-scripted adjustments to a team's system of member roles that contribute to team effectiveness.

Team adaptation was conceptually analyzed and a model was put forth by Burke, Stagl, Salas, Pierce, and Kendall (2006). They define *team adaptation* as the change in team performance, in response to a cue, which leads to an effective outcome. Team adaptation is centered around the development of a new action or the modification of existing actions. These actions may be behavioral or cognitive in nature.

Under uncertain and novel events, the aspects of team adaptation that have been discussed as being critical are: the team's ability to adjust to these novel situations, the effectiveness and smoothness of their reorientation, and the extent to which they take reasonable action (Pulakos, Arad, Donovan, & Plamondon, 2000). The team's ability to adjust includes both behavioral adjustment and cognitive adjustment. Both cognitive and behavioral fixation on one particular action will prohibit the team from

adapting to a novel event and from taking reasonable action to solve the dilemma.

As illustrated in Figure 41.2, team adaptation emerges from a series of cognitive and behavioral actions. As Burke and colleagues (2006) depict in their cross-level mixed determinants model of team adaptation, team members utilize their individual and shared resources to detect, frame, and act on a cue. The cue is the team's signal to change. The cue can be either a change event during a typical situation (e.g., a firefighting team detects that the floor of a building is too soft and may require immediate evacuation), or the cue may be the detection that the situation is novel.

Looking Ahead to a Cross-Fertilization of Approaches

Each of the above-mentioned approaches has made unique contributions to NDM research and practice. These approaches are complimentary in nature, despite differences in origins and application in some instances. The bulk of NDM research represents a synthesis between several theoretical perspectives. The RPD model is tightly aligned with cognitive psychology views of expertise, focusing on the internal mechanisms of the decision maker that produce expert performance. However, NDM research also emphasizes the distributed nature of cognition, especially with external representations in the form of information displays and team cognition. In the future, further integration between perspectives may prove fruitful. For example, four general descriptive themes are apparent from the preceding discussion, illustrating fundamental compatibilities between the theories reviewed in this chapter.

SPECIALIZATION AND ADAPTATION

There is no such thing as general decision-making expertise. Expert decision making involves an attunement of the person to the task and environment. This is explicit in the ideas of expertise research wherein decision makers develop specialized knowledge and skill, the RPD model wherein past experience drives future decisions, and the ecological decision-making perspective where decision makers develop ways of taking advantage of the information structure in the environment.

EMBEDDEDNESS

Decision making does not happen in a vacuum. The social, environmental, cultural, and technological contexts of decision making are crucial parts of

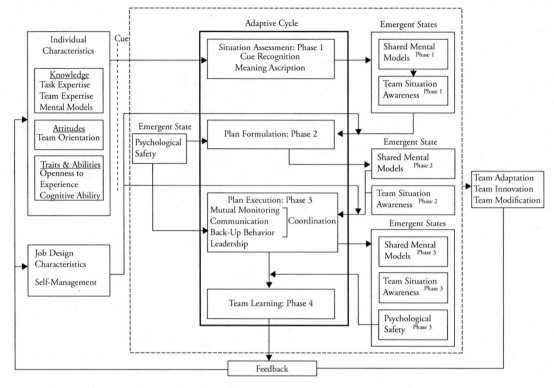

Figure 41.2 Model of Adaptive Team Performance From Burke et al. (2006)

understanding how decisions are made. The tools that people use and the organization and distribution of work among people and machines are part of the decision-making process. This is explicit in the distributed cognition and SMM theory traditions, where decision making is viewed as an activity occurring at a unit of analysis larger than the individual.

FRUGALITY

Experts make the most out of the least. In time-pressured and uncertain settings, experts make good decisions by pursuing the first acceptable course of action in lieu of attempting to find the best solution. This is fundamental to the RPD model as well as the ecological decision-making tradition. Decision-making expertise involves coping with the limitations of the human information processing system as well as the constraints in the environment.

INTERDEPENDENCE

Decision makers frequently do not work alone. They pool information from each other to form better assessments of the situation and rely on one another's expertise to generate, evaluate, and implement better courses of action. Team cognition, leadership, and team adaptation all emphasize this component of decision making in real-world settings.

In addition to the cross-fertilization of approaches within NDM, there are opportunities for synergy between NDM and traditional perspectives. The NDM tradition grew from dissatisfaction with the ability of the dominant decision-making perspectives to address complex real-world situations. However, the dominant decision-making perspectives have evolved over the years into forms that are much more compatible with the NDM perspective. For example, dual process theories of decision making and reasoning seek to integrate models of deliberative and intuitive cognition (e.g., Hodgkinson, Langan-Fox, & Sadler-Smith, 2008; Lieberman, 2000; Sloman, 2002). This approach is much more aligned with the NDM perspective than were its predecessors, providing an opportunity for synergy between NDM and more basic science approaches to decision making.

Methodological Approaches to NDM Research and Practice

NDM researchers have adopted a wide range of methodologies that span the breadth of a continuum from naturalism to empiricism (Hoffman & Militello, 2009). While qualitative and descriptive field research is central to NDM, laboratory research methods have been adopted as well (Lipshitz et al., 2006). However, uncovering the specific knowledge and skills that enable expert decision making is at the heart of every NDM research project. To this end, a broad range of knowledge elicitation and representation approaches have been adapted from cognitive psychology, ethnography, and other perspectives. These methods are loosely grouped under the heading of cognitive task analysis (CTA). This section provides an overview of a prototypical CTA project, as well as a discussion of relevant methodological challenges in the NDM community. For a more comprehensive treatment of methods used in NDM research, we refer the reader to Crandall, Klein, and Hoffman (2006), and Hoffman and Militello (2009).

A General CTA Process

In this section, the general process of conducting a CTA is described in terms of five core phases: exploring and defining what to analyze, knowledge elicitation strategy selection, the knowledge elicitation, data analysis, and knowledge representation (Chipman, Schraagen, & Shalin, 2000; Crandall et al., 2006; Rosen, Salas, Lazzara, & Lyons, in press). Variations in the overall purpose of the project, practical constraints, and the methods employed undoubtedly influence the CTA process; however, the overview provided here is a general framework that maps onto most applications. Table 41.1 provides a summary of the phases of the CTA processes, as well as examples of tasks and outcomes for each phase. Each phase is discussed below in more detail.

Table 41.1 High Level General Framework of a CTA Effort

CTA Phase	Representative Activities	Output of Phase

Preliminary phase (exploring and defining what to analyze)	• Define the scope and purpose of the CTA
	  • Clearly articulate the question the CTA must answer for sponsoring the organization(s)
	• Determine which tasks warrant a CTA
	  • Use standard methods (e.g., informal interviews, questionnaires) to determine the importance and complexity of tasks
	• Identify experts (proficiency scaling)
	• Gain commitments of time and effort from identified experts
	• "Bootstrapping" (bringing the analyst up to speed on the task domain)
	  • Analysis of existing task related documentation (if available), including traditional task analyses, training materials, and standard operating procedures
	  • Informal interviews with experts
		• A set of deliverables, ultimate products of the CTA
		• A statement of purpose for the CTA
		• A basic understanding of the tasks and the target domain
		• Access to subject matter experts
		• Focus for the CTA effort
		  • A set of tasks where CTA can make the biggest impact

Identifying knowledge representations	• Determine the abstract nature of knowledge involved in the task
	• Choose the CTA methods and techniques that are most likely to be effective
	  • Match methods to (1) characteristics of the work domain, (2) purpose of the CTA, (3) cognitive style of the expert, (4) pragmatics (e.g., access, time constraints)
		• The CTA strategy
		  • Set of knowledge elicitation, analysis, and representation techniques to be used

(Continued)

Table 41.1 (Continued)

CTA Phase	Representative Activities	Output of Phase

Knowledge elicitation	• Data collection (asking questions and making observations)
	  • Interviews
	  • Field observations
	  • Process tracing techniques
	  • Simulations
	  • Automated data capture
	  • Questionnaires
		• "Raw" data
		  • Transcriptions of interviews
		  • Video/audio recordings and notes from observations
		  • Self-report data

Data analysis	• Decomposing data
	  • Reducing quantity, but maintaining content, of large amounts of protocol data
	  • Extracting process (or cognitive trace) information from data
	  • Making inferences about knowledge and processes not directly represented in data
	• Creating a big picture
	  • Look for themes and trends between large units of analysis (multiple experts, tasks, etc.)
		• An explanation of how complex cognitive work is accomplished
		  • Models of the domain of work
		  • Models of the experts' knowledge in the domain
		  • Models of expert processes and reasoning
		  • Chronologies
		  • Process diagrams

Putting knowledge representations to use	• Communicate findings effectively to sponsors, system and training designers.
	• Create impact; provide representations that can be used to meet the overall goals of the CTA
		• Input to:
		  • Training development
		  • Socio-technical system design
		  • Interface and display design
		• Knowledge preservation

Adapted from Rosen, Salas, Lazzara, & Lyons (in press)

EXPLORING AND DEFINING WHAT TO ANALYZE

The first step of a CTA involves exploring the task domain and defining what to analyze. More specifically, this entails defining a clear vision to guide the project, defining boundaries around key aspects of tasks, identifying experts and building their support, and "boot strapping" (i.e., becoming familiar with the basic information of the domain). Crandall and colleagues (2006) propose using a clear and concise statement of the questions to be answered in the project (i.e., a "kernel statement") to guide decisions throughout the CTA (Annett, 2000). This includes identifying aspects of performance where CTA can have the most impact (Gordon & Gill, 1997; Militello & Hutton, 1998; Shepherd & Stammers, 2005), as well as identifying relevant subject matter experts. Being able to identify experts is a fundamental prerequisite for conducting a CTA. This, however, is a challenging task in many situations of interest. Objective performance measures are the true basis for identifying an expert, but these are frequently unavailable or of low quality in the

types of complex and ill-structured environments (Austin & Crespin, 2006). Researchers have developed proxy measures (Weiss & Shanteau, 2003), and have employed methods using social network analysis and other techniques to identify the individuals recognized as experts within an organization (Stein, 1997). In order to facilitate communication and understanding throughout the CTA, the analyst or knowledge elicitor must develop a fundamental understanding of the knowledge and specialized vocabulary within a domain (Flach, 2000; Hoffman et al., 1995). This can be achieved through document review (e.g., training materials, documented procedures), interviews, and questionnaires.

KNOWLEDGE ELICITATION STRATEGY SELECTION

After the initial phase of the CTA has been completed and a clear vision for the project has been articulated, decisions about knowledge elicitation strategies can be made. In addition to the purpose and nature of the task (Klein & Militello,

2001), practical constraints (e.g., time and access to experts) will influence the choice of methods. Hoffman and Lintern (2006) discuss the concept of differential utility in knowledge elicitation techniques. That is, different methods will be more or less useful, given differences in the work domain, purpose of the project, and individual differences in the experts. However, much more work is needed to develop a systematic mapping of different strategies to different contexts. General categories of methods are discussed in the following section.

KNOWLEDGE ELICITATION

During this phase of the CTA, raw data from the experts are collected. The complete breadth of elicitation techniques is outside the scope of this chapter. In general, however, methods can be grouped into four categories: process tracing, interview and observation, indirect conceptual methods, and simulations of representative tasks. Process-tracing techniques, such as protocol analysis (Ericsson & Simon, 1993) or eye tracking, involve creating or capturing a detailed record of the external aspects of performance such that good inferences are afforded about the internal cognitive processes involved (Ford, Schmitt, Schechtman, Hults, & Doherty, 1989). These methods produce very rich data sets, but data reduction and analysis can be time consuming. Interview and observation approaches provide insight into the full range of social and organizational factors in which experts make decisions. The critical decision method (CDM; Klein, Calderwood, & MacGregor, 1989) and methods from cognitive anthropology (Hutchins, 1995) are examples of techniques used to elicit knowledge through interview and field observation. These methods are frequently limited by practical issues of access to field settings for safety or security reasons. Indirect and conceptual methods of knowledge elicitation (e.g., concept mapping, paired comparison ratings) are designed to assess the structure and organization of knowledge underlying expert performance (Hoffman & Lintern, 2006). Finally, simulations of representative tasks are a way of balancing experimental controls, which is usually impossible in field settings with the richness of real-world tasks. They are particularly useful for observing low-frequency and high-criticality events, which generally cannot be observed in the field (Ward, Williams, & Hancock, 2006). These types of events are particularly useful for understanding expert performance. However, simulations can be costly to develop, and no matter how much effort is dedicated to replicating critical aspects of the real world, there will be some differences between the real world and the simulation that may influence decision-making performance. Any one CTA project will likely employ multiple methods in order to balance the strengths and weaknesses of each approach. For a detailed review of techniques, see Hoffman & Militello (2009).

DATA ANALYSIS

The relationship between data collection and analysis differs by the method employed. For example, concept mapping is an iterative process in which collection and analysis are interleaved, while protocol analysis data can be collected and analyzed many different ways at a later date. Several researchers in CTA and traditional task analysis caution against providing just a description. In order to move beyond description, data analysis must answer specific research questions and must be guided by the overall purpose of the CTA effort (Annett, 2000). In general, though, the types of CTA outcomes include a listing of cognitive functions involved in task performance, a set of the cues and corresponding performance processes, and a thorough explanation of how the cognitive work of a task is accomplished (Klein & Militello, 2001).

Methodological Challenges

NDM is concerned both with advancing the scientific knowledge of decision making and related phenomenon as well as improving performance and effectiveness in organizations. This requires balancing practical constraints and issues of methodological rigor. Many of the methods employed by NDM researchers tend to be qualitative and exploratory in nature. As is the case with methods of this nature, there are always questions about the validity of results, especially in terms of replicability and validity. NDM deals with the expertise of decision makers. Expertise is highly task- and domain-dependent. This creates challenges in generalizing findings from one domain—or even from one setting within a domain—to another. NDM researchers are keenly aware of these methodological issues, and are continually searching for techniques for addressing these issues. For example, the comparative CTA approach (Kirschenbaum, Trafton, & Pratt, 2007) involves sampling experts from various organizations within a domain in order to produce more generalizable knowledge about decision-making performance. Additionally, Hoffman and Militello (2009) discuss criteria by which the quality of a CTA can be evaluated (i.e., how can you tell a good CTA from a bad CTA?). These criteria include the degree to which the methods employed represent ecologically valid and relevant aspects of the domain of work, the degree to which methods are scientifically rooted, the degree to which results of the project can be practically applied, and the degree to which results inform the scientific understanding of a phenomenon. Beyond the traditional methodological concern, NDM is faced with additional unique challenges, such as the "moving target" phenomenon (i.e., work practices in dynamic domains are frequently not stable), as well as the complexity of studying cognitive systems (people and their tools) in the field.

What Does Expert Decision Making Look Like?: Themes in NDM Findings

As discussed throughout this chapter, expertise effectiveness and decision-making effectiveness in real-world settings are inextricably linked. Additionally, the mechanisms of expertise differ across task domains. In the following sections, we provide a prototype view of expert decision making in individuals and teams. That is, we discuss trends that have emerged from the expertise and NDM literatures that describe the types of adaptations in performance processes underlying expert decision-making performance in different domains.

Individuals

The following section provides a set of mechanisms that support expert decision making in complex environments (adapted from Salas & Rosen, 2010). These mechanisms are based on a review of the NDM literature, as well as related fields investigating proficient decision making by professionals. Table 41.2 provides an overview of key mechanisms of expert decision making on the individual level.

DOMAIN KNOWLEDGE

While it may seem obvious that experts know more than non-experts about a given domain, there are more subtle differences between experts and novices than the amount of knowledge about a domain. Specifically, experts differ from novices in terms of the organization of their knowledge. This manifests in two primary ways: the level of abstraction and the interrelatedness of knowledge. First, experts differ from non-experts in how they conceptualize aspects of their knowledge, with experts tending to organize their knowledge around deeper conceptual relationships than non-experts (Bordage & Zacks, 1984;

Zeitz, 1997). Conversely, novices tend to categorize information based on superficial features. Second, experts maintain more and stronger links between their concepts (Feltovich, Johnson, Moller, & Swanson, 1984). The strength of the link may be due to the mere exposure that they have had (Stanovich & Cunningham, 1992, 1993) or the interest in the domain (Alexander, Jetton, & Kulikowich, 1995; Alexander, Kulikowich, & Schulze, 1994). In sum, in comparison to non-experts, experts possess more knowledge, organize it at a deeper conceptual level, and maintain more interrelations between the components of their knowledge.

PATTERN RECOGNITION

The importance of pattern recognition was discussed above in the section on the RPD model. This is one of the fundamental mechanisms of expert decision making. Because experts possess superior domain knowledge, they are able to perceive patterns of cues in the environment that go undetected by non-experts (Gobet, 1997). The first general theory of human expertise—chunking theory—was rooted in the notion of expert pattern recognition (Chase & Simon, 1973). Chunking theory proposes that inherent in expertise is the ability to rapidly recognize important features of the problem. These chunks, which are stored in an expert's memory, make it quicker and easier to retrieve the information.

SITUATION AND PROBLEM REPRESENTATIONS

In addition to differences in stable or long-term knowledge structures described above, experts and non-experts differ in terms of their dynamic understanding of situations. Essentially, experts create more functional and abstract representations of problems and situations than do non-experts (Feltovich, Prietula, & Ericsson, 2006). Better problem representations facilitate expert decision making in two fundamental ways. First, a good representation of the problem facilitates pattern recognition and recall of information from past situations that may be relevant in the present context. Second, good problem representations also provide the support necessary for the evaluation of possible problem solutions (see Zeitz, 1997). The ability for experts to generate higher quality situation and problem representations is linked in part to a deeper conceptual understanding of the domain, but also to routines of performance. Specifically, experts spend more time developing an understanding of a specific problem, whereas non-experts spend more

Table 41.2 Mechanisms of Expertise and Individual Decision Making

Expert Decision Makers...

Are tightly coupled to cues and contextual features of the environment:
They develop psychological and physiological adaptations to the task environment.
They are sensitive to and leverage contextual patterns of cues in decision making.

Have a larger knowledge base and organize it different from non-experts:
They have a more conceptually organized knowledge base.
They have more robust connections between aspects of their knowledge.
They have a more abstracted and functional knowledge base.

Engage in pattern recognition:
They perceive larger and more meaningful patterns in the environment.
They are able to detect subtle cue configurations.
They are able to retrieve courses of action based on situation/action matching rules.

Engage in deliberate and guided practice:
They devote time and effort to improving knowledge and skills.
They have high motivation to learn and long term learning goals.

Seek diagnostic feedback:
They seek out input from other experts.
They self-diagnose their performance, identify weaknesses in their knowledge and processes, and correct them.

Have better situation assessment and problem representations:
They spend more time evaluating the situation.
They create deeper, more conceptual, more functional, and more abstracted situation representations.

Have specialized memory skills:
They functionally increase their ability to handle large amounts of information.
They anticipate what information will be needed in the decision making.

Automate the small steps:
They quickly and effortlessly do what requires large amounts of attention for non-experts.
They have more cognitive resources available for dealing with more complex aspects of decision making.

Self-regulate and monitor their processes:
They evaluate their own understanding of a situation.
They judge the consistency, reliability, and completeness of their information.
They make good decisions about when to stop evaluating the situation.

Adapted from Rosen et al. (2008)

time developing possible solutions (Randel, Pugh, & Reed, 1996). The expert's performance advantage then stems from the deep understanding of the situation.

SKILLED MEMORY

There are well-documented limitations to the human information-processing system (e.g., Miller, 1956, magical number seven). We understand that for memory to exist, learning must occur. Equally important to understanding memory is the required coordination of certain activities to not only store information into memory but also the retrieval of this information. A detailed discussion of the cognitive functioning of memory is beyond the scope of this chapter. However, we will touch briefly on how an expert—based on the notion that we all have a limit on our cognitive resources and the activities that must occur to store and retrieve information into memory—has a more highly skilled memory than a non-expert. As we stated above, experts chunk information (see chunking theory, Chase & Simon, 1973). This strategy allows for more efficient use of an individual's resources. That is, since an expert is able to assess a situation and take in information as "chunks" rather than individual pieces of information, they are able to evaluate more cues than a novice.

AUTOMATICITY

As efficiency is frequently a measure by which expertise is evaluated, it is not surprising that experts are able to rapidly and effortlessly perform components of a task. Automaticity is the ability to accomplish things without occupying the mind with the low-level details required for the task (automatic and controlled processing; see Schneider & Shiffrin, 1977). For experts, processes are automated, that is, they execute certain actions without thought or effort (Sternberg, 1997). Consequently, an expert can divide his or her attention among tasks, which in typical naturalistic decision-making settings is critical.

METACOGNITION AND SELF-REGULATION

Metacognition is the knowledge of one's own knowledge, cognitive processes, and performance (Flavell, 1979). An expert is aware of what she knows and how she uses the knowledge that she has. Moreover, experts are capable of evaluating their performance. They do this so that they can evaluate their understanding of the situation. Experts, in a sense, are automatic learners. They understand the knowledge that they have, and they self-regulate in order to determine how well their assessment and implementation of a course of action is. For this

reason, an expert's knowledge domain grows at a faster rate than that of a novice.

In sum, the basis of expert performance can be described in terms of a set of mechanisms or adaptations to the performance domain. The prominent mechanisms described above can be thought of as a "prototype" of expertise (Sternberg, 1997). Expert performers utilize these mechanisms when in their domain.

Teams

The preceding mechanisms support expert decision making at the individual level; however, as discussed earlier, decision making frequently occurs in team settings. Just as individuals develop performance adaptations to reach high levels of effectiveness, there is an identifiable set of expert team mechanisms (Rosen, Salas, Lyons, & Fiore, 2008; Salas et al., 2006). As on the individual level, these mechanisms represent a prototype of team expertise wherein the importance of any one mechanism will depend on the features of the task domain. These mechanisms are briefly reviewed below, and a summary is presented in Table 41.3.

LEARN AND ADAPT

Similar to the ways in which individuals practice self-regulation and engage in continuous learning in order to develop and maintain performance capacities, teams too must learn and adapt. For

Table 41.3 Prototypical Mechanisms of Expert Team Performance and Decision Making

Members of Expert Teams…
Develop shared mental models:
They anticipate each other's needs and actions.
They can communicate implicitly.
They interpret cues in a complimentary manner.
Learn and adapt:
They self-correct.
They learn from past decision-making episodes.
They adapt coordinating processes to dynamic environments.
They compensate for each other.
Maintain clear roles and responsibilities:
They mange expectations.
They understand each others' roles and how they fit together.
They maintain clarity of roles while maintaining flexibility.
Possess clear, valued, and shared vision:
They develop their goals with a shared sense of purpose.
They guide their decisions with a common set of values.

Table 41.3 (Continued)

Members of Expert Teams...

Develop a cycle of pre-brief → performance → debrief:
They regularly provide individual- and team-level feedback to one another.
They establish and revise team goals and plans.
They dynamically set priorities.
They anticipate and review issues/problems of members.
They periodically diagnose team decision-making "effectiveness," including its results and processes.

Are lead by strong team leaders:
They are led by someone with good leadership skills and not just technical competence.
They believe the leaders care about them.
Leaders of expert teams provide situation updates.
Leaders of expert teams foster teamwork, coordination, and cooperation.
Leaders of expert teams self-correct first.

Have a strong sense of "collective," trust, teamness, and confidence:
They manage conflict well; they confront each other effectively.
They have a strong sense of team orientation.
They trust other team members' "intentions."
They strongly believe in the team's collective ability to succeed.

Cooperate and coordinate:
They identify teamwork and task work requirements.
They ensure that, through staffing and/or development, the team possesses the right mix of competencies.
They consciously integrate new team members.
They distribute and assign work thoughtfully.
They examine and adjust the team's physical workplace to optimize communication and coordination.

Adapted from Salas et al. (2006)

example, Edmondson, Bohmer, and Pisano (2001) demonstrated that surgical teams who successfully implemented new technology solutions did so by supporting the collective learning process. A team may accomplish this by learning about others' roles (Levine & Moreland, 1999), improvising (Orlikowski & Hofman, 1997), and making small adjustments to existing performance strategies (Leonard-Barton & Deschamps, 1988). Furthermore, teams must be able to adapt to novel situations. Burke and colleagues (2006) have proposed a model of team adaptation comprising four process-oriented phases: (a) situation assessment, (b) plan formulation, (c) plan execution, and (d) team learning. Their model illustrates the series of phases that unfold over time and constitute the core processes (and emergent states) that underlie adaptive team performance. Team learning and adaptation are important research topics in the industrial and organizational (I/O) and management literatures (e.g., Kozlowski & Bell, 2008; Wilson, Goodman, & Cronin, 2007) and consequently represent a potential for productive collaboration with the NDM community.

CLEAR ROLES AND RESPONSIBILITIES

An expert team is composed of individuals who are very knowledgeable in their domain; that is, an expert team is composed of expert members. However, an expert team is not merely a group of experts. Individual team members are also very aware of the roles and responsibilities of their teammates. This awareness of their teammates' roles and responsibilities is crucial for their ability to anticipate each other's actions and needs. Expert teams do not let role clarity interfere with their ability to learn and adapt as a team. Roles are clear, but they are not rigid in the face of changing demands. For example, Eisenstat and Cohen (1990) found that the highest performing top management teams were characterized by an ability to accept whatever change in team member roles occurred as long as these roles were clearly articulated.

PREBRIEF AND DEBRIEF CYCLE

The use of a prebrief and debrief affords teams a mechanism of decision-making effectiveness, but in the short term as well as from a longer term developmental perspective. First, the prebrief provides an opportunity to ensure that the roles and responsibilities of the team are clear, but also it allows the leader to provide any information that will help the team's performance in a high-stakes situation (Inzana, Driskell, Salas, & Johnston, 1996). Second, feedback is critical to the development of expertise, and the debrief provides the team with a structured way to review their performance and establish areas for improvement.

STRONG TEAM LEADERS

Team leaders of expert teams are not only strong technically (i.e., are experts in their individual taskwork), but they also possess strong leadership skills. The team leader conveys that he cares about the team members; he also provides situation updates and fosters teamwork (Day, Gronn, & Salas, 2004; Salas, Burke, & Stagl, 2004), and by doing so, is able to increase team performance levels (Tannenbaum, Smith-Jentsch, & Behson, 1998). Leaders of expert teams must learn to manage the team through ups and downs, and must be able to learn from these experiences, both in terms of their own technical skills and their leadership skills. What is most critical and difficult for a team leader to do is to play both the roles of a team member with a high level of technical knowledge, skills, and attitudes, but also the role of leader who must act as the force that directs the team. Zaccaro, Rittman, and Marks (2001), in their article on team leadership, focused on the importance of functional leadership. From this perspective, effective team leaders take on roles and tasks or direct others to take on roles and tasks necessary to accomplish the team's goals. Their responsibility is to identify the gaps and fulfill them as needed, either by them or any of the team's members. This function of the leader rings equally true in expert teams.

STRONG SENSE OF TEAM ORIENTATION

Much research has been conducted on the impact that team level affect has on performance processes and outcomes. Research has demonstrated that psychological safety fosters learning behavior in work teams (Edmondson, 1999). Furthermore, mutual trust (Bandow, 2001), collective efficacy (Gibson, 2003), and collective orientation (Driskell & Salas, 1992) have all been shown to be critical for team effectiveness. However, it is inevitable that there will be tension in a group. Expert teams have high levels of collective orientation, but they also engage in appropriate tension/conflict management. An NDM setting can be classified as an extreme context; thus, understanding how to deal with conflict effectively and quickly is critical for the team's effectiveness.

COORDINATION AND COOPERATION

Teamwork is grounded in the notion of cooperation and coordination. To produce high levels of team performance, teams must be able to organize team members' activities to successfully reach their goals (Cannon-Bowers et al., 1995). Coordination is dependent on the timeliness of actions and the contributions of all team members (Kozlowski & Bell, 2003). Cooperation is equally important for expert teams. However, cooperation is the cognitive mechanism behind effective teamwork, whereas coordination is the behavioral mechanism. Cooperation is the motivational force that team members have to coordinate. Wilson, Salas, Priest, and Andrews (2007) argue that the source of coordination failure should be sought out in the attitudes (i.e., cooperation) of team members.

In summary, the previous sections have provided an overview of individual- and team-level mechanisms underlying expert decision making. The mechanisms outlined above are based on investigations of individuals and teams in naturalistic settings and represent a prototype of expert decision making. In the following section, examples of how this research has been translated into increased performance in organizations are discussed.

Improving Decision-Making Performance

NDM research is use-inspired research; the impetus for understanding real-world decision making is frequently pragmatic in that NDM researchers are interested in improving decision-making performance within a given domain. By developing contextualized models of real-world decision making, NDM can contribute to performance improvement in two primary ways: the development of training to accelerate the acquisition of expertise, and the design of better socio-technical systems to support expert decision making. Ideally, these two approaches work in concert, such that expert decision making is supported by the design of organizational structures and technological tools as much as possible, and training interventions are provided to accelerate the development of new experts in the domain. NDM research seeking to support expert decision making through improved socio-technical system design is realized through the design of information systems, interfaces, and organizational structures that "play to the strengths" of human adaptation to complexity. The topic of system design based upon naturalistic understandings of human performance is large, and interested readers are referred to the numerous sources available (Hollnagel, Woods, & Levenson, 2006; Vicente, 1999). The following section focuses on NDM work in the area of training system design and delivery.

Training

Training programs rooted in classical decision making have met with limited success at best. Programs have been developed to train decision-making processes rooted in the formulas of subjective-expected utility theory (von Neumann & Morgenstern, 1947) and designed to correct for the biases identified in rationalist research (Mann, Beswick, Allouache, & Ivey, 1989; Yates & Estin, 1996). These types of training programs seek to impose a prescriptive conceptualization of decision making with underlying core assumptions that are met rarely in modern organizations (March & Simon, 1958).

However, training programs developed from the naturalistic tradition do not attempt to "de-bias" decision makers or train processes rooted in impractical prescriptive models; instead, they focus on building knowledge and skills underlying expert decision making. This perspective values the natural adaptive capacity of human expertise and seeks to cultivate practically applicable decision-making strategies. As Cohen, Freeman, and Thompson (1997) note, "if a house is basically sound, it can be better to renovate than to tear down and rebuild from scratch" (p. 257). This embodies the NDM perspective on training in that human decision making is not fundamentally flawed; the processes of expert decision making should be supported, not replaced.

Numerous specific training programs (e.g., Cohen, Freeman, & Thompson, 1998; Pounds & Fallesen, 1994), as well as general methods for training design (e.g., Pliske, McCloskey, & Klein, 2006; Ross, Lussier, & Klein, 2005), have been developed from NDM research. The following section discusses the implications of NDM research for training program content and delivery. These implications are summarized in Table 41.4. Subsequently, we provide a set of general principles for developing expertise in organizations.

Content

As described earlier in this chapter, a naturalistic view of decision making emphasizes the role of pattern recognition, a rapid and largely unconscious process. This begs the question, how do you train something that is performed in a largely unconscious

Table 41.4 Overview of Implications of NDM Research for Training

Implications for Training Content	*Decision making skills*—Train the mechanisms of expertise.	• Metacognitive skills • Reasoning skills • Domain-specific problem-solving skills • Mental simulation skills • Risk assessment skills • Situation assessment skills • Knowledge organization • Teamwork
	Developmental processes—Train the process of becoming an expert; facilitate learning from experience.	• Build an awareness of what expertise is and how it is developed. • Observational skills • Speculation skills • Testing skills • Generalization skills • Practice
Implications for Training Delivery	*Simulation-based Training*—Experience is the heart of the matter; provide carefully engineered practice activities.	• Emphasize cognitive fidelity • Use diagnostic measurement tools • Provide corrective feedback
	On-the-job Training—Provide access to mentors and coaches to structure learning on the job.	• Train existing experts on the processes of mentoring and coaching.

manner by the decision maker (Ross, Lussier, & Klein, 2005)? Domain knowledge underlies pattern recognition abilities, but acquiring enough domain knowledge to produce expert decision making in ill-structured environments can take years of experience. Imparting all of this knowledge in a formal training system will infrequently be a viable option. NDM researchers have addressed this issue in relation to training content in two distinct ways. First, there are sets of competencies related to the actual decision-making processes that experts use beyond pattern recognition. Training programs of this type attempt to directly train the mechanisms of expert decision-making performance. Second, because expertise is the product of experience within a domain, developing experts can be trained in processes that will facilitate learning from experience. Essentially, this approach seeks to maximize the value of experience and practice activities, ultimately accelerating the development of a robust and well-organized knowledge base. These two perspectives are complementary, rather than exclusive. Each is described in more detail below.

TRAINING DECISION-MAKING SKILLS

While naturalistic decision making is largely recognitional in nature, there are further components to the process that can be directly trained. Cohen et al. (1998) describe these skills as meta-recognitional in nature. That is, these skills involve strategies for developing a better understanding or awareness of the situation and evaluation of generated courses of action. In this vein, Cannon-Bowers and Bell (1997) identified several categories of competencies for improving decision-making effectiveness in NDM-like environments. These seven areas are tightly aligned with both the mechanisms of expert decision-making performance outlined above, as well as features of the NDM environment. These competencies include metacognitive skills, reasoning skills, domain-specific problem solving skills, mental simulation skills, risk assessment skills, situation assessment skills, and knowledge organization. For example, metacognition is a fundamental mechanism of expertise, and consequently metacognitive skills are suggested as competencies for training programs. Expert decision makers are better able to monitor their own processes throughout a performance episode. Novices use domain-independent metacognitive strategies (Veenman, Elshout, & Meijer, 1997); however, expertise can involve developing specialized strategies for regulating internal cognitive and affective processes,

as well as overt behavioral aspects of performance (Zimmerman, 2006). Therefore, both general and domain-specific metacognitive skills can be targeted competencies in a training program. Additionally, while general problem-solving strategies such as hill-climbing have been found to be characteristic of novice problem-solving processes and therefore not a good way of creating expert decision makers, training programs can be developed around specialized problem-solving strategies used by experts. For example, Pounds and Fallesen (1994) developed a training program based on an informal problem-solving strategy used by expert U.S. Army officers.

While the above competency areas are illustrative of the implications of NDM research for individual decision makers, decision making frequently occurs in teams. There are several implications of NDM research for team decision making (TDM) training content as well. Specifically, Salas, Rosen, Burke, Nicholson, and Howse (2007) advanced a set of guidelines for team decision-making training. These include: (a) basing TDM training in theory; (b) adopting a systems approach to design; (c) creating learner-centered TDM training; (d) using information provision, demonstration, and practice-based methods, and incorporating diagnostic performance measurement; (e) guiding practice performance; (f) clarifying expectations early; (g) setting a climate for learning; (h) encouraging participation in the learning process during feedback sessions with trainees; (i) providing opportunities to perform; and (j) employing dynamic assessment of performance. Perhaps one of the greatest success stories related to NDM is the development of crew resource management (CRM) training programs in military and civilian aviation. These training programs target specific teamwork competencies underlying effective team decision making (e.g., communication, assertiveness).

TRAINING DEVELOPMENTAL PROCESSES

An additional approach to training decision-making performance attempts to improve how people learn from experience. The fundamental premise of this approach is that by increasing the ability of a person to learn from experience, the acquisition of a large and well-organized knowledge base underlying expert performance can be accelerated. The problem-based learning (PBL) tradition in medical education is rooted in part in this notion of training developmental processes. That is, in addition to the basic knowledge of a domain and the processes of performance, experts must develop the ability to continuously learn from experience (Rosen, Fiore, & Salas, 2009). The PBL approach grew out of the concern that much of what medical students learned in well-structured academic coursework was not transferring to the ill-structured clinical context of performance. The proposed solution to this problem is rooted in experiential learning, such that the structure of the learning and transfer environments are as similar as possible.

While there are far fewer examples of empirically validated training programs that adopt this approach in isolation from training decision-making skills, specifications for such an approach have been articulated. For example, Hogarth (2001) has proposed a framework for developing intuition consisting of three central components: building awareness, acquiring specific learning skills (i.e., observation, speculation, testing, and generalization), and practice. While intuition and expertise are distinct, they share important similarities, and the development of intuition (as discussed by Hogarth, 2001) closely parallels the development of pattern recognition abilities. The process outlined above is deliberative in nature; it describes a conscious and reflective evaluation of one's own performance and environment. This may seem at odds with the nature of expert decision making described throughout this chapter. However, the development of the mechanisms underlying rapid and intuitive decision making is facilitated by focused attention on learning from experience.

There is perhaps more evidence of the effectiveness of training developmental processes on the team level in naturalistic contexts than on the individual level. For example, team self-correction training has been shown to increase team decision making and coordination (Smith-Jentsch et al., 2008; Smith-Jentsch, Zeisig, et al., 1998). Additionally, Henderson (2008) discusses the use of an experiential learning strategy in surgical teams. The fundamental approach in these programs is to instantiate a process (e.g., a prebrief, debrief routine) and tools (e.g., structured debrief aides) so that teams are able to diagnose their own performance and make plans for improvement by generating lessons learned.

Delivery

While NDM training programs have taken many forms, there are expert decision makers who have achieved their superior performance abilities through extensive experience in a given domain. Simulation-based training (SBT) is viewed as a method for replicating these experiences in a safe manner and accelerating the development expertise. In many domains, the type and amount of experiences that a person has are determined by random opportunities. This is exemplified in medical residency programs, where learning experiences are determined by the types of patients available. Additionally, on-the-job training cannot be ignored when discussing expertise within organizations. While this is not a formal training delivery method, organizations can support this activity and can help systematize and improve the value of learning on the job.

SIMULATION

For similar reasons that make simulation a good tool for NDM research, simulation-based training (SBT) in different forms is a key training method of training delivery in NDM. SBT is a methodology of training delivery that incorporates opportunities to learn in the form of practice opportunities (Salas et al., 2006). These practice activities can be conducted using technology (i.e., simulators) of various levels and types of fidelity (Hays & Singer, 1989). The distinction between cognitive fidelity (i.e., the degree to which a decision maker has to perform the same cognitive operations as in the real task) and physical fidelity (i.e., the degree to which the simulator replicates in detail the physical detail of task environment) has proven valuable. Cognitive fidelity is emphasized over physical fidelity in many NDM training programs. In SBT, the "scenario is the curriculum" (Salas, Guthrie, & Burke, 2007, p. 228); that is, the events in the practice activity are the embodiment of the training objectives.

OJT: APPRENTICESHIPS AND MENTORS

It has been noted that the majority of training within organizations is informal rather than formal. On-the-job training (OJT) is estimated to account for up to 60% of organizational training efforts (Wehrenberg, 1987). This type of training is no doubt invaluable to the development of an expert decision maker. The uniqueness of on-the-job training is that it affords the trainee an opportunity to develop her skills while conducting and practicing the skills of the job. On-the-job training is a hands-on form of training that requires the trainee to become actively involved in the learning process. Moreover, when done correctly, on-the-job training assigns an expert to lead the training. The trainer's role is to ensure that the trainee is acquiring the relevant knowledge, skills, and attitudes to become an expert. On-the-job training comes in many forms.

For example, mentoring or coaching programs and apprenticeships are closely related to on-the-job training (Hunt & Michael, 1983). Mentors or coaches are the trainers, and protégés are the trainees. Mentors and coaches can offer both psychosocial and career development advice. The advice that is provided to the trainee assists the knowledge-building process (Hunt & Michael, 1983). Mentors are individuals who have well-developed communication, observational, and problem-solving skills (Head, Reiman, & Thies-Sprinthall, 1992). Moreover, the mentors have been given the role of cognitive coaches; this translates into the role of a mentor as a developer of a protégé's mental processing (Costa & Garmston, 1994).

Using on-the-job training as a method of training individual's decision making performance is useful because of the exposure to on-the-job situations. It is an unfortunate truth that completion of a training program does not produce competent performance. It is the on-the-job experiences that build knowledge and connections that have the potential to lead to competent performance (Cornford, & Athanasou, 1995). The exposure not only helps to develop their ability to make decisions, but it is also the practice that they are afforded in these situations that helps them become experts. Moreover, these experiences provide the trainee with an arsenal of events to use when prompted by an unknown situation. It is critical to understand that we are not suggesting that practice is enough. On the contrary, feedback about the practice is required, as well as providing the trainee with guided practice (Salas, Guthrie, & Burke, 2007). On-the-job training, although it is one of the simplest methods of designing training, should not be exempt from the characteristics of training that make a training program effective.

Inherent in a well-designed on-the-job training program is the direction provided to the trainee by the expert on the job. The expert's job as the trainer is to develop the individual to be proficient in the task. The trainer can provide guided practice and feedback, which will help develop the trainee. Furthermore, if done properly, the trainer can teach the trainee to utilize such NDM techniques as pattern recognition or mental representation when making decisions on the job.

Principles for Developing Expertise in Organizations

Salas and Rosen (2010) have proposed an initial set of principles for training rooted in the science of expertise. These principles summarize much of the preceding discussion and are detailed in Table 41.5. These principles are organized around

Table 41.5 Summary of Principles for Developing Expertise in Organizations

Characteristic of Expertise	Principle
Deliberate and guided practice	1. Enable learning and development through diagnostic feedback of work performance.
	2. Provide safe environments to make mistakes.
	3. Provide opportunities for practice inside and outside work performance.
	4. Provide pre-practice tools for learning activities.
	5. Draw explicit connections between new and previously held knowledge and skills.
	6. Use guided errors to accelerate learning and conceptual understanding.
	7. Provide variability in learning activities.
	8. Objective performance is the "brass ring" for evaluating expertise.
Continuous learning	9. Provide information on likely future directions for the organization and skill sets and knowledge bases of value to the organization.
	10. Support changing learning needs throughout the course of development: – Provide "phase appropriate" scaffolding for beginning learners – Provide training on independent learning and self-monitoring for intermediate learners – Provide access to guidance from mentors for advanced learners.

Table 41.5 (Continued)

Characteristic of Expertise	Principle
Motivation	11. Reward performance improvements instead of performance levels.
	12. Frame learning experiences to improve self-efficacy.
	13. Reinforce learning goals.
	14. Create "empowering" work environments.
Feedback seeking	15. Provide organizational goals and performance criteria at a level that enables feedback.
	16. Encourage feedback-seeking behavior.
	17. Provide feedback that affords the determination of the causes of performance outcomes.

Adapted from Salas & Rosen (2010)

four mechanisms of acquiring expertise in a domain: practice, continuous learning, motivation and learning goals, and feedback.

First, experts engage in deliberate and guided practice. There is no substitute for prolonged experience within a given domain. However, as described above, not all experiences are equal, and not all people learn equally well from experience. Therefore, important questions about how to engineer practice opportunities and maximize learning from experience become salient. Principles related to this aspect of development involve providing diagnostic feedback, as well as opportunities to practice and make mistakes in safe environments. Second, experts engage in continuous learning; that is, expertise is not a destination, but a journey. Without continued performance and practice, expertise fades. Additionally, developing experts will have different needs as they progress (Dreyfus & Dreyfus, 1986). Consequently, principles for training related to continuous learning involve supporting instructional approaches to support changing learning needs. Additionally, because expertise takes large amounts of time to develop, learners need to have an idea of what skill sets they should be developing so that they are able to support the organization's needs in the years to come. Third, experts have a high motivation to learn, and they have long-term learning goals. The expert's level of motivation has been described as a "rage to master" (Winner, 1996). In order to promote this motivation and goal orientation, reward systems should focus on performance improvements versus set levels. Fourth, experts engage in feedback seeking behaviors. In order to support this, organizations should provide goals by

which employees can gauge their performance, as well as appropriate feedback.

Future Directions for NDM

This chapter has outlined some of the core features of NDM as a field of inquiry and a community of practice. In a relatively short amount of time, NDM has emerged as a powerful approach for understanding and improving decision-making performance in complex and high-stakes environments. However, there is still much to be done in terms of growth as a field of scientific inquiry, as well as the breadth of domains served by the NDM community. This section discusses future direction for NDM, both as an emerging scientific field as well as a community of practitioners. These are summarized in Table 41.6, along with some key challenges and research needs.

First, NDM researchers will continue to expand the types of work domains. The majority of NDM research to date has been within the military and aviation communities. However, other critical safety domains, such as power generation and health care, have been investigated as well. As described earlier, these NDM domains have been stressful, complex, and frequently very dangerous. The ubiquitous nature of the types of cognitive work and situational variables of interest to NDM researchers means that there are many domains that have yet to be explored—domains where the potential for impact and improvement of safety and effectiveness is great. However, this raises important theoretical and practical challenges that must be addressed. Expertise is inherently task- or domain-dependent. The specialized performance mechanisms developed

Table 41.6 Summary of Future Directions for NDM

Future Directions	Challenges and Research Needs
Extend to new domains of work	• Expertise is task/domain specific. • Theory for understanding what aspects of expertise are generalizable to which contexts.
Move beyond a focus on decision making to consider more complex forms of cognitive work and collaboration	• Increasingly complex types of performance will demand more complex theories. • NDM studies examining planning, problem solving, causal reasoning, sense making, and collaboration. • Move beyond a decision-making paradigm to a more inclusive macrocognition paradigm.
Refine and grow the methodological repertoire of NDM researchers	• NDM research is frequently opportunistic (e.g., access to experts, "naturally occurring" experiments) and its methods have not traditionally been widely accessible. • More sophisticated approaches to measuring complex cognitive work in field settings as well as formalization and standardization of NDM methodologies. • Continued development of cognitive engineering techniques and an integration between design, training, and selection approaches.
Expanded cross-fertilization between NDM and other communities	• NDM has evolved in relative isolation from mainstream decision making and other relevant academic traditions. • NDM researchers will increasingly draw from new lines of research complimenting the NDM perspective (e.g., intuition and affect in DM, team learning and problem solving)

by an expert within one domain will not transfer to another. Consequently, the degree to which findings from one domain are directly relevant in others is always a concern. NDM has only begun to consider these issues in an explicit and systematic way. In the future, the efficacy of NDM as an applied research tradition will rest in large part on its ability to develop methods for accurately gauging the generalizability of its findings, of reusing the products of field studies for new purposes.

Second, the NDM community began with a focus on decision making; however, the types of performance processes investigated by NDM researchers have grown increasingly diverse. Now, topics such as causal reasoning and sense making are increasingly commonplace. This work extends beyond decision-making performance and includes processes such as planning and problem solving. Macrocognition is an emerging perspective within the NDM community that addresses this more complex cognitive work, including individual and collaborative problem solving and planning (e.g., Fiore, Smith-Jentsch, Salas, Warner, & Letsky, 2010; Klein, Ross, Moon, Klein, Hoffman, & Hollnagel,

2003; Schraagen, Militello, Ormerod, & Lipshitz, 2008). On the team level, *macrocognition* has been defined as "the process of transforming internalized team knowledge into externalized team knowledge through individual and team knowledge building processes" (Fiore et al., 2010). This perspective focuses on understanding how groups effectively collaborate to solve problems in unique situations. This is representative of trends in the NDM community, where the emphasis is increasingly moving beyond routine aspects of team decision making to look at how teams collaborate in unique situations. Addressing these issues will be a major theoretical challenge for the NDM community, but much work has already begun. By focusing on more complex aspects of performance, theories developed by NDM researchers will necessarily grow in complexity as well. This will raise new methodological challenges, requiring more sophisticated measurement techniques and ways of testing the hypotheses generated from field studies.

Third, and building from the previous points, the NDM community will expand and refine its methodological toolbox. This involves, among other things, an increased emphasis on developing new measurement techniques to capture complex cognitive and collaborative processes in a systematic manner. In order to test the new theories that will be needed to understand more complex cognitive work, more diagnostic and robust measurement systems will need to be developed. In addition to new measurement techniques, NDM researchers need to make the existing methods more accessible. Cognitive engineering (e.g., designing sociotechnical systems that capitalize on human abilities to increase effectiveness) is a core concern for many NDM researchers. If the NDM community is to continue broadening its impact, more practitioners are needed. These practitioners must be trained in the use of a standardized set of methods for eliciting and representing the cognitive work of professionals. To date, these techniques have been somewhat esoteric in nature, though progress has been made in formalizing NDM techniques (e.g., Crandall et al., 2006). Additionally, comprehensive approaches that consider system design, training, and selection need to be developed. Presently, these activities are most commonly considered in isolation.

Fourth, the NDM community will become less isolated from related traditions. The initial impetus for NDM was dissatisfaction with the applicability of mainstream or traditional decision-making research to many real-world situations. However, since this time, the mainstream decision-making research has progressed dramatically. New theories, particularly those addressing intuition and affect in decision making are conceptually consistent with findings from NDM (see Salas, Rosen, & DiazGranados, 2010). Additionally, other domains, including group communication theory, human factors and industrial organizational psychology, management, and computer science, to name a few, have profited from and have contributed to NDM work. This cross-fertilization between disciplines is likely to continue and accelerate in the coming years.

Concluding Remarks

The naturalistic decision making movement is a young science, one that needs to evolve and mature as more robust studies are conducted and more deep and precise theories are developed. But, we are optimistic and the signs are there—the literature now reports more studies, discussions, and debates about NDM. We have documented just two short decades of NDM science, and much has been learned. This is indeed encouraging, and there is more to come.

We hope that this chapter motivates more naturalistic studies of expertise and team decision making. We hope that it generates more theoretical frameworks to understand the context of expert performance at work. We hope that building from what we have highlighted in this chapter, NDM becomes a science that offers practical contributions to the acceleration and maintenance of expertise in individuals and teams.

Acknowledgment

We would like to thank Gary Klein for comments on an earlier version of this chapter. The views herein are those of the authors and do not necessarily reflect those of the organizations with which they are affiliated or their sponsoring agencies. This research was supported by the Office of Naval Research Collaboration and Knowledge Interoperability (CKI) Program and ONR MURI Grant #N000140610446 (Dr. Michael Letsky, Program Manager) as well as Grant Number SBE0350345 from the National Science Foundation awarded to Eduardo Salas and Stephen M. Fiore, and by Grant Number SES0527675 from the National Science Foundation awarded to Glenn Harrison, Stephen M. Fiore, Charlie Hughes, and Eduardo Salas.

References

Alexander, P. A., Jetton, T. L., & Kulikowich, J. M. (1995). Interrelationship of knowledge, interest, and recall: Assessing a model of domain learning. *Journal of Educational Psychology, 87*(4), 559–575.

Alexander, P. A., Kulikowich, J. M., & Schulze, S. K. (1994). How subject-matter knowledge affects recall and interest. *American Educational Research Journal, 31,* 313–337.

Annett, J. (2000). Theoretical and pragmatic influences on task analysis methods. In J. M. Schraagen, S. F. Chipman, & V. L. Shalin (Eds.), *Cognitive task analysis* (pp. 25–39). Mahwah, NJ: Erlbaum.

Austin, J. T., & Crespin, T. R. (2006). Problems of criteria in industrial and organizational psychology: Progress, problems, and prospects. In W. Bennet, Jr., C. E. Lance, & D. J. Woehr (Eds.), *Performance measurement: Current perspectives and future challenges* (pp. 9–48). Mahwah, NJ: Erlbaum.

Bandow, D. (2001). Time to create sound teamwork. *The Journal for Quality and Participation, 24,* 41–47.

Beach, L. R. (1993). Broadening the definition of decision making: The role of prechoice screening of options. *Psychological Science, 4*(4), 215–220.

Beach, L. R., & Mitchell, T. R. (1987). Image theory: Principles, goals, and plans in decision making. *Acta Psychologica, 66*(3), 201–220.

Beach, L. R., Smith, B., Lundell, J., & Mitchell, T. R. (1988). Image theory: Descriptive sufficiency of a simple rule for the compatibility test. *Journal of Behavioral Decision Making, 1*(1), 17–28.

Beach, L. R., & Strom, E. (1989). A toadstool among the mushrooms: Screening decisions and image theory's compatibility test. *Acta Psychologica, 72*(1), 1–12.

Bedard, J., & Chi, M. T. H. (1992). Expertise. *Current Directions in Psychological Science, 1*(4), 135–139.

Benner, P. (2004). Using the Dreyfus model of Skull acquisition to describe and interpret Skull acquisition and clinical judgment in nursing practice and education. *Bulletin of Science, Technology, & Society, 24*, 188–199.

Bernoulli, D. (1738). Specimen theoriae novae de mensura sortis. *Commentarii Academiae Scientrum Imperialis Petropolitanae, 5*, 175–192.

Bordage, G., & Zacks, R. (1984). The structure of medical knowledge in the memories of medical students and general practitioners: Categories and prototypes. *Medical Education, 18*, 406–416.

Brehmer, B., & Hagafors, R. (1986). Use of experts in complex decision making: A paradigm for the study of staff work. *Organizational Behavior and Human Decision Processes, 38*(2), 181–195.

Buchanan, B. G., Davis, R., & Feigenbaum, E. A. (2006). *Expert systems: A perspective from computer science.* New York: Cambridge University Press.

Burke, C. S., Stagl, K., Salas, E., Pierce, L., & Kendall, D. (2006). Understanding team adaptation: A conceptual analysis and model. *Journal of Applied Psychology, 91*(6), 1189–1207.

Calderwood, R., Crandall, B., & Klein, G. (1987). *Expert and novice fireground command decisions* (No. MDA903-85-C-0327). Alexandria, VA: U.S. Army Research Institute.

Canas, J. J., Antoli, A., Fajardo, I., & Salmeron, L. (2005). Cognitive inflexibility and the development and use of strategies for solving complex dynamic problems: Effects of different types of training. *Theoretical Issues in Ergonomics Science, 6*(1), 95–108.

Cannon-Bowers, J. A., & Bell, H. H. (1997). Training decision makers for complex environments: Implications of the naturalistic decision making perspective. In C. E. Zsambok & G. Klein (Eds.), *Naturalistic decision making* (pp. 99–110). Mahwah, NJ: Erlbaum.

Cannon-Bowers, J. A., & Salas, E. (Ed.). (1998). *Making decisions under stress: Implications for individual and team training.* Washington, DC: American Psychological Association.

Cannon-Bowers, J. A., Salas, E., & Converse, S. (1993). Shared mental models in expert team decision making. In N. J. J. Castellan (Ed.), *Individual and group decision making* (pp. 221–246). Hillsdale, NJ: Erlbaum.

Cannon-Bowers, J. A., Salas, E., & Pruitt, J. S. (1996). Establishing the boundaries of a paradigm for decision-making research. *Human Factors, 38*(2), 193–205.

Cannon-Bowers, J. A., Tannenbaum, S. I., Salas, E., & Volpe, C. E. (1995). Defining competencies and establishing team training requirements. In R. Guzzo, & E. Salas (Eds.), *Team effectiveness and decision making in organizations* (pp. 333–380). San Francisco: Jossey-Bass.

Cellier, J. M., Eyrolle, H., & Marine, C. (1997). Expertise in dynamic environments. *Ergonomics, 40*(1), 28–50.

Chase, W. G., & Simon, H. A. (1973). Perception in chess. *Cognitive Psychology, 4*, 55–81.

Chipman, S. F., Schraagen, J. M., & Shalin, V. L. (2000). *Cognitive task analysis.* Mahwah, NJ: Erlbaum.

Christensen, E. J., & Redd, S. B. (2004). Bureaucrats versus the ballot box in foreign policy decision making. *The Journal of Conflict Resolution, 48*, 69–90.

Cohen, M. S. (1993). Three paradigms for viewing decision biases. In G. Klein, J. Orasanu, R. Calderwood, & C. E. Zsambok (Eds.), *Decision making in action: Models and methods* (pp. 36–50). Norwood, NJ: Ablex.

Cohen, M. S., Freeman, J. T., & Thompson, B. B. (1997). Training the naturalistic decision maker. In C. E. Zsambok & G. Klein (Eds.), *Naturalistic decision making* (pp. 257–268). Mahwah, NJ: Erlbaum.

Cohen, M. S., Freeman, J. T., & Thompson, B. B. (1998). Critical thinking skills in tactical decision making: A model and a training strategy. In J. A. Cannon-Bowers & E. Salas (Eds.), *Decision making under stress: Implications for training and simulation* (pp. 155–189). Washington, DC: American Psychological Association.

Cooke, N. J., Salas, E., Kiekel, P. A., & Bell, B. (2004). Advances in measuring team cognition. In E. Salas & S. M. Fiore (Eds.), *Team cognition: Understanding the factors that drive process and performance* (pp. 83–106). Washington, DC: American Psychological Association.

Cooksey, R. W. (1996). The methodology of social judgment theory. *Thinking & Reasoning, 2*(2–3), 141–173.

Costa, A. L., & Garmston, R. J. (1994). *Cognitive coaching: A foundation for renaissance schools.* Berkeley, CA: The Institute for Intelligent Behavior.

Cornford, I., & Athanasou, J. (1995). Developing expertise through training. *Industrial and Commericial Training, 27*(2), 10.

Crandall, B., & Calderwood, R. (1989). *Clinical assessment skills of experienced neonatal intensive care nurses.* Yellow Springs, OH: Klein Associates.

Crandall, B., Klein, G., & Hoffman, R. R. (2006). *Working minds: A practitioner's guide to cognitive task analysis.* Cambridge, MA: MIT Press.

Dacey, R., & Carlson, L. J. (2004). Traditional decision analysis and the poliheuristic theory of foreign policy decision making. *Journal of Conflict Resolution, 48*(1), 38–55.

Day, D. V., Gronn, P., & Salas, E. (2004). Leadership capacity in teams. *Leadership Quarterly, 15*(6), 857–880.

de Groot, A. ([1946] 1978). *Thought and choice in chess* (2nd ed.). The Hague: Mouton De Gruyter.

Devine, D. J., & Kozlowski, S. W. J. (1995). Domain-specific knowledge and task characteristics in decision making. *Organizational Behavior and Human Decision Processes, 64*(3), 294–306.

Doyle, J. (1999). Bounded rationality. In R. A. Wilson & F. C. Keil (Eds.), *The MIT encycolpedia of the cognitive sciences* (pp. 92–93). Cambridge, MA: The MIT Press.

Dreyfus, H. L., & Dreyfus, S. E. (1986). *Mind over machine: The power of human intuition and expertise in the era of the computer.* New York: The Free Press.

Driskell, J. E., & Salas, E. (1992). Collective behavior and team performance. *Human Factors, 34*(3), 277–288.

Eccles, D. W., & Feltovich, P. J. (2008). Implications of domain-general psychological support skills for transfer of skill and acquisition of expertise. *Performance Improvement Quarterly, 21*(1), 43–60.

Edmondson, A. C. (1999). Psychological safety and learning behavior in work teams. *Administrative Science Quarterly, 44*, 350–383.

Edmondson, A. C., Bohmer, R. M., & Pisano, G. P. (2001). Disrupted routines: Team learning and new technology implementation in hospitals. *Administrative Science Quarterly, 46*(4), 685–716.

Eisenstat, R. A., & Cohen, S. G. (1990). Summary: Top management groups. In J. R. Hackman (Ed.), *Groups that work (and those that don't): Creating conditions for effective teamwork* (pp. 78–86). San Francisco: Jossey-Bass.

Endsley, M. R. (1997). The role of situation awareness in naturalistic decision making. In C. E. Zsambok, & G. Klein (Eds.), *Naturalisitc decision making*. Hillsdale, NJ: Erlbaum.

Engestrom, Y., & Middleton, D. (1998). Introduction: Studying work as mindful practice. In Y. Engestrom & D. Middleton (Eds.), *Cognition and communication at work* (pp. 1–14). Cambridge, UK: Cambridge University Press.

Ericsson, K. A. (1998). The scientific study of expert levels of performance: General implications for optimal learning and creativity. *High Ability Studies, 9*(1), 75–100.

Ericsson, K. A. (2004). Deliberate practice and the acquisition and maintenance of expert performance in medicine and related domains. *Academic Medicine, 79*(10), S70-S81.

Ericsson, K. A., & Charness, N. (1994). Expert performance: Its structure and acquisition. *American Psychologist, 49*(8), 725–747.

Ericsson, K. A., Krampe, R. T., & Tesch-Romer, C. (1993). The role of deliberate practice in the acquisition of expert performance. *Psychological Review, 100*(3), 363–406.

Ericsson, K. A., & Lehmann, A. C. (1996). Expert and exceptional performance: Evidence of maximal adaptation to task constraints. *Annual Review of Psychology, 47*, 273–305.

Ericsson, K. A., & Simon, H. A. (1993). *Protocol analysis: Verbal reports as data* (Rev. ed.). Cambridge, MA: MIT Press.

Ericsson, K. A., & Smith, J. (Eds.). (1991). *Toward a general theory of expertise: Prospects and limits*. Cambridge, UK: Cambridge University Press.

Evetts, J., Mieg, H. A., & Felt, U. (2006). *Professionalization, scientific expertise, and elitism: A sociological perspective*. New York: Cambridge University Press.

Feltovich, P. J., Johnson, P. E., Moller, J. H., & Swanson, L. C. S. (1984). The role and development of medical knowledge in diagnostic expertise. In W. J. Clancey, & E. H. Shortliffe (Eds.), *Readings in medical artificial intelligence* (pp. 275–319). Reading, MA: Addison-Wesley.

Feltovich, P. J., Prietula, M. J., & Ericsson, K. A. (2006). Studies of expertise from psychological perspectives. In K. A. Ericsson, N. Charness, P. J. Feltovich, & R. R. Hoffman (Eds.), *Cambridge handbook of expertise and expert performance* (pp. 41–67). New York: Cambridge University Press.

Feltovich, P. J., Spiro, R. J., & Coulson, R. L. (1997). Issues of expert flexibility in contexts characterized by complexity and change. In P. J. Fletovich, K. M. Ford, & R. R. Hoffman (Eds.), *Expertise in context* (pp. 125–146). Menlo Park, CA: The AAAI Press/MIT Press.

Fiore, S. M., Smith-Jentsch, K. A., Salas, E., Warner, N., & Letsky, M. (2010). Macrocognition in teams: Developing and defining complex collaborative processes and products. *Theoretical Issues in Ergonomics Science, 11*(4), 250–271.

Fitts, P. M., & Posner, M. I. (1967). *Human performance*. Monterrey, CA: Brooks Cole.

Flach, J. (2000). Discovering situated meaning: An ecological approach to task analysis. In J. M. Schraagen, S. F. Chipman, & V. L. Shalin (Eds.), *Cognitive task analysis* (pp. 87–100). Mahwah, NJ: Erlbaum.

Flavell, J. H. (1979). Metacognition and cognitive monitoring: A new area of cognitive-development inquiry. *American Psychologist, 34*(10), 906–911.

Fleming, P. J., Wood, G. M., Dudley, N. M., Bader, P. K., & Zaccaro, S. J. (2003, April). An adaptation training program for military leaders and teams. In E. D. Pulakos (Chair), *Mission critical: Developing adaptive performance in U.S. Army Special Forces*. Symposium conducted at the 18th annual conference of the Society for Industrial and Organizational Psychology, Orlando, Florida.

Ford, J. K., Schmitt, N., Schechtman, S. L., Hults, B. M., & Doherty, M. L. (1989). Process tracing methods: Contributions, problems, and neglected research questions. *Organizational Behavior and Human Decision Processes, 43*(1), 75.

Gardner, G. H. (1983). The psychology of career consciousness: Temporal experience and leisure decision-making attitudes. Ph.D. dissertation, Kent State University. *Dissertation Abstracts International*, 8400968.

Gibson, C. B. (2003). The efficacy advantage: Factors related to the formation of group efficacy. *Journal of Applied Social Psychology, 33*(10), 2153–2186.

Gigerenzer, G. (1996). On narrow norms and vague heuristics: A reply to Kahneman and Tversky (1996). *Psychological Review, 103*(3), 592–596.

Gigerenzer, G., & Kurz, E. (2001). Vicarious functioning reconsidered: A fast and frugal lens model. In K. R. Hammond & T. R. Stewart (Eds.), *The essential Brunswik: Beginnings, explications, applications* (pp. 342–347). New York: Oxford University Press.

Gigerenzer, G., & Selten, R. (Eds.). (2001). *Bounded rationality: The adaptive toolbox*. Cambridge, MA: The MIT Press.

Gigerenzer, G., Todd, P. M., & Group, T. A. R. (1999). *Simple heuristics that make us smart*. Oxford: Oxford University Press.

Gladwell, M. (2005). *Blink: The power of thinking without thinking*. New York: Little, Brown.

Gobet, F. (1997). A pattern-recognition theory of search in expert problem solving. *Thinking and Reasoning, 3*(4), 291–313.

Gordon, S. E., & Gill, R. T. (1997). *Cognitive task analysis*. Hillsdale, NJ: Erlbaum.

Groopman, J. (2007). *How doctors think*. New York: Houghton Mifflin Company.

Hammond, K. R. (1996). *Human judgment and social policy: Irreducible uncertainty, inevitable error, unavoidable injustice*. New York: Oxford University Press.

Hammond, K. R., & Stewart, T. R. (2001). *The essential Brunswik: Beginnings, explications, applications*. New York: Oxford University Press.

Hatano, G., & Inagaki, K. (1986). Two courses of expertise. In H. W. Stevenson & H. Azuma (Eds.), *Child development and education in Japan* (pp. 262–272). New York: W. H. Freeman.

Hays, R. T., & Singer, M. J. (1989). *Simulation fidelity in training system design*. New York: Springer-Verlag.

Head, F. A., Reiman, A. J., & Thies-Sprinthall, L. (1992). The reality of mentoring: Complexity in its process and function. In T. M. Bey & C. T. Holmes (Eds.), *Mentoring: Contemporary principles and issues* (pp. 5–24). Reston, VA: Association of Teachers Educators.

Henderson, S. (2008). Macrocognition and experimental learning in surgical teams. In J. M. Schraagen, L. G. Militello, T. Ormerod, & R. Lipshitz (Eds.), *Naturalistic decision making and macrocognition* (pp. 221–250). Aldershot, UK: Ashgate.

Hinsz, V. B., Tindale, R. S., & Vollrath, D. A. (1997). The emerging conceptualization of groups as information processors. *Psychological Bulletin, 121*(1), 43–64.

Hodgkinson, G. P., Langan-Fox, J., & Sadler-Smith, E. (2008). Intuition: A fundamental bridging construct in the behavioral sciences. *British Journal of Psychology, 99*(1), 1–27.

Hoffman, R. R. (Ed.). (2007). *Expertise out of context*. Mahwah, NJ: Erlbaum.

Hoffman, R. R., & Lintern, G. (2006). *Eliciting and representing the knowledge of experts*. New York: Cambridge University Press.

Hoffman, R. R., & Militello, L. G. (2009). *Perspectives on cognitive task analysis*. New York: Psychology Press.

Hoffman, R. R., Shadbolt, N. R., Burton, A. M., & Klein, G. (1995). Eliciting knowledge from experts: A methodological analysis. *Organizational Behavior and Human Decision Processes, 62*, 128–158.

Hogarth, R. M. (2001). *Educating intuition*. Chicago: University of Chicago Press.

Hollan, J., H., Hutchins, E., & Kirsh, D. (1999). Distributed cognition: A new foundation for human-computer interaction research. *ACM Transactions on Human-Computer Interaction: Special Issue on Human-Computer Interaction in the New Millennium, 7*, 174–196.

Hollenbeck, J. R., Ilgen, D. R., Sego, D. J., Hedlund, J., Major, D. A., & Phillips, J. (1995). Multilevel theory of team decision making: Decision performance in teams incorporating distributed expertise. *Journal of Applied Psychology, 80*(2), 292–316.

Hollnagel, E., Woods, D. D., & Levenson, N. (Eds.). (2006). *Resilience engineering: Concepts and precepts*. Aldershot, UK: Ashgate.

Holyoak, K. J. (1991). Symbolic connectionism: Toward third-generation theories of expertise. In K. A. Ericsson & J. Smith (Eds.), *Toward a general theory of expertise: Prospects and limits* (pp. 301–335). Cambridge, UK: Cambridge University Press.

Hunt, D. M., & Michael, C. (1983). Mentorship: A career training and development tool. *Academy of Management Review, 8*(3), 475–485.

Hutchins, E. (1995). *Cognition in the wild*. Cambridge, MA: The MIT Press.

Hutchins, E. (1996). Learning to navigate. In S. Chaiklin & J. Lave (Eds.), *Understanding practice: Perspectives on activity and context* (pp. 35–63). Cambridge, UK: Cambridge University Press.

Hutchins, E., & Klausen, T. (1996). Distributed cognition in an airline cockpit. In Y. Engestrom & D. Middleton (Eds.), *Cognition and communication at work* (pp. 15–34). Cambridge, UK: Cambridge University Press.

Inzana, C. M., Driskell, J. E., Salas, E., & Johnston, J. H. (1996). Effects of preparatory information on enhancing performance under stress. *Journal of Applied Psychology, 81*(4), 429–435.

Johnson-Laird, P. N. (1983). *Mental models: Towards a cognitive science of language, inference, and consciousness*. Cambridge, MA: Harvard University Press.

Kahneman, D., Slovic, P., & Tversky, A. (1982). *Judgment under uncertainty: Heuristics and biases*. New York: Cambridge University Press.

Keller, J. W., & Yang, Y. E. (2008). Leadership style, decision context, and the Poliheuristic theory of decision making: An experimental analysis. *Journal of Conflict Resolution, 52*(2), 687–712.

Kirlik, A. (2006). Introduction. In A. Kirlik (Ed.), *Adaptive perspectives on human-technology interaction: Methods and models for cognitive engineering and human-computer interaction* (pp. 89–90). Oxford: Oxford University Press.

Kirschenbaum, S. S., Trafton, J. G., & Pratt, E. (2007). Comparative cognitive task analysis. In R. Hoffman (Ed.), *Expertise out of context: Proceedings of the sixth International Conference on Naturalistic Decision Making* (pp. 327–336). Mahwah, NJ: Erlbaum.

Klein, G. A. (1993). A recognition-primed decision (RPD) model of rapid decision making. In G. A. Klein, & J. Orasanu (Eds.), *Decision making in action: Models and methods* (pp. 138–147). Westport, CT: Ablex.

Klein, G. A. (1997). The current status of naturalistic decision making framework. In E. S. R. Flin, M. E. Strub, & L. Martin (Eds.), *Decision making under stress: Emerging themes and applications* (pp. 11–28). Aldershot, UK: Ashgate.

Klein, G. A. (1998). *Sources of power: How people make decisions*. Cambridge, MA: MIT Press.

Klein, G. A., Calderwood, R., & MacGregor, D. (1989). Critical decision method for eliciting knowledge. *IEEE Transactions on Systems, Man, and Cybernetics, 19*(3), 462–472. Klein, G. A., & Militello, L. (2001). Some guidelines for conducting a cognitive task analysis. In: E. Salas (Ed.), *Advances in Human Performance and Cognitive Engineering Research* (pp. 163–197). New York: JAI Press.

Klein, G. A., Orasanu, J., Calderwood, R., & Zsambok, C. E. (1993). *Decision making in action*. Norwood, NJ: Ablex.

Klein, G. A., & Pierce, L. (2001). *Adaptive teams*. Paper presented at the Proceedings of the Sixth ICCRTS Collaboration in the Information Age Track 4: C2 Decision Making and Cognitive Analysis.

Klein, G. A., Ross, K. G., Moon, B. M., Klein, D. E., Hoffman, R. R., & Hollnagel, E. (2003). Macrocognition. *IEEE Intelligent Systems, 18*(3), 81–85.

Klimoski, R. J., & Mohammed, S. (1994). Team mental model: Construct or metaphor? *Journal of Management, 20*, 403–437.

Kozlowski, S. W. J. (1998). *Training and developing adaptive teams: Theory, principles, and research*. Washington, DC: American Psychological Association.

Kozlowski, S. W. J., & Bell, B. S. (2003). Work groups and teams in organizations. In W. C. Borman & D. R. Ilgen (Eds.), *Handbook of psychology: Industrial and organizational psychology* (Vol. 12, pp. 333–375). New York: John Wiley & Sons.

Kozlowski, S. W. J., & Bell, B. S. (2008). Team learning, development, and adaptation. In V. I. Sessa & M. London (Eds.), *Group learning* (pp. 15–44). Mahwah, NJ: Erlbaum.

Kozlowski, S. W. J., Gully, S. M., Salas, E., & Cannon-Bowers, J. A. (1996). *Team leadership and development: Theory, principles, and guidelines for training leaders and teams*. Greenwich, CT; JAI Press.

Kozlowski, S. W. J., Gully, S. M., McHugh, P. P., Salas, E., & Cannon-Bowers, J. A. (1996). A dynamic theory of leadership and team effectiveness; Developmental and task contingent leader roles. In G. R. Ferris (Ed.), *Research and personnel and human resources management* (Vol. 14, pp. 253–305). Greenwich, CT; JAI Press.

Kozlowski, S. W. J., Gully, S. M., Nason, E. R., & Smith, E. M. (1999). Developing adaptive teams: A theory of compilation and performance across levels and time. In D. R. Ilgen & E. D. Pulakos (Eds.), *The changing nature of work* and performance: Implications for staffing personnel actions and development (pp. 240–292). San Francisco: Jossey-Bass.

Kozlowski, S.W.J., Toney, R.J., Mullins, M.E., Weissbein, D.A., Brown, K.G., & Bell, B.S. (2001). Developing adaptability: A theory for the design of integrated-embedded training systems. In E. Salas (Ed.), Advances in human performance and cognitive engineering research (Vol. 1, pp. 59–123). Amsterdam: JAI/Elsevier Science.

Krampe, R. T., & Ericsson, K. A. (1996). Maintaining excellence: Deliberate practice and elite performance in young and older pianists. *Journal of Experimental Psychology: General, 125*(4), 331–359.

Leonard-Barton, D., & Deschamps, I. (1988). Managerial influence in the implementation of new technology. *Management Science, 34*(10), 1252–1265.

LePine, J. A. (2003). Team adaptation and postchange performance: Effects of team composition in terms of members' cognitive ability and personality. *Journal of Applied Psychology, 88*(1), 27–39.

Letsky, M. P., Warner, N., Fiore, S., & Smith, C. A. P. (2008). *Macrocognition in complex team problem solving.* Paper presented at the 12th National Command and Control Research and Technology Symposium, Washington, DC.

Levine, J. M., & Moreland, R. L. (1999). *Knowledge transmission in work groups: Helping newcomers to succeed.* Mahwah, NJ: Erlbaum.

Lieberman, M. D. (2000). Intuition: A social cognitive neuroscience approach. *Psychological Bulletin, 126*(1), 109–137.

Lipshitz, R. (2005). There is more to seeing than meets the eyeball: The art and science of observation. In H. Montgomery, R. Lipshitz, & B. Brehmer (Eds.), *How professionals make decisions* (pp. 365–378). Mahwah, NJ: Erlbaum.

Lipshitz, R., Klein, G., & Carroll, J. S. (2006). Naturalistic decision making and organizational decision making: Exploring the intersections. *Organization Studies, 27*(7), 917–923.

Lipshitz, R., Klein, G., Orasanu, J., & Salas, E. (2001a). Rejoinder: A welcome dialogue—and the need to continue. *Journal of Behavioral Decision Making, 14,* 385–389.

Lipshitz, R., Klein, G., Orasanu, J., & Salas, E. (2001b). Taking stock of naturalistic decision making. *Journal of Behavioral Decision Making, 14*(5), 331–352.

Mann, L., Beswick, G., Allouache, P., & Ivey, M. (1989). Decision workshops for the improvement of decision-making skills and confidence. *Journal of Counseling & Development, 67*(8), 478–481.

March, J. G., & Simon, H. A. (1958). *Organizations.* New York: Wiley.

Mieg, H. A. (2001). *The social psychology of expertise: Case studies in research, professional domains, and expert roles.* Mahwah, NJ: Erlbaum.

Miller, G. A. (1956). The magical number seven, plus or minus two: Some limits on our capacity for processing information. *Psychological Review, 63,* 81–97.

Militello, L., & Hutton, R. J. B. (1998). Applied cognitive task analysis: A practitioner's toolkit for understanding cognitive task demands. *Ergonomics, 41,* 1618–1641.

Mintz, A. (1993). The decision to attack Iraq: A noncompensatory theory of decision making. *Journal of Conflict Resolution, 37*(4), 595–618.

Mintz, A. (2003). The method-of-analysis problem in international relations. Photocopy, United Nations Studies, Yale University.

Mintz, A. (2004). How do leaders make decisions?: A poliheuristic perspective. *Journal of Conflict Resolution, 48*(1), 3–13.

Mitchell, T. R., Rediker, K., & Beach, L. R. (1986). *Image theory and its implications for policy and strategic decision making.* San Francisco: Jossey-Bass.

Mohammed, S., & Dumville, B. C. (2001). Team mental models in a team knowledge framework: Expanding theory and measure across disciplinary boundaries. *Journal of Organizational Behavior, 22*(2), 89–103.

Montgomery, H., LIpshitz, R., & Brehmer, B. (2005). *How professionals make decisions.* Mahwah, NJ: Erlbaum.

Moors, A., & De Houwer, J. (2006). Automaticity: A theoretical and conceptual analysis. *Psychological Bulletin, 132*(2), 297–326.

Newell, A., & Simon, H. A. (1972). *Human problem solving.* Englewood Cliffs, NJ: Prentice-Hall.

Orasanu, J., & Connolly, T. (1993). The reinvention of decision making. In G. A. Klein, J. Orasanu, R. Calderwood, & C. E. Zsambok (Eds.), *Decision making in action: Models and methods* (pp. 3–20). Norwood, CT: Ablex.

Orlikowski, W. J., & Hofman, J. D. (1997). An improvisational model of change management: The case of groupware technologies. *Sloan Management Review, 38*(2), 11–21.

Perry, M. (2003). Distributed cognition. In J. M. Carroll (Ed.), *HCI models, theories, and frameworks: Toward an interdisciplinary science* (pp. 193–223). San Francisco: Morgan Kaufmann.

Potter, R. E., & Beach, L. R. (1994). Decision making when the acceptable options become unavailable. *Organizational Behavior and Human Decision Processes, 57,* 468–483.

Pounds, J. F., & Fallesen, J. F. (1994). *Understanding problem solving strategies.* (Army Research Institute Rep. No. 1020). Alexandria, VA: U.S. Army Research Institute for the Behavioral and Social Sciences.

Pulakos, E. D., Arad, S., Donovan, M. A., & Plamondon, K. E. (2000). Adaptability in the workplace: Development of a taxonomy of adaptive performance. *Journal of Applied Psychology, 85*(4), 612–624.

Randel, J. M., Pugh, H. L., & Reed, S. K. (1996). Differences in expert and novice situation awareness in naturalistic decision making. *International Journal of Human-Computer Studies, 45*(5), 579–597.

Rediker, K. J., Mitchell, T. R., Beach, L. R., & Beard, D. W. (1993). The effects of strong belief structures on information-processing evaluations and choice. *Journal of Behavioral Decision Making, 6*(2), 113–132.

Rosen, M. A., Fiore, S., & Salas, E. (2009). *Managing uncertainty in macrocognition: A multidisciplinary review and integration.* Paper presented at the 9th International Conference on Naturalistic Decision Making, London.

Rosen, M. A., Salas, E., Lyons, R., & Fiore, S. (2008). Expertise and naturalistic decision making in organizations: Mechanisms of effective decision making. In G. P. Hodgkinson & W. H. Starbuck (Eds.), *The Oxford handbook of organizational decision making* (pp. 211–230). Oxford: Oxford University Press.

Rosen, M. A., Salas, E., Lazzara, E. H., & Lyons, R. (in press). Cognitive task analysis: Methods for capturing and leveraging expertise in the workplace. In W. Bennett, G. M. Alliger, W. J. Strickland, & J. L. Mitchell (Eds.), *Job analysis: Studying the world of work in the 21st century.*

Ross, K. G., Lussier, J. W., & Klein, G. (2005). *From the recognition primed decision model to training*. Mahwah, NJ: Erlbaum.

Ross, K. G., Shafer, J. L., & Klein, G. (2006). Professional judgment and naturalistic decision making. In K. A. Ericsson, N. Charness, P. J. Feltovich, & R. R. Hoffman (Eds.), *The Cambridge handbook of expertise and expert performance* (pp. 403–419). Cambridge, UK: Cambridge University Press.

Salas, E., Burke, C. S. & Stagl, K. C. (2004). Developing teams and team leaders: Strategies and principles. In D. Day, S. J. Zaccaro, & S. M. Halpin (Eds.), *Leader development for transforming organizations: Growing leaders for tomorrow* (pp. 325–355). Mahwah, NJ: Erlbaum.

Salas, E., & Fiore, S. M. (Eds.). (2004). *Team cognition*. Washington, DC: American Psychological Association.

Salas, E., Guthrie, J., & Burke, S. (2007). *Why training team decision making is not as easy as you think: Guiding principles and needs*. Aldershot, UK: Ashgate.

Salas, E., & Klein, G. (Eds.). (2001). *Linking expertise and naturalisitc decision making*. Mahwah, NJ: Erlbaum.

Salas, E., & Rosen, M. A. (2010). Experts at work: Principles developing expertise in organizations. In S. W. J. Kozlowski, & E. Salas (Eds.), *Learning, training, and development in organizations*. Mahwah, NJ: Erlbaum.

Salas, E., Rosen, M. A., Burke, C. S., Goodwin, G. F., & Fiore, S. (2006). The making of a dream team: When expert teams do best. In K. A. Ericsson, N. Charness, P. J. Feltovich, & R. R. Hoffman (Eds.), *The Cambridge handbook of expertise and expert performance* (pp. 439–453). New York: Cambridge University Press.

Salas, E., Rosen, M. A., Burke, C. S., Nicholson, D., & Howse, W. R. (2007). Markers for enhancing team cognition in complex environments: The power of team performance diagnosis. *Aviation, Space, and Environmental Medicine Special Supplement on Operational Applications of Cognitive Performance Enhancement Technologies, 78*(5), B77–85.

Salas, E., Rosen, M. A., & DiazGranados, D. (2010). Expertise-based intuition and decision making in organizations. *Journal of Management, 36*, 941–973.

Salomon, G. (Ed.). (1993). *Distributed cognitions: Psychological and educational considerations*. Cambridge, UK: Cambridge University Press.

Savage, L. J. (1954). *The foundations of statistics*. New York: Wiley.

Schneider, W. & Shiffrin, R. M. (1977). Controlled and automatic human information processing: I. Detection, search, and attention. *Psychological Review, 84*(1), 1–66.

Schraagen, J. M., Militello, L. G., Ormerod, T., & Lipshitz, R. (Eds.). (2008). *Naturalistic decision making and macrocognition*. Aldershot, UK: Ashgate.

Schunn, C. D., McGregor, M. U., & Saner, L. D. (2005). Expertise in ill-defined problem-solving domains as effective strategy use. *Memory and Cognition, 33*(8), 1377–1387.

Serfaty, D., MacMillan, J., & Deckert, J. C. (1991). *Toward a theory of tactical decision making expertise* (Tech. Rep. No. 496-1). Burlington, MA: Alphatech, Inc.

Serfaty, D., MacMillan, J., Entin, E. E., & Entin, E. B. (1997). The decision-making expertise of battle commanders, In C. Zsambok & G. Klein (Eds.), *Naturalistic decision making* (pp. 233–246). Mahwah, NJ: Erlbaum.

Serfaty, D., & Michel, R. R. (1990). Toward a theory of tactical decision making expertise. *Proceedings of the 1990 symposium on Command and Control Research*. Naval Postgraduate School: Monterrey, CA.

Shanteau, J. (1992). Competence in experts: The role of task characteristics. *Organizational Behavior and Human Decision Processes, 53*, 252–266.

Shepherd, A., & Stammers, R. B. (2005). *Evaluation of human work: A practical ergonomics methodology*. Boca Raton, FL: CRC Press.

Sloman, S. (2002). Two systems of reasoning. In T. Gilovich, D. Griffin, & D. Kahneman (Eds.), *Heuristics and biases: The psychology of intuitive judgment* (pp. 379–396). New York: Cambridge University Press.

Smith, E. M., Ford, J. K., & Kozlowski, S. W. J. (1997). Building adaptive expertise: Implications for training design strategies. In M. A. Quiñones & A. Ehrenstein (Eds.), *Training for a rapidly changing workplace: Applications of psychological research* (pp. 89–118). Washington, DC: American Psychological Association.

Smith-Jentsch, K. A., Cannon-Bowers, J. A., Tannenbaum, S. I., & Salas, I. (2008). Guided team self-correction: Impacts on team mental models, processes, and effectiveness. *Small Group Research, 39*(3), 303–327.

Smith-Jentsch, K. A., Johnston, J. A., & Payne, S. C. (1998). Measuring team-related expertise in complex environments. In J. A. Cannon-Bowers & E. Salas (Eds.), *Making decisions under stress: Implications for individual and team training* (pp. 61–87). Washington, DC: American Psychological Association.

Smith-Jentsch, K. A., Zeisig, R. L., Acton, B., & McPherson, J. A. (1998). Team dimensional training: A strategy for guided team self-correction. In J. A. Cannon-Bowers & E. Salas (Eds.), *Making decisions under stress: Implications for individual and team training* (pp. 271–297). Washington, DC: American Psychological Association.

Stanovich, K. E., & Cunningham, A. E. (1992). Studying the consequences of literacy within a literate society: The cognitive correlates of print exposure. *Memory & Cognition, 20*(1), 51–68.

Stanovich, K. E., & Cunningham, A. E. (1993). Where does knowledge come from? Specific associations between print exposure and information acquisition. *Journal of Educational Psychology, 85*(2), 211–229.

Stein, E. W. (1997). A look at expertise from a social perspective. In P. J. Feltovich, K. M. Ford, & R. R. Hoffman (Eds.), *Expertise in context* (pp. 181–194). Menlo Park, CA: AAAI Press/MIT Press.

Sternberg, R. J. (1997). Cognitive conceptions of expertise. In P. J. Fletovich, K. M. Ford, & R. R. Hoffman (Eds.), *Expertise in context* (pp. 149–162). Menlo Park, CA: AAAI Press/MIT Press.

Sternberg, R. J., & Frensch, P. A. (1991). On being an expert: A cost-benefit analysis. In R. R. Hoffman (Ed.), *The psychology of expertise: Cognitive research and empirical AI* (pp. 191–203). Mahwah, NJ: Erlbaum.

Stout, R. J., Cannon-Bowers, J. A., & Salas, E. (1996). The role of shared mental models in developing team situational awareness: Implications for training. *Training Research Journal, 2*, 85–116.

Tannenbaum, S. I., Smith-Jentsch, K. A., & Behson, S. J. (1998). Training team leaders to facilitate team learning and performance. In J. A. Cannon-Bowers, & E. Salas (Eds.), *Making decisions under stress: Implications for individual and team training* (pp. 247–270). Washington, DC: American Psychological Association.

Tichy, N., & Bennis, W. (November 19, 2007). Judgment: How winning leaders make great calls. *Businessweek, 4059*, 68–72.

Todd, P. M., & Gigerenzer, G. (2001). Putting naturalistic decision making into the adaptive toolbox. *Journal of Behavioral Decision Making, 14*, 353–384.

Tolman, E. C., & Brunswik, E. (1935). The organism and the causal texture of the environment. *Psychological Review, 42*(1), 43–77.

Tubbs, M. E., & Eckeberg, S. E. (1991). The role of intentions in work motivation: Implications for goal-setting theory and research. *Academy of Management Review, 16*(1), 180–199.

Veenman, M. V. J., Elshout, J. J., & Meijer, J. (1997). The generality vs domain-specificity of metacognitive skills in novice learning across domains. *Learning and Instruction, 7*(2), 187–209.

Vicente, K. J. (1999). *Cognitive work analysis: Toward safe, productive, and healthy computer-based work.* Mahwah, NJ: Erlbaum.

von Neumann, J., & Morgenstern, O. (1947). *Theory of games and economic behavior* (2nd rev. ed.). Princeton: Princeton University Press.

Ward, P., Williams, A. M., & Hancock, P. A. (2006). Simulation for performance and training. In K. A. Ericsson, N. Charness, P. J. Feltovich & R. R. Hoffman (Eds.), *The Cambridge handbook of expertise and expert performance* (pp. 243–262). Cambridge, UK: Cambridge University Press.

Wehrenberg, S. B. (1987). Supervisors as trainers: The long-term gains of OJT. *Personnel Journal, 66*(4), 48–51.

Weiss, D. J., & Shanteau, J. (2003). Empirical assessment of expertise. *Human factors, 45*(1), 104–114.

Wilson, J. M., Goodman, P. S., & Cronin, M. A. (2007). Group learning. *Academy of Management Review, 32*(4), 1041–1059.

Wilson, K. A., Salas, E., Priest, H. A., & Andrews, D. (2007). Errors in the heat of battle: Taking a closer look at shared cognition breakdowns through teamwork. *Human Factors, 49*(2), 243–256.

Winner, E. (1996). The rage to master: The decisive role of talent in the visual arts. In K. Ericsson (Ed.), *The road to excellence: The acquisition of expert performance in the arts and sciences, sports and games* (pp. 271–301). Mahwah, NJ: Erlbaum.

Yates, J. F., & Estin, P. (1996). *Training good judgment.* Proceedings of the paper presented at the annual meetings of the Society for Judgment and Decision Making, Chicago.

Zaccaro, S. J., Rittman, A. L., & Marks, M. A. (2001). Team leadership. *Leadership Quarterly, 12*, 451–483.

Zeitz, C. M. (1997). Some concrete advantages of abstraction: How experts' representations facilitate reasoning. In P. J. Feltovich, K. M. Ford, & R. R. Hoffman (Eds.), *Expertise in context* (pp. 43–65). Menlo Park, CA: AAAI Press/MIT Press.

Zhang, J. J. (1997). The nature of external representations in problem solving. *Cognitive Science, 21*, 179–217.

Zhang, J. J., & Norman, D. A. (1994). Representations in distributed cognitive tasks. *Cognitive Science: A Multidisciplinary Journal, 18*(1), 87–122.

Zimmerman, B. J. (2006). Development and adaptation of expertise: The role of self-regulatory processes and beliefs. In K. A. Ericsson, N. Charness, P. J. Feltovich, & R. R. Hoffman (Eds.), *The Cambridge handbook of expertise and expert performance* (pp. 705–722). New York: Cambridge University Press.

Zsambok, C. E. (1997). Naturalisitc decision making: Where are we now? In C. E. Zsambok & G. Klein (Eds.), *Naturalistic decision making* (pp. 3–16). Mahwah, NJ: Erlbaum.

Postscript

On the Horizon

Steve W. J. Kozlowski

Abstract

The collection of chapters in this handbook document the evolution of industrial and organizational (I/O) psychology as a science and practice, our foundational methods for generating knowledge, and the broad range of actionable knowledge created by our science that can be applied to enrich employee well-being and to enhance the effectiveness of individuals, teams, and organizations. Each of the chapters provides an agenda for continued scientific progress and evidence to support practical applications. In that sense, the future of I/O psychology is solid. In this closing chapter, I advocate four desirable evolutionary themes that I believe would enhance the potential, relevance, and impact of the field going forward. It should strengthen its scientific foundation, increase its multi- and interdisciplinary linkages, focus on multilevel system dynamics as core capabilities, and improve the translation of I/O psychological science into evidence-based practice.

Key Words: Future of I/O psychology, evolutionary themes, strengthen I/O science, improve inter-disciplinary linkages, focus on mulitlevel system dynamics, translate I/O psychological science

> Prediction is very difficult, especially if it's about the future.
> —*Niels Bohr*

Overview

The quote from Niels Bohr aptly frames the challenge of trying to anticipate what the future might hold for the field of industrial and organizational psychology (I/O) as we move deeper into the twenty-first century. If I imagine the vantage point of its early pioneers and think about what they might have predicted 25, 50, or even 100 years out, I wonder how well they would have projected how the field would develop, evolve, and mature across the span of the twentieth century. Would they have anticipated the influence on the development of the field of two world wars, the social movements for equal rights, the evolution of team-based work

systems, and the cultural interconnections sparked by globalization (among many others)? Doubtful, but it really does not matter. I do not intend to try to predict the future because there are too many unknowns that are likely to shape the continued evolution of work, organizations, and I/O psychology. It is the future generations of scientists and practitioners, and the events that shape their world, who will determine the nature of organizational psychology going forward.

On the other hand, if I think about how I would like to see the field develop, then reflecting on desirable evolutionary themes is much more tractable. So, I will take this opportunity in these brief concluding comments to suggest four evolutionary themes that I believe would help to strengthen the science and practice of organizational psychology, and enhance its relevance to society:

- Strengthen its scientific foundation;
- Increase its multi- and interdisciplinary linkages;
- Focus on multilevel system dynamics as core capabilities;
- Improve the translation of I/O psychological science into evidence-based practice.

Desirable Evolutionary Themes
STRENGTHEN THE SCIENTIFIC FOUNDATION OF I/O PSYCHOLOGY

I do not mean to imply that I/O psychology does not do good science—we do—but the science we do can be substantially improved. There are many ways in which we can strengthen our science. However, here I will briefly sketch three primary ways to address this issue: (a) expand our perspective, (b) conduct more systematic research, and (c) increase our connections to basic sciences. First, I/O psychology needs to expand its perspective beyond "the organization" to also engage in tackling big problems that span across systems and multiple organizations—problems that have broad societal impact. We have an aging population who will live longer and work longer. We need to be conducting research that will help society keep these high-knowledge and high-value employees working in productive, healthy, and fulfilling ways. Think about other challenging problems our society faces: delivering health care, pioneering new forms of renewable energy, stimulating innovation, fostering sustainability, and improving education, to name just a few. These problems are *not* organization-specific; they transcend single organizations and implicate much bigger *systems* of interconnected organizations, government agencies, and other key stakeholders. We need to *focus our science on big problems*, not just on problems in this or that organization.

Second, we need to do a better job of conducting research that is *systematic*, not just research that is *thematic*. Historically, much of the organizational psychology, human resource management (HRM), and organizational behavior (OB) research conducted within organizations is based on data collected within single organizational settings—an *n* of one organization. This makes it difficult for our science to capture contextual differences

across organizations and to think about problems more broadly across contexts. Yet, this is one place where organizational psychology should be developing research-based principles. Gaining access to organizational samples, which is difficult and often facilitated by entry for problem-solving, is a big contributor to this problem. In general, organizations do not support research per se. Rather, they want problems solved; often, some research can be accomplished while the problem is addressed. However, one consequence of this approach is that much research in I/O psychology, HRM, and OB is thematic rather than systematic. That is, investigators study a topic area—a theme—but the specifics of the research are often constrained and influenced by the negotiated access to the organizational sample. Over time with multiple studies, a collage of thematic findings may yield useful scientific knowledge about the topic area. Meta-analytic methods may be able to summarize what has been learned about the problem area and contingencies that influence basic relationships (if the primary studies allow). But focused, disciplined, and systematic research would get us there quicker and with more precision. We can build a stronger scientific foundation if organizations could be persuaded to support basic research that would be of broad interest, mutual benefit, and wide applicability; if organizational psychology and related disciplines pursued more federal funding to conduct systematic research on big problems; and if more researchers focused their efforts on fundamentally important problems.

Third, organizational psychology and related disciplines need to increase connections to more basic sciences. As an applied science, much of the important research that is conducted in organizational psychology is *translational*. That is, our research typically does not reveal the mechanisms of a basic psychological phenomenon; rather, we draw on the theoretical principles and research findings of basic psychological research and apply it to contextualized or situated problems in organizations. But the range of theory that we consider is somewhat restricted. Organizational psychology, HRM, and OB draw on social psychology to a large extent and on other basic sciences (psychological and otherwise) much less. This observation is not meant to suggest that there is something wrong with our reliance on social psychological principles. A substantial range of behavior at work is inherently social in nature. Rather, the point is that other basic sciences in psychology, such as cognitive, developmental, behavioral decision making, and even cognitive neuroscience, have the potential to enrich our theories, models, and applications. We need to *develop a broader scientific foundation in basic psychology*.

INCREASE MULTI- AND INTERDISCIPLINARY LINKAGES

I/O psychology has long had multidisciplinary linkages with related fields of study in management such as HRM (essentially "I" psychology), and OB (essentially "O" psychology), and, increasingly, organizational strategy. These are natural affiliations and, to some extent, reflect the ongoing migration of I/O psychologists to academic homes other than psychology departments. That is to be expected and will likely continue.[1] However, we draw on the same theories, share the same research interests, and possess essentially the same methodological knowledge and skills. This sort of "multidisciplinary" activity does not expand our theoretical perspective, methodologies, or research paradigms. Arguably, it is not truly multidisciplinary.

I advocate that I/O psychology should strengthen its connections with other applied, translational sciences that interface with organizations and complex systems, disciplines like human factors, cognitive engineering, and computer science. Moreover, relative to our sister disciplines in management, we are uniquely well suited to make and leverage these connections. We have a common foundation in psychological science and methods; we interface well around systems phenomena of common interest. Furthermore, we should also link with other disciplines that transcend psychology. The big problems highlighted previously also implicate the fields of communications, education, engineering, and medicine. We have unique capabilities, but so, too, do these other fields. Related to point two, there is a real push in the United States to focus on strengthening science, technology, engineering, and math (STEM sciences). Psychology is not currently viewed by the federal government as a STEM science, and the field is working to shift that policy perspective. Arguably, organizational psychology is uniquely well suited to help create the organizational supports to help foster interdisciplinary research across the STEM sciences, but currently we are not involved in a meaningful way. Regardless, big societal problems cannot be addressed by single disciplines. I/O psychology has a tendency to be insular and it needs to better link with other disciplines so we can better leverage our unique capabilities.

FOCUS ON MULTILEVEL SYSTEM DYNAMICS AS CORE CAPABILITIES

In the opening chapter of this handbook, I made a case for multilevel systems, teams, and dynamic phenomena as trends that have emerged in organizational psychology over the last couple of decades or so. I think that research that incorporates multilevel theory and/or focuses on team effectiveness are well represented in mainstream research published in top journals. The focus on dynamic phenomena is more nascent, but it is an important—I would argue critical—aspect of enhancing our unique capabilities. In that sense, rather than just trends, I think the field of organizational psychology—and our sister disciplines of HRM, OB, and labor and industrial relations (LIR)—should focus graduate training on strengthening theory, methods paradigms, and analytics to make these our core research capabilities.

We are doing fine, but we could do much better. Too much of our science is based on cross-sectional (i.e., static design) survey data (i.e., self-reported, retrospective perceptions, attitudes, affect, etc.) collected in single organizations. This is a well used and, yes, very useful approach to gain an understanding of human behavior and performance in the workplace. But, it is just one approach, and it does come with significant limitations. I think that I/O psychology should focus on tackling big problems that encompass human cognition; work motivation, affect, and behavior—and individual, team, and higher level performance—in complex, technology-enabled, organizational, and trans-organizational systems. Aside from the multilevel aspects of such a focus, it necessitates attention to cognitive, motivational-affective, and behavioral dynamics; we are not going to get meaningful dynamic data by just relying on retrospective self-reports to questionnaires. We need to be more creative and resourceful.

For example, I conduct much of my research (e.g., individual and team learning, decision making, and performance) using computer-based laboratory simulations. I will not recite all the advantages and disadvantages of this type of paradigm, but I will highlight two key advantages. We are able to collect precise behavioral indicators of basic psychological constructs, rather than relying *solely* on self-reports. And, we capture dynamic processes. Over restricted time frames, yes, but within a meaningful chunk of activity we create a movie, not just a snapshot, of the phenomena of interest. We can examine dynamics.

How is this relevant to field research? Computer technology is penetrating all aspects of the workplace. It is not everywhere yet, but it encompasses many jobs and interconnected work systems. Streams of behavioral data are being generated, collected, and retained on an increasing basis. Organizations—now—use such data to monitor employee behavior and performance. I recognize that such practices have Orwellian implications that have to be acknowledged…and monitored. But such data also have legitimate and potentially frame-breaking uses for scientific research—not just the commercial research that is already being conducted—that can be used to enhance human performance *and* employee well-being. Moreover, people have shown a willingness to use a wide range of social media to share extraordinary amounts of personal information about themselves, including ongoing, contextualized, self-reports (e.g., Twitter). There is potential to harness these technologies to create new research paradigms that can fuse dynamic behavioral, perceptual, and affective data to draw powerful and meaningful inferences about human performance in the workplace—and beyond. Organizational psychology should be on the cutting edge, exploring the frontier of these new paradigms for research.

IMPROVE THE TRANSLATION OF I/O PSYCHOLOGICAL SCIENCE INTO EVIDENCE-BASED PRACTICE

Finally, I close this set of thematic observations about improving the future of I/O psychology with an issue that represents an increasing challenge for the field. Many observers have noted what is often viewed as a growing gap between the science and practice of I/O psychology—two poles among many dialectal tensions. This one is particularly important, however, because it goes to our core identity (our birth, history, triumphs) as a translational, applied science. I am not going to review the observations about the nature of the gap, how big it is, why it exists, and so forth. I will just make a simple point that echoes what I asserted in the introductory chapter. I/O psychological science and practice need each other. As work and organizations evolve, new challenges and problems arise that provide gist for the mill of applied psychological science. Good translational science yields principles, tools, and techniques that are evidence-based. Evidence-based practice is what distinguishes I/O practice from the fads and outright frauds that populate the marketplace for consulting services aimed at organizations.

Anyone can be a consultant to organizations. Good I/O psychology practice is based on solid science. That is a major competitive advantage.

Nonetheless, we need to do a much better job of translating the findings of I/O science into knowledge that is useful, accessible, and actionable for enhancing practice. Some suggest that scientific journals should be more concerned about enhancing practical impact. As editor for the *Journal of Applied Psychology*, I can tell you that what publishes in top tier journals is oriented toward scientific contribution; translation is not going to get addressed in such journals because it falls outside the mission. On the other hand, specialized journals, periodicals, and books are good mechanisms for compiling findings, identifying what we know about a phenomenon, and pushing evidence closer to practical application.

I think it is also useful to bear in mind that the idealized model of the "scientist/practitioner" that is targeted at the individual level can be usefully generalized to the community level. That is, while not everyone in the field is a scientist/practitioner in the idealized sense, at the community level we have scientists who primarily conduct basic research, scientist/practitioners who are more centered in the translation process, and practitioners who primarily solve problems. The key is to do a better job of linking the end points of this community through problem- or topic-focused conferences, books, and specialized journals. We need to recognize that there is a range of translation activities as well, and there are many ways that we can each contribute to the translation process to strengthen the links between science and practice. It depends on everyone, but it does not depend on everyone fitting to the same "one size fits all" model.

Concluding Comments

I have no crystal ball that reveals what the future holds for I/O psychology as a science, area of scholarship in psychology, and a practice. The twentieth century provided many opportunities for the growth, development, and evolution of the field. As documented in the chapters of this handbook, organizational psychology—and our sister disciplines of HRM, OB, and strategy—have generated a wide array of actionable knowledge that can be applied to enrich employee well-being and to enhance the effectiveness of individuals, teams, and organizations. As we embark more deeply into the twenty-first century, I hope that organizational psychology as a field will become more visible and influential. To accomplish that, I have advocated that it should strengthen its scientific foundation, increase its multi- and interdisciplinary linkages, focus on multilevel system dynamics as core capabilities, and improve the translation of I/O psychological science into evidence-based practice. I hope that 100 years from now, at the dawn of the twenty-second century, a handbook editor will be looking back and commenting on how the field has continued to be vibrant, adaptive, and relevant.

Acknowledgment

I gratefully acknowledge the Office of Naval Research (ONR), Command Decision Making (CDM) Program (N00014-09-1-0519, S. W. J. Kozlowski and G. T. Chao, Principal Investigators) and the National Aeronautics and Space Administration (NASA, NNX09AK47G, S. W. J. Kozlowski, Principal Investigator) for support that, in part, assisted the composition of this chapter. Any opinions, findings, and conclusions or recommendations expressed are those of the authors and do not necessarily reflect the views of ONR or NASA.

Note

1. Of course, the long-term prospects of a continuous "brain drain" are not very good for the future of I/O psychology. But that is for another discussion.

INDEX

Note: Page numbers followed by "*f*" and "*t*" refer to figures and tables, respectively.

A

AA. *See* affirmative action
AAAP. *See* American Association of
    Applied Psychology
ability
    diversity and, 1012–13
    entity theory of, 288
    extroversion and, 150
    general, 340–41
    HPWS and, 779
    incremental theory of, 288
    malleability of, 288
    neuroticism and, 150
    PFC and, 1185
    stability over time of, 147
    testing of, 8
ability, cognitive, 270
    aging and, 1253–55
    continuous learning and, 1254
    crystallized, 1253, 1256
    dynamic performance and, 554–55
    fluid, 1253, 1256
    gender and, 1253
    performance and, 149
    for selection, 229–31
    stability over time of, 147
    training and, 340–41, 1254–55
ability, KSAOs, 221–41
    adverse impact and, 1055, 1058
    predictor composites with, 229–33
ability, KSAs, 60
    brand equity and, 214
    developmental interaction and, 333
    JCM and, 253
    knowledge transfer of, 332
    PE and, 386
    recruitment and, 213
    self-regulation and, 334–35
    self-selection and, 212–13
    from training, 331
    as training objectives, 346

work design and, 270
ability, physical
    adverse impact and, 1060
    aging and, 1252–53, 1262
    safety and, 1231
    in selection, 233
ability-demand theory, 377
    fit and, 379
absenteeism
    aging and, 1257
    autonomous work groups and, 251
    diversity and, 1016
    JCM and, 253
    from physical demands, 262
    scientific management and, 250
    social support and, 264
    stress and, 1235
    in teams, 919
    work design and, 257
absorptive capacity, 946
    OD and, 969–71
    research on, 977*t*
Academy of Management (AOM), 25*t*,
    43, 411, 416, 428
Academy of Management Executive (*AME*),
    430
Academy of Management Journal (*AMJ*),
    410, 414, 1105
*Academy of Management Learning and
    Education* (*AMLE*), 437
accidents, 19
    aging and, 1256
    psychological contracts and, 1238
accident-prone individuals, 1230–31
accommodation
    for disabilities, 1040
    in learning, 1214
    PE and, 395–96
    for religion, 1041–42
    in socialization, 587–88
    in work-family interface, 1187

accountability, 1107
    situational, 264
achievement
    culture and, 1121–22
    GO and, 289
    individual empowerment and, 774–75
    nAch, 206, 270
achievement-oriented leadership behavior,
    708
Achilles, Paul S., 41
ACM SIGCHI. *See* Association for
    Computing Machinery Special
    Interest Group on Computer-
    Human Interaction
ACP. *See* Association of Consulting
    Psychologists
acquired immunodeficiency syndrome
    (AIDS), 1083–84
acrobats, in work-family interface, 1187
ACs. *See* assessment centers
action
    continuous learning and, 1203
    goals, 5
    in interdisciplinary research, 1308
    processes, 771
    research, 982–83
actional-personal learning barrier, 975
action phases, dynamic performance in,
    563
action-regulation
    emergent states and, 869
    in team learning, 865–69, 866*f*
active context, 936–37
active learning
    motivation and, 477
    work design and, 269
active performance, 183–84, 551*t*
activity theory, 1311
ACT* model of learning, 334
ADA. *See* Americans with Disabilities Act
Adams, J. Stacey, 52

(see above)

autonomy (*Contd.*)
  meta-analysis for, 260
  PE and, 374
  team empowerment and, 769
  vertical, 747–48
  work design and, 260
  with work schedules, 260
aversive racism, 1050
Aviation Cadet Qualifying Examination, 45
Aviation Psychology Unit of the Army Air Forces, 25*t*, 45
avoidance/denial, 1066
avoidance motivation, 468
avoid performance, 266
awareness. *See also* situation awareness
  CSCW and, 1328
  product, 203–4, 209
  training for, 1250
Ayres, I., 437

B
baby boom, 1246–47
Bacon, Francis, 29
balanced scorecards, 289
Balmer, Thomas L., 34
Bandura, Albert, 51, 52
Bannon, Liam, 1340
BARS. *See* Behaviorally Anchored Rating Scales
Bartlett, C.J., 47
Bartlett, Frederick, 1310
BAS. *See* behavioral activation system
Bayesian approach, 95
Bayesian information criterion (BIC), 135
behaviors. *See also specific behaviors or behavior types*
  affect and, 519n1
  age discrimination and, 1250
  in Kirkpatrick's typology, 353–54
  in leadership, 704–6, 708
  motivation and, 457
  organizational culture and, 657
  organizational learning and, 935
  performance and, 549, 913
  of protégé, 625
  in safety climate, 1233
  satisfaction and, 499–500
  self-esteem and, 149
  SH and, 1064
  team effectiveness and, 913
  in team empowerment, 772
  team learning and, 869
behavioral activation system (BAS), 468
behavioral engagement, 772
Behavioral Expectation Scales (BES), 27*t*, 54
behavioral inhibition system (BIS), 468
Behaviorally Anchored Rating Scales (BARS), 27*t*, 54
behavioral management programs, 306
Behavioral Observation Scales (BOS), 27*t*, 54

behavioral observation training, 188
behavioral performance unit, 563
behavioral team processes, 1129
A Behavioral Theory of the Firm (Cyert and March), 939
Behavior Description Questionnaire, 170
behaviorism, 39, 40, 44–45
behavior modification, 27*t*
Bell System, Management Progress Study by, 46
belonging, 16
  fairness and, 534
  mentoring and, 631–32
  PE and, 398
  socialization and, 584
  in team spatial interdependence, 758
  work design and, 270
benefits packages, 8–9
  aging and, 1266
  discrimination in, 1036
  recruitment and, 199
Bennis, Warren G., 1349
BES. *See* Behavioral Expectation Scales
best practices, for virtual teams, 835
"Best Practices Project," 1114
best sellers, 427
BFOQ. *See* bona fide occupational qualification
BIAS map, 1044
BIC. *See* Bayesian information criterion
bidirectional causal models, 83
Big Five personality model, 703–4
  aging and, 1259–60
  discrimination and, 1048
Bills, Marion A., 37, 37*f*
Binet-Simon intelligence test, 33
Bingham, Walter, 36, 151
biodata, 234, 1059
biological clock, 561
biological work design, 254, 254*t*
BIS. *See* behavioral inhibition system
bisexual, 1042
bivariate dynamic models, 119, 119*f*
Blink: The Power of Thinking Without Thinking (Gladwell), 419
block modeling, 671
blood pressure, 1182
"Blue Books," 25*t*, 45
BMI. *See* body mass index
bobo doll, 124
body mass index (BMI), 1043
Bohr, Niels, 9, 1385
bona fide occupational qualification (BFOQ), 1250
boredom, 47
  leadership and, 708
  scientific management and, 250
  stress and, 1235
BOS. *See* Behavioral Observation Scales
bottom-up influence, culture and, 1141–42
Bovet, Pierre, 40
Boy Scout organizational personality, 206

brain-computer interface, 1316–17
brainstorming, 796, 814
brand equity
  attitudes and, 212–13
  expectations and, 214
  factors in, 203–4
  familiarity and, 209
  fit and, 212–13
  individuals and, 212–14
  KSAs and, 214
  OCB and, 214
  organizational culture and, 214
  outcomes and, 210
  performance and, 213–14
  presocialization and, 214
  product awareness and, 203–4
  recruitment and, 197–216
  reputation and, 201–5
  theory of, 202–3
  turnover and, 213
Bregman, Elsie Oschrin, 24*t*, 38
bridge jobs, aging and, 1263–64
bridges, in social networks, 680–81, 681*f*
bridging leadership theories, 710–11
broaden and build theory, of positive emotions, 567
broad-mindedness, 659
brokerage-performance relationship, 676
Brown, C.W., 50
Brown, Ken, 436
Brown v. Board of Education, 44
bubble hypothesis, 111
Building an Interdisciplinary Science of Organizations (Roberts, Hulin, and Rousseau), 11
Bureau of Retail Training, 36
burnout, 19, 1239
  insomnia and, 1236
  situational accountability and, 264
Burns, J.M., 169
Burt, R.S., 685
Burtt, Harold, 40
business psychology, 22
business trips, 594
Businessweek, 210

C
caffeine
  in Coca-Cola, 34
  stress and, 1235
California Psychological Inventory (CPI), 1258
Calvinism, 6
"Cambridge Cockpit," 1310
Campbell Causal Model (CCM), 79–80, 89–101, 111
  RCM and, 103
Campbell et al. model, for performance, 163–65
Canadian Journal of Behavioral Science, 1236
Canadian Pacific (CP), 994
capacity

fit in, 1114
in-group/out-group in, 1117, 1128
interdependence in, 1119
loyalty in, 1120
motivation in, 1119
outcomes in, 1122
performance appraisals in, 1117
promotion in, 1118
recruitment in, 1114
self-actualization in, 1120
self-efficacy in, 1125
virtual teams and, 797
culture, individualistic, 311
autonomy in, 500
charisma in, 1134
equity theory and, 1122
fairness in, 1132
motivation in, 1119
performance appraisals in, 1117
recruitment in, 1114
satisfaction in, 1126
self-actualization in, 1119
self-determination in, 1119, 1120
virtual teams and, 797
culture, power distance, 312
equity theory and, 1122
job definitions in, 1116
leadership in, 1135
SMWT and, 1128–29
teams and, 1128
culture blind, 1104
culture bound, 1104
currency, 5
Current Population Survey, 1040
curvilinear changes, in performance,
567–68
custodial roles, 590
customer service, 7, 795, 922
CWB. *See* counterproductive work
behavior
cybernetics, 1310
cycle time, 289
Cyert, R.M., 939

D

Darwin, Charles, 30, 421–22, 678
data aggregation, 11
*Daubert v. Merrell Dow Pharmaceuticals,
Inc.*, 410
Dawkins, Richard, 422
Day, David, 428
DDI. *See* Development Dimensions
International
Dearborn Conference Group, 49
debate and dissent processes, 1129–30
debriefings
NDM and, 1367–68
in training, 350
decentralization
knowledge creation and, 939
OD and, 934
in virtual teams, 849
decision bias, 1131

decision making. *See also* naturalistic
decision making
absorptive capacity and, 971
autonomy in, 260
CDM, 1351
in collectivistic cultures, 1136
continuous learning and, 1222
diversity and, 1016
ecological, 1356
formal-empiricist, 1351
information-processing in, 872
jury, 420–21
macrocognition and, 875
ODM, 1351
PDM, 263, 770–71, 777, 1136
rationalist, 1351
TDM, 1370
by TMTs, 1019
in virtual teams, 825, 830, 843, 846
in work-family interface, 1187
*Decision Sciences Journal of Innovative
Education (DSJIE)*, 437
decline in homeostasis, 1252
deep-level diversity, 1013
Defense Manpower Data Center
(DMDC), 1067
deliberate and guided practice, 357
demands-control model, employee-
employer relationships and, 1238
demographics
aging and, 1246
economic security and, 1246–47
in-group/out-group and, 1051
interindividual variability and, 153–54
IPO and, 1028
mentoring and, 622t
performance and, 1018–19
in recruitment, 198
of retirement, 1246–47
of TMTs, 1019
demographic changes, 7
aging and, 1245–76
discrimination and, 1046
fertility and, 1246
foundations of, 1246
immigration and, 1246
life expectancy, 1246
morality and, 1246
work and, 249, 1246–47
demonstrating effort, 165
demonstration research, 80
deontic model, 534–35
Department of Homeland Security, 56
dependability, aging and, 1259
dependent care, 1176–77
dependent variable (DV), 160–61
causation and, 80, 87, 88–89
depreciation model, 1271–72
depression, 117, 259, 738
psychological contracts and, 1238
retirement planning and, 1271
stress and, 1235
DeSanctis, G., 1337, 1337f

descriptive norms, in culture, 1110–11
determinism, 421
SMWT and, 1128–29
development, 17–18. *See also*
organizational development
with continuous learning, 1201,
1209–13, 1210t–1211t
definition of, 331–33
of expertise, 1372–73, 1372t–1373t
future research on, 364t
mentoring and, 617–18, 636n1
motivation and, 475–77, 485
organizational change and, 357–58
in performance management, 295–99
personal, 919
self-development, 167
with team learning, 862–63
of virtual teams, 801, 806–8, 823, 832
zone of proximal development, 1212
developmental approach, to readiness for
change, 965–66
developmental interaction, KSAs and, 333
developmental models, of team
effectiveness, 912, 924–25
developmental psychology, 9, 14
Development Dimensions International
(DDI), 55
deviation amplification, 559–60
dialectic tensions, 7–8, 8f
dialectic theory, 963
dialogue theory, 845
Dictionary of Occupational Titles (DOT),
39, 58, 180
differential psychology, 8
differentiation
of individuals, 399
of informational justice, 529
of interpersonal justice, 529
in organizational justice, 527–34
digital technology, 248
dilution effect, 824
direct consensus models, 99–100
direct fit, 233, 381–83
directive leadership behavior, 708
direct-tie networks, 676
disability
aging and, 1041
performance appraisal discrimination
by, 1072–73
disability discrimination, 1040
perceived, 1083–84
disability leave, discrimination in, 1036
discrepancy
PE and, 375–77
readiness for change and, 967
discrepancy-effort cycle, 128
discretionary tasks, 865
discriminant validity, 222
discrimination, 18, 1034–89
causes of, 1086–87
cognition and, 1043–47
as compliance, 1054
conservatism and, 1049

loosely coupled systems, 127, 734
loosely coupled teams, 735, 760–61
loyalty, 167, 1114, 1120
LPC. *See* least preferred coworker
LSH. *See* Likelihood to Sexually Harass
LTA. *See* latent transition analysis
Luther, Martin, 5–6

M

Maastricht Aging Study, 1254
MacArthur Foundation National Survey
    of Midlife Development in the
    United States (MIDUS), 1043, 1170
macrocognition, 901*t*
    collective knowledge and, 894–96
    meta-model of, 875–76, 876*f*
    NDM and, 1374
    team knowledge typology and,
        894–96
    team learning and, 875–77, 894–96
maintenance stages, 557
majority influence, 818, 1013
Malcolm X, 50
Management and Organizational Review,
    1105
management-by-exception (MBE), 710
management by objectives (MBO), 51,
    289
management capacity, 310
management information systems (MIS),
    1330–31
management performance
    dimensions of, 171*t*
    factors in, 173*t*
    individual performance and, 181–82
    leadership and, 700
Management Progress Study, 46
Managerial Grid, 169
Managerial Practice Survey, 170
manifest approach, to readiness for
    change, 965
manifest measures, construct validity and,
    98–99
March, J.G., 939
Marey, E.J., 31
Marrow, A., 50
Marxism, 6
Maslow, Abraham, 47, 304, 584, 960,
    1119–20, 1229
Massachusetts Institute of Technology
    (MIT), 48, 1205–6
mastery learning, 1208–9, 1215
matrix approach, to SEM, 121
maximum likelihood estimator (MLE),
    135
Mayflower Group, 55
Mayo, Elton, 64n16
MBE. *See* management-by-exception
MBO. *See* management by objectives
McClelland's typology of needs, 1121
McGrath, J.E., 1337–39, 1338*f*
McGregor, Douglas, 26*t*, 47, 49, 52
McHenry, Jeff, 438

meaning
    creation of, 16–17
    personal, 1202
meaningfulness
    experienced meaningfulness of the
        work, 265
    team empowerment and, 769
measurement error, 226–27
*The Measurement of Satisfaction in Work
    and Retirement* (Smith, Kendall, and
    Hulin), 53
mechanistic work design, 254, 254*t*
median naturalness theory, 843
media richness theory, 204
    CSCW and, 1342
    virtual teams and, 813, 822, 832, 841,
        847
media spaces, 1325
media synchronicity theory, 822, 837
mediated relationships, 126–27
mediation, 126–27
    by artifacts, 1311
Medical Research Council (MRC), 49
member-member social network
    knowledge creation and, 941
    knowledge retention and, 943–44
    knowledge transfer and, 946
member-task network
    knowledge creation and, 942–43
    knowledge retention and, 944
    knowledge transfer and, 947
memory. *See also* transactive memory
    systems
    NDM and, 1365–66
mental stimulation, in RPD, 1355–56
mental test, 31
mentoring, 16–17, 615–36
    attitudes and, 624
    belonging and, 631–32
    context and, 629–30
    contextual performance and, 307
    decline in, 628–29
    development and, 617–18, 636n1
    dissimilarity with, 631
    diversity and, 1022
    fit and, 390–91
    future research on, 633–36
    gender and, 619, 623–24
    initiation of, 618–21, 622*t*
    for learning, 356
    maturation in, 621–25, 627*t*
    methodological issues with, 632–33
    NDM and, 1371–72
    organizational culture and, 659
    outcomes with, 356, 620, 622*t*, 625
    perceptions with, 629
    phases of, 616–17
    problems in, 625–26
    promotions and, 624–25
    race and, 619, 624
    recruitment and, 629
    redefinition phase in, 628–29
    SET and, 631

similarity and, 623–24, 630–31
socialization and, 629
willingness to provide, 620–21
merit pay, 304, 314
meta-analysis, 27*t*
    for accident-prone individuals, 1231
    for adverse impact, 1055, 1057
    for age discrimination, 1249
    for aging, 1265
    for agreeableness/conscientiousness,
        145–46
    for autonomy, 260
    for behavioral management programs,
        306
    for conservatism, 1049
    for contextual performance, 307–8
    for cross-cultural psychology, 1105
    for diversity, 1017, 1018–19
    for dynamic performance, 552
    for EMT, 477
    for forced distributions, 303
    for GO, 878
    for goals, 288
    for goal setting, 864–65
    for interdependence, 263
    for interindividual variability, 145
    for JCM, 253–54
    for leadership, 703–4
    for MBO, 289
    for mentoring, 356, 625
    for organizational climate, 645
    for organizational image, 209–10
    for outcomes, 501*t*
    for path-goal theory, 708
    for PE, 387
    for performance, 161, 188, 501*t*
    for recruitment, 199
    for safety, 1234
    for safety climate, 1233
    for safety training, 1231
    for SDO, 1048
    for socialization, 593
    for stress, 1236, 1240
    for training, 296, 332, 1265
    for training/motivation, 345–46
    for transformational leadership, 650
    for unit-level satisfaction, 516
    for wellness programs, 1237
metacognition, 1366
meta-competency, 334–35
meta-model, of macrocognition, 875–76,
    876*f*
met expectations theory, 587
metrix distance matching, 103
Meyer, Herb, 54
Michigan State Leadership Studies, 705
microaggressions, 1078
middle adulthood, 1213
Middle Ages, 5
MIDUS. *See* MacArthur Foundation
    National Survey of Midlife
    Development in the United States
Mill, John Stuart, 87–88

organizational learning management,
933–49
organizational reference groups, 758
organizational reputation
familiarity and, 208–10
self-concept and, 207–8
trait inferences and, 209
organizational socialization. *See*
socialization
organizational support, contextual
performance and, 307
Organizational Tolerance for Sexual
Harassment (OTSH), 1064
organizational wellness programs. *See*
wellness programs
organization change recipients belief scale,
966
Organization Science, 972
OSHA. *See* Occupational Safety and
Health Administration
OSS. *See* Office of Strategic Services
other orientation, 270
OTSH. *See* Organizational Tolerance for
Sexual Harassment
OU. *See* Open University
outcomes
assimilation and, 399
brand equity and, 210
in collectivistic cultures, 1122
with continuous learning, 1206, 1222
CQ and, 1134
distributive justice and, 528, 538
diversity and, 1015, 1016
fairness and, 533
of feedback, 293
fit and, 392–97
happiness and, 538
for individuals, 781–82, 918–19
individual differences and, 152–53
interdependence and, 748–53
JCM and, 253
of learning, 332–33
with mentoring, 356, 620, 622*t*, 625
meta-analysis for, 501*t*
misfits and, 392–97
of motivation, 457
motivation to learn and, 357
objective fit and, 383–84, 383*f*
OD and, 959–60
for organizations, 782
perceived discrimination and, 1088
performance and, 186–87, 286, 501*t*,
549, 913
with recruitment, 205–12, 215
safety and, 1234
satisfaction and, 1126
of SH, 1066
social networks and, 681–85
for strategic human resource
management, 1000
subjective fit and, 383–84, 383*f*
for teams, 780–81
team effectiveness and, 918

for team empowerment, 780–82
team knowledge typology and, 901–2,
901*t*
of team learning, 886–902
for team participation, 780–82
with WFC, 1168–69, 1181–82
with WFE, 1170–71
work design and, 257–58
outcome evaluation and retrieval phase,
of macrocognition, 877
Overcoming Resistance to Change
(Coch and French), 50
overconfidence, 560
over-eating, 1235
overtime, 39

P

PA. *See* positive affect
pakikisama (group involvement), 1106
parsimony, in organizational justice,
530–31
partial inclusion, 1186
partial mediation, 127
participant dual-career families, 1187
participation
in continuous learning, 1206
goals and, 413
MLT and, 17
in performance appraisals, 313
in SMWT, 771
participation, team
antecedents of, 774
definition of, 771–72
future research on, 782–85, 784*t*
HPWS and, 779
multilevel model for, 783
OCB in, 770–71
organization climate and, 779–80
outcomes for, 780–82
proactive behavior in, 770–71, 913
participative decision making (PDM),
263, 770–71, 777, 1136
participative leadership behavior, 708,
1136
part-time work, aging and, 1263
passive/defensive organizational culture,
659
Pasteur's Quadrant (Stokes), 9
paternalism, 1079, 1128
culture and, 1138
Paternalistic Leadership Questionnaire
(PLQ), 1138
path-goal theory, 52, 168–69, 708
Patrizi, L.O., 32
PATs. *See* physical ability tests
pattern recognition, in RPD, 1355, 1364
pay
aging and, 1266
discrimination with, 1075–78
by gender, 1038
mentoring and, 356
merit, 304, 314
personality and, 206–7

recruitment and, 199
skill-based pay plans, 305
for work, 5
in work-family interface, 1165
pay-for-performance, 303–7
expectancy theory and, 1123
PE and, 379
research on, 305–6
PBL. *See* problem-based learning
PDAs. *See* personal digital assistants
PDM. *See* participative decision making
PDRI. *See* Personnel Decisions Research
Institute
PE. *See* person-environment fit
Pearson, Egon, 91
Pearson, Karl, 30
peer management performance, 182
pension plans, 1266, 1272
perceived age discrimination, 1081–82
perceived disability discrimination,
1083–84
perceived discrimination, 1080–84, 1088
perceived fit. *See* direct fit
perceived gender discrimination, 1081
perceived racial discrimination, 1080–81
perceived sexual orientation
discrimination, 1082–83
perceptions
on age, 1249
of burnout, 1239
with diversity, 1023, 1029
FSOP, 1178
of leadership, 27*t*, 698, 713
with mentoring, 629
of motivation, 1121
organizational climate and, 644–48, 649
psychological contracts and, 1238
for retirement, 1272
of SH, 1063–64
shared, 645, 649–50, 651
in team empowerment, 772
perceptual accuracy, for fit, 388–90
perceptual/motor work design, 254, 254*t*
performance, 14–15, 223
action-regulation and, 865–68
active, 183–84, 551*t*
adaptive, 183–84, 185*t*
adverse impact and, 1061–63
aging and, 1255–56
avoid, 266
behavioral performance unit, 563
behaviors and, 549, 913
brand equity and, 213–14
brokerage-performance relationship,
676
Campbell et al. model for, 163–65
change and, 183, 559
cognitive, 258–59, 262
cognitive ability and, 149
collective efficacy and, 882
complexity and, 559
context and, 166–67, 286–87, 307–8,
550, 1056

strategic human resource management (SHRM) (*Contd.*)
outcomes for, 1000
RBV for, 997–99, 1001*t*
recent theory for, 997–1000
value added and, 1002–3
strategy mapping, 999
stress, 19. *See also* burnout
adaptive performance and, 287
aging and, 1267
antecedents of, 1236
attitudes and, 1236
career and, 1236
catecholamines and, 1185
from employee-employer relationships, 1238
from goals, 288
groups and, 1237–38
health and, 1235–38
individual differences and, 1236
from interpersonal relationships, 1236
job design and, 1267
meta-analysis for, 1236, 1240
needs-supply theory and, 375
organizations and, 1237–38
PE and, 1236
policies and procedures and, 1237–38
preferences and, 1236
promotion and, 1236
recovery from, 1236–37
regulatory focus and, 1236
relationships and, 1235, 1236, 1240
from role ambiguity, 1236
roles and, 1240
from role conflict, 1236
values and, 1236
in work-family interface, 1181–82, 1237
Strong, E.K., Jr., 42
Strong Vocational Interest Blank, 37–38
structural empowerment, 768
structural equation modeling (SEM), 27*t*, 117–18, 121
structural equivalence, 671
Structural Holes (Burt), 685
structural interdependence, 17
structuralism, 30, 33, 39, 649
structural-organizational learning barrier, 975
structure-oriented inputs, for teams, 778
STS. *See* socio-technical systems theory
studies audit, 1036–37
Style organizational personality, 206
subgroup differences, 228–29
adverse impact and, 1058–59
range restriction and, 154
in virtual teams, 803
subgroup fault-line, 840
subjective culture, 1110–11
subjective fit, 380–81
direct fit and, 382

objective fit and, 388–92
outcomes and, 383–84, 383*f*
subject matter expert (SME), 163, 225, 340
substantially limits test, 1040
subtle discrimination, 1078–80
suicide, 1235
Sun Tzu, 1103
Super Crunchers (Ayres), 437
supervisory control, 1294
supervisory justice, 529
supplementary fit, 378–79
support, 168
contextual performance and, 286–87, 307
for continuous learning, 1216–22
GDSS, 797, 799, 1323
organizational climate and, 644
readiness for change and, 967, 968
for safety, 1233
stress and, 1236
in work-family interaction, 1177–78
supportive leadership behavior, 708
support-seeking, 1066
SUR. *See* seemingly unrelated regressions
surface-level diversity, 1013
Survey of Organizations, 705
survival analysis, 107
sustainability
of competitive advantage, 240
through human capital, 221–41
organizational change and, 984–86
RBV for, 240
symbolic attributes, 205–6
symbolic interactionism, 649
Symbolic Racism Scale, 1050
symmetry breaking, 962
systems
archetypes, 979–80
cognitive engineering and, 1311–14
equilibria in, 124–25
stability, 124–25
systematic reviews, 436
system dynamics. *See also* linear dynamic systems
organizational change and, 979–80
in research design, 108–10
systemic fit, 994–95, 998*t*
System Justification Theory, 1052–53

T

Tactical Decision Making Under Stress (TADMUS), 61, 1350
TADMUS. *See* Tactical Decision Making Under Stress
tangible outputs, team effectiveness and, 913, 914–17
tasks
analysis, 339–40, 1312–13
cognitive engineering and, 1311–14
compilation, 871
complexity of, 82*f,* 557
consistency of, 557

decomposition, 737–39
diversity and, 1017–18
expertise with, 1354–55
identity, 253, 261
interdependence with, 751
performance and, 82, 82*f,* 286–87, 308, 550, 551*t,* 1056
significance, 253, 261
socialization and, 602–3
statements, 339–40, 340*t*
variety, 261
virtual teams and, 791
in work design, 260–62
task-media fit, 830
tasks/task network
knowledge creation and, 941
knowledge retention and, 944
knowledge transfer and, 946
task-technology fit, 837
TAT. *See* Thematic Apperception Test
Tavistock Institute of Human Relations, 26*t,* 48, 251
Taylor, Frederick Winslow, 33–34, 250, 1309
TDM. *See* team decision making
Tead, O., 25*t*
teams, 7, 17. *See also* virtual teams
absenteeism in, 919
adaptation in, 1359, 1360*f*
adaptive performance and, 315
with agreeableness, 145–46
coaching of, 297
with conscientiousness, 145–46
cross-cultural psychology and, 1105
cross-functional, 741–42
culture and, 1127–30
definition of, 911
diversity in, 1028
emergent states of, 877–85
empowerment in, 768–69, 919
formation of, 28*t,* 871
FTF, 789
horizontal interdependence in, 736–42
human-agent, 1315–16
individuals in, 734, 918–19
individual performance in, 563
interdependence in, 734–63, 774
leadership of, 176, 715–19
mental models, 888–91, 901*t*
motivation in, 477, 484, 868, 868*f*
multicultural, 1130
NDM and, 1366–68, 1366*f*
organizational climate and, 779–80
organizational culture and, 659
outcomes for, 780–81
outcome interdependence in, 748–53
participation in, 767–85
pay-for-performance for, 304
performance of, 868*f*
power distance cultures and, 1128
rise of, 12
skills of, 177